Real Ethics
for
Real Lawyers

Real Ethics
for
Real Lawyers

Second Edition

Daniel R. Coquillette

J. Donald Monan, S.J. University Professor,
Boston College Law School
Charles Warren Visiting Professor of American Legal History,
Harvard Law School
Reporter, Committee on Rules of Practice and Procedure,
Judicial Conference of the United States

Carolina Academic Press
Durham, North Carolina

ISBN 978-1-59460-597-0
LCCN 2011922296

CAROLINA ACADEMIC PRESS
700 Kent St.
Durham, NC 27701
Telephone (919) 489-7486
Fax (919) 493-5668
www.cap-press.com

To My Parents, Who Taught Real Ethics.

Contents

Table of Cases

(Primary cases are listed in **bold** typeface.)

Foreword

Real Ethics for Real Lawyers is designed to teach professional responsibility by solving practical problems.[1] This approach is informed by my experience as a litigation partner in a major law firm, and my experience advising real law firms and lawyers about actual ethical dilemmas.

Too often "legal ethics" are taught in a vacuum, as if they were somehow technical subjects that stand apart from the moral values that you grew up with. This is dangerous. "Legal ethics" are, in the end, about fundamental responsibility. This book deliberately links issues of "legal ethics" directly to such fundamental values, i.e. "real ethics." But the book does not overlook the economics of the profession, nor those topics of particular concern to new lawyers, such as how to start a law practice, bar admissions, bar discipline and malpractice liability.

There is a big emphasis here on preparing problems for oral argument, just as real lawyers would, and on solving difficult dilemmas by asking questions and debating options, again, just like real lawyers. Long experience in teaching professional responsibility in four law schools has taught me that class debate is the best way to learn the rules, and, more importantly, prepares you for what awaits in practice. It is also more fun.

This book can be used as a free-standing professional responsibility course, but can also be paired with another short book, Coquillette, Cassidy, McMorrow, *Lawyers and Fundamental Moral Responsibility* (2d ed., Lexis Nexis, San Francisco, 2010) (Hereafter "*Fundamental Moral Responsibility*"). The two books together can be covered in a three-hour course. *Real Ethics for Real Lawyers* teaches the relevant rules and legal doctrines. *Fundamental Moral Responsibility* addresses practical problems from the perspective of ethical philosophy, and provides a philosophical "tool box" for resolving moral dilemmas. Taken together, the books provide the new lawyer with both a legal and an ethical framework for resolving the real problems of practice.

This book can also be paired with other special perspectives. For example, it could be combined with a book by my distinguished colleague and friend, R. Michael Cassidy, *Prosecutorial Ethics* (Thompson/West, St. Paul, 2005). There are many other possibilities.

Unlike many other texts, this book does include selected professional rules, including an appendix containing the *Massachusetts Rules of Professional Conduct*. Obviously, these

---

1. For a leading philosophical basis of this approach, see John M. Rist, *Real Ethics: Reconsidering the Foundations of Morality* (Cambridge, 2002). "The major issues in moral philosophy, as Plato realized, are comparatively simple and cannot be fudged." *Id.*, p. 8. This book also lends itself to another approach that derives from early Jesuit philosophy, and has been ably advocated by a most valued friend and colleague, Paul R. Tremblay. This is casuistry, "a form of ethical reasoning that involves the close analysis of particular cases, seeking ethical guidance in an inductive manner, rather than deductively through the application of theory." See Paul R. Tremblay, "Shared Norms, Bad Lawyers, and the Virtues of Casuistry," 36 *University of San Francisco L. Rev.* 659, 661 (2002).

rules change, and may have to be updated, but the convenience for students of an integrated book is very great. Occasional supplements, such as the latest ABA rule pamphlet, are easy to provide.

As with almost every teacher in this field, I am deeply indebted to my special friend and colleague, Andrew L. Kaufman. His original edition of *Problems in Professional Responsibility* (Boston, 1976) essentially invented this genre. I have borrowed many ideas from that great classic, and its subsequent editions, including the excellent new edition prepared with another most valued friend and colleague, David B. Wilkins.

Andrew Kaufman's example as a teacher, a scholar, a true friend, and a lawyer dedicated to the standards of his beloved profession, has been an inspiration to me for more than forty years. His admirers are legion, and his influence for the good has been profound.

Another special friend has been my colleague Judith A. McMorrow, co-author with me of the *Federal Law of Attorney Conduct* (Lexis Nexis, San Francisco, 2011). She teaches responsibility, honesty and loyalty by example. Such teachers and friends are priceless, and I owe more to my colleagues at both Boston College and Harvard than I can ever say. It has been a great privilege to know them, and to learn from their wisdom and idealism.

Essential to this book has been the enthusiasm and invaluable insights of my Boston College research assistants, James-Ryan Fagan '06, Kristen A. Johnson '06, James E. Kruzer '07, Michael E. Pastore '07, and Andrew Choe '12, and the generous support of my Dean, John H. Garvey. I would also like to specially thank Charles Riordan, Editorial Assistant to the Monan Professor, for his tireless efforts in preparing these materials. His intelligence and hard work are evident on every page.

Acknowledgments

Page

21   Andrew L. Kaufman, "Who Should Make the Rules Governing Conduct of Lawyers in Federal Matters," originally published in 75 *Tul. L. Rev.* 149-164 (2000). Reprinted with permission of the *Tulane Law Review* Association and Andrew L. Kaufman.

31 ff.   American Bar Association, *Model Rules of Professional Conduct* (2004). Selected rules. Reprinted with permission of the American Bar Association. Copies of ABA *Model Rules of Professional Conduct, 2004* are available from Service Center, American Bar Association, 750 North Clark Street, Chicago, IL, 60610, 1-800-285-2221.

34 ff.   American Bar Association, *Model Code of Professional Responsibility* (1983). Selected sections. Reprinted with permission of the American Bar Association. Copies of ABA *Model Code of Professional Responsibility* are available from Service Center, American Bar Association, 321 North Clark Street, Chicago, IL 60610, 1-800-285-2221.

51   Coquillette, Daniel R. and McMorrow, Judith P., "Toward an Ecclesiastical Professional Ethic: Lessons from the Legal Profession," *Church Ethics and Its Organizational Context: Learning From the Sex Abuse Scandal in the Catholic Church*, edited by Jean Bartunek, Mary Ann Hinsdale and James F. Keenan (Rowman & Littlefield Publishers, Inc., 2005). Reprinted with permission.

77   Frank, John P., "The Legal Ethics of Louis D. Brandeis," 17 *Stanford L. Rev.* 683 (1965). Reprinted with permission of the *Stanford Law Review*.

90   Berenson, Alex, "A Caldron of Ethics and Asbestos," *New York Times*, March 12, 2003, p. c.1. © 2003 by the New York Times Co. Reprinted with permission. Photograph of Joseph F. Rice, © Douglas Levere Photo. Reproduced with permission.

92   Donovan, Karen, "When Big Law Firms Trip Over Their Own Clients," *New York Times*, October 3, 2004, p. 5. © 2004 by the New York Times Co. Reprinted with permission.

95   Association of the Bar of the City of New York, Formal Opinion No. 2003-03. Reprinted with permission of the Committee on Professional and Judicial Ethics of the Association of the Bar of the City of New York.

190   Nelson, Bryce, "Ethical Dilemma: Should Lawyers Turn in Clients?" Copyright *Los Angeles Times*, July 2, 1974, p. 1, col. 1. Reprinted with permission.
      Maine Board of Overseers of the Bar Ethics Opinion 146 (December 9, 1994). Reprinted with permission. Maine Bar Ethics Opinion ¶ 146 has been overruled and withdrawn, and replaced by Opinion ¶ 172, issued March 7, 2000.

223   American Bar Association Formal Ethics Opinion 05-437.

239   American Law Institute, *Restatement of the Law Third, The Law Governing Lawyers*, § 98. Copyright 2000 by the American Law Institute. Reprinted with permission. All rights reserved.

Page

260   Freedman, Monroe, "The Professional Responsibility of the Criminal Defense Lawyer: The Three Hardest Questions," 64 *Mich. L. Rev.* 1469 (1966). Reprinted with permission of the author and the publisher. [Professor Freedman has considerably expanded and updated his views in Monroe Freedman & Abbe Smith, *Understanding Lawyers' Ethics* (3rd ed., 2004) (Matthew Bender).]

270   Frankel, Marvin, "The Search for Truth: An Umpireal View," 123 *U. Pa. L. Rev.* 1031 (1975). Reprinted with permission of the *University of Pennsylvania Law Review* and the Williams S. Hein & Company, Inc.

282   Rubin, Alvin, "A Causerie on Lawyer's Ethics in Negotiation," 35 *La. L. Rev.* 577 (1975). Reprinted with permission of the *Louisiana Law Review*.

294   Fried, Charles, *The Lawyer as Friend: The Moral Foundations of the Lawyer-Client Relation*

353   Federal Bar Association, Professional Ethics Committee, Opinion 73-1 "The Government Client and Confidentiality," 32 *Fed. B.J.* 71 (1973). Reprinted with permission.

357   District of Columbia Opinion 323 (2004). Reprinted with permission.

361   Sommer, A.A., "The Emerging Responsibilities of the Securities Lawyer," 1974-75, Fed Sec. L. Rep. ¶ 79, 631. © 1974-1975, CCH INCORPORATED. All Rights Reserved. Reprinted with permission from (FEDERAL SECURITY LAW REPORTER).

365   Diemer, Mary S., "SEC Continues Considering 'Noisy Withdrawal' Rule," 28 *Litigation News*, Vol. 28, No. 6, September 2003. Reprinted by Permission.

367   Simon, William H., "The Kaye Scholer Affair: The Lawyer's Duty of Candor and the Bar's Temptations of Evasion and Apology," *Law and Social Inquiry* (1998) pp. 243-282. Reprinted with permission of the author and the University of Chicago Press.

379   Judson, George, "Hostility to Whistle-Blowers Is Cited in A-Plant Problems," *New York Times* (August 8, 1996), Metropolitan Desk, Section B., p. 7. © 1996 by the New York Times Co. Reprinted with permission.

381   Zacharias, Fred, "Lawyers as Gatekeepers," 41 *San Diego L. Rev.* 1387. Copyright 2004 San Diego Law Review. Reprinted with permission of the author and the *San Diego Law Review*.

395   Stone, Alan A., "The Myth of Advocacy," *Hospital & Community Psychiatry*, Dec. 1979; 12: 819-822. Reprinted with permission from Hospital and Community Psychiatry, Copyright 1979. American Psychiatric Association.

400   Committee on Professional Judicial Ethics, Association of the Bar of the City of New York, Opinion No. 80-23. Reprinted with permission of the Committee on Professional and Judicial Ethics of the Association of the Bar of the City of New York.

405   Van Natta, Don, Jr., "Agents' Talk with Ex-Intern Provokes Angry Exchanges," *New York Times*, January 24, 1998, p. A10. © 1998 by the New York Times Co. Reprinted with permission.

407   Boynton, Paul D., "Talking to Manager in Bias Suit Not Unethical," 29 *Massachusetts Lawyer's Weekly*, 1, 31 (December 18, 2000). Reprinted with permission.

456   James E. Morgan, "Internet Advertising Raises Ethical Concerns," *Litigation News*, Vol. 26, No. 6, September, 2001. Reprinted with permission of the author and the American Bar Association.

Page

500   Rattigan, David, "Would you know this man if you saw him?" *Massachusetts Bar Association Lawyers Journal*, p. B1, B9 (October, 1999). Reprinted with permission.

507   Notice, "How to Start and Run a Successful Solo or Small-Firm Practice," MBA-MCLE (May, 2004), p. 1. Reprinted with permission.

508   Lawrence J. Fox, "Dan's World: A Free Enterprise Dream; An Ethics Nightmare," *The Business Lawyer*, Vol. 55, No. 4, August 2000. Reprinted with permission.

627   Massachusetts Board of Overseers, "How to File a Complaint," published on http://www.mass.gov/obcbbo/complaint.htm (site visited August 3, 2010). Reprinted with permission.

631   Massachusetts Client Security Board Announcement (2004). Reprinted by permission of The Massachusetts Clients' Security Board of the Supreme Judicial Court.

633   ABA Committee on Evaluation of Disciplinary Enforcement, "Problem 31—Reluctance on the Part of Lawyers and Judges to Report Instances of Professional Misconduct," published in Problems and Recommendations in Disciplinary Enforcement ("The Clark Report"), 1970. Reprinted with permission.

637   American Bar Association Formal Opinion 03-431 (August, 2003). Reprinted by permission of the American Bar Association. Copies of ABA Ethics Opinions are available from Service Center, American Bar Association, 321 North Clark Street, Chicago, IL 60610, 1-800-285-2221.

Real Ethics
for
Real Lawyers

Chapter I

Regulating the Profession

Problem

Problem 1

Select sides and set up the case of *In Re Ruffalo*, set out at Chapter I-5, *infra*, for oral argument. One team will represent Attorney Ruffalo, and the other the case against him brought by the Mahoning County Bar Association. Assume the case is before the Ohio Board of Commissioners on Grievances and Discipline. How would you argue the case under the "conduct unbecoming a member of the bar" standard? Under the standard of *ABA Code* DR-1-102? Under *ABA Model Rule* 8.4? How do these standards differ? Which do you prefer? What if *Massachusetts Rule* 7.3 had been in effect? Do you like the Massachusetts rule? See *Appendix for Massachusetts Rules*. Are any of these rules actually rules of "ethics," or is this really a matter of economic regulation? If the latter, is there any moral reason to obey them, except for fear of punishment?

Compare *In re Ruffalo* to *In re S. (A Barrister)*, *infra*. "S" was disbarred for handing out his card to an electrician doing work on his house, for accepting legal employment directly without going through a solicitor (required by the bifurcated English bar), and for accepting services rather than money as payment for legal work. Are these moral violations? In the *Crossen* case, *infra*, Gary Crossen argued that he was wrongly disciplined, in part because some of the rules were "vague." What do you think of that case? Could Crossen be disciplined under a "conduct unbecoming a member of the bar" standard?

I-1. Introduction: What Are "Professional Ethics?"

Bernard Williams observed that your profession "is a personal fact" about you. In other words, it inevitably changes how you relate to the rest of the world.[1] Some have even argued that certain acts that would be "fairly horrible" in themselves actually become desirable if "done in a professional role, in the name of a desirable system."[2] Whatever you think of this argument, the converse is certainly true. Once you become a lawyer, acts that would be excusable, or even praiseworthy if you were a layperson, can result in suspension or disbarment. For example, as we will see, lawyers are expected to

---

1. Bernard Williams, "Politics and Moral Character" from *Public and Private Morality*, S. Hampshire, ed., (Cambridge, 1978), pp. 66–71, set out at Coquillette, Cassidy, McMorrow, *Lawyers and Fundamental Moral Responsibility* (San Francisco, 2010), p. 320. (Hereafter, "Coquillette, Cassidy, McMorrow, *Fundamental Moral Responsibility*").
2. *Id.*, p. 320–321.

keep certain client confidences, even when that is clearly harmful to innocent third parties. In the course of this book, we will see many other examples.

For a new lawyer, or a law student, this can be a stressful idea, but even very experienced attorneys often find themselves wrestling with what defines "professional ethics," and how that definition sets lawyers apart. The answers are not easy, and are a product of the long historical evolution of the Anglo-American legal profession itself, which goes back nearly a thousand years. One thing is certain, however. Once you raise your hand in court and take the oath of attorney, you will be governed by rules and standards that are different, and more demanding, than those of ordinary citizens. Many lawyers have been acquitted of all criminal charges, only to be disbarred or suspended for the same conduct. Two modern Presidents of the United States have discovered this fact the hard way.

There are many courses in law school that are important to your future, but none as important as this one. Relying on your inherent sense of virtue will not save you from serious trouble if you are ignorant of what is in this book. Most courses are about honing your professional skills. This course is about professional survival.

Some would also say it is about another kind of survival, one that is even more important. How do you survive as a true professional, in a tough professional world, and also survive as a good person? Throughout this book, we will be discussing this central question. It is a deep question, about your moral soul. But ignorance about professional norms, how they have evolved historically and how they are enforced, certainly is not the answer. Genuine resolution of such "core" issues comes from knowledge, experience, and reflection.

A. The Jurisprudential Context

"Professional ethics" are, in practice, "rule driven." In other words, when you are admitted to practice law, you will be governed by specific sets of rules, such as the *Massachusetts Rules of Professional Conduct* (hereafter, "*Mass. Rules*") that form an Appendix to this book. As we will see, if you are admitted to more than one state bar, or are admitted to the bars of federal courts, or practice before certain state or federal agencies, you could be, in theory at least, subject to several different sets of professional rules. For this reason, every chapter in this book begins with examples of the relevant professional rules.

But to say that "professional ethics" are defined by professional rules is simplistic and unrealistic. To begin with, there is no deputy of the Bar Counsel's Office lurking under your desk. It is an empirical fact that most professional rules are self-enforced, and that fear of punishment alone would hardly suffice to create an ethical bar. This leads to an important question. If you obey professional rules voluntarily, even when it prejudices your client or yourself and even when it would be easy to go undetected, why do you do it? The reasons why you, or anyone, voluntarily obeys rules are called "deep theories." If your profession "is a personal fact" about you, your "deep theories" are even more so.

Some of the genuinely unethical lawyers are experts at what the rules say and how to evade them. They would get an excellent grade in professional responsibility, and some have. But they are genuinely dangerous, as they have no real allegiance to the spirit of the rule system or to the core value of the profession. Thus we begin this book with "Professionalism: The Deep Theory," an article which challenges you to define why you obey rules.

B. The Historical Context

Most professional rules are adopted by courts as rules of court. Usually, these courts are the supreme court of each state, although federal courts also adopt rules regulating attorneys, as do some legislatures and executive agencies. A good example of the latter is the SEC Standards of Professional Conduct promulgated on January 23, 2003, pursuant to the Sarbanes-Oxley Act, 17 CFR 205, which we will examine at length in Chapter VI. But, in general, legislatures and executive agencies have deferred to the courts in establishing professional rules. Why?

This is a question you might well ask if you were a corporate lawyer who specialized in commercial transactions. You may never appear in a court in your life, unless it is to take your oath of admission to the bar. The law you practice may be entirely a creature of legislatures and agencies. Or you may have a global practice, and your life may be governed by international trade practice, treaties, or even foreign legal systems. But your acts will, nevertheless, usually be governed by the state supreme court in the jurisdiction where you were admitted, and the bar discipline agencies appointed by those courts could bring your law practice to an abrupt end.

What is more, you may be suspended or disbarred for acts that have nothing to do with your law practice. The comments to the *Mass. Rules*, for example, state clearly that "willful failure to file an income tax return" is a violation of Rule 8.4 (b), even if that is entirely a personal matter, and your law practice is exemplary. Attorney General Richard C. Kleindienst was suspended for lying under oath in a matter that had nothing to do with his law practice. See *State Bar of Arizona* v. *Richard C. Kleindienst*, set out in Chapter IX-3, *infra*. The same happened to President William J. Clinton.

The explanation for the courts' control over the legal profession is not logical, but historical. Lawyers, at least those in the Anglo-American tradition, have always been subject to three conflicting professional ideals. The oldest, dating back to the dawn of time, could be called the "attorney" ideal. It began when the first bright, articulate young tribal "mouth piece" stood up to defend a less articulate, or bright, kinsman.[3] Under this ideal, the lawyer owes a first loyalty to the client, and "stands in the client's shoes." Indeed, this ideal could even be made to justify the lawyer doing things to protect a client that would be wrong for the lawyer to do for himself or herself.[4]

But, beginning at least as early as the thirteenth century, lawyers had a second ideal, the "officer of the court" ideal. As courts began to supervise the training and conduct of lawyers, they began to demand a loyalty in return, not just to the client, but to the legal system itself and to the state that protects it. This loyalty can, and sometimes does, conflict directly with the duty to the client. For example, the Department of Defense had put restraints on the representation of alleged terrorists at Guantanamo Bay in the name of protecting the state.[5] While these have proven controversial, few would argue that a lawyer has no obligation to protect the system of justice. As we will see, the issue is

---

3. See the discussion in Daniel R. Coquillette, *The Anglo-American Legal Heritage* (2d ed., Durham, N.C., 2004) pp. 265–272. "Attorney" actually came from the Law French meaning "to transfer or assign" or "appoint."

4. See, for example, Charles Fried's provocative article, "The Lawyer as Friend," 85 *Yale L.J.* 1060, (1975–1976) set out in Chapter V-3, *infra*.

5. See Department of Defense, MCI No. 5, "Qualification of Civilian Defense Counsel," Annex B, April 30, 2003.

how much of an obligation exists, and where "trade offs" with other values should be made.

But these two conflicting ideals are not the end of the story. As early as the fourteenth century, lawyers began to organize themselves into guilds, the most famous being the Inns of Court in London. With these increasingly powerful organizations came a new idea, that lawyers are not just defined by their duties to their clients or to the state, but also a duty to their profession. This "guild ideal" also remains strong today, at the local, state and national level. For example, many Massachusetts lawyers belong to the Boston Bar Association, the Massachusetts Bar Association, and the American Bar Association, and perhaps a specialty bar, like the National Association of Criminal Defense Lawyers ("NACDL"), as well. All of these are powerful, politically and professionally, and the American Bar Association is, today, the largest voluntary professional organization in the world.

We will discover that most professional rules, although adopted by courts, are actually based on "model" rules developed by the American Bar Association (the "ABA"), the most famous being the ABA *Code*, first promulgated in 1969, and the ABA *Model Rules* (hereafter the "*Model Rules*") first adopted in 1983. Very few non-lawyers were ever involved in drafting these rules, and, of course, the courts that adopted them were all comprised of lawyers, many of whom also belonged to the ABA. In addition, the state and local bar associations lobby hard for particular rules. As we will see, these rules may serve the interest of the profession, and not that of the clients or the justice system. The "guild ideal" is certainly alive and well in American bar today.

Because of the importance historically of these competing ideals, both to the rule systems and to their application in practice, we have included essays on the history of "Legal Professionalism" and "Professional Education: The Inns of Court," together with a famous article by Andrew Kaufman, "Who Should Make the Rules Governing Conduct of Lawyers in Federal Matters," which brilliantly, and critically, examines the roles of the guilds.

C. The Sources of Professional Ethics Today

We have already talked about rule systems. They are complicated. Despite the ABA "models," many states, including some of the most legally important, have adopted variants of the ABA "models." Some, at least for now, still follow the format of the old ABA *Code* of 1969. For example, New York abandoned the ABA *Code* of 1969 only in 2008. Others, such as Massachusetts, have changed from the old ABA *Code* format, but have not exactly adopted the new *Model Rules*. Indeed, as we will see, Massachusetts has made some major changes to the *Model Rules*. California has a very different system. Even in states that follow the *Model Rules*, the federal courts in the same state may follow a different version.[6] Efforts to persuade all federal courts to follow automatically the rules of the state in which they are located have so far been unsuccessful, although many federal courts have adopted "dynamic conformity" rules which do, automatically, track the state

---

6. See the discussion in Judith A. McMorrow, Daniel R. Coquillette, *The Federal Law of Attorney Practice* (San Francisco, 2010) issued with *Moore's Federal Practice* (4th ed., San Francisco, 2011) at pp. 802–6 to 802–54. (Hereafter, "*McMorrow, Coquillette*.")

rules.[7] Federal Courts of Appeal can include several states, making "dynamic conformity" even more difficult.[8]

In this book, the relevant sections from the latest version [at publication date] of the *Model Rules* head each chapter, together, where appropriate, with the relevant section of the old ABA *Code*. [Warning: the *Model Rules* change! Always consult the latest ABA edition.] But these "models" are not automatically adopted in any state or federal court. They are just guides. A version (as of 2011) of a "real" set of rules, the Massachusetts Rules of Professional Conduct (hereafter "*Massachusetts Rules*"), is included as an Appendix. This is partly because the author served in 1998 on the committee named by the Supreme Judicial Court of Massachusetts to assist in adopting these rules, but also because the Massachusetts Rules are an interesting, and typical, variant on the *Model Rules*. And at least they are the actual "law" somewhere. Of course, these rules are constantly updated, and, in practice, you must be sure you have the latest version.

As complex as they are, the rule systems are not the end of the regulatory process. To begin with, they are regularly interpreted by the courts, and many of the cases reproduced in this book do just that. As most rules are actually adopted by the courts themselves, they are actually "interpreting" their own "legislation." Some believe that this puts a special burden on the courts not to change the rules judicially, as they can always change them by the rule making process prospectively—which gives lawyers more notice.[9]

The courts also tend to interpret the rules in three very different contexts. The first is disciplinary actions. Usually these are initiated by a bar counsel, who is a prosecutor appointed by the state supreme court. In big states, the bar counsel's office can have a very large staff. There are over seventy in Massachusetts. This staff is usually paid by the annual dues payable to renew a bar membership. The investigations initiated by bar counsel are usually heard by a hearing committee appointed by a board of bar overseers. This board is also appointed by the state supreme court, but it sits in a judicial capacity, whereas the bar counsel is a prosecutor. Appeals from decisions of the board of bar overseers go to the courts. These cases, obviously, involve professional discipline, such as disbarment or suspension. Because the consequences can be severe, the courts examine carefully the proceedings below, to be sure the accused lawyer receives fair consideration. These court reviews are frequently reported, and many are in this book.

The second category is disqualification motions. These usually involve conflict of interest allegations, and will be discussed at length in Chapter 2 and 3, *infra*. Here the true sanction is that the disqualified lawyer may forfeit all the fees for the work for the client to date. It also forces the client to hire a new lawyer in the middle of the case, a great strategic nuisance. Increasingly, disqualification motions have been brought to harass opposing counsel. For this reason, and for reasons of judicial economy, courts "balance the equities" in granting such motions, trying to deter serious conflicts of interest, while avoiding waste. These cases are also frequently reported.

---

7. See *id.*, pp. 802-8 to 802-10.
8. See *id.*, pp. 803-1 to 803-66.
9. This issue was presented with regard to a comment to Mass. Rule 4.2 in the case of *Messing, Rudavsky & Weliky P.C. v. President and Fellows of Harvard College* 436 Mass. 347 (2002) (hereafter "*Messing*"). See the discussion at Chapter VI-I "*Introduction: Handling Difficulty Clients and Client Communication*," *infra*. The case itself is set out at Chapter VI-3.

Finally, there are malpractice actions. In theory, the professional rules are for disciplinary actions, not to establish standard of care for tort actions. The Preamble to the ABA *Model Rules* says so. "Violation of a Rule should not itself give rise to a cause of action against a lawyer nor should it create any presumption in such a case that a legal duty has been breached."[10] For that matter, "violation of a Rule does not necessarily warrant any other nondisciplinary remedy, such as disqualification of a lawyer in pending litigation."[11] Nevertheless, the rules are routinely looked to by courts as evidence of the minimum standards of care owed to clients, and, therefore, are routinely invoked and construed in malpractice cases, as we shall see. "[S]ince the Rules do establish standards of conduct by lawyers, a lawyer's violation of a Rule may be evidence of breach of the applicable standard of conduct." "Preamble," *supra*, paragraph [20]. Often, malpractice cases involve millions of dollars. While the lawyer defendants do not have their "license at risk," and while most have malpractice insurance, there are large deductibles, and a careless lawyer can only find reinsurance at high rates, if at all.

But it is not just the courts that construe the professional rules. Hopefully many of you will be considered for judgeships, or other distinguished positions. Confirmation hearings give opponents the opportunity to question the professional ethics of the appointee. One such example is included in the book—a very famous example—the confirmation hearing of Justice Louis D. Brandeis.[12] In theory, at least, the standards for such a confirmation should be extremely high, much higher than needed to avoid professional discipline, disqualification or malpractice. After all, this could be a life appointment to the highest court in the country. In addition, as mentioned before, many executive agencies, including the SEC, the INS, and the Patent Office, have adopted their own professional rules. Here the ultimate sanction is to be barred from practice before the agency. Some of these rules could conflict with state professional rules, such as an agency rule which requires disclosure that a state rule may prohibit.[13] It is an ongoing controversy as to how desirable such "extra" agency regulation really is.

Many bar associations, including the ABA, have established "Ethics Committees" or "Committees on Professional Responsibility." These committees issue opinions whose legal effect is merely "persuasive." But, in fact, these opinions can be quite important. To begin, boards of bar overseers are reluctant to discipline lawyers who follow such opinions in good faith, even if the board and the courts eventually disagree. Further, such opinions are evidence of good practice, and can thus be relevant evidence in malpractice cases. Many states, like Massachusetts, have emergency procedures, where a troubled lawyer can get advice from a "duty member" at short notice. When this author was Chair of the Massachusetts Bar Association Committee on Professional Responsibility, there was even an emergency request from a lawyer seeking to break the attorney duty of confidentiality to prevent a client suicide! Such services can be invaluable to new attorneys, or to solo practitioners. Bar association ethics opinions are frequently published, including the *Opinion of the ABA Standing Committee on Ethics and Professional Responsibility* (hereafter, *ABA Ethics Opinions*).

Finally, there are a number of leading treatises on Professional Ethics, such as the *American Law Institute* (hereafter, "ALI") *Restatement of the Law Governing Lawyers*,

---

10. See *Model Rules*, "Preamble," "Scope," paragraph [20].

11. *Id.*, paragraph [20].

12. See John P. Frank, "The Legal Ethics of Louis D. Brandeis," 17 *Stan. L. Rev.* 683 (1965) set out at Chapter II-3, *infra*.

13. See *McMorrow, Coquillette, supra*, at pp. 801-18 to 801-19.

published in the fall of 2000. The author of this book was an Advisor to that *Restatement*. As you doubtless recall from first year in law school, such ALI *Restatements* have no direct legal effect. They are "authoritative" sources to which the courts may look to guidance, particularly in malpractice cases, but they are not "binding" like rules and court decisions.

The materials in this book include all of the above "sources" of professional ethics. Some would also include "moral" authorities, including the Talmud and the Bible.[14] It is important to stay alert to which of these many sources are being invoked. In addition, the type of proceeding may make a big difference. Thus, the application of a professional rule by a trial court to decide a disqualification motion may be very different from that in a proceeding for professional discipline, such as disbarment.

These "sources" of professional ethics and their application are as complex as the "deep theories" and the rule systems themselves. This is not the fault of the teacher of your course. Legal ethics is a complex and multi-layered study. Reality is complicated. This book is designed to help make a subject easier for you, but it is, at its core, a very difficult subject to study.

D. The Danger of Rules

There remains one more caution. Rules are seductive as a focus of study because they are so concrete. They also lend themselves to bar examinations, such as the Multistate Professional Responsibility Examination (the "MPRE"), and to law school examinations. You clearly need to know them. But, as a lifelong rule maker and Reporter to the Committee on Rules of Practice and Procedure of the Judicial Conference of the United States, I can assure you that rules are useless when divorced from an appropriate professional culture. In fact, reliance on rules alone can be dangerous, as the accounting profession has discovered. This is particularly true when rules are only used to encourage minimal behavior, or encourage "technical" compliance, which is really evasion.

There have been attempts to draft "catch all" rules that anticipate everything, such as ABA Model Rule 8.4 (d), ("It is professional misconduct for a lawyer to … engage in conduct that is prejudicial to the administration of justice.") Or see, the old ABA *Code* DR-1-102 A (3), ("engage in illegal conduct involving moral turpitude.") The latter rule requires importing the judge's moral philosophy directly into the rule system! In extreme cases, such subjective generality can cause constitutional problems, as described by Justice Byron White's opinion in *In Re Ruffalo*, set out at Chapter I-5, *infra*. At best, such general rules offer only "fuzzy" guidance.

The truth is that rulemaking is a limited tool in addressing professional problems. For example, following the sexual abuse scandal, leaders within the Catholic Church considered using rules to establish an "Ecclesiastical Professional Ethic." At a Church in the Twenty-First Century Conference at Boston College, Judith McMorrow and I warned that those involved should learn from the Legal Profession, and be careful in using rules. Included in Chapter I-5, *infra*, is our presentation "Toward an Ecclesiastical Professional Ethic: Lessons from the Legal Profession." It concludes with a very useful bibliography for those concerned about rulemaking and its dangers.

---

14. See Coquillette, "Professionalism: The Deep Theory," 72 *North Carolina Law Review* 1271, 1271–1277 (1994), set out at Chapter I-2, *infra*.

I-2. Professionalism

Professionalism: The Deep Theory
Daniel R. Coquillette
72 *North Carolina Law Review* 1271, 1271–1277 (1994)

Recently I went to a little shop in Georgetown to buy my wife a teapot. The owner was a charming old lady with a sweet smile. We started talking, and she asked me what I did.

"Oh," I said, "I'm a law professor."

She smiled again and asked, "Does that mean you train lawyers?"

"Why yes," I replied.

"Well," she said, "perhaps you can help me answer this question: if a litigator, a divorce lawyer, and a corporate counsel all jump at the same time from a ten story window, who hits the ground first?"

"Gosh," I said, "I don't know!"

With the same sweet smile she looked up and said, "Who cares?"

The profession of being a lawyer has been the focus of my academic work as a legal historian and as a specialist in legal ethics. More important, it has been the business of my life, as it has been the business of your lives. I have taught for twelve years in four law schools and have practiced law for ten years. I believe that my profession, and your profession, is in deep trouble today. The question is, "Who cares?"

Notice my choice of words. It is not our "occupation," our "career," or our "vocation" that is in trouble. It is our "profession." There is a big difference among these terms. "Occupation," from the Latin *occupatio*, refers to "means of passing one's time"[1] — simply a way to pass the time each day. I hope we all are doing more than this! "Career" is somewhat more elevated. It comes from the Latin *carraria*, or "vehicle," and refers to a forward motion through life.[2] It shares the same root word as "careen"[3] — the way vehicles are driven in Boston. Some of us are certainly "careening" through life, and yet, there should be more. Finally, there is "vocation," from the Latin *vocare*, meaning "to call."[4] Historically, it refers to a divine call in the sense of being fit for something, talented in something.[5]

Simply passing your time in an occupation, or careening through life in a career, or even being called by your talent to a particular job does not require anything from *you*. But being a "professional" most certainly does. Here the root is the Latin *professio*, or "declaration,"[6] referring to a vow, a declaration of belief—an avowal made by *you*. All of you have taken "professional" oaths. These oaths require you to uphold the rule of law and to obey the regulations of the bar. They are not equivocal. You took these oaths in open court. If your word means anything, you are committed to this formal "profession" of obedience and to other "professional" duties.

---

1. The Concise Oxford Dictionary Of Current English 702 (J.B. Sykes ed., 7th ed. 1982).
2. *Id.* at 139.
3. *Id.*
4. *Id.* at 1202.
5. *Id.*
6. *Id.* at 821; *see* D.P. Simpson, Cassell's New Latin Dictionary 477 (1959).

This obligation is a deeply personal one. It is a delusion of young, inexperienced lawyers to think that they can separate their personal from their professional lives and their personal from their professional morality. The current jargon refers to this dichotomy as "role-defined" ethics. It is true intellectual rubbish. As Aristotle observed:

> The man, then, must be a perfect fool who is unaware that people's characters take their bias from the steady direction of their activities. If a man, well aware of what he is doing, behaves in such a way that he is bound to become unjust, we can only say that he is voluntarily unjust.[7]

You cannot be a bad person and a good lawyer, nor can you be a good person and a lawyer with sharp practices. A lawyer who behaves like a jerk in court is not an "aggressive advocate" with an "assertive strategy," but a jerk.

I was told that W.C. Fields once paused by a tombstone that read, "Here lies a lawyer and an honest man" and remarked, "How did they get two bodies under there?" We can't split ourselves down the middle. Indeed, the word "integrity" itself comes from the Latin root *integritas*, as in "integral" and "integration."[8] It means "wholeness" or "oneness." There is just one of each of us.

This means our professional identity as lawyers is at the center of our personal morality. And where do we get this identity? From our legal education, both at law school and, equally importantly, from the bar itself. Some of the most important lessons I have learned about professional ethics came not from my law professors but from my law partners and, indeed, from my professional adversaries in the heat of trial.

I believe our profession is in crisis today not because the American Bar Association has a bad media strategy, but because we have lost sight of the "deep theory" of professionalism in the classroom, in the office, and in the courtroom. What is a "deep theory?" Let me explain.

"Deep theory" focuses on our ultimate motivation for obeying rules.[9] There are three common categories: "goal-based," "rights-based," and "duty-based." Goal-based deep theories focus solely on political or economic outcomes. Examples include Marxism, fascism, and utilitarianism. If obedience to a rule promotes your goal, then obey it. If it doesn't, then don't, unless you might get caught. Suppose you obey the *ABA Model Rules* because if you don't, you might get disbarred, and you won't be able to afford that new car. That's a goal-based deep theory. From Marx to Machiavelli, goal-based theories have been easy to understand and implement. Best of all, they require no intrinsic test of the means that you employ to achieve your goal.

Recent developments in legal education, particularly legal realism and critical legal theory, have emphasized the function of law as an "instrument" to achieve particular political, social, or economic ends.[10] This is legal education with a goal-based deep theory. The older ideals of a "neutral" rule of law have been debunked as, at best, a pious myth, and, at worst, a deliberate effort by the powerful to exploit the weak under an illusion of "fairness" of principle. Many students become convinced that professionalism

---

7. ARISTOTLE, THE ETHICS OF ARISTOTLE 91 (J.A.K. Thompson trans., Penguin Books 1955) (1953).

8. THE CONCISE OXFORD DICTIONARY, *supra* note 1, at 521.

9. For a discussion of "goal-based," "rights-based," and "duty-based" "deep theories," *see* RONALD DWORKIN, TAKING RIGHTS SERIOUSLY 172–73 (1977).

10. *See* Roger C. Cramton, *The Ordinary Religion of the Law School Classroom*, 29 J. LEGAL EDUC. 247, 250 (1978).

means being willing to pursue the ends of others, irrespective of the means. It ultimately puts the client, for good or bad, in the driver's seat, and the ideal of justice becomes secondary.

This goal-based deep theory of education is very old. Indeed, it goes back to Greek philosophical schools known as the "Pre-Socratics."[11] One of these schools taught that all morality is relative: What's good for you is good for you, and my notion of goodness is entirely personal as well. There is no objective standard of a good person or of good conduct. This school was called the Cynics, from which we derive the pejorative word "cynical." The Pre-Socratics, however, did not treat such notions of moral relativism as inherently bad, and neither do many modern American law teachers.

If you subscribe to the School of Cynics, or moral relativism, your goal in teaching is to equip each student to pursue as ably and effectively as possible her individual view of what is good. The Greek Pre-Socratics called this doctrine the Sophist School. The Sophists taught rhetoric, logic, and advocacy. If you used these skills to promote a military dictatorship, such as Sparta, well fine. If you used them to support a democracy, such as Athens, fine again. If your view of the good led you to become a swindler, well, that was your business, too. Cynicism and Sophism, in the classical Greek sense, are alive and well in American law schools today. Moral relativism and its corollary—a theory of "professional" teaching that equips each future lawyer to pursue whatever ends she or her client may choose—may be found everywhere. Thus, moral relativism and goal-based deep theories go hand in hand.

In the final analysis, however, democracies are poor settings for goal-based deep theories. As you may have noticed, democracies have trouble getting anything done efficiently. At least in the short run, totalitarian regimes—even very evil regimes—can pursue some ends better than democracies. Our faith in a democratic rule of law cannot be solely instrumental. Consequently, most democratic systems, including our own, have historically been founded on rights-based deep theories rather than goal-based theories. The focus in a rights-based deep theory is on human freedom. Perhaps the most famous modern rights-based deep theory is that of John Rawls. He asks us to imagine ourselves in an "original position," a kind of meeting before we are born—ignorant of our sex, race, size, health, intelligence, social, or economic class.[12] What ground rules would we all agree to? Rawls postulates at least two. Put roughly by Ronald Dworkin they are "that every person must have the largest political liberty compatible with a like liberty for all" and "that inequalities in power, wealth, income, and other resources must not exist except insofar as they work to the absolute benefit of the worst-off members of society."[13] These so-called "principles of justice" in turn become touchstones to test the validity of all positive laws.

The trouble with rights-based deep theories is that they are excellent for defining the parameters of personal freedoms, but are less helpful in making critical choices within our own area of freedom. We can live an almost totally depraved life in complete accord with the Constitution and laws of the United States. Indeed, one could argue that we have a legal "right" to lead a depraved life. Put bluntly, rights-based deep theories are

---

11. For an engaging, if elementary, introduction to the Pre-Socratics, *see* BERTRAND RUSSELL, A HISTORY OF WESTERN PHILOSOPHY 3–81 (1945). *See also* ALASDAIR MACINTYRE, A SHORT HISTORY OF ETHICS 14–25 (1966).

12. *See* DWORKIN, *supra* note 9, at 150–181. Dworkin provides an excellent introduction to John Rawls's great but difficult book, A THEORY OF JUSTICE (1971).

13. DWORKIN, *supra* note 9, at 150.

powerful tools for defending the freedoms of clients and of other people in general. As professionals, however, they do not really help us *personally*, because they fail to answer the affirmative questions such as what exactly we must *do* to be a good person and a good lawyer.

This leaves us with duty-based deep theories. Many of them have fancy names, like "Neo-Platonism," "Neo-Kantianism," and "Neo-Thomism." In fact, duty-based deep systems are familiar because they are founded on the great classical and religious traditions that we so widely share.[14]

A key tenet of a duty-based system is that good acts do not necessarily lead to good results, at least not in this life. All great religions put us on notice that a good, even holy, life will not necessarily be free from cruel blows and bitter disappointments. If we measure our success by achievement, such as political or economic power, or by glory, we cannot ensure these results by being virtuous. Indeed, goal-based philosophers such as Machiavelli argue that we actually can be rewarded for doing evil, particularly if we pretend to do good in public and do evil in secret.[15]

Here is a true historical irony. If we go back to the origins of our professional traditions in the Inns of Court, or to the foundations of the American legal profession and the first American law schools, we will discover a duty-based deep theory for the formalization of legal education in the Anglo-American tradition. Law was initially taught as a humanistic study in both American and English universities.[16] The Inns of Court—the ultimate source of the "barrister ideal" in English law—strengthened the identification of individual lawyers with the system of justice.[17] Maintaining this identity was seen

---

14. *See* F.H. Bradley, Ethical Studies 162–74 (1990); A.C. Ewing, Ethics 49–61 (1965); *cf.* Bernard Williams, *Politics and Moral Character, in* Public and Private Morality 55, 66–71 (Stuart Hampshire ed., 1978) (discussing the desirability of immoral acts to reach legal or political ends). For an explanation of duty theory from the master himself, *see* Immanuel Kant, *Theory and Practice Concerning the Common Saying: This May Be True in Theory But Does Not Apply in Practice*, in The Philosophy of Kant 412, 412–29 (Carl J. Friedrich ed., 1949).

15. *See* Niccolo Machiavelli, The Prince 43–49 (W.K. Marriott trans., 1958).

16. For a discussion of the role of humanism in early English university study of law, *see* Harold J. Berman, Law and Revolution: The Formation of the Western Legal Tradition 120–64 (1983); Daniel R. Coquillette, The Civilian Writers of Doctors' Commons, London 24–27 (1988); Francis de Zulueta & Peter Stein, The Teaching of Roman Law in England Around 1200, at xiii–xxvii (1990); Alan Harding, A Social History of English Law 185–90 (1965); 1 Sir Frederick Pollock & Frederic W. Maitland, The History of English Law Before the Time of Edward I 118–19 (2d ed. 1898).

For a discussion of the role of humanism in early American legal education, *see* Lawrence M. Friedman, A History of American Law 84–85, 278–82 (1973); Daniel R. Coquillette, *Justinian in Braintree: John Adams, Civilian Learning, and Legal Elitism*, 1758–1775, in Law in Colonial Massachusetts 359, 359–418 (Daniel R. Coquillette et al. eds., 1984).

17. For an introduction to the importance of the Inns of Court, see J.H. Baker, An Introduction to English Legal History 187, 194–96 (3d ed. 1990); Sir Robert Megarry, Inns Ancient and Modern 3–14, 48–50 (1972); E.W. Ives, *The Common Lawyers, in* Profession, Vocation and Culture in Later Medieval England 181, 181–217 (Cecil H. Clough ed., 1982). For more detailed studies, *see* J.H. Baker, *The Inns of Court in 1388*, in *The Legal Profession and the Common Law* 3, 3–6 (1986); J.H. Baker, *Learning Exercises in the Medieval Inns of Court and Chancery*, in The Legal Profession and the Common Law, *supra*, at 7, 7–24; E.W. Ives, The Common Lawyers of Pre-Reformation England 7–89 (1983); David S. Lemmings, Gentlemen and Barristers: The Inns of Court and the English Bar 1680–1730 (1990); Wilfred R. Prest, The Inns of Court Under Elizabeth I and the Early Stuarts 1590–1640 (1972); Wilfred R. Prest, The Rise of the Barristers: A Social History of the English Bar 1590–1640 (1986); J.H. Baker, *Introduction to 2 Readings* and Moots at the Inns of Court in the Fifteenth Century at xv, xv–xxxiii (Samuel E. Thorne & J.H. Baker eds., 1990).

as a professional duty. The diaries and legal papers of early American lawyers, including John Adams, Thomas Jefferson, and Alexander Hamilton, show that they shared these ideals.

I do not have time here to trace the details of how American legal education left its roots for the more modern emphasis on goal instrumentalism. But I do believe this shift lies at the heart of our identity crisis as a profession. This is not a superficial problem. It cannot be solved by required ethics courses or media consultants. It requires a major re-examination of what we, as lawyers, are doing with our lives every day.

Now here is the good news. While the task of refocusing legal education on its humanistic roots and on the duties of professionalism is a vast one, we, as individual lawyers, can act now.[18] These are, after all, our lives and our profession.

Let me close with a true story. The ABA Ethics Committee usually spends its time wrestling with complex cases of conflict of interest or confidentiality. Last spring, however, we had a case that was simplicity itself. A lawyer's secretary was out sick, and the "temp" erroneously put a top secret client report into an envelope addressed to the opposing attorney. (The demand letter that was supposed to go to the opposing attorney went into the client's envelope.) The lawyer discovered the mistake after the mail had been dispatched but before it had been delivered. He called the lawyer on the other side and asked him to please return the envelope unopened, as it contained privileged, confidential client material. The other attorney refused to return the letter without his client's consent and the client said, "Open it."

The ABA Ethics Committee argued about this case for two days.[19] Twenty years ago, I experienced a similar incident. The senior partner of my firm mistakenly received a top secret report from the opposing side. He took two minutes to return the letter unopened, observing that the integrity of the legal process rested in mutual trust between lawyers and that "we could lose any client, but not our self-respect."

Self-respect demands that we get away from the intellectual tyranny of instrumentalism. We are not just means to someone else's ends. We have a far prouder heritage, which, unfortunately, has been obscured in the classroom. This heritage is founded on our ancient duties: to protect the rule of law as an ideal, to serve the system of justice on which our democracy is based, and to study and promote humanism — the mutual bonds of our humanity on which peace itself ultimately depends.

I will be happy to answer your questions about what I, as a legal educator, am trying to do about this in the law school setting.[20] But there is a more important point. This

---

18. Let me be clear about one possible point of misunderstanding. No sane legal historian wishes to return to the past. Many aspects of both the early English and American bars were unattractive and unjust. What I wish to do is to revive certain ideals of professional duty. This exercise, by its nature, focuses on the best achievements of the past. It ignores the worst, and even the typical.

19. In the end, the committee decided that the lawyer should return the envelope. *See* ABA Comm. on Ethics and Professional Responsibility, Formal Op. 92-368 (1992). Note: This position has now been reversed, at least in part. See ABA Opinion 05-437 and the new version of *Model Rule* 4.4(b) at Chapter V, *infra*.

20. One step currently underway at Boston College Law School is to require both introductory and advanced courses in legal ethics. The latter are for the third-year students and are taught in relatively small classes with a personal emphasis. I have just completed materials for such a course that applies the classical methodologies of Western ethical philosophy to practical, professional problems. *See* Daniel R. Coquillette, Lawyers and Fundamental Moral Responsibility (forthcoming 1994). [Note: this book has been republished in a second edition, Coquillette, Cassidy, McMorrow, Lawyers and Fundamental Moral Responsibility (2d ed. LexisNexis, San Francisco, 2010).]

profession does not belong to the law professors. It belongs to you and me as lawyers. Each day, and each hour, in our own professional lives, we possess the power to return to our profession's fundamental duties and roots. In countless small acts, such as returning envelopes, we can return the dignity. We can return the sense of self-respect. The ultimate answer to the question "Who cares?" has to be, "We do."

I-3. The Historical and Modern Context

The Birth of the English Legal Profession and English Legal Education

Daniel R. Coquillette, from *The Anglo-American Legal Heritage: Introductory Materials* (2d ed. 2004), Chapter IX, pp. 265–272 (Carolina Academic Press) [Some footnotes omitted. Remaining footnotes renumbered.]

A. Legal Professionalism

* * *

Despite the great diversity of the American legal profession, being "a lawyer" today has a fairly specific meaning. Most lawyers attend an accredited law school, often associated with a university. Almost all are licensed by their state of practice, and are usually supervised by the highest court of that state. Many are also members of the bar of federal courts, as well.

The past was very different. The first "lawyers," in the sense of persons who represented others in legal proceedings, were called "attorneys," from the medieval Latin "*attornatus*," ("substituted") and the Norman French "*attorner*" ("to transfer or assign"). They probably were no more than particularly articulate and bright kinsmen, or assistants, who were "assigned" by a party to speak on the party's behalf, not unlike the "eloquent and forceful" Mord at the Law Rock in *Njal's Saga*. See Chapter II, *Materials*, *supra*. These "attornies" literally "stood in the shoes" of a litigant, very much the way a power of attorney operates today. As Edward Coke observed, attorney "signifies one that is set in the turne, stead, or place of another." *Coke on Littleton*, fol. 128a.

Along with the role of the "attorney" there was the ancient idea of the "counselor." This also derived from an old French term, "*conseiller*," and ultimately came from the Latin "*consilium*" (referring to the giving of "advice" or "counsel"). This term also appeared very early, usually in reference to the King's advisors who were learned in the law. These he would consult ("*pur conseiller*") in legal matters. Originally, such learned advisors were available in both a public and private capacity, but by the twelfth century a clear distinction was developing between "counselors" to the Crown, who increasingly acted as judges in disputes, and "counselors" to private persons, who acted as "attorneys." After the development of the centralized Norman courts in the thirteenth century, the "justicars" to the Crown were a well defined elite group. This division between the function of the private representative, the "attorney," and the representative of the state, the "judge," still persists today.

It is no accident, therefore, that our two oldest models of legal professionalism, the "counselor" and the "attorney," have Norman French names. They were products of the new Norman-Angevin bureaucracy and court systems. Although the function of legal advisor and legal advocate clearly go back to the "Law Rock" of the Anglo-Saxons, as does the word "law" in "lawyer" itself, the Normans brought an entirely new dimension of training and expertise. They introduced the idea of the "professional," the judge or advocate who was more than just a learned and talented amateur, rather one who had a permanent identity and business with the law. As early as the treatise *Glanvill* (*circa* 1187 A.D.), the word "attorney" appears to be used in a way that implies a professional representative, not just a kinsman or a volunteer to stand in "your shoes." See *Materials, infra*. This coincided with the evolution of a formulary system and, indeed, *Glanvill* is basically a collection of legal forms, clearly designed for use by such a practitioner. By the time of *Bracton* (*circa* 1236 A.D.), there was a clearly understood office of royal "justicar." Indeed, *Bracton's* purpose was to instruct "the unwise and unlearned who ascend the judgment seat before they have learned the laws." The evolving formulary system, the growing central royal courts and assize system, and the sophisticated new modes of trial and remedies, including Henry II's possessory assizes, all required experts to function properly.

As we have seen, the reign of Edward I brought even more sophistication, including the major statutes of *De Donis* and *Quia Emptores*. The complexity of these statutes—and the list of abuses set out in their prologues—testified to a growing class of legal professionals. By 1292, the professional judges of the royal courts began to take responsibility for "lawful and ready learners" who "shall attend the court, enter into a business, and no other."[1] Eventually, lawyers trained directly by the royal courts to be advocates in these courts became known as "barristers," because they could plead at the "bar" of the court. The term first appears in 1455, but the idea of a litigation specialist directly under the supervision of the royal judges was, as we have seen, much older. Not surprisingly, it became customary to choose royal judges from the ranks of these "barrister" specialists.

Another distinct group continued in the "attorney" tradition of managing their client's affairs day to day. They also became regulated directly by the bench and were subject to professional oaths, but their close association with their clients created a contrast with the barrier elite, who were more identified with the courts themselves. Eventually, the attorneys became known as "solicitors," and no client could employ a barrister directly, but only through a solicitor. This "bifurcated" legal profession, split between barristers and solicitors, still exists in England. It reflects a division of legal skills many centuries old.

It originally represented more. Younger sons disinherited by primogeniture needed a way to make a living, but trade was beneath them. The "honorable" professions were three: the Church, the Army, and the Bar, to which was later added colonial governance. The "barrister class" reflected a social aristocracy, while the busy solicitors became a symbol of middle class advancement. When I studied law in England in the 1960s, these class distinctions still persisted. Even today, it is considered rude to discuss legal fees directly with a barrister, rather than the barrister's "clerk."

Above the barristers was an even older class, dating from at least the fourteenth century. These "serjeants at law" had a monopoly in the Common Pleas, and—until the

---

1. In 1292, the following royal writ [*Rot. Parl.* I, 84] was sent to the Common Pleas: "Concerning attorneys and learners ('apprentices') the lord King enjoined Mettingham and his fellows to provide and ordain at their discretion a certain number, from every country, of the better, worthier and more promising students..., and that those so chosen should follow the court and take part in its business; and no others."

See the discussion at T.F.T. Plucknett, *A Concise History of the Common Law, supra*, 217–218.

sixteenth century—were the exclusive source of new royal judges. With their character-istic hoods and "coifs," or head coverings, serjeants at law were certainly an admired elite, "leaders of the bar by natural, judicial, and royal selection."[2] Perhaps their greatest importance was as a "bridge" between the judiciary and the private advocates. In other legal culture, such as that of Germany and France, the private bar and the judiciary came to be trained separately, and were really different professions. It is of great impor-tance, even today, that a different tradition arose in England, and spread to all common law countries. Serjeants at law not only represented private clients, but took on royal commissions as assize judges when there was a shortage of judicial labor.

Chaucer left us a wonderful picture of this elite professional in "The Prologue" to *Canterbury Tales* (*circa* 1390 A.D.). Chaucer's serjeant at law "often had been justice of Assize, by letters patent, and in full commission," and "[h]is fame and learning and his high positions, had won him many a robe and many a fee." But Chaucer had it in for this pompous lawyer. "Discreet he was, a man to reverence, *or so he seemed*, his sayings were so wise ... Nowhere there was so busy a man as he; *But he was less busy than he seemed to be*." Busy or not, the serjeants gradually declined in influence, and became ex-tinct in 1921. Today their memory survives in American law schools through an hon-orary society, the "Order of the Coif."

Even today, the dominant norm of the legal profession reflects this past. Although there is no bifurcated bar in America, the division between litigation and business spe-cialties certainly persists—as does the practice of choosing new judges primarily from the ranks of experienced litigators. Perhaps most important, the "attorney" ideal of "stepping in the shoes" of your client for legal purposes—with its associated values of loyalty and confidentiality—dominates the American profession. But this "attorney" role also continues to be checked by the "counselor" role of cautious advice and by "offi-cer of the court" duties to the supervising courts of the jurisdiction, and to the justice system generally.

B. Professional Education: The Inns of Court

There is one additional "professional" norm besides loyalty to the client and to the court. That norm is loyalty to the profession itself as a guild with some very pronounced ethical and political values. The "legal" guild has always defined itself by its special edu-cation. This was first achieved in England by the Inns of Court.

The earliest legal study in England was associated with the ancient Universities of Oxford and Cambridge, where teachers taught Roman law as early as 1149 A.D. As seen before, canon law was also taught in the universities before the suppression by Henry VIII. But the common law of the royal courts was not a university subject until the eigh-teenth century and Blackstone's lectures. So the model of legal education so familiar to us today, the university law school, had very little to do with the common law for nearly six centuries.

One of the major reasons for this extraordinary fact was the Inns of Court. Located conveniently in London, between the law courts at Westminster and the commercial districts of the city proper, this center of legal education combined the characteristics of a powerful trade guild with that of a university. All common law barristers, serjeants, and judges were "graduates" and members. As an Elizabethan observer remarked, the Inns of Court were "A whole university ... of students, practices or pleaders, and judges

---

2. J.H. Baker, *An Introduction to English Legal History* (3d ed., London, 1990), *supra*, 180.

of the laws of this realm, not living of common stipends, as in other universities ... but of their own private maintenance ... for that the younger sort are either gentlemen, or the sons of gentlemen, or of other most wealthy persons ..."[3] By 1600, one of the distinctions between a barrister or a serjeant and a plain "attorney" was that the former were trained in the Inns of Court, and—increasingly—the latter were barred from the premises. As mentioned before, this legal elite was an acceptable occupation for gentry—particularly the younger sons disinherited by primogeniture—and the distinction between serjeants and barristers, as opposed to attorneys or "solicitors," became one of function reinforced by class.

The early history of the Inns is still somewhat mysterious. The name, "inns," probably comes from the hospices that filled western London for the benefit of government officials, supplicants, agents and, during term time, lawyers and clients. By 1350 some of these hospices had hit on the idea of housing apprentices at law, perhaps the apprentices mentioned in Edward I's royal writ of 1292 as under the supervision of the courts. This provided tenants for the "slack" periods when the courts were out of session, and also business for experienced lawyers at these slow times—as teachers and supervisors. Some of the students stayed in the large homes of prominent lawyers, or occupied the under-utilized city mansions of nobles who rarely come to London.[4] Other students stayed in the houses of Chancery clerks, which became collectively known as "Inns of Chancery," although there was no direct connection with the Court of Chancery itself. Perhaps these students learned the drafting of legal writs from these clerks, a valuable skill for a common lawyer.

By 1400, four "inns" began to establish a dominant position. Two were named from nobles who either owned or sponsored the original houses: "Gray's Inn," a house of the Lords Grey, and "Lincoln's Inn," which either was named for Henry de Lacy, Earl of Lincoln, or Thomas de Lincoln, a prominent serjeant at law.[5] Two others were founded in the defunct London premises of the powerful Knights Templar, and became known as "Middle Temple" and "Inner Temple." By 1450, these four "inns" were professional schools, with the exclusive right to train common law barristers and serjeants, and the Inns of Chancery—of which there were nine or more—became "feeders," or schools for young students who wished to enter one of the four Inns of Court. Finally, for the very elite who became serjeants, there were two "Serjeant's Inns," although these were more like small clubs than educational institutions. Over time, the Inns of Chancery diminished and disappeared, and the Serjeant's Inns died in that order at the end of the 19th century. The four Inns of Court, however, not only remain, but are among the wealthiest and most powerful institutions in London. Although they have now coordinated their educational and regulatory functions into the Consolidated Inns of Court, they are still four separate entities, with magnificent libraries, gardens, dining halls, and common rooms. Three, the Inner and Middle Temple and Lincoln's Inn, also house the

---

3. This was John Stow. See Alan Harding, *A Social History of English Law* (London, 1960) 185–186.

4. See J.H. Baker, "Introduction," *Readings and Moots at the Inns of Court in the Fifteenth Century*, vol. 2 (eds. S.E. Thorne, J.H. Baker) (London, 1990), Selden Society vol. 105, xxv–xxxi; Samuel E. Thorne "The Early History of the Inns of Court," (1959) 50 *Graya* 79–96, reprinted S.E. Thorne, *Essays in English Legal History* (1985) 137–154.

5. Baker believes it was the latter, despite tradition favoring the Earl. See Baker, *Introduction, supra*, 183.

"chambers," or offices, of most practicing London barristers. (The fourth, Gray's Inn, is largely filled with solicitor's offices.) Despite heavy bomb damage during the war, many sixteenth and seventeenth-century features survive.[6]

In the sixteenth and seventeenth centuries, the Inns of Court not only trained young lawyers, but were centers of political influence, literature, and even art. Some of Shakespeare's plays were first performed in the dining halls of Gray's Inn and Middle Temple, and Francis Bacon composed poetry for magnificent "masques," which featured lovely costumes and stage settings—and attracted the grandest people in the kingdom, including the sovereign personally.[7] The quadrangles were familiar to Ben Johnson, Oliver Goldsmith and Charles Dickens alike, and former students routinely occupied the greatest political positions in the land.

One of our best contemporary pictures of this extraordinary "legal university" comes from Sir John Fortescue (?1394–?1476). Fortescue became Chief Justice of the King's Bench in 1442, but followed the exiled House of Lancaster to France, where he was a tutor to Edward, Prince of Wales. In exile, he apparently had the office of Lord Chancellor to the Lancastrian monarchs. See Illustration 9-5. Fortescue's efforts to explain to the Prince differences between the French and English legal system resulted in a little book, *De laudibus legum angliae*, written about 1470, and first printed in 1545–46.[8] It is very significant that, along with trial by jury, precedent justice, and lack of torture, Fortescue emphasized the importance of the professional training of lawyers in the independent Inns of Court.

Of course, the mode of legal training changed across the centuries. In the sixteenth century, promising students like Thomas More would either go directly into the Inns of Chancery, at age fifteen or less, or would spend a few years at Oxford and Cambridge, and then enroll. After about two or three years in the Inns of Chancery, one would enter one of the four Inns of Court as a student. After three or four years, the student would be admitted as "utter barrister," and by six or seven years, at about age twenty-two or twenty-three, could be "called to the bar."[9]

The nature of legal education within the Inns has only recently received careful study.[10] Its three most important characteristics certainly make an interesting contrast with modern legal education. First, the faculty were almost exclusively practicing lawyers. They had been trained as common lawyers themselves through the same sys-

---

6. Parts of two "Inns of Chancery" also can still be seen, Barnard's Inn and Staples Inn. The latter, close to Gray's Inn on High Holborn, has been heavily, but beautifully, restored, and today houses the Society of Actuaries.

7. See Daniel R. Coquillette, *Francis Bacon* (Edinburgh, 1992), *supra*, 31–35.

8. See S.B. Chrimes, "General Preface," *Sir John Fortescue. De Laudibus Legum Angliae* (Cambridge, 1942), ix–liii.

9. Francis Bacon (1561–1626) was a good example of a very bright young man on a "fast track." He matriculated at Trinity College, Cambridge, at age 12 (1573), left Trinity at age 14 (1575) and was admitted at Gray's Inn, Inns of Court, at age 15 (1576). (By this time, the Inns of Chancery were in abeyance. A century earlier, they might have substituted for Cambridge.) At age 21 (1582), he was admitted "utter barrister," and by age 25 (1586) he was made "bencher" at Gray's Inn, and began reading to students. In 1594, at age 33, he reached the highest standard levels within the bar, being called "within the bar" and named "Queen's Counsel, Extraordinary" at age 34 (1595), a position at least equivalent to serjeant in precedence. By 1607, at age 46, he was Solicitor General; at age 52 (1613) he was Attorney General, and at age 57 (1618), he was finally appointed Lord Chancellor. By 1621 (age 60), he was impeached, and disgraced. Altogether, the entire process of "higher" education leading to a professional law certification was about seven to eight years, not that far from the typical American "path" through the B.A. to the J.D., although in the past, the process started at an earlier age.

10. See, for example, J.H. Baker, "Introduction" to *Readings and Moots at the Inns of Court in the Fifteenth Century* (ed. S.E. Thorne, J.H. Baker, London, 1990) vol. II, Selden Society, vol. 105.

tem. Providing "readings" on statutes and supervising the exercises within the Inn were part of the duties of those seeking advancement from barrister to benches. The benchers were also expected to sit on "the bench" at moot court exercises, and to critique the student participants.

The second important characteristic of this educational system was the required exercises, the "moots," or public pleading exercises, and the "bolts," similar exercises held in private. These combined learning by rote and "learning by doing," under close personal supervision. The moots and bolts encouraged "thinking on your feet" and the kind of quick ingenuity that was the essence of the pleader's skill. This skill remains important to litigators today.

The final characteristic was the most important. The Inns were a compulsory society, where keeping commons with your colleagues was required. To this day eating a substantial number of dinners at your Inn of Court is required to be called to the bar. I would have regarded this compulsory collegiality as trivial had I not undergone it myself for over three years at Gray's Inn. I can still recall the moots argued in Hall, after dinner, before demanding benchers. Then there were "name games," such as the compulsory toasts, naming all in the "messes" below and above at the table. Missing a name resulted in a "fine" of a bottle of port. And then there were the debates, where quick minds were praised, and the reflective, but awkward, student assisted. To say this "society" built a sense of professional identity and value was certainly true, even in the more democratic and diverse days of 1966–1969. There is every evidence that in the sixteenth century this was true with a vengeance, a fact that had both juristic and political consequences. Even today, the "cultural" and "social" values of legal education are more significant than we like to acknowledge, and there is even an "American Inns of Court" organization which seeks to restore some of the advantages of past centuries.

After the English Civil War, the educational function of the Inns deteriorated. Only recently has the Consolidated Inns of Court revived serious educational programs. Today, most students at the Inns of Court will also get university degrees. As we have seen, this was not uncommon, even in the fifteenth and sixteenth centuries. More remarkable, however, to an American law student is the fact that many of those students will not take a university law degree, but will study "greats" (classics), "P.P.E." (politics, philosophy, and economics) or English literature. Law, likewise, is taught routinely as an undergraduate degree, and many with this degree do not become professional lawyers at all. While many young English barristers today do have university law degrees, the technical separation between university legal study and professional legal qualification continues.

It is important to emphasize the historical importance of this separation. As Baker has observed,

> "The strength and unity of this profession explain how the reasoning of a small group of men in Westminster Hall grew into one of the world's two greatest systems of law. For this peculiarly English professional structure was wholly independent of the university law faculties, where only Canon law and Roman Civil law were taught, and this factor as much as any other ensured the autonomous character of English law and its isolation from the influence of Continental jurisprudence."[11]

---

11. Baker, *Introduction, supra,* 177.

It could be argued that legal education in America, with powerful university law faculties as early as the mid-nineteenth century, presents a different picture. In fact, the separation of the legal curriculum from the humanities, which isolates legal study in graduate schools, has created a very similar situation. Law is taught as a professional subject, primarily for future practitioners. The study is not well integrated with economics, philosophy, politics, history, or cultural comparative work. The result is a highly provincial approach to most legal problems, and a lack of knowledge of the comparative or international context. Interestingly enough, American law schools are accredited by a professional organization of lawyers, the American Bar Association, as well as by an academic group, the American Association of Law Schools. Such accreditation is a delegated power of the state supreme courts, which largely regulate the bar. Thus, ultimate supervision by the practicing bench and bar, similar to that of the Inns of Court, has persisted in most American states. This "professionalism" of legal education in America is directly related to attitudes that can be traced back to the Inns of Court themselves.[12]

Who Should Make the Rules Governing Conduct of Lawyers in Federal Matters

Andrew L. Kaufman*
(The 2000 McGlinchey Lecture), 75 *Tulane Law Review* 149 (2000)

* * *

I hope that Dermot McGlinchey would be pleased by my choice of topic. It concerns fundamental issues about the conduct of lawyers, especially lawyers engaged in trial practice. It is a drama involving a pressing issue of federalism that is not yet well known in the profession. The subject of the drama is the governing rules of professional conduct. The problem begins with the federal courts, but the solution chosen could control the rules in the state courts as well. Here is the cast of characters: first, the federal judiciary, represented by the 94 federal district courts of the United States, the Judicial Conference of the United States, its Committee on Rules of Practice and Procedure, and its Subcommittee on Attorney Conduct, with representation from all the major committees of the Judicial Conference; second, the federal executive, represented by the Department of Justice (DOJ); third, the federal legislature which is, of course, the Congress of the United States; fourth, the state judiciaries, in their role as lawmakers and law enforcers in the field of attorney conduct, represented by the Conference of Chief Justices, an organization—as its name suggests—of the state court chief justices; and finally, the private bar, currently represented by the American Bar Association (ABA). Before the drama is over, the private bar will perhaps also be represented by local bar associations in every state, most of which might be expected to rally to the support of the state judiciaries, but they are only just beginning to wake up to the problem.

---

12. See Daniel R. Coquillette, "Introduction: The 'Countenance of Authorite'" in *Law in Colonial Massachusetts* (eds. Coquillette, Brink, Menand, Boston, 1984) xxvi–lxii, 359–418.

* Charles Stebbins Fairchild Professor of Law, Harvard University. At the outset, I should disclose that I have acted as unpaid advisor to a subcommittee of the Conference of Chief Justices in connection with the work of the Subcommittee on Attorney Conduct of the Committee on Rules of Practice and Procedure of the Judicial Conference of the United States. Its work is the main topic of this Lecture. I do not speak for the Conference of Chief Justices or its subcommittee, and the views expressed herein are mine alone. This Lecture was delivered as the McGlinchey Lecture at Tulane Law School on April 6, 2000. I have not altered the lecture style except to add some identifying footnotes. [Reproduced with the kind permission of Professor Kaufman and the *Tulane Law Review*.]

Our drama arises from the wide disparity in the stated rules that govern the professional responsibilities of lawyers in the 94 federal district courts of the United States. A study conducted in 1995 by the Subcommittee on Rules of Attorney Conduct disclosed the disarray at the federal district court level: Forty-eight districts, including Louisiana's three federal districts, have adopted state court rules based on, but not identical to, the ABA's 1983 Model Rules of Professional Conduct; twelve districts have adopted state rules based on, but not identical to, the ABA's 1969 Model Code of Professional Responsibility; ten districts have adopted the ABA's Model Code or Model Rules directly and not their respective state's amended version; ten districts have adopted simultaneously both an ABA model and their own state's rules; eleven districts have not adopted any rule, although some of those districts have confusing standing orders about the district's policy; two of California's four federal districts have adopted the California Rules of Professional Conduct and the other two have adopted both the state rules and the ABA Model Code; and the Northern District of Illinois has adopted its own version of the ABA Model Rules, which is very different from both the ABA model and the Illinois Supreme Court's rules.[1]

The result is that the standards of attorney conduct in the federal courts are not uniform horizontally across the federal system and are uniform vertically within the federal and state systems in some jurisdictions but not in others. Thus, for federal government attorneys who practice in federal courts across the country, the rules of professional conduct that govern their daily lives may change—and change substantially—as they cross state lines. On the other hand, in some states, the rules for private attorneys with both a state and a federal practice may change not only as they cross the street to go from one courthouse to another, but also as they sit in their offices putting down one transaction folder and picking up another. In light of the above inconsistencies, the Subcommittee on Attorney Conduct must decide whether to recommend horizontal or vertical conformity, some mixture of the two, or just to leave the entire problem alone, on the theory that any change may make the situation even worse.

How have lawyers been able to live such a schizophrenic existence for so long? The answer is related to the answer to another question: Why was there so little substantive professional responsibility law in this country until the second half of the twentieth century, when the standards of professional responsibility had been discussed for at least the previous century? The answer is that until those issues became the subject of litigation, and therefore came to have bite, they were not much noticed. The conflicting rules of professional responsibility within the federal system and between the state and federal systems also went unnoticed. The initial bite did not arise from conflicting rules of federal and state conduct. It arose from a federal court decision applying a state rule to the criminal investigatory activity of the DOJ.

This part of the drama is the story of Rule 4.2 of the Model Rules of Professional Conduct, which, in one version or another, is part of the attorney conduct rules in almost every state and federal court in the United States. Rule 4.2 forbids a lawyer from communicating with an adverse party and many of the employees of an adverse organization, known to be represented by counsel, without the consent of that counsel.[2] The rule is controversial in civil litigation between private parties. But in *United States v.*

---

1. Daniel R. Coquillette, *Report on Local Rules Regulating Attorney Conduct in the Federal Courts* (July 5, 1995), *in* Working Papers of the Committee on the Rules of Practice and Procedure, Special Studies of Federal Rules Governing Attorney Conduct 3–6 (1997).

2. Model Rules of Prof'l Conduct R. 4.2 (1998).

Hammad, the Court of Appeals for the Second Circuit dealt with the applicability of the anticontact rule to federal prosecutors in a criminal setting.[3] In *Hammad*, a prosecutor supplied an informant with a fictitious subpoena and then "wired" him and recorded his conversation with the defendant, knowing that the defendant was represented by counsel.[4] The Second Circuit agreed with the district court that the anticontact rule applied at the investigation stage.[5] While the court regarded the legitimate use of informants as falling within the "authorized by law" exception to the anticontact rule, it held that the use of a counterfeit grand jury subpoena with a false signature of the clerk of the court was egregious misconduct, making the informant the "alter ego" of the prosecutor.[6] Hence, the court found that the prosecutor had violated the anticontact rule. The court held that suppression of evidence would be an appropriate remedy for an anticontact rule violation, but it reversed the suppression in *Hammad* itself because the law had previously been so unsettled.[7] The court did announce a general rule that, absent egregious misconduct, the use of informants in preindictment, noncustodial situations would usually not constitute a violation of the anticontact rule.[8] But *Hammad* upset government counsel a great deal because it held that the anticontact rule applied to criminal investigations even in the preindictment stage and that, at least in some instances, investigative conduct by nonlawyers could be imputed to a government lawyer for purposes of the anticontact rule.

The DOJ has argued that the application of the anticontact rule to its investigative efforts hampers law enforcement efforts greatly, especially when applied to prearrest investigations. It responded to *Hammad* and other similar cases with a variety of efforts to prevent the application of the anticontact rule to its lawyers. The most far-reaching effort began in 1989 when Attorney General Richard Thornburgh issued a memorandum declaring that DOJ lawyers were exempt from both state and federal anticontact rules.[9] This memorandum provoked considerable controversy. Nevertheless, even with a change in administration, the DOJ maintained its course and promulgated its own regulations, known as the Reno Rules, that govern the circumstances under which its attorneys may contact represented persons and parties.[10]

The United States Court of Appeals for the Eighth Circuit considered the validity of the Reno Rules in *United States ex rel. O'Keefe v. McDonnell Douglas Corp.*[11] The Conference of Chief Justices filed a brief as amicus curiae urging that the DOJ lacked authority to preempt the state rules of professional responsibility.[12] The Eighth Circuit agreed, holding that the DOJ had no such authority.[13] The court enjoined DOJ lawyers from violating the anticontact provisions embodied in the local federal district court rules, which mirrored the relevant state court rules of professional conduct.[14]

---

3. 846 F.2d 854, *reh'g denied*, 855 F.2d 36, *opinion revised by* 858 F.2d 834 (2d Cir. 1988).
4. *See id.* at 836.
5. *See id.* at 840.
6. *Id.*
7. *Id.* at 840–42.
8. *Id.* at 840.
9. Memorandum from Richard Thornburgh, United States Attorney General, to Justice Department Litigators (June 8, 1989) (*reprinted in In re Doe*, 801 F. Supp 478, 489–93 (D.N.M. 1992)).
10. Ethical Standards for Attorneys for the Government, 28 C.F.R. pt. 77 (1999).
11. 132 F.3d 1252, 1253–58 (8th Cir. 1998).
12. *See id.* at 1254.
13. *Id.* at 1257.
14. *See id.*

The battle over Rule 4.2 has become entangled in the effort of the Judicial Conference of the United States to impose some order on the wildly inconsistent local rules of the federal district courts, especially those pertaining to lawyers. That effort, which I described at the beginning of this Lecture, immediately ran up against both the issue of what kind of order should be imposed and the more specific issue of what to do about Rule 4.2. Five model solutions to the diversity of district court attorney conduct rules have been suggested, ranging from Model 1 at one extreme, which would change nothing, to Model 5 at the other extreme, which would establish a complete set of federal rules of professional conduct. Between these extremes are three other proposed models. One is Model 2, which proposes so-called "dynamic conformity" of federal and state rules of professional responsibility. Dynamic conformity is the name given to federal court rules for attorney conduct that adopt not only state rules currently in force in their respective states but also any subsequent state amendments to those rules. That is the solution that has been adopted by two of the three federal district courts in Louisiana.[15]

In addition to those already discussed, two other models have been suggested so far: Model 3, which adopts dynamic conformity with state rules in some matters, but a federal solution with respect to the professional responsibility issues that most often arise in federal courts; and Model 4, which endorses dynamic conformity combined with control by the federal courts over their own procedure, leaving open the possibility of future specialized rules of professional conduct in particular situations, such as bankruptcy, or matters in which federal government lawyers are involved.

The Judicial Conference's Subcommittee on Attorney Conduct produced a tentative discussion document adopting the hybrid solution of Model 3, with some dynamic conformity and some federal rules.[16] One major problem with the Model 3 solution was that it promised to generate confusion for lawyers who dealt with matters that had both state and federal ramifications, because those attorneys would be faced with conflicting federal and state rules of conduct.[17] The Model 3 proposal met with strong criticism and, for the moment, has disappeared from the scene.[18]

While the Subcommittee was considering what to do next, two developments complicated matters further. First, the Conference of Chief Justices and the DOJ negotiated concerning a possible revision of Rule 4.2 to recommend to the states.[19] The purpose was to ease the concerns of both the DOJ and state and local prosecutors faced with similar problems arising out of application of the anticontact rule. The ABA was also considering Rule 4.2 as part of its Ethics 2000 Project, the current revision of the Model Rules of Professional Conduct being prepared for recommendation to the states.[20] ABA representatives, however, were not part of the discussions between the Conference on Chief Justices and the DOJ. At a point when agreement seemed near, the Chief Justices

---

15. E.D. La. Local Rule 83.2.4; W.D. La. Local Rule 83.2.4.

16. Note, *Uniform Rules of Federal Attorney Conduct: A Flawed Proposal*, 111 Harv. L. Rev. 2063, 2073 (1998).

17. *See id.* at 2079.

18. *See id.* at 2078–80.

19. *Chief Justices May Consider Proposal to Revise Rule* 4.2, 13 ABA/BNA Law. Manual Prof'l Conduct 427, 427–29 (1997) [hereinafter *Chief Justices*].

20. American Bar Association, Ethics 2000 Project, *at* http://www.abanet.org/cpr/ethics2k.html (last visited Aug. 25, 2000).

and the DOJ made their proposed revisions to Rule 4.2 public.[21] Various ABA representatives expressed opposition to those revisions, and, as a result, the Conference on Chief Justices and the DOJ halted talks.[22] Subsequently, the ABA's Standing Committee on Ethics and Professional Responsibility and the Ethics 2000 Commission proposed its own version of a changed Rule 4.2, but more recently, the Commission has decided that the text of Rule 4.2 does not need any change at all insofar as it applies to government prosecutors.[23] The DOJ is undoubtedly unhappy with that outcome, although the change in Comment 6 to Rule 4.2, removing the restriction against communicating with persons whose statement may constitute an admission on the part of the organization, allows conversation with some employees that a cautious government lawyer might avoid under the current Comment to Model Rule 4.2.[24]

Second, in 1998, the drama unfolded even further with the entry of another major actor. Quite precipitously, Congress made an appearance on stage, enacting the so-called McDade Amendment.[25] The statute was named for its sponsor, Congressman Joseph McDade, whom the DOJ once prosecuted unsuccessfully for campaign donation fraud. The McDade Amendment makes government attorneys "subject to State laws and rules, and local Federal court rules, governing attorneys in each State where such attorney engages in that attorney's duties, to the same extent and in the same manner as other attorneys in that State."[26] It thus puts the federal legislature into the attorney conduct regulation business in a big way. However, the statute is quite ambiguous, to put it mildly, and has created enormous problems not only of interpretation but also of defining the limits of legislative, judicial, and executive authority at the federal and state levels.[27] Not the least of these problems is that the statute subjects government attorneys to both state laws and rules and federal court rules without explaining how to reconcile these provisions when they conflict.[28]

Some who have considered the confusion regarding the rules of attorney conduct believe that the federal system itself is the problem, and that the appropriate solution would be for Congress to enact a single set of rules of attorney conduct applicable to all courts, both state and federal.[29] Others, perhaps thinking that the Commerce Clause

---

21. *Chief Justices, supra* note 19, at 427–28.

22. *ABA Ethics Groups Recommend Changes to Model Rules on Ex Parte Communications*, 15 ABA/BNA Law. Manual Prof'l Conduct 347, 347–50 (1999); *Chief Justices Defer Vote on Rule 4.2 to Allow More Time for Public Comment*, 14 ABA/BNA Law. Manual Prof'l Conduct 20, 20 (1998); *Uncertainties Dog Efforts to Reform Rule on Contacts with Represented Persons*, 14 ABA/BNA Law. Manual Prof'l Conduct 264, 264–68 (1998); *Chief Justices, Citing Lack of Consensus, Put Off Vote on Proposal for New Rule 4.2*, 14 ABA/BNA Law. Manual Prof'l Conduct 459, 459 (1998).

23. American Bar Association, Ethics 2000 Commission, Model Rule 4.2—Reporter's Explanation of Changes (Feb. 21, 2000), *available at* http:// www.abanet.org/cpr/rule42memo.html (last visited Aug. 25, 2000).

24. *See id.*

25. 28 U.S.C. § 530B(a) (Supp. IV 1998).

26. *Id.*

27. *See* Fred C. Zacharias & Bruce A. Green, *The Uniqueness of Federal Prosecutors*, 88 Geo. L.J. 207, 245–59 (2000) (analyzing the McDade Amendment and evaluating the problems with the rules governing attorney conduct in the federal courts).

28. *See id.* at 247–59 (discussing who has the power to regulate attorney conduct and highlighting the problem that no single set of rules has clear preemptory authority).

29. *See* Linda S. Mullenix, *Multiforum Federal Practice: Ethics and Erie*, 9 Geo. J. Legal Ethics 89, 126–27 (1995) (discussing the difficulty that attorneys have ascertaining the appropriate standards of professional conduct); Fred C. Zacharias, *Federalizing Legal Ethics*, 73 Tex. L. Rev. 335, 379–80

might not sustain such a thoroughgoing solution, believe that if uniform federal rules of attorney conduct were enacted, they would rather quickly supersede state rules at the demand of lawyers who would not wish to be subject to both state and federal attorney conduct rules. Such a solution might well please some national law firms, some national accounting firms who want to sweep away obstacles to their practice of law, perhaps the DOJ, and also theorists who like neat solutions.

I do not have the time here to do much more than state that I do not like the solution of Congress enacting a single set of rules for both state and federal courts. I happen to like our federal system for its diffusion of power. Of course there are many problems in our society today that demand national solutions at the hands of Congress. I do not think that the conduct of attorneys all over the country is one of them. I do not think that legislators are the preferred regulators of lawyers' conduct. Another branch of government, the judiciary, has more experience with the problems of lawyer conduct, and has traditionally been the ultimate regulator through the adoption and enforcement of the rules. Without pushing the issue of where, as a matter of the law of federal and state division and separation of power, the final authority ought to be constitutionally located, historically legislatures and judiciaries have avoided confrontation and, by and large, legislatures have left attorney conduct to the judiciary. Admittedly, when the judiciary fails to solve a major problem itself, and important interests are affected, then the temptation arises for the legislature to intervene. The result can be disastrous, particularly if the legislation is ill-considered, as was the case with the McDade Amendment.

There is yet another aspect to the problem. As I have mentioned, for the last several years the ABA has been engaged in its Ethics 2000 Project, revising its Model Rules of Professional Conduct for recommendation to the states.[30] In my view, that very process is in need of revision. During the twentieth century, the ABA several times performed the very useful task of revising the professional rules for consideration by the various state and federal rulemaking authorities.[31] There was a vacuum of power. We should be grateful that the ABA stepped in to do the job, for otherwise it might not have been done at all. The state courts, which have been the principal legislators of the professional rules, have not had the apparatus, or perhaps even the will, to undertake the arduous task of revision. They have been content to let the ABA do it.

This is not the occasion to analyze all the reasons why the ABA chose to involve itself in revising the professional rules of conduct.[32] It is enough to say that it did so. But each successive revision has become more and more contentious. Lawyers and some of their clients have come to realize that, as with some of the major projects of the American Law Institute, a good deal is at stake for both lawyers and clients in the formulation of ethics rules, and that a great deal of law can be put in near final form out of the public eye in a forum where many affected interests are not even formally represented.[33] While it is true that the ABA only recommends rules—it does not enact them—the ABA knows what every good lawyer knows: the one who does the first draft of a document

---

(1994) (discussing the growing need for federal codification of professional standards due to the increasing nationalization of legal practice).

30. *See* American Bar Association, *supra* note 20, *at* http:// www.abanet.org/cpr/ethics2k.html.

31. *See* Deborah L. Rhode, *Why the ABA Bothers: A Functional Perspective on Professional Codes*, 59 Tex L. Rev. 689, 693 (1981).

32. For one attempt at answering that question, *see id.* at 689–721.

33. *Id.* at 694.

usually sets the parameters of the discussion. Whether or not the ABA used to be more nonpartisan, more impartial when it came to drafting professional rules, the fact is that in today's ABA, as in the American Law Institute, it does not seem that lawyers, or at least many lawyers, can be counted on to leave their clients behind them at the door. Their clients' interests tend to be in the room with them.

What does that say for the process of professional rulemaking in both the federal and state systems? Change is in the air, and more change is called for. When the ABA recommended the Model Code of Professional Conduct to the states in 1969, state courts tended to adopt the proposals unchanged in most respects. When the ABA recommended the Model Rules of Professional Responsibility in 1980, the state courts scrutinized the proposals more closely. Few, if any, states adopted the 1980 proposals unchanged, and a majority of states have rejected the critical proposals on confidentiality. Indeed, the longer particular states waited, the more changes they made. My own state, Massachusetts, changed a majority of the provisions, and then rewrote the Comments substantially.[34] The downside of this heightened scrutiny by individual state courts is that the hoped-for uniformity among the states has not been accomplished. The upside, however, is that this history demonstrates that many state courts have begun to take seriously their legislative responsibility regarding the governing rules of attorney conduct. The state courts' realization of what is at stake, and perhaps, their growing awareness that interest group battles within the ABA have helped shape the outcomes of its debates, have led them to reclaim, to some extent, their lawmaking power from the ABA.

I suggest that they do more. Indeed, the very fact that the current major revision of the governing rules of attorney conduct is being performed once again by the ABA demonstrates the need for judges to consider their role in the process. It is true that the ABA is aware of its volunteer status in the rulemaking process. It has sought to be more inclusive of the judiciary by appointing a state judge as chair and a federal judge as a member of its Ethics 2000 project.[35] But the ABA is still running the show, and nothing will be recommended without the approval of the ABA House of Delegates.[36] I think that the time has come for the judiciary to run the show, just as the Judicial Conference controls the process of federal court rulemaking, with the ABA and other groups playing important roles as consultants.

The state courts now have their own administrative structure. The Conference of Chief Justices has been established, and it has begun to be heard on a variety of important issues involving the country's judiciary. It has its own administrative support in the Center for State Courts.[37] At the moment, however, those organizations do not have the funding or the administrative capacity to play the role in the life of the state judiciaries that the Federal Judicial Center and the Judicial Conference of the United States play in the life of the federal judiciary. The latter two institutions have grown in recent years to make the federal judiciary an effective force, not just in managing judicial affairs, but also in dealing with the other two branches of the federal government. The state judici-

---

34. I should disclose that I was a member of the committee appointed by the Supreme Judicial Court of Massachusetts to make recommendations regarding adoption of the Model Rules.

35. E. Norman Veasey, Chief Justice of the Delaware Supreme Court, is chair of the Commission, and Judge Patrick Higginbotham of the United States Court of Appeals for the Fifth Circuit is a member.

36. American Bar Association Constitution and Bylaws §§ 6, 31 (2000).

37. National Center for State Courts, About the National Center for State Courts, *available at* http://www.ncsc.dni.us/About.html (last visited Sept. 20, 2000).

aries must find a way to function in a similar fashion, not only to enable them to deal effectively at home and vis-a-vis their federal counterparts, but also to help reclaim primary lawmaking authority from those private entities like the ABA that have moved into an existing vacuum of power and sought, in important ways, to exercise state judicial authority.

Indeed, in my view, much of the confusion that currently exists with respect to the rules of attorney conduct in federal courts is an outgrowth of the current system of lawmaking regarding attorney conduct. There is an ongoing struggle for lawmaking power, and the failure of lawmakers themselves to take charge of the process has invited others—both private parties like the ABA, and other branches of government, like Congress—to intervene.

A key to the solution of the process problem is the will of the respective state judiciaries to organize themselves, to create the necessary structure, and then to energize it, in order to take greater control of the lawmaking process with regard to attorney conduct. If such a mechanism were developed, state judiciaries could be running the Ethics 2000 Project, perhaps with the ABA and other interested parties acting in an advisory capacity. In the twenty-first century it should become clear that a project like Ethics 2000 should be the state judiciaries' project, not the private bar's project.

Mobilization of the state judiciaries, however, is only a piece of the solution. The other piece of the solution relates to the issue with which I began—the rules of attorney professional conduct that govern in the federal courts. That there is an issue of horizontal versus vertical uniformity is one of the prices we pay for our federal system. Where the conduct of attorneys who practice in many different settings in tens of thousands of communities all across the country is at stake, I, for one, am willing to pay the price of vertical uniformity, at least as a starting point.

Those who want a national solution, imposed by Congress, the Judicial Conference, or the federal courts themselves through common law adjudication, argue forcefully that the growing nationalization and internationalization of legal practice is hampered by the multiplicity of different rules governing attorney conduct in different states.[38] But the great bulk of lawyers do not practice all over the country. Clients, with the advice of lawyers, deal with differences in substantive law throughout the country all the time. And so do ordinary people, for example, as we all do when we drive our cars from one state to another, and, indeed, from one community to another.

Local control and decentralization have their virtues, too. Local control over lawyers has been the tradition; it is ingrained in every aspect of the profession. We lawyers organize ourselves locally, by community and by state, because we think we can exert some influence over the operation of the profession. To take just one example, the discipline of lawyers is carried out locally, through a large administrative apparatus that interprets and enforces the state law of professional responsibility. I doubt that that apparatus would be ready, willing, or able to enforce a federal law of professional responsibility. For myself, I think someone would have to demonstrate empirically that the present system, which tolerates some substantive differences among state professional responsibil-

---

38. *See, e.g.*, Mullenix, *supra* note 29, at 126–27 (discussing the difficulty that attorneys have ascertaining the appropriate standards of professional conduct); Zacharias, *supra* note 29, at 379–80 (discussing the growing need for federal codification of professional standards due to the increasing nationalization of legal practice).

ity laws, has created so many serious problems that it needs to be altered in favor of a national solution.

If we can tolerate, at least for the time being, the current diversity in state professional responsibility law, then why not the current diversity among the federal district courts? There is some virtue in a national solution that attempts to remedy the current state of confusion in the local rules of those courts. One hears anecdotally that district courts sometimes deal with the confusion by simply ignoring their own rules when they prove troublesome. That does not seem like a wonderful solution. Even if the number of instances in which problems actually arise is small, the confusion is nevertheless troublesome because it means that lawyers who are trying to avoid trouble have no sure place even to begin looking for guidance. This may be one of those problems that isn't much of a problem when it is largely unnoticed, but becomes one just by reason of its discovery.

For me, the long-term solution begins with my instinct, which has no empirically proven basis, that there are many more private lawyers who practice in both the federal and state systems in their states than who practice in the federal system in many different states. If that is the case, then it seems that the better solution to the local federal rule problem begins with vertical uniformity between the federal and state courts in a given jurisdiction under the principle of dynamic conformity. In that fashion, most lawyers will not have to master two sets of professional rules, which will occasionally be conflicting and will therefore cause problems for lawyers in litigation and transaction matters that have both state and federal aspects.

Even the most ardent advocate of dynamic conformity recognizes that such a solution does not mean that federal courts surrender control of the operation of their courtrooms, nor does it threaten the well-established rule that matters of procedure are matters of federal law. Lawyers and especially academics may worry about the possibility of a lawyer being disciplined for conduct that is permitted or even required as a matter of federal procedural law. The line between matters of procedure and matters of professional responsibility may not be easy to draw and perhaps a common law development would be the preferable solution. Let me give one example by way of illustration. A lawyer undertakes a matter in apparent violation of the ethics rules governing conflicts of interest. In the midst of a federal trial, the violation is noticed and becomes the subject of a motion to disqualify. The court decides that the trial itself would not be tainted by any conflict, that the trial has proceeded very far, and that it would be a waste of judicial resources to interrupt it by disqualifying one of the participating lawyers. Motion denied. Should a state disciplinary agency be precluded or preempted from disciplining the lawyer if the conflict was egregious? I think not. The federal court did not adjudicate whether the lawyer committed a serious violation, or, indeed, *any* violation of the conflict of interest rules. It only decided that, as a matter of procedure, it would not disqualify the lawyer. Some courts reaching that result even say that the question of ethical violation, if any, should be adjudicated elsewhere.[39] The result should be different if the federal court had adjudicated the ethical violation question and concluded that there was none.

I have thus far not discussed the DOJ's concerns about the effect of certain interpretations of the anticontact rule on its law enforcement responsibilities. I believe that

---

39. *See* Bd. of Educ. v. Nyquist, 590 F.2d 1241, 1247–48 (2d Cir. 1979); Universal City Studios, Inc. v. Reimerdes, 98 F. Supp. 2d 449, 456 (S.D.N.Y. 2000).

those concerns are reasonable. I also understand the DOJ's belief that a national solution, achieved by its own rules, by congressional action, or by national federal judicial rules, is the most efficient way to alleviate its concerns. However, the DOJ's solution of making its own rules by memorandum or regulation has thus far failed in the courts, as the Eighth Circuit's recent decision indicates.[40] The solution of congressional action was turned against it in the McDade Amendment. Even if the DOJ succeeds in having the McDade Amendment repealed, and even if it persuades Congress to adopt its preferred solution, the lesson of the McDade Amendment is that one can lose everything with a national solution that is the product of hasty and ill-considered action. I think that a congressional solution is the worst idea I have heard. Congress simply does not have time to deal thoughtfully with all the nuances that need to be considered in adjusting the interests of clients, lawyers, and the system of justice and to keep adjusting them as problems appear. The danger with a congressional solution is that these delicate issues will be left to committee staffs and the lobbyists for the best financed or best organized interests.

That leaves the possibility of national rules of attorney conduct imposed by the federal judiciary for federal matters. Those are still a real possibility, especially for some special issues that are strong federal concerns, such as some of the rules for government lawyers and perhaps also some of the rules of bankruptcy practice. One problem with crafting rules for federal government lawyers, however, is that their work very often is performed in a context where there is a private lawyer adversary. To avoid the problem of having different professional rules apply to lawyers in a single transaction or litigation, federal professional rules would have to govern private lawyers too, thus imposing on private lawyers the potential of having two different sets of professional rules apply simultaneously in matters with state and federal ramifications.

A further question is whether the problems of DOJ lawyers, or federal lawyers generally, are unique, or whether state government lawyers face similar problems. DOJ lawyers are sometimes considered unique because, compared to state attorney general office lawyers, they work much more closely with investigating officers, and their work involves large complex litigation with nationwide implications.[41] But local prosecutors often work just as closely with police and face similar problems with interpretations of the anticontact rule. As far as nationwide activity is concerned, private law firms currently cope with issues similar to those encountered by the DOJ.

A good deal of the furor surrounding the remedy for the diversity of rules in the federal district courts derives from the DOJ's concern with Rule 4.2. The cry ought to be taken up by state and local prosecutors as well, because they are potentially affected in quite similar ways. There is no doubt that the matter of Rule 4.2 needs to be solved, but it needs to be solved at both the state and the federal level.

That brings me to complete the circle. I have urged that in the matter of the diverse federal district court rules, the solution ought to be one of dynamic conformity, with an explicit acknowledgment that federal courts control their own procedure. But federal courts also need to be involved in another way. It is appropriate to recognize the histor-

---

40. *See* United States *ex rel.* O'Keefe v. McDonnell Douglas Corp., 132 F.3d 1252, 1253–58 (8th Cir. 1998).

41. Zacharias & Green, *supra* note 27, at 235–43.

ical lodging of control of attorney behavior in the state systems, but reciprocity should follow such recognition. State courts, meanwhile, need to recognize that dynamic conformity means that federal courts have an interest in the professional conduct of lawyers practicing in federal courts in a given jurisdiction. That interest should be accommodated by bringing federal judges in each jurisdiction into the process of formulating those standards of conduct. State courts ought to take the lead in figuring out how, consistent with the respective operation of their courts, to include the federal courts in their jurisdiction in the process of making the rules that govern the conduct of lawyers in both state and federal courts.

I also believe that there should be more global cooperation between the state and federal judiciaries. The Conference of State Court Chief Justices, in cooperation with the relevant committees of the federal Judicial Conference, ought to figure out how to superintend, or even to operate, the process of rewriting the rules of professional conduct—a task that the ABA has taken upon itself. This joint venture could then propose model rules of professional conduct that would be applicable in both the federal and state systems. Such model rules would, in my view, be more likely to command nationwide respect and thus lead to greater nationwide uniformity than rules recommended by the ABA.

* * *

I-4. Professionalism: The Rules

ABA Model Rules

PREAMBLE: A LAWYER'S RESPONSIBILITIES

SCOPE

[14] The Rules of Professional Conduct are rules of reason. They should be interpreted with reference to the purposes of legal representation and of the law itself. Some of the Rules are imperatives, cast in the terms "shall" or "shall not." These define proper conduct for purposes of professional discipline. Others, generally cast in the term "may," are permissive and define areas under the Rules in which the lawyer has discretion to exercise professional judgment. No disciplinary action should be taken when the lawyer chooses not to act or acts within the bounds of such discretion. Other Rules define the nature of relationships between the lawyer and others. The Rules are thus partly obligatory and disciplinary and partly constitutive and descriptive in that they define a lawyer's professional role. Many of the Comments use the term "should." Comments do not add obligations to the Rules but provide guidance for practicing in compliance with the Rules.

[15] The Rules presuppose a larger legal context shaping the lawyer's role. That context includes court rules and statutes relating to matters of licensure, laws defining specific obligations of lawyers and substantive and procedural law in general. The Comments are sometimes used to alert lawyers to their responsibilities under such other law.

[16] Compliance with the Rules, as with all law in an open society, depends primarily upon understanding and voluntary compliance, secondarily upon reinforcement by peer and public opinion and finally, when necessary, upon enforcement through disciplinary proceedings. The Rules do not, however, exhaust the moral and ethical consider-

ations that should inform a lawyer, for no worthwhile human activity can be completely defined by legal rules. The Rules simply provide a framework for the ethical practice of law.

[17] Furthermore, for purposes of determining the lawyer's authority and responsibility, principles of substantive law external to these Rules determine whether a client-lawyer relationship exists. Most of the duties flowing from the client-lawyer relationship attach only after the client has requested the lawyer to render legal services and the lawyer has agreed to do so. But there are some duties, such as that of confidentiality under Rule 1.6, that attach when the lawyer agrees to consider whether a client-lawyer relationship shall be established. See Rule 1.18. Whether a client-lawyer relationship exists for any specific purpose can depend on the circumstances and may be a question of fact.

[18] Under various legal provisions, including constitutional, statutory and common law, the responsibilities of government lawyers may include authority concerning legal matters that ordinarily reposes in the client in private client-lawyer relationships. For example, a lawyer for a government agency may have authority on behalf of the government to decide upon settlement or whether to appeal from an adverse judgment. Such authority in various respects is generally vested in the attorney general and the state's attorney in state government, and their federal counterparts, and the same may be true of other government law officers. Also, lawyers under the supervision of these officers may be authorized to represent several government agencies in intragovernmental legal controversies in circumstances where a private lawyer could not represent multiple private clients. These Rules do not abrogate any such authority.

[19] Failure to comply with an obligation or prohibition imposed by a Rule is a basis for invoking the disciplinary process. The Rules presuppose that disciplinary assessment of a lawyer's conduct will be made on the basis of the facts and circumstances as they existed at the time of the conduct in question and in recognition of the fact that a lawyer often has to act upon uncertain or incomplete evidence of the situation. Moreover, the Rules presuppose that whether or not discipline should be imposed for a violation, and the severity of a sanction, depend on all the circumstances, such as the willfulness and seriousness of the violation, extenuating factors and whether there have been previous violations.

[20] Violation of a Rule should not itself give rise to a cause of action against a lawyer nor should it create any presumption in such a case that a legal duty has been breached. In addition, violation of a Rule does not necessarily warrant any other nondisciplinary remedy, such as disqualification of a lawyer in pending litigation. The Rules are designed to provide guidance to lawyers and to provide a structure for regulating conduct through disciplinary agencies. They are not designed to be a basis for civil liability. Furthermore, the purpose of the Rules can be subverted when they are invoked by opposing parties as procedural weapons. The fact that a Rule is a just basis for a lawyer's self-assessment, or for sanctioning a lawyer under the administration of a disciplinary authority, does not imply that an antagonist in a collateral proceeding or transaction has standing to seek enforcement of the Rule. Nevertheless, since the Rules do establish standards of conduct by lawyers, a lawyer's violation of a Rule may be evidence of breach of the applicable standard of conduct.

[21] The Comment accompanying each Rule explains and illustrates the meaning and purpose of the Rule. The Preamble and this note on Scope provide general orientation. The Comments are intended as guides to interpretation, but the text of each Rule is authoritative.

RULE 8.4: MISCONDUCT

It is professional misconduct for a lawyer to:

(a) violate or attempt to violate the Rules of Professional Conduct, knowingly assist or induce another to do so, or do so through the acts of another;

(b) commit a criminal act that reflects adversely on the lawyer's honesty, trustworthiness or fitness as a lawyer in other respects;

(c) engage in conduct involving dishonesty, fraud, deceit or misrepresentation;

(d) engage in conduct that is prejudicial to the administration of justice;

(e) state or imply an ability to influence improperly a government agency or official or to achieve results by means that violate the Rules of Professional Conduct or other law; or

(f) knowingly assist a judge or judicial officer in conduct that is a violation of applicable rules of judicial conduct or other law.

Comment

[1] Lawyers are subject to discipline when they violate or attempt to violate the Rules of Professional Conduct, knowingly assist or induce another to do so or do so through the acts of another, as when they request or instruct an agent to do so on the lawyer's behalf. Paragraph (a), however, does not prohibit a lawyer from advising a client concerning action the client is legally entitled to take.

[2] Many kinds of illegal conduct reflect adversely on fitness to practice law, such as offenses involving fraud and the offense of willful failure to file an income tax return. However, some kinds of offenses carry no such implication. Traditionally, the distinction was drawn in terms of offenses involving "moral turpitude." That concept can be construed to include offenses concerning some matters of personal morality, such as adultery and comparable offenses, that have no specific connection to fitness for the practice of law. Although a lawyer is personally answerable to the entire criminal law, a lawyer should be professionally answerable only for offenses that indicate lack of those characteristics relevant to law practice. Offenses involving violence, dishonesty, breach of trust, or serious interference with the administration of justice are in that category. A pattern of repeated offenses, even ones of minor significance when considered separately, can indicate indifference to legal obligation.

[3] A lawyer who, in the course of representing a client, knowingly manifests by words or conduct, bias or prejudice based upon race, sex, religion, national origin, disability, age, sexual orientation or socioeconomic status, violates paragraph (d) when such actions are prejudicial to the administration of justice. Legitimate advocacy respecting the foregoing factors does not violate paragraph (d). A trial judge's finding that peremptory challenges were exercised on a discriminatory basis does not alone establish a violation of this rule.

[4] A lawyer may refuse to comply with an obligation imposed by law upon a good faith belief that no valid obligation exists. The provisions of Rule 1.2(d) concerning a good faith challenge to the validity, scope, meaning or application of the law apply to challenges of legal regulation of the practice of law.

[5] Lawyers holding public office assume legal responsibilities going beyond those of other citizens. A lawyer's abuse of public office can suggest an inability to fulfill the professional role of lawyers. The same is true of abuse of positions of private trust such as trustee, executor, administrator, guardian, agent and officer, director or manager of a corporation or other organization.

ABA Code

EC 1-1 A basic tenet of the professional responsibility of lawyers is that every person in our society should have ready access to the independent professional services of a lawyer of integrity and competence. Maintaining the integrity and improving the competence of the bar to meet the highest standards is the ethical responsibility of every lawyer.

EC 1-5 A lawyer should maintain high standards of professional conduct and should encourage fellow lawyers to do likewise. He should be temperate and dignified, and he should refrain from all illegal and morally reprehensible conduct. Because of his position in society, even minor violations of law by a lawyer may tend to lessen public confidence in the legal profession. Obedience to law exemplifies respect for law. To lawyers especially, respect for the law should be more than a platitude.

DR 1-102 Misconduct.

(A) A lawyer shall not:

(1) Violate a Disciplinary Rule.

(2) Circumvent a Disciplinary Rule through actions of another.

(3) Engage in illegal conduct involving moral turpitude.

(4) Engage in conduct involving dishonesty, fraud, deceit, or misrepresentation.

(5) Engage in conduct that is prejudicial to the administration of justice.

(6) Engage in any other conduct that adversely reflects on his fitness to practice law.

Federal Rules of Appellate Procedure

Rule 46. Attorneys

* * *

(c) Discipline. A court of appeals may discipline an attorney who practices before it for conduct unbecoming a member of the bar or for failure to comply with any court rule. First, however, the court must afford the attorney reasonable notice, an opportunity to show cause to the contrary, and, if requested, a hearing.

(As amended Mar. 10, 1986, eff. July 1, 1986; Apr. 24, 1998, eff. Dec. 1, 1998.)

I-5. Cases and Materials

In re Ruffalo

U.S. Supreme Court, 390 U.S. 544
Certiorari to the United States Court of Appeals for the Sixth Circuit
No. 73. [Footnotes omitted]
Argued March 4, 1968
Decided April 8, 1968

MR. JUSTICE DOUGLAS delivered the opinion of the Court.

Petitioner was ordered indefinitely suspended from the practice of law by the Supreme Court of Ohio on two findings of alleged misconduct. Mahoning County Bar

Assn. v. Ruffalo, 176 Ohio St. 263, 199 N. E. 2d 396. That order became final and is not here on review. The Federal District Court, after ordering petitioner to show cause why he should not be disbarred, found that there was no misconduct. In re Ruffalo, 249 F. Supp. 432 (D.C. N. D. Ohio). The Court of Appeals likewise ordered petitioner to show cause why he should not be stricken from the roll of that court on the basis of Ohio's disbarment order. The majority held that while one of the two charges might not justify discipline, the other one did; and it disbarred petitioner from practice in that Court. 370 F.2d 447 (C. A. 6th Cir.). The dissenting judge thought that neither charge justified suspension from practice. Id., at 460. The case is here on a writ of certiorari. 389 U.S. 815.

Petitioner was an active trial lawyer who handled many Federal Employers' Liability Act cases. The Association of American Railroads investigated his handling of claims and referred charges of impropriety to the President of the Mahoning County Bar Association who was also local counsel for the Baltimore & Ohio Railroad Co. See In re Ruffalo, 249 F. Supp. 432, 435, n. 3. The Mahoning County Bar Association then filed the charges against petitioner.

In the state court proceedings, upon which the decision of the Court of Appeals relied (see Rule 6 (3) of the United States Court of Appeals for the Sixth Circuit), the Ohio Board of Commissioners on Grievances and Discipline originally charged petitioner with 12 counts of misconduct. Charges Nos. 4 and 5 accused petitioner of soliciting FELA plaintiffs as clients through an agent, Michael Orlando. At the hearings which followed, both Orlando and petitioner testified that Orlando did not solicit clients for petitioner but merely investigated FELA cases for him. It was brought out that some of Orlando's investigations involved cases where his employer, the Baltimore & Ohio Railroad, was defendant. Immediately after hearing this testimony, the Board, on the third day of hearings, added a charge No. 13 against petitioner based on his hiring Orlando to investigate Orlando's own employer. Counsel for petitioner objected, stating:

> "Oh, I object to that very highly. There is nothing morally wrong and there is nothing legally wrong with it.... When does the end of these amendments come? I mean the last minute you are here, [counsel for the county Bar Association] may bring in another amendment. I think this gentleman [petitioner] has a right to know beforehand what the charges are against him and be heard on those charges."

Motion to strike charge No. 13 was denied, but the Board gave petitioner a continuance in order to have time to respond to the new charge.

The State Board found petitioner guilty of seven counts of misconduct, including No. 13. On review, the Supreme Court of Ohio found the evidence sufficient to sustain only two charges, one of them being No. 13, but concluded that the two violations required disbarment. The only charge on which the Court of Appeals acted was No. 13, which reads as follows:

> "That Respondent did conspire with one, Michael Orlando, and paid said Michael Orlando moneys for preparing lawsuits against the B. & O. Railroad, the employer of said Michael Orlando, during all the periods of time extending from 1957 to July of 1961, well knowing that said practice was deceptive in its nature and was morally and legally wrong as respects the employee, Michael Orlando, toward his employer, the B. & O. Railroad Company."

Though admission to practice before a federal court is derivative from membership in a state bar, disbarment by the State does not result in automatic disbarment by the federal court. Though that state action is entitled to respect, it is not conclusively binding on the federal courts. Theard v. United States, 354 U.S. 278, 281–282.

Petitioner, active in the trial of FELA cases, hired a railroad man to help investigate the cases. He was Orlando, a night-shift car inspector for the Baltimore & Ohio Railroad Co. There was no evidence that Orlando ever investigated a case in the yard where he worked as inspector. There was no evidence that he ever investigated on company time. Orlando had no access to confidential information; and there was no claim he ever revealed secret matters or breached any trust. It is clear [390 U.S. 544, 548] from the record that petitioner chose a railroad man to help him investigate those claims because Orlando knew railroading.

One federal guidepost in this field is contained in 10 of the Federal Employers' Liability Act, as amended, 53 Stat. 1404, 45 U.S.C. 60, which was enacted to encourage employees of common carriers to furnish information "to a person in interest," as to facts incident to the injury or death of an employee.*

The Ohio Supreme Court, however, concluded that "one who believes that it is proper to employ and pay another to work against the interests of his regular employer is not qualified to be a member of the Ohio Bar." 176 Ohio St., at 269, 199 N. E. 2d, at 401.

We are urged to hold that petitioner's efforts to conceal this employment relationship and the likelihood of a conflict of interest require the federal courts to respect the decision of the Ohio Supreme Court as being within the range of discretion.

We do not pursue that inquiry. Nor do we stop to inquire whether the proceeding was defective because the Bar Association, the agency that made the charges against petitioner, was headed by counsel for the Baltimore & Ohio Railroad Co. against which petitioner filed several of his claims. For there is one other issue dispositive of the case which requires reversal.

As noted, the charge (No. 13) for which petitioner stands disbarred was not in the original charges made against him. It was only after both he and Orlando had testified that this additional charge was added. Thereafter, no additional evidence against petitioner relating to charge No. 13 was taken. Rather, counsel for the county bar association said:

> "We will stipulate that as far as we are concerned, the only facts that we will introduce in support of Specification No. 13 are the statements that Mr. Ruffalo has made here in open court and the testimony of Mike Orlando from the witness stand. Those are the only facts we have to support this Specification No. 13."

There was no de novo hearing before the Court of Appeals. Rather, it rested on the Ohio court's record and findings:

> "We have before us, and have reviewed, the entire record developed by the Ohio proceedings, but think it proper to dispose of the matter primarily upon

---

* Editor's note: Section 60 of the FELA now reads "any contract, rule, regulation ... the purpose, intent, or effect of which shall be to prevent employees of any common carrier from furnishing voluntarily information ... as to the facts incident to the injury or death of any employee, shall be void.... 45 U.S.C. 60.

the charges on which the Ohio Court disciplined Mr. Ruffalo. The facts as to these are not in dispute. We consider whether we find insupportable the Ohio Court's determination that such facts disclosed unprofessional conduct warranting the discipline imposed and whether they warrant similar discipline by us." 370 F.2d, at 449.

The Court of Appeals proceeded to analyze the "admitted facts of Charge No. 13" as found by the Ohio court and the Ohio court's ruling on those facts. Id., at 450–452.

If there are any constitutional defects in what the Ohio court did concerning Charge 13, those defects are reflected in what the Court of Appeals decided. The Court of Appeals stated:

"We do not find in the record of the state proceedings, 'Such an infirmity of proof as to the facts found to have established the want of … [Ruffalo's] fair private and professional character' to lead us to a conviction that we cannot, consistent with our duty, 'accept as final the conclusion' of the Supreme Court and the Ohio bar." Id., at 453.

We turn then to the question whether in Ohio's procedure there was any lack of due process.

Disbarment, designed to protect the public, is a punishment or penalty imposed on the lawyer. Ex parte Garland, 4 Wall. 333, 380; Spevack v. Klein, 385 U.S. 511, 515. He is accordingly entitled to procedural due process, which includes fair notice of the charge. See In re Oliver, 333 U.S. 257, 273. It was said in Randall v. Brigham, 7 Wall. 523, 540, that when proceedings for disbarment are "not taken for matters occurring in open court, in the presence of the judges, notice should be given to the attorney of the charges made and opportunity afforded him for explanation and defence." Therefore, one of the conditions this Court considers in determining whether disbarment by a State should be followed by disbarment here is whether "the state procedure from want of notice or opportunity to be heard was wanting in due process." Selling v. Radford, 243 U.S. 46, 51.

In the present case petitioner had no notice that his employment of Orlando would be considered a disbarment offense until after both he and Orlando had testified at length on all the material facts pertaining to this phase of the case. As Judge Edwards, dissenting below, said, "Such procedural violation of due process would never pass muster in any normal civil or criminal litigation." 370 F.2d, at 462.

These are adversary proceedings of a quasi-criminal nature. Cf. In re Gault, 387 U.S. 1, 33. The charge must be known before the proceedings commence. They become a trap when, after they are underway, the charges are amended on the basis of testimony of the accused. He can then be given no opportunity to expunge the earlier statements and start afresh.

How the charge would have been met had it been originally included in those leveled against petitioner by the Ohio Board of Commissioners on Grievances and Discipline no one knows.

This absence of fair notice as to the reach of the grievance procedure and the precise nature of the charges deprived petitioner of procedural due process.

Reversed.

MR. JUSTICE BLACK, for reasons stated in the Court's opinion and many others, agrees with the Court's judgment and opinion.

MR. JUSTICE STEWART took no part in the decision of this case.

MR. JUSTICE HARLAN, concurring in the result.

I see no need to decide whether the notice given petitioner of the charge that formed the basis of his subsequent federal disbarment was adequate to afford him constitutional due process in the state proceedings. For I think that Theard v. United States, 354 U.S. 278, leaves us free to hold, as I would, that such notice should not be accepted as adequate for the purposes of disbarment from a federal court. On that basis, I concur in the judgment of the Court.

MR. JUSTICE WHITE, with whom MR. JUSTICE MARSHALL joins, concurring in the result.

The Court reverses petitioner's disbarment by the Court of Appeals for the Sixth Circuit because petitioner had inadequate notice prior to his earlier state disbarment proceeding of the charges which the Mahoning County Bar Association was bringing against him at that proceeding. The state disbarment, however, is not before us. We denied a petition for certiorari seeking review of it. Ruffalo v. Mahoning County Bar Assn., 379 U.S. 931 (1964). Our writ in the instant case extends only to petitioner's disbarment by the Court of Appeals for the Sixth Circuit. The question therefore is whether the defective notice in petitioner's state disbarment proceeding so infected that federal proceeding that justice requires reversal of the federal determination.

In answering that question we must inquire into the nature of the proceeding that took place in the Court of Appeals. That court was obligated to determine for itself the facts of the attorney's conduct and whether that conduct had been so grievous as to require disbarment. Theard v. United States, 354 U.S. 278 (1957). The Court of Appeals asked petitioner to "show cause if any he has ... why he should not be stricken from the roll of counsel of this Court." In response to that order petitioner filed a response and brief. The Ohio State Bar Association filed a brief also, urging petitioner's disbarment. The cause was argued orally to a panel of the Court of Appeals.

In his brief and oral argument, petitioner did not take issue with the determinations of fact that had been made by the Ohio Supreme Court. The Court of Appeals gave petitioner a full opportunity to assert that the state court had not accurately determined the facts of his conduct—and to assert, had he wished to do so, that the late point at which he learned that employing car inspector Orlando would be one ground for disbarment had prejudiced the factual record formed in the state court. Petitioner, not disputing the lower court's factual conclusions, made no such objection. Instead petitioner's response in the Court of Appeals was that the agreed facts of his conduct were not a sufficient basis for disbarment. In reaching its conclusion on that question the Court of Appeals properly gave weight to the views of the state court judges who had passed on the issue. Petitioner, however, had full and fair opportunity to put to the Court of Appeals his contrary view. I must therefore conclude that no procedural defect supports reversal of the decision of the Court of Appeals, and that the asserted defect relied upon by the Court, since not raised by petitioner below or here, is not properly before us. I am therefore constrained to deal with the central question posed by this case, whether it was proper for the Court of Appeals, in making the independent determination of petitioner's fitness to remain a member of its bar mandated by Theard v. United States, supra, to disbar petitioner for having hired an employee of the B. & O. Railroad to investigate facts relevant to damage suits against the railroad brought by other employees who had retained petitioner to represent them. We must determine whether the Court of Appeals satisfied its duty "not to disbar except upon the conviction that, under the principles of right and justice, [it is] constrained so to do." Selling v. Radford, 243 U.S. 46, 51 (1917).

A relevant inquiry in appraising a decision to disbar is whether the attorney stricken from the rolls can be deemed to have been on notice that the courts would condemn the conduct for which he was removed. The Court of Appeals for the Sixth Circuit had provided petitioner and the other members of its bar with a general standard for disbarment:

> "When it is shown to the court that any member of its bar has been suspended or disbarred from practice in any other court of record, or has been guilty of conduct unbecoming a member of the bar of the court, the member will be forthwith suspended from practice before the court and notice of his suspension will be mailed to him, and unless he shows good cause to the contrary within 40 days thereafter, he will be further suspended or disbarred from practice before the court." Rule 6 (3), Court of Appeals for the Sixth Circuit.

Even when a disbarment standard is as unspecific as the one before us, members of a bar can be assumed to know that certain kinds of conduct, generally condemned by responsible men, will be grounds for disbarment. This class of conduct certainly includes the criminal offenses traditionally known as malum in se. It also includes conduct which all responsible attorneys would recognize as improper for a member of the profession.

The conduct for which the Court of Appeals disbarred petitioner cannot, however, be so characterized. Some responsible attorneys, like the judge who refused to order petitioner disbarred from practice in the Northern District of Ohio, 249 F. Supp. 432 (1965), would undoubtedly find no impropriety at all in hiring a railroad worker, a man with the knowledge and experience to select relevant information and appraise relevant facts, to "moonlight" — work on his own time — collecting data. On the other hand some, like the officials of the Mahoning County and Ohio State Bar Associations, would believe that encouraging a man to do work arguably at odds with his chief employer's interests is unethical. The appraisal of petitioner's conduct is one about which reasonable men differ, not one immediately apparent to any scrupulous citizen who confronts the question. I would hold that a federal court may not deprive an attorney of the opportunity to practice his profession on the basis of a determination after the fact that conduct is unethical if responsible attorneys would differ in appraising the propriety of that conduct. I express no opinion about whether the Court of Appeals, as part of a code of specific rules for the members of its bar, could proscribe the conduct for which petitioner was disbarred.

In re S. (A Barrister)

[VISITORS TO THE INNER TEMPLE]

1981	March 20; April 15	Vinelott, McNeill and Anthony Lincoln JJ.

Barrister — Discipline — Disciplinary tribunal — Committee of General Council of Bar preferring charges of misconduct against barrister — Hearing before disciplinary tribunal of Senate — Tribunal consisting of members of Senate and practising barristers — Inclusion of lay member — Whether bias in membership of tribunal

Figure 1. Barristers in traditional wigs and gowns in Hong Kong. The professional traditions of the British bar have had a profound effect throughout the former British colonies, including Hong Kong, Australia, Canada, New Zealand, Nigeria, Kenya, India, Bermuda, Pakistan, South Africa and, some might say, the United States (David Turnley, Corbis).

APPEAL from the decision of the Disciplinary Tribunal of the Senate of the Inns of Court and the Bar.

The Professional Conduct Committee preferred a number of charges alleging professional misconduct against the appellant, S., a barrister and a member of the Inner Temple. The charges were heard and determined by a disciplinary tribunal on behalf of the Senate which considered the charges, found three of the categories of misconduct proved and ordered that he should be disbarred and expelled from his Inn.

By his petition of appeal, the appellant contended that the constitution of the disciplinary tribunal infringed the principal *nemo judex in causa sua* and its findings were a nullity. The grounds of the contention were (a) that the Senate was legislator, investigator, prosecutor, judge and jury; (b) that a tribunal made up primarily of members of the Senate which included the Bar Council, a committee of which was under a duty to investigate and prefer charges heard by the tribunal, would not be viewed by ordinary, informed members of the public as unbiased and unprejudiced and its findings should not be allowed to stand; (c) that since the majority of members of the tribunal were practising barristers it could not be capable of considering fairly a charge of misconduct against a fellow barrister. He further contended that the tribunal's findings were unsafe and unsatisfactory having regard to the evidence before it. He also contended that the sentence was unduly severe having regard to his record and to sentences imposed in other cases.

The appeal was heard in private but judgment was given in open court.

Louis Blom-Cooper Q.C. and Alan Newman for the appellant.
Stephen Powles for the respondent, Professional Conduct Committee.
Cur. adv. vult.
April 15.

VINELOTT J: read the following decision of the visitors. In this appeal we sit not as a court of law but as visitors to the Inns of Court. The Lord Chancellor and all the judges of the High Court of Justice are visitors to the Inns of Court and as visitors it is their duty to hear appeals by barristers who have been found guilty of professional misconduct and who have been disbarred or disciplined by suspension from practice for a period or by the imposition of a fine or who have been reprimanded. Under rules made on behalf of all the judges of the High Court by the Lord Chancellor, the Lord Chief Justice, the President and the Vice-Chancellor, appeals to the judges as visitors are heard by not fewer than three judges nominated by the Lord Chief Justice after consultation with the Lord Chancellor. We have been so nominated to hear an appeal by a barrister who has been found guilty by the disciplinary tribunal of the Senate of the Inns of Court and the Bar of very serious charges of misconduct. He was sentenced to be disbarred and expelled from the Inn of Court of which he was a member. Normally, the visitors sit and give their decision in private. In this case we heard the appeal in private, but, as a question of principle has been raised by Mr. Blom-Cooper Q.C., who appeared for the appellant, we have decided, with the consent of counsel for the appellant and the Professional Conduct Committee, to pronounce our findings in public.

* * *

In our opinion ... the objections raised by Mr. Blom-Cooper to the constitution of the disciplinary tribunal are wholly without substance.

The charges which the tribunal found proved fall into three categories. First the tribunal found that on two separate occasions the appellant gave to a man who had done some electrical work at his house a number of visiting cards showing both his chambers and home addresses with telephone numbers without having been asked for them or for the information printed on them with a view to their distribution and in doing so was guilty of touting for instructions. Secondly, the tribunal found that the appellant had on two separate occasions without the intervention of a solicitor demanded and accepted a fee from a lay client whom he subsequently represented in court. Thirdly, the tribunal found that the appellant had required a client whom he had represented at a Crown Court to execute building and decorating work at his home in lieu of payment for part of his fee for representing him.

Mr. Blom-Cooper stressed that the appellant came here in 1965, when he was 26 years old, from Bangladesh where he was born and brought up. He took his degree in law at the University of Dacca. He was admitted a student of the Inner Temple in April 1965 and was called in 1970. He did not undertake a pupillage until 1975 and did not commence his practice until January 1976. All the offences with which he was charged occurred during his first year of practice or shortly thereafter. Mr. Blom-Cooper pointed out that in Bangladesh there is a single fused profession and that as a necessary consequence there is no rule prohibiting a member of the legal profession from dealing directly with and accepting payment from a member of the public even in relation to a matter in which he is instructed as an advocate. He submitted that given his background the appellant might not have appreciated fully the very very serious nature of the offences with which he was charged even though, as Mr. Blom-Cooper accepts, he must be taken to have known that the offences, or at least those within the second and third categories, were breaches of the code of conduct governing members of the Bar.

It is possible that if the appellant had admitted his guilt and had put these matters fairly before the tribunal, the tribunal might have been persuaded not to go to the length of deciding that the appellant should be disbarred and expelled from his Inn. The tribunal heard the appellant and could have evaluated the sincerity of his explanation. We are in no position to do so, although it is relevant to point out that when the appellant started to practise here he had been here for 11 years and that he had spent five years as a student at his Inn and had completed a year's pupillage. However, this explanation was not put before the tribunal. The case put before the tribunal, in particular in relation to the charges in the second and third categories, was that the evidence of the witnesses called to substantiate those charges was fabricated and that they had fabricated this evidence because of the grievance they felt at the fact that his advocacy had not resulted in an acquittal. Any force which this plea by Mr. Blom-Cooper might have had is destroyed by the nature of the defence relied on by the appellant. Although the appellant was not found guilty of all the charges made against him, the misconduct of which he was found guilty, in particular bargaining for and accepting a fee from a lay client without the intervention of a solicitor, was of the gravest nature and strikes at the root of the independence of the Bar and of the barrister on which the courts and the public are entitled to rely.

In these circumstances the disciplinary tribunal in our opinion had no alternative but to order that this appellant be disbarred and expelled from his Inn.

We were informed by Mr. Blom-Cooper that the appellant is a polio victim and in addition in October 1980 suffered a serious coronary heart attack and will shortly have to return to hospital for major heart surgery. It is, of course, a serious and distressing thing that a member of the Bar should be disbarred and expelled from his Inn and deprived of the prospect of success in his profession. We are not indifferent to the consequences to the appellant. At the same time we have to consider the wider interests of the profession and the public.

Appeal dismissed.

Solicitors: *Bernard Sheridan & Co.*

[Reported by MISS EILEEN O'GRADY, Barrister-at-Law]

In the Matter of Gary C. Crossen

Supreme Judicial Court of Massachusetts, 450 Mass. 533
[Footnotes omitted]
Argued Oct. 4, 2007
Decided Feb. 6, 2008

MARSHALL, C.J.

Attorney Gary C. Crossen contests an information filed in the county court by the Board of Bar Overseers (board) recommending that Crossen be disbarred for his part in an intricate plan to discredit a Superior Court judge presiding in an ongoing matter in which he represented some of the litigants. The aim of the plan was to influence the outcome of the litigation by forcing the judge's recusal and obtaining reversal of her prior rulings against Crossen's clients. In furtherance of the scheme, Crossen, with his own investigators posing as corporate executives, set up and secretly made a tape recording of a sham job interview for a former law clerk of the judge, during which the law clerk repeatedly was questioned about the judge's personal and professional character and her decision-making process in the ongoing matter involving Crossen's clients. Although the "interview" with the law clerk did not yield the information Crossen had hoped, Crossen did not change course. He redoubled his efforts to malign the judge for the benefit of his clients by using a tape recording of the interview to coax and then threaten the law clerk into providing sworn statements damaging to the judge, which the law clerk otherwise would not have made.

Bar counsel alleged that Crossen's conduct violated S.J.C. Rule 3:07, Canon 1, DR 1-102(A)(2) and (4)-(6), as appearing in 382 Mass. 769 (1981), and Canon 7, DR 7-102(A)(5) and (7), as appearing in 382 Mass. 785 (1981). The matter was tried to a special hearing officer appointed by the board. The board adopted, with minor exceptions, the special hearing officer's extensive findings and conclusions, as well as her recommendation that Crossen be disbarred. A single justice reserved and reported the matter to the full court.

We adopt the board's recommendation. The record leaves no doubt that Crossen was a willing participant, and at times a driving force, in a web of false, deceptive, and threatening behavior designed to impugn the integrity of a sitting judge in order to obtain a result favorable to his clients. The scope of this misconduct has scant parallel in the disciplinary proceedings of this Commonwealth. This was not conduct on the uncertain border between zealous advocacy and dishonorable tactics, a border about which reasonable minds may differ. It struck at the heart of the lawyer's professional obligations of good faith and honesty. Crossen's conduct was so egregious and extensive that no reasonable attorney could have believed it comported with the solemn ethical obligations of attorneys. It caused harm to the orderly administration of justice, as well as to the law clerk, the judge, and their families, and it harmed public confidence in the legal profession.

We reject Crossen's argument that the prevailing ethical standards at the time were at best ambiguous about the propriety of attorney participation in the kind of "sting" operation at the center of this case. Nor do we credit Crossen's contentions that the special hearing officer was obligated to accept the testimony of Crossen's expert on legal ethics; that Crossen was improperly singled out for disciplinary action; that he was otherwise deprived of due process of law; or that the sanction of disbarment is markedly disparate from sanctions for similar conduct. We remand the case to the county court where a judgment of disbarment shall enter.

* * *

a. *Demoulas family litigation.*

As with its companion case, *Matter of Curry,* 450 Mass. 503, 506, 880 N.E.2d 388 (2008) (*Curry*), this disciplinary proceeding is one more offspring of a family dispute among members of the Demoulas family, recounted at length in *Demoulas v. Demoulas Super Markets, Inc.,* 424 Mass. 501, 504–509, 677 N.E.2d 159 (1997), and *Demoulas v. Demoulas,* 432 Mass. 43, 732 N.E.2d 875 (2000). See also *Demoulas v. Demoulas,* 428 Mass. 555, 703 N.E.2d 1149 (1998). For a summary of the issues in these family disputes, see *Curry, supra.*

We turn now to the key events in this disciplinary proceeding against Crossen.

b. *Preparations for a sham interview.*

On June 8, 1997, a Sunday, Crossen met with Arthur T. Demoulas (Arthur T.) at the latter's request at the Demoulas corporate offices in Tewksbury. There Crossen learned for the first time that, in 1995, Arthur T. had hired attorney Kevin Curry and two investigators, Ernest Reid and Richard LaBonte, to conduct a "pretext investigation … to figure out who wrote the Demoulas decision." Arthur T. told Crossen that Curry and LaBonte, using assumed identities, had met with a former law clerk of Judge Lopez (law clerk) in Halifax, Nova Scotia, under the pretext of interviewing the law clerk for a position as in-house counsel for a sham multinational corporation. Arthur T. reported that the law clerk claimed to have written the entire *Demoulas* decision, and that Judge Lopez had signed the decision without reading it. More significantly, Arthur T. told Crossen that the law clerk had said that Judge Lopez had told him (the law clerk) who the winners and losers, the "good guys" and the "bad guys," were going to be before the shareholder derivative suit began. Crossen dismissed as "not that big a deal" the information concerning authorship of the *Demoulas* decision, but he was troubled by the information that Judge Lopez had prejudged his clients' case.

That same day Crossen met with Arthur T. and another attorney for the defendants, Richard K. Donahue, to discuss the import of the Halifax interview. Crossen testified before the special hearing officer that he considered his only options at the time to be ignoring the information, incorporating it into a motion or pleading or complaint, or investigating further to determine the truth. At the time, Crossen testified, he did not "give[ ] a whole lot of thought to the issue of the propriety" of Curry's communications with the law clerk.

Some time after the June 8 meetings, Crossen received a signed affidavit from Curry in which the latter averred that during the Halifax "interview," the law clerk on four separate occasions had disclosed Judge Lopez's predisposition against Crossen's clients; that the law clerk claimed to have written the *Demoulas* decision himself; and that the law clerk had submitted a letter attesting his fitness for admission to the Massachusetts bar that was written by someone whom the law clerk did not know. See *Curry, supra* at 515 n. 19, 880 N.E.2d 388. Soon after receiving Curry's affidavit, Crossen decided to procure tape-recorded statements of the law clerk by interviewing and secretly tape recording him in a jurisdiction that permits one-party consent, which Massachusetts does not. See G.L. c. 272, § 99(B)(4) & (C)(1).

Crossen then set about to implement his plan. He directed an associate at his law firm to review the laws of Canada and a Caribbean jurisdiction (either Bermuda or the Bahamas) to determine whether one-party consent to tape recording communications was permitted in either jurisdiction. To assess Curry's credibility, Crossen also directed the associate to discover what he could about Curry. In addition, Crossen met personally with Curry to discuss the information Curry claimed he had learned from the law clerk, and what to do with it. Among other things, the two men discussed continuing the ruse and secretly tape recording the law clerk's statements in a one-party consent jurisdiction such as New York or Bermuda. At some point in early June, Crossen also discussed the surreptitious tape-recording plan with Donahue. Donahue questioned Crossen about the propriety of such an investigation; he testified before the special hearing officer that Crossen "said he was having [the matter] looked into, and that he was not concerned with it and that basically I shouldn't be."

Between June 9 and June 12, Crossen consulted about the planned subterfuge with Donahue, Curry, and others, including two private investigators who were working with Crossen on the Charles Restaurant investigation, Stewart Henry and Joseph McCain. The group decided that the law clerk would be asked to go to the Four Seasons Hotel in New York, a one-party-consent jurisdiction, for a "further interview" for an in-house counsel position with a phantom multinational reinsurance firm, British Pacific Surplus

Risks, Ltd. (British Pacific). See *Curry, supra* at 512, 516–517, 880 N.E.2d 388. Unbeknownst to the law clerk, the interview would be tape recorded. The group's plan was to catch the law clerk unawares by having him repeat the assertions Curry claimed he had made in Halifax concerning Judge Lopez's predispositions about the *Demoulas* decision. At that point, Crossen would "brace," or aggressively confront, the law clerk with the tape recorded-statements in order to gain his cooperation in giving an affidavit or sworn testimony against Judge Lopez.

The group decided that Reid, resuming his guise as a job consultant, see *Curry, supra* at 510–511, 880 N.E.2d 388, would contact the law clerk about interviewing with some British Pacific "decision makers." In New York LaBonte, reprising his role in Halifax as British Pacific employee Richard LaBlanc, would be one of the interviewers. See *Curry, supra* at 516, 880 N.E.2d 388. The part of "Peter O'Hara," a "principal" in British Pacific, would be played by Joseph Peter Rush, a private investigator who previously had worked as a United States Secret Service special agent-in-charge in Boston. Crossen and Henry would "monitor" developments from an adjoining room. A tape-recording technician would complete the New York contingent. Crossen was to be the sole decision maker on whether to "brace" the law clerk once the law clerk uttered the "magic words" concerning Judge Lopez's predisposition.

Other members of Crossen's team besides Donahue felt uncomfortable with their intended methods. During the planning process, Rush asked Crossen whether the New York interview was ethical and legal. Rush was particularly concerned to know whether it was permissible for him, as a private citizen, to conduct a sham interview and secretly make a tape recording of the interview with the law clerk, another private citizen. Crossen assured Rush that, in Rush's words, Crossen "had researched the legalities and ethics of it and that it was legal." Crossen also reassured Rush that, again in Rush's words, "it's been cleared by ethics." Rush testified that he "took that to believe [Crossen's] firm had an ethical committee, and it had been run through them and they had okayed it." "In fact," the special hearing officer found, "Crossen never discussed any issue regarding the Demoulas case with [his] firm's committee on conflicts and professional responsibility." Based on Crossen's assurances that, in Rush's words, the "legal and ethical bases had been touched," Rush agreed to participate in the sham interview.

Crossen, Henry, LaBonte, and Rush decided that Rush would carry a concealed tape recorder in the pocket of a spare jacket and that Crossen and Henry would monitor the interview by silent videotape recording in the adjacent room of the suite.

c. *The sham interview in New York.*

Prior to the interview, Reid delivered airplane tickets, one hundred dollars in cash, and O'Hara's name to the law clerk. When he arrived in New York, the law clerk was met by a chauffeur who drove him to the hotel in a Mercedes limousine.

The ruse interview lasted approximately one and one-half hours. Rush, as O'Hara, began by (falsely) explaining the nature of British Pacific's reinsurance business and its opportunities for travel and interesting work. Rush then explained (again falsely) that Shaw was unable to attend the interview but had been "very laudatory" about the law clerk's writing skills. He reassured the law clerk that the law clerk's speech impediment, see *Curry, supra* at 513, 880 N.E.2d 388, would not be a barrier to his employment by British Pacific because the company was most concerned with hiring "new blood" who could "write the facts in a manner which is favorable to our partnership...." Rush also raised the law clerk's submission of a letter of support for his bar application written by an attorney who falsely claimed to know the law clerk. See *Curry, supra* at 515 n. 19, 880 N.E.2d 388.

Conversation then turned to what Rush called the "Demopolis" case. The law clerk explained that he was able to write the decision on his own because he had sat through the trial and he and Judge Lopez had discussed the witnesses at the end of each day of the trial. He also told his interlocutors that he had begun writing the decision shortly before the trial ended. The law clerk's responses to questions concerning Judge Lopez's alleged predisposition were decidedly more equivocal and weaker than they were alleged to have been in Halifax.

At one point during the interview, Rush took a break and went to the adjoining suite to tell Crossen and Henry that he believed the law clerk's statements to be "very weak." Crossen instructed Rush to resume the interview and attempt to "clarify the issue of" Judge Lopez's predisposition. Soon thereafter, LaBonte was summoned out of the room because Rush was afraid that he was being so persistent about the *Demoulas* decision that the law clerk would become suspicious. When LaBonte went to the room where Crossen and Henry were viewing the videotape recording, he told them that the law clerk was stuttering badly, and that they would give the law clerk a "heart attack" if they were to "brace" him. Crossen replied that they "would see." The law clerk was not "braced" that day.

* * *

On July 24, Reid made reservations for "Peter O'Hara" at the Four Seasons Hotel in Boston for an August 2 meeting with the law clerk. On August 1, Crossen, Curry, Donahue, Arthur T., Rush, Reid, McCain, and Henry met at the offices of Crossen's law firm to discuss strategy for this upcoming meeting. The participants knew that Reid had told the law clerk that this meeting would be his final "interview" for the British Pacific job. They decided on a free-form interview that would (1) apprise the law clerk of the ruse, (2) serve to determine whether the law clerk would verify the statements attributed to him in Halifax and parts of his New York interview, and (3) gauge the law clerk's willingness to cooperate with defendants' counsel by confirming the statements in an affidavit or otherwise. The group also decided to have the law clerk followed after the meeting in case the law clerk attempted to contact Judge Lopez or the Demoulas plaintiffs' counsel. McCain and his associates were given the job of surveillance.

e. *Confrontation of the law clerk.*

Soon after the law clerk arrived at the appointed suite in the Four Seasons Hotel in Boston, Rush told the law clerk to listen carefully because he would hear something that would send him on the "roller coaster of [his] life" and elicit a range of emotions and "concern for the future." But, Rush added, "if you cooperate with us, it will be okay." Rush then laid out for the dumbfounded law clerk the details of the British Pacific ruse. The law clerk almost immediately connected the dupery with the *Demoulas* decision and with Crossen, whom he had earlier seen in the lobby. Rush explained to the law clerk, who by this time was enraged, who his clients were.

Crossen then entered the room. He and the law clerk had words about the motion to recuse, and the ruse. The law clerk yelled at Crossen for doing nothing to stop the chicanery, and Crossen replied that, while he was not entirely comfortable with the tape recording, he had "inherited the ruse" and it was not something he could stop. He told the law clerk that the present meeting was not being tape recorded because this was not legal in Massachusetts, but that Halifax and New York were one-party consent jurisdictions. Crossen did nothing to dispel the impression conveyed by Rush that tape recordings had been made of both the Halifax and New York sham interviews. The law clerk angrily denied that he had written the entire *Demoulas* decision and claimed to have been "puffing" when he previously had proclaimed otherwise. He also refused to answer repeated questions about Judge Lopez's predisposition, saying that the *Demoulas* defendants had received a fair trial.

Crossen told the law clerk that he could not control what his clients would do with the information they had; that if the law clerk did not "help him" there would be a "missile" fired "that's out of my control and it's off, and I don't know where it goes and what it ends up doing"; that he, Crossen, needed a "candid conversation" with the law clerk "about what really happened here"; and other statements that the special hearing officer, in our view, characterized correctly as threats. Donahue told the law clerk that, if he did not cooperate with them, the false letter submitted with his bar application would be made public.

The law clerk asked numerous times to hear the "tapes" or read transcripts of the Halifax and New York tape recordings himself, but Crossen refused to permit this. After some forty minutes, the law clerk got up to leave. Crossen told the law clerk to retain a lawyer, talk the matter over with his wife, and to telephone either Donahue or Crossen on Monday.

f. *Further threats and surveillance.*

The law clerk was so visibly shaken and upset when he left the meeting that McCain, who was following him, thought he might be suicidal. The law clerk went to the offices of his employer where named law partner Robert Sullivan found him alone in a conference room, crying. The law clerk told Sullivan what happened. Sullivan promptly contacted attorney Harry Manion, who agreed to represent the law clerk. The law clerk then went home to see his wife. A delivery person appeared at their door with a pizza the couple had not ordered. The law clerk noticed a man with a mobile telephone sitting on a bench across from his apartment house, the same man who had been there when the law clerk had left for work in the morning.

On Manion's advice, the law clerk began drafting an affidavit. On August 4, the law clerk met with agents of the Federal Bureau of Investigation (FBI), a meeting Manion had arranged. The law clerk's affidavit and a supplemental affidavit were given to the FBI and also provided to Judge Lopez and her attorney. The Federal agents told the law clerk that his affidavit did not provide substantial evidence of what had occurred and urged him to agree to wear a recording device to capture Crossen's statements that he had the "tapes," as well as Crossen's threats to the law clerk. After some hesitation, the law clerk agreed to do so.

On August 20, after exchanging several telephone calls, the law clerk and Crossen met at the latter's office. There they had a lengthy conversation, which was secretly tape recorded by the law clerk for the FBI. The law clerk repeatedly asked Crossen whether he could listen to the "tapes," claiming that he did not recall some of the statements attributed to him in the sham interviews, and that listening to the tape recordings would help him determine his next steps. Crossen adamantly refused, telling him "that is just not going to happen." Crossen did tell the law clerk that the information about Judge Lopez's predisposition would "come out one way or the other," and he again urged the law clerk to have a "candid conversation" with him about Judge Lopez's predisposition. Crossen told the law clerk that, while he (Crossen) could not guarantee that the false bar application letter would not be made public by other counsel, he would do his best to see that the letter was not introduced in evidence or to minimize the damage if it were.

The special hearing officer found that the law clerk understood from Crossen's comments that "if he helped Crossen, Crossen would not bring up the bar letter."

The special hearing officer also determined that the "candid conversation" Crossen was urging meant a conversation in which the law clerk stated that Judge Lopez was predisposed against Crossen's clients: no other statement from the law clerk would have satisfied Crossen. The meeting concluded on a note of urgency. While the special hearing officer did not summarize the remainder of the conversation, the transcript entered in evidence establishes that Crossen told the law clerk that a hearing on the interlocutory appeal of Judge Lopez's denial of the Charles Restaurant recusal motion was scheduled to take place in five days before a single justice of the Appeals Court. As a result, he said, he and the client were "making strategic decisions day to day." Crossen stated that "the client knows the information is there" and might direct the attorneys to use the information at or before the Appeals Court hearing. Crossen told the law clerk to get back to him within twenty-four hours.

The following day, Crossen and the law clerk spoke by telephone. Again, the law clerk secretly tape recorded the conversation at the request of the FBI. The law clerk and Crossen repeated their respective, contradictory demands about the "tapes." After the law clerk again refused to help Crossen without hearing the tape recordings, Crossen told the law clerk that "you're going to find yourself in a situation that is gonna be very troublesome to you and the lawyers that recommended you" for admission to the bar. He urged the law clerk to hire independent counsel, saying: "It's, it's gonna be a very harmful road for you, you [ought to] talk to somebody before this hits." After more wrangling about the tape recordings, Crossen offered to let the law clerk listen to a "small segment" to satisfy himself that the tape recordings existed. The law clerk agreed to the proposal. They agreed to meet the next day at Crossen's office. Prior to the meeting, Crossen and Donahue decided to play the portion of the New York tape recording dealing with the false bar letter because, in the words of the special hearing officer, "they knew that it was [the law clerk's] Achilles heel, and they intended to use that to pressure and intimidate [the law clerk] into cooperating with them by giving them an affidavit on Judge Lopez's alleged predisposition in the [s]hareholder [d]erivative [c]ase."

* * *

On August 28, the law clerk left Crossen a voice mail message saying he was going out of town and would contact Crossen when he returned. On August 29, the FBI served grand jury subpoenas on McCain, LaBonte, Rush, and Reid. On that day, Crossen learned that the FBI also was investigating his contacts with the law clerk. The law clerk and Manion held a press conference about the matter on September 17, 1997.

2. *Bar disciplinary proceedings.*

In January, 2002, bar counsel filed a three-count petition for discipline against Crossen, Curry, and Donahue in connection with the law clerk matter. Among other things, the petition alleged that Crossen: "plann[ed], execut[ed], and participat[ed] in a scheme to induce a former law clerk to travel to New York under the pretext of a job interview in order to tape record a conversation with him without his knowledge or consent," in violation of Canon 1, DR 1-102(A)(2) and (4)-(6), and Canon 7, DR 7-102(A)(5) and (7); "plann[ed], execut[ed], and participat[ed] in a scheme to induce a former law clerk to make damaging or compromising statements about himself or about the judge for whom he clerked with the false inducement of a lucrative employment … in order to force the judge's recusal or undermine her decisions in an ongoing case," in violation of Canon 1, DR 1-102(A)(2) and (4)-(6) and Canon 7, DR 7-102(A)(5) and (7); "communicat[ed] falsely to [the law clerk] that [he] had in [his] possession a tape of the Halifax meeting," in violation of Canon 1, DR 1-102(A)(4) and (6), and Canon 7, DR 7-102(A)(5) and (7); "attempt[ed] to get [the law clerk] to state under oath that Judge Lopez had predetermined the outcome of the stockholder derivative trial and had told him from the outset how the case was to be decided under the threat of disclosing the supposed contents of the tape and embarrassing and compromising statements [the law clerk] made at the pretext job interviews," in violation of Canon 1, DR 1-102(A)(4)-(6), and Canon 7, DR 7-102(A)(5) and (7); "attempt[ed] to get [the law clerk] to state under oath that Judge Lopez had predetermined the outcome of the stockholder derivative trial and had told him from the outset how the case was to be decided under the threat of disclosing that he and his friends had submitted with his petition for admission to the bar a recommendation from a lawyer whom he personally did not know," in violation of Canon 1, DR 1-102(A)(4)-(6), and Canon 7, DR 7-102(A)(5) and (7); "[had the law clerk] and his wife put under surveillance and [had the law clerk's] personal circumstances investigated," in violation of Canon 1, DR 1-102(A)(5) and (6); and "[denied] to [the law clerk] that [the law clerk] was under surveillance," in violation of Canon 1, DR 7-102(A)(4) and (6).

Pursuant to S.J.C. Rule 4:01, §3(2), as amended, 430 Mass. 1314 (1999), and Rule 3.19(a) of the Rules of the Board of Bar Overseers (2007), the board designated a special hearing officer to take evidence and make findings of fact, conclusions, and recommendations. Her report issued on May 11, 2005. By a vote of nine to two, the board adopted the special hearing officer's recommendation that Crossen be disbarred.

3. *Standard of review.*

Our standard of review in bar discipline cases is well established, and is set out in *Curry, supra* at 519, 880 N.E.2d 388. We apply this settled standard to Crossen's threefold appeal. He contends, first, that judged by professional standards as they existed in 1997, his actions were not only proper but "required" in order to represent his clients zealously and to protect the integrity of the judicial system. He was acting, he claims, as would any "courageous advoca[te]." Second, he argues that the procedures followed by the special hearing officer deprived him of due process. Last, he claims that the sanction of disbarment is markedly harsher than sanctions imposed for similar conduct. We consider each argument in turn.

4. *Violations of the Rules of Professional Responsibility.*

a. *Contemporary ethical standards.*

Crossen does not argue, nor could he, that the disciplinary rules forbidding a lawyer from engaging in dishonest or deceitful behavior, through his own professional conduct or through an emissary, are unclear or ambiguous. See DR 1-102(A)(2) and (4) and DR 7-102(A)(5) and (7). To the contrary, the disciplinary rules are written in terms that any attorney bound by them should readily understand. See *Matter of the Discipline of an Attorney,* 442 Mass. 660, 669, 815 N.E.2d 1072 (2004), quoting *Matter of Keiler,* 380 A.2d 119, 126 (D.C.1977) (because disciplinary rules are written "by and for lawyers," they "need not meet the precise standards of clarity that might be required of rules of conduct for laymen").

Nor does he argue as a general matter that his conduct in the law clerk matter would be appropriate professional conduct in all circumstances. Rather, Crossen argues that the professional norms prevalent in 1997 obligated him to vindicate his clients' interests by investigating allegations of judicial misconduct, and, further, that he reasonably believed at the time that as a private attorney he was empowered to use the same investigative techniques that would have been available to government attorneys, including the ploy of a "pretextual" interview where ascertaining the truth by less covert means likely would not be possible. We are not persuaded.

* * *

5. *Due process.*

Crossen argues that the procedures followed by the special hearing officer denied him an adequate opportunity to defend himself because Canon 1, DR 1-102(A)(5) (conduct prejudicial to administration of justice), is "so broad" that it raises a due process concern about "potential random application"; the special hearing officer did not permit Crossen's expert witness or the expert witnesses of his corespondents to testify; the special hearing officer struck Crossen's affirmative defense of selective prosecution; and the special hearing officer refused to issue certain subpoenas that Crossen sought. We have considered each of these objections and, for the reasons below, conclude that each is without merit.

a. *Vagueness of DR 1-102(A)(5).*

An attorney must be afforded due process of law, including fair notice of the charges and an opportunity to be heard, before he can be deprived of his constitutionally protected interest in his license to practice law. *Matter of Kenney,* 399 Mass. 431, 435, 504 N.E.2d 652 (1987). See *In re Ruffalo,* 390 U.S. 544, 550, 88 S.Ct. 1222, 20 L.Ed.2d 117 (1968). Due process requires fair notice of the proscribed conduct, meaning that attorneys may not be subject to rules that are so broad that they implicate concerns about "potential random application or unclear meaning," i.e., rules that are unconstitutionally vague. *Matter of Discipline of an Attorney,* 442 Mass. 660, 668, 815 N.E.2d 1072 (2004).

Crossen argues that DR 1-102(A)(5) is a "catch all" provision that is so vague as to raise due process concerns "at least when it forms the sole basis of discipline." The argument is unavailing here, because DR 1-102(A)(5) is *not* the sole, or even the dominant, basis of discipline. And Crossen's argument that the rule is unconstitutionally vague as a stand-alone basis for sanctions was considered and rejected in *Matter of the Discipline of Two Attorneys,* 421 Mass. 619, 629, 660 N.E.2d 1093 (1996), where we limited the reach of the rule, as the sole basis of discipline, to those activities that are so "egregious" as to "undermine the legitimacy of the judicial process." "Egregious" meant in 1997 what it means today: "Extremely or remarkably bad; flagrant." Black's Law Dictionary 534 (8th ed.2004). While we need not and do not consider Crossen's conduct under DR 1-102(A)(5) alone, we agree with the board that prior bar disciplinary law and prevailing professional norms, as well as his own colleagues' understandable misgivings about his conduct, placed Crossen on notice that, in the board's words, "such outrageous conduct" was proscribed.

We conclude as well that, acting with reason, Crossen should have known that his efforts to intimidate the law clerk with threats of disclosure unless the law clerk produced sworn statements damaging to Judge Lopez was prejudicial to the administration of justice: it was intended or was likely to produce from the law clerk testimony more critical of Judge Lopez than the law clerk otherwise would or could have given.

* * *

[The case was remanded to the county court for entry of a judgment of disbarment.]

Toward an Ecclesiastical Professional Ethics:
Lessons from the Legal Profession

Daniel R. Coquillette and Judith A. McMorrow, appearing in
J. Bartunek, M. A. Hinsdale, and J. F. Keenan (eds), *Church Ethics and Its
Organizational Context: Learning from the Sex Abuse Scandal in the
Catholic Church*, (Rowman & Littlefield, 2005)
[Citations in parentheses are to the works listed at the end.]

The sexual abuse crisis in the American Catholic Church has thrust us into a social drama. Where social drama occurs in the United States, lawyers are sure to be present. Adding a few dozen lawyers to any stressful situation inevitably has interesting consequences. The advocacy ethic of lawyers, which is captured in our *Rules of Professional Conduct*, not only encourages but compels the lawyer to function as a zealous advocate for the client. That assures that the client's point of view is strongly presented. From the perspective of some observers, that adversarial ethic encourages distortion and elevation of the interests of the individual over that of the collective. Whatever the challenges of having the legal system—and lawyers—involved in the current crisis, it has had the benefit of identifying individual, and to a lesser extent institutional, failures.

The experience of lawyers may offer assistance beyond the representation of both the victims and the Catholic Church. Lawyers, like clergy, are professionals with professional norms and ethical requirements. There are obviously huge differences in these two professions. But as priests to our secular religion of law, lawyers are "called forth and mandated by a competent authority" to function in a specific and defined role, the specifics of which are reflected in part in *Rules of Professional Conduct* (cf., Gula). Lawyers' long and storied history with professional codes offers a cautionary tale to those exploring an ecclesiastical code of ethics

The rules of the legal profession were originally designed to encourage good conduct. The first set of rules, *The ABA Canons of Ethics*, promulgated in 1908, was largely aspirational, and spoke generally of loyalty and character. As aspirational guides, the Canons were available for review if a lawyer happened to know of their existence. But many of the aspirational provisions were part of the culture of lawyering and did not need a formal code for weight or credibility.

The second effort to codify lawyer conduct occurred in 1969, when the American Bar Association passed the *Model Code of Professional Responsibility* (1969). The *Model Code* contained nine broad canons, such as "A lawyer should assist in maintaining the integrity and competence of the legal profession" (Canon 1) and "A lawyer should exercise independent professional judgment on behalf of the client" (Canon 5). These broad canons were followed by somewhat more specific, but still heavily aspirational, *Ethical Considerations* (which became known colloquially as "ECs") and very specific *Disciplinary Rules* ("DRs"). The *Ethical Considerations* offered somewhat more guidance, but maintained an aspirational focus. For example, "A lawyer should maintain high standards of professional conduct and should encourage fellow lawyers to do likewise. He should be temperate and dignified, and he should refrain from all illegal and morally reprehensible conduct." (EC 1-5). The *Disciplinary Rules* were designed to be enforced in disciplinary contexts and provided the bottom-line requirements, violation of which could subject the lawyer to professional discipline by the state body authorized to control the admission and expulsion of lawyers. For example, DR 1-102(A)(4) states that "A lawyer shall not engage in conduct involving dishonesty, fraud, deceit, or misrepresentation."

The 1969 *Code of Professional Responsibility* did not work well in its dual role of offering both broad ethical pronouncements and specific prohibitions. Some of the *Ethical Considerations* appeared to be inconsistent with the *Disciplinary Rules*, important non-litigation issues that affect the day-to-day life of lawyers were not addressed and the code continued to contain provisions, such as limitations on advertising, that were seen as advancing the economic interests of the profession.

The 1969 Code of Professional Responsibility was in existence a bare 10 years before the lawyers reevaluated the Code. Like the current crisis in the Catholic Church, moral and professional failures of lawyers, including Watergate, inspired the return to the drafting table. In 1983 the American Bar Association promulgated the *Model Rules of Professional Conduct*. The *Model Rules* presented, as its name indicates, specific rules of conduct, designed to be clearer and more easily enforced in disciplinary contexts. The natural tendency when crafting a code during a time of crisis is to offer more guidance and direction, rather than less. After all, moral failures arose because the prior guidance was, by definition, insufficient to stop the lapses (cf. Nielsen). As with the current discussions of an ecclesiastical code, using the code as a vehicle to build public trust is an understandable and potentially positive use of a code. That goal, however, also pushes the code in the direction of setting baselines for behavior.

The evolution in the names of the lawyer codes over the last 100 years reflects this more directive trend. Lawyers moved from broad canons (1908), to a code (1969), to rules (1983). And the focus of these codifications similarly changed from a broad articulation of ethics (1908), to responsibility (1969), to a specific focus on conduct (1983). While the *Rules of Professional Conduct*, recently refined in 2000, are somewhat better vehicles to punish through a disciplinary system, no one suggests that they capture the normative whole of what it means to be lawyer. Indeed, the Chair of the 2000 revisions panel, was quite open that "Our objective [in Ethics 2000 revision of Model Rules of Professional Conduct] was also to resist the temptation to preach aspirationally about 'best practices' or professionalism concepts. Valuable as the profession might find such guidance, sermonizing about best practices would not have—and should not be mis-perceived as having—a regulatory dimension." (Veazy). As St. Thomas Aquinas observed, punishment does not create high character and virtue, it merely deters evil conduct. (Coquillette). Codes, particularly when drawn during times of crisis with an eye to deterring wrongful conduct, have a very specific utility—a vehicle for control and punishment. Presumably an ecclesiastical code would be more receptive to "sermonizing" and a tone that might "preach," but the hydraulic pressure of crisis-inspired codes will be toward specificity.

As codes tend to move to greater level of specificity, the language of values and the broader norms that undergird the specific prohibition often get subsumed into the specific prohibitions. For example, the *Model Rules of Professional Conduct* for lawyers starts out with a preamble that invokes the larger values of the profession. But the weight of the lawyer code focuses on the specifics of prohibited conduct. For example, the importance of the fiduciary relationship, the value of which infuses so many specific provisions, is rarely mentioned in the *Rules* themselves.

Accepting for purposes of discussion that there will be a pressure toward specificity in any ecclesiastical code, with a corresponding danger of losing sight of the fundamental values that drive the code, we can identify some additional challenges and opportunities to a code of conduct. Based on the experience of lawyers, we would predict that the challenges to an ecclesiastical code fall into five broad areas. First, who gets to craft the first draft, quite apart from the complex question of adoption, will reveal much about the goals and likely success of a code. Second, such a code must acknowledge and confront the inherent limitations of all rules: identifying the optimum level of discretion and understanding the role of fact-finding within a code. Third, drafters must understand—as they inevitably do—the necessity of ethical awareness as a precondition for the effectiveness of any code. Fourth, as a code articulates the contours of the role-differentiated behavior of the professional, it must be sufficiently flexible to reflect the challenges of role-differentiated behavior. Finally, and perhaps most importantly, a code of conduct by its nature focuses on the function of the individual professional and can be an awkward, and often ineffective, vehicle for addressing the need for changes in the institutional structures within which the professional functions. Against these challenges sits a huge and incredibly important benefit—education.

Who Gets to Draft the Code

Who crafts the first draft of a code reveals who is entitled to sit at the table, whose input is important, and what points of view are most likely to be reflected in the code. Lawyers are regulated at the state level, and these model versions of the lawyer Code and Rules also reflect the challenge of who should have the power of shaping the first draft. By a process largely of default, the "model" versions of the lawyer codes have been crafted by the American Bar Association (ABA). Since the ABA is a voluntary trade association, it has no meaningful power to regulate lawyers. (Violating the code would only get you ousted from the ABA. For most lawyers, that would mean only losing your subscription to the *ABA Journal*.) The real power of the Rules of Conduct is infused when the rules were sent to the state courts, which then could take the first draft and shape it to reflect the values of the state. This process has come under increasing scrutiny. Some question whether the ABA is sufficiently representative of all who are affected by the lawyer codes. (Wolfram; Kaufman) There is concern about capture by the more elitist members of the bar. There is always the lurking suspicion that the fox is guarding the chicken coop. As other authors have noted, the same credibility challenges face the drafters of an ecclesiastical code.

As the *Rules of Professional Conduct* moved from aspirational to regulatory, the states increasingly have modified the specific rules to make changes in the text on issues such as the duty of confidentiality, candor required to a court, whether lawyers should be mandatory reporters of professional wrongdoing and the like. Changes sharpened the differences between those who proposed the first draft and those who have the power to adopt the final version. This process can provide a vehicle for shared discussion, or highlight the differences and tensions between the competing perspectives.

The Inherent Limitation of Rules

Professional Codes and Rules also share the inherent limitation of all rules. Rules typically have as their goal to identify clear lines of conduct. Their function is to limit discretion and increase perceived consistency. To achieve that goal, they must become more specific. But the more specific the rule, the less the ability to tailor the rule to new circumstances, and this increases the possibility of unfairness in application. (Shauer)

Even assuming the rule is crafted with an optimum level of specificity, there is still inevitable discretion required. The application of any code or rule requires a decision-maker to analyze what rule applies, engage in fact-finding to see if the circumstances of the case are covered by the rule, and make a decision about remedies. (Alexander & Sherwin). Fact-finding (or self-assessment about facts) is a huge challenge in any ethical deliberation. How many actors in the Church crisis did not take aggressive action because they were not sure that wrongdoing was taking place, were hesitant about their competence to find facts, or were uncertain about whether someone else—more properly placed to take action—had intervened? In many cases the factual uncertainty and requisite fact-finding can appear benign. For example, lawyers who are required by both our fiduciary obligations and our *Rules of Professional Conduct* to avoid representing conflicting interests must make factual determinations, such as whether the interest of two clients are "directly adverse" or whether the lawyer's judgment will be "materially limited." The focus on these precise questions can cause the lawyer to lose sight of the important values at stake in this fact-finding.

Rules also tend, over time, to encourage those bound by the rules to take a legalistic approach to their interpretation. The ethical rules for lawyers have become, in many instances, just another tool in the arsenal of lawyers in litigation with an opposing side. (Wilkins). There is also a tendency, over time, to see that everything not forbidden is allowed. We are not surprised that lawyers might take a legalistic approach to their own code of conduct. But this tendency is not unique to lawyers. Since accountability is likely to be a goal of an ecclesiastical code (Gula), those whose conduct is held up to scrutiny under the code will quite naturally be put in a defensive posture.

All these concerns about the limits of codes are not startling new insights. The Catholic Church has a rich and impressive legal system, including canon law scholars who understand the complexity of doctrinal interpretation and the challenge of words as a constraining force. An ecclesiastical code will not be exempt from these same challenges.

Ethical Awareness and the Values behind the Rules

Rules also require initial cognitive awareness of their possible application. Those bound by the rules need ethical awareness to understand when they are moving into conduct that encroaches on a value behind the rules. But that ethical awareness flows not from the rules themselves, but from the underlying moral values or principles that presumably serve as the foundation for the specific code or rule. Kohlberg's theory of moral development is illustrative. Kohlberg hypothesized six stages of moral development. Choosing to act according to rules because of a concern for punishment reflects a low stage of moral development. Choosing to act according to rules in order to do one's duty, respect authority and maintain social order rates higher on the scale, but still reflects what Kohlberg characterized as "conventional" approach. More complex moral development requires the person making decisions to understand the values behind the rules and recognize the need to thoughtfully consider the competing claims to right behavior. (Dallas)

Enron is a classic example. With a relentless corporate culture of profit maximization, individual professionals became caught up in the corporate goals. In house lawyers, who were asked to prepare the paper work for questionable transactions, often went through the formal process of receiving appropriate corporate approval. They often acted with formal compliance with the rules. But the essence of the transactions was highly questionable. Why didn't more lawyers within the corporation speak out? From what we have gleaned from that experience, they became caught up in a corporate culture that saw legal questioning of a transaction as an indication that the individual lawyer was just not sufficiently clever to figure out how to get the transaction done. That same corporate culture gave tangible rewards to those clever folks who worked around obstacles. There was a slow stretching of what was seen as tolerable. That last clever deal became the median point, not the outer bounds, of what was appropriate.

The corporate culture blunted the ethical awareness of many, but not all, of the lawyers. This was a process of seduction, not a conscious embracing of wrongdoing. It is quite telling that the two high profile in-house professionals who most strongly questioned Enron's activities were a lawyer and an accountant who had transferred into a division known for questionable activities. The lawyer and accountant had came from outside that "20th floor." They were able to recognize that something was seriously amiss. Because they had not been part of the slow deadening of professional judgment, they could see what was obvious, including what was obvious to outside reviewers during the post-mortem of Enron: *i.e.*, a few individuals were engaged in serious wrongdoing, and a large number of other individuals acquiesced, either through active assistance or a decision to stay silent.

The parallels between Enron and the crisis in the Catholic Church are striking. Both the executives at Enron and the abusive clergy were engaged in clear wrongdoing. Both criminal and corporate law had ample provisions to prohibit the worst of the activities in Enron. Similarly, both criminal law and canon law provided ample support to censure the wrongdoing of the individual church actors. No code of ethics will prevent such knowing wrongdoing. As we are well aware, in both Enron and within the Catholic Church, the most painful failures were systematic failures that flowed from tunnel vision of many of those around the wrongdoers. A culture of silence impaired ethical decision-making. A code of conduct does not magically create ethical awareness. Education is required to achieve that goal.

Role-Differentiated Behavior

Professional codes purport to identify rules of conduct that are specific, that cannot be derived from general moral principles applicable to all. Often called *role-differentiated behavior*, the notion is that lawyers and priests and others who function in a professional role have specific obligations that flow from their professional roles. (Wasserstrom) For example, the strong obligation of confidentiality shared by both priests and lawyers derives from the professional role. We expect both priests and lawyers to maintain confidentiality, even in the face of competing claims that right behavior for non-priests and non-lawyers would require disclosure. The professional obligation is grounded in an assessment that the greater good is achieved by maintaining confidentiality. While the duty of confidentiality is often the subject of dramatic television shows, the reality of the life of most lawyers—and priests—is that the duty of loyalty and ethic of care that flow from the fiduciary obligation causes the greatest ethical challenges.

We all engage in role-differentiated behavior, whether as a spouse, parent, lawyer, doctor, or minister. The challenge comes when the individual sees the role (like compliance with rules) as a complete identification of how they should behave. Role-differentiated behavior was a significant culprit in both Enron and the Catholic Church crises. Many individuals saw questioning as outside their role, sometimes understandably so. There was, in both cases, an assumption that others were in a superior position of both power and fact-finding.

Role-differentiated behavior is an endemic challenge. For example, one of our students was standing on a station platform of the "T," the public subway, in Boston. To his surprise, a 12 year old kid grabbed the purse of an old lady. There were fifty people on the platform, but no one intervened. The student reported that, inspired by a class discussion about Aristotelian responsibility, he unsuccessfully rushed after the purse-snatcher. When the student finally found a policeman at the top of the station stairs, the officer pointed out that he was a City of Boston policeman, and that the student would have to call the MBTA police. Too many rules, too much occupational specialization, as Max Weber observed, can get in the way of seeing your true responsibility in a clear way.

The Relationship between Codes and the Systems within Which They Function

An ecclesiastical code of conduct may have an important role in sharpening values important in professional functioning. But codes of professional conduct are directed toward *individual* misconduct, and their utility can drown under conflicting signals sent by the institutions and structures within which the professional functions. As Professor Richard Nielsen notes, "external environments and internal organization systems and traditions can support and encourage unethical behavior." (Nielsen)

Again, the lawyer codes are illustrative. They prohibit the individual lawyer from overbilling, lying to the court, fabricating evidence, representing conflicting interests, and the like. But all the punishment is directed at the individual lawyer. A few jurisdictions have flirted with the 800 pound gorilla in the room: structural systems, such as law firm policies and the adversary system itself, that tolerate and sometimes even encourage unethical behavior. For example, it is a violation of the lawyer's code to state to your client that you have put in 100 hours when, in fact, you have worked only 50. That false statement involves both lying to, and stealing from, your client. Lawyers are occasionally sanctioned, some quite seriously, for such misconduct. But law firms that require 2200 hours per year by associates—a work level that strongly pushes toward padding of time sheets—receive no disciplinary scrutiny.

The problems of the American Catholic Church demonstrate, as so many chapters in this volume attest, that the systems within which the professional functions can have a huge impact on professional choices. Certainly we do not want a defense that "the system made me do it." Such defenses have been decried since Nuremberg. But the systems within which both lawyers and clergy function can blunt ethical awareness or, more often, create a sense of powerlessness on the part of the individual professional. (Nielsen) And many aspects of the system are not addressed in the professional codes.

This problem is shared by all professionals. Physicians, nurses and other health care professionals struggle with the tension between their professional ethic and the reality of managed care and limited resources. Teachers struggle with professional obligations, in the face of increasing expectation of schools to solve complex social issues with inadequate resources. Business managers must confront the relentless pressure of profit maximization. A code of conduct can highlight norms and values, but as all authors who have touched on this subject recognize, it cannot cure institutional failures.

The *Rules of Professional Conduct* for lawyers could not function against the corporate culture in Enron. It is difficult to envision rules, certainly more specific rules, that would have stopped the professional failures. Similarly, an ecclesiastical code could not have corrected the numbing of ethical awareness, the discounting of the possibility of recurrence, and the awareness of the effects on victims.

Professional codes cannot function in isolation. To be effective, a code must interact and be harmonious with the aspirational goals of the systems in which the professional functions. As Robert Hinings has shown, organizational structure, such as the adversary system of justice, can either facilitate or prevent moral failure. Specialization by function and occupational hierarchies can be both highly desirable and dangerous. In Professor Hining's words, "our form of social organization [may] prevent us from recognizing our moral responsibility in the first place." (Hinings) This is great danger.

The Value of Codes

Codification of ethical norms can offer some advantages. To achieve those advantages, drafters must approach the process with great humility and caution. The process of crafting the rules, if inclusive, can facilitate a conversation about shared norms. Rules can help clarify best practices in recurring situations. If reinforced by the corporate culture, rules can be part of the norm setting within the institutions. Rules can be one part of a larger educational process.

But we must recognize that rules can, as many of the essays in this volume suggest, occasionally get in the way of virtue. Here is an example we use in class. It is an ethical dilemma drawn from life, not a sterile hypothetical. A corporate client authorized $800,000 to settle a terrible accident in which it was clearly at fault. The victims, a poor immigrant family, could not speak English. The victim's lawyer demanded "$400,000, and not a penny less." He was incompetent and did not know the value of his own case. What should the client's lawyer have done? The usual answer, in light of the confidentiality and zealousness rules, is to offer "$250,000, and not a penny more!" Now our students are good young men and women. Many are religious devout, and know well the Sermon on the Mount and the Talmud. But occupational rules, which enforce professional minimums, get in the way of their better intuitions. For them law school is like a bramble bush. As Karl Llewellyn observed, they jump in "and scratched out both [their] eyes." (Llewellyn).

We often take that blindness, the role, as inevitable. But we forget the rest of the poem that inspired Karl Llewellyn's famous book. "[A]nd when he saw that he was blind, with all his might and main he jumped into another one and scratched them in again." A professional may be guided by a code of conduct, even sanctioned for failure to comply with it. But such a code must be constantly examined in light of larger moral principles. Those larger principles have been developed, under the inspiration of the Church, by some of the greatest philosophical minds. Hopefully, efforts to develop an ecclesiastical profession will be more successful than the legal profession in fully embracing this moral foundation.

The Value of Education

The dominant theme of this collection of essays is that the root of effective reform is cultural, not technical or legal. And culture is about education, both for the clergy and the laity. We are not experts on seminary education, but our hope for the legal profession is that, through education, we can improve the professional culture. We spend much of our professional lives working with the lawyer codes and can appreciate the important, but limited, utility of rules. We have no faith in rules alone. They are a small part of the much larger question of the exercise of discretion.

Formal education within a law school, seminary or for the laity is one part of the educational process. That education must include not simply analysis of the norms, but much more rigorous and thoughtful education about how to facilitate conversation and exercise discretion. Too often formal education treats the professional with an ethical dilemma as an autonomous individual with no communal support in assessing right behavior. We must teach students the skills of outreach in ethical discussions. We must constantly remind ourselves that the greatest risk comes from cultures that silence discussion about right behavior.

We also need education in context. This is the case for casuistry—a context-driven decision-making that brings moral theory to life. (Tremblay) Education in context recognizes a role for deductive decisions from larger moral theory and virtue ethics, but validates the messiness of real-life decisions. We need to be constantly teaching each other how to deal with the real-life pressures to stay in role, ignore uncomfortable facts, and embrace deliberate ignorance. This education does not end when the diploma is granted. It is a life-long necessity. A final example might bring this into sharper focus. One of the authors of this essay adheres to a religious tradition of pacifism, yet actively supports the education of commanding officers at the Naval War College in Newport through the Naval War College Foundation, and participate in its programs. Why? Because in an era of terrorism, where there are no neat uniforms to mark combatants, the first line of defense against evil conduct, genocide, or war crimes is, at least on our part, the culture of our professional military. That culture is based on their professional education. The War College teaches its graduates critical judgment, the judgment necessary to abstain from evil conduct and not to tolerate it in others, regardless of the provocation or justification. The same should be true of lawyers and for the church as well.

Larry Alexander & Emily Sherwin, *The Deceptive Nature of Rules*, 142 U. Pa. L. Rev. 1191 (1994).

Daniel R. Coquillette, *Lawyers and Fundamental Moral Responsibility*, (Cincinnati: Anderson, 1995), 90–96.

Lynne L. Dallas, *A Preliminary Inquiry Into the Responsibility of Corporations and Their Officers and Directors For Corporate Climate: The Psychology of Enron's Demise*, 35 Rutgers L. J. 1, 13–17 (2003).

Heidi Li Feldman, *Codes and Virtues: Can Good Lawyers Be Good Ethical Deliberators?*, 69 S. Cal. L. Rev. 885, 932 (1996).

Robert W. Gordan, *A New Role for Lawyers?: The Corporate Counselor After Enron*, 35 Conn. L. Rev. 1185 (2003).

Andrew L. Kaufman, *Ethics 2000—Some Heretical Thoughts*, 2001 The Professional Lawyer 1.

Karl N. Llewellyn, *The Bramble Bush*. (New York: Oceana, 1960), iii.

Lisa H. Nicholson, *Sarbox 307's Impact on Subordinate In-House Counsel: Between a Rock and a Hard Place*, 2004 Mich. St. L. Rev. 559 (2004).

Fredrick Schauer, *Playing by the Rules: A Philosophical Examination of Rule-Based Decision-Making in Law and in Life* (1991).

Paul R. Tremblay, *The New Casuistry*, 12 Geo. J. Legal Ethics 489 (1999).

E. Norman Veazey, *Ethics 2000: Thoughts and Comments on Key Issues of Professional Responsibility in the Twenty-First Century*, 5 Del. L. Rev. 1, 4 (2002).

Richard Wasserstrom, *Lawyers as Professionals: Some Moral Issues*, 5 Human Rights 1 (1975).

David B. Wilkins, *Legal Realism for Lawyers*, 104 Harv. L. Rev. 469 (1990).

Charles Wolfram, *Modern Legal Ethics* (St. Paul, MN: West 1986) § 2.6.2.

Chapter II

Loyalty to Present Clients: Concurrent Conflicts of Interest

Problems

Problem 2

Select sides and set up the confirmation hearing of Louis Brandeis for adversary oral argument, addressing each of the three charges against him. One team should represent his challengers; the other, his defenders. Should the outcome depend on the professional rules then in effect? Remember, this is not a disciplinary hearing, but a confirmation hearing for the nation's highest judicial office. Should that make a difference? Do you agree with John Frank's conclusions? See his controversial article, set out at Chapter II-3, *infra*. What conflict of interest rules would apply today? Do you agree with them?

Problem 3

Select sides and argue the motion to disqualify the law firm of Parker, Coulter in the case of *McCourt* v. *FPC*, set out at Chapter II-3, *infra*. Do you think the Massachusetts doctrine is too strict? The case was originally decided when Massachusetts still followed DR 5-105(C) of the old *ABA Code*. Massachusetts changed to the new Mass. Rule 1.7 on January 1, 1998. Should that make a difference? What if the question was liability for legal malpractice, rather than a motion for disqualification?

Problem 4

While in practice, I represented a telephone company. One of their employees was present at the scene of a serious accident. Assume the company asked me to investigate the legal consequences of the accident, and to interview the employee. Exactly how should I do this? My interview could have resulted in problems with the employee's union. Why? What practical considerations, outside of the professional rules, should a lawyer in this situation have firmly in mind?

II-1. Introduction: "Professional Loyalty"

In examining professional rules and doctrines, it is always worth asking, "what is the underlying value being protected?" Take, for example, the *In Re Ruffalo* case, set out at Chapter I-5, *supra*. What values were being protected there? Were the efforts to punish Ruffalo for "solicitation" motivated by genuine concern for his clients and the justice system, or by the economic self-interest of the Mahoning County Bar Association, or both? With conflict of interest rules, the initial answer is easy, it is the moral value of "loyalty" that is being protected.

But loyalty alone can be an ambiguous value. We have punished severely people who were loyal to the "families" of organized crime, or to terrorist groups, or to leaders like Hitler. And the lawyer's duty of loyalty is not justified by the "goodness" of the client. It is owed to clients who are dangerous criminals. Nothing in *Model Rule* 1.7, the basic conflict of interest rule, says a word about the client's virtue or the justness of the client's cause. "Professional" loyalty, and the conflict of interest rules, are a direct result of the historical "attorney ideal," discussed in Chapter I-1, *infra*, and our commitment to the adversary system. It also is designed to encourage client trust in the lawyer and the system. It is this professional context, and this context alone, that justifies attorney loyalty.

A. Practical Problems of Enforcing Loyalty

A very large number of professional malpractice cases, and almost all disqualification motions, involve allegations of conflict of interest, i.e. violations of the attorney's loyalty obligations. Professional malpractice insurers, such as "ALAS," the Attorneys' Liability Assurance Society, have learned to fear conflict of interest cases. Juries understand violations of loyalty. I heard a witness in one case say to the jury, "There was one thing I never learned in business school. What do you do when your lawyer stabs you in the back?" The jury was very sympathetic.

But it can be difficult to detect conflicts of interest. Even in small firms, there are hundreds of clients. What is worse, their affairs change daily. Suppose you have a client who builds and operates drug stores in the north of Boston. Another lawyer has a client who operates hardware stores south of Boston. But that client may decide to go into the drug store business. If firms "screened" all incoming clients for any potential conflicts, they would have little new business, and lawyers very much want new business. Perhaps more important, such a rigid screen would discourage economic delivery of legal services or, worse, permit certain big clients to "lock up" legal talent, as actually occurred in *Emle Industries, Inc.* v. *Patentex*, set out at Chapter III-3, *infra*. Disqualification motions can be particularly disruptive, and can entail, if successful, great additional costs to client and lawyer alike.

Now imagine a big law firm, with hundreds of lawyers and hundreds of thousands of clients, and possibly a dozen branch offices. Most such firms have rigorous "conflicts checks" on taking in new clients, and some have full-time lawyers that do little else. But, even so, with constant change in client activities and plans, preventing all conflicts of interest is incredibly hard. See Association of the Bar of the City of New York, Formal Opinion 2003-03, at Chapter II-3, *infra*.

For this reason, the rules do not prohibit all implicit conflicts of interests. To begin, where you are no longer representing a client, the rules only prohibit your "knowingly represent[ing] a person in the same or substantially related matter in which that person's interests are materially adverse to the interests of the former client unless the former client gives informed consent, confirmed in writing." *Model Rule* 1.9 (a). Such a conflict of interest is called a "successive" conflict, and will be discussed in the next chapter, together with some different issues of imputed and vicarious conflicts. Notice that such a "successive" conflict can be waived by the former client.[1] It is hard enough to keep track of existing clients, so the rules only require that you be aware of what you actually did for the former client. In addition to protecting loyalty values, successive conflict rules also protect confidentiality, as we will see in Chapter IV.

B. The "Two-Pronged Test"

The standards are tougher for "concurrent" or "simultaneous" conflicts. *Model Rule* 1.7 is "triggered" whenever "the representation of one client will be directly adverse to another client" or "there is a significant risk that the representation of one or more clients will be materially limited by the lawyer's responsibility to another client, a former client or a third person or by a personal interest of the lawyer." *Model Rule* 1.7 (a) (2). Note that conflicts of interest can occur, not just between clients, but between the client and the lawyer! This is specifically addressed by Model Rule 1.8. See the Massachusetts version of this rule, *Mass. Rule* 1.8, set out in an appendix to this book.

But even if Model Rule 1.7 is "triggered," the lawyer can still continue to represent "each affected client" if the "two-pronged" test of Rule 1.7 (b) is met. The first part of the "prong" requires the "informed" consent of each client. The new version of *Model Rule* 1.7 requires that this consent be "confirmed in writing," although *Mass. Rule* 1.7, as of the date of this book, does not. The second "prong" is sometimes called the "objective" or "reasonableness" prong. Even if "informed" client consent is obtained in writing, the concurrent representation is not permitted unless "the lawyer will be able to provide competent and diligent representation to each affected client." *Model Rule* 1.7 (b)(1).

This is sometimes called the "objective" test because "reasonableness" is not just a question of what the lawyer believed to be the case at the time. In practice, "reasonableness" is determined by the trier of fact, after the fact, and with "twenty-twenty" hindsight of what went wrong. Like the "reasonable man" of tort negligence, this is not a subjective question of the lawyer's good or bad intentions, but rather an objective standard of professional conduct, established by much case law.

C. Evolution of Rules

It is worth comparing the existing *Model Rule* 1.7 with the *Mass. Rule* 1.7 and the old ABA *Code* of 1969. This is not just because the *Code* is still in effect in some states, or because it still applies to a diminishing number of cases dating from before the *Model Rules* were adopted. (In Massachusetts, these would be cases involving attorney conduct before January 1, 1998). The comparison is also important because it shows how rules evolve over time.

For example, the "trigger" for the old ABA *Code* concurrent conflict rule, DR-5-105(A), was not "directly adverse" interests, as in *Model Rule* 1.7, but "differing interests," with the latter defined in the Definition Section of the *Code* as including "every in-

---

1. *Model Rule* 1.7 also governs if there is "a significant risk that the representation of one or more clients will be materially limited by the lawyer's responsibility to ... a former client." *Model Rule* 1.7 (a)(2). Such a conflict under Rule 1.7 can only be waived if the lawyer "reasonably believes that the lawyer will be able to provide competent and diligent representation...," and both the former and present clients give informed consent in writing.

terest that will adversely affect either the judgment or the loyalty of a lawyer to a client, whether it be a conflicting, inconsistent, diverse, or other interest." (Note, both the ABA *Code* and the *Model Rules* (Rule 1.0) have definition sections. Be sure to check them!) This seems to be a significantly more rigorous standard than *Model Rule* 1.7. In addition, the "two-pronged" test under DR-5-105 (c) requires client consent "after full disclosure" and that "it is obvious that he [the lawyer] can adequately represent the interests of each." Is this "obviousness" standard tougher than *Mode Rule* 1.7's "reasonableness" standard? It would appear so.[2]

But the new *Model Rule* 1.7 is tougher in other ways. For example, it requires "consent confirmed in writing." It also has added bars against representations "prohibited by law" or "involving the assertion of a claim by one client against another client represented by the lawyer in the same litigation or other proceedings before a tribunal," not found in the *Mass. Rule* 1.7, although Massachusetts case law had reached similar conclusions. See *The McCourt Company, Inc.* v. *FPC Properties, Inc.*, 386 Mass. 145 (1982), set out at Chapter II-3, *infra*. In short, the conflicts rules not only exist in differing forms in different jurisdictions, they also evolve over time.

D. "Issue" Conflicts

Lawyers are taught to argue both sides of a legal question. Moot court teams do it all the time. Traditionally, there has been no requirement that you actually believe your legal argument, made as an advocate, should prevail if you were the judge. Everyone with any sophistication understands that lawyers are not expected just to make the arguments they believe should win. Rather, they should do their best to argue for the client, as long as the arguments are not frivolous, false, fraudulent, or intended for harassment. This is a keystone of the adversary system. (There is one important limitation to this principle which we will discuss in Chapter V. You must disclose legal authority in the controlling jurisdiction "known to the lawyer to be directly adverse to the position of the client and not disclosed by opposing counsel." *Model Rule* 3.3).

From this it follows that a lawyer can stand up in court on one day and make argument "X" for one client, and stand up at a different time and make argument "Y" for another client. In general, courts and rule makers have not regarded such "issue conflicts" as constituting prohibited conflicts of interest that go to professional loyalty, unless some economic or other non-theoretical adversity exists between the clients. But both the *Model Rule* 1.7 and *Mass. Rule* 1.7 have attached "comments" that address this issue. These comments are different! *Mass. Rule* 1.7 Comment [9] reads:

> "[9] A lawyer may ordinarily represent parties having antagonistic positions on a legal question that has arisen in different matters. However, the antagonism may relate to an issue that is so crucial to the resolution of a matter as to require that the clients be advised of the conflict and their consent obtained. On rare occasions, such as the argument of both sides of a legal question before the same court at the same time, the conflict may be so severe that a lawyer could nor continue the representation even with client consent."

---

2. See *T.C. & Theatre Corp.* v. *Warner Bros. Pictures*, 113 F. Supp. 265 (S.D.N.Y., 1953). Interestingly, the old ABA *Code* had no rule governing "successive" conflicts of interest, like *Model Rule* 1.9, at all! But similar standards were established by case law.

Model Rule 1.7 comment [24] reads:

> "[24] Ordinarily a lawyer may take inconsistent legal positions in different tribunals at different times on behalf of different clients. The mere fact that advocating a legal position on behalf of one client might create precedent adverse to the interests of a client represented by the lawyer in an unrelated matter does not create a conflict of interest. A conflict of interest exists, however, if there is a significant risk that a lawyer's action on behalf of one client will materially limit the lawyer's effectiveness in representing another client in a different case; for example, when a decision favoring one client will create a precedent likely to seriously weaken the position taken on behalf of the other client. Factors relevant in determining whether the clients need to be advised of the risk include: where the cases are pending, whether the issue is substantive or procedural, the temporal relationship between the matters, the significance of the issue to the immediate and long-term interests of the clients involved and the clients' reasonable expectations in retaining the lawyer. If there is significant risk of material limitation, then absent informed consent of the affected clients, the lawyer must refuse one of the representations or withdraw from one or both matters."

As you study the rules, you will notice that the "Comments" often are more specific and more directive than the rules themselves. It is clearly a bad idea not to read them, even if the rule seems clear on its face. But is this good rulemaking? As mentioned before, the Massachusetts Supreme Judicial Court has even disapproved a comment that it promulgated itself. See *Messing, Rudavsky & Weliky P.C. v. President and Fellows of Harvard College*, in Chapter I-1, footnote 9, *supra*. This case is set out in full at Chapter VI-3.

In any event, practicing lawyers have no choice. It is important to read the comments, just as it is important to check the "Definitions" sections of both the *Model Rules* and the *Code*.

II-2. Concurrent Conflicts of Interest: The Rules

ABA Model Rules

RULE 1.7: CONFLICT OF INTEREST: CURRENT CLIENTS

(a) Except as provided in paragraph (b), a lawyer shall not represent a client if the representation involves a concurrent conflict of interest. A concurrent conflict of interest exists if:

(1) the representation of one client will be directly adverse to another client; or

(2) there is a significant risk that the representation of one or more clients will be materially limited by the lawyer's responsibilities to another client, a former client or a third person or by a personal interest of the lawyer.

(b) Notwithstanding the existence of a concurrent conflict of interest under paragraph (a), a lawyer may represent a client if:

(1) the lawyer reasonably believes that the lawyer will be able to provide competent and diligent representation to each affected client;

(2) the representation is not prohibited by law;

(3) the representation does not involve the assertion of a claim by one client against another client represented by the lawyer in the same litigation or other proceeding before a tribunal; and

(4) each affected client gives informed consent, confirmed in writing.

Comment

General Principles

[1] Loyalty and independent judgment are essential elements in the lawyer's relationship to a client. Concurrent conflicts of interest can arise from the lawyer's responsibilities to another client, a former client or a third person or from the lawyer's own interests. For specific Rules regarding certain concurrent conflicts of interest, see Rule 1.8. For former client conflicts of interest, see Rule 1.9. For conflicts of interest involving prospective clients, see Rule 1.18. For definitions of "informed consent" and "confirmed in writing," see Rule 1.0(e) and (b).

[2] Resolution of a conflict of interest problem under this Rule requires the lawyer to: 1) clearly identify the client or clients; 2) determine whether a conflict of interest exists; 3) decide whether the representation may be undertaken despite the existence of a conflict, i.e., whether the conflict is consentable; and 4) if so, consult with the clients affected under paragraph (a) and obtain their informed consent, confirmed in writing. The clients affected under paragraph (a) include both of the clients referred to in paragraph (a)(1) and the one or more clients whose representation might be materially limited under paragraph (a)(2).

[3] A conflict of interest may exist before representation is undertaken, in which event the representation must be declined, unless the lawyer obtains the informed consent of each client under the conditions of paragraph (b). To determine whether a conflict of interest exists, a lawyer should adopt reasonable procedures, appropriate for the size and type of firm and practice, to determine in both litigation and non-litigation matters the persons and issues involved. See also Comment to Rule 5.1. Ignorance caused by a failure to institute such procedures will not excuse a lawyer's violation of this Rule. As to whether a client-lawyer relationship exists or, having once been established, is continuing, see Comment to Rule 1.3 and Scope.

[4] If a conflict arises after representation has been undertaken, the lawyer ordinarily must withdraw from the representation, unless the lawyer has obtained the informed consent of the client under the conditions of paragraph (b). See Rule 1.16. Where more than one client is involved, whether the lawyer may continue to represent any of the clients is determined both by the lawyer's ability to comply with duties owed to the former client and by the lawyer's ability to represent adequately the remaining client or clients, given the lawyer's duties to the former client. See Rule 1.9. See also Comments [5] and [29].

[5] Unforeseeable developments, such as changes in corporate and other organizational affiliations or the addition or realignment of parties in litigation, might create conflicts in the midst of a representation, as when a company sued by the lawyer on behalf of one client is bought by another client represented by the lawyer in an unrelated matter. Depending on the circumstances, the lawyer may have the option to withdraw from one of the representations in order to avoid the conflict. The lawyer must seek court approval where necessary and take steps to minimize harm to the clients. See Rule 1.16. The lawyer must continue to protect the confidences of the client from whose representation the lawyer has withdrawn. See Rule 1.9(c).

Identifying Conflicts of Interest: Directly Adverse

[6] Loyalty to a current client prohibits undertaking representation directly adverse to that client without that client's informed consent. Thus, absent consent, a lawyer may not act as an advocate in one matter against a person the lawyer represents in some other matter, even when the matters are wholly unrelated. The client as to whom the representation is directly adverse is likely to feel betrayed, and the resulting damage to the client-lawyer relationship is likely to impair the lawyer's ability to represent the client effectively. In addition, the client on whose behalf the adverse representation is undertaken reasonably may fear that the lawyer will pursue that client's case less effectively out of deference to the other client, i.e., that the representation may be materially limited by the lawyer's interest in retaining the current client. Similarly, a directly adverse conflict may arise when a lawyer is required to cross-examine a client who appears as a witness in a lawsuit involving another client, as when the testimony will be damaging to the client who is represented in the lawsuit. On the other hand, simultaneous representation in unrelated matters of clients whose interests are only economically adverse, such as representation of competing economic enterprises in unrelated litigation, does not ordinarily constitute a conflict of interest and thus may not require consent of the respective clients.

[7] Directly adverse conflicts can also arise in transactional matters. For example, if a lawyer is asked to represent the seller of a business in negotiations with a buyer represented by the lawyer, not in the same transaction but in another, unrelated matter, the lawyer could not undertake the representation without the informed consent of each client.

Identifying Conflicts of Interest: Material Limitation

[8] Even where there is no direct adverseness, a conflict of interest exists if there is a significant risk that a lawyer's ability to consider, recommend or carry out an appropriate course of action for the client will be materially limited as a result of the lawyer's other responsibilities or interests. For example, a lawyer asked to represent several individuals seeking to form a joint venture is likely to be materially limited in the lawyer's ability to recommend or advocate all possible positions that each might take because of the lawyer's duty of loyalty to the others. The conflict in effect forecloses alternatives that would otherwise be available to the client. The mere possibility of subsequent harm does not itself require disclosure and consent. The critical questions are the likelihood that a difference in interests will eventuate and, if it does, whether it will materially interfere with the lawyer's independent professional judgment in considering alternatives or foreclose courses of action that reasonably should be pursued on behalf of the client.

Lawyer's Responsibilities to Former Clients and Other Third Persons

[9] In addition to conflicts with other current clients, a lawyer's duties of loyalty and independence may be materially limited by responsibilities to former clients under Rule 1.9 or by the lawyer's responsibilities to other persons, such as fiduciary duties arising from a lawyer's service as a trustee, executor or corporate director.

Personal Interest Conflicts

[10] The lawyer's own interests should not be permitted to have an adverse effect on representation of a client. For example, if the probity of a lawyer's own conduct in a transaction is in serious question, it may be difficult or impossible for the lawyer to give a client detached advice. Similarly, when a lawyer has discussions concerning possible employment with an opponent of the lawyer's client, or with a law firm representing the

opponent, such discussions could materially limit the lawyer's representation of the client. In addition, a lawyer may not allow related business interests to affect representation, for example, by referring clients to an enterprise in which the lawyer has an undisclosed financial interest. See Rule 1.8 for specific Rules pertaining to a number of personal interest conflicts, including business transactions with clients. See also Rule 1.10 (personal interest conflicts under Rule 1.7 ordinarily are not imputed to other lawyers in a law firm).

[11] When lawyers representing different clients in the same matter or in substantially related matters are closely related by blood or marriage, there may be a significant risk that client confidences will be revealed and that the lawyer's family relationship will interfere with both loyalty and independent professional judgment. As a result, each client is entitled to know of the existence and implications of the relationship between the lawyers before the lawyer agrees to undertake the representation. Thus, a lawyer related to another lawyer, e.g., as parent, child, sibling or spouse, ordinarily may not represent a client in a matter where that lawyer is representing another party, unless each client gives informed consent. The disqualification arising from a close family relationship is personal and ordinarily is not imputed to members of firms with whom the lawyers are associated. See Rule 1.10.

[12] A lawyer is prohibited from engaging in sexual relationships with a client unless the sexual relationship predates the formation of the client-lawyer relationship. See Rule 1.8(j).

Interest of Person Paying for a Lawyer's Service

[13] A lawyer may be paid from a source other than the client, including a co-client, if the client is informed of that fact and consents and the arrangement does not compromise the lawyer's duty of loyalty or independent judgment to the client. See Rule 1.8(f). If acceptance of the payment from any other source presents a significant risk that the lawyer's representation of the client will be materially limited by the lawyer's own interest in accommodating the person paying the lawyer's fee or by the lawyer's responsibilities to a payer who is also a co-client, then the lawyer must comply with the requirements of paragraph (b) before accepting the representation, including determining whether the conflict is consentable and, if so, that the client has adequate information about the material risks of the representation.

Prohibited Representations

[14] Ordinarily, clients may consent to representation notwithstanding a conflict. However, as indicated in paragraph (b), some conflicts are nonconsentable, meaning that the lawyer involved cannot properly ask for such agreement or provide representation on the basis of the client's consent. When the lawyer is representing more than one client, the question of consentability must be resolved as to each client.

[15] Consentability is typically determined by considering whether the interests of the clients will be adequately protected if the clients are permitted to give their informed consent to representation burdened by a conflict of interest. Thus, under paragraph (b)(1), representation is prohibited if in the circumstances the lawyer cannot reasonably conclude that the lawyer will be able to provide competent and diligent representation. See Rule 1.1 (competence) and Rule 1.3 (diligence).

[16] Paragraph (b)(2) describes conflicts that are nonconsentable because the representation is prohibited by applicable law. For example, in some states substantive law provides that the same lawyer may not represent more than one defendant in a capital case,

even with the consent of the clients, and under federal criminal statutes certain representations by a former government lawyer are prohibited, despite the informed consent of the former client. In addition, decisional law in some states limits the ability of a governmental client, such as a municipality, to consent to a conflict of interest.

[17] Paragraph (b)(3) describes conflicts that are nonconsentable because of the institutional interest in vigorous development of each client's position when the clients are aligned directly against each other in the same litigation or other proceeding before a tribunal. Whether clients are aligned directly against each other within the meaning of this paragraph requires examination of the context of the proceeding. Although this paragraph does not preclude a lawyer's multiple representation of adverse parties to a mediation (because mediation is not a proceeding before a "tribunal" under Rule 1.0(m)), such representation may be precluded by paragraph (b)(1).

Informed Consent

[18] Informed consent requires that each affected client be aware of the relevant circumstances and of the material and reasonably foreseeable ways that the conflict could have adverse effects on the interests of that client. See Rule 1.0(e) (informed consent). The information required depends on the nature of the conflict and the nature of the risks involved. When representation of multiple clients in a single matter is undertaken, the information must include the implications of the common representation, including possible effects on loyalty, confidentiality and the attorney-client privilege and the advantages and risks involved. See Comments [30] and [31] (effect of common representation on confidentiality).

[19] Under some circumstances it may be impossible to make the disclosure necessary to obtain consent. For example, when the lawyer represents different clients in related matters and one of the clients refuses to consent to the disclosure necessary to permit the other client to make an informed decision, the lawyer cannot properly ask the latter to consent. In some cases the alternative to common representation can be that each party may have to obtain separate representation with the possibility of incurring additional costs. These costs, along with the benefits of securing separate representation, are factors that may be considered by the affected client in determining whether common representation is in the client's interests.

Consent Confirmed in Writing

[20] Paragraph (b) requires the lawyer to obtain the informed consent of the client, confirmed in writing. Such a writing may consist of a document executed by the client or one that the lawyer promptly records and transmits to the client following an oral consent. See Rule 1.0(b). See also Rule 1.0(n) (writing includes electronic transmission). If it is not feasible to obtain or transmit the writing at the time the client gives informed consent, then the lawyer must obtain or transmit it within a reasonable time thereafter. See Rule 1.0(b). The requirement of a writing does not supplant the need in most cases for the lawyer to talk with the client, to explain the risks and advantages, if any, of representation burdened with a conflict of interest, as well as reasonably available alternatives, and to afford the client a reasonable opportunity to consider the risks and alternatives and to raise questions and concerns. Rather, the writing is required in order to impress upon clients the seriousness of the decision the client is being asked to make and to avoid disputes or ambiguities that might later occur in the absence of a writing.

Revoking Consent

[21] A client who has given consent to a conflict may revoke the consent and, like any other client, may terminate the lawyer's representation at any time. Whether revoking

consent to the client's own representation precludes the lawyer from continuing to represent other clients depends on the circumstances, including the nature of the conflict, whether the client revoked consent because of a material change in circumstances, the reasonable expectations of the other client and whether material detriment to the other clients or the lawyer would result.

Consent to Future Conflict

[22] Whether a lawyer may properly request a client to waive conflicts that might arise in the future is subject to the test of paragraph (b). The effectiveness of such waivers is generally determined by the extent to which the client reasonably understands the material risks that the waiver entails. The more comprehensive the explanation of the types of future representations that might arise and the actual and reasonably foreseeable adverse consequences of those representations, the greater the likelihood that the client will have the requisite understanding. Thus, if the client agrees to consent to a particular type of conflict with which the client is already familiar, then the consent ordinarily will be effective with regard to that type of conflict. If the consent is general and open-ended, then the consent ordinarily will be ineffective, because it is not reasonably likely that the client will have understood the material risks involved. On the other hand, if the client is an experienced user of the legal services involved and is reasonably informed regarding the risk that a conflict may arise, such consent is more likely to be effective, particularly if, e.g., the client is independently represented by other counsel in giving consent and the consent is limited to future conflicts unrelated to the subject of the representation. In any case, advance consent cannot be effective if the circumstances that materialize in the future are such as would make the conflict nonconsentable under paragraph (b).

Conflicts in Litigation

[23] Paragraph (b)(3) prohibits representation of opposing parties in the same litigation, regardless of the clients' consent. On the other hand, simultaneous representation of parties whose interests in litigation may conflict, such as coplaintiffs or codefendants, is governed by paragraph (a)(2). A conflict may exist by reason of substantial discrepancy in the parties' testimony, incompatibility in positions in relation to an opposing party or the fact that there are substantially different possibilities of settlement of the claims or liabilities in question. Such conflicts can arise in criminal cases as well as civil. The potential for conflict of interest in representing multiple defendants in a criminal case is so grave that ordinarily a lawyer should decline to represent more than one codefendant. On the other hand, common representation of persons having similar interests in civil litigation is proper if the requirements of paragraph (b) are met.

[24] Ordinarily a lawyer may take inconsistent legal positions in different tribunals at different times on behalf of different clients. The mere fact that advocating a legal position on behalf of one client might create precedent adverse to the interests of a client represented by the lawyer in an unrelated matter does not create a conflict of interest. A conflict of interest exists, however, if there is a significant risk that a lawyer's action on behalf of one client will materially limit the lawyer's effectiveness in representing another client in a different case; for example, when a decision favoring one client will create a precedent likely to seriously weaken the position taken on behalf of the other client. Factors relevant in determining whether the clients need to be advised of the risk include: where the cases are pending, whether the issue is substantive or procedural, the temporal relationship between the matters, the significance of the issue to the immediate and long-term interests of the clients involved and the clients' reasonable expecta-

tions in retaining the lawyer. If there is significant risk of material limitation, then absent informed consent of the affected clients, the lawyer must refuse one of the representations or withdraw from one or both matters.

[25] When a lawyer represents or seeks to represent a class of plaintiffs or defendants in a class-action lawsuit, unnamed members of the class are ordinarily not considered to be clients of the lawyer for purposes of applying paragraph (a)(1) of this Rule. Thus, the lawyer does not typically need to get the consent of such a person before representing a client suing the person in an unrelated matter. Similarly, a lawyer seeking to represent an opponent in a class action does not typically need the consent of an unnamed member of the class whom the lawyer represents in an unrelated matter.

Nonlitigation Conflicts

[26] Conflicts of interest under paragraphs (a)(1) and (a)(2) arise in contexts other than litigation. For a discussion of directly adverse conflicts in transactional matters, see Comment [7]. Relevant factors in determining whether there is significant potential for material limitation include the duration and intimacy of the lawyer's relationship with the client or clients involved, the functions being performed by the lawyer, the likelihood that disagreements will arise and the likely prejudice to the client from the conflict. The question is often one of proximity and degree. See Comment [8].

[27] For example, conflict questions may arise in estate planning and estate administration. A lawyer may be called upon to prepare wills for several family members, such as husband and wife, and, depending upon the circumstances, a conflict of interest may be present. In estate administration the identity of the client may be unclear under the law of a particular jurisdiction. Under one view, the client is the fiduciary; under another view the client is the estate or trust, including its beneficiaries. In order to comply with conflict of interest rules, the lawyer should make clear the lawyer's relationship to the parties involved.

[28] Whether a conflict is consentable depends on the circumstances. For example, a lawyer may not represent multiple parties to a negotiation whose interests are fundamentally antagonistic to each other, but common representation is permissible where the clients are generally aligned in interest even though there is some difference in interest among them. Thus, a lawyer may seek to establish or adjust a relationship between clients on an amicable and mutually advantageous basis; for example, in helping to organize a business in which two or more clients are entrepreneurs, working out the financial reorganization of an enterprise in which two or more clients have an interest or arranging a property distribution in settlement of an estate. The lawyer seeks to resolve potentially adverse interests by developing the parties' mutual interests. Otherwise, each party might have to obtain separate representation, with the possibility of incurring additional cost, complication or even litigation. Given these and other relevant factors, the clients may prefer that the lawyer act for all of them.

Special Considerations in Common Representation

[29] In considering whether to represent multiple clients in the same matter, a lawyer should be mindful that if the common representation fails because the potentially adverse interests cannot be reconciled, the result can be additional cost, embarrassment and recrimination. Ordinarily, the lawyer will be forced to withdraw from representing all of the clients if the common representation fails. In some situations, the risk of failure is so great that multiple representation is plainly impossible. For example, a lawyer cannot undertake common representation of clients where contentious litigation or negotiations between them are imminent or contemplated. Moreover, because the lawyer

is required to be impartial between commonly represented clients, representation of multiple clients is improper when it is unlikely that impartiality can be maintained. Generally, if the relationship between the parties has already assumed antagonism, the possibility that the clients' interests can be adequately served by common representation is not very good. Other relevant factors are whether the lawyer subsequently will represent both parties on a continuing basis and whether the situation involves creating or terminating a relationship between the parties.

[30] A particularly important factor in determining the appropriateness of common representation is the effect on client-lawyer confidentiality and the attorney-client privilege. With regard to the attorney-client privilege, the prevailing rule is that, as between commonly represented clients, the privilege does not attach. Hence, it must be assumed that if litigation eventuates between the clients, the privilege will not protect any such communications, and the clients should be so advised.

[31] As to the duty of confidentiality, continued common representation will almost certainly be inadequate if one client asks the lawyer not to disclose to the other client information relevant to the common representation. This is so because the lawyer has an equal duty of loyalty to each client, and each client has the right to be informed of anything bearing on the representation that might affect that client's interests and the right to expect that the lawyer will use that information to that client's benefit. See Rule 1.4. The lawyer should, at the outset of the common representation and as part of the process of obtaining each client's informed consent, advise each client that information will be shared and that the lawyer will have to withdraw if one client decides that some matter material to the representation should be kept from the other. In limited circumstances, it may be appropriate for the lawyer to proceed with the representation when the clients have agreed, after being properly informed, that the lawyer will keep certain information confidential. For example, the lawyer may reasonably conclude that failure to disclose one client's trade secrets to another client will not adversely affect representation involving a joint venture between the clients and agree to keep that information confidential with the informed consent of both clients.

[32] When seeking to establish or adjust a relationship between clients, the lawyer should make clear that the lawyer's role is not that of partisanship normally expected in other circumstances and, thus, that the clients may be required to assume greater responsibility for decisions than when each client is separately represented. Any limitations on the scope of the representation made necessary as a result of the common representation should be fully explained to the clients at the outset of the representation. See Rule 1.2(c).

[33] Subject to the above limitations, each client in the common representation has the right to loyal and diligent representation and the protection of Rule 1.9 concerning the obligations to a former client. The client also has the right to discharge the lawyer as stated in Rule 1.16.

Organizational Clients

[34] A lawyer who represents a corporation or other organization does not, by virtue of that representation, necessarily represent any constituent or affiliated organization, such as a parent or subsidiary. See Rule 1.13(a). Thus, the lawyer for an organization is not barred from accepting representation adverse to an affiliate in an unrelated matter, unless the circumstances are such that the affiliate should also be considered a client of the lawyer, there is an understanding between the lawyer and the organizational client that the lawyer will avoid representation adverse to the client's affiliates, or the lawyer's obli-

gations to either the organizational client or the new client are likely to limit materially the lawyer's representation of the other client.

[35] A lawyer for a corporation or other organization who is also a member of its board of directors should determine whether the responsibilities of the two roles may conflict. The lawyer may be called on to advise the corporation in matters involving actions of the directors. Consideration should be given to the frequency with which such situations may arise, the potential intensity of the conflict, the effect of the lawyer's resignation from the board and the possibility of the corporation's obtaining legal advice from another lawyer in such situations. If there is material risk that the dual role will compromise the lawyer's independence of professional judgment, the lawyer should not serve as a director or should cease to act as the corporation's lawyer when conflicts of interest arise. The lawyer should advise the other members of the board that in some circumstances matters discussed at board meetings while the lawyer is present in the capacity of director might not be protected by the attorney-client privilege and that conflict of interest considerations might require the lawyer's recusal as a director or might require the lawyer and the lawyer's firm to decline representation of the corporation in a matter.

RULE 1.8: CONFLICT OF INTEREST: CURRENT CLIENTS: SPECIFIC RULES

(a) A lawyer shall not enter into a business transaction with a client or knowingly acquire an ownership, possessory, security or other pecuniary interest adverse to a client unless:

(1) the transaction and terms on which the lawyer acquires the interest are fair and reasonable to the client and are fully disclosed and transmitted in writing in a manner that can be reasonably understood by the client;

(2) the client is advised in writing of the desirability of seeking and is given a reasonable opportunity to seek the advice of independent legal counsel on the transaction; and

(3) the client gives informed consent, in a writing signed by the client, to the essential terms of the transaction and the lawyer's role in the transaction, including whether the lawyer is representing the client in the transaction.

(b) A lawyer shall not use information relating to representation of a client to the disadvantage of the client unless the client gives informed consent, except as permitted or required by these Rules.

(c) A lawyer shall not solicit any substantial gift from a client, including a testamentary gift, or prepare on behalf of a client an instrument giving the lawyer or a person related to the lawyer any substantial gift unless the lawyer or other recipient of the gift is related to the client. For purposes of this paragraph, related persons include a spouse, child, grandchild, parent, grandparent or other relative or individual with whom the lawyer or the client maintains a close, familial relationship.

(d) Prior to the conclusion of representation of a client, a lawyer shall not make or negotiate an agreement giving the lawyer literary or media rights to a portrayal or account based in substantial part on information relating to the representation.

(e) A lawyer shall not provide financial assistance to a client in connection with pending or contemplated litigation, except that:

(1) a lawyer may advance court costs and expenses of litigation, the repayment of which may be contingent on the outcome of the matter; and

(2) a lawyer representing an indigent client may pay court costs and expenses of litigation on behalf of the client.

(f) A lawyer shall not accept compensation for representing a client from one other than the client unless:

(1) the client gives informed consent;

(2) there is no interference with the lawyer's independence of professional judgment or with the client-lawyer relationship; and

(3) information relating to representation of a client is protected as required by Rule 1.6.

(g) A lawyer who represents two or more clients shall not participate in making an aggregate settlement of the claims of or against the clients, or in a criminal case an aggregated agreement as to guilty or nolo contendere pleas, unless each client gives informed consent, in a writing signed by the client. The lawyer's disclosure shall include the existence and nature of all the claims or pleas involved and of the participation of each person in the settlement.

(h) A lawyer shall not:

(1) make an agreement prospectively limiting the lawyer's liability to a client for malpractice unless the client is independently represented in making the agreement; or

(2) settle a claim or potential claim for such liability with an unrepresented client or former client unless that person is advised in writing of the desirability of seeking and is given a reasonable opportunity to seek the advice of independent legal counsel in connection therewith.

(i) A lawyer shall not acquire a proprietary interest in the cause of action or subject matter of litigation the lawyer is conducting for a client, except that the lawyer may:

(1) acquire a lien authorized by law to secure the lawyer's fee or expenses; and

(2) contract with a client for a reasonable contingent fee in a civil case.

(j) A lawyer shall not have sexual relations with a client unless a consensual sexual relationship existed between them when the client-lawyer relationship commenced.

(k) While lawyers are associated in a firm, a prohibition in the foregoing paragraphs (a) through (i) that applies to any one of them shall apply to all of them.

ABA Code

DR 5-105 Refusing to Accept or Continue Employment if the Interests of Another Client May Impair the Independent Professional Judgment of the Lawyer.

(A) A lawyer shall decline proffered employment if the exercise of his independent professional judgment in behalf of a client will be or is likely to be adversely affected by the acceptance of he proffered employment, or if it would be likely to involve him in representing differing interests, except to the extent permitted under DR 5-105(C).

(B) A lawyer shall not continue multiple employment if the exercise of his independent professional judgment in behalf of a client will be or is likely to be adversely affected by his representation of another client, or if it would be likely to involve him in representing differing interests, except to the extent permitted under DR 5-105(C).

(C) In the situations covered by DR 5-105(A) and (B), a lawyer may represent multiple clients if it is obvious that he can adequately represent the interest of each and if each consents to the representation after full disclosure of the possible effect of such representation on the exercise of his independent professional judgment on behalf of each.

II-3. Concurrent Conflicts of Interest: Cases and Materials

The McCourt Company v. FPC Properties et al.

386 Mass. 145
Suffolk. Argued Jan. 6, 1982–Decided May 6, 1982
[Some footnotes omitted. Remaining footnotes renumbered.]
Present: Hennessey, C.J., Wilkins, Abrams, Lynch & O'Connor, JJ.

WILKINS, J. A law firm that represents client A in the defense of an action may not, at the same time, be counsel for a plaintiff in an action brought against client A, at least without the consent of both clients. It does not matter that the law firm represents client A as a defendant because it was selected as A's counsel by A's liability insurer. See Opinion 80-10, Opinions of the Committee on Professional Ethics of the Massachusetts Bar Association, 66 Mass.L.Rev. 50 (1981). The law firm is attorney for the insured as well as the insurer. See *Imperiali* v. *Pica*, 338 Mass. 494, 499, 156 N.E.2d 44 (1959). Nor does it matter that client A is a corporation or that client A consists, collectively, of a parent corporation and various wholly owned subsidiaries. It is also irrelevant that the lawsuits are unrelated in subject matter and that it appears probable that client A will not in fact be prejudiced by the concurrent participation of the law firm in both actions. The undivided loyalty that a lawyer owes to his clients forbids him, without the clients' consent, from acting for client A in one action and at the same time against client A in another. If there are any special circumstances in which an exception to this general rule should be recognized, no such circumstances have been demonstrated here, and we are aware of no case in which such an exception has been recognized and applied.

The provisions of Disciplinary Rules 5-105(B) and 5-105(C), appearing in S.J.C. Rule 3:07, as amended, ___ Mass. ___ (effective January 1, 1981), explicitly forbid one attorney from acting for a client in the defense of one action and against that same client as counsel in a second action unless each client consents. "A lawyer shall not continue multiple employment ... if it would be likely to involve him in representing differing interests, except to the extent permitted under DR 5-105(C)." DR 5-105(B). Acting for a client in one action and against the same client in another action constitutes "representing differing interests" within the meaning of DR 5-105(B). "Differing interests" does not mean "conflicting interests." See A. L. Kaufman, Problems in Professional Responsibility at 37 (1976). Rule DR 5-105(C) states that "a lawyer may represent multiple clients if it is obvious that he can adequately represent the interest of each *and if each consents to the representation* after full disclosure of the possible effect of such representation on the exercise of his independent professional judgment on behalf of each" (emphasis supplied). Even if it is clear that the attorney can adequately represent the interests of each client where he represents differing interests, he may not do so without the consent of each.

This action, brought on behalf of the McCourt Company (McCourt) on April 2, 1981, seeks specific performance of an option agreement and damages against FPC

Properties, Inc., a wholly owned subsidiary of Cabot, Cabot & Forbes Co., with respect to certain property in the Fort Point Channel area of Boston. We shall refer to Cabot, Cabot & Forbes Co. and its wholly owned subsidiaries collectively as CC & F. On April 22, 1981, attorneys for the Boston law firm of Parker, Coulter, Daley & White (Parker, Coulter) entered an appearance for McCourt. By an amended complaint, the parent corporation, Cabot, Cabot & Forbes Co., was named as a defendant as guarantor of certain obligations of FPC Properties, Inc. Cabot, Cabot & Forbes Co. has a substantial interest in the litigation. It is not merely a nominal party.

In May, 1981, counsel for the defendants moved to disqualify Parker, Coulter from representing McCourt on the ground that Parker, Coulter had represented CC & F as defense counsel in numerous personal injury cases throughout the Commonwealth and that Parker, Coulter continued to so represent CC & F. Parker, Coulter and CC & F have agreed that at all material times Parker, Coulter has represented CC & F in the defense of personal injury actions, and that Aetna Life and Casualty Insurance Company, insurer for CC & F, selected Parker, Coulter to represent CC & F. Four such tort actions were pending on October 26, 1981, one of which CC & F's insurer apparently referred to Parker, Coulter after this action was commenced.

In opposition to the motion to disqualify it, Parker, Coulter argued that disqualification is not required in every simultaneous representation case. It argued that, in this case, there is no actual or apparent conflict of loyalties or obligations; that it has been entrusted with no confidences or secrets that could be used against CC & F; and that it is unlikely that any adverse effect on its independent judgment on behalf of CC & F would result from its adversary posture toward CC & F in this action. We assume, although the record does not show it, that McCourt has consented to both (1) Parker, Coulter's representation of it in an action against another client of Parker, Coulter (CC & F) and (2) Parker, Coulter's representation of CC & F in a personal injury action referred to Parker, Coulter after this action was commenced.

The Superior Court judge who heard the motion essentially accepted this argument and denied the motion to disqualify Parker, Coulter. He concluded that the facts warranted an exception to the general rule because (1) Parker, Coulter's independent professional judgment in its representation of CC & F would not be adversely affected; (2) Parker, Coulter was not representing differing interests (which he defined as "conflicting, inconsistent, diverse or otherwise discordant"); and (3) CC & F had not shown that Parker, Coulter would not represent CC & F properly. We transferred CC & F's appeal here on our own motion. For reasons we have already stated, the standards and burden of proof applied by the judge were not the appropriate ones. The motion to disqualify Parker, Coulter should have been allowed.

In other jurisdictions where the propriety of simultaneous representation of a client in one action and of his opponent in another action, involving an unrelated subject, has been considered, courts have viewed DR 5-105, and the attorney's ethical obligations, as we have stated them. See *International Business Machs. Corp.* v. *Levin*, 579 F.2d 271, 280 (3rd Cir. 1978) ("We think, however, that it is likely that some 'adverse effect' on an attorney's exercise of his independent judgment on behalf of a client may result from the attorney's adversary posture toward that client in another legal matter"); *Fund of Funds, Ltd.* v. *Arthur Andersen & Co.*, 567 F.2d 225, 232–233 (2d Cir. 1977); *Cinema 5, Ltd.* v. *Cinerama, Inc.*, 528 F.2d 1384, 1386 (2d Cir. 1976) ("Under the Code (of Professional Responsibility), the lawyer who would sue his own client, asserting in justification the lack of 'substantial relationship' between the litigation and the work he has undertaken to perform for that client, is leaning on a slender reed indeed. Putting it as mildly as we can, we think it would be questionable conduct for an attorney to participate in any lawsuit against his own client without the knowledge and consent of all concerned"); *Pennwalt Corp.* v. *Plough, Inc.*, 85 F.R.D. 264, 271 (D.Del.1980); *Jeffry* v. *Pounds*, 67 Cal.App.3d 6, 10–12, 136 Cal.Rptr. 373 (1977); *Grievance Comm. of the Bar of Hartford County* v. *Rottner*, 152 Conn. 59, 65, 203 A.2d 82 (1964). See also Note, Developments in the Law: Conflicts of Interest in the Legal Profession, 94 Harv.L.Rev. 1244, 1293–1294, 1302–1303 (1981).

Although Parker, Coulter argues that opinions elsewhere are not apt in this case and that some leave room in their language for an exception to the general rule, its basic argument is that this court should fashion an exception to the general rule where a commercial corporation is involved.[1] No other court has recognized such an exception. There does not appear to be any tendency in favor of such an exception. The ABA Model Rules of Professional Conduct (Proposed Final Draft, 1981) advanced by the so called Kutak Commission make no distinction between clients who are natural persons and those that are corporations. See Rule 1.7, set forth in the margin.[2] The Kutak Commission's comment on Rule 1.7 includes statements that are wholly consistent with our view of DR 5-105(B) and DR 5-105(C).[3]

Parker, Coulter points to language appearing in Opinion No. 75-7 at 7–8 (March 13, 1975), issued by the Committee on Professional Ethics of the Massachusetts Bar Association. That opinion, which is quoted in relevant part in the margin,[4] recognized that a

---

1. Cases involving interests of a former client, of course, stand on a different footing. It seems that the Cinema 5, Ltd., and International Business Machs. cases, cited immediately above, dealt with versions of DR 5-105(B) parallel to that which existed in the ABA Code of Professional Responsibility just prior to its amendment in 1974. As it then appeared, the disciplinary rule did not forbid simultaneous representation of "differing interests," but only simultaneous representation likely to adversely affect the lawyer's independent professional judgment. Because of this circumstance, the conclusions of the Second and the Third Circuit Courts of Appeals are perhaps even more persuasive in support of the result we reach.

2. "RULE 1.7 CONFLICT OF INTEREST: GENERAL RULE

"(a) A lawyer shall not represent a client if the lawyer's ability to consider, recommend or carry out a course of action on behalf of the client will be adversely affected by the lawyer's responsibilities to another client or to a third person, or by the lawyer's own interests.

"(b) When a lawyer's own interests or other responsibilities might adversely affect the representation of a client, the lawyer shall not represent the client unless:

"(1) The lawyer reasonably believes the other responsibilities or interests involved will not adversely affect the best interest of the client; and

"(2) The client consents after disclosure. When representation of multiple clients in a single matter is undertaken, the disclosure shall include explanation of the implications of the common representation and the advantages and risks involved."

3. "Ordinarily, a lawyer may not act as advocate against a person the lawyer represents in some other matter, even if the other matter is wholly unrelated. However, there are circumstances in which a lawyer may act as advocate against a client. For example, a lawyer engaged in a suit against an enterprise with diverse operations may accept employment by the enterprise in an unrelated matter if doing so will not affect the lawyer's conduct of the suit and if both clients consent upon disclosure." Rule 1.7 supra at 49.

…."Absent client consent, a lawyer cannot undertake representation adverse to a current client even in an entirely unrelated matter. E.g., IBM Corp. v. Levin, 579 F.2d 271 (3d Cir. 1978); Chateau de Ville Productions v. Tams-Whitmark Music Library, 474 F.Supp. 223 (S.D.N.Y.1979); Grievance Comm. v. Rottner, 152 Conn. 59, 203 A.2d 82 (1964); In re Gillard, 271 N.W.2d 785 (Minn.1978); In re Cohn, 46 N.J. 202, 216 A.2d 1 (1966); In re Hansen, 586 P.2d 413 (Utah 1978)." Rule 1.7 supra at 54.

4. "It seems to be a generally accepted standard of ethical conduct that a lawyer should not take a case against a present client of himself or his firm, unless the client consents, at least where the client is an individual person.

lawyer should not take a case against a present client unless the client consents, at least where the client is an individual person. The committee expressed concern that, where a client is a large corporation, the corporation may distribute its legal business with the view to barring any local attorney from handling cases against the corporation. However, the Committee of Professional Ethics did not pass on this question because the issue was not presented on the facts before it. Similarly, we need not pass on the question because Parker, Coulter has not shown any such anticipatorily defensive behavior by CC & F.

We conclude by noting that this case does not involve any reprehensibly unethical conduct. It represents an honest disagreement concerning the appropriate application of the Code of Professional Responsibility. CC & F has not objected, as far as the record discloses, to Parker, Coulter's continuing representation of it in the various personal injury actions brought against CC & F.

We recognize that McCourt has an interest in having counsel of its own choosing, but McCourt's interest cannot predominate in all instances. That right is not absolute and must yield in these circumstances. See *International Business Machs. Corp.* v. *Levin*, 579 F.2d 271, 283 (3rd Cir. 1978); *Silver Chrysler Plymouth, Inc.* v. *Chrysler Motors Corp.*, 518 F.2d 751, 757 (2d Cir. 1975). In the absence of consent by CC & F (and McCourt), DR 5-105(B) and DR 5-105(C) bar Parker, Coulter from representing McCourt in this action while Parker, Coulter is acting as counsel for CC & F in other matters.

The order of the Superior Court judge denying the motion to disqualify Parker, Coulter is vacated. An order allowing that motion should be entered on such conditions as seem appropriate, in the discretion of the judge, concerning Parker, Coulter's cooperation over a limited transitional period with successor counsel for McCourt and concerning delivery of appropriate documents to successor counsel. The process of promptly disengaging Parker, Coulter from this case should be carried out with fair consideration of the interests of McCourt, as well as, of course, the interests of CC & F.

So ordered.

"....

"However, we are concerned with the implications of the (Grievance Comm. v.) Rottner (152 Conn. 59, 203 A.2d 82 (1964)) rationale (i.e., that a client is entitled to the undivided loyalty of his lawyer) if it is extended to large commercial clients. It is obvious that a large bank, insurance company, or industrial company which has a considerable volume of legal work may find it advantageous to spread that work among a number of local lawyers or law firms in the expectation that none of them then will be left free to handle cases against the company.

"If both clients give informed consent, we believe that a lawyer properly may undertake an adversary matter against such a commercial client even if it is his present client. We express no opinion at this time as to whether or not the lawyer could undertake such a case without the consent of the commercial client, preferring to defer consideration of that matter until it is put to us in a specific factual context."

Baldasarre v. Butler

132 N.J. 278
Supreme Court of New Jersey
Argued Dec. 1, 1992
Decided March 11, 1993
[Footnotes omitted.]

Vendors brought action against purchaser and attorney, alleging legal and equitable fraud and seeking rescission of contract and compensatory and punitive damages. Purchaser brought counterclaim seeking damages for tortious interference with prospective economic advantage and seeking to compel vendors to convey property. The Superior Court, Chancery Division, Somerset County, required vendors to close title and subsequently rejected vendors' fraud claim and found for purchaser on counterclaim. Appeals were taken. The Superior Court, Appellate Division, 254 N.J.Super. 502, 604 A.2d 112, reversed and remanded in part and vacated in part. Attorney, his law firm, and purchaser petitioned for certification, which was granted. The Supreme Court, Garibaldi, J., held that: (1) purchaser was not vicariously liable for any fraud of attorney, who represented both vendors and purchaser, and (2) vendors were not liable to purchaser for tortious interference with purchaser's contract to resell property.

Affirmed in part, reversed in part, and remanded.

[EXCERPT]
Page 467
IV

This case graphically demonstrates the conflicts that arise when an attorney, even with both clients' consent, undertakes the representation of the buyer and the seller in a complex commercial real estate transaction. The disastrous consequences of Butler's dual representation convinces us that a new bright-line rule prohibiting dual representation is necessary in commercial real estate transactions where large sums of money are at stake, where contracts contain complex contingencies, or where options are numerous. The potential for conflict in that type of complex real estate transaction is too great to permit even consensual dual representation of buyer and seller. Therefore, we hold that an attorney may not represent both the buyer and the seller in a complex commercial real estate transaction even if both give their informed consent.

The Legal Ethics of Louis D. Brandeis

John P. Frank, from 17 *Stan. L. Rev.* 683 (1964–1965) [Excerpted]
[Some footnotes omitted. Remaining footnotes renumbered.]

There is a common though rueful impression that if Jesus were to return to this earth, he would be arrested for vagrancy, disorderly conduct, or inciting to revolution. Louis D. Brandeis was no saint, but he gives us a case in point on a very human scale. Brandeis did guide his life by a standard more severe and exacting than most of us, and his appointment to the United States Supreme Court came close to being a rendezvous for a lynching.

* * *

I

The Brandeis appointment raised no question of competence. The long-time head of a great New England firm was clearly able. After extended hearings, however, the Republican minority of the Judiciary Committee reported adversely to Brandeis. They adopted as their own the conclusion of six former presidents of the American Bar Association, including Taft, that Brandeis was "not a fit person to be a member of the Supreme Court of the United States." The minority listed, in summary, twelve specific counts of ethical unfitness on which they based this grave conclusion. Of these twelve charges, five do not in retrospect warrant more than most casual discussion. [Note: what follows is Frank's discussion of the three most serious charges.]

* * *

4. The Warren Matter

Charge:

That he for a long time represented and collected fees from two clients whose interests were diametrically opposed to each other and when they, later, went to law over those same conflicting interests he took employment for one of them against the other.

Facts: The actual event has only a remote resemblance to the charge so succinctly stated. In 1888 and before, Brandeis and his partner, Sam Warren, were counsel for S. D. Warren and Company, a paper manufacturing concern dominated by Sam Warren's father. In 1888 the elder Warren died, leaving a wife, a daughter, and four sons—Sam, Fiske, Henry, and Edward, commonly referred to as Ned. The estate covered all the investment in the paper mills except the very substantial portion owned by a person named Mason.

The Brandeis firm represented the estate, as well as the entire family. It was apparent that only Sam and Mason could make the business prosper; Ned, for example, preferred to live in England where he was engaged in the antique business. An arrangement was finally made—with the full and complete concurrence of every member of the family—whereby the properties were placed in trust, the three trustees being the mother, Mason, and Sam Warren. The trustees leased the property to a newly formed company of which Sam and Mason were the principal members. As the mills prospered, the lessees were entitled to keep a portion of the revenue for their services. Another portion passed to the trustees as payment on the lease and was distributed by the trustees among the various beneficiaries, of whom Ned was one.

This arrangement continued throughout the last decade of the nineteenth century. Sam Warren resigned from the law firm to devote himself entirely to his business, though his name was included in the firm name until 1897. The Brandeis firm continued to handle the legal problems of the trustees and the lessees.

After 1900, Ned Warren began to grow discontent with his brother's management of the family affairs. Finally, in 1909 he brought an action to void the lease and to secure an accounting. Ned was not a trustee, and all trustees—indeed all other members of the family—stood by Sam and supported the arrangement. In the resulting litigation the Brandeis firm represented the lessees. Any individual member of the family who became involved separately had individual counsel. In the course of the litigation, Sam Warren died. Ned's interest in the trust was bought out by the other members of the family, and the litigation was abandoned.

Ethical Problem: As this matter was presented to the Committee, there were essentially two charges. The first did not survive the investigation; and yet had it not been made, the second probably would never have been explored.

The first charge of the counsel who had represented Ned in the intra-family litigation was that the entire trust-lease arrangement had been a fraud upon their client and that the accounting methods used by Sam Warren were part of this fraud.

No one on the Committee, and no one likely to look into it at any subsequent time, could find any merit in this charge. The business prospered admirably under the direction of Sam Warren and Mason, and all interests seem to have been most fairly treated. Even the minority members of the Committee went out of their way to eliminate this issue.

The second charge, involving the true problem of legal ethics, was that the Brandeis firm could not properly represent the lessees in an action brought by a beneficiary of the trust. If there had been a dispute between the trustees and the lessees, the Brandeis firm could, of course, represent neither. There is an inherent possibility of conflict between the trustees and the lessees, it being the duty of the trustees to gain as much from the property as possible, and the natural inclination of the lessees to pay as little as possible. To this relationship, which involves a troublesome problem, we must return.

The Committee, however, did not raise this problem. To the criticism it did see fit to make there is little merit. The Committee report asserts that Brandeis represented two clients "whose interests were diametrically opposed to each other and when they, later, went to law over those same conflicting interests he took employment for one of them against the other." This is reckless talk. The only parties who ever "went to law" against each other were Ned and the lessees. Except as a member of the family group which had a common interest in the total situation, Ned was never represented by Brandeis. His interests as an heir in 1888 were represented in the sense that he was a member of a family which was making a common arrangement to deal with a common problem. Assuming that at that stage Ned's interest was technically in conflict with that of the lessees, Canon 6 expressly provides that one is not "to represent conflicting interests, except by express consent of all concerned given after a full disclosure of the facts." Ned, whose dealings were essentially with his brother Sam, completely consented to the whole arrangement and executed papers to that effect. As an individual he never paid a nickel to Brandeis. After 1890, except for drawing a will for Ned on one of his visits to Boston, Brandeis never — even in a technical sense — represented Ned or had any dealings with him.

We are here clearly concerned with three separate interests: those of the beneficiaries, the trust and the lessees. Simply because one of several beneficiaries becomes dissatisfied with the policies which a trust has been following and seeks to have them set aside does not require counsel to abandon the trustees who have employed him. As the majority of the Judiciary Committee said, "It would have been virtually a desertion if the counsel for the trustee and his firm had failed to act." Senator Walsh, noting that Ned had made no disclosures to the firm, confidential or otherwise, asked:

> Can it be that when the title of the trustee or his administration of the trust is attacked by one of the beneficiaries the attorney for the trustee can not represent him because, forsooth, the former has been drawing pay out of funds which belong equitably in part to the suing cestui? Is an attorney for a corporation precluded from defending its directors when assailed in court for malad-

ministration? Is the attorney for an executor or an administrator? The suggestion must have been made unreflectingly.[1]

The real problem is not whether Brandeis could properly represent either the trustees or the lessees against Ned, but whether he could ethically represent both the trustees and the lessees simultaneously. This was the principal matter that troubled Senator Works; his concern was not that Brandeis should have abandoned the representation in 1909, but that he erred in permitting the firm to represent both the trustee and the lessees in 1889. For a twenty-year period he was paid for services to both; and at the beginning of the relationship he represented the heirs as well.

Except where consent is given it is poor practice for an attorney to represent both a trust and someone leasing property from a trust. In Opinion No. 60 of the American Bar Association Committee on Legal Ethics, a trust company was trustee for an estate which it held for the life of *A*, with remainder over to various other persons. The remainder men can be considered to be in a position roughly similar to that of the beneficiaries under the Warren trust. The trust company, having sold property to *C*, filed an action seeking a court order declaring this sale legal. The remainder-men objected to the sale. The same lawyer represented the trust company, the purchaser, and the life tenant. This was held to be a clear violation of Canon 6 on Conflicts of Interest. The Committee said:

> The attorney for the purchaser ... could not properly also act for the trustee.
>
> The litigation that followed was caused by the different estimates of value placed on the property by the purchasers and the beneficiaries of the trust funds. The real question then was one between the purchaser and the beneficiaries of the trust. It was the duty of the trustee, inherent in its fiduciary capacity, to protect the interest of these beneficiaries. That duty could not be performed for it by an attorney who represented an adverse interest.

Assuming Opinion No. 60 to be correct, it differs from the Warren case first, as has been noted, because of the element of consent. It differs even more fundamentally because of the family nature of the transaction. When the elder Warren died, the Warren family faced a problem together. There is no canon of legal ethics which requires each of the relatives of the deceased to take different counsel to the funeral: if a half-dozen heirs were required to pay a half-dozen counsel, they would indeed have additional grounds for grief. Sherman L. Whipple, trial counsel for Ned in the 1909 litigation, testified at the 1916 hearing that given a situation of "perfect understanding and accord among all the members of the family" at the time the trust and lease arrangement was established, there could be no criticism of Brandeis's role. "[I]f that was so, and all parties assented, there was no violation of trust; and there was no moral wrong."

Presumably the reason the Republican minority did not rest its argument on the original multiple representations was that Senator Cummins rejected the suggestion that "it was improper for Mr. Brandeis to represent the heirs, trustees, and lessees in the original arrangement, because there were or might be conflicting interests ..." Senator Works, however, saw the problem differently. While his position is ambiguous, he

---

1. II *Hearings*, 227. Certainly Brandeis had no obligation to represent Ned, and it is equally certain that his obligation was to the trustees. In Trimble Estate, 392 Pa. 277, 140 A.2d 609 (1958), the court suggests that once an attorney has accepted the representation of a trust in an estate situation, it is unethical to represent a beneficiary in any manner adverse to the trust.

seemed to think it was a "bad practice" to represent a group in this situation. Moorefield Storey—a distinguished Boston attorney, a regular adversary of Brandeis, and a former president of the American Bar Association—was one of Ned Warren's counsel. Storey on the one hand seemed to agree with Works that this was a "bad practice," and yet he testified, "[I]f I had been in Mr. Brandeis's shoes when that situation came up, I think I would have taken the same course."

Once the facts of family representation and general consent of all parties to the basic arrangement are recognized as the essentials of the situation, the Warren charge evaporates. Granting that, as a fresh matter under Opinion No. 60, a scrupulous attorney might not enter such a situation after conflicts have already arisen, once he is innocently in the situation, there is no direction to go but forward. The lawyer cannot lightly withdraw from a representation once undertaken; as Canon 44 provides, he "should not throw up the unfinished task to the detriment of his client except for reasons of honor or self-respect." From 1889 to 1903, Ned Warren, both by express writing and by complete absence of objection, accepted the trust and lease arrangements. In 1903 he obtained independent counsel and was well represented at all subsequent times.

In 1909 he brought a lawsuit. For Brandeis to have failed to defend against that suit would have been, as the majority concluded, desertion of a plain duty.

5. *The Lennox Case*

Charge:

> That he took employment from a client, advised him to make an assignment for the benefit of his creditors, had his own partner appointed the assignee and afterwards denied that he had ever been employed by the client. That at the time he took the employment and gave the advice he was the attorney of one of the largest creditors of the client and for whose benefit the assignment was made, and in connection with the question whether the assignment should be made or not, was advising another of the large creditors. That later he repudiated his employment by his client and prosecuted a petition in bankruptcy against him alleging, as an act of bankruptcy, the making of the assignment that he himself had advised him to make. Out of this course of conduct he made for himself and his firm fees amounting to $43,852.

Facts: Patrick Lennox and his son James operated a tannery. The business was substantial, amounting to around a million dollars a year or more, but the debts of the enterprise amounted to a million dollars too. As of the morning of September 4, 1907, Brandeis had never seen or heard of the Lennoxes and their problems, nor did he know Moses Stroock, New York counsel for one of the Lennox creditors. Brandeis was, however, regular counsel for still a third concern, which in fact did have some money owing from Lennox, though Brandeis at that point had no knowledge of this fact.

Mr. Stroock came to Massachusetts to investigate the situation for his own client. After meeting with James Lennox he arranged an appointment with Brandeis, whom he knew by repute, to consider what could be done. Stroock and James Lennox kept their appointment on the afternoon of September 4. The conference was fully and completely recorded, and the notes make a fascinating account of Brandeis's method of swiftly extracting information. It was apparent that the company was hopelessly insolvent, and Brandeis suggested an assignment for the benefit of creditors. He then asked Lennox and Stroock what they wanted his firm to do—did they want him to represent Lennox; did they want him to represent Stroock's client; or did they want him to do something else? He insisted that the conference be adjourned overnight so that James Lennox could discuss the matter with his father to be absolutely sure that there was complete agreement on the course of conduct.

There are passages in the many pages of notes which permit the impression that Brandeis was to represent Lennox. There are other passages which make it clear that Lennox was retaining Brandeis to be trustee of the property for the benefit of creditors. Brandeis expressly said that under this plan, "an assignment would be made and a trustee appointed of your and your father's property for the purpose of liquidating them and distributing to creditors." This was not simply a casual phrase — it was discussed in great detail.

Toward the end of the conversation, as the plan crystallized, James Lennox said in response to an observation by Stroock, "You are speaking now of Mr. Brandeis acting as my counsel?" To this Brandeis replied, "Not altogether as your counsel, but as a trustee of your property."

Thereupon, a trust instrument was prepared whereby George R. Nutter, a partner in the Brandeis firm, was given an assignment for benefit of creditors, signed by both Lennoxes and P. Lennox & Company.

The matter proceeded with friction, but with considerable long-run success. James Lennox, for his assistance in managing the property, wanted payment by the trustee of $500 a week; Nutter, in view of the total situation, would agree to no more than $100. The elder Lennox did not wish to disclose certain hidden assets, and Nutter was required to press him sharply. Moreover, the creditors were unwilling to accept the assignment, and bankruptcy finally became necessary. Nevertheless, the creditors of the individual Lennoxes were paid off 100 cents on the dollar, and the creditors of the company about 40 cents.

Ethical Problem: The essence of this complaint is that Brandeis undertook to represent the Lennoxes, and that in fact he served not their interests but the interests of the creditors.

The first assertion is that Brandeis "took employment from a client and afterwards denied that he had ever been employed by the client." But the fact is that Brandeis did not take employment from Lennox. He never purported to represent Lennox, never billed Lennox, never was tendered any fee by Lennox. The conclusion is inescapable that the Lennoxes were caught stealing; indeed, there was a criminal proceeding against them for concealing assets. It is an unhappy part of the legal tradition that many a so-called "friendly" trustee or "friendly" receiver has permitted the debtor to loot the estate for the benefit of the debtor and at the expense of the creditors. Brandeis did not permit this; in the course of the original interview he repeatedly said that if he undertook the matter there would be a square deal for everyone, with no favoritism to any. The younger Lennox clearly heard this, but did not believe it. When the Lennoxes sought to line their pockets or hide assets and Brandeis would not allow it, they were angry. Whosever ethics this reflects upon, it is not Brandeis's.

Nonetheless, the episode does raise the question of the ethical obligation of a lawyer who has made a general canvas of a situation before he agrees to represent anyone. In the normal situation counsel is solicited by only one party. In the routine auto accident case, for instance, an injured party goes to his lawyer, the other party goes to his lawyer, and the two have at it.

But there is also the frequent, though less usual, situation in which a group of persons with a common problem all come to a lawyer for counsel. In the simplest case, the so-called consent divorce, husband and wife both want a divorce and may go to counsel together to discuss the problem. At some point in such a conversation, the lawyer must say to the two, "Well, which of you am I to represent?"[2] A much more complex variant generally arises in a conference among one or more debtors and their creditors.

In such circumstances, when does representation begin? There is general conversation. The lawyer is asked by the group what directions are open to it; because of their general trust and confidence in him they may wish his suggestions, which he may give if he cares to. There will be no one to bill because he has not yet agreed to represent anyone. At this point, he is really more of a traffic director than a lawyer. Once he has been given and accepts his assignment, if any subsequent conflicts should develop between the interest he has agreed to represent and that of anyone else in the original group, he must be careful not to represent both.

Thus, in the Lennox situation, it was expressly agreed at the basic meeting that Brandeis could consider the interests of Stroock's client only so long as they did not conflict with those of the trust, and that if such a conflict arose that client would have to obtain independent counsel. This is precisely what in fact happened later. The elder Lennox also obtained independent counsel in the course of subsequent proceedings. The same principle would apply if an independent creditor of Lennox, whom Brandeis might reasonably expect to represent, should have a problem over the assignment.

There is no discussion at any point in the report as to why it was unethical, if the Judiciary Committee so conceived it, to utilize the assignment as an act of bankruptcy. The assignment was, of course, an act of bankruptcy, readily and properly utilized for the purpose of solving the problems between the creditors and the bankrupt.

A good share of any embarrassment Brandeis suffered over the Lennox case is due to his own use of what must have been one of the most unfortunate phrases he ever casually uttered. Sherman L. Whipple represented James Lennox in the bankruptcy proceedings. Whipple reported that when he asked Brandeis for whom the latter was counsel when he advised the assignment, Brandeis replied, "I should say that I was counsel for the situation."

This is a misty phrase which could have meant one thing to Brandeis, another to Whipple, and might mean something else again to today's lawyer. Lawyers are not retained by situations, and the adversary system assumes that they faithfully represent one interest at a time. The family in the Warren case in 1888 and 1889 was a true unit; one

---

2. I personally handle very few divorces, but I find myself facing this problem about once a year. I very pointedly tell such a couple at the beginning of the conversation that I want it understood that I have not agreed to represent either of them. We then take such time together as may be necessary to explore the possibility of reconciliation. If this fails, I may agree to represent one or the other, and I insist that any property settlement agreement be approved in writing by independent counsel on behalf of the party not represented by me before it is signed and before judgment is taken on it. A highly experienced lawyer of my acquaintance takes the opposite view. He believes that if two persons in this situation approach the lawyer, he must accept one as a client before any discussion.

The problem is particularly common in the creditors' rights field. For example, both an insolvent debtor and a buyer of his property recently consulted the head of the Creditors' Rights Section of my own office. He necessarily heard both of them in the identical fashion as did Brandeis in the Lennox case. After about forty-five minutes, he excused the buyer, consulted with the debtor for an additional hour, and then met again with both. In this latter meeting he made it clear that he was representing the interest only of the debtor. However, in the first forty-five minutes it would have been impossible to know what his representation should have been, and yet of course some information was exchanged and obtained during that introductory interview. There appears to be no other good solution to some of these debtor-creditor situations than to hear the story in this manner.

could properly represent the family. But representation of a "situation" is too vague to be intelligible. When Brandeis suggested a course of action for the consideration of his visitors, he had not yet agreed to represent anyone. The matter was merely exploratory until the suggestion was adopted.

Whipple believed that Brandeis was open to no ethical criticism, but that he was open to the criticism of not having made it clear enough to Lennox just what an assignment would entail:

> [H]e did not make it clear, so that a layman would understand just what he was talking about. When a lawyer talks to a business man about being charged with the responsibility of an equitable division of the estate among all who may be interested, such talk, I think, goes right over the head of the ordinary business man who does not understand clearly the fiduciary duties of a man in that position, and who does not understand the clear and fine definition of the fiduciary duty in its different aspects.

This is justifiable criticism. Although Brandeis worded the plan over and over again in terms of a square deal to the creditors, he may very well have failed to make Lennox understand that he really meant it. Brandeis also thought of the matter as a misunderstanding. As he wrote to Whipple in 1907,

> The present difficulty with Mr. James T. Lennox has arisen from the fact that although at the time Mr. Lennox desired that the situation should be worked out in the way I suggested, he apparently did not clearly see that he might afterwards be unwilling to give this plan his cooperation, and that in such case there must necessarily arise a time when his attitude would be inconsistent with that of the assignee.

Any misunderstanding, if such there was, may at this late date be put aside as a common human problem of communication between the Lennoxes and Brandeis. From a strictly ethical standpoint, there is no problem. If a debtor and creditors call on counsel to discuss a course of action to handle the debts, if at this meeting it is determined that there should be an assignment for the benefit of creditors and that counsel should represent the assignee, and if thereafter counsel does with scrupulous care carry forward his fiduciary duty to the creditors, he is doing precisely what he is supposed to do.

6 and 7. *The United Shoe Matter*

Of the twelve charges, eleven deal with separate matters. The United Shoe matter appealed to the minority on the Committee so strongly that it was divided in half and charged twice.

Charges:

> That, after serving a client and upholding and defending its manner of doing business and the form of its contracts with its customers, he, in the interest of its competitors in business, and, as he claimed, in the public interest attacked the former client and assailed the same contracts he had approved and defended, denounced theni as in violation of law and endeavored to secure legislation against them.

* * *

> That he made believe that he was appearing and contesting these contracts in the public interests and without pay when he was acting directly for and in the interest of private individuals, and his firm, other than himself, accepted and received a large fee for the services rendered by him in this behalf.

Facts: There were two major branches of the shoe industry in Massachusetts: the manufacturers of shoe machinery and the manufacturers of shoes. The latter, of course, used the machinery. Brandeis was a director of one of the companies which in 1899 merged into the United Shoe Machinery Company. He then became a director of United with a minor role in its legal representation. He also represented a number of shoe manufacturers.

United and its predecessors had for many years, prior to the adoption of the Sherman Act, leased their machinery for use by the shoe manufacturers. The lease agreements contained "tying clauses" that required a person who leased machinery from United to use it in conjunction only with other United machinery. Since much of the machinery was patented, the addition of this tying clause to the patent license gave a considerable monopolistic advantage to United.

In 1906, a bill was introduced in the Massachusetts Legislature to restrict tying clauses. Brandeis was asked to appear before the Massachusetts Legislature by United Shoe in opposition to this proposal. This position created no conflict for him because while his shoe manufacturer clients were hostile to the tying clauses, assurances had been exchanged between United and the shoe manufacturers that, if the industry should succeed in defeating the bill, United and the shoe manufacturers could work the matter out on a mutually satisfactory basis. With this understanding in mind Brandeis did appear for United, and helped to vindicate the United lease system.

It is possible, by narrow distinctions and careful qualifications, to distinguish the position Brandeis took on this matter in 1906 from his later position on tying clauses. But rapid changes in economic and legal circumstances intervened to cause Brandeis to change his stand fundamentally.

The change came fairly quickly. In the first place, United and the shoe manufacturers did not peacefully work out their differences. Brandeis was not involved in such negotiations, but he was aware of them. Secondly, during the legislative session of 1906, the tying clause had not appeared to be illegal under existing law, but later that year an opinion of a federal district court in Wisconsin cast great doubt upon the legality of such arrangements. Brandeis called this opinion to the attention of counsel for United and expressed his own doubts. These doubts intensified as he studied the matter more closely. Still later in 1906 he resigned as a director of United Shoe expressly because of his doubts about the validity of the leasing practices, and except for cleaning up minor matters, he did nothing further for United Shoe after 1907. In that year legislation directed against these leases and tying clauses passed the Massachusetts Legislature with Brandeis not participating. Between 1906 and 1910 Supreme Court decisions gave vigor to the Sherman Act and increased the doubts as to the legality of such practices. By 1910 Brandeis was able to give an opinion to another shoe machinery manufacturer that the tying clauses were illegal under the then existing law.

Starting in 1911, Brandeis began his representation of the Shoe Manufacturers' Alliance. The Alliance paid him 2,500 dollars which he forwarded to his firm; then he contributed 2,500 dollars back to the Shoe Alliance. 1911, 1912, and 1913 Brandeis supported the legislation that became the Clayton Act—legislation clearly directed against such activities as the tying practices of United Shoe Machinery. This position did not involve an ethical conflict; there had been too much legal development since the time he had represented United. But certainly in spirit his position did conflict with the position he took as an advocate in 1906.

This Brandeis freely acknowledged. In 1906 he had supposed that it was possible for there to be a "good trust" as well as a "bad trust"; this illusion had vanished with the years.

Ethical Problems: The charge that Brandeis in his congressional appearances in support of the Clayton legislation "made believe that he was appearing and contesting these contracts in the public interests and without pay when he was acting directly for and in the interest of private individuals" is another of those remarkable conflicts between the report of the minority of the Judiciary Committee and the reports of its individual members, who also signed the overall report. Senator Works, in his individual report, expressly quoted Brandeis as telling the House Judiciary Committee that: "I represent primarily myself, Mr. Chairman, but I have also acted for a certain number of gentlemen known as the Shoe Manufacturers' Alliance, who had specifically objected to the methods and policies of the Shoe Machinery Corporation, who are therefore interested in this bill ..." So far as the "large fee" was concerned, this was the 2,500 dollars which he himself paid for the privilege of representing the Shoe Manufacturers' Alliance.

The charge just discussed is so clearly a product of passion and unreason that it may obscure the one genuine and serious question lurking in the United matter. Under what circumstances, if any, may a lawyer reverse himself and oppose the interests of a client whom he formerly represented? The answer requires the making of nice distinctions.

A retainer does not bind forever, and a lawyer who has represented a client in one matter is perfectly free, after the representation is terminated, to oppose him in another, so long as the matter is separate and so long as no confidences are involved. Canon 6 declares that the lawyer may not accept subsequent "retainers or employment from others in matters adversely affecting any interest of the client with respect to which confidence has been reposed." Numerous cases hold that "one may sue a former client if his representation is ended and the matter does not involve confidential communications." This freedom for the lawyer is essential; otherwise a casual or episodic representation would limit his freedom for life. Senator Walsh hit very hard on this:

> Mr. Winslow [of United Shoe Machinery] seems to be possessed with the idea that because Brandeis had taken fees from the Shoe Machinery Co. he bound himself forever not to criticize its policy or its practices — that in a way he had violated his fealty. It is not an uncommon view on the part of those who manage great industries and command many men that they may insure the support of lawyers on public questions by putting them on the payroll or paying them from time to time for legal services. In the case of Brandeis the assumption seems not to have been well founded. In that he did something to dispel that notion, he deserves well of his profession.

Whether the question is "public" or not, the lawyer may not take a position adverse to his earlier client if he utilizes confidences gained in that earlier representation? Just what is a confidence and just what is its abuse is the subject of much refined law? But in the instant case, these refinements need not be considered. There is no specific suggestion that Brandeis utilized in his later activities in favor of the Clayton legislation anything in the slightest degree confidential gained from his earlier representation of United. The leases under attack were a matter of public concern, and so was the law. The concept of confidence does not refer in this context to the miscellaneous expansion of one's education that comes from every representation. Here there was no transference of confidential knowledge.

The hardest question remains. The better view—one that has developed considerably since the early part of the twentieth century—is that the attorney may not take a position in opposition to a former client on the same matter, even if no confidences are involved. It is the view that "irrespective of actual conflict of interest, maintenance of public confidence requires a lawyer not appear both for and against the same party in the same controversy."

The issue then becomes whether the United Shoe matter had become sufficiently "different" so that the "same matter" rule would not apply. None of the precedents fits. The situation was substantially changed by the numerous events occurring between 1906 and 1910. Putting all the circumstances together, one must depend on intuition rather than authority. Because of the legal evolution, my own opinion is that the later legislation should not be considered the "same controversy," as that phrase is used in the passage just quoted. Nonetheless, the episode is marginal, and reasonable attorneys can certainly differ about it.

III

The story of the Brandeis appointment and confirmation has lessons for our time.

The mere putting together of these scattered episodes from a law practice covering 1878 to 1916 is bound to be misleading. One's main impression is surprise that the powers of wealth and political position, which had been hitting at Brandeis for years and searching for every possible ground of complaint, should have found so little to work with. As Georgia's Senator Hoke Smith asked, 'What lawyer with thirty-five years of experience at the bar can go over what he has done during that period without feeling that it would have been better not to have done some of the things that he has done?" The majority recognized that Brandeis after a lifetime of contests on vital matters, "would indeed be a human prodigy if he had not aroused some bitter antagonisms."

While one's thoughts can range wide on the Brandeis appointment, and his career, I restrict myself here to a few observations on legal ethics.

(I) There is forthright talk in the record on the subjectivity of legal ethics. Sherman L. Whipple thought that if Mr. Brandeis had been a different sort of man, not so aloof, not so isolated, with more of the comradery of the bar, gave his confidence to more men, and took their confidence, said to him, when he was charged with anything that was doubtful, "Boys, what do you think about it?" and talked it over with them—you would not have heard the things you have heard in regard to him.

Arthur Hill, a Republican Boston lawyer and professor of great ability and character, who supported Brandeis, put it bluntly:

[A]mong a considerable proportion of the lawyers here he has the reputation of … one who is unscrupulous in regard to his professional conduct. Many of his opponents are my personal friends and I understand and respect their point of view, though I believe they are mistaken. At the same time, I believe that the reputation to which I have referred is not founded so much on anything Mr. Brandeis has done as it is on other causes. He is a radical and has spent a large part, not only of his public, but of his professional career, in attacking established institutions, and this alone would, in my judgment, account for a very large part of his unpopularity. It would be difficult, if not impossible, for a radical to be generally popular with Boston lawyers, or escape severe adverse criticisms of his motives and conduct. Certainly I have never heard of anybody, from Joseph Story down, who has ever succeeded in doing so.

This is inescapably true. On the simpler questions of legal ethics, personality and personal relations make little difference, because the answers are fairly clear. But those who commingle trust funds are not likely to be proposed for the highest judicial office. The kinds of matters which crop up at that level—or in any appraisal of the ethics of significant leaders of the bar—are more subtle. They may depend on motive, on detail, on nuance. A bar has predispositions towards its members, and these inescapably color ethical judgments.

It follows that the liberals (Hill on review of his 1916 letter in 1944 thought "radical" a poorly chosen word) have to try a little harder. The bar is largely conservative, and its members may well—not in wickedness but in common human failing—tend to be ungenerous toward those with whom they happen to disagree.

One can agree with this argument and act upon it, without also agreeing with Whipple that a little clubbishness by Brandeis would have made any difference. His enemies would have sought to cut him to shreds whether or not he had been the gayest of the lads at the Lawyers' Club. The New Haven Railroad, the United Shoe Company, and President Taft had felt the full lethal force of Brandeis's power. They could not be expected to like it. They did not like it; and, together with all those seeking to regain the Presidency for their party in 1916, they could reasonably be expected to be partisan. The liberal will do well to be extra careful to turn corners squarely; but no amount of care can guarantee freedom from a little character assassination now and then.

It also follows that the lawyer with a duty or a desire to express ethical judgments on his fellows has a heavy obligation to find a solid basis before he speaks. The case lost by the advocate may too easily become the case stolen by his adversary. One too rarely hears the ethical problem considered from the other fellow's point of view. Overly lusty moral criticism very nearly cost the country one of the most useful Justices it ever had. How many lawyers of worth have failed to be appointed to the Bench, at some level, because talk is cheap and charge is easy?

(2) If I may share a purely personal lesson, the greatest caution to be gained from study of the Brandeis record is, never be "counsel for a situation." A lawyer is constantly confronted with conflicts which he is frequently urged to somehow try to work out. I have never attempted this without wishing I had not, and I have given up attempting it. Particularly when old clients are at odds, counsel may feel the most extreme pressure to solve their problems for them. It is a time-consuming, costly, unsuccessful mistake, which usually results in disaffecting both sides.

(3) While the role of Brandeis in United Shoe was not, in any technical sense, unethical, he would have used better judgment had he stayed out of the subsequent controversies. Obviously he came to believe that he had erred badly by making his 1906 appearance, as indeed he had. But it is part of the cost of the profession that some errors may be irredeemable. Had Brandeis in his 1911–1913 advocacy of the Clayton Act not represented the Shoe Alliance, he would not have been open to fair criticism. It was a purposeless representation; for practical purposes he took no fee. By accepting the representation he exposed himself to the charge of representing an interest adverse to the earlier one.

The unhappy fact is that some of a lawyer's mistakes must be borne, and lived with, and are not redeemable: When a practitioner is in doubt on an ethical question, the best answer is usually No, and perhaps Brandeis should have given that answer when the reformer's ardor seized him to tilt against the tying clause.

(4) For all these cautions, the Brandeis experience also teaches fearlessness and incisiveness in ethical matters, as well as in all the other problems of the law. The business of living and of law must be got on with. Decisions must be made, actions taken. Something had to be done with the Warren estate and the management of the Warren properties in 1889; the matter would not wait until brother Ned saw fit to come home from Europe. When James Lennox and Moses Stroock arrived in the Brandeis office, a program was needed at once — critical notes would come due the very next day.

The good lawyer should also be able to tell private from public duty. He should be able to represent the corporation which hires him and still advocate the public interest as he sees it, either in his voting or in his private conversations or in his community leadership.

He must have a sense of the right, and confidence to act on it. Brandeis did.

A Caldron of Ethics and Asbestos

Alex Berenson, *The New York Times*, March 12, 2003,
Section C; Column 2; Business/Financial Desk; Pg. 1*

Joseph F. Rice, a leading class-action lawyer, has agreed to accept a $20 million fee from the parent of a company that he is suing in addition to the fees that he will collect from his clients for settling their claims against that very company.

Legal ethicists said the payment raised serious ethical concerns because he was in effect being paid by both sides in the dispute, and several class-action lawyers criticized the payment.

Mr. Rice said he did not believe that the fee was a conflict of interest, and a lawyer for ABB, the Swiss company that will pay the fee, said it was justified and fair.

The fee is part of a proposed settlement for the bankruptcy of Combustion Engineering, a United States company owned by ABB that faces 220,000 claims from people who say they were injured by asbestos in its boilers. Mr. Rice is being paid for helping to broker a settlement with other lawyers handling asbestos claims against the company.

Under the settlement, people who develop asbestos-related disease because of their exposure to the boilers will receive a fixed payout from a trust being created by the companies. They will not be allowed to sue ABB or Combustion Engineering.

If the trust is overwhelmed with claims, as expected, people badly injured by asbestos — representing a small fraction of the claimants — may receive less money than if they could pursue their cases in court, lawyers for those plaintiffs say. But the trust will pay lightly injured plaintiffs quickly, producing a windfall for a handful of lawyers who represent thousands of those claimants.

Figure 2. Joseph F. Rice, a leading class-action lawyer. (Douglas Levere)

Some lawyers who represent seriously injured plaintiffs are protesting the creation of the trust, and similar structures that other companies, including Honeywell and Halliburton, are trying to create.

The disclosure of Mr. Rice's fee in a letter discussing the bankruptcy has further provoked those lawyers, as well as legal ethicists, who say Mr. Rice should not be paid by the company he is suing. The fee creates a conflict of interest for Mr. Rice and his firm, said Susan P. Koniak, a Boston University law professor and expert on legal ethics.

"They're representing people who were ostensibly allegedly injured by products produced by these companies," she said. "And they're taking money from the other side to get a deal through that the other side wants too? What does one need to say?"

George Kuhlman, ethics counsel for the American Bar Association, said the group did not have absolute rules that bar lawyers from being paid by both sides in a case. "We have very complex rules on lawyers and conflicts of interest," Mr. Kuhlman said. "There are things that you are supposed to avoid, but it does not boil down to that you are supposed to avoid a fee from someone you are otherwise suing."

He said he would have to do much more research to determine whether this case passed muster.

Mr. Rice, whose South Carolina firm, Ness Motley, rose to prominence because of his work suing tobacco companies, said the arrangement had been favorable for his clients.

He does not see a conflict because his $20 million fee, a portion of which he said he had already received, was coming from ABB, which owns all of Combustion Engineering, rather than Combustion Engineering itself.

"I'm not taking the fee from anybody that I'm suing," he said in a phone interview yesterday. "I did a business transaction." In addition, Mr. Rice said he and his firm did not advise any clients on whether to vote in favor of the agreement, which was approved by outside experts including lawyers representing future claimants against Combustion Engineering.

"The agreement was good for both sides," Mr. Rice said. ABB "had its independent problems that needed to get solved, and in solving their problems my asbestos clients came out ahead of the game."

Lawyers representing the states in the global tobacco settlement were paid by the tobacco companies rather than by the states. Those fees, however, were negotiated before any settlement and took the place of fees from the states.

Claimants typically pay a contingency fee to lawyers like Mr. Rice, a fee that generally ranges from 25 to 40 percent of the total. In addition, Mr. Rice has consulting arrangements with other law firms under which he receives a portion of the fees that they bill their clients in exchange for his work on their cases.

David Bernick, outside counsel for ABB, said he considered Mr. Rice's fee for brokering the settlement reasonable. Mr. Rice worked hard to negotiate the deal, which was completed in a matter of months last fall, with ABB and Combustion Engineering on the verge of bankruptcy.

Mr. Rice played a crucial role in explaining the agreement to other plaintiffs' lawyers and winning them over, Mr. Bernick said.

"Why shouldn't he get paid for brokering a deal?" Mr. Bernick said.

John Brett, general counsel for ABB in the United States, said ABB believed that most lawyers approved of the settlement, including the fee. For the deal to be passed, more than 75 percent of all claimants must vote in favor of it, and the bankruptcy judge overseeing the case must approve the agreement. "We believe that we have more than adequate votes for its approval," Mr. Brett said.

The case was filed in bankruptcy court in Delaware but will be heard by Judith Fitzgerald, a federal bankruptcy judge in Pittsburgh.

Combustion Engineering was forced into bankruptcy because of claims from people who say they were injured by asbestos-lined boilers made before 1972. Most of those people are not seriously hurt, and many have no injuries at all, aside from plaque in their lungs that does not affect their ability to breathe.

But both ABB and plaintiffs' lawyers agree that the combined cost of the claims is more than Combustion Engineering can afford to pay, making bankruptcy the only alternative. To keep the bankruptcy relatively short and inexpensive, ABB began negotiating with plaintiffs' lawyers about the structure of a trust that would be created from the filing, as well as the amount of money ABB would put into the trust.

Under the deal, ABB agreed to contribute all of Combustion Engineering's assets, valued at about $800 million, to the trust, which will be used to pay current and future claims of asbestos-related injury. ABB will also contribute $250 million in cash and $50 million in shares to the trust, and it may contribute $100 million more in the future.

Honeywell International and Halliburton are trying similar legal tactics to relieve themselves of asbestos liability by putting subsidiaries into bankruptcy, and lawyers for both plaintiffs and defendants say the process will probably become more common as big companies seek a way to put asbestos lawsuits behind them.

Halliburton said it would not pay a success fee like Mr. Rice's as part of its settlement, and Honeywell declined to comment.

The $20 million fee for Mr. Rice is equal to almost 7 percent of the cash and stock that ABB is initially contributing to the settlement, and nearly 2 percent of the overall value of the trust. That amount is too much, said Bill Connelly, a partner at Richardson, Patrick, a Charleston, S.C., firm formed by lawyers who left Mr. Rice's firm last year.

"David Bernick at a meeting in Houston before 40 or 50 lawyers said that before he even started negotiating, he offered $20 million if Rice could put this package together," Mr. Connelly said.

Lawyers who generally represent lightly injured claimants say that Mr. Rice should not be paid by ABB. "It makes Joe Rice look bad," said Fred Baron, a Dallas lawyer whose firm represents about 8,000 people who have sued Combustion Engineering and other companies because of asbestos exposure.

Mr. Baron said the fee was particularly inappropriate because the total cost of settling all ABB claims at full face value would far outstrip the $1.1 billion to $1.3 billion that will be available for payment. As a result, many claimants will be paid a fraction of the face value of their claims. "Virtually everybody I've talked to has said that it would be unseemly for the $20 million to be paid if 100 cents on the dollar are not being paid," Mr. Baron said.

But Mr. Baron said he was not opposed in principle to allowing lawyers to be paid directly by companies they were suing. And some other class-action lawyers defended Mr. Rice's fee.

"You're being paid a facilitating fee," said Perry Weitz, whose firm represents 35,000 asbestos claimants, including 20,000 that have sued Combustion Engineering. "The court's got to approve it."

Mr. Weitz said he planned to ask for similar fees in future bankruptcy settlements. "I would have no reservations," he said.

When Big Law Firms Trip Over Their Own Clients

Karen Donovan, *The New York Times*, October 3, 2004,
Section 3; Column 1; Sunday Business, Pg. 5*

Weil, Gotshal & Manges is a law firm known for its top-flight bankruptcy practice and its aggressive litigators. The firm, based in New York, has more than 1,000 lawyers in 18 offices from Silicon Valley to Singapore, and was ranked eighth in The American Lawyer's latest annual survey of the 100 top-grossing law firms, with an estimated $801 million in 2003 revenue.

Like every firm of its size and stature, Weil Gotshal has an elaborate system to safe-guard against client conflicts—that is, against representing clients who have or could

---

have conflicting interests. To prevent such problems, it requires its lawyers to fill out "new matter" forms for new clients, explaining why they are hiring the firm and what people or companies may be a source of conflicts. A computer runs through the information, looking for matches.

Despite this effort, Weil Gotshal is embroiled in two lawsuits by former clients who contend that the firm breached its duty to provide them with its undivided loyalty, as state rules on ethics require. The cases—one by the owners of a luxury shop, now defunct, in the Mall at Short Hills, N.J., and one by the pop singer Michael Bolton—stem from very different circumstances. But each case is a cautionary tale for big law firms, experts say.

As law firms have consolidated in recent years, conflicts have become a thornier issue. David G. Briscoe of the legal consulting firm Altman Weil in Newtown Square, Pa., says that as firms expand worldwide and as the level of organizational complexity goes "through the roof," some firms have started running conflict checks as often as twice a day.

Busy partners at law firms have a lot of leeway in how they fulfill their administrative duties, Mr. Briscoe said: "If there isn't strong central control and authority, that can be something that gets you in trouble."

But giving lawyers much of the burden of weeding out conflicts "just doesn't work," said C.Evan Stewart, a partner at Brown Raysman Millstein Felder & Steiner in New York, who teaches legal ethics at two law schools in the city. Lawyers are compensated based on the fees they generate, he said, and checking for conflicts does not generate fees. "That's not how law firms make money," he said.

Some firms now have partners whose job is to help lawyers follow the rules without becoming too distracted from business. "I've seen the doctrines become increasingly complex and almost inscrutable, and that's why lawyers need lawyers to help them stay safe," said Stephen Gillers, an ethics expert and a professor at the New York University School of Law.

Richard J. Davis, a Weil Gotshal senior partner who advises the firm on ethical issues, said the firm viewed both of the cases against it as without merit. But like any other business in these litigious times, it is spending a fair amount of time and money to defend itself against them in court.

A state appeals court in Manhattan reinstated a malpractice case against Weil Gotshal in August, allowing the owners of the mall store, Fashion Boutique of Short Hills, to pursue their contention that the law firm represented them in a suit against the fashion house Fendi even as it also agreed to represent Prada in another case. A few months earlier, Prada had teamed up with LVMH Moet Hennessy Louis Vuitton to buy a 51 percent stake in Fendi.

Weil Gotshal did not tell the owners, Annette C. Fischer and her daughter, Randi Fischer, that it was also representing Fendi's new owner until seven months after it started working with Prada; by then, a jury was already deliberating the Fischers' contention that Fendi had used unfair business practices to run them out of business to protect its new flagship store on Fifth Avenue in Manhattan. In the case against Weil Gotshal, Fashion Boutique is seeking $15.5 million, an estimate of the value of lost business.

Mr. Bolton, meanwhile, sued Weil Gotshal in New York Supreme Court in Manhattan last December, seeking $30 million. The firm had defended him, along with his publisher, Warner-Chappell Music Ltd. of Britain, and his record label, Sony Music Entertainment Inc., in a 1994 suit contending that Mr. Bolton had infringed someone else's copyright with his 1991 hit "Love Is a Wonderful Thing." When a jury found that the song was too much like a 1964 tune of the same name by the Isley Brothers, the defendants were ordered to pay more than $5 million in damages. Mr. Bolton, however, soon learned that he was personally responsible for the entire judgment because his contracts with both Warner-Chappell and Sony said that he would indemnify them in the event of a judgment of copyright infringement.

He contends that a Weil Gotshal partner, Robert G. Sugarman, failed to reveal the "nature or scope" of these contracts to him, according to the complaint, and that Mr. Sugarman "took instructions" from Warner-Chappell's insurer, which was paying him as is customary in such defense suits. The insurance company, Mr. Bolton added, had a "secret agenda" to go to trial rather than settle, because the contract protected it only in the event of a trial judgment.

Mr. Bolton says in his suit that Mr. Sugarman hid opportunities to settle the case and misrepresented how Mr. Bolton would be affected when the co-author of the song, Andy Goldmark, reached a settlement. By not going to trial, Mr. Goldmark avoided the risk of having to pay half of a multimillion-dollar judgment; his insurance company paid his share of the settlement.

Weil Gotshal contends that Mr. Bolton was "fully aware" of his obligation to accept full responsibility for copyright infringement and that his personal lawyer lobbied to have Mr. Sugarman handle the case. Weil Gotshal says Mr. Bolton had confidence in Mr. Sugarman because he had successfully defended him in an earlier copyright infringement suit.

Weil Gotshal's joint representation of Mr. Bolton, his publisher and his record label raised another tricky problem when Mr. Bolton and his lawyers discussed whether to settle the case, experts said. One lawyer often represents all the defendants at a copyright trial. But Laurence F. Pulgram, a copyright lawyer at Fenwick & West in San Francisco, said lawyers must be "extremely meticulous" in ensuring that all parties are aware of the potential for conflict. That would have meant having Mr. Bolton sign a waiver indicating he understood the conflicting interests, he said.

Experts are divided on whether Weil Gotshal crossed a line in the Prada case. Professor Gillers of N.Y.U. said it did not do so because the conflict rules "get vague" when clients have a stake in another company but do not own it outright.

Others are less sympathetic. Professor Roger C. Cramton of Cornell Law School, author of a legal ethics textbook, said he took a "dim view" of the risks that New York firms in particular were willing to take to get and retain business. "The New York firms are some of the biggest risk-takers that I run into," he said.

When a Weil Gotshal partner, Michael A. Epstein, took on Prada as a client, Fendi did not come up as an adverse party in the firm's check for client conflicts "because it had nothing to do with Fendi," Mr. Davis said. Prada never became an important client, he added. The Weil Gotshal lawyer who had represented Fashion Boutique, Helene D. Jaffe, testified that she "just didn't" look at the new-matter sheets that came across her desk in December 1999. At least four of them listed Prada as a client in an unrelated matter.

When she and Mr. Epstein made the connection during the Fashion Boutique trial, they consulted Mr. Davis. Ms. Jaffe has testified that Mr. Davis told her that there was no formal conflict, but that it would be appropriate to tell the Fischers that the firm also represented Prada.

Randi Fischer said Ms. Jaffe characterized the firm's representation of Prada as "no big deal," but she said she had been floored by the news. "It was one of those moments in your life you never forget," Ms. Fischer said.

Mr. Davis said he was keeping tabs on the Fashion Boutique case as early as May 1999, when the firm tried to withdraw from it over what it called "irreconcilable" differences with the store owners. The judge would not allow it, so now, even as the Fischers are suing Weil Gotshal, the firm is suing them for $2.7 million in unpaid fees.

Geoffrey C. Hazard Jr., an ethics expert who is a professor at the University of Pennsylvania Law School, said the suits pending against Weil Gotshal were an unfortunate result of the intense competition for new business. "You've got to keep those new cases coming in," he said. And as firms have become more focused on "one-shot engagements," he said, trust has deteriorated on both sides of the relationship: "Lawyers are dealing with clients they don't trust, and clients are dealing with lawyers they don't trust."

The Association of the Bar of the City of New York
Formal Opinion 2003-03
Checking for Conflicts of Interest

Topic: Conflicts of Interest; Recordkeeping, Policies, and Systems for Conflicts-Checking Purposes

Digest: Under DR 5-105(e) of the New York Code of Professional Responsibility, all law firms must keep records and must have policies and systems in place to check for conflicts of interest to the extent necessary to render effective assistance to the lawyers in the firm in avoiding imputed conflicts under DR 5-105(d) based on current or prior engagements. What records the firm must keep, and what policies and systems the firm must implement, depends on a number of factors, including (a) the size of the firm, (b) where the firm practices, and (c) the nature of the firm's practice.

Code: DR 5-105(d); DR 5-105(e)

Question

What records must a law firm keep, and what policies and systems must a law firm implement for checking proposed engagements against current and previous engagements, to comply with New York's mandatory conflict-checking rule, DR 5-105(e)?

Opinion

On May 22, 1996, effective immediately, the Appellate Divisions adopted DR 5-105(e) of the New York Code of Professional Responsibility. In essence, the rule requires every New York law firm to keep records and implement policies and systems that effectively assist the firm in complying with New York's imputed conflicts rule, DR 5-105(d), with respect to conflicts caused by the firm's current and previous engagements.

DR 5-105(e) was drafted by the courts sua sponte. It was not based on any formal proposal by the Bar. It was adopted as part of the package of new and amended rules (also including DR 1-102 and DR 1-104) that made law firms as entities subject to discipline in New York. The requirements of the rule are not well defined or understood. The New York State Bar Association has not adopted any Ethical Considerations to explain DR 5-105(e); not a single court case has discussed the rule; and only one bar association ethics committee opinion has discussed DR 5-105(e) at any length — see N.Y. State Opinion No. 720 (1999), 1999 WL 692571. The rule is unique to New York — no other jurisdiction has adopted a rule anything like it—so other jurisdictions provide minimal guidance. At least one article has been written about the rule—see Roy Simon, Checking for Conflicts Under DR 5-105(e), New York Professional Responsibility Report, November 2002—but little formal guidance is available about the rule and its requirements. Accordingly, this Committee has been asked to render guidance to the Bar regarding the requirements imposed on law firms by DR 5-105(e).

Discussion

The three sentences of DR 5-105(e) (which we quote verbatim below but break into separate paragraphs for greater clarity) provide as follows:

• "A law firm shall keep records of prior engagements, which records shall be made at or near the time of such engagements and shall have a policy implementing a system by which proposed engagements are checked against current and previous engagements, so as to render effective assistance to lawyers within the firm in complying with DR 5-105(d)."

• "Failure to keep records or to have a policy which complies with this subdivision, whether or not a violation of DR 5-105(d) occurs, shall be a violation by the firm."

• "In cases in which a violation of this subdivision by the firm is a substantial factor in causing a violation of DR 5-105(d) by a lawyer, the firm, as well as the individual lawyer, shall also be responsible for the violation of DR 5-105(d)."

The text of DR 5-105(d), to which DR 5-105(e) refers four times, provides as follows:

"While lawyers are associated in a law firm, none of them shall knowingly accept or continue employment when any one of them practicing alone would be prohibited from doing so under DR 5-101(a), DR 5-105(a) or (b), DR 5-108(a) or (b), or DR 9-101(b) except as otherwise provided therein. "

This opinion will focus only on the first sentence of DR 5-105(e), with particular emphasis on the type and quality of records that a law firm must keep and the policies and systems the law firm must implement for checking proposed engagements against current and previous engagements.

What is a "law firm"?

Because DR 5-105(e) applies only to a "law firm," we begin by briefly exploring the scope of the term "law firm." The New York Code of Professional Responsibility (the "Code") (at 22 N.Y.C.R.R. § 1200.01) defines the term "law firm" as follows:

"'Law firm'" includes, but is not limited to, a professional legal corporation, a limited liability company or partnership engaged in the practice of law, the legal department of a corporation or other organization and a qualified legal assistance organization."

This definition of course encompasses large law firms, corporate legal departments, governmental legal departments, and non-profit law firms. We also believe that a solo law practice, whether or not it is organized as a professional corporation or a limited liability company, is a "law firm" within the meaning of DR 5-105(e).

In addition, since the definition of "law firm" in the Code "is not limited to" traditional law firms and legal departments, the term has been applied for conflicts purposes to other practice arrangements. For example, as this Committee and other ethics committees have opined, lawyers in some practice arrangements must check for conflicts of interest as if they were a single law firm. See, e.g., ABCNY Opinion No. 80-63 (1980) (two firms that shared offices could not represent opposing parties in litigation because of the "strong likelihood" that the separate law firms could not maintain the confidences and secrets of their respective clients); N.Y. County Opinion No. 680 (1990), 1990 WL 677022, *2 ("Even though lawyers who share office space are not partners, they may be treated as if they were partners for some purposes under the Code (particularly the provisions for vicarious disqualification in the event of a conflict of interest)" if they share confidential information.) ABCNY Opinion No. 1995-8 (1995) (when law firms are "of counsel" to each other one-unit conflicts checking is required); ABCNY Formal Op. 1996-08, 1996 WL 416301, *3 ("'of counsel' relationships are treated as if the 'counsel' and the firm are one unit").

We think DR 5-105(e) applies to these "constructive" law firms as well as to more traditional firms. In short, we believe DR 5-105(e) applies to a wide range of practice arrangements. We concentrate the remainder of this opinion on private law firms, but the principles and concepts discussed here apply in some fashion to other types of law firms as well, including the legal departments of corporations and government agencies.

Fundamentals of DR 5-105(e)

The essence of the first sentence of DR 5-105(e) is to require every law firm to do two things: (1) create a record of each new engagement at or near the time the engagement commences; and (2) have a policy implementing a system for checking proposed engagements against current and previous engagements. The rule does not specify what records a firm must keep, or what type of policy and system a firm must implement to check proposed engagements against current and previous engagements. Rather, the rule indicates simply that whatever systems are adopted should "render effective assistance to lawyers within the firm" in complying with their obligation to avoid conflicts that would violate DR 5-105(d).

At a minimum, to assist in complying with DR 5-105(d), we think that all firms should have mechanisms for assisting lawyers in identifying and resolving two types of conflicts arising from current or previous engagements that are expressly covered by DR 5-105(d):

• Conflicts among current clients, whether the conflicts arise before or during the engagement—see DR 5-105(a) and (b); and

• Conflicts with former clients, including the former clients of laterals and their former firms—see DR 5-108(a) and (b).

DR 5-105(d) also embraces conflicts that arise under DR 9-101(b) when a private law firm hires lawyers who formerly served as public officers or employees. However, because conflicts with former government lawyers are complicated by laws and rules governing grand jury secrecy, the secrecy of investigative information acquired by the government, governmental privileges, and other factors that make public officers and employees substantially different from private lawyers, this opinion does not address systems for checking the conflicts of former public officers and employees.

What kind of system is required to check for conflicts with current and former clients will turn on the nature of each law firm. In particular, the specific measures that DR 5-105(e) requires will depend on factors such as: (a) the size and structure of the firm; (b) the nature of the firm's practice; (c) the number and location of the firm's offices; (d) the relationship among the firm's separate offices; and (e) other characteristics of the law firm and its operations. The records, policies, and systems will vary from law firm to law firm. But all law firms, whatever their particular characteristics—large or small, urban or rural, litigation or transactional, governmental or private—must keep certain minimum records and implement certain minimum policies and systems suitable to provide effective assistance to the firm's lawyers in avoiding conflicts arising from current or former engagements and that will be imputed to the firm under DR 5-105(d).

Recordkeeping Requirements

The first sentence of DR 5-105(e) begins with a mandate for recordkeeping. It provides, in part, that a law firm "shall keep records of prior engagements ... made at or near the time of such engagements...." The expressly stated purpose of this recordkeeping requirement is to assist lawyers in the firm in avoiding conflicts of interest that will be imputed to the entire firm under DR 5-105(d) (discussed above). The rule raises a number of questions, which we address one at a time.

1. What are "records"?

To get one preliminary point out of the way quickly, we think the term "records" refers to written or electronic records. Information inside a lawyer's head that has not been written down does not qualify as "records." Thus, even solo practitioners must keep written or electronic records to comply with DR 5-105(e).

Moreover, those records must be maintained in a way that allows them to be quickly and accurately checked for possible conflicts. Thus, the mere fact that the law firm has information about clients and engagements written down in the individual files pertaining to each matter does not satisfy the "records" requirement. It is simply not realistic to think that a law firm can search through every paper file and folder to look for conflicts each time the firm considers a proposed new engagement. However, if the law firm opens electronic files on all of the law firm's clients and prospective clients, and if those records are electronically searchable (as all word processing programs and law practice management programs appear to be), then those electronic files will qualify as "records" for purposes of DR 5-105(e). In other words, the key characteristic that qualifies information as "records" under DR 5-105(e) is that the information can be systematically and accurately checked when the law firm is considering a proposed new engagement.

2. When must the required records be made?

DR 5-105(e) provides that the required records of prior engagements "shall be made at or near the time of such engagements...." We think this language is largely self explanatory. If the records are made at the inception of a new engagement, that obviously satisfies the rule. If the records are not made at the inception of a new engagement, however, DR 5-105(e) allows them to be made "near" the time the engagement begins. To satisfy that alternative requirement, we think the records must ordinarily be made in time to assist in checking for conflicts by the next time a proposed new engagement comes along. In many law firms, proposed new engagements (including new matters for existing clients) come along every day or every few days. Thus, we think DR 5-105(e) requires that law firms make the necessary records within days, not weeks, after commencing a new engagement. The best practice is to make the records at the time engagements commence, but the rule allows some leeway by using the word "near." In addition, even though it is not required by DR 5-105(e), the best practice would also be to update the records periodically with additional parties or other pertinent information, for example where a complaint is amended to add new parties or where there are other developments with respect to a matter that might create a conflict under another rule. However, the Committee expresses no view in this opinion on whether other rules require such updating.

3. How far back in time must records go?

DR 5-105(e) took effect on May 22, 1996. Since that date, law firms have been obligated to "keep records of prior engagements...." However, nothing in the rule suggests that law firms were required to develop a comprehensive list of prior engagements going backward in time from May 22, 1996. As a practical matter, the rule contemplated only that law firms would begin keeping records of all engagements (including engagements already underway on May 22, 1996) starting on the rule's effective date. With these records in place the firm can determine whether it needs to fill in gaps in past records to provide effective assistance to the firm in avoiding conflicts.

4. How must the records be organized?

Merely recording information about current and previous engagements will not accomplish anything unless the information is readily accessible. The Committee therefore believes that the required records must be kept in a way that permits efficient access to the information they contain. Many methods are possible, but one straightforward method would be to list clients and former clients (perhaps alphabetically) and to list engagements undertaken for each client (perhaps in chronological order) under each client name. Regarding adverse parties, a firm should probably maintain a list, cross-referenced to the client and matter in which the adverse parties were involved. But a law firm may use any method that makes it possible for the firm to check the records in a timely fashion, and the type and organization of the records may depend largely on, among other things, the software and search engine employed to create and check the records.

5. What records must a law firm keep?

Unfortunately, DR 5-105(e) is silent about the type of records that a firm must maintain. It says only that the records are to provide "effective assistance" to lawyers within the firm in avoiding new engagements that would create a conflict of interest based on other current engagements or previous engagements. We therefore now address what records we think DR 5-105(e) requires.

The nature of the records needed to render effective assistance to lawyers in the conflict clearing process will vary depending on the size, structure, history, and nature of the law practice at issue. An example of a law firm near one end of the spectrum is a solo practitioner, concentrating solely in plaintiffs' personal injury matters, who has just begun to practice law. Such a law firm has relatively few clients and former clients and may need only the simplest written records to jog the lawyer's memory sufficiently to recognize and avoid conflicts. Toward the other end of the spectrum, presenting different and more complex problems, is an established law firm with hundreds of lawyers practicing in multiple domestic and foreign offices. Such a firm typically has thousands or tens of thousands of clients and former clients, many of them large corporate clients with affiliates and subsidiaries and with names that may have changed over time. In such a firm, fairly complex records will be needed to check effectively for conflicts. Somewhere in the middle of the spectrum are law firms with five or ten or twenty lawyers that have been in business for a decade or more. The nature of the records needed to check for conflicts in these mid-sized firms will depend on many factors.

As an initial matter, we note that several options are theoretically open regarding recordkeeping requirements. One option is a standard recordkeeping requirement specifying in detail the precise data that all firms must keep. We reject that option because it would ignore the substantial differences among firms. An alternative option is to adopt a variable recordkeeping requirement so that the nature of the required records depends on the size and nature of the law firm, its practice, and its lawyers. We adopt that option because a variable requirement takes into account the differences among firms and recognizes that firms may have to change the nature of their records as they grow and change. However, this Committee is not capable of specifying in detail the nature of the records that each type and size of firm must keep. Rather, we specify in general terms only the rock-bottom minimum records that we think all law firms must keep, no matter how small or specialized. But we caution that as law firms grow larger and more complex, they will find it increasingly difficult to fulfill their conflict checking duties unless they keep more than the minimum records that we believe are mandated by DR 5-105(e). (We address additional desirable information that might be maintained toward the end of the opinion, when we discuss systems for checking particular types of conflicts.)

Against this background, and for the reasons given below, the Committee believes that the following records are the minimum that any lawyer or private law firm must keep in order to comply with DR 5-105(e):

1. **Client names.** The full and precise name of each client the firm currently represents.

2. **Adverse party names.** The precise names of parties involved in a matter whose interests are materially adverse to each party the firm represents.

3. **Description of engagement.** A brief description of each engagement or prospective engagement.

With this basic information at hand, a law firm should be able to detect most potential conflicts involving clients or former clients before accepting any proposed new engagement. With less information in its records, many conflicts could not be detected. For example, without the client information, the remaining firm data would be useless in assisting lawyers in avoiding conflicts. Without adverse party information, a firm could not determine whether it was already acting adversely to the interests of a person or entity it later might seek to represent. Without a brief description of each engagement, a law firm could not judge whether a proposed new engagement would create conflicts with former clients. Of course, after identifying a potential conflict, a law firm may need to conduct factual and legal investigation to determine whether a prohibited conflict actually exists or is likely to develop. But the basic information outlined above should render effective assistance to most firms in putting them on notice that possible conflicts exist and that further study may be required.

We have not interpreted DR 5-105(e) to require records of the financial, business, property, or personal interests that may create conflicts under DR 5-101(a). Personal conflicts are not current or previous "engagements," so they are not within the scope of DR 5-105(e). We do not address whether any other provision of the Code requires a law firm to check for conflicts arising under DR 5-101.

Regarding records of prior engagements, we note that since March 4, 2002, a new court rule entitled "Written Letter of Engagement" (22 N.Y.C.R.R. Part 1215) has required all New York lawyers to provide written letters of engagement to clients in every matter where fees are expected to be $3,000 or more unless the client has previously paid the attorney for services "of the same general kind" or the matter is a domestic relations matter (in which case a written retainer agreement is required — see 22 N.Y.C.R.R. § 1400.3). For firms that do not have many repeat clients, such as firms that handle personal injury work, the written engagement letters required by Part 1215 will, in the normal course, identify the client and describe the nature of the representation in enough detail to satisfy the basic recordkeeping requirements we have set out above. (The firm will either have to record adverse parties separately or add that information to the engagement letters, however.) More elaborate engagement letters may also define who is not the client (e.g., "The firm does not represent any of the client's affiliates or subsidiaries" or "The firm represents you but not your spouse even though you and your spouse own your home as joint tenants"). Indexing or cataloging engagement letters may be one way to keep records of prior engagements at or near the time of the engagements. But engagement letters will not provide information about each new engagement if firms do not issue new engagement letters to clients who have previously paid for legal services of the same general kind, or for clients whose matters were never expected to generate $3,000 or more in legal fees.

While much additional information could be maintained to assist in the conflicts research process, it is difficult to argue that DR 5-105(e) requires information beyond the basic information necessary to put lawyers on notice that a potential problem exists. What law firms do with that basic information — what "system" they use to check for conflicts — is a separate and more difficult question, to which we now turn.

Policies and Systems for Checking for Possible Conflicts

In addition to mandating that law firms keep records, DR 5-105(e) requires every law firm to have "a policy implementing a system by which proposed engagements are checked against current and previous engagements," again with the stated aim of rendering "effective assistance to lawyers within the firm in complying with" DR 5-105(e)'s purpose to avoid conflicts arising from current or previous engagements.

1. What is a "system"?

An initial question is: What is a "system" within the meaning of DR 5-105(e)? The wording of DR 5-105(e) is curious: While the rule requires law firms to maintain "records of prior engagements," it does not expressly require the law firm to check those records when checking proposed engagements for conflicts. Rather, DR 5-105(e) simply requires a law firm to establish a policy and system "by which proposed engagements are checked against current and prior engagements ..." (We do not believe that the word "policy" adds anything significant to the word "system," so we focus only on the meaning of the word "system.") Taken literally, a "system" for checking proposed engagements against current and previous engagements would not necessarily require checking the written records. No doubt some solo practitioners use a "system" of consulting their memories alone, and some small law firms (and perhaps even some mid-sized law firms) use a "system" of talking to a partner with a good memory or asking around the firm (orally or via email or memo) to find out whether anyone knows of a conflict with a proposed engagement.

This Committee does not believe that any of those relatively informal methods of checking for conflicts would qualify as a "system" within the meaning of DR 5-105(e). Rather, we think DR 5-105(e) requires that a "system" of checking for conflicts within the meaning of DR 5-105(e) must include systematically consulting the "records" that must be kept to satisfy the opening clause of the rule. Less formal methods of checking for conflicts may of course be used (and may have to be used) to supplement a systematic check against those records, but we think it would be pointless to require a law firm to maintain written "records" but not require the law firm to consult those records as part of its conflict checking "system."

2. Essential elements of a "system."

We have just said that a "system" must include systematically consulting the "records" required by DR 5-105(e). What else must a system include to meet the requirements of DR 5-105(e)?

Because law firms vary in size, structure, practice areas, and history, the systems that will provide "effective assistance" in checking for conflicts within the meaning of DR 5-105(e) will depend on many factors. Sole practitioners and very small firms (five lawyers or less, all practicing in a single location) may not need to do much more than check their records and consult with other lawyers in the firm about any questions triggered by the records. As firms grow larger and build up a larger base of prior engagements, and as their practices grow more diverse, law firms may need to install software systems to check the records for conflicts rather than checking the records in a rudimentary fashion. See Pennwalt Corp. v. Plough, Inc., 85 F.R.D. 264 (D. Del. 1980) (law firms should make maximum use of technology to aid in avoiding conflicts). Some firms will be able to use commercial software programs "off-the-rack," but other firms, especially those with larger or more complex practices, may need to seek technical assistance to tailor the software program to the firm's particular needs.

If consulting the records leads to missing too many potential conflicts, and thus is not providing "effective assistance" to the firm in ferreting out conflicts with current and previous engagements, the firm will need to supplement the records check. Small firms may be able to do this through personal communications among key partners (or all partners) at the firm, either in writing or orally. Larger firms, especially those with more than one office, may need to supplement their records with email, formal written memos circulated throughout the firm, or other communication methods — electronic and traditional — designed to reach lawyers who may have relevant information about possible conflicts.

Many law firms (perhaps most firms) will be able to satisfy DR 5-105(e) by implementing a system that checks only the basic information that the rule requires (client names, adverse party names, and brief description of each engagement), supplemented by other types of communications and records checks to resolve any questions and detect certain types of conflicts not readily discoverable through a records check alone. In larger or more complex practices, however, an effective system will depend not only on a check of the records database but also on the ability of lawyers in the firm to communicate with others in the firm who have relevant information, to gain access to the firm's client files or other information regarding particular engagements, and to obtain more information readily upon request.

We believe that most firms afford access to information relevant to client engagements (except to the extent certain files have been screened off from particular lawyers). We also believe that virtually all large firms make it easy for a lawyer in the firm to communicate with other lawyers in the firm by email or other means. The more difficult question is the third element: What other information must be readily available upon request to supplement the basic records that all firms must keep? We turn to that complex question.

Systems for Checking Particular Types of Conflicts

In this section we discuss special considerations that may affect the system a law firm uses to check for conflicts arising under DR 5-105 and DR 5-108. We note, however, that we believe that the fact that a law firm is disqualified from a matter under these (or any other) rules does not necessarily mean that the law firm violated DR 5-105(e), and, furthermore, that keeping records required by DR 5-105(e) is not, in and of itself, a defense to a disqualification motion under DR 5-105, DR 5-108, or any other rules.

1. Conflicts with current clients.

The law is well established in New York that a law firm may not oppose a current client in any matter—even a totally unrelated matter—unless the law firm satisfies the "disinterested lawyer" test and obtains the informed consent of each client affected by the conflict. See, e.g., DR 5-105; Cinema 5, Ltd. v. Cinerama, Inc., 528 F.2d 1384 (2d Cir. 1976). Moreover, whenever two or more of a law firm's current clients are involved in the same litigation or transaction, even on the same side, the potential for conflict—and for a violation of DR 5-105(d)—is present. The records that include the names of all current clients, plus information available to the person checking the proposed engagement for conflicts, should usually be sufficient. That information will ordinarily be enough to alert the firm to investigate potential conflicts that arise when a law firm is opposing a current client, or when more than one current client is involved in the same transaction or litigation. However, concurrent client conflicts come in so many varieties that no single system of checking for conflicts will detect them all. We therefore address here some special situations that illustrate the practice-specific nature of conflict-checking systems.

(a) Corporate family conflicts.

When a law firm desires to oppose an entity that belongs to a current client's corporate family (e.g., an affiliate, subsidiary, parent, or sister corporation of a current corporate client), a concurrent client conflict may arise. Whether such a conflict is disqualifying will depend on many factors, including the relationship between the two corporations and the relationship between the work the law firm is doing for the current client and the work the law firm wishes to undertake in opposition to the client's corporate family member. See, e.g., Discotrade Ltd. v. Wyeth-Ayerst Int'l, Inc., 200 F. Supp. 2d 355 (S.D.N.Y. 2002) (granting motion to disqualify); JPMorgan Chase Bank v. Liberty Mutual Ins. Co., 189 F. Supp. 2d 20 (S.D.N.Y. 2002) (granting motion to disqualify); Brooklyn Navy Yard Cogeneration Partners L.P. v. PMNC, 254 A.D.2d 447, 679 N.Y.S.2d 312 (2d Dep't 1998) (denying motion to disqualify); see generally ABA Formal Opinion No. 95-390 (1995) (no automatic disqualification when a law firm opposes a corporate client's affiliate); N.Y. County Opinion 684 (1991), 1991 WL 755940 (attorney may, under certain circumstances, accept employment in a matter adverse to a subsidiary of a corporate client if the adverse action would not materially affect the corporate client's interests).

We would not require a law firm to maintain records showing every corporate affiliate of every current client. However, if a law firm frequently represents corporations that belong to large corporate families, then the firm should have some system for alerting the firm to potential conflicts with the members of the corporate client's family. One possibility is to explore the corporate family tree of proposed new adversaries to determine whether the adversary is related to other current clients of the firm. This search may require the law firm to maintain its own database of corporate family members; or the firm may decide to use a commercial service for that purpose; or the firm may directly ask its current clients. If the firm discovers a potential conflict with a corporate family member, the firm can conduct the appropriate research to determine whether the current client's consent is necessary. Not all law firms need such a system, but some kind of system will be necessary to render effective conflict-checking assistance to firms whose clients have many affiliates, subsidiaries, and other corporate relatives. (The same research will often be required to determine whether a proposed engagement will create a conflict with a former client—see the discussion of former client conflicts below.)

(b) Corporate constituents.

When a law firm represents an entity, DR 5-109(a) provides that the law firm "is the lawyer for the organization and not for any of the constituents." The first sentence of EC 5-18 of the Code is even more explicit: "A lawyer employed or retained by a corporation or similar entity owes allegiance to the entity and not to a shareholder, director, officer, employee, representative, or other person connected with the entity."

Nevertheless, especially when a law firm represents a small or closely held corporation with few shareholders, or when the law firm appears on behalf of individual officers or employees but bills the corporate client for the legal services, an attorney-client relationship does or may develop — intentionally or unintentionally — between the law firm and one or more individual constituents of the entity. See, e.g., Rosman v. Shapiro, 653 F. Supp. 1441 (S.D.N.Y. 1987) (50% shareholder of a closely held corporation was a client of law firm that represented the corporation); Cooke v. Laidlaw, Adams & Peck, Inc., 126 A.D.2d 453, 510 N.Y.S.2d 597 (1st Dep't 1987) (corporate officer was considered client of law firm that represented corporation because law firm appeared on behalf of officer in an SEC proceeding). Accordingly, a law firm that represents corporate clients may need a system for determining whether the law firm has an attorney-client relationship with individual constituents of a client organization and, if so, should add the names of those clients to its records database.

(c) Trade association members.

A law firm that represents a trade association ordinarily represents only the trade association and not the members of the trade association. However, an attorney-client relationship between the law firm and a member may arise if a member provides the law firm with confidential information. In that instance, the law firm will be restricted in its freedom to oppose the member. See, e.g., Glueck v. Jonathan Logan, Inc., 653 F.2d 746 (2d Cir. 1981) (trade association member may be a "vicarious" client); Westinghouse Elec. Corp. v. Kerr-McGee Corp., 580 F.2d 1311 (7th Cir. 1978) (a client is no longer merely a person who walks through the door); ABA Formal Opinion 92-365 (1992) (whether a lawyer for a trade association also represents members of the association is a question of fact). If a law firm represents a trade association, its conflict-checking system should enable attorneys to determine whether members of the trade association are also clients. If so, the law firm should add the member's name to the records identifying the firm's clients.

2. Conflicts with former clients.

(a) The law firm's own former clients.

Under DR 5-108(a) (entitled "Conflict of Interest — Former Client"), except with the consent of a former client after full disclosure, or in compliance with the special provisions of DR 9-101(b) for former public servants, a lawyer who has formerly represented a client in a matter shall not thereafter "represent another person in the same or a substantially related matter in which that person's interests are materially adverse to the interests of the former client." In short, absent the former client's informed consent, or absent an information screen and other procedures mandated by DR 9-101(b) for conflicts involving former public servants, a lawyer may not oppose a former client in the same or a substantially related matter.

Because conflicts with former clients are common, we think every law firm must have a system for discovering such conflicts. If the law firm consistently maintains its database of clients and former clients, then checking each proposed engagement against that list should be adequate. If a probable adverse party turns out to be one of the firm's former clients, the firm will know that it should look further into the situation to see whether the former client's consent is required.

Unfortunately, it will not always be clear whether a particular person is a current client or a former client. See, e.g., Oxford Sys. Inc. v. CellPro, Inc. 45 F. Supp. 2d 1055 (W.D. Wash. 1999); SWS Financial Fund A v. Salomon Bros., Inc., 790 F. Supp. 1392 (N.D. Ill. 1992); Lama Holding Co. v. Shearman & Sterling, 758 F. Supp. 159 (S.D.N.Y. 1991). This is not the place for a comprehensive discussion of the factors that will enable a law firm to distinguish between current clients and former clients, or to tell when a current client has become a former client.

However, to provide effective assistance to the firm in avoiding conflicts with current clients, a law firm's conflict-checking system should include some means of determining whether a client remains a current client or has become a former client.

(b) The former clients of laterals.

When a lawyer moves from one private law firm to another private law firm, the clients that the lawyer personally represented at his or her prior law firm are potential sources of conflict for the new law firm. See, e.g., Kassis v. Teachers Ins. and Annuity Ass'n, 93 N.Y.2d 611, 695 N.Y.S. 2d 515 (1999) (disqualifying a firm that hired a lawyer who had actively worked on litigation in which the old and new firms were opposing counsel, where the litigation was still pending when the lawyer changed firms); N.Y. State Opinion 723 (1999) (discussing the DR 5-108); (N.Y. State Opinion 720 (1999), 1999 WL 692571, at *2 ("[W]e believe that the intent of [DR 5-105(e)] can only be effected if a firm adds to its system information about the representations of lawyers who join the firm."). Under DR 5-108(b), absent the former client's informed consent, a law firm that hires a lateral may be disqualified from acting adversely to a client of the lateral's former law firm in a matter substantially related to the former firm's representation of that client if the lateral, while at the former firm, "acquired information protected by DR 4-101(b) that is material to the matter," even if the lateral never personally represented the client in question at the former firm.

Accordingly, since DR 5-105(e) specifically applies only to prior engagements of the law firm itself, if a law firm hires lawyers laterally from other law firms, the hiring firm should include in its conflict-checking system a means for determining which clients the lateral lawyer personally represented while at his or her former firm. At the same time, while it is not required under DR 5-505(e), it would be prudent for the firm to consider what, if any, other steps it might take with regard to other matters about which the lateral lawyer acquired protected information while at the former firm. In either event, the information from the lateral's former firm should be obtained only insofar as it is possible to do so in a manner that is consistent with the lateral's obligations to his or her former firm and its clients. See, e.g., N.Y. State Opinion 720 (1999) 1999 WL 692571 (discussing lateral's duties to protect former clients' confidences and secrets, as well as contractual or fiduciary restrictions the lateral may be subject to regarding the disclosure of information proprietary to the lawyer's former firm).

Types of Conflicts Not Addressed in This Opinion

The subject of conflicts of interest is vast, and we have discussed only a small portion of the field. There are many other areas that we have not discussed but that law firms may have to consider when checking for conflicts pursuant to DR 5-105(e). These include (a) conflicts arising in class actions; (b) conflicts that arise when lawyers in a firm invest in client ventures (either directly or in lieu of fees—see ABCNY Opinion 2000-3 (2000),

2000 WL 33769162; (c) conflicts that arise when lawyers in the firm serve on a client's Board of Directors; (d) conflicts that arise in connection with an insurance triangle; (e) conflicts with nonlawyers (such as paralegals and secretaries), especially those who have previously worked at another law firm (including the legal department of a corporate adversary); (f) conflicts arising from the use of temporary lawyers who concurrently work or have in the past worked at other law firms; (g) conflicts that arise when lawyers represent or are represented by other lawyers; (h) conflicts that arise when a current client is an adverse witness; (i) conflicts involving former public servants; and (j) the special conflict issues that may arise in connection with beauty contests or other business development activities. Each firm should survey the extent to which these special varieties of conflicts are pertinent to the firm's practice and should adopt measures to detect and deal with them.

Conclusion

Under DR 5-105(e) of the New York Code of Professional Responsibility, all law firms must keep records and must have policies and systems in place to check for conflicts of interest to the extent necessary to render effective assistance to the lawyers in the firm in complying with New York's rule on imputed conflicts, DR 5-105(d). The records each firm must keep, and the policies and systems each firm must implement, will depend on each law firm's particular nature, structure, practice, history, personnel, and other factors. However, all law firms must keep certain minimum written or electronic records of each new or prospective engagement and must consult those records when checking proposed new engagements for conflicts of interest.

Issued: October, 2003

Chapter III

Loyalty to Past Clients: Successive and Imputed Conflicts of Interest

Problems

Problem 5

Select sides and argue the motion to disqualify David Rabin, Esq. as described in *Emle Industries, Inc.* v. *Patentex, Inc.*, set out at Chapter III-3, *infra*. Would it make a difference if the case were governed by the *ABA Model Rules* or the *Mass. Rules*? Be sure to argue the policy issues inherent in this decision. Do you like the outcome of the Second Circuit Court of Appeals? Rubin was the partner of a small "boutique" specialty firm. What does this case say about that career option?

Problem 6

Select sides and argue the motion to disqualify Dale Schreiber, Esq., as described in the *Silver Chrysler Plymouth* case, set out at Chapter III-3, *infra*. Would it make a difference which rule system was in effect? What do you think of the conduct of Kelley, Drye, Warren, Clark, Carr & Ellis? Was the case properly decided? Could this case influence your career decisions? Schreiber was a former associate at a big "corporate" firm. What does this case say about that career option?

Problem 7

Select sides and argue the motion to disqualify the Rabinowitz Law Firm as described in *Hull* v. *Celanese Corporation*, set out at Chapter III-3, *infra*. Does the choice of rule system make a difference? Could this case affect your career choices? This case involved Donata A. Delulio, an "in-house" counsel at Celanese Corporation. What does this case say about that career option?

Problem 8

Select sides and argue the motion to disqualify George D. Reycroft, Esq., as described in *General Motors Corp.* v. *City of New York*, set out at Chapter III-3, *infra*. Why does General Motors have the right to object, as Reycraft was always on the other side? Do you like this outcome? Does it make any difference which rule system was in effect? Could this case influence your career choice? Reycraft was a former government lawyer who then went into public practice. What does this case say abut that career option?

Problem 9

Assume you will pursue a career in a major law firm. Do you think that the issues raised in cases such as *Emle Industries*, *infra*, *Silver Chrysler Plymouth*, *infra*, and *Analytica, Inc.*

v. *NPD Research, Inc.*, set out at Chapter III-3, *infra*, have been satisfactory resolved in the latest version of the *ABA Model Rules*? Could this influence your career?

III-1. Introduction: Living with the "Hand of the Past" and Legal Fictions

Loyalty to past clients and imputed conflicts of interest may seem like very technical subjects until you begin to think about your own career. Many new lawyers today move from firm to firm. Their careers often depend on it. Each firm has thousands of clients. You may think, once you leave the firm, those clients do not matter. Wrong. Or, you may think, "only those clients I know a lot about matter." Wrong again. Loyalty to past clients of your former firms can have a direct impact on your professional life.

Clients can be in a poor position to know who in a firm knows their secrets, or worked on their matters. So the doctrine evolved that if one lawyer in a firm had a conflict of interest, everyone did. This was the rule under the old ABA *Code* DR 5-105(D). It is still the rule. *Mass. Rule* 1.10 (a) reads:

> "(a) While lawyers are associated in a firm, none of them shall knowingly represent a client when any one of them practicing alone would be prohibited from doing so by Rules 1.7, 1.8(c), or 1.9. A lawyer employed by the Public Counsel Division of the Committee for Public Counsel Services and a lawyer assigned to represent clients by the Private Counsel Division of the Committee are not considered to be associated. Lawyers are not considered to be associated merely because they have each individually been assigned to represent clients by the Committee for Public Counsel Services through its Private Counsel Division."

(The provisions distinguishing Public Counsel Services was clearly necessary to encourage such service). The new ABA *Model Rule* 1.10(a) adds an exemption where the conflict is based "on a personal interest of the prohibited lawyer" or where there is no "significant risk" of limiting the representation by the other lawyers. The new *Model Rule* 1.10(b) also provides a major exception where a lawyer is "timely screened" and "is apportioned no part of the fee therein" and proper screening procedures are adopted. This rule has not been adopted by many states, for reasons discussed below.

A. Legal Fictions

This type of conflict of interest is called "imputed conflict of interest" because another lawyer's conflict is imputed to you. "Imputed conflict of interest" is a "legal fiction." Legal fictions are a common tool in the Anglo-American tradition.[1] They occur whenever we assume something is true, for theoretical or policy reasons, when we know, in fact, that it may not be true at all. Thus we assume Queen Elizabeth II is "sovereign"

---

1. See Daniel R. Coquillette, *Anglo-American Legal Heritage* (2d ed., Durham, N.C., 2004), pp. 282–283, 303–309.

of England, or that the Supreme Court of the United States does not legislate, but merely applies an eighteenth century document as written. But these are fictions. Some jurists, like Jeremy Bentham or Jerome Frank, have resisted legal fictions, but most of us find them a comfortable way of making incremental reforms, or promoting policies.[2]

Assume a Boston firm with 100 lawyers, governed by *Mass. Rule* 1.10(a). Most of these lawyers will know nothing about any particular client but, as a policy matter, they are presumed to share the confidential knowledge and loyalty obligations of the few that do. Now take this fiction one step further. Assume an associate of that firm leaves and joins another firm of over 100 lawyers. Does the fiction now "impute" that associate's knowledge, which could already be a fiction, to all the other lawyers in the second firm, a "fiction on a fiction?" The consequences of this to the associate's career would, however, not be a fiction. It would be very real. Now imagine a lawyer who worked for the federal government! Without special exemption, imputed conflicts could make hiring such a lawyer a real danger to a firm's business. In the crude language of the profession, such a lawyer is called a "Typhoid Mary."

For this reason, the drafters of the *Model Rules* built in important exceptions to *Model Rule* 1.10(a). First, imputed disqualification only occurs when the lawyer's "had acquired information protected by Rule 1.6 and 1.9(c) that is material to the matter." (Confidentiality of Rule 1.6 and Rule 1.9(c) are discussed in Chapter IV, *infra*). Second, it has to be the "same or substantially related" matter, and the new client's interests must be "materially adverse to the interests of the former client." *Model Rule* 1.9(b)(1). Finally, the former client can always remove the bar by giving "informed consent, confirmed in writing." *Model Rule* 1.9(a).

In addition, special rules have traditionally been established for a former "public officer or employee of the government." If such a lawyer "participated personally and substantially" in a matter for the government, informed consent, "confirmed in writing," is required before that lawyer can represent a client in a related matter. But other lawyers in the same firm can undertake such a representation if "the disqualified lawyer is timely screened from any participation in the matter and is apportioned no part of the fee therefore" and "written notice is promptly given to the appropriate government agency." *Model Rule* 1.11(b)(1) and (2). There are also measures to protect "confidential government information." *Model Rule* 1.11 (c). Failure to meet these standards can disqualify an entire firm. See *United States* v. *Philip Morris, Inc.*, 312 F. Supp. 2d 27 (D.C. 2004).

B. Screening

So why is "screening" not the answer to all problems of imputed conflicts of interest? This is a very controversial subject and, for obvious reasons, big law firms have pressured the ABA for such a change. In Massachusetts, *Mass. Rule* 1.10 has been amended to provide for screening where "the personally disqualified lawyer" has "neither substantial involvement nor substantial material information relating to the matter." *Mass. Rule*

---

2. Jerome Frank was cautioned, quoting Valhinger, "One must guard against the vice of assuming that, because a fiction is useful, it therefore was objective validity. The bulk between reality and fiction must always be stressed"; one must avoid "the fundamental error of converting fiction into reality." See Jerome Frank, *Law and the Modern Mind* (New York, 1963), 338–339.

1.10(d)(2). The ABA has recently gone much further, and has completely reversed its original position, which was against any screening, except former government employees. The new Model Rule 1.10(a)(2) permits a general screening remedy. It extends screening privileges previously reserved for former government attorneys to all attorneys that are "timely screened" and "apportioned no part of the fee therein...." See *Model Rule* 1.10(b)(1) and (2). So far, however, the new ABA rule has been resisted by many states.The problem is that clients are suspicious of "screening." If there is a "leak" of information or unauthorized assistance from their former lawyer to an adversary in a related matter, who is likely to tell them? To encourage government careers, many states make a special exception for former government lawyers, but the general use of screening to avoid imputed conflicts of interest has not been widely accepted. As of 2009, only twenty-four states had adopted the new ABA Model Rule 1.10 with regards to screening. Screens, however, are frequently used to obtain the consent of former clients under *Model Rule* 1.9 to what would otherwise be an impermissible representation. But that is a very different matter from automatic protection through screens, because, where consent is required, the former client is still in control.

III-2. Successive and Imputed Conflicts of Interest: The Rules

ABA Model Rules

RULE 1.9: DUTIES TO FORMER CLIENTS

(a) A lawyer who has formerly represented a client in a matter shall not thereafter represent another person in the same or a substantially related matter in which that person's interests are materially adverse to the interests of the former client unless the former client gives informed consent, confirmed in writing.

(b) A lawyer shall not knowingly represent a person in the same or a substantially related matter in which a firm with which the lawyer formerly was associated had previously represented a client

(1) whose interests are materially adverse to that person; and

(2) about whom the lawyer had acquired information protected by Rules 1.6 and 1.9(c) that is material to the matter;

unless the former client gives informed consent, confirmed in writing.

(c) A lawyer who has formerly represented a client in a matter or whose present or former firm has formerly represented a client in a matter shall not thereafter:

(1) use information relating to the representation to the disadvantage of the former client except as these Rules would permit or require with respect to a client, or when the information has become generally known; or

(2) reveal information relating to the representation except as these Rules would permit or require with respect to a client.

Comment

[1] After termination of a client-lawyer relationship, a lawyer has certain continuing duties with respect to confidentiality and conflicts of interest and thus may not represent

another client except in conformity with this Rule. Under this Rule, for example, a lawyer could not properly seek to rescind on behalf of a new client a contract drafted on behalf of the former client. So also a lawyer who has prosecuted an accused person could not properly represent the accused in a subsequent civil action against the government concerning the same transaction. Nor could a lawyer who has represented multiple clients in a matter represent one of the clients against the others in the same or a substantially related matter after a dispute arose among the clients in that matter, unless all affected clients give informed consent. See Comment [9]. Current and former government lawyers must comply with this Rule to the extent required by Rule 1.11.

[2] The scope of a "matter" for purposes of this Rule depends on the facts of a particular situation or transaction. The lawyer's involvement in a matter can also be a question of degree. When a lawyer has been directly involved in a specific transaction, subsequent representation of other clients with materially adverse interests in that transaction clearly is prohibited. On the other hand, a lawyer who recurrently handled a type of problem for a former client is not precluded from later representing another client in a factually distinct problem of that type even though the subsequent representation involves a position adverse to the prior client. Similar considerations can apply to the reassignment of military lawyers between defense and prosecution functions within the same military jurisdictions. The underlying question is whether the lawyer was so involved in the matter that the subsequent representation can be justly regarded as a changing of sides in the matter in question.

[3] Matters are "substantially related" for purposes of this Rule if they involve the same transaction or legal dispute or if there otherwise is a substantial risk that confidential factual information as would normally have been obtained in the prior representation would materially advance the client's position in the subsequent matter. For example, a lawyer who has represented a businessperson and learned extensive private financial information about that person may not then represent that person's spouse in seeking a divorce. Similarly, a lawyer who has previously represented a client in securing environmental permits to build a shopping center would be precluded from representing neighbors seeking to oppose rezoning of the property on the basis of environmental considerations; however, the lawyer would not be precluded, on the grounds of substantial relationship, from defending a tenant of the completed shopping center in resisting eviction for nonpayment of rent. Information that has been disclosed to the public or to other parties adverse to the former client ordinarily will not be disqualifying. Information acquired in a prior representation may have been rendered obsolete by the passage of time, a circumstance that may be relevant in determining whether two representations are substantially related. In the case of an organizational client, general knowledge of the client's policies and practices ordinarily will not preclude a subsequent representation; on the other hand, knowledge of specific facts gained in a prior representation that are relevant to the matter in question ordinarily will preclude such a representation. A former client is not required to reveal the confidential information learned by the lawyer in order to establish a substantial risk that the lawyer has confidential information to use in the subsequent matter. A conclusion about the possession of such information may be based on the nature of the services the lawyer provided the former client and information that would in ordinary practice be learned by a lawyer providing such services.

Lawyers Moving Between Firms

[4] When lawyers have been associated within a firm but then end their association, the question of whether a lawyer should undertake representation is more complicated.

There are several competing considerations. First, the client previously represented by the former firm must be reasonably assured that the principle of loyalty to the client is not compromised. Second, the rule should not be so broadly cast as to preclude other persons from having reasonable choice of legal counsel. Third, the rule should not unreasonably hamper lawyers from forming new associations and taking on new clients after having left a previous association. In this connection, it should be recognized that today many lawyers practice in firms, that many lawyers to some degree limit their practice to one field or another, and that many move from one association to another several times in their careers. If the concept of imputation were applied with unqualified rigor, the result would be radical curtailment of the opportunity of lawyers to move from one practice setting to another and of the opportunity of clients to change counsel.

[5] Paragraph (b) operates to disqualify the lawyer only when the lawyer involved has actual knowledge of information protected by Rules 1.6 and 1.9(c). Thus, if a lawyer while with one firm acquired no knowledge or information relating to a particular client of the firm, and that lawyer later joined another firm, neither the lawyer individually nor the second firm is disqualified from representing another client in the same or a related matter even though the interests of the two clients conflict. See Rule 1.10(b) for the restrictions on a firm once a lawyer has terminated association with the firm.

[6] Application of paragraph (b) depends on a situation's particular facts, aided by inferences, deductions or working presumptions that reasonably may be made about the way in which lawyers work together. A lawyer may have general access to files of all clients of a law firm and may regularly participate in discussions of their affairs; it should be inferred that such a lawyer in fact is privy to all information about all the firm's clients. In contrast, another lawyer may have access to the files of only a limited number of clients and participate in discussions of the affairs of no other clients; in the absence of information to the contrary, it should be inferred that such a lawyer in fact is privy to information about the clients actually served but not those of other clients. In such an inquiry, the burden of proof should rest upon the firm whose disqualification is sought.

[7] Independent of the question of disqualification of a firm, a lawyer changing professional association has a continuing duty to preserve confidentiality of information about a client formerly represented. See Rules 1.6 and 1.9(c).

[8] Paragraph (c) provides that information acquired by the lawyer in the course of representing a client may not subsequently be used or revealed by the lawyer to the disadvantage of the client. However, the fact that a lawyer has once served a client does not preclude the lawyer from using generally known information about that client when later representing another client.

[9] The provisions of this Rule are for the protection of former clients and can be waived if the client gives informed consent, which consent must be confirmed in writing under paragraphs (a) and (b). See Rule 1.0(e). With regard to the effectiveness of an advance waiver, see Comment [22] to Rule 1.7. With regard to disqualification of a firm with which a lawyer is or was formerly associated, see Rule 1.10.

RULE 1.10: IMPUTATION OF CONFLICTS OF INTEREST: GENERAL RULE

(a) While lawyers are associated in a firm, none of them shall knowingly represent a client when any one of them practicing alone would be prohibited from doing so by Rules 1.7 or 1.9, unless

(1) the prohibition is based on a personal interest of the disqualified lawyer and does not present a significant risk of materially limiting the representation of the client by the remaining lawyers in the firm; or

(2) the prohibition is based upon Rule 1.9(a) or (b) and arises out of the disqualified lawyer's association with a prior firm, and

(i) the disqualified lawyer is timely screened from any participation in the matter and is apportioned no part of the fee therefrom;

(ii) written notice is promptly given to any affected former client to enable the former client to ascertain compliance with the provisions of this Rule, which shall include a description of the screening procedures employed; a statement of the firm's and of the screened lawyer's compliance with these Rules; a statement that review may be available before a tribunal; and an agreement by the firm to respond promptly to any written inquiries or objections by the former client about the screening procedures; and

(iii) certifications of compliance with these Rules and with the screening procedures are provided to the former client by the screened lawyer and by a partner of the firm, at reasonable intervals upon the former client's written request and upon termination of the screening procedures.

(b) When a lawyer has terminated an association with a firm, the firm is not prohibited from thereafter representing a person with interests materially adverse to those of a client represented by the formerly associated lawyer and not currently represented by the firm, unless:

(1) the matter is the same or substantially related to that in which the formerly associated lawyer represented the client; and

(2) any lawyer remaining in the firm has information protected by Rules 1.6 and 1.9(c) that is material to the matter.

(c) A disqualification prescribed by this rule may be waived by the affected client under the conditions stated in Rule 1.7.

(d) The disqualification of lawyers associated in a firm with former or current government lawyers is governed by Rule 1.11.

Comment

Definition of "Firm"

[1] For purposes of the Rules of Professional Conduct, the term "firm" denotes lawyers in a law partnership, professional corporation, sole proprietorship or other association authorized to practice law; or lawyers employed in a legal services organization or the legal department of a corporation or other organization. See Rule 1.0(c). Whether two or more lawyers constitute a firm within this definition can depend on the specific facts. See Rule 1.0, Comments [2]–[4].

Principles of Imputed Disqualification

[2] The rule of imputed disqualification stated in paragraph (a) gives effect to the principle of loyalty to the client as it applies to lawyers who practice in a law firm. Such situations can be considered from the premise that a firm of lawyers is essentially one lawyer for purposes of the rules governing loyalty to the client, or from the premise that each lawyer is vicariously bound by the obligation of loyalty owed by each lawyer with whom the lawyer is associated. Paragraph (a)(1) operates only among the lawyers cur-

rently associated in a firm. When a lawyer moves from one firm to another, the situation is governed by Rules 1.9(b) 1.10(a)(2) and 1.10(b).

[3] The rule in paragraph (a) does not prohibit representation where neither questions of client loyalty nor protection of confidential information are presented. Where one lawyer in a firm could not effectively represent a given client because of strong political beliefs, for example, but that lawyer will do no work on the case and the personal beliefs of the lawyer will not materially limit the representation by others in the firm, the firm should not be disqualified. On the other hand, if an opposing party in a case were owned by a lawyer in the law firm, and others in the firm would be materially limited in pursuing the matter because of loyalty to that lawyer, the personal disqualification of the lawyer would be imputed to all others in the firm.

[4] The rule in paragraph (a) also does not prohibit representation by others in the law firm where the person prohibited from involvement in a matter is a nonlawyer, such as a paralegal or legal secretary. Nor does paragraph (a) prohibit representation if the lawyer is prohibited from acting because of events before the person became a lawyer, for example, work that the person did while a law student. Such persons, however, ordinarily must be screened from any personal participation in the matter to avoid communication to others in the firm of confidential information that both the nonlawyers and the firm have a legal duty to protect. See Rules 1.0(k) and 5.3.

[5] Rule 1.10(b) operates to permit a law firm, under certain circumstances, to represent a person with interests directly adverse to those of a client represented by a lawyer who formerly was associated with the firm. The Rule applies regardless of when the formerly associated lawyer represented the client. However, the law firm may not represent a person with interests adverse to those of a present client of the firm, which would violate Rule 1.7. Moreover, the firm may not represent the person where the matter is the same or substantially related to that in which the formerly associated lawyer represented the client and any other lawyer currently in the firm has material information protected by Rules 1.6 and 1.9(c).

[6] Rule 1.10(c) removes imputation with the informed consent of the affected client or former client under the conditions stated in Rule 1.7. The conditions stated in Rule 1.7 require the lawyer to determine that the representation is not prohibited by Rule 1.7(b) and that each affected client or former client has given informed consent to the representation, confirmed in writing. In some cases, the risk may be so severe that the conflict may not be cured by client consent. For a discussion of the effectiveness of client waivers of conflicts that might arise in the future, see Rule 1.7, Comment [22]. For a definition of informed consent, see Rule 1.0(e).

[7] Rule 1.10(a)(2) similarly removes the imputation otherwise required by Rule 1.10(a), but unlike section (c), it does so without requiring that there be informed consent by the former client. Instead, it requires that the procedures laid out in sections (a)(2)(i)–(iii) be followed. A description of effective screening mechanisms appears in Rule 1.0(k). Lawyers should be aware, however, that, even where screening mechanisms have been adopted, tribunals may consider additional factors in ruling upon motions to disqualify a lawyer from pending litigation.

[8] Paragraph (a)(2)(i) does not prohibit the screened lawyer from receiving a salary or partnership share established by prior independent agreement, but that lawyer may not receive compensation directly related to the matter in which the lawyer is disqualified.

[9] The notice required by paragraph (a)(2)(ii) generally should include a description of the screened lawyer's prior representation and be given as soon as practicable after

the need for screening becomes apparent. It also should include a statement by the screened lawyer and the firm that the client's material confidential information has not been disclosed or used in violation of the Rules. The notice is intended to enable the former client to evaluate and comment upon the effectiveness of the screening procedures.

[10] The certifications required by paragraph (a)(2)(iii) give the former client assurance that the client's material confidential information has not been disclosed or used inappropriately, either prior to timely implementation of a screen or thereafter. If compliance cannot be certified, the certificate must describe the failure to comply.

[11] Where a lawyer has joined a private firm after having represented the government, imputation is governed by Rule 1.11(b) and (c), not this Rule. Under Rule 1.11(d), where a lawyer represents the government after having served clients in private practice, nongovernmental employment or in another government agency, former-client conflicts are not imputed to government lawyers associated with the individually disqualified lawyer.

[12] Where a lawyer is prohibited from engaging in certain transactions under Rule 1.8, paragraph (k) of that Rule, and not this Rule, determines whether that prohibition also applies to other lawyers associated in a firm with the personally prohibited lawyer.

RULE 1.11: SPECIAL CONFLICTS OF INTEREST FOR FORMER AND CURRENT GOVERNMENT OFFICERS AND EMPLOYEES

(a) Except as law may otherwise expressly permit, a lawyer who has formerly served as a public officer or employee of the government:

(1) is subject to Rule 1.9(c); and

(2) shall not otherwise represent a client in connection with a matter in which the lawyer participated personally and substantially as a public officer or employee, unless the appropriate government agency gives its informed consent, confirmed in writing, to the representation.

(b) When a lawyer is disqualified from representation under paragraph (a), no lawyer in a firm with which that lawyer is associated may knowingly undertake or continue representation in such a matter unless:

(1) the disqualified lawyer is timely screened from any participation in the matter and is apportioned no part of the fee therefrom; and

(2) written notice is promptly given to the appropriate government agency to enable it to ascertain compliance with the provisions of this rule.

(c) Except as law may otherwise expressly permit, a lawyer having information that the lawyer knows is confidential government information about a person acquired when the lawyer was a public officer or employee, may not represent a private client whose interests are adverse to that person in a matter in which the information could be used to the material disadvantage of that person. As used in this Rule, the term "confidential government information" means information that has been obtained under governmental authority and which, at the time this Rule is applied, the government is prohibited by law from disclosing to the public or has a legal privilege not to disclose and which is not otherwise available to the public. A firm with which that lawyer is associated may undertake or continue representation in the matter only if the disqualified lawyer is timely screened from any participation in the matter and is apportioned no part of the fee therefrom.

(d) Except as law may otherwise expressly permit, a lawyer currently serving as a public officer or employee:

(1) is subject to Rules 1.7 and 1.9; and

(2) shall not:

(i) participate in a matter in which the lawyer participated personally and substantially while in private practice or nongovernmental employment, unless the appropriate government agency gives its informed consent, confirmed in writing; or

(ii) negotiate for private employment with any person who is involved as a party or as lawyer for a party in a matter in which the lawyer is participating personally and substantially, except that a lawyer serving as a law clerk to a judge, other adjudicative officer or arbitrator may negotiate for private employment as permitted by Rule 1.12(b) and subject to the conditions stated in Rule 1.12(b).

(e) As used in this Rule, the term "matter" includes:

(1) any judicial or other proceeding, application, request for a ruling or other determination, contract, claim, controversy, investigation, charge, accusation, arrest or other particular matter involving a specific party or parties, and

(2) any other matter covered by the conflict of interest rules of the appropriate government agency.

Comment

[1] A lawyer who has served or is currently serving as a public officer or employee is personally subject to the Rules of Professional Conduct, including the prohibition against concurrent conflicts of interest stated in Rule 1.7. In addition, such a lawyer may be subject to statutes and government regulations regarding conflict of interest. Such statutes and regulations may circumscribe the extent to which the government agency may give consent under this Rule. See Rule 1.0(e) for the definition of informed consent.

[2] Paragraphs (a)(1), (a)(2) and (d)(1) restate the obligations of an individual lawyer who has served or is currently serving as an officer or employee of the government toward a former government or private client. Rule 1.10 is not applicable to the conflicts of interest addressed by this Rule. Rather, paragraph (b) sets forth a special imputation rule for former government lawyers that provides for screening and notice. Because of the special problems raised by imputation within a government agency, paragraph (d) does not impute the conflicts of a lawyer currently serving as an officer or employee of the government to other associated government officers or employees, although ordinarily it will be prudent to screen such lawyers.

[3] Paragraphs (a)(2) and (d)(2) apply regardless of whether a lawyer is adverse to a former client and are thus designed not only to protect the former client, but also to prevent a lawyer from exploiting public office for the advantage of another client. For example, a lawyer who has pursued a claim on behalf of the government may not pursue the same claim on behalf of a later private client after the lawyer has left government service, except when authorized to do so by the government agency under paragraph (a). Similarly, a lawyer who has pursued a claim on behalf of a private client may not pursue the claim on behalf of the government, except when authorized to do so by paragraph (d). As with paragraphs (a)(1) and (d)(1), Rule 1.10 is not applicable to the conflicts of interest addressed by these paragraphs.

[4] This Rule represents a balancing of interests. On the one hand, where the successive clients are a government agency and another client, public or private, the risk exists that power or discretion vested in that agency might be used for the special benefit of the other client. A lawyer should not be in a position where benefit to the other client might affect performance of the lawyer's professional functions on behalf of the government. Also, unfair advantage could accrue to the other client by reason of access to confidential government information about the client's adversary obtainable only through the lawyer's government service. On the other hand, the rules governing lawyers presently or formerly employed by a government agency should not be so restrictive as to inhibit transfer of employment to and from the government. The government has a legitimate need to attract qualified lawyers as well as to maintain high ethical standards. Thus a former government lawyer is disqualified only from particular matters in which the lawyer participated personally and substantially. The provisions for screening and waiver in paragraph (b) are necessary to prevent the disqualification rule from imposing too severe a deterrent against entering public service. The limitation of disqualification in paragraphs (a)(2) and (d)(2) to matters involving a specific party or parties, rather than extending disqualification to all substantive issues on which the lawyer worked, serves a similar function.

[5] When a lawyer has been employed by one government agency and then moves to a second government agency, it may be appropriate to treat that second agency as another client for purposes of this Rule, as when a lawyer is employed by a city and subsequently is employed by a federal agency. However, because the conflict of interest is governed by paragraph (d), the latter agency is not required to screen the lawyer as paragraph (b) requires a law firm to do. The question of whether two government agencies should be regarded as the same or different clients for conflict of interest purposes is beyond the scope of these Rules. See Rule 1.13 Comment [9].

[6] Paragraphs (b) and (c) contemplate a screening arrangement. See Rule 1.0(k) (requirements for screening procedures). These paragraphs do not prohibit a lawyer from receiving a salary or partnership share established by prior independent agreement, but that lawyer may not receive compensation directly relating the lawyer's compensation to the fee in the matter in which the lawyer is disqualified.

[7] Notice, including a description of the screened lawyer's prior representation and of the screening procedures employed, generally should be given as soon as practicable after the need for screening becomes apparent.

[8] Paragraph (c) operates only when the lawyer in question has knowledge of the information, which means actual knowledge; it does not operate with respect to information that merely could be imputed to the lawyer.

[9] Paragraphs (a) and (d) do not prohibit a lawyer from jointly representing a private party and a government agency when doing so is permitted by Rule 1.7 and is not otherwise prohibited by law.

[10] For purposes of paragraph (e) of this Rule, a "matter" may continue in another form. In determining whether two particular matters are the same, the lawyer should consider the extent to which the matters involve the same basic facts, the same or related parties, and the time elapsed.

ABA Code

DR 5-105 Refusing to Accept or Continue Employment if the Interests of Another Client May Impair the Independent Professional Judgment of the Lawyer.

* * *

(D) If a lawyer is required to decline employment or to withdraw from employment under a Disciplinary Rule, no partner, or associate, or any other lawyer affiliated with him or his firm, may accept or continue such employment.

III-3. Imputed Disqualification and Successive Conflicts of Interest: Cases and Materials

Emle Industries, Inc. v. Patentex, Inc.

478 F.2d 562
United States Court of Appeals, Second Circuit
Argued April 3, 1973
Decided May 9, 1973
[Some footnotes omitted. Footnotes renumbered.]

Before KAUFMAN, ANDERSON and OAKES, Circuit Judges.

IRVING R. KAUFMAN, Circuit Judge:

We are called upon today to decide a question of acute sensitivity and importance, touching upon vital concerns of the legal profession and the public's interest in the scrupulous administration of justice. At issue is the disqualification of David Rabin, Esq., on the ground that his representation of the plaintiffs in the underlying actions below constituted a breach of Canon 4 of the Code of Professional Responsibility, which governs the conduct of lawyers.[1]

The complaints in these actions sought declaratory judgments that patents held by Patentex, Inc., were invalid and unenforceable. The complaints alleged unlawful manipulation and control of Patentex by its part-owner, Burlington Industries, Inc., and charged Burlington with directing Patentex to improperly acquire and illegally use the patents in question to control prices in the yarn processing and knitting industry. Lead counsel for the plaintiffs, and self-acknowledged architect of all but one of the seven complaints in these actions, was David Rabin, a specialist in textile patent litigation. In the years between 1958 and 1962, however, Rabin had represented Burlington in another patent suit, referred to as the *Supp-hose* case, which also called into question the nature and scope of Burlington's control over Patentex. Patentex, therefore, moved for Rabin's disqualification, asserting that Rabin's present adversarial posture might result in disclosure or conscious or unintentional use of confidential information acquired by

---

1. Canon 4 of the Code of Professional Responsibility provides that "A lawyer should preserve the confidences and secrets of a client."

him during the *Supp-hose* litigation. Judge Motley, in the district court, granted the motion, and this appeal followed.

We approach our task as a reviewing court in this case conscious of our responsibility to preserve a balance, delicate though it may be, between an individual's right to his own freely chosen counsel and the need to maintain the highest ethical standards of professional responsibility. This balance is essential if the public's trust in the integrity of the Bar is to be preserved. Moreover, we are mindful that ethical problems cannot be resolved in a vacuum. To affirm the order below will, to be sure, deprive plaintiffs of highly qualified counsel of their own choosing and may foreclose Rabin's participation in future actions brought against Burlington and Patentex. There can be no doubt, however, that we may not allow Rabin to press these claims against Patentex if, in doing so, he might employ information disclosed to him in confidence during his prior defense of Burlington. Such a result would work a serious injustice upon Burlington and Patentex and would tend to undermine public confidence in the Bar. Thus, even an appearance of impropriety requires prompt remedial action by the court. After thorough consideration, we conclude that Rabin's earlier defense of Burlington against charges that it controlled Patentex for illegal purposes precludes him from pressing similar claims in the instant suits. Accordingly, we affirm.

I.

At the outset, it is useful to identify the central characters in this litigation. Burlington Industries Inc., whose executive offices are located in Greensboro, North Carolina, is, we are told, the world's largest textile company. As such, it is a major force in the yarn processing and knitting industry. Chadbourn Gotham, Inc., headquartered in Charlotte, North Carolina, is also a primary competitor in this field. These two companies each own fifty percent of the voting stock of Patentex, Inc. According to a Dun & Bradstreet report, Burlington and Chadbourn created Patentex in 1955 "to acquire title [from them] to patents and methods of manufacturing women's stretch stockings and processing yarns used in their manufacture.... [Patentex] license[d] other hosiery manufacturers under their patents and in turn receive[d] royalties for their use." Thus, in return for royalty payments, Burlington and Chadbourn allowed their competitors to employ knitting technology which they had patented.

* * *

Finally, David Rabin is a patent attorney who specializes in textile patents. In addition to both a bachelor's and a master's degree in law, his professional background includes a degree in mechanical engineering from Duke University and a period of employment in the United States Patent Office, where he specialized in yarn and knitting technology. His present office is in Greensboro, an area correctly categorized as "the heart of the textile industry."

* * *

B. *The Present Actions*

Our discussion of the instant controversy is, perforce, a limited one, since other than the submission of affidavits and depositions pertaining to the motion for disqualification, and the filing of the parties' complaints and answers, there has been little activity directed towards resolving the merits of the underlying dispute. Emle and three affiliated companies, represented by Rabin, filed their complaint in May 1968, naming as defendants both Patentex and Burlington. Of particular interest is paragraph 12 of the complaint, prepared entirely by Mr. Rabin, which alleges that

Defendant Patentex, Inc. is a patent holding and licensing company controlled by defendant Burlington Industries, Inc. and holds numerous patents pooled together from various sources for the purpose of controlling the manufacture and sale of stretchable knitted fabrics, including hosiery, the method of manufacture thereof, and the processing of yarns to impart torque characteristics, among other products. *Defendant Burlington Industries, Inc., through management of Patentex, Inc.*, has acquired competing patents through the resolution of interference proceedings in the United States Patent Office, and otherwise, and has endeavored to license the entire yarn processing industry and knitting industry, of which Burlington Industries, Inc. is a major entity, through preferential and discriminatory agreements, with the resolution of such proceedings occurring without regard to the first and true inventor of the alleged inventions, and have misused such patents. [emphasis supplied]

The complaint sought "an adjudication that defendants have misused their patents ... and that such patents are unenforceable." Patentex's answer, apart from admitting that it was a company holding title to patents acquired from various sources, denied all other allegations in paragraph 12. As indicated by that portion of paragraph 12 that we have underscored for emphasis, the issue of Burlington's control of Patentex was contested in the present action just as it was in the *Supp-hose* case.

* * *

Aside from a few requests for admissions and interrogatories served by Patentex and Burlington in the Emle action, these matters lay dormant until May, 1971. On May 25 of that year, however, Burlington moved to dismiss the Emle complaint under Rule 12(b)(6), F.R.Civ.P., for failure to allege the existence of an actual controversy between the Emle plaintiffs and Burlington. In order to prepare a defense to this motion, Rabin sought to depose Kobos, still Assistant to the President of Patentex and its Secretary. Rabin had only begun questioning Kobos on his duties at Patentex when counsel for Patentex instructed Kobos not to respond to any further questions. Subsequently, on September 27, 1971, Patentex filed a motion to disqualify Rabin from representing the plaintiff in each action on the ground that Rabin's involvement constituted a breach of professional ethics. As we have noted, the actions were consolidated for the purposes of deciding this motion and came before Judge Motley. She concluded that "the issues of the control of Patentex by Burlington and the business relationships between Patentex and Burlington were present in the *Supp-Hose* Case and are also present in the instant cases" and accordingly granted the motions to disqualify Rabin. This appeal followed.

II.

As previously indicated, Canon 4 of the Code of Professional Responsibility provides that "A lawyer should preserve the confidences and secrets of a client." We take as our guidepost in applying the language of Canon 4 to this case the standard articulated by Judge Weinfeld in T.C. Theatre Corp. v. Warner Bros. Pictures, 113 F.Supp. 265 (S.D.N.Y. 1953). There, the court said:

> I hold that the former client need show no more than that the matters embraced within the pending suit wherein his former attorney appears on behalf of his adversary are *substantially related* to the matters or cause of action wherein the attorney previously represented him, the former client. The Court will assume that during the course of the former representation confidences were disclosed to the attorney bearing on the subject matter of the representation. It will not inquire into their nature and extent. Only in this manner can

the lawyer's duty of absolute fidelity be enforced and the spirit of the rule relating to privileged communications be maintained.[2]

113 F.Supp. at 268–269 (emphasis supplied). The "substantially related" test has been approved and followed by subsequent decisions, *see, e.g.*, Consolidated Theatres v. Warner Bros., 216 F.2d 920 (2d Cir. 1954); Doe v. A. Corp., 330 F. Supp. 1352 (S.D.N.Y.1971), aff'd, 453 F.2d 1375 (2d Cir. 1972) (per curiam); Empire Linotype School v. United States 143 F.Supp. 627 (S.D.N.Y.1956); United States v. Standard Oil Company, 136 F.Supp. 345 (S.D.N.Y.1955), and has been embraced by both sides in this proceeding.

Canon 4 implicitly incorporates the admonition, embodied in old Canon 6, that "The [lawyer's] obligation to represent the client with undivided fidelity and not to divulge his secrets or confidences forbids also the subsequent acceptance of retainers or employment from others in matters adversely affecting any interest of the client with respect to which confidence has been reposed." Without strict enforcement of such high ethical standards, a client would hardly be inclined to discuss his problems freely and in depth with his lawyer, for he would justifiably fear that information he reveals to his lawyer on one day may be used against him on the next. A lawyer's good faith, although essential in all his professional activity, is, nevertheless, an inadequate safeguard when standing alone. Even the most rigorous self-discipline might not prevent a lawyer from unconsciously using or manipulating a confidence acquired in the earlier representation and transforming it into a telling advantage in the subsequent litigation. Or, out of an excess of good faith, a lawyer might bend too far in the opposite direction, refraining from seizing a legitimate opportunity for fear that such a tactic might give rise to an appearance of impropriety. In neither event would the litigant's or the public's interest be well served. The dynamics of litigation are far too subtle, the attorney's role in that process is far too critical, and the public's interest in the outcome is far too great to leave room for even the slightest doubt concerning the ethical propriety of a lawyer's representation in a given case. These considerations require application of a strict prophylactic rule to prevent any possibility, however slight, that confidential information acquired from a client during a previous relationship may subsequently be used to the client's disadvantage.

Moreover, the court need not, indeed cannot, inquire whether the lawyer did, *in fact*, receive confidential information during his previous employment which might be used to the client's disadvantage. Such an inquiry would prove destructive of the weighty policy considerations that serve as the pillars of Canon 4 of the Code, for the client's ultimate and compelled response to an attorney's claim of non-access would necessarily be to describe in detail the confidential information previously disclosed and now sought to be preserved. Thus, where "it can reasonably be said that in the course of the former representation the attorney *might* have acquired information related to the subject matter of his subsequent representation," T.C. Theatre Corp., *supra*, at 269, (emphasis supplied), it is the court's duty to order the attorney disqualified. Nowhere is Shakespeare's

---

2. At the time of Judge Weinfield's decision, preservation of a client's confidences was governed by Canons 6 and 37 of the Canons of Professional Ethics, whereas the motion to disqualify in the instant case was made under Canon 4 of the Code of Professional Responsibility, which superseded the Canons on January 1, 1970. The difference is immaterial, however, since "Canon 4 and its subjoined rules make no changes in settled principles of ethics involving the preservation of confidential cliental information. These precepts have been traditional in the relationship of client and lawyer in the art of legal ethics, preserved by old Canons 6, 11, and 37...." R. Wise, Legal Ethics 65 (1970).

observation that "there is nothing either good or bad but thinking makes it so," more apt than in the realm of ethical considerations. It is for this reason that Canon 9 of the Code of Professional Responsibility cautions that "A lawyer should avoid even the appearance of professional impropriety" and it has been said that a "lawyer should avoid representation of a party in a suit against a former client, where there may be the appearance of a possible violation of confidence, even though this may not be true in fact." American Bar Association, Standing Committee on Professional Ethics, Informal Opinion No. 885 (Nov. 2, 1965).

Examination of the issues in the *Supp-hose* case and in the present actions, in light of the "substantial relationship" test, leads inexorably to the conclusion that Rabin properly was disqualified from representing the plaintiffs in the present actions. Each proceeding involves a claim that Burlington controls Patentex and uses this control for an illegal purpose. In the *Supp-hose* case, Kayser-Roth argued that Burlington's control was used to destroy the *Supp-hose* patent and, also, that this control justified imputing to Burlington an admission made by Patentex. In the present suits, plaintiffs alleged that such control permitted Burlington, through Patentex, to fix prices within an industry in which Burlington is the dominant factor.

* * *

It is urged that the fact of Burlington's control of Patentex was widely known throughout the industry and that such notoriety removes that issue from the case. We do not understand what this "notoriety" argument proves. Henry Drinker, a leading authority in the field of legal ethics, notes that the client's privilege in confidential information disclosed to his attorney "is not nullified by the fact that the circumstances to be disclosed are part of a public record, or that there are other available sources for such information, or by the fact that the lawyer received the same information from other sources." H. Drinker, Legal Ethics 135 (1953).[3] Here, even assuming *arguendo* that Burlington's control of Patentex was "notorious" within the industry, it can hardly be contended that "trade gossip" is sufficiently reliable such as to constitute the basis of formal proof. The issue of control—its nature and scope—remained to be developed at trial, and Rabin, were he permitted to represent the plaintiffs in any further proceedings, might make use of confidential information establishing Burlington's alleged control over Patentex. Thus, industry "notoriety" of Burlington's control does not bear even one iota upon the ethical considerations here involved.

* * *

Lastly, it is urged that Burlington's motion to disqualify Rabin is barred by the doctrine of laches. This claim too must fail. Since, as we have noted, disqualification is in the public interest, the court cannot act contrary to that interest by permitting a party's delay in moving for disqualification to justify the continuance of a breach of the Code of Professional Responsibility. *See* United States v. Standard Oil Co., *supra*, 136 F.Supp. at 351 n. 6. Accordingly, "the Court's duty and power to regulate the conduct of attor-

---

3. This reasoning also explains why Rabin is barred from these actions despite his claim that he became aware of Burlington's control of Patentex during a previous defense of Bossong Hosiery Mills in a patent infringement action brought against it by Patentex. Rabin asserts that he became familiar with Burlington's relationship with Patentex in order to prosecute Bossong's counterclaim that Patentex misused its patents "in the exercise of a concerted effort to monopolize illegally the field of stretch yarn production...." This representation cannot destroy the inference that during his subsequent attorney-client relationship with Burlington, Rabin became privy to confidential information not disclosed during the Bossong action.

neys practicing before it, in accordance with the Canons, cannot be defeated by the laches of a private party or complainant." *Empire Linotype School, supra,* 143 F.Supp. at 631. Although in an extreme case a party's delay in making a motion for disqualification may be given some weight, *see* Marco v. Dulles, 169 F.Supp. 622, 632 (S.D.N.Y.1959) (nineteen year delay), such extenuating circumstances are not present here. The three-year gap between filing of the Emle action in 1968 and Patentex's motion to disqualify Rabin in 1971 is not extraordinary. Moreover, plaintiffs themselves allowed the actions to remain virtually dormant and they have not demonstrated that Patentex's delay has caused them any prejudice. Indeed, whatever delay may have accompanied Patentex's motion to disqualify Mr. Rabin has, if anything, worked to its disadvantage and not to that of the plaintiffs. Appellants themselves suggest that the delay has rendered Patentex's claim of prejudice under Canon 4 moot because Mr. Rabin has been associated with this matter for over five years. If that is true, it can hardly be argued that appellants would have been better situated if Patentex had moved for disqualification at an earlier time, for had they done so appellants would have been deprived of Rabin's services altogether. Laches is an equitable remedy and the court will not bar a claim on that ground where no prejudice has resulted from the delay.

IV.

In light of all we have said, we conclude that the issue of Burlington's control over Patentex was a disputed matter in the *Supp-hose* case and is a core subject of the controversy in the present actions. Since Rabin defended Burlington against such a claim in the *Supp-hose* case he must be barred from asserting a "substantially related" claim against Burlington on behalf of the present plaintiffs. For the reasons set forth above, we need not inquire whether Rabin in fact had access to confidential information when he represented Burlington in the *Supp-hose* case. We realize, of course, that Rabin's disqualification may inconvenience plaintiffs, who undoubtedly chose Rabin in the belief that he was the best attorney to prosecute their claims. Moreover, without impugning its motives, we are not so naive as to believe that Patentex will be displeased to see Rabin, effective advocate that he is, removed from these proceedings. But the possibility that Patentex may benefit from Rabin's disqualification cannot alter our conclusion that his continued participation in these proceedings would constitute a serious breach of professional ethics. Furthermore, we are certain that despite his considerable talents, Rabin is not the only member of the patent bar qualified to capably represent these plaintiffs.

It is argued that to disqualify Rabin from these actions in an excess of ethical zeal will permit the defendant to monopolize patent counsel. We can only note, however, that it is hardly appropriate to cast aside ethical responsibilities out of an excess of antimonopolistic fervor. Reduced to basics, this argument would permit Rabin to represent plaintiffs only by carving out a special exception to the strictures of Canon 4 for situations in which a motion for disqualification has been made by a large corporate litigant against an attorney who has crossed sides to represent smaller interests. Nothing in the Code of Professional Responsibility or in the teaching of prior cases warrants such ethical relativity, for the Code, like its predecessor the Canons of Professional Ethics, "set[s] up a high moral standard, akin to that applicable to a fiduciary.... Without firm judicial support, the Canons of Ethics would be only reverberating generalities." Empire Linotype School v. United States, 143 F.Supp. 627, 633 (S.D.N.Y.1956). We have said that our duty in this case is owed not only to the parties—who by chance consist of a group of smaller competitors arrayed against the industry giant—but to the public as well. These interests require this court to exercise its leadership to insure that nothing, not even the appearance of impropriety, is permitted to tarnish our judicial process. The stature of the profession and the courts, and the esteem in which they are held, are dependent upon the complete absence of even a semblance of improper conduct. We conclude, therefore, that the substantial relationship between matters contested in the *Supp-hose* litigation and issues raised in the present actions requires that Rabin be barred from further participation in these proceedings.

Accordingly, the order of the district court is affirmed.

Silver Chrysler Plymouth, Inc. v. Chrysler Motors Corporation
518 F.2d 751
United States Court of Appeals, Second Circuit
Argued Sept. 16, 1974
Decided May 23, 1975
[Some footnotes omitted. Remaining footnotes renumbered.]

Before MOORE, ADAMS* and MULLIGAN, Circuit Judges.

MOORE, Circuit Judge: An action is pending before Judge Weinstein in the Eastern District of New York entitled *Silver Chrysler Plymouth, Inc. v. Chrysler Motors Corporation and Chrysler Realty Corporation.* It awaits trial. The controversy alleged therein essentially is whether Silver Chrysler's dealership agreement with Chrysler was for five years (the term specified in a written lease executed between the parties in 1968) as asserted by Chrysler or for twenty-five years as alleged by Silver Chrysler on the basis of a 1967 agreement. This seemingly simple breach of contract complaint also contains a cause of action under the so-called Dealers' Day in Court Act, 15 U.S.C. s 1221 *et seq.* The claim alleges threats amounting to coercion or intimidation which forced Silver Chrysler under threat of eviction to sign a new agreement at a higher rental in May 1973 (the expiration date of the five-year term). This brief recital of the nature of the action is required only as a background to the issue on this appeal, which is disqualification of counsel.

Chrysler for many years has been represented by the law firm of Kelley Drye Warren Clark Carr & Ellis (Kelley Drye) and its predecessors, which also represents Chrysler in this action. Although many other law firms represent Chrysler on various matters throughout the country, only Kelley Drye is listed on Chrysler's annual reports as "Counsel." Silver Chrysler is represented by the firm of Hammond & Schreiber, P. C. Dale Schreiber of that firm had been employed as an associate by Kelley Drye, and while there worked on certain Chrysler matters. Because of this fact Kelley Drye by motion sought to disqualify both Schreiber and his firm from representing Silver Chrysler in this action. In support of, and in opposition to, the motion respectively, the parties submitted voluminous affidavits, copies of pleadings in cases in which Schreiber had allegedly worked, and extensive memoranda of law. With this material before him and after oral argument, the Judge proceeded to analyze the motion on the theory that "[d]ecision turns on whether, in the course of the former 'representation,' the associate acquired information reasonably related to the particular subject matter of the subsequent representation." The Judge reviewed the subject matter of the cases on which Schreiber was claimed to have worked and the law as it appears in this Circuit from decided cases and in a comprehensive opinion (reported at 370 F.Supp. 581), concluded

---

* Of the Third Circuit, sitting by designation.

that "[d]isqualification of plaintiff's counsel is not warranted." From this decision Chrysler appeals.

Our task on review is to endeavor to ascertain those general precepts which may influence or even control our decision and then relate them to the particular facts of this case. Fortunately, we have the benefit of recent pronouncements in the area by this Circuit. *Emle Industries, Inc. v. Patentex, Inc.*, 478 F.2d 562 (2d Cir. 1973). *See also Hull v. Celanese Corporation*, 513 F.2d 568 No. 74-2126 (2d Cir. 1975); *Ceramco, Inc. v. Lee Pharmaceuticals*, 510 F.2d 268 (2d Cir. 1975); *General Motors Corp. v. City of New York*, 501 F.2d 639 (2d Cir. 1974). As in *Emle*, we recognize "our responsibility to preserve a balance, delicate though it may be, between an individual's right to his own freely chosen counsel and the need to maintain the highest ethical standards of professional responsibility." 478 F.2d at 564–65.

A starting point is of necessity the Code of Professional Responsibility. Canon 4 provides: "A Lawyer Should Preserve the Confidences and Secrets of a Client." Canon 9 also cautions that "A Lawyer Should Avoid Even the Appearance of Professional Impropriety." But "ethical problems cannot be resolved in a vacuum." *Emle, supra*, at 565. Thorough consideration of the facts, as more elaborately set forth in the opinion below, is required.[1] Nor can judges exclude from their minds realities of which fair decision would call for judicial notice.

Upon graduation from law school in 1965, Dale Schreiber was hired by Kelley Drye to commence work in September 1965. He worked at the firm briefly before accepting a position as a law clerk to a federal judge. His work at Kelley Drye began again in September 1966 and continued to February 1969.

Kelley Drye is one of New York's larger law firms, having had at the time some 30 partners and 50 associates. Several of New York's firms have well over 100 associates and over 50 partners. Many firms hire a dozen or more law graduates each year and it has now become the practice to hire for summer work (usually between their second and third years at law school) a substantial number of law students. These "summer associates" most frequently perform tasks assigned to them by supervising associates or partners. Many of the summer students do not return to the same firms with which they have been associated or even remain in New York City. Even after an initial association with a firm upon graduation, it is not uncommon for young lawyers to change their affiliation once or even several times. It is equally well known that the larger firms in the metropolitan areas have hundreds (collectively thousands) of clients. It is unquestionably true that in the course of their work at large law firms, associates are entrusted with the confidences of some of their clients. But it would be absurd to conclude that immediately upon their entry on duty they become the recipients of knowledge as to the names of all the firm's clients, the contents of all files relating to such clients, and all confidential disclosures by client officers or employees to any lawyer in the firm. Obviously such legal osmosis does not occur. The mere recital of such a proposition should be self-refuting. And a rational interpretation of the Code of Professional Responsibility

---

1. As a district judge, now Chief Judge Kaufman, the author of the *Emle* opinion, said in *United States v. Standard Oil Company*, 136 F.Supp. 345, 367 (S.D.N.Y.1955), while refusing to disqualify an attorney:

> When dealing with ethical principles, it is apparent that we cannot paint with broad strokes. The lines are fine and must be so marked. Guide-posts can be established when virgin ground is being explored, and the conclusion in a particular case can be reached only after painstaking analysis of the facts and precise application of precedent.

does not call for disqualification on the basis of such an unrealistic perception of the practice of law in large firms.

Fulfilling the purpose of the disqualification remedy, "namely the need to enforce the lawyer's duty of absolute fidelity and to guard against the danger of inadvertent use of confidential information" *Ceramco, Inc.* v. *Lee Pharmaceuticals, supra*, 510 F.2d at 271, does not require such a blanket approach. Nor are such broad measures required to maintain "in the public mind, a high regard for the legal profession" *General Motors Corp.* v. *City of New York, supra*, 501 F.2d at 649. Thus, while this Circuit has recognized that an inference may arise that an attorney formerly associated with a firm himself received confidential information transmitted by a client to the firm, that inference is a rebuttable one. *Laskey Bros. of W. Va., Inc.* v. *Warner Bros. Pictures*, 224 F.2d 824, 827 (2d Cir. 1955), *cert. denied*, 350 U.S. 932, 76 S.Ct. 300, 100 L.Ed.2d 814 (1956); *United States* v. *Standard Oil Co.*, 136 F.Supp. 345, 364 (S.D.N.Y.1955). And in *Laskey*, the court cautioned that:

> It will not do to make the presumption of confidential information rebuttable and then to make the standard of proof for rebuttal unattainably high. This is particularly true where, as here, the attorney must prove a negative, which is always a difficult burden to meet.

224 F.2d at 827. The importance of not unnecessarily constricting the careers of lawyers who started their practice of law at large firms simply on the basis of their former association underscores the significance of this language. *See generally* Note, *Unchanging Rules in Changing Times: The Canons of Ethics and Intra-firm Conflicts of Interest*, 73 Yale L.J. 1058 (1964).

The Circuit has also adhered to the rule enunciated by Judge Weinfeld in *T. C. Theatre Corp.* v. *Warner Bros. Pictures, Inc.*, 113 F.Supp. 265, 268 (S.D.N.Y.1953), that "where any substantial relationship can be shown between the subject matter of a former representation and that of a subsequent adverse representation, the latter will be prohibited." And as to proof, Judge Weinfeld continued: "the former client need show no more than that the matters embraced within the pending suit wherein his former attorney appears on behalf of his adversary are substantially related to the matters or cause of action wherein the attorney previously represented him, the former client" (p. 268). This case was the genesis of the now so-called "substantially related" test. But as the present Chief Judge of the Second Circuit Court of Appeals noted twenty years ago in *United States* v. *Standard Oil Company*, 136 F.Supp. 345, 355 (S.D.N.Y.1955): "[u]nfortunately, the cases furnish no applicable guide as to what creates a 'substantial' relationship." The cases available at that time were cases in which the relationship was "patently clear."[2] *Id.*

Over the intervening years the cases in which disqualification has been granted have also fallen into, or have come close to, the "patently clear" category. A review of some of the more recent decisions is illustrative.

In *Hull* v. *Celanese Corp., supra*, an attorney who had worked in defense of the same case in the legal department of Celanese sought to join forces (albeit as a client) with the group suing Celanese and to be represented by the very law firm she had been opposing.

---

2. The court noted that "[n]o such glaringly obvious relationship exists in this case" and, applying a substantial relationship test, refused to disqualify counsel. 136 F.Supp. at 355–59.

The trial court initially denied the motion of the attorney to intervene, and little wonder that both trial and appellate court considered the opportunity for disclosure of confidential information to require disqualification of the law firm, Judge Tenney saying on appeal: "Also, here the matter at issue is not merely 'substantially related' to the previous representation, rather, it is exactly the same litigation." 513 F.2d at 571.

In *General Motors Corp.* v. *City of New York, supra*, Reycraft, the attorney whose disqualification was in issue, while formerly serving with the Department of Justice in Washington, undisputedly "had substantial responsibility" in initiating a Government suit against General Motors alleging monopolization or attempted monopolization of the nationwide market for sale of buses. After returning to private practice, Reycraft sought to represent the City of New York in an antitrust suit against General Motors also claiming monopolization of bus sales. This court found that his subsequent action was "sufficiently similar to the 1956 *Bus* (United States v. General Motors No. 15816, E.D.Mich.1956) case to be the same 'matter' under DR 9-101(B)."[3] 501 F.2d at 650. Therefore disqualification was properly directed.[4] Recently in *Ceramco, Inc.* v. *Lee Pharmaceuticals, supra*, we interpreted the facts in *General Motors Corp.* as a case wherein the "matter ... was almost identical to the dispute for which (Reycraft's) retention was sought." 510 F.2d at 271.

In *Emle Industries, Inc.* v. *Patentex, Inc., supra*, this court used the "substantially related" test as a guidepost in applying Canon 4 and disqualified the lawyer who first represented Burlington Industries, Inc. as a client and then turned about to represent a client suing a Burlington subsidiary. The court found that "there are matters in controversy in each case—both the nature and scope of control, if any, exercised by Burlington, over Patentex—that are not merely 'substantially related,' but are in fact identical." 478 F.2d at 572.

In *Richardson* v. *Hamilton International Corp.*, 469 F.2d 1382 (3d Cir. 1972), *cert. denied*, 411 U.S. 986, 93 S.Ct. 2271, 36 L.Ed.2d 964 (1973), Richardson had been an associate at a law firm representing Hamilton in connection with an SEC investigation of possible securities law violations. He had been vested with substantial responsibility in the matter, having interviewed Hamilton's officers and directors, discussed their forthcoming testimony, and mapped the strategy for presentation of the case. Quite obviously he had been the recipient of such information that he was not free to represent persons suing Hamilton on matters pertaining to a false and misleading proxy statement.

In *Chugach Elec. Ass'n* v. *United States District Court*, 370 F.2d 441 (9th Cir. 1966), disqualification was ordered where for some years the attorney involved had been General Counsel for Chugach. This attorney then appeared as counsel in an antitrust action against Chugach. This situation is "patently clear."

In *Motor Mart, Inc.* v. *Saab Motors, Inc.*, 359 F.Supp. 156, 157 (S.D.N.Y.1973), Motor Mart's attorney, in the course of his former service as Saab's counsel, had represented

---

3. DR 9-101(B) directs:
  A lawyer shall not accept private employment in a matter in which he had substantial responsibility while he was a public employee.
  4. However, the court recognized that: "If, for example, Reycraft had not worked on the 1956 *Bus* case, but was simply a member of the Antitrust Division at that time, a case not unlike *Esso Export* (136 F.Supp. 345) would be before us." 501 F.2d at 652.

Saab in "essentially the same type of suit" (unlawful termination of an automobile deal-ership). He thus had had an opportunity to learn of Saab's policies, practices and proce-dures. It would have been a violation of his ethical obligations to turn this acquired knowledge against his former client.[5]

In contrast to the foregoing decisions, quite a different situation is presented here. Schreiber was not counsel for Chrysler in the sense that the disqualified attorneys were in those cases. Although Kelley Drye had pervasive contacts with Chrysler, Schreiber's relationship cannot be considered co-extensive with that of his firm. The evidence sub-mitted to Judge Weinstein on the motion was admittedly somewhat conflicting. By affi-davits submitted by the head of the litigation department at Kelley Drye, Chrysler sought to show not only the purportedly "substantially related" cases upon which Schreiber worked but also the extensive amount of Chrysler-dealer litigation in the of-fice and in which Schreiber was concededly not involved. Schreiber responded by affi-davit, detailing his responsibilities in Chrysler matters upon which he recalled working. Schreiber also obtained, amongst other things, supporting affidavits of Clark J. Gurney (the associate who handled the bulk of Chrysler dealer matters) and Hugh M. Baum, two former colleagues at Kelley Drye (presently employed elsewhere).

As we recently recognized in *Hull* v. *Celanese Corp.*, *supra*:

> The district court bears the responsibility for the supervision of the members of its bar.... The dispatch of this duty is discretionary in nature and the finding of the district court will be upset only upon a showing that an abuse of discre-tion has taken place.

513 F.2d at 571. *See also Richardson* v. *Hamilton International Corp.*, 469 F.2d 1382, 1386 (3d Cir. 1972), *cert. denied*, 411 U.S. 986, 93 S.Ct. 2271, 36 L.Ed.2d 964 (1973). Judge Weinstein was well aware of the tests to be applied. He examined (370 F.Supp. at 585–86) *Checker* v. *Chrysler*, an antitrust action and Schreiber's principal Chrysler case while at Kelley Drye, and concluded that the case was not substantially related to this litiga-tion. As to other matters that Schreiber recalled working on, the judge was entitled to conclude that they also were not substantially related (*Ezzes* v. *Ackerman*; *Abikkarm* v. *Chrysler*; *Chrysler Motors Corp.* v. *Toffany*; *Polk* v. *Cross & Brown*). With respect to still others (*Bayside Motors, Inc.* v. *Chrysler*; *Long Island Motors, Inc.* v. *Chrysler*; *DiCarlo Dodge, Inc.* v. *Chrysler*; *Rocco Motors* v. *Chrysler*; *Buono Sales, Inc.* v. *Chrysler Motors Corp.*; *Chrysler Motors Corp.* v. *Estree Co.*) there was ample basis for crediting Schreiber's denial of having worked on them and concluding that Schreiber's involvement was, at

---

5. Our attention has been drawn to three district court cases, each dealing with the same attor-ney and his former association with a Los Angeles law firm that had represented Shell Oil Company in certain matters. *Gas-A-Tron of Arizona* v. *Union Oil Company of California*, No. Civ. 73-292-TUC-WCF (D.Ariz., decided Aug. 27, 1974) (consolidated for purposes of memorandum and order with *Petrol Stops Northwest* v. *Continental Oil Co.*, No. Civ. 73-212-TUC-JAW); *Redd* v. *Shell Oil Co.*, Civil No. C-104-71 (D.Utah, decided Dec. 2, 1974); *Bonus Oil Co.* v. *American Petrofina Co.*, No. CV73-L-165 (D.Neb., decided May 1, 1974). The court in *Gas-A-Tron* granted a motion to disqualify the at-torney and his new law firm. The courts in *Redd* and *Bonus Oil Co.* declined to do so. These three cases were similar in nature, and all three courts purported to apply the "substantially related" test. The evidence introduced pertaining to the activities of the attorney at his former firm was appar-ently nearly identical in each case, however, the *Gas-A-Tron* court characterized it quite differently than the other two. Without examining the full records in these cases, we would not care to hazard a conclusion as to which result was more appropriate.

most, limited to brief, informal discussions on a procedural matter or research on a specific point of law. The affidavits of Gurney and Baum provided support for such a conclusion. In this respect we do not believe that there is any basis for distinguishing between partners and associates on the basis of title alone both are members of the bar and are bound by the same Code of Professional Responsibility. *See Consolidated Theatres* v. *Warner Bros. Circuit Management Corp.*, 216 F.2d 920, 927 (2d Cir. 1954). But there is reason to differentiate for disqualification purposes between lawyers who become heavily involved in the facts of a particular matter and those who enter briefly on the periphery for a limited and specific purpose relating solely to legal questions. In large firms at least, the former are normally the more seasoned lawyers and the latter the more junior. This is not to say that young attorneys in large firms never become important figures in certain matters but merely to recognize that some of their work is often of a far more limited variety. Under the latter circumstances the attorney's role cannot be considered "representation" within the meaning of *T. C. Theatre Corp.* and *Emle* so as to require disqualification. Those cases and the Canons on which they are based are intended to protect the confidences of former clients when an attorney has been in a position to learn them. To apply the remedy when there is no realistic chance that confidences were disclosed would go far beyond the purpose of those decisions. Chrysler was in a position here conclusively to refute Schreiber's position that his role in these cases had been non-existent or fleeting. Through affidavits of those who supervised Schreiber on particular matters or perhaps through time records, the issue was capable of proof. Chrysler instead chose to approach the matter in largely conclusory terms.[6] We cannot realistically subscribe to the contention that proof submitted for this limited purpose, by time records or otherwise, would have necessitated disclosure of any confidences entrusted to Kelley Drye.

Judge Weinstein also concluded that Schreiber had rebutted any inference, arising merely from his former association with Kelley Drye, that he possessed confidences that can be used against Chrysler in this lawsuit. We think the district judge was plainly correct. There may have been matters within the firm which, had Schreiber worked on them, would have compelled disqualification here. But Schreiber denied having been entrusted with any such confidences. He was supported in this respect by the affidavits of Gurney and Baum. This was sufficient. See *Laskey Bros. of W. Va., Inc.* v. *Warner Bros. Pictures, Inc.*, *supra*, at 827.

Finally, in view of the conclusion that Schreiber's work at Kelley Drye does not necessitate disqualification, we agree with the district court that refusal to disqualify Schreiber and his firm will not create an appearance of impropriety. Neither Chrysler nor any other client of a law firm can reasonably expect to foreclose either all lawyers formerly at the firm or even those who have represented it on unrelated matters from subsequently representing an opposing party. Although Canon 9 dictates that doubts should be resolved in favor of disqualification, *Hull* v. *Celanese Corp.*, *supra*, 513 F.2d at 571, it is not intended completely to override the delicate balance created by Canon 4 and the decisions thereunder.

---

6. Example from a Kelley Drye (Chrysler) affidavit:
   "[Schreiber] obtained unmeasurable confidential information regarding the practices, procedures, methods of operation, activities, contemplated conduct, legal problems, and litigations of [Chrysler]." J.A. 29a.

A decision to sustain Judge Weinstein's denial of the motion does not diminish the force of our decisions which hold that the right of the public to counsel of its choice or the possibility of a reduction of "both the economic mobility of employees and their personal freedom to follow their own interests." (Blake, *Employee Agreements not to Compete*, 73 Harv.L.Rev. 625, 627 (1960)), must be secondary considerations to the paramount importance of "maintaining the highest standards of professional conduct and the scrupulous administration of justice." *Hull* v. *Celanese Corp., supra*, 513 F.2d at 569.[7]

Judge Weinstein has seen and heard counsel for the litigants and appraised the worth of their proofs and arguments. He has suggested that "[t]he parties should endeavor to complete preparations for trial so that this simple case can be speedily disposed of...." If during such further preparation, or even during the trial itself, there should appear indications that confidential information not apparent from the proof submitted thus far is being used, the trial judge will be available for such action as may be appropriate.[8]

Order affirmed.

ADAMS, *Circuit Judge* (concurring):

In this case the plaintiff, Silver Chrysler Plymouth, Inc., presents breach of contract claims against Chrysler Motors Corp. based on diversity jurisdiction and on the Dealers Day in Court Act. Chrysler Motors seeks to disqualify plaintiff's attorney, Dale A. Schreiber, formerly an associate in the law firm that is, and for an extended period of time has been, counsel to Chrysler Motors ("Kelley Drye"). During his tenure at Kelley Drye, Mr. Schreiber worked on numerous matters relating to Chrysler Motors, and Chrysler alleges that, deriving from such association, Mr. Schreiber acquired confidential information that would make his continuation on the present case unethical under the Code of Professional Responsibility.

Our role as an appellate tribunal is, of course, a limited one. We are asked to review the facts found below to determine whether they are clearly in error, and to ascertain whether the legal tests applied are correctly formulated.

Like the majority and the trial court, I believe that the relevant test for disqualification of an attorney under Canons Four and Nine of the Code of Professional Responsibility is the test articulated by Judge Weinfeld in *T. C. Theatre Corp.* v. *Warner Brothers*

---

7. We cannot endorse Judge Weinstein's comments appearing at 370 F.Supp. at 591 pertaining to the possible antitrust implications of limitations on the ability of associates to represent interests opposing clients of former firms. The Supreme Court presently has pending before it a question of the Sherman Act's application to the legal profession and, in particular, minimum fee schedules. *Goldfarb* v. *Virginia State Bar*, No. 74-70 (420 U.S. 944, 95 S.Ct. 1323, 43 L.Ed.2d 422) (argued April 1, 1975). Whatever the decision in that case, we would think it inappropriate to relax ethical standards directed at preserving a sound attorney-client relationship in the name of the antitrust laws. As long as the "substantially related" test is employed, we perceive no conflict between the two.

8. In *W. E. Bassett Company* v. *H. C. Cook Company*, 201 F.Supp. 821 (D.Conn.1962), *aff'd*, 302 F.2d 268 (2nd Cir. 1962), the trial court became alerted to the possibility of conflict as the result of a motion made pursuant to Rule 34 of the Federal Rules of Civil Procedure seeking disclosure of certain documents. (Items 12 and 13.) The Rule 34 motion brought to the forefront, by the nature of the material requested, the fact that the challenged attorney had individually represented Bassett prior to becoming a partner of the firm which represented Cook. Disqualification was ordered because "a *present* partner of [the challenged attorney] had actually represented one of the defendants in connection with some of the very same issues raised by the very same plaintiff." 201 F.Supp. at 824 (emphasis in original.)

Pictures, Inc., and reaffirmed on a number of occasions by this Court:[9] "Where any substantial relationship can be shown between the subject matter of the former representation and that of a subsequent adverse representation, the latter will be prohibited."[10]

In this context, the question of "a substantial relationship" between the two matters is not one whose dimensions are delineated with mathematical precision. However, a case presenting an apt frame of comparison to the present suit is *Motor Mart, Inc. v. Saab Motors, Inc.*[11] There, disqualification of plaintiff's attorney was ordered in a Dealers Day in Court case. The challenged attorney had previously represented Saab "as its counsel on a regular basis" for a five-year period, during which time he had defended Saab in a state action characterized as "essentially the same type of suit" as the *Motor Mart* case.[12]

Surely, were the proof to disclose that, while at Kelley Drye, Mr. Schreiber had worked in any significant respect on a case implicating issues "essentially the same" as those in dispute here, his disqualification would appear to be mandated. This is so because, given the identity of issues between the earlier and present cases, Mr. Schreiber would be unable to overcome the inference that he was privy to client disclosures germane to the case here, and the appearance of impropriety would be sufficiently strong so as to prohibit his continued subsequent representation.

The district court investigated, thoroughly and meticulously, the serious charges brought forward by Chrysler against Mr. Schreiber. Chrysler did not persuade the district court that Mr. Schreiber, as a Kelley Drye associate, had maintained any but a peripheral involvement in a Chrysler matter bearing a substantial relationship to the matters at issue here. Based on the proof, the district court undertook to catalog Mr. Schreiber's professional work while at Kelley Drye. The evidence credited by the district court included two affidavits, one by Mr. Schreiber himself, recollecting his cumulative participation in Chrysler matters, and the other by Mr. Clark J. Gurney, a former associate at Kelley Drye who, at the time in question, was the senior associate primarily responsible for Chrysler dealer litigation. These two affidavits complemented each other and disclosed that, generally, cases with which Mr. Schreiber was concerned raised factual and legal issues remote from the allegations in the present case. Mr. Gurney stated that Mr. Schreiber "did not work directly or indirectly on Chrysler dealer cases with the possible exception of researching a few specific points of law that may have been involved in a dealer case." One example of such legal research had been documented in the affidavit by Mr. Schreiber.

Chrysler was at liberty to substantiate its broad claims that Mr. Schreiber had acquired confidences requiring disqualification. Evidence of his participation in any material aspect of a dealer litigation might well have provided support sufficient to sustain the defendant's disqualification motion. The district judge suggested possible methods by which Chrysler might counter the affidavits, without breaching the very confidences that it was attempting to preserve. In particular, supportive data might have included the production of time sheets maintained by Kelley Drye that would disclose in detail Mr. Schreiber's work on Chrysler matters related to the case at hand. No such evidence was forthcoming. Considering all the testimony and other material before it, the district

---

9. *Hull* v. *Celanese Corp.*, No. 74-2126, 513 F.2d 568 (2d Cir. 1975); *Ceramco, Inc.* v. *Lee Pharmaceuticals*, 510 F.2d 268 (2d Cir. 1975); *General Motors Corp.* v. *City of New York*, 501 F.2d 639 (2d Cir. 1974); *Emle Industries, Inc.* v. *Patentex, Inc.*, 478 F.2d 562 (2d Cir. 1973).

10. 113 F.Supp. 265, 268 (S.D.N.Y.1953).

11. 359 F.Supp. 156 (S.D.N.Y.1973).

12. *Id.* at 157.

judge made a finding that "the evidence demonstrates that there was no actual knowledge" by Mr. Schreiber of pertinent, confidential information from Chrysler.

Having found that Mr. Schreiber obtained no actual knowledge that would operate to disqualify him, the district court proceeded to acknowledge its obligation to guard against an appearance of impropriety in a case such as this. Public confidence in the integrity of legal institutions serves as an over-arching consideration beneath which attorneys practice their profession. The semblance of unethical behavior by practitioners may well be as damaging to the public image as improper conduct itself. Thus, charges of potential abuse of client communications merit close scrutiny by courts. In questions such as these, judges are in effect the caryatids charged with upholding the highest of ethical standards in the legal profession.

It cannot be gainsaid that in a civil suit[13] disqualification is in order where any inference can reasonably be maintained that client confidences may have been, or will be, violated. Here Kelley Drye has demonstrated only tangential involvement by Mr. Schreiber in any case related to the matter here. Therefore, Kelley Drye's allegations would be tantamount to a claim that a showing of previous work by an attorney for a client would, without more, preclude any subsequent representation antagonistic to that client by the attorney. While the courts must apply the Canons broadly, and are admonished to draw the line at the first hint of unethical behavior, it would not appear appropriate to disqualify attorneys in such a sweeping and speculative fashion.

Rather, disqualification would seem to depend on a more refined assessment of the earlier and later cases. This analysis must be done, in the first instance, by the trial court. The trial judge should focus on the similarities between the two factual situations, the legal questions posed, and the nature and extent of the attorney's involvement with the cases. As part of its review, the court should examine the time spent by the attorney on the earlier cases, the type of work performed, and the attorney's possible exposure to formulation of policy or strategy. Where a threshold quantum of similarity exists between the prior and current representations, courts must be scrupulous to ensure that even the appearance of impropriety is avoided.

The district court stated that, in order to justify disqualification, "Actual activities on specific cases by Schreiber must be demonstrated which would make it reasonable to infer that he gained some information about his former client of some value to his present client."[14] However, following a careful and conscientious review of the facts before it, the district court determined that the requisite showing of such a relationship was absent. I cannot conclude that such finding is erroneous.

Accordingly, I concur in the judgment affirming the district court. In so doing, however, candor requires that I express misgivings respecting the wisdom of attorneys accepting representations when former clients are involved. Although it was not established that the representation here warrants disqualification, my concurrence should not be understood as an approval of the practice, a practice which ofttimes necessitates an examination of the obligation due a former law firm and client, and imposes on the court the duty to probe the outer reaches of the Canons of Ethics.

---

13. Additional, constitutional considerations are present in the criminal field. *See, United States* v. *Wisniewski*, 478 F.2d 274 (2d Cir. 1973); *United States* v. *Sheiner*, 410 F.2d 337 (2d Cir.), *cert. denied*, 396 U.S. 825, 90 S.Ct. 68, 24 L.Ed.2d 76 (1969).

14. 370 F.Supp. at 589.

Hull v. Celanese Corporation

513 F.2d 568
United States Court of Appeals, Second Circuit
Argued Jan. 30, 1975
Decided March 26, 1975
[Some footnotes omitted. Remaining footnotes renumbered.]

Before OAKES and GURFEIN, Circuit Judges, and TENNEY,* District Judge.

TENNEY, District Judge.

This Court today hears the appeal from an order of disqualification of plaintiff's counsel, the law firm of Rabinowitz, Boudin & Standard ("the Rabinowitz firm").[1] The question at issue is whether a law firm can take on, as a client, a lawyer for the opposing party in the very litigation against the opposing party. Factually, the case is novel and we approach it mindful of the important competing interests present. It is incumbent upon us to preserve, to the greatest extent possible, both the individual's right to be represented by counsel of his or her choice and the public's interest in maintaining the highest standards of professional conduct and the scrupulous administration of justice.

The complaint in this action was brought by plaintiff-appellant Joan Hull ("Hull"), an employee of Celanese Corporation ("Celanese"), against Celanese alleging sex-based discrimination in employment in violation of Title VII of the Civil Rights Act of 1964, 42 U.S.C.A. s 2000e et seq. In its answer, Celanese denied the material allegations of the complaint. Thereafter, the Rabinowitz firm filed a motion seeking leave for five other women to intervene as plaintiffs in the action. One of the proposed intervenors was Donata A. Delulio, an attorney on the corporate legal staff of Celanese. Celanese opposed the proposed intervention and additionally sought the disqualification of the Rabinowitz firm based on the risk that confidential information received by Delulio as Celanese's attorney might be used by the Rabinowitz firm against Celanese in the prosecution of the joint Hull-Delulio claims.

The trial court denied Delulio's motion to intervene and subsequently ordered the disqualification of the Rabinowitz firm.

Judge Owen premised the denial of intervention on the fact that Delulio had been active in the defense of this very action, thus raising a serious risk of disclosure of confidential information. He found the opportunity for even inadvertent disclosure to be ever-present.[2]

In granting the motion to disqualify the Rabinowitz firm, Judge Owen clearly recognized three competing interests: (1) Hull's interest in freely selecting counsel of her choice, (2) Celanese's interest in the trial free from the risk of even inadvertent disclosures of confidential information, and (3) the public's interest in the scrupulous administration of justice. In balancing these competing interests, the trial court acknowledged the right of Hull to counsel of her choice, but held the interests of Celanese and the

---

* United States District Judge for the Southern District of New York, sitting by designation.

1. 73 Civ. 3725 (S.D.N.Y., July 12, 1974).

2. The trial court noted an interchange of correspondence between Delulio and the Association of the Bar of the City of New York wherein Delulio sought advice regarding, *inter alia*, the propriety of her intervention in the Hull case. The Association advised against intervention. *See* 73 Civ. 3725 (S.D.N.Y., May 6, 1974), at 2–3. These letters are set out in full in the Joint Appendix at 125a–132a.

public to be predominant. Based upon the relationship between Delulio and the Rabinowitz firm, the preparation by the Rabinowitz firm on the motion to intervene, supporting affidavits, and amended complaint, and the contents of those documents, Judge Owen concluded:

> "The foregoing contents of affidavits prepared by Delulio and the Rabinowitz office are some evidence, in my opinion, of the possibility that Delulio, unquestionably possessed of information within the attorney-client privilege, did in fact transmit some of it to the Rabinowitz firm, consciously or unconsciously."

The trial court felt that the continued retention of the Rabinowitz firm would create at least the appearance of impropriety due to the on-going possibility for improper disclosure.[3] For the reasons stated *infra*, we must affirm.

The unusual factual situation presented here bears repetition in some detail. Hull's employment by Celanese began in 1963; Delulio's employment there began in July 1972. In September of 1972, Hull filed charges with the Equal Employment Opportunity Commission ("EEOC") against Celanese alleging sex-based discrimination in employment. Delulio was assigned to work on the defense of the *Hull* case in February of 1973 and her work on the case continued until September 1973.[4] In the interim, the complaint herein was filed.

It was during September of 1973 that Hull and Delulio met socially for the first time. Two months later Delulio approached Hull to ascertain the name of the law firm representing Hull. As a result of this conversation, Delulio contacted the Rabinowitz firm on November 9, and on November 15, 1973 the Rabinowitz firm filed sex discrimination charges on behalf of Delulio with the EEOC. Delulio thereafter consulted with the Association of the Bar of the City of New York regarding, *inter alia*, the propriety of her intervention in the *Hull* action. By letter dated March 12, 1974, the Association of the Bar of the City of New York advised Delulio against intervention. Subsequently, the motion herein seeking intervention on behalf of Delulio and four other women was filed. Two weeks later Celanese cross-moved to deny intervention and to disqualify the Rabinowitz firm.

Jurisdiction

The order of disqualification has been held by this Court to be a "final order" and hence appealable pursuant to 28 U.S.C. s 1291. Silver Chrysler Plymouth, Inc. v. Chrysler Motors Corp., 496 F.2d 800 (2d Cir. 1974) (en banc). *See also* General Motors

---

3. Judge Owen initially considered holding a hearing to determine whether there had been actual disclosures, but decided in the negative. He concluded that "a hearing would be self-defeating since it would be necessary to reveal to the Rabinowitz firm in some specificity the extent of Celanese's disclosures to Miss Delulio in the course of ascertaining to what extent, if any, that information reached them." *Id.* at 6.

4. Delulio characterized her work on the *Hull* case as follows:

> "During the six months that I worked on that case I studied the general regulations of the Equal Employment Opportunities Commission, its procedures and the law on sex discrimination generally. I obtained specific information from the personnel department at the division concerning salaries and hiring practices. I attended on (sic) interview of the employee's (Hull's) superior, and attended one interview of another division employee. I participated in a conference with outside consultants hired by the corporation to prepare statistical information regarding employment within the division. I obtained inter-office memoranda and prepared a memorandum myself regarding the case."

73 Civ. 3725 (S.D.N.Y., July 12, 1974), at 3.

Corporation v. City of New York, 501 F.2d 639, 644 (2d Cir. 1974). Therefore, jurisdiction to review the order below is clearly in this Court.

Analysis

The district court bears the responsibility for the supervision of the members of its bar. Handelman v. Weiss, 368 F.Supp. 258, 263 (S.D.N.Y.1973); E. F. Hutton & Company v. Brown, 305 F.Supp. 371, 378 (S.D.Tex.1969). The dispatch of this duty is discretionary in nature and the finding of the district court will be upset only upon a showing that an abuse of discretion has taken place. Richardson v. Hamilton International Corporation, 469 F.2d 1382, 1385–86 (3d Cir. 1972), cert. denied, 411 U.S. 986, 93 S.Ct. 2271, 36 L.Ed.2d 964 (1973). Moreover, in the disqualification situation, any doubt is to be resolved in favor of disqualification. Fleischer v. A. A. P., Inc., 163 F.Supp. 548, 553 (S.D.N.Y.1958), appeal dismissed, 264 F.2d 515 (2d Cir.), cert. denied, 359 U.S. 1002, 79 S.Ct. 1139, 3 L.Ed.2d 1030 (1959).

Factually, this case is distinguishable from our decision in Emle Industries, Inc. v. Patentex, Inc., 478 F.2d 562 (2d Cir. 1973). However, the conclusions reached in that case apply with equal validity here.

In *Emle*, a lawyer who had previously represented Burlington Industries, Inc. was disqualified when he attempted to represent Emle in litigation against Patentex, a Burlington subsidiary. The matters at issue in the two suits were deemed to be "substantially related." *Id.* at 571, citing T.C. Theatre Corp. v. Warner Bros. Pictures, 113 F.Supp. 265 (S.D.N.Y.1953). In that instance the court felt that the invocation of Canon 9 of the Code of Professional Responsibility was particularly appropriate.[5]

In the instant case we have a divergence from the more usual situation of the lawyer switching sides to represent an interest adverse to his initial representation (as in *Emle*). Here, the in-house counsel for Celanese switched sides to become a plaintiff (rather than a lawyer) on the other side. Also, here the matter at issue is not merely "substantially related" to the previous representation, rather, it is exactly the same litigation. Thus, while the cases are factually distinguishable, the admonition of Canon 9 is equally appropriate here. This is, in short, one of those cases in which disqualification is "a necessary and desirable remedy … to enforce the lawyer's duty of absolute fidelity and to guard against the danger of inadvertent use of confidential information…." *See* Ceramco, Inc. v. Lee Pharmaceuticals, 510 F.2d 268, 271 (2d Cir. 1975).

The Rabinowitz firm argues that they had never worked for Celanese and therefore never had direct access to any confidences of Celanese. They maintain that they carefully cautioned Delulio not to reveal any information received in confidence as an attorney for Celanese, but rather to confine her revelations to them to the facts of her own case. This, they contend would avoid even an indirect transferral of confidential information. They conclude that since they never got any information either directly or indirectly, they could not use the information either consciously or unconsciously.

---

5. Canon 9 of the Code of Professional Responsibility states: "A lawyer should avoid even the appearance of professional impropriety."

While the Code of Professional Responsibility has not been formally adopted in the Southern District, its salutary provisions have consistently been relied upon by the courts of this district and circuit in evaluating the ethical conduct of attorneys. *See, e. g.*, General Motors Corporation v. City of New York, 501 F.2d 639 (2d Cir. 1974); Emle Industries, Inc. v. Patentex, Inc., 478 F.2d 562 (2d Cir. 1973); Handelman v. Weiss, 368 F.Supp. 258 (S.D.N.Y.1973).

This argument, somewhat technical in nature, seems to overlook the spirit of Canon 9 as interpreted by this Court in *Emle*. We credit the efforts of the Rabinowitz firm to avoid the receipt of any confidence. Nonetheless, *Emle* makes it clear that the court need not "inquire whether the lawyer did, *in fact*, receive confidential information...." Emle Industries, Inc. v. Patentex, Inc., *supra*, 478 F.2d at 571. Rather, "where 'it can reasonably be said that in the course of the former representation the attorney *might* have acquired information related to the subject matter of his subsequent representation,' *T.C. Theatre Corp.*, *supra* (113 F.Supp.), at 269 (emphasis supplied), it is the court's duty to order the attorney disqualified." *Id.* at 571. The breach of confidence would not have to be proved; it is presumed in order to preserve the spirit of the Code.

The Rabinowitz firm had notice that Delulio had worked on the defense of the *Hull* case and should have declined representation when approached. Had Delulio joined the firm as an assistant counsel in the *Hull* case, they would have been disqualified. Here she joined them, as it were, as a client. The relation is no less damaging and the presumption in *Emle* should apply.

Our holding herein is distinguishable from the result reached in Meyerhofer v. Empire Fire and Marine Insurance Co., 497 F.2d 1190 (2d Cir.), cert. denied, 419 U.S. 998, 95 S.Ct. 314, 42 L.Ed.2d 272 (1974). There it was held that disqualification was unnecessary since the lawyer had acted properly in defending himself "against 'an accusation of wrongful conduct.'" *Id.* 497 F.2d at 1194–95.

The novel factual situation presented here dictates a narrow reading of this opinion. This decision should not be read to imply that either Hull or Delulio cannot pursue her claim of employment discrimination based on sex. The scope of this opinion must, of necessity, be confined to the facts presented and not read as a broad-brush approach to disqualification.

The preservation of public trust both in the scrupulous administration of justice and in the integrity of the bar is paramount. Recognizably important are Hull's right to counsel of her choice and the consideration of the judicial economy which could be achieved by trying these claims in one lawsuit. These considerations must yield, however, to considerations of ethics which run to the very integrity of our judicial process.

Accordingly, the order of the district court is affirmed.

General Motors Corp. v. City of New York

501 F.2d 639
United States Court of Appeals, Second Circuit
Argued June 3, 1974
Decided June 28, 1974
[Some notes omitted. Remaining notes renumbered.]

Before KAUFMAN, Chief Judge, MANSFIELD and MULLIGAN, Circuit Judges.

IRVING R. KAUFMAN, Chief Judge: Suits involving large damage claims inevitably spark intensive pretrial skirmishing, as the litigants bombard each other and the district court with a variety of motions. In this case, brought by the City of New York [City], which alone has a $12,000,000 claim, as a class action alleging that General Motors Corporation [GM] has violated the antitrust laws principally by monopolizing or attempting to monopolize the nationwide market for city buses, we face appeals by GM from interlocutory orders deciding two bitterly contested pretrial, although unrelated, motions. The first is the City's successful motion to permit the suit to proceed as a class action; the second, GM's unsuccessful motion to have the City's privately-retained counsel, George D. Reycraft, disqualified for breach of the ethical precepts embodied in Canon 9 of the Code of Professional Responsibility.[1] After carefully applying the *Cohen*[2] collateral order doctrine to separate the appealable from the non-appealable order, we dismiss the appeal from the court's order determining that this action may proceed as a class action because in the context of this case that order is not appealable. With respect to the motion to disqualify counsel, however, we conclude, without intending to suggest any actual impropriety on the part of Reycraft, that his disqualification is required to 'avoid even the appearance of professional impropriety.'[3] Accordingly, the court's order denying disqualification of Reycraft is reversed.

I. FACTUAL BACKGROUND

The facts necessary to an understanding of our disposition of these appeals have been gleaned, in the main, from the complaint and from the affidavits filed by the parties in support of and in opposition to the respective motions at issue. They are, thankfully, rather straightforward and, in all material respects, undisputed.

On October 4, 1972, the City filed a complaint alleging that GM had violated Section 2 of the Sherman Act by attempting to monopolize and monopolizing "trade and commerce in the manufacture and sale of city buses." The complaint contained, as a second cause of action, the allegation that GM had breached Section 7 of the Clayton Act by acquiring, in 1925, a controlling interest in Yellow Truck & Coach Manufacturing Co. [Yellow Coach] — an acquisition which purportedly "threatens substantially to lessen competition and to tend to create a monopoly in the manufacture and sale of buses within the United State...." The action, furthermore, was commenced on behalf of a class consisting of "all non-federal governmental units and instrumentalities in the United States which have purchased or have contributed to the purchase of city buses or city bus parts...." The relief sought was, *inter alia*, for appropriate divestiture, treble damages, costs and attorneys' fees.

According to Reycraft's affidavit, filed in opposition to the disqualification motion, he was asked by the Office of the Corporation Counsel, sometime in July 1972, to assist in the preparation of the complaint. When approached by the Corporation Counsel, then J. Lee Rankin, Reycraft responded by informing Rankin of his prior and substantial involvement in an action brought by the United States against GM, under Section 2 of the Sherman Act, based on GM's alleged monopolization of a nation-wide market for the manufacture and sale of city and intercity buses. United States v. General Motors (No. 15816, E.D.Mich.1956) [1956 *Bus* case].

In his affidavit, Reycraft described his participation in the 1956 *Bus* case, and his work for the Antitrust Division of the Department of Justice, in these words:

> I was employed as an attorney for the Antitrust Division of the Department of Justice from the end of December, 1952 through the end of December, 1962. From sometime during the middle of 1954 through the end of 1962 I was employed in the Washington Office of the Antitrust Division. My initial assign-

---

1. Canon 9 of the Code of Professional Responsibility provides that "A lawyer should avoid even the appearance of professional impropriety." More particularly, Disciplinary Rule (DR) 9-101(B), prohibits "A lawyer ... [from accepting] private employment in a matter in which he had substantial responsibility while he was a public employee."

2. Cohen v. Beneficial Industrial Loan Corp., 337 U.S. 541, 69 S.Ct. 1221, 93 L.Ed. 1528 (1949).

3. Canon 9, *supra* note 1.

ment in the Washington Office of the Antitrust Division in 1954 was as a trial attorney in the General Litigation Section.

One of my first assignments as a member of the General Litigation Section was to work on an investigation of alleged monopolization by General Motors of the city and intercity bus business. The chief counsel in that matter from at least 1954 until the case was settled by Consent Decree in 1965 was Walter D. Murphy. At no time was I in active charge of the case. *That investigation culminated in the Complaint filed on July 6, 1956 which I signed and in the preparation of which I participated substantially.*

In 1958, I became Chief of the Special Trial Section of the Antitrust Division and no longer had any direct or indirect involvement with the 1956 *Bus* case. Subsequently in 1961 I became Chief of Section Operations of the Antitrust Division and had technical responsibility for all matters within the Washington Office of the Antitrust Division, including the 1956 *Bus* case. I have no recollection of any active participation on my part in the 1956 *Bus* case from 1958 through the time I departed from the Antitrust Division in December of 1962. The case was in the charge of Walter D. Murphy from its inception and he continued in charge until the Consent Decree was entered on December 31, 1965.

In light of his substantial involvement as an employee of the Department of Justice in a matter which, at the very least, was similar to the dispute for which his retention was sought, Reycraft initially consulted his partners in the firm of Cadwalader, Wickersham & Taft and, subsequently, requested the advice of the Antitrust Division on the applicability of the Federal conflict of interest statute.[4] That statute, we note, is penal in nature and its prohibitory rules, only two in number, must therefore be specifically defined and strictly construed. With that in mind, the Justice Department had little difficulty in concluding that the statute placed no bar on Reycraft's employment by the City. Its response to Reycraft states, in pertinent part:

It is clear that section 207(b) [which applies for only one year after separation from government employ] has no bearing on your case. As for section 207(a) [which applies only where the United States is a party or has a direct and substantial interest in the matter], although it appears that you participated personally and substantially in the case brought by the United States against General Motors, the Antitrust Division advises us that the United States will not be a party to or have a direct and substantial interest in the private antitrust suit by the City of New York against General Motors. Therefore, section 207(a) has no application.

Accordingly, with Cadwalader's approval and the absence of any barrier posed by federal law, Reycraft agreed to represent the City on a contingent fee basis, a not infrequent arrangement in actions where recovery is at the same time uncertain but potentially great.

On February 22, 1973, the City moved before Judge Carter for a determination that its suit could proceed as a class action pursuant to Fed.R.Civ.P. 23(a) and 23(b)(3). GM responded by opposing the class determination and, in turn, moved for the disqualification of Reycraft. Argument on both motions was subsequently heard by the court.

* * *

In August 1973, Judge Carter entered his order, and filed an accompanying memorandum opinion, granting the City's motion for class action status and denying GM's

---

4. 18 U.S.C. § 207.

motion to disqualify Reycraft. Rejecting GM's twofold contention that the requirements of Rule 23(b)(3) had not been met, the district judge concluded: (1) "that the common underlying issue of liability pursuant to an unlawful, nationwide monopoly predominates over any questions as to the varying nature or amount of damages;" and (2) that the class action mechanism was the superior method for resolving this controversy because "it is ... inconceivable that other governmental units will not pursue such claims [of monopolization] in the event that the class action motion is denied and the suit brought by the City of New York is, or appears likely to be, successful."

Turning to the disqualification motion, the district court recognized that DR9-101(b) requires[5] Reycraft's disqualification, in order to avoid "even the appearance of impropriety," if his participation in this action would constitute "private employment in a matter in which he had substantial responsibility while he was a public employee." Since it was virtually conceded that Reycraft had "substantial responsibility" over the 1956 *Bus* case, the only questions which remained were whether his engagement to represent the City was "private employment," and whether the City's antitrust action was, for purposes of DR9-101(B), the same "matter" as to the 1956 *Bus* case. Judge Carter answered both questions in the Negative.

* * *

III. DISQUALIFICATION OF COUNSEL

We turn now to GM's unsuccessful motion to disqualify the City's privately-retained counsel, George Reycraft. It is necessary that we begin our discussion by focusing again on the language of Canon 9 of the Code of Professional Responsibility:

> A lawyer should avoid even the appearance of professional impropriety.

Providing a measure of specificity to this general caveat, DR9-101(B) commands:

> A lawyer shall not accept private employment in a matter in which he had substantial responsibility while he was a public employee.

The purpose behind this plain interdiction is not difficult to discern. Indeed, the City recognizes its salutary goal, as stated by the ABA Comm. on Professional Ethics, Opinions, No. 37 (1931)[6] to be:

> [to avoid] the manifest possibility that ... [a former Government lawyer's] action as a public legal official might be influenced (or open to the charge that it had been influenced) by the hope of later being employed privately to *uphold* or *upset* what he had done.

Id. at 124. Viewed in this light, the question before us is whether Reycraft's decision to represent the City on a contingent fee basis in an antitrust suit strikingly similar, though perhaps not identical in every respect, to an antitrust action brought over his signature by the Department of Justice would raise an "appearance of impropriety," as private em-

---

5. The Preliminary Statement of the Code of Professional Responsibility recites: "[t]he Disciplinary Rules ... are mandatory in character ... [and] state the minimum level of conduct below which no lawyer can fall without being subject to disciplinary action." Although, as noted by the lower court, 60 F.R.D. 393, 397 n. 3, no statutory authority undergirds judicial enforcement of the Code, the court's inherent power to assure compliance with these prophylactic rules of ethical conduct has not been questioned at any stage of these proceedings.

6. Opinion 37 was a commentary principally on Canon 36 of the Canons of Professional Ethics. The Canons of Professional Ethics were superseded by the Code of Professional Responsibility on January 1, 1970. Canon 9, and DR9-101(B), with which we deal, however, carry forward the ethical principles embodied in old Canon 36. *See* R. Wise, Legal Ethics 122 n. 2 (1970).

ployment "to uphold ... what he had done" as a Government lawyer. Unlike the court below, we are constrained to answer in the affirmative.

Before we commence our analysis, we would do well to recall the following description of our task:

> We approach our task as a reviewing court in this case conscious of our responsibility to preserve a balance, delicate though it may be, between an individual's right to his own freely chosen counsel [we do not presume the City to have a lesser right] and the need to maintain the highest ethical standards of professional responsibility. This balance is essential if the public's trust in the integrity of the Bar is to be preserved.

Emle Industries, Inc. v. Patentex, Inc., 478 F.2d 562, 564–565 (2d Cir. 1973).

Indeed, the "public's trust" is the raison d'etre for Canon 9's "appearance-of-evil" doctrine. Now explicitly incorporated in the profession's ethical Code,[7] this doctrine is directed at maintaining, in the public mind, a high regard for the legal profession. The standard it sets—i.e. what creates an appearance of evil—is largely a question of current ethical-legal mores. See Kaufman, The Former Government Attorney and the Canons of Professional Ethics, 70 Harv.L.Rev. 657, 660 (1957).

Nor can we overlook that the Code of Professional Responsibility is not designed for Holmes' proverbial "bad man" who wants to know just how many corners he may cut, how close to the line he may play, without running into trouble with the law. Holmes, The Path of the Law, in Collected Legal Papers 170 (1920). Rather, it is drawn for the "good man," as a beacon to assist him in navigating an ethical course through the sometimes murky waters of professional conduct. Accordingly, without in the least even intimating that Reycraft himself was improperly influenced while in Government service, or that he is guilty of any actual impropriety in agreeing to represent the City here, we must act with scrupulous care to avoid any *appearance* of impropriety lest it taint both the public and private segments of the legal profession.

It is undisputed that Reycraft had "substantial responsibility" in initiating the Government's Sherman §2 claim against GM for monopolizing or attempting to monopolize the nationwide market for city and intercity buses. Thus, we are left to determine whether the City's antitrust suit is the same "matter" as the Government's action and whether Reycraft's contingent fee arrangement with the City constitutes "private employment."

Directing our attention to the simpler question first, we are convinced beyond doubt that Reycraft's and, indeed, his firm's opportunity to earn a substantial fee for Reycraft's services is plainly "private employment" under DR9-101(B). The district judge apparently grounded his contrary decision on the rationale that Reycraft "has not changed sides"—i.e. "there is nothing antithetical in the postures of the two governments in the actions in question ..." But, as we have already noted, Opinion No. 37 of the ABA Commission on Professional Ethics unequivocally applies the ethical precepts of Canon 9 and DR9-101(B) irrespective of the side chosen in private practice.[8] *And see* Allied Re-

---

7. Although Canon 36 of the old Canons of Professional Ethics was uniformly interpreted to espouse the "appearance-of-evil" doctrine, *see e.g.* United States v. Standard Oil Co. (N.J.), 136 F.Supp. 345, 359 (D.C.N.Y. 1955); H. Drinker, Legal Ethics 130, it was not until the adoption of Canon 9 of the Code of Professional Responsibility that the canons of ethics expressly enunciated that doctrine.

8. Indeed, the question of "side-switching," and of the conflict of interest which is almost certain to arise when counsel changes sides, is one addressed by Canon 4 and not Canon 9. *Compare* Emle Industries, Inc. v. Patentex, Inc., *supra*. The ethical problem raised here, we repeat, does not stem

alty of St. Paul v. Exchange Nat. Bank of Chicago, 283 F. Supp. 464, 466 (D.Minn. 1968). We believe, moreover, that this is as it should be for there lurks great potential for lucrative returns in following into private practice the course already charted with the aid of governmental resources. And, with such a large contingent fee at stake, we could hardly accept "pro bono publico" as a proper characterization of Reycraft's work, simply because the keeper of the purse is the City of New York or other governmental entities in the class.

It is manifest also, from an examination of the respective complaints (see the appendix to this opinion), that the City's antitrust action is sufficiently similar to the 1956 *Bus* case to be the same "matter" under DR9-101(B). Indeed, virtually every *overt* act of attempted monopolization alleged in the City's complaint is lifted in *haec verba* from the Justice Department complaint. We cite, merely by way of illustration, paragraphs appearing in both complaints alleging the withdrawal of more than 20 companies from bus manufacturing, the coincidence of directors on the boards of GM and another bus manufacturer, the Flxible Company, and GM's acquisition of a controlling stock interest in Yellow Coach in 1925.

To be sure, as the City urges, the four-year statute of limitations, embodied in 15 U.S.C. § 15b, requires the City to focus on market conditions since 1968, some ten years after Reycraft ceased his involvement in the *Bus* case.[9] But, an equally essential element in proving a violation of Section 2 of the Sherman Act is either an intent to monopolize or an abuse of monopoly power. *See* United States v. Grinnell Corp., 384 U.S. 563, 570–571, 86 S.Ct. 1698, 16 L.Ed.2d 778 (1966); Coniglio v. Highwood Services, Inc., 495 F.2d 1286, 1293 (2d Cir. 1974); United States v. Aluminum Co. of America, 148 F.2d 416, 429–430 (2d Cir. 1945). Moreover, to decide the question whether GM is a passive recipient of monopoly power, a history of its operations will be imperative. *See e.g.* United States v. Aluminum Co. of America, *supra*(included an exhaustive study of Alcoa's operations from 1902 to the date of the lawsuit). Accordingly, at the very forefront of the City's case will be proof of alleged predatory practices amassed by the United States, with the substantial participation of Reycraft, when the Justice Department built its case against GM in 1956.

The addition of the Clayton Act claim, based solely on the same 1925 Yellow Coach acquisition which was part of the Sherman Act violation alleged by both the United States and the City, hardly alters the nuclear identity of these two suits.[10] Both, after all, allege monopolization or attempted monopolization of the *same* product line[11] — city

---

from the breach of confidentiality bred by a conflict of interest but from the possibility that a lawyer might wield Government power with a view toward subsequent private gain.

9. Although we recognize that the passage of time is a factor to consider in determining the applicability of Canon 9, *compare* Control Data Corp. v. International Business Mach. Corp., 318 F.Supp. 145 (D.Minn. 1970) *with* Hilo Metals Co. v. Learner Co., 258 F.Supp. 23 (D.Hawaii 1966), we also note that the Canon and its subjoined Disciplinary Rules contain no explicit temporal limitation. Indeed, the lawyer whose conduct was the subject of Opinion No. 37, discussed in the text, was himself *ten years* removed from the matter over which he had substantial responsibility while in public employ at the time he accepted the private engagement relating to the same matter.

10. As to this, the district court set forth the proper test (60 F.R.D. at 402): In determining whether this case involves the same matter as the 1956 *Bus* case, the most important consideration is not whether the two actions rely for their foundation upon the same section of the law, but whether the facts necessary to support the two claims are sufficiently similar.

11. In light of the identity of product markets here, this case presents a sharp contrast to Control Data Corp. v. International Business Mach. Corp., *supra*, heavily relied upon by the City as well as by the court below. In *Control Data*, the court concluded that where the Government suit involved tab-

buses—and, in the *same* geographic market—the United States. The subtleties of differential proof will not obviate the "appearance of impropriety" to an unsophisticated public. We opined in *Emle*:

> Nowhere is Shakespeare's observation that "there is nothing either good or bad but thinking makes it so," more apt than in the realm of ethical considerations.

Emle Industries, Inc. v. Patentex, Inc., *supra*, 478 F.2d at 571.

The City maintains, in the end, that if we reverse the court below and disqualify Reycraft, we will chill the ardor for Government service by rendering worthless the experience gained in Government employ. Indeed, the author of this opinion is hardly unaware of this claim, for he has cautioned:

> If the government service will tend to sterilize an attorney in too large an area of law for too long a time, or will prevent him from engaging in the practice of a technical specialty which he has devoted years in acquiring, and if that sterilization will spread to the firm with which he becomes associated, the sacrifice of entering government service will be too great for most men to make.

Kaufman, *supra*, 70 Harv.L.Rev. at 668. But, in that commentary, and the case upon which it was based (United States v. Standard Oil Co. (N.J.), 136 F.Supp. 345 (S.D.N.Y. 1955)—Esso Export Case), the accommodation between maintaining high ethical standards for former Government employees, on the one hand, and encouraging entry into Government service, on the other, was struck under far different circumstances. Unlike the instant case, in which Reycraft's "substantial responsibility" in the *Bus* case is undisputed, the writer of this opinion concluded in *Esso Export* that the lawyer:

> never investigated or passed upon the subject matter of the pending case ... never rendered or had any specific duty to render any legal advice in relation to the regulations involved in the litigation.

Kaufman, *supra*, 70 Harv.L.Rev. at 664. More to the point, therefore, is another admonition voiced in that article:

> If there was a likelihood that information *pertaining* to the pending matter reached the attorney, although he did not "investigate" or "pass upon" it, ... there would undoubtedly be an appearance of evil if he were not disqualified.

Id. at 665.

Esso Export unquestionably presented a case for the cautious application of the "appearance-of-evil doctrine," because the former Government lawyer's connection with the matter at issue was the tenuous one of mere employment in the same Government agency. If, for example, Reycraft had not worked on the 1956 *Bus* case, but was simply a member of the Antitrust Division at that time, a case not unlike *Esso Export* would be before us. To the contrary, however, Reycraft not only participated in the *Bus* case, but he signed the complaint in that action and admittedly had "substantial responsibility" in its investigatory and preparatory stages. Where the overlap of issues is so plain, and the

---

ulating machines and the subsequent private antitrust suit focused on electronic computers and data processing machines, and, furthermore, where the "entire business of the computer industry has so completely changed ... since 1955 (the year counsel had left Government service)," *id.* at 147, "[c]ertainly the claimed illegal acts of which IBM is now accused are nothing which Mr. Hoffman 'investigated or passed upon' in 1955...." *Id.* Here, to the contrary, we would be hard pressed to conclude that the "claimed illegal acts of which GM is now accused are nothing which Mr. Reycraft 'investigated or passed upon' from 1954–1958."

involvement while in Government employ so direct, the resulting appearance of impropriety must be avoided through disqualification.

Accordingly, we dismiss the appeal from the order granting class action status, and reverse the court's order denying disqualification of Reycraft.

Analytica, Inc. v. NPD Research, Inc.

708 F.2d 1263
United States Court of Appeals, Seventh Circuit
Argued Sept. 17, 1982
Decided May 31, 1983
Rehearing and Rehearing En Banc Denied Aug. 24, 1983
[Footnotes omitted.]

Before POSNER and COFFEY, Circuit Judges, and CAMPBELL, Senior District Judge.

POSNER, Circuit Judge.

Two law firms, Schwartz & Freeman and Pressman and Hartunian, appeal from orders disqualifying them from representing Analytica, Inc. in an antitrust suit against NPD, Inc. Schwartz & Freeman also appeals from an order directing it to pay NPD some $25,000 in fees and expenses incurred in prosecuting the disqualification motion; and NPD cross-appeals from this order, contending it should have got more.

John Malec went to work for NPD, a closely held corporation engaged in market research, in 1972. His employment agreement allowed him to, and he did, buy two shares of NPD stock, which made him a 10 percent owner. It also gave him an option to buy two more shares. He allowed the option to expire in 1975, but his two co-owners, in recognition of Malec's substantial contributions to the firm (as executive vice-president and manager of the firm's Chicago office), decided to give him the two additional shares—another 10 percent of the company—anyway and they told Malec to find a lawyer who would structure the transaction in the least costly way. He turned to Richard Fine, a partner in Schwartz & Freeman. Fine devised a plan whereby the other co-owners would each transfer one share of stock back to the corporation, which would then issue the stock to Malec together with a cash bonus. Because the stock and the cash bonus were to be deemed compensation for Malec's services to the corporation, the value of the stock, plus the cash, would be taxable income to Malec (the purpose of the cash bonus was to help him pay the income tax that would be due on the value of the stock), and a deductible business expense to the corporation. A value had therefore to be put on the stock. NPD gave Fine the information he needed to estimate that value—information on NPD's financial condition, sales trends, and management—and Fine fixed a value which the corporation adopted. Fine billed NPD for his services and NPD paid the bill, which came to about $850, for 11 1/2 hours of Fine's time plus minor expenses.

While the negotiations over the stock transfer were proceeding, relations between Malec and his co-owners were deteriorating, and in May 1977 he left the company and sold his stock to them. His wife, who also had been working for NPD since 1972, left NPD at the same time and within a month had incorporated Analytica to compete with NPD in the market-research business. She has since left Analytica; Mr. Malec apparently never had a position with it.

In October 1977, several months after the Malecs had left NPD and Analytica had been formed, Analytica retained Schwartz & Freeman as its counsel. Schwartz & Freeman forthwith complained on Analytica's behalf to the Federal Trade Commission, charging that NPD was engaged in anticompetitive behavior that was preventing Analytica from establishing itself in the market. When the FTC would do nothing, Analytica decided to bring its own suit against NPD, and it authorized Schwartz & Freeman to engage Pressman and Hartunian as trial counsel. The suit was filed in June 1979 and charges NPD with various antitrust offenses, including abuse of a monopoly position that NPD is alleged to have obtained before June 1977.

In January 1980 NPD moved to disqualify both of Analytica's law firms. Evidentiary hearings on the motion were held intermittently between April 1980 and May 1981. At one stage the law firms voluntarily withdrew, but when the judge told them that he was minded to make them pay the fees and expenses that NPD had incurred in prosecuting the motion they moved to vacate the order granting their motion to withdraw. The motion to vacate was granted and the hearings resumed. In June 1981 the judge disqualified both firms and ordered Schwartz & Freeman to pay NPD's fees and expenses. Analytica has not appealed the orders of disqualification, having retained substitute counsel to prosecute its suit against NPD.

* * *

For rather obvious reasons a lawyer is prohibited from using confidential information that he has obtained from a client against that client on behalf of another one. But this prohibition has not seemed enough by itself to make clients feel secure about reposing confidences in lawyers, so a further prohibition has evolved: a lawyer may not represent an adversary of his former client if the subject matter of the two representations is "substantially related," which means: if the lawyer could have obtained confidential information in the first representation that would have been relevant in the second. It is irrelevant whether he actually obtained such information and used it against his former client, or whether — if the lawyer is a firm rather than an individual practitioner — different people in the firm handled the two matters and scrupulously avoided discussing them. See, e.g., *Emle Industries, Inc. v. Patentex, Inc.*, 478 F.2d 562, 570–71 (2d Cir.1973); *Cinema 5, Ltd. v. Cinerama, Inc.*, 528 F.2d 1384, 1386 (2d Cir.1976); *Trone v. Smith*, 621 F.2d 994, 998 (9th Cir.1980); *Duncan v. Merrill Lynch, Pierce, Fenner & Smith*, 646 F.2d 1020, 1028 (5th Cir.1981), and in this circuit *Cannon v. U.S. Acoustics Corp.*, 532 F.2d 1118, 1119 (7th Cir.1976) (per curiam), aff'g 398 F.Supp. 209, 223–24 (N.D.Ill.1975); *Schloetter v. Railoc of Indiana, Inc.*, 546 F.2d 706, 710 (7th Cir.1976); *Westinghouse Elec. Corp. v. Gulf Oil Corp.*, 588 F.2d 221, 223–25 (7th Cir.1978).

There is an exception for the case where a member or associate of a law firm (or government legal department) changes jobs, and later he or his new firm is retained by an adversary of a client of his former firm. In such a case, even if there is a substantial relationship between the two matters, the lawyer can avoid disqualification by showing that effective measures were taken to prevent confidences from being received by whichever lawyers in the new firm are handling the new matter. See *Novo Terapeutisk Laboratorium A/S v. Baxter Travenol Laboratories, Inc.*, 607 F.2d 186, 197 (7th Cir.1979) (en banc); *Freeman v. Chicago Musical Instrument Co., supra*, 689 F.2d at 722–23; *LaSalle Nat'l Bank v. County of Lake*, 703 F.2d 252 (7th Cir.1983). The exception is inapplicable here; the firm itself changed sides.

Schwartz & Freeman's Mr. Fine not only had access to but received confidential financial and operating data of NPD in 1976 and early 1977 when he was putting together the deal to transfer stock to Mr. Malec. Within a few months, Schwartz & Freeman popped up as counsel to an adversary of NPD's before the FTC, and in that proceeding and later in the antitrust lawsuit advanced contentions to which the data Fine received might have been relevant. Those data concerned NPD's profitability, sales prospects, and general market strength—all matters potentially germane to both the liability and damage phases of an antitrust suit charging NPD with monopolization. The two representations are thus substantially related, even though we do not know whether any of the information Fine received would be useful in Analytica's lawsuit (it might just duplicate information in Malec's possession, but we do not know his role in Analytica's suit), or if so whether he conveyed any of it to his partners and associates who were actually handling the suit. If the "substantial relationship" test applies, however, "it is not appropriate for the court to inquire into whether actual confidences were disclosed," *Westinghouse Elec. Corp. v. Gulf Oil Corp., supra,* 588 F.2d at 224, unless the exception noted above for cases where the law firm itself did not switch sides is applicable, as it is not here. *LaSalle Nat'l Bank v. County of Lake, supra,* 703 F.2d at 257–58.

Consistently with this distinction, *Westinghouse Elec. Corp. v. Kerr-McGee Corp.,* 580 F.2d 1311, 1321 (7th Cir.1978)—like this a case where the same law firm represented adversaries in substantially related matters—states that it would have made no difference whether "actual confidences were disclosed" even if the law firm had set up a "Chinese wall" between the teams of lawyers working on substantially related matters, though the two teams were in different offices of the firm, located hundreds of miles apart. Now Schwartz & Freeman has never, in this litigation, contended that it created a "Chinese wall" between Fine and the lawyers working for Analytica against NPD. The offer of proof that it made in the district court was an offer to prove that the individuals in Schwartz & Freeman who were handling Analytica's case against NPD had not received any relevant confidential information about NPD from Fine. This proof would not have established the existence of a "Chinese wall." In *LaSalle Nat'l Bank,* where this court just the other day upheld the disqualification of a law firm that hired a former county lawyer and later was retained to bring a suit against the county, it was not enough that the lawyer "did not disclose to any person associated with the firm any information ... on any matter relevant to this litigation," for "no specific institutional mechanisms were in place to insure that that information was not shared, even if inadvertently," until the disqualification motion was filed—months after the lawyer had joined the firm. 703 F.2d at 259. We contrasted the absence of such mechanisms with a case in which the lawyer "was denied access to relevant files and did not share in the profits or fees derived from the representation in question; discussion of the suit was prohibited in his presence and no members of the firm were permitted to show him any documents relating to the case; and both the disqualified attorney and others in his firm affirmed these facts under oath," and with another case where "all other attorneys in the firm were forbidden to discuss the case with the disqualified attorney and instructed to prevent any documents from reaching him; the files were kept in a locked file cabinet, with the keys controlled by two partners and issued to others only on a 'need to know' basis." *Id.* at 258–59. Schwartz & Freeman has never offered to prove—has never so much as intimated—that any "institutional mechanisms" were in place in this case. But we emphasize that even if they were, this would not help Schwartz & Freeman; a law firm is not permitted to switch sides if its former representation was substantially related to its new representation, no matter what screens it sets up.

Schwartz & Freeman argues, it is true, that Malec rather than NPD retained it to structure the stock transfer, but this is both erroneous and irrelevant. NPD's three co-owners retained Schwartz & Freeman to work out a deal beneficial to all of them. All agreed that Mr. Malec should be given two more shares of the stock; the only question was the cheapest way of doing it; the right answer would benefit them all. Cf. Coase, *The Problem of Social Cost*, 3 J. Law & Econ. 1 (1960). The principals saw no need to be represented by separate lawyers, each pushing for a bigger slice of a fixed pie and a fee for getting it. Not only did NPD rather than Malec pay Schwartz & Freeman's bills (and there is no proof that it had a practice of paying its officers' legal expenses), but neither NPD nor the co-owners were represented by counsel other than Schwartz & Freeman. Though Millman, an accountant for NPD, did have a law degree and did do some work on the stock-transfer plan, he was not acting as the co-owners' or NPD's lawyer in a negotiation in which Fine was acting as Malec's lawyer. As is common in closely held corporations, Fine was counsel to the firm, as well as to all of its principals, for the transaction. If the position taken by Schwartz & Freeman prevailed, a corporation that used only one lawyer to counsel it on matters of shareholder compensation would run the risk of the lawyer's later being deemed to have represented a single shareholder rather than the whole firm, and the corporation would lose the protection of the lawyer-client relationship. Schwartz & Freeman's position thus could force up the legal expenses of owners of closely held corporations.

But it does not even matter whether NPD or Malec was the client. In Westinghouse's antitrust suit against Kerr-McGee and other uranium producers, Kerr-McGee moved to disqualify Westinghouse's counsel, Kirkland & Ellis, because of a project that the law firm had done for the American Petroleum Institute, of which Kerr-McGee was a member, on competition in the energy industries. Kirkland & Ellis's client had been the Institute rather than Kerr-McGee but we held that this did not matter; what mattered was that Kerr-McGee had furnished confidential information to Kirkland & Ellis in connection with the law firm's work for the Institute. *Westinghouse Elec. Corp. v. Kerr-McGee Corp., supra.* As in this case, it was not shown that the information had actually been used in the antitrust litigation. The work for the Institute had been done almost entirely by Kirkland & Ellis's Washington office, the antitrust litigation was being handled in the Chicago office, and Kirkland & Ellis is a big firm. The connection between the representation of a trade association of which Kerr-McGee happened to be a member and the representation of its adversary thus was rather tenuous; one may doubt whether Kerr-McGee really thought its confidences had been abused by Kirkland & Ellis. If there is any aspect of the *Kerr-McGee* decision that is subject to criticism, it is this. The present case is a much stronger one for disqualification. If NPD did not retain Schwartz & Freeman—though we think it did—still it supplied Schwartz & Freeman with just the kind of confidential data that it would have furnished a lawyer that it had retained; and it had a right not to see Schwartz & Freeman reappear within months on the opposite side of a litigation to which that data might be highly pertinent.

We acknowledge the growing dissatisfaction, illustrated by Lindgren, *Toward a New Standard of Attorney Disqualification*, 1982 Am. Bar Foundation Research J. 419, with the use of disqualification as a remedy for unethical conduct by lawyers. The dissatisfaction is based partly on the effect of disqualification proceedings in delaying the underlying litigation and partly on a sense that current conflict of interest standards, in legal representation as in government employment, are too stringent, particularly as applied to large law firms—though there is no indication that Schwartz & Freeman is a large firm. But we cannot find any authority for withholding the remedy in a case like this, even if we assume contrary to fact that Schwartz & Freeman is as large as Kirkland & Ellis. NPD thought Schwartz & Freeman was its counsel and supplied it without reserve with the sort of data—data about profits and sales and marketing plans—that play a key role in a monopolization suit—and lo and behold, within months Schwartz & Freeman had been hired by a competitor of NPD's to try to get the Federal Trade Commission to sue NPD; and later that competitor, still represented by Schwartz & Freeman, brought its own suit against NPD. We doubt that anyone would argue that Schwartz & Freeman could resist disqualification if it were still representing NPD, even if no confidences were revealed, and we do not think that an interval of a few months ought to make a critical difference.

The "substantial relationship" test has its problems, but conducting a factual inquiry in every case into whether confidences had actually been revealed would not be a satisfactory alternative, particularly in a case such as this where the issue is not just whether they have been revealed but also whether they will be revealed during a pending litigation. Apart from the difficulty of taking evidence on the question without compromising the confidences themselves, the only witnesses would be the very lawyers whose firm was sought to be disqualified (unlike a case where the issue is what confidences a lawyer received while at a former law firm), and their interest not only in retaining a client but in denying a serious breach of professional ethics might outweigh any felt obligation to "come clean." While "appearance of impropriety" as a principle of professional ethics invites and maybe has undergone uncritical expansion because of its vague and open-ended character, in this case it has meaning and weight. For a law firm to represent one client today, and the client's adversary tomorrow in a closely related matter, creates an unsavory appearance of conflict of interest that is difficult to dispel in the eyes of the lay public—or for that matter the bench and bar—by the filing of affidavits, difficult to verify objectively, denying that improper communication has taken place or will take place between the lawyers in the firm handling the two sides. Clients will not repose confidences in lawyers whom they distrust and will not trust firms that switch sides as nimbly as Schwartz & Freeman.

* * *

Pressman and Hartunian's appeal from the order disqualifying it is dismissed for lack of jurisdiction. The order assessing fees and expenses against Schwartz & Freeman is affirmed. No costs will be awarded in this court.

SO ORDERED.

COFFEY, Circuit Judge, dissenting.

I am compelled to write separately and dissent as I believe the majority inexplicably refuses to accept or follow the mandates of the court's three most recent decisions on the subject of attorney disqualification. The majority's decision casts aside, without a valid legal basis, this court's reasoning set forth in the recent cases of *LaSalle National Bank v. County of Lake,* 703 F.2d 252 (7th Cir.1983), *Freeman v. Chicago Musical Instrument Co.,* 689 F.2d 715 (7th Cir.1982), and *Novo Terapeutisk, etc. v. Baxter Travenol Lab,* 607 F.2d 186 (7th Cir.1979), in which this court took a more enlightened perspective, contemporaneous with the modern practice of law, on the law of attorney disqualification, rejecting the irrebuttable presumption that the knowledge of one attorney in a law firm is shared with the entire firm, and holding that the presumption of intra-firm sharing of confidences is rebuttable. The majority has incorrectly distinguished the holdings of *LaSalle National Bank, Freeman* and *Novo* and instead has reverted to the same oversimplified analysis that existed prior to our three most recent decisions in the area of attorney disqualification. By attempting to distinguish rather than applying the thoughtful rationale of *LaSalle National Bank, Freeman* and *Novo*, the majority's analysis in this case unnecessarily creates a conflict with our prior precedent and therefore can only generate problems and confusion for our district courts and for law firms as they attempt to deal with and reconcile our most recent pronouncements.

Prior to *LaSalle National Bank, Novo* and *Freeman*, the accepted analysis in attorney disqualification matters was summary in nature, and thus if a substantial relationship existed between the prior representation and the present litigation, disqualification would and must automatically follow. *See Westinghouse Elec. Corp. v. Kerr-McGee Corp.,* 580 F.2d 1311 (7th Cir.1978). This harsh iron-clad rule, however, was modified in *Novo* and *Freeman.* In *Novo,* this court agreed that the presumption that every attorney in the law firm has knowledge of the confidences and secrets of the firm's clients is rebuttable. *Novo,* 607 F.2d at 197. This conclusion is necessary, as we noted in *Freeman,* just four and a half months ago, because "the possible appearance of impropriety … is simply too weak and too slender a reed on which to rest a disqualification order.…" 689 F.2d at 723. We went on in *Freeman* to address the question of the quality of proof required to rebut the presumption and held that "if an attorney can clearly and effectively show that he had no knowledge of the confidences and secrets of the client, disqualification is unnecessary.…" Disqualification motions, as we noted, are drastic measures which courts should hesitate to impose except when absolutely necessary. 689 F.2d at 721.

A review of the facts and holding of this court's most recent decision on attorney disqualification, *LaSalle National Bank,* clearly demonstrates, contrary to the majority's interpretation, that that case does not support an irrebuttable presumption of shared confidences. In *LaSalle National Bank,* the defendant County of Lake brought a motion seeking disqualification of the plaintiff's law firm, on the grounds that one of the firm's associates had formerly been employed as a State's Attorney in Lake County. After determining that there was a "substantial relationship" between the present litigation and the associate's previous work for the County, this court properly determined that the individual associate was precluded from representing the plaintiff according to the guidelines reaffirmed in this opinion. The court then turned to the question of whether the disqualification of one associate automatically required the disqualification of the whole firm,

> "Having found that Mr. Seidler was properly disqualified from representation of the plaintiffs in this case, we must now address whether this disqualification should be extended to the entire law firm of Rudnick & Wolfe. Although the knowledge possessed by one attorney in a law firm is presumed to be shared with the other attorneys in the firm, *Schloetter,* 546 F.2d at 710–11, *this court has held that this presumption may be rebutted. Novo Terapeutisk,* 607 F.2d at 197. The question arises here whether this presumption may be effectively rebutted by establishing that the 'infected' attorney was 'screened', or insulated, from all participation in and information about a case, thus avoiding disqualification of an entire law firm based on the prior employment of one member."

Id. at 257 (emphasis added). The court went on to hold that a law firm defending against a disqualification motion *may* rebut the presumption of intra-firm sharing of confidences by demonstrating that a timely and effective "Chinese Wall" has been established to insulate against the flow of confidences from the tainted lawyer to his colleagues in the law firm.

* * *

The irrebuttable presumption that all information is shared among every attorney in a firm ignores the practical realities of modern day legal practice. The practice of law has changed dramatically in recent years, with many lawyers working in firms consisting of 20, 30, 60, 100 or even 300 or more attorneys, and with some firms having offices located throughout the country or even throughout the world. Additionally, the trend within law firms has been toward greater specialization and departmentalization. Surely, it defies logic and common sense to establish a presumption, with no opportunity for rebuttal, that every individual lawyer in such a multi-member and multi-specialized firm has *substantial knowledge* of the confidences of each of the firm's clients. Recognizing these realities of the modern practice of law, we must continue to take a more realistic view toward the law of attorney disqualification by allowing the presumption that confidences have been shared throughout a firm to be rebuttable, as we have held in *Freeman* and *Novo*. The district court's decision to automatically disqualify the entire law firm based on an irrebuttable presumption is unreasonable and unrealistic and is directly contrary to our holdings in *LaSalle National Bank, Freeman* and *Novo*.

Recognizing that the district court's decision directly contradicts the mandates of the *LaSalle National Bank, Freeman* and *Novo* holdings, the majority feebly attempts to distinguish those cases and states that they do not apply when the firm itself opposes a prior client and, in effect, "changes sides," but apply only to situations where an individual member of a law firm changes employment. This is "poppycock," a distinction without a difference and one which defies both logic and the practical realities of our modern legal system. First, reason tells us that a law firm is indeed nothing more than a group of individual attorneys who have formed an association to further the practice of law. A clear understanding of *LaSalle National Bank, Novo* and *Freeman* establishes that once the appearance of impropriety has arisen, the law firm, as well as an individual attorney, must be given the opportunity to demonstrate an absence of professional impropriety or misconduct. The point the majority overlooks is that it is irrelevant when analyzing the allegations of impropriety whether the potential conflict emanates from one new associate or from several partners or even, for that matter, the entire law firm. The governing legal principle must be the same regardless of whether the alleged conflict arises from the firm itself changing sides or from an individual attorney changing employment; a lawyer or law firm must be given an opportunity to rebut the inference of professional impropriety by demonstrating that the former client's confidences have not been shared with the individuals involved in the current litigation. Why must a lawyer or law firm be disqualified if in fact, they have no substantial knowledge of the former client's confidences because of the out-dated irrebuttable presumption? The mere existence of a possible conflict of interest is of such serious magnitude that the trial judge must afford the litigants (law firms) a hearing and explore the ethical questions in their entirety, unless there are unrebutted facts in the pleadings on file supporting disqualification.

More importantly, however, the majority's analysis ignores a basic principle of law, fairness to all litigants. I believe that fairness requires that any law firm and/or individual lawyer accused of professional impropriety, questionable ethics, or misconduct be given the opportunity to rebut any and all adverse inferences which may have arisen by virtue of a prior representation, and this court so held in *LaSalle National Bank* and *Freeman*. A law firm should not be disqualified with only a summary proceeding conducted by a judge on a sparse factual record such as in this case. To disqualify a lawyer or law firm, and besmirch their professional reputation, based on a sparse and inadequate factual record and an antiquated irrebuttable presumption is to trip lightly through the valley of due process since due process guarantees, at the very least, fundamental fairness to litigants. *See e.g. Lassiter v. Dept. of Social Services,* 452 U.S. 18, 24, 101 S.Ct. 2153, 2158, 68 L.Ed.2d 640 (1981).

* * *

The majority attempts to justify the irrebuttable presumption by stating "clients will not ... trust firms that switch sides as nimbly as Schwartz & Freeman." If we accept this as true, the "test of the market" and the law of economics will prevail. A fair and just result will be obtained since the concerned client will select other counsel if he does not trust the present firm. *Cf. Merritt v. Faulkner,* 697 F.2d 761 at 769–770 (7th Cir.1983) (Posner, J., concurring in part and dissenting in part); *McKeever v. Israel,* 689 F.2d 1315, 1325 (7th Cir.1982) (Posner, J., dissenting).

The majority makes a second attempt to justify the irrebuttable presumption of intra-firm sharing of confidences by stating that a law firm's "interest not only in retaining a client but in denying a serious breach of professional ethics might outweigh any felt obligation to 'come clean.'" Evidently, the majority believes that lawyers generally are not to be trusted to honor their ethical obligations. I, on the other hand, believe that the great majority of attorneys, as officers of the court, will and do live up to their ethical duties and "come clean" *if given an opportunity to do so. See generally,* Hazard, *The Lawyer's Obligation to be Trustworthy when Dealing with Opposing Parties,* 33 S.C.L.Rev. 181 (1981). As for those attorneys who chose not to "come clean," the district court distinguishes between the meritorious and the frivolous on a regular basis in other types of cases, and I see no reason why the courts cannot perform that task equally well in the context of attorney disqualification, without relying on an ancient out-dated irrebuttable presumption.

I wish to emphasize there are indeed situations where orders of disqualification are both legitimate, necessary and proper. The attorney-client relationship has been most properly described as sacrosanct and "[i]t is part of a court's duty to safeguard the sacrosanct privacy of the attorney-client relationship." *Freeman,* 689 F.2d at 721. However, the majority's irrebuttable presumption that all confidences are shared among every lawyer in a law firm, even a large multi-office firm, ignores the fact that in many firms, particularly large firms, there is little exchange of confidences between, for example, the antitrust, personal injury, tax, patent, securities or corporate sections of a firm because of the work load and the varied nature of the different department's practices. The majority's analysis fails to give Schwartz & Freeman or even contemplate in the future giving other law firms, large or small, the opportunity to demonstrate to the court the absence of impropriety. By analogy, the solution I advocate has worked well in our jury selection procedure for years. Where a juror states that he/she has information concerning a case, they are not automatically disqualified, but it is a trigger for further questioning to ascertain the degree of involvement, potential relationships or formed opinions in the matter. In essence, we are trusting the judge to perform a fact finding process that has been performed successfully for years. Why in our legal system is a juror entitled to more protection than an officer of the court who has dedicated himself to the highest ideals of our legal profession? Why should not a judge conduct a meaningful factual inquiry rather than merely relying on an antiquated irrebuttable presumption?

* * *

In short, the distinction the majority has drawn in this case unnecessarily deviates from the standard we set forth in *LaSalle National Bank, Novo* and *Freeman*. I believe the distinction advocated by the majority is unwarranted, unworkable, and will only confuse the law of attorney disqualification, a developing area of fundamental importance not only to the legal community, but to our society. We are not in a position, based on the incomplete record developed in the trial court, to decide conclusively whether or not Schwartz & Freeman should be disqualified. Accordingly, I would remand this case to the district court to allow Schwartz & Freeman an opportunity to demonstrate, if possible, that (1) Fine has not disclosed NPD's confidences to any Schwartz & Freeman attorney involved in the monopolization suit; and (2) that some meaningful effective plan has been instituted to ensure that such a disclosure will not occur in the future. Finally, I would not assess attorney's fees against Schwartz & Freeman.

Hitachi, Ltd. v. Tatung Company, et al.

419 F. Supp.2d 1158
United States District Court, N.D. California
March 3, 2006

MEMORANDUM AND ORDER RE: MOTION TO
DISQUALIFY GREENBERG TRAURIG, LLP

BREYER, District Judge.

Plaintiff, Hitachi, Ltd. ("Hitachi"), filed a complaint alleging that defendants, Tatung Co. and Tatung Co. of America, Inc. (collectively "Tatung"), infringed three Hitachi patents. Plaintiff now moves to disqualify defense counsel, Greenberg Traurig, LLP, on the ground that Greenberg's representation of defendants constitutes a conflict of interest under Rule 3-310(E) of the Rules of Professional Conduct of the State Bar of California.

BACKGROUND

Hitachi alleges that Tatung infringed three Hitachi patents, U.S. Patent Nos. 6,247,090 (filed March 10, 1999), 6,513,088 (filed Dec. 8, 2000), and 6,549,970 (filed Dec. 8, 2000). Hitachi is represented by McDermott, Will & Emery LLP ("McDermott").

Between December 2003 and November 2004, McDermott represented Hitachi in *Top Victory Electronics, et al. v. Hitachi, Ltd.,* Case No. C 03-5792 WHA (N.D.Cal.) (dismissed on November 16, 2004 per settlement agreement) ("TVP case"). In the TVP case, Hitachi asserted the *same three patents* asserted in this lawsuit against Tatung. Hitachi claims that the accused products in the TVP case operate virtually identically to the accused Tatung products. Further, the defenses alleged in the TVP case were substantively identical to those raised by Tatung in this case.

Until mid-October 2005, Mr. Jong P. Hong was an associate at McDermott. He represented Hitachi in the TVP case and billed 340 hours to the case over six months, until the time the case settled. The parties dispute the extent of Mr. Hong's involvement in the TVP case. Tatung claims Mr. Hong had limited knowledge of the TVP case which primarily was derived from document review. Hitachi claims, however, that Mr. Hong was involved with most areas of the case and even attended meetings concerning case strategy and preparations for mediation.

McDermott filed the present action on behalf of Hitachi in June 2005. Although Mr. Hong was still employed at McDermott until October 2005, he did not work on the present matter and billed no time to it.

Tatung originally retained a different firm, Baum and Weems, as counsel in this case. Tatung substituted Greenberg Traurig, LLP ("Greenberg") as counsel in this case in January 2006. Tatung claims it chose Greenberg because it is familiar with Tatung's intellectual property and its products. Greenberg has represented Tatung in seventeen matters in the last four years. Further, Tatung claims to have chosen Greenberg for this matter to consolidate its patent litigation into one team, already familiar with its technology and strategy, thus saving costs.

Mr. Hong is currently an associate at Greenberg. Mr. Hong began working at Greenberg in October 2005, before Tatung retained Greenberg in this matter. Greenberg has 28 offices and four affiliate offices. Most of the work relating to the present matter, however, is being conducted out of the Silicon Valley office, where Mr. Hong is located. Only 14 attorneys are listed on the Greenberg website as being in the Greenberg Silicon Valley intellectual property department. Only six attorneys are listed as being a member of only the intellectual property or intellectual property litigation groups, of which Mr. Hong is one. Another attorney listing only intellectual property and intellectual property litigation as areas of practice is Mr. Korea, one of three attorneys of record for Tatung.

Prior to entering an appearance in this case, Greenberg implemented an ethical wall. The firm notified Mr. Hong that his employment would be terminated if he shared any confidential information related to Hitachi with anyone at Greenberg. The firm's information technology ("IT") department set up a separate "library" to house documents in the case, which Mr. Hong cannot access. Further, the firm sent a memorandum highlighting the conflict and screening procedures to the entire Silicon Valley office, the intellectual property and records department in the Los Angeles office, and the entire intellectual property department firmwide. The firm instituted a "closed door" policy when their attorneys are discussing the Tatung matter. Finally, Mr. Hong has declared that he has not disclosed any confidential information related to, derived from, or in any way connected to his representation of Hitachi.

* * *

II. DISQUALIFICATION OF MR. HONG: SUBSTANTIALLY RELATED REPRESENTATION

Mr. Hong must be disqualified from representing Tatung in this matter. Rule 3-310(E) of the Rules of Professional Conduct of the State Bar of California states:

> A member shall not, without the informed written consent of the client or former client, accept employment adverse to the client or former client where, by reason of the representation of the client or former client, the member has obtained confidential information material to the employment.

Prof.Conduct, Rule 3-310(E). Further, where an attorney violates this rule by "successively represent[ing] clients with adverse interest, and where the subjects of the two representations are substantially related, the need to protect the first client's confidential information requires that the attorney be disqualified from the second representation." *SpeeDee Oil*, 20 Cal.4th at 1146, 86 Cal.Rptr.2d 816, 980 P.2d 371. Because Tatung does not dispute that this case constitutes a substantially related matter to the TVP case, Mr. Hong must be disqualified from representing Tatung in this matter. Tatung does not dispute Mr. Hong's disqualification.

III. DISQUALIFICATION OF GREENBERG: ETHICAL WALLS

A. Legal Background

The established rule in California is that where an attorney is disqualified from representing a client because that attorney had previously represented a party with adverse interests in a substantially related matter that attorney's entire firm must be disqualified as well, regardless of efforts to erect an ethical wall. *Klein v. Superior Court*, 198 Cal.App.3d 894, 912–14, 244 Cal.Rptr. 226 (1988); *Henriksen v. Great American Savings & Loan*, 11 Cal.App.4th 109, 117, 14 Cal.Rptr.2d 184 (1992); *Flatt v. Superior Court*, 9 Cal.4th 275, 283, 36 Cal.Rptr.2d 537, 885 P.2d 950 (1994). Nonetheless, recent California and Federal decisions may indicate an increased willingness in California to allow timely and effective ethical walls to prevent vicarious disqualification. *See* Ronald St. John, *Screened Out: When an Ethical Screen Can Be Used to Avoid Vicarious Disqualification of a Law Firm Remains Unsettled*, 27-Feb L.A. Law. 29, 32–35 (2005). No California case, however, has yet expressly altered the established rule.

In *Klein*, the California Court of Appeals for the Sixth District reversed a trial court's order allowing the use of an ethical wall. *Klein*, 198 Cal.App.3d at 913–14, 244 Cal.Rptr. 226. There, a partner in the plaintiff's firm had formerly represented the defendant in similar matters. *Id.* at 905–06, 244 Cal.Rptr. 226. The trial court disqualified the partner and ordered an ethical wall to screen the disqualified partner from the rest of the firm. *Id.* at 906, 244 Cal.Rptr. 226. The California appellate court reversed and ordered the entire firm disqualified. *Id.* at 913–14, 244 Cal.Rptr. 226. In *Klein*, unlike the present case, there was no attempt to screen the disqualified attorney from the litigation at hand, *id.* at 914, 244 Cal.Rptr. 226, and the disqualified attorney even appeared on the complaint in the current action. *Id.* at 906, 244 Cal.Rptr. 226. Commenting on the use of ethical walls, however, the court noted:

> Clearly, the California precedent has not rushed to accept the concept of disqualifying the attorney but not the firm, nor has it enthusiastically embarked upon erecting [ethical] walls. Aside from two limited exceptions—the former government attorney [ ] and the punitive disqualification, not for conflict of interest but for improper communication [ ]—no California case appears to have permitted disqualification of the individual attorney for a conflict without disqualifying his law firm.

Id. at 912–13, 244 Cal.Rptr. 226. Thus, the court held that the use of an ethical wall would not prevent vicarious disqualification. *Id.* at 913–14, 244 Cal.Rptr. 226.

In *Henriksen*, the California Court of Appeal for the First District relying on *Klein* again rejected the use of an ethical wall to screen non-governmental attorneys. *Henriksen*, 11 Cal.App.4th at 117, 14 Cal.Rptr.2d 184. There, an attorney who formally worked on the matter at issue for the defendant's firm joined the plaintiff's firm during the pendency of litigation. *Id.* at 115, 14 Cal.Rptr.2d 184. In opposition to a motion to disqualify the entire plaintiff's firm, the plaintiffs alleged that the disqualified attorney was ethically walled from the matter from the point at which he joined the firm. *Id.* at 112, 14 Cal.Rptr.2d 184. Rejecting this option the court noted:

> we believe the rule to be quite clear cut in California: where an attorney is disqualified because he formerly represented and therefore possesses confidential information regarding the adverse party in the current litigation, vicarious disqualification of the entire firm is compelled as a matter of law.

Id. at 117, 14 Cal.Rptr.2d 184. Thus, the court vicariously disqualified the entire firm. *Id.*

In *Flatt*, the California Supreme Court addressed the issue of vicarious disqualification. *Flatt*, 9 Cal.4th at 283, 36 Cal.Rptr.2d 537, 885 P.2d 950. *Flatt* involved the duty to advise a client of the impending statute of limitations when the attorney must withdraw because of concurrent conflict of interest. *Id.* at 278, 36 Cal.Rptr.2d 537, 885 P.2d 950. The court, in analyzing the issue presented, looked to the area of vicarious disqualification and repeated the "compelled as a matter of law" rule of *Henriksen*. *Id.* at 283, 36 Cal.Rptr.2d 537, 885 P.2d 950 ("Where the requisite substantial relationship between the subjects of the prior and the current representations can be demonstrated, access to confidential information by the attorney in the course of the first representation (relevant, by definition, to the second representation) is *presumed* and disqualification of the attorney's representation of the second client is mandatory; indeed, *the disqualification extends vicariously to the entire firm.*") (underlined emphasis added).

Tatung relies on a more recent California Supreme Court case and a Ninth Circuit opinion to evince a shift toward an increased willingness in California to allow ethical walls. *SpeeDee Oil*, 20 Cal.4th at 1151–52, 86 Cal.Rptr.2d 816, 980 P.2d 371; *County of Los Angeles*, 223 F.3d at 995–996. The Court finds that these cases, though indicating the possibility of a future shift in California law, have not altered the established rule of vicarious disqualification.

The California Supreme Court in *SpeeDee Oil* used language seemingly consistent with the *possibility* of ethical walls. *SpeeDee Oil*, 20 Cal.4th at 1152–53, 86 Cal.Rptr.2d 816, 980 P.2d 371. There a number of attorneys from the firm representing the defendants discussed the matter with an attorney representing an adverse party. *Id.* at 1140–43, 86 Cal.Rptr.2d 816, 980 P.2d 371. The court stated:

> In any event, we need not consider whether an attorney can rebut a presumption of shared confidences, and avoid disqualification, by establishing that the firm imposed effective screening procedures. The declarations the Shapiro firm submitted fail to demonstrate that any formal screening procedure prevented attorneys working on respondents' behalf from being exposed to Mobil's confidences.

Id. at 1152–53, 86 Cal.Rptr.2d 816, 980 P.2d 371. Commentators have argued that if the *Henriksen* "clear cut rule" was truly the law in California, the court would not have needed to even examine the efficacy of the ethical wall. St. John, *supra*, at 32. But the mere failure of the California Supreme Court to address the issue of whether ethical walls are permissible to preclude vicarious disqualification does not overrule the established rule. Thus, *SpeeDee Oil* did not overrule *Henriksen* or *Flatt*.

The facts of *County of Los Angeles* lend no support to the present case because *County of Los Angeles* dealt with a former settlement judge entering private practice and not a private attorney moving from one firm to another. *County of Los Angeles*, 223 F.3d at 992; *see also Chambers v. Superior Court*, 121 Cal.App.3d 893, 902–03, 175 Cal.Rptr. 575 (1981) (allowing law firms that employ former government lawyers to use ethical walls to prevent vicarious disqualification). Further, the two matters at issue in *County of Los Angeles* were not as similar as they are here. *See County of Los Angeles*, 223 F.3d at 992. There, the two matters involved two unrelated incidents of police brutality while here the two cases involve the same patents. *Id.* As for the Ninth Circuit's treatment of the law of ethical walls, the Ninth Circuit addressed the impact of *SpeeDee Oil*, asserting:

> the [California Supreme Court] left open the possibility that screening can rebut the presumption of shared confidences within the firm. We read *SpeeDee*

Oil as sending a signal that the California Supreme Court *may well adopt* a more flexible approach to vicarious disqualification.

Id. at 995 (emphasis added). Thus, the *County of Los Angeles* court interpreted *SpeeDee Oil* as indicating a move in California toward a rejection of the "clear cut rule" of *Henriksen*. But even the Ninth Circuit's flexible interpretation of *SpeeDee Oil,* however, only indicates that California "may well adopt a more flexible approach" *in the future. Id.* Thus, although *County of Los Angeles* indicates the possibility of a future shift in California law, the established law outlined in *Klein, Henriksen,* and *Flatt* remains intact.

Finally, Tatung points to two district court cases allowing the use of ethical walls to prevent vicarious disqualification. *Nichols Institute Diagnostics, Inc. v. Scantibodies Clinical Labs., Inc.,* Civ. No. 02-0046-B (LAB) (S.D.Cal. Mar. 21, 2002), aff'd 37 Fed.Appx. 510 (Fed.Cir.2002) (allowing the use of an ethical wall where partner was disqualified for having received confidential information while meeting a prospective client); *Visa, U.S.A., Inc. v. First Data Corp.,* 241 F.Supp.2d 1100 (N.D.Cal.2003) (allowing the use of an ethical wall where the adverse client prospectively waived conflicts). However, a more recent District Court Case has rejected the flexible approach of *Nichols* and *Visa. I-Enterprise Co. v. Draper Fisher Jurvetson Management Co.,* No. C-03-1561 (MMC), 2005 WL 757389 (N.D.Cal. April 4, 2005) (rejecting the broad reading of *County of Los Angeles* and *SpeeDee Oil* and holding ethical walls may not prevent disqualification where an attorney moves from one private firm to another).

The established law in California rejects ethical walls and neither *SpeeDee Oil* nor *County of Los Angeles* reverse *Klein, Henriksen,* or *Flatt.* Although the combined force of *SpeeDee Oil* and *County of Los Angeles* may indicate a move toward increased flexibility, this has yet to happen; district courts have not universally rushed to adopt the more flexible approach foretold in *County of Los Angeles.* Finally, Tatung can point to no California state court case after *Henriksen* that has expressly allowed the use of an ethical wall where an attorney moves from one private firm to another. Thus, although the law in California may be at a critical shift, this Court is bound to follow California law as it presently exists. Accordingly, as a matter of California law, the Court finds that Greenberg's ethical screening procedures cannot prevent vicarious disqualification and Greenberg is disqualified from representing Tatung in this matter.

B. Even if Ethical Walls Were Permissible the Court Would Still Disqualify Greenberg

Even if California law permitted ethical walls to prevent disqualification where an attorney moves from one private firm to another, in the particular circumstances of this case, the Court, in its discretion, would disqualify Greenberg.

As set forth above, Greenberg promptly recognized and attempted to resolve the ethical conflict. Greenberg immediately initiated an ethical wall, instituting its screening procedures prior entering an appearance in this case without being compelled by Hitachi. Greenberg isolated Mr. Hong from the present case by warning him and other members of the firm, denied him access to case files, and instituted a closed door policy for discussions relating to the present case. Short of transferring the matter to another office, which they have offered if the Court finds necessary, Greenberg could not substantially improve the efficacy of their ethical screening procedures.

Nonetheless, the Court finds that disqualification is warranted, in part because this action and the action in which Mr. Hong represented Hitachi are so substantially related-indeed, they are nearly identical. The same patents are at issue in both cases. In a patent infringement action the patent holder's strategy with respect to claim construction is critical. This strategy often depends more on how the patent is written, the statements made in obtaining the patent, and prior art than with the accused infringer's products. Further, Tatung has not cited a single case in which a court held that an ethical wall prevented the vicarious disqualification of a firm where the two matters were as closely related as the two at issue here, and where the disqualified attorney had billed such a significant amount of time on the earlier matter.

The Court also finds it troubling that the present case is handled primarily out of the same office that Mr. Hong is located. It is not proximity, but financial incentive, that has led past courts to render ethical walls insufficient in the private firm context. *City of Santa Barbara v. Superior Court,* 122 Cal.App.4th 17, 24, 18 Cal.Rptr.3d 403 (2004). In the context of the disqualification of government attorneys, for example, courts regularly disqualify a government attorney without disqualifying the attorney's particular office. *Id.* However, the close proximity of Mr. Hong and the attorneys handling the Tatung matter undoubtedly increases the unease of Hitachi that their confidential information will be improperly disclosed. Moreover, the close proximity increases the actual risk of intentional or unintentional disclosure of Hitachi confidential information.

The small size of Greenberg's Silicon Valley intellectual property department exacerbates the problem of proximity and leads the Court to conclude that the ethical wall is insufficient. Because of the small number attorneys practicing intellectual property in Greenberg's Silicon Valley office, and the even smaller number of attorneys practicing only intellectual property and intellectual property litigation, Mr. Hong likely has substantial contact with the Greenberg intellectual property attorneys handling this case. Further, although Greenberg has instituted a "closed door" policy when their attorneys are discussing the Tatung matter, Greenberg has not otherwise isolated Mr. Hong from the Tatung legal team.

Ultimately, balancing the relative interests of the parties with the need to preserve ethical standards favors the disqualification of Greenberg. Although Tatung has a substantial relationship with Greenberg, having handled seventeen patent litigation matters for Tatung since 2002, the risk of the improper disclosure of Hitachi confidential information is too great. Moreover, Greenberg was not Tatung's first choice to handle this matter. While recognizing that Greenberg promptly instituted screening procedures to protect Hitachi confidential information, the Court is concerned by the small size of the Greenberg Silicon Valley intellectual property department and substantial contact between Mr. Hong and the Greenberg attorneys handling the Tatung matter.

Tatung's offer to move the handling of the present case to another Greenberg office is also insufficient to prevent Greenberg's disqualification. Moving the matter to another office would reduce the contact that Mr. Hong would have with the attorneys handling this case and could relieve some of the Court's concerns while preserving Tatung's interest of having effective counsel of their choice. The offer to move the case here, however, is similar to the offer to create an ethical wall that the California Supreme Court rejected in *SpeeDee Oil. See SpeeDee Oil,* 20 Cal.4th at 1151–52, 86 Cal.Rptr.2d 816, 980 P.2d 371. Moving the matter to another office is too late as Mr. Hong already has had significant contact with the attorneys handling this matter during the pendency of the litigation. The time to have moved the matter would have been when the ethical conflict was discovered, not after losing a motion to disqualify. Thus, Tatung's offer to move the handling of the present case to another Greenberg office is insufficient.

IV. CONCLUSION

Mr. Hong must be disqualified from the present matter as he previously represented Hitachi in a substantially related matter. Greenberg must also be disqualified. The vicarious disqualification of Mr. Hong's entire firm is compelled as a matter of California law. Further, even if the Court were to accept a more flexible approach to the use of ethical walls, in the particular circumstances of this case the screening procedures utilized in this case are insufficient to adequately protect Hitachi confidential information and prevent the appearance of impropriety.

IT IS SO ORDERED.

Chapter IV

Confidentiality

Problems

Problem 10

One of my former students is a criminal defense lawyer. A few years back, she called in obvious distress. A client, accused of dealing drugs, had arrived in her office with $10,000 in "Benjies" ($100 bills, which, in case you have forgotten, have Benjamin Franklin engraved portraits). The client said, "Deduct the fees I owe you, and use the rest as the down payment on a motorboat, which I want you to buy on my behalf." I asked my former student where the money was. She said it was in a filing cabinet in her office. I asked if it was under "C" for "Cash." She was not amused. What should I have told her?

Problem 11

Imagine you are counsel for a celebrity accused of murdering his wife. He was suspected of using a knife, but no weapon was found. At one of the attorney-client conferences, he carefully hands a knife to you, using a glove. It appears "cleaned up." He says he is sure the police will find it if he leaves it in his house. What do you do? Does it make any difference if you are convinced that he is innocent? Could you suggest that he be sure the knife is "completely clean"?

Problem 12

Select sides and argue the disqualification motion against Stuart Charles Goldberg, Esq. and the Berenson firm as described in *Meyerhofer* v. *Empire Fire And Marine Insurance Co.*, set out at Chapter IV-3, *infra*.

Problem 13

One of my former students called me, late at night, to say she had uncovered evidence of a fraud committed by a client of her firm. She was convinced that lawyers in the firm had assisted the fraud. She was now actually standing in the office of the supervising partner. Her intention was to resign from the firm the next day, but she was sure these lawyers would claim that she, too, was involved. She asked if she could copy certain documents and take them with her, to prove her innocence. What should I have told her? Should I also have thanked her for calling me from the office phone, since the call could certainly have been traced to me when the act was discovered?

Problem 14

Select sides and argue the issue of whether Frank Armani, Esq., and Francis Belge, Esq. should be disciplined by the New York bar authorities for their conduct during their representation of Robert Garrow, as described in *People* v. *Belge*, set out at Chapter IV-3, *infra*, and Bryce Nelson's article in the *Los Angeles Times* of July 2, 1974, *infra*. Would it make a difference to you if a relative of one of the victims was in the class? See also *McClure* v. *Thompson*, 323 F. 3d 1233 (9th Cir., 2003), set out at Chap. IV-3, *infra*. What do you think of the anonymous phone call "solution" in the *McClure* case?

Problem 15

The lawyer on the other side of the case hit the "reply all" key on his computer by mistake. Good job! The attachment contains the highly confidential settlement strategy he has worked out with his client. He has no idea he copied you. What should you do? Do you need your client's consent?

IV-1. Introduction: Keeping Secrets

My first effort at teaching professional ethics was a class at Boston University Law School. Among the cases covered was the "Syracuse Cave Case." See *Problem 14, infra*, the *Los Angeles Times* article by Bryce Nelson and *People* v. *Belge*, 50 A.D. 2d 1088, 376 N.Y.S. 2s 771 (4th Dept., 1975), set out at Section IV-3, *infra*. As it happened, a close friend of one of the murdered victims of Robert Garrow was in the class. When another student asserted that professional ethics rules required that the two lawyers representing Garrow should not tell the woman's parents of her death and the location of her body, the friend slammed down his casebook and said, "I never want to be a lawyer if that's what it means!"

The confidentiality rules present some of the most acute dilemmas between personal morality and professional ethics. On the one hand, we all understand that clients will never confide in a lawyer if the lawyer will use the information against the client, and it becomes very hard to give good legal advice to a client who will not tell you the truth. On the other hand, everyone wants to see justice done, vulnerable third parties protected and harm averted. But keeping professional secrets can, at least in the short run, work against all of that.

A. Confusing and Different Types of Professional Confidentiality: "Information Relating to the Representation," "Confidential" Information, "Secrets," and "Privileged" Information

Confidential professional information can be roughly divided into two categories: (1) information that is subject to the attorney-client privilege and (2) information that is governed by the professional rules limiting disclosure by a lawyer. Information subject to the evidentiary privilege usually may not be used as evidence in court. Information governed by the professional rules usually may not be voluntarily disclosed by a lawyer to anyone without client consent, but is usually not protected against court-ordered disclosure. See *Formal Opinion* 2002-106, *Pennsylvania Bar Association*. The evidentiary privilege is established by rules of evidence and court evidentiary doctrines. Professional confidentiality is established by professional rules. The two categories have different functions and scope.

The scope of the evidentiary privilege is much narrower than the scope of the information protected by the professional rules. In general, the privilege only applies to information communicated between a lawyer and a client in confidence for the purpose of getting legal advice. Such information is permanently protected from disclosure by the lawyer or the client as evidence, unless the client has waived the privilege in some way, including involving the lawyer in a fraud. See § 2292 of 8 *Wigmore on Evidence* set out at Section IV-2, *infra*. DR-4-101 of the *Code* calls information protected by the attorney client privilege "confidences," and calls "secrets," all "other information gained in the professional relationship that the client has requested by held inviolate or the disclosure of which would be embarrassing or would likely to be detrimental to the client." DR-4-101(A). Both "confidences" and "secrets" are protected by DR-4-101(B) against disclosure by the lawyer.

The *Model Rule* 1.6, which defines the scope of professional confidentiality, is even broader. It protects any "information relating to the representation of a client." *Model Rule* 1.6(a). The Massachusetts version of *Model Rule* 1.6 is a little less broad, protecting only "confidential information relating to representation of a client." Massachusetts Comment [5B] explains the difference. "The exclusion of generally known or widely available information from the information protected by this rule explains the addition of the word "confidential" before the word "information" in Rule 1.6(a) as compared to the comparable ABA Model Rule."

Mass. Rule 1.6, Comment [5B] continues:

"It also explains the elimination of the words "or is generally known" in Rule 1.9(c)(1) as compared to the comparable ABA Model Rule. The elimination of such information from the concept of protected information in that subparagraph has been achieved more generally throughout the rules by the addition of the word "confidential" in this rule. It might be misleading to repeat the concept in just one specific subparagraph. Moreover, even information that is generally known may in some circumstances be protected, as when the client instructs the lawyer that generally known information, for example, spousal infidelity, not be revealed to a specific person, for example, the spouse's parent who does not know of it."

The Massachusetts version of Comment [5] also explains the difference between professional confidentiality and evidentiary privilege.

"[5] The principle of confidentiality is given effect in two related bodies of law, the attorney-client privilege (and the related work product doctrine) in the law of evidence and the rule of confidentiality established in professional ethics. The attorney-client privilege applies in judicial and other proceedings in which a lawyer may be called as a witness or otherwise required to produce evidence concerning a client. The rule of client-lawyer confidentiality applies in situations other than those where evidence is sought from the lawyer through compulsion in law. The confidentiality rule applies not merely to matters communicated in confidence by the client but also to virtually all information relating to the representation, whatever its source. The term "confidential information" relating to representation of a client therefore includes information described as "confidences" and "secrets" in former DR-4-101(A) but without the limitation in the prior rules that the information be "embarrassing" or "detrimental" to the client."

One might think that information covered by the evidentiary privilege could be described as a subset of the larger world of confidential information, but that is not necessarily the case. As we will see, sometimes client information can be revealed by a lawyer because it falls within one of the exceptions to the confidentiality rules, but is found to be privileged when an attempt is made to use the disclosure of evidence in a court proceeding. This is exactly what happened in *Purcell* v. *District Attorney for Suffolk District*, 424 Mass. 109 (1999), set out at Section IV-3, *infra*. But there is obviously a large universe of information relating to a representation that is covered by the confidentiality rules, but that is not privileged. This is usually because the information comes from a source other than the client.

It is also important to remember that confidentiality is protected by rules other than *Model Rule* 1.6. In particular, *Model Rule* 1.9, the duty to past clients rule, and *Model Rule* 1.10, the imputed conflict rule, are designed to protect confidentiality as well as loyalty.

B. Exceptions

Equally confusing are the different formulations of exceptions to the confidentiality rules. For example, the old *Code* DR-4-101(C) gave the lawyer discretion to disclose ("may reveal") "the intention of his client to commit a crime and the information necessary to prevent a crime." In theory, this could include a parking offense. The existing *Mass. Rule* 1.6(b)(2) permits disclosure to "prevent the commission of a criminal or fraudulent act that the lawyer reasonably believes is likely to result in death or substantial bodily harm, or to prevent the wrongful execution or incarceration of another." As originally adopted by the ABA, *Model Rule* 1.6 only permitted disclosure "to prevent reasonably certain death or substantial bodily harm." Now recent amendments permit a lawyer to disclose "to prevent the client from committing a crime or fraud that is reasonably certain to result in substantial injury to the financial interests or property of another" or to "prevent, mitigate, or rectify" such injury, but in both cases only where the client "has used the lawyer's service" to further the crime or fraud.

Another controversial exception is the so-called lawyer's "self-defense" exception. The other exceptions to the "attorney ideal" of loyalty and confidentiality to the client are justified because they prevent harm and advance justice. But *Model Rule* 1.9(b)(5) is different. It permits disclosure "to establish a claim or defense on behalf of the lawyer in a controversy between the lawyer and the client, to establish a defense to a criminal charge or civil claim against the lawyer based upon conduct in which the client was involved, or to respond to allegations in an proceeding concerning the lawyer's representation of the client." (*Mass. Rule* 1.6(b)(2) is essentially identical). The old *Code* DR-4-101(B)(4) gave discretion to reveal "[c]onfidences or secrets necessary to establish or collect his fee or to defend himself or his employees ... against an accusation of wrongful conduct."

What justifies these exceptions? Certainly not the client's interests, and not necessarily the interests of the justice system or the state. These are "guild" rules primarily adopted by lawyers to protect themselves. What do you think of *Meyerhofer* v. *Empire Fire and Marine Ins. Co.*, set out at Section IV-3, *infra*? That case is a good example of the outer limits of the "self-defence" exception.

C. Inadvertent Disclosure

A classic problem occurs when privileged or confidential information is inadvertently disclosed by opposing Counsel. This can happen by a push of a button on a computer or a fax machine, and happens many times. Suppose the opposing side doesn't know of the mistake. Do you have to disclose the error, or can you use the information for your client's advantage? Do you have to return the document or information? Do you need to ask your client for permission? In some cases, the courts have disqualified counsel who have used such information, particularly when the other side is unaware of the mistake. See *Rico v. Mitsubishi Motors Corp.*, 10 Cal. Reptr. 3d 601 (Ct. App. 2004), set out at Chapter IV-3, *infra*. In other cases, where the attorney has promptly notified the opposing side, the courts have been more lenient about adverse use of such inadvertently disclosed information, in light of a lawyer's duty to "zealously represent" a client. See *In re Kagan*, 351 F.3d 1157 (D.C. Cir. 2003). Finally, there is the different, but related issue of waiver of privilege. That is governed by procedural and evidentiary rules. See, for example, Rule 26(b)(5) of the Federal Rules of Civil Procedure. This problem also involves issues of attorney conduct. See Opinion #146 (1994) Board of Overseers of Maine, set out at Chapter IV-3, *infra*.

We have mentioned before that private bar associations often issue "Opinions" for the guiding of practicing attorneys. See Chapter I-3, *supra*. These are not necessarily binding on courts or disciplinary authorities, but complying with such "neutral" advice does protect an attorney to some extent. As to inadvertent disclosure, the ABA originally issued ABA Formal Opinion 92-368 which stated: "A lawyer who receives materials that on their face appear to be subject to the attorney-client privilege or otherwise confidential, under circumstances where it is clear they were not intended for the receiving lawyer, should refrain from examining the materials, notify the sending lawyer and abide the instructions of the lawyer who sent them."

Other bar ethics opinions disagreed. See The Professional Ethics Commission of the Board of Overseers of the Bar (Maine), Opinion #146, December 7, 1994, set out at Section IV-3, *infra*. That opinion, arguably binding because it was issued by a public disciplinary authority, held that all a lawyer need do is notify the opposing counsel, and then may use the documents "as permitted by the rules of procedure and evidence." There was a fierce dissent, which actually cited this author. Later, the Maine Board of Overseers changed its mind, withdrew Opinion #146, and issued a new Opinion #172, restricting use of the materials. The ABA then changed its mind (the other way!), redrafting Model Rule 4.4, to require only notification, and withdrew the formal Opinion 92-368. See ABA Formal Ethics Opinion 05-437, set out at Section IV-3, *infra*. It concludes, "Where a lawyer is not required by applicable law to do so, the decision to voluntarily return such a document is a matter of professional judgment ordinarily reserved to the lawyer. See Rules 1.2 and 1.4."

How helpful is this conclusion? What do you think should be the rule? What would you do in such circumstances?

D. Physical Evidence

Almost every state has "tampering with evidence" statutes such as Alaska Title II, Chap. 56, Article 4, *infra*, or Massachusetts General Laws, Chap. 274, Sec. 4, *infra*. These statutes prohibit anyone from hiding or tampering with evidence, or being an accessory to crime. How such an obligation can be balanced against a lawyer's duty of loyalty and confidentiality can be an interesting issue. *Model Rule* 3.4(a) attempts to resolve this dilemma by stating that a lawyer shall not "unlawfully obstruct another party's access to evidence" or "unlawfully alter, destroy or conceal a document or other material having potential evidentiary value."[1] Of course, this rule, by its terms, incorporates the substantive law. Comment [2] to the rule is also helpful.

> "[2] Documents and other items of evidence are often essential to establish a claim or defense. Subject to evidentiary privileges, the right of an opposing party, including the government, to obtain evidence through discovery or subpoena is an important procedural right. The exercise of that right can be frustrated if relevant material is altered, concealed or destroyed. Applicable law in many jurisdictions makes it an offense to destroy material for the purpose of impairing its availability in a pending proceeding or one whose commencement can be foreseen. Falsifying evidence is also generally a criminal offense. Paragraph (a) applies to evidentiary material generally, including computerized information. Applicable law may permit a lawyer to take temporary possession of physical evidence of client crimes for the purpose of conducting a limited examination that will not alter or destroy material characteristics of the evidence. In such a case, applicable law may require the lawyer to turn the evidence over to the police or other prosecuting authority, depending on the circumstances."

But, in practice, these distinctions can be difficult, particularly when a document is created to assist with legal advice, or when a client asks for return of a piece of evidence, and the lawyer does not know what the client intends. How helpful is the "depending on the circumstances" language that concludes Comment [2]?

E. Controversy

As you can see from the variations in the rules and the cases interpreting them, duties of professional confidentiality and their exceptions remain a very controversial and difficult area. A good example is *McClure v. Thompson, infra,* 323 F.3d 1233 (9th Cir. 2003), set out at Chapter IV-3, where two lives may have been at stake. There will continue to be rule changes here. Some will involve the special problems of electronic evidence, including deletion of computer evidence. See *Report to the Chief Justice of the United States on the 2010 Conference on Civil Litigation,* Section III(B), "Discovery." (Administrative Office of the U.S. Courts, 2010). It is worth thinking through your own views carefully. Not only may you be involved in such a dilemma in practice, a very likely prospect, but you may find yourself debating proposed rule changes in your bar association.

---

1. The *Code,* DR-7-102(A)(3), (6) requires that a lawyer "shall not ... [c]onceal or knowingly fail to disclose that which he is required by law to reveal" and shall not "[p]articipate in the creation or preservation of evidence when he knows or it is obvious that the evidence is false."

IV-2. Confidentiality: The Rules

ABA Model Rules

RULE 1.6: CONFIDENTIALITY OF INFORMATION

(a) A lawyer shall not reveal information relating to the representation of a client unless the client gives informed consent, the disclosure is impliedly authorized in order to carry out the representation or the disclosure is permitted by paragraph (b).

(b) A lawyer may reveal information relating to the representation of a client to the extent the lawyer reasonably believes necessary:

(1) to prevent reasonably certain death or substantial bodily harm;

(2) to prevent the client from committing a crime or fraud that is reasonably certain to result in substantial injury to the financial interests or property of another and in furtherance of which the client has used or is using the lawyer's services;

(3) to prevent, mitigate or rectify substantial injury to the financial interests or property of another that is reasonably certain to result or has resulted from the client's commission of a crime or fraud in furtherance of which the client has used the lawyer's services;

(4) to secure legal advice about the lawyer's compliance with these Rules;

(5) to establish a claim or defense on behalf of the lawyer in a controversy between the lawyer and the client, to establish a defense to a criminal charge or civil claim against the lawyer based upon conduct in which the client was involved, or to respond to allegations in any proceeding concerning the lawyer's representation of the client; or

(6) to comply with other law or a court order.

Comment

[1] This Rule governs the disclosure by a lawyer of information relating to the representation of a client during the lawyer's representation of the client. See Rule 1.18 for the lawyer's duties with respect to information provided to the lawyer by a prospective client, Rule 1.9(c)(2) for the lawyer's duty not to reveal information relating to the lawyer's prior representation of a former client and Rules 1.8(b) and 1.9(c)(1) for the lawyer's duties with respect to the use of such information to the disadvantage of clients and former clients.

[2] A fundamental principle in the client-lawyer relationship is that, in the absence of the client's informed consent, the lawyer must not reveal information relating to the representation. See Rule 1.0(e) for the definition of informed consent. This contributes to the trust that is the hallmark of the client-lawyer relationship. The client is thereby encouraged to seek legal assistance and to communicate fully and frankly with the lawyer even as to embarrassing or legally damaging subject matter. The lawyer needs this information to represent the client effectively and, if necessary, to advise the client to refrain from wrongful conduct. Almost without exception, clients come to lawyers in order to determine their rights and what is, in the complex of laws and regulations, deemed to be legal and correct. Based upon experience, lawyers know that almost all clients follow the advice given, and the law is upheld.

[3] The principle of client-lawyer confidentiality is given effect by related bodies of law: the attorney-client privilege, the work product doctrine and the rule of confidentiality

established in professional ethics. The attorney-client privilege and work-product doctrine apply in judicial and other proceedings in which a lawyer may be called as a witness or otherwise required to produce evidence concerning a client. The rule of client-lawyer confidentiality applies in situations other than those where evidence is sought from the lawyer through compulsion of law. The confidentiality rule, for example, applies not only to matters communicated in confidence by the client but also to all information relating to the representation, whatever its source. A lawyer may not disclose such information except as authorized or required by the Rules of Professional Conduct or other law. See also Scope.

[4] Paragraph (a) prohibits a lawyer from revealing information relating to the representation of a client. This prohibition also applies to disclosures by a lawyer that do not in themselves reveal protected information but could reasonably lead to the discovery of such information by a third person. A lawyer's use of a hypothetical to discuss issues relating to the representation is permissible so long as there is no reasonable likelihood that the listener will be able to ascertain the identity of the client or the situation involved.

Authorized Disclosure

[5] Except to the extent that the client's instructions or special circumstances limit that authority, a lawyer is impliedly authorized to make disclosures about a client when appropriate in carrying out the representation. In some situations, for example, a lawyer may be impliedly authorized to admit a fact that cannot properly be disputed or to make a disclosure that facilitates a satisfactory conclusion to a matter. Lawyers in a firm may, in the course of the firm's practice, disclose to each other information relating to a client of the firm, unless the client has instructed that particular information be confined to specified lawyers.

Disclosure Adverse to Client

[6] Although the public interest is usually best served by a strict rule requiring lawyers to preserve the confidentiality of information relating to the representation of their clients, the confidentiality rule is subject to limited exceptions. Paragraph (b)(1) recognizes the overriding value of life and physical integrity and permits disclosure reasonably necessary to prevent reasonably certain death or substantial bodily harm. Such harm is reasonably certain to occur if it will be suffered imminently or if there is a present and substantial threat that a person will suffer such harm at a later date if the lawyer fails to take action necessary to eliminate the threat. Thus, a lawyer who knows that a client has accidentally discharged toxic waste into a town's water supply may reveal this information to the authorities if there is a present and substantial risk that a person who drinks the water will contract a life-threatening or debilitating disease and the lawyer's disclosure is necessary to eliminate the threat or reduce the number of victims.

[7] Paragraph (b)(2) is a limited exception to the rule of confidentiality that permits the lawyer to reveal information to the extent necessary to enable affected persons or appropriate authorities to prevent the client from committing a crime or fraud, as defined in Rule 1.0(d), that is reasonably certain to result in substantial injury to the financial or property interests of another and in furtherance of which the client has used or is using the lawyer's services. Such a serious abuse of the client-lawyer relationship by the client forfeits the protection of this Rule. The client can, of course, prevent such disclosure by refraining from the wrongful conduct. Although paragraph (b)(2) does not require the lawyer to reveal the client's misconduct, the lawyer may not counsel or assist the client in conduct the lawyer knows is criminal or fraudulent. See Rule 1.2(d). See also Rule

1.16 with respect to the lawyer's obligation or right to withdraw from the representation of the client in such circumstances, and Rule 1.13(c), which permits the lawyer, where the client is an organization, to reveal information relating to the representation in limited circumstances.

[8] Paragraph (b)(3) addresses the situation in which the lawyer does not learn of the client's crime or fraud until after it has been consummated. Although the client no longer has the option of preventing disclosure by refraining from the wrongful conduct, there will be situations in which the loss suffered by the affected person can be prevented, rectified or mitigated. In such situations, the lawyer may disclose information relating to the representation to the extent necessary to enable the affected persons to prevent or mitigate reasonably certain losses or to attempt to recoup their losses. Paragraph (b)(3) does not apply when a person who has committed a crime or fraud thereafter employs a lawyer for representation concerning that offense.

[9] A lawyer's confidentiality obligations do not preclude a lawyer from securing confidential legal advice about the lawyer's personal responsibility to comply with these Rules. In most situations, disclosing information to secure such advice will be impliedly authorized for the lawyer to carry out the representation. Even when the disclosure is not impliedly authorized, paragraph (b)(4) permits such disclosure because of the importance of a lawyer's compliance with the Rules of Professional Conduct.

[10] Where a legal claim or disciplinary charge alleges complicity of the lawyer in a client's conduct or other misconduct of the lawyer involving representation of the client, the lawyer may respond to the extent the lawyer reasonably believes necessary to establish a defense. The same is true with respect to a claim involving the conduct or representation of a former client. Such a charge can arise in a civil, criminal, disciplinary or other proceeding and can be based on a wrong allegedly committed by the lawyer against the client or on a wrong alleged by a third person, for example, a person claiming to have been defrauded by the lawyer and client acting together. The lawyer's right to respond arises when an assertion of such complicity has been made. Paragraph (b)(5) does not require the lawyer to await the commencement of an action or proceeding that charges such complicity, so that the defense may be established by responding directly to a third party who has made such an assertion. The right to defend also applies, of course, where a proceeding has been commenced.

[11] A lawyer entitled to a fee is permitted by paragraph (b)(5) to prove the services rendered in an action to collect it. This aspect of the rule expresses the principle that the beneficiary of a fiduciary relationship may not exploit it to the detriment of the fiduciary.

[12] Other law may require that a lawyer disclose information about a client. Whether such a law supersedes Rule 1.6 is a question of law beyond the scope of these Rules. When disclosure of information relating to the representation appears to be required by other law, the lawyer must discuss the matter with the client to the extent required by Rule 1.4. If, however, the other law supersedes this Rule and requires disclosure, paragraph (b)(6) permits the lawyer to make such disclosures as are necessary to comply with the law.

[13] A lawyer may be ordered to reveal information relating to the representation of a client by a court or by another tribunal or governmental entity claiming authority pursuant to other law to compel the disclosure. Absent informed consent of the client to do otherwise, the lawyer should assert on behalf of the client all nonfrivolous claims that the order is not authorized by other law or that the information sought is protected

against disclosure by the attorney-client privilege or other applicable law. In the event of an adverse ruling, the lawyer must consult with the client about the possibility of appeal to the extent required by Rule 1.4. Unless review is sought, however, paragraph (b)(6) permits the lawyer to comply with the court's order.

[14] Paragraph (b) permits disclosure only to the extent the lawyer reasonably believes the disclosure is necessary to accomplish one of the purposes specified. Where practicable, the lawyer should first seek to persuade the client to take suitable action to obviate the need for disclosure. In any case, a disclosure adverse to the client's interest should be no greater than the lawyer reasonably believes necessary to accomplish the purpose. If the disclosure will be made in connection with a judicial proceeding, the disclosure should be made in a manner that limits access to the information to the tribunal or other persons having a need to know it and appropriate protective orders or other arrangements should be sought by the lawyer to the fullest extent practicable.

[15] Paragraph (b) permits but does not require the disclosure of information relating to a client's representation to accomplish the purposes specified in paragraphs (b)(1) through (b)(6). In exercising the discretion conferred by this Rule, the lawyer may consider such factors as the nature of the lawyer's relationship with the client and with those who might be injured by the client, the lawyer's own involvement in the transaction and factors that may extenuate the conduct in question. A lawyer's decision not to disclose as permitted by paragraph (b) does not violate this Rule. Disclosure may be required, however, by other Rules. Some Rules require disclosure only if such disclosure would be permitted by paragraph (b). See Rules 1.2(d), 4.1(b), 8.1 and 8.3. Rule 3.3, on the other hand, requires disclosure in some circumstances regardless of whether such disclosure is permitted by this Rule. See Rule 3.3(c).

Acting Competently to Preserve Confidentiality

[16] A lawyer must act competently to safeguard information relating to the representation of a client against inadvertent or unauthorized disclosure by the lawyer or other persons who are participating in the representation of the client or who are subject to the lawyer's supervision. See Rules 1.1, 5.1 and 5.3.

[17] When transmitting a communication that includes information relating to the representation of a client, the lawyer must take reasonable precautions to prevent the information from coming into the hands of unintended recipients. This duty, however, does not require that the lawyer use special security measures if the method of communication affords a reasonable expectation of privacy. Special circumstances, however, may warrant special precautions. Factors to be considered in determining the reasonableness of the lawyer's expectation of confidentiality include the sensitivity of the information and the extent to which the privacy of the communication is protected by law or by a confidentiality agreement. A client may require the lawyer to implement special security measures not required by this Rule or may give informed consent to the use of a means of communication that would otherwise be prohibited by this Rule.

Former Client

[18] The duty of confidentiality continues after the client-lawyer relationship has terminated. See Rule 1.9(c)(2). See Rule 1.9(c)(1) for the prohibition against using such information to the disadvantage of the former client.

RULE 1.18: DUTIES TO PROSPECTIVE CLIENT

(a) A person who discusses with a lawyer the possibility of forming a client-lawyer relationship with respect to a matter is a prospective client.

(b) Even when no client-lawyer relationship ensues, a lawyer who has had discussions with a prospective client shall not use or reveal information learned in the consultation, except as Rule 1.9 would permit with respect to information of a former client.

(c) A lawyer subject to paragraph (b) shall not represent a client with interests materially adverse to those of a prospective client in the same or a substantially related matter if the lawyer received information from the prospective client that could be significantly harmful to that person in the matter, except as provided in paragraph (d). If a lawyer is disqualified from representation under this paragraph, no lawyer in a firm with which that lawyer is associated may knowingly undertake or continue representation in such a matter, except as provided in paragraph (d).

(d) When the lawyer has received disqualifying information as defined in paragraph (c), representation is permissible if:

(1) both the affected client and the prospective client have given informed consent, confirmed in writing; or

(2) the lawyer who received the information took reasonable measures to avoid exposure to more disqualifying information than was reasonably necessary to determine whether to represent the prospective client; and

(i) the disqualified lawyer is timely screened from any participation in the matter and is apportioned no part of the fee therefrom; and

(ii) written notice is promptly given to the prospective client.

Comment

[1] Prospective clients, like clients, may disclose information to a lawyer, place documents or other property in the lawyer's custody, or rely on the lawyer's advice. A lawyer's discussions with a prospective client usually are limited in time and depth and leave both the prospective client and the lawyer free (and sometimes required) to proceed no further. Hence, prospective clients should receive some but not all of the protection afforded clients.

[2] Not all persons who communicate information to a lawyer are entitled to protection under this Rule. A person who communicates information unilaterally to a lawyer, without any reasonable expectation that the lawyer is willing to discuss the possibility of forming a client-lawyer relationship, is not a "prospective client" within the meaning of paragraph (a).

[3] It is often necessary for a prospective client to reveal information to the lawyer during an initial consultation prior to the decision about formation of a client-lawyer relationship. The lawyer often must learn such information to determine whether there is a conflict of interest with an existing client and whether the matter is one that the lawyer is willing to undertake. Paragraph (b) prohibits the lawyer from using or revealing that information, except as permitted by Rule 1.9, even if the client or lawyer decides not to proceed with the representation. The duty exists regardless of how brief the initial conference may be.

[4] In order to avoid acquiring disqualifying information from a prospective client, a lawyer considering whether or not to undertake a new matter should limit the initial interview to only such information as reasonably appears necessary for that purpose. Where the information indicates that a conflict of interest or other reason for non-representation exists, the lawyer should so inform the prospective client or decline the representation. If the prospective client wishes to retain the lawyer, and if consent is possi-

ble under Rule 1.7, then consent from all affected present or former clients must be obtained before accepting the representation.

[5] A lawyer may condition conversations with a prospective client on the person's informed consent that no information disclosed during the consultation will prohibit the lawyer from representing a different client in the matter. See Rule 1.0(e) for the definition of informed consent. If the agreement expressly so provides, the prospective client may also consent to the lawyer's subsequent use of information received from the prospective client.

[6] Even in the absence of an agreement, under paragraph (c), the lawyer is not prohibited from representing a client with interests adverse to those of the prospective client in the same or a substantially related matter unless the lawyer has received from the prospective client information that could be significantly harmful if used in the matter.

[7] Under paragraph (c), the prohibition in this Rule is imputed to other lawyers as provided in Rule 1.10, but, under paragraph (d)(1), imputation may be avoided if the lawyer obtains the informed consent, confirmed in writing, of both the prospective and affected clients. In the alternative, imputation may be avoided if the conditions of paragraph (d)(2) are met and all disqualified lawyers are timely screened and written notice is promptly given to the prospective client. See Rule 1.0(k) (requirements for screening procedures). Paragraph (d)(2)(i) does not prohibit the screened lawyer from receiving a salary or partnership share established by prior independent agreement, but that lawyer may not receive compensation directly related to the matter in which the lawyer is disqualified.

[8] Notice, including a general description of the subject matter about which the lawyer was consulted, and of the screening procedures employed, generally should be given as soon as practicable after the need for screening becomes apparent.

[9] For the duty of competence of a lawyer who gives assistance on the merits of a matter to a prospective client, see Rule 1.1. For a lawyer's duties when a prospective client entrusts valuables or papers to the lawyer's care, see Rule 1.15.

RULE 3.4: FAIRNESS TO OPPOSING PARTY AND COUNSEL

A lawyer shall not:

(a) unlawfully obstruct another party' s access to evidence or unlawfully alter, destroy or conceal a document or other material having potential evidentiary value. A lawyer shall not counsel or assist another person to do any such act;

(b) falsify evidence, counsel or assist a witness to testify falsely, or offer an inducement to a witness that is prohibited by law;

(c) knowingly disobey an obligation under the rules of a tribunal except for an open refusal based on an assertion that no valid obligation exists;

(d) in pretrial procedure, make a frivolous discovery request or fail to make reasonably diligent effort to comply with a legally proper discovery request by an opposing party;

(e) in trial, allude to any matter that the lawyer does not reasonably believe is relevant or that will not be supported by admissible evidence, assert personal knowledge of facts in issue except when testifying as a witness, or state a personal opinion as to the justness of a cause, the credibility of a witness, the culpability of a civil litigant or the guilt or innocence of an accused; or

(f) request a person other than a client to refrain from voluntarily giving relevant information to another party unless:

(1) the person is a relative or an employee or other agent of a client; and

(2) the lawyer reasonably believes that the person's interests will not be adversely affected by refraining from giving such information.

Comment

[1] The procedure of the adversary system contemplates that the evidence in a case is to be marshalled competitively by the contending parties. Fair competition in the adversary system is secured by prohibitions against destruction or concealment of evidence, improperly influencing witnesses, obstructive tactics in discovery procedure, and the like.

[2] Documents and other items of evidence are often essential to establish a claim or defense. Subject to evidentiary privileges, the right of an opposing party, including the government, to obtain evidence through discovery or subpoena is an important procedural right. The exercise of that right can be frustrated if relevant material is altered, concealed or destroyed. Applicable law in many jurisdictions makes it an offense to destroy material for purpose of impairing its availability in a pending proceeding or one whose commencement can be foreseen. Falsifying evidence is also generally a criminal offense. Paragraph (a) applies to evidentiary material generally, including computerized information. Applicable law may permit a lawyer to take temporary possession of physical evidence of client crimes for the purpose of conducting a limited examination that will not alter or destroy material characteristics of the evidence. In such a case, applicable law may require the lawyer to turn the evidence over to the police or other prosecuting authority, depending on the circumstances.

[3] With regard to paragraph (b), it is not improper to pay a witness's expenses or to compensate an expert witness on terms permitted by law. The common law rule in most jurisdictions is that it is improper to pay an occurrence witness any fee for testifying and that it is improper to pay an expert witness a contingent fee.

[4] Paragraph (f) permits a lawyer to advise employees of a client to refrain from giving information to another party, for the employees may identify their interests with those of the client. See also Rule 4.2.

RULE 4.4: RESPECT FOR RIGHTS OF THIRD PERSONS

(b) A lawyer who receives a document relating to the representation of the lawyer's client and knows or reasonably should know that the document was inadvertently sent shall promptly notify the sender.

Comment

[1] Responsibility to a client requires a lawyer to subordinate the interests of others to those of the client, but that responsibility does not imply that a lawyer may disregard the rights of third persons. It is impractical to catalogue all such rights, but they include legal restrictions on methods of obtaining evidence from third persons and unwarranted intrusions into privileged relationships, such as the client-lawyer relationship.

[2] Paragraph (b) recognizes that lawyers sometimes receive documents that were mistakenly sent or produced by opposing parties or their lawyers. If a lawyer knows or reasonably should know that such a document was sent inadvertently, then this Rule requires the lawyer to promptly notify the sender in order to permit that person to take protective measures. Whether the lawyer is required to take additional steps, such as returning the original document, is a matter of law beyond the scope of these Rules, as is the question of whether the privileged status of a document has been waived. Similarly,

this Rule does not address the legal duties of a lawyer who receives a document that the lawyer knows or reasonably should know may have been wrongfully obtained by the sending person. For purposes of this Rule, "document" includes e-mail or other electronic modes of transmission subject to being read or put into readable form.

[3] Some lawyers may choose to return a document unread, for example, when the lawyer learns before receiving the document that it was inadvertently sent to the wrong address. Where a lawyer is not required by applicable law to do so, the decision to voluntarily return such a document is a matter of professional judgment ordinarily reserved to the lawyer. See Rules 1.2 and 1.4.

ABA Code

DR 4-101—Preservation of Confidences and Secrets of a Client.

(A) "Confidence" refers to information protected by the attorney-client privilege under applicable law, and "secret" refers to other information gained in the professional relationship that the client has requested be held inviolate or the disclosure of which would be embarrassing or would be likely to be detrimental to the client.

(B) Except when permitted under DR 4-101(C), a lawyer shall not knowingly:

(1) Reveal a confidence or secret of his client.

(2) Use a confidence or secret of his client to the disadvantage of the client.

(3) Use a confidence or secret of his client for the advantage of himself or of a third person, unless the client consents after full disclosure.

(C) A lawyer may reveal:

(1) Confidences or secrets with the consent of the client or clients affected, but only after a full disclosure to them.

(2) Confidences or secrets when permitted under Disciplinary Rules or required by law or court order.

(3) The intention of his client to commit a crime and the information necessary to prevent the crime.

(4) Confidences or secrets necessary to establish or collect his fee or to defend himself or his employees or associates against an accusation of wrongful conduct.

(D) A lawyer shall exercise reasonable care to prevent his employees, associates, and others whose services are utilized by him from disclosing or using confidences or secrets of a client, except that a lawyer may reveal the information allowed by DR 4-101(C) through an employee.

8 *Wigmore on Evidence* § 2292

From: John Henry Wigmore, *Evidence in Trials at Common Law*
(rev. J.T. McNaughton, Little Brown, Boston, 1961), vol. 8, pp. 554–555

Attorney-Client Privilege

§ 2292. General principle, Statutory definitions. The phrasing of the general principle so as to represent all its essentials, but only essentials, and to group them in natural sequence is a matter of some difficulty. The following form seems to accomplish this:

(1) Where legal advice of any kind is sought (2) from a professional legal adviser in his capacity as such, (3) the communications relating to that purpose, (4) made in confidence (5) by the client, (6) are at his instance permanently protected (7) from disclosure by himself or by the legal adviser, (8) except the protection be waived.

Alaska "Tampering" Statutes

From: Alaska Statutes 1962 (November, 2002) (Lexis Nexis), vol. 3,
Title 11, Chapter 56, Article 4, Sec. 11.56.610

[Current through all 2010 Sessions, Annotations through Opinions Decided
as of June 3, 2010.

Copyright 2004, Alaska Statutes, 2004 by The State of Alaska and Matthew Bender
& Company, Inc. a member of the LexisNexis Group.]

Sec. 11.56.610. Tampering with physical evidence. (a) A person commits the crime of tampering with physical evidence if the person

(1) destroys, mutilates, alters, suppresses, conceals, or removes physical evidence with intent to impair its verity or availability in an official proceeding or a criminal investigation;

(2) makes, presents, or uses physical evidence, knowing it to be false, with intent to mislead a juror who is engaged in an official proceeding or a public servant who is engaged in an official proceeding or a criminal investigation;

(3) prevents the production of physical evidence in an official proceeding or a criminal investigation by the use of force, threat, or deception against anyone; or

(4) does any act described by (1), (2), or (3) of this subsection with intent to prevent the institution of an official proceeding.

(b) Tampering with physical evidence is a class C felony. (§ 6 ch 166 SLA 1978)

ANNOTATIONS

Opinions of attorney general.—Where an operator of a motor vehicle which was involved in an accident, fails to render assistance to an injured person, an act which is punishable as a felony under AS 28.35.060(c); the Alaska state troopers investigate the incident and during the course of the investigation an attorney contacts the troopers, stating that a client has informed him that the client has committed the act and wishes to make restitution to the victim for medical expenses; and the attorney requests the troopers' assistance in making the payment, but refuses to disclose to the troopers the name of his client, such refusal to divulge the client's identity is neither illegal nor unethical. November 27, 1979, Op. Att'y Gen.

Massachusetts "Accessories After Fact" Statute
Massachusetts General Laws
Chapter 274, Sec. 4

§ 4. Accessories after fact; punishment; relationship as defence; cross-examination; impeachment

Whoever, after the commission of a felony, harbors, conceals, maintains or assists the principal felon or accessory before the fact, or gives such offender any other aid, knowing that he has committed a felony or has been accessory thereto before the fact, with intent that he shall avoid or escape detention, arrest, trial or punishment, shall be an accessory after the fact, and, except as otherwise provided, be punished by imprisonment in the state prison for not more than seven years or in jail for not more than two and one half years or by a fine of not more than one thousand dollars. The fact that the defendant is the husband or wife, or by consanguinity, affinity or adoption, the parent or grandparent, child or grandchild, brother or sister of the offender, shall be a defence to a prosecution under this section. If such a defendant testifies solely as to the existence of such relationship, he shall not be subject to cross examination on any other subject matter, nor shall his criminal record, if any, except for perjury or subornation of perjury, be admissible to impeach his credibility.

Amended by St.1943, c. 488, § 1.

IV-3. Confidentiality: Cases and Materials

Note: The following case, *In re Ryder,* predates the ABA *Code* of 1969 and refers to the old ABA *Canon of Ethics,* first promulgated in 1908, and adopted by the Supreme Court of Appeals of Virginia pursuant to 1940 legislation. The 47 Canons were relatively concise and general. What do you think of them? What do you think of Richard Ryder's efforts to get ethical advice?

In re Ryder

263 F.Supp. 360

United States District Court E.D. Virginia, Richmond Division

Jan. 23, 1967

Before HOFFMAN, Chief Judge, and LEWIS and BUTZNER, Judges.

MEMORANDUM

PER CURIAM.

This proceeding was instituted to determine whether Richard R. Ryder should be removed from the roll of attorneys qualified to practice before this court. Ryder was admitted to this bar in 1953. He formerly served five years as an Assistant United States Attorney. He has an active trial practice, including both civil and criminal cases.

* * *

On August 24, 1966 a man armed with a sawed-off shotgun robbed the Varina Branch of the Bank of Virginia of $7,583. Included in the currency taken were $10 bills known as 'bait money,' the serial numbers of which had been recorded.

On August 26, 1966 Charles Richard Cook rented safety deposit box 14 at a branch of the Richmond National Bank. Later in the day Cook was interviewed at his home by agents of the Federal Bureau of Investigation, who obtained $348 from him. Cook telephoned Ryder, who had represented him in civil litigation. Ryder came to the house and advised the agents that he represented Cook. He said that if Cook were not to be placed under arrest, he intended to take him to his office for an interview. The agents left. Cook insisted to Ryder that he had not robbed the bank. He told Ryder that he had won the money, which the agents had taken from him, in a crap game. At this time Ryder believed Cook.

Later that afternoon Ryder telephoned one of the agents and asked whether any of the bills obtained from Cook had been identified as a part of the money taken in the bank robbery. The agent told him that some bills had been identified. Ryder made inquiries about the number of bills taken and their denominations. The agent declined to give him specific information but indicated that several of the bills were recorded as bait money.

The next morning, Saturday, August 27, 1966, Ryder conferred with Cook again. He urged Cook to tell the truth, and Cook answered that a man, whose name he would not divulge, offered him $500 on the day of the robbery to put a package in a bank lockbox. Ryder did not believe this story. Ryder told Cook that if the government could trace the money in the box to him, it would be almost conclusive evidence of his guilt. He knew that Cook was under surveillance and he suspected that Cook might try to dispose of the money.

That afternoon Ryder telephoned a former officer of the Richmond Bar Association to discuss his course of action. He had known this attorney for many years and respected his judgment. The lawyer was at home and had no library available to him when Ryder telephoned. In their casual conversation Ryder told what he knew about the case, omitting names. He explained that he thought he would take the money from Cook's safety deposit box and place it in a box in his own name. This, he believed, would prevent Cook from attempting to dispose of the money. The lawyers thought that eventually F.B.I. agents would locate the money and that since it was in Ryder's possession, he could claim a privilege and thus effectively exclude it from evidence. This would prevent the government from linking Ryder's client with the bait money and would also destroy any presumption of guilt that might exist arising out of the client's exclusive possession of the evidence.

Ryder testified:

> 'I had sense enough to know, one, at that time that apparently the F.B.I. did have the serial numbers on the bills. I had sense enough to know, from many, many years of experience in this court and in working with the F.B.I. and, in fact, in directing the F.B.I. on some occasions, to know that eventually the bank—that the F.B.I. would find that money if I left that money in the bank. There was no doubt in my mind that eventually they would find it. The only thing I could think of to do was to get the money out of Mr. Cook's possession. * * * The idea was that I assumed that if anybody tried to go into a safety deposit box in my name, the bank officials would notify me and that I would get an opportunity to come in this court and argue a question of whether or not they could use that money as evidence.'

The lawyers discussed and rejected alternatives, including having a third party get the money. At the conclusion of the conversation Ryder was advised, 'Don't do it surreptitiously and to be sure that you let your client know that it is going back to the rightful owners.'

On Monday morning Ryder asked Cook to come by his office. He prepared a power of attorney, which Cook signed. . . .

Ryder did not follow the advice he had received on Saturday. He did not let his client know the money was going back to the rightful owners. He testified about his omission:

> 'I prepared it myself and told Mr. Cook to sign it. In the power of attorney, I did not specifically say that Mr. Cook authorized me to deliver that money to the appropriate authorities at any time because for a number of reasons. One,

in representing a man under these circumstances, you've got to keep the man's confidence, but I also put in that power of attorney that Mr. Cook authorized me to dispose of that money as I saw fit, and the reason for that being that I was going to turn the money over to the proper authorities at whatever time I deemed that it wouldn't hurt Mr. Cook.'

Ryder took the power of attorney which Cook had signed to the Richmond National Bank. He rented box 13 in his name with his office address, presented the power of attorney, entered Cook's box, took both boxes into a booth, where he found a bag of money and a sawed-off shotgun in Cook's box. The box also contained miscellaneous items which are not pertinent to this proceeding. He transferred the contents of Cook's box to his own and returned the boxes to the vault. He left the bank, and neither he nor Cook returned.

Ryder testified that he had some slight hesitation about the propriety of what he was doing. Within a half-hour after he left the bank, he talked to a retired judge and distinguished professor of law. He told this person that he wanted to discuss something in confidence. Ryder then stated that he represented a man suspected of bank robbery. The judge recalled the main part of the conversation:

> '* * * And that he had received from this client, under a power of attorney, a sum (of) money which he, Mr. Ryder, suspected was proceeds of the robbery, although he didn't know it, but he had a suspicion that it was; that he had placed this money in a safety deposit vault at a bank; that he had received it with the intention of returning it to the rightful owner after the case against his client had been finally disposed of one way or the other; that he considered that he had received it under the privilege of attorney and client and that he wanted responsible people in the community to know of that fact and that he was telling me in confidence of that as one of these people that he wanted to know of it. 'Q. Did he say anything to you about a sawed-off shotgun? 'A. I don't recall. If Mr. Ryder says he did, I would not deny it, but I do not recall it, because the—my main attention in what he was saying was certainly drawn to the fact that the money was involved, but I just cannot answer the question emphatically, but if Mr. Ryder says he told me, why, I certainly wouldn't deny it.'

Ryder testified that he told about the shotgun. The judge also testified that Ryder certainly would not have been under the impression that he—the judge—thought that he was guilty of unethical conduct.

The same day Ryder also talked with other prominent persons in Richmond—a judge of a court of record and an attorney for the Commonwealth. Again, he stated that what he intended to say was confidential. He related the circumstances and was advised that a lawyer could not receive the property and if he had received it he could not retain possession of it.

On September 7, 1966 Cook was indicted for robbing the Varina Branch of the Bank of Virginia. A bench warrant was issued and the next day Ryder represented Cook at a bond hearing. Cook was identified as the robber by employees of the bank. He was released on bond. Cook was arraigned on a plea of not guilty on September 9, 1966.

On September 12, 1966 F.B.I. agents procured search warrants for Cook's and Ryder's safety deposit boxes in the Richmond National Bank. They found Cook's box empty. In Ryder's box they discovered $5,920 of the $7,583 taken in the bank robbery and the sawed-off shotgun used in the robbery.

On September 23, 1966 Ryder filed a motion to suppress the money obtained from Cook by the agents on August 26, 1966. The motion did not involve items taken from Ryder's safety deposit box. The motion came on to be heard October 6, 1966. Ryder called Cook as a witness for examination on matters limited to the motion to suppress. The court called to Ryder's attention papers pertaining to the search of the safety deposit boxes. Ryder moved for a continuance, stating that he intended to file a motion with respect to the seizure of the contents of the lockbox.

On October 14, 1966 the three judges of this court removed Ryder as an attorney for Cook; suspended him from practice before the court until further order; referred the matter to the United States Attorney, who was requested to file charges within five days; set the matter for hearing November 11, 1966; and granted Ryder leave to move for vacation or modification of its order pending hearing.

The United States Attorney charged Ryder with violations of Canons 15 and 32 of the Canons of Professional Ethics of the Virginia State Bar. Ryder did not move for vacation or modification of the order, and the case was heard as scheduled by the court en banc. After the transcript was prepared and the case briefed, the court heard the argument of counsel on December 27, 1966.

At the outset, we reject the suggestion that Ryder did not know the money which he transferred from Cook's box to his was stolen. We find that on August 29 when Ryder opened Cook's box and saw a bag of money and a sawed-off shotgun, he then knew Cook was involved in the bank robbery and that the money was stolen. Ryder knew that the man who had robbed the bank used a sawed-off shotgun. He disbelieved Cook's story about the source of the money in the lockbox. He knew that some of the bills in Cook's possession were bait money.

Judge Learned Hand observed in United States v. Werner, 160 F.2d 438, 441 (2d Cir. 1947):

> 'The defendants ask us to distinguish between 'knowing' that goods are stolen and merely being put upon an inquiry which would have led to discovery; but they have misconceived the distinction which the decisions have made. The receivers of stolen goods almost never 'know' that they have been stolen, in the sense that they could testify to it in a court room.'

Judge Hand then went on to say (160 F.2d 442):

> 'But that the jury must find that the receiver did more than infer the theft from the circumstances has never been demanded, so far as we know; and to demand more would emasculate the statute * * *.'

In Melson v. United States, 207 F.2d 558, 559 (4th Cir. 1953), the court said:

> 'It is well settled that knowledge that goods have been stolen may be inferred from circumstances that would convince a man of ordinary intelligence that this is the fact.'

We also find that Ryder was not motivated solely by certain expectation the government would discover the contents of his lockbox. He believed discovery was probable. In this event he intended to argue to the court that the contents of his box could not be revealed, and even if the contents were identified, his possession made the stolen money and the shotgun inadmissible against his client. He also recognized that discovery was not inevitable. His intention in this event, we find, was to assist Cook by keeping the stolen money and the shotgun concealed in his lockbox until after the trial. His conversations, and the secrecy he enjoined, immediately after he put the money and the gun in his box, show that he realized the government might not find the property.

We accept his statement that he intended eventually to return the money to its rightful owner, but we pause to say that no attorney should ever place himself in such a position. Matters involving the possible termination of an attorney-client relationship, or possible subsequent proceedings in the event of an acquittal, are too delicate to permit such a practice.

We reject the argument that Ryder's conduct was no more than the exercise of the attorney-client privilege. The fact that Cook had not been arrested or indicted at the time Ryder took possession of the gun and money is immaterial. Cook was Ryder's client and was entitled to the protection of the lawyer-client privilege. Continental Oil Co. v. United States, 330 F.2d 347 (9th Cir, 1964).

Regardless of Cook's status, however, Ryder's conduct was not encompassed by the attorney-client privilege. A frequently quoted definition of the privilege is found in United States v. United Shoe Mach. Corp., 89 F.Supp. 357, 358 (D.Mass.1950):

> 'The privilege applies only if (1) the asserted holder of the privilege is or sought to become a client; (2) the person to whom the communication was made (a) is a member of the bar of a court, or his subordinate and (b) in connection with this communication is acting as a lawyer; (3) the communication relates to a fact of which the attorney was informed (a) by his client (b) without the presence of strangers (c) for the purpose of securing primarily either (i) an opinion on law or (ii) legal services or (iii) assistance in some legal proceeding, and not (d) for the purpose of committing a crime or tort; and (4) the privilege has been (a) claimed and (b) not waived by the client.'

The essentials of the privilege have been stated in 8 Wigmore, Evidence § 2292 (McNaughton Rev.1961):

> '(1) Where legal advice of any kind is sought (2) from a professional legal adviser in his capacity as such, (3) the communications relating to that purpose, (4) made in confidence (5) by the client, (6) are at his instance permanently protected (7) from disclosure by himself or by the legal adviser, (8) except the protection be waived.'

It was Ryder, not his client, who took the initiative in transferring the incriminating possession of the stolen money and the shotgun from Cook. Ryder's conduct went far beyond the receipt and retention of a confidential communication from his client. Counsel for Ryder conceded, at the time of argument, that the acts of Ryder were not within the attorney-client privilege.

Ryder's reliance upon United States v. Judson, 322 F.2d 460 (9th Cir. 1963) and Schwimmer v. United States, 232 F.2d 855 (8th Cir. 1956), cert. denied 352 U.S. 833, 77 S.Ct. 48, 1 L.Ed.2d 52 (1956), is unfounded. In both of these cases subpoenas duces tecum were served upon lawyers requiring them to produce papers deposited with them by their clients. Judson turns upon the application of the Fifth Amendment. The court said at 322 F.2d 466:

> 'Clearly, if the taxpayer in this case * * * had been subpoenaed and directed to produce the documents in question, he could have properly refused. The government concedes this. But instead of closeting himself with his myriad tax data drawn up around him, the taxpayer retained counsel. quite predictably, in the course of the ensuing attorney-client relationship the pertinent records

were turned over to the attorney. The government would have us hold that the taxpayer walked into his attorney's office unquestionably shielded with the Amendment's protection, and walked out with something less.

* * *

'The thrust of the Fifth Amendment is that 'prosecutors are forced the search for independent evidence instead of relying upon proof extracted from individuals by force of law.' United States v. White, supra, 322 U.S. (694,) at 698 (64 S.Ct. 1248, 88 L.Ed. 1542).'

Schwimmer (232 F.2d 855) concerned papers which had been contained in a lawyer's files. The lawyer had discontinued his practice and had stored the papers with a manufacturing company. The court recognized that the lawyer had standing to quash a subpoena duces tecum. The case turned upon the Fourth Amendment. The court recognized that production of one's private books and papers by subpoena duces tecum for use against him in a criminal proceeding is prohibited by the Amendment. The fact that the papers were in the constructive possession of the attorney did not remove them from its protection. The court also recognized that the attorney had sufficient interest in the papers to be permitted to take a part in the proceedings to determine their admissibility.

Not all papers in a lawyer's file are immune. The rule is summarized in McMormick, Evidence, § 93 at p. 188 (1954):

> 'If a document would be subject to an order for production if it were in the hands of a client, it would be equally subject if it is in the hands of an attorney.'

The basic difficulty with Ryder's reliance upon Judson and Schwimmer is that this proceeding is not concerned with the concealment of Cook's papers or other articles of an evidentiary nature. Neither Cook nor his attorney could be compelled to produce merely evidentiary articles nor could such articles be seized in a legal search. Cf. Hayden v. Warden, 363 F.2d 647 (4th Cir. 1966), cert. granted, 385 U.S. 926, 87 S.Ct. 290, 17 L.Ed.2d 210 (1966) (No. 480, 1966 Term). In Harris v. United States, 331 U.S. 145, 154, 67 S.Ct. 1098, 1103, 91 L.Ed. 1399 (1947), Mr. Chief Justice Vinson said:

> 'This Court has frequently recognized the distinction between merely evidentiary materials, on the one hand, which may not be seized either under the authority of a search warrant or during the course of a search incident to arrest, and on the other hand, those objects which may validly be seized including the instrumentalities and means by which a crime is committed, the fruits of crime such as stolen property, weapons by which escape of the person arrested might be effected, and property the possession of which is a crime.'

Ryder, an experienced criminal attorney, recognized and acted upon the fact that the gun and money were subject to seizure while in the possession of Cook.

In Clark v. United States, 289 U.S. 1, 15, 53 S.Ct. 465, 469, 77 L.Ed. 993 (1933), Mr. Justice Cardozo expressed a dictum, which is apt to the aid Ryder gave Cook:

> 'We turn to the precedents in the search for an analogy, and the search is not in vain. There is a privilege protecting communications between attorney and client. The privilege takes flight if the relation is abused. A client who consults an attorney for advice that will serve him in the commission of a fraud will have no help from the law. He must let the truth be told.'

* * *

We conclude that Ryder violated Canons 15 and 32. His conduct is not sanctioned by Canons 5 or 37. In providing for the adoption and enforcement by the Supreme Court of Appeals of Virginia of rules and regulations prescribing a code of ethics to govern professional conduct of attorneys, the General Assembly of Virginia stated that 'the Supreme Court of Appeals shall not adopt or promulgate rules or regulations prescribing a code of ethics * * * (for) attorneys * * * which shall be inconsistent with any statute * * *.' Va.Acts of Assembly 1940, ch. 314 at 508 (Mar. 28, 1940).

* * *

The money in Cook's box belonged to the Bank of Virginia. The law did not authorize Cook to conceal this money or withhold it from the bank. His larceny was a continuing offense. Cook had no title or property interest in the money that he lawfully could pass to Ryder. The Act of Assembly authorizing the promulgation of the Canons of Ethics in Virginia forbids inconsistency with § 18.1-107 Code of Virginia, 1950, which provides:

> 'If any person buy or receive from another person, or aid in concealing, any stolen goods or other thing, knowing the same to have been stolen, he shall be deemed guilty of larceny thereof, and may be proceeded against, although the principal offender be not convicted.'

No canon of ethics or law permitted Ryder to conceal from the Bank of Virginia its money to gain his client's acquittal.

Cook's possession of the sawed-off shotgun was illegal. 26 U.S.C. § 5851. Ryder could not lawfully receive the gun from Cook to assist Cook to avoid conviction of robbery. Cook had never mentioned the shotgun to Ryder. When Ryder discovered it in Cook's box, he took possession of it to hinder the government in the prosecution of its case, and he intended not to reveal in pending trial unless the government discovered it and a court compelled its production. No statute or canon of ethics authorized Ryder to take possession of the gun for this purpose.

Canon 15 states in part:

> '* * * The great trust of the lawyer is to be performed within and not without the bounds of law. The office of attorney does not permit, much less does it demand of him for any client, violation of law or any manner of fraud or chicane. He must obey his own conscience and not that of his client.'

In helping Cook to conceal the shotgun and stolen money, Ryder acted without the bounds of law. He allowed the office of attorney to be used in violation of law. The scheme which he devised was a deceptive, legalistic subterfuge—rightfully denounced by the canon as chicane.

* * *

There is much to be said, however, for mitigation of the discipline to be imposed. Ryder intended to return the bank's money after his client was tried. He consulted reputable persons before and after he placed the property in his lockbox, although he did not precisely follow their advice. Were it not for these facts, we would deem proper his permanent exclusion from practice before this court. In view of the mitigating circumstances, he will be suspended from practice in this court for eighteen months effective October 14, 1966.

* * *

Purcell v. District Attorney for Suffolk District

424 Mass. 109
Suffolk. October 9, 1996–January 13, 1997
[Some footnotes omitted. Remaining footnotes renumbered.]

Present: Wilkins, C.J., Abrams, Lynch, O'Connor, Greaney, & Fried, JJ.

WILKINS, C.J. On June 21, 1994, Joseph Tyree, who had received a court order to vacate his apartment in the Allston section of Boston, consulted the plaintiff, Jeffrey W. Purcell, an attorney employed by Greater Boston Legal Services, which provides representation to low income individuals in civil matters. Tyree had recently been discharged as a maintenance man at the apartment building in which his apartment was located. On the day that Tyree consulted Purcell, Purcell decided, after extensive deliberation, that he should advise appropriate authorities that Tyree might engage in conduct harmful to others. He told a Boston police lieutenant that Tyree had made threats to burn the apartment building.

The next day, constables, accompanied by Boston police officers, went to evict Tyree. At the apartment building, they found incendiary materials, containers of gasoline, and several bottles with wicks attached. Smoke detectors had been disconnected, and gasoline had been poured on a hallway floor. Tyree was arrested and later indicted for attempted arson of a building.

In August, 1995, the district attorney for the Suffolk district subpoenaed Purcell to testify concerning the conversation Purcell had had with Tyree on June 21, 1994. A Superior Court judge granted Purcell's motion to quash the subpoena. The trial ended in a mistrial because the jury was unable to reach a verdict.

The Commonwealth decided to try Tyree again and once more sought Purcell's testimony. Another Superior Court judge concluded that Tyree's statements to Purcell were not protected by the attorney-client privilege, denied Purcell's motion to quash an anticipated subpoena, and ordered Purcell to testify. Purcell then commenced this action, pursuant to G.L. c. 211, § 3 (1994 ed.), in the single justice session of this court. The parties entered into a stipulation of facts, and a single justice reserved and reported the case to the full court.

There is no question before this court, directly or indirectly, concerning the ethical propriety of Purcell's disclosure to the police that Tyree might engage in conduct that would be harmful to others. As bar counsel agreed in a memorandum submitted to the single justice, this court's disciplinary rules regulating the practice of law authorized Purcell to reveal to the police "[t]he intention of his client to commit a crime and the information necessary to prevent the crime." S.J.C. Rule 3:07, Canon 4, DR 4-101(C)(3), as appearing in 382 Mass. 778 (1981).[1] The fact that the disciplinary code permitted

---

1. The same conclusion would be reached under Rule 1.6(b)(1) of the Proposed Massachusetts Rules of Professional Conduct, now pending before the Justices. Under rule 1.6(b)(1), as now proposed, a lawyer may reveal confidential information relating to a client "to prevent the commission of a criminal or fraudulent act that the lawyer reasonably believes is likely to result in death or substantial bodily harm, or in substantial injury to the financial interests or property of another." Unlike DR 4-101(C)(3), which allows disclosure of a client's intention to commit any crime, disclosure of a client's intention to commit a crime is permissible under proposed rule 1.6(b)(1) only as to crimes threatening substantial consequences, and disclosure is permitted based on an attorney's reasonable belief of the likely existence of the threat rather than, as is the case under DR 4-101(C)(3), a known intention of the client to commit a crime.

Purcell to make the disclosure tells us nothing about the admissibility of the information that Purcell disclosed. See *Kleinfeld v. State*, 568 So.2d 937, 939–940 (Fla.Dist.Ct.App.1990).

The district attorney does not press the fact that Purcell may not be entitled to relief under G.L. c. 211, § 3, because he could resist testifying, be held in contempt, and then appeal. A single justice has reported this case, implicitly indicating that a discretionary exercise of authority under G.L. c. 211, § 3, in Purcell's favor would be appropriate if his legal position is sound.

The attorney-client privilege is founded on the necessity that a client be free to reveal information to an attorney, without fear of its disclosure, in order to obtain informed legal advice. *Matter of a John Doe Grand Jury Investigation*, 408 Mass. 480, 481–482, 562 N.E.2d 69 (1990). It is a principle of long standing. See *Foster v. Hall*, 29 Mass. 89, 12 Pick. 89, 93 (1831). The debate here is whether Tyree is entitled to the protection of the attorney-client privilege in the circumstances.

The district attorney announces the issue in his brief to be whether a crime-fraud exception to the testimonial privilege applies in this case. He asserts that, even if Tyree's communication with Purcell was made as part of his consultation concerning the eviction proceeding, Tyree's communication concerning his contemplated criminal conduct is not protected by the privilege. We shall first consider the case on the assumption that Tyree's statements to Purcell are protected by the attorney-client privilege unless the crime-fraud exception applies.

"It is the purpose of the crime-fraud exception to the attorney-client privilege to assure that the 'seal of secrecy'... between lawyer and client does not extend to communications 'made for the purpose of getting advice for the commission of a fraud' or crime" (citation omitted). *United States v. Zolin*, 491 U.S. 554, 563, 109 S.Ct. 2619, 2626, 105 L.Ed.2d 469 (1989), quoting *O'Rourke v. Darbishire*, [1920] App. Cas. 581, 604 (P.C.). There is no public interest in the preservation of the secrecy of that kind of communication. See *United States v. Zolin*, supra at 562–563, 109 S.Ct. at 2625–2626; *Matter of John Doe Grand Jury Investigation*, supra at 486, 562 N.E.2d 69.

Our cases have not defined a crime-fraud exception to the attorney-client privilege with any precision. In *Matter of John Doe Grand Jury Investigation*, supra at 486, 562 N.E.2d 69, the court stated that there was "no legitimate interest of a client and no public interest would be served by a rule that would preserve the secrecy of" a conversation between attorney and client in a conference related to the possible future defrauding of an insurance company. We cited *Commonwealth v. Dyer*, 243 Mass. 472, 138 N.E. 296, cert. denied, 262 U.S. 751, 43 S.Ct. 700, 67 L.Ed. 1214 (1923), in which we said that "[t]here is no privilege between attorney and client where the conferences concern the proposed commission of a crime by the client." *Id.* at 505–506, 138 N.E. 296. The cases cited in our *Dyer* opinion and the facts of that case — the attorney was alleged to be part of the conspiracy — demonstrate that the exception asserted concerned conferences in which the attorney's advice was sought in furtherance of a crime or to obtain advice or assistance with respect to criminal activity.

We, therefore, accept the general principle of a crime-fraud exception. The Proposed Massachusetts Rules of Evidence adequately define the crime-fraud exception to the lawyer-client privilege set forth in rule 502(d)(1) as follows: "If the services of the lawyer were sought or obtained to enable or aid anyone to commit or plan to commit what the client knew or reasonably should have known to be a crime or fraud." We need not at this time consider seemingly minor variations of the exception expressed in various sources. See Restatement (Third) of the Law Governing Lawyers § 132, and authorities cited in Reporter's Note at 465–466 (Proposed Final Draft No. 1 1996). The applicability of the exception, like the existence of the privilege, is a question of fact for the judge.

The district attorney rightly grants that he, as the opponent of the application of the testimonial privilege, has the burden of showing that the exception applies. See M.A. Larkin, Federal Testimonial Privileges § 2:07, at 2-150 (1995); P.R. Rice, Attorney-Client Privilege in the United States § 8:3, at 571–572 (1993); S.N. Stone & R.K. Taylor, Testimonial Privileges § 1.65, at 1-173–1-174 (2d ed.1995). In its *Zolin* opinion, the Supreme Court did not have to decide what level of showing the opponent of the privilege must make to establish that the exception applies. See *United States v. Zolin, supra* at 563–564 n. 7, 109 S.Ct. at 2626–2627 n. 7. We conclude that facts supporting the applicability of the crime-fraud exception must be proved by a preponderance of the evidence. However, on a showing of a factual basis adequate to support a reasonable belief that an in camera review of the evidence may establish that the exception applies, the judge has discretion to conduct such an in camera review. *United States v. Zolin, supra* at 572, 109 S.Ct. at 2630–2631. Once the judge sees the confidential information, the burden of proof normally will be unimportant.

In this case, in deciding whether to conduct a discretionary in camera review of the substance of the conversation concerning arson between Tyree and Purcell, the judge would have evidence tending to show that Tyree discussed a future crime with Purcell and that thereafter Tyree actively prepared to commit that crime. Without this evidence, the crime of arson would appear to have no apparent connection with Tyree's eviction proceeding and Purcell's representation of Tyree. With this evidence, however, a request that a judge inquire in camera into the circumstances of Tyree's apparent threat to burn the apartment building would not be a call for a "fishing expedition," and a judge might be justified in conducting such an inquiry. The evidence in this case, however, was not sufficient to warrant the judge's finding that Tyree consulted Purcell for the purpose of obtaining advice in furtherance of a crime. Therefore, the order denying the motion to quash because the crime-fraud exception applied cannot be upheld.

There is a consideration in this case that does not appear in other cases that we have seen concerning the attorney-client privilege. The testimony that the prosecution seeks from Purcell is available only because Purcell reflectively made a disclosure, relying on this court's disciplinary rule which permitted him to do so. Purcell was under no ethical duty to disclose Tyree's intention to commit a crime. He did so to protect the lives and property of others, a purpose that underlies a lawyer's discretionary right stated in the disciplinary rule. The limited facts in the record strongly suggest that Purcell's disclosures to the police served the beneficial public purpose on which the disciplinary rule was based.

We must be cautious in permitting the use of client communications that a lawyer has revealed only because of a threat to others. Lawyers will be reluctant to come forward if they know that the information that they disclose may lead to adverse consequences to their clients. A practice of the use of such disclosures might prompt a lawyer to warn a client in advance that the disclosure of certain information may not be held confidential, thereby chilling free discourse between lawyer and client and reducing the prospect that the lawyer will learn of a serious threat to the well-being of others. To best promote the purposes of the attorney-client privilege, the crime-fraud exception should apply only if the communication seeks assistance in or furtherance of future criminal conduct. When the opponent of the privilege argues that the communication itself may show that the exception applies and seeks its disclosure in camera, the judge, in the exercise of discretion on the question whether to have an in camera proceeding, should consider if the public interest is served by disclosure, even in camera, of a communication whose existence is known only because the lawyer acted against his client's interests under the authority of a disciplinary rule. The facts of each situation must be considered.

It might seem that this opinion is in a posture to conclude by stating that the order denying the motion to quash any subpoena to testify is vacated and the matter is to be remanded for further proceedings concerning the application of the crime-fraud exception. However, the district attorney's brief appears to abandon its earlier concession that all communications between Tyree and Purcell should be treated as protected by the attorney-client privilege unless the crime-fraud exception applies. The question whether the attorney-client privilege is involved at all will be open on remand. We, therefore, discuss the issue.

The attorney-client privilege applies only when the client's communication was for the purpose of facilitating the rendition of legal services. See Rule 502(b) of the Proposed Massachusetts Rules of Evidence; Restatement (Third) of the Law Governing Lawyers § 118 (Proposed Final Draft No. 1 1996) (communication "for the purpose of obtaining or providing legal assistance"); 8 J. Wigmore, Evidence § 2292, at 554 (McNaughton rev. ed.1961) (communication relating to seeking legal advice). See also *In re Richard Roe, Inc.*, 68 F.3d 38, 40 (2d Cir.1995) ("the crime-fraud exception does not apply simply because privileged communications would provide an adversary with evidence of a crime or fraud"); *United States v. United Shoe Mach. Corp.*, 89 F.Supp. 357, 358 (D.Mass.1950) (communication "for the purpose of securing primarily either [i] an opinion on law or [ii] legal services or [iii] assistance in some legal proceeding"); *People v. Clark*, 50 Cal.3d 583, 622, 268 Cal.Rptr. 399, 789 P.2d 127, cert. denied, 498 U.S. 973, 111 S.Ct. 442, 112 L.Ed.2d 425 (1990) (crime-fraud exception "permits disclosure only of communications made to *enable* or *aid* anyone to commit or plan to commit a crime or fraud"). The burden of proving that the attorney-client privilege applies to a communication rests on the party asserting the privilege. *United States v. Harrelson*, 754 F.2d 1153, 1167 (5th Cir.), cert. denied, 474 U.S. 908, 106 S.Ct. 277, 88 L.Ed.2d 241, and cert. denied, 474 U.S. 1034, 106 S.Ct. 599, 88 L.Ed.2d 578 (1985); M.A. Larkin, Federal Testimonial Privileges § 2.05[2], at 2-98 (1995); P.R. Rice, Attorney-Client Privilege in the United States § 11:9, at 971 (1993); S.N. Stone & R.K. Taylor, Testimonial Privileges § 1.61, at 1-161 (2d ed.1995). The motion judge did not pass on the question whether the attorney-client privilege applied to the communication at all but rather went directly to the issue of the crime-fraud exception, although not using that phrase.

A statement of an intention to commit a crime made in the course of seeking legal advice is protected by the privilege, unless the crime-fraud exception applies. That exception applies only if the client or prospective client seeks advice or assistance in furtherance of criminal conduct. It is agreed that Tyree consulted Purcell concerning his impending eviction. Purcell is a member of the bar, and Tyree either was or sought to become Purcell's client. The serious question concerning the application of the privilege is whether Tyree informed Purcell of the fact of his intention to commit arson for the purpose of receiving legal advice or assistance in furtherance of criminal conduct. Purcell's presentation of the circumstances in which Tyree's statements were made is likely to be the only evidence presented.

This is not a case in which our traditional view that testimonial privileges should be construed strictly should be applied. See *Three Juveniles v. Commonwealth*, 390 Mass. 357, 359–360, 455 N.E.2d 1203 (1983), cert. denied sub nom. *Keefe v. Massachusetts*, 465

U.S. 1068, 104 S.Ct. 1421, 79 L.Ed.2d 746 (1984); *Commonwealth v. O'Brien,* 377 Mass. 772, 775, 388 N.E.2d 658 (1979). A strict construction of the privilege that would leave a gap between the circumstances in which the crime-fraud exception applies and the circumstances in which a communication is protected by the attorney-client privilege would make no sense. The attorney-client privilege "is founded upon the necessity, in the interest and administration of justice, of the aid of persons having knowledge of the law and skilled in its practice, which assistance can only be safely and readily availed of when free from the consequences or the apprehension of disclosure." *Matter of a John Doe Grand Jury Investigation,* 408 Mass. 480, 481–482, 562 N.E.2d 69 (1990), quoting *Hunt v. Blackburn,* 128 U.S. 464, 470, 9 S.Ct. 125, 127, 32 L.Ed. 488 (1888). Unless the crime-fraud exception applies, the attorney-client privilege should apply to communications concerning possible future, as well as past, criminal conduct, because an informed lawyer may be able to dissuade the client from improper future conduct and, if not, under the ethical rules may elect in the public interest to make a limited disclosure of the client's threatened conduct.

POLICY

A judgment should be entered in the county court ordering that the order denying the motion to quash any subpoena issued to Purcell to testify at Tyree's trial is vacated and that the matter is remanded for further proceedings consistent with this opinion. *So ordered.*

Meyerhofer v. Empire Fire and Marine Ins. Co.
497 F. 2d 1190 (2d Cir. 1974), cert. denied, 419 U.S. 998 (1974)
United States Court of Appeals, Second Circuit
Argued Jan. 16, 1974
Decided June 10, 1974
[Some footnotes omitted. Remaining footnotes renumbered.]

Before MOORE, FRIENDLY and ANDERSON, Circuit Judges.

MOORE, Circuit Judge:

This is an appeal by Dietrich Meyerhofer and Herbert Federman, plaintiffs, and their counsel, Bernson, Hoeniger, Freitag & Abbey, from an order of the United States District Court for the Southern District of New York, dated August 23, 1973, (a) dismissing without prejudice plaintiffs' action against defendants, (b) enjoining and disqualifying plaintiffs' counsel, Bernson, Hoeniger, Freitag & Abbey, and Stuart Charles Goldberg from acting as attorneys for plaintiffs in this action or in any future action against defendant Empire Fire and Marine Insurance Company (Empire) involving the same transactions, occurrences, events, allegations, facts or issues, and (c) enjoining Bernson, Hoeniger, Freitag & Abbey and Stuart Charles Goldberg from disclosing confidential information regarding Empire to others. Intervenor Stuart Charles Goldberg also appeals from said order.

Defendants Empire, Gross, Kaplan, Phillips, Kratky, Lalich, Swick, Jennings, Jr., Sitomer, Sitomer & Porges, A. L. Sitomer, S. J. Sitomer and Robert E. Porges cross-appeal from the order insofar as that order failed to disqualify plaintiffs, Meyerhofer and Federman, from acting as class representatives of those who purchased the common stock of Empire, or to enjoin them from disclosing confidential information learned either from Bernson, Hoeniger, Freitag & Abbey or from Stuart Charles Goldberg.

The full import of the problems and issues presented on this appeal cannot be appreciated and analyzed without an initial statement of the facts out of which they arise.

Empire Fire and Marine Insurance Company on May 31, 1972, made a public offering of 500,000 shares of its stock, pursuant to a registration statement filed with the Securities and Exchange Commission (SEC) on March 28, 1972. The stock was offered at $16 a share. Empire's attorney on the issue was the firm of Sitomer, Sitomer & Porges. Stuart Charles Goldberg was an attorney in the firm and had done some work on the issue.

Plaintiff Meyerhofer, on or about January 11, 1973, purchased 100 shares of Empire stock at $17 a share. He alleges that as of June 5, 1973, the market price of his stock was only $7 a share—hence, he has sustained an unrealized loss of $1,000. Am'd Compl. P9a. Plaintiff Federman, on or about May 31, 1972, purchased 200 shares at $16 a share, 100 of which he sold for $1,363, sustaining a loss of some $237 on the stock sold and an unrealized loss of $900 on the stock retained.

On May 2, 1973, plaintiffs, represented by the firm of Bernson, Hoeniger, Freitag & Abbey (the Bernson firm), on behalf of themselves and all other purchasers of Empire common stock, brought this action alleging that the registration statement and the prospectus under which the Empire stock had been issued were materially false and misleading. Thereafter, an amended complaint, dated June 5, 1973, was served. The legal theories in both were identical, namely, violations of various sections of the Securities Act of 1933, the Securities Exchange Act of 1934, Rule 10b-5, and common law negligence, fraud and deceit. Damages for all members of the class or rescission were alternatively sought.

The lawsuit was apparently inspired by a Form 10-K which Empire filed with the SEC on or about April 12, 1973. This Form revealed that 'The Registration Statement under the Securities Act of 1933 with respect to the public offering of the 500,000 shares of Common Stock did not disclose the proposed $200,000 payment to the law firm as well as certain other features of the compensation arrangements between the Company (Empire) and such law firm (defendant Sitomer, Sitomer and Porges).' Later that month Empire disseminated to its shareholders a proxy statement and annual report making similar disclosures.

The defendants named were Empire, officers and directors of Empire, the Sitomer firm and its three partners, A. L. Sitomer, S. J. Sitomer and R. E. Porges, Faulkner, Dawkins & Sullivan Securities Corp., the managing underwriter, Stuart Charles Goldberg, originally alleged to have been a partner of the Sitomer firm, and certain selling stockholders of Empire shares.

On May 2, 1973, the complaint was served on the Sitomer defendants and Faulkner. No service was made on Goldberg who was then no longer associated with the Sitomer firm. However, he was advised by telephone that he had been made a defendant. Goldberg inquired of the Bernson firm as to the nature of the charges against him and was informed generally as to the substance of the complaint and in particular the lack of disclosure of the finder's fee arrangement. Thus informed, Goldberg requested an opportunity to prove his non-involvement in any such arrangement and his lack of knowledge thereof. At this stage there was unfolded the series of events which ultimately resulted in the motion and order thereon now before us on appeal.

Goldberg, after his graduation from Law School in 1966, had rather specialized experience in the securities field and had published various books and treatises on related subjects. He became associated with the Sitomer firm in November 1971. While there Goldberg worked on phases of various registration statements including Empire, although another associate was responsible for the Empire registration statement and prospectus. However, Goldberg expressed concern over what he regarded as excessive fees, the nondisclosure or inadequate disclosure thereof, and the extent to which they might include a 'finder's fee,' both as to Empire and other issues.

The Empire registration became effective on May 31, 1972. The excessive fee question had not been put to rest in Goldberg's mind because in middle January 1973 it arose in connection with another registration (referred to as 'Glacier'). Goldberg had worked on Glacier. Little purpose will be served by detailing the events during the critical period January 18 to 22, 1973, in which Goldberg and the Sitomer partners were debating the fee disclosure problem. In summary Goldberg insisted on a full and complete disclosure of fees in the Empire and Glacier offerings. The Sitomer partners apparently disagreed and Goldberg resigned from the firm on January 22, 1973. ↩

On January 22, 1973, Goldberg appeared before the SEC and placed before it information subsequently embodied in his affidavit dated January 26, 1973, which becomes crucial to the issues now to be considered.

Some three months later, upon being informed that he was to be included as a defendant in the impending action, Goldberg asked the Bernson firm for an opportunity to demonstrate that he had been unaware of the finder's fee arrangement which, he said, Empire and the Sitomer firm had concealed from him all along. Goldberg met with members of the Bernson firm on at least two occasions. After consulting his own attorney, as well as William P. Sullivan, Special Counsel with the Securities and Exchange Commission, Division, of Enforcement, Goldberg gave plaintiffs' counsel a copy of the January 26th affidavit which he had authored more than three months earlier. He hoped that it would verify his nonparticipation in the finder's fee omission and convince the Bernson firm that he should not be a defendant. The Bernson firm was satisfied with Goldberg's explanations and, upon their motion, granted by the court, he was dropped as a defendant. After receiving Goldberg's affidavit, the Bernson firm amended plaintiffs' complaint. The amendments added more specific facts but did not change the theory or substance of the original complaint.

By motion dated June 7, 1973, the remaining defendants moved 'pursuant to Canons 4 and 9 of the Code of Professional Responsibility, the Disciplinary Rules and Ethical Considerations applicable thereto, and the supervisory power of this Court' for the order of disqualification now on appeal.

By memorandum decision and order, the District Court ordered that the Bernson firm and Goldberg be barred from acting as counsel or participating with counsel for plaintiffs in this or any future action against Empire involving the transactions placed in issue in this lawsuit and from disclosing confidential information to others.

The complaint was dismissed without prejudice. The basis for the Court's decision is the premise that Goldberg had obtained confidential information from his client Empire which, in breach of relevant ethical canons, he revealed to plaintiffs' attorneys in their suit against Empire. The Court said its decision was compelled by 'the broader obligations of Canons 4 and 9.'[1]

---

1. Code of Professional Responsibility
Canon 4
A lawyer Should Preserve the Confidence and Secrets of a Client Ethical Considerations
EC 4-1 Both the fiduciary relationship existing between lawyer and client and the proper functioning of the legal system require the preservation by the lawyer of confidences and secrets of one who has employed or sought to employ him.
EC 4-4 The attorney-client privilege is more limited than the ethical obligation of a lawyer to guard

There is no proof—not even a suggestion—that Goldberg had revealed any information, confidential or otherwise, that might have caused the instigation of the suit. To the contrary, it was not until after the suit was commenced that Goldberg learned that he was in jeopardy. The District Court recognized that the complaint had been based on Empire's—not Goldberg's—disclosures, but concluded because of this that Goldberg was under no further obligation 'to reveal the information or to discuss the matter with plaintiffs' counsel.'

Despite the breadth of paragraphs EC 4-4 and DR 4-101(B), DR 4-101(C) recognizes that a lawyer may reveal confidences or secrets necessary to defend himself against 'an accusation of wrongful conduct.' This is exactly what Goldberg had to face when, in their original complaint, plaintiffs named him as a defendant who wilfully violated the securities laws.

The charge, of knowing participation in the filing of a false and misleading registration statement, was a serious one. The complaint alleged violation of criminal statutes and civil liability computable at over four million dollars. The cost in money of simply defending such an action might be very substantial. The damage to his professional reputation which might be occasioned by the mere pendency of such a charge was an even greater cause for concern.

---

the confidences and secrets of his client. The ethical precept, unlike the evidentiary privilege, exists without regard to the nature or source of information or the fact that others share the knowledge. A lawyer should endeavor to act in a manner which preserves the evidentiary privilege....

EC 4-5 A lawyer should not use information acquired in the course of the representation of a client to the disadvantage of the client and a lawyer should not use, except with the consent of his client after full disclosure, such information for his own purposes....

EC 4-6 The obligation of a lawyer to preserve the confidences and secrets of his client continues after the termination of his employment.... Disciplinary Rules

DR 4-101 Preservation of Confidences and Secrets of a Client.

(A) 'Confidence' refers to information protected by the attorney-client privilege under applicable law, and 'secret' refers to other information gained in the professional relationship that the client has requested be held inviolate or the disclosure of which would be embarrassing or would be likely to be detrimental to the client.

(B) Except when permitted under DR 4-101(C), a lawyer shall not knowingly:

(1) Reveal a confidence or secret of his client.

(2) Use a confidence or secret of his client to the disadvantage of the client.

(3) Use a confidence or secret of his client for the advantage of himself or of a third person, unless the client consents after full disclosure.

(C) A lawyer may reveal:

(4) Confidences or secrets necessary to establish or collect his fee or to defend himself or his employees or associates against an accusation of wrongful conduct.

Canon 9

A Lawyer Should Avoid Even the Appearance of Professional Impropriety Ethical Considerations

EC 9-1 Continuation of the American concept that we are to be governed by rules of law requires that the people have faith that justice can be obtained through our legal system. A lawyer should promote public confidence in our system and in the legal profession.

EC 9-6 Every lawyer owes a solemn duty to uphold the integrity and honor of his profession: to encourage respect for the law and for the courts and the judges thereof; to observe the Code of Professional Responsibility; to act as a member of a learned profession, one dedicated to public service; to cooperate with his brother lawyers in supporting the organized bar through the devoting of his time, efforts, and financial support as his professional standing and ability reasonably permit; to conduct himself so as to reflect credit on the legal profession and to inspire the confidence, respect, and trust of his clients and of the public; and to strive to avoid not only professional impropriety but also the appearance of impropriety.

Under these circumstances Goldberg had the right to make an appropriate disclosure with respect to his role in the public offering. Concomitantly, he had the right to support his version of the facts with suitable evidence.

The problem arises from the fact that the method Goldberg used to accomplish this was to deliver to Mr. Abbey, a member of the Bernson firm, the thirty page affidavit, accompanied by sixteen exhibits, which he had submitted to the SEC. This document not only went into extensive detail concerning Goldberg's efforts to cause the Sitomer firm to rectify the nondisclosure with respect to Empire but even more extensive detail concerning how these efforts had been precipitated by counsel for the underwriters having come upon evidence showing that a similar nondisclosure was contemplated with respect to Glacier and their insistence that full corrective measures should be taken. Although Goldberg's description reflected seriously on his employer, the Sitomer firm and, also, in at least some degree, on Glacier, he was clearly in a situation of some urgency. Moreover, before he turned over the affidavit, he consulted both his own attorney and a distinguished practitioner of securities law, and he and Abbey made a joint telephone call to Mr. Sullivan of the SEC. Moreover, it is not clear that, in the context of this case, Canon 4 applies to anything except information gained from Empire. Finally, because of Goldberg's apparent intimacy with the offering, the most effective way for him to substantiate his story was for him to disclose the SEC affidavit. It was the fact that he had written such an affidavit at an earlier date which demonstrated that his story was not simply fabricated in response to plaintiffs' complaint.

The District Court held: 'All that need be shown ... is that during the attorney-client relationship Goldberg had access to his client's information relevant to the issues here.' See Emle Industries, Inc. v. Patentex, Inc., 478 F.2d 562 (2d Cir. 1973). However, the irrebutable presumption of Emle Industries has no application to the instant circumstances because Goldberg never sought to 'prosecute litigation,' either as a party, compare Richardson v. Hamilton International Corp., 62 F.R.D. 413 (E.D.Pa. 1974), or as counsel for a plaintiff party. Compare T.C. Theatre Corporation v. Warner Brothers Pictures, 113 F.Supp. 265 (S.D.N.Y.1953). At most the record discloses that Goldberg might be called as a witness for the plaintiffs but that role does not invest him with the intimacy with the prosecution of the litigation which must exist for the Emle presumption to attach.

In addition to finding that Goldberg had violated Canon 4, the District Court found that the relationship between Goldberg and the Bernson firm violated Canon 9 of the Code of Professional Responsibility which provides that:

EC 9-6 Every lawyer (must) strive to avoid not only professional impropriety but also the appearance of impropriety.

The District Court reasoned that even though there was no evidence of bad faith on the part of either Goldberg or the Bernson firm, a shallow reading of the facts might lead a casual observer to conclude that there was an aura of complicity about their relationship. However, this provision should not be read so broadly as to eviscerate the right of self-defense conferred by DR4-101(C)(4).

Nevertheless, Emle Industries, Inc. v. Patentex, Inc., supra, requires that a strict prophylactic rule be applied in these cases to ensure that a lawyer avoids representation of a party in a suit against a former client where there may be the appearance of a possible violation of confidence. To the extent that the District Court's order prohibits Goldberg from representing the interests of these or any other plaintiffs in this or similar actions, we affirm that order. We also affirm so much of the District Court's order as enjoins Goldberg from disclosing material information except on discovery or at trial.

The burden of the District Court's order did not fall most harshly on Goldberg; rather its greatest impact has been felt by Bernson, Hoeniger, Freitag & Abbey, plaintiffs' counsel, which was disqualified from participation in the case. The District Court based its holding, not on the fact that the Bernson firm showed bad faith when it received Goldberg's affidavit, but rather on the fact that it was involved in a tainted association with Goldberg because his disclosures to them inadvertently violated Canons 4 and 9 of the Code of Professional Responsibility. Because there are no violations of either of these Canons in this case, we can find no basis to hold that the relationship between Goldberg and the Bernson firm was tainted. The District Court was apparently unpersuaded by appellees' salvo of innuendo to the effect that Goldberg 'struck a deal' with the Bernson firm or tried to do more than prove his innocence to them. Since its relationship with Goldberg was not tainted by violations of the Code of Professional Responsibility, there appears to be no warrant for its disqualification from participation in either this or similar actions. A fortiori there was no sound basis for disqualifying plaintiffs or dismissing the complaint.

Order dismissing action without prejudice and enjoining Bernson, Hoeniger, Freitag & Abbey from acting as counsel for plaintiffs herein reversed. Upon cross-appeal by Empire, Gross, Kaplan, Phillips, Kratky, Lalich, Swick and Jennings, Jr., and cross-appeal by Sitomer, Sitomer and Porges, A. L. Sitomer, S. J. Sitomer and R. E. Porges insofar as said orders failed to enjoin plaintiffs from disclosing confidential information regarding Empire and to disqualify plaintiffs from representing themselves or a similar class of Empire stockholders, appeals dismissed. To the extent that the orders appealed from prohibit Goldberg from acting as a party or as an attorney for a party in any action arising out of the facts herein alleged, or from disclosing material information except on discovery or at trial, they are affirmed.

Ethical Dilemma: Should Lawyers Turn In Clients?

Bryce Nelson, *The Los Angeles Times*
July 2, 1974

Are there limits to a lawyer's pledge to keep strictly confidential information given to him by his client? For instance, should the lawyer notify authorities if his client says that he plans to dynamite a building or shoot someone?

Or does a lawyer have an obligation to report the existence of the undiscovered bodies of his client's victims to authorities — or to the anxious parents of the missing persons?

The issue of client-attorney confidentiality received wide attention in recent days after it was disclosed that two Syracuse, N.Y., lawyers, Frank Armani and Francis Belge, had known for six months the location of the bodies of two young women who had been killed but felt legally obligated to keep silent — because they got the information from their client.

Although many legal authorities say Armani and Belge acted properly in keeping their client's information secret, the two court-appointed lawyers have found themselves battered by protests and investigations that could lead to disbarment or criminal prosecution.

"Very rarely are lawyers put to these kinds of tests," Armani commented in an interview.

The case brings into sharp focus the ethical quandary of lawyers trying to protect the confidences of a client—a problems that faces doctors, psychiatrists, accountants, ministers, social workers and journalists also.

According to legal experts, the case promises to become one of the most studied examples of confidentiality privilege.

"Any lawyer with any guts who knew what he was doing would have done the same thing," Armani said, "but the law profession is composed of many different lawyers."

Confidentiality is a privilege more easily defended in the tranquility of a law school than in the outside world.

"Citizens are in an absolute rage here," said John K. Holcombe, prosecutor of Onondaga County (Syracuse). Syracuse Police Chief Thomas J. Sardino has asked Holcombe to report on whether the lawyers should be prosecuted. Holcombe said he would announce his decision today.

William Hauck, father of one of the murdered girls, has filed a complaint against the lawyers with the Onondaga County Bar Assn., which had referred it to the appellate division of the State Supreme Court, which has, in turn, asked for an investigation by the State Bar Assn.

The two lawyers may well be in a fight for their professional lives, and not all their fellow lawyers support the stand they have taken.

"It's outrageous," said leading Minneapolis attorney, "They should both be put in jail. You have to report a crime if you know about it."

But the Syracuse lawyers have their supporters, too.

"The only way this New York case is different," said George P. Lynch, a leading Chicago criminal lawyer, "is that the evidence is composed of human bodies. I recognize the unappealing position the lawyers were in, but the lawyer is duty-bound to remain silent about information from his client. If you reveal such information, you should be disbarred."

The client who put Armani and Belge on the spot is Robert Garrow, a 38-year-old Syracuse mechanic who has admitted that he killed four persons in upstate New York last summer.

Garrow was arrested Aug. 9 and indicted on charges of murdering 18-year-old Philip Domblewski. The court appointed Belge and Armani as Garrow's attorneys. In his conversations with the lawyers, Garrow told of the other murders he had committed.

One was that of Alicia Hauck, 16, a Syracuse high school student who had disappeared in July; the lawyers later found her body in a Syracuse cemetery. The other murders were those of Daniel Porter, a 22-year-old Harvard student, whose body had been found on July 20; and of Susan Petz, 21, of Skokie, Ill., a Boston University journalism student who had been Porter's camping companion in the Adirondack Mountains.

Following Garrow's directions, the two lawyers found and photographed the bodies of Miss Petz and Miss Hauck—but they said nothing to authorities.

Miss Hauck's family thought she might have run away from home. The Petz family—knowing that their daughter's companion had been killed—feared the worst.

With the knowledge that the two Syracuse lawyers represented a client charged with a killing in the Adirondacks, Earl Petz, Susan's father, went to Syracuse to talk to Belge. The lawyer has since said he felt obligated not to tell Petz anything—and didn't—adding that his silence caused him "many, many sleepless nights."

The bodies of both girls were found accidentally last winter by students.

When Garrow testified at his trial about the other three killings he said he committed, the lawyers felt they had been released from their obligation of secrecy and disclosed they had known the locations of the bodies.

Garrow was convicted of Domblewski's murder Thursday. He was sentenced Monday to the maximum penalty of 25 years to life.

Roberta Petz, mother of Susan, angrily asked for the prosecution of the two attorneys.

She said, as have several lawyers, that she could not understand why the attorneys could not have given the information to the police anonymously, so that the parents could have been spared their troubled and seemingly interminable wait for information on their daughters.

One answer, say legal scholars, is that even an anonymous disclosure, if given without the client's permission, would be a breach of lawyer-client confidentiality. In addition, evidence obtained from or near the bodies, such as fingernail scrapings or footprints, might incriminate the client.

Armani and Belge understand from personal experience the anxieties caused by a death in the family. Belge suffered the death of a 12-year-old son. And Armani's brother was lost during an Air Force reconnaissance mission over the North Sea. The body was never recovered.

"We feel for these parents," Armani said. "I know what torment my mother went through in never having my brother's body returned. We know what hell these parents were going through.

"We both have daughters the same age as the girls who were killed … We just couldn't figure any other way to do it.

"You have your duty to your state, to your law and order, but my primary duty is to my client—so long as I don't jeopardize anybody's life or property. If the girl had been alive, then we would have had the duty to save her life, because life is primary. A body is a sacred thing but I couldn't give it life, and I figured somebody is going to find it."

After their client had told them about the killing last summer, it took a while for the two attorneys to find the abandoned mineshaft in which Susan Petz's body had been left.

The bodies of Miss Petz and of Miss Hauck, which was left in the woods of the Syracuse cemetery, were found months after they had been located by the lawyers but well before Garrow's disclosures in court.

One aspect of the case that has raised questions is the lawyers' attempt to plea bargain with the Hamilton County district attorney and police investigators of four other upstate New York counties.

In September, after the two lawyers had found Miss Petz's body, they offered to help the district attorney and the police solve the Petz and Hauck murders if their client, Garrow, was placed in a mental institution. The district attorney rejected their offer and went ahead with the prosecution of Garrow for the murder of Domblewski.

Bernard B. Meltzer, a University of Chicago law professor, thinks this plea bargaining raises "very serious questions." An attempt, he said, "to exploit the desire of investigating officers to solve the crimes by making a deal makes their motives seem less worthy than they otherwise would be."

Several leading prosecutors interviewed, however, said that the New York lawyers had acted properly both in their refusal to divulge information about the bodies and in their attempt to bargain with the prosecutor.

"I'm in complete agreement with these lawyers," said Samuel Skinner, head of the criminal division of the U.S. attorney's office in Chicago. "They operated in accordance with the highest traditions of the legal profession at a time when the profession is in great trouble."

Confidentiality between client and lawyer is a privilege established in legal history, written in the code of professional responsibility for the American Bar Assn. and adopted as law in 48 of the 50 states.

The oath of admission to the bar—proposed by the ABA and adopted in many states—requires lawyers to "solemnly swear" that "I will maintain the confidence and preserve inviolate the secrets of my client." Violation of the oath can lead to disbarment.

But the lawyer-client confidentiality relationship is not clear-cut, and judges and officials investigating bodies sometimes have a different view from that of a defense lawyer. A Chicago judge recently held a lawyer in contempt for continued refusal to divulge a fact about his relationship with his client.

Some lawyers say that they are under increasing pressure from agencies such as the Internal Revenue Service, the Securities and Exchange Commission, the FBI and police departments to divulge confidences.

From his study of decisions in the federal courts, Warren D. Wolfson, a leading Chicago defense attorney, has concluded that lawyers have not been able to withstand IRS efforts to obtain records.

Wolfson advises his clients to keep their own records so that they can retain their Fifth Amendment privilege against self-incrimination when asked to produce documents.

"I could not function as a lawyer without this (confidentiality) privilege," Wolfson said. "Very simply, it's based on the supposition that the government must prove that the defendant is guilty.

"If you're a man with a problem, you want to know that you can speak to your lawyer honestly with the knowledge that what you say will not be repeated without your approval. If you don't have that assurance, you won't be open with your lawyer and he can't give you the proper legal advice."

Lawyers point out that if the privilege did not exist, they would be put in the "impossible" situation of being continually subpoenaed to testify against their own clients.

Among the exceptions to the confidentiality rule in the ABA code are that the lawyer "may reveal" confidences with the consent of the client and that he also "may reveal the intention of his client to commit a crime and the information necessary to prevent that crime."

"If a client tells you that he has planted a bomb in an office building to go off in four days, I think the canons of ethics require disclosure," said federal prosecutor Skinner.

"The people who drew up the code didn't expect lives to be lost because of the confidentiality privilege."

When asked about their legally protected confidentiality privilege with clients, lawyers point out that no citizen is legally required to report crimes and that it would be especially harmful to ask lawyers to divulge such information given to them by their clients.

A comment by Wolfson is representative of such opinions: "If lawyers become stool pigeons and informers, our system of justice is down the drain."

People v. Belge
50 A.D. 2d 1088
Supreme Court, Appellate Division, Fourth Department, New York
December 17, 1975

From order of the Onondaga County Court, Ormand N. Gale, J., dismissing indictment charging defendant with violating and interfering with rights of burial and failure to give notice of death without medical attendance. People appealed. The Supreme Court, Appellate Division, held that attorney-client privilege attached insofar as the communications were to advance a client's interests.

Order affirmed.

Before MOULE, J.P., and CARDAMONE, SIMONS, MAHONEY and DEL VECCHIO, JJ.

MEMORANDUM:

We affirm the order of the trial court which properly dismissed the indictments laid against defendant for alleged violations of section 4200 (duty of a decent burial) and section 4143 (requirement to report death occurring without medical attendance) of the Public Health Law. We believe that the attorney-client privilege attached insofar as the communications were to advance a client's interests, and that the privilege effectively shielded the defendant attorney from his actions which would otherwise have violated the Public Health Law.

In view of the fact that the claim of absolute privilege was proffered, we note that the privilege is not all-encompassing and that in a given case there may be conflicting considerations. We believe that an attorney must protect his client's interests, but also must observe basic human standards of decency, having due regard to the need that the legal system accord justice to the interests of society and its individual members.

We write to emphasize our serious concern regarding the consequences which emanate from a claim of an absolute attorney-client privilege. Because the only question presented, briefed and argued on this appeal was a legal one with respect to the sufficiency of the indictments, we limit our determination to that issue and do not reach the ethical questions underlying this case.

Order affirmed.

All concur, except DEL VECCHIO, J., not participating.

McClure v. Thompson

323 F.3d 1233 (9th Cir. 2003)
United States Court of Appeals, Ninth Circuit
Argued and Submitted July 8, 2002
Filed April 2, 2003
[Some footnotes omitted. Remaining footnotes renumbered.]

Appeal from the United States District Court for the District of Oregon; Ann L. Aiken, District Judge, Presiding. D.C. No. CV-97-06182-ALA.

Before FERGUSON, W. FLETCHER, Circuit Judges, and KING,* District Judge.

Opinion by Judge WILLIAM A. FLETCHER; Dissent by Judge FERGUSON.

OPINION

WILLIAM W. FLETCHER, Circuit Judge: Oregon state prisoner Robert A. McClure appeals the district court's denial of his 28 U.S.C. § 2254 habeas corpus petition challenging his jury trial conviction for three aggravated murders. McClure's original defense attorney, Christopher Mecca, placed an anonymous telephone call to law enforcement officials directing them to the locations of what turned out to be the bodies of two children whom McClure was ultimately convicted of killing. The district court rejected McClure's arguments that the disclosure constituted ineffective assistance of counsel, holding there was no breach of the duty of confidentiality and no actual conflict of interest. We affirm.

I. Background
A. Offense, Arrest and Conviction

On Tuesday, April 24, 1984, the body of Carol Jones was found in her home in Grants Pass, Oregon. She had been struck numerous times on the head, arms and hands with a blunt object. A gun cabinet in the home had been forced open and a .44 caliber revolver was missing. Two of Jones' children—Michael, age 14, and Tanya, age 10—were also missing. The fingerprints of Robert McClure, a friend of Jones, were found in the blood in the home. On Saturday, April 28, McClure was arrested in connection with the death of Carol Jones and the disappearance of the children.

That same day, McClure's mother contacted attorney Christopher Mecca and asked him to represent her son. As discussed in more detail below, sometime in the next three days, under circumstances described differently by McClure and Mecca, McClure revealed to Mecca the separate remote locations where the children could be found. On Tuesday, May 1, Mecca, armed with a map produced during his conversations with McClure, arranged for his secretary to place an anonymous phone call to a sheriff's department telephone number belonging to a law enforcement officer with whom Mecca had met earlier.

Later that day and the following day, sheriff's deputies located the children's bodies, which were in locations more than 60 miles apart. The children had each died from a single gunshot wound to the head. Mecca then withdrew from representation. On May 3, McClure was indicted for the murders of Carol Jones and her children. At trial, the prosecution produced extensive evidence that stemmed from the discovery of the chil-

---

* The Honorable George H. King, United States District Judge for the Central District of California, sitting by designation.

dren's bodies and introduced testimony regarding the anonymous phone call. McClure was found guilty of all three murders and was sentenced to three consecutive life sentences with 30-year minimums. On direct appeal, his conviction was affirmed without opinion. *State v. McClure,* 80 Or.App. 461, 721 P.2d 482 (1986), *rev. denied,* 302 Or. 158, 727 P.2d 128 (1986).

* * *

III. Discussion

McClure's single claim is that habeas relief is appropriate because he received ineffective assistance of counsel under the Sixth Amendment. He asserts three independent grounds on which ineffectiveness could be found. The first two are based on alleged breaches of Mecca's professional duty to maintain client confidentiality. McClure argues that this duty was breached both by a failure to obtain informed consent prior to the disclosure of confidential information and by a failure to inquire thoroughly before concluding that disclosure was necessary to prevent the deaths of the children. The third ground is that the primacy of Mecca's concern for the victims constituted a conflict of interest that rendered Mecca's counsel constitutionally ineffective.

The overarching standard for a claim of ineffective assistance of counsel is set out in *Strickland v. Washington,* 466 U.S. 668, 104 S.Ct. 2052, 80 L.Ed.2d 674 (1984), in which the Supreme Court emphasized that a successful claim must establish both (1) deficient performance, such that "counsel was not functioning as the 'counsel' guaranteed the defendant by the Sixth Amendment," and (2) prejudice resulting from that deficiency. *Id.* at 687, 104 S.Ct. 2052. The Court in *Strickland* noted that the Sixth Amendment "relies on the legal profession's maintenance of standards sufficient to justify the law's presumption that counsel will fulfill the role in the adversary process that the Amendment envisions," and that "[t]he proper measure of attorney performance" is "reasonableness under prevailing professional norms." *Id.* at 688, 104 S.Ct. 2052. The Court specified a limited number of "basic duties" that are essential components of reasonable performance by criminal defense counsel, including "a duty of loyalty" and "a duty to avoid conflicts of interest," but held that this list was not exhaustive and that every case will involve an inquiry into "whether counsel's assistance was reasonable considering all the circumstances." *Id.* "Prevailing norms of practice as reflected in American Bar Association standards and the like ... are guides to determining what is reasonable, but they are only guides." *Id.; see also Nix v. Whiteside,* 475 U.S. 157, 165, 106 S.Ct. 988, 89 L.Ed.2d 123 (1986) ("Under the *Strickland* standard, breach of an ethical standard does not necessarily make out a denial of the Sixth Amendment guarantee of assistance of counsel.").

The Court has yet to "define with greater precision the weight to be given to recognized canons of ethics, the standards established by the state in statutes or professional codes, and the Sixth Amendment" in defining the proper scope of and limits on attorney conduct for *Strickland* purposes. *Whiteside,* 475 U.S. at 165, 106 S.Ct. 988. It has, however, suggested that when "virtually all of [those] sources speak with one voice" as to what constitutes reasonable attorney performance, departure from ethical canons and ABA guidelines "make[s] out a deprivation of the Sixth Amendment right to counsel." *Id.* at 166, 171, 106 S.Ct. 988.

We examine each of McClure's three assertions of deficient performance in turn.

A. The Duty of Confidentiality

McClure contends that Mecca's disclosure of McClure's confidential statements about the location of the children violated McClure's Sixth Amendment right to effective assistance of counsel. ABA Model Rule of Professional Conduct 1.6 sets forth a widely recognized duty of confidentiality: "A lawyer shall not reveal information relating to representation of a client[.]" Our legal system is premised on the strict adherence to this principle of confidentiality, and "[t]he Supreme Court has long held attorneys to stringent standards of loyalty and fairness with respect to their clients." *Damron v. Herzog*, 67 F.3d 211, 214 (9th Cir.1995). There are few professional relationships "involving a higher trust and confidence than that of attorney and client," and "few more anxiously guarded by the law, or governed by sterner principles of morality and justice." *Id.* (quoting *Stockton v. Ford*, 52 U.S. (11 How.) 232, 13 L.Ed. 676 (1850)).

As critical as this confidential relationship is to our system of justice, the duty to refrain from disclosing information relating to the representation of a client is not absolute. The ABA Model Rule provides a list of well-established exceptions to the general principle of confidentiality, two of which are pertinent to the present case. First, a lawyer may reveal confidential information if "the client consents after consultation." Second, "[a] lawyer may reveal such information to the extent the lawyer reasonably believes necessary to prevent the client from committing a criminal act that the lawyer believes is likely to result in imminent death or substantial bodily harm[.]" ABA Model Rule of Professional Conduct 1.6(b)(1) (1983). The relevant provisions of the Oregon Code of Professional Responsibility echo both the general principle of confidentiality and these particular exceptions. *See* Oregon Code of Prof. Resp. D.R. 4-101.[1]

The parties, apparently agreeing that these consistently recognized ethical standards provide important guidance as to whether Mecca's counsel was deficient under the first prong of *Strickland*, focus much of their dispute on the reasonableness of Mecca's actions in light of these exceptions to the general principle of confidentiality. We agree that this approach is proper. The duty of an attorney to keep his or her client's confidences in all but a handful of carefully defined circumstances is so deeply ingrained in our legal system and so uniformly acknowledged as a critical component of reasonable representation by counsel that departure from this rule "make[s] out a deprivation of the Sixth Amendment right to counsel." *Whiteside*, 475 U.S. at 171, 106 S.Ct. 988. With this uncontested premise as our starting point, we examine whether the circumstances surrounding Mecca's revelation of a confidential client communication excused his disclosure, such that his performance could have been found by the state court and the district court to be constitutionally adequate. Specifically, we look to see if Mecca's client "consent[ed] after consultation" or if Mecca "reasonably believe[d] [the revelation was] necessary to prevent the client from committing a criminal act that [Mecca] believe[d][was] likely to result in imminent death or substantial bodily harm[.]" We conclude that the first of these exceptions does not apply to justify Mecca's behavior, but that the second does.

1. Consent After Consultation

McClure argues that Mecca rendered constitutionally ineffective assistance because he breached his duty of confidentiality by not obtaining McClure's informed consent

---

1. A lawyer may reveal:

(1) Confidences or secrets with the consent of the client or clients affected, but only after full disclosure to the client or clients.

* * *

(3) The intention of the lawyer's client to commit a crime and the information necessary to prevent the crime.

Oregon Code Prof. Resp. D.R. 4-101.

before disclosure. The professional standard that allows disclosure of confidential communications when "the client consents after consultation" has two distinct parts: consent by the client, and consultation by the counsel. Our required deference to both the state court's factual findings and the district court's credibility determination leads us to hold that the first of these elements was met. However, despite this deference, we hold that the second element was not met.

a. Consent

The state court made the following finding: "Trial counsel received petitioner's permission to anonymously disclose the whereabouts of the children to the authorities." AEDPA demands that this finding of consent be presumed correct and accepted as true unless McClure rebuts the presumption with clear and convincing evidence to the contrary. 28 U.S.C. § 2254(e)(1). The district court, whose credibility determinations are given great weight, and whose findings of fact are reviewed only for clear error, explicitly accepted that finding, and stated that it did "not find credible petitioner's assertion that he did not consent to the disclosure of the information contained in the map." It found that McClure "voluntarily drew the map and gave it to Mecca," and that, even in the absence of the words "I consent," Mecca could infer consent from the circumstances and from McClure's conduct. It stated that it found Mecca's testimony "entirely credible and corroborated by his contemporaneous notes which state specifically that petitioner consented to the disclosure."

There is evidence in the record to cast doubt on these consent findings—indeed, enough evidence that if we were sitting as trier of fact, we might find that McClure did not give consent. McClure repeatedly denied that he consented, and certainly would have had good reason not to consent. The state court determination that McClure had consented was made before Mecca clarified that the consent was implied and not express. Moreover, it was based on Mecca's unconditional affirmative response, in his state-court deposition, to the question of whether permission to reveal the information was granted. Only later, in the federal habeas proceeding, did it come to light that Mecca had merely inferred McClure's consent.

Further, Mecca's account of the circumstances from which he inferred McClure's consent changed over the years. His initial account stated that he inferred consent from the fact that McClure called him at home, drew the map, and gave it to him. It is a significant leap to infer McClure's consent to disclose the map to law enforcement authorities from the fact that McClure gave the map to Mecca. Virtually all clients provide information to their attorneys, but they do so assuming that the attorneys will not breach their duty of confidentiality. Further, Mecca's behavior at the time of the disclosure suggested that he thought he lacked the kind of informed consent that would give him the legal authority to act.

However, the findings reached by the state and district courts are not so "[im]plausible"—particularly in light of the district court's credibility determinations—that they produce a "definite and firm conviction that a mistake has been committed." *Easley,* 532 U.S. at 242, 121 S.Ct. 1452; *Doe,* 155 F.3d at 1074; *Phoenix Eng'g & Supply Inc.,* 104 F.3d at 1141. The district court believed Mecca's account at the evidentiary hearing, disbelieved McClure's, and found the discrepancies in Mecca's testimony to be "minor." Because there are "two permissible views of the evidence, the factfinder's choice between them cannot be clearly erroneous." *Working,* 224 F.3d at 1102. We therefore hold that McClure gave his consent to the disclosure.

b. Consultation

However, the mere fact of consent is not sufficient to excuse what would otherwise be a breach of the duty of confidentiality. Consent must also be informed. That is, the client can provide valid consent only if there has been appropriate "consultation" with his or her attorney. Mecca's consultation with McClure regarding his consent to disclosure was addressed in the state court and district court findings. Both courts found that Mecca did not advise McClure about the potential harmful consequences of disclosure. The state court found that "[b]efore petitioner authorized trial counsel to reveal the childrens' [sic] locations to authorities, trial counsel did not advise petitioner that if authorities located the children, he could be further implicated in the criminal activity and the evidence against him would be stronger." The district court found that "Mecca admits that he did not ... advise petitioner [of all potential adverse consequences]."

Emphasizing that McClure was "fully engaged" in his defense and that he was told that the obligation to disclose the children's location arose only if the children were alive, the district court held that "[u]nder the circumstances, Mecca's failure to advise petitioner of all possible adverse consequences was not unreasonable." We believe this holding is inconsistent with the consultation requirement because it does not attach sufficient importance to the role that an attorney's advice plays in the attorney-client relationship. It is not enough, as the district court suggests, that McClure "did not dissuade Mecca from his intentions" to share the map with authorities. The onus is not on the client to perceive the legal risks himself and then to dissuade his attorney from a particular course of action. The district court's statement that Mecca was relieved of his duty to counsel his client because "common sense dictate[d] that petitioner understood the consequences of his actions" fails to acknowledge the seriousness of those consequences and the importance of good counsel regarding them. See Strickland, 466 U.S. at 688, 104 S.Ct. 2052. Even in cases in which the negative ramifications seem obvious — for example, when criminal defendants opt for self-representation — we require that a criminal defendant's decision be made on the basis of legal guidance and with full cautionary explanation. See, e.g., Faretta v. California, 422 U.S. 806, 835, 95 S.Ct. 2525, 45 L.Ed.2d 562 (1975). We disagree with the district court's conclusion that this case was so exceptional that the attorney's basic consultation duties did not apply. It is precisely because the stakes were so high that Mecca had an obligation to consult carefully with his client. In the absence of some other exception to the duty of confidentiality, his failure to obtain informed consent would demonstrate constitutionally deficient performance under the Sixth Amendment.

2. Prevention of Further Criminal Acts

The State contends that, even if Mecca did not have informed consent, his revelation of client confidences did not amount to ineffective assistance of counsel because he reasonably believed that disclosing the location of the children was necessary in order to prevent further criminal acts. That is, Mecca reasonably believed that revealing the children's locations could have prevented the escalation of kidnapping to murder. This is not a traditional "prevention of further criminal acts" case, because all of the affirmative criminal acts performed by McClure had been completed at the time Mecca made his disclosure. Mecca was thus acting to prevent an earlier criminal act from being transformed by the passage of time into a more serious criminal offense. Nonetheless, we believe that where an attorney's or a client's omission to act could result in "imminent death or substantial bodily harm" constituting a separate and more severe crime from the one already committed, the exception to the duty of confidentiality may be triggered. ABA Model Rule 1.6(b)(1).

This exception, however, requires that an attorney reveal confidences only to the extent that he "reasonably believes necessary to prevent" those criminal acts and imminent harms. *Id.* In assessing the effectiveness of McClure's counsel in light of this standard, the first step is to determine what a constitutionally effective counsel should be required to do before making a disclosure. That is, we must determine what basis the attorney had for believing that the precondition to disclosure was present, and how much investigation he or she must have undertaken before it was "reasonabl[e]" to "believ[e][it] necessary" to make the disclosure to prevent the harm. The second step is to apply that standard to the facts surrounding Mecca's decision to disclose.

There is remarkably little case law addressing the first analytical step. Citing cases dealing with a separate confidentiality exception allowing attorneys to reveal intended perjury on the part of their clients, McClure argues that a lawyer must have a "firm factual basis" before adopting a belief of impending criminal conduct. *See, e.g., United States v. Omene,* 143 F.3d 1167, 1171 (9th Cir.1998); *United States v. Scott,* 909 F.2d 488, 493–94 & n. 10 (11th Cir.1990); *United States v. Long,* 857 F.2d 436, 444–45 (8th Cir. 1988). However, we are not persuaded that the perjury cases provide the proper standard.

McClure is correct that our inquiry must acknowledge the importance of the confidential attorney-client relationship and the gravity of the harm that results from an unwarranted breach of that duty. However, the standard applied in the professional responsibility code asks only if the attorney "*reasonably* believes" disclosure is necessary to prevent the crime. ABA Model Rule 1.6(b)(1) (emphasis added). Further, the *Strickland* standard likewise focuses on "whether counsel's assistance was *reasonable* considering all the circumstances." 466 U.S. at 688, 104 S.Ct. 2052 (emphasis added). Accordingly, we hold that the guiding rule for purposes of the exception for preventing criminal acts is objective reasonableness in light of the surrounding circumstances.

Reasonableness of belief may be strongly connected to adequacy of investigation or sufficiency of inquiry in the face of uncertainty. Significantly, as indicated above, *Strickland* explicitly imposes a duty on counsel "to make reasonable investigations or to make a reasonable decision that makes particular investigations unnecessary." 466 U.S. at 691, 104 S.Ct. 2052. In any ineffectiveness of counsel case, "a particular decision not to investigate must be directly assessed for reasonableness in all the circumstances, applying a heavy measure of deference to counsel's judgments." *Id.* Thus, in determining whether Mecca's disclosure of confidential client information constituted ineffective assistance of counsel, we must examine whether Mecca "reasonably believed" that the precondition for disclosure existed and whether, in coming to that belief, Mecca conducted a reasonable investigation and inquiry.

The parties vigorously debate both the reasonableness of Mecca's belief that the children were alive and the reasonableness of his level of investigation and inquiry on that point. McClure argues that any conclusion that Mecca had a reasonable belief is unsupported because Mecca himself indicated that he harbored doubts as to the children's state, and yet failed to inquire further. He points to evidence in the record that Mecca, at least at some stages of his representation of McClure, did not believe the children were alive — or that he, at the least, suspected that they were dead. It is indisputable that this evidence exists, and that most of this evidence is contained in statements by Mecca himself, whom the district court found "highly credible." Mecca's notes state that, after Mc-

Clure drew the map, Mecca "felt in my own mind that the children were dead, but, of course, I wasn't sure." He testified in the district court evidentiary hearing that the conclusion he came to was that, "without telling me, [McClure had] told me he had killed three people." And he stated in this same testimony that, at the time he had his secretary place the anonymous call, he thought there was a "possibility," but not a "strong possibility," that the children were alive.

McClure argues that the statement Mecca says abruptly changed his mind about the status of the children — McClure's comment that "Jesus saved the kids" — was so vague and ambiguous that it was not a sufficient basis for a "reasonable belief" that disclosure was necessary. Despite Mecca's acknowledgment that this comment led him only to "assume" that McClure was saying the children were alive, Mecca never directly asked a question that could have confirmed or refuted that assumption. Mecca repeatedly testified that he never squarely asked about the condition of the children or whether McClure had killed them. Accordingly, McClure argues, any finding that Mecca believed the children were alive is not sufficient to establish effective assistance of counsel, because Mecca's failure to engage in a reasonable level of investigation and inquiry rendered that belief unreasonable.

Given the implicit factual findings of the state court, and the explicit factual findings of the district court, which are at least plausible in light of the record viewed in its entirety, *Phoenix Eng'g & Supply Inc.,* 104 F.3d at 1141, we disagree. The ultimate question of the reasonableness of Mecca's belief is a question of law, which we review de novo. In answering that question, however, we look to the facts and circumstances of the case, and as to these facts, we give great deference to the findings of the state court and the district court.

The district court made a number of specific findings regarding the factual basis for Mecca's belief that the children were alive. It found that only McClure knew the true facts and that he deliberately withheld them, leading Mecca to believe the children were alive. It found that McClure controlled the flow of information, and that when Mecca informed McClure that he had an obligation to disclose the children's whereabouts if there were a chance they were alive, McClure did not tell him they were dead. It specifically rejected McClure's assertion that Mecca in fact believed that the children were dead or that he lacked information that they were alive, noting that at the time there was no evidence, other than their disappearance and the passage of time, that they had been injured or killed.

The district court also made specific factual findings regarding the nature of Mecca's investigation and inquiry. It found that "Mecca attempted to discern whether the children were alive" and "that Mecca investigated to the best of his ability under extremely difficult circumstances." McClure argues that these findings are clearly erroneous, and that "arguments that Mr. McClure was manipulative and difficult are essentially irrelevant to the lawyer's obligations." But *Strickland* holds otherwise. The *Strickland* Court emphasized that "[t]he reasonableness of counsel's actions may be determined or substantially influenced by the defendant's own statements or actions." *Strickland,* 466 U.S. at 691, 104 S.Ct. 2052. More specifically, it held that "what investigation decisions are reasonable depends critically" on the "information supplied by the defendant." *Id.*

This is a close case, even after we give the required deference to the state and district courts. The choices made by McClure's counsel give us significant pause, and, were we deciding this case as an original matter, we might decide it differently. But we take as true the district court's specific factual findings as to what transpired — including what

McClure said and did, and what actions Mecca took and why he took them—and we conclude that Mecca made the disclosure "reasonably believ[ing] [it was] necessary to prevent the client from committing a criminal act that [Mecca] believe[d] [was] likely to result in imminent death or substantial bodily harm[.]" ABA Model Rule 1.6(b)(1). Mecca therefore did not violate the duty of confidentiality in a manner that rendered his assistance constitutionally ineffective.

B. Conflict of Interest

In addition to his claim that Mecca breached his duty of confidentiality, McClure claims that Mecca was not functioning as the "counsel" guaranteed by the Sixth Amendment because he suffered from a "fatal conflict of interest." McClure argues that Mecca was acting primarily out of concern for the welfare of possible victims rather than in his client's best interests. A conflict of interest constitutes a constructive denial of counsel altogether and is legally presumed to result in prejudice. *See Strickland,* 466 U.S. at 692, 104 S.Ct. 2052.

It is clear that Mecca's actions were at least partially driven by concern for the lives of the children. He forthrightly indicated as much under oath on more than one occasion. McClure suggests that Mecca's candid statements amount to "a direct admission of an actual conflict." But this is not necessarily so. *Strickland* recognizes both the "wide range of professionally competent assistance" and the need for great leeway for tactical determinations by counsel. 466 U.S. at 690, 104 S.Ct. 2052. Accepting the district court's factual findings as true, Mecca had some basis for believing that the children would be found alive if a prompt search were undertaken, and that this would be beneficial to McClure. Mecca also made an attempt to make a deal with the State in return for the information. His testimony, which the district court regarded as highly credible, repeatedly referred to his concern that McClure's kidnapping charges could become murder charges if the children were allowed to die. The district court specifically found that Mecca "believed the disclosure could have avoided two additional aggravated murder charges and was the best strategic decision for petitioner under the circumstances," and that Mecca "sought to avoid further harm to the children *and* his client's case." (Emphasis added.) Moreover, even if Mecca was acting to preserve the lives of the children rather than to protect the interests of his client, the ethical rule requiring an attorney to act to prevent a crime means that such an action, if based on a reasonable belief, is not inconsistent with the attorney's ethically prescribed duty of loyalty.

To prove an ineffectiveness claim premised on an alleged conflict of interest a petitioner must "establish that an actual conflict of interest adversely affected his lawyer's performance." *Cuyler v. Sullivan,* 446 U.S. 335, 350, 100 S.Ct. 1708, 64 L.Ed.2d 333 (1980). The client must demonstrate that his attorney made a choice between possible alternative courses of action that impermissibly favored an interest in competition with those of the client. Because McClure cannot identify specific evidence in the record that suggests that his interests were impermissibly impaired or compromised for the benefit of another party, he cannot demonstrate that his counsel "actively represented a conflicting interest." *Id.* at 350, 100 S.Ct. 1708. Without this factual showing of inconsistent interests, the conflict is merely possible or speculative. Under *Cuyler,* 446 U.S. at 350, 100 S.Ct. 1708, such a conflict is "insufficient to impugn a criminal conviction."

Conclusion

For the foregoing reasons, we conclude that McClure did not receive constitutionally ineffective assistance of counsel. Accordingly, the district court's denial of McClure's petition for writ of habeas corpus is
AFFIRMED.

FERGUSON, Circuit Judge, dissenting:

I respectfully dissent. The majority erred when it held that the disclosure of the location of two of McClure's victims' bodies by his defense attorney did not constitute deficient performance under *Strickland v. Washington,* 466 U.S. 668, 104 S.Ct. 2052, 80 L.Ed.2d 674 (1984). McClure's attorney, Christopher Mecca, breached one of the most sacred obligations of the attorney-client relationship, the duty of confidentiality, and in turn violated McClure's Sixth Amendment right to counsel. Based on an utterly unreasonable interpretation of the events surrounding the disclosure at issue in this case, the majority finds that Mecca met an exception to the duty of confidentiality. As a result, the majority holds that it was reasonable for Mecca to believe that two missing children were alive but dying, when he disclosed their location to authorities, without McClure's consent, without asking McClure directly whether he had killed them, and without conducting any investigation to find out.

* * *

I

The notion that lawyers are obligated to safeguard a client's secrets and confidences is well established. An attorney's duty of confidentiality emanates from the profession's ethical rules, the evidentiary attorney-client and work product privileges, and the Sixth Amendment.[2] One of the oldest and most sacrosanct duties of an attorney, the duty of confidentiality in the United States dates back to 1908 and the first incantation of the ethical rules for lawyers, the American Bar Association's Canons of Professional Ethics. Canon 6 provided that lawyers had an "obligation to represent the client with undivided fidelity and not to divulge his secrets or confidences." While the duty of confidentiality has evolved as our profession has evolved, the underlying principle remains steadfast: an attorney should not reveal his client's confidences without first obtaining their informed consent.

The duty to guard a client's confidences is, of course, not absolute, and the ethical rules recognize as much. Because an attorney's duty of confidentiality must be balanced against the public's interest in safety and justice, Model Rule 1.6 carves out two exceptions. Both exceptions allow an attorney to disclose a client's confidences "to the extent [he or she] reasonably believes necessary,"[3] either "to prevent the client from commit-

---

2. Other ethical rules relevant to the duty of confidentiality in this case are DR 4-101 of the Oregon Code of Professional Responsibility, entitled "Preservation of Confidences and Secrets of a Client," which reads in relevant part:
  (B) Except when permitted under DR 4-101(C), a lawyer shall not knowingly:
  (1) Reveal a confidence or secret of the lawyer's client.
  (2) Use a confidence or secret of the lawyer's client to the disadvantage of the client.
  (3) Use a confidence or secret of the lawyer's client for the advantage of the lawyer or of a third person, unless the client consents after full disclosure.
  (C) A lawyer may reveal:
  ...
  (3) The intention of the lawyer's client to commit a crime and the information necessary to prevent the crime.
In addition, Oregon Revised Statute § 9.460 entitled "Duties of Attorneys," states in relevant part:
  An attorney shall:
  ...
  (3) Maintain the confidences and secrets of the attorney's clients consistent with the rules of professional conduct established pursuant to ORS 9.490...."
3. ABA Model Rule 1.6(b).

ting a criminal act that the lawyer believes is likely to result in imminent death or substantial bodily harm," or "to establish a claim or defense on behalf of the lawyer" in particular controversies. The majority erroneously finds that the first exception applies in this case, thereby justifying Mecca's disclosure of the location of the bodies of two of McClure's victims, Michael and Tanya Jones.

The Supreme Court has made clear that an attorney's duty of confidentiality intersects with the Sixth Amendment right to counsel. "[The Sixth Amendment] obviously involves the right to keep the confidences of the client from the ear of the Government which these days seeks to learn more and more of the affairs of men." *Russo v. Byrne*, 409 U.S. 1219, 1221, 93 S.Ct. 21, 34 L.Ed.2d 30 (1972). As such, an attorney's unwarranted breach of the duty of confidentiality is not only an ethical violation, but also implicates the Sixth Amendment right to effective assistance of counsel.

II

Identifying the relevant rules and governing standard is merely the first part of the analysis. As the majority correctly notes, the next logical step is determining what constitutes an objectively reasonable belief under the first exception to Model Rule 1.6 and for purposes of *Strickland*. In a somewhat distinct but related context, Justice O'Connor has commented that the word unreasonable "is no doubt difficult to define. That said, it is a common term in the legal world and, accordingly, federal judges are familiar with its meaning." *Williams v. Taylor*, 529 U.S. 362, 410, 120 S.Ct. 1495, 146 L.Ed.2d 389 (2000) (interpreting AEDPA's requirement that a state court adjudication be "contrary to, or involve an unreasonable application of clearly established law."). Thus, the majority's failure to give meaning to the standard in this case is not excused by the inherent difficulty attached to the task.

As a general matter, Mecca's behavior should be judged against that of a "reasonable attorney."[4] In other words, what would a reasonable attorney in Mecca's position have done, if anything, with the information that McClure gave him? Framed in accordance with *Strickland* and Model Rule 1.6, was Mecca's belief that the children were alive reasonable and was disclosure reasonable under the circumstances?

* * *

Mecca purportedly believed the children were alive; however, his words and actions at the time of the disclosure indicate that his belief was pallid. Since Mecca testified in hindsight about his belief that the children were alive, the majority emphasizes the lower courts' credibility determination in favor of Mecca. Even accepting that veracity of Mecca's belief, examining the strength of that belief betrays the government's assertions that it was reasonable. It is true that Model Rule 1.6 does not indicate what is required beyond a "reasonable belief[,]" but surely an inkling alone cannot suffice to support a reasonable belief.

The majority omits a number of undisputed facts about the events leading up to Mecca's disclosure that show Mecca was not as certain about the children's vitality at the time of the disclosure as he is today. First, Mecca repeatedly used the word "bodies"

---

4. The Restatement (Second) of Torts provides that

   [u]nless he represents that he has greater or less skill or knowledge, one who undertakes to render services in the practice of a profession or trade is required to exercise the skill and knowledge normally possessed by members of that profession or trade in good standing in similar communities.

Restatement (Second) of Torts § 299A (1965).

when referring to the children in his notes taken shortly after the disclosure. For example, Mecca wrote: "'McClure related to me ... one place where a body might be' and then 'described [where] the other body would be located.'" Maj. Op. at 1236. Additionally, Mecca recorded the following after the prosecutor had refused to negotiate a plea for McClure: "'The only option I had, as far as I was concerned, was to disclose the whereabouts of the body [sic].'" *Id.* at 1237. Mecca also wrote, "'I arranged to have the information released anonymously to the Sheriff's Department with directions to the bodies.'" *Id.* at 1237. Although Mecca attempted to explain his choice of words by explaining that he made the notes after the bodies were located, this answer is unsatisfying.

Examining Mecca's mental state around the time of the disclosure is also illuminating. After his conversation with McClure on Monday, Mecca testified, "'[t]he conclusion I came to was that, without telling me, he told me he had killed three people.'" *Id.* at 1238. When discussing McClure's comment that "'Satan killed Carol, but Jesus saved the kids[,]'" Mecca stated that he "'kind of felt that[McClure] was talking about a sexual thing, but, in any event, [he] wasn't sure.'" *Id.* at 1237. In addition, Mecca stated the following regarding the Jesus/Satan comment: "'I allowed myself to believe that these kids might somehow be alive.'" *Id.* at 1239. Mecca's own words suggest the absurdity of this belief—he *allowed* himself to believe it because it was so incredulous. Finally, Mecca practically admitted that his belief was weak in discussing the possibility that the children were alive. He testified that he "'felt it was a possibility. I wouldn't say a strong possibility.'" *Id.*

Finally, Mecca attempted to negotiate a deal with the prosecution in exchange for the information about the children's bodies. If Mecca strongly believed the children were alive but dying, and his concern for their welfare was as great as he claims, why would he continue to jeopardize their lives by first trying to strike a deal for his client?

While it is true that the events leading up to Mecca's disclosure unfolded rapidly and were no doubt incredibly stressful, it is not unfair to expect a reasonable criminal defense attorney to be capable of competently dealing with these types of situations. It was not such a brief period of time[5] that Mecca's lack of investigation and rash disclosure can be justified. In short, Mecca had agreed to represent an individual who was accused of killing a woman whose children were missing. Over the course of a few days, McClure revealed himself to be a mentally disturbed individual who fantasized about sex with young girls and enlisted his attorney's help in destroying evidence related to the murders. Perhaps Mecca is correct that there was no way to be 100% certain at the time whether the children were alive or dead, and perhaps we should not question whether he truly personally believed that the children were alive. But as a criminal defense attorney, Mecca had a responsibility to inform himself, investigate, and support his belief by facts before taking the extreme step of disclosing McClure's confidential information to the police. When an attorney falls below this standard, courts should not be afraid to name the problem: deficient performance under the Sixth Amendment guarantee of effective assistance of counsel.

In the end, it is clear that not only did Mecca lack a "firm factual basis" for his belief that the children were alive, he had virtually no basis whatsoever, nor did he make a reasonable effort to gain one—at best, Mecca's "investigation" can be characterized as pal-

---

5. Mecca represented McClure for three days before he made the disclosure. During this period, they met seven times and spoke via telephone numerous times.

try. The danger of the majority's decision is that it risks making Mecca's conduct the standard for attorneys who may find themselves in a similar predicament in the future.

III

I too sympathize with Mecca for being concerned with the welfare of the children, as do the majority, the District Court and the state court. It would scarcely be wrong to criticize him for, as the District Court stated, being "a human being." However, because at the time of the disclosure Mecca was playing a critical and unique role as McClure's defense attorney, I cannot sanction his behavior. It seems that the time has come for Mecca to take responsibility for the choice he made to breach his client's confidence and for a court, *this court,* to recognize that whether or not Mecca did the "right" thing does not diminish the fact that his doing so constituted an abdication of his professional duties and rendered his performance as McClure's defense attorney deficient under the Sixth Amendment. Mecca's concern for the children is certainly understandable and laudable, however, it does not negate the infirmity of McClure's conviction. Therefore, I must dissent.

Rico v. Mitsubishi Motors Corp.

10 Cal. Rptr. 3d 601 (Cal. App. 4 Dist. 2004)
Court of Appeal, Fourth District, Division 2, California
Feb. 25, 2004
[Footnotes omitted]

OPINION

GAUT, J.

1. *Introduction*

In a sports utility vehicle (SUV) rollover case with serious injuries and death, counsel for plaintiffs obtained a document that provided a summary, in dialogue form, of a defense conference between attorneys and defense experts in which the participants discussed the strengths and weaknesses of the defendants' technical evidence. Despite the fact that the notes were clearly the confidential work product of defense counsel, plaintiffs' counsel made no effort to notify defense counsel of his possession of the document and instead examined, disseminated, and used the notes to impeach the testimony of defense experts during their deposition, all in contravention of the legal and ethical standards established in *State Comp. Ins. Fund v. WPS, Inc.*

Although the document did not implicate the attorney-client privilege, we uphold the court's finding that defense counsel's notes did constitute attorney work product. We also uphold the court's disqualification order because substantial evidence supported the court's finding that the dissemination and use of the document placed defendants at a significant disadvantage that could not have been removed by lesser sanctions. We affirm the court's order.

2. *Factual and Procedural History*

On March 15, 1999, plaintiffs Zerlene Rico, Estate of Denise Rico, Fernando Rico, and Silvia Rico, individually or through a guardian ad litem or administrator, filed a complaint for various causes of actions including negligence, strict liability, and breach of warranties, against Mitsubishi Motors Corporation, Mitsubishi Motor Sales of America, Inc. (collectively Mitsubishi or defendants), the California Department of Transportation (the Department), Lenette Rico-Abassi, and Michael Abassi. On June 16, 1999, plaintiffs Lenette Rico-Abassi and Michael Abassi filed a complaint with similar claims against Mitsubishi and the Department. By the parties' stipulation, the trial court consolidated the two cases. In their complaint, the plaintiffs alleged that, on June 21, 1998, Lenette Rico-Abassi drove a Mitsubishi Montero along Interstate 10 and, when Rico-Abassi maneuvered the vehicle, the vehicle overturned, resulting in both fatal and debilitating injuries to the other plaintiffs who were passengers in the vehicle.

On September 18, 2002, defendants filed a motion to disqualify plaintiffs' legal team and experts on the grounds that plaintiffs' attorney obtained and used confidential and privileged materials prepared by defense counsel.

Plaintiffs' attorney Raymond Johnson obtained the notes of one of the defense attorneys, James Yukevich, after a deposition with Yukevich and defense expert, Anthony Sances. While Johnson stated that a court reporter accidentally delivered the document to Johnson, Yukevich claimed that the document was taken from his files when Johnson temporarily commandeered the deposition room for a personal meeting.

The document, later identified as exhibit 52, has the following heading:

"August 28, 2002

"LEC

"10:30"

The 12-page document is written in the form of a dialogue between the defense attorneys, including Yukevich and Alexander Calfo, and the defense experts. All the participants are referred to by their initials only. The document also contains a few handwritten notes or comments.

Yukevich testified that, under his instructions, James Rowley, a case manager for Mitsubishi who had worked with Yukevich for three years, drafted the document during an August 28, 2002 legal engineering meeting (LEC). During the breaks and after the meeting, Yukevich edited the typewritten notes and later added his own handwritten comments. At some point before Sances's deposition, Yukevich printed one copy of these notes for his own personal use.

When Johnson received the document, he knew that Yukevich had unintentionally left it in the deposition room. Realizing that he had in his hand a "powerful impeachment document," Johnson made a copy for himself before returning the original to the court reporter. Johnson then made additional copies and sent them to plaintiffs' experts and the other attorneys.

On September 16, 2002, Johnson used the document for impeachment purposes during the deposition of defense expert Geoffrey Germane. During the deposition, Johnson showed Germane a copy of the document and proceeded to ask questions concerning the comments attributed to Germane (JG) in the document. Yukevich did not attend Germane's deposition, but cocounsel Calfo was present. Calfo did not know the source of the document or its significance. Although he did not object to the document as confidential or privileged, Calfo raised several objections on other grounds, including lack of foundation, hearsay, and inaccuracy. Johnson provided no explanation as to the source of the document, except to say that, "[i]t was put in Dr. Sances' file."

On the day after Germane's deposition, Yukevich, after discovering that Johnson had a copy of his personal notes, accused Johnson of reading and using a privileged document. Yukevich demanded all copies of the document and advised Johnson of his intent to request that the court disqualify Johnson, Anthony Sances, and any other experts who had seen the document.

As threatened, on September 18, 2002, Yukevich filed a motion to disqualify plaintiffs' attorney and experts. Yukevich argued that Johnson failed to comply with the ethical requirement of advising opposing counsel of his receipt of the confidential document.

After a lengthy hearing on the motion, the trial court granted the motion. The trial court made the following factual findings: Rowley acted as Yukevich's paralegal in preparing the notes; Yukevich created the document for his own personal use; Johnson obtained the document inadvertently; Johnson provided copies to attorneys Robert Balbuena and Jack Mattingly and experts Sances and Robert Anderson; the document is protected under both the attorney-client privilege and the attorney work product doctrine; Johnson violated his ethical duty by failing to notify opposing counsel and using the document; and, as a result of the unmitigatable prejudice, disqualification was the appropriate remedy. The court then continued the case to provide the plaintiffs an opportunity to retain new counsel.

3. Standard of Review

Generally, appellate courts review a trial court's decision to grant a disqualification motion for an abuse of discretion. A court abuses its discretion when it acts arbitrarily or without reason. In applying the abuse of discretion standard in this context, we carefully review the record to make the following determinations: whether the court's factual findings were supported by substantial evidence; whether the court properly exercised its discretion in reaching its ultimate factual conclusions; and whether, based on our independent review, the court properly understood and applied the law.

4. Privileged Document

Plaintiffs claim that the trial court erred in finding that the document was protected as both an attorney-client communication and as attorney work product. For the reasons provided below, we conclude that the document was not protected by the attorney-client privilege. The document was, however, confidential and privileged as attorney work product. Therefore, while the court misapplied the attorney-client privilege, the court did not abuse its discretion in reaching the ultimate conclusion that the document was privileged.

A. Attorney-Client Privilege

Plaintiffs argue that the document did not constitute a confidential communication under Evidence Code section 952.

Evidence Code section 952 defines a "confidential communication" as "information transmitted between a client and his or her lawyer in the course of that relationship and in confidence by a means which, so far as the client is aware, discloses the information to no third persons other than those who are present to further the interest of the client in the consultation or those to whom disclosure is reasonably necessary for the transmission of the information or the accomplishment of the purpose for which the lawyer is consulted, and includes a legal opinion formed and the advice given by the lawyer in the course of that relationship." As the holder of the privilege, the client may refuse to disclose and prevent others from disclosing confidential communications. The privilege safeguards the confidential relationship between the client and his attorney and allows the two to engage in full and open discussion about the facts and legal strategies.

These general principles envision some communication or transmission of information between an attorney and his client. The document in this case, however, does not fall within this general description. The document did not memorialize any attorney-client communication and, contrary to defendants' argument, the document was not transmitted between an attorney and his client.

First, the conversation encapsulated in the 12-page document was not a communication between an attorney and his client. The dialogue was primarily between defense attorneys and defense experts. While the privilege may extend to the client's agents and employees, the privilege attaches to the client's communication as relayed by the representative, not to communication originating from the representative. An attorney-client privilege does not attach to a communication that has no connection to the client. A conference between attorneys and experts, who are simply stating their own opinions, is not protected by the attorney-client privilege.

Moreover, even if the expert's communication is somehow protected, any privilege is lost once the expert is called to testify at trial. During cross-examination, the opposing party is entitled to delve into all matters relied on or considered by the expert in reaching his conclusions.

Second, the document in this case was not the instrument through which the client or the attorney transmitted confidential information. Defendants argue that the document was a communication between Yukevich and Rowley, Mitsubishi's representative and case manager. Defendants note that privileged information may be communicated by electronic means. Defendants therefore contend that, as Rowley entered the notes into Yukevich's personal computer and Yukevich edited the notes during the August 28, 2002 conference, they were exchanging confidential information.

The trial court found, however, that Rowley, in summarizing and transcribing the comments made during the conference, assumed the role of Yukevich's paralegal. Substantial evidence supports the court's finding. Yukevich testified that Rowley was acting under his directions. Rowley merely included information that Yukevich wanted in the document. Rowley confirmed that he was acting under Yukevich's directions to take notes of specific subject areas addressed during the conference. Under these facts, Rowley was not acting in his capacity as Mitsubishi's representative. Rowley also was not providing nor receiving information on Mitsubishi's behalf. The exchange was simply between an attorney and an individual acting as the attorney's paralegal.

We conclude therefore that neither the document nor the subject matter of the document involved an attorney-client communication. While the court was correct concerning the foundational facts, the court erred in reaching its ultimate conclusion that the document was privileged as an attorney-client communication.

B. *Attorney Work Product*

Plaintiffs also argue that the trial court erred in concluding that the document, which contained notes from a conference between defense attorneys and defense experts, was protected by the absolute work product privilege. Plaintiffs specifically argue that the document was no longer privileged after defendants designated the same defense experts as witnesses at trial. Plaintiffs also argued that defendants waived their right to assert the work product privilege by failing to raise an objection on this specific ground during Germane's deposition on September 16, 2002.

In regards to the waiver argument, plaintiffs explain that they are not claiming waiver based on any inadvertent disclosure of the document. Rather, plaintiffs claim that defendants failed to raise a timely objection during Germane's deposition. Plaintiffs note that, although Yukevich did not attend Germane's deposition, Calfo represented the defense during the deposition and had ample opportunity to object to the offending document. Generally, waiver is the intentional relinquishment of a right with knowledge of the facts. The burden is on the party claiming waiver to prove the existence of an intentional and knowing waiver.

Calfo did not attend the meeting at which the document was created and he did not recognize it when plaintiffs' counsel began to cross-examine defendants' expert. It was not until after the deposition that Calfo concluded that the document was privileged on its face. Calfo testified that he had no opportunity to read the document, but only peered over Germane's shoulder. The excerpted transcript of Germane's deposition shows that, while Calfo did not know what to make of the document, he clearly objected to its use in cross-examining the witness. He first asked about the source of the document, to which Johnson vaguely responded, "It was put in Dr. Sances' file." Calfo then challenged any statement in the document as being "attributed to Mr. Germane." He objected on the ground that there was "no foundation for this document." He objected to Johnson's attempt to use a quote from the document as Germane's actual words. As he continued to raise one objection after another, Calfo asserted that he objected "to the exhibit as a whole." As Johnson again attempted to use the document, Calfo interrupted with, "I don't even know where this exhibit came from." Johnson continued his question as Calfo continued his onslaught of objections. Calfo objected "to this whole line of inquiry with respect to an unknown document." We cannot fault defendants for failing to object to a document that was sprung on the defense at the deposition, that was erroneously identified by plaintiffs' counsel, and that was not recognized by defense counsel.

After the deposition, Johnson handed Calfo a copy of the document. Calfo informed Yukevich and Yukevich immediately sent a letter to Johnson stating that the document consisted of personal notes reflecting his thoughts and impressions. Two days after the deposition, defendants filed their motion to disqualify plaintiffs' counsel on various grounds, including that Johnson violated the attorney work product privilege. Based on Calfo's objections to the unknown document during the deposition and Yukevich's formal objection shortly thereafter, the record flies in the face of plaintiffs' waiver argument.

In the absence of waiver, we turn to a determination of whether the document was immune from discovery under the attorney work product doctrine. Code of Civil Procedure section 2018 codifies the attorney's work product privilege doctrine. That provision states in part:

"(a) It is the policy of the state to: (1) preserve the rights of attorneys to prepare cases for trial with that degree of privacy necessary to encourage them to prepare their cases thoroughly and to investigate not only the favorable but the unfavorable aspects of those cases; and (2) to prevent attorneys from taking undue advantage of their adversary's industry and efforts.

"(b) Subject to subdivision (c), the work product of an attorney is not discoverable unless the court determines that denial of discovery will unfairly prejudice the party seeking discovery in preparing that party's claim or defense or will result in an injustice.

"(c) Any writing that reflects an attorney's impressions, conclusions, opinions, or legal research or theories shall not be discoverable under any circumstances."

While subdivision (b) sets forth the conditional or qualified privilege, subdivision (c) provides an absolute privilege for certain writings.

An attorney's notes containing his impressions, conclusions, opinions, or legal theories regarding a witness' prior statement is absolutely immune from discovery. There is a significant difference between a witness' statement and an attorney's notes concerning that prior statement. While the former may be discoverable, the latter is protected from discovery based on its derivative or interpretive nature. The materials no longer consist solely of the witness' statements, but they also expose the attorney's impressions, including his evaluation of the strengths and weaknesses of the case. When the notes consist an attorney's impressions concerning the witness' statement, the notes are protected absolutely under the attorney work product doctrine.

This rule applies equally to lay and expert witnesses despite the discovery rules set forth in Code of Civil Procedure section 2034. Code of Civil Procedure section 2034, subdivision (a)(3) provides: "Any party may also include a demand for the mutual and simultaneous production for inspection and copying of all discoverable reports and writings, if any, made by an expert described in paragraph (2) in the course of preparing that expert's opinion." Under Code of Civil Procedure section 2034, the attorney's work product privilege does not apply to an expert's pretrial statements once that expert is designated as a witness at trial. The statute, however, only pertains to various items including the expert's reports, writings, and declarations. The provision does not require the production of an attorney's personal notes concerning the expert's pretrial statements. While the statute specifically requires that the item be "discoverable," an attorney's work product is privileged and, hence, not discoverable.

An attorney's derivative or interpretive notes, including notes pertaining to an expert's prior statements or opinions, are absolutely privileged and protected from discovery. "[A]ny such notes or recorded statements taken by defendant's counsel would be protected by the absolute work product privilege because they would reveal counsel's 'impressions, conclusions, opinions, or legal research or theories' within the meaning of Code of Civil Procedure section 2018, subdivision (c). [Citation.]"

Here, the document was not merely a transcript of the August 28, 2002 conference. As found by the court, Rowley, who was acting under Yukevich's instructions, summarized the important points addressed during the meeting. Substantial evidence supported the court's finding. Rowley testified that he did not record the statements verbatim, but only noted the important points. The conference lasted for about six hours including breaks beginning at about 10:30 a.m. and ending at about 4:00 p.m. Although the attorneys and experts met for several hours, Rowley only produced 12 pages of notes. This evidence alone suggests that the notes were not a transcript of the conference, but the product of a selective screening process. Both Yukevich and Rowley testified that the notes reflected Yukevich's desired content. Johnson also agreed that the notes consisted of major points, rather than a verbatim transcript. Yukevich's thoughts and expectations were the screening process for gathering specific data, or, to use the trial court's language, "the filter through which all the discussions and the conference were passed through on the way to the page."

The court correctly concluded that the 12-page document was attorney work product. Although the document was written in dialogue format with information provided by Mitsubishi experts, the above evidence shows that the document was not simply an expert's report, writings, declaration, or deposition testimony. Instead, the document contained Yukevich's thoughts and impressions concerning the evidence and the case.

Furthermore, contrary to plaintiffs' argument, the fact that Rowley primarily drafted the notes did not affect the character of the document. The attorney's work product doctrine covers documents created not only by an attorney, but also his agents or employees, including his paralegal. As the evidence established, Rowley wore multiple hats. During the August 28, 2002 hearing, he assisted Yukevich as his paralegal. The evidence indicated that, in addition to essentially guiding Rowley's hand, Yukevich also edited the notes and finalized the document before printing a hard copy. Yukevich testified that he deleted certain language and added several sentences. Although the document was created by Yukevich and Rowley's joint efforts, it was Yukevich's work product.

As Yukevich's work product containing his thoughts and impressions of the case, the document was not discoverable under any circumstances.

5. *Attorney's Ethical Duty in Regards to a Privileged Document*

The question in this case is what was Johnson's ethical duty once he received the privileged document.

Throughout the proceedings here and below, plaintiffs have relied on the *Aerojet-General Corp. v. Transport Indemnity, Inc.* (hereafter *Aerojet*). case for the rule that, upon inadvertently discovering a privileged document, plaintiffs were duty-bound to use the nonprivileged portions of the document to their client's advantage. In stark contrast, defendants, relying on *State Comp. Ins. Fund v. WPS, Inc.*, claim that Johnson, upon happening upon the privileged document, was required immediately to notify defendants without even reading beyond what was necessary to ascertain the privileged nature of the materials.

In *Aerojet*, several liability insurers sued Aerojet over a dispute regarding insurance coverage after an incident involving the widespread contamination at or near an *Aerojet* facility. During a break in the discovery process, an attorney for the plaintiffs received a packet of documents from an Aerojet employee, who had received the packet from Aerojet's insurance brokers. Among the documents was a memorandum revealing the existence of a witness, an independent insurance adjuster who had investigated a prior industrial accident at the same facility, and the attorney's assessment of that witness's potential. Upon discovering the memorandum, the plaintiffs' attorney reviewed the document and did not notify opposing counsel or the court of his find.

In reversing the trial court's monetary sanction order, the appellate court concluded the plaintiffs' attorney could not be faulted for examining the memorandum based on the volume of documents involved in the case and the inconspicuous nature of the unmarked document. The document was on plain paper without any identifying characteristics. The court found that, without reviewing the document, it would be impossible to discern what counsel had in his possession.

The *Aerojet* court focused primarily on two essential considerations. First, the court noted that the Aerojet had failed to demonstrate any specific prejudice. "They did not claim any specific damage or harm to their case based on the disclosure of the documents, nor did they seek sanctions for such." The secreted witness never testified at trial. And the jury decided the case in their favor.

The court also noted that Aerojet should have disclosed certain information that was neither privileged as attorney-client communication or attorney work product. "The attorney-client privilege is a shield against deliberate intrusion; it is not an insurer against inadvertent disclosure. Further, not all information that passes privately between attorney and client is entitled to remain confidential in the literal sense. The most obvious example is information that is required to be disclosed in response to discovery, such as the identification of potential witnesses. Consequently, whether the existence and identity of a witness or other nonprivileged information is revealed through formal discovery or inadvertence, the end result is the same: the opposing party is entitled to the use of that witness or information."

The court went on to say, "'[T]he attorney-client privilege only protects disclosure of communications; it does not protect disclosure of the underlying facts upon which the communications are based [citations]' [citation], 'and it does not extend to independent witnesses [citations]' [citation] or their discovery. [Citations.] Nor can 'the identity and location of persons having knowledge of relevant facts' be concealed under the attorney work product rule of Code of Civil Procedure section 2018. [Citations.]" The court made clear that, while the packet may have contained privileged materials, the targeted information, the existence of a potential witness, was not privileged.

The court held that the plaintiffs' attorney was duty bound to use the information. "Once he had acquired the information in a manner that was not due to his own fault or wrongdoing, he cannot purge it from his mind. Indeed, his professional obligation demands that he utilize his knowledge about the case on his client's behalf."

Therefore, under *Aerojet,* an attorney who inadvertently discovers a privileged document has no duty to inform opposing counsel, but instead has a duty to use any unprivileged information contained in the document that would be advantageous to his client. Notably, the court conditioned its holding on the grounds that, "[t]here is no State Bar rule of professional conduct, no rule of court nor any statute specifically addressing this situation and mandating or defining any duty under such circumstances." At the end of its opinion, the court again conditioned its holding, as follows: "In the absence of any clear statutory, regulatory or decisional authority imposing a duty of immediate disclosure of the inadvertent receipt of privileged information, we conclude the sanction order cannot stand."

In retrospect, the court had good reason for caution in formulating its holding. In *State Fund,* National Commercial Recovery, Inc., State Fund's assignee, sued WPS, Inc. for underpaying its workers' compensation insurance premiums. The defendant cross-complained for bad faith. After the discovery cutoff date, plaintiff sent defendant's attorney three boxes of documents that were identical to the documents provided during the discovery, with the exception of 273 pages of forms entitled, "Civil Litigation Claims Summary." These inadvertently included documents were marked as "Attorney-Client Communication/Attorney Work Product" and with the admonition, "Do Not Circulate or Duplicate." The forms were created by plaintiff's legal department to identify litigation issues and to assist outside cocounsel in their understanding of the strengths and weakness of the cases. One of the forms involved the subject of the litigation. When the plaintiff's attorney realized the mistake, he contacted the defendant's attorney and demanded the return of the documents. The defendant's attorney refused and plaintiff sought relief from the court. The trial court found the defendant's attorney violated his ethical obligations in refusing to return the documents. The trial court relied on American Bar Association (ABA) Formal Ethics Opinion No. 92-368 (Nov. 10, 1992). In finding a breach of counsel's ethical obligations, the court imposed monetary sanctions.

In reviewing the trial court's decision, the appellate court phrased the issue as follows: "what is a lawyer to do when he or she receives through the inadvertence of opposing counsel documents plainly subject to the attorney-client privilege?" After preliminarily concluding that the documents were privileged and that inadvertent disclosure did not waive the privilege, the court discussed an attorney's obligation after inadvertently discovering privileged documents. The court distinguished the *Aerojet* case based on the plainly privileged nature of the State Fund documents and the specific demonstration of resulting prejudice.

In *State Fund,* the appellate court disagreed with the trial court's application of the ABA opinion. Although the court acknowledge that the ABA Model Rules of Professional Conduct may provide guidance in resolving ethical questions, the court found that defendant's attorney could not have been found to have acted in bad faith when there was no decision, statute, or ethical rule applicable in California. Nevertheless, the appellate court found the analysis in the ABA opinion useful in formulating a standard for future cases. The court established the following standard: "When a lawyer who receives materials that obviously appear to be subject to an attorney-client privilege or otherwise clearly appear to be confidential and privileged and where it is reasonably apparent that the materials were provided or made available through inadvertence, the lawyer receiving such materials should refrain from examining the materials any more than is essential to ascertain if the materials are privileged, and shall immediately notify the sender that he or she possesses material that appears to be privileged. The parties may then proceed to resolve the situation by agreement or may resort to the court for guidance with the benefit of protective orders and other judicial intervention as may be justified."

A significant consideration in determining the appropriate judicial remedy is whether the injured party can demonstrate specific damages. The court explained, "'Mere exposure to the confidences of an adversary does not, standing alone, warrant disqualification. Protecting the integrity of judicial proceedings does not require so draconian a rule. Such a rule would nullify a party's right to representation by chosen counsel any time inadvertence or devious design put an adversary's confidences in an attorney's mailbox. Nonetheless, we consider the means and sources of breaches of attorney-client confidentiality to be important considerations.' [Citation.] Having so noted, however, we do not rule out the possibility that in an appropriate case, disqualification might be justified if an attorney inadvertently receives confidential materials and fails to conduct himself or herself in the manner specified above, assuming other factors compel disqualification."

Although the *State Fund* court did not expressly disapprove the *Aerojet* case, it severely limited its holding. While unnecessarily broad in its holding, *Aerojet* was right in its narrow application. In regards to its application, the case essentially involved non-privileged information, namely, a witness' identity, which was never used to the other party's detriment. In regards to its holding, *State Fund* provided the decisional authority that was lacking in *Aerojet.* For cases following *State Fund,* there is an ethical duty immediately to disclose inadvertently received privileged information. More precisely, an attorney who inadvertently receives plainly privileged documents must refrain from examining the materials any more than is necessary to determine that they are privileged, and must immediately notify the sender, who may not necessarily be the opposing party, that he is in possession of potentially privileged documents.

Although *State Fund* specifically involved documents that were privileged as attorney-client communications, the court did not limit its holding to only those documents that are covered under the attorney-client privilege. The *State Fund* rule applies to not only materials that obviously appear to be covered under "an attorney-client privilege," but also materials that "otherwise clearly appear to be confidential and privileged."

Like the attorney-client privilege, the work product privilege is equally fundamental to the justice system. "'Historically, a lawyer is an officer of the court and is bound to work for the advancement of justice while faithfully protecting the rightful interests of his clients. In performing his various duties, however, it is essential that a lawyer work with a certain degree of privacy, free from unnecessary intrusion by opposing parties and their counsel. Proper preparation of a client's case demands that he assemble information, sift what he considers to be the relevant from the irrelevant facts, prepare his legal theories and plan his strategy without undue and needless interference. That is the historical and the necessary way in which lawyers act within the framework of our system of jurisprudence to promote justice and to protect their clients' interests. This work is reflected, of course, in interviews, statements, memoranda, correspondence, briefs, mental impressions, personal beliefs, and countless other tangible and intangible ways—aptly though roughly termed by the Circuit Court of Appeals in this case [citation] as the "Work product of the lawyer." Were such materials open to opposing counsel on mere demand, much of what is now put down in writing would remain unwritten. An attorney's thoughts, heretofore inviolate, would not be his own. Inefficiency, unfairness and sharp practices would inevitably develop in the giving of legal advice and in the preparation of cases for trial. The effect on the legal profession would be demoralizing. And the interests of the clients and the cause of justice would be poorly served.' [Citation.]"

There is no reasonable basis for drawing a distinction between the attorney-client privilege and the work product privilege in this context. The *State Fund* court certainly did not draw such a distinction. The *State Fund* standard applies to documents that are plainly privileged and confidential, regardless of whether they are privileged under the attorney-client privilege, the work product privilege, or any other similar doctrine that would preclude discovery based on the confidential nature of the document.

In applying the *State Fund* standard to the present case, we conclude that Johnson, upon his discovery of Yukevich's notes, which were plainly privileged, should not have examined the document any more than was necessary to determine that it was privileged, and should have notified Yukevich immediately to avoid any potential prejudice. While markings, including "Confidential," "Privileged," or "Attorney Work Product," would have made light work of examining the document, the absence of such markings does not make the document any less obviously privileged. Yukevich's notes were not intended for an audience. Thus, if Yukevich alone intended to use his own notes, it does not strain logic to understand why he did not mark the document. Even without such markings, a brief examination of the document would reveal its confidential nature. Johnson should have known that he was not entitled to the document that he had in his possession.

A brief look and a simple phone call could have resolved the matter. Instead, Johnson, as the court found, "studied the document carefully, made his own notes on it, dispensed the information to his associates and experts, discussed the meaning of the notes with the experts and based his litigation strategy and expert witness cross-examination upon the information contained in the document."

The court's finding was supported by substantial evidence. According to his own testimony, after receiving the document from the court reporter, Johnson studied and analyzed the document. Without informing the court reporter, Johnson copied the document, keeping the copy and returning the original to the court reporter. After examining the document, Johnson showed it to cocounsel, Balbuena and Mattingly, and faxed copies to plaintiffs' experts.

Johnson's testimony and his copy of Yukevich's notes indicate that he meticulously examined the document, noting potential inconsistencies and weaknesses in defendants' case. Johnson consulted with plaintiffs' experts on the document's technical content. Johnson then used the document to prepare questions and impeach the defense experts during their depositions.

Relying on the *Aerojet* case, and without further inquiry into his ethical responsibilities, Johnson decided to conceal his possession of the document and use the information to his clients' advantage. The record shows that, rather than informing opposing counsel of his inadvertent discovery, Johnson surreptitiously copied the document, disseminated it to the key players of plaintiffs' legal team, and made full use of the privileged document. Johnson's conduct constituted a breach of the ethical standards established in *State Fund*.

6. *Remedy for Breach of Ethical Duty*

After concluding that Johnson breached his ethical obligations, we must now determine whether the trial court's disqualification order was the proper remedy.

The trial court settled on disqualification as the proper remedy because of the unmitigable damage caused by Johnson's dissemination and use of the document. The court noted that beyond mere exposure to the documents, Johnson fully exploited the document's potential to damage the defense case. Disqualification, the court concluded, was necessary to insure a fair trial.

As previously stated, we review the trial court's disqualification decision for an abuse of discretion. "Our task is to decide, as a question of law, whether under applicable legal principles the trial court acted beyond the allowable scope of its judicial discretion in determining disqualification of plaintiff[s'] counsel was the appropriate remedy under the circumstances of this case."

A judge may disqualify an attorney under Code of Civil Procedure section 128, subdivision (b). "A judge's authority to disqualify an attorney has its origins in the inherent power of every court in the furtherance of justice to control the conduct of ministerial officers and other persons in pending judicial proceedings. [Citations.] In [*People ex. rel. Dept. of Corporations v. SpeeDee Oil Change Systems, Inc.*], the Supreme Court held: 'Ultimately, disqualification motions involve a conflict between the clients' right to counsel of their choice and the need to maintain ethical standards of professional responsibility. [Citation.] The paramount concern must be to preserve public trust in the scrupulous administration of justice and the integrity of the bar. The important right to counsel of one's choice must yield to ethical considerations that affect the fundamental principles of our judicial process. [Citations.]'"

The court properly concluded that the damage was irreversible and, hence, disqualification was justified. "[I]n an appropriate case, disqualification might be justified if an attorney inadvertently receives confidential materials and fails to conduct himself or herself in the manner specified above, assuming other factors compel disqualification."

As discussed in the previous section, the record shows that Johnson not only failed to conduct himself as required under the *State Fund* case, but also acted unethically in making full use of the confidential document. The liability issues hinged on the technical evidence and the expert opinions based on that evidence. Johnson's use of the document to undermine the defense experts' opinions placed defendants at a great disadvantage.

As the court found, the damage could not have been undone. Even if the court omitted all references to the document from the record, the court recognized the practical realities that plaintiffs' counsel and experts had information that inevitably would have been used in preparing for trial. We conclude that the trial court did not abuse its discretion in determining that disqualification was necessary to insure a fair trial.

In reaching this conclusion, we have given serious thought to plaintiffs' accusations that the defense experts provided false testimony during their earlier depositions. Plaintiffs repeatedly note that the statements attributed to the defense experts in Yukevich's notes contradicted their earlier deposition statements. Plaintiffs accuse the defense experts of lying about the technical evidence involved in the case.

In affirming the court's order to disqualify plaintiffs' attorneys, this court's intention is not to reward any wrongdoing. Nevertheless, when a writing is protected under the absolute attorney work product privilege, courts do not invade upon the attorney's thought processes by evaluating the content of the writing. Once an unintended reader ascertains that the writing contains an attorney's impressions, conclusions, opinions, legal research or theories, the reading stops and the contents of the document for all practical purposes are off limits. In the same way, once the court determines that the writing is absolutely privileged, the inquiry ends. Courts do not make exceptions based on the content of the writing. Unlike with the attorney-client privilege, there is no crime-fraud exception to the attorney work product rule. The absolute attorney work product privilege is just that, absolute.

In preserving this fundamental principle of our justice system, while the goal of justice is to unearth the truth, this goal cannot be achieved through means that deprive its participants of a fair process. A process that recognizes the state's policy to "preserve the rights of attorneys to prepare cases for trial with that degree of privacy necessary to encourage them to prepare their cases thoroughly and to investigate not only the favorable but the unfavorable aspects of those cases." In this case, regardless of its potential impeachment value, Yukevich's personal notes should never have been subject to opposing counsel's scrutiny and use.

We recognize the potentially serious effect of the court's order on plaintiffs' case. Plaintiffs themselves have done nothing to cause the disqualification. In accordance with the trial court's order, plaintiffs must be given ample opportunity to retain new counsel and experts, who in turn should be afforded every opportunity to complete discovery and prepare for trial.

7. Disposition

We affirm the trial court's disqualification order. Defendants shall recover their costs on appeal, and, in the interests of justice, plaintiffs' attorneys shall be liable for such costs.

We concur: RAMIREZ, P.J., and McKINSTER, J.

The Professional Ethics Commission of the Board of Overseers of the Bar [Maine]

Opinion #146

Issued 12/9/1994*

[Some footnotes omitted. Remaining footnotes renumbered.]

Facts

Pursuant to Maine Bar Rule 11(c)(1), Bar Counsel has requested an opinion based on the following set of facts.

Counsel A and Counsel Z represented adverse parties in a lawsuit. In the course of pretrial discovery, Counsel Z received a number of documents from Counsel A. Among those items was a copy of a document that is clearly privileged. According to the facts posed by Bar counsel, Counsel Z knew or should have known[1] that the disclosure of the document was inadvertent.

Questions

Bar counsel poses the following questions:

1. May Counsel Z use the privileged memorandum or the information in the privileged memorandum in representing her client and if so to what extent?

2. Must Counsel Z notify Counsel A of his error?

Opinion

At the outset, we note that the discoverability and admissibility of the document in question are governed by the Rules of Civil and Criminal Procedure and Evidence. Interpretation and application of those rules are beyond the jurisdiction of this Commission. Under the rules governing this Commission as established by the Supreme Judicial Court, the sole consideration for us is whether there are any ethical limitations in the Maine Bar Rules on Counsel Z's use of the document.

For the reasons stated herein, the Commission concludes that Counsel Z may use the document and the information contained in it to the extent permitted by the rules of procedure and evidence, but that she should notify Counsel A, the sending lawyer, of the fact that the document has been received and provide a copy of the document to Counsel A on request.

In so holding, we are mindful that the ABA Standing Committee on Ethics and Professional Responsibility reached a contrary result in Formal Opinion 92-368. We do not find that Opinion to be persuasive. The ABA Committee was unable to cite any specific provision of the Model Rules of Professional Conduct in support of its conclusion. Indeed, Committee Opinion 92-368 expressly acknowledged that it was not based on any

---

* [Editor's note: This opinion is reproduced by permission of the Maine Board of Overseers on condition that it be noted that Opinion #146 was withdrawn and vacated, and superseded by Opinion #172, issued 3/7/2000. In light of the Dissent, do you agree with this change in position? Ironically, ABA Formal Opinion 92-368, which was not followed by the majority in the initial opinion, has itself been withdrawn. See ABA Formal Opinion 05-437 *infra*. What do you think of all this change? Why do you think these opinions shift so much?]

1. In requesting this Opinion Bar Counsel has not indicated the grounds for the factual statement that Counsel Z "should have known" that the disclosure by Counsel A was "inadvertent." Nevertheless, the Commission answers this Request based on the facts as posed by Bar Counsel. We do not express any view as to the circumstances under which an attorney "should know" of another attorney's inadvertent error.

"black letter of the Model Rules." Instead, the ABA Committee's analysis referred to other general principles and rules of law, including the rules regarding attorney-client privilege, the substantive law regarding inadvertent waiver of the attorney-client privilege, the law of bailments, and what it characterized as other unspecified "ethical restraints on uncontrolled advocacy," to conclude that the receiving lawyer had a professional obligation to return the privileged documents to opposing counsel and that failure to do so was an ethical violation.

More recently the Ohio Supreme Court Board of Commissioners on Grievances and Discipline in opinion 93-11 (December 3, 1993) expressed disagreement with ABA opinion 92-368. The Ohio Board stated that it "was not persuaded by A.B.A. Formal Opinion 92-368" which was based on an interpretation of the ABA Model Rules of Professional Responsibility. However, the Ohio Board went on to state that the receiving lawyer, while free to use the information and to disclose the same to his client, was obligated to inform opposing counsel of the disclosure of the confidential information. The Ohio Opinion did not cite any Rule in support of its conclusion.

We disagree with the ABA Opinion and agree with the Ohio Board, although for different reasons. In our view, the standards of ethical conduct in Maine are to be drawn from the codified provisions of the Maine Bar Rules. This Commission is limited to rendering advisory Opinions "on matters involving the interpretation and application of the Code of Professional Responsibility." Maine Bar Rule 11(c). We are not free to read into those Rules limitations on conduct that have not been stated expressly. However theoretically appealing we might find the conclusion reached by the ABA Committee or the sentiments expressed by the other members of this Commission, we believe that the approach to interpretation and application of the Maine Bar Rules adopted by both the ABA Opinion and the other Commission members are not appropriate for this Commission. "In fairness to attorneys who look to [the Bar Rules] for guidance, the Rules must provide a clear and consistent articulation of what constitutes appropriate professional standards." *Board of Overseers v. Rodway*, 470 A.2d 790, 791 (Me.1984). The fundamental purpose behind the creation of the Bar Rules was to establish a clear codified set of standards for attorneys, the violation of which could result in professional sanctions. With that purpose and the Law Court's directive in *Rodway* in mind, we strongly believe that this Commission is not free to add ethical limitations not expressed by the Bar Rules.

In reviewing the Maine Bar Rules, the only applicable provisions are Bar Rules 3.2(f)(3) and 3.2(f)(4). Rule 3.2(f)(3) states that a lawyer shall not "engage in conduct involving dishonesty, fraud, deceit or misrepresentation."

Nothing in the history at Rule 3.2(f)(3) indicates that it was intended to prohibit a lawyer from retaining and using a document voluntarily but mistakenly provided by opposing counsel. We do not believe it is dishonest, fraudulent or deceitful within the meaning of this rule to take advantage of the mistake of opposing counsel. In the recent decision of *Aerojet General Corporation v. Transport Indemnity Insurance*, 22 Cal.Rptr. 862 (1993) involving a similar fact situation, a California court similarly concluded that the receiving lawyer was permitted to retain the mistakenly sent document and was not required to notify the sending lawyer of the receipt of the document. In so holding, that court said:

> "There is no State Bar rule of professional conduct, no rule of court nor any statute specifically addressing this situation and mandating or defining any duty under such circumstances."

Rule 3.2(f)(4) states that "A lawyer shall not:

... (4) engage in conduct that is prejudicial to the administration of justice."

While that rule is very broad, nothing in its history suggests that the language of the Rule on its face would apply to the question before us. So long as use of the memorandum is permitted by the Rules of Evidence or Procedure,[2] use of the memorandum cannot be said to be prejudicial to our adversary system of litigation. We do not believe that Rule 3.2(f)(4), standing alone, requires Counsel Z to return the document to the sending lawyer, nor does that rule prohibit a lawyer from taking advantage of any other mistake of opposing counsel such as the failure to (1) plead an affirmative defense, (2) assert a counterclaim, (3) argue a theory of law, (4) assert an evidentiary objection at trial, (5) introduce an essential piece of evidence or (6) demand an important provision during contract negotiations.

Although we believe that Rules 3.2(f)(3) and (4) do not on their face require return of the document in issue, we are mindful that in interpreting the Bar Rules we cannot ignore the substantive law of Maine, specifically Title 17-A M.R.S.A. § 356. That statute makes it a crime to retain mistakenly delivered property of another. It is unclear to the Commission how that statute would apply to the present facts. Reasonable arguments can be made as to whether that law applies to documents obtained in pretrial discovery. Unfortunately there is no judicial guidance on its application to facts such as those posed to us. However, we must acknowledge the real possibility that this law could apply. If the statute did apply to these facts, then we believe that it would necessarily follow that to retain documents in violation of state law would be "dishonest" under Rule 3.2(f)(3). Further, we think that a violation of Section 356 would also violate Rule 3.2(f)(2) ("A lawyer shall not ... engage in illegal conduct that adversely reflects on the lawyer's honesty, trustworthiness or fitness as a lawyer in other respects.").

Since the jurisdiction of this Commission is by rule expressly limited to interpretation of the Bar Rules, and since we have consistently declined to interpret statutes, we are unable to determine whether Section 356 would apply in this case. However, because of the possibility that the statute could apply to documents received in discovery, we conclude that the prudent course is to advise the receiving lawyer to notify the sending lawyer of the receipt of privileged documents. Further, if requested by the sending lawyer, the receiving lawyer should send a copy of the document to the sending lawyer in order to ensure that there is no misunderstanding about the document in issue. Such notification will afford the sending attorney the opportunity to take any action deemed appropriate, including for example moving for return of the document or seeking a judicial construction of the application of Section 356, and will negate the possibility that the receiving lawyer "intended to deprive the owner" of property within the meaning of § 356(2). Accordingly, on the facts of the case presented to us, we hold that Counsel Z may retain the inadvertently delivered privileged document and use it in any way permitted by the Rules of Evidence and Procedure, but Counsel Z should notify Counsel A of the receipt of the document and send a copy of the document to opposing counsel on request.

---

2. The Commission is aware that at least one court in this jurisdiction has expressly held that inadvertent disclosure of privileged documents constitutes a waiver of any privilege. See the unreported opinion of the U.S. District Court in F.D.I.C. v. Singh, et al. Civil No. 91-0057-P-C (January 10, 1992). Such holding, however, appears to be the minority view. See W. Ayers, Attorney Client Privilege: The Necessity of Intent to Waive the Privilege in Inadvertent Disclosure Cases, 18 Pac.L.J. 59 (1986).

We are aware that a single Justice of the Supreme Judicial Court has held that the intentional and surreptitious removal and photocopying of trial materials of opposing counsel is a violation of Bar Rules 3.4(f)(3) and 3.4(f)(4), the same rules at issue in this opinion. *Board of Overseers of the Bar v.Ebitz*, BAR 92-10 (1992). However, the facts in *Ebitz* are very different from those considered in this Opinion. Attorney Z has not engaged in any affirmative misconduct to obtain the privileged document, but rather has been the passive beneficiary of opposing counsel's error.[3] On the facts before us, the document came into the hands of Counsel Z from opposing counsel. In such a circumstance the Maine Bar Rules do not prohibit Counsel Z from retaining and using the documents so long as she notifies Counsel A of the inadvertent disclosure and provides a copy of the document to Counsel A on request.

We recognize that the other members of the Commission would go further and require Counsel Z to return the inadvertently sent documents.[4] That position and the ABA Committee Opinions are based in part on the view that lawyers owe to each other a level of courtesy that obligates them to return an inadvertently disclosed privileged document. That general philosophy also appears to form the foundation for the views of the other Commission members. However appealing such rationale is in theory, we find no support for that conclusion in the Maine Bar Rules. As the court stated in *Aerojet General:*

> The attorney-client privilege is a shield against deliberate intrusion; it is not an insurer against inadvertent disclosure.

22 Cal. Rptr. at 866. We agree.

We join the other Commission members in their concern for maintaining and improving the level of civility, honor and common courtesy in the profession, however we do not believe that we can enforce those values through the Bar Rules in the absence of specific provisions to that effect in those Rules. Nonetheless, we think that this reading of the Bar Rules in conjunction with § 356 will also help to promote those values.

* * *

Four members of the eight member Professional Ethics Commission subscribe to the foregoing opinion. One member of the Commission concurs in the result reached, but is of the view that the obligation of the receiving lawyer to inform the sending lawyer of receipt of the document and provide a copy of the document to the sending lawyer on request is supported by Bar Rule 3.2(f)(3) (prohibiting conduct "that involves dishon-

---

3. The conclusion expressed in this Opinion is expressly limited to the facts presented. We specifically decline to indicate our view on other facts, for example: (1) if Attorney Z received a call from Attorney A telling her that he had sent a package of discovery documents which inadvertently contained a privileged document and asking Attorney Z to return the package or destroy the document without reading it or (2) if Attorney Z received a package of discovery documents which included privileged documents and was aware that the privileged documents were surreptitiously placed in the package by a disgruntled employee of Attorney A who was attempting to sabotage A or his client.

4. The view expressed by the other Commission members would also mean that other "inadvertently" disclosed documents would also have to be returned. Thus, for example, under their analysis, if Counsel Z served a document request seeking certain specified categories of documents, and if Attorney A provided some additional non-privileged documents beyond the scope of Z's request, Attorney Z would be ethically required to return to Attorney A those extra non-privileged but voluntarily furnished documents. In addition, their analysis would shift the burden of vigilance from the producing attorney to the receiving attorney. Such a shifting of responsibility finds no basis in the Bar Rules.

esty") regardless of 17-A M.R.S.A. § 356, and notes that in any event, following such disclosure by the receiving lawyer, either party may file a motion with the court with respect to the use of the document in litigation or otherwise under the circumstances of the particular case.

Dissent

Three members of the Commission dissent from the plurality opinion authorizing the use of the inadvertently obtained privileged materials.

In the debate about how the ethical question discussed in the majority opinion should be resolved, several Commission members indicated that, acting as individuals, they would return the papers as requested. However, absent any specific disciplinary rule which required otherwise, these members felt constrained to follow the client's wishes that they retain the documents even though they would have preferred to do otherwise.

In an article entitled "Uncivil Law" appearing in the winter, 1994, edition of the *Boston College Magazine*, former B.C. Law School Dean Dan Coquillette states that the "legal culture" must change before the public's perception of lawyers will improve. He suggests that attorneys cannot separate their private views of justice and morality from the standards which they practice as professionals:

> One lawyer I talked to who was very embarrassed about the profession said to me, "You know, one thing I keep telling myself is that being a lawyer is what I do. It's not what I am." I said, "You've got it wrong. Aristotle said you are what you do every day. You are the product of what you do day in, day out, hour in, hour out. You can't say that being a lawyer is what you do and not what you are … There's no way you can split these roles. If you act like a jerk in court, you're not an aggressive advocate pursuing an assertive strategy—you're just a jerk." *Id* at p. 42.

These views led Dean Coquillette to conclude that an attorney who had been asked by opposing counsel to return unopened a missent confidential letter could not ethically permit himself to be guided by his client's desire that he not do so. Indeed, Dean Coquillette attributes much of the profession's present image problem to its failure to maintain a proper balance between the duty to uphold the system of justice embodied in the lawyers' oath, and the obligation to promote the interests of individual clients.

The foregoing considerations suggest that conduct which attorneys would find repugnant in their private lives, e.g., refusing to return something which clearly belongs to another, should not be tolerated on a professional level. It must be conceded that no disciplinary rule can be cited which specifically requires that the documents be returned in this case over the client's objection. However, the Commission's reluctance to rely on generalized rules of conduct to resolve specific ethical questions should not deter us in this instance from holding that failure to return the confidential letter in this case would be "prejudicial to the administration of justice" and therefore violate Rule 3.2(f)(4). See also Me. Bar R. 3.1(a).

Our inability to identify a specific rule condemning such conduct would presumably not prevent the majority from requiring that the document be returned if it had been taken from Attorney A's file by a disgruntled staff member and sent to Attorney Z, or if it had been picked up from counsel table and copied by the opposing attorney. See *Board of Overseers v. Ebitz*, BAR 92-10 (1992). It is obvious, therefore, that the majority would at least in *some* cases be willing to condemn professional conduct even without benefit of a specific rule upon which to base its conclusion. Since we are, therefore, engaged in an exercise in line-drawing to determine what circumstances would require the return of the confidential material even though no disciplinary rule specifically requires it, these dissenting members would draw the line at holding that the privileged information must be returned in those cases in which it is clear from the circumstances that the disclosure was unintended.

Although we would resolve the hypothetical presented to the Commission by Bar Counsel in this case by requiring Attorney Z to return the privileged documents and make no further use of them in the litigation, it is conceded that cases may arise in which Attorney Z's ethical obligation will not be so clear. After all, Attorney Z should not be expected to rectify every mistake made by opposing counsel in the course of litigation. In those situations in which an attorney is unclear whether an opponent's inadvertent disclosure gives rise to an ethical duty to keep the information confidential, the attorney should request the court having jurisdiction of the matter for instruction as to how to proceed.

American Bar Association Formal Ethics Opinion 05-437
Inadvertent Disclosure of Confidential Materials:
Withdrawal of Formal Opinion 92-368
October 1, 2005

A lawyer who receives a document from opposing parties or their lawyers and knows or reasonably should know that the document was inadvertently sent should promptly notify the sender in order to permit the sender to take protective measures. To the extent that Formal Opinion 92-368 opined otherwise, it is hereby withdrawn.

On November 10, 1992, the Committee issued Formal Opinion 92-368, "Inadvertent Disclosure of Confidential Materials," in which we opined as follows:

> A lawyer who receives materials that on their face appear to be subject to the attorney-client privilege or otherwise confidential, under circumstances where it is clear they were not intended for the receiving lawyer, should refrain from examining the materials, notify the sending lawyer and abide the instructions of the lawyer who sent them.

The opinion covered the circumstances where a lawyer received information subject to the attorney-client privilege or that could otherwise be deemed confidential in a situation where it was clear that the information was inadvertently sent. In that instance, the Committee opined that the receiving lawyer had three obligations: (1) to refrain from examining the materials; (2) to notify the sending lawyer of the receipt of the materials; and (3) to abide by the instructions of the sending lawyer.

In February 2002, the ABA Model Rules of Professional Conduct[1] were amended pursuant to the recommendations of the ABA Commission on Evaluation of the Rules of Professional Conduct. The amendment to Rule 4.4,"Respect for Rights of Third Persons," not only directly addressed the precise issue discussed in Formal Opinion 92-368, but narrowed the obligations of the receiving lawyer. The amendment added Rule 4.4(b), which states that "[a] lawyer who receives a document relating to the representa-

---

1. This opinion is based on the Model Rules of Professional Conduct as amended by the ABA House of Delegates through August 2003. The laws, court rules, regulations, rules of professional conduct, and opinions promulgated in the individual jurisdictions are controlling.

tion of the lawyer's client and knows or reasonably should know that the document was inadvertently sent shall promptly notify the sender."

Rule 4.4(b) thus only obligates the receiving lawyer to notify the sender of the inadvertent transmission promptly. The rule does not require the receiving lawyer either to refrain from examining the materials or to abide by the instructions of the sending lawyer. Comment [2] to Rule 4.4 explains, "[w]hether the lawyer is required to take additional steps, such as returning the original document, is a matter of law beyond the scope of these Rules, as is the question of whether the privileged status of a document has been waived." Comment [3] goes on to state the following:

> Some lawyers may choose to return a document unread, for example, when the lawyer learns before receiving the document that it was inadvertently sent to the wrong address. Where a lawyer is not required by applicable law to do so, the decision to voluntarily return such a document is a matter of professional judgment ordinarily reserved to the lawyer. See Rules 1.2 and 1.4.

Thus, because the conclusion of Formal Opinion 92-368 presently conflicts with amended Rule 4.4, the opinion is hereby withdrawn.

ABA Formal Op. 05-437.

Chapter V

Truthfulness

Problems

Problem 16

Several drafts of the "USA Patriot Act" (Pub. L. No. 107-56, 115 Stat. 272 (2001) (passed October 26, 2001) contained provisions that would have exempted some government lawyers, including Department of Justice lawyers, from state and federal court adoptions of certain ABA *Model Rules*, including Rule 8.4 and Rule 4.2. (The latter we will discuss in Chapter VI). The explanation was the need for government lawyers to pursue terrorists by designing and supervising "sting" operations involving FBI agents and others. What are your views on this proposed exemption? See D.C. Ethics Opinion 323 (2004), set out at Chapter VI-3, *infra*.

Problem 17

Select sides and set Monroe Freedman's "Three Hardest Questions" for oral argument. What are the "answers" to Freedman's "Questions" under the different rule systems? Do you agree with these "answers"? See Monroe Freedman, "The Professional Responsibility of the Criminal Defense Lawyer: The Three Hardest Questions," 64 *Mich. L. Rev.* 1469 (1966), set out at Chapter V-3, *infra*. How would Charles Fried resolve these issues? See "The Lawyer as Friend: The Moral Foundation of the Lawyer-Client Relation," 85 *Yale L. J.* 1060 (1976), *infra*, Section V-C. Do you agree with Fried that there is a "moral liberty of a lawyer to make his life out of what personal scraps and shards of motivation his inclination and character suggest: idealism, greed, curiosity, love of luxury, love of travel, a need for adventure or repose; only so long as these lead him to give wise and faithful counsel"?

Problem 18

Mass. Rule 3.3 provides more protection for a lying defendant than that required by the constitutional safeguards established by *Nix* v. *Whiteside*, set out at Chapter V-3 *infra*. I was on the Committee that recommended these differences. Does this additional protection for criminal defendants make any sense?

Problem 19

Marvin Frankel argues that a lawyer has an affirmative duty to ensure a fair, truthful trial, and even proposes a disciplinary rule requiring it. Do you agree with this? Alvin Rubin extends this duty to ensuring a fair, truthful negotiation. Do you agree with that? See the relevant articles, set out at Chapter V-3, *infra*. In a courtroom, lawyers are under the supervision of a neutral third party, the judge. In a negotiation, they are unsupervised. Should their responsibilities in the courtroom be more, or less, than in a negotiation? What do the rules say? Do you agree? (Notice that both Frankel and Rubin were judges when they wrote these articles, not practicing lawyers!)

Problem 20

Assume that you represent a corporation that had a major dispute with another about a product defect. Although a lawsuit was filed and discovery has commenced, the case is almost certain to "settle." Through the carelessness of opposing counsel, a major fact that would directly affect the settlement has gone undiscovered, although your client was fully cooperative with all discovery requests. There was a laboratory report, prepared by another company, that if known to the other side would cause them to demand much more in damages. You and your client have a copy of the report, but the other side inexplicably has failed to ask for it. What should you do? Suppose the other side also has facts, unknown to you, that would have assisted your case? Efforts to amend *F. Rule Civ. P. Rule* 26 to require parties to reveal damaging information "automatically" have been largely unsuccessful. In a Congressional hearing on such a proposed rule, where I was present, a lawyer testifying against the change argued that "[he] had a right to be opposed by incompetent counsel!" What do you think? How can negotiation ever lead to fair results if the parties fail to disclose such information?

Problem 21

Assume you represent a tire manufacturer. After a particularly bad accident, in which a child was killed, your client authorized a generous settlement. The opposing plaintiff's lawyer, who was eager to obtain a large contingency fee with little work, "demanded" only half what you were permitted to pay. (This unethical practice is called "low balling"). What should you do? Would it make a difference if you suspect that the plaintiffs are poor, cannot speak English, and may be "illegal" immigrants?

Problem 22

One night your doorbell rings unexpectedly. It is a friend, a retired teacher, who has just lost her husband. She says that she was going to "lose her house" because her husband's estate is in a "tax escrow," and there is no money to pay the mortgage. The story sounds implausible, and a review by your partner, an estate and trust specialist, soon leads to a confrontation with the deceased husband's lawyer. He quickly admitted that he has taken the money, "but she will get it all back if we don't report him." If we do report him, "we will soon discover he is close to bankruptcy, and she will get only a few cents on the dollar." It is clear that he will get the money to pay your friend by stealing from other clients. What should you do? What if your friend urges you to accept the "deal," because "all she wants is to get her money back?" Do you owe any duty to the other victims?

(The above is a fictional adaptation of a real case that took place long before the Massachusetts Supreme Judicial Court adopted the new *Mass. Rule* 8.3, that would require lawyers to report to the Bar Counsel "a violation of the Rules of Professional Conduct that raises a substantial question as to that lawyer's honesty, trustworthiness or fitness as a lawyer in other respects ..." But that rule "does not require disclosure of information otherwise protested by Rule 1.6." The old ABA Code DR-1-103 excluded "privileged knowledge," which, as we have seen in Chapter III, is a narrower category. In Massachusetts before January 1, 1998, there was no mandatory duty to disclose, as Massachusetts did not adopt DR-1-103 at all. See the Report of Special Master, Justice John V. Spalding, April 13, 1972, set out at Chapter IX-3, *infra*. In your opinion, would a mandatory reporting rule have helped in the above situation? We will discuss this issue in Chapter IX, *infra*, "*Bar Discipline*.")

V-1. Introduction: Being an Honest Lawyer

There is a great W.C. Fields joke. Apparently, he was standing transfixed before a tomb on which was carved "Here lies a lawyer and an honest man." When asked what so interested him, W.C. Fields replied, "I cannot figure out how they got two bodies under there!"

But lawyers are highly regulated for honesty, at least in theory. Under the *Code*, DR-1-102(A), a lawyer is prohibited from "conduct involving dishonesty, fraud, deceit or misrepresentation," with no limitation to law practice. There are further prohibitions in DR-7-102(A) that state that "in his representation of a client, a lawyer shall not ... knowingly make a false statement of law or fact." The *Model Rules* are equally tough. *Model Rule* 8.4 states it is "professional misconduct for a lawyer to ... engage in conduct involving dishonesty, fraud, deceit or misrepresentation." *Model Rule* 3.3 states that "a lawyer shall not knowingly ... make a false statement of fact or law to a tribunal or fail to correct a false statement of material fact or law previously made to the tribunal by the lawyer." *Model Rule* 4.1 states that "[i]n the course of representing a client a lawyer shall not knowingly make a false statement of material fact or law to a third party; or fail to disclose a material fact when disclosure is necessary to avoid a criminal or fraudulent act by a client, unless disclosure is prohibited by Rule 1.6."

If you are a lawyer, knowingly telling serious lies is always prohibited. Under *Model Rule* 8.4, this is arguably true even outside your professional role. As seen in the Introduction to Chapter I, attempts to relieve Department of Justice lawyers of the prohibition of *Model Rule* 8.4 through direct legislation, so that they could supervise "sting" operations against terrorists, and others, have been defeated. The theoretical controversies are about whether "puffing" and negotiation tactics really constitute lying—particularly where they are established by custom[1]—and when a lawyer must do more than just not lie. In particular, when does a lawyer have an affirmative obligation to correct negotiation misunderstandings, or lies by the client, or mistakes of fact by a court, particularly if this involves disclosing otherwise protected client confidences?

A. Affirmative Duties of Honesty before a Tribunal

Let us assume that you will not knowingly tell lies. "Affirmative" duties of honesty are when you must do more than that. Here is a simple illustration. You know your client has a prior conviction. Obviously, it would be wrong—and a professional dereliction—if you told a sentencing judge, or anyone else, that your client "did not have a prior conviction." But suppose your client tells the judge just that. Or that the court simply makes a mistake on its own. What should you do? Would it make a difference if it was not a court mistake, but a simple reference check, outside of a court proceeding for an important position of trust? Should you just say nothing?

Under the rules, it makes a big difference whether you are before a "tribunal." *Model Rule* 3.3(a)(1) states that "a lawyer shall not knowingly ... make a false statement of fact or law to a tribunal or fail to correct a false statement of material fact or law previously

---

1. For a discussion of "accepted conventions in negotiation," see Comment [2] to Model Rule 4.1. See also James J. White, "Machiavelli and the Bar: Ethical Limits on Lying in Negotiation," 1980 *Am. Bar Foundation J.*, p. 926.

made to the tribunal by the lawyer." In addition, as mentioned before, a lawyer has an affirmative duty to disclose controlling legal authority "directly adverse to the position of the client." *Model Rule* 3.3(a)(2). This obligation is taken seriously. See *Precision Specialty Metals Inc. v. United States*, 315 F.3d 1346 (Fed. Cir. 2003). Finally, and most importantly, a lawyer has an affirmative duty to "take reasonable remedial measures, including, if necessary disclosure to the tribunal" if the lawyer knows or learns that false evidence has been offered by his client or a witness called by the lawyer, or if the lawyer learns that any person "intends to engage, is engaging or has engaged in criminal or fraudulent conduct related to the proceeding." *Model Rule* 3.3(a)(3), (b). These duties "continue to the conclusion of the proceeding," and apply even if the information is "otherwise protected by Rule 1.6," the professional confidentiality rule. The *Model Rules* are stronger in their duty than the old *Code* DR-7-102(B)(1), which, had an exception for "information ... protected as a privileged communication," which was later construed by some as including all professional confidences, although it could be argued that some such communication would not be protected due to the "crime-fraud" exception to the privilege. Once again, the comments help explain the policy. Comment [11] to *Model Rule* 3.3 states:

> "[11] The disclosure of a client's false testimony can result in grave consequences to the client, including not only a sense of betrayal but also loss of the case and perhaps a prosecution for perjury. But the alternative is that the lawyer cooperate in deceiving the court, thereby subverting the truth-finding process which the adversary system is designed to implement. See Rule 1.2(d). Furthermore, unless it is clearly understood that the lawyer will act upon the duty to disclose the existence of false evidence, the client can simply reject the lawyer's advice to reveal the false evidence and insist that the lawyer keep silent. Thus the client could in effect coerce the lawyer into being a party to fraud on the court."

It is important, also, to check the definition section of the *Model Rules*, *Model Rule* 1.0, or the equivalent section in the *Code* to see if an important term is defined. "Tribunal," for example, is a defined term.

> (m) "Tribunal" denotes a court, an arbitrator in a binding arbitration proceeding or a legislative body, administrative agency or other body acting in an adjudicative capacity. A legislative body, administrative agency or other body acts in an adjudicative capacity when a neutral official, after the presentation of evidence or legal argument by a party or parties, will render a binding legal judgment directly affecting a party's interests in a particular matter." ABA *Model Rule* 1.0(m).

Finally, as we will see, some administrative agencies have imposed their own affirmative duty on lawyers. The best example is the SEC Standards of Professional Conduct, promulgated pursuant to the Sarbanes-Oxley Act, 17 CFR 205 (January 23, 2003), that are set out in the next Chapter, Chapter VI, but there are many others, including the IRS, the INS, and the Patent and Trademark Office.[2]

There remains one very special problem of affirmative honesty for attorneys, perjury by a criminal defendant client. In *Nix* v. *Whiteside*, 475 U.S. 157 (1986), included in Sec-

---

2. See the discussion in Judith A. McMorrow, Daniel R. Coquillette, *The Federal Law of Attorney Conduct, Moore's Federal Practice* (3rd ed.), (San Francisco, Lexis Nexis, 2010), pp. 801-18–801-19 and note 27. (Hereafter, "*McMorrow, Coquillette*").

tion V-3, *infra*, the Supreme Court held that the constitutional rights of such a defendant do not include a right to give perjured testimony, but some jurisdictions, including Massachusetts, make a special allowance for a criminal defendant. Comment [7] of *Model Rule* 3.3 indicates that the "obligation of the advocate under the Rules of Professional Conduct is subordinate to such requirements." In Massachusetts, *Mass. Rule* 3.3 has been changed from the *Model Rules* to include a new section "(e)" that specifically covers this situation.

> "(e) In a criminal case, defense counsel who knows that the defendant, the client, intends to testify falsely may not aid the client in constructing false testimony, and has a duty strongly to discourage the client from testifying falsely, advising that such a course is unlawful, will have substantial adverse consequences, and should not be followed. If a lawyer discovers this intention before accepting representation of the client, the lawyer shall not accept the representation; if the lawyer discovers this intention before trial, the lawyer shall seek to withdraw from the representation, requesting any required permission. Disclosure of privileged or prejudicial information shall be made only to the extent necessary to effect the withdrawal. If disclosure of privileged or prejudicial information is necessary, the lawyer shall make an application to withdraw *ex parte* to a judge other than the judge who will preside at the trial and shall seek to be heard in camera and have the record of the proceeding, except for an order granting leave to withdraw, impounded. If the lawyer is unable to obtain the required permission to withdraw, the lawyer may not prevent the client from testifying. If a criminal trial has commenced and the lawyer discovers that the client intends to testify falsely at trial, the lawyer need not file a motion to withdraw from the case if the lawyer reasonably believes that seeking to withdraw will prejudice the client. If, during the client's testimony or after the client has testified, the lawyer knows that the client has testified falsely, the lawyer shall call upon the client to rectify the false testimony and, if the client refuses or is unable to do so, the lawyer shall not reveal the false testimony to the tribunal. In no event may the lawyer examine the client in such a manner as to elicit any testimony from the client the lawyer knows to be false, and the lawyer shall not argue the probative value of the false testimony in closing argument or in any other proceedings, including appeals."

Do you like this change? Needless to say, affirmative disclosure obligations remain controversial, even before a tribunal.

B. Other Affirmative Duties of Honesty

As seen before, *Model Rule* 4.1 specifically prohibits making "false statements of material fact or law to a third person" while "in the course of representing a client." But it also affirmatively requires a lawyer to "disclose a material fact when disclosure is necessary to avoid assisting a criminal or fraudulent act by a client, unless disclosure is prohibited by Rule 1.6." *Model Rule* 4.1(b). Notice that *Model Rule* 1.6 duties of confidentiality trump such obligations to third parties, but do not apply to disclosures to a tribunal under *Model Rule* 3.3.

Nevertheless, *Model Rule* 4.1 must be taken very seriously. In some jurisdictions, including Massachusetts, Rule 1.6 has been amended to *require* disclosure where information "may" be disclosed as an exception to Rule 1.6 and is required to be disclosed by

Rule 3.3, Rule 4.1(b), or Rule 8.3. (The latter rule, the "Reporting Professional Misconduct" rule, also establishes affirmative duties, which will be discussed in Chapter IX.) For example, *Mass. Rule* 1.6(b)(1) permits disclosure of information "to prevent the commission of a … fraudulent act that the lawyer reasonably believes is likely to result in … substantial injury to the financial interests or property of another." Now assume that the lawyer is in a position where disclosure of "a material fact to a third person" is necessary to avoid assisting a criminal or fraudulent act by a client," under *Rule* 4.1(b) and the information may be disclosed under *Mass. Rule* 1.6(b)(1) because it involves fraud likely to cause "substantial" financial injury. Because the lawyer "may" reveal the information under *Mass. Rule* 1.6(b)(1), the lawyer *must* reveal the information under *Mass. Rule* 4.1(b). The lawyer is *affirmatively* required to make the disclosure. Note that the meaning of "assistance" is carefully defined by Comment [3] to *Mass. Rule* 4.1.[3]

Model Rule 4.1 can also be important in negotiations. Comment [1] defined the scope of the "honesty."

> "[1] A lawyer is required to be truthful when dealing with others on a client's behalf, but generally has no affirmative duty to inform an opposing party of relevant facts. A misrepresentation can occur if the lawyer incorporates or affirms a statement of another person that the lawyer knows is false. Misrepresentations can also occur by partially true but misleading statements or omissions that are equivalent of affirmative false statements. For dishonest conduct that does not amount to a false statement or for misrepresentations by a lawyer other than in the course of representing a client, see Rule 8.4."

Note that "omissions that are the equivalent of affirmative false statements" are included. *Mass. Rule* 4.1 Comment [1] has similar, but different, language. "Misrepresentation can also occur by failure to act." What this means in practice can be unclear.

Finally, there is the whole issue of "accepted conventions in negotiation," sometimes called "puffing." You say "my client won't settle for a penny less than $100,000," although you know, and I know, that the client would be happy with much less. I offer "$50,000 … not a penny more!" That is "puffing." Is it lying, governed by *Model Rule* 4.1? What if I say, "my case is rock solid," although I know it is weak, or "Mass. Law supports my client," although I know it does not? When do I cross the line? Surely the line is crossed if I say my chief witness is "alive and well," knowing she died last night. What if I just don't mention it, and say, "I've got great corroborating evidence" instead, knowing, I have, in fact, none?

Comment [2] to *Model Rule* 4.1 tries to deal with this problem.

> "[2] This Rule refers to statements of fact. Whether a particular statement should be regarded as one of fact can depend on the circumstances. Under generally accepted conventions in negotiation, certain types of statements ordinarily are not taken as statements of material fact. Estimates of price or value

---

3. Comment [3] to the *Model Rule* 4.1 notes that "ordinarily, a lawyer can avoid assisting a client's crime or fraud from withdrawing from the representation. Sometimes it may be necessary for the lawyer to give notice of the fact of withdrawal to disaffirm an opinion, document, affirmation or the like. In extreme cases, substantive law may require a lawyer to disclose information relating to the representation to avoid being deemed to have assisted the client's crime or fraud." But the comment still says such disclosure if required "unless the disclosure is prohibited by Rule 1.6."

placed on the subject of a transaction and a party's intentions as to an acceptable settlement of claim are ordinarily in this category, and so is the existence of an undisclosed principal except where nondisclosure of the principal would constitute fraud. Lawyers should be mindful of their obligations under applicable law to avoid criminal and tortious misrepresentation."

See also James J. White's famous article "Machiavelli and the Bar: Ethical Limits on Lying in Negotiation," 1980 *Am. Bar Foundation J.*, p. 920–926. But it is obvious that such conventions are a "slippery slope." Also, it is unclear that they advance efficient, economic negotiations. Quaker merchants were famous for never using "puff," but they reached fair deals, efficiently, once the ground rules of strict honesty were understood by their customers.

In the next chapter, we will discuss *Model Rule* 1.13, which also imposes affirmative duties on lawyers to take certain steps with regard to organizational clients when the individuals who normally would guard that clients interests, such as corporate officers, are behaving badly. In Massachusetts this can include "disclosures consistent with *Rule* 1.6, *Rule* 3.3, *Rule* 4.1 and *Rule* 8.3." See *Mass. Rule* 1.13(c).

Note one very important fact about all of these "honesty" obligations. Where the rules either permit or require disclosure, failure to take such actions may result in more than just professional discipline. For example, dishonesty in negotiations runs the risk of an action for fraud. See *Shafer* v. *Berger* et al., set out at Chapter V-3, *infra*. You may also be sued by injured third parties, or even by your own client. The latter often happens when corrupt officers are replaced in an organization by honest ones, and the lawyer has failed to defend the organization. Of course, such malpractice actions must establish the usual tort requirements of duty of care, causation and damages, but they are very unpleasant to defend.

In light of all of this, do you regard the requirements of professional honesty going too far? Not far enough? Would your views change if you were a layperson?

V-2. Truthfulness: The Rules

ABA Model Rules

RULE 3.3: CANDOR TOWARD THE TRIBUNAL

(a) A lawyer shall not knowingly:

(1) make a false statement of fact or law to a tribunal or fail to correct a false statement of material fact or law previously made to the tribunal by the lawyer;

(2) fail to disclose to the tribunal legal authority in the controlling jurisdiction known to the lawyer to be directly adverse to the position of the client and not disclosed by opposing counsel; or

(3) offer evidence that the lawyer knows to be false. If a lawyer, the lawyer's client, or a witness called by the lawyer, has offered material evidence and the lawyer comes to know of its falsity, the lawyer shall take reasonable remedial measures, including, if necessary, disclosure to the tribunal. A lawyer may refuse to offer evidence, other than the testimony of a defendant in a criminal matter, that the lawyer reasonably believes is false.

(b) A lawyer who represents a client in an adjudicative proceeding and who knows that a person intends to engage, is engaging or has engaged in criminal or fraudulent conduct related to the proceeding shall take reasonable remedial measures, including, if necessary, disclosure to the tribunal.

(c) The duties stated in paragraphs (a) and (b) continue to the conclusion of the proceeding, and apply even if compliance requires disclosure of information otherwise protected by Rule 1.6.

(d) In an ex parte proceeding, a lawyer shall inform the tribunal of all material facts known to the lawyer that will enable the tribunal to make an informed decision, whether or not the facts are adverse.

Comment

[1] This Rule governs the conduct of a lawyer who is representing a client in the proceedings of a tribunal. See Rule 1.0(m) for the definition of "tribunal." It also applies when the lawyer is representing a client in an ancillary proceeding conducted pursuant to the tribunal's adjudicative authority, such as a deposition. Thus, for example, paragraph (a)(3) requires a lawyer to take reasonable remedial measures if the lawyer comes to know that a client who is testifying in a deposition has offered evidence that is false.

[2] This Rule sets forth the special duties of lawyers as officers of the court to avoid conduct that undermines the integrity of the adjudicative process. A lawyer acting as an advocate in an adjudicative proceeding has an obligation to present the client's case with persuasive force. Performance of that duty while maintaining confidences of the client, however, is qualified by the advocate's duty of candor to the tribunal. Consequently, although a lawyer in an adversary proceeding is not required to present an impartial exposition of the law or to vouch for the evidence submitted in a cause, the lawyer must not allow the tribunal to be misled by false statements of law or fact or evidence that the lawyer knows to be false.

Representations by a Lawyer

[3] An advocate is responsible for pleadings and other documents prepared for litigation, but is usually not required to have personal knowledge of matters asserted therein, for litigation documents ordinarily present assertions by the client, or by someone on the client's behalf, and not assertions by the lawyer. Compare Rule 3.1. However, an assertion purporting to be on the lawyer's own knowledge, as in an affidavit by the lawyer or in a statement in open court, may properly be made only when the lawyer knows the assertion is true or believes it to be true on the basis of a reasonably diligent inquiry. There are circumstances where failure to make a disclosure is the equivalent of an affirmative misrepresentation. The obligation prescribed in Rule 1.2(d) not to counsel a client to commit or assist the client in committing a fraud applies in litigation. Regarding compliance with Rule 1.2(d), see the Comment to that Rule. See also the Comment to Rule 8.4(b).

Legal Argument

[4] Legal argument based on a knowingly false representation of law constitutes dishonesty toward the tribunal. A lawyer is not required to make a disinterested exposition of the law, but must recognize the existence of pertinent legal authorities. Furthermore, as stated in paragraph (a)(2), an advocate has a duty to disclose directly adverse authority in the controlling jurisdiction that has not been disclosed by the opposing party. The underlying concept is that legal argument is a discussion seeking to determine the legal premises properly applicable to the case.

Offering Evidence

[5] Paragraph (a)(3) requires that the lawyer refuse to offer evidence that the lawyer knows to be false, regardless of the client's wishes. This duty is premised on the lawyer's obligation as an officer of the court to prevent the trier of fact from being misled by false evidence. A lawyer does not violate this Rule if the lawyer offers the evidence for the purpose of establishing its falsity.

[6] If a lawyer knows that the client intends to testify falsely or wants the lawyer to introduce false evidence, the lawyer should seek to persuade the client that the evidence should not be offered. If the persuasion is ineffective and the lawyer continues to represent the client, the lawyer must refuse to offer the false evidence. If only a portion of a witness's testimony will be false, the lawyer may call the witness to testify but may not elicit or otherwise permit the witness to present the testimony that the lawyer knows is false.

[7] The duties stated in paragraphs (a) and (b) apply to all lawyers, including defense counsel in criminal cases. In some jurisdictions, however, courts have required counsel to present the accused as a witness or to give a narrative statement if the accused so desires, even if counsel knows that the testimony or statement will be false. The obligation of the advocate under the Rules of Professional Conduct is subordinate to such requirements. See also Comment [9].

[8] The prohibition against offering false evidence only applies if the lawyer knows that the evidence is false. A lawyer's reasonable belief that evidence is false does not preclude its presentation to the trier of fact. A lawyer's knowledge that evidence is false, however, can be inferred from the circumstances. See Rule 1.0(f). Thus, although a lawyer should resolve doubts about the veracity of testimony or other evidence in favor of the client, the lawyer cannot ignore an obvious falsehood.

[9] Although paragraph (a)(3) only prohibits a lawyer from offering evidence the lawyer knows to be false, it permits the lawyer to refuse to offer testimony or other proof that the lawyer reasonably believes is false. Offering such proof may reflect adversely on the lawyer's ability to discriminate in the quality of evidence and thus impair the lawyer's effectiveness as an advocate. Because of the special protections historically provided criminal defendants, however, this Rule does not permit a lawyer to refuse to offer the testimony of such a client where the lawyer reasonably believes but does not know that the testimony will be false. Unless the lawyer knows the testimony will be false, the lawyer must honor the client's decision to testify. See also Comment [7].

Remedial Measures

[10] Having offered material evidence in the belief that it was true, a lawyer may subsequently come to know that the evidence is false. Or, a lawyer may be surprised when the lawyer's client, or another witness called by the lawyer, offers testimony the lawyer knows to be false, either during the lawyer's direct examination or in response to cross-examination by the opposing lawyer. In such situations or if the lawyer knows of the falsity of testimony elicited from the client during a deposition, the lawyer must take reasonable remedial measures. In such situations, the advocate's proper course is to remonstrate with the client confidentially, advise the client of the lawyer's duty of candor to the tribunal and seek the client's cooperation with respect to the withdrawal or correction of the false statements or evidence. If that fails, the advocate must take further remedial action. If withdrawal from the representation is not permitted or will not undo the effect of the false evidence, the advocate must make such disclosure to the tribunal as is reasonably necessary to remedy the situation, even if doing so requires the

lawyer to reveal information that otherwise would be protected by Rule 1.6. It is for the tribunal then to determine what should be done—making a statement about the matter to the trier of fact, ordering a mistrial or perhaps nothing.

[11] The disclosure of a client's false testimony can result in grave consequences to the client, including not only a sense of betrayal but also loss of the case and perhaps a prosecution for perjury. But the alternative is that the lawyer cooperate in deceiving the court, thereby subverting the truth-finding process which the adversary system is designed to implement. See Rule 1.2(d). Furthermore, unless it is clearly understood that the lawyer will act upon the duty to disclose the existence of false evidence, the client can simply reject the lawyer's advice to reveal the false evidence and insist that the lawyer keep silent. Thus the client could in effect coerce the lawyer into being a party to fraud on the court.

Preserving Integrity of Adjudicative Process

[12] Lawyers have a special obligation to protect a tribunal against criminal or fraudulent conduct that undermines the integrity of the adjudicative process, such as bribing, intimidating or otherwise unlawfully communicating with a witness, juror, court official or other participant in the proceeding, unlawfully destroying or concealing documents or other evidence or failing to disclose information to the tribunal when required by law to do so. Thus, paragraph (b) requires a lawyer to take reasonable remedial measures, including disclosure if necessary, whenever the lawyer knows that a person, including the lawyer's client, intends to engage, is engaging or has engaged in criminal or fraudulent conduct related to the proceeding.

Duration of Obligation

[13] A practical time limit on the obligation to rectify false evidence or false statements of law and fact has to be established. The conclusion of the proceeding is a reasonably definite point for the termination of the obligation. A proceeding has concluded within the meaning of this Rule when a final judgment in the proceeding has been affirmed on appeal or the time for review has passed.

Ex Parte Proceedings

[14] Ordinarily, an advocate has the limited responsibility of presenting one side of the matters that a tribunal should consider in reaching a decision; the conflicting position is expected to be presented by the opposing party. However, in any ex parte proceeding, such as an application for a temporary restraining order, there is no balance of presentation by opposing advocates. The object of an ex parte proceeding is nevertheless to yield a substantially just result. The judge has an affirmative responsibility to accord the absent party just consideration. The lawyer for the represented party has the correlative duty to make disclosures of material facts known to the lawyer and that the lawyer reasonably believes are necessary to an informed decision.

Withdrawal

[15] Normally, a lawyer's compliance with the duty of candor imposed by this Rule does not require that the lawyer withdraw from the representation of a client whose interests will be or have been adversely affected by the lawyer's disclosure. The lawyer may, however, be required by Rule 1.16(a) to seek permission of the tribunal to withdraw if the lawyer's compliance with this Rule's duty of candor results in such an extreme deterioration of the client-lawyer relationship that the lawyer can no longer competently represent the client. Also see Rule 1.16(b) for the circumstances in which a lawyer will be permitted to seek a tribunal's permission to withdraw. In connection with a request for

permission to withdraw that is premised on a client's misconduct, a lawyer may reveal information relating to the representation only to the extent reasonably necessary to comply with this Rule or as otherwise permitted by Rule 1.6.

RULE 4.1: TRUTHFULNESS IN STATEMENTS TO OTHERS

In the course of representing a client a lawyer shall not knowingly:

(a) make a false statement of material fact or law to a third person; or

(b) fail to disclose a material fact to a third person when disclosure is necessary to avoid assisting a criminal or fraudulent act by a client, unless disclosure is prohibited by Rule 1.6.

Comment

Misrepresentation

[1] A lawyer is required to be truthful when dealing with others on a client's behalf, but generally has no affirmative duty to inform an opposing party of relevant facts. A misrepresentation can occur if the lawyer incorporates or affirms a statement of another person that the lawyer knows is false. Misrepresentations can also occur by partially true but misleading statements or omissions that are the equivalent of affirmative false statements. For dishonest conduct that does not amount to a false statement or for misrepresentations by a lawyer other than in the course of representing a client, see Rule 8.4.

Statements of Fact

[2] This Rule refers to statements of fact. Whether a particular statement should be regarded as one of fact can depend on the circumstances. Under generally accepted conventions in negotiation, certain types of statements ordinarily are not taken as statements of material fact. Estimates of price or value placed on the subject of a transaction and a party's intentions as to an acceptable settlement of a claim are ordinarily in this category, and so is the existence of an undisclosed principal except where nondisclosure of the principal would constitute fraud. Lawyers should be mindful of their obligations under applicable law to avoid criminal and tortious misrepresentation.

Crime or Fraud by Client

[3] Under Rule 1.2(d), a lawyer is prohibited from counseling or assisting a client in conduct that the lawyer knows is criminal or fraudulent. Paragraph (b) states a specific application of the principle set forth in Rule 1.2(d) and addresses the situation where a client's crime or fraud takes the form of a lie or misrepresentation. Ordinarily, a lawyer can avoid assisting a client's crime or fraud by withdrawing from the representation. Sometimes it may be necessary for the lawyer to give notice of the fact of withdrawal and to disaffirm an opinion, document, affirmation or the like. In extreme cases, substantive law may require a lawyer to disclose information relating to the representation to avoid being deemed to have assisted the client's crime or fraud. If the lawyer can avoid assisting a client's crime or fraud only by disclosing this information, then under paragraph (b) the lawyer is required to do so, unless the disclosure is prohibited by Rule 1.6.

RULE 4.3 DEALING WITH UNREPRESENTED PERSON

In dealing on behalf of a client with a person who is not represented by counsel, a lawyer shall not state or imply that the lawyer is disinterested. When the lawyer knows or reasonably should know that the unrepresented person misunderstands the lawyer's role in the matter, the lawyer shall make reasonable efforts to correct the misunderstanding. The lawyer shall not give legal advice to an unrepresented person, other than the advice to secure counsel, if the lawyer knows or reasonably should know that the interests of such a person are or have a reasonable possibility of being in conflict with the interests of the client.

Comment

[1] An unrepresented person, particularly one not experienced in dealing with legal matters, might assume that a lawyer is disinterested in loyalties or is a disinterested authority on the law even when the lawyer represents a client. In order to avoid a misunderstanding, a lawyer will typically need to identify the lawyer's client and, where necessary, explain that the client has interests opposed to those of the unrepresented person. For misunderstandings that sometimes arise when a lawyer for an organization deals with an unrepresented constituent, see Rule 1.13(f).

[2] The Rule distinguishes between situations involving unrepresented persons whose interests may be adverse to those of the lawyer's client and those in which the person's interests are not in conflict with the client's. In the former situation, the possibility that the lawyer will compromise the unrepresented person's interests is so great that the Rule prohibits the giving of any advice, apart from the advice to obtain counsel. Whether a lawyer is giving impermissible advice may depend on the experience and sophistication of the unrepresented person, as well as the setting in which the behavior and comments occur. This Rule does not prohibit a lawyer from negotiating the terms of a transaction or settling a dispute with an unrepresented person. So long as the lawyer has explained that the lawyer represents an adverse party and is not representing the person, the lawyer may inform the person of the terms on which the lawyer's client will enter into an agreement or settle a matter, prepare documents that require the person's signature and explain the lawyer's own view of the meaning of the document or the lawyer's view of the underlying legal obligations.

RULE 4.4 RESPECT FOR RIGHTS OF THIRD PERSONS

(a) In representing a client, a lawyer shall not use means that have no substantial purpose other than to embarrass, delay, or burden a third person, or use methods of obtaining evidence that violate the legal rights of such a person.

(b) A lawyer who receives a document relating to the representation of the lawyer's client and knows or reasonably should know that the document was inadvertently sent shall promptly notify the sender.

Comment

[1] Responsibility to a client requires a lawyer to subordinate the interests of others to those of the client, but that responsibility does not imply that a lawyer may disregard the rights of third persons. It is impractical to catalogue all such rights, but they include legal restrictions on methods of obtaining evidence from third persons and unwarranted intrusions into privileged relationships, such as the client-lawyer relationship.

[2] Paragraph (b) recognizes that lawyers sometimes receive documents that were mistakenly sent or produced by opposing parties or their lawyers. If a lawyer knows or reasonably should know that such a document was sent inadvertently, then this Rule requires the lawyer to promptly notify the sender in order to permit that person to take protective measures. Whether the lawyer is required to take additional steps, such as returning the original document, is a matter of law beyond the scope of these Rules, as is

the question of whether the privileged status of a document has been waived. Similarly, this Rule does not address the legal duties of a lawyer who receives a document that the lawyer knows or reasonably should know may have been wrongfully obtained by the sending person. For purposes of this Rule, "document" includes e-mail or other electronic modes of transmission subject to being read or put into readable form.

[3] Some lawyers may choose to return a document unread, for example, when the lawyer learns before receiving the document that it was inadvertently sent to the wrong address. Where a lawyer is not required by applicable law to do so, the decision to voluntarily return such a document is a matter of professional judgment ordinarily reserved to the lawyer. See Rules 1.2 and 1.4.

ABA Code

DR 7-102 Representing a Client Within the Bounds of the Law.

(A) In his representation of a client, a lawyer shall not:

(1) File a suit, assert a position, conduct a defense, delay a trial, or take other action on behalf of his client when he knows or when it is obvious that such action would serve merely to harass or maliciously injure another.

(2) Knowingly advance a claim or defense that is unwarranted under existing law, except that he may advance such claim or defense if it can be supported by good faith argument for an extension, modification, or reversal of existing law.

(3) Conceal or knowingly fail to disclose that which he is required by law to reveal.

(4) Knowingly use perjured testimony or false evidence.

(5) Knowingly make a false statement of law or fact.

(6) Participate in the creation or preservation of evidence when he knows or it is obvious that the evidence is false.

(7) Counsel or assist his client in conduct that the lawyer knows to be illegal or fraudulent.

(8) Knowingly engage in other illegal conduct or conduct contrary to a Disciplinary Rule.

(B) A lawyer who receives information clearly establishing that:

(1) His client has, in the course of the representation, perpetrated a fraud upon a person or tribunal shall promptly call upon his client to rectify the same, and if his client refuses or is unable to do so, he shall reveal the fraud to the affected person or tribunal, except when the information is protected as a privileged communication.

(2) A person other than his client has perpetrated a fraud upon a tribunal shall promptly reveal the fraud to the tribunal.

DR 7-104 (A) (2) Communicating With One of Adverse Interest.

(A) During the course of his representation of a client a lawyer shall not:

* * *

(2) Give advice to a person who is not represented by a lawyer, other than the advice to secure counsel, if the interests of such person are or have a reasonable possibility of being in conflict with the interests of his client.

V-3. Truthfulness: Cases and Materials

Statement of the Acting Solicitor General, May 20, 2011

(from "The Justice Blog," United States Department of Justice,
available at http://blogs.usdoj.gov/blog/archives/1346)

It has been my privilege to have served as Acting Solicitor General for the past year and to have served as Principal Deputy Solicitor General before that. The Solicitor General is responsible for overseeing appellate litigation on behalf of the United States, and with representing the United States in the Supreme Court. There are several terrific accounts of the roles that Solicitors General have played throughout history in advancing civil rights. But it is also important to remember the mistakes. One episode of particular relevance to AAPI Heritage Month is the Solicitor General's defense of the forced relocation and internment of Japanese-American during World War II.

Following the attack on Pearl Harbor, the United States uprooted more than 100,000 people of Japanese descent, most of them American citizens, and confined them in internment camps. The Solicitor General was largely responsible for the defense of those policies.

By the time the cases of Gordon Hirabayashi and Fred Korematsu reached the Supreme Court, the Solicitor General had learned of a key intelligence report that undermined the rationale behind the internment. The Ringle Report, from the Office of Naval Intelligence, found that only a small percentage of Japanese Americans posed a potential security threat, and that the most dangerous were already known or in custody. But the Solicitor General did not inform the Court of the report, despite warnings from Department of Justice attorneys that failing to alert the Court "might approximate the suppression of evidence." Instead, he argued that it was impossible to segregate loyal Japanese Americans from disloyal ones. Nor did he inform the Court that a key set of allegations used to justify the internment, that Japanese Americans were using radio transmitters to communicate with enemy submarines off the West Coast, had been discredited by the FBI and FCC. And to make matters worse, he relied on gross generalizations about Japanese Americans, such as that they were disloyal and motivated by "racial solidarity."

The Supreme Court upheld Hirabayashi's and Korematsu's convictions. And it took nearly a half century for courts to overturn these decisions. One court decision in the 1980s that did so highlighted the role played by the Solicitor General, emphasizing that the Supreme Court gave "special credence" to the Solicitor General's representations. The court thought it unlikely that the Supreme Court would have ruled the same way had the Solicitor General exhibited complete candor. Yet those decisions still stand today as a reminder of the mistakes of that era.

Today, our Office takes this history as an important reminder that the "special credence" the Solicitor General enjoys before the Supreme Court requires great responsibility and a duty of absolute candor in our representations to the Court. Only then can we fulfill our responsibility to defend the United States and its Constitution, and to protect the rights of all Americans.

Neal Katyal is the Acting Solicitor General of the United States.

American Law Institute Restatement of
The Law Governing Lawyers (Philadelphia, 2000)
Ch. 6, pp. 58–61

§ 98. Statements to a Nonclient

A lawyer communicating on behalf of a client with a nonclient may not:

(1) knowingly make a false statement of material fact or law to the nonclient,

(2) make other statements prohibited by law; or

(3) fail to make a disclosure of information required by law.

Comment:

a. Scope and cross-references. This Section considers misrepresentations by a lawyer in the course of representing a client. Its rules may apply in representing a client in litigation, such as when negotiating a settlement, as well as in nonlitigation situations. On remedies, see Comment *g* hereto and § 51 and § 56, Comment *f*; see also generally § 6. For liability with respect to erroneous statements in an opinion letter or similar evaluation, see § 51(2) and Comment *e* thereto and § 95. On more stringent requirements for statements in some representations of a client before a legislative or administrative body, see § 104. The Section does not purport to state rules of liability under state and federal securities legislation.

On the standard of truthfulness for statements to clients, see §§ 16, 20, and 56. On the standard for communications with a tribunal, see § 120(1)(b). See also § 112 (ex parte and similar proceedings).

On warning a potential victim of certain criminal or fraudulent activities of a client, see §§ 66–67. On a lawyer's right to withdraw when the client engages in criminal or fraudulent conduct, see § 32(3)(d). On a lawyer's duty to protect confidential information of a client, see § 60. A lawyer's obligation not to make statements that mislead an unrepresented nonclient is addressed in § 103.

b. Rationale. A lawyer communicating with a nonclient on behalf of a client is not privileged to make a material misrepresentation of fact or law to the nonclient. See generally Restatement Second, Agency §§ 343 and 348. The law governing misrepresentation by a lawyer includes the criminal law (theft by deception), the law of misrepresentation in tort law and of mistake and fraud in contract law, and procedural law governing statements by an advocate (see § 120, Comment *f*). Compliance with those obligations meets social expectations of honesty and fair dealing and facilitates negotiation and adjudication, which are important professional functions of lawyers. Corresponding duties are stated in lawyer codes, which are generally based on the requirements of criminal and civil law.

This Section applies equally to statements made to a sophisticated person, such as to a lawyer representing another client, as well as to an unsophisticated person. However, the sophistication in similar transactions of a person to whom a representation is made is relevant in determining such issues as the reasonableness of the person's reliance on the representation.

c. Knowing misrepresentation. The law of misrepresentation applies to lawyers. See generally Restatement Second, Contracts § 159 and following; Restatement Second, Torts § 525 and following. For purposes of common-law damage recovery, reckless as well as knowing misrepresentation by a lawyer may be actionable. On negligent misrepresentation, see also § 51(2). A misrepresentation can occur through direct statement or through affirmation of a misrepresentation of another, as when a lawyer knowingly affirms a client's false or misleading statement. A statement can also be false because only partially true. If constrained from conveying specific information to a nonclient, for example due to confidentiality obligations to the lawyer's client, the lawyer must either make no representation or make a representation that is not false.

For purposes of professional discipline, the lawyer codes generally incorporate the definition of misrepresentation employed in the civil law of tort damage liability for knowing misrepresentation, including the elements of falsity, scienter, and materiality. However, for disciplinary purposes, reliance by and injury to another person are not required. The lawyer codes of many jurisdictions also prohibit a lawyer from engaging in "conduct involving dishonesty, fraud, deceit, or misrepresentation" (see § 5, Comment *c*). Some courts have interpreted these provisions to impose a more exacting standard of disclosure than the prohibition against knowing misrepresentation (compare id.).

A knowing misrepresentation may relate to a proposition of fact or law. Certain statements, such as some statements relating to price or value, are considered nonactionable hyperbole or a reflection of the state of mind of the speaker and not misstatements of fact or law (see Restatement Second, Contracts § 168; Restatement Third, Unfair Competition § 3, Comment *d*). Whether a misstatement should be so characterized depends on whether it is reasonably apparent that the person to whom the statement is addressed would regard the statement as one of fact or based on the speaker's knowledge of facts reasonably implied by the statement or as merely an expression of the speaker's state of mind. Assessment depends on the circumstances in which the statement is made, including the past relationship of the negotiating persons, their apparent sophistication, the plausibility of the statement on its face, the phrasing of the statement, related communication between the persons involved, the known negotiating practices of the community in which both are negotiating, and similar circumstances. In general, a lawyer who is known to represent a person in a negotiation will be understood by nonclients to be making nonimpartial statements, in the same manner as would the lawyer's client. Subject to such an understanding, the lawyer is not privileged to make misrepresentations described in this Section.

A lawyer may also be liable under civil or criminal law for aiding and abetting a client's misrepresentation (see § 8). A lawyer representing a client in a transaction with respect to which the client has made a misrepresentation is not free, after the lawyer learns of the misrepresentation, to continue providing assistance to the client as if the misrepresentation had not been made when the lawyer's continued representation of the client would induce the nonclient reasonably to believe that no such misrepresentation has occurred.

Illustration:

1. Client has contracted to sell interests in Client's business to Buyer. As part of the arrangement, Lawyer for Client prepares an offering statement to be presented to Buyer. Lawyer knows that information in the statement, provided by Client, is materially misleading; the information shows Client's business as profitable and growing, but Lawyer knows that its assets are heavily encumbered, business is declining and unprofitable, and the company has substantial debts. Lawyer's knowing actions assisted Client's fraud.

d. Subsequently discovered falsity. A lawyer who has made a representation on behalf of a client reasonably believing it true when made may subsequently come to know of its falsity. An obligation to disclose before consummation of the transaction ordinarily arises, unless the lawyer takes other corrective action. See Restatement Second, Agency § 348, Comment *c*; Restatement Second, Contracts § 161(a) (nondisclosure as equivalent to assertion when person "knows that disclosure of the fact is necessary to prevent some previous assertion from being a misrepresentation or from being fraudulent or material"). Disclosure, being required by law (see § 63), is not prohibited by the general rule of confidentiality (see § 60). Disclosure should not exceed what is required to comply with the disclosure obligation, for example by indicating to recipients that they should not rely on the lawyer's statement. On permissive disclosure to prevent or rectify a client's wrongful act, see §§ 66–67.

e. Affirmative disclosure. In general, a lawyer has no legal duty to make an affirmative disclosure of fact or law when dealing with a nonclient. Applicable statutes, regulations, or common-law rules may require affirmative disclosure in some circumstances, for example disciplinary rules in some states requiring lawyers to disclose a client's intent to commit life-threatening crimes or other wrongful conduct (see § 66, Comment *b*, and Reporter's Note thereto; on permissive disclosure, see §§ 66–67).

On the duty to disclose the lawyer's role as representative of a client to avoid misleading an unrepresented nonclient, see § 103. With respect to a duty to disclose legal authority to a tribunal, see § 111. On the absence of a general duty to disclose facts to a tribunal, see § 120, Comment *b*. See also § 112 on disclosure requirements in ex parte and similar proceedings. On the duty to disclose false evidence to a tribunal, see § 120(2) and Comment *i*.

f. Other wrongful statements. Beyond the law of misrepresentation, other civil or criminal law may constrain a lawyer's statements, for example, the criminal law of extortion. In some jurisdictions, lawyer codes prohibit a lawyer negotiating a civil claim from referring to the prospect of filing criminal charges against the opposing party. On the extent of lawyer liability for defamatory statements concerning nonclients, see § 57(1).

g. Remedies. In general, a lawyer who makes fraudulent misrepresentation is subject to liability to the injured person when the other elements of the tort are established (see Restatement Second, Agency § 348; see generally § 56). On remedies for nonnegligent misrepresentation, see Restatement Second, Torts § 552C (difference in values represented and those in fact existing). A lawyer's misrepresentation may also be a basis for setting aside or reforming a contract, as well as other contractual remedies (see Restatement Second, Contracts § 345).

The types of misstatements prohibited in the lawyer codes are different in certain important respects from the definitions of false statement for the purposes of many kinds of civil actions, for example because the disciplinary standard does not require third-party reliance or actual harm (see Comment *c* hereto). Conversely, a lawyer's merely negligent misrepresentation (see § 51(2)) may constitute grounds for liability to an injured party but not for discipline for fraud.

A. Constitutional Requirements

Nix v. Whiteside

475 U.S. 157
U.S. Supreme Court
Argued November 5, 1985
Decided February 26, 1986
[Some footnotes omitted. Remaining footnotes renumbered.]

BURGER, C. J., delivered the opinion of the Court, in which WHITE, POWELL, REHN-QUIST, and O'CONNOR, JJ., joined. BRENNAN, J., filed an opinion concurring in the judgment. BLACKMUN, J., filed an opinion concurring in the judgment, in which BRENNAN, MARSHALL, and STEVENS, JJ., joined. STEVENS, J., filed an opinion concurring in the judgment.

CHIEF JUSTICE BURGER delivered the opinion of the Court.

We granted certiorari to decide whether the Sixth Amendment right of a criminal defendant to assistance of counsel is violated when an attorney refuses to cooperate with the defendant in presenting perjured testimony at his trial.[1]

I

A

Whiteside was convicted of second-degree murder by a jury verdict which was affirmed by the Iowa courts. The killing took place on February 8, 1977, in Cedar Rapids, Iowa. Whiteside and two others went to one Calvin Love's apartment late that night, seeking marihuana. Love was in bed when Whiteside and his companions arrived; an argument between Whiteside and Love over the marihuana ensued. At one point, Love directed his girlfriend to get his "piece," and at another point got up, then returned to his bed. According to Whiteside's testimony, Love then started to reach under his pillow and moved toward Whiteside. Whiteside stabbed Love in the chest, inflicting a fatal wound.

Whiteside was charged with murder, and when counsel was appointed he objected to the lawyer initially appointed, claiming that he felt uncomfortable with a lawyer who had formerly been a prosecutor. Gary L. Robinson was then appointed and immediately began an investigation. Whiteside gave him a statement that he had stabbed Love as the latter "was pulling a pistol from underneath the pillow on the bed." Upon questioning by Robinson, however, Whiteside indicated that he had not actually seen a gun, but that he was convinced that Love had a gun. No pistol was found on the premises; shortly after the police search following the stabbing, which had revealed no weapon, the victim's family had removed all of the victim's possessions from the apartment. Robinson interviewed Whiteside's companions who were present during the stabbing, and none

---

1. Although courts universally condemn an attorney's assisting in presenting perjury, Courts of Appeals have taken varying approaches on how to deal with a client's insistence on presenting perjured testimony. The Seventh Circuit, for example, has held that an attorney's refusal to call the defendant as a witness did not render the conviction constitutionally infirm where the refusal to call the defendant was based on the attorney's belief that the defendant would commit perjury. United States v. Curtis, 742 F.2d 1070 (1984). The Third Circuit found a violation of the Sixth Amendment where the attorney could not state any basis for her belief that defendant's proposed alibi testimony was perjured. United States ex rel. Wilcox v. Johnson, 555 F.2d 115 (1977). See also Lowery v. Cardwell, 575 F.2d 727 (CA9 1978) (withdrawal request in the middle of a bench trial, immediately following defendant's testimony).

had seen a gun during the incident. Robinson advised Whiteside that the existence of a gun was not necessary to establish the claim of self-defense, and that only a reasonable belief that the victim had a gun nearby was necessary even though no gun was actually present.

Until shortly before trial, Whiteside consistently stated to Robinson that he had not actually seen a gun, but that he was convinced that Love had a gun in his hand. About a week before trial, during preparation for direct examination, Whiteside for the first time told Robinson and his associate Donna Paulsen that he had seen something "metallic" in Love's hand. When asked about this, Whiteside responded:

"[I]n Howard Cook's case there was a gun. If I don't say I saw a gun, I'm dead."

Robinson told Whiteside that such testimony would be perjury and repeated that it was not necessary to prove that a gun was available but only that Whiteside reasonably believed that he was in danger. On Whiteside's insisting that he would testify that he saw "something metallic" Robinson told him, according to Robinson's testimony:

"[W]e could not allow him to [testify falsely] because that would be perjury, and as officers of the court we would be suborning perjury if we allowed him to do it; ... I advised him that if he did do that it would be my duty to advise the Court of what he was doing and that I felt he was committing perjury; also, that I probably would be allowed to attempt to impeach that particular testimony." App. to Pet. for Cert. A-85.

Robinson also indicated he would seek to withdraw from the representation if Whiteside insisted on committing perjury.[2]

Whiteside testified in his own defense at trial and stated that he "knew" that Love had a gun and that he believed Love was reaching for a gun and he had acted swiftly in self-defense. On cross-examination, he admitted that he had not actually seen a gun in Love's hand. Robinson presented evidence that Love had been seen with a sawed-off shotgun on other occasions, that the police search of the apartment may have been careless, and that the victim's family had removed everything from the apartment shortly after the crime. Robinson presented this evidence to show a basis for Whiteside's asserted fear that Love had a gun.

The jury returned a verdict of second-degree murder, and Whiteside moved for a new trial, claiming that he had been deprived of a fair trial by Robinson's admonitions not to state that he saw a gun or "something metallic." The trial court held a hearing, heard testimony by Whiteside and Robinson, and denied the motion. The trial court made specific findings that the facts were as related by Robinson.

The Supreme Court of Iowa affirmed respondent's conviction. State v. Whiteside, 272 N. W. 2d 468 (1978). That court held that the right to have counsel present all appropriate defenses does not extend to using perjury, and that an attorney's duty to a client does not extend to assisting a client in committing perjury. Relying on DR 7-102(A)(4) of the Iowa Code of Professional Responsibility for Lawyers, which expressly prohibits an attorney from using perjured testimony, and Iowa Code 721.2 (now Iowa Code 720.3 (1985)), which criminalizes subornation of perjury, the Iowa court concluded that not

---

2. Whiteside's version of the events at this pretrial meeting is considerably more cryptic: "Q. And as you went over the questions, did the two of you come into conflict with regard to whether or not there was a weapon? "A. I couldn't—I couldn't say a conflict. But I got the impression at one time that maybe if I didn't go along with—with what was happening, that it was no gun being involved, maybe that he will pull out of my trial." App. to Pet. for Cert. A-70.

only were Robinson's actions permissible, but were required. The court commended "both Mr. Robinson and Ms. Paulsen for the high ethical manner in which this matter was handled."

B

Whiteside then petitioned for a writ of habeas corpus in the United States District Court for the Southern District of Iowa. In that petition Whiteside alleged that he had been denied effective assistance of counsel and of his right to present a defense by Robinson's refusal to allow him to testify as he had proposed. The District Court denied the writ. Accepting the state trial court's factual finding that Whiteside's intended testimony would have been perjurious, it concluded that there could be no grounds for habeas relief since there is no constitutional right to present a perjured defense.

The United States Court of Appeals for the Eighth Circuit reversed and directed that the writ of habeas corpus be granted. Whiteside v. Scurr, 744 F.2d 1323 (1984). The Court of Appeals accepted the findings of the trial judge, affirmed by the Iowa Supreme Court, that trial counsel believed with good cause that Whiteside would testify falsely and acknowledged that under Harris v. New York, 401 U.S. 222 (1971), a criminal defendant's privilege to testify in his own behalf does not include a right to commit perjury. Nevertheless, the court reasoned that an intent to commit perjury, communicated to counsel, does not alter a defendant's right to effective assistance of counsel and that Robinson's admonition to Whiteside that he would inform the court of Whiteside's perjury constituted a threat to violate the attorney's duty to preserve client confidences. According to the Court of Appeals, this threatened violation of client confidences breached the standards of effective representation set down in Strickland v. Washington, 466 U.S. 668 (1984). The court also concluded that Strickland's prejudice requirement was satisfied by an implication of prejudice from the conflict between Robinson's duty of loyalty to his client and his ethical duties. A petition for rehearing en banc was denied, with Judges Gibson, Ross, Fagg, and Bowman dissenting. Whiteside v. Scurr, 750 F.2d 713 (1984). We granted certiorari, 471 U.S. 1014 (1985), and we reverse.

II
* * *
C

We turn next to the question presented: the definition of the range of "reasonable professional" responses to a criminal defendant client who informs counsel that he will perjure himself on the stand. We must determine whether, in this setting, Robinson's conduct fell within the wide range of professional responses to threatened client perjury acceptable under the Sixth Amendment.

In Strickland, we recognized counsel's duty of loyalty and his "overarching duty to advocate the defendant's cause." Ibid. Plainly, that duty is limited to legitimate, lawful conduct compatible with the very nature of a trial as a search for truth. Although counsel must take all reasonable lawful means to attain the objectives of the client, counsel is precluded from taking steps or in any way assisting the client in presenting false evidence or otherwise violating the law. This principle has consistently been recognized in most unequivocal terms by expositors of the norms of professional conduct since the first Canons of Professional Ethics were adopted by the American Bar Association in 1908. The 1908 Canon 32 provided:

> "No client, corporate or individual, however powerful, nor any cause, civil or political, however important, is entitled to receive nor should any lawyer render any service or advice involving disloyalty to the law whose ministers we are, or

disrespect of the judicial office, which we are bound to uphold, or corruption of any person or persons exercising a public office or private trust, or deception or betrayal of the public.... He must ... observe and advise his client to observe the statute law...."

Of course, this Canon did no more than articulate centuries of accepted standards of conduct. Similarly, Canon 37, adopted in 1928, explicitly acknowledges as an exception to the attorney's duty of confidentiality a client's announced intention to commit a crime:

"The announced intention of a client to commit a crime is not included within the confidences which [the attorney] is bound to respect."

These principles have been carried through to contemporary codifications[3] of an attorney's professional responsibility. Disciplinary Rule 7-102 of the Model Code of Professional Responsibility (1980), entitled "Representing a Client Within the Bounds of the Law," provides:

"(A) In his representation of a client, a lawyer shall not:

....

"(4) Knowingly use perjured testimony or false evidence.

....

"(7) Counsel or assist his client in conduct that the lawyer knows to be illegal or fraudulent."

This provision has been adopted by Iowa, and is binding on all lawyers who appear in its courts. See Iowa Code of Professional Responsibility for Lawyers (1985). The more recent Model Rules of Professional Conduct (1983) similarly admonish attorneys to obey all laws in the course of representing a client:

"RULE 1.2 Scope of Representation

....

"(d) A lawyer shall not counsel a client to engage, or assist a client, in conduct that the lawyer knows is criminal or fraudulent...."

Both the Model Code of Professional Responsibility and the Model Rules of Professional Conduct also adopt the specific exception from the attorney-client privilege for disclosure of perjury that his client intends to commit or has committed. DR 4-101(C)(3) (intention of client to commit a crime); Rule 3.3 (lawyer has duty to disclose falsity of evidence even if disclosure compromises client confidences). Indeed, both the Model Code and the Model Rules do not merely authorize disclosure by counsel of

---

3. There currently exist two different codifications of uniform standards of professional conduct. The Model Code of Professional Responsibility was originally adopted by the American Bar Association in 1969, and was subsequently adopted (in many cases with modification) by nearly every state. The more recent Model Rules of Professional Conduct were adopted by the American Bar Association in 1983. Since their promulgation by the American Bar Association, the Model Rules have been adopted by 11 States: Arizona, Arkansas, Delaware, Minnesota, Missouri, Montana, Nevada, New Hampshire, New Jersey, North Carolina, and Washington. See 1 ABA/BNA Lawyers' Manual on Professional Conduct 334 (1984–1985) (New Jersey); id., at 445 (Arizona); id., at 855 (Montana, Minnesota); id., at 924 (Missouri); id., at 961 (Delaware, Washington); id., at 1026 (North Carolina); id., at 1127 (Arkansas); 2 id., at 14 (1986) (New Hampshire, Nevada). Iowa is one of the States that adopted a form of the Model Code of Professional Responsibility, but has yet to adopt the Model Rules. See Iowa Code of Professional Responsibility for Lawyers (1985).

client perjury; they require such disclosure. See Rule 3.3(a)(4); DR 7-102(B)(1); Committee on Professional Ethics and Conduct of Iowa State Bar Assn. v. Crary, 245 N. W. 2d 298 (Iowa 1976).

These standards confirm that the legal profession has accepted that an attorney's ethical duty to advance the interests of his client is limited by an equally solemn duty to comply with the law and standards of professional conduct; it specifically ensures that the client may not use false evidence.[4] This special duty of an attorney to prevent and disclose frauds upon the court derives from the recognition that perjury is as much a crime as tampering with witnesses or jurors by way of promises and threats, and undermines the administration of justice. See 1 W. Burdick, Law of Crime 293, 300, 318–336 (1946).

The offense of perjury was a crime recognized at common law, id., at p. 475, and has been made a felony in most states by statute, including Iowa. Iowa Code 720.2 (1985). See generally 4 C. Torcia, Wharton's Criminal Law 631 (14th ed. 1981). An attorney who aids false testimony by questioning a witness when perjurious responses can be anticipated risks prosecution for subornation of perjury under Iowa Code 720.3 (1985).

It is universally agreed that at a minimum the attorney's first duty when confronted with a proposal for perjurious testimony is to attempt to dissuade the client from the unlawful course of conduct. Model Rules of Professional Conduct, Rule 3.3, Comment; Wolfram, Client Perjury, 50 S. Cal. L. Rev. 809, 846 (1977). A statement directly in point is found in the commentary to the Model Rules of Professional Conduct under the heading "False Evidence":

> "When false evidence is offered by the client, however, a conflict may arise between the lawyer's duty to keep the client's revelations confidential and the duty of candor to the court. Upon ascertaining that material evidence is false, the lawyer should seek to persuade the client that the evidence should not be offered or, if it has been offered, that its false character should immediately be disclosed." Model Rules of Professional Conduct, Rule 3.3, Comment (1983) (emphasis added).

The commentary thus also suggests that an attorney's revelation of his client's perjury to the court is a professionally responsible and acceptable response to the conduct of a client who has actually given perjured testimony. Similarly, the Model Rules and the commentary, as well as the Code of Professional Responsibility adopted in Iowa, expressly permit withdrawal from representation as an appropriate response of an attorney when the client threatens to commit perjury. Model Rules of Professional Conduct, Rule 1.16(a)(1), Rule 1.6, Comment (1983); Code of Professional Responsibility, DR 2-110(B), (C) (1980). Withdrawal of counsel when this situation arises at trial gives rise to many difficult questions including possible mistrial and claims of double jeopardy.[5]

---

4. The brief of amicus American Bar Association, which supports petitioner, makes this point, referring to the history of codes of professional conduct which it has promulgated. The preamble to the most current version of the ethical standards recognizes the difficult choices that may confront an attorney who is sensitive to his concurrent duties to his client and to the legal system: "Within the framework of these Rules many difficult issues of professional discretion can arise. Such issues must be resolved through the exercise of sensitive professional and moral judgment guided by the basic principles underlying the Rules." Preamble, Model Rules of Professional Conduct, p. 10 (1983).

5. In the evolution of the contemporary standards promulgated by the American Bar Association, an early draft reflects a compromise suggesting that when the disclosure of intended perjury is made during the course of trial, when withdrawal of counsel would raise difficult questions of a mistrial holding, counsel had the option to let the defendant take the stand but decline to affirma-

The essence of the brief amicus of the American Bar Association reviewing practices long accepted by ethical lawyers is that under no circumstance may a lawyer either advocate or passively tolerate a client's giving false testimony. This, of course, is consistent with the governance of trial conduct in what we have long called "a search for truth." The suggestion sometimes made that "a lawyer must believe his client, not judge him" in no sense means a lawyer can honorably be a party to or in any way give aid to presenting known perjury.

D

Considering Robinson's representation of respondent in light of these accepted norms of professional conduct, we discern no failure to adhere to reasonable professional standards that would in any sense make out a deprivation of the Sixth Amendment right to counsel. Whether Robinson's conduct is seen as a successful attempt to dissuade his client from committing the crime of perjury, or whether seen as a "threat" to withdraw from representation and disclose the illegal scheme, Robinson's representation of Whiteside falls well within accepted standards of professional conduct and the range of reasonable professional conduct acceptable under Strickland.

The Court of Appeals assumed for the purpose of the decision that Whiteside would have given false testimony had counsel not intervened; its opinion denying a rehearing en banc states:

"[W]e presume that appellant would have testified falsely.

. . .

"... Counsel's actions prevented [Whiteside] from testifying falsely. We hold that counsel's action deprived appellant of due process and effective assistance of counsel.

. . .

"Counsel's actions also impermissibly compromised appellant's right to testify in his own defense by conditioning continued representation by counsel and confidentiality upon appellant's restricted testimony." 750 F.2d., at 714–715.

While purporting to follow Iowa's highest court "on all questions of state law," 744 F.2d., at 1330, the Court of Appeals reached its conclusions on the basis of federal constitutional due process and right to counsel.

The Court of Appeals' holding that Robinson's "action deprived [Whiteside] of due process and effective assistance of counsel" is not supported by the record since Robinson's action, at most, deprived Whiteside of his contemplated perjury. Nothing counsel

---

tively assist the presentation of perjury by traditional direct examination. Instead, counsel would stand mute while the defendant undertook to present the false version in narrative form in his own words unaided by any direct examination. This conduct was thought to be a signal at least to the presiding judge that the attorney considered the testimony to be false and was seeking to disassociate himself from that course. Additionally, counsel would not be permitted to discuss the known false testimony in closing arguments. See ABA Standards for Criminal Justice, Proposed Standard 4-7.7 (2d ed. 1980). Most courts treating the subject rejected this approach and insisted on a more rigorous standard, see, e. g., United States v. Curtis, 742 F.2d 1070 (CA7 1984); McKissick v. United States, 379 F.2d 754 (CA5 1967); Dodd v. Florida Bar, 118 So.2d 17, 19 (Fla. 1960). The Eighth Circuit in this case and the Ninth Circuit have expressed approval of the "free narrative" standards. Whiteside v. Scurr, 744 F.2d 1323, 1331 (CA8 1984); Lowery v. Cardwell, 575 F.2d 727 (CA9 1978). The Rule finally promulgated in the current Model Rules of Professional Conduct rejects any participation or passive role whatever by counsel in allowing perjury to be presented without challenge.

did in any way undermined Whiteside's claim that he believed the victim was reaching for a gun. Similarly, the record gives no support for holding that Robinson's action "also impermissibly compromised [Whiteside's] right to testify in his own defense by conditioning continued representation … and confidentiality upon [Whiteside's] restricted testimony." The record in fact shows the contrary: (a) that Whiteside did testify, and (b) he was "restricted" or restrained only from testifying falsely and was aided by Robinson in developing the basis for the fear that Love was reaching for a gun. Robinson divulged no client communications until he was compelled to do so in response to Whiteside's post-trial challenge to the quality of his performance. We see this as a case in which the attorney successfully dissuaded the client from committing the crime of perjury.

Paradoxically, even while accepting the conclusion of the Iowa trial court that Whiteside's proposed testimony would have been a criminal act, the Court of Appeals held that Robinson's efforts to persuade Whiteside not to commit that crime were improper, first, as forcing an impermissible choice between the right to counsel and the right to testify; and, second, as compromising client confidences because of Robinson's threat to disclose the contemplated perjury.[6]

Whatever the scope of a constitutional right to testify, it is elementary that such a right does not extend to testifying falsely. In Harris v. New York, we assumed the right of an accused to testify "in his own defense, or to refuse to do so" and went on to hold:

> "[T]hat privilege cannot be construed to include the right to commit perjury. See United States v. Knox, 396 U.S. 77 (1969); cf. Dennis v. United States, 384 U.S. 855 (1966). Having voluntarily taken the stand, petitioner was under an obligation to speak truthfully...." 401 U.S., at 225.

In Harris we held the defendant could be impeached by prior contrary statements which had been ruled inadmissible under Miranda v. Arizona, 384 U.S. 436 (1966). Harris and other cases make it crystal clear that there is no right whatever—constitutional or otherwise—for a defendant to use false evidence. See also United States v. Havens, 446 U.S. 620, 626–627 (1980).

The paucity of authority on the subject of any such "right" may be explained by the fact that such a notion has never been responsibly advanced; the right to counsel includes no right to have a lawyer who will cooperate with planned perjury. A lawyer who would so cooperate would be at risk of prosecution for suborning perjury, and disciplinary proceedings, including suspension or disbarment.

Robinson's admonitions to his client can in no sense be said to have forced respondent into an impermissible choice between his right to counsel and his right to testify as he proposed for there was no permissible choice to testify falsely. For defense counsel to take steps to persuade a criminal defendant to testify truthfully, or to withdraw, deprives the defendant of neither his right to counsel nor the right to testify truthfully. In United States v. Havens, supra, we made clear that "when defendants testify, they must testify

---

6. The Court of Appeals also determined that Robinson's efforts to persuade Whiteside to testify truthfully constituted an impermissible threat to testify against his own client. We find no support for a threat to testify against Whiteside while he was acting as counsel. The record reflects testimony by Robinson that he had admonished Whiteside that if he withdrew he "probably would be allowed to attempt to impeach that particular testimony," if Whiteside testified falsely. The trial court accepted this version of the conversation as true.

truthfully or suffer the consequences." Id., at 626. When an accused proposed to resort to perjury or to produce false evidence, one consequence is the risk of withdrawal of counsel.

On this record, the accused enjoyed continued representation within the bounds of reasonable professional conduct and did in fact exercise his right to testify; at most he was denied the right to have the assistance of counsel in the presentation of false testimony. Similarly, we can discern no breach of professional duty in Robinson's admonition to respondent that he would disclose respondent's perjury to the court. The crime of perjury in this setting is indistinguishable in substance from the crime of threatening or tampering with a witness or a juror. A defendant who informed his counsel that he was arranging to bribe or threaten witnesses or members of the jury would have no "right" to insist on counsel's assistance or silence. Counsel would not be limited to advising against that conduct. An attorney's duty of confidentiality, which totally covers the client's admission of guilt, does not extend to a client's announced plans to engage in future criminal conduct. See Clark v. United States, 289 U.S. 1, 15 (1933). In short, the responsibility of an ethical lawyer, as an officer of the court and a key component of a system of justice, dedicated to a search for truth, is essentially the same whether the client announces an intention to bribe or threaten witnesses or jurors or to commit or procure perjury. No system of justice worthy of the name can tolerate a lesser standard.

The rule adopted by the Court of Appeals, which seemingly would require an attorney to remain silent while his client committed perjury, is wholly incompatible with the established standards of ethical conduct and the laws of Iowa and contrary to professional standards promulgated by that State. The position advocated by petitioner, on the contrary, is wholly consistent with the Iowa standards of professional conduct and law, with the overwhelming majority of courts, and with codes of professional ethics. Since there has been no breach of any recognized professional duty, it follows that there can be no deprivation of the right to assistance of counsel under the Strickland standard.

E

We hold that, as a matter of law, counsel's conduct complained of here cannot establish the prejudice required for relief under the second strand of the Strickland inquiry. Although a defendant need not establish that the attorney's deficient performance more likely than not altered the outcome in order to establish prejudice under Strickland, a defendant must show that "there is a reasonable probability that, but for counsel's unprofessional errors, the result of the proceeding would have been different." 466 U.S., at 694. According to Strickland, "[a] reasonable probability is a probability sufficient to undermine confidence in the outcome." Ibid. The Strickland Court noted that the "benchmark" of an ineffective-assistance claim is the fairness of the adversary proceeding, and that in judging prejudice and the likelihood of a different outcome, "[a] defendant has no entitlement to the luck of a lawless decisionmaker." Id., at 695.

Whether he was persuaded or compelled to desist from perjury, Whiteside has no valid claim that confidence in the result of his trial has been diminished by his desisting from the contemplated perjury. Even if we were to assume that the jury might have believed his perjury, it does not follow that Whiteside was prejudiced.

In his attempt to evade the prejudice requirement of Strickland, Whiteside relies on cases involving conflicting loyalties of counsel. In Cuyler v. Sullivan, 446 U.S. 335 (1980), we held that a defendant could obtain relief without pointing to a specific prejudicial default on the part of his counsel, provided it is established that the attorney was "actively represent[ing] conflicting interests." Id., at 350.

Here, there was indeed a "conflict," but of a quite different kind; it was one imposed on the attorney by the client's proposal to commit the crime of fabricating testimony without which, as he put it, "I'm dead." This is not remotely the kind of conflict of interests dealt with in Cuyler v. Sullivan. Even in that case we did not suggest that all multiple representations necessarily resulted in an active conflict rendering the representation constitutionally infirm. If a "conflict" between a client's proposal and counsel's ethical obligation gives rise to a presumption that counsel's assistance was prejudicially ineffective, every guilty criminal's conviction would be suspect if the defendant had sought to obtain an acquittal by illegal means. Can anyone doubt what practices and problems would be spawned by such a rule and what volumes of litigation it would generate?

Whiteside's attorney treated Whiteside's proposed perjury in accord with professional standards, and since Whiteside's truthful testimony could not have prejudiced the result of his trial, the Court of Appeals was in error to direct the issuance of a writ of habeas corpus and must be reversed.

Reversed.

JUSTICE BRENNAN, concurring in the judgment.

This Court has no constitutional authority to establish rules of ethical conduct for lawyers practicing in the state courts. Nor does the Court enjoy any statutory grant of jurisdiction over legal ethics.

Accordingly, it is not surprising that the Court emphasizes that it "must be careful not to narrow the wide range of conduct acceptable under the Sixth Amendment so restrictively as to constitutionalize particular standards of professional conduct and thereby intrude into the state's proper authority to define and apply the standards of professional conduct applicable to those it admits to practice in its courts." Ante, at 165. I read this as saying in another way that the Court cannot tell the States or the lawyers in the States how to behave in their courts, unless and until federal rights are violated.

Unfortunately, the Court seems unable to resist the temptation of sharing with the legal community its vision of ethical conduct. But let there be no mistake: the Court's essay regarding what constitutes the correct response to a criminal client's suggestion that he will perjure himself is pure discourse without force of law. As JUSTICE BLACK-MUN observes, that issue is a thorny one, post, at 177–178, but it is not an issue presented by this case. Lawyers, judges, bar associations, students, and others should understand that the problem has not now been "decided."

I join JUSTICE BLACKMUN's concurrence because I agree that respondent has failed to prove the kind of prejudice necessary to make out a claim under Strickland v. Washington, 466 U.S. 668 (1984).

JUSTICE BLACKMUN, with whom JUSTICE BRENNAN, JUSTICE MARSHALL, and JUSTICE STEVENS join, concurring in the judgment.

How a defense attorney ought to act when faced with a client who intends to commit perjury at trial has long been a controversial issue.[7] But I do not believe that a federal

---

7. See, e. g., Callan & David, Professional Responsibility and the Duty of Confidentiality: Disclosure of Client Misconduct in an Adversary System, 29 Rutgers L. Rev. 332 (1976); Rieger, Client Perjury: A Proposed Resolution of the Constitutional and Ethical Issues, 70 Minn. L. Rev. 121 (1985); compare, e. g., Freedman, Professional Responsibility of the Criminal Defense Lawyer: The Three Hardest Questions, 64 Mich. L. Rev. 1469 (1966), and ABA Standards for Criminal Justice, Proposed Standard 4-7.7 (2d ed. 1980) (approved by the Standing Committee on Association Standards for Criminal Justice, but not yet submitted to the House of Delegates), with Noonan, The Purposes of

habeas corpus case challenging a state criminal conviction is an appropriate vehicle for attempting to resolve this thorny problem. When a defendant argues that he was denied effective assistance of counsel because his lawyer dissuaded him from committing perjury, the only question properly presented to this Court is whether the lawyer's actions deprived the defendant of the fair trial which the Sixth Amendment is meant to guarantee. Since I believe that the respondent in this case suffered no injury justifying federal habeas relief, I concur in the Court's judgment.

* * *

The Court of Appeals erred in concluding that prejudice should have been presumed. Strickland v. Washington found such a presumption appropriate in a case where an attorney labored under "'an actual conflict of interest [that] adversely affected his ... performance,'" id., at 692, quoting Cuyler v. Sullivan, 446 U.S., at 348. In this case, however, no actual conflict existed. I have already discussed why Whiteside had no right to Robinson's help in presenting perjured testimony. Moreover, Whiteside has identified no right to insist that Robinson keep confidential a plan to commit perjury. See Committee on Professional Ethics and Conduct of Iowa State Bar Assn. v. Crary, 245 N. W. 2d 298, 306 (Iowa 1976). The prior cases where this Court has reversed convictions involved conflicts that infringed a defendant's legitimate interest in vigorous protection of his constitutional rights. See, e. g., Wood v. Georgia, 450 U.S. 261, 268–271 (1981) (defense attorney paid by defendants' employer might have pursued employer's interest in litigating a test case rather than obtaining leniency for his clients by co-operating with prosecution); Glasser v. United States, 315 U.S. 60, 72–75 (1942) (defense attorney who simultaneously represented two defendants failed to object to certain potentially inadmissible evidence or to cross-examine a prosecution witness in an apparent attempt to minimize one codefendant's guilt). Here, Whiteside had no legitimate interest that conflicted with Robinson's obligations not to suborn perjury and to adhere to the Iowa Code of Professional Responsibility.

In addition, the lawyer's interest in not presenting perjured testimony was entirely consistent with Whiteside's best interest. If Whiteside had lied on the stand, he would have risked a future perjury prosecution. Moreover, his testimony would have been contradicted by the testimony of other eyewitnesses and by the fact that no gun was ever found. In light of that impeachment, the jury might have concluded that Whiteside lied as well about his lack of premeditation and thus might have convicted him of first-degree murder. And if the judge believed that Whiteside had lied, he could have taken Whiteside's perjury into account in setting the sentence. United States v. Grayson, 438 U.S. 41, 52–54 (1978).[8] In the face of these dangers, an attorney could reasonably conclude that dissuading his client from committing perjury was in the client's best interest and comported with standards of professional responsibility.[9] In short, Whiteside failed to show the kind of conflict that poses a danger to the values of zealous and loyal repre-

---

Advocacy and the Limits of Confidentiality, 64 Mich. L. Rev. 1485 (1966), and ABA Model Rules of Professional Conduct, Rule 3.3 and comment, at 66–67 (1983).

8. In fact, the State apparently asked the trial court to impose a sentence of 75 years, see Tr. 4 (Aug. 26, 1977), but the judge sentenced Whiteside to 40 years' imprisonment instead.

9. This is not to say that an attorney's ethical obligations will never conflict with a defendant's right to effective assistance. For example, an attorney who has previously represented one of the State's witnesses has a continuing obligation to that former client not to reveal confidential information received during the course of the prior representation. That continuing duty could conflict with his obligation to his present client, the defendant, to cross-examine the State's witnesses zealously. See Lowenthal, Successive Representation by Criminal Lawyers, 93 Yale L. J. 1 (1983).

sentation embodied in the Sixth Amendment. A presumption of prejudice is therefore unwarranted.

C

In light of respondent's failure to show any cognizable prejudice, I see no need to "grade counsel's performance." Strickland v. Washington, 466 U.S., at 697. The only federal issue in this case is whether Robinson's behavior deprived Whiteside of the effective assistance of counsel; it is not whether Robinson's behavior conformed to any particular code of legal ethics.

Whether an attorney's response to what he sees as a client's plan to commit perjury violates a defendant's Sixth Amendment rights may depend on many factors: how certain the attorney is that the proposed testimony is false, the stage of the proceedings at which the attorney discovers the plan, or the ways in which the attorney may be able to dissuade his client, to name just three. The complex interaction of factors, which is likely to vary from case to case, makes inappropriate a blanket rule that defense attorneys must reveal, or threaten to reveal, a client's anticipated perjury to the court. Except in the rarest of cases, attorneys who adopt "the role of the judge or jury to determine the facts," United States ex rel. Wilcox v. Johnson, 555 F.2d 115, 122 (CA3 1977), pose a danger of depriving their clients of the zealous and loyal advocacy required by the Sixth Amendment.[10]

I therefore am troubled by the Court's implicit adoption of a set of standards of professional responsibility for attorneys in state criminal proceedings. See ante, at 168–171. The States, of course, do have a compelling interest in the integrity of their criminal trials that can justify regulating the length to which an attorney may go in seeking his client's acquittal. But the American Bar Association's implicit suggestion in its brief amicus curiae that the Court find that the Association's Model Rules of Professional Conduct should govern an attorney's responsibilities is addressed to the wrong audience. It is for the States to decide how attorneys should conduct themselves in state criminal proceedings, and this Court's responsibility extends only to ensuring that the restrictions a State enacts do not infringe a defendant's federal constitutional rights. Thus, I would follow the suggestion made in the joint brief amici curiae filed by 37 States at the certiorari stage that we allow the States to maintain their "differing approaches" to a complex ethical question. Brief for State of Indiana et al. as Amici Curiae 5. The signal merit of asking first whether a defendant has shown any adverse prejudicial effect before inquiring into his attorney's performance is that it avoids unnecessary federal interference in a State's regulation of its bar. Because I conclude

---

10. A comparison of this case with Wilcox is illustrative. Here, Robinson testified in detail to the factors that led him to conclude that respondent's assertion he had seen a gun was false. See, e.g., Tr. 38–39, 43, 59 (July 29, 1977). The Iowa Supreme Court found "good cause" and "strong support" for Robinson's conclusion. State v. Whiteside, 272 N. W. 2d 468, 471 (1978). Moreover, Robinson gave credence to those parts of Whiteside's account which, although he found them implausible and unsubstantiated, were not clearly false. See Tr. 52–53 (July 29, 1977). By contrast, in Wilcox, where defense counsel actually informed the judge that she believed her client intended to lie and where her threat to withdraw in the middle of the trial led the defendant not to take the stand at all, the Court of Appeals found "no evidence on the record of this case indicating that Mr. Wilcox intended to perjure himself," and characterized counsel's beliefs as "private conjectures about the guilt or innocence of [her] client." 555 F.2d, at 122.

that the respondent in this case failed to show such an effect, I join the Court's judgment that he is not entitled to federal habeas relief.

JUSTICE STEVENS, concurring in the judgment.

Justice Holmes taught us that a word is but the skin of a living thought. A "fact" may also have a life of its own. From the perspective of an appellate judge, after a case has been tried and the evidence has been sifted by another judge, a particular fact may be as clear and certain as a piece of crystal or a small diamond. A trial lawyer, however, must often deal with mixtures of sand and clay. Even a pebble that seems clear enough at first glance may take on a different hue in a handful of gravel.

As we view this case, it appears perfectly clear that respondent intended to commit perjury, that his lawyer knew it, and that the lawyer had a duty—both to the court and to his client, for perjured testimony can ruin an otherwise meritorious case—to take extreme measures to prevent the perjury from occurring. The lawyer was successful and, from our unanimous and remote perspective, it is now pellucidly clear that the client suffered no "legally cognizable prejudice."

Nevertheless, beneath the surface of this case there are areas of uncertainty that cannot be resolved today. A lawyer's certainty that a change in his client's recollection is a harbinger of intended perjury—as well as judicial review of such apparent certainty—should be tempered by the realization that, after reflection, the most honest witness may recall (or sincerely believe he recalls) details that he previously overlooked. Similarly, the post-trial review of a lawyer's pretrial threat to expose perjury that had not yet been committed—and, indeed, may have been prevented by the threat—is by no means the same as review of the way in which such a threat may actually have been carried out. Thus, one can be convinced—as I am—that this lawyer's actions were a proper way to provide his client with effective representation without confronting the much more difficult questions of what a lawyer must, should, or may do after his client has given testimony that the lawyer does not believe. The answer to such questions may well be colored by the particular circumstances attending the actual event and its aftermath.

Because JUSTICE BLACKMUN has preserved such questions for another day, and because I do not understand him to imply any adverse criticism of this lawyer's representation of his client, I join his opinion concurring in the judgment.

Commonwealth v. Curtis Mitchell

438 Mass. 535
Supreme Judicial Court of Massachusetts
Argued Dec. 6, 2002
Decided Jan. 24, 2003
[Some footnotes omitted. Remaining footnotes renumbered.]

Present: MARSHALL, C.J., GREANEY, IRELAND, SPINA, COWIN, SOSMAN, & CORDY, JJ.

GREANEY, J. A jury convicted the defendant of two indictments charging murder in the first degree by reason of deliberate premeditation and extreme atrocity or cruelty. The defendant's motion for a new trial was denied by the trial judge, on the basis of affidavits, without an evidentiary hearing. The defendant is represented on appeal by the counsel who represented him in connection with his motion for a new trial. The defendant argues that he was denied constitutionally effective assistance of counsel (and incurred violations of other constitutional rights) when his trial counsel, relying on Mass. R. Prof. C. 3.3(e), 426 Mass. 1383 (1998), set forth below,[1] advised the judge at trial that the defendant would testify and present false testimony to the jury, that counsel had attempted to persuade the defendant from testifying falsely, that counsel had decided that he would not seek to withdraw from representing the defendant in the ongoing trial, and that counsel needed instruction from the judge on how to proceed before the jury. After receiving instruction, counsel presented the defendant's testimony in narrative form and made a closing argument that reflected his understanding of his ethical obligations. The defendant also argues that the judge erred by (a) denying a motion to dismiss the indictments because potentially exculpatory evidence had been lost; (b) rejecting his other contentions concerning the effectiveness of his trial counsel; and (c) denying his motion for funds to interview potentially exculpatory witnesses. We find no basis in any of the defendant's arguments to order a new trial. We also conclude that there is no reason to exercise our authority under G.L. c. 278, § 33E, to grant the defendant relief. Accordingly, we affirm the judgments of conviction and the orders denying the motion for a new trial and the motion for funds.

* * *

e. It is of no consequence that the defendant's trial counsel informed the judge, in the prosecutor's presence, of his intention to invoke rule 3.3(e). The defendant's trial counsel did not disclose what expected testimony he believed would be perjurious. Had the defendant's trial counsel left the prosecutor out of his discussions with the judge, the defendant's subsequent testimony in narrative form likely would have been met with strong objection from the prosecutor, thereby drawing the jury's attention to the procedure.

f. The narrative form of testimony was properly directed. This approach was adopted by the ABA in 1971. See ABA Standards for Criminal Justice 4-7.7 (Approved Draft 1971). Although the ABA later rejected this approach and currently suggests that the lawyer may examine as to truthful testimony, and although the approach has been criticized, see *United States v. Long*, 857 F.2d 436, 446 n. 7 (8th Cir.1988), "the narrative [approach] continues to be a commonly accepted method of dealing with client perjury," *Shockley v. State*, 565 A.2d 1373, 1380 (Del.1989). See *Butler v. United States*, 414 A.2d 844, 850 (D.C.1980); *Sanborn v. State*, 474 So.2d 309, 313 & n. 3

---

1. Paragraph (e) of Rule 3.3 of the Massachusetts Rules of Professional Conduct, 426 Mass. 1383 (1998), entitled, "Candor Toward the Tribunal," provides, in pertinent part:

"In a criminal case, defense counsel who knows that the defendant, the client, intends to testify falsely may not aid the client in constructing false testimony, and has a duty strongly to discourage the client from testifying falsely, advising that such a course is unlawful, will have substantial adverse consequences, and should not be followed.... If a criminal trial has commenced and the lawyer discovers that the client intends to testify falsely at trial, the lawyer need not file a motion to withdraw from the case if the lawyer reasonably believes that seeking to withdraw will prejudice the client. If, during the client's testimony or after the client has testified, the lawyer knows that the client has testified falsely, the lawyer shall call upon the client to rectify the false testimony and, if the client refuses or is unable to do so, the lawyer shall not reveal the false testimony to the tribunal. In no event may the lawyer examine the client in such a manner as to elicit any testimony from the client the lawyer knows to be false, and the lawyer shall not argue the probative value of the false testimony in closing argument or in any other proceedings, including appeals." The rule has separate requirements when the issue arises prior to trial.

(Fla.Dist.Ct.App.1985); *People v. Bartee,* 208 Ill.App.3d 105, 108, 153 Ill.Dec. 5, 566 N.E.2d 855 (1991). The defendant suggests that his trial counsel should have conducted a direct examination with respect to the "non-suspect" portions of his testimony and should also have argued the truthful portions of the defendant's testimony in his closing argument. The former suggestion has been justifiably criticized by the Criminal Justice Section of the ABA: "[T]his is the worst approach of all.... This [approach] would be far worse for the client than saying nothing, not to mention it would be virtually impossible to control once the client takes the stand. And what about cross? How can you possibly prepare your clients for that? Tell them not to answer any questions that they do not like?" ABA Criminal Justice Section, Ethical Problems Facing the Criminal Defense Lawyer at 162 (1995). The latter suggestion is impractical, as it may call attention to testimony of the defendant that is not argued by trial counsel, and would likely lead to counsel's making an incoherent final argument. We shall not impose these requirements on counsel. Further, to permit the defendant to make an unsworn statement or his own closing argument would allow him to do what rule 3.3(e) prohibits his counsel from doing, arguing perjured testimony to the jury. The defendant's testimony was placed before the jury, and his trial counsel made a persuasive, well-reasoned closing argument to the jury. The judge correctly concluded that the defendant was not "denude[d]" of a defense.

* * *

A summary of our disposition of this issue is now in order. The duties imposed on a criminal defense lawyer (zealous advocacy, preservation of client confidences, avoidance of a conflict of interest) and the constitutional rights granted a defendant (effective legal representation, opportunity to testify in his own defense, right to a fair trial) are circumscribed by what we demand of honorable lawyers and the core principle of our judicial system that seeks to make a trial a search for truth. The rights of a defendant are not so exclusive that justice can be subrogated to the defendant's perceived interests thereby dismissing or ignoring the interests of victims and the Commonwealth. Perjury, a most serious common-law felony, is antithetical to these values. In Massachusetts it is punishable in a noncapital case by up to twenty years' imprisonment, and in a capital case by possible life imprisonment. G.L. c. 268, § 1.

The standard set forth in rule 3.3(e) "confirm[s] that the legal profession has accepted that an attorney's ethical duty to advance the interests of his client is limited by an equally solemn duty to comply with the law and standards of professional conduct; it specifically ensures that the client may not use false evidence. This special duty of an attorney to prevent and disclose frauds upon the court derives from the recognition that perjury is as much a crime as tampering with witnesses or jurors by way of promises and threats, and undermines the administration of justice." (Footnote and citation omitted.) *Nix v. Whiteside, supra* at 168–169, 106 S.Ct. 988. The standard in no way abridges constitutional rights of a defendant. There is no constitutional or permissible right of a defendant to testify falsely. When defense counsel attempts to persuade a defendant to testify truthfully, counsel is not depriving the defendant of his right to counsel nor the right to testify truthfully. "In short, the responsibility of an ethical lawyer, as an officer of the court and a key component of a system of justice, dedicated to a search for truth, is essentially the same whether the client announces an intention to bribe or threaten witnesses or jurors or to commit or procure perjury. No system of justice worthy of the name can tolerate a lesser standard." *Id.* at 174, 106 S.Ct. 988.

* * *

B. Prohibited Conduct

In re Beiny

132 A.D.2d 190

Supreme Court, Appellate Division, First Department, New York

December 9, 1987

[Footnotes omitted.]

Before MURPHY, P.J., and KUPFERMAN, MILONAS and KASSAL, JJ.

Murphy, P.J. We refer this proceeding to the Departmental Disciplinary Committee for investigation, including an inquiry by the Committee into the August 3, 1987 report of the Wall Street Journal that Donald Christ, a member of Sullivan & Cromwell, allegedly assaulted an attorney for trustee Beiny in the Surrogate's Court at a conference in this case.

* * *

In ending this appeal, it might be useful to trace the lines of certain features of the case for they show how this court, faced each morning with matters involving profound issues of liberty and property, can be burdened by an appeal such as that at bar, an appeal that is before us solely because of the misconduct of lawyers in pursuit of a fee. We speak of the matter because it extends beyond the ownership and transfer of porcelains, and well beyond the interest of a law firm in its reputation. Our consideration of the case is enlarged by issues involving the ethical norms required of attorneys as advocates.

Petitioner's counsel, Sullivan & Cromwell, believing that the liquidator of the law firm of Greenbaum, Wolff & Ernst had factual information concerning the property at issue, served a subpoena duces tecum and notice of deposition directing the liquidator to appear for examination with all the papers concerning certain clients, including trustee Beiny. No notice was given by Sullivan & Cromwell to the other parties. The subpoena was knowingly aimed at privileged materials, and no court would have sustained its broad demand. In order to give the subpoena a sharper edge, Sullivan & Cromwell enclosed it in a letter that deceptively represented to the liquidator that Sullivan & Cromwell's client, petitioner Wynyard, was the executor of the estate of a former client of the Greenbaum firm. Sullivan & Cromwell, having thereafter received from the liquidator the mass of papers to which no law but only its deceit entitled it, then canceled the day fixed for the liquidator's examination. Within weeks, the trustee, ignorant of the raid upon Greenbaum's papers, was examined in London by Sullivan & Cromwell who not only used those papers to surprise her but refused to disclose how the papers had been obtained. When the trustee's counsel learned how Sullivan & Cromwell had obtained the papers, they asked for their production, but Sullivan & Cromwell refused, unless the trustee made concessions in discovery. Only after the trustee was driven to obtain an order of the Surrogate in December 1985, granting the trustee access to the papers, did the trustee learn the extent of Sullivan & Cromwell's massive intrusion into the trustee's privileged papers; and not until July 1986 did the trustee have in hand an order of the Surrogate suppressing all but 7 of 114 documents as to which the trustee claimed privilege.

In consequence of Sullivan & Cromwell's conduct, this court has had placed before five of its Justices about 1,700 pages of record and briefs, to say nothing of paper footage given to motions that have since slid into the dark of appellate memory. Petitioner Wynyard's case, which may be one having substantial merit, has been delayed by about 2 Ω years given over to the legal debris that now lies before us. He has been left by Sullivan & Cromwell's conduct to search for other counsel who will probably bill him for the reading of the lengthy record generated by Sullivan & Cromwell's misconduct. Trustee Beiny has been driven down a legal gauntlet, arched by fees of expensive counsel and hedged by the anxiety to which Bench and Bar are often insensible. In short, upon facts that should have led Sullivan & Cromwell to a prompt, practical resolution, one that would have avoided delay, fees and the worrying of court and clients, Sullivan & Cromwell chose instead to drive the trustee toward the steps of the Surrogate's Court and, ultimately, both petitioner and the trustee to the steps of this court. Having arrived in this court, Sullivan & Cromwell, in protection of its reputation, then set about the making of arguments that, startlingly curious in design, required the time of this much pressed court to identify and answer. We will describe only several of these arguments. Cousins to them, equally strange looking, may be found sitting in the briefs.

Sullivan & Cromwell argued on the appeal that its associate, Garrard Beeney, who had engineered the acquisition of the now suppressed documents, was procedurally correct in his obtaining of the papers without notice to the parties. The argument was notable if only because it might have caused an applicant's failure upon the Bar examination, to say nothing of its use against Sullivan & Cromwell by its adversaries in other actions. On reargument, petitioner's additional counsel, retained for the motions at bar, made for safer waters, conceding that Beeney was in error but that Beeney had acted innocently. In short, Beeney had known what he was doing but did not know that it was wrong. As far as our research has gone this is the first instance, at least in this court, in which a breach of the Civil Practice Law and Rules has been met with the defense raised in 1843 in *M'Naghten's Case* (8 Eng Rep 718), a fact that would have startled poor M'Naghten as he stood acquitted in the dock. The record shows that Beeney indeed knew what he was about when he palmed off petitioner as the executor of the estate of a decedent whose will was never probated, and when he canceled a deposition that he never intended to conduct. The record shows that even though Donald Christ, a senior partner at Sullivan & Cromwell, must have known at the very least of the way Beeney had acquired the privileged papers, still nothing was done to right what must have seemed to Mr. Christ to have been wrong. Instead, Sullivan & Cromwell in their prosecution of the case thereafter used the papers against the trustee. As for the argument that the liquidator was in substance a volunteer in need of a subpoena as a kind of receipt for his files, we give to it the same value that we have given to Beeney's singular belief that petitioner was the executor of an estate unknown to any probate court.

Petitioner's claim that the trustee and he had been jointly represented by the Greenbaum firm, a claim unproved before the Surrogate, can hardly be a foothold in justification of Sullivan & Cromwell's raid upon the Greenbaum files. Our cachet of approval upon such a primitive notion of discovery, to say nothing of the extension of such a principle throughout our law, would entice the invasive, disorderly mind in an area in which rights must be judicially or consensually fixed before parties proceed in the gathering of facts.

Last, it is disingenuous for petitioner's counsel to argue that we did not find that the suppressed documents were substantially related to the issues. We suppose that petitioner's counsel read our statement that "among the matters to which the documents refer are transactions involving the disposition of the very assets whose ownership is at issue in this proceeding" (129 AD2d 126, 142), or if they did not read our plain statement, they surely must have recalled their own repeated statements concerning the probative value of the suppressed documents. Nor do we think it an exercise in candor for petitioner's counsel to say on this motion that the suppressed documents are not substantially related to the issues before us when the record shows that, among other things, petitioner's counsel themselves characterized those documents as proof that the trustee unlawfully transferred the property at issue to entities in her control, defrauded the petitioner, violated her fiduciary duties to him, and is a perjurer.

In sum, this appeal is an example of the accidental subversion of the interests of a client by his own advocates who acted as if the law did not apply to them. For this court to have done less than disqualify Sullivan & Cromwell for its misconduct in this case, for this court to have chosen a lower standard that both diminishes the integrity of the judicial process and cuts into the heart of the attorney-client privilege, might be congenial to casual temperaments at home in the shade. Courts, however, must make law as they did anciently, in the open and in the sun where those who have eyes may see and those who have ears may listen.

Shafer v. Berger

107 Cal.App.4th 54
Court of Appeal, Second District, Division 1, California
March 18, 2003
As Modified on Denial of Rehearing April 8, 2003
Review Denied July 16, 2003

MALLANO, J. This appeal presents the question of whether an attorney, who is retained by an insurance company to provide coverage advice in a lawsuit against its insured, may be held liable to the plaintiff in that lawsuit for making a fraudulent statement about coverage. We answer that question in the affirmative because deceit undermines the administration of justice.

* * *

The relationship of attorney and client is one of agent and principal. (See *CPI Builders, Inc. v. Impco Technologies, Inc.* (2001) 94 Cal.App.4th 1167, 1174, 114 Cal.Rptr.2d 851; *Caro v. Smith* (1997) 59 Cal.App.4th 725, 731, 69 Cal.Rptr.2d 306; see also *Levy v. Superior Court* (1995) 10 Cal.4th 578, 583–584, 41 Cal.Rptr.2d 878, 896 P.2d 171.) As with other types of agency relationships, "[t]he law of misrepresentation applies to lawyers." (Rest.3d, Law Governing Lawyers (2000) § 98, com. c, p. 59.) "Lawyers are subject to the general law. If activities of a nonlawyer in the same circumstances would render the nonlawyer civilly liable..., the same activities by a lawyer in the same circumstances generally render the lawyer liable...." (*Id.,* § 56, com. b, p. 416.)

"A lawyer communicating on behalf of a client with a nonclient may not ... [¶] ... knowingly make a false statement of material fact ... to the nonclient...." (Rest.3d, Law Governing Lawyers, § 98, p. 58.) "The law governing misrepresentation by a lawyer includes the criminal law (theft by deception), *the law of misrepresentation in tort law* and of mistake and fraud in contract law, and procedural law governing statements by an advocate.... Compliance with those obligations meets social expectations of honesty and fair dealing and facilitates negotiation and adjudication, which are important professional functions of lawyers." (*Id.,* com. b, pp. 58–59, citation omitted, italics added.) "A misrepresentation can occur through direct statement or through affirmation of a misrepresentation of another, as when a lawyer knowingly affirms a client's false or misleading statement." (*Id.,* com. c, p. 59.)

* * *

Turning to the present case, under California law, "[f]raud is an intentional tort, the elements of which are (1) misrepresentation; (2) knowledge of falsity; (3) intent to defraud, i.e., to induce reliance; (4) justifiable reliance; and (5) resulting damage." (*Cicone, supra,* 183 Cal.App.3d at p. 200, 227 Cal.Rptr. 887; accord, 5 Witkin, Summary of Cal. Law (9th ed. 1988) Torts, § 676, p. 778.) LaBelle argues that his statement about insurance coverage was not a representation of fact but a nonactionable legal opinion. He also contends that he did not owe the Shafers a duty to make truthful statements about coverage and that they did not justifiably rely on any statements he made. Based on the allegations of the first amended complaint, we disagree.

* * *

The Shafers justifiably relied on LaBelle's alleged false statements. They had no reason to doubt him. They did not know that LaBelle had sent DeMay's attorney two reservation of rights letters, nor did they know the contents of either one. Like the plaintiffs in *Fire Ins. Exchange, supra,* 643 N.E.2d 310, *Hansen, supra,* 630 N.W.2d 818, and *Slotkin, supra,* 614 F.2d 301, the Shafers reasonably relied on the coverage representations made by counsel for an insurance company.

In a March 16, 1994 letter to the Shafers' attorney, LaBelle stated that "[Truck] reserves its rights under California case and statutory law, and in accordance with California public policy which precludes indemnity for damages based upon a finding of fraud." As alleged in the operative complaint, "[the Shafers'] reliance on [LaBelle's] fraudulent concealment was well justified.... [W]ithout the reservation of rights letters, [the Shafers] had no real choice but to rely on [LaBelle's] pronouncements about lack of coverage for intentional acts. [The Shafers'] attorneys understood that intentional misconduct by an insured precludes coverage under any policy of insurance. What they did not know, and what [LaBelle] failed to reveal..., was that the manner in which [Truck] had reserved its rights under the policy tacitly expanded coverage to include intentional misconduct by the insured...." Elsewhere in the amended complaint, the Shafers alleged that they did not obtain evidence about the fraudulent nature of LaBelle's statements until late 1998 and early 1999, during discovery in related litigation.

If the Shafers had known or suspected the truth — that Truck had agreed to provide coverage for willful acts — they would have aggressively sought full payment of the judgment at the outset instead of accepting a payment of $120,000 in March 1994. But the Shafers believed LaBelle. They did not file suit until June 2000 — six years and eight months after the entry of judgment — when they learned about the alleged fraud. In the meantime, the Shafers allegedly incurred economic and noneconomic damages.

Further, LaBelle's relationship vis-à-vis the Shafers was not that of an *opposing* participant or party. Under section 11580, Truck had to pay the Shafers the amount of the judgment, subject to the terms and limitations of the insurance policy, including any reservation of rights. (See Croskey et al., Cal. Practice Guide: Insurance Litigation, *supra,* ¶¶ 15:1123 to 15:1136, pp. 15-200.1 to 15-200.2.) In that sense, the Shafers were to be treated as the insureds. Section 11580 "inure[s] to the benefit of any and every person who might be negligently injured by the assured as completely as if *such injured person had been specifically named in the policy.*" (*Malmgren v. Southwestern A. Ins. Co.* (1927) 201 Cal. 29, 33, 255 P. 512, italics added; construing Stats.1919, ch. 367, § 1, p. 776, now section 11580, see Historical Note, 43 West's Ann. Ins.Code (1988 ed.) foll. § 11580, p. 242.) And, as stated, the Shafers were third party beneficiaries of the insurance policy. (See, e.g., *Murphy, supra,* 17 Cal.3d at pp. 942–943, 132 Cal.Rptr. 424, 553 P.2d 584.)

We also observe that LaBelle is trying to have his cake and eat it too. He advised Truck to provide coverage for willful acts so that Truck would not have to pay for *Cumis* counsel. Yet, LaBelle represented to the Shafers that willful acts were not covered so that Truck would not have to pay the total amount due on the judgment.

LaBelle's case authority does not support his position that the Shafers could not justifiably rely on his word. In *Goodman v. Kennedy, supra,* 18 Cal.3d 335, 134 Cal.Rptr. 375, 556 P.2d 737, the plaintiffs (nonclients) sued an attorney for erroneous advice about purchasing stock from his clients. But "[t]here [was] no allegation that the advice was ever communicated to plaintiffs and hence no basis for any claim that they relied upon it in purchasing or retaining the stock." (*Id.* at p. 343, 134 Cal.Rptr. 375, 556 P.2d 737; see *Bily v. Arthur Young & Co.* (1992) 3 Cal.4th 370, 411, 11 Cal.Rptr.2d 51, 834 P.2d 745 [discussing *Goodman*].) Here, LaBelle made the misrepresentations directly to the Shafers, and they relied on his statements in failing to seek full payment on the judgment.

* * *

Counsel retained by an insurer has an obligation to be truthful in describing insurance coverage to a third party beneficiary. The litigation privilege is not a license to deceive an injured party who steps into the shoes of the insured. (See pt. II.A.2., *ante.*) Section 11580 grants an injured party the right to file suit in order to recover under the insurance policy. Coverage counsel may not commit fraud in an attempt to defeat that right. And to the extent there is a conflict between an injured party's rights under section 11580 and coverage counsel's reliance on the litigation privilege (Civ.Code, § 47, subd. (b)), the rights of the injured party prevail as they arise under the more specific of the two statutes. (See *Schoendorf v. U.D. Registry* (2002) 97 Cal.App.4th 227, 243, 118 Cal.Rptr.2d 313.)

* * *

DISPOSITION

The judgment is reversed. Appellants are entitled to costs on appeal.

We concur: SPENCER, P.J., and MIRIAM A. VOGEL, J.

C. The Academic Controversy

Professional Responsibility of the Criminal Defense Lawyer: The Three Hardest Questions

Monroe H. Freedman,* 64 *Michigan Law Review* 1469 (1966)

In almost any area of legal counseling and advocacy, the lawyer may be faced with the dilemma of either betraying the confidential communications of his client or participating to some extent in the purposeful deception of the court. This problem is nowhere more acute than in the practice of criminal law, particularly in the representation of the indigent accused. The purpose of this article is to analyze and attempt to resolve three of the most difficult issues in this general area:

---

* Professor Freedman was Dean of Hofstra Law School from 1973–1977. This article appears with his kind permission and that of the *Michigan Law Review*. He has considerably expanded and updated his views in Monroe Freedman and Abbe Smith, *Understanding Lawyers' Ethics* (3rd. ed., 2004) (Matthew Bender).

1. Is it proper to cross-examine for the purpose of discrediting the reliability or credibility of an adverse witness whom you know to be telling the truth?

2. Is it proper to put a witness on the stand when you know he will commit perjury?

3. Is it proper to give your client legal advice when you have reason to believe that the knowledge you give him will tempt him to commit perjury?

These questions present serious difficulties with respect to a lawyer's ethical responsibilities. Moreover, if one admits the possibility of an affirmative answer, it is difficult even to discuss them without appearing to some to be unethical.[1] It is not surprising, therefore, that reasonable, rational discussion of these issues has been uncommon and that the problems have for so long remained unresolved. In this regard it should be recognized that the Canons of Ethics, which were promulgated in 1908 "as a general guide,"[2] are both inadequate and self-contradictory.

I. The Adversary System and the Necessity for Confidentiality

At the outset, we should dispose of some common question-begging responses. The attorney is indeed an officer of the court, and he does participate in a search for truth. These two propositions, however, merely serve to state the problem in different words: As an officer of the court, participating in a search for truth, what is the attorney's special responsibility, and how does that responsibility affect his resolution of the questions posed above?

The attorney functions in an adversary system based upon the presupposition that the most effective means of determining truth is to present to a judge and jury a clash between proponents of conflicting views. It is essential to the effective functioning of this system that each adversary have, in the words of Canon 15, "entire devotion to the interest of the client, warm zeal in the maintenance and defense of his rights and the exertion of his utmost learning and ability." It is also essential to maintain the fullest uninhibited communication between the client and his attorney, so that the attorney can most effectively counsel his client and advocate the latter's cause. This policy is safeguarded by the requirement that the lawyer must, in the words of Canon 37, "preserve his client's confidences." Canon 15 does, of course, qualify these obligations by stating that "the office of attorney does not permit, much less does it demand of him for any client, violations of law or any manner of fraud or chicane." In addition, Canon 22 requires candor toward the court.

The problem presented by these salutary generalities of the Canons in the context of particular litigation is illustrated by the personal experience of Samuel Williston, which was related in his autobiography.[3] Because of his examination of a client's correspondence file, Williston learned of a fact extremely damaging to his client's case. When the judge announced his decision, it was apparent that a critical factor in the favorable judgment for Williston's client was the judge's ignorance of this fact. Williston remained

---

1. The substance of this paper was recently presented to a Criminal Trial Institute attended by forty-five members of the District of Columbia Bar. As a consequence, several judges (none of whom had either heard the lecture or read it) complained to the Committee on Admissions and Grievances of the District Court for the District of Columbia, urging the author's disbarment or suspension. Only after four months of proceedings, including a hearing, two meetings, and a de novo review by eleven federal district court judges, did the Committee announce its decision to "proceed no further in the matter."

2. American Bar Association, Canons of Professional Ethics, Preamble (1908).

3. Williston, Life and Law 271 (1940).

silent and did not thereafter inform the judge of what he knew. He was convinced, and Charles Curtis[4] agrees with him, that it was his duty to remain silent.

In an opinion by the American Bar Association Committee on Professional Ethics and Grievances, an eminent panel headed by Henry Drinker held that a lawyer should remain silent when his client lies to the judge by saying that he has no prior record, despite the attorney's knowledge to the contrary.[5] The majority of the panel distinguished the situation in which the attorney has learned of the client's prior record from a source other than the client himself. William B. Jones, a distinguished trial lawyer and now a judge in the United States District Court for the District of Columbia, wrote a separate opinion in which he asserted that in neither event should the lawyer expose his client's lie. If these two cases do not constitute "fraud or chicane" or lack of candor within the meaning of the Canons (and I agree with the authorities cited that they do not), it is clear that the meaning of the Canons is ambiguous.

The adversary system has further ramifications in a criminal case. The defendant is presumed to be innocent. The burden is on the prosecution to prove beyond a reasonable doubt that the defendant is guilty. The plea of not guilty does not necessarily mean "not guilty in fact," for the defendant may mean "not legally guilty." Even the accused who knows that he committed the crime is entitled to put the government to its proof. Indeed, the accused who knows that he is guilty has an absolute constitutional right to remain silent.[6] The moralist might quite reasonably understand this to mean that, under these circumstances, the defendant and his lawyer are privileged to "lie" to the court in pleading not guilty. In my judgment, the moralist is right. However, our adversary system and related notions of the proper administration of criminal justice sanction the lie.

Some derive solace from the sophistry of calling the lie a "legal fiction," but this is hardly an adequate answer to the moralist. Moreover, this answer has no particular appeal for the practicing attorney, who knows that the plea of not guilty commits him to the most effective advocacy of which he is capable. Criminal defense lawyers do not win their cases by arguing reasonable doubt. Effective trial advocacy requires that the attorney's every word, action, and attitude be consistent with the conclusion that his client is innocent. As every trial lawyer knows, the jury is certain that the defense attorney knows whether his client is guilty. The jury is therefore alert to, and will be enormously affected by, any indication by the attorney that he believes the defendant to be guilty. Thus, the plea of not guilty commits the advocate to a trial, including a closing argument, in which he must argue that "not guilty" means "not guilty in fact."[7]

---

4. Curtis, It's Your Law 17–21 (1954). See also Curtis, The Ethics of Advocacy, 4 Stan. L. Rev. 3, 9–10 (1951); Drinker, *Some Remarks on Mr. Curtis' "The Ethics of Advocacy,"* 4 Stan. L. Rev. 349, 350–51 (1952).

5. Opinion 287, Committee on Professional Ethics and Grievances of the American Bar Association (1953).

6. Escobedo v. Illinois, 378 U.S. 478, 485, 491 (1964).

7. "The failure to argue the case before the jury, while ordinarily only a trial tactic not subject to review, manifestly enters the field of incompetency when the reason assigned is the attorney's conscience. It is as improper as though the attorney had told the jury that his client had uttered a falsehood in making the statement. The right to an attorney embraces effective representation throughout all stages of the trial, and where the representation is of such low caliber as to amount to no representation, the guarantee of due process has been violated." Johns v. Smyth, 176 F. Supp. 949, 953 (E.D. Va. l959); Schwartz, Cases on Professional Responsibility and the Administration of Criminal Justice 79 (1962).

There is, of course, a simple way to evade the dilemma raised by the not guilty plea. Some attorneys rationalize the problem by insisting that a lawyer never knows for sure whether his client is guilty. The client who insists upon his guilt may in fact be protecting his wife, or may know that he pulled the trigger and that the victim was killed, but not that his gun was loaded with blanks and that the fatal shot was fired from across the street. For anyone who finds this reasoning satisfactory, there is, of course, no need to think further about the issue.

It is also argued that a defense attorney can remain selectively ignorant. He can insist in his first interview with his client that, if his client is guilty, he simply does not want to know. It is inconceivable, however, that an attorney could give adequate counsel under such circumstances. How is the client to know, for example, precisely which relevant circumstances his lawyer does not want to be told? The lawyer might ask whether his client has a prior record. The client, assuming that this is the kind of knowledge that might present ethical problems for his lawyer, might respond that he has no record. The lawyer would then put the defendant on the stand and, on cross-examination, be appalled to learn that his client has two prior convictions for offenses identical to that for which he is being tried.

Of course, an attorney can guard against this specific problem by telling his client that he must know about the client's past record. However, a lawyer can never anticipate all of the innumerable and potentially critical factors that his client, once cautioned, may decide not to reveal. In one instance, for example, the defendant assumed that his lawyer would prefer to be ignorant of the fact that the client had been having sexual relations with the chief defense witness. The client was innocent of the robbery with which he was charged, but was found guilty by the jury—probably because he was guilty of fornication, a far less serious offense for which he had not even been charged.

The problem is compounded by the practice of plea bargaining. It is considered improper for a defendant to plead guilty to a lesser offense unless he is in fact guilty. Nevertheless, it is common knowledge that plea bargaining frequently results in improper guilty pleas by innocent people. For example, a defendant falsely accused of robbery may plead guilty to simple assault, rather than risk a robbery conviction and a substantial prison term. If an attorney is to be scrupulous in bargaining pleas, however, he must know in advance that his client is guilty, since the guilty plea is improper if the defendant is innocent. Of course, if the attempt to bargain for a lesser offense should fail, the lawyer would know the truth and thereafter be unable to rationalize that he was uncertain of his client's guilt.

If one recognizes that professional responsibility requires that an advocate have full knowledge of every pertinent fact, it follows that he must seek the truth from his client, not shun it.[8] This means that he will have to dig and pry and cajole, and, even then, he will not be successful unless he can convince the client that full and confidential disclosure to his lawyer will never result in prejudice to the client by any word or action of the lawyer. This is, perhaps, particularly true in the case of the indigent defendant, who meets his lawyer for the first time in the cell block or the rotunda. He did not choose the lawyer, nor does he know him. The lawyer has been sent by the judge and is part of the system that is attempting to punish the defendant. It is no easy task to persuade this client that he can talk freely without fear of prejudice. However, the inclination to mis-

---

8. "[C]ounsel cannot properly perform their duties without knowing the truth." Opinion 28, Committee on Professional Ethics and Grievances of the American Bar Association (1930).

lead one's lawyer is not restricted to the indigent or even to the criminal defendant. Randolph Paul has observed a similar phenomenon among a wealthier class in a far more congenial atmosphere:

> The tax adviser will sometimes have to dynamite the facts of his case out of the unwilling witnesses on his own side—witnesses who are nervous, witnesses who are confused about their own interest, witnesses who try to be too smart for their own good, and witnesses who subconsciously do not want to understand what has happened despite the fact that they must if they are to testify coherently.[9]

Paul goes on to explain that the truth can be obtained only by persuading the client that it would be a violation of a sacred obligation for the lawyer ever to reveal a client's confidence. Beyond any question, once a lawyer has persuaded his client of the obligation of confidentiality, he must respect that obligation scrupulously.

II. The Specific Questions

The first of the difficult problems posed above will now be considered: Is it proper to cross-examine for the purpose of discrediting the reliability or the credibility of a witness whom you know to be telling the truth? Assume the following situation. Your client has been falsely accused of a robbery committed at 16th and P Streets at 11:00 p.m. He tells you at first that at no time on the evening of the crime was he within six blocks of that location. However, you are able to persuade him that he must tell you the truth and that doing so will in no way prejudice him. He then reveals to you that he was at 15th and P Streets at 10:55 that evening, but that he was walking east, away from the scene of the crime, and that, by 11:00 p.m., he was six blocks away. At the trial, there are two prosecution witnesses. The first mistakenly, but with some degree of persuasion, identifies your client as the criminal. At that point, the prosecution's case depends on this single witness, who might or might not be believed. Since your client has a prior record, you do not want to put him on the stand, but you feel that there is at least a chance for acquittal. The second prosecution witness is an elderly woman who is somewhat nervous and who wears glasses. She testifies truthfully and accurately that she saw your client at 15th and P Streets at 10:55 p.m. She has corroborated the erroneous testimony of the first witness and made conviction virtually certain. However, if you destroy her reliability through cross-examination designed to show that she is easily confused and has poor eyesight, you may not only eliminate the corroboration, but also cast doubt in the jury's mind on the prosecution's entire case. On the other hand, if you should refuse to cross-examine her because she is telling the truth, your client may well feel betrayed, since you knew of the witness's veracity only because your client confided in you, under your assurance that his truthfulness would not prejudice him.

The client would be right. Viewed strictly, the attorney's failure to cross-examine would not be violative of the client's confidence because it would not constitute a disclosure. However, the same policy that supports the obligation of confidentiality precludes the attorney from prejudicing his client's interest in any other way because of knowledge gained in his professional capacity. When a lawyer fails to cross-examine only because his client, placing confidence in the lawyer, has been candid with him, the basis for such confidence and candor collapses. Our legal system cannot tolerate such a result.

---

9. Paul, *The Responsibilities of the Tax Adviser*. 63 Harv. L. Rev. 877, 383 (1950).

> The purposes and necessities of the relation between a client and his attorney require, in many cases, on the part of the client, the fullest and freest disclosures to the attorney of the client's objects, motives and acts.... To permit the attorney to reveal to others what is so disclosed, would be not only a gross violation of a sacred trust upon his part, but it would utterly destroy and prevent the usefulness and benefits to be derived from professional assistance.[10]

The client's confidences must "upon all occasions be inviolable," to avoid the "greater mischiefs" that would probably result if a client could not feel free "to repose [confidence] in the attorney to whom he resorts for legal advice and assistance."[11] Destroy that confidence, and "a man would not venture to consult any skillful person, or would only dare to tell his counsellor half his case."[12]

Therefore, one must conclude that the attorney is obligated to attack, if he can, the reliability or credibility of an opposing witness whom he knows to be truthful. The contrary result would inevitably impair the "perfect freedom of consultation by client with attorney," which is "essential to the administration of justice."[13]

The second question is generally considered to be the hardest of all: Is it proper to put a witness on the stand when you know he will commit perjury? Assume, for example, that the witness in question is the accused himself, and that he has admitted to you, in response to your assurances of confidentiality, that he is guilty. However, he insists upon taking the stand to protest his innocence. There is a clear consensus among prosecutors and defense attorneys that the likelihood of conviction is increased enormously when the defendant does not take the stand. Consequently, the attorney who prevents his client from testifying only because the client has confided his guilt to him is violating that confidence by acting upon the information in a way that will seriously prejudice his client's interests.

Perhaps the most common method for avoiding the ethical problem just posed is for the lawyer to withdraw from the case, at least if there is sufficient time before trial for the client to retain another attorney.[14] The client will then go to the nearest law office, realizing that the obligation of confidentiality is not what it has been represented to be, and withhold incriminating information or the fact of his guilt from his new attorney. On ethical grounds, the practice of withdrawing from a case under such circumstances is indefensible, since the identical perjured testimony will ultimately be presented. More important, perhaps, is the practical consideration that the new attorney will be ignorant of the perjury and therefore will be in no position to attempt to discourage the client from presenting it. Only the original attorney, who knows the truth, has that opportunity, but he loses it in the very act of evading the ethical problem.

---

10. 2 Mechem, Agency § 2297 (2d ed. 1914).

11. Opinion 150, Committee on Professional Ethics and Grievances of the American Bar Association (1936), quoting Thornton, Attorneys at Law § 94 (1914). See also Opinion 23, supra note 8.

12. Greenough v. Gaskell, 1 Myl. & K. 98, 103, 39 Eng. Rep. 618, 621 (Ch. 1833) (Lord Chancellor Brougham).

13. Opinion 91, Committee on Professional Ethics and Grievances of the American Bar Association (1933).

14. See Orkin, *Defense of One Known To Be Guilty*, 1 Crim. L.Q. 170, 174 (1958). Unless the lawyer has told the client at the outset that he will withdraw if he learns that the client is guilty, "it is plain enough as a matter of good morals and professional ethics" that the lawyer should not withdraw on this ground. Opinion 90, Committee on Professional Ethics and Grievances of the American Bar Association (1982). As to the difficulties inherent in the lawyer's telling the client that he wants to remain ignorant of crucial facts, see note 8 *supra* and accompanying text.

The problem is all the more difficult when the client is indigent. He cannot retain other counsel, and in many jurisdictions, including the District of Columbia, it is impossible for appointed counsel to withdraw from a case except for extraordinary reasons. Thus, appointed counsel, unless he lies to the judge, can successfully withdraw only by revealing to the judge that the attorney has received knowledge of his client's guilt. Such a revelation in itself would seem to be a sufficiently serious violation of the obligation of confidentiality to merit severe condemnation. In fact, however, the situation is far worse, since it is entirely possible that the same judge who permits the attorney to withdraw will subsequently hear the case and sentence the defendant. When he does so, of course, he will have had personal knowledge of the defendant's guilt before the trial began.[15] Moreover, this will be knowledge of which the newly appointed counsel for the defendant will probably be ignorant.

The difficulty is further aggravated when the client informs the lawyer for the first time during trial that he intends to take the stand and commit perjury. The perjury in question may not necessarily be a protestation of innocence by a guilty man. Referring to the earlier hypothetical of the defendant wrongly accused of a robbery at 16th and P, the only perjury may be his denial of the truthful, but highly damaging, testimony of the corroborating witness who placed him one block away from the intersection five minutes prior to the crime. Of course, if he tells the truth and thus verifies the corroborating witness, the jury will be far more inclined to accept the inaccurate testimony of the principal witness, who specifically identified him as the criminal.[16]

If a lawyer has discovered his client's intent to perjure himself, one possible solution to this problem is for the lawyer to approach the bench, explain his ethical difficulty to the judge, and ask to be relieved, thereby causing a mistrial. This request is certain to be denied, if only because it would empower the defendant to cause a series of mistrials in the same fashion. At this point, some feel that the lawyer has avoided the ethical problem and can put the defendant on the stand. However, one objection to this solution, apart from the violation of confidentiality, is that the lawyer's ethical problem has not been solved, but has only been transferred to the judge. Moreover, the client in such a case might well have grounds for appeal on the basis of deprivation of due process and denial of the right to counsel, since he will have been tried before, and sentenced by, a judge who has been informed of the client's guilt by his own attorney.

A solution even less satisfactory than informing the judge of the defendant's guilt would be to let the client take the stand without the attorney's participation and to omit reference to the client's testimony in closing argument. The latter solution, of course,

---

15. The judge may infer that the situation is worse than it is in fact. In the case related in note 25 *infra*, the attorney's actual difficulty was that he did not want to permit a plea of guilty by a client who was maintaining his innocence. However, as is commonly done, he told the judge only that he had to withdraw because of "an ethical problem." The judge reasonably inferred that the defendant had admitted his guilt and wanted to offer a perjured alibi.

16. One lawyer, who considers it clearly unethical for the attorney to present the alibi in this hypothetical case, found no ethical difficulty himself in the following case. His client was prosecuted for robbery. The prosecution witness testified that the robbery had taken place at 10:15, and identified the defendant as the criminal. However, the defendant had a convincing alibi for 10:00 to 10:30. The attorney presented the alibi, and the client was acquitted. The alibi was truthful, but the attorney knew that the prosecution witness had been confused about the time, and that his client had in fact committed the crime at 10:45.

would be as damaging as to fail entirely to argue the case to the jury, and failing to argue the case is "as improper as though the attorney had told the jury that his client had uttered a falsehood in making the statement."[17]

Therefore, the obligation of confidentiality, in the context of our adversary system, apparently allows the attorney no alternative to putting a perjurious witness on the stand without explicit or implicit disclosure of the attorney's knowledge to either the judge or the jury. Canon 37 does not proscribe this conclusion; the canon recognizes only two exceptions to the obligation of confidentiality. The first relates to the lawyer who is accused by his client and may disclose the truth to defend himself. The other exception relates to the "announced intention of a client to commit a crime." On the basis of the ethical and practical considerations discussed above, the Canon's exception to the obligation of confidentiality cannot logically be understood to include the crime of perjury committed during the specific case in which the lawyer is serving. Moreover, even when the intention is to commit a crime in the future, Canon 37 does not require disclosure, but only permits it. Furthermore, Canon 15, which does proscribe "violation of law" by the attorney for his client, does not apply to the lawyer who unwillingly puts a perjurious client on the stand after having made every effort to dissuade him from committing perjury. Such an act by the attorney cannot properly be found to be subornation — corrupt inducement — of perjury. Canon 29 requires counsel to inform the prosecuting authorities of perjury committed in a case in which he has been involved, but this can only refer to perjury by opposing witnesses. For an attorney to disclose his client's perjury "would involve a direct violation of Canon 37."[18] Despite Canon 29, therefore, the attorney should not reveal his client's perjury "to the court or to the authorities."[19]

Of course, before the client testifies perjuriously, the lawyer has a duty to attempt to dissuade him on grounds of both law and morality. In addition, the client should be impressed with the fact that his untruthful alibi is tactically dangerous. There is always a strong possibility that the prosecutor will expose the perjury on cross-examination. However, for the reasons already given, the final decision must necessarily be the client's. The lawyer's best course thereafter would be to avoid any further professional relationship with a client whom he knew to have perjured himself.

The third question is whether it is proper to give your client legal advice when you have reason to believe that the knowledge you give him will tempt him to commit perjury. This may indeed be the most difficult problem of all, because giving such advice creates the appearance that the attorney is encouraging and condoning perjury.

If the lawyer is not certain what the facts are when he gives the advice, the problem is substantially minimized, if not eliminated. It is not the lawyer's function to prejudge his client as a perjurer. He cannot presume that the client will make unlawful use of his advice. Apart from this, there is a natural predisposition in most people to recollect facts, entirely honestly, in a way most favorable to their own interest. As Randolph Paul has observed, some witnesses are nervous, some are confused about their own interests, some try to be too smart for their own good, and some subconsciously do not want to

---

17. See note 7 *supra*.

18. Opinion 287, Committee on Professional Ethics and Grievances of the American Bar Association (1953).

19. *Ibid.*

understand what has happened to them.[20] Before he begins to remember essential facts, the client is entitled to know what his own interests are.

The above argument does not apply merely to factual questions such as whether a particular event occurred at 10:15 or at 10:45.[21] One of the most critical problems in a criminal case, as in many others, is intention. A German writer, considering the question of intention as a test of legal consequences, suggests the following situation.[22] A young man and a young woman decide to get married. Each has a thousand dollars. They decide to begin a business with these funds, and the young lady gives her money to the young man for this purpose. Was the intention to form a joint venture or a partnership? Did they intend that the young man be an agent or a trustee? Was the transaction a gift or a loan? If the couple should subsequently visit a tax attorney and discover that it is in their interest that the transaction be viewed as a gift, it is submitted that they could, with complete honesty, so remember it. On the other hand, should their engagement be broken and the young woman consult an attorney for the purpose of recovering her money, she could with equal honesty remember that her intention was to make a loan.

Assume that your client, on trial for his life in a first-degree murder case, has killed another man with a penknife but insists that the killing was in self-defense. You ask him, "Do you customarily carry the penknife in your pocket, do you carry it frequently or infrequently, or did you take it with you only on this occasion?" He replies, "Why do you ask me a question like that?" It is entirely appropriate to inform him that his carrying the knife only on this occasion, or infrequently, supports an inference of premeditation, while if he carried the knife constantly, or frequently, the inference of premeditation would be negated. Thus, your client's life may depend upon his recollection as to whether he carried the knife frequently or infrequently. Despite the possibility that the client or a third party might infer that the lawyer was prompting the client to lie, the lawyer must apprise the defendant of the significance of his answer. There is no conceivable ethical requirement that the lawyer trap his client into a hasty and ill-considered answer before telling him the significance of the question.

A similar problem is created if the client has given the lawyer incriminating information before being fully aware of its significance. For example, assume that a man consults a tax lawyer and says, "I am fifty years old. Nobody in my immediate family has lived past fifty. Therefore, I would like to put my affairs in order. Specifically, I understand that I can avoid substantial estate taxes by setting up a trust. Can I do it?" The lawyer informs the client that he can successfully avoid the estate taxes only if he lives at least three years after establishing the trust or, should he die within three years, if the trust is found not to have been created in contemplation of death. The client then might ask who decides whether the trust is in contemplation of death. After learning that the determination is made by the court, the client might inquire about the factors on which such a decision would be based.

At this point, the lawyer can do one of two things. He can refuse to answer the question, or he can inform the client that the court will consider the wording of the trust instrument and will hear evidence about any conversations which he may have or any letters he may write expressing motives other than avoidance of estate taxes. It is likely that

---

20. See Paul, *supra* note 9.

21. Even this kind of "objective fact" is subject to honest error. See note 16 *supra*.

22. Wurzel, Das Juristische Denken 82 (1904), translated in Fuller, Basic Contract Law 67 (1964).

virtually every tax attorney in the country would answer the client's question, and that no one would consider the answer unethical. However, the lawyer might well appear to have prompted his client to deceive the Internal Revenue Service and the courts, and this appearance would remain regardless of the lawyer's explicit disclaimer to the client of any intent so to prompt him. Nevertheless, it should not be unethical for the lawyer to give the advice.

In a criminal case, a lawyer may be representing a client who protests his innocence, and whom the lawyer believes to be innocent. Assume, for example, that the charge is assault with intent to kill, that the prosecution has erroneous but credible eyewitness testimony against the defendant, and that the defendant's truthful alibi witness is impeachable on the basis of several felony convictions. The prosecutor, perhaps having doubts about the case, offers to permit the defendant to plead guilty to simple assault. If the defendant should go to trial and be convicted, he might well be sent to jail for fifteen years; on a plea of simple assault, the maximum penalty would be one year, and sentence might well be suspended.

The common practice of conveying the prosecutor's offer to the defendant should not be considered unethical, even if the defense lawyer is convinced of his client's innocence. Yet the lawyer is clearly in the position of prompting his client to lie, since the defendant cannot make the plea without saying to the judge that he is pleading guilty because he is guilty. Furthermore, if the client does decide to plead guilty, it would be improper for the lawyer to inform the court that his client is innocent, thereby compelling the defendant to stand trial and take the substantial risk of fifteen years' imprisonment.[23]

Essentially no different from the problem discussed above, but apparently more difficult, is the so-called *Anatomy of a Murder* situation.[24] The lawyer, who has received from his client an incriminating story of murder in the first degree, says, "If the facts are as you have stated them so far, you have no defense, and you will probably be electrocuted. On the other hand, if you acted in a blind rage, there is a possibility of saving your life. Think it over, and we will talk about it tomorrow." As in the tax case, and as in the case of the plea of guilty to a lesser offense, the lawyer has given his client a legal opinion that might induce the client to lie. This is information which the lawyer himself would have, without advice, were he in the client's position. It is submitted that the client is entitled to have this information about the law and to make his own decision as to whether to act upon it. To decide otherwise would not only penalize the less well-educated defen-

---

23. In a recent case, the defendant was accused of unauthorized use of an automobile, for which the maximum penalty is five years. He told his court-appointed attorney that he had borrowed the car from a man known to him only as "Junior," that he had not known the car was stolen, and that he had an alibi for the time of the theft. The defendant had three prior convictions for larceny, and the alibi was weak. The prosecutor offered to accept a guilty plea to two misdemeanors (taking property without right and petty larceny) carrying a combined maximum sentence of eighteen months. The defendant was willing to plead guilty to the lesser offenses, but the attorney felt that, because of his client's alibi, he could not permit him to do so. The lawyer therefore informed the judge that he had an ethical problem and asked to be relieved. The attorney who was appointed in his place permitted the client to plead guilty to the two lesser offenses, and the defendant was sentenced to nine months. The alternative would have been five or six months in jail while the defendant waited for his jury trial, and a very substantial risk of conviction and a much heavier sentence. Neither the client nor justice would have been well served by compelling the defendant to go to trial against his will under these circumstances.

24. See Traver, Anatomy of a Murder (1958).

dant, but would also prejudice the client because of his initial truthfulness in telling his story in confidence to the attorney.

III. Conclusion

The lawyer is an officer of the court, participating in a search for truth. Yet no lawyer would consider that he had acted unethically in pleading the statute of frauds or the statute of limitations as a bar to a just claim. Similarly, no lawyer would consider it unethical to prevent the introduction of evidence such as a murder weapon seized in violation of the fourth amendment or a truthful but involuntary confession, or to defend a guilty man on grounds of denial of a speedy trial.[25] Such actions are permissible because there are policy considerations that at times justify frustrating the search for truth and the prosecution of a just claim. Similarly, there are policies that justify an affirmative answer to the three questions that have been posed in this article. These policies include the maintenance of an adversary system, the presumption of innocence, the prosecution's burden to prove guilt beyond a reasonable doubt, the right to counsel, and the obligation of confidentiality between lawyer and client.

The Search for Truth: An Umpireal View[*]

Marvin E. Frankel,[†]
123 *University of Pennsylvania Law Review* 1031 (1975)

What I have written for the thirty-first Benjamin N. Cardozo Lecture makes no pretense to be polished or finished wisdom. In the words of an imposingly great predecessor, Judge Charles E. Clark, beginning the fifth of these lectures in 1945, I propose "to suggest problems and raise doubts, rather than to resolve confusion; to disturb thought, rather than to dispense legal or moral truth."[1] Probably more rash than Judge Clark, I do not experience "trepidation"[2] for offering questions rather than answers; honest exploration in any province of the law is surely no dishonor to the questing spirit of Judge Cardozo.

My questions, briefly stated, have to do with some imperfections in our adversary system. My purposes are to recall some perennial problems, to touch upon one or two familiar ideas for improvement, and to sketch some tentative lines along which efforts to reform our law might proceed.

Because I plan to focus on recurrent criticisms of the activity to which my professional life is and has been devoted, I find it fortifying and prudent, if not heroic, to ex-

---

25. *Cf.* Kamisar, *Equal Justice in the Gatehouses and Mansions of American Criminal Procedure*, in Criminal Justice in Our Time 77–78 (Howard ed. 1965):

> Yes, the presence of counsel in the police station may result in the suppression of truth, just as the presence of counsel at the trial may, when a client is advised not to take the stand, or when an objection is made to the admissibility of trustworthy, but illegally seized, "real" evidence. If the subject of police interrogation not only cannot be "coerced" into making a statement, but need not volunteer one, why shouldn't he be so advised? And why shouldn't court-appointed counsel, as well as retained counsel, so advise him?

* 31st Annual Benjamin N. Cardozo Lecture, delivered before the Association of the Bar of the City of New York, December 16, 1974.

† District Judge, United States District Court for the Southern District of New York. A.B. 1943, Queens College; LL.B. 1949, Columbia University.

1. Clark, *State Law in the Federal Courts: The Brooding Omnipresence of Erie v. Tompkins*, 55 YALE L.J. 267, 268–69 (1946).

2. *Id.* 268.

tend this introduction with a few deprecatory words. The business of the American trial courtroom seems to me in many ways to be instructive, creative, and sometimes even noble. As for the task of judging, it is nearly always a rich and satisfying challenge. The work produces fascinations and rewards that my imagination had failed to picture in advance. The trial court is a scene of drama, wit, humor, and humanity, along with the sorrows and the stretches of boredom. Even the periods of tedium are charged with the awareness of important stakes. There are daily choices that compel the judge to confront himself or herself, not less than those who will be affected, in stark and moving ways. There is power and there is, often more satisfying, the opportunity to forego the exercise of power.[3]

If I question the adequacy of our trial processes, it is not to serve the judges. It is to serve the ends of justice, for the furtherance of which all in our profession are commissioned. As is so often the case, Holmes said it better:

> I take it for granted that no hearer of mine will misinterpret what I have to say as the language of cynicism.... I trust that no one will understand me to be speaking with disrespect of the law, because I criticise it so freely. I venerate the law, and especially our system of law, as one of the vastest products of the human mind.... But one may criticise even what one reveres. Law is the business to which my life is devoted, and I should show less than devotion if I did not do what in me lies to improve it....[4]

I. The Judicial Perspective

My theme, to be elaborated at some length, is that our adversary system rates truth too low among the values that institutions of justice are meant to serve. Having worked for nine years at judging, and having evolved in that job the doubts and questions to be shared with you, I find it convenient to move into the subject with some initial reminders about our judges: who they are, how they come to be, and how their arena looks to them.

Except when we rely upon credentials even more questionable, we tend to select our trial judges from among people with substantial experience as trial lawyers. Most of us have had occasion to think of the analogy to the selection of former athletes as umpires for athletic contests. It may not press the comparison too hard to say it serves as a reminder that the "sporting theory"[5] continues to infuse much of the business of our trial courts. Reflective people have suggested from time to time that qualities of detachment and calm neutrality are not necessarily cultivated by long years of partisan combat.[6] Merely in passing, because it is not central to my theme, I question whether we are wise to have rejected totally the widespread practice in civil law countries of having career

---

3. *Cf.* C. Bok, I Too, Nicodemus 330 (1946).

4. O.W. Holmes, *The Path of the Law*, in Collected Legal Papers 167, 194 (1920).

The quotation was used in a similar setting by Judge Jerome Frank. J. Frank, Courts on Trial 3 (1950). As will be seen, this lecture follows in more pervasive respects positions urged in that engaging and valuable book. That the positions have not prevailed might discourage people more impatient than those who believe in the possibility of law reform.

5. The phrase was undoubtedly a cliche when Roscoe Pound used it in a famous address in 1906. Pound, *The Causes of Popular Dissatisfaction with the Administration of Justice*, 29 ABA Rep. 395, 404 (1906). Like other cliches, it still tells an important story. It also shares with many cliches the quality of referring to a widely known, deeply troublesome problem which has become entombed in a phrase so that it does not seem to require much active attention as a live concern.

6. *See, e.g.*, B. Shientag, the Personality of the Judge 19 (1944) (3d Annual Benjamin N. Cardozo Lecture).

magistrates, selected when relatively young to function in the role of impartial adjudicators. Reserving a fuller effort for another time, I wonder now whether we might benefit from some admixture of such magistrates to leaven or test our trial benches of elderly lawyers.

In any event, our more or less typical lawyer selected as a trial judge experiences a dramatic change in perspective as he moves to the other side of the bench. It is said, commonly by judges, that "[t]he basic purpose of a trial is the determination of truth...."[7] Justice David W. Peck identified "truth and ... the right result" as not merely "basic" but "the sole objective of the judge...."[8]

These are not questionable propositions as a matter of doctrine or logic. Trials occur because there are questions of fact. In principle, the paramount objective is the truth. Nevertheless, for the advocate turned judge this objective marks a sharp break with settled habits of partisanship. The novelty is quickly accepted because it has been seen for so long from the other side. But the novelty is palpable, and the change of role may be unsettling. Many judges, withdrawn from the fray, watch it with benign and detached affection, chuckling nostalgically now and then as the truth suffers injury or death in the process.[9] The shop talk in judges' lunchrooms includes tales, often told with pleasure, of wily advocates who bested the facts and prevailed. For many other judges, however, probably a majority at one time or another, the habit of adversariness tends to be rechanneled, at least in some measure, into a combative yearning for truth. With perhaps a touch of the convert's zeal, they may suffer righteously when the truth is being blocked or mutilated, turn against former comrades in the arena, feel (and sometimes yield to) the urge to spring into the contest with brilliant questions that light the way.

However the trial judge reacts, in general or from time to time, the bench affords a changed and broadened view of the adversary process. "Many things look different from the bench. Being a judge is a different profession from being a lawyer."[10] In the strictest sense I can speak only for myself, but I believe many other trial judges would affirm that the different perspective helps to arouse doubts about a process that there had been neither time nor impetus to question in the years at the bar. It becomes evident that the search for truth fails too much of the time. The rules and devices accounting for the failures come to seem less agreeable and less clearly worthy than they once did. The skills of the advocate seem less noble, and the place of the judge, which once looked so high, is lowered in consequence. There is, despite the years of professional weathering that went before the assumption of the judicial office, a measure of disillusionment.

The disillusionment is, as I indicated at the outset, only a modest element of the judicial experience. It is relevant here, however. It accounts for recurrent judicial expressions that seem critical of the bar when they probably stem from more basic dissatisfactions. In any event, it is undoubtedly part of the genesis of this essay.

---

7. Tehan v. United States *ex rel.* Shott, 382 U.S. 406, 416 (1966).

8. D. PECK, THE COMPLEMENT OF COURT AND COUNSEL 9 (1954) (13th Annual Benjamin N. Cardozo Lecture).

9. As in the sentence just ended, this essay will be laced with general statements about matters of fact that are neither quantified nor tightly documented. These rest variously upon introspection, observation, reading, and conversations with fellow judges. They are believed to be accurate, but they are undoubtedly debatable in many instances.

10. H. LUMMUS, THE TRIAL JUDGE 39 (1937). *See also* Medina, *Some Reflections on the Judicial Function: A Personal Viewpoint*, 38 A.B.A.J. 107 (1952).

II. The Adversarial Posture

The preceding comments on the transition from bar to bench have touched explicitly upon the role of the advocate. That role is not, however, a matter of sharp and universally agreed definition. The conception from which this paper proceeds must now be outlined.

In a passage partially quoted above, Presiding Justice David W. Peck said:

> The object of a lawsuit is to get at the truth and arrive at the right result. That is the sole objective of the judge, and counsel should never lose sight of that objective in thinking that the end purpose is to win for his side. Counsel exclusively bent on winning may find that he and the umpire are not in the same game.[11]

Earlier, stating his theme that court and counsel "complement" each other, Justice Peck said:

> Unfortunately, true understanding of the judicial process is not shared by all lawyers or judges. Instead of regarding themselves as occupying a reciprocal relationship in a common purpose, they are apt to think of themselves as representing opposite poles and exercising divergent functions. The lawyer is active, the judge passive. The lawyer partisan, the judge neutral. The lawyer imaginative, the judge reflective.[12]

Perhaps unfortunately, and certainly with deference, I find myself leaning toward the camp the Justice criticized. The plainest thing about the advocate is that he is indeed partisan, and thus exercises a function sharply divergent from that of the judge. Whether or not the judge generally achieves or maintains neutrality, it is his assigned task to be nonpartisan and to promote through the trial an objective search for the truth. The advocate in the trial courtroom is not engaged much more than half the time—and then only coincidentally—in the search for truth. The advocate's prime loyalty is to his client, not to truth as such. All of us remember some stirring and defiant declarations by advocates of their heroic, selfless devotion to The Client—leaving the nation, all other men, and truth to fend for themselves. Recall Lord Brougham's familiar words:

> [A]n advocate, in the discharge of his duty, knows but one person in all the world, and that person is his client. To save that client by all means and expedients, and at all hazards and costs to other persons, and, among them, to himself, is his first and only duty; and in performing this duty he must not regard the alarm, the torments, the destruction which he may bring upon others. Separating the duty of a patriot from that of an advocate, he must go on reckless of consequences, though it should be his unhappy fate to involve his country in confusion.[13]

Neither the sentiment nor even the words sound archaic after a century and a half. They were invoked not longer than a few months ago by a thoughtful and humane scholar answering criticisms that efforts of counsel for President Nixon might "involve his

---

11. D. PECK, *supra* note 8, at 9.
12. *Id.* 7.
13. 2 TRIAL OF QUEEN CAROLINE 8 (J. Nightingale ed. 1821).

country in confusion."[14] There are, I think, no comparable lyrics by lawyers to The Truth.

This is a topic on which our profession has practiced some self-deception. We proclaim to each other and to the world that the clash of adversaries is a powerful means for hammering out the truth. Sometimes, less guardedly, we say it is "best calculated to getting out all the facts...."[15] That the adversary technique is useful within limits none will doubt. That it is "best" we should all doubt if we were able to be objective about the question. Despite our untested statements of self-congratulation, we know that others searching after facts—in history, geography, medicine, whatever—do not emulate our adversary system. We know that most countries of the world seek justice by different routes. What is much more to the point, we know that many of the rules and devices of adversary litigation as we conduct it are not geared for, but are often aptly suited to defeat, the development of the truth.

We are unlikely ever to know how effectively the adversary technique would work toward truth if that were the objective of the contestants. Employed by interested parties, the process often achieves truth only as a convenience, a byproduct, or an accidental approximation. The business of the advocate, simply stated, is to win if possible without violating the law. (The phrase "if possible" is meant to modify what precedes it, but the danger of slippage is well known.) His is not the search for truth as such. To put that thought more exactly, the truth and victory are mutually incompatible for some considerable percentage of the attorneys trying cases at any given time.

Certainly, if one may speak the unspeakable, most defendants who go to trial in criminal cases are not desirous that the whole truth about the matters in controversy be exposed to scrutiny. This is not to question the presumption of innocence or the prosecution's burden of proof beyond a reasonable doubt. In any particular case, because we are unwilling to incur more than a minimal risk of convicting the innocent, these bedrock principles must prevail. The statistical fact remains that the preponderant majority of those brought to trial did substantially what they are charged with. While we undoubtedly convict some innocent people, a truth horrifying to confront, we also acquit a far larger number who are guilty, a fact we bear with much more equanimity.[16]

One reason we bear it so well is our awareness that in the last analysis truth is not the only goal. An exceedingly able criminal defense lawyer who regularly serves in our court makes a special point of this. I have heard him at once defy and cajole juries with the re-

---

14. Freedman, *The President's Advocate and the Public Interest*, N.Y.L.J., Mar. 27, 1974, at 1, col. 1. Dean Freedman went on to explain that the system contemplates an equally single-minded "advocate on the other side, and an impartial judge over both." *Id.* 7, col. 2.

15. D. PECK, *supra* note 8, at 9.

16. One of our greatest jurists has observed:

"What bothers me is that almost never do we have a genuine issue of guilt or innocence today. The system has so changed that what we are doing in the courtroom is trying the conduct of the police and that of the prosecutor all along the line. Has there been a misstep at this point? at that point? You know very well that the man is guilty; there is no doubt about the proof. But you must ask, for example: Was there something technically wrong with the arrest? You're always trying something irrelevant. The case is determined on something that really hasn't anything to do with guilt or innocence. To the extent you are doing that to preserve other significant values, I think it is unobjectionable and must be accepted. But with a great many derailing factors there is either no moral justification or only a very minimal justification."

McDonald, *A Center Report: Criminal Justice*, THE CENTER MAGAZINE, Nov. 1968, at 69, 76 (remarks of Judge Walter V. Schaefer).

minder that the question is not at all "guilt or innocence," but only whether guilt has been shown beyond a reasonable doubt. Whether that is always an astute tactic may be debated. Its doctrinal soundness is clear.

Whatever doctrine teaches, it is a fact of interest here that most criminal defense counsel are not at all bent upon full disclosure of the truth. To a lesser degree, but stemming from the same ethos, we know how fiercely prosecutors have resisted disclosure, how often they have winked at police lapses, how mixed has been their enthusiasm for the principle that they must seek justice, not merely convictions.[17] While the patterns of civil cases are different, and variable, we may say that it is the rare case in which either side yearns to have the witnesses, or anyone, give *the whole truth*. And our techniques for developing evidence feature devices for blocking and limiting such unqualified revelations.

The devices are too familiar to warrant more than a fleeting reminder. To begin with, we leave most of the investigatory work to paid partisans, which is scarcely a guarantee of thorough and detached exploration. Our courts wait passively for what the parties will present, almost never knowing—often not suspecting—what the parties have chosen not to present. The ethical standards governing counsel command loyalty and zeal for the client, but no positive obligation at all to the truth. Counsel must not knowingly break the law or commit or countenance fraud. Within these unconfining limits, advocates freely employ time-honored tricks and stratagems to block or distort the truth.

As a matter of strict logic, in the run of cases where there are flatly contradictory assertions about matters of fact, one side must be correct, the other wrong. Where the question is "Did the defendant pass a red light?" or "Does the plaintiff have a scarred retina?" or "Was the accused warned of the reasons why anyone of sound mind would keep quiet and did he then proceed nevertheless like a suicidal idiot to destroy himself by talking?" the "facts" are, or were, one way or the other. To be sure, honest people may honestly differ, and we mere lawyers cannot—actually, must not—set ourselves up as judges of the facts. That is the great release from effective ethical inhibitions. We are not to pass judgment, but only to marshal our skills to present and test the witnesses and other evidence—the skills being to make the most of these for our side and the least for the opposition. What will out, we sometimes tell ourselves and often tell others, is the truth. And, if worse comes to worst, in the end who really knows what is truth?

There is much in this of cant, hypocrisy, and convenient overlooking. As people, we know or powerfully suspect a good deal more than we are prepared as lawyers to admit or explore further. The clearest cases are those in which the advocate has been informed directly by a competent client, or has learned from evidence too clear to admit of genuine doubt, that the client's position rests upon falsehood. It is not possible to be certain, but I believe from recollection and conversation such cases are far from rare. Much more numerous are the cases in which we manage as counsel to avoid too much knowledge. The sharp eye of the cynical lawyer becomes at strategic moments a demurely averted and filmy gaze. It may be agreeable not to listen to the client's tape recordings of vital conversations that may contain embarrassments for the ultimate goal of vindicating the client. Unfettered by the clear prohibitions actual "knowledge" of the truth might impose, lawyers may be effective and exuberant in employing the familiar skills:

---

17. Among the most recent and highly publicized examples of prosecutors subordinating truth and fairness to the lust after victory are the dismissals of indictments in the Wounded Knee and Ellsberg cases. United States v. Banks, 383 F. Supp. 389 (D.S.D. 1974); United States v. Russo, No. 9373-CD-WMB (C.D. Cal., May 11, 1973).

techniques that make a witness look unreliable although the look stems only from counsel's artifice, cunning questions that stop short of discomfiting revelations, complaisant experts for whom some shopping may have been necessary. The credo that frees counsel for such arts is not a doctrine of truth-seeking.

The litigator's devices, let us be clear, have utility in testing dishonest witnesses, ferreting out falsehoods, and thus exposing the truth. But to a considerable degree these devices are like other potent weapons, equally lethal for heroes and villains. It is worth stressing, therefore, that the gladiator using the weapons in the courtroom is not primarily crusading after truth, but seeking to win. If this is banal, it is also overlooked too much and, in any event, basic to my thesis.

Reverting to the time before trial, our unlovely practice of plea bargaining—substantially unique to the United States—reflects as one of its incidents the solemn duty of defense counsel to seek the acquittal of guilty people. Plea negotiations must begin, in principles governing all but some exotic cases, with the understanding that the defendant is guilty. Plea negotiations should not otherwise be happening. But the negotiations break down in many cases, most often because there is no mutually acceptable deal on the sentence, the key concern.[18] When that occurs, the defendant goes to trial, and the usual measures to prevent conviction are to be taken by his advocate. The general, seemingly principled, view would hold his tendered plea and attendant discussions inadmissible at trial.[19] Does all this make sense? Is it comfortable? All of us in the law have explained patiently to laymen that "guilty" means not simply that "he did it"; it means nothing less than that he has been "found-guilty-beyond-a-reasonable-doubt-by-a-unanimous-jury-in-accordance-with-law-after-a-fair-trial." Despite the sarcastic hyphens, all of us mean that and live by it. But when a fair trial entails a trial so tortured and obstacle-strewn as our adversary process, we make the system barely tolerable, if not widely admired, only by contriving that most of those theoretically eligible get no trial at all. The result suggests we might inquire how things work on the European continent, where the guilty plea, at least in technical strictness, is scarcely known and the plea bargain seems to be truly nonexistent.

Our relatively low regard for truth-seeking is perhaps the chief reason for the dubious esteem in which the legal profession is held. The temptation to quote poetical diatribes is great. Before fighting it off altogether, let us recall only Macaulay on Francis Bacon, purporting not to

> inquire ... whether it be right that a man should, with a wig on his head, and a band round his neck, do for a guinea what, without those appendages, he would think it wicked and infamous to do for an empire; whether it be right that, not merely believing but knowing a statement to be true, he should do all that can be done by sophistry, by rhetoric, by solemn asseveration, by indignant exclamation, by gesture, by play of features, by terrifying one honest witness, by perplexing another, to cause a jury to think that statement false.[20]

---

18. The discussion here applies quite generally, but not universally. "Sentence bargaining," probably a better label, is almost entirely unknown in the Southern District of New York. It happens with varying frequency in other federal courts—the Agnew case comes to mind, cf. Hoffman, *Plea Bargaining and the Role of the Judge*, 53 F.R.D. 499 (1971)—and appears to be widespread in the state courts of New York and elsewhere.

19. *See* ABA Project on Minimum Standards for Criminal Justice, Pleas of Guilty § 3.4 (Approved Draft (1968)).

20. 6 T. Macaulay, The Works of Lord Macaulay 135, 163 (H. Trevelyan ed. 1900).

Less elegant than Macaulay but also numbered among the laymen who do not honor us for our dealings with the truth are many beneficiaries of such stratagems. One of the least edifying, but not uncommon, of trial happenings is the litigant exhibiting a special blend of triumph, scorn, complicity, and moral superiority when his false position has scored a point in artful cross-examination or some other feat of advocacy. This is a kind of fugitive scene difficult to document in standard ways, but described here in the belief that courtroom habitués will confirm it from their own observations.

I am among those who believe the laity have ground to question our service in the quest for truth. The ranks of lawyers and judges joining in this rueful stance are vast. Many have sought over the years to raise our standards and our functioning, not merely our image. There has been success. Liberalized discovery has helped, though the struggles over that, including the well-founded fears of tampering with the evidence, highlight the hardy evils of adversary management. We have, on the whole, seemed to become better over time, occasional lapses notwithstanding. At any rate, the main object of this talk is not merely to bewail, but to participate in the ongoing effort to improve. Modest thoughts on that subject, respectively negative and positive, occupy the two sections that follow.

* * *

IV. Some Proposals

Having argued that we are too much committed to contentiousness as a good in itself and too little devoted to truth, I proceed to some prescriptions of a general nature for remedying these flaws. Simply stated, these prescriptions are that we should:

(1) modify (not abandon) the adversary ideal,

(2) make truth a paramount objective, and

(3) impose upon the contestants a duty to pursue that objective.

A. Modifying the Adversary Ideal

We should begin, as a concerted professional task, to question the premise that adversariness is ultimately and invariably good. For most of us trained in American law, the superiority of the adversary process over any other is too plain to doubt or examine. The certainty is shared by people who are in other respects widely separated on the ideological spectrum. The august *Code of Professional Responsibility*, as has been mentioned, proclaims, in order, the "*Duty of the Lawyer to a Client*,"[55] then the "*Duty of the Lawyer to the Adversary System of Justice*."[56] There is no announced "Duty to the Truth" or "Duty to the Community." Public interest lawyers, while they otherwise test the law's bounds, profess a basic commitment "to the adversary system itself" as the means of giving "everyone affected by corporate and bureaucratic decisions ... a voice in those decisions...."[57] We may note similarly the earnest and idealistic scholar who brought the fury of the (not necessarily consistent) establishment upon himself when he wrote, reflecting upon experience as devoted defense counsel for poor people, that as an advocate you must (a) try to destroy a witness "whom you know to be telling the truth," (b) "put a witness on the stand when you know he will commit perjury," and (c) "give your client legal advice when you have reason to believe that the knowledge you give him will tempt

---

55. *Id.* (heading preceding EC 7-4).
56. *Id.* (heading preceding EC 7-19).
57. Halpern & Cunningham, *Reflections on the New Public Interest Law*, 59 GEO. L.J. 1095, 1109 (1971).

him to commit perjury."[58] The "policies" he found to justify these views, included, as the first and most fundamental, the maintenance of "an adversary system based upon the presupposition that the most effective means of determining truth is to present to a judge and jury a clash between proponents of conflicting views."[59]

Our commitment to the adversary or "accusatorial" mode is buttressed by a corollary certainty that other, alien systems are inferior. We contrast our form of criminal procedure with the "inquisitorial" system, conjuring up visions of torture, secrecy, and dictatorial government. Confident of our superiority, we do not bother to find out how others work. It is not common knowledge among us that purely inquisitorial systems exist scarcely anywhere; that elements of our adversary approach exist probably everywhere; and that the evolving procedures of criminal justice, in Europe and elsewhere, are better described as "mixed" than as strictly accusatorial or strictly inquisitorial.[60]

In considering the possibility of change, we must open our minds to the variants and alternatives employed by other communities that also aspire to civilization. Without voting firmly, I raise the question whether the virginally ignorant judge is always to be preferred to one with an investigative file. We should be prepared to inquire whether our arts of examining and cross-examining, often geared to preventing excessive outpourings of facts, are inescapably preferable to safeguarded interrogation by an informed judicial officer.[61] It is permissible to keep asking, because nobody has satisfactorily answered, why our present system of confessions in the police station versus no confessions at all is better than an open and orderly procedure of having a judicial official question suspects.[62]

If the mention of such a question has not exhausted your tolerance, consider whether our study of foreign alternatives might suggest means for easing the unending tension surrounding the privilege against self-incrimination as it frequently operates in criminal trials. It would be prudent at least to study closely whether our criminal defendant, privileged to stay suspiciously absent from the stand or to testify subject to a perjury prosecution or "impeachment" by prior crimes, is surely better off than the European defendant who cannot escape questioning both before and at trial, though he may refuse to answer, but is free to tell his story without either the oath or the impeachment pretext for using his criminal record against him.[63] Whether or not the defendant is better off, the question remains open whether the balance we have struck is the best possible.

To propose only one other topic for illustration, we need to study whether our elaborate struggles over discovery, especially in criminal cases, may be incurable symptoms of pathology inherent in our rigid insistence that the parties control the evidence until it is all "prepared" and packaged for competitive manipulation at the eventual continuous trial. Central in the debates on discovery is the concern of the ungenerous that the evi-

---

58. Freedman, *Professional Responsibility of the Criminal Defense Lawyer: The Three Hardest Questions*, 64 MICH. L. REV. 1469 (1966).

59. *Id.* 1470. *See also id.* 1471, 1477–78, 1482.

60. W. SCHAEFER, THE SUSPECT AND SOCIETY 71 (1967); Damaska, *Evidentiary Barriers to Conviction and Two Models of Criminal Procedure: A Comparative Study*, 121 U. PA. L. REV. 506, 557–61, 569–70 (1973).

61. *Cf.* Watts v. Indiana, 338 U.S. 49, 54–55 (1949).

62. *See* W. SCHAEFER, *supra* note 60; *cf.* Friendly, *The Fifth Amendment Tomorrow: The Case for Constitutional Change*, 37 U. CIN. L. REV. 671, 685, 700–01, 713–16 (1968).

63. *See* Damaska, *supra* note 60, at 527–28.

dence may be tainted or alchemized between the time it is discovered and the time it is produced or countered at the trial. The concern, though the debaters report it in differing degrees, is well founded. It is significant enough to warrant our exploring alternative arrangements abroad where investigation "freezes" the evidence (that is, preserves usable depositions and other forms of relatively contemporaneous evidence) for use at trial, thus serving both to inhibit spoilage and to avoid pitfalls and surprises that may defeat justice.[64]

Such illustrative lines of study and comparison are tendered here only as the beginning of a suggested agenda. For myself, I plan to go back to law school with them by proposing their consideration as topics for seminars I shall be privileged to "give" (more aptly, to share) during the coming year. It is my hope that some of those who read this may wish to embark upon comparable efforts.

B. Making Truth the Paramount Objective

We should consider whether the paramount commitment of counsel concerning matters of fact should be to the discovery of truth rather than to the advancement of the client's interest. This topic heading contains for me the most debatable and the least thoroughly considered of the thoughts offered here. It is a brief suggestion for a revolution, but with no apparatus of doctrine or program.

We should face the fact that the quality of "hired gun"[65] is close to the heart and substance of the litigating lawyer's role. As is true always of the mercenary warrior, the litigator has not won the highest esteem for his scars and his service. Apart from our image, we have had to reckon for ourselves in the dark hours with the knowledge that "selling" our stories rather than striving for the truth cannot always seem, because it is not, such noble work as befits the practitioner of a learned profession. The struggle to win, with its powerful pressures to subordinate the love of truth, is often only incidentally, or coincidentally, if at all, a service to the public interest.

We have been bemused through the ages by the hardy (and somewhat appealing) notion that we are to serve rather than judge the client. Among the implications of this theme is the idea that lawyers are not to place themselves above others and that the client must be equipped to decide for himself whether or not he will follow the path of truth and justice. This means quite specifically, whether in *Anatomy of a Murder*[66] or in

---

64. In the depths of the cold war, Mr. Justice Jackson reported a comparison that should be no more offensive in a time of even tremulous detente:

> [T]he Soviet Delegation objected to our practice on the ground that it is not fair to defendants. Under the Soviet System when an indictment is filed every document and the statement of every witness which is expected to be used against the defendant must be filed with the court and made known to the defense. It was objected that under our system the accused does not know the statements of accusing witnesses nor the documents that may be used against him, that such evidence is first made known to him at the trial too late to prepare a defense, and that this tends to make the trial something of a game instead of a real inquest into guilt. It must be admitted that there is a great deal of truth in this criticism. We reached a compromise by which the Nürnberg indictment was more informative than in English or American practice but less so than in Soviet and French practice.

Bull, *Nurnberg Trial*, 7 F.R.D. 175, 178 (n.d.) (quoting Justice Jackson, source not indicated).

65. *See* H. PACKER & T. EHRLICH, NEW DIRECTIONS IN LEGAL EDUCATION 33 (1972).

66. R. TRAVER, ANATOMY OF A MURDER (1958). For those who did not read or have forgotten it, the novel, by a state supreme court justice, involved an eventually successful homicide defense of impaired mental capacity with the defendant supplying the requisite "facts" after having been told in advance by counsel what type of facts would constitute the defense.

Dean Freedman's altruistic sense of commitment,[67] that the client must be armed for effective perjury as well as he would be if he were himself legally trained. To offer anything less is arrogant, elitist, and undemocratic.

It is impossible to guess closely how prevalent this view may be as a practical matter. Nor am I clear to what degree, if any, received canons of legal ethics give it sanction. My submission is in any case that it is a crass and pernicious idea, unworthy of a public profession. It is true that legal training is a source of power, for evil as well as good, and that a wicked lawyer is capable of specially skilled wrongdoing. It is likewise true that a physician or pharmacist knows homicidal devices hidden from the rest of us. Our goals must include means for limiting the numbers of crooked and malevolent people trained in the vital professions. We may be certain, notwithstanding our best efforts, that some lawyers and judges will abuse their trust. But this is no reason to encourage or facilitate wrongdoing by everyone.

Professional standards that placed truth above the client's interests would raise more perplexing questions. The privilege for client's confidences might come in for reexamination and possible modification. We have all been trained to know without question that the privilege is indispensable for effective representation. The client must know his confidences are safe so that he can tell all and thus have fully knowledgeable advice. We may want to ask, nevertheless, whether it would be an excessive price for the client to be stuck with the truth rather than having counsel allied with him for concealment and distortion. The full development of this thought is beyond my studies to date. Its implications may be unacceptable. I urge only that it is among the premises in need of examination.

If the lawyer is to be more truth-seeker than combatant, troublesome questions of economics and professional organization may demand early confrontation. How and why should the client pay for loyalties divided between himself and the truth? Will we not stultify the energies and resources of the advocate by demanding that he judge the honesty of his cause along the way? Can we preserve the heroic lawyer shielding his client against all the world—and not least against the State—while demanding that he honor a paramount commitment to the elusive and ambiguous truth? It is strongly arguable, in short, that a simplistic preference for the truth may not comport with more fundamental ideals—including notably the ideal that generally values individual freedom and dignity above order and efficiency in government.[68] Having stated such issues too broadly, I leave them in the hope that their refinement and study may seem worthy endeavors for the future.

C. A Duty to Pursue the Truth

The rules of professional responsibility should compel disclosures of material facts and forbid material omissions rather than merely proscribe positive frauds. This final

---

67. *See* text accompanying note 58 *supra*. In M. FREEDMAN, LAWYERS' ETHICS IN AN ADVERSARY SYSTEM, ch. 6 (forthcoming), Dean Freedman reports a changed view on this last of his "three hardest questions." He would under some circumstances (including the case in *Anatomy of a Murder*) condemn the lawyer's supplying of the legal knowledge to promote perjury. Exploring whether the Dean's new position is workable would transcend even the wide leeway I arrogate in footnotes.

68. Two previous Cardozo Lecturers have been among the line of careful thinkers cautioning against too single-minded a concern for truth. "While our adversary system of litigation may not prove to be the best means of ascertaining truth, its emphasis upon respect for human dignity at every step is not to be undermined lightly in a democratic state." Botein, *The Future of the Judicial Process*, 15 RECORD OF N.Y.C.B.A. 152, 166 (1960). *See also* Shawcross, *The Functions and Responsibilities of an Advocate*, 13 RECORD OF N.Y.C.B.A. 483, 498, 500 (1958).

suggestion is meant to implement the broad and general proposition that precedes it. In an effort to be still more specific, I submit a draft of a new disciplinary rule that would supplement or in large measure displace existing disciplinary rule 7-102 of the *Code of Professional Responsibility.*[69] The draft says:

(1) In his representation of a client, unless prevented from doing so by a privilege reasonably believed to apply, a lawyer shall:

(a) Report to the court and opposing counsel the existence of relevant evidence or witnesses where the lawyer does not intend to offer such evidence or witnesses.

(b) Prevent, or when prevention has proved unsuccessful, report to the court and opposing counsel the making of any untrue statement by client or witness or any omission to state a material fact necessary in order to make statements made, in the light of the circumstances under which they were made, not misleading.

(c) Question witnesses with a purpose and design to elicit the whole truth, including particularly supplementary and qualifying matters that render evidence already given more accurate, intelligible, or fair than it otherwise would be.

(2) In the construction and application of the rules in subdivision (1), a lawyer will be held to possess knowledge he actually has or, in the exercise of reasonable diligence, should have.

Key words in the draft, namely, in (1)(b), have been plagiarized, of course, from the Securities and Exchange Commission's rule 10b-5.[70] That should serve not only for respectability; it should also answer, at least to some extent, the complaint that the draft would impose impossibly stringent standards. The morals we have evolved for business clients cannot be deemed unattainable by the legal profession.

Harder questions suggest themselves. The draft provision for wholesale disclosure of evidence in litigation may be visionary or outrageous, or both. It certainly stretches out of existing shape our conception of the advocate retained to be partisan. As against the yielding up of everything, we are accustomed to strenuous debates about giving a supposedly laggard or less energetic party a share in his adversary's litigation property safe-

---

69. The affected portions of DR 7-102 are:
   (A) In his representation of a client, a lawyer shall not:
   ....
   (3) Conceal or knowingly fail to disclose that which he is required by law to reveal.
   (4) Knowingly use perjured testimony or false evidence.
   (5) Knowingly make a false statement of law or fact.
   (6) Participate in the creation or preservation of evidence when he knows or it is obvious that the evidence is false.
   (7) Counsel or assist his client in conduct that the lawyer knows to be illegal or fraudulent.
   ....
   (B) A lawyer who receives information clearly establishing that:
   (1) His client has, in the course of the representation, perpetrated a fraud upon a person or tribunal shall promptly call upon his client to rectify the same, and if his client refuses or is unable to do so, he shall reveal the fraud to the affected person or tribunal.
   (2) A person other than his client has perpetrated a fraud upon a tribunal shall promptly reveal the fraud to the tribunal.
70. 17 C.F.R. § 240.10b-5 (1974).

guarded as "work product."[71] A lawyer must now surmount partisan loyalty and disclose "information clearly establishing" frauds by his client or others.[72] But that is a far remove from any duty to turn over all the fruits of factual investigation,[73] as the draft proffered here would direct. It has lately come to be required that some approach to helpful disclosures be made by prosecutors in criminal cases; "the suppression by the prosecution of evidence favorable to an accused upon request violates due process where the evidence is material either to guilt or to punishment, irrespective of the good faith or bad faith of the prosecution."[74] One may be permitted as a respectful subordinate to note the awkward placement in the quoted passage of the words "upon request," and to imagine their careful insertion to keep the duty of disclosure within narrow bounds. But even that restricted rule is for the *public* lawyer. Can we, should we, adopt a far broader rule as a command to the bar generally?

That question touches once again the most sensitive nerve of all. A bar too tightly regulated, too conformist, too "governmental," is not acceptable to any of us. We speak often of lawyers as "officers of the court" and as "public" people. Yet our basic conception of the office is of one essentially private—private in political, economic, and ideological terms—congruent with a system of private ownership, enterprise, and competition, however modified the system has come to be.[75] It is not necessary to recount here the contributions of a legal profession thus conceived to the creation and maintenance of a relatively free society. It is necessary to acknowledge those contributions and to consider squarely whether, or how much, they are endangered by proposed reforms.

If we must choose between truth and liberty, the decision is not in doubt. If the choice seemed to me that clear and that stark, this essay would never have reached even the tentative form of its present submission. But I think the picture is quite unclear. I lean to the view that we can hope to preserve the benefits of a free, skeptical, contentious bar while paying a lesser price in trickery and obfuscation.

A Causerie on Lawyers' Ethics in Negotiation

Alvin B. Rubin,* 35 *Louisiana Law Review* 577 (1975)

I asked him whether, as a moralist, he did not think that the practice of the law, in some degree, hurt the nice feeling of honesty. JOHNSON: 'Why no, sir, if you act properly. You are not to deceive your clients with false representations of your opinion: you are not to tell lies to a judge.' 2 *Boswell's Life of Johnson* 47 (G.B. Hill ed. 1934).

The philosopher of Mermaid Tavern did not discuss the morality expected when lawyers deal with other lawyers or with laymen. When a lawyer buys or sells a house or a

---

71. *See* 4 J. MOORE, FEDERAL PRACTICE ¶ 26.64 (2d ed. 1974).

72. ABA CODE OF PROFESSIONAL RESPONSIBILITY, DR 7-102(B).

73. *Cf.* AMERICAN COLLEGE OF TRIAL LAWYERS, CODE OF TRIAL CONDUCT R. 15(b):

    A lawyer should not suppress any evidence that he or his client has a legal obligation to reveal or produce. He should not advise or cause a person to secrete himself or to leave the jurisdiction of a tribunal for the purpose of making himself unavailable as a witness therein. However, except when legally required, it is not his duty to disclose any evidence or the identity of any witness.

74. Brady v. Maryland, 373 U.S. 83, 87 (1963).

75. Cf. Damaska, *supra* note 60, at 565–69, 584–87.

  * Judge, United States District Court, E.D. Louisiana.

horse or a used car, he is expected to bargain. When he becomes a Secretary of State—like Dean Acheson or John Foster Dulles—or a Governor, or a Senator, or a Congressman or a legislator, he will negotiate and compromise.

In such activities lawyers may be acting for themselves as principals, or they may be representing constituents. But they are not practicing their profession as attorneys-at-law. It may be assumed that the lawyer who is buying or selling a farm on his own behalf is expected to behave no differently from any other member of his society, that no special ethical principles command his adherence or govern his conduct. And while the lawyer-diplomat or lawyer-politician may conceive of himself as a professional, rather than as an amateur, he will not be practicing a profession, as that term is generally understood.

When the lawyer turns to his law practice and begins to represent his clients as attorney or advocate, he assumes the role of a professional. What constitutes a profession is difficult to define comprehensively, but all attempts include reference to a store of special training, knowledge, and skills and to the adoption of ethical standards governing the manner in which these should be employed. When acting as an advocate, the lawyer professes a complex set of ethical principles that regulate his conduct toward the courts, his own clients, other lawyers and their clients.

Litigation spawns compromise, and courtroom lawyers engage almost continually in settlement discussions in civil cases and plea bargains in criminal cases. We do not know what proportion of civil claims is settled by negotiation before the filing of suit, but it must be vastly greater than the number of cases actually filed. Neither does institution of suit mean an end to negotiations; 91% of all cases filed in the United States District Courts for the fiscal year ending June 30, 1974 were disposed of prior to the beginning of a trial on the merits, most of them by some sort of negotiated compromise. In the same year only 15% of the defendants in criminal cases in the federal courts went to trial; 61% of the charges terminated in pleas of guilty or nolo contendere and 24% were nol prossed or dismissed for some other reason.[1] In almost all of the cases that were disposed of without trials, there were likely negotiations of one kind or another, such as plea bargains or exchanges of information.

Although less than one fourth of the lawyers in practice today devote a majority of their time to litigation, and most spend none at all in the traditional courtroom,[2] there are few lawyers who do not negotiate regularly, indeed daily, in their practice. Some lawyers who handle little conventional litigation persist in saying that they do not act as negotiators. If there are a few at the bar who do not, they are *rarae aves*. Patent lawyers, tax counselors and securities specialists and all those who perform the myriad tasks of office law practice may not dicker about the value of a case—though some assuredly do; but they constantly negotiate the settlement of disputed items.

Neither the Code of Professional Responsibility nor most of the writings about lawyers' ethics specifically mention any precepts that apply to this aspect of the profession. The few references to the lawyer's conduct in settlement negotiations relate to ob-

---

1. *See* Reports of the Proceedings of the Judicial Conference of the United States-Annual Report of the Director of the Administrative Office of the United States Courts 1973; 1974 Semi-Annual Report of the Director-Administrative Office of the United States Courts.

2. This "fact" is derived from personal observation, conversation with lawyers, and discussions with managing partners of larger law firms, who usually report that about 25% of their lawyers are in the litigation section.

taining client approval[3] and disclosing potentially conflicting interests.[4] It is scant comfort to observe here, as apologists for the profession usually do, that lawyers are as honest as other men.[5] If it is an inevitable professional duty that they negotiate, then as professionals they can be expected to observe something more than the morality of the market place.

In 1969, after five years of study, the American Bar Association, to which 192,000 of the nation's more than 300,000 lawyers belong, adopted a Code of Professional Responsibility, superseding the archaic Canons of Ethics. The Code has, with minor changes, been adopted in forty-nine states and the District of Columbia.[6] It purports to set forth the ethical standards that apply to the lawyer's professional conduct. It is lengthy and intricate. Its style is forbidding and is only slightly more lucid than the more formidable parts of the Internal Revenue Code. But its complex structure and apparent effort to be comprehensive induce the belief that it sets forth those general principles to which lawyers should adhere in every aspect of their professional engagements.

Its nine canons are preceptual; they purport to state "axiomatic norms,"[7] and to express "in general terms the standards of professional conduct expected of lawyers in their relationships with the public, with the legal system, and with the legal profession."[8] From the Canons are derived 137 Ethical Considerations that are "aspirational in character."[9] Both Canons and Ethical Considerations (EC) are reinforced by 38 mandatory Disciplinary Rules (DR), each with subparts, that set forth the sanctions for proscribed conduct. But these scriptures contain nothing that deals directly with the propriety of a lawyer's conduct or his ethical responsibilities when dealing as a negotiator with another lawyer, a layman or a government agency. Indeed, there are only a few texts that can be used to construct precepts by analogy.

The superseded Canons of Ethics contained a fine homiletic sentence: "The conduct of the lawyer before the Court *and with other lawyers* should be characterized by candor and fairness."[10] The admonitions of duty to the Court—at least in some respects—remain explicit and elaborated in the Code; the general statement of a duty to other lawyers no longer appears.[11] The Code does not speak directly to the duty of a lawyer in dealing with laymen.

There are a few rules designed to apply to other relationships that touch peripherally the area we are discussing. A lawyer shall not:

---

3. ABA Code of Professional Responsibility, EC 7-7. The ABA Code, as adopted in Louisiana, is found in Articles of Incorporation, Louisiana State Bar Ass'n art. XVI, La. R.S. 37, ch. 4, app.

4. ABA Code of Professional Responsibility, EC 5-16, 5-17.

5. Ferdinand Lunberg, *quoted in* M.Bloom, The Trouble with Lawyers 17 (1968).

6. California adopted new Rules of Professional Conduct on January 1, 1975. They are based in part on the Disciplinary Rules of the new code but do not include the ethical considerations.

7. *Preliminary Statement* to ABA Code of Professional Responsibility.

8. *Id.*

9. *Id.*

10. ABA Canons of Professional Ethics No. 22 (emphasis added).

11. ABA Code of Professional Responsibility, EC 7-38 speaks to the lawyer's relationship with other lawyers in litigation: "A lawyer should be courteous to opposing counsel and should accede to reasonable requests regarding court proceedings, setting continuances, waiver of procedural formalities and similar matters which do not prejudice the rights of his client." It concludes: "A lawyer should be *punctual* in fulfilling all professional commitments." (Emphasis added.)

–knowingly make a false statement of law or fact.[12]

–participate in the creation or preservation of evidence when he knows or it is obvious that the evidence is false.[13]

–counsel or assist his client in conduct that the lawyer knows to be illegal or fraudulent,[14] or

–knowingly engage in *other illegal conduct* or conduct contrary to a Disciplinary Rule.[15]

–conceal or knowingly fail to disclose that which he is *required by law* to reveal.[16]

In addition, he "should be temperate and dignified and ... refrain from all illegal and morally reprehensible conduct."[17] The lawyer is admonished "to treat with consideration all persons involved in the legal process and to avoid the infliction of needless harm."[18]

Taken together, these rules, interpreted in the light of that old but ever useful candle, *ejusdem generis*, imply that a lawyer shall not himself engage in illegal conduct, since the meaning of assisting a client in fraudulent conduct is later indicated by the proscription of *other* illegal conduct. As we perceive, the lawyer is forbidden to make a false statement of law or fact *knowingly*. But nowhere is it ordained that the lawyer owes any general duty of candor or fairness to members of the bar or to laymen with whom he may deal as a negotiator, or of honesty or of good faith insofar as that term denotes generally scrupulous activity.

Is the lawyer-negotiator entitled, like Metternich, to depend on "cunning, precise calculation, and a willingness to employ whatever means justify the end of policy"?[19] Few are so bold as to say so. Yet some whose personal integrity and reputation are scrupulous have instructed students in negotiating tactics that appear tacitly to countenance that kind of conduct. In fairness it must be added that they say they do not "endorse the *propriety*" of this kind of conduct and indeed even indicate "grave reservations"[20] about such behavior; however, this sort of generalized disclaimer of sponsorship hardly appears forceful enough when the tactics suggested include:

–Use two negotiators who play different roles. (Illustrated by the "Mutt and Jeff" police technique; "Two lawyers for the same side feign an internal dispute ...")

–Be tough — especially against a patsy.

–Appear irrational when it seems helpful.

–Raise some of your demands as the negotiations progress.

---

12. ABA Code of Professional Responsibility, DR 7-102(A)(5).

13. ABA Code of Professional Responsibility, DR 7-102(A)(6).

14. ABA Code of Professional Responsibility, DR 7-102(A)(7). Presumably this implies, a fortiori, that a lawyer must not himself do anything fraudulent.

15. ABA Code of Professional Responsibility, DR 7-102(A)(8). (emphasis added).

16. ABA Code of Professional Responsibility, DR 7-102(A)(3). (emphasis added).

17. ABA Code of Professional Responsibility, EC 1-5.

18. ABA Code of Professional Responsibility, EC 7-10.

19. Lapham, *The Easy Chair*, Harper's, November, 1954, at 30.

20. M. Meltsner & P. Schrag, Public Interest Advocacy; Materials for Clinical Legal Education 232 (1974) (emphasis in original).

–*Claim* that you do not have authority to compromise. (Emphasis supplied.)

–After agreement has been reached, have your client reject it and raise his demands.[21]

Another text used in training young lawyers commendably counsels sincerity, capability, preparation, courage and flexibility. But it also suggests "a sound set of tools or tactics and the know-how to use (or not to use) them."[22] One such tactic is, "Make false demands, bluffs, threats; even use irrationality."[23]

Occasionally, an experienced legal practitioner comments on the strain the custom of the profession puts on conscience. An anonymous but reputedly experienced Delaware lawyer is quoted as saying, "The practice of tax law these days requires the constant taking of antiemetics."[24]

The concern of lawyers with problems that do not ostensibly involve either ethics or negotiations reveals assumptions regarding what attorneys assume to be professionally proper. Thus, the American Bar Association suggests that a major problem is raised by the question, "Must Attorneys Tell All to Accountants?"[25]

> The problem revolves around the growing demand by accountants auditing corporate books that they be informed by corporate lawyers when a mutual client is facing or could be facing contingent liabilities through involvement in potentially costly lawsuits, possible tax claims, and so on.[26]

This is not a negotiation situation, but the resistance to telling an auditor the truth about his client's affairs arises, we are told, "because revelations could weaken cases already in court …"[27] Since the disclosure would certainly not be admissible in evidence, we must assume that the apprehended "weakening" is a softening of settlement posture if the real truth were told.

Honesty, as the oath administered to witnesses makes clear, implies not only telling literal truth but also disclosing the whole truth. The lawyer has no ethical duty to disclose information to an adversary that may be harmful to his client's cause; most lawyers shrink from the notion that morality requires a standard more demanding than duty to clients. EC 4-5 prohibits a lawyer from using information acquired in the representation of a client to the client's disadvantage, and this, together with the partisan nature of the lawyer's employment, indicates to the practitioner that nondisclosure is both a duty to the client and consistent with ethical norms.

While the lawyer who appears in court is said to owe a duty to disclose relevant legal authorities even if they harm his client's position, he need not disclose, and indeed most would say that he must conceal, evidence damaging to the client's cause. This fine analysis of what a lawyer should reveal to the judge in court doubtless inspired the observation by the Italian jurist, Piero Calamandrei, who, in his celebrated *Eulogy of Judges,* asked:

---

21. *Id.* at 236–38. Regarding the tactic of having the client reject the agreement and raise his demand, the authors add, "This is the most ethically dubious of the tactics listed here, but there will be occasions where a lawyer will have to defend against it or even to employ it." *Id.* at 238.

22. H. Freeman & H. Weihofer, Clinical Law Training 122 (1972).

23. *Id.*

24. Hawley, *Morality v. Legality,* Pas. Bar Ass'n Q. 230, 235 (1956).

25. American Bar Association News, September, 1974, at 9.

26. *Id.*

27. *Id.*

Why is it that when a judge meets a lawyer in a tram or in a café and converses with him, even if they discuss a pending case, the judge is more disposed to believe what the lawyer says than if he said the same thing in court during the trial? Why is there greater confidence and spiritual unity between man and man than between judge and lawyer?[28]

Let us consider the proper role for a lawyer engaged in negotiations when he knows that the opposing side, whether as a result of poor legal representation or otherwise, is assuming a state of affairs that is incorrect. Hypothesize: *L.*, a lawyer, is negotiating the sale of his client's business to another businessman, who is likewise represented by counsel. Balance sheets and profit and loss statements prepared one month ago have been supplied. In the last month, sales have fallen dramatically. Counsel for the potential buyer has made no inquiry about current sales. Does *L* have a duty to disclose the change in sales volume?

Some lawyers say, "I would notify my client and advise him that *he* has a duty to disclose," not because of ethical considerations but because the client's failure to do so might render the transaction voidable if completed. If the client refused to sanction disclosure, some of these lawyers would withdraw from representing him *in this matter* on ethical grounds. As a practical matter, (*i.e.*, to induce the client to accept their advice) they say, in consulting with the client, the lawyer is obliged to present the problem as one of possible fraud in the transaction rather than of lawyers' ethics.

In typical law school fashion, let us consider another hypothetical. *L*, the lawyer is representing *C*, a client, in a suit for personal injuries. There have been active settlement negotiations with *LD*, the defendant's lawyer. The physician who has been treating *C* rendered a written report, containing a prognosis stating that it is unlikely that *C* can return to work at his former occupation. This has been furnished to *LD*. *L* learns from *C* that he has consulted another doctor, who has given him a new medication. *C* states that he is now feeling fine and thinks he can return to work, but he is reluctant to do so until the case is settled or tried. The next day *L* and *LD* again discuss settlement. Does *L* have a duty either to guard his client's secret or to make a full disclosure? Does he satisfy or violate either duty if, instead of mentioning *C's* revelation he suggests that *D* require a new medical examination?[29]

Some lawyers avoid this problem by saying that it is inconceivable that a competent *LD* would not ask again about *C's* health. But if the question as to whether *L* should be frank is persistently presented, few lawyers can assure that they would disclose the true facts.

Lawyers whose primary practice is corporate tend to distinguish the two hypotheticals, finding a duty to disclose the downturn in earnings but not the improvement in health. They may explain the difference by resorting to a discussion of the lower standards (expectations?) of the bar when engaged in personal injury litigation. "That's why I stay away from that kind of work," one lawyer said. The esteem of a lawyer for his own profession must be scant if he can rationalize the subclassifications this distinction implies. Yet this kind of gradation of professional ethics appears to permeate the bar.

Lawyers from Wall Street firms say that they and their counterparts observe scrupulous standards, but they attribute less morality to the personal injury lawyer, and he, in

---

28. P. Calamandrei, Eulogy of Judges 39 (1942).

29. "[P]laintiff should disclose as much information as he possibly can without harming his own case." H. Baer & A. Broder, How to Prepare and Negotiate Cases for Settlement 91 (1967).

turn, will frequently point out the inferiority of the standards of those who spend much time in criminal litigation. The gradation of the ethics of the profession by the area of law becomes curiouser and curiouser the more it is examined, if one may purloin the words of another venturer in wonderland.

None would apparently deny that honesty and good faith in the sale of a house or a security implies telling the truth and not withholding information. But the Code does not exact that sort of integrity from lawyers who engage in negotiating the compromise of a law suit or other negotiations. Scant impetus to good faith is given by EC 7-9, which states, "When an action in the best interest of his client seems to him to be unjust, [the lawyer] may ask his client for permission to forego such action," for such a standard means that the client sets the ultimate ethical parameter for the lawyer's conduct. Neither is there much guidance for the negotiator in EC 7-10, "The duty of a lawyer to represent his client with zeal does not militate against his concurrent obligation to treat with consideration all persons involved in the legal process and to avoid infliction of needless harm." EC 7-27 also palters with the issue: "Because it interferes with the proper administration of justice, a lawyer should not *suppress* evidence that he or his client has a *legal* obligation to reveal or produce."[30] In context, this obviously applies to the presentation of evidence before a tribunal and not to out-of-court conversations. It likewise begs our present inquiry, for the issue in regard to EC 7-27 is whether there is a *legal* rather than an ethical obligation to reveal or produce the evidence.

The professional literature contains many instances indicating that, in the general opinion of the bar, there is no requirement that the lawyer disclose unfavorable evidence in the usual litigious situation.[31] The *racontes* of lawyers and judges with their peers are full of tales of how the other side failed to ask the one key question that would have revealed the truth and changed the result, or how one side cleverly avoided producing the critical document or the key witness whom the adversary had not discovered. The feeling that, in an adversary encounter, each side should develop its own case helps to insulate counsel from considering it a duty to disclose information unknown to the other side. Judge Marvin Frankel, an experienced and perceptive observer of the profession, comments, "Within these unconfining limits [of the Code] advocates freely employ time-honored tricks and strategems to block or distort the truth."[32]

The United States Supreme Court has developed a rule that requires the disclosure by the prosecutor in a criminal case of evidence favorable to the accused. But this is a duty owed by the government as a matter of due process, not a duty of the prosecutor as a lawyer. In all other respects in criminal cases, and in almost every aspect of the trial of civil cases, client loyalty appears to insulate the lawyer's conscience. Making fidelity to client the ultimate loyalty and the client himself the authority served appears to sanction the abdication of personal ethical responsibility, a kind of behavior described by

---

30. ABA Code of Professional Responsibility, EC 7-27 (in pertinent part) (emphasis added).

31. "[I]n ordinary litigious controversy the bar has been told that it is entitled and perhaps required to take a tough, unyielding attitude with respect to the revelation of distasteful evidence...." Maguire, *Conscience and Propriety in Lawyer's Tax Practice*, 6 Tax Counselor's Q. 493 (1962). In a footnote, Maguire continues: "Instance after instance can be adduced. Williston, Life and Law 271–272 (1940) (refraining from correcting judge's statement of fact, although Mr. Williston did and his opponents did not know the truth); Opinion 309, NYCLA 708 (1933) (not improper to refrain from revealing presence in court of eye witness vital to case of client's opponent, a three year old child).... cf. Opinion 307, NYCLA 706 (1933) (not improper to refrain from warning witness whose testimony would be helpful to client that witness by testifying may expose himself to prosecution)...."

32. Frankel, *The Search for Truth—An Umpireal View*, 30 The Record of the Association of the Bar of the City of New York 21 (1975).

psychologist Stanley Milgrim in *Obedience to Authority*. He discusses a series of experiments in which people are induced to inflict apparent physical pain on another person because someone in authority orders it. The lawyer permits obedience to the client's interest to provide the moral authority as well as the rationalized justification for his conduct.

Do the lawyer's ethics protest more strongly against giving false information? DR 7-102(A)(5), already quoted,[33] forbids the lawyer to "knowingly make" a false statement of law or fact. Most lawyers say it would be improper to prepare a false document to deceive an adversary or to make a factual statement known to be untrue with the intention of deceiving him. But almost every lawyer can recount repeated instances where an adversary of reasonable repute dealt with facts in such an imaginative or hyperbolic way as to make them appear to be different from what he knew they were.

Interesting answers are obtained if lawyers are asked whether it is proper to make false statements that concern negotiating strategy rather than the facts in litigation. Counsel for a plaintiff appears quite comfortable in stating, when representing a plaintiff, "My client won't take a penny less than $25,000," when in fact he knows that the client will happily settle for less; counsel for the defendant appears to have no qualms in representing that he has no authority to settle, or that a given figure exceeds his authority, when these are untrue statements. Many say that, as a matter of strategy, when they attend a pre-trial conference with a judge known to press settlements, they disclaim any settlement authority both to the judge and adversary although in fact they do have settlement instructions; estimable members of the bar support the thesis that a lawyer may not misrepresent a fact in controversy but may misrepresent matters that pertain to his authority or negotiating strategy because this is expected by the adversary.[34]

To most practitioners it appears that anything sanctioned by the rules of the game is appropriate. From this point of view, negotiations are merely, as the social scientists have viewed it, a form of game; observance of the expected rules, not professional ethics, is the guiding precept. But gamesmanship is not ethics.

Consider the problems raised when a lawyer represents a client before a government agency, for example the Internal Revenue Service. Here special rules are thought to be applicable. A formal opinion of the ABA Committee on Ethics states:

> In practice before the Internal Revenue Service, which is itself an adversary party rather than a judicial tribunal, the lawyer is under a duty not to mislead the Service, either by misstatement, silence, or through his client, but is under no duty to disclose the weaknesses of his client's case. He must be candid and fair, and his defense of his client must be exercised within the bounds of the law and without resort to any manner of fraud or chicane.[35]

The committee states that a lawyer engaged in handling a case before the Internal Revenue Service is not held to the principles of ethics that would apply to litigation in court because he is dealing with the IRS, which is the representative of one of the parties. The lawyer has an "absolute duty not to make false assertions of fact" but this does not "require the disclosure of weaknesses in the client's case ... unless the facts in the attorney's possession indicate beyond reasonable doubt that a crime will be committed. A wrong,

---

33. *See* text at note 12 *supra.*

34. *See, e.g.,* Voorhies, *Law Office Training: The Art of Negotiation,* 13 Prac. Law., no. 4, at 61 (April, 1967).

35. American Bar Association, Opinions of the Committee on Professional Ethics, Formal Opinion 314, at 690 (April 27, 1965).

or indeed sometimes an unjust, tax result in the settlement of a controversy is not a crime."[36] This kind of juxtaposition of the permissible and the criminal leads inevitably to the conclusion that all that is not criminal is acceptable.

A different distinction is drawn by Calamandrei:

> The difference between the true lawyer and those men who consider the law merely a trade is that the latter seek to find ways to permit their clients to violate the moral standards of society without overstepping the letter of the law, while the former look for principles which will persuade their clients to keep within the limits of the spirit of the law in common moral standards.[37]

The courts have seldom had occasion to consider these ethical problems, for disciplinary proceedings have rarely been invoked on any charge of misconduct in the area. But where settlements have in fact been made when one party acted on the basis of a factual error known to the other and this error induced the compromise, courts have set releases aside[38] on the basis of mistake, or, in some cases, fraud.

In Louisiana "fraud" is defined as "an assertion of what is false, or a suppression of what is true...."[39] Such assertion or suppression embraces "not only an affirmation or negation by words either written or spoken, but any other means calculated to produce a belief of what is false, or an ignorance or disbelief of what is true."[40] This codification is much the same as the prevailing view at common law.[41] It is embraced within the concept of good faith in the negotiation and performance of contracts under the Uniform Commercial Code.[42] Obviously a contract negotiated on the basis of misrepresentation of fact may be set aside; there is precedent, too, for invalidating the release of a personal injury claim entered into as a result of misrepresentation of matters of law.[43] These authorities fix limits on the conduct of the principal whether he acts in person or through a lawyer.

The profession seldom confronts the necessity Vern Countryman and Ted Finman say the attorney-at-law must consider: "the need, if conflicting interests are to be protected, for the lawyer to serve as a source of restraint on his client, and, indeed, on himself."[44] The lawyer is a professional because his role is not merely to represent his client as a mercenary in the client's war; he is also "a guardian of society's interests."[45]

In an unpublished paper, Dean Murray L. Schwartz, of the University of California Law School,[46] succinctly proposed three possible standards of the relationship of the lawyer's value structure to that of his client:

> (1) A lawyer should do everything for his client that is lawful and that the client would do for himself if he had the lawyer's skill;

---

36. *Id.* At 691.

37. P. Calamandrei, Eulogy of Judges 62 (1942).

38. *See, e.g.,* Cole v. Lumbermens Mut. Cas. Co., 160 So. 2d 785 (La. App. 3d Cir. 1964).

39. La. Civ. Code art. 1847(5).

40. La. Civ. Code art. 1847(6).

41. Summers,*"Good Faith" in General Contract Law and the Sales Provisions of the Uniform Commercial Code,* 54 Va. L. Rev. 195 (1968).

42. *See* Uniform Commercial Code §§ 1-201, 1-203, 2-103.

43. Annot., 21 A.L.R.2d 272 (1952). *See also* Annot., 71 A.L.R.2d (1960). In addition, there may be a tort claim against the person who induces the release. *See* Annot., 58 A.L.R.2d 500 (1958).

44. V. Countryman & T. Finman, The Lawyer in Modern Society 185 (1966).

45. *Id.* At 186.

46. M. Schwartz, *Moral Development, Ethics and the Professional Education of Lawyers,* October 14, 1974 (unpublished paper on file in office of *Louisiana Law Review*).

(2) A lawyer *need not* do for his client that which the lawyer thinks is unfair, unconscionable or over-reaching, even if lawful;

(3) A lawyer *must not* do for his client that which the lawyer thinks is unfair, unconscionable or over-reaching, even if lawful.[47]

"It will be giving away no professional secrets," he continues, "to tell you that the first standard of behavior is the one that is largely applied in a contested judicial matter."[48] He thinks that the second standard is "officially recognized as appropriate for non-litigated matters"[49] though the authorities cited in this paper and my own experience make me think this observation overly generous to the profession. The third, he correctly finds, "no part of official doctrine."[50]

A lawyer should not be restrained only by the legal inhibitions on his client. He enjoys a monopoly on the practice of law protected by sanctions against unauthorized practice. Through a subpart of the profession, lawyer-educators, the lawyer controls access to legal education. He licenses practitioners by exacting bar examinations. He controls access to the courts save in those limited instances when a litigant may appear *pro se*, and then he aptly characterizes this litigant as being his own lawyer, hence having a fool for his client.

The monopoly on the practice of law does not arise from the presumed advantages of an attorney's education or social status: it stems from the concept that, as professionals, lawyers serve society's interests by participating in the process of achieving the just termination of disputes. That an adversary system is the basic means to this end does not crown it with supreme value. It is means, not end.[51]

If he is a professional and not merely a hired, albeit skilled hand, the lawyer is not free to do anything his client might do in the same circumstances. The corollary of that proposition does set a minimum standard: the lawyer must be at least as candid and honest as his client would be required to be. The agent of the client, that is, his attorney-at-law, must not perpetrate the kind of fraud or deception that would vitiate a bargain if practiced by his principal. Beyond that, the profession should embrace an affirmative ethical standard for attorneys' professional relationships with courts, other lawyers and the public: *The lawyer must act honestly and in good faith.* Another lawyer, or a layman, who deals with a lawyer should not need to exercise the 'same degree of caution that he would if trading for reputedly antique copper jugs in an oriental bazaar. It is inherent in the concept of an ethic, as a principle of good conduct, that it is morally binding on the conscience of the professional, and not merely a rule of the game adopted because other players observe (or fail to adopt) the same rule. Good conduct exacts more than mere convenience. It is not sufficient to call on personal self-interest; this is the standard created by the thesis that the same adversary met today may be faced again tomorrow, and one had best not prejudice that future engagement.

Patterson and Cheatham[52] correctly assert that the basic standard for the negotiator is honesty. "In terms of the standards of the profession, honesty is candor...."[53] Candor

---

47. *Id.* at 7.

48. *Id.*

49. *Id.*

50. *Id.*

51. For a recent illuminating reappraisal of the adversary process as a means to truth, see Frankel, *supra* note 32.

52. L. Patterson & E. Cheatham, The Profession of Law 121 (1971).

53. *Id.* at 123.

is not inconsistent with striking a deal on terms favorable to the client,[54] for it is known to all that, at least within limits, that is the purpose to be served. Substantial rules of law in some areas already exact of principals the duty to perform legal obligations honestly and in good faith. Equivalent standards should pervade the lawyer's professional environment. The distinction between honesty and good faith need not be finely drawn here; all lawyers know that good faith requires conduct beyond simple honesty.

Since bona fides and truthfulness do not inevitably lead to fairness in negotiations, an entirely truthful lawyer might be able to make an unconscionable deal when negotiating with a government agency, or a layman or another attorney who is representing his own client. Few lawyers would presently deny themselves and their clients the privilege of driving a hard bargain against any of these adversaries though the opponent's ability to negotiate effectively in his own interest may not be equal to that of the lawyer in question. The American Bar Association Committee on Ethics does not consider it improper for a lawyer to gain an unjust result in a tax controversy. Young lawyers, among the most idealistic in the profession, about to represent indigents, are advised that they be tough, especially against a patsy.[55]

There is an occasional Micah crying in the wilderness:

> One should go into conference realizing that he is an instrument for the furtherance of justice and is under no obligation to aid his client in obtaining an unconscionable advantage. Of course, in the zone of doubt an attorney may and probably should get all possible for his client.[56]

This raises the problem inevitable in an adversary profession if one opponent obeys a standard the other defies. As Countryman and Finman inquire,

> How is a lawyer who looks at himself as 'an instrument for the furtherance of justice' likely to fare when pitted against an attorney willing to take whatever he can get and use any means he can get away with?[57]

In criminal trial matters, *Brady v. Maryland*[58] imposes constraints on the prosecutor as a matter of constitutional due process by requiring that he divulge evidence favorable to the accused. The only limitations in the Code of Professional Responsibility on sharp practice in plea bargaining are on the public prosecutor, who

> shall make timely disclosure to counsel for the defendant ... of the existence of evidence, known to the prosecutor or other government lawyer, that tends to negate the guilt of the accused, mitigate the degree of the offense, or reduce the punishment.[59]

It is obvious, as has already been pointed out, that this does not stem from an ethical standard for lawyers but on the duty of the government, a duty the government's lawyer performs as alter ego for his employer.

---

54. *Id.*

55. *See* text at notes 20–21, *supra.*

56. Herrington, *Compromise v. Contest in Legal Controversies,* 16 A.B.A.J. 795, 798 (1930).

57. V. Countryman & T. Finman, The Lawyer in Modern Society 281 (1966). *See also* Mathews, *Negotiation: A Pedagogical Challenge,* 6 J. Legal Ed. 93, 95 (1953), observing that in negotiation a lawyer "endowed with shrewdness and a sportive sense of outmaneuvering his opponent" has "an opportunity to indulge his proclivity almost devoid of risk of detection" provided he limits himself to "sharp practice" and does not step over into fraud, coercion or violations of law "or public policy." *See* Note, 112 U. Pa. L. Rev. 865 (1964).

58. 373 U.S. 83 (1962).

59. ABA Code of Professional Responsibility, DR 7-103(B).

While it might strain present concepts of the role of the lawyer in an adversary system, surely the professional standards must ultimately impose upon him a duty not to accept an unconscionable deal. While some difficulty in line-drawing is inevitable when such a distinction is sought to be made, there must be a point at which the lawyer cannot ethically accept an arrangement that is completely unfair to the other side, be that opponent a patsy or a tax collector. So I posit a second precept: *The lawyer may not accept a result that is unconscionably unfair to the other party.*[60]

A settlement that is unconscionable may result from a variety of circumstances. There may be a vast difference in the bargaining power of the principals so that, regardless of the adequacy of representation by counsel, one party may simply not be able to withstand the expense and bear the delay and uncertainty inherent in a protracted suit. There may be a vast difference in the bargaining skill of counsel so that one is able to manipulate the other virtually at will despite the fact that their framed certificates of admission to the bar contain the same words.

The unconscionable result in these circumstances is in part created by the relative power, knowledge and skill of the principals and their negotiators. While it is the unconscionable result that is to be avoided, the question of whether the result is indeed intolerable depends in part on examination of the relative status of the parties. The imposition of a duty to tell the truth and to bargain in good faith would reduce their relative inequality, and tend to produce negotiation results that are within relatively tolerable bounds.

But part of the test must be in result alone: whether the lesion is so unbearable that it represents a sacrifice of value that an ethical person cannot in conscience impose upon another. The civil law has long had a principle that a sale of land would be set aside if made for less than half its value, regardless of circumstance.[61] This doctrine, called lesion beyond moiety, looks purely to result. If the professional ethic is *caveat negotiator*, then we could not tolerate such a burden. But there certainly comes a time when a deal is too good to be true, where what has been accomplished passes the line of simply-a-good-deal and becomes a cheat.

The lawyer should not be free to negotiate an unconscionable result, however pleasing to his client, merely because it is possible, any more than he is free to do other reprobated acts. He is not to commit perjury or pay a bribe or give advice about how to commit embezzlement. These examples refer to advice concerning illegal conduct, but we do already, in at least some instances, accept the principle that some acts are proscribed though not criminal: the lawyer is forbidden to testify as a witness in his client's cause,[62] or to assert a defense merely to harass his opponent;[63] he is enjoined to point out to his client "those factors that may lead to a decision that is morally just."[64] Whether a mode of conduct available to the lawyer is illegal or merely unconscionably unfair, the attorney must refuse to participate. This duty of fairness is one owed to the profession and to society; it must supersede any duty owed to the client.

One who has actively practiced law for over 20 years and been a federal trial judge for eight years knows that the theses he has set forth are vulnerable to charges that they are

---

60. *Compare* Summers, *"Good Faith" in General Contract Law and the Sales Provisions of the Uniform Commercial Code*, 54 Va. L. Rev. 195 (1968).

61. *See, e.g.,* LA. CIV. CODE. Art. 2589.

62. ABA Code of Professional Responsibility, DR 5-102(A). *See also* EC 5-9, DR 5-101(B).

63. ABA Code of Professional Responsibility, DR 7-102(A)(1).

64. ABA Code of Professional Responsibility, EC 7-8.

impractical, visionary, or radical. Old friends will shake their heads and say that years on the bench tend to addle brains and lead to doddering homilies.

But, like other lawyers, judges hear not only of the low repute the public has for the bench but also of the even lower regard it has for the bar. We have been told so in innumerable speeches but, more important, our friends, neighbors and acquaintances tell us on every hand that they think little of the morality of our profession. They like us; indeed some of their best friends are lawyers. But they deplore the conduct of our colleagues. This is not merely an aftermath of Watergate: it is, in major part, because many members of the public, not without some support in the facts, view our profession as one that adopts ethics as cant, pays lip service to DR's and on behalf of clients stoops to almost any chicane that is not patently unlawful. We will not change that attitude by Law Days alone. It is to serve society's needs that professions are licensed and the unlicensed prohibited from performing professional functions. It is inherent in the concept of professionalism that the profession will regulate itself, adhering to an ethos that imposes standards higher than mere law observance. Client avarice and hostility neither control the lawyer's conscience nor measure his ethics. Surely if its practitioners are principled, a profession that dominates the legal process in our law-oriented society would not expect too much if it required its members to adhere to two simple principles when they negotiate as professionals: Negotiate honestly and in good faith; and do not take unfair advantage of another—regardless of his relative expertise or sophistication. This is inherent in the oath the ABA recommends be taken by all who are admitted to the bar: "I will employ for the purpose of maintaining the causes confided to me such means only as are consistent with truth and honor."[65]

The Lawyer as Friend:
The Moral Foundations of the Lawyer-Client Relation[1]
Charles Fried[2], 85 *Yale L.J.* 1060 (1976)
Copyright © 1976 by the Yale Law Journal Company, Inc.; Charles Fried

Advocatus sed non ladro,
Res miranda populo....

Medieval anthem
honoring St. Ives

Can a good lawyer be a good person? The question troubles lawyers and law students alike. They are troubled by the demands of loyalty to one's client and by the fact that one can win approval as a good, maybe even great, lawyer even though that loyalty is engrossed by over-privileged or positively distasteful clients. How, they ask, is such loyalty compatible with that devotion to the common good characteristic of high moral princi-

---

65. Oath of Admission recommended by ABA, modeled after the one in use in the State of Washington.

1. Copyright © 1976 by Charles Fried (used here by personal permission of Professor Fried). This essay is part of a larger work on right and wrong, supported by the National Science Foundation under grant number SOC75-13506. Research assistance and suggestions were provided by Dan Polster and Jerrold Tannenbaum, students at the Harvard Law School. I am grateful for the comments of Gary Bellow, Sissela Bok, Alan Dershowitz, Philip Heymann, Andrew Kaufman, Robert Keeton, Thomas Nagel, Charles Nesson, Albert Sacks, and David Shapiro. I am especially grateful to the editors of the *Yale Law Journal* for their understanding, help, and encouragement. I wonder if any of them agree with what I say here. The National Science Foundation, of course, underwrites only the effort, not the conclusion.

2. Professor of Law, Harvard University.

ples? And whatever their views of the common good, they are troubled because the willingness of lawyers to help their clients use the law to the prejudice of the weak or the innocent seems morally corrupt. The lawyer is conventionally seen as a professional devoted to his client's interests and as authorized, if not in fact required, to do some things (though not anything) for that client which he would not do for himself.[3] In this essay I consider the compatibility between this traditional conception of the lawyer's role and the ideal of moral purity-the ideal that one's life should be lived in fulfillment of the most demanding moral principles, and not just barely within the law. So I shall not be particularly concerned with the precise limits imposed on the lawyer's conduct by positive rules of law and by the American Bar Association's *Code of Professional Responsibility*[4] except as these provide a background. I assume that the lawyer observes these scrupulously. My inquiry is one of morals: Does the lawyer whose conduct and choices are governed only by the traditional conception of the lawyer's role, which these positive rules reflect, lead a professional life worthy of moral approbation, worthy of respect-ours and his own?

I. The Challenge to the Traditional Conception

A. *The Two Criticisms*

Two frequent criticisms of the traditional conception of the lawyer's role attack both its ends and its means. First, it is said that the ideal of professional loyalty to one's client permits, even demands, an allocation of the lawyer's time, passion, and resources in ways that are not always maximally conducive to the greatest good of the greatest number.[5] Interestingly, this criticism is leveled increasingly against doctors[6] as well as lawyers. Both professions affirm the principle that the professional's primary loyalty is to his client,[7] his patient. A "good" lawyer will lavish energy and resources on his existing client, even if it can be shown that others could derive greater benefit from them.

---

3. *See, e.g.,* J. AUERBACH, UNEQUAL JUSTICE (1976); M. GREEN, THE OTHER GOVERNMENT (1975).

Lord Brougham stated the traditional view of the lawyer's role during his defense of Queen Caroline:

[A]n advocate, in the discharge of his duty, knows but one person in all the world, and that person is his client. To save that client by all means and expedients, and at all hazards and costs to other persons, and, among them, to himself, is his first and only duty; and in performing this duty he must not regard the alarm, the torments, the destruction which he may bring upon others. Separating the duty of a patriot from that of an advocate, he must go on reckless of consequences, though it should be his unhappy fate to involve his country in confusion.

2 TRIAL OF QUEEN CAROLINE 8 (J. Nightingale ed. 1821). A sharply contrasting view was held by law professors at the University of Havana who said that "the first job of a revolutionary lawyer is not to argue that his client is innocent, but rather to determine if his client is guilty and, if so, to seek the sanction which will best rehabilitate him." Berman, *The Cuban Popular Tribunals,* 09 COLUM. L. REV. 1317, 1341 (1969). And a Bulgarian attorney has been quoted as saying, "'In a Socialist state there is no division of duty between the judge, prosecutor and defense counsel ... the defense must assist the prosecution to find the objective truth in a case." J. KAPLAN, CRIMINAL JUSTICE: INTRODUCTORY CASES AND MATERIALS 204–65 (1973).

4. The American Bar Association approved a revised *Code of Professional Responsibility* in 1969. In part that revision was a response to the criticism that the legal profession, by failing to make legal services more widely available, had not met its public responsibilities. J. AUERBACH, *supra* note 1, at 285–86. *See also Preface,* ABA CODE OF PROFESSIONAL RESPONSIBILITY.

5. *See* M. GREEN, *supra* note 1, at 268–69, 285–89.

6. *See* V. FUCHS, WHO SHALL LIVE? 60 (1974); Havighurst & Blumstein, *Coping With Quality/Cost Trade-Offs in Medical Care: The Role of PSROs,* 70 Nw. U. L. REV. 6, 25–28 (1975). *But see* Fried, *Equality and Rights in Medical Care,* 6 HASTINGS CENTER REP. 29, 33–34 (1976).

7. *See* ABA CODE OF PROFESSIONAL RESPONSIBILITY CANON 7.

The professional ideal authorizes a care for the client and the patient which exceeds what the efficient distribution of a scarce social resource (the professional's time) would dictate.

That same professional ideal has little or nothing to say about the initial choice of clients or patients. Certainly it is laudable if the doctor and lawyer choose their clients among the poorest or sickest or most dramatically threatened, but the professional ideal does not require this kind of choice in any systematic way—the choice of client remains largely a matter of fortuity or arbitrary choice. But once the client has been chosen, the professional ideal requires primary loyalty to the client whatever his need or situation. Critics contend that it is wasteful and immoral that some of the finest talent in the legal profession is devoted to the intricacies of, say, corporate finance or elaborate estate plans, while important public and private needs for legal services go unmet. The immorality of this waste is seen to be compounded when the clients who are the beneficiaries of this lavish attention use it to avoid their obligations in justice (if not in law) to society and to perpetuate their (legal) domination of the very groups whose greater needs these lawyers should be meeting.[8]

The second criticism applies particularly to the lawyer. It addresses not the misallocation of scarce resources, which the lawyer's exclusive concern with his client's interests permits, but the means which this loyalty appears to authorize, tactics which procure advantages for the client at the direct expense of some identified opposing party. Examples are discrediting a nervous but probably truthful complaining witness[9] or taking advantage of the need or ignorance of an adversary in a negotiation. This second criticism is, of course, related to the first, but there is a difference. The first criticism focuses on a social harm: the waste of scarce resources implicit in a doctor caring for the hearts of the sedentary managerial classes or a lawyer tending to the estates and marital difficulties of the rich. The professional is accused of failing to confer benefits wisely and efficiently. By the second criticism the lawyer is accused not of failing to benefit the appropriate, though usually unidentified, persons, but of harming his identified adversary.[10]

---

8. For a description of the growth of such criticisms, see J. AUERBACH, *supra* note 1, at 275–88.

9. For a defense of an attorney's use of such tactics, see M. FREEDMAN, LAWYERS' ETHICS IN AN ADVERSARY SYSTEM 43–49 (1975). *See also* Curtis, *The Ethics of Advocacy*, 4 STAN. L. REV. 3 (1951).

10. The point really carries further than the distinction between benefit and harm. In the former case, though some particular person may have benefited had the distribution been efficient, it does not seem correct to say that for that reason this person had a right to the benefit which he was denied, or that this person was wronged by not receiving the benefit. Individuals do not acquire lights under policies which are dictated purely by considerations of efficiency. *See generally* Dworkin, *Hard Cases,* 88 HARV. L. REV. 1057, 1058–78 (1975).

Professor Anscombe makes the following suggestive argument: If saving the life of one patient requires a massive dose of a drug that could be divided up and used to save five other people, not one of those five can claim that he has been wronged, that the smaller dose of the drug was owed to him.

Yet all can reproach me if I gave it to none. It was there, ready to supply human need, and human need was not supplied. So any one of them can say: you ought to have used it to help us who needed it; and so all are wronged. But if it was used for someone, as much as he needed it to keep him alive, no one has any ground for accusing me of having wronged *himself.*—Why, just because he was one of five who could have been saved, is he wronged in not being saved, if someone is supplied with it who needed it? What is *his* claim, except the claim that what was needed go to him rather than be wasted? But it was not wasted. So he was not wronged. So who was wronged? And if no one was wronged, what injury did I do?

. . . .

B. *Examples*

Consider a number of cases which illustrate the first criticism: A doctor is said to owe a duty of loyalty to his patient, but how is he to react if doing his very best for his patient would deplete the resources of the patient's family, as in the case of a severely deformed baby who can only be kept alive through extraordinarily expensive means? Should a doctor prescribe every test of distinct but marginal utility for every patient on public assistance, even if he knows that in the aggregate such a policy will put the medical care system under intolerable burdens?[11] Should he subject his patients to prudent testing of new remedies because he knows that only in this way can medicine make the strides that it has in the past?[12]

These problems are analogous to problems which are faced by the lawyer. The lawyer who advises a client how to avoid the effects of a tax or a form of regulation, though it is a fair tax or a regulation in the public interest, is facing the same dilemma and resolving it in favor of his client. So does the public defender who accedes to his client's demands and takes a "losing" case to trial, thereby wasting court time and depleting the limited resources of his organization. We tolerate and indeed may applaud the decision of a lawyer who vigorously defends a criminal whom he believes to be guilty and dangerous.[13] And I for one think that a lawyer who arranges the estate of a disagreeable dowager or represents one of the parties in a bitter matrimonial dispute must be as assiduous and single-minded in fulfilling his obligation to that client as the lawyer who is defending the civil liberties case of the century.

Illustrative of the second criticism (doing things which are offensive to a particular person) are familiar situations such as the following: In a negotiation it becomes clear to the lawyer for the seller that the buyer and his lawyer mistakenly believe that somebody else has already offered a handsome price for the property. The buyer asks the seller if this is true, and the seller's lawyer hears his client give an ambiguous but clearly encouraging response.[14] Another classic case is the interposition of a technical defense such as the running of the statute of limitations to defeat a debt that the client admits he owes.[15]

I do not mean that 'because they are more' isn't a good reason for helping these and not that one, or these rather than those. It is a perfectly intelligible reason. But it doesn't follow from that that a man acts badly if he doesn't make it his reason. He acts badly if human need for what is in his power to give doesn't work in him as a reason. He acts badly if he chooses to rescue rich people rather than poor ones, having ill regard for the poor ones because they are poor. But he doesn't act badly if he uses his resources to save X, or X, Y and Z, *for no bad reason,* and is not affected by the consideration that he could save a larger number of people. For, once more: who can say he is wronged? And if no one is wronged, how does the rescuer commit any wrong?

Anscombe, *Who is Wronged?*, 5 OXFORD REV. 16, 16–17 (1967) (emphasis in original).

11. *See generally* V. FUCHS, *supra* note 4, at 94–95; Fried, *Rights and Health Care Beyond Equity and Efficiency,* 293 NEW ENGLAND J. MEDICINE 241, 244 (1975).

12. For discussions of this dilemma, sec A. COCHRANE, EFFECTIVENESS AND EFFICIENCY (1972); C. FRIED, MEDICAL EXPERIMENTATION: PERSONAL INTEGRITY AND SOCIAL POLICY (1974).

13. *See* M. FREEDMAN, *supra* note 7, at 43–49.

14. DR 7-102(A)(5) of the *Code of Professional Responsibility* states that a lawyer shall not knowingly make a false statement of law or fact in his representation of a client. The issue is how to apply this admonition in the context of negotiation, where deception is commonplace. *See* M. MELTSNER & P. SCHRAG, PUBLIC INTEREST ADVOCACY: MATERIALS FOR CLINICAL LEGAL EDUCATION 231–39 (1974).

15. For a striking example, see *Zabella v. Pakel*, 242 F.2d 452 (7th Cir. 1957), where the debtor asserting the technical defenses was a savings and loan association president, and the creditor was a man who had worked for him as a carpenter and had lent him money in earlier, less fortunate days.

There is another class of cases which does not so unambiguously involve the lawyer's furthering his client's interests at the direct expense of some equally identified, concrete individual, but where furthering those interests does require the lawyer to do things which are personally offensive to him. The conventional paradigms in the casuistic literature deal with criminal defense lawyers who are asked improper questions by the trial judge ("Your client doesn't have a criminal record, does he?" or "Your client hasn't offered to plead guilty to a lesser offense, has he?"), a truthful answer to which would be damningly prejudicial to the client, but which the lawyer cannot even refuse to answer without running the risk of creating the same prejudice. There are those who say the lawyer must lie in defense of his client's interests even though lying is personally and professionally offensive to him.[16] The defense lawyer who cross-examines a complaining rape victim (whom he knows to be telling the truth) about her chastity or lack thereof in order to discredit her accusing testimony faces a similar moral difficulty. In some respects these cases might be taken to illustrate both principal criticisms of the traditional conception. On the one hand, there is harm to society in making the choice to favor the client's interests: a dangerous criminal may escape punishment or an appropriately heavy sentence. On the other hand, this social harm is accomplished by means of acting towards another human being—the judge, the complaining witness—in ways that seem demeaning and dishonorable.

II. The Lawyer as Friend

A. *The Thesis*

In this essay I will consider the moral status of the traditional conception of the professional. The two criticisms of this traditional conception, if left unanswered, will not put the lawyer in jail, but they will leave him without a moral basis for his acts. The real question is whether, in the face of these two criticisms, a decent and morally sensitive person can conduct himself according to the traditional conception of professional loyalty and still believe that what he is doing is morally worthwhile.

It might be said that anyone whose conscience is so tender that he cannot fulfill the prescribed obligations of a professional should not undertake those obligations. He should not allow his moral scruples to operate as a trap for those who are told by the law that they may expect something more. But of course this suggestion merely pushes the inquiry back a step. We must ask then not how a decent lawyer may behave, but whether a decent, ethical person can ever be a lawyer. Are the assurances implicit in assuming the role of lawyer such that an honorable person would not give them and thus would not enter the profession? And, indeed, this is a general point about an argument from obligation:[17] It may be that the internal logic of a particular obligation demands

---

16. Although Charles Curtis explicitly denounces lying to the court, his observation that the propriety of lying might depend on whether the question is asked "by someone who has a right to ask it" at least implies a possible qualification in the case of improper questioning by the court. Curtis, *supra* note 7. at 7–9. Monroe Freedman does not specifically address this problem, but his argument that an attorney's duty to safeguard the attorney-client privilege requires the attorney to introduce his client's perjurious testimony would seem to extend to this situation. M. FREEDMAN, *supra* note 7, at 27–41. *Cf.* ABA COMM. ON PROFESSIONAL ETHICS, OPINIONS NO. 287 (1967) (if attorney for defendant learns of previous criminal record through his communications with his client, he has no duty to correct misapprehension on part of court that client has no record).

17. That one assumes obligations to persons which cannot always be overridden by the benefits which would accrue from aiding some third person is a standard objection to utilitarianism. *See, e.g.,* W. Ross, THE RIGHT AND THE GOOD 17–19 (1930).

certain forms of conduct (*e.g.,* honor among thieves), but the question remains whether it is just and moral to contract such obligations.

I will argue in this essay that it is not only legally but also morally right that a lawyer adopt as his dominant purpose the furthering of his client's interests—that it is right that a professional put the interests of his client above some idea, however valid, of the collective interest. I maintain that the traditional conception of the professional role expresses a morally valid conception of human conduct and human relationships, that one who acts according to that conception is to that extent a good person. Indeed, it is my view that, far from being a mere creature of positive law, the traditional conception is so far mandated by moral right that any advanced legal system which did not sanction this conception would be unjust.

The general problem raised by the two criticisms is this: How can it be that it is not only permissible, but indeed morally right, to favor the interests of a particular person in a way which we can be fairly sure is either harmful to another particular individual or not maximally conducive to the welfare of society as a whole?[18]

The resolution of this problem is aided, I think, if set in a larger perspective. Charles Curtis made the perspicacious remark that a lawyer may be privileged to lie for his client in a way that one might lie to save one's friends or close relatives.[19] I do not want to underwrite the notion that it is justifiable to lie even in those situations, but there is a great deal to the point that in those relations—friendship, kinship—we recognize an authorization to take the interests of particular concrete persons more seriously and to give them priority over the interests of the wider collectivity. One who provides an expensive education for his own children surely cannot be blamed because he does not use these resources to alleviate famine or to save lives in some distant land. Nor does he blame himself. Indeed, our intuition that an individual is authorized to prefer identified persons standing close to him over the abstract interests of humanity finds its sharpest expression in our sense that an individual is entitled to act with something less than impartiality to that person who stands closest to him—the person that he is. There is such a thing as selfishness to be sure, yet no reasonable morality asks us to look upon ourselves as merely plausible candidates for the distribution of the attention and resources which we command, plausible candidates whose entitlement to our own concern is no greater in principle than that of any other human being. Such a doctrine may seem edifying, but on reflection it strikes us as merely fanatical.

This suggests an interesting way to look at the situation of the lawyer. As a professional person one has a special care for the interests of those accepted as clients, just as his friends, his family, and he himself have a very general claim to his special concern. But I concede this does no more than widen the problem. It merely shows that in claiming this authorization to have a special care for my clients I am doing something which I do in other contexts as well.

---

18. I have discussed this problem elsewhere. C. FRIED, AN ANATOMY OF VALUES 207–36 (1970); C. FRIED, *supra* note 10, at 132–37. *Cf.* Schelling, *The Life You Save May Be Your Own,* in PROBLEMS IN PUBLIC EXPENDITURE ANALYSIS 127, 129–30 (S. Chase ed. 1968) (also discussing our greater concern for known, as opposed to unknown, individuals).

19. Curtis, *supra* note 7, at 8. Analogizing the lawyer to a friend raises a range of problems upon which I shall not touch. These have to do with the lawyer's benevolent and sometimes not so benevolent tyranny over and imposition on his client, seemingly authorized by the claim to be acting in the client's interests. Domineering paternalism is not a normal characteristic of friendship. This point is due to Jay Katz.

B. *The Utilitarian Explanation*

I consider first an argument to account for fidelity to role, for obligation, made most elaborately by the classical utilitarians, Mill[20] and Sidgwick.[21] They argued that our propensity to prefer the interests of those who are close to us is in fact perfectly reasonable because we are more likely to be able to benefit those people. Thus, if everyone is mainly concerned with those closest to him, the distribution of social energies will be most efficient and the greatest good of the greatest number will be achieved. The idea is that the efforts I expend for my friend or my relative are more likely to be effective because I am more likely to know what needs to be done. I am more likely to be sure that the good I intend is in fact accomplished. One might say that there is less overhead, fewer administrative costs, in benefiting those nearest to us. I would not want to ridicule this argument, but it does not seem to me to go far enough. Because if that were the sole basis for the preference, then it would be my duty to determine whether my efforts might not be more efficiently spent on the collectivity, on the distant, anonymous beneficiary. But it is just my point that *this* is an inquiry we are not required, indeed sometimes not even authorized, to make. When we decide to care for our children, to assure our own comforts, to fulfill our obligations to our clients or patients, we do not do so as a result of a cost-benefit inquiry which takes into account the ease of producing a good result for our friends and relations.

Might it not be said, however, that the best means of favoring the abstract collectivity is in certain cases not to try to favor it directly but to concentrate on those to whom one has a special relation? This does not involve tricking oneself, but only recognizing the limitations of what an individual can do and know. But that, it seems to me, is just Mill's and Sidgwick's argument all over again. There is no trickery involved, but this is still a kind of deliberate limitation of our moral horizon which leaves us uncomfortable. Do I know in a particular case whether sticking to the narrow definition of my role will *in that case* further the good of all? If I know that it will not further the general good, then why am I acting as the role demands? Is it to avoid setting a bad example? But for whom? I need not tell others—whether I tell or not could enter into my calculation. For myself then? But that begs the question, since if short-circuiting the role-definition of my obligation and going straight for the general good is the best thing to do in that case, then the example I set myself is not a bad example, but a good example. In short, I do not see how one can at the same time admit that the general good is one's only moral standard, while steadfastly hewing to obligations to friends, family, and clients. What we must look for is an argument which shows that giving some degree of special consideration to myself, my friends, my clients is not merely instrumentally justified (as the utilitarians would argue) but to some degree intrinsically so.[22]

I think such an argument can be made. Instead of speaking the language of maximization of value over all of humanity, it will speak the language of rights. The stubborn ethical datum affirming such a preference grows out of the profoundest springs of morality: the concepts of personality, identity, and liberty.

---

20. Mill, *Utilitarianism,* in THE PHILOSOPHY OF JOHN STUART MILL 321, 342–44 (M. Cohen ed. 1961).

21. H. SIDGWICK, THE METHODS OF ETHICS 252 (7th ed. 1907).

22. *See generally* D. LYONS, FORMS AND LIMITS OF UTILITARIANISM (1965); J. SMART & B. WILLIAMS, UTILITARIANISM: FOR AND AGAINST (1973); Harrod, *Utilitarianism Revised,* 45 MIND 137 (1936); Mabbott, *Punishment,* 48 MIND 152 (1939).

C. *Self, Friendship, and Justice*

Consider for a moment the picture of the human person that would emerge if the utilitarian claim were in fact correct. It would mean that in all my choices I must consider the well-being of all humanity—actual and potential—as the range of my concern. Moreover, every actual or potential human being is absolutely equal in his claims upon me. Indeed, I myself am to myself only as one of this innumerable multitude. And that is the clue to what is wrong with the utilitarian vision. Before there is morality there must be the person. We must attain and maintain in our morality a concept of personality such that it makes sense to posit choosing, valuing entities—free, moral beings. But the picture of the moral universe in which my own interests disappear and are merged into the interests of the totality of humanity is incompatible with that,[23] because one wishes to develop a conception of a responsible, valuable, and valuing agent, and such an agent must first of all be dear to himself. It is from the kernel of individuality that the other things we value radiate. The Gospel says we must love our neighbor as ourselves, and this implies that any concern for others which is a *human* concern must presuppose a concern for ourselves.[24] The human concern which we then show others is a concern which first of all recognizes the concrete individuality of that other person just as we recognize our own.

It might be objected that the picture I sketch does not show that each individual, in order to maintain the integral sense of himself as an individual, is justified in attributing a greater value to his most essential interests than he ascribes to the most essential interests of all other persons. Should not the individual generalize and attribute in equal degree to all persons the value which he naturally attributes to himself? I agree with those who hold that it is the essence of morality for reason to push us beyond inclination to

---

23. *See generally* C. FRIED, AN ANATOMY OF VALUES, 203–06; Rawls, *The Independence of Moral Theory*, 48 AM. PHIL. ASS'N 17–20 (1975) (Kantian theory, as compared to utilitarianism, takes seriously basic moral fact of primacy of notion of individual personality).

24. .... It is written (Lev. xix. 18, Matth. xxii. 39); *Thou shalt love thy neighbor* (Lev. *loc. cit.,-friend) as thyself*. Whence it seems to follow that man's love for himself is the model of his love for another. But the model exceeds the copy. Therefore, out of charity, a man ought to love himself more than his neighbor.

...

We must, therefore, say that, even as regards the affection we ought to love one neighbor more than another. The reason is that, since the principle of love is God, and the person who loves, it must needs be that the affection of love increases in proportion to the nearness to one or the other of those principles.

...

... As stated above ... we ought out of charity to love those who are more closely united to us more, both because our love for them is more intense, and because there are more reasons for loving them....

Accordingly we must say that friendship among blood relations is based upon their connection by natural origin, the friendship of fellow-citizens on their civic fellowship, and the friendship of those who are fighting side by side on the comradeship of battle. Wherefore in matters pertaining to nature we should love our kindred most, in matters concerning relations between citizens, we should prefer our fellow-citizens, and on the battlefield our fellow-soldiers....

...

If however we compare union with union, it is evident that the union arising from natural origin is prior to, and more stable than, all others, because it is something affecting the very substance, whereas other unions supervene and may cease altogether.

II THOMAS AQUINAS, SUMMA THEOLOGICA 1297–1301 (Fathers of the English Dominican Province trans. 1947).

the fair conclusion of our premises.[25] It *is* a fair conclusion that as my experience as a judging, valuing, choosing entity is crucial to me, I must also conclude that for other persons their own lives and desires are the center of their universes. If morality is transcendent, it must somehow transcend particularity to take account of this general fact. I do not wish to deny this. On the contrary, my claim is that the kind of preference which an individual gives himself and concrete others is a preference which he would in exactly this universalizing spirit allow others to exhibit as well. It is not that I callously overlook the claim of the abstract individual, but indeed I would understand and approve were I myself to be prejudiced because some person to whom I stood in a similar situation of abstraction preferred his own concrete dimensions.

Finally, the concreteness which is the starting point of my own moral sensibility, the sense of myself, is not just a historical, biographical fact. It continues to enter into and condition my moral judgments because the effects which I can produce upon people who are close to me are qualitatively different from those produced upon abstract, unknown persons. My own concreteness is important not only because it establishes a basis for understanding what I and what all other human beings might be, but because in engaging that aspect of myself with the concrete aspects of others, I realize special values for both of us. Quite simply, the individualized relations of love and friendship (and perhaps also their opposites, hatred and enmity) have a different, more intense aspect than do the cooler, more abstract relations of love and service to humanity in general. The impulse I describe, therefore, is not in any sense a selfish impulse. But it does begin with the sense of self as a concrete entity. Those who object to my thesis by saying that we must generalize it are not wholly wrong; they merely exaggerate. Truly I must be ready to generalize outward all the way. That is what justice consists of. But justice is not all of morality; there remains a circle of intensity which through its emphasis on the particular and the concrete continues to reflect what I have identified as the source of all sense of value — our sense of self.

Therefore, it is not only consonant with, but also required by, an ethics for human beings that one be entitled first of all to reserve an area of concern for oneself and then to move out freely from that area if one wishes to lavish that concern on others to whom one stands in concrete, personal relations. Similarly, a person is entitled to enjoy this extra measure of care from those who choose to bestow it upon him without having to justify this grace as either just or efficient. We may choose the individuals to whom we will stand in this special relation, or they may be thrust upon us, as in family ties. Perhaps we recognize family ties because, after all, there often has been an element of choice, but also because — by some kind of atavism or superstition — we identify with those who share a part of our biological natures.

In explicating the lawyer's relation to his client, my analogy shall be to friendship, where the freedom to choose and to be chosen expresses our freedom to hold something of ourselves in reserve, in reserve even from the universalizing claims of morality. These personal ties and the claims they engender may be all-consuming, as with a close friend or family member, or they may be limited, special-purpose claims, as in the case of the client or patient.[26] The special-purpose claim is one in which the beneficiary, the client,

---

25. *See* G. WARNOCK, THE OBJECT OF MORALITY 79–80 (1971); Nagel, Book Review, 85 YALE L.J. 136, 140 (1975).

26. This argument is, of course, just a fragment which must be fitted into a larger theory. This larger theory would have to explain, among other things, what the precise contents of the various personal roles might be and how conflicts between personal roles are to be resolved. My later discussion of permissible and impermissible tactics in legal representation deals with this conflict in one

is entitled to all the special consideration *within* the limits of the relationship which we accord to a friend or a loved one. It is not that the claims of the client are less intense or demanding; they are only more limited in their scope. After all, the ordinary concept of friendship provides only an analogy, and it is to the development of that analogy that I turn.

D. *Special-Purpose Friends*

How does a professional fit into the concept of personal relations at all? He is, I have suggested, a limited-purpose friend. A lawyer is a friend in regard to the legal system. He is someone who enters into a personal relation with you—not an abstract relation as under the concept of justice. That means that like a friend he acts in your interests, not his own; or rather he adopts your interests as his own. I would call that the classic definition of friendship. To be sure, the lawyer's range of concern is sharply limited. But within that limited domain the intensity of identification with the client's interests is the same. It is not the specialized focus of the relationship which may make the metaphor inapposite, but the way in which the relation of legal friendship comes about and the one-sided nature of the ensuing "friendship." But I do insist upon the analogy, for in overcoming the arguments that the analogy is false, I think the true moral foundations of the lawyer's special role are illuminated and the utilitarian objections to the traditional conception of that role overthrown.

* * *

Yet the unease persists. Is it that while I have shown that the lawyer has a right to help the "unworthy" client, I have not shown that whenever the lawyer exercises this right he does something which is morally worthy, entitling him to self-respect? I may have shown that the law is obliged to allow the "unworthy" client to seek legal help and the lawyer to give it. But have I also shown that every lawyer who avails himself of this legal right (his and the client's legal right) performs a *morally worthy* function? Can a good lawyer be a good person?

The lawyer acts morally because he helps to preserve and express the autonomy of his client vis-à-vis the legal system. It is not just that the lawyer helps his client accomplish a particular lawful purpose. Pornography may be legal, but it hardly follows that I perform a morally worthy function if I lend money or artistic talent to help the pornographer flourish in the exercise of this right. What is special about legal counsel is that whatever else may stop the pornographer's enterprise, he should not be stopped because he mistakenly believes there is a legal impediment. There is no wrong if a venture fails for lack of talent or lack of money—no one's rights have been violated. But rights *are* violated if, through ignorance or misinformation about the law, an individual refrains from pursuing a wholly lawful purpose. Therefore, to assist others in understanding and realizing their legal rights is always morally, worthy. Moreover, the legal system, by instituting the role of the legal friend, not only assures what it in justice must—the due lib-

---

context. A complete theory would also have to spell out the relation between personal roles and duties to the larger collectivity. These latter duties to man in the abstract as opposed to concrete persons are the subject of principles of justice. I have no doubt that such abstract duties exist and that they can be very demanding. Roughly, I would adopt something like the principles put forward in J. RAWLS, A THEORY OF JUSTICE 54–117 (1971). I would require, however, that these principles of justice leave sufficient scope for the free definition and inviolability of personal relations—to a greater extent perhaps than Rawls allows. These systematic concerns are the subject of a larger work from which the present essay is drawn. The relation of principles of justice to other aspects of right and wrong is a principal concern of that larger work.

erty of each citizen before the law—but does it by creating an institution which exemplifies, at least in a unilateral sense, the ideal of personal relations of trust and personal care which (as in natural friendship) are good in themselves.

Perhaps the unease has another source. The lawyer does work for pay. Is there not something odd about analogizing the lawyer's role to friendship when in fact his so-called friendship must usually be bought? If the lawyer is a public purveyor of goods, is not the lawyer-client relationship like that underlying any commercial transaction? My answer is "No." The lawyer and doctor have obligations to the client or patient beyond those of other economic agents. A grocer may refuse to give food to a customer when it becomes apparent that the customer does not have the money to pay for it. But the lawyer and doctor may not refuse to give additional care to an individual who cannot pay for it if withdrawal of their services would prejudice that individual.[30] Their duty to the client or patient to whom they have made an initial commitment transcends the conventional quid pro quo of the marketplace. It is undeniable that money is usually what cements the lawyer-client relationship. But the content of the relation is determined by the client's needs, just as friendship is a response to another's needs. It is not determined, as are simple economic relationships, by the mere coincidence of a willingness to sell and a willingness to buy. So the fact that the lawyer works for pay does not seriously undermine the friendship analogy.

3. *Institutional Clients*

Another possible objection to my analysis concerns the lawyer in government or the lawyer for a corporation. My model posits a duty of exclusive concern (within the law) for the interests of the client. This might be said to be inappropriate in the corporate area because larger economic power entails larger social obligations, and because the idea of friendship, even legal friendship, seems peculiarly far-fetched in such an impersonal context. After all, corporations and other institutions, unlike persons, are creatures of the state. Thus, the pursuit of their interests would seem to be especially subject to the claims of the public good. But corporations and other institutions are only formal arrangements of real persons pursuing their real interests. If the law allows real persons to pursue their interests in these complex forms, then why are they not entitled to loyal legal assistance, "legal friendship," in this exercise of their autonomy just as much as if they pursued their interests in simple arrangements and associations?

The real problem in these cases is that the definition of the client is complicated and elusive. The fundamental concepts remain the same, but we must answer a question which so far we could treat as straight-forward: Who is the client? It is the corporation. But because the corporation is an institutional entity, institutional considerations enter into both the definition of the entity to whom the loyalty is owed and the substance of that loyalty. This is dramatically so in the case of a government lawyer, since his client might be thought to be the government of the United States, or the people of the United States, mediated by an intricate political and institutional framework. So it is said that a United States attorney is interested (unlike an ordinary lawyer) not only in winning his case but also in seeing that "justice is done," because his client's interests are served only if justice is done. Since more and more lawyers have only institutional clients, the introduction of institutional concerns into the definition of the representational obligation is virtually pervasive. From this some would conclude that my argument is inappropriate

---

30. *See* ABA COMM. ON PROFESSIONAL ETHICS, OPINIONS 56 (1967) (Informal Opinion No. 334); ABA CODE OF PROFESSIONAL RESPONSIBILITY EC 2-31, 2-32. *Compare id.* DR. 2-110 (C)(1)(f) *with id.* DR 2-110(A)(2).

or at least anachronistic. I insist that my analogy is the correct one, that it is applicable to the institutional client, but that it must be combined in a complicated though wholly coherent way with other arguments about who one's client is and how that client's interests are to be identified.

* * *

B. The Choice of Means

More difficult problems are posed by the conflict between the interests of the client and the interests of some other concrete and specified person to whom the client stands in opposition. How does my friendship analogy help to resolve the conflict which a lawyer must feel if his client asks him to lie, to oppress, or to conceal—to do something which is either illegal or felt by the lawyer to be immoral?

1. Staying Within the Law

I have defined the lawyer as a client's legal friend, as the person whose role it is to insure the client's autonomy within the law. Although I have indicated that the exercise of that autonomy is not always consonant with the public interest, it does not at all follow that the exercise of that autonomy, therefore, must also violate the law. If the legal system is itself sensitive to moral claims, sensitive to the rights of individuals, it must at times allow that autonomy to be exercised in ways that do not further the public interest. Thus, the principle that the lawyer must scrupulously contain his assistance and advocacy within the dictates of the law seems to me perfectly consistent with my view of the lawyer as the client's friend, who maintains the client's interests even against the interests of society.

To be sure, there may have been and may still be situations where the law grossly violates what morality defines as individual rights; and there have been lawyers who have stood ready to defy such laws in order to further their client's rights—the rights which the law should, but did not, recognize. Whatever might be said about those cases, the lawyer's conduct in them travels outside the bounds of legal friendship and becomes political friendship, political agitation, or friendship *tout court*. But that is not the case I am examining. The moral claims which a client has on his lawyer can be fully exhausted though that lawyer contains his advocacy strictly within the limits of the law.

A critic who fails to see the importance of the lawyer's moral status in assisting the autonomy of his client, may also be inclined to complain that the constraints of the law restrain his advocacy of truly just causes too much. Such a critic has things wrong at both ends. Just as it is false to argue that the lawyer is morally reprehensible if he furthers the interests of some clients and not others or some purposes and not others, so it is false to assume that the lawyer fails to have the proper zeal if he does for his client only what the law allows. The distinction between the role of the lawyer as a personal adviser and that of the lawyer as a citizen and member of the community should be quite clear. It is by controlling what the law is and by varying the interests that clients may lawfully pursue that social policy should be effectuated; it is not by deforming the role of the lawyer as the client's legal friend and asking him to curb his advocacy in that relationship.

This explains why in a reasonably just system which properly commands the lawyer's loyalty, he must confine his advocacy to what the rules of advocacy permit. He may not counsel his client to commit a crime, nor to destroy evidence, nor to perjure himself on the witness stand. Of course, here as elsewhere there will be borderline problems. It may not be a crime to lie to the judge who has asked the improper and prejudicial question of the defense attorney, but the implicit or quasi-official rules defining the limits of the lawyer's advocacy may nonetheless forbid this. Nothing in my model should discourage the lawyer from observing such limits scrupulously.

A very difficult question would arise if the law imposed upon the lawyer an obligation first to seek and then to betray his client's trust, an obligation to do that which seems outrageous and unjust. I do not mean to say that the resolution of this question would be easy, but myanalys is at least clearly locates the area in which a resolution should be sought. For such laws, if they are to be opposed, ought to be opposed as are other unjust laws, and not because the lawyer is in general entitled to travel outside the constraints of the law in protecting his client's interests. Maybe in such a dilemma a conscientious lawyer would keep his client's confidence as would a priest or a natural friend; but if conscientiousness requires this, it requires it as an act of disobedience and resistance to an unjust law, rather than as a necessary entailment of some extreme view of the lawyer's general role.

2. *Immoral Means*

I come to what seems to me one of the most difficult dilemmas of the lawyer's role. It is illustrated by the lawyer who is asked to press the unfair claim, to humiliate a witness, to participate in a distasteful or dishonorable scheme. I am assuming that in none of these situations does the lawyer do anything which is illegal or which violates the ethical canons of his profession; the dilemma arises if he acts in a way which seems to him personally dishonorable, but there are no sanctions—legal or professional—which he need fear.

This set of issues is difficult because it calls on the same principles which provide the justification for the lawyer's or the friend's exertions on behalf of the person with whom he maintains a personal relation. Only now the personal relation is one not of benefit but of harm. In meeting the first criticism, I was able to insist on the right of the lawyer as friend to give this extra weight to the interests of his client when the only competing claims were the general claims of the abstract collectivity. But here we have a specific victim as well as a specific beneficiary. The relation to the person whom we deceive or abuse is just as concrete and human, just as personal, as to the friend whom we help.

It is not open to us to justify this kind of harm by claiming that personal relations must be chosen, not thrust upon us. Personal relations are indeed typically chosen. If mere proximity could place on us the obligations of friendship, then there would soon be nothing left of our freedom to bestow an extra measure of care over and above what humanity can justly claim. But there is a personal relation when we inflict intentional harm; the fact that it is intentional reaches out and particularizes the victim. "Who is my neighbor?" is a legitimate question when affirmative aid is in question; it is quite out of order in respect to the injunction "Do not harm your neighbor." Lying, stealing, degrading, inflicting pain and injury are personal relations too. They are not like failing to benefit, and for that reason they are laid under a correspondingly stricter regime than abstract harms to the collectivity.[36] If I claim respect for my own concrete particularity, I

---

36. This point is discussed in detail in Fried, *Right and Wrong—Preliminary Considerations,* 5 J. LEGAL STUD. (June, 1976; forthcoming). The notion that abstention from harming particular persons is a special kind of duty is expressed in Ross's concept of nonmaleficencc. *See* W. Ross, *supra* note 15, at 21–22.

must accord that respect to others. Therefore, what pinches here is the fact that the lawyer's personal engagement with the client is urging him to do that to his adversary which the very principles of personal engagement urge that he not do to anyone.

It is not wrong but somewhat lame to argue that the lawyer like the client has autonomy. From this argument it follows that the lawyer who is asked to do something personally distasteful or immoral (though perfectly legal) should be free either to decline to enter into the relationship of "legal friendship" or to terminate it.[37] And if the client can find a lawyer to do the morally nasty but legally permissible thing for him, then all is well—the complexities of the law have not succeeded in thwarting an exercise of autonomy which the law was not entitled to thwart. So long as the first lawyer is reasonably convinced that another lawyer can be found, I cannot see why he is less free to decline the morally repugnant case than he is the boring or poorly paid case. True, but lame, for one wants to know not whether one *may* refuse to do the dirty deed, but whether one is morally *bound* to refuse—bound to refuse even if he is the last lawyer in town and no one else will bail him out of his moral conundrum.

If personal integrity lies at the foundation of the lawyer's right to treat his client as a friend, then surely consideration for personal integrity—his own and others'—must limit what he can do in friendship. Consideration for personal integrity forbids me to lie, cheat, or humiliate, whether in my own interests or those of a friend, so surely they prohibit such conduct on behalf of a client, one's legal friend. This is the general truth, but it must be made more particular if it is to do service here. For there is an opposing consideration. Remember, the lawyer's special kind of friendship is occasioned by the right of the client to exercise his full measure of autonomy within the law. This suggests that one must not transfer uncritically the whole range of personal moral scruples into the arena of legal friendship. After all, not only would I not lie or steal for myself or my friends, I probably also would not pursue socially noxious schemes, foreclose on widows or orphans, or assist in the avoidance of just punishment. So we must be careful lest the whole argument unravel on us at this point.

Balance and structure are restored if we distinguish between kinds of moral scruples. Think of the soldier. If he is a citizen of a just state, where foreign policy decisions are made in a democratic way, he may well believe that it is not up to him to question whether the war he fights is a just war. But he is personally bound not to fire dum-dum bullets, not to inflict intentional injury on civilians, and not to abuse prisoners. These are personal wrongs, wrongs done by his person to the person of the victim.[38] So also, the lawyer must distinguish between wrongs that a reasonably just legal system permits to be worked by its rules and wrongs which the lawyer personally commits. Now I do not offer this as a rule which is tight enough to resolve all borderline questions of judg-

---

37. DR 2-110(B)(1) of the *Code of Professional Responsibility* makes withdrawal *mandatory* if the attorney "knows or it is obvious that his client is bringing the legal action, conducting the defense, or asserting a position in the litigation, or is otherwise having steps taken for him, merely for the purpose of harassing or maliciously injuring any person." DR 2-110(C)(1)(c) and (1)(d) *permit* a lawyer to seek withdrawal if the client either "[i]nsists that the lawyer pursue a course of conduct that is illegal or that is prohibited under the Disciplinary Rules" or "[b]y other conduct renders it unreasonably difficult for the lawyer to carry out his employment effectively." For an argument that an attorney should make his own moral judgments about whether and how to represent clients, sec M. GREEN, *supra* note 1, at 268–89. *See also* J. AUERBACH, *supra* note 1, at 279–82.

38. *See* Nagel, *War and Massacre*, 1 PHILOSOPHY & PUB. AFF. 123, 133–34, 136 (1972); Fried, *supra* note 34.

ment. We must recognize that the border is precisely the place of friction between competing moral principles. Indeed, it is unreasonable to expect moral arguments to dispense wholly with the need for prudence and judgment.

Consider the difference between humiliating a witness or lying to the judge on one hand, and, on the other hand, asserting the statute of limitations or the lack of a written memorandum to defeat what you know to be a just claim against your client. In the latter case, if an injustice is worked, it is worked because the legal system not only permits it, but also defines the terms and modes of operation. Legal institutions have created the occasion for your act. What you do is not personal; it is a formal, legally-defined act. But the moral quality of lying or abuse obtains both without and within the context of the law. Therefore, my general notion is that a lawyer is morally entitled to act in this formal, representative way even if the result is an injustice, because the legal system which authorizes both the injustice (*e.g.*, the result following the plea of the statute of limitations) and the formal gesture for working it insulates him from personal moral responsibility. I would distinguish between the lawyer's own wrong and the wrong of the system used to advantage by the client.

The clearest case is a lawyer who calls to the attention of the court a controlling legal precedent or statute which establishes his client's position even though that position is an unjust one. (I assume throughout, however, that this unjust law is part of a generally just and decent system. I am not considering at all the moral dilemmas of a lawyer in Nazi Germany or Soviet Russia.) Why are we inclined to absolve him of personal moral responsibility for the result he accomplishes? I assert it is because the wrong is wholly institutional; it is a wrong which does not exist and has no meaning outside the legal framework. The only thing preventing the client from doing this for himself is his lack of knowledge of the law or his lack of authority to operate the levers of the law in official proceedings. It is to supply that lack of knowledge or of formal capacity that the lawyer is in general authorized to act; and the levers he pulls are all legal levers.

Now contrast this to the lawyer who lies to an opposing party in a negotiation. I assume that (except in extreme cases akin to self-defense) an important lie with harmful consequences is an offense to the victim's integrity as a rational moral being, and thus the liar affirms a principle which denigrates his own moral status.[39] Every speech act invites belief, and so every lie is a betrayal. However, may a lawyer lie in his representative capacity? It is precisely my point that a man cannot lie just in his representative capacity; it is like stabbing someone in the back "just" in a representative capacity. The injury and betrayal are not worked by the legal process, but by an act which is generally harmful quite apart from the legal context in which it occurs.

There is an important class of cases which might be termed "lying in a representative capacity." An example is the lawyer presenting to the court a statement by another that he knows to be a lie, as when he puts a perjurious client-defendant on the stand. There is dispute as to whether and when the positive law of professional responsibility permits this,[40] but clearly in such instances it is not the lawyer who is lying. He is like a letter car-

---

39. Here I follow Augustine, *Lying*, in TREATISES ON VARIOUS SUBJECTS (R. Deferrari ed. 1952), and I. KANT, THE METAPHYSICAL PRINCIPLES OF VIRTUE 90–93 (J. Ellington trans. 1964).

40. *Compare M.* FREEDMAN, *supra* note 7, at 27–41 *with* Noonan, *The Purposes of Advocacy and the Limits of Confidentiality,* 64 MICH. L. REV. 1485 (1966).

rier who delivers the falsehood. Whether he is free to do that is more a matter of legal than personal ethics.

A test that might make the distinction I offer more palpable is this: How would it be if it were known in advance that lawyers would balk at the practice under consideration? Would it not be intolerable if it were known that lawyers would not plead the defense of the Statute of Frauds or of the statute of limitations? And would it not be quite all right if it were known in advance that you cannot get a lawyer to lie for you, though he may perhaps put you on the stand to lie in your own defense?

A more difficult case to locate in the moral landscape is abusive and demeaning cross-examination of a complaining witness. Presumably, positive law and the canons of ethics restrict this type of conduct, but enforcement may be lax or interpretation by a trial judge permissive. So the question arises: What is the lawyer *morally* free to do? Here again I urge the distinction between exposing a witness to the skepticism and scrutiny envisaged by the law and engaging in a personal attack on the witness. The latter is a harm which the lawyer happens to inflict in court, but it is a harm quite apart from the institutional legal context. It is perhaps just a matter of style or tone, but the crucial point is that the probing must not imply that the lawyer believes the witness is unworthy of respect.

The lawyer is not morally entitled, therefore, to engage his own person in doing personal harm to another, though he may exploit the system for his client even if the system consequently works injustice. He may, but must he? This is the final issue to confront. Since he may, he also need not if there is anyone else who will do it. Only if there is no one else does the agony become acute. If there is an obligation in that case, it is an institutional obligation that has devolved upon him to take up a case, to make arguments when it is morally permissible but personally repugnant to him to do so. Once again, the inquiry is moral, for if the law enjoins an obligation against conscience, a lawyer, like any conscientious person, must refuse and pay the price.

The obligation of an available lawyer to accept appointment to defend an accused is clear. Any moral scruples about the proposition that no man should be accused and punished without counsel are not morally well-founded. The proposition is intended to enhance the autonomy of individuals within the law. But if you are the last lawyer in town, is there a moral obligation to help the finance company foreclose on the widow's refrigerator? If the client pursues the foreclosure in order to establish a legal right of some significance, I do not flinch from the conclusion that the lawyer is bound to urge this right. So also if the finance company cannot foreclose because of an ideological boycott by the local bar. But if all the other lawyers happen to be on vacation and the case means no more to the finance company than the resale value of one more used refrigerator, common sense says the lawyer can say no. One should be able to distinguish between establishing a legal right and being a cog in a routine, repetitive business operation, part of which just happens to play itself out in court.

Conclusion

I do not imagine that what I have said provides an algorithm for resolving some of these perennial difficulties. Rather, what I am proposing is a general way of looking at the problem, a way of understanding not so much the difficult borderline cases as the central and clear ones, in the hope that the principles we can there discern will illuminate our necessarily approximate and prudential quest for resolution on the borderline. The notion of the lawyer as the client's legal friend, whatever its limitations and difficulties, does account for a kind of callousness toward society and exclusivity in the service of the client which otherwise seem quite mysterious. It justifies a kind of scheming which we would deplore on the part of a lay person dealing with another lay person — even if he were acting on behalf of a friend.

But these special indulgences apply only as a lawyer assists his client in his legal business. I do not owe my client my political assistance. I do not have to espouse his cause when I act as a citizen. Indeed, it is one of the most repellent features of the American legal profession — one against which the barrister-solicitor split has to some extent guarded the English profession — that many lawyers really feel that they are totally bought by their clients, that they must identify with their clients' interests far beyond the special purpose of advising them and operating the legal system for them. The defendants' antitrust lawyer or defendants' food and drug lawyer who writes articles, gives speeches, and pontificates generally about the evils of regulation may believe these things, but too often he does so because it is good for business or because he thinks that such conduct is what good representation requires.[41] In general, I think it deplorable that lawyers have specialized not only in terms of subject matter — that may or may not be a good thing — but in terms of plaintiffs or defendants, in terms of the position that they represent.[42]

There is a related point which cuts very much in the opposite direction. It is no part of my thesis that the *client* is not morally bound to avoid lying to the court, to pay a just debt even though it is barred by the statute of limitations, to treat an opposite party in a negotiation with humanity and consideration for his needs and vulnerability, or to help the effectuation of policies aimed at the common good. Further, it is no part of my argument to hold that a lawyer must assume that the client is not a decent, moral person, has no desire to fulfill his moral obligations, and is asking only what is the minimum that he must do to stay within the law. On the contrary, to assume this about anyone is itself a form of immorality because it is a form of disrespect between persons. Thus in very many situations a lawyer will be advising a client who wants to effectuate his purposes within the law, to be sure, but who also wants to behave as a decent, moral person. It would be absurd to contend that the lawyer must abstain from giving advice that takes account of the client's moral duties and his presumed desire to fulfill them. Indeed, in these situations the lawyer experiences the very special satisfaction of assisting the client not only to realize his autonomy within the law, but also to realize his status as a moral being. I want to make very clear that my conception of the lawyer's role in no way disentitles the lawyer from experiencing this satisfaction. Rather, it has been my purpose to explicate the less obvious point that there is a vocation and a satisfaction

---

41. The implications of this idea are particularly important for the so-called Washington lawyer (wherever he might be) who is hired to represent his client before agencies and legislatures contemplating new law. This may put us on one of the borderlines I do not pretend to resolve definitively, yet I think we can get an idea of how to think about these cases too. To the extent that such representation involves participation in a formal proceeding in which laws or regulations are drafted and technical competence is required, the task is *closer* to the traditional task of the lawyer as I have sketched it, and the legal friend concept is more appropriate. To the extent that the representation involves (wholly lawful) deployment of political pressures, inducements, and considerations, it is closer to being political action, and thus to requiring the kind of overriding concern for the common good that should motivate all political actors. Certainly it is absurd that a man should seek to be insulated from moral judgment of his accomplishments as a political string-puller or publicist by the defense that he was only doing it for money.

42. In England barristers are regularly hired by the government in all manner of litigation, thereby accomplishing the many-sidedness I call for here. *See* Q. JOHNSTONE & D. HOPSON, LAWYERS AND THEIR WORK 374–75 (1967). Why should this not be done in the United States? Perhaps there is fear that this might simply become the occasion for a suspect form of patronage.

even in helping Shylock obtain his pound of flesh or in bringing about the acquittal of a guilty man.[43]

Finally, I would like to return to the charge that the morality of role and personal relationship I offer here is almost certain to lead to the diversion of legal services from areas of greatest need. It is just my point, of course, that when we fulfill the office of friend—legal, medical, or friend *tout court*—we do right, and thus it would be a great wrong to place us under a general regime of always doing what will "do the most good." What I affirm, therefore, is the moral liberty of a lawyer to make his life out of what personal scraps and shards of motivation his inclination and character suggest: idealism, greed, curiosity, love of luxury, love of travel, a need for adventure or repose; only so long as these lead him to give wise and faithful counsel. It is the task of the social system as a whole, and of all its citizens, to work for the conditions under which everyone will benefit in fair measure from the performance of doctors, lawyers, teachers, and musicians. But I would not see the integrity of these roles undermined in order that the millennium might come sooner. After all, it may never come, and then what would we be left with?

---

43. This point is due to Albert Sacks and Richard Stewart.

Chapter VI

Difficult Clients and Communications: Responsibility for Corporations, the Government, the Incompetent and the Trusting

Problems

Problem 23

Assume you are a trusted in-house counsel at a major utility. One day, at lunch, one of the engineers expresses a concern to you. There are microscopic cracks in the cooling pipes of one of the major nuclear reactors. It is unclear whether this presents a serious danger or not. Your client is a publicly traded corporation. It is also regulated by the Nuclear Regulatory Agency. How do you handle this? Does it make a difference which system of rules apply? What if you subsequently learned that the reactor is about to be sold to another utility without disclosure of the cracks? That the reactor may have to be shut down at great expense? That the cracks may be dangerous? (I used to represent a utility with nuclear reactors, but this is *not* a true story. On the other hand, at a different utility, it could have been. See the *New York Times* article of August 8, 1996, set out at Chapter VI-3, *infra*.)

Problem 24

As a U.S. Attorney, you have been instructed to concentrate on immigration violations and potential terrorist organizations. But the neighborhood organizations in your state have strongly petitioned your office to focus on gun control violations, civil rights abuses, and drug offenses. You are fully aware that there is a local crisis of teenage shootings that are a direct result of *de facto* segregated schools, lax gun controls, and a thriving drug business. But instructions from Washington are explicit. Who is your client?

Problem 25

As an Assistant U.S. Attorney, you have been assigned to "breaking" a major drug ring. You believe one of the key suspects could be "turned" against his colleagues. Unfortunately, you know he is represented by one of the state's leading criminal defense lawyers, who also represents other members of "the family." What do you do? Would it make a difference if you were investigating a terrorist plot? Would it be different if you were investigating civil rights abuses within a large corporation? Environmental crimes? As discussed before in Problem 15, *supra*, the Department of Justice has sought exemption from the full rigors of *ABA Model Rule* 4.2. Do you agree? What about plaintiff's lawyers seeking to prove sexual discrimination within a large corporation? What if you were a special prosecutor investigating the President? See "Questioning of Ex-Intern [Monica Lewinsky] Provoked Angry Words," set out at Chapter VI-3, *infra*.

Problem 26

This is a "true story." My fellow associate decided that he wanted to do *pro bono* work for "people who are really down and out." He was assigned to represent homeless people who were being involuntarily committed because of mental illness. One old lady seemed particularly stubborn. My friend admired her, but feared for her safety as winter approached. She insisted that he do "all he can to keep her free!" What are my friend's responsibilities? Does it make a difference which rule systems apply? What *should* the law be? See Dr. Alan Stone's article "The Myth of Advocacy," set out at Chapter VI-3, *infra*.

Problem 27

This happens to almost every lawyer. Two old friends from college, Bob and Mary, make an appointment. They were college sweethearts and have been married ten years now. You were at the wedding. They now have two adorable kids. "It's just not working," they say. "But we want an *amicable* divorce. What's important is our kids Katy and Ted. We want to cooperate for *their* sake. You're the only lawyer we trust."

Assume Mary is a sophisticated businesswoman with a major bank position. Bob "dropped out" and has became a carpenter. Their financial affairs are also complicated. Bob brought most of the money into the marriage through inheritance. What can you do for your friends? Does the rule system make a difference? Do you like the current rules?

VI-1. Introduction: The Responsibility for Handling Difficult Clients and Client Communications

Communication with clients can be very difficult, even under ideal conditions. This is why most good lawyers take pains to use clear engagement letters, withdrawal letters, reporting letters, and detailed bills. *Model Rule* 1.4 requires good communication, including explanations to clients "to the extent reasonably necessary to permit the client to make informed decisions ..." *Model Rule* 1.4(b). But some kinds of clients always present special difficulties.

While in law practice, I represented some very large corporations. In general, I got clear direction from my "contact" person, usually an in-house lawyer. But many times I did not get good guidance or, even worse, I got conflicting directions. How do you talk to a company like IBM when you are confused about what it wants? Sometimes I felt like walking into a closet, shutting the door, and trying to communicate with the "spirit" of an organization! Because organizations, including corporations and government entities, present special communication problems, they are governed by a special rule, *Model Rule* 1.13.

There are other types of clients who are hard to talk to about their legal affairs. Minors and the very elderly can present problems. So can the mentally disabled. *Model Rule* 1.14 attempts to deal with some of these issues. Interestingly enough, clients who are very trusting, and wish to have you mediate with spouses and loved ones, or act as a "neutral," can also present problems. *Model Rule* 2.4 deals with this.

But one thing is certain. None of these problems relieve the lawyer of the need to try to communicate as clearly as possible, and to seek to learn the goals of the client, as the client sees them. One of my daughters, as a very small girl, became ill and had to undergo a dangerous operation. While my wife and I stood nervously in the corridor, I could hear the surgeon, a very distinguished doctor, talking in the room. I became impatient, and later asked what he was doing. "Talking to your daughter," he replied, "she's the patient." My daughter thankfully recovered, and I will never forget that lesson in professionalism.

A. Organizational Clients

The *Model Rules* make it clear that a lawyer representing a corporation or government agency represents the entity itself "acting through its duly authorized constituents." *Model Rule* 1.13. If the lawyer also represents an officer, the officer will be a separate individual client, and care must be taken that there is no conflict of interest. This can get confusing. I was an expert in a case where one woman was both CEO and sole shareholder of a valuable corporation. She was also the executor and primary beneficiary of her husband's estate, which included the corporation. One lawyer represented her in all three capacities: as an individual, as CEO of the corporation, and as executor of the estate. He also represented the corporation. She later accused him of conflict of interest. Although he was only talking to one person—indeed, only *could* talk to one person—he was representing different clients. I believed there were no conflicts of interest, but it was a difficult case for the lawyer.

Now let us assume that I represent a corporation, and become convinced that some of the individuals that act for the corporation are actually engaged in activity that could cause "substantial injury" to the corporation, at least in my view. What do I do? It would be nice to think that this would be a very rare occurrence, but recent corporate scandals indicate otherwise. In my own experience, I have seen senior officers deliberately violate the antitrust laws, causing great financial and criminal risk for the corporation and its owners. These officers believed they were "doing a good job." I have also seen major utilities (not my clients) evade their responsibilities to their shareholder, the public, and the Nuclear Regulatory Agency. See the newspaper article set out at Chapter VI-3.

Model Rule 1.13 was designed to deal with these problems. It represents one of the major changes over the old *Code*, which never dealt with these issues in a disciplinary rule, and mentioned them only in passing in an "EC," an "aspirational only" guideline called an "Ethical Consideration." See *Code*, EC-5-18. Perhaps it is a sign of the times that such issues now require extensive explicit regulation.

Model Rule 1.13 should be read carefully. In general, it requires a lawyer to go "up the corporate ladder" if the activity "is a violation of a legal obligation to the organization or a violation of law that reasonably might be imputed to the organization and that is likely to result in substantial injury to the organization" and otherwise "proceed as is reasonably necessary in the best interest of the organization." As of the ABA August 2003 Annual Meeting, *Model Rule* 1.13(c) was amended to permit, but not require, the disclosure of client confidences "to prevent substantial injury to the organization."

Now whether this is, in theory, an exception to the confidentiality rules, is a nice point. After all, would not the corporate client "consent" to such disclosure to prevent serious harm to itself? But the officers who normally would give this consent may be part of the danger. Can the lawyer get the "consent" directly from the "spirit" of the corporation—say by walking into the closet I mentioned before?

In practice, however, there is no doubt that this is seen as subject to client confidentiality. Earlier versions of *Model Rule* 1.13 permitted "reporting up," but only the remedy of withdrawal, not disclosure, if nothing happened. *Mass. Rule* 1.13, however, permits limited disclosure when all else fails "consistent with Rule 1.6, Rule 3.3. Rule 4.1 and Rule 8.3," which, as seen, could include the "crime-fraud" exceptions to Rule 1.6. This provision made it clear that *Mass. Rule* 1.13 did not limit the lawyer's discretion to reveal under these provisions. See *Mass. Rule* 1.13, Comment [5].

In August 2003, the ABA House of Delegates amended *Rule* 1.13(c) to permit, but not require, lawyer disclosures where the requirements of *Rule* 1.13(b) are met "whether or not Rule 1.6 permits such disclosure, but only if and to the extent the lawyer reasonably believes necessary to prevent substantial injury to the organization." This major change did not happen in a vacuum. On January 23, 2003, the SEC had promulgated *Standards of Professional Conduct* pursuant to the Sarbanes-Oxley Act, an act aimed at the corporate corruption evident in scandals. As originally proposed, those standards would have required "reporting up the corporate ladder" for a wide range of internal and external corporate lawyers, where substantial SEC Act violations were involved. They would also have required mandatory reporting to the SEC if the internal response was unsatisfactory. Major lobbying by the ABA and other professional groups prevented the adoption of the rules in that severe form. In particular, *mandatory* lawyer reporting was defeated. But the ABA then amended its own *Model Rule* 1.13(c) to permit *discretionary* reporting. Do you think this is a good result? Read the *SEC Standards of Professional Conduct*, set out at Chapter VI-2, with care. Note the breadth of their application. Not just securities lawyer are included, but any lawyer with information relevant to SEC compliance.

Note also that *Mass. Rule* 1.13 applies to government agencies. Usually, the practice is for a government lawyer to regard the specific agency as the client. But suppose your agency is dominated by a corrupt official, or decides to pursue an illegal or unconstitutional policy. Can you inform other government officials in another agency, say the FBI or the Attorney General, of the danger to the government? Comment [9] to *Model Rule* 1.13 has been carefully drafted to assist with these issues.[1] Nevertheless, it is obvious that thorny issues remain. Some of these issues came to a head in the 1998 investigation by Independent Counsel Kenneth W. Starr into allegations about President Clinton. In *In re Lindsey,* Section VI-3, *infra,* the Court of Appeals for the District of Columbia held

---

1. "[9] The duty defined in this Rule applies to governmental organizations. Defining precisely the identity of the client and prescribing the resulting obligations of such lawyers may be more difficult in the government context and is a matter beyond the scope of these Rules. See Scope [18]. Although in some circumstances the client may be a specific agency, it may also be a branch of government, such as the executive branch, or the government as a whole. For example, if the action or failure to act involves the head of a bureau, either the department of which the bureau is a part or the relevant branch of government may be the client for purposes in this Rule. Moreover, in a matter involving the conduct of government officials, a government lawyer may have authority under applicable law to question such conduct more extensively than that of a lawyer for a private organization in similar circumstances. Thus, when the client is a governmental organization, a different balance may be appropriate between maintaining confidentiality and assuring that the wrongful act is prevented or rectified, for public business is involved. In addition, duties of lawyers employed by the government or lawyers in military service may be defined by statutes and regulation. This Rule does not limit that authority. See Scope." *Model Rule* 1.13.

that Deputy White House Counsel Bruce R. Lindsey represented "The Office of the President" and not Clinton personally, and that communication between Clinton and Lindsey was not automatically privileged. How do you represent "the Office of the President" when you are uncertain when you can talk to the President in absolute confidence?

B. Communications Problems

1) The Model Rule 4.2 Controversy

The rules and materials set out in Sections VI-2 and VI-3 above are largely self-explanatory with regard to clients who are very young, very old, or suffering from a mental disability. But there are other related "communications" matters that have caused much controversy. The first is the Model Rule 4.2 controversy.

For example, most large corporations and other big organizations have corporate counsel. For evidentiary privilege reasons, these counsel often represent employees as well as the corporations assuming, of course, no conflict of interest. Now assume that such an organization is being investigated for sex discrimination, or environmental violations, or other illegal activity, or is the potential target for a private plaintiff's action. The plaintiff's investigators will obviously want to contact key people within the organization, and they will want to do it confidentially. But *Model Rule* 4.2 prohibits any such contact to "a person the lawyer knows to be represented by another lawyer in the matter, unless the lawyer has the consent of the other lawyer or is authorized to do so by law or a court order."

Both plaintiffs' lawyers and government agencies, such as the Department of Justice, have long sought to change, or evade, this rule. Once corporate counsel knows of the intended contact, the employee is unlikely to cooperate! The Department of Justice even tried to adopt an internal rule system to "trump" state and local federal court rules, largely to avoid *Rule* 4.2. This was rejected by the Eighth Circuit in *U.S.* v. *McDonnell Douglas Corporation*, 133 F. 3d, 1252, 1256 (8th Cir. 1998). There are strong emotions on all sides. See John Leubsdorf's excellent article, "Communicating with Another Lawyer's Client: The Lawyer's Veto and the Client's Interests," 127 *U. Pa. L. Rev.* 683 (1979), and the discussion at *McMorrow, Coquillette, supra*, pp. 802–75.

Recently, there were two major *Rule* 4.2 cases in Massachusetts, *Messing, Rudavsky & Weliky, P.C.* v. *President and Fellows of Harvard College*, 436 Mass. 347 (2002), (hereafter "*Messing*") and *Patriarca* v. *Center for Living & Working, Inc.*, 438 Mass. 132 (2002), (hereafter "*Patriarca*"). *Messing* had been set out in full in Chapter VI-3. It took a narrow view of the scope of *Rule* 4.2, holding the rule "to ban contact only with those employees who have authority to 'commit the organization to a position regarding the subject matter of representation.'" *Messing, supra*, p. 357, quoting *Johnson* v. *Cadillac Plastic Group, Inc.*, 930 F. Supp. 1437, 1442 (D. Colo., 1996). This was despite the Court having promulgated a Comment 4 to *Mass. Rule* 4.2 that also included persons "whose act or omission in connection with that matter may be imputed to the organization for purposes of civil or criminal liability" or "whose statement may constitute an admission on the part of the organization." *Mass. Rule* 4.2, *Comment* 4, (original version). The opinion of the court admitted that its decision was "a retrenchment from the broad prohibition on employee contact endorsed by the Comment," but applied the different interpretation anyway to the case at hand. *Messing, supra*, p. 357. What does this tell you about rulemaking through the "Comments"? Should not the Court have changed the Comment, and then applied it prospectively only? (The Court did change the Comment [4] in June of 2003, after *Messing*, to the version in the *Appendix* of this book). An excellent article by Professor Gerald J. Clark, "Navigating the Investigation Quagmire after *Messing* and *Patriarca*," 88 *Mass. L. Rev.* (2003) 62 (hereafter "*Clark*") suggests "that the policing of attorneys' ethics by the judiciary in the heat of litigation is inappropriate!" *Id.*, p. 62. While he agrees with the outcome of *Messing*, Professor Clark also criticizes the opinion of the court as "confusing and internally contradictory." *Id.*, p. 72. Do you agree?

Soon after *Messing*, the Supreme Judicial Court decided *Patriarca*, which asked whether Rule 4.2 covered *former* employees. The trial judge said it did, but the Supreme Judicial Court reversed on the grounds that there was no real attorney-client relationship between institutional counsel and these former employees even if they had been still working at the organization at the time involved in the case. Professor Clark argues that this is a clearer and better focus than *Messing* itself. See *Clark, supra*, p. 72. Do you agree?

2) The "Neutral" Lawyer Controversy

Another "communications" controversy occurs when clients want to step out of the adversary posture altogether, and to use a lawyer as a "neutral" or "mediator." Given the expense and stress of litigation, this is very understandable, but it has created much practical difficulty. Actually, as with the *Rule* 4.2 controversy, we could argue that the "difficulty" has more to do with the legal profession itself than with the clients.

Lawyers like to think in "categories." You are my client, or you are not. I represent you, or I don't. If I represent you, I have an obligation to pursue your lawful interests diligently and, in Massachusetts, "zealously." See *Mass. Rule* 1.3. I do not want to agree to go "half way" or seek a "fair solution for all." It is not what I am trained to do, and the professional rule reflects this culture.

The ABA *Code* had a simple solution. If a lawyer is asked to be "an impartial arbitrator or mediator," the lawyer can play that role. But she or he must stop acting as a lawyer, and "should not thereafter represent in the dispute any of the parties involved." ABA *Code* EC-5-20. This "solves" the difficulty professionally, but it hardly serves the clients' interests. They may have to go out and hire a new lawyer or several new lawyers, who will represent them in the same "adversarial" way as before.

The *Model Rules* tried a new approach. Originally, the ABA adopted a *Model Rule* 2.2, "Intermediary," that permitted a lawyer to act on behalf of more than one client as a "neutral" under very strict conditions. The rule was never adopted in Massachusetts, and was regarded as such a disaster that it was repealed by the ABA House of Delegates at its February, 2002 meeting. It was replaced by *Model Rule* 2.4 "Lawyer Serving a Third-Party Neutral," which has now been adopted by Massachusetts with some changes to comments 2 and 4. *Model Rule* 2.4 goes back to the old ABA *Code* solution. If you are a "third-party neutral," you are not representing anybody involved, and if anybody involved is not represented by another lawyer, the lawyer "neutral" must "inform unrepresented parties that the lawyer is not representing them."

What do you think of this "solution"? If any unrepresented party to such a process "does not understand the lawyer's role in the matter, the lawyer shall explain the difference between the lawyer's role as a third-party neutral and a lawyer's role as one who represents a client." *Model Rule* 2.4(b). But what kind of a lawyer represents no clients? It is a judge. Essentially, *Model Rule* 2.4 turns its back on any professional role for lawyers in "alternative dispute resolution" except as adversaries in the traditional mode or, as a "rent-a-judge," also in a traditional mode. This solves the "communication" and "client" problems, but at what cost? Of course, this too remains hotly debated. What are your views?

C. Withdrawal

"Difficult" clients and "communication" problems inherently bring up one solution, terminating the representation. It is a very common misconception, even among experienced lawyers, that representation is a matter of mutual consent and can be terminated on both sides with appropriate notice. This is exactly half true. Representation can always be terminated by the client, for any reason. *Model Rule* 1.6(a)(3). Indeed, in-house counsel may find themselves in danger of losing wrongful discharge remedies, because their employer is their client, and can discharge them for any reason. (In *Spratley* v. *State Farm Mutual Insurance Co.*, 78 P.3d 603 (Utah 2003) the court held that the terminated in-house lawyers could sue for wrongful discharge because of the self-defense exception to *Model Rule* 1.6).

But the opposite is *not* true. Lawyers cannot fire their clients "at will." There are only two types of allowed withdrawal by a lawyer from a representation: "mandatory" and "permissive." Unless the termination fits one of these two categories, set out by *Model Rule* 1.16, the lawyer cannot resign. The "mandatory" category is simple. There are only three basic grounds: (1) that the representation "will result in violation of the rules of professional conduct or other law," i.e., will result in a conflict of interest, assistance in a fraud, etc.; (2) that the lawyer's "physical or mental condition materially impairs the lawyer's ability to represent the client"; or (3) the lawyer is "discharged" by the client. (The second ground does *not* mean that the lawyer can resign if the client "makes him sick.") These mandatory grounds offer little discretion for the lawyer.

The "permissive grounds" are also restrictive. They include failure to pay the bills, *Model Rule* 1.16(b)(6), or that "the client persists in a course of action involving the lawyer's services that the lawyer reasonably believes is criminal or fraudulent," *Model Rule* 1.16(b)(2). The most flexible grounds are in *Model Rule* 1.16(b)(4), "the client insists on taking action that the lawyer considers repugnant or with which the lawyer has a fundamental disagreement" or *Model Rule* 1.16(b)(6), "the representation will result in an unreasonable financial burden on the lawyer or has been rendered unreasonably difficult by the client." A lawyer may also withdraw "if withdrawal can be accomplished without material adverse effect on the interests of the client." *Model Rule* 1.16(b)(1). Note that "reasonable" is a defined word in the *Model Rules*, and is an objective test, "denotes the conduct of a reasonably prudent and competent lawyer," not a subjective standard. See *Model Rule* 1.0. As a lawyer, you cannot just terminate a representation because you feel like it, unless it makes no real difference to the client.

Even if the withdrawal is permitted, the lawyer has an affirmative duty to protect the client. If the client "has severely diminished capacity," there are special duties set out in *Model Rule* 1.6, Comment [6]. In all cases, "a lawyer shall take steps to the extent reasonably practicable to protect a client's interest," including "time for employment of other counsel." Where a lawyer has been appointed to represent a client, court approval is often required. "Even if the lawyer has been unfairly discharged by the client, a lawyer must take all reasonable steps to mitigate the consequences to the client." *Model Rule 1.16*, Comment [9].

In short, unless the termination has no "material adverse" effect on the client's interests, it is not easy to walk away from even a very difficult client. In practice, this makes lawyers careful about whom they accept as clients, but economic pressures or professional duty can sometimes leave them little choice. This is particularly true of the moral duty to represent worthy, but indigent clients, or clients accused of serious crimes who have a constitutional right to counsel, or other court appointments. In short, dealing with "difficult clients," or clients that present serious communication problems, is not always avoidable, and doing it right is part of the challenge of being a good, responsible, ethical lawyer.

VI-2. "Difficult" Clients and Communications: The Rules

ABA Model Rules

RULE 1.2: SCOPE OF REPRESENTATION AND ALLOCATION OF AUTHORITY BETWEEN CLIENT AND LAWYER

(a) Subject to paragraphs (c) and (d), a lawyer shall abide by a client's decisions concerning the objectives of representation and, as required by Rule 1.4, shall consult with the client as to the means by which they are to be pursued. A lawyer may take such action on behalf of the client as is impliedly authorized to carry out the representation. A lawyer shall abide by a client's decision whether to settle a matter. In a criminal case, the lawyer shall abide by the client's decision, after consultation with the lawyer, as to a plea to be entered, whether to waive jury trial and whether the client will testify.

(b) A lawyer's representation of a client, including representation by appointment, does not constitute an endorsement of the client's political, economic, social or moral views or activities.

(c) A lawyer may limit the scope of the representation if the limitation is reasonable under the circumstances and the client gives informed consent.

(d) A lawyer shall not counsel a client to engage, or assist a client, in conduct that the lawyer knows is criminal or fraudulent, but a lawyer may discuss the legal consequences of any proposed course of conduct with a client and may counsel or assist a client to make a good faith effort to determine the validity, scope, meaning or application of the law.

Comment

Allocation of Authority between Client and Lawyer

[1] Paragraph (a) confers upon the client the ultimate authority to determine the purposes to be served by legal representation, within the limits imposed by law and the lawyer's professional obligations. The decisions specified in paragraph (a), such as whether to settle a civil matter, must also be made by the client. See Rule 1.4(a)(1) for the lawyer's duty to communicate with the client about such decisions. With respect to the means by which the client's objectives are to be pursued, the lawyer shall consult with the client as required by Rule 1.4(a)(2) and may take such action as is impliedly authorized to carry out the representation.

[2] On occasion, however, a lawyer and a client may disagree about the means to be used to accomplish the client's objectives. Clients normally defer to the special knowledge and skill of their lawyer with respect to the means to be used to accomplish their objectives, particularly with respect to technical, legal and tactical matters. Conversely, lawyers usually defer to the client regarding such questions as the expense to be incurred and concern for third persons who might be adversely affected. Because of the varied nature of the matters about which a lawyer and client might disagree and because the actions in question may implicate the interests of a tribunal or other persons, this Rule does not prescribe how such disagreements are to be resolved. Other law, however, may be applicable and should be consulted by the lawyer. The lawyer should also consult with the client and seek a mutually acceptable resolution of the disagreement. If such efforts are unavailing and the lawyer has a fundamental disagreement with the client, the lawyer may withdraw from the representation. See Rule 1.16(b)(4). Conversely, the client may resolve the disagreement by discharging the lawyer. See Rule 1.16(a)(3).

[3] At the outset of a representation, the client may authorize the lawyer to take specific action on the client's behalf without further consultation. Absent a material change in circumstances and subject to Rule 1.4, a lawyer may rely on such an advance authorization. The client may, however, revoke such authority at any time.

[4] In a case in which the client appears to be suffering diminished capacity, the lawyer's duty to abide by the client's decisions is to be guided by reference to Rule 1.14.

Independence from Client's Views or Activities

[5] Legal representation should not be denied to people who are unable to afford legal services, or whose cause is controversial or the subject of popular disapproval. By the same token, representing a client does not constitute approval of the client's views or activities.

Agreements Limiting Scope of Representation

[6] The scope of services to be provided by a lawyer may be limited by agreement with the client or by the terms under which the lawyer's services are made available to the client. When a lawyer has been retained by an insurer to represent an insured, for example, the representation may be limited to matters related to the insurance coverage. A limited representation may be appropriate because the client has limited objectives for the representation. In addition, the terms upon which representation is undertaken may exclude specific means that might otherwise be used to accomplish the client's objectives. Such limitations may exclude actions that the client thinks are too costly or that the lawyer regards as repugnant or imprudent.

[7] Although this Rule affords the lawyer and client substantial latitude to limit the representation, the limitation must be reasonable under the circumstances. If, for example, a client's objective is limited to securing general information about the law the client needs in order to handle a common and typically uncomplicated legal problem, the lawyer and client may agree that the lawyer's services will be limited to a brief telephone consultation. Such a limitation, however, would not be reasonable if the time allotted was not sufficient to yield advice upon which the client could rely. Although an agreement for a limited representation does not exempt a lawyer from the duty to provide competent representation, the limitation is a factor to be considered when determining the legal knowledge, skill, thoroughness and preparation reasonably necessary for the representation. See Rule 1.1.

[8] All agreements concerning a lawyer's representation of a client must accord with the Rules of Professional Conduct and other law. See, e.g., Rules 1.1, 1.8 and 5.6.

Criminal, Fraudulent and Prohibited Transactions

[9] Paragraph (d) prohibits a lawyer from knowingly counseling or assisting a client to commit a crime or fraud. This prohibition, however, does not preclude the lawyer from giving an honest opinion about the actual consequences that appear likely to result from a client's conduct. Nor does the fact that a client uses advice in a course of action that is criminal or fraudulent of itself make a lawyer a party to the course of action. There is a critical distinction between presenting an analysis of legal aspects of questionable conduct and recommending the means by which a crime or fraud might be committed with impunity.

[10] When the client's course of action has already begun and is continuing, the lawyer's responsibility is especially delicate. The lawyer is required to avoid assisting the client, for example, by drafting or delivering documents that the lawyer knows are fraudulent or by suggesting how the wrongdoing might be concealed. A lawyer may not continue assisting a client in conduct that the lawyer originally supposed was legally proper but then discovers is criminal or fraudulent. The lawyer must, therefore, withdraw from the representation of the client in the matter. See Rule 1.16(a). In some cases, withdrawal alone might be insufficient. It may be necessary for the lawyer to give notice of the fact of withdrawal and to disaffirm any opinion, document, affirmation or the like. See Rule 4.1.

[11] Where the client is a fiduciary, the lawyer may be charged with special obligations in dealings with a beneficiary.

[12] Paragraph (d) applies whether or not the defrauded party is a party to the transaction. Hence, a lawyer must not participate in a transaction to effectuate criminal or fraudulent avoidance of tax liability. Paragraph (d) does not preclude undertaking a criminal defense incident to a general retainer for legal services to a lawful enterprise. The last clause of paragraph (d) recognizes that determining the validity or interpretation of a statute or regulation may require a course of action involving disobedience of the statute or regulation or of the interpretation placed upon it by governmental authorities.

[13] If a lawyer comes to know or reasonably should know that a client expects assistance not permitted by the Rules of Professional Conduct or other law or if the lawyer intends to act contrary to the client's instructions, the lawyer must consult with the client regarding the limitations on the lawyer's conduct. See Rule 1.4(a)(5).

RULE 1.4: COMMUNICATION

(a) A lawyer shall:

(1) promptly inform the client of any decision or circumstance with respect to which the client's informed consent, as defined in Rule 1.0(e), is required by these Rules;

(2) reasonably consult with the client about the means by which the client's objectives are to be accomplished;

(3) keep the client reasonably informed about the status of the matter;

(4) promptly comply with reasonable requests for information; and

(5) consult with the client about any relevant limitation on the lawyer's conduct when the lawyer knows that the client expects assistance not permitted by the Rules of Professional Conduct or other law.

(b) A lawyer shall explain a matter to the extent reasonably necessary to permit the client to make informed decisions regarding the representation.

Comment

[1] Reasonable communication between the lawyer and the client is necessary for the client effectively to participate in the representation.

Communicating with Client

[2] If these Rules require that a particular decision about the representation be made by the client, paragraph (a)(1) requires that the lawyer promptly consult with and secure the client's consent prior to taking action unless prior discussions with the client have resolved what action the client wants the lawyer to take. For example, a lawyer who receives from opposing counsel an offer of settlement in a civil controversy or a proffered plea bargain in a criminal case must promptly inform the client of its substance unless the client has previously indicated that the proposal will be acceptable or unacceptable or has authorized the lawyer to accept or to reject the offer. See Rule 1.2(a).

[3] Paragraph (a)(2) requires the lawyer to reasonably consult with the client about the means to be used to accomplish the client's objectives. In some situations—depending on both the importance of the action under consideration and the feasibility of consulting with the client—this duty will require consultation prior to taking action. In other circumstances, such as during a trial when an immediate decision must be made, the exigency of the situation may require the lawyer to act without prior consultation. In such cases the lawyer must nonetheless act reasonably to inform the client of actions the lawyer has taken on the client's behalf. Additionally, paragraph (a)(3) requires that the lawyer keep the client reasonably informed about the status of the matter, such as significant developments affecting the timing or the substance of the representation.

[4] A lawyer's regular communication with clients will minimize the occasions on which a client will need to request information concerning the representation. When a client makes a reasonable request for information, however, paragraph (a)(4) requires prompt compliance with the request, or if a prompt response is not feasible, that the lawyer, or a member of the lawyer's staff, acknowledge receipt of the request and advise the client when a response may be expected. Client telephone calls should be promptly returned or acknowledged.

Explaining Matters

[5] The client should have sufficient information to participate intelligently in decisions concerning the objectives of the representation and the means by which they are to be pursued, to the extent the client is willing and able to do so. Adequacy of communication depends in part on the kind of advice or assistance that is involved. For example, when there is time to explain a proposal made in a negotiation, the lawyer should review all important provisions with the client before proceeding to an agreement. In litigation a lawyer should explain the general strategy and prospects of success and ordinarily should consult the client on tactics that are likely to result in significant expense or to injure or coerce others. On the other hand, a lawyer ordinarily will not be expected to describe trial or negotiation strategy in detail. The guiding principle is that the lawyer should fulfill reasonable client expectations for information consistent with the duty to act in the client's best interests, and the client's overall requirements as to the character of representation. In certain circumstances, such as when a lawyer asks a client to consent to a representation affected by a conflict of interest, the client must give informed consent, as defined in Rule 1.0(e).

[6] Ordinarily, the information to be provided is that appropriate for a client who is a comprehending and responsible adult. However, fully informing the client according to this standard may be impracticable, for example, where the client is a child or suffers from diminished capacity. See Rule 1.14. When the client is an organization or group, it is often impossible or inappropriate to inform every one of its members about its legal affairs; ordinarily, the lawyer should address communications to the appropriate officials of the organization. See Rule 1.13. Where many routine matters are involved, a system of limited or occasional reporting may be arranged with the client.

Withholding Information

[7] In some circumstances, a lawyer may be justified in delaying transmission of information when the client would be likely to react imprudently to an immediate communication. Thus, a lawyer might withhold a psychiatric diagnosis of a client when the examining psychiatrist indicates that disclosure would harm the client. A lawyer may not withhold information to serve the lawyer's own interest or convenience or the interests or convenience of another person. Rules or court orders governing litigation may provide that information supplied to a lawyer may not be disclosed to the client. Rule 3.4(c) directs compliance with such rules or orders.

RULE 1.13: ORGANIZATION AS CLIENT

(a) A lawyer employed or retained by an organization represents the organization acting through its duly authorized constituents.

(b) If a lawyer for an organization knows that an officer, employee or other person associated with the organization is engaged in action, intends to act or refuses to act in a matter related to the representation that is a violation of a legal obligation to the organization, or a violation of law that reasonably might be imputed to the organization, and that is likely to result in substantial injury to the organization, then the lawyer shall proceed as is reasonably necessary in the best interest of the organization. Unless the lawyer reasonably believes that it is not necessary in the best interest of the organization to do so, the lawyer shall refer the matter to higher authority in the organization, including, if warranted by the circumstances to the highest authority that can act on behalf of the organization as determined by applicable law.

(c) Except as provided in paragraph (d), if

(1) despite the lawyer's efforts in accordance with paragraph (b) the highest authority that can act on behalf of the organization insists upon or fails to address in a timely and appropriate manner an action, or a refusal to act, that is clearly a violation of law, and

(2) the lawyer reasonably believes that the violation is reasonably certain to result in substantial injury to the organization,

then the lawyer may reveal information relating to the representation whether or not Rule 1.6 permits such disclosure, but only if and to the extent the lawyer reasonably believes necessary to prevent substantial injury to the organization.

(d) Paragraph (c) shall not apply with respect to information relating to a lawyer's representation of an organization to investigate an alleged violation of law, or to defend the organization or an officer, employee or other constituent associated with the organization against a claim arising out of an alleged violation of law.

(e) A lawyer who reasonably believes that he or she has been discharged because of the lawyer's actions taken pursuant to paragraphs (b) or (c), or who withdraws under circumstances that require or permit the lawyer to take action under either of those paragraphs, shall proceed as the lawyer reasonably believes necessary to assure that the organization's highest authority is informed of the lawyer's discharge or withdrawal.

(f) In dealing with an organization's directors, officers, employees, members, shareholders or other constituents, a lawyer shall explain the identity of the client when the lawyer knows or reasonably should know that the organization's interests are adverse to those of the constituents with whom the lawyer is dealing.

(g) A lawyer representing an organization may also represent any of its directors, officers, employees, members, shareholders or other constituents, subject to the provisions of Rule 1.7. If the organization's consent to the dual representation is required by Rule 1.7, the consent shall be given by an appropriate official of the organization other than the individual who is to be represented, or by the shareholders.

Comment

The Entity as the Client

[1] An organizational client is a legal entity, but it cannot act except through its officers, directors, employees, shareholders and other constituents. Officers, directors, employees and shareholders are the constituents of the corporate organizational client. The duties defined in this Comment apply equally to unincorporated associations. "Other constituents" as used in this Comment means the positions equivalent to officers, directors, employees and shareholders held by persons acting for organizational clients that are not corporations.

[2] When one of the constituents of an organizational client communicates with the organization's lawyer in that person's organizational capacity, the communication is protected by Rule 1.6. Thus, by way of example, if an organizational client requests its lawyer to investigate allegations of wrongdoing, interviews made in the course of that investigation between the lawyer and the client's employees or other constituents are covered by Rule 1.6. This does not mean, however, that constituents of an organizational client are the clients of the lawyer. The lawyer may not disclose to such constituents information relating to the representation except for disclosures explicitly or impliedly authorized by the organizational client in order to carry out the representation or as otherwise permitted by Rule 1.6.

[3] When constituents of the organization make decisions for it, the decisions ordinarily must be accepted by the lawyer even if their utility or prudence is doubtful. Decisions concerning policy and operations, including ones entailing serious risk, are not as such in the lawyer's province. Paragraph (b) makes clear, however, that when the lawyer knows that the organization is likely to be substantially injured by action of an officer or other constituent that violates a legal obligation to the organization or is in violation of law that might be imputed to the organization, the lawyer must proceed as is reasonably necessary in the best interest of the organization. As defined in Rule 1.0(f), knowledge can be inferred from circumstances, and a lawyer cannot ignore the obvious.

[4] In determining how to proceed under paragraph (b), the lawyer should give due consideration to the seriousness of the violation and its consequences, the responsibility in the organization and the apparent motivation of the person involved, the policies of the organization concerning such matters, and any other relevant considerations. Ordinarily, referral to a higher authority would be necessary. In some circumstances, however, it may be appropriate for the lawyer to ask the constituent to reconsider the matter; for example, if the circumstances involve a constituent's innocent misunderstanding

of law and subsequent acceptance of the lawyer's advice, the lawyer may reasonably conclude that the best interest of the organization does not require that the matter be referred to higher authority. If a constituent persists in conduct contrary to the lawyer's advice, it will be necessary for the lawyer to take steps to have the matter reviewed by a higher authority in the organization. If the matter is of sufficient seriousness and importance or urgency to the organization, referral to higher authority in the organization may be necessary even if the lawyer has not communicated with the constituent. Any measures taken should, to the extent practicable, minimize the risk of revealing information relating to the representation to persons outside the organization. Even in circumstances where a lawyer is not obligated by Rule 1.13 to proceed, a lawyer may bring to the attention of an organizational client, including its highest authority, matters that the lawyer reasonably believes to be of sufficient importance to warrant doing so in the best interest of the organization.

[5] Paragraph (b) also makes clear that when it is reasonably necessary to enable the organization to address the matter in a timely and appropriate manner, the lawyer must refer the matter to higher authority, including, if warranted by the circumstances, the highest authority that can act on behalf of the organization under applicable law. The organization's highest authority to whom a matter may be referred ordinarily will be the board of directors or similar governing body. However, applicable law may prescribe that under certain conditions the highest authority reposes elsewhere, for example, in the independent directors of a corporation.

Relation to Other Rules

[6] The authority and responsibility provided in this Rule are concurrent with the authority and responsibility provided in other Rules. In particular, this Rule does not limit or expand the lawyer's responsibility under Rules 1.8, 1.16, 3.3 or 4.1. Paragraph (c) of this Rule supplements Rule 1.6(b) by providing an additional basis upon which the lawyer may reveal information relating to the representation, but does not modify, restrict, or limit the provisions of Rule 1.6(b)(1)–(6). Under paragraph (c) the lawyer may reveal such information only when the organization's highest authority insists upon or fails to address threatened or ongoing action that is clearly a violation of law, and then only to the extent the lawyer reasonably believes necessary to prevent reasonably certain substantial injury to the organization. It is not necessary that the lawyer's services be used in furtherance of the violation, but it is required that the matter be related to the lawyer's representation of the organization. If the lawyer's services are being used by an organization to further a crime or fraud by the organization, Rules 1.6(b)(2) and 1.6(b)(3) may permit the lawyer to disclose confidential information. In such circumstances Rule 1.2(d) may also be applicable, in which event, withdrawal from the representation under Rule 1.16(a)(1) may be required.

[7] Paragraph (d) makes clear that the authority of a lawyer to disclose information relating to a representation in circumstances described in paragraph (c) does not apply with respect to information relating to a lawyer's engagement by an organization to investigate an alleged violation of law or to defend the organization or an officer, employee or other person associated with the organization against a claim arising out of an alleged violation of law. This is necessary in order to enable organizational clients to enjoy the full benefits of legal counsel in conducting an investigation or defending against a claim.

[8] A lawyer who reasonably believes that he or she has been discharged because of the lawyer's actions taken pursuant to paragraph (b) or (c), or who withdraws in circum-

stances that require or permit the lawyer to take action under either of these paragraphs, must proceed as the lawyer reasonably believes necessary to assure that the organization's highest authority is informed of the lawyer's discharge or withdrawal.

Government Agency

[9] The duty defined in this Rule applies to governmental organizations. Defining precisely the identity of the client and prescribing the resulting obligations of such lawyers may be more difficult in the government context and is a matter beyond the scope of these Rules. See Scope [18]. Although in some circumstances the client may be a specific agency, it may also be a branch of government, such as the executive branch, or the government as a whole. For example, if the action or failure to act involves the head of a bureau, either the department of which the bureau is a part or the relevant branch of government may be the client for purposes of this Rule. Moreover, in a matter involving the conduct of government officials, a government lawyer may have authority under applicable law to question such conduct more extensively than that of a lawyer for a private organization in similar circumstances. Thus, when the client is a governmental organization, a different balance may be appropriate between maintaining confidentiality and assuring that the wrongful act is prevented or rectified, for public business is involved. In addition, duties of lawyers employed by the government or lawyers in military service may be defined by statutes and regulation. This Rule does not limit that authority. See Scope.

Clarifying the Lawyer's Role

[10] There are times when the organization's interest may be or become adverse to those of one or more of its constituents. In such circumstances the lawyer should advise any constituent, whose interest the lawyer finds adverse to that of the organization of the conflict or potential conflict of interest, that the lawyer cannot represent such constituent, and that such person may wish to obtain independent representation. Care must be taken to assure that the individual understands that, when there is such adversity of interest, the lawyer for the organization cannot provide legal representation for that constituent individual, and that discussions between the lawyer for the organization and the individual may not be privileged.

[11] Whether such a warning should be given by the lawyer for the organization to any constituent individual may turn on the facts of each case.

Dual Representation

[12] Paragraph (g) recognizes that a lawyer for an organization may also represent a principal officer or major shareholder.

Derivative Actions

[13] Under generally prevailing law, the shareholders or members of a corporation may bring suit to compel the directors to perform their legal obligations in the supervision of the organization. Members of unincorporated associations have essentially the same right. Such an action may be brought nominally by the organization, but usually is, in fact, a legal controversy over management of the organization.

[14] The question can arise whether counsel for the organization may defend such an action. The proposition that the organization is the lawyer's client does not alone resolve the issue. Most derivative actions are a normal incident of an organization's affairs, to be defended by the organization's lawyer like any other suit. However, if the claim involves serious charges of wrongdoing by those in control of the organization, a conflict

may arise between the lawyer's duty to the organization and the lawyer's relationship with the board. In those circumstances, Rule 1.7 governs who should represent the directors and the organization.

RULE 1.14: CLIENT WITH DIMINISHED CAPACITY

(a) When a client's capacity to make adequately considered decisions in connection with a representation is diminished, whether because of minority, mental impairment or for some other reason, the lawyer shall, as far as reasonably possible, maintain a normal client-lawyer relationship with the client.

(b) When the lawyer reasonably believes that the client has diminished capacity, is at risk of substantial physical, financial or other harm unless action is taken and cannot adequately act in the client's own interest, the lawyer may take reasonably necessary protective action, including consulting with individuals or entities that have the ability to take action to protect the client and, in appropriate cases, seeking the appointment of a guardian ad litem, conservator or guardian.

(c) Information relating to the representation of a client with diminished capacity is protected by Rule 1.6. When taking protective action pursuant to paragraph (b), the lawyer is impliedly authorized under Rule 1.6(a) to reveal information about the client, but only to the extent reasonably necessary to protect the client's interests.

Comment

[1] The normal client-lawyer relationship is based on the assumption that the client, when properly advised and assisted, is capable of making decisions about important matters. When the client is a minor or suffers from a diminished mental capacity, however, maintaining the ordinary client-lawyer relationship may not be possible in all respects. In particular, a severely incapacitated person may have no power to make legally binding decisions. Nevertheless, a client with diminished capacity often has the ability to understand, deliberate upon, and reach conclusions about matters affecting the client's own well-being. For example, children as young as five or six years of age, and certainly those of ten or twelve, are regarded as having opinions that are entitled to weight in legal proceedings concerning their custody. So also, it is recognized that some persons of advanced age can be quite capable of handling routine financial matters while needing special legal protection concerning major transactions.

[2] The fact that a client suffers a disability does not diminish the lawyer's obligation to treat the client with attention and respect. Even if the person has a legal representative, the lawyer should as far as possible accord the represented person the status of client, particularly in maintaining communication.

[3] The client may wish to have family members or other persons participate in discussions with the lawyer. When necessary to assist in the representation, the presence of such persons generally does not affect the applicability of the attorney-client evidentiary privilege. Nevertheless, the lawyer must keep the client's interests foremost and, except for protective action authorized under paragraph (b), must to look to the client, and not family members, to make decisions on the client's behalf.

[4] If a legal representative has already been appointed for the client, the lawyer should ordinarily look to the representative for decisions on behalf of the client. In matters involving a minor, whether the lawyer should look to the parents as natural guardians may depend on the type of proceeding or matter in which the lawyer is representing the minor. If the lawyer represents the guardian as distinct from the ward, and is aware that

the guardian is acting adversely to the ward's interest, the lawyer may have an obligation to prevent or rectify the guardian's misconduct. See Rule 1.2(d).

Taking Protective Action

[5] If a lawyer reasonably believes that a client is at risk of substantial physical, financial or other harm unless action is taken, and that a normal client-lawyer relationship cannot be maintained as provided in paragraph (a) because the client lacks sufficient capacity to communicate or to make adequately considered decisions in connection with the representation, then paragraph (b) permits the lawyer to take protective measures deemed necessary. Such measures could include: consulting with family members, using a reconsideration period to permit clarification or improvement of circumstances, using voluntary surrogate decisionmaking tools such as durable powers of attorney or consulting with support groups, professional services, adult-protective agencies or other individuals or entities that have the ability to protect the client. In taking any protective action, the lawyer should be guided by such factors as the wishes and values of the client to the extent known, the client's best interests and the goals of intruding into the client's decisionmaking autonomy to the least extent feasible, maximizing client capacities and respecting the client's family and social connections.

[6] In determining the extent of the client's diminished capacity, the lawyer should consider and balance such factors as: the client's ability to articulate reasoning leading to a decision, variability of state of mind and ability to appreciate consequences of a decision; the substantive fairness of a decision; and the consistency of a decision with the known long-term commitments and values of the client. In appropriate circumstances, the lawyer may seek guidance from an appropriate diagnostician.

[7] If a legal representative has not been appointed, the lawyer should consider whether appointment of a guardian ad litem, conservator or guardian is necessary to protect the client's interests. Thus, if a client with diminished capacity has substantial property that should be sold for the client's benefit, effective completion of the transaction may require appointment of a legal representative. In addition, rules of procedure in litigation sometimes provide that minors or persons with diminished capacity must be represented by a guardian or next friend if they do not have a general guardian. In many circumstances, however, appointment of a legal representative may be more expensive or traumatic for the client than circumstances in fact require. Evaluation of such circumstances is a matter entrusted to the professional judgment of the lawyer. In considering alternatives, however, the lawyer should be aware of any law that requires the lawyer to advocate the least restrictive action on behalf of the client.

Disclosure of the Client's Condition

[8] Disclosure of the client's diminished capacity could adversely affect the client's interests. For example, raising the question of diminished capacity could, in some circumstances, lead to proceedings for involuntary commitment. Information relating to the representation is protected by Rule 1.6. Therefore, unless authorized to do so, the lawyer may not disclose such information. When taking protective action pursuant to paragraph (b), the lawyer is impliedly authorized to make the necessary disclosures, even when the client directs the lawyer to the contrary. Nevertheless, given the risks of disclosure, paragraph (c) limits what the lawyer may disclose in consulting with other individuals or entities or seeking the appointment of a legal representative. At the very least, the lawyer should determine whether it is likely that the person or entity consulted with will act adversely to the client's interests before discussing matters related to the client. The lawyer's position in such cases is an unavoidably difficult one.

Emergency Legal Assistance

[9] In an emergency where the health, safety or a financial interest of a person with seriously diminished capacity is threatened with imminent and irreparable harm, a lawyer may take legal action on behalf of such a person even though the person is unable to establish a client-lawyer relationship or to make or express considered judgments about the matter, when the person or another acting in good faith on that person's behalf has consulted with the lawyer. Even in such an emergency, however, the lawyer should not act unless the lawyer reasonably believes that the person has no other lawyer, agent or other representative available. The lawyer should take legal action on behalf of the person only to the extent reasonably necessary to maintain the status quo or otherwise avoid imminent and irreparable harm. A lawyer who undertakes to represent a person in such an exigent situation has the same duties under these Rules as the lawyer would with respect to a client.

[10] A lawyer who acts on behalf of a person with seriously diminished capacity in an emergency should keep the confidences of the person as if dealing with a client, disclosing them only to the extent necessary to accomplish the intended protective action. The lawyer should disclose to any tribunal involved and to any other counsel involved the nature of his or her relationship with the person. The lawyer should take steps to regularize the relationship or implement other protective solutions as soon as possible. Normally, a lawyer would not seek compensation for such emergency actions taken.

RULE 1.16 DECLINING OR TERMINATING REPRESENTATION

(a) Except as stated in paragraph (c), a lawyer shall not represent a client or, where representation has commenced, shall withdraw from the representation of a client if:

(1) the representation will result in violation of the rules of professional conduct or other law;

(2) the lawyer's physical or mental condition materially impairs the lawyer's ability to represent the client; or

(3) the lawyer is discharged.

(b) Except as stated in paragraph (c), a lawyer may withdraw from representing a client if:

(1) withdrawal can be accomplished without material adverse effect on the interests of the client;

(2) the client persists in a course of action involving the lawyer's services that the lawyer reasonably believes is criminal or fraudulent;

(3) the client has used the lawyer's services to perpetrate a crime or fraud;

(4) the client insists upon taking action that the lawyer considers repugnant or with which the lawyer has a fundamental disagreement;

(5) the client fails substantially to fulfill an obligation to the lawyer regarding the lawyer's services and has been given reasonable warning that the lawyer will withdraw unless the obligation is fulfilled;

(6) the representation will result in an unreasonable financial burden on the lawyer or has been rendered unreasonably difficult by the client; or

(7) other good cause for withdrawal exists.

(c) A lawyer must comply with applicable law requiring notice to or permission of a tribunal when terminating a representation. When ordered to do so by a tribunal, a lawyer shall continue representation notwithstanding good cause for terminating the representation.

(d) Upon termination of representation, a lawyer shall take steps to the extent reasonably practicable to protect a client's interests, such as giving reasonable notice to the client, allowing time for employment of other counsel, surrendering papers and property to which the client is entitled and refunding any advance payment of fee or expense that has not been earned or incurred. The lawyer may retain papers relating to the client to the extent permitted by other law.

Comment

[1] A lawyer should not accept representation in a matter unless it can be performed competently, promptly, without improper conflict of interest and to completion. Ordinarily, a representation in a matter is completed when the agreed-upon assistance has been concluded. See Rules 1.2(c) and 6.5. See also Rule 1.3, Comment [4].

Mandatory Withdrawal

[2] A lawyer ordinarily must decline or withdraw from representation if the client demands that the lawyer engage in conduct that is illegal or violates the Rules of Professional Conduct or other law. The lawyer is not obliged to decline or withdraw simply because the client suggests such a course of conduct; a client may make such a suggestion in the hope that a lawyer will not be constrained by a professional obligation.

[3] When a lawyer has been appointed to represent a client, withdrawal ordinarily requires approval of the appointing authority. See also Rule 6.2. Similarly, court approval or notice to the court is often required by applicable law before a lawyer withdraws from pending litigation. Difficulty may be encountered if withdrawal is based on the client's demand that the lawyer engage in unprofessional conduct. The court may request an explanation for the withdrawal, while the lawyer may be bound to keep confidential the facts that would constitute such an explanation. The lawyer's statement that professional considerations require termination of the representation ordinarily should be accepted as sufficient. Lawyers should be mindful of their obligations to both clients and the court under Rules 1.6 and 3.3.

Discharge

[4] A client has a right to discharge a lawyer at any time, with or without cause, subject to liability for payment for the lawyer's services. Where future dispute about the withdrawal may be anticipated, it may be advisable to prepare a written statement reciting the circumstances.

[5] Whether a client can discharge appointed counsel may depend on applicable law. A client seeking to do so should be given a full explanation of the consequences. These consequences may include a decision by the appointing authority that appointment of successor counsel is unjustified, thus requiring self-representation by the client.

[6] If the client has severely diminished capacity, the client may lack the legal capacity to discharge the lawyer, and in any event the discharge may be seriously adverse to the client's interests. The lawyer should make special effort to help the client consider the consequences and may take reasonably necessary protective action as provided in Rule 1.14.

Optional Withdrawal

[7] A lawyer may withdraw from representation in some circumstances. The lawyer has the option to withdraw if it can be accomplished without material adverse effect on the

client's interests. Withdrawal is also justified if the client persists in a course of action that the lawyer reasonably believes is criminal or fraudulent, for a lawyer is not required to be associated with such conduct even if the lawyer does not further it. Withdrawal is also permitted if the lawyer's services were misused in the past even if that would materially prejudice the client. The lawyer may also withdraw where the client insists on taking action that the lawyer considers repugnant or with which the lawyer has a fundamental disagreement.

[8] A lawyer may withdraw if the client refuses to abide by the terms of an agreement relating to the representation, such as an agreement concerning fees or court costs or an agreement limiting the objectives of the representation.

Assisting the Client upon Withdrawal

[9] Even if the lawyer has been unfairly discharged by the client, a lawyer must take all reasonable steps to mitigate the consequences to the client. The lawyer may retain papers as security for a fee only to the extent permitted by law. See Rule 1.15.

RULE 2.1 ADVISOR

In representing a client, a lawyer shall exercise independent professional judgment and render candid advice. In rendering advice, a lawyer may refer not only to law but to other considerations such as moral, economic, social and political factors, that may be relevant to the client's situation.

Comment

Scope of Advice

[1] A client is entitled to straightforward advice expressing the lawyer's honest assessment. Legal advice often involves unpleasant facts and alternatives that a client may be disinclined to confront. In presenting advice, a lawyer endeavors to sustain the client's morale and may put advice in as acceptable a form as honesty permits. However, a lawyer should not be deterred from giving candid advice by the prospect that the advice will be unpalatable to the client.

[2] Advice couched in narrow legal terms may be of little value to a client, especially where practical considerations, such as cost or effects on other people, are predominant. Purely technical legal advice, therefore, can sometimes be inadequate. It is proper for a lawyer to refer to relevant moral and ethical considerations in giving advice. Although a lawyer is not a moral advisor as such, moral and ethical considerations impinge upon most legal questions and may decisively influence how the law will be applied.

[3] A client may expressly or impliedly ask the lawyer for purely technical advice. When such a request is made by a client experienced in legal matters, the lawyer may accept it at face value. When such a request is made by a client inexperienced in legal matters, however, the lawyer's responsibility as advisor may include indicating that more may be involved than strictly legal considerations.

[4] Matters that go beyond strictly legal questions may also be in the domain of another profession. Family matters can involve problems within the professional competence of psychiatry, clinical psychology or social work; business matters can involve problems within the competence of the accounting profession or of financial specialists. Where consultation with a professional in another field is itself something a competent lawyer would recommend, the lawyer should make such a recommendation. At the same time, a lawyer's advice at its best often consists of recommending a course of action in the face of conflicting recommendations of experts.

Offering Advice

[5] In general, a lawyer is not expected to give advice until asked by the client. However, when a lawyer knows that a client proposes a course of action that is likely to result in substantial adverse legal consequences to the client, the lawyer's duty to the client under Rule 1.4 may require that the lawyer offer advice if the client's course of action is related to the representation. Similarly, when a matter is likely to involve litigation, it may be necessary under Rule 1.4 to inform the client of forms of dispute resolution that might constitute reasonable alternatives to litigation. A lawyer ordinarily has no duty to initiate investigation of a client's affairs or to give advice that the client has indicated is unwanted, but a lawyer may initiate advice to a client when doing so appears to be in the client's interest.

RULE 2.4 LAWYER SERVING AS THIRD-PARTY NEUTRAL

(a) A lawyer serves as a third-party neutral when the lawyer assists two or more persons who are not clients of the lawyer to reach a resolution of a dispute or other matter that has arisen between them. Service as a third-party neutral may include service as an arbitrator, a mediator or in such other capacity as will enable the lawyer to assist the parties to resolve the matter.

(b) A lawyer serving as a third-party neutral shall inform unrepresented parties that the lawyer is not representing them. When the lawyer knows or reasonably should know that a party does not understand the lawyer's role in the matter, the lawyer shall explain the difference between the lawyer's role as a third-party neutral and a lawyer's role as one who represents a client.

Comment

[1] Alternative dispute resolution has become a substantial part of the civil justice system. Aside from representing clients in dispute-resolution processes, lawyers often serve as third-party neutrals. A third-party neutral is a person, such as a mediator, arbitrator, conciliator or evaluator, who assists the parties, represented or unrepresented, in the resolution of a dispute or in the arrangement of a transaction. Whether a third-party neutral serves primarily as a facilitator, evaluator or decisionmaker depends on the particular process that is either selected by the parties or mandated by a court.

[2] The role of a third-party neutral is not unique to lawyers, although, in some court-connected contexts, only lawyers are allowed to serve in this role or to handle certain types of cases. In performing this role, the lawyer may be subject to court rules or other law that apply either to third-party neutrals generally or to lawyers serving as third-party neutrals. Lawyer-neutrals may also be subject to various codes of ethics, such as the Code of Ethics for Arbitration in Commercial Disputes prepared by a joint committee of the American Bar Association and the American Arbitration Association or the Model Standards of Conduct for Mediators jointly prepared by the American Bar Association, the American Arbitration Association and the Society of Professionals in Dispute Resolution.

[3] Unlike nonlawyers who serve as third-party neutrals, lawyers serving in this role may experience unique problems as a result of differences between the role of a third-party neutral and a lawyer's service as a client representative. The potential for confusion is significant when the parties are unrepresented in the process. Thus, paragraph (b) requires a lawyer-neutral to inform unrepresented parties that the lawyer is not representing them. For some parties, particularly parties who frequently use dispute-resolution processes, this information will be sufficient. For others, particularly those

who are using the process for the first time, more information will be required. Where appropriate, the lawyer should inform unrepresented parties of the important differences between the lawyer's role as third-party neutral and a lawyer's role as a client representative, including the inapplicability of the attorney-client evidentiary privilege. The extent of disclosure required under this paragraph will depend on the particular parties involved and the subject matter of the proceeding, as well as the particular features of the dispute-resolution process selected.

[4] A lawyer who serves as a third-party neutral subsequently may be asked to serve as a lawyer representing a client in the same matter. The conflicts of interest that arise for both the individual lawyer and the lawyer's law firm are addressed in Rule 1.12.

[5] Lawyers who represent clients in alternative dispute-resolution processes are governed by the Rules of Professional Conduct. When the dispute-resolution process takes place before a tribunal, as in binding arbitration (see Rule 1.0(m)), the lawyer's duty of candor is governed by Rule 3.3. Otherwise, the lawyer's duty of candor toward both the third-party neutral and other parties is governed by Rule 4.1.

RULE 4.2: COMMUNICATION WITH PERSON REPRESENTED BY COUNSEL

In representing a client, a lawyer shall not communicate about the subject of the representation with a person the lawyer knows to be represented by another lawyer in the matter, unless the lawyer has the consent of the other lawyer or is authorized to do so by law or a court order.

Comment

[1] This Rule contributes to the proper functioning of the legal system by protecting a person who has chosen to be represented by a lawyer in a matter against possible overreaching by other lawyers who are participating in the matter, interference by those lawyers with the client-lawyer relationship and the uncounselled disclosure of information relating to the representation.

[2] This Rule applies to communications with any person who is represented by counsel concerning the matter to which the communication relates.

[3] The Rule applies even though the represented person initiates or consents to the communication. A lawyer must immediately terminate communication with a person if, after commencing communication, the lawyer learns that the person is one with whom communication is not permitted by this Rule.

[4] This Rule does not prohibit communication with a represented person, or an employee or agent of such a person, concerning matters outside the representation. For example, the existence of a controversy between a government agency and a private party, or between two organizations, does not prohibit a lawyer for either from communicating with nonlawyer representatives of the other regarding a separate matter. Nor does this Rule preclude communication with a represented person who is seeking advice from a lawyer who is not otherwise representing a client in the matter. A lawyer may not make a communication prohibited by this Rule through the acts of another. See Rule 8.4(a). Parties to a matter may communicate directly with each other, and a lawyer is not prohibited from advising a client concerning a communication that the client is legally entitled to make. Also, a lawyer having independent justification or legal authorization for communicating with a represented person is permitted to do so.

[5] Communications authorized by law may include communications by a lawyer on behalf of a client who is exercising a constitutional or other legal right to communicate with the government. Communications authorized by law may also include investigative activities of lawyers representing governmental entities, directly or through investigative agents, prior to the commencement of criminal or civil enforcement proceedings. When communicating with the accused in a criminal matter, a government lawyer must comply with this Rule in addition to honoring the constitutional rights of the accused. The fact that a communication does not violate a state or federal constitutional right is insufficient to establish that the communication is permissible under this Rule.

[6] A lawyer who is uncertain whether a communication with a represented person is permissible may seek a court order. A lawyer may also seek a court order in exceptional circumstances to authorize a communication that would otherwise be prohibited by this Rule, for example, where communication with a person represented by counsel is necessary to avoid reasonably certain injury.

[7] In the case of a represented organization, this Rule prohibits communications with a constituent of the organization who supervises, directs or regularly consults with the organization's lawyer concerning the matter or has authority to obligate the organization with respect to the matter or whose act or omission in connection with the matter may be imputed to the organization for purposes of civil or criminal liability. Consent of the organization's lawyer is not required for communication with a former constituent. If a constituent of the organization is represented in the matter by his or her own counsel, the consent by that counsel to a communication will be sufficient for purposes of this Rule. Compare Rule 3.4(f). In communicating with a current or former constituent of an organization, a lawyer must not use methods of obtaining evidence that violate the legal rights of the organization. See Rule 4.4.

[8] The prohibition on communications with a represented person only applies in circumstances where the lawyer knows that the person is in fact represented in the matter to be discussed. This means that the lawyer has actual knowledge of the fact of the representation; but such actual knowledge may be inferred from the circumstances. See Rule 1.0(f). Thus, the lawyer cannot evade the requirement of obtaining the consent of counsel by closing eyes to the obvious.

[9] In the event the person with whom the lawyer communicates is not known to be represented by counsel in the matter, the lawyer's communications are subject to Rule 4.3.

ABA Code

EC 5–20 A lawyer is often asked to serve as an impartial arbitrator or mediator in matters which involve present or former clients. He may serve in either capacity if he first discloses such present or former relationships. After a lawyer has undertaken to act as an impartial arbitrator or mediator, he should not thereafter represent in the dispute any of the parties involved.

SEC Standards of Professional Conduct Press Release and CFR Part 205

SEC Adopts Attorney Conduct Rule Under Sarbanes-Oxley Act
FOR IMMEDIATE RELEASE
2003-13
[Note: Warning! Like ABA and bar rules, SEC rules can change!
Always consult the current version in practice.]

Washington, D.C., January 23, 2003—The Securities and Exchange Commission today adopted final rules to implement Section 307 of the Sarbanes-Oxley Act by setting "standards of professional conduct for attorneys appearing and practicing before the Commission in any way in the representation of issuers." In addition, the Commission approved an extension of the comment period on the "noisy withdrawal" provisions of the original proposed rule and publication for comment of an alternative proposal.

On Nov. 6, 2002, the Commission voted to propose the standards of professional conduct in a new Part 205 of 17 CFR. That proposal defined who is appearing and practicing before the Commission in the representation of an issuer. Attorneys were required to report evidence of a material violation "up-the-ladder" within an issuer. In addition, under certain circumstances, these provisions permitted or required attorneys to effect a so-called "noisy withdrawal"—that is, to withdraw from representing an issuer and notify the Commission that they have withdrawn for professional reasons.

The rules adopted by the Commission today will

- require an attorney to report evidence of a material violation, determined according to an objective standard, "up-the-ladder" within the issuer to the chief legal counsel or the chief executive officer of the company or the equivalent;

- require an attorney, if the chief legal counsel or the chief executive officer of the company does not respond appropriately to the evidence, to report the evidence to the audit committee, another committee of independent directors, or the full board of directors;

- clarify that the rules cover attorneys providing legal services to an issuer who have an attorney-client relationship with the issuer, and who have notice that documents they are preparing or assisting in preparing will be filed with or submitted to the Commission;

- provide that foreign attorneys who are not admitted in the United States, and who do not advise clients regarding U.S. law, would not be covered by the rule, while foreign attorneys who provide legal advice regarding U.S. law would be covered to the extent they are appearing and practicing before the Commission, unless they provide such advice in consultation with U.S. counsel;

- allow an issuer to establish a "qualified legal compliance committee" (QLCC) as an alternative procedure for reporting evidence of a material violation. Such a QLCC would consist of at least one member of the issuer's audit committee, or an equivalent committee of independent directors, and two or more independent board members, and would have the responsibility, among other things, to recommend that an issuer implement an appropriate response to evidence of a material violation. One way in which an attorney could satisfy the rule's reporting obligation is by reporting evidence of a material violation to a QLCC;

- allow an attorney, without the consent of an issuer client, to reveal confidential information related to his or her representation to the extent the attorney reasonably believes necessary (1) to prevent the issuer from committing a material violation likely to cause substantial financial injury to the financial interests or property of the issuer or investors; (2) to prevent the issuer from committing an illegal act; or (3) to rectify the consequences of a material violation or illegal act in which the attorney's services have been used;

- state that the rules govern in the event the rules conflict with state law, but will not preempt the ability of a state to impose more rigorous obligations on attorneys that are not inconsistent with the rules; and

- affirmatively state that the rules do not create a private cause of action and that authority to enforce compliance with the rules is vested exclusively with the Commission.

In addition, the final rules modify the definition of the term "evidence of a material violation," which defines the trigger for an attorney's obligation to report up-the-ladder within an issuer. The revised definition confirms that the Commission intends an objective, rather than a subjective, triggering standard, involving credible evidence, based upon which it would be unreasonable, under the circumstances, for a prudent and competent attorney not to conclude that it is reasonably likely that a material violation has occurred, is ongoing or is about to occur.

The Commission voted to extend for 60 days the comment period on the "noisy withdrawal" and related provisions originally included in proposed Part 205. Given the significance and complexity of the issues involved, including the implications of a reporting out requirement on the relationship between issuers and their counsel, the Commission decided to continue to seek comment and give thoughtful consideration to these issues.

The Commission also voted to propose an alternative to "noisy withdrawal" that would require attorney withdrawal, but would require an issuer, rather than an attorney, to publicly disclose the attorney's withdrawal or written notice that the attorney did not receive an appropriate response to a report of a material violation. Specifically, an issuer that has received notice of an attorney's withdrawal would be required to report the notice and the circumstances related thereto on form 8-K, 20-F or 40-F, as applicable, within two days of receiving the attorney's notice. Accordingly, the proposal includes proposed amendments to forms 8-K, 20-F, and 40-F to require issuers to report an attorney's written notice under the proposed rule. The proposing release also will seek comment on whether there are circumstances in which an issuer should be permitted not to disclose an attorney's written notice.

The proposed rules also would permit an attorney, if an issuer has not complied with the disclosure requirement, to inform the Commission that the attorney has withdrawn from representing the issuer or provided the issuer with notice that the attorney has not received an appropriate response to a report of a material violation.

The final rules will become effective 180 days after publication in the *Federal Register* to provide issuers, attorneys, and law firms sufficient time to put in place procedures to comply with their requirements, and to allow the Commission the opportunity to consider the adoption of the proposed noisy withdrawal provision or the alternative disclosure procedure proposed today.

The full text of detailed releases concerning each of these items will be posted to the SEC Web site as soon as possible.

http://www.sec.gov/news/press/2003-13.htm

17 C.F.R. § 205.1

Code of Federal Regulations
Title 17: Commodity and Securities Exchanges
Chapter II: Securities and Exchange Commission
Part 205: Standards of Professional Conduct for Attorneys Appearing and
Practicing Before the Commission in the Representation of an Issuer
Current through April 14, 2011; 76 FR 21167

§ 205.1 Purpose and scope.

This part sets forth minimum standards of professional conduct for attorneys appearing and practicing before the Commission in the representation of an issuer. These standards supplement applicable standards of any jurisdiction where an attorney is admitted or practices and are not intended to limit the ability of any jurisdiction to impose additional obligations on an attorney not inconsistent with the application of this part. Where the standards of a state or other United States jurisdiction where an attorney is admitted or practices conflict with this part, this part shall govern.

* * *

§ 205.3 Issuer as client.

(a) Representing an issuer. An attorney appearing and practicing before the Commission in the representation of an issuer owes his or her professional and ethical duties to the issuer as an organization. That the attorney may work with and advise the issuer's officers, directors, or employees in the course of representing the issuer does not make such individuals the attorney's clients.

(b) Duty to report evidence of a material violation.

(1) If an attorney, appearing and practicing before the Commission in the representation of an issuer, becomes aware of evidence of a material violation by the issuer or by any officer, director, employee, or agent of the issuer, the attorney shall report such evidence to the issuer's chief legal officer (or the equivalent thereof) or to both the issuer's chief legal officer and its chief executive officer (or the equivalents thereof) forthwith. By communicating such information to the issuer's officers or directors, an attorney does not reveal client confidences or secrets or privileged or otherwise protected information related to the attorney's representation of an issuer.

(2) The chief legal officer (or the equivalent thereof) shall cause such inquiry into the evidence of a material violation as he or she reasonably believes is appropriate to determine whether the material violation described in the report has occurred, is ongoing, or is about to occur. If the chief legal officer (or the equivalent thereof) determines no material violation has occurred, is ongoing, or is about to occur, he or she shall notify the reporting attorney and advise the reporting attorney of the basis for such determination. Unless the chief legal officer (or the equivalent thereof) reasonably believes that no material violation has occurred, is ongoing, or is about to occur, he or she shall take all reasonable steps to cause the issuer to adopt an appropriate response, and shall advise the reporting attorney thereof. In

lieu of causing an inquiry under this paragraph (b), a chief legal officer (or the equivalent thereof) may refer a report of evidence of a material violation to a qualified legal compliance committee under paragraph (c)(2) of this section if the issuer has duly established a qualified legal compliance committee prior to the report of evidence of a material violation.

(3) Unless an attorney who has made a report under paragraph (b)(1) of this section reasonably believes that the chief legal officer or the chief executive officer of the issuer (or the equivalent thereof) has provided an appropriate response within a reasonable time, the attorney shall report the evidence of a material violation to:

(i) The audit committee of the issuer's board of directors;

(ii) Another committee of the issuer's board of directors consisting solely of directors who are not employed, directly or indirectly, by the issuer and are not, in the case of a registered investment company, "interested persons" as defined in section 2(a)(19) of the Investment Company Act of 1940 (15 U.S.C. 80a-2(a)(19)) (if the issuer's board of directors has no audit committee); or

(iii) The issuer's board of directors (if the issuer's board of directors has no committee consisting solely of directors who are not employed, directly or indirectly, by the issuer and are not, in the case of a registered investment company, "interested persons" as defined in section 2(a)(19) of the Investment Company Act of 1940 (15 U.S.C. 80a-2(a)(19))).

(4) If an attorney reasonably believes that it would be futile to report evidence of a material violation to the issuer's chief legal officer and chief executive officer (or the equivalents thereof) under paragraph (b)(1) of this section, the attorney may report such evidence as provided under paragraph (b)(3) of this section.

* * *

(d) Issuer confidences.

(1) Any report under this section (or the contemporaneous record thereof) or any response thereto (or the contemporaneous record thereof) may be used by an attorney in connection with any investigation, proceeding, or litigation in which the attorney's compliance with this part is in issue.

(2) An attorney appearing and practicing before the Commission in the representation of an issuer may reveal to the Commission, without the issuer's consent, confidential information related to the representation to the extent the attorney reasonably believes necessary:

(i) To prevent the issuer from committing a material violation that is likely to cause substantial injury to the financial interest or property of the issuer or investors;

(ii) To prevent the issuer, in a Commission investigation or administrative proceeding from committing perjury, proscribed in 18 U.S.C. 1621; suborning perjury, proscribed in 18 U.S.C. 1622; or committing any act proscribed in 18 U.S.C. 1001 that is likely to perpetrate a fraud upon the Commission; or

(iii) To rectify the consequences of a material violation by the issuer that caused, or may cause, substantial injury to the financial interest or property of the issuer or investors in the furtherance of which the attorney's services were used.

§ 205.4 Responsibilities of supervisory attorneys.

(a) An attorney supervising or directing another attorney who is appearing and practicing before the Commission in the representation of an issuer is a supervisory attorney. An issuer's chief legal officer (or the equivalent thereof) is a supervisory attorney under this section.

(b) A supervisory attorney shall make reasonable efforts to ensure that a subordinate attorney, as defined in § 205.5(a), that he or she supervises or directs conforms to this part. To the extent a subordinate attorney appears and practices before the Commission in the representation of an issuer, that subordinate attorney's supervisory attorneys also appear and practice before the Commission.

(c) A supervisory attorney is responsible for complying with the reporting requirements in § 205.3 when a subordinate attorney has reported to the supervisory attorney evidence of a material violation.

(d) A supervisory attorney who has received a report of evidence of a material violation from a subordinate attorney under § 205.3 may report such evidence to the issuer's qualified legal compliance committee if the issuer has duly formed such a committee.

§ 205.5 Responsibilities of a subordinate attorney.

(a) An attorney who appears and practices before the Commission in the representation of an issuer on a matter under the supervision or direction of another attorney (other than under the direct supervision or direction of the issuer's chief legal officer (or the equivalent thereof)) is a subordinate attorney.

(b) A subordinate attorney shall comply with this part notwithstanding that the subordinate attorney acted at the direction of or under the supervision of another person.

(c) A subordinate attorney complies with § 205.3 if the subordinate attorney reports to his or her supervising attorney under § 205.3(b) evidence of a material violation of which the subordinate attorney has become aware in appearing and practicing before the Commission.

(d) A subordinate attorney may take the steps permitted or required by § 205.3(b) or (c) if the subordinate attorney reasonably believes that a supervisory attorney to whom he or she has reported evidence of a material violation under § 205.3(b) has failed to comply with § 205.3.

§ 205.6 Sanctions and discipline.

(a) A violation of this part by any attorney appearing and practicing before the Commission in the representation of an issuer shall subject such attorney to the civil penalties and remedies for a violation of the federal securities laws available to the Commission in an action brought by the Commission thereunder.

(b) An attorney appearing and practicing before the Commission who violates any provision of this part is subject to the disciplinary authority of the Commission, regardless of whether the attorney may also be subject to discipline for the same conduct in a jurisdiction where the attorney is admitted or practices. An administrative disciplinary proceeding initiated by the Commission for violation of this part may result in an attorney being censured, or being temporarily or permanently denied the privilege of appearing or practicing before the Commission.

(c) An attorney who complies in good faith with the provisions of this part shall not be subject to discipline or otherwise liable under inconsistent standards imposed by any state or other United States jurisdiction where the attorney is admitted or practices.

(d) An attorney practicing outside the United States shall not be required to comply with the requirements of this part to the extent that such compliance is prohibited by applicable foreign law.

§ 205.7 No private right of action.

(a) Nothing in this part is intended to, or does, create a private right of action against any attorney, law firm, or issuer based upon compliance or noncompliance with its provisions.

(b) Authority to enforce compliance with this part is vested exclusively in the Commission.

VI-3. "Difficult" Clients and Communications: Cases and Materials

A. The Government

In re Lindsey

158 F.3d 1263

United States Court of Appeals, District of Columbia Circuit
Argued June 29, 1998
Decided July 27, 1998
Order Filed Oct. 9, 1998 [certiorari denied Nov. 9, 1998]
[Some footnotes omitted. Remaining footnotes renumbered.]

Before: RANDOLPH, ROGERS, and TATEL, Circuit Judges.

Opinion for the Court filed PER CURIAM.

Opinion dissenting from Part II and concurring in part and dissenting in part from Part III filed by Circuit Judge TATEL.

PER CURIAM:

In these expedited appeals, the principal question is whether an attorney in the Office of the President, having been called before a federal grand jury, may refuse, on the basis of a government attorney-client privilege, to answer questions about possible criminal conduct by government officials and others. To state the question is to suggest the answer, for the Office of the President is a part of the federal government, consisting of government employees doing government business, and neither legal authority nor policy nor experience suggests that a federal government entity can maintain the ordinary common law attorney-client privilege to withhold information relating to a federal criminal offense. The Supreme Court and this court have held that even the constitutionally based executive privilege for presidential communications fundamental to the operation of the government can be overcome upon a proper showing of need for the evidence in criminal trials and in grand jury proceedings. *See United States v. Nixon,* 418 U.S. 683, 707–12, 94 S.Ct. 3090, 41 L.Ed.2d 1039 (1974); *In re Sealed Case (Espy),* 121 F.3d 729, 736–38 (D.C.Cir.1997). In the context of federal criminal investigations and trials, there is no basis for treating legal advice differently from any other advice the Office of the President receives in performing its constitutional functions. The public interest in honest government and in exposing wrongdoing by government officials, as well as the tradition and practice, acknowledged by the Office of the President and by former White House Counsel, of government lawyers reporting evidence of federal criminal offenses whenever such evidence comes to them, lead to the conclusion that a government attorney may not invoke the attorney-client privilege in response to grand jury questions seeking information relating to the possible commission of a federal crime. The extent to which the communications of White House Counsel are privileged against disclosure to a federal grand jury depends, therefore, on whether the communications contain information of possible criminal offenses. Additional protection may flow from executive privilege and such common law privileges as may inhere in the relationship between White House Counsel and the President's personal counsel.

I.

On January 16, 1998, at the request of the Attorney General, the Division for the Purpose of Appointing Independent Counsels issued an order expanding the prosecutorial jurisdiction of Independent Counsel Kenneth W. Starr. Previously, the main focus of Independent Counsel Starr's inquiry had been on financial transactions involving President Clinton when he was Governor of Arkansas, known popularly as the Whitewater inquiry. The order now authorized Starr to investigate "whether Monica Lewinsky or others suborned perjury, obstructed justice, intimidated witnesses, or otherwise violated federal law" in connection with the civil lawsuit against the President of the United States filed by Paula Jones. *In re Motions of Dow Jones & Co.*, 142 F.3d 496, 497–98 (D.C.Cir.), (quoting order). "Thereafter, a grand jury here began receiving evidence about Monica Lewinsky and President Clinton, and others...." *Id.* at 498.

On January 30, 1998, the grand jury issued a subpoena to Bruce R. Lindsey, an attorney admitted to practice in Arkansas. Lindsey currently holds two positions: Deputy White House Counsel and Assistant to the President. On February 18, February 19, and March 12, 1998, Lindsey appeared before the grand jury and declined to answer certain questions on the ground that the questions represented information protected from disclosure by a government attorney-client privilege applicable to Lindsey's communications with the President as Deputy White House Counsel, as well as by executive privilege, and by the President's personal-attorney-client privilege. Lindsey also claimed work product protections related to the attorney-client privileges.

On March 6, 1998, the Independent Counsel moved to compel Lindsey's testimony. The district court granted that motion on May 4, 1998. The court concluded that the President's executive privilege claim failed in light of the Independent Counsel's showing of need and unavailability. *See In re Sealed Case (Espy)*, 121 F.3d at 754. It rejected Lindsey's government attorney-client privilege claim on similar grounds, ruling that the President possesses an attorney-client privilege when consulting in his official capacity with White House Counsel, but that the privilege is qualified in the grand jury context and may be overcome upon a sufficient showing of need for the subpoenaed communications and unavailability from other sources. The court also ruled the President's personal attorney-client privilege and work product immunity inapplicable to Lindsey's testimony.

Both the Office of the President and the President in his personal capacity appealed the order granting the motion to compel Lindsey's testimony, challenging the district court's construction of both the government attorney-client privilege and President Clinton's personal attorney-client privilege. The Independent Counsel then petitioned the Supreme Court to review the district court's decision on those issues, among others, before judgment by this court. On June 4, 1998, the Supreme Court denied certiorari, while indicating its expectation that "the Court of Appeals will proceed expeditiously to decide this case." *United States v. Clinton,* 524 U.S. 912, 118 S.Ct. 2079, 141 L.Ed.2d 155 (1998). Following an expedited briefing schedule, on June 29, 1998, this court heard argument on the attorney-client issues. Neither the Office of the President nor the President in his personal capacity has appealed the district court's ruling on executive privilege. In Part II we address the availability of the government attorney-client privilege; in Part III we address the President's personal attorney-client privilege claims.

II.

The attorney-client privilege protects confidential communications made between clients and their attorneys when the communications are for the purpose of securing legal advice or services. *See In re Sealed Case,* 737 F.2d 94, 98–99 (D.C.Cir.1984). It "is one of the oldest recognized privileges for confidential communications." *Swidler & Berlin v. United States,* 524 U.S. 399, [403], 118 S.Ct. 2081, 2084, 141 L.Ed.2d 379 (1998).

The Office of the President contends that Lindsey's communications with the President and others in the White House should fall within this privilege both because the President, like any private person, needs to communicate fully and frankly with his legal advisors, and because the current grand jury investigation may lead to impeachment proceedings, which would require a defense of the President's official position as head of the executive branch of government, presumably with the assistance of White House Counsel. The Independent Counsel contends that an absolute government attorney-client privilege would be inconsistent with the proper role of the government lawyer and that the President should rely only on his private lawyers for fully confidential counsel.

Federal courts are given the authority to recognize privilege claims by Rule 501 of the Federal Rules of Evidence, which provides that

> [e]xcept as otherwise required by the Constitution of the United States or provided by Act of Congress or in rules prescribed by the Supreme Court pursuant to statutory authority, the privilege of a witness, person, government, State, or political subdivision thereof shall be governed by the principles of the common law as they may be interpreted by the courts of the United States in the light of reason and experience.

Fed.R.Evid. 501. Although Rule 501 manifests a congressional desire to provide the courts with the flexibility to develop rules of privilege on a case-by-case basis, *see Trammel v. United States,* 445 U.S. 40, 47, 100 S.Ct. 906, 63 L.Ed.2d 186 (1980), the Supreme Court has been "disinclined to exercise this authority expansively," *University of Pa. v. EEOC,* 493 U.S. 182, 189, 110 S.Ct. 577, 107 L.Ed.2d 571 (1990). "[T]hese exceptions to the demand for every man's evidence are not lightly created nor expansively construed, for they are in derogation of the search for truth." *Nixon,* 418 U.S. at 710, 94 S.Ct. 3090; *see also Trammel,* 445 U.S. at 50, 100 S.Ct. 906. Consequently, federal courts do not recognize evidentiary privileges unless doing so "promotes sufficiently important interests to outweigh the need for probative evidence." *Id.* at 51, 100 S.Ct. 906.

The Supreme Court has not articulated a precise test to apply to the recognition of a privilege, but it has "placed considerable weight upon federal and state precedent," *In re Sealed Case (Secret Service),* 148 F.3d 1073, 1076 (D.C.Cir.1998), *petition for cert. filed,* 67 USLW 3083 (U.S. July 16, 1998) (No. 98-93), and on the existence of "a 'public good transcending the normally predominant principle of utilizing all rational means for ascertaining the truth." *Jaffee v. Redmond,* 518 U.S. 1, 9, 116 S.Ct. 1923, 135 L.Ed.2d 337 (1996) (quoting *Trammel,* 445 U.S. at 50, 100 S.Ct. 906 (quoting *Elkins v. United States,*

364 U.S. 206, 234, 80 S.Ct. 1437, 4 L.Ed.2d 1669 (1960) (Frankfurter, J., dissenting))). That public good should be shown "with a high degree of clarity and certainty." *In re Sealed Case (Secret Service),* 148 F.3d at 1076.

A.

Courts, commentators, and government lawyers have long recognized a government attorney-client privilege in several contexts. Much of the law on this subject has developed in litigation about exemption five of the Freedom of Information Act ("FOIA"). *See* 5 U.S.C. § 552(b)(5) (1994). Under that exemption, "intra-agency memorandums or letters which would not be available by law to a party other than an agency in litigation with the agency" are excused from mandatory disclosure to the public. *Id.; see also* s.Rep. No. 89-813, at 2 (1965) (including within exemption five "documents which would come within the attorney-client privilege if applied to private parties"). We have recognized that "Exemption 5 protects, as a general rule, materials which would be protected under the attorney-client privilege." *Coastal States Gas Corp. v. Department of Energy,* 617 F.2d 854, 862 (D.C.Cir. 1980). "In the governmental context, the 'client' may be the agency and the attorney may be an agency lawyer." *Tax Analysts v. IRS,* 117 F.3d 607, 618 (D.C.Cir.1997); *see also Brinton v. Department of State,* 636 F.2d 600, 603–04 (D.C.Cir.1980). In Lindsey's case, his client—to the extent he provided legal services— would be the Office of the President.[1]

Exemption five does not itself create a government attorney-client privilege. Rather, "Congress intended that agencies should not lose the protection traditionally afforded through the evidentiary privileges simply because of the passage of the FOIA." *Coastal States,* 617 F.2d at 862. In discussing the government attorney-client privilege applicable to exemption five, we have mentioned the usual advantages:

> the attorney-client privilege has a proper role to play in exemption five cases.... In order to ensure that a client receives the best possible legal advice, based on a full and frank discussion with his attorney, the attorney-client privilege assures him that confidential communications to his attorney will not be disclosed without his consent. We see no reason why this same protection should not be extended to an agency's communications with its attorneys under exemption five.

Mead Data Cent., Inc. v. United States Dep't of Air Force, 566 F.2d 242, 252 (D.C.Cir. 1977). Thus, when "the Government is dealing with its attorneys as would any private party seeking advice to protect personal interests, and needs the same assurance of confidentiality so it will not be deterred from full and frank communications with its counselors," exemption five applies. *Coastal States,* 617 F.2d at 863.

Furthermore, the proposed (but never enacted) Federal Rules of Evidence concerning privileges, to which courts have turned as evidence of common law practices, *see, e.g., United States v. Gillock,* 445 U.S. 360, 367–68, 100 S.Ct. 1185, 63 L.Ed.2d 454 (1980); *In re Bieter Co.,* 16 F.3d 929, 935 (8th Cir.1994); *Linde Thomson Langworthy Kohn & Van*

---

1. Charles F.C. Ruff, the current White House Counsel, stated in an affidavit that he provides legal advice to the President regarding a wide variety of matters relating to his constitutional, statutory, ceremonial, and other official duties. He also provides legal advice to the President regarding the effective functioning of the Executive Branch. Lindsey's affidavit stated that the "White House Counsel's Office provides confidential counsel to the President in his official capacity, to the White House as an institution, and to senior advisors about legal matters that affect the White House's interests, including investigative matters. To this end, the Counsel's Office, in which I serve as Deputy, receives confidential communications from individuals about matters of institutional concern."

Dyke v. Resolution Trust Corp., 5 F.3d 1508, 1514 (D.C.Cir.1993); *United States v. (Under Seal),* 748 F.2d 871, 874 n. 5 (4th Cir.1984); *United States v. Mackey,* 405 F.Supp. 854, 858 (E.D.N.Y.1975), recognized a place for a government attorney-client privilege. Proposed Rule 503 defined "client" for the purposes of the attorney-client privilege to include "a person, public officer, or corporation, association, or other organization or entity, either public or private." Proposed Fed.R.Evid. 503(a)(1), *reprinted in* 56 F.R.D. 183, 235 (1972). The commentary to the proposed rule explained that "[t]he definition of 'client' includes governmental bodies." *Id.* advisory committee's note. The Restatement also extends attorney-client privilege to government entities. *See* Restatement (Third) of the Law Governing Lawyers § 124 (Proposed Final Draft No. 1, 1996) [hereinafter Restatement].

The practice of attorneys in the executive branch reflects the common understanding that a government attorney-client privilege functions in at least some contexts. The Office of Legal Counsel in the Department of Justice concluded in 1982 that

> [a]lthough the attorney-client privilege traditionally has been recognized in the context of private attorney-client relationships, the privilege also functions to protect communications between government attorneys and client agencies or departments, as evidenced by its inclusion in the FOIA, much as it operates to protect attorney-client communications in the private sector.

Theodore B. Olsen, Assistant Attorney General, Office of Legal Counsel, *Confidentiality of the Attorney General's Communications in Counseling the President,* 6 Op. Off. Legal Counsel 481, 495 (1982). The Office of Legal Counsel also concluded that when government attorneys stand in the shoes of private counsel, representing federal employees sued in their individual capacities, confidential communications between attorney and client are privileged. *See* Antonin Scalia, Assistant Attorney General, Office of Legal Counsel, *Disclosure of Confidential Information Received by U.S. Attorney in the Course of Representing a Federal Employee* (Nov. 30, 1976); Ralph W. Tarr, Acting Assistant Attorney General, Office of Legal Counsel, *Duty of Government Lawyer Upon Receipt of Incriminating Information in the Course of an Attorney-Client Relationship with Another Government Employee* (Mar. 29, 1985); *see also* 28 C.F.R. § 50.15(a)(3) (1998).

B.

Recognizing that a government attorney-client privilege exists is one thing. Finding that the Office of the President is entitled to assert it here is quite another.

* * *

We therefore turn to the question whether an attorney-client privilege permits a government lawyer to withhold from a grand jury information relating to the commission of possible crimes by government officials and others. Although the cases decided under FOIA recognize a government attorney-client privilege that is rather absolute in civil litigation, those cases do not necessarily control the application of the privilege here. The grand jury, a constitutional body established in the Bill of Rights, "belongs to no branch of the institutional Government, serving as a kind of buffer or referee between the Government and the people," *United States v. Williams,* 504 U.S. 36, 47, 112 S.Ct. 1735, 118 L.Ed.2d 352 (1992), while the Independent Counsel is by statute an officer of the executive branch representing the United States. For matters within his jurisdiction, the Independent Counsel acts in the role of the Attorney General as the country's chief law enforcement officer. *See* 28 U.S.C. § 594(a) (1994). Thus, although the traditional privilege between attorneys and clients shields private relationships from inquiry in either civil litigation or criminal prosecution, competing values arise when the Office of the President resists demands for information from a federal grand jury and the nation's chief law enforcement officer. As the drafters of the Restatement recognized, "More particularized rules may be necessary where one agency of government claims the privilege in resisting a demand for information by another. Such rules should take account of the complex considerations of governmental structure, tradition, and regulation that are involved." RESTATEMENT § 124 cmt. b. For these reasons, others have agreed that such "considerations" counsel against "expansion of the privilege to all governmental entities" in all cases. 24 CHARLES ALAN WRIGHT & KENNETH W. GRAHAM, JR., FEDERAL PRACTICE AND PROCEDURE § 5475, at 125 (1986).

The question whether a government attorney-client privilege applies in the federal grand jury context is one of first impression in this circuit, and the parties dispute the import of the lack of binding authority. The Office of the President contends that, upon recognizing a government attorney-client privilege, the court should find an *exception* in the grand jury context only if practice and policy require. To the contrary, the Independent Counsel contends, in essence, that the justification for any *extension* of a government attorney-client privilege to this context needs to be clear. These differences in approach are not simply semantical: they represent different versions of what is the status quo. To argue about an "exception" presupposes that the privilege otherwise applies in the federal grand jury context; to argue about an "extension" presupposes the opposite. In *Swidler & Berlin,* the Supreme Court considered whether, as the Independent Counsel contended, it should create an exception to the personal attorney-client privilege allowing disclosure of confidences after the client's death. *See Swidler & Berlin,* at [400], 118 S.Ct. at 2083. After finding that the Independent Counsel was asking the Court "not simply to 'construe' the privilege, but to narrow it, contrary to the weight of the existing body of caselaw," the Court concluded that the Independent Counsel had not made a sufficient showing to warrant the creation of such an exception to the settled rule. *Id.* at [411], 118 S.Ct. at 2088.

In the instant case, by contrast, there is no such existing body of caselaw upon which to rely and no clear principle that the government attorney-client privilege has as broad a scope as its personal counterpart. Because the "attorney-client privilege must be 'strictly confined within the narrowest possible limits consistent with the logic of its principle,'" *In re Sealed Case,* 676 F.2d 793, 807 n. 44 (D.C.Cir.1982) (quoting *In re Grand Jury Investigation,* 599 F.2d 1224, 1235 (3d Cir.1979)); *accord Trammel,* 445 U.S. at 50, 100 S.Ct. 906, and because the government attorney-client privilege is not recognized in the same way as the personal attorney-client privilege addressed in *Swidler & Berlin,* we believe this case poses the question whether, in the first instance, the privilege extends as far as the Office of the President would like. In other words, pursuant to our authority and duty under Rule 501 of the Federal Rules of Evidence to interpret privileges "in light of reason and experience," Fed.R.Evid. 501, we view our exercise as one in defining the particular contours of the government attorney-client privilege.

When an executive branch attorney is called before a federal grand jury to give evidence about alleged crimes within the executive branch, reason and experience, duty, and tradition dictate that the attorney shall provide that evidence. With respect to investigations of federal criminal offenses, and especially offenses committed by those in government, government attorneys stand in a far different position from members of the private bar. Their duty is not to defend clients against criminal charges and it is not to protect wrongdoers from public exposure. The constitutional responsibility of the President, and all members of the Executive Branch, is to "take Care that the Laws be faithfully executed." U.S. Const. art. II, § 3. Investigation and prosecution of federal crimes is one of the most important and essential functions within that constitutional responsibility. Each of our Presidents has, in the words of the Constitution, sworn that he "will faithfully execute the Office of President of the United States, and will to the best of [his] Ability, preserve, protect and defend the Constitution of the United States." *Id.* art. II, § 1, cl. 8. And for more than two hundred years each officer of the Executive Branch has been bound by oath or affirmation to do the same. *See id.* art. VI, cl. 3; *see also* 28 U.S.C. § 544 (1994). This is a solemn undertaking, a binding of the person to the cause of constitutional government, an expression of the individual's allegiance to the principles embodied in that document. Unlike a private practitioner, the loyalties of a government lawyer therefore cannot and must not lie solely with his or her client agency.[2]

The oath's significance is underscored by other evocations of the ethical duties of government lawyers.[3] The Professional Ethics Committee of the Federal Bar Association has described the public trust of the federally employed lawyer as follows:

> [T]he government, over-all and in each of its parts, is responsible to the people in our democracy with its representative form of government. Each part of the government has the obligation of carrying out, in the public interest, its assigned responsibility in a manner consistent with the Constitution, and the applicable laws and regulations. In contrast, the private practitioner represents the client's personal or private interest.... [W]e do not suggest, however, that the public is the client as the client concept is usually understood. It is to say that the lawyer's employment requires him to observe in the performance of his professional responsibility the public interest sought to be served by the governmental organization of which he is a part.

Federal Bar Association Ethics Committee, The Government Client and Confidentiality: Opinion 73-1, 32 FED. B.J. 71, 72 (1973). Indeed, before an attorney in the Justice Department can step into the shoes of private counsel to represent a federal employee sued in his or her individual capacity, the Attorney General must determine whether the representation would be in the interest of the United States. *See* 28 C.F.R. § 50.15(a). The obligation of a government lawyer to uphold the public trust reposed in him or her strongly militates against allowing the client agency to invoke a privilege to prevent the lawyer from providing evidence of the possible commission of criminal offenses within the government. As Judge Weinstein put it, "[i]f there is wrongdoing in government, it must be exposed.... [The government lawyer's] duty to the people, the law, and his own

---

2. We recognize, as our dissenting colleague emphasizes, that every lawyer must take an oath to enter the bar of any court. But even after entering the bar, a government attorney must take another oath to enter into government service; that in itself shows the separate meaning of the government attorney's oath. Moreover, the oath is significant to our analysis only to the extent that it underlies the fundamental differences in the roles of government and private attorneys—of particular note, the fact that private attorneys cannot take official actions.

3. Indeed, the responsibilities of government lawyers to the public have long governed the actions they can take on behalf of their "client":

> The United States Attorney is the representative not of an ordinary party to a controversy, but of a sovereignty whose obligation to govern impartially is as compelling as its obligation to govern at all; and whose interest ... is not that it shall win a case, but that justice shall be done.

Berger v. United States, 295 U.S. 78, 88, 55 S.Ct. 629, 79 L.Ed. 1314 (1935). In keeping with these interests, prosecutors must disclose to the defendant exculpatory evidence, see Brady v. Maryland, 373 U.S. 83, 87, 83 S.Ct. 1194, 10 L.Ed.2d 215 (1963), and must try to "seek justice, not merely to convict," MODEL CODE OF PROFESSIONAL RESPONSIBILITY EC 7-13 (1980). Similarly, the government lawyer in a civil action must "seek justice" and avoid unfair settlements or results. Id. EC 7-14.

conscience requires disclosure...." Jack B. Weinstein, *Some Ethical and Political Problems of a Government Attorney*, 18 MAINE L.REV. 155, 160 (1966).

This view of the proper allegiance of the government lawyer is complemented by the public's interest in uncovering illegality among its elected and appointed officials. While the President's constitutionally established role as superintendent of law enforcement provides one protection against wrongdoing by federal government officials, *see United States v. Valenzuela-Bernal*, 458 U.S. 858, 863, 102 S.Ct. 3440, 73 L.Ed.2d 1193 (1982), another protection of the public interest is through having transparent and accountable government.[4] As James Madison observed,

> [a] popular Government, without popular information, or the means of acquiring it, is but a Prologue to a Farce or a Tragedy; or, perhaps both. Knowledge will forever govern ignorance: And a people who mean to be their own Governors, must arm themselves with the power which knowledge gives.

Letter from James Madison to W.T. Barry (Aug. 4, 1822), *in* 9 THE WRITINGS OF JAMES MADISON 103 (Gaillard Hunt ed., 1910). This court has accordingly recognized that "openness in government has always been thought crucial to ensuring that the people remain in control of their government." *In re Sealed Case (Espy)*, 121 F.3d at 749. Privileges work against these interests because their recognition "creates the risk that a broad array of materials in many areas of the executive branch will become 'sequester[ed]' from public view." *Id.* (quoting *Wolfe v. Department of Health & Human Servs.*, 815 F.2d 1527, 1533 (D.C.Cir.1987)). Furthermore, "to allow any part of the federal government to use its in-house attorneys as a shield against the production of information relevant to a federal criminal investigation would represent a gross misuse of public assets." *In re Grand Jury Subpoena Duces Tecum*, 112 F.3d 910, 921 (8th Cir.), *cert. denied*, 521 U.S. 1105, 117 S.Ct. 2482, 138 L.Ed.2d 991 (1997).

Examination of the practice of government attorneys further supports the conclusion that a government attorney, even one holding the title Deputy White House Counsel, may not assert an attorney-client privilege before a federal grand jury if communications with the client contain information pertinent to possible criminal violations. The Office of the President has traditionally adhered to the precepts of 28 U.S.C. §535(b), which provides that

> [a]ny information ... received in a department or agency of the executive branch of the Government relating to violations of title 18 involving Government officers and employees shall be expeditiously reported to the Attorney General.

28 U.S.C. §535(b) (1994). We need not decide whether section 535(b) alone requires White House Counsel to testify before a grand jury.[5] The statute does not clearly apply to the Office of the President. The Office is neither a "department," as that term is de-

---

4. Congress has clearly indicated, as a matter of policy, that federal employees should not withhold information relating to possible criminal misconduct by federal employees on any basis. We discuss at more length Congress's recognition of these concerns below in our discussion of 28 U.S.C. §535(b).

5. 28 U.S.C. §535(a) authorizes the Attorney General to "investigate any violation of title 18 [the federal criminal code] involving Government officers and employees." The Independent Counsel fills the shoes of the Attorney General in this regard because Congress has given the Independent Counsel "with respect to all matters in [his] prosecutorial jurisdiction ... full power and independent authority to exercise all investigative and prosecutorial functions and powers of ... the Attorney General." 28 U.S.C. §594(a); see In re Sealed Case (Secret Service), 148 F.3d at 1078.

fined by the statute, *see* 5 U.S.C. § 101 (1994); 28 U.S.C. § 451 (1994); *Haddon v. Walters,* 43 F.3d 1488, 1490 (D.C.Cir.1995) (per curiam), nor an "agency," *see Kissinger v. Reporters Comm. for Freedom of the Press,* 445 U.S. 136, 156, 100 S.Ct. 960, 63 L.Ed.2d 267 (1980) (FOIA case); *see also Armstrong v. Executive Office of the President,* 1 F.3d 1274, 1295 (D.C.Cir.1993) (per curiam); *National Sec. Archive v. Archivist of the United States,* 909 F.2d 541, 545 (D.C.Cir.1990) (per curiam). However, at the very least "[section] 535(b) evinces a strong congressional policy that executive branch employees must report information" relating to violations of Title 18, the federal criminal code. *In re Sealed Case (Secret Service),* 148 F.3d at 1078. As the House Committee Report accompanying section 535 explains, "[t]he purpose" of the provision is to "require the reporting by the departments and agencies of the executive branch to the Attorney General of information coming to their attention concerning any alleged irregularities on the part of officers and employees of the Government." h.R.Rep. No. 83-2622, at 1 (1954). Section 535(b) suggests that all government employees, including lawyers, are duty-bound not to withhold evidence of federal crimes.

Furthermore, government officials holding top legal positions have concluded, in light of section 535(b), that White House lawyers cannot keep evidence of crimes committed by government officials to themselves. In a speech delivered after the *Kissinger* FOIA case was handed down, Lloyd Cutler, who served as White House Counsel in the Carter and Clinton Administrations, discussed the "rule of making it your duty, if you're a Government official as we as lawyers are, a statutory duty to report to the Attorney General any evidence you run into of a possible violation of a criminal statute." Lloyd N. Cutler, *The Role of the Counsel to the President of the United States,* 35 RECORD OF THE ASS'N OF THE BAR OF THE CITY OF NEW YORK No. 8, at 470, 472 (1980). Accordingly, "[w]hen you hear of a charge and you talk to someone in the White House ... about some allegation of misconduct, almost the first thing you have to say is, 'I really want to know about this, but anything you tell me I'll have to report to the Attorney General.'" *Id.* Similarly, during the Nixon administration, Solicitor General Robert H. Bork told an administration official who invited him to join the President's legal defense team: "A government attorney is sworn to uphold the Constitution. If I come across evidence that is bad for the President, I'll have to turn it over. I won't be able to sit on it like a private defense attorney." *A Conversation with Robert Bork,* D.C. BAR REP., Dec. 1997–Jan. 1998, at 9.

* * *

The Supreme Court's recognition in *United States v. Nixon* of a qualified privilege for executive communications severely undercuts the argument of the Office of the President regarding the scope of the government attorney-client privilege. A President often has private conversations with his Vice President or his Cabinet Secretaries or other members of the Administration who are not lawyers or who are lawyers, but are not providing legal services. The advice these officials give the President is of vital importance to the security and prosperity of the nation, and to the President's discharge of his constitutional duties. Yet upon a proper showing, such conversations must be revealed in federal criminal proceedings. *See Nixon,* 418 U.S. at 713, 94 S.Ct. 3090; *In re Sealed Case (Espy),* 121 F.3d at 745. Only a certain conceit among those admitted to the bar could explain why legal advice should be on a higher plane than advice about policy, or politics, or why a President's conversation with the most junior lawyer in the White House Counsel's Office is deserving of more protection from disclosure in a grand jury investigation than a President's discussions with his Vice President or a Cabinet Secretary. In short, we do not believe that lawyers are more important to the operations of government than all other officials, or that the advice lawyers render is more crucial to the functioning of the Presidency than the advice coming from all other quarters.

The district court held that a government attorney-client privilege existed and was applicable to grand jury proceedings, but could be overcome, as could an applicable executive privilege, upon a showing of need and unavailability elsewhere by the Independent Counsel. While we conclude that an attorney-client privilege may not be asserted by Lindsey to avoid responding to the grand jury if he possesses information relating to possible criminal violations, he continues to be covered by the executive privilege to the same extent as the President's other advisers. Our analysis, in addition to having the advantages mentioned above, avoids the application of balancing tests to the attorney-client privilege—a practice recently criticized by the Supreme Court. *See Swidler & Berlin,* at [409], 118 S.Ct. at 2087.

In sum, it would be contrary to tradition, common understanding, and our governmental system for the attorney-client privilege to attach to White House Counsel in the same manner as private counsel. When government attorneys learn, through communications with their clients, of information related to criminal misconduct, they may not rely on the government attorney-client privilege to shield such information from disclosure to a grand jury.

III.

* * *

B.

The President also contends that Lindsey is within the protection of his personal attorney-client privilege under the "common interest" doctrine. As a usual rule, disclosure of attorney-client or work product confidences to third parties waives the protection of the relevant privileges; however, when the third party is a lawyer whose client shares an overlapping "common interest" with the primary client, the privileges may remain intact. *See In re Sealed Case,* 29 F.3d 715, 719 (D.C.Cir.1994); *United States v. AT&T,* 642 F.2d 1285, 1300–01 (D.C.Cir.1980). Finding that the President and the Office of the President do not share any legally cognizable common interest, the district court denied Lindsey's invocation of the President's personal attorney-client privilege through the common interest doctrine. The President contends that the district court erred and that Lindsey's interactions with the President's private counsel should be protected under the doctrine.

Although it has long been recognized that the President in his private persona shares some areas of common interest with the Office of the President, *see, e.g., United States v. Burr,* 25 F. Cas. 187, 191–92 (No. 14,694) (C.C.D.Va. 1807) (Marshall, C.J.), and although the Office of the President contends persuasively that the threat of impeachment, if nothing else, presents a common interest between the President in his personal capacity and the Office of the President,[6] the existence of a common interest does not end our analysis.

---

6. Impeachment may remove the person, but no one could reasonably controvert that it affects the Office of the President as well. Even if there will always be a President and an Office of the President, it is unrealistic to posit that the Presidency will not be diminished by an impeachment. See, e.g., Michael Stokes Paulsen,The Most Dangerous Branch: Executive Power to Say What the Law Is, 83 Geo. L.J. 217, 323 (1994); see also William H. Rehnquist, The Impeachment Clause: A Wild Card in the Constitution, 85 Nw. U. L.Rev. 903, 917–18 (1991). The possibility of impeachment implicates institutional concerns of the White House, and White House Counsel, representing the Office

As we have established, government officials have responsibilities not to withhold evidence relating to criminal offenses from the grand jury. *See supra* section II.B. The President cannot bring Lindsey within his personal attorney-client privilege as he could a private citizen, for Lindsey is in a fundamentally different position. Unlike in his role as an intermediary, *see supra* section III.A, Lindsey necessarily acts as a government attorney functioning in his official capacity as Deputy White House Counsel in those instances when the common interest doctrine might apply, just as in those instances when the government attorney-client privilege might apply. His obligation not to withhold relevant information acquired as a government attorney remains the same regardless of whether he acquired the information directly from the President or from the President's personal counsel. Thus, his status before the federal grand jury does not allow him to withhold evidence obtained in his official role under either the government attorney-client privilege or the President's personal attorney-client privilege applied through the common interest doctrine.

If the President wishes to discuss matters jointly between his private counsel and his official counsel, he must do so cognizant of the differing responsibilities of the two counsel and tailor his communications appropriately; undoubtedly, his counsel are alert to this need as well. Although his personal counsel remain fully protected by the absolute attorney-client privilege, a Deputy White House Counsel like Lindsey may not assert an absolute privilege in the face of a grand jury subpoena, but only the more limited protection of executive privilege. Consequently, although the President in his personal capacity has at least some areas of common interest with the Office of the Presidency, and although there may thus be reason for official and personal counsel to confer, the overarching duties of Lindsey in his role as a government attorney prevent him from withholding information about possible criminal misconduct from the grand jury.

IV.

Accordingly, for the reasons stated in this opinion, we affirm in part and reverse in part.

In accordance with the Supreme Court's expectation that "the Court of Appeals will proceed expeditiously to decide this case," *Clinton,* at [912], 118 S.Ct. at 2079, any petition for rehearing or suggestion for rehearing *in banc* shall be filed within seven days after the date of this decision.

It is so ordered.

TATEL, Circuit Judge, dissenting from Part II and concurring in part and dissenting in part from Part III.

The attorney-client privilege protects confidential communication between clients and their lawyers, whether those lawyers work for the private sector or for government. Although I have no doubt that government lawyers working in executive departments and agencies enjoy a reduced privilege in the face of grand jury subpoenas, I remain unconvinced that either "reason" or "experience" (the tools of Rule 501) justifies this court's abrogation of the attorney-client privilege for lawyers serving the Presidency. This court's far-reaching ruling, moreover, may have been unnecessary to give this grand jury access to Bruce Lindsey's communications with the President, for on this

---

of the President, would presumably play an important role in defending the institution of the Presidency.

record it is not clear whether those communications involved official legal advice that would be protected by the attorney-client privilege. Before limiting the attorney-client privilege not just for this President, but for all Presidents to come, the court should have first remanded this case to the district court to recall Lindsey to the grand jury to determine the precise nature of his communications with the President.

I

* * *

Preserving the official presidential attorney-client privilege would not place the President above the law, as the Independent Counsel implies. To begin with, by enabling clients—including Presidents—to be candid with their lawyers and lawyers to advise clients confidentially, the attorney-client privilege promotes compliance with the law. *See Upjohn,* 449 U.S. at 389, 101 S.Ct. 677. Independent Counsels, moreover, have powerful weapons to combat abuses of the attorney-client privilege. If evidence suggested that a President used White House counsel to further a crime, the crime-fraud exception would abrogate the privilege. *See United States v. Zolin,* 491 U.S. 554, 562–63, 109 S.Ct. 2619, 105 L.Ed.2d 469 (1989). If an Independent Counsel had evidence that White House counsel's status as an attorney was used to protect non-legal materials from disclosure, those materials would not be protected. *See State v. Philip Morris Inc.,* No. C1-94-8565, 1998 WL 257214, at *7 (Minn.Dist.Ct. Mar.7, 1998) (releasing documents as penalty for bad faith claim of privilege). "The privilege takes flight," Justice Benjamin Cardozo wrote, "if the [attorney-client] relation is abused." *Clark v. United States,* 289 U.S. 1, 15, 53 S.Ct. 465, 77 L.Ed. 993 (1933). Or if an Independent Counsel presented evidence that a White House counsel committed a crime, a grand jury could indict that lawyer. *See* George Lardner, Jr., *Dean Guilty in Cover-Up: Nixon Ex-Aide Pleads to Count of Conspiracy,* Wash. Post, Oct. 20, 1973, at A1. This Independent Counsel has never alleged that any of these abuses occurred.

To be sure, a properly exercised attorney-client privilege may deny a grand jury access to information, *see Swidler,* at [407], 118 S.Ct. at 2086 (justifying the burden placed on the truthseeking function by the privilege), but Presidents remain accountable in other ways, *see Fitzgerald,* 457 U.S. at 757, 102 S.Ct. 2690 (checks on Presidential action include impeachment, press scrutiny, congressional oversight, need to maintain prestige, and concern for historical stature). An Independent Counsel, moreover, can always report to Congress that a President has denied critical information to a grand jury. *See* 28 U.S.C. § 595(a)(2), (c). If the President continues to exercise his attorney-client privilege in the face of a congressional subpoena, and if Congress believes that the President has committed "high Crimes and Misdemeanors," U.S. Const. art. II, § 4, Congress can always consider impeachment. *See* H. Rep. No. 93-1305, at 4, 187–213 (1974) (recommending impeachment of President Nixon based on his refusal to turn over information in response to congressional subpoenas).

* * *

III

I concur in Part III.A of the court's opinion. For the reasons stated in Parts I and II of my published dissent, I cannot join Part III.B. Since I believe that the Presidency's confidential attorney-client privilege covers communications with White House counsel, I would hold that the common interest doctrine protects communications between White House counsel and a President's private counsel where the attorneys share an overlapping common interest.

The Government Client and Confidentiality
Opinion 73-1

Professional Ethics Committee, Federal Bar Association
The Honorable Charles Fahy, Chairman

At the outset of his Presidency of the Association Mr. Poirier submitted to the Committee under date of October 8, 1971, the following questions:

1. Under what circumstances may a federally employed lawyer disclose information concerning a Government official of any rank which would reveal corrupt, illegal, or grossly negligent conduct?

2. If disclosure may be properly made, to whom may it be made?

3. Who is the client of a Government attorney in the Executive or Legislative branches of Government?

A draft of proposed opinion was submitted to Mr. Poirier by the Committee, as then constituted, in June, 1972. It was circulated by him for their comments among a number of federally employed lawyers of high rank in Washington. Numerous comments were made. It was also discussed by the National Council of the Association at its meeting in September, 1972. At that meeting, at the suggestion of the Chairman of the Ethics Committee, the matter was referred again to the Committee for reconsideration in light of the comments and discussion. The Committee now submits the result of its further consideration.

A few remarks as to terminology are in order. Thus, the "federally employed lawyer," for purposes of this opinion, is considered to be the lawyer employed by the federal government in a legal capacity. This opinion may at times refer to him as the government lawyer, or simply as the lawyer or attorney, without repetition that he is "federally employed." In defining the terms "corrupt, illegal or grossly negligent" conduct, as used in the opinion, and in judging whether particular conduct comes within those terms, special care is required. The "corrupt" conduct referred to in the request for an opinion was construed to be venal conduct in violation of law and duty, engaged in for personal gain or the gain of another, the gain ordinarily being of a pecuniary or other valuable nature which is measurable. Defining "illegal" conduct was not so easy for such conduct is often subject to reasonable differences of opinion as to its legality. The profession as well as the courts are constantly troubled and at odds about whether particular conduct is legal or not. For purposes of this opinion "illegal" conduct is divided into two general categories. One consists of the willful or knowing disregard of or breach of law, other than of a corrupt character, the latter type of illegal conduct having been separately defined. The second category of illegal conduct was considered to be that about which the lawyer may hold a firm position as to its illegality but which he nevertheless recognizes is in an area subject to reasonable differences of professional opinion as to its legality. Conduct which is "grossly negligent" would seem not to lend itself to greater clarification than those words themselves indicate.

One further general comment seems desirable. The federally employed lawyer in reaching a conclusion that the type of conduct referred to has occurred must be fully aware of the circumstances and exercise care commensurate of the need always to avoid an unjust or mistaken derogatory characterization of the conduct of another.

Assuming the described conduct to have occurred, answers to the three questions can be more clearly developed by considering first the question posed as to who is the client of the federally employed lawyer in the Executive and Legislative branches of the government. Problems of disclosure involved in the other questions should be considered in light of the answer to the client question.

The client problem also divides according to the duties involved. There is the government lawyer who is designated to represent another in government service against whom proceedings are brought of a disciplinary, administrative or personnel character, including a court-martial. The answer to the client question in these situations seems clear. The person the lawyer is designated to represent is the client. The usual attorney-client relationship arises, with its privilege and professional responsibility to protect and defend the interest of the one represented.

The more usual situation of the federally employed lawyer, however, is that of the lawyer who is a principal legal officer of a department, agency or other legal entity of the Government, or a member of the legal staff of the department, agency, or entity.[1] This lawyer assumes a public trust, for the government, over-all and in each of its parts, is responsible to the people in our democracy with its representative form of government. Each part of the government has the obligation of carrying out, in the public interest, its assigned responsibility in a manner consistent with the Constitution, and the applicable laws and regulations. In contrast, the private practitioner represents the client's personal or private interest. In pointing out that the federally employed lawyer thus is engaged professionally in the furtherance of a particular governmental responsibility we do not suggest, however, that the public is the client as the client concept is usually understood. It is to say that the lawyer's employment requires him to observe in the performance of his professional responsibility the public interest sought to be served by the governmental organization of which he is a part.

Proceeding upon the foregoing background, the client of the federally employed lawyer, using the term in the sense of where lies his immediate professional obligation and responsibility, is the agency where he is employed, including those charged with its administration insofar as they are engaged in the conduct of the public business. The relationship is a confidential one, an attribute of the lawyer's profession which accompanies him in his government service. This confidential relationship is usually essential to the decision-making process to which the lawyer brings his professional talents. Moreover, it encourages resort to him for consultation and advice in the on-going operations of the agency.

The relationship above described gives rise to the question whether or to what degree the attorney-client privilege known to private practice attaches with respect to those to whom the government lawyer is professionally obligated in the conduct of the public business. No all-inclusive answer to the problem of the privilege is attempted herein, not only because no concrete factual situation has been posed, but also because the questions as submitted call for consideration of the privilege only as it bears upon the problem of disclosure. In that context the following is submitted.

The Committee does not believe there are any circumstances in which corrupt conduct may not be disclosed by the federally employed lawyer, apart from those situations to which we have referred in which the lawyer has been designated to defend an individual in a proceeding against him with respect to a personal problem.

---

1. In the course of this opinion when we use the term "agency" as a matter of convenience to include "Department" or other governmental entity.

In other instances of corruption the ethical aspect of the answer merges with the legal. Section 535 of Title 28 of the United States Code provides:

(b) Any information, allegation, or complaint received in a department or agency of the executive branch of the Government relating to violations Title 18 [the federal criminal code] involving Government officers and employees shall be expeditiously reported to the Attorney General by the head of the department or agency, unless—

(1) the responsibility to perform an investigation with respect thereto is specifically assigned otherwise by another provision of law; or

(2) as to any department or agency of the Government, the Attorney General directs otherwise with respect to a specified class of information, allegation, or complaint.

(c) This section does not limit—

(1) the authority of the military departments to investigate persons or offenses over which the armed forces have jurisdiction under the Uniform Code of Military Justice (chapter 47 of Title 10); or

(2) the primary authority of the Postmaster General to investigate postal offenses.

In addition to this statute, there is House Concurrent Resolution No. 175 of July 11, 1958, 72 Stat. B12, entitled "Code of Ethics for Government Service." Its provisions have been made applicable to the entire Executive branch by Regulations of the Civil Service Commission, 5 C.F.R. § 735.10.[2] The Resolution provides: "Any person in the Government service should: 9. Expose corruption wherever discovered." ...[3]

Reading section 535 of Title 28 of the United States Code with the Joint Resolution and the Civil Service Commission Regulations, corrupt conduct and other illegal conduct of a criminal character, that is, the willful or knowing disregard of or breach of law, in either the Legislative or Executive branch may be disclosed by the federally employed lawyer, that is, reported to the "head of the department or agency" or other governmental entity, who shall report it to the Attorney General. If the head officer referred to is involved, the report in our opinion may be made directly to the Attorney General, or other appropriate official of the Department of Justice.[4]

With respect to the second category of illegal conduct, conduct about which there may be reasonable differences of opinion as to its legality, and grossly negligent conduct, the Committee considers the problem to be different. Ordinarily there is no need of dis-

---

2. The legislative history of the Resolution (S. Rep. No. 1812, 85th Cong., 2d Sess. (1958)) states it is intended only as a guide and "creates no new law ... and established no legal restraints on anyone."

3. *Id.*

4. The Committee adds at this point a strong recommendation that the federally employed lawyer, for himself personally and for his ability to assist others in his agency, acquaint himself with the full content of 5 C.F.R. § 735.10. This section provides that each employee shall acquaint himself with each statute that relates to his ethical and other conduct as an employee of his agency and of the Government, and that the agency itself shall direct the attention of its employees, by specific reference in agency regulations issued under this Part 735, which is concerned with employee responsibilities and conduct, to each statue relating to the ethical and other conduct of employees of that agency, as well as to a listed number of provisions respecting employee conduct, including Chapter 11 of Title 18 U.S.C., which is concerned, *inter alia,* with conflicts of interest.

closure of such conduct beyond the personnel of the agency where it arises. Differences of opinion as to the legality of action are often unavoidable in the process of arriving at a course of action to be recommended or adopted. The lawyer may not deem the decision reached or the action taken to be legally sound, but in the situations in which the question arises it may not be misconduct at all. Moreover, when we turn particular conduct may be accidental by a person ordinarily careful. There should usually be an adequate remedy in the public interest calling for no disclosure beyond the immediate persons involved, including if need be other members of the agency. In all of these matters there may be regulations of the agency pointing to the course which should be followed. These should be observed unless for some very good reason the lawyer deems them inapplicable. In any event, the opportunity to correct these matters should first be within the agency itself.

Something more needs to be said. The confidential relationship of the lawyer with those entitled to consult with and be advised by him varies in degree according to the subject matter. It is one thing in the area of national security or the conduct of foreign affairs, for example, and quite another if there is involved, for example, a dispute over the validity of a particular order of the National Labor Relations Board. The diversity of situations is almost innumerable. It is to be borne in mind throughout that ours is an open society insofar as compatible with the orderly and effective conduct of government. This follows from the nature of the relationship of our Government with the people, and it has been given legislative recognition in recent years by the Freedom of Information Act, with its limited exemptions from the obligation of disclosure. Moreover, the government lawyer cannot be a refuge for the corrupt or looked upon as a secret repository for illegal or grossly negligent conduct of the business of the Government. There is a dividing line between conduct which falls in the area of strict confidentiality and that which falls within the area of appropriate public knowledge. This line cannot accurately be drawn except upon consideration of a particular factual situation, and even then not always easily or accurately drawn, certainly not to the satisfaction of all. Accordingly, the Committee feels obliged to limit its answer respecting disclosure to acceptance of the principle that disclosure beyond the confines of the agency or other law enforcing or disciplinary authorities of the Government is warranted only in the case when the lawyer, as a reasonable and prudent man, conscious of his professional obligation of care, confidentiality and responsibility, concludes that these authorities have without good cause failed in the performance of their own obligation to take remedial measures required in the public interest. In the absence of a concrete situation upon which to pass judgment as to the ethical course which should be followed we go no further than to adopt the above stated ethical principle. We think it appropriate for us to affirm the position that honesty and faithfulness is the prevailing rule in the Government service, and we warn against applying the principle we have stated to any situation without that care and sense of responsibility which is the hallmark of the legal profession at its best. Such care would call for resort by the lawyer himself to a trustworthy advisor as to the course to be followed. The ultimate decision, however, remains with him.

One final comment. The Committee has not considered it relevant to the present inquiries to embrace the subject of classified material or the Executive privilege.

The opinion has the unanimous approval of the Committee, composed as follows in alphabetical order: Circuit Judge Arlin M. Adams, Third Circuit; Superior Court Judge Sylvia Bacon, District of Columbia; Judge Earl Chudoff of the Court of Common Pleas, Philadelphia; Justin Dingfelder, Esquire, Office of the General Counsel, Federal Trade Commission; Senior Circuit Judge Charles Fahy, District of Columbia Circuit; Axel

Kleiboemer, Esquire, Department of Justice, Washington, D.C.; Joseph G. O'Neill, Jr., Esquire, Assistant Legislative Counsel, Central Intelligence Agency; Honorable Harold E. Stassen, Philadelphia; Major Charles A. White, Jr., Judge Advocate General's School, U.S. Army, Charlottesville.

District of Columbia Ethics Opinion 323
2004

Misrepresentation by an Attorney Employed by a Government Agency as Part of Official Duties

Lawyers employed by government agencies who act in a non-representational official capacity in a manner they reasonably believe to be authorized by law do not violate Rule 8.4 if, in the course of their employment, they make misrepresentations that are reasonably intended to further the conduct of their official duties.

Applicable Rules

- Rule 8.4 (Misconduct)

Inquiry

The Committee has received an inquiry on a matter relating to the obligation of an attorney under Rule 8.4(c). We are asked to determine whether attorneys who are employed by a national intelligence agency violate the Rules of Professional Conduct if they engage in fraud, deceit, or misrepresentation in the course of their non-representational official duties.

Discussion

Rule 8.4(c) of the Rules of Professional Responsibility makes it professional misconduct for a lawyer to "engage in conduct involving fraud, deceit, or misrepresentation." This prohibition applies to attorneys in whatever capacity they are acting—it is not limited to conduct occurring during the representation of a client and is, therefore, facially applicable to the conduct of attorneys in a non-representational context. See ABA Formal Op. No. 336 (1974) (lawyer must comply with applicable disciplinary rules at all times).[1] The prohibition on misrepresentation would, therefore, facially apply to attorneys conducting certain activities that are part of their official duties as officers or employees of the United States when the attorneys are employed in an intelligence or national security capacity. Thus, though the inquirer asked specifically about misrepresentations made by intelligence officers acting in their official capacity as authorized by law, the principles enunciated in this opinion are equally applicable to other governmental officers who are attorneys and whose duties require the making of misrepresentations as authorized by law as part of their official duties.

Such employees may, on occasion, be required to act deceitfully in the conduct of their official duties on behalf of the United States, as authorized by law. It is easy, for ex-

---

1. This opinion applies only to the conduct of attorneys acting in a non-representational capacity. It does not address potentially applicable requirements under Rule 4.1 (communication with clients), or Rule 4.3 (dealing, on behalf of clients, with unrepresented parties) which, inter alia, prohibits attorneys from making a false statement of material fact to a third party "in the course of representing a client."

ample, to imagine attorneys whose work for the CIA might require their personal clandestine work and falsification of their identity, employment status, or fidelity to the United States. We are confronted with the question whether such misrepresentations run afoul of Rule 8.4's anti-deceit prohibition.[2]

For three reasons, we conclude that Rule 8.4 does not prohibit conduct of the nature described.

First, our conclusion is premised on our understanding of the purposes for which Rule 8.4 was adopted. The prohibition against engaging in conduct "involving dishonesty, fraud, deceit, or misrepresentation" applies, in our view, only to conduct that calls into question a lawyer's suitability to practice law. The Comments to Rule 8.4 discuss why the current version discarded earlier references to a prohibition on conduct involving "moral turpitude" (as the conduct that had been proscribed was referred to in our former Code of Professional Responsibility). Comment [1] explains that this somewhat archaic formulation,

> can be construed to include offenses concerning some matters of personal morality, such as adultery and comparable offenses, that have no specific connection to fitness for the practice of law. Although a lawyer is personally answerable to the entire criminal law, a lawyer should be professionally answerable only for offenses that indicate lack of those characteristics relevant to law practice.

D.C. Rule 8.4, Comment [1]; see also In re White, 815 P.2d 1257 (Or. 1991) (concluding that Rule applies to conduct in violation of criminal law if it "reflects adversely on the lawyer's honesty, trustworthiness or fitness as a lawyer in other respects").

Thus, in rejecting the formulation of "moral turpitude" and substituting the current anti-deceit formulation, the District of Columbia Court of Appeals has indicated its intention to limit the scope of Rule 8.4 to conduct which indicates that an attorney lacks the character required for bar membership. As the Comments elaborate, this may include "violence, dishonesty, breach of trust, or serious interference with the administration of justice." D.C. Rule 8.4, Comment [1].[3] But, clearly, it does not encompass all acts of deceit—for example, a lawyer is not to be disciplined professionally for committing adultery, or lying about the lawyer's availability for a social engagement.

Given this understanding of Rule 8.4, in our judgment the category of conduct proscribed by the Rule does not include misrepresentations made in the course of official conduct as an employee of an agency of the United States if the attorney reasonably believes that the conduct in question is authorized by law. An attorney's professional competence and ability are not called into question by service in our intelligence or national

---

2. Rule 8.4(c) prohibits a lawyer from engaging in conduct "involving dishonesty, fraud, deceit, or misrepresentation." And "fraud" is, of course, separately defined by the Rules. See D.C. Rules of Prof. Conduct, Terminology (defining "fraud" and "fraudulent" as "conduct having a purpose to deceive"). For convenience sake, we refer to Rule 8.4(c) as the anti-deceit provision, while recognizing that the scope of the prohibition may depend upon a close analysis of the meaning of each of the four related prohibitions.

3. In March 2003, the Virginia Supreme Court made this connection explicit by amending the Virginia version of Rule 8.4(c) to prohibit "dishonesty, fraud, deceit or misrepresentation which reflects adversely on a lawyer's fitness to practice law." Va. R. Prof. Cond. 8.4(c).

security agencies in conformance with legal authorization, nor is it called into question by the use of effective covert means to achieve legitimate national security goals. Cf. Apple Corps Ltd. v. International Collectors Society, 15 F. Supp. 2d 456, 476 (D.N.J. 1998) (concluding that investigator's and tester's misrepresentation of identity is not a misrepresentation of "such gravity as to raise questions as to a person's fitness to be a lawyer"). As a consequence, we do not believe that Rule 8.4(c) is intended to reach lawful, authorized official conduct, even if there is a deceitful component to that conduct.

Second, our conclusion in this regard is buttressed by an analogous provision of the Rules and its construction within this jurisdiction. Rule 4.2 prohibits certain communications between a lawyer and an opposing party who is represented by counsel. This jurisdiction has construed the Rule to permit lawful law enforcement activity. Thus, our Commentary says that:

> This Rule is not intended to enlarge or restrict the law enforcement activities of the United States or the District of Columbia which are authorized and permissible under the Constitution and the laws of the United States or the District of Columbia. The "authorized by law" proviso to Rule 4.2(a) is intended to permit government conduct that is valid under this law.

Rule 4.2, Comment [8].[4] The Virginia Standing Committee on Legal Ethics recently recognized the parallel between law enforcement and intelligence activity in an opinion that is consistent with our views. In Va. Legal Ethics Opinion 1738 (2000), the Virginia Standing Committee considered whether the ethical rule prohibiting non-consensual tape recording then in effect in Virginia applied to law enforcement undercover activities. The Virginia Standing Committee concluded that it did not. In Va. Legal Ethics Opinion 1765 (2003), the Virginia Standing Committee then considered whether the policies animating the exception for law enforcement undercover activities expressed in Opinion 1738 also authorized the use of non-consensual tape recording and other covert activities by attorneys working for a federal intelligence agency. Reasoning by analogy to its earlier decision concerning law enforcement undercover activities, the Committee agreed that covert intelligence activities also serve "important and judicially-sanctioned social policies." Accordingly Opinion 1765 concluded that "when an attorney employed by the federal government uses lawful methods such as the use of 'alias identities' and non-consensual tape-recording, as part of his intelligence or covert activities, those methods cannot be seen as reflecting adversely on his fitness to practice law; therefore such conduct will not violate the prohibition in Rule 8.4(c)." That reasoning is equally persuasive to this Committee.

To be sure, Rule 8.4 does not have an "authorized by law" proviso, like that in Rule 4.2, and the absence of such a provision authorizing deceit in the intelligence, national security, or other foreign representational context might be construed as indicating that such conduct is not permitted. Nonetheless, we agree with Virginia that the treatment of law enforcement activity is instructive of the proper treatment of intelligence activity. A better construction is to view Comment [8] to Rule 4.2 as expressing a general approval

---

4. Some other jurisdictions have construed this provision to preclude law enforcement agents, acting at the direction of a lawyer, from conducting covert, undercover activity against individuals who are represented by counsel. Cf. In re Gatti, 8 P.3d 966 (Or. 2000), overruled, Or. DR 1-102(D) & Or. Formal Op. 2003-173.

of lawful undercover activity by government agents and the failure to mention the myriad ways in which the issue might arise simply reflects the drafters' focus on the more immediate issue of law enforcement activity that was before them. We do not think that the Court of Appeals intended to authorize legitimate law enforcement undercover activity while proscribing covert activity in aid of our national security; we would not impute so illogical an intent to the drafters absent far stronger evidence.

Third, "[t]he Rules of Professional Conduct are rules of reason. They should be interpreted with reference to the purposes of legal representation and of the law itself." D.C. Rules, Scope, Comment [1]. Some activities conducted on behalf of the United States necessarily involve circumstances where disclosure of one's identity or purpose would be inappropriate—and, indeed, potentially dangerous. We do not think that the Rules of Professional Conduct require lawyers to choose between their personal safety or compliance with the law, on the one hand,[5] and maintenance of their bar licenses, on the other. See Utah State Bar Ethics Advisory Committee Op. No. 02-05 (2002) (relying on "rule of reasons" provision to conclude that government attorneys' "lawful participation in a lawful government operation" does not violate Rule 8.4 if deceit is "required in the successful furtherance" of the undercover or covert operation).

For these several reasons we are convinced that the anti-deceit provisions of Rule 8.4 do not prohibit attorneys from misrepresenting their identity, employment or even allegiance to the United States if such misrepresentations are made in support of covert activity on behalf of the United States and are duly authorized by law.[6]

Finally, we emphasize the narrow scope of this opinion. It applies only to misrepresentations made in the course of official conduct when the employee (while acting in a non-representational capacity, see supra n.1), reasonably believes that applicable law authorizes the misrepresentations. It is not blanket permission for an attorneys employed by government agencies to misrepresent themselves. Nor does it authorize misrepresentation when a countervailing legal duty to give truthful answers applies. Thus, for example, false testimony under oath in a United States court or before the Congress is prohibited, see In re Abrams, 689 A.2d 6 (D.C. 1997) (en banc), notwithstanding any countervailing intelligence or national security justification. And, of course, this opinion does not authorize deceit for non-official reasons, or where an attorney could not, objectively, have a reasonable belief that applicable law authorizes the actions in question.

With that limitation, our conclusion is as follows: Lawyers employed by government agencies who act in a non-representational official capacity in a manner they reasonably believe to be authorized by law do not violate Rule 8.4 if, in the course of their employment, they make misrepresentations that are reasonably intended to further the conduct of their official duties. Inquiry No. 01-11-25

Adopted: March 29, 2004

---

5. In some circumstances, federal law affirmatively prohibits disclosure of information relating to the identity of covert agents, for example. See, e.g., 50 U.S.C. § 421.

6. This Committee lacks the expertise to precisely identify, for example, which covert activities are authorized by law. Moreover, such an enumeration would exceed our charter, which ordinarily limits our opinions to interpretations of the District of Columbia Rules of Professional Conduct. We emphasize, however, that for conduct to come within the safe-harbor of this opinion the lawyer must reasonably believe that the conduct in question was both authorized by law and reasonably intended to further the attorney's official duties.

B. Corporate

The Emerging Responsibilities of the Securities Lawyer

A.A. Sommer, Jr.*
Securities and Exchange Commission
Washington, D.C.
1974 Federal Securities Law Reports, pp. 79, 631**

For many years the sponsors of securities institutes and programs have been blessed with innumerable occasions to promote their wares; attorneys have flocked to programs on Rule 10b-5, then the *Texas Gulf Sulphur* complaint (at this point we all ceased to wait for the decisions and spent endless hours and days discussing simply the *charges*) was the focus, then *BarChris*, accountant's liabilities, and innumerable subtopics and variations of these. All of these and others have now been subordinated in interest to a single topic: the legal exposures of lawyers under the securities laws administered by the Securities and Exchange Commission. Anyone organizing a program to which he expects to entice lawyers in substantial numbers cannot safely omit this topic. The topic is, in the vernacular, hot, a best seller.

The event which triggered this interest, of course, was the filing of the complaint by the Commission against National Student Marketing Corp., its accountants, several of its executives, and most importantly from the standpoint of attorneys, two outstanding and prestigious law firms, one in New York, and the other in Chicago, and partners in the firms.

It was not just the filing of a complaint naming attorneys that triggered this intense and tense interest, for, after all, other attorneys had been named in Commission complaints, frequently because of conduct during their representations of clients and not because of other roles—director, officer, and so on. Clearly the interest was heightened by the fact that for the first time old firms of recognized competence and integrity were named as defendants. I think many attorneys had read the travails of other less well-known counsel with the thought that these were not really relevant because of their obscurity and the absence of recognition of their firms as expert and knowledgeable, whereas the naming of firms of national prominence hinted that no one was immune. Everyone who worked in securities law suddenly felt vulnerable and exposed. Lawyers began to experience the trepidation and concern and uneasiness that began to afflict their accounting brethren many years ago as they began to realize that prestige, name, proud history, did not afford immunity against civil and even criminal action.

It is something of an understatement to say that the complaint in *National Student Marketing* had excited lively interest in the legal profession. Innumerable articles, notes, student comments, lectures have now been published analyzing the complaint, dis-

---

* The Securities and Exchange Commission, as a matter of policy, disclaims responsibility for any private publication or speech by any of its members or employees. The views expressed here are my own and do not necessarily reflect the views of the Commission or of my fellow Commissioners.

** Copyright © 1974–1975 CCH Incorporated. All rights reserved. Reprinted with permission from Federal Securities Law Reporter.

cussing the applicable law, proposing means of swiftly eliminating the questions in the collective stomach of the securities bar.

The apprehension of securities and corporate attorneys was, of course, increased by the complaint in the *Vesco* case which, while not naming a firm, nonetheless named attorneys associated with a prominent firm. And another measure of disturbance was added when the Court of Appeals for the Second Circuit in the *Spectrum* case suggested that simple negligence in the rendering of an opinion concerning exemption from registration might expose counsel at least to Commission injunctive action.

It would not, I'm sure you realize, be appropriate for me to comment on any of this pending litigation or say anything which would sound like prejudgment, or argument of the case, or suggestion to the various courts involved of the manner in which they should view these charges. And it is not my purpose to discuss at length the legal theories concerning counsel liability, the subtleties of the Code of Professional Responsibilities and its relationship to the problem; the sources on these matters are plentiful. However, I think I can with propriety discuss the milieu, if you will, in which these cases arise, some of the broader implications of them, and make a few very personal observations concerning their significance.

Attorneys have since the earliest days of the federal securities laws been at the heart of the scheme that developed in response to those laws. While their formal participation mandated by the '33 and '34 Acts was limited — the only reference to counsel was in Item (23) of Schedule A to the 1933 Act which required the inclusion in registration statements of "the names and addresses of counsel who have passed on the legality of the issue ..." — nonetheless, the registration statement has always been a lawyer's document and with very, very rare exceptions the attorney has been the field marshall who coordinated the activities of others engaged in the registration process, wrote (or at least rewrote) most of the statement, made the judgments with regard to the inclusion or exclusion of information on the grounds of materiality, compliance with registration form requirements, necessities of avoiding omission of disclosure necessary to make those matters stated not misleading. The auditors have been able to point to clearly identifiable parts of the registration statements as their responsibility and they have successfully warded off efforts to extend their responsibility beyond the financial statements with respect to which they opine. With the exception of the financial statements, virtually everything else in the registration statement bears the imprint of counsel.

Counsel have been involved in many other ways with the federal securities laws. They are frequently called upon to give opinions with respect, principally, to the availability of exemptions from the requirements for registration and use of a statutory prospectus. None would deny the importance of these opinions: millions upon millions of dollars of securities have been put into the channels of commerce — not just sold once, but permanently into the trading markets — in reliance upon little more than the professional judgment of an attorney. In many, perhaps most, instances these opinions have been confined to questions concerning the technical availability of the exemption and have not been concerned with questions of disclosure, compliance with the somewhat amorphous mandates of Rule 10B-5 and other anti-fraud provisions of the federal securities laws.

Attorneys' opinions have played other roles as well: They are customarily rendered in connection with the closing of registered public offerings, both by issuer and underwriter counsel, and in those opinions conclusions with respect to disclosure begin to emerge. In opining that a registration statement complies as to "form" with the requirements of the Securities Act of 1933, often counsel may be saying more about the contents of the statement than he realizes and if his opinion goes to the question of the legality of the offering as distinguished from the securities, certainly clear questions concerning the adequacy of disclosure are raised.

Of course, the attorney appears in many other contexts: often he appears in court or before the Commission as an advocate in formal proceedings; his advocacy may also be discerned in various discussions with the staff. For the moment I would put those matters aside and suggest that the resolution of the responsibilities of the advocate, as distinguished from the counselor, registration statement writer and opinion giver, are somewhat more amenable to resolution with traditional notions.

In a word, and the word is Professor Morgan Shipman's, the professional judgment of the attorney is often the "passkey" to securities transactions. If he gives an opinion that an exemption is available, securities get sold; if he doesn't give the opinion, they don't get sold. If he judges that certain information must be included in a registration statement, it gets included (unless the client seeks other counsel or the attorney crumbles under the weight of client pressure); if he concludes it need not be included, it doesn't get included.

Securities lawyers have since the adoption of the 1933 Act stoutly urged that they play a limited role in this process, even to the point of continuing to insist, despite the requirement of Form S-1, among others, that there be submitted as a part of the registration statement an opinion of counsel concerning the legality of the securities being registered, that they are in no way "experts" within the meaning of Section 11. Beyond that, they have gloried in the occasional judicial acknowledgment of the limitations of their role. How often have we been reminded that In *Escott v. BarChris* Judge McLean specifically rejected the suggestion that the attorneys involved in the preparation of the contested registration statement were experts with respect to all of it except the financial statements and concluded that some of the attorneys had liability only because of their roles as director and officer of the issuer?

We are consistently reminded that historically the attorney has been an advocate, that his professional ethics have over the years defined his function in those terms, that such a role includes unremitting loyalty to the interests of his client (short of engaging in or countenancing fraud). Whenever the effort is made to analogize the responsibilities of the attorney to those of the independent auditor, one is reminded that the federal securities law system conceives of the auditor as independent and defines his role specifically, whereas the attorney is not and cannot be independent in the same sense in which an auditor is independent. It has been asserted by very eminent counsel that, "The law, so far [this was in 1969] is very clear. The lawyers' responsibility is exclusively to their own client." If this distinction is clear to lawyers, it is less clear to others. Last week two of the most eminent leaders of the accounting profession asked me why it was that the attorneys named in the Commission's *National Student Marketing* complaint were not indicted while the auditors were. This sort of inquiry is increasingly asked, not only by auditors, but others as well.

I would suggest that the security bar's *conception* of its role too sharply contrasts with the *reality* of its role in the securities process to escape notice and attention—and in such situations the reality eventually prevails. Lawyers are not paid in the amounts they are to put the representations of their clients in good English, or give opinions which assume a pure state of facts upon which any third year law student could confidently express an opinion.

We live in the age of the consumer. All of the old articles of faith which frustrated him in efforts to achieve equity have fallen or are falling: cognovit notes are repudiated in most places; the sale of installment paper no longer immunizes the paper purchaser from responsibility for the shoddiness of the merchandise; people pressured into purchases on their doorstep have time to think over their decision; the real cost of borrowing and purchases on installments must be disclosed. This pervading judicial and legislative concern for the interests of the consumer which has for forty years been present in large measure in the securities field (the securities laws may have been the first federal consumer legislation) is affecting and will affect increasingly the securities field—and those involved in it.

Consequently, I would suggest that all the old verities and truisms about attorneys and their roles are in question and in jeopardy—and, unless you are ineradicably dedicated to the preservation of the past, that is not all bad.

I would suggest that in securities matters (other than those where advocacy is clearly proper) the attorney will have to function in a manner more akin to that of the auditor than to that of the advocate. This means several things. It means he will have to exercise a measure of independence that is perhaps uncomfortable if he is also the close counselor of management in other matters, often including business decisions. It means he will have to be acutely cognizant of his responsibility to the public who engage in securities transactions that would never have come about were it not for his professional presence. It means he will have to adopt the healthy skepticism toward the representations of management which a good auditor must adopt. It means he will have to do the same thing the auditor does when confronted with an intransigent client—resign.

This may seem shocking to many ears, but I would suggest that these conclusions are already implicit in what the courts and the Commission have already said; more important, their foundations lie deep in the past.

As long ago as 1934 William O. Douglas lamented an absence of social-mindedness in business lawyers and opined that this was "evidenced by the almost perverted singleness of purpose with which they have championed the cause of their clients, whether it be in the drafting of a deposit agreement, the handling of a merger, the conduct of a reorganization, or the marketing of securities. It resulted in getting accomplished what clients wanted but without regard for the long-term consequences of those accomplishments. That singleness of purpose has been wholly incompatible with the use of these aggregations of capital for either the welfare of the investor or for the good of the public ..."

More recently, the Court of Appeals for the Second Circuit in 1964 said the familiar words, "In our complex society the accountant's certificate and the lawyer's opinion can be instruments for inflicting pecuniary loss more potent than the chisel or the crowbar."

Two years earlier the commission, in discussing the practices of attorneys in rendering opinions concerning securities matters, said:

> "An attorney's opinion based upon hypothetical facts is worthless if the facts are not as specified, or if unspecified but vital facts are not considered. Because of this, it is the practice of responsible counsel not to furnish an opinion concerning ... the availability of an exemption from registration ... unless such counsel have themselves carefully examined all of the relevant circumstances and satisfied themselves, to the extent possible, that the contemplated transaction is, in fact, not a part of an unlawful distribution."

Another manifestation to the trends of the law with respect to the role of lawyers is, in my estimation, clearly discerned in the case which has been a consolation to many, the *BarChris* case. The outside counsel for the company was sued as a director of the company under Section 11 of the 1933 Act and the court made clear that its determination of his liability was as a director. But the discussion by the court of his liability is interesting: it all relates to his activities as lawyer in the preparation of the registration statement. For instance, the court said:

> "It is claimed that a lawyer [note the court says lawyer, *not director*] is entitled to rely on the statements of his client and that to require him to verify their accuracy would set an unreasonably high standard. This is too broad a generalization. It is all a matter of degree. To require an audit would obviously be unreasonable. On the other hand, to require a check of matters easily verifiable is not unreasonable. Even honest clients make mistakes."

I would suggest that had this director been sued *qua* lawyer under Rule 10b-5, the court would have reached the same conclusion for the same reasons. Implicit in the language of the court is the thought that a lawyer preparing a registration statement has an obligation to do more than simply act as the blind scrivener of the thoughts of his client.

* * *

I would suggest that the sort of reexamination of the historic role of counsel is not inconsistent with the broader responsibilities of the bar to its clients. Much of what I have said was expressed in the Preface of the American Bar Association's Code of Professional Responsibility:

> "Before the Bar can function at all as a guardian of the public interests committed to its care, there must be appraisal and comprehension of the new conditions, and the changed relationship of the lawyer to his clients, to his professional brethren and to the public. That appraisal must pass beyond the petty details of form and manners which have been so largely the subject of our Codes of Ethics, to more fundamental consideration of the way in which our professional activities affect the welfare of society as a whole. Our canons of ethics for the most part are generalizations designed for an earlier era."

I would urge that as lawyers we not be hesitant in representing our clients, but let us not be hesitant, either, in protecting those who rely, sometimes rather blindly, upon the protections of professional judgment. Corporate law lawyers are paid well, ultimately by society, for doing a professional job and assuming professional responsibility. Let us not, I urge, appear to society fearful and hesitant as we adapt to the emerging responsibilities of this age where consumer is king.

SEC Continues Considering Mandatory
"Noisy Withdrawal" Rules

Both the ABA and the Section of Litigation weigh in against SEC proposals
Mary S. Diemer, *Litigation News* (A Publication of the Section of Litigation),
American Bar Association, September 2003 Vol. 28, No. 6

In the wake of the Enron, WorldCom, Adelphia and other corporate scandals shaking consumer confidence in the markets, the Securities and Exchange Commission is considering a rule that would require attorneys to report corporate misconduct "up the chain" and to resign publicly from further representation while disavowing improper filings by the issuer. A comment letter recently filed by the American Bar Association again urges the SEC to delete the "noisy withdrawal" requirement from the SEC's rules of attorney conduct.

Under the proposed rule, the SEC will require attorneys to report evidence of a material violation of securities law, breach of fiduciary duty, or other material violation of law by an issuer "up the ladder" within the company to the chief legal officer or chief executive officer. In the absence of an appropriate response from these corporate officers addressing the violations, the attorney is required to report the illegal activity to the company's audit committee or the board of directors. If such efforts are unsuccessful in bringing the company into compliance, the attorney must withdraw from further representation, notify the SEC, and disaffirm filings made by the company.

Section 307 of the Sarbanes-Oxley Act charged the SEC with drafting minimum standards of professional conduct for attorneys. The SEC issued implementing regulations in January. It extended the comment period, however, as to the noisy withdrawal requirement. This requirement continues to be the focus of the ABA's and the Section of Litigation's objections.

In response to the initial rules of attorney practice proposed by the SEC, Section Chair Scott J. Atlas, Houston, TX, formed an ad hoc working group to assist the ABA Task Force on Implementation of Section 307 of the Sarbanes-Oxley Act of 2002 in drafting comments for submission to the SEC.

The ABA's supplemental comments draw heavily on text prepared by the Section of Litigation. They reaffirm the view that mandatory withdrawal and disclosure will erode the attorney-client privilege and fundamentally change the role that lawyers play in representing public companies. Implementation of a noisy withdrawal rule will: (1) destroy the issuer's trust in their attorneys by creating conflicts between the attorney's personal interest in avoiding potential discipline and the desire of management to operate the business; (2) discourage companies from consulting counsel on sensitive issues, or cause companies to withhold necessary facts; (3) hinder attorney flexibility in responding to compliance questions; and (4) encourage premature withdrawal by counsel to avoid application of the "reporting out" rule.

The ABA continues to support permissive withdrawal and limited "up the chain" reporting of issuer misconduct. The comment letter notes that this approach is less intrusive upon the attorney-client relationship and permits the client to rely on the attorney's professional judgment without concern of violating a mandatory federal rule of professional conduct. Otherwise, the client will view the attorney as a potential adversary and exclude the attorney from critical deliberations regarding how to maintain compliance with the law. Permissive withdrawal also permits the attorney to work with the client to achieve the right compliance decision. Finally, permissive withdrawal permits the SEC to assess the effectiveness of corporate governance and accounting practices imposed under Sarbanes-Oxley and other laws without requiring lawyers to breach the privilege.

The noisy withdrawal rules bring concern from both outside counsel and corporate clients who worry that the attorney-client privilege will be irrevocably damaged, notes Koji Francis Fukumura, San Diego, CA, Co-Chair of the Section's Securities Litigation Committee and a member of the Section's ad hoc group contributing to the ABA comment letters. "My principal concern—and I've heard this from corporations too—is that the rule chills communications between a corporation and its counsel. If a corporation needs to 'vet' an issue internally before running it by counsel," Fukumura adds, "the proposed rule certainly undermines the privilege and the reasons it is sacrosanct to our jurisprudence."

An attorney's reporting obligations would be triggered when the attorney should become aware of a material violation by the company or its officers. As a consequence, attorneys may feel pressured to divulge client communications to the SEC to avoid liability for themselves, "putting the lawyer's interest in avoiding prosecution ahead of the client's interests," Fukumura comments.

Although it continues to support permissive withdrawal and limited "up the chain" reporting of issuer misconduct, the ABA also recommended several changes and clarifications to the noisy withdrawal rule to lessen the SEC's intrusion into the attorney-client privilege.

Resource: The full text of the ABA's Comment Letter, prepared by the Task Force on Implementation of the Sarbanes-Oxley Act of 2002, is available at www.abanet.org/ poladv/new.html.

From the Trenches and Towers: The Kaye Scholer Affair

William H. Simon,* *Law and Social Inquiry*, Spring, 1998
[Most footnotes omitted. Remaining footnoted renumbered.]

The charges brought by the Office of Thrift Supervision against the law firm of Kaye, Scholer, Fierman, Hays, and Handler, in 1992 generated the most prominent legal ethics controversy of the decade. Despite massive attention to the case, the substance of the OTS charges has received little analysis and has been often mischaracterized. This article analyzes the charges and the bar's response to them. It concludes that the charges were plausible prima facie. It argues, further, that the response by bar organizations and leaders has been pervasively disingenuous and irresponsible. It also identifies and analyzes some broad ethical issues raised by the case about the participation of lawyers in financial scandals. The article concludes with an appendix reporting and assessing Kaye Scholer's response to the charges.

For three years, lawyers from the New York firm of Kaye, Scholer, Fierman, Hays, & Handler devoted themselves to keeping the government off the back of Charles Keating while he engaged in financial and political exploits that eventuated in criminal convictions for Keating and several of his associates, billions of dollars in civil liability for Keating and a larger group of associates, formal criticism by the United States Senate of five of its members, and a loss to the federal banking insurance system estimated at $3.4 billion (Resolution Trust Corporation 1994, 5–6, 26–29; Thompson 1990, 37–43).

* William H. Simon is Kenneth and Harle Montgomery Professor of Public Interest Law, Stanford University. The author is grateful for advice from Ken Scott, Marc Franklin, Fred Zacharias, Steve Pepper, Lewis Segal, Deborah Rhode, Richard Painter, Philip Lewis, Patrick Crawford, Gregory Keating, Jennifer Arlen, Eric Talley, Ed Rubin, and Tom Ehrlich. Peter Fishbein of the Kaye Scholer firm made documents available and commented on an earlier draft. Some of these people disagreed strongly with some of the things I say here. [William H. Simon is now Arthur Levitt Professor at Columbia University School of Law. This article reproduced with the kind permission of Professor Simon and *Law and Social Inquiry*.]

Of course, this fact alone is no discredit to the lawyers. The legality of Keating's conduct was then—and in some aspects remains today—a matter of dispute. (Both Keating's own criminal convictions have been reversed, though billions of dollars in civil judgments against him and various civil and criminal judgments against his associates still stand [Sterngold 1996; Zagorin 1997]). Moreover, as the bar often reminds us, "unpopular" people are entitled to representation too, even people who are unpopular because they are crooks.[1]

But this case took an unusual turn. Succeeding Keating to ownership of the defunct Lincoln Savings & Loan, the banking agencies found themselves with access to records of confidential communications between the Keating crowd and the Kaye Scholer lawyers and, from this intimate vantage point, concluded that some of the lawyers' conduct went beyond the legitimate bounds of representation. The Office of Thrift Supervision (OTS) charged the lawyers with misconduct in a case the firm settled for $41 million and injunctive relief.

Although widely publicized, these charges against the best-known lawyers for the most notorious figure in the largest financial scandal in American history have received little direct discussion within the profession. Not that the bar doesn't have a lot to say about Kaye Scholer. Lawyers like to talk about the "freeze" of the firm's assets that OTS, on questionable grounds, mandated. They like to talk about how the agency's authority to regulate lawyers relates to that of the bar and the courts. They like to talk about what the case has done to insurance rates. But they don't particularly care to talk about what OTS alleged Kaye Scholer did and whether such conduct is wrong.

Unpleasant as some may find the prospect, there are good reasons to consider the charges against Kaye Scholer in detail. First, the effort can help clarify the issues. OTS's charges were widely portrayed as radical and, in particular, as challenging traditional notions of confidentiality. In fact, as I show in part I, though the charges were occasionally ambiguous and innovative, most rested in substantial part on the notion that a lawyer who cannot do anything for a client that would not further his frauds should withdraw. This proposition is in no way radical, but the Kaye Scholer debate has left great confusion as to whether the mainstream bar rejects it as a matter of principle, disputes its applicability to the particulars of the Kaye Scholer matter, or simply emotionally resists its enforcement against prominent lawyers.

Second, the bar's performance in the Kaye Scholer affair should be counted as a large mark against it in the current debate over the appropriate allocation of regulatory responsibilities between public authorities and professional institutions (see generally Wilkins 1992). Kaye Scholer indicates limitations on the profession's willingness and ability to set and enforce plausible standards of practice. Its instincts throughout the affair appear to have been self-protective rather than self-regulatory. Part II shows that a broad range of professional leaders and institutions failed to seriously confront the issues raised by the OTS complaint, instead producing a panoply of evasions.

Third, the case raised important issues about the participation of lawyers in the kinds of events that turn out to be major scandals. Professional responsibility discussions most often focus on discrete episodes of lawyer behavior in relatively clearly and

---

1. ABA 1969, EC 2-27 ("a lawyer should not decline representation because a client or cause is unpopular").

narrowly defined practice contexts. Issues that arise from lawyer involvement in financial and political scandals typically involve longer courses of conduct in broader and more ambiguous contexts. In such situations, disputes can arise both about the proper characterization of relevant norms and conduct and about allocations of responsibility to individual lawyers for outcomes that result from complex interactions of many people. Kaye Scholer's partisans deserve credit for raising a variety of issues of this sort that are rarely discussed, but as I show in part III, their arguments have been often unpersuasive.

A major obstacle to appraising Kaye Scholer's conduct that may have inhibited discussion, especially by those inclined to be sympathetic to the charges, is that we have limited knowledge of the facts. Thus, one risks both doing an injustice to Kaye Scholer and looking foolish in the event one's inferences prove mistaken. Nevertheless, the issues are too important to pass over. The stakes in the immediate case are large; the charges are representative of those found in several S&L failures, and the alleged conduct is emblematic for many of a morally disturbing style of professional conduct.

I. OTS'S DUTY-OF-CANDOR CHARGES AGAINST KAYE SCHOLER

* * *

B. The Allegations

The Kaye Scholer litigators were asked to represent Lincoln in its dealings with the Bank Board in June 1986, after examiners had raised what turned out to be largely valid concerns about the soundness of the bank and the propriety of some of its practices. They represented the bank until it was finally seized in 1989. Kaye Scholer immediately set an aggressive tone and asserted a degree of control that everyone agrees was unusual in the bank examination process. It wrote the Bank Board insisting that all requests for information be funneled through its lawyers. The firm billed Lincoln $13 million for work done between 1985 and 1989 (OTS, ¶¶ 6–10, 16–19).

Here are the principal specific instances of misconduct toward the Bank Board alleged in OTS's Notice of Charges.

1. *The "Grandfathered" Loans.* Kaye Scholer made misleading representations regarding whether certain otherwise-prohibited Lincoln investments were allowed under a "grandfathering" exception. Whether the investments were grandfathered depended on whether Lincoln had made "definitive plans" for them by a cutoff date. Many documents Lincoln used to support its grandfathering claim had been prepared after the cutoff date in a manner designed to give the impression that they were contemporaneous records of a pre-cutoff decision. They were backdated and written in the present tense. Unauthorized signatures were appended to some documents, and some falsely recited that other documents had been presented to the Board prior to the cutoff date.

Beside its general participation in the examination, Kaye Scholer associated itself with Lincoln's fraud in two specific ways. First, it gave Lincoln an opinion, which it knew Lincoln intended to use to shore up its position with the Bank Board, that various investments met the "definite plans" requirement of the grandfathering exception. The opinion recited as grounds for its conclusion that the "Board of Directors had directed" that the investments be made prior to the relevant date. In fact, the documentation of Board action provided to the examiners consisted of the written consents that were prepared after the grandfathering date but backdated to before it. Second, the lawyers transmitted the misleading documents to the Bank Board and asserted repeatedly that they supported Lincoln's position, again without disclosing the circumstances of their preparation (OTS, ¶¶ 22–33, 140–51).

2. *The Arthur Andersen Resignation.* Kaye Scholer transmitted a Lincoln SEC "8-K" filing requested by the Bank Board that reported the resignation of its accounting firm, Arthur Andersen, and stated that the resignation "was not the result of any concern by AA [Arthur Andersen] with [ACC/Lincoln's] operations ... or asset/liability management." Although the Arthur Andersen firm approved this statement, members of the firm had expressed concerns about operations and asset/liability management, and Kaye Scholer was aware of at least one of these statements. A few days before transmitting the form to the Bank Board, Fishbein wrote to Keating, enclosing a memorandum of a conversation with a senior Andersen partner named Joseph Kresse, which he characterized as containing "some insight into what may have motivated Andersen's decision [to resign]." The memo reports various reservations about Lincoln's operations, for example, "Lincoln looks like most of the other S&L's that have failed.... Andersen views Lincoln as a high risk client." Kaye Scholer did not disclose this statement in connection with its transmission of the SEC form. (OTS, ¶¶ 37–42).

3. *The "Linked" Transactions.* Keating inflated the book value of Lincoln's assets by a series of "linked" transactions. He would sell property to an ally for a price higher than Lincoln had paid for it, recording the increase as a capital gain. In fact, Lincoln or ACC sometimes had loaned the ally the money to buy the property, promised to repurchase it, or simultaneously purchased an overvalued property from the ally. The records of the sale would be separated from the records of the loan, repurchase obligation, or concurrent purchase in the hope that the regulators would not notice the "link." These practices were a major focus of the criminal charges that resulted in Keating's federal conviction, as well as various civil charges against Lincoln executives (Granelli 1992; SEC 1991).

Kaye Scholer was aware of this activity and repeatedly expressed concern internally that the regulators would discover it, once for example referring to "Linked transactions" as "a powder keg which could explode if FHLBB analyzes them carefully." The firm made general representations to the Bank Board about Lincoln's financial circumstances that were misleading without disclosure of the links. For example, they argued that the earnings figures on Lincoln's financial statements demonstrated "managerial skill" and "prudent underwriting," knowing that these figures reflected the "linked transactions" (OTS, ¶¶ 58–71).

4. *Underwriting Defects.* Kaye Scholer's study of Lincoln's records revealed a pattern of loans made without formal loan applications, with little or no analysis of collateral, with unexplained negative-credit-verification material, and without appraisals or cash-flow histories. In an internal memo, a firm lawyer characterized one set of loan files as running "the spectrum from disaster to non-existent." Yet in defending the firm's underwriting to the Bank Board, the firm made statements such as the following: "In making real estate loans, Lincoln has always undertaken very careful and thorough procedures to analyze the collateral and the borrower. What is unusual about Lincoln's underwriting is its particular emphasis on, and the thoroughness of, its underwriting of the collateral."

Similarly, Kaye Scholer lawyers had privately concluded that Lincoln's junk bond underwriting was "very weak, and there is little or no evidence in the files of proper underwriting." Yet they made representations to the Board to the effect that there was "no basis for the … conclusion that Lincoln's high yield bond underwriting is inadequate." The lawyers used as examples two junk bond investments that they had selected privately "to show Lincoln's underwriting in its best possible light" but represented to the Board that "a similar process is undertaken for all of Lincoln's investments" (OTS, ¶¶ 76–103).

5. *The Doctored Loan Files.* Kaye Scholer knew but failed to disclose that Lincoln had altered loan documentation files produced for the examiners. Information that reflected negatively on loans had been removed. Information supporting the loans had been added subsequent to the decisions to make them. Much of this information had not been obtained from borrowers or verified in accordance with customary underwriting practices but had been pulled from the borrowers' advertising and the public media. "Repayment analyses" coinciding with the payment obligations of the loan were invented without analysis and verification of the borrowers' actual circumstances. Underwriting summaries prepared after the decisions were written in the present tense, as if they were contemporaneous with the loan decision, and placed, undated, in the files.

Kaye Scholer transmitted some of the misleading documents to the Board and made numerous representations defending Lincoln's underwriting without disclosing these facts (though the Notice of Charges concedes that the principal written responses to the 1986 examination report did acknowledge briefly that some material had been added to some files subsequent to the loans) (OTS, ¶¶ 74–93).

6. *Rancho Vistoso.* Kaye Scholer made misleading representations about a large land development transaction that Lincoln had classified as a loan in an effort to comply with limits on equity investments. In fact, Kaye Scholer knew facts suggesting that the classification was improper, and many people within Lincoln had expressed doubts about it.

Arthur Andersen and its successor, Arthur Young, had signed off on the classification, but Kaye Scholer knew that they did so in ignorance of the facts, first, that Lincoln controlled the project, and second, that the putative borrower was dependent on further uncollateralized loans and "sham land 'purchases'" by Lincoln in order to make the payments. Without noting either these facts or the accountants' lack of awareness of them, Kaye Scholer repeatedly asserted that the opinions of the accountants, whom they described as having "carefully reviewed" and "closely scrutinized" the transactions, established the validity of the classifications (OTS, ¶¶ 107–35).

7. *Hotel Pontchartrain.* Kaye Scholer made misrepresentations about a $20 million line of credit granted by a Lincoln subsidiary to a limited partnership formed by Keating and other ACC insiders to hold the Hotel Pontchartrain. The loan was an illegal "affiliated transaction." It was made without collateral to an entity experiencing serious operating losses at a below-market interest rate. A Kaye Scholer internal memo reported these facts and noted that the "[f]ile lacks virtually all required materials" and the "loan has serious problems concerning (a) safety and soundness and (b) affiliate transactions."

Kaye Scholer securities lawyers prepared SEC filings, which by law had to be filed with the Board as well, from which several specific facts reflecting on the quality and legality of the loan were misleadingly omitted. These facts included the liberal terms of the loan, which the internal memo had suggested might make it a "gift of assets," and the severe operating losses and negative net worth of the borrower.

When the California Department of Savings and Loan questioned Lincoln's disclosure, Kaye Scholer wrote a letter insisting that it was adequate and specifically referring to a letter from Lincoln that asserted that the borrower was running an operating profit, when in a nearly contemporaneous in-house memo one of its lawyers noted that "although an 'operating profit' of $60,037 was achieved, this failed to account for $2,192,760 of expenses for interest, property taxes, depreciation, management fees and other expenses.... It seems disingenuous to fail to deduct [these expenses] when the relevant figures are so easily obtainable" (OTS, ¶¶ 153–69).

* * *

II. EVASION

Although Kaye Scholer did dispute the OTS allegations, the main emphasis of its campaign of self-exoneration, executed with the help of a public relations firm (Goldberg 1992, 51), was to characterize OTS's charges as a radical departure from established norms and as an assertion of disclosure duties that would infringe confidentiality. These characterizations fit poorly with the specifics of the allegations, but many prominent lawyers proved happy to talk about the case with little or no reference to the specifics.

The resulting literature often either crudely misstates or delicately sidesteps the key allegations of the case. At the same time, it shows a concern with the "asset freeze" so obsessive and parochial as to call to mind a discussion of the sinking of the Titanic preoccupied with a claim for overtime pay by the navigator. Throughout much of it, we find barely a hint of concern that lawyers might have contributed to the worst financial disaster in American history.

* * *

III. APOLOGY

When the bar did reach the merits, it was usually to excuse Kaye Scholer with arguments whose plausibility was rarely proportionate to the eminence of their proponents. The proponents offered various apologies: The rules weren't clear; Kaye Scholer was acting as "litigation" rather than "regulatory" counsel; everybody else was doing the same thing; they didn't do any harm; the "government" was the real culprit; confidentiality forced them to do what they did.

Aside from implausibility, these arguments have in common that they point to aspects of ambiguity in the assessment of individual conduct in large scandals. Scandals generally involve both innovative behavior and complex interaction. The primary wrongdoers typically think that their schemes make some improvement over the failed chicanery of the past, and the consequences of wrongdoing typically depend on the conduct, not just of the prime mover, but also of many knowing and inadvertent collaborators. In a strictly libertarian system, it would be impossible to hold anyone responsible under such circumstances. Libertarianism requires that norms be fully specified in advance and liability be imposed only where a definite link between individual action and harmful consequence is demonstrated, neither of which is possible in the type of case we are considering. However, our legal system is not libertarian. Its standard analytical practices are more than adequate to deal with the problems of innovation and collective action posed by scandals.

A. The Rules Weren't Clear

A leitmotif of the Working Group report is bewilderment and distress at the perceived novelty and indeterminacy of OTS's interpretation of counsel's responsibilities.

Where the analysis does not flat out disagree with OTS, it throws out rhetorical questions about the meaning of its interpretation in innumerable circumstances. It repeatedly demands that OTS specify just how the standards would apply in various circumstances and that it use various procedures, especially administrative rule making, to specify the standards (ABA Working Group 1993, 143–50, 153–54, 202–04, 212, 220–23).

The dominant theme of the discussion is not an effort to make the standards more workable, but rather to suggest that the novelty of OTS's view makes its prior applications illegitimate and that the indeterminacy of its standards makes their coherent elaboration impossible. You would think that the group had never heard of the common law! Case-by-case reinterpretation and elaboration of general standards is, of course, the essence of the common law process. Retroactivity and indeterminacy are the age-old complaints of those whose innovative wrongdoing the common law has caught up with. They are the prices we pay for flexibility and adaptability. OTS's complaints were based on statutes and regulations, but these statutes and regulations incorporated familiar common law terms and were of a sort routinely developed by courts and regulators in the manner of the common law.

Of course, notice is a legitimate concern, but in our system, notice has never meant certainty, and it has connoted advance knowledge of governing principles, not prior specification of how they will apply in every particular situation. This seems especially appropriate in the case of a group of professionals who often characterize themselves in terms of a superior capacity for complex contextual judgment.

At least with respect to the duty-of-candor claims, what was new in the Lincoln case was not the principles but the circumstances. Those who speak about the novelty of OTS's approach do not point to past bank failures of comparable magnitude involving similar conduct in which lawyers were treated more leniently. There was nothing radical about the notion that lawyers ought not to assist fraud. What was new, other perhaps than the degree of aggression of Kaye Scholer's advocacy, was the banking system's vulnerability to fraud. The disastrous changes of the 1980s had exacerbated the system's long-standing precariousness. A lawyer operating in the 1980s on automatic pilot might have been surprised to find that the risk that improper conduct might implicate her in a huge disaster was as high as it turned out to be. Some such experience may explain the otherwise mistaken sentiments of many insurers that the case created a new ball game. But a lawyer who, before the fiasco, gave some thought to how traditional responsibility and disclosure norms should apply in the changed circumstances of the day would not have been surprised.

B. They Were "Litigation Counsel"

While the assertion that OTS's claims were radical was grossly exaggerated, one prominent claim in the Kaye Scholer debate was extremely radical. This was the firm's and Geoffrey Hazard's argument that because the firm was "litigation" rather than "regulatory" counsel, it had a lower standard of responsibility to the Bank Board.

The argument had two parts. The first was that although a bank examination is not itself litigation, the Kaye Scholer lawyers should be considered "litigation" counsel because Keating designated the lawyers as such and hired them in plausible anticipation of litigation with the Bank Board. The second part of the argument was that since they were litigation counsel, the propriety of their statements and responses to the Bank Board should be judged under the standard of Model Rule 3.1, which applies to the lawyer as "advocate" rather than as "counselor" and asserts that in a "proceeding" the lawyer shall not "assert or controvert an issue therein, unless there is a good faith basis for doing so that is not frivolous." Fortunately for the dignity of the bar, this argument has been widely dismissed (for example, ABA Standing Committee 1993, 10). Skepticism has focused, however, on the first part, whereas the most disturbing and implausible feature is the second.

With respect to the first part, if any important ethical consequences turn on designation as litigation counsel, that designation cannot reasonably turn on either the client's characterization or the likelihood of litigation. The client should not be given the power to determine unilaterally the lawyer's obligations to third parties. And since the likelihood of litigation is strongly correlated with whether the client has behaved wrongfully, the argument comes far too close to asserting that the more clearly the client has misbehaved, the lower the counsel's responsibilities to third parties.

In any event, characterization as litigation counsel would have been helpful to Kaye Scholer only if one accepted the further claim that its conduct would then be judged under the Rule 3.1 "not frivolous" standard. Under this standard, any Kaye Scholer action would be permissible as long as the firm could come up with a nonfrivolous argument that the response was truthful and complete. This approach would give Kaye Scholer latitude in exploiting ambiguities in the examiners' requests to withhold information they knew the examiners would regard as material and ambiguities in their own statements that they knew would mislead the examiners.

Suppose an examiner asked a Kaye Scholer lawyer for the "underwriting documents for loan X," and the lawyer handed over a file, knowing but not disclosing that the file had been recently altered to remove negative information present at the time the loan was authorized and to add favorable information obtained since authorization. Suppose further that the lawyer knew or should have known that this response would mislead the examiner because the examiner understood this request to call for *all* the *contemporaneous* underwriting documents and would interpret the lawyer's response in the light of this understanding. (Assume further that the examiner's understanding was reasonable and consistent with bank auditing practice.) Under the Kaye Scholer/Hazard position, the fact that Kaye Scholer knew the examiner would be misled is irrelevant as long as there was some nonfrivolous interpretation under which its response would not be misleading. Kaye Scholer would contend that it would not be "frivolous" to interpret "underwriting documents for loan X" to mean "whatever documents happened to be in the X file at the time of the request," and thus its response was not misleading (PLI 1992, ¶¶ 3–6).

Professional responsibility doctrine provides no support for this position whether or not we call the lawyers "litigation counsel." The argument's spurious force depends entirely on its disregard for the distinction between factual assertion and argument. Rule 3.1 and its "not frivolous" standard applies to the latter; it governs positions that counsel takes, not assertions containing *information*. In a pleading, brief, or argument in court, the lawyer refers to evidence that has been or will be presented to the tribunal. Argument involves assertions as to how this evidence should be interpreted or characterized. Since the evidence is, or will be, of record, opposing counsel is equally able to argue for an interpretation, and the judge or jury can make its own assessment of the arguments by comparing them to the evidence. The dangers of deception are limited, and counsel can be given wide latitude.

Note also that argument is usually optional. Typically, neither lawyers nor clients are under a duty to third parties to raise legal issues or provide legal theories and characterizations.

The situation is different if the lawyer provides information, especially under a disclosure duty. This can occur both outside and inside litigation. For example, within litigation the discovery process creates a broad range of disclosure duties, and even though the information rights of the Bank Board were stronger than the discovery rights of the typical civil litigant, there are in fact some analogies between Kaye Scholer's role in responding to the examiners' requests and "litigation counsel's" role in responding to civil discovery requests. In these situations, counsel's task does not consist of suggesting characterizations for evidence of record but rather of providing information within their control in response to the other party's requests. When counsel represent expressly or implicitly that they have provided all the information responsive to the request, they put their credibility in issue in ways that they do not in argument. Moreover, while the record provides a safeguard against distortions in argument, there is no analogous check on inadequate discovery compliance. The process depends heavily on honesty of counsel.

It should thus not be surprising that the courts have consistently rejected suggestions that the adequacy of litigation counsel's responses to discovery requests should be measured by anything resembling the "not frivolous" argument standard. On the contrary, they consistently condemn "incomplete," "evasive," and "misleading" responses.[2]

The ethics rule most relevant to Kaye Scholer's conduct is not Model Rule 3.1 on positions, but Rule 8.4(c), which forbids "conduct involving ... fraud ... or misrepresentation." These terms are not defined in the rules, but they have a familiar common law meaning different from the "not frivolous" standard. For example, the *Restatement of Torts* puts it this way:

> A representation that the maker knows to be capable of two interpretations, one of which he knows to be false and the other true is fraudulent if it is made:
>
> (a) with the intention that it be understood in the sense that it is false, or
>
> (b) without any belief or expectation as to how it will be understood, or
>
> (c) with reckless indifference as to how it will be understood. (1977 § 527)

Responding to the distinction between argument and factual assertion, Kaye Scholer suggests that much of its work for Lincoln more resembled trial argument than discovery compliance. Several of the OTS charges were based on statements in memoranda Kaye Scholer produced to respond to the examiners' reports of their examinations. At this point, the examiners already had had extensive access to Lincoln's records and personnel. The point of the memoranda was not to provide new information but to assess the inferences to be drawn from evidence the examiners had seen, they say.

---

2. *Pilling v. General Motors* (1968, 369); *Dollar v. Long Mfg.* (1977); *Miller v. Doctor's Gen. Hosp.* (1977); see also the Advisory Committee notes to the 1993 amendments to Federal Rule of Civil Procedure 37, 146 F.R.D. at 690 ("Interrogatories should not be read or interpreted in an artificially restrictive or hypertechnical manner to avoid disclosure of information fairly covered by the discovery request."). The Washington Supreme Court recently rebuffed an effort by the firm of Bodle and Gates, also with the assistance of Geoffrey Hazard, to justify withholding vital discovery information on a theory similar to Kaye Scholer's. *Washington State Physicians Ins. Exch. & Ass'n v. Fisons Corp.* (1993).

I find this unpersuasive. The bank examination did not involve a circumscribed record, and the Kaye Scholer statements OTS objected to did not purport to be characterizations of evidence of record. They appeared to be statements of fact. The formal, adversarial norms of the trial had not been prevalent previously in the examination process, and lawyers had no traditional distinctive role in this process. It thus seems likely that the examiners reasonably believed that lawyers were as bound as anyone else by the norms prohibiting knowingly misleading, even if "not frivolous," statements.

C. Everybody Was Doing It

Some have suggested that Kaye Scholer's conduct did not differ materially from that of many other lawyers in banking and analogous regulatory contexts. It is far from clear that this is factually correct. The Kaye Scholer lawyers were litigators without prior banking experience, and even the Working Group report concedes that it was unusual for counsel to take control of a bank audit to the extent that Kaye Scholer did (1993, 155). Nevertheless, Howell Jackson suggests that it can be inferred from the large number of lawyers charged with misconduct that "a substantial segment of the legal community—much more than a few bad apples—operated throughout the 1980s under a different conception of professional obligations from the one the government now advances" (1993, 1024).

If this is true, it is not insignificant but should not weigh heavily. One consideration is whether the lawyers engaging in this conduct did so under the impression that it was proper. Contrary to Jackson's assumption, it does not follow from the fact that many people engage in an activity that they think they are justified in doing so. For example, among restaurant workers, the practice of underreporting tip income to the IRS is so widespread that you often hear it said that "everybody does it." But when someone gets caught, he doesn't expect to be excused on these grounds because while everybody may have been doing it, everybody also knew it was wrong.

Even if we grant that the practices were both widespread and legitimate within the profession, the claim of the Working Group and others that only prospective reform would be appropriate is not well supported by the dominant judicial practices in the area of civil liability. In situations where, as Learned Hand put it, "a whole calling [has] unduly lagged" behind the norms of the surrounding society, we do impose liability retroactively. Some actions, Hand continued, "are so imperative that even their universal disregard will not excuse their omission."

Finally, the appeal to long-standing practice is least plausible where the institutional setting of the practice has changed. This happened with a vengeance in the S&L field in the 1980s. The stakes were much higher, and the government's interests as insurer were much more vulnerable than they had been before. Those who appeal to custom in such circumstances ought to have some responsibility to assess whether the customary practices serve their traditional purposes in their altered settings.

D. They Didn't Do Any Harm

Kaye Scholer has seemed understandably ambivalent about defending its conduct on the ground that it caused no harm. The harm alleged by OTS is the delaying of the seizure of Lincoln, and it's indisputable that Kaye Scholer was trying to do that. If the lawyers didn't have any effect, what were they charging all that money for?

However, others have felt less constrained to push this line of argument. Notably, Jonathan Macey and Geoffrey Miller argue that even if Kaye Scholer misbehaved, its conduct did not aggravate the public's losses. Their point is that despite the lawyers' obfuscations, the Bank Board indicated that it had determined that Lincoln was insolvent by April 1987; yet the institution was not seized until nearly two years later. "These facts make it clear that bureaucratic timidity and ineptitude, rather than Kaye, Scholer's machinations, are primarily to blame for the unconscionable delays in closing Lincoln" (Macey and Miller 1993, 1119; see also Moore 1992; Douglas and Train 1992).

To their great credit, Macey and Miller are among the few lawyers willing to discuss directly whether conduct the OTS charged was wrongful, and their discussion concludes that on some points it was. Moreover, their primary concern is with the efficacy of the "freeze" order in protecting the financial interests of the insurance system. Nevertheless, particularly given the moralistic, conclusory denunciations of public officials that pervade it, their discussion implies some exoneration of Kaye Scholer, and as such, there are two objections to it.

First, Kaye Scholer may indeed have delayed the seizure. Perhaps without Kaye Scholer's efforts, the agency would have made its determination before April 1987, and the earlier determination would have led to an earlier seizure. Kaye Scholer had been working to forestall seizure for nearly a year before April 1987. The Bank Board's field-office regulators who first pushed for action against Lincoln asserted that Kaye Scholer's efforts "played a major role in preventing the government from seizing Lincoln until … some 23 months after San Francisco first sounded the alarm" (Beck 1990, 40).

The fact that the agency "knew" of Lincoln's insolvency in April 1987 does not mean that Kaye Scholer's efforts had no effect in delaying action. Government officials, especially "timid," "inept" ones (Macey's and Miller's characterizations) often lack the confidence to act on their beliefs. The fact that highly paid, highly credentialed lawyers from a prestigious law firm were vigorously disputing their determination might have led them to hesitate or wait for more substantiation before proceeding.

* * *

E. The "Government" Was Responsible

Macey and Miller and Daniel Fischel argue that Kaye Scholer (and in Fischel's case, most of the defendants in the other S&L suits) were "scapegoats" for a government trying to divert attention from its own responsibility for the fiasco.

In their accounts, the government's irresponsibility dwarfs anything Kaye Scholer or even (in Fischel's account) Charles Keating might have done wrong. "In the early days of the crisis," Macey and Miller write, "many believed that fraud, incompetence and corruption within the banking system were to blame. But by 1991, it was clear to all that the regulatory system itself was at fault" (1993, 1137).

It was the government that decided in the early 1980s to run the huge risks of maintaining an obsolete and precarious industry dependent on federal insurance. Trying to placate various interest groups and avoid recognizing short-term losses to the insurance fund, the government encouraged the banks to understate their financial weakness and make riskier investments. It tolerated and even promoted increased competition in the industry, ignoring that the new conditions created even greater pressures for the banks to take risks that were implicitly subsidized by the public. After these developments predictably attracted more aggressive and less principled financiers who used the deposits as personal slush funds and gambling stakes, the government continued to forbear for fear of aggravating its short-term fiscal problems or offending influential constituents.

Although the critique these authors make of public policies toward the industry is largely plausible, their arguments about responsibility seem unconvincing in several respects. Macey and Miller and especially Fischel decry the conclusory, moralistic denunciation of Kaye Scholer and others by the press and politicians as mindless demagoguery; yet their own discussions are full of conclusory moralistic denunciations of public officials. They provide no substantiation for their assertion that the "real reason" OTS prosecuted Kaye Scholer was that, in Macey's and Miller's words, "it needed a convenient scapegoat that it could confront in a dramatic gesture designed to help it regain prestige" (1993, 1138; for nearly identical language, see Fischel 1995, 232).

The logic of the charge is far from self-evident. In 1989 Congress came to share these critics' judgment of the Bank Board and responded by abolishing it. The OTS was a new agency with a strong interest, not in vindicating its predecessor, but in distancing itself from it. Neither of the men most responsible for the prosecution, OTS director Timothy Ryan and General Counsel Harris Weinstein (who are not identified in the Fischel and Macey-Miller accounts), were connected to the Bank Board. Both were scions of the establishment corporate bar who could have anticipated that they would take a good deal of grief for their effort, which of course they did.

Macey and Miller also repeat allegations that banking officials were corrupt without substantiation (1993, 1136). In one of many hyperbolic excesses, Fischel treats the S&L crisis as an epiphenomenon of what his title calls a "conspiracy to destroy Michael Milken," but the book provides not a word of evidence or analysis to substantiate anything that a lawyer should call a conspiracy.

The force of Fischel's moral indictment depends heavily on a literary trope that he shares with Macey and Miller. When he discusses the popularly designated private-sector villains of the S&L affair, Fischel identifies them by name, often gives personal information about them, often describes their activities in detail, and analyzes the charges against them in a rather skeptical legalistic manner. In doing so, he creates a receptive setting for the rules-weren't-clear, everybody-was-doing-it, and harmless-error excuses, which he often invokes on their behalf.

On the other hand, when he discusses his own villain—the "government"—he usually paints it as a faceless monolith. He describes broad policies and nefarious motives, but the policies and motives are usually attributed to an abstraction rather than to particular people and conduct.

* * *

IV. CONCLUSION

We do not know enough about the facts to pass confident judgment on Kaye Scholer's performance in the Lincoln case, but most of the OTS charges seem facially well grounded. We are in a better position to assess the bar's response to Kaye Scholer's performance in the Lincoln case, and the only plausible judgment is condemnation. If only because of the magnitude of the stakes in the S&L crisis and Lincoln in particular, investigation and assessment of the OTS charges should have been a high priority. Even more important, the case was an occasion for clarifying substantive ambiguity about lawyers' duties of candor in banking and other contexts. Finally, the case strikingly raised issues about individual lawyer responsibility in situations of broad institutional breakdown. The bar failed to meet these challenges, and indeed spent considerable energy and ingenuity in evading them. Its performance has intensified the ambiguity about the relevant standards of professional responsibility and fueled doubts about its capacity for self-regulation.

Hostility to Whistle-Blowers
Is Cited in A-Plant Problems

George Judson, *The New York Times*, August 8, 1996,
Metropolitan Desk, Section B, p. 7*

WATERFORD, Conn., Aug. 7 Northeast Utilities's hostility toward employees who raised safety concerns at its Millstone Point nuclear plants contributed to the breakdown in standards that eventually led to their shutdown by the Nuclear Regulatory Commission, a commission panel reported today.

"Top management historically condoned a hostile work environment" toward whistle-blowers, John N. Hannon, the head of the panel, which is reviewing the utility's dealings with employees, told the utility's executives at a public meeting at Millstone Point.

The hostility was so longstanding, he said, that Northeast Utilities must now not only repair the effects of years of lax maintenance and procedures, but restore the trust that a nuclear plant operator must have from its employees and the public.

Just as the utility must prove to the commission that all of its safety features and procedures meet high standards before it can restart the plants, panel members said today, it must demonstrate that it has resolved management's "longstanding cultural problems" in dealing with employees. The panel's report will be considered by the commission when the company applies for permission to restart the reactors.

"Historically, Northeast Utilities management has not been supportive of employees' raising safety concerns," Mr. Hannon said, reporting his panel's conclusions after studying nine whistle-blower cases and interviewing more than 40 people. "Many employees said they do not trust the recent management shake-up, because they say it's a shuffle of the same people."

The utility's chief nuclear officer, Ted C. Feigenbaum, responded today that the utility was already addressing many of the problems identified by the panel. The number of cases that resulted in whistle-blower disputes, he said, "is a small percentage of the total number of problems that do get resolved."

Few of the issues swirling around the commission's shutdown of the Millstone plants, once considered among the best in the country, have been more emotional than the company's treatment of employees who came forward with safety concerns.

To many residents and Millstone employees, the whistle-blowers have become heroes, and the Nuclear Regulatory Commission has become a villain for not listening to them sooner. When the public was allowed to comment today, nearly as many people called for the resignation of commission officials as demanded the dismissal of Northeast Utilities's top executives.

"These people have not done their jobs," Gary Verdone, who was Millstone's site maintenance supervisor until he and 103 other employees were laid off in January, said of the utility's executives.

Mr. Hannon faulted his own agency, too, for contributing to the distrust of Northeast Utilities among employees and the public.

The panel, he said, had found several areas where the agency had not shown sensitivity to whistle-blowers who brought their allegations to it, had failed to recognize the hostile environment at Millstone, and had failed to enforce its own regulations.

As late as 1993, Mr. Hannon said, "the N.R.C. may have underreacted to Northeast Utilities's continued denial of discrimination or a hostile environment."

The Millstone Nuclear Power Station in Waterford, Connecticut, 1990. © Roger Ressmeyer/CORBIS.

Lawyers as Gatekeepers

Fred Zacharias,* 41 *San Diego Law Review* 1387 (2004)

Three recent legislative and regulatory proposals seek to enlist lawyers in thwarting crime.[1] Outraged opponents have relied on flamboyant rhetoric.[2] They challenge the

---

* Herzog Research Professor of Law, University of San Diego School of Law; LL.M. 1981, Georgetown University; J.D. 1977, Yale University; B.A. 1974, Johns Hopkins University. [This article reproduced with the kind permission of Professor Zacharias and the *San Diego Law Review.*]

1. These proposals are in varying stages of existence. The American Bar Association (ABA) recently adopted an amendment to its model rule on confidentiality that would allow lawyers to disclose information "to prevent the client from committing a crime or fraud that is reasonably certain to result in substantial injury to the financial interests or property of another and in furtherance of which the client has used or is using the lawyer's services." *ABA Amends Ethics Rules on Confidentiality, Corporate Clients, to Allow More Disclosures*, 19 ABA/BNA Law. Manual Prof'l Conduct 467, 467 (2003) [hereinafter *ABA Amends Ethics Rules*] (reporting the adoption of Model Rule 1.6(b)(2)). The ABA adopted a parallel provision allowing lawyers to disclose to "prevent, mitigate or rectify substantial injury" caused by the prohibited conduct in the past. *Id.* (reporting the adoption of Model Rule 1.6(b)(3)). States have yet to respond to the new model rules, which are, in effect, proposals for state action.

In 2002, Congress required the Securities and Exchange Commission (SEC) to promulgate some regulations governing securities lawyers. Sarbanes-Oxley Act of 2002, Pub. L. No. 107-204, § 307, 116 Stat. 745, 784 ("[T]he Commission shall issue rules ... setting forth minimum standards of professional conduct for attorneys appearing and practicing before the Commission."). In response, the SEC adopted rules that require securities lawyers who become aware of "credible evidence" that a client is violating a federal or state securities law or is materially breaching a fiduciary duty arising under federal or state law to report the matter to the chief legal officer, the chief executive, or to a legal compliance committee, and ultimately to take further steps. 17 C.F.R. §§ 205.1(b)(2), (e), 205.3(b) (2003) [hereinafter SEC Final Rule]. The SEC proposed, but held in abeyance pending further comment, a rule that would require attorneys who have gone up the ladder within a corporation and who still "believe that the reported material violation is ongoing or is about to occur and is likely to result in substantial injury to the financial interest of the issuer or of investors ... to withdraw from the representation, notify the Commission of their withdrawal, and disaffirm any submission to the Commission that they have participated in preparing which is tainted by the violation." Implementation of Standards of Professional Conduct for Attorneys, 67 Fed. Reg. 71,674 (proposed Dec. 2, 2002) [hereinafter Proposed Rule]; *see* Implementation of Standards of Professional Conduct for Attorneys, 68 Fed. Reg. 6296 (Feb. 6, 2003) [hereinafter Final Rule Discussion Section] (noting deferral of implementation and stating "[w]e are still considering the 'noisy withdrawal' provisions of our original proposal under section 307"). *See generally* Roger C. Cramton et al., *Legal and Ethical Duties of Lawyers After Sarbanes-Oxley*, 49 Vill. L. Rev. 725 (2004) (analyzing in comprehensive fashion the Sarbanes-Oxley controversy).

The ABA's most recent revisions to the Model Rules includes a revised Model Rule 1.13, discussed *infra* notes 58 & 87, that parallels the adopted and proposed SEC regulations. Revised Model Rule 1.13(c) is a permissive provision that would allow organizational lawyers who have gone up the ladder to disclose information, but only when disclosure is necessary to prevent "'substantial injury' to the organization." *ABA Amends Ethics Rules, supra*, at 468.

Finally, an international task force is considering a range of proposals that would, in some form, enlist the help of lawyers in reporting client money laundering and other unlawful activity. *See* authorities cited *infra* note 94. American agencies have postponed their own consideration of regulations to the same effect pending the task force's report.

2. *See, e.g.,* Jonathan Peterson, *SEC Wants Attorneys to Stand Up to Companies' Misconduct*, L.A. Times, May 19, 2003, at C1 ("Critics are using such terms as 'orwellian' to describe the [Sarbanes-Oxley] proposal."); Seth Stern, *... And Attorneys Face New Rules on Secrets*, Christian Sci. Monitor, Aug. 13, 2003, at 2 (quoting William Paul, former ABA President, as stating that the recently adopted ABA rules paralleling the Sarbanes-Oxley proposals are "bartering away a piece of our professional soul to gain some hoped-for public approval"); *ABA Amends Ethics Rules, supra* note 1, at 469 (quoting Lawrence Fox's claim that proposed rules requiring a corporate lawyer to respond to client misconduct make the lawyer an "*uberdirector*"); *id.* (quoting Judah Best's characterization of the pro-

notion that lawyers should act as gatekeepers[3]—which some of the opponents deem equivalent to operating like the "secret police in Eastern European countries."[4]

This article makes a simple, and ultimately uncontroversial, point.[5] Lawyers are gatekeepers and always have been. Whatever one's position on the merits of the specific reforms currently being proposed, it is important to avoid the misconception that lawyers have no role to play in preventing client misconduct.

At its root, the gatekeeper rhetoric conflates several separate concepts. At one level, everyone will agree that lawyers are clients' agents and that lawyers' traditional role in the adversary system is to help clients pursue lawful goals through those lawful means that are available. That, however, is quite different from saying that lawyers should do whatever clients want, that lawyers should assist clients in achieving illegal pursuits, or that lawyers have no business shaping client ends.

Let us consider, as a starting point, the famous statement of Elihu Root that "half of the practice of a decent lawyer consists in telling would-be clients that they are damned fools and should stop."[6] We should remember that Root, among his other accomplishments, was a high-powered attorney noted for representing notorious corporate and

---

posed 1.13(c) as "utterly wicked"); *ABA Update of Model Ethics Rules All But Completed in Philadelphia*, 18 ABA/BNA Law. Manual Prof'l Conduct 99, 101 (2002) ("Stephen A. Saltzburg ... told the delegates that the 'gatekeeper initiative' is the 'single most alarming threat to the attorney-client privilege to be seen in a long time.'"); *cf.* W. Bradley Wendel, *How I Learned to Stop Worrying and Love Lawyer-Bashing: Some Post-Conference Reflections*, 54 S.C. L. Rev. 1027, 1044 (2003) ("Debevoise & Plimpton worried that 'the [SEC] would be using the attorney as the Commission's eyes and ears to build a case against the client.'").

3. Howard Stock, *S-O's Lawyer Rule May Chill Information Flow*, Investor Rel. Bus., Aug. 18, 2003 (quoting Professor Jill Fisch to the effect that "[t]here are plenty of watchdogs already in place, and lawyers are poorly positioned to be gatekeepers"); David E. Rovella, *Going from Bad to Worse: Defense Bar Fears Jail over Tainted Fees*, Nat'l L.J., Mar. 11, 2002, at A1 (quoting practitioners who argue that efforts "to make lawyers 'gatekeepers' of the financial system may further impede the ability of criminal defense lawyers to properly represent their clients"); *cf. Corporate Counsel Critique SEC Proposal On Lawyer Reporting Mandated by New Law*, 18 ABA/BNA Law. Manual Prof'l Conduct 698, 698 (2002) (reporting the criticism that, in close cases, the Sarbanes-Oxley regulations put attorneys "in the role of judge rather than advocate").

4. *Programs Explore Concern that Government is 'Federalizing' Professional Ethics Rules*, 19 ABA/BNA Law. Manual Prof'l Conduct 320, 322 (2003) [hereinafter *Programs Explore Concern*] (quoting comment regarding the proposed gatekeeper initiative "Doesn't that conjure up a sort of East German notion of reporting all 'suspicious' behavior?"); *see also* Bruce Moyer, *The Dawn of Federal Regulation of Attorney Conduct?*, 50 Fed. Law. 5, 5 (2003) ("Corporate law firms and bar associations had levied a barrage of criticism at the SEC's proposed 'noisy withdrawal' rule, saying it threatened to turn lawyers into a police force."); Wendel, *supra* note 2, at 1044 ("Sullivan and Cromwell resists the [SEC's alleged] requirement that lawyers 'police and pass judgment on their clients.'"); *ABA Amends Ethics Rules, supra* note 1, at 467 ("[William Paul] charged that the [proposed Model Rule] changes threaten to turn lawyers into 'policemen, prosecutors, judges, and regulators.'"); *cf.* John C. Elam, *Lawyers Shouldn't Be Police Agents: ABA Must Preserve Client Confidentiality*, Nat'l L.J., Aug. 1, 1983, at 37 ("[A]n attorney should ... not be cast in the role of policeman or watchman over his client.").

5. Indeed, the point may be so uncontroversial that some readers will perceive the article as erecting and knocking down a strawman. The notion that lawyers sometimes must intervene in client misconduct, particularly in transactional representation, hardly requires support. *See, e.g.*, Rutherford B. Campbell, Jr. & Eugene B. Gaetke, *The Ethical Obligation of Transactional Lawyers to Act as Gatekeepers*, 56 Rutgers L. Rev. 9, 14 (2004) (proposing steps "to invigorate the transactional lawyer's role as gatekeeper further"). Nevertheless, misuse of the term "gatekeeper" and the heated rhetoric surrounding the recent reform proposals have tended to muddy the waters. These developments justify reiteration and clarification of lawyers' traditional gatekeeping role.

6. 1 Philip C. Jessup, Elihu Root 133 (1938).

political clients.[7] One biographer has characterized Root's practice as "tempered by a failure to regard the law as a living organism and by a reluctance to look beyond its letter to its implications for society as a whole."[8] In one famous case, Root and his co-counsel were nearly held in contempt for representing a corrupt politician and were lectured by the presiding judge as follows:

> I ask you young gentlemen, to remember that good faith to a client never can justify or require bad faith to your own consciences, and that however good a thing it may be, to be known as successful and great lawyers, it is even a better thing, to be known as honest men.[9]

Root, to his death, protested the importance of aggressive advocacy. In a speech to graduates of Columbia Law School, he stated: "One obligation I want to impress upon you.... You must support the law even when in particular cases its justice seems doubtful. The inviolability of constitutional and statutory rights is more valuable than the punishment of any one criminal."[10] Given this commitment to partisanship, what did Root mean when emphasizing the duty to stand in the way of client conduct and how did he anticipate that lawyers should accomplish the half of their practice that consists of telling their clients "no"?

There are four broad aspects of lawyers' traditional role that necessarily involve lawyers in regulating client conduct. Each will be discussed below. Categorized broadly, the lawyer functions that might require a lawyer to seek to prevent client behavior include: (1) advising clients, (2) screening cases and legal arguments, (3) avoiding personal participation in improper behavior, and (4) disclosing confidences, when permitted by rule, to serve interests that trump the client's.

I. The Advising Function

Lawyers' alliance with clients and lawyers' duty to serve client interests do not require lawyers either to agree with client aims[11] or to assume that clients always wish to maximize their own economic interests.[12] Thomas Shaffer[13] and others[14] have written that

---

7. *See* Richard W. Leopold, Elihu Root and the Conservative Tradition 12, 14–18 (Oscar Handlin ed., 1954) (discussing Root's participation in defending Boss Tweed and noting that this "did brand Root for all time as the defender of a corrupt boss and persuaded many persons that he would accept anyone as a client").

8. *Id.* at 19.

9. 1 Jessup, *supra* note 6, at 88.

10. *Id.* at 93.

11. Model Rules of Prof'l Conduct R. 1.2(b) (2002) [hereinafter Model Rules] ("A lawyer's representation of a client ... does not constitute an endorsement of the client's political, economic, social or moral views or activities."). Citations throughout this Article are to the new version of the Model Rules adopted in 2002. References to provisions that were subsequently amended are specifically identified.

12. *See* Fred C. Zacharias, *Reconciling Professionalism and Client Interests*, 36 Wm. & Mary L. Rev. 1303, 1341 (1995) (questioning the practice of lawyers who "assume that their sole mission is to maximize the clients' chances of obtaining their desired results"); *see also* Robert L. Nelson, *Ideology, Practice, and Professional Autonomy: Social Values and Client Relationships in the Large Law Firm*, 37 Stan. L. Rev. 503, 504–05, 538 (1985) (finding that lawyers in large law firms enthusiastically seek the maximization of client interests without attempting to discuss the goals first); William H. Simon, *The Ideology of Advocacy: Procedural Justice and Professional Ethics*, 1978 Wis. L. Rev. 29, 30 (discussing the framework from which lawyers approach client counseling).

13. *E.g.*, Thomas L. Shaffer, *Legal Ethics and the Good Client*, 36 Cath. U. L. Rev. 319, 328 (1987); Thomas L. Shaffer, *The Practice of Law as Moral Discourse*, 55 Notre Dame Law. 231 (1979).

14. *See, e.g.*, Stephen L. Pepper, *The Lawyer's Amoral Ethical Role: A Defense, A Problem, and Some Possibilities*, 1986 Am. B. Found. Res. J. 613, 630–32 (discussing the importance of moral dis-

lawyers have both a right and an obligation to engage in a moral dialogue with their clients.[15] At a minimum, lawyers owe clients information, including information that suggests that the clients' proposed or completed conduct is criminal (or wrongful in other respects).[16] Especially when a client may initially be uninformed, lawyers owe it to the client to identify and explain all the ramifications of particular behavior, including the moral consequences for the client and the effects of the behavior on third persons who may subsequently blame the client.[17] Many professional codes make the duty to keep clients informed explicit.[18] Presumably, the option of acting ethically is one that a client might wish to consider.[19]

The spirit of the codes goes further, however—encouraging lawyers to express their own moral positions[20] and to attempt to persuade clients to act well.[21] One of the traditional justifications for strict attorney-client confidentiality and privilege is that the guarantee of secrecy enhances a lawyer's ability to learn what the client plans to do and facilitates the lawyer's task of encouraging law compliance.[22] Other aspects of the codes emphasize the importance of lawyers maintaining independent judgment[23] and avoiding giving any assistance to illegal and fraudulent client conduct.[24] The essence of these provisions is that lawyers should not act simply as clients' alter egos. Lawyer independence can help serve client interests, but it comes freighted with personal moral responsibility that lawyers must exercise within the confines of the rules governing confidentiality and loyalty.[25]

---

course for lawyers who emphasize client autonomy in decisionmaking); Zacharias, *supra* note 12, at 1357–62 (discussing the possibility of codifying a duty to engage in a moral discourse with clients).

15. Even Monroe Freedman, the strongest proponent of partisan lawyering, acknowledges the importance of discussing objectives with clients. *See* Monroe H. Freedman, *Personal Responsibility in a Professional System*, 27 Cath. U. L. Rev. 191, 200 (1977) (warning lawyers against "assum[ing] the worst regarding the client's desires"); Monroe H. Freedman, *Professional Responsibility of the Criminal Defense Lawyer: The Three Hardest Questions*, 64 Mich. L. Rev. 1469, 1478 (1966) (arguing that lawyers have a duty to remonstrate with clients who wish to commit perjury).

16. The client must know this information at least in order to make informed judgments regarding whether pursuing the objective is worth the potential consequences.

17. A lawyer who fails to do so ultimately may subject the client to reactions that disadvantage the client and that the client did not anticipate.

18. *See, e.g.*, Model Rules, *supra* note 11, R. 1.4 (requiring communication with clients).

19. *See* Robert F. Cochran, Jr. et al., *Symposium: Client Counseling and Moral Responsibility*, 30 Pepp. L. Rev. 591, 608 (2003) ("Survey evidence suggests that lawyers significantly underestimate the extent to which clients would welcome non-legal advice.").

20. Many jurisdictions follow Model Rules, *supra* note 11, R. 1.7(a)(2), which requires a lawyer to obtain a conflict waiver when her representation might be limited "by a personal interest of the lawyer," including her moral interests.

21. For example, Model Rules, *supra* note 11, R. 2.1 provides: "In representing a client, a lawyer shall exercise independent professional judgment and render candid advice. In rendering advice, a lawyer may refer not only to law but to other considerations such as moral, economic, social and political factors, that may be relevant to the client's situation."

22. *See* Upjohn Co. v. United States, 449 U.S. 383, 392 (1981) (justifying attorney-client privilege by reference to the need to facilitate lawyers' ability to promote law compliance by clients).

23. *E.g.*, Model Rules, *supra* note 11, R. 2.1.

24. *E.g.*, Model Rules, *supra* note 11, R. 1.2(d) & cmt.

25. *Cf.* Cochran, Jr. et al., *supra* note 19, at 608 ("As officers of the court and gatekeepers in imperfect regulatory processes, lawyers have obligations that transcend those owed to any particular client.... [N]either legal nor market systems can function effectively if lawyers lack a basic sense of social responsibility for the consequences of their professional acts.").

One recent case suggests that a lawyer's responsibility to counteract client misconduct has legal ramifications as well. Traditionally, the crime-fraud exception to attorney-client privilege has been interpreted to mean that client communications are unprivileged when uttered for the purpose of involving, or using, the attorney in committing a crime or fraud.[26] In In re *Public Defender Service*, the District of Columbia Court of Appeals held that the crime-fraud exception applies only when a lawyer has been unsuccessful in dissuading the client from committing the intended misconduct.[27] In other words, by exercising the gatekeeping function of dissuasion, the lawyer can retroactively convert potentially damaging discoverable statements into privileged communications. Consider the ramifications of the court's conception: if the court's analysis is correct, lawyers in these circumstances arguably have a professional *obligation* to dissuade, rooted in competency requirements, because that is the only way to maintain the client's legal rights.[28]

To be clear, let me neither understate nor overstate my position. There is a hard question; namely, the extent to which lawyers should investigate clients' motives and conduct in an effort to uncover illegality that they should counteract. Robert Gordon recently has written a forceful argument that lawyers' conscious efforts to avoid learning the true facts are what made lawyers complicit in the Enron scandal.[29] The effect that an investigative role might have on the lawyer-client relationship underlies the legitimate controversy surrounding the Gatekeeper Initiative, which may ultimately require lawyers to investigate or report suspicious client activity.[30] I focus here, however, on the simpler question of whether lawyers have any gatekeeper role to play.

The lawyer's role, and all of the lawyer's professional obligations, should be read against the backdrop of agency law. As clients' employees and agents, lawyers have significant responsibility to serve their masters.[31] Yet agency law also sets boundaries, recognizing limitations concerning what agents must do for their masters and authorizing agents to react to superior third party interests.[32] The lawyer codes fine tune agency law for the special functions lawyers serve, but the codes do not change the underlying axiom: principals are not entitled to the help of their agents in committing wrongs, and agents' personal moral responsibility is not extinguished by virtue of their agency status.

---

26. *See, e.g.*, Cal. Evid. Code § 956 (West 1995) ("There is no privilege … if the services of the lawyer were … obtained to enable or aid anyone to commit or plan to commit a crime or a fraud.").

27. 831 A.2d. 890, 902 (D.C. Cir. 2003) ("[A]n ill-motivated client communication that 'goes nowhere'—as where the client consults an attorney with an evil purpose but the attorney quashes the venture …—is not sufficiently in furtherance of a crime or fraud to fall within the crime-fraud exception.").

28. *Cf. id.* at 901 ("[T]he attorney-client privilege encourages clients to make … unguarded and ill-advised suggestions to their lawyers. The lawyer *is then obliged, in the interests of justice and the client's own long-term best interests*, to urge the client … to abandon illegal conduct or plans.") (emphasis added).

29. Robert W. Gordon, *A New Role for Lawyers?: The Corporate Counselor After Enron*, 35 Conn. L. Rev. 1185, 1199–200 (2003); *cf.* Kenneth Mann, Defending White Collar Crime: A Portrait of Attorneys at Work 17, 103–05 (1985) (discussing the conscious practice of criminal defense lawyers of avoiding learning the actual facts).

30. *See infra* text accompanying notes 94–96.

31. *See* Restatement (Third) of Agency § 1.01 cmt. e (Tentative Draft No. 2, 2001) ("[A]n agent must act in the principal's interest as well as on the principal's behalf.").

32. Restatement (Second) of Agency § 395 cmt. f (1958) ("An agent is privileged to reveal information confidentially acquired by him in the course of his agency in the protection of a superior interest of himself or of a third person.").

II. The Screening Function

Lawyers serve most clearly as gatekeepers in screening the legal claims clients make.[33] There are various aspects to the screening function, all of which have been recognized explicitly in the professional codes or other law.

Lawyers must, for example, screen the filings clients make before courts[34] and administrative agencies.[35] If they do not, the lawyers themselves are subject to sanction. Sanctions can take the form of personal civil liability,[36] discipline,[37] or fines.[38]

Post-filing, tribunals continue to rely upon lawyers to screen client arguments, perceiving that to be an essential aspect of efficient judicial administration. At the simplest level, lawyers may not take frivolous positions.[39] But the dependence on lawyers as gatekeepers goes further. Rules like Rule 11 of the Federal Rules of Civil Procedure anticipate that lawyers should also prevent clients from filing nonfrivolous claims for an improper purpose.[40] Courts expect lawyers to cull the arguments clients wish them to pursue, in deference to the need for judicial efficiency in responding to the arguments.[41] And the professional codes impose candor to tribunal regulations that sometimes re-

---

33. Lawyers, of course, screen client claims for a variety of reasons, some of which rest on economic self-interest and some of which rest on their obligation to exercise independent judgment. *Cf.* Teresa Stanton Collett, *The Common Good and the Duty to Represent: Must the Last Lawyer in Town Take Any Case?*, 40 S. Tex. L. Rev. 137, 171–72 (1999) (arguing that a lawyer may reject a case for moral and political reasons even if he is the "last lawyer in town"); Herbert M. Kritzer, *Contingency Fee Lawyers as Gatekeepers in the Civil Justice System*, 81 Judicature 22, 26, 29 (1997) ("[C]ontingency fee lawyers generally turn down at least as many cases as they accept, ... most often because those potential clients do not have a basis for the case.").

34. *See, e.g.*, Fed. R. Civ. P. 11(b) ("By presenting to the court ... a pleading, written motion, or other paper, an attorney ... is certifying that ... (1) it is not being presented for any improper purpose, ... (2) the claims, defenses, and other legal contentions therein are warranted by existing law ... (3) the allegations and other factual contentions have evidentiary support or ... are likely to have evidentiary support ... and (4) the denials of factual contentions are warranted on the evidence or ... are reasonably based on a lack of information or belief."); *see also* Evan A. Davis, *The Meaning of Professional Independence*, 103 Colum. L. Rev. 1281, 1283 (2003) ("Even a litigator is a gatekeeper who typically makes a representation of due inquiry and colorable merit when he or she signs a pleading.").

35. Some of the federal regulations requiring lawyers to screen positions taken before agencies are collected and discussed in Fred C. Zacharias, *Understanding Recent Trends in Federal Regulation of Lawyers*, 2003 Symp. Issue Prof'l Lawyer (forthcoming 2004) (on file with author).

36. The SEC has always treated attorneys who participate in the preparation of documents that violate federal securities laws as aiders and abettors. *E.g.*, SEC v. Nat'l Student Mktg. Corp., 457 F. Supp. 682, 715 (D. D.C. 1978); *cf.* Cent. Bank v. First Interstate Bank, 511 U.S. 164, 191 (1994) (holding attorneys civilly liable under Rule 10b-5 when they are "primary" violators of the rule). In the notorious *Kaye, Scholer* case, the Office of Thrift Supervision imposed financial liability upon attorneys, establishing its position that lawyers who file documents as agents for clients assume the clients' reporting obligations. *See* Zacharias, *supra* note 35. Other federal agencies have followed suit. *See id.*

37. *See, e.g.*, *In re* Scott, 4 Cal. St. B. Ct. Rptr. 446 (2002) (suspending attorney for filing a frivolous lawsuit); *cf.* Model Rules, *supra* note 11, R. 3.1 (forbidding lawyers from asserting frivolous positions).

38. *See, e.g.*, Fed. R. Civ. P. 11(c)(2) (authorizing monetary penalties for violations of Rule 11).

39. Model Rules, *supra* note 11, R. 3.1.

40. Fed. R. Civ. P. 11(b)(1) (prohibiting filing court documents "presented for any improper purpose").

41. *See, e.g.*, Jones v. Barnes, 463 U.S. 745, 746 (1983) (noting the importance of allowing lawyers to "winnow" the arguments made to the court, even when the client disagrees).

quire lawyers to disclose information that clients want to keep secret.[42] In some instances, the lawyer must turn on the client directly in order to preserve interests that society has deemed more important than the client's interests.[43]

III. The Personal Separation Function

There are both broad and narrow legal principles that impose on lawyers the obligation to separate themselves from unlawful or fraudulent client activity. In doing so, lawyers influence client conduct. The lawyer's refusal to take a particular action on a client's behalf, such as filing a fraudulent claim, can effectively prevent the client from succeeding in the action. The lawyer's threat of withdrawal, or actual withdrawal, may be enough to prevent the client from pursuing his plan.[44] In some instances, the lawyer's ability to disavow actions that she[45] has taken or documents that she has prepared is tantamount to allowing the lawyer to disclose a client's wrongdoing.

The professional codes do not mince words. Lawyers may not engage in dishonest behavior.[46] More specifically, they may not participate in or assist illegal conduct[47]—and the ABA has interpreted the term "assist" very broadly.[48] To the extent the client insists upon a lawyer's participation in forbidden conduct, the lawyer must withdraw.[49] After withdrawing, she may also disavow documents that reflect her unwitting complicity in improper actions.[50]

The professional codes are only the tip of the iceberg. Criminal laws apply to lawyers as well.[51] Lawyers may not conspire with clients,[52] aid or abet illegal conduct,[53] or participate directly in client crimes or frauds.[54] Moreover, fees they receive that are a product

---

42. *E.g.*, Model Rules, *supra* note 11, R. 3.3(a).

43. *E.g.*, Model Rules, *supra* note 11, R. 3.3(b).

44. *See* Reinier H. Kraakman, *Gatekeepers: The Anatomy of a Third-Party Enforcement Strategy*, 2 J. L., Econ., & Org. 53 (1986) (considering whether liability should be imposed on lawyers for failing to "disrupt misconduct by withholding their cooperation from wrongdoers").

45. To avoid confusion, this essay refers to lawyers as female and to other actors in the system as male.

46. Model Rules, *supra* note 11, R. 8.4(c) (forbidding "conduct involving dishonesty").

47. *Id*. R. 1.2(d).

48. ABA Comm. on Ethics and Prof'l Responsibility, Formal Op. 87-353 (1987) (interpreting the term "assisting" broadly to include more than "criminal law concepts of aiding and abetting or subornation"); *see also* ABA Comm. on Ethics and Prof'l Responsibility, Formal Op. 93-376 (1993) (reaffirming Formal Op. 87-353's broad interpretation of "assisting").

49. Model Rules, *supra* note 11, R. 1.16(a)(1).

50. *Id.* R. 1.6 cmt.

51. *See, e.g.*, Bruce A. Green, *The Criminal Regulation of Lawyers*, 67 Fordham L. Rev. 327, 330–52 (1998) (discussing the interaction of criminal law and professional regulation); Charles W. Wolfram, *Lawyer Crimes: Beyond the Law?*, 36 Val. U. L. Rev. 73, 79–91 (2001) (analyzing the notion that lawyers' professional activities are "beyond the law"); Zacharias, *supra* note 35 (noting that lawyers have always been subject to criminal prosecution for criminal acts related to their practice).

52. *See, e.g.*, United States v. Cueto, 151 F.3d 620 (7th Cir. 1998) (upholding a lawyer's conviction for conspiracy to defraud the government); United States v. Enstam, 622 F.2d 857 (5th Cir. 1980) (upholding a lawyer's conviction for conspiracy to defraud the government by impairing the collection of taxes).

53. *See, e.g.*, United States v. Kaplan, 832 F.2d 676 (1st Cir. 1987) (upholding a conviction for aiding and abetting mail fraud); United States v. Arrington, 719 F.2d 701 (4th Cir. 1983) (upholding a lawyer's conviction for aiding and abetting a conspiracy to receive and sell stolen property).

54. *See, e.g.*, United States v. Feaster, No. 87-1340, 1988 WL 33814 (6th Cir. Apr. 15, 1988) (unpublished opinion) (upholding a conviction of a lawyer for participating in the preparation of false tax returns); United States v. Cintolo, 818 F.2d 980 (1st Cir. 1987) (upholding a lawyer's conviction for obstruction of justice).

of illegal conduct may be subject to seizure.[55] Again, therefore, lawyers are required to make themselves aware of the nature of client conduct[56] and, by their reactions, play a significant role in shaping subsequent client behavior.

IV. The Direct Gatekeeper Function

In certain situations, the professional codes already impose upon lawyers the precise type of gatekeeper function that has proven so controversial in the recent reform proposals. Corporate and other organizational lawyers, for example, are required to "take remedial measures" upon learning of corporate illegality and certain other kinds of wrongdoing.[57] In most jurisdictions, the implementation of this obligation is subject to significant discretion on the part of the lawyer.[58] Unlike under some of the recent proposals,[59] a lawyer typically may not disclose corporate wrongdoing to authorities outside the organization.[60] But the implication nonetheless is clear: the lawyer does play a significant role in preventing client misconduct.[61]

More importantly, the general issue of whether a lawyer should have a direct gatekeeper role in preventing client misconduct is a red herring. The attorney-client privilege has always excluded client communications made for the purpose of involving a lawyer in a criminal or fraudulent enterprise.[62] All American jurisdictions recognize that society's need to prevent particular kinds of client conduct sometimes trumps the client's interests in confidentiality and his lawyer's loyalty.[63] All lawyer codes have confi-

---

55. *See, e.g.,* Comprehensive Forfeiture Act of 1984, 21 U.S.C. §853(a), (c) (1982 & Supp. IV 1986) (providing, *inter alia,* for the forfeiture to the U.S. of property derived from particular crimes and rendering transfers of such property to attorneys subject to seizure by the government); Caplin & Drysdale, Chartered v. United States, 491 U.S. 617, 623–35 (1989) (holding that the forfeiture of fees paid to an attorney was consistent with §853 of the Comprehensive Forfeiture Act of 1982 and was constitutional).

56. *See, e.g.,* United States v. Monsanto, 491 U.S. 600, 604 (1989) (rejecting the argument that attorneys who do not know a client's property is subject to forfeiture should be allowed to retain fees paid with forfeitable assets); United States v. Raimondo, 721 F.2d 476, 478 (4th Cir. 1983) (holding that an attorney should have known that his client's property and profits might be subject to forfeiture by virtue of the client's indictment).

57. *E.g.,* Model Rules, *supra* note 11, R. 1.13(b).

58. Under rules like Model Rule 1.13(b), lawyers are given a menu of possible actions that they can take. Some jurisdictions expand the menu, or make certain actions mandatory. *See, e.g.,* Md. Rules of Prof'l Conduct, R. 1.13(c) (2004) (allowing some disclosures of otherwise confidential information); Mich. Rules of Prof'l Conduct, R. 1.13(c) (2004) (allowing some disclosures); Minn. Rules of Prof'l Conduct, R. 1.13(c) (2004) (allowing disclosure of criminal conduct); N.J. Rules of Prof'l Conduct, R. 1.13(c) (2004) (providing that remedial action may, under some circumstances, include disclosure of confidential information).

59. *E.g.,* Proposed Rule, *supra* note 1.

60. *E.g.,* Model Rules, *supra* note 11, R. 1.13 cmt.; Cal. Rules of Prof'l Conduct, R. 3-600(B)(2) (2003). As stated in note 58 *supra,* a few jurisdictions do allow disclosure.

61. *See generally* Campbell & Gaetke, *supra* note 5 (discussing the gatekeeping role of transactional lawyers).

62. *See* Restatement of the Law Governing Lawyers § 82 (2000) (identifying the crime-fraud exception to attorney client privilege).

63. *See* Charles W. Wolfram, Modern Legal Ethics § 6.7.3 at 301 (1986) ("[T]he normal expectation of lawyer loyalty to a client's interests is hardly an absolute. It does not purport to be a reason why a lawyer must always maintain silence regardless of the claims and interests of third persons."); Fred C. Zacharias, *Limits on Client Autonomy in Legal Ethics Regulation,* 81 B.U. L. Rev. 199, 211 (2001) (discussing "'social compact rules,' under which third party or societal interests simply trump client autonomy").

dentiality exceptions[64]—some discretionary,[65] some mandatory.[66] In either event, the differences among the code provisions are only a matter of degree. They do not vary on the question of whether a lawyer may ever disclose client misconduct, but simply distinguish among the situations in which disclosure is appropriate.

V. The Recent Criticisms and the Modern Reforms

The observations above illustrate that the modern critics are wrong in the rhetoric they have selected. Requiring lawyers to respond to client misconduct is not automatically equivalent to enlisting lawyers as secret police.[67] Indeed, the lawyer's role has always included a substantial gatekeeper aspect.[68]

Older conceptions of professionalism probably envisioned greater involvement by lawyers in preventing client wrongdoing[69] than the partisan conceptions that developed in the 1970s.[70] But even the latter, and their developed forms that are encapsulated in modern professional codes, had lawyer gatekeeping in mind. The modern tradition of ultra-partisan criminal defense lawyering may encourage lawyers to think of their relationship with clients primarily in terms of an alliance. Yet, upon reflection, even the most active partisan advocates should be willing to concede that the alliance has limits.[71]

---

64. Until recently, California's confidentiality provision seemed to be absolute. Cal. Bus. & Prof. Code §6068(e) (West 2003); *see* San Diego County Bar Ass'n Legal Ethics and Unlawful Practices Comm., Op. 1990-1, at 3 (1990) *available at* http://www.sdcba.org/ethics/ethicsopinion90-1.html (interpreting §6068(e) as being absolute). *See generally* Fred C. Zacharias, *Privilege and Confidentiality in California*, 28 U.C. Davis L. Rev. 367 (1994) (analyzing the status of confidentiality and privilege in California). The provision was recently amended, however, to include a future crime exception roughly similar to the one in the pre-2003 Model Rules. *See* A.B. 1101, 2003–04 Leg., Reg. Sess. (Cal. 2003) (amending §6068(e) of California's Business and Professions Code to allow an attorney to "reveal confidential information to the extent that the attorney reasonably believes disclosure is necessary to prevent a criminal act likely to result in death or substantial bodily harm to an individual") (effective July 1, 2004).

65. *E.g.*, Model Rules, *supra* note 11, R. 1.6(b) (allowing certain disclosures); Model Code of Prof'l Responsibility, DR 4-101(C)(3) (1969) (allowing disclosure of client's intent to commit a future crime or fraud) [hereinafter Model Code].

66. *E.g.*, Fla. Rules of Court, R. 4-1.6(b) (2003) (requiring the disclosure of information necessary to prevent a crime or serious bodily harm); Ill. Court Rules & Proc., R. 1.6(b) (2003) (requiring disclosure to prevent certain harms); N.J. Rules of Court, R. 1.6(b) (2004) (requiring disclosure to prevent certain criminal and fraudulent acts).

67. *See supra* text accompanying note 4.

68. For an interesting discussion of the constraints upon lawyers in exercising their gatekeeper role with respect to "strategic litigation" by clients, *see generally* Ronald J. Gilson, *The Devolution of the Legal Profession: A Demand Side Perspective*, 49 Md. L. Rev. 869, 885 (1990).

69. *See* Susan D. Carle, *Lawyers' Duty to Do Justice: A New Look at the History of the 1908 Canons*, 24 L. & Soc. Inquiry 1, 10–12 (1999) (characterizing David Hoffman's 1836 "Resolutions for Professional Deportment" as being based, in part, on the notion that a lawyer should act as a "gatekeeper"); Gordon, *supra* note 29, at 1208–09 (citing the 1908 ABA Canons for the proposition that a lawyer must "observe and advise his client[s] to [follow] the … law" and discussing conceptions of the corporate lawyer as a "wise-counselor-lawyer-statesman" that endured until the 1970s); Russell G. Pearce, *Rediscovering the Republican Origins of the Legal Ethics Codes*, 6 Geo. J. Legal Ethics 241, 241–42 (1992) (suggesting the limitations on partisanship in early American professional norms).

70. *See* Zacharias, *supra* note 12, at 1314–27 (discussing the evolution of partisanship in lawyering and the changing emphases on objectivity during different periods of American history) and authorities cited at 1319–20 nn.54–57.

71. *See supra* note 15; *see also* Davis, *supra* note 34, at 1283 (opposing recent reform proposals, but conceding that lawyers sometimes act as gatekeepers); *Lessons from Enron: A Symposium on Corporate Governance*, 54 Mercer L. Rev. 683, 719 (2003) ("Now, Sol said a couple of things that re-

Which brings us to the real, important question—one from which the modern rhetoric deflects attention. Assuming that lawyers sometimes have some role to play in shaping or responding to illegal or improper conduct, what is that role? More specifically, where on the spectrum of potential lawyer gatekeeping do the recently proposed reforms fall? Do they, in fact, require anything new or anything that is inconsistent with the essential attorney-client relationship that society should wish to protect?

To the extent criticism of the proposals is fair, it must fall in one of two categories. First, it may be that one or the other proposal simply goes too far in emphasizing the gatekeeping role. In other words, the proposals may weigh societal interests in disclosure or preventing client misconduct too heavily, or may shortchange the societal benefits achieved by safeguarding partisanship. The second possible criticism is related to the first. The proposals may undermine essential aspects of the lawyer-client relationship in a way that unduly interferes with the lawyer's ability to fulfill the functions that the adversarial system depends upon her to undertake and accomplish.

Consider, for example, the change to Model Rule 1.6 recently adopted by the ABA, based on a recommendation by the ABA Corporate Responsibility Task Force.[72] The new rule effectuates one significant change. It would *permit* lawyers whose services are being, or have been, used to perpetuate a financial crime or fraud upon a third person to disclose the fraud *to the extent necessary* to prevent or rectify the injury.[73] Is this a revolutionary change? Does it, as one opponent has asserted, "turn lawyers into the new cops on the beat, auditors of their clients, whistleblowers for the government ... [and] destroy the very core values that preserve the lawyer-client relationship"?[74]

Hardly. The ABA's 1969 Model Code of Professional Responsibility, which used to apply in most states, allowed disclosure for ongoing or future financial crimes.[75] The comments to the 1983 Model Rules already allow lawyers to "disavow" documents in circumstances similar to those contemplated by the new rule.[76] The current change was only narrowly defeated both when the 1983 rules were initially proposed[77] and again

---

minded me that lawyers are not only gatekeepers; lawyers are watchdogs. We fill both roles.") (comments of former ABA President A. P. Carlton).

72. *See ABA Amends Ethics Rules, supra* note 1 (reporting the amendments); *see also ABA Task Force Revised Recommendations on Model Rule Changes Generally Welcomed*, 19 ABA/BNA Law. Manual Prof'l Conduct 263 (2003) (reporting the ABA Task Force proposals to amend the model rules).

73. Model Rules, *supra* note 11, R. 1.6(b)(2) (2003 version) (permitting lawyers to disclose "to prevent the client from committing a crime or fraud that is reasonably certain to result in substantial injury to the financial interests or property of another and in furtherance of which the client has used or is using the lawyer's services"); *see also* Model Rules, *supra*, R. 1.6(b)(3) (2003 version) (permitting lawyers to disclose "to prevent, mitigate or rectify substantial injury to the financial interests or property of another that is reasonably certain to result or has resulted from the client's commission of a crime or fraud in furtherance of which the client has used the lawyer's services").

74. Lawrence J. Fox, *On the Proposed Changes in ABA Model Rules: Frontal Assaults on the Profession*, 229 Legal Intelligencer 7 (Aug. 6, 2003).

75. Model Code, *supra* note 65, DR 4-101(C)(3) (allowing lawyers to disclose a client's intention to commit any crime).

76. Model Rules, *supra* note 11, R. 1.6 cmt.

77. *See* Lisa H. Nicholson, *A Hobson's Choice For Securities Lawyers in the Post-Enron Environment: Striking a Balance Between the Obligation of Client Loyalty and Market Gatekeeper*, 16 Geo. J. Legal Ethics 91, 141–44 (2002) (noting that, in February 1983, "the ABA House of Delegates voted to eliminate from Model Rule 1.6 the two provisions relating to the prevention and rectification of client fraud, by a vote of 207 to 129").

two years ago, when a similar amendment was proposed to the ABA House of Delegates.[78]

Moreover, the change is narrow. It is discretionary. It does not allow lawyers to blow the whistle on client frauds or crimes unless the lawyers' services are being or have been used, essentially, to make the lawyers co-conspirators. The permitted disclosures are limited to those necessary to prevent the injury. They parallel disclosures permitted under the crime-fraud exception to the attorney-client privilege,[79] so clients have no right to perceive the information to be sacrosanct. In short, in most situations, the attorney-client relationship continues as usual. The client simply must be forewarned that there are limits to what he can expect the lawyer to do for, or with, him.

Consider next the recently adopted Sarbanes-Oxley regulations, which have been echoed, in part, in a new version of Model Rule 1.13 just adopted by the ABA.[80] In essence, the SEC regulations require corporate lawyers[81] who are aware of particular types of prospective corporate misconduct[82] to report the issues to the organization's "chief legal officer ... or to both the [organization's] chief legal officer and its chief executive officer"[83] or to a "qualified legal compliance committee."[84] Lawyers who do not receive an "appropriate response"—one that avoids the misconduct or convinces the lawyer that her assessment was erroneous—must refrain from participating in the misconduct and continue to report up the ladder. In some cases, they also may disclose information to the SEC.[85]

---

78. *ABA Stands Firm On Client Confidentiality, Rejects 'Screening' For Conflicts of Interest*, 17 ABA/BNA Law. Manual Prof'l Conduct 492 (2001) (reporting the rejection of proposed revisions to the Model Rules).

79. *See supra* text accompanying note 62.

80. Model Rules, *supra* note 11, R. 1.13(b), (c) (2003 version) (requiring lawyers who know that a corporate officer is engaging in a violation of law that is likely to substantially injure the organization to take remedial steps and permitting the lawyers to disclose outside the organization under certain circumstances).

81. The proposed rule's definition of the term "attorney" seemed to broadly encompass nonsecurities lawyers who simply prepare or review limited portions of a filing, lawyers who respond to auditors' letters or prepare work product unrelated to securities matters that may later be used in connection with filings, and lawyers preparing documents that eventually may be filed as exhibits. Proposed Rule, *supra* note 1, at 71,676, 71,678. The final rule provides that, to be covered, an attorney must at least have notice that his work will be submitted to the Commission. Final Rule Discussion Section, *supra* note 1, General Overview, at 6298 ("[A]n attorney must have notice that a document he or she is preparing or assisting in preparing will be submitted to the Commission to be deemed to be 'appearing and practicing' under the revised definition.").

82. The covered misconduct is not limited to violations of federal securities laws. The regulations address broader breaches of fiduciary duties, particularly breaches of duties to pension funds. SEC Final Rule, *supra* note 1, § 205.2(d).

83. *Id.* § 205.3(b).

84. *Id.* § 205.3(b), (c).

85. The SEC's rule provides:

An attorney appearing and practicing before the Commission in the representation of an issuer may reveal to the Commission, without the issuer's consent, confidential information related to the representation to the extent the attorney reasonably believes necessary:

(i) To prevent the issuer from committing a material violation that is likely to cause substantial injury to the financial interest or property of the issuer or investors;

(ii) To prevent the issuer, in a Commission investigation or administrative proceeding from committing perjury ... ; suborning perjury ... ; or committing any act proscribed in 18 U.S.C. 1001 that is likely to perpetrate a fraud upon the Commission; or

(iii) To rectify the consequences of a material violation by the issuer that caused, or may cause, substantial injury to the financial interest or property of the issuer or investors in

These gatekeeping requirements are extensions of rules that already exist. They require specific remedial action by lawyers,[86] whereas most state codes only require some action and leave the specific response to lawyer discretion.[87] They make the duty not to participate in wrongdoing explicit, but that duty already exists under the professional codes.[88] To the extent that the gatekeeping requirements represent statements by the federal agency that lawyers are personally responsible for statements they make in filings before the agency, that also is nothing new at all.[89] The most that critics can fairly argue about these new rules is that their extensions of existing requirements go too far and are bad public policy.

That is different than what might be argued, for example, with respect to the provision of the Sarbanes-Oxley regulations that the SEC has held in abeyance, pending further comment.[90] This provision would require lawyers "who reasonably believe that the reported material violation is ongoing or is about to occur and is likely to result in substantial injury to the financial interest of the issuer or of investors ... [to] notify the Commission of their withdrawal, and disaffirm any submission to the Commission that they have participated in preparing which is tainted by the violation."[91] The ABA recently has adopted a revision to Model Rule 1.13 that puts a somewhat similar, but permissive, requirement into effect.[92]

These reforms are more than a matter of degree. The SEC proposal, in particular, potentially changes the lawyer-client relationship because the lawyer is almost required to blackmail the client into law compliance; if the client does not abide by the lawyer's view of correct behavior, the lawyer effectively must notify the SEC of the dispute, subjecting

---

the furtherance of which the attorney's services were used.

Id. § 205.3(d)(2). For an interesting recent discussion of the likely effects of the SEC regulations, see generally Jill E. Fisch and Kenneth M. Rosen, *Is There a Role for Lawyers in Preventing Future Enrons?*, 48 Vill. L. Rev. 1097 (2003).

86. SEC Final Rules, *supra* note 1, § 205.3(b)(1), (3), (9) (imposing mandatory internal reporting requirements on attorneys with knowledge of a potential violation); *Id.* § 205.3(d) (authorizing some disclosures to the SEC).

87. *See, e.g.*, Model Rules, *supra* note 11, R. 1.13 (requiring the lawyer to "proceed as is reasonably necessary in the best interest of the organization" and providing examples of possible remedial measures). Of course, the recent amendments to Model Rule 1.13 making certain actions mandatory are likely to influence some states to adopt a similar change for their own professional codes.

88. *E.g.*, Model Rules, *supra* note 11, R. 1.2(d), R. 1.16(a).

89. *See Programs Explore Concern, supra* note 4, at 320 ("Although Sarbanes-Oxley certainly presents new nuances and challenges, [Bryan J. Redding] said, it is for all intents and purposes 'just another aiding and abetting problem.'"); Zacharias, *supra* note 35 (discussing various federal regulations imposing personal responsibility on lawyers for their federal filings); *cf.* Davis, *supra* note 34, at 1283 ("As for the idea of the securities lawyer as gatekeeper, the general concept is noncontroversial since, under typical contractual arrangements, securities issuances cannot go forward without a host of opinions from the attorneys involved.").

90. Although the SEC envisioned a relatively short comment period, the resulting controversy has led to a prolonged deferral and reconsideration of the proposal. *See Federal Lawmakers Get Earful at Hearing On SEC's Proposed 'Noisy Withdrawal' Rules*, 20 ABA/BNA Law. Manual Prof'l Conduct 69 (2004) (discussing a congressional hearing regarding the proposed regulation).

91. Proposed Rule, *supra* note 1, *deferred by* SEC Final Rule Discussion Section, *supra* note 1. In-house attorneys would not be required to withdraw, but would have to "disaffirm any tainted submission they have participated in preparing." *Id.*

92. *See ABA Amends Ethics Rules, supra* note 1, at 468 (reporting the adoption of a provision stating that an organizational lawyer who has not received an appropriate response to an up-the-ladder report "may reveal information relating to the representation whether or not Rule 1.6 permits such disclosure, but only if and to the extent the lawyer reasonably believes necessary to prevent substantial injury to the organization").

the client to investigation and likely sanction. Although this type of blackmail is possible under the traditional (and new) exceptions to attorney-client confidentiality, those exceptions cover far more limited and extreme circumstances. And because the traditional exceptions typically are discretionary, like the existing SEC disclosure rule,[93] they do not envision the lawyer adopting the dominant role as routinely as the proposal would. Nevertheless, the fair criticism of this proposal, again, is not that it is unique in requiring gatekeeping conduct, but rather that its effect would unduly interfere with the lawyer's traditional role as confidant and advisor.

Perhaps the most interesting of the recent reform proposals is the so-called Gatekeeper Initiative.[94] It is fair to say that the impetus for the initiative is to change lawyers from client allies to sources of information for government agents investigating terrorism and money laundering. Accordingly, an ABA task force has already gone on record as opposing any proposal that would require the disclosure of confidential information "or otherwise compromise the lawyer-client relationship or the independence of the bar."[95]

What is interesting about the ABA Task Force's noble sentiments is that they have been expressed *before* any proposal actually has issued. One can imagine *possible* proposals that would undermine the role of lawyers—such as a rule requiring lawyers to investigate clients and report any suspicious activity to law enforcement authorities, including suspicions about past wrongdoing.[96] In contrast, if all that the reforms ultimately require is for lawyers to avoid aiding and abetting client crimes, this conduct already is required.[97] The intermediate possibility—that lawyers may be asked to report future crimes—easily would fit within the traditional conception of the lawyer's role,[98] but (like all confidentiality exceptions) should be subjected to a policy analysis of its countervailing benefits for society and its costs to clients and the efficiency of the adversary system. None of the possible formulations are vulnerable to the criticism that the proposed reforms are per se invalid because they turn lawyers into gatekeepers.

---

93. SEC Final Rule, *supra* note 1, § 205.3(d)(2), quoted *supra* note 85.

94. The Gatekeeper Initiative is described in Sally Baghdasarian, Comment, *Gatekeepers: How the Broad Application of Anti-Money Laundering Statutes and Strategies May Open An Attorney's Gates to Prosecution*, 32 Sw. U. L. Rev. 721, 725–26 (2003); Kevin L. Shepherd, *USA PATRIOT Act and the Gatekeeper Initiative: Surprising Implications for Transactional Lawyers*, 16 Prob. & Prop. 26, 27 (2002); Zacharias, *supra* note 35; Bruce Zagaris, *Gatekeepers Initiative: Seeking Middle Ground Between Client and Government*, 16 Crim. Just. 26, 30 (2002).

95. *ABA Delegates Vote Opposition to Proposals to Make Attorneys Report Shady Transactions*, 19 ABA/BNA Law. Manual Prof'l Conduct 99 (2003).

96. Some observers, based in part on the reactions of other countries to the Gatekeeper Initiative, have assumed that the forthcoming proposals for U.S. lawyers might well include a requirement that lawyers inquire into or report suspicious transactions by their clients or both. *E.g.*, Baghdasarian, *supra* note 94, at 726; Susan R. Martyn, *In Defense of Client-Lawyer Confidentiality ... And Its Exceptions...*, 81 Neb. L. Rev. 1320, 1348–49 (2003); Zagaris, *supra* note 94, at 28; *ABA Creates Task Force on Gatekeeper Regulation and the Profession*, 17 Crim. Just. 31 (2002); *cf.* Nicole M. Healy, *The Impact of September 11th on Anti-money Laundering Efforts, and the European Union and Commonwealth Gatekeeper Initiatives*, 36 Int'l Law. 733, 735 (2002) ("The effects of [European] directives on U.S. lawyers practicing or doing business in EU or Commonwealth nations will bear watching, because these gatekeeper initiatives may conflict with U.S. lawyers' ethical obligations of confidentiality.").

97. *See supra* text accompanying notes 48 and 51.

98. *See supra* text accompanying note 75.

VI. Conclusions

At root, it is a good thing for lawyers to screen client misconduct. It keeps lawyers themselves honest. It serves societal interests in preventing harm. It enhances judicial administration. And it makes lawyers think about the morality and legality of clients' conduct as well as their own, thus encouraging lawyers to help clients recognize and pursue appropriate behavior. All of these are valid functions for lawyers, and they have always been understood to play a part in the lawyer's everyday dealings with clients. The recent reform proposals simply address some regulators' perceptions that lawyers' own understanding and implementation of these functions has not been adequate in recent times.

But gatekeeping is only one part, and a relatively small part, of the lawyer's role. If lawyers are to put the adversary system into effect—with all its societal benefits—society must protect lawyers' ability to obtain information, ally themselves with lawful client ends, and serve even unpopular client causes. Indeed, lawyers' ability to act as gatekeepers, in some respects, depends on their partisanship.[99]

The key to evaluating reform proposals that emphasize gatekeeping is to avoid rhetoric that ignores both aspects of the balance. Characterizing any shift as an end to lawyering as we know it only serves to strengthen the case for reform. That characterization suggests that its proponents misunderstand the limits of partisanship and themselves require reforms that will reeducate them about those limits.[100]

Elihu Root was an aggressive, ultrapartisan lawyer.[101] Yet he warned us that the lawyer's job consists as much of standing in the way of misguided client pursuits as of implementing client desires. No one except misguided practitioners and cynical criminal clients truly envision the lawyer's role as assisting wrongful ends. We are gatekeepers, and we should never forget it.

---

99. This is one of the standard justifications for strict attorney-client confidentiality. Arguably, only if the client understands that the lawyer is a complete ally and will not disclose confidences will the client inform the lawyer of intended misconduct and thereby provide an opportunity for the lawyer to dissuade the client. *See* Fred C. Zacharias, *Rethinking Confidentiality*, 74 Iowa L. Rev. 351, 359 (1989) (reviewing the justifications for strict confidentiality); *cf.* John C. Coffee, Jr., *The Attorney as Gatekeeper: An Agenda for the SEC*, 103 Colum. L. Rev. 1293, 1307 (2003) (justifying a gatekeeper role for lawyers, in part, on the basis that "the ultimate goal of the law is to achieve law compliance, not to maximize uninhibited communications between the attorney and client. Client confidentiality is a means to an end, not an end in itself. Thus, the law has long placed some limitations on attorney-client communications....").

100. An interesting example of this phenomenon is discussed in Baghdasarian, *supra* note 94, at 731, which suggests that one of the two reasons not to emphasize lawyer gatekeeping is the mere fact that such an emphasis might lead to the government pursuing "criminal sanctions against an attorney." Of course, there is nothing inherent in the lawyer's role that should immunize lawyers from prosecution for aiding and abetting client crimes. *See* authorities cited *supra* notes 48 and 51.

101. *See* Leopold, *supra* note 7, at 18 ("[W]hile he would not prostitute himself to abet illegal action, he did believe he should help businessmen operate to the fullest advantage within the letter of the law.").

C. Clients with Diminished Capacity

The Myth of Advocacy

Alan A. Stone, M.D.*

30 *Hospital & Community Psychiatry* 819 (No. 12, December, 1979)

President, American Psychiatric Association

In an era in which advocacy has become a buzzword, both psychiatry and the legal profession have climbed aboard the advocacy bandwagon. Yet the American Psychiatric Association's notion of advocacy—championing the medical needs of patients—is often in direct conflict with the lawyers' notion of advocacy—championing the legal rights of their clients. The author observes that psychiatry has proved to be a weak adversary for patients' legal advocates: the result has been a one-sided advocacy system that has advanced patients' rights at the expense of their needs. He believes that if the APA is to become an effective advocate for patients, it must hire lawyers and work with them to reverse the trend of turning rights into needs.

Several years ago, a congressman wrote to me asking if I would testify on behalf of a bill he had filed. His staff, with the assistance of the Department of Health, Education, and Welfare and the Library of Congress, had determined that it would cost $60 million a year to provide every psychiatric inpatient in the United States with a lawyer. In his letter, he claimed that he had read my book, *Mental Health and Law: A System in Transition*[1], and he was confident that I would support his bill on behalf of patient advocates. I responded by return mail that I would be delighted to testify if he would amend his bill to ask for $120 million so that there would be good legal representation on both sides. I never heard from the congressman again. But recently legislation providing for federally funded advocates for patients has surfaced again in Congress, with no recognition of the need for legal representation on the other side.

This is the era of advocacy. We have consumer advocates, child advocates, and patient advocates. The American Psychiatric Association has even amended its constitution and bylaws so that psychiatry too has an advocacy mission. Like the Congress, we want to climb on the bandwagon; we want the public to know we are for advocacy. Advocacy is by no means a new idea. One of the eponyms for Jesus Christ was "the Advocate," but surely his version of salvation was different than the one the lawyers have recently proposed for our patients and for us. It is time to unpack this buzzword, this slogan of advocacy.

The APA's notion of advocacy is that we will champion the medical needs of our patients. The lawyers' notion of advocacy is that they will champion the legal rights of their clients. Where we want the best treatment setting for our patients, they want the least restrictive alternative. Where we want careful treatment planning and continuity of care, they want immediate deinstitutionalization and maximum liberty. Where we are

---

* Dr. Stone, 108th president of APA, is professor of law and psychiatry at Harvard University in Cambridge, Massachusetts. This paper is the address he gave at the 31st Institute on Hospital & Community Psychiatry, held September 3–6, 1979, in New Orleans. [Dr. Stone is now Touroff-Glueck Professor of Law and Psychiatry at Harvard Law School. This paper is reprinted with the kind permission of Professor Stone and the American Psychiatric Association.]

1. A.A. Stone, *Mental Health and Law: A System in Transition*, National Institute of Mental Health, Rockville, Maryland, 1975.

concerned about access to treatment, they are concerned about stigma and the right to refuse treatment. Where we are trying to salvage what is salvageable in the state hospital system, they are trying to close down the state hospital system. Where we want to advocate the medical model, they want to advocate the legal model. Our advocacy and theirs conflict more often than not, but for those who know little about the mental health system, the buzzword "advocacy" suggests both kinds with no conflict.

The root problem of the conflict is only understood when the last difference I mentioned, the legal model versus the medical model, is examined not in terms of goals but of procedures. The lawyers' notion of advocacy comes naturally; it is part of the Anglo-American adversarial system of justice. Each side is meant to have a zealous advocate. The work of the court advances as these advocates joust with each other.

The lawyers' canons of ethics give great importance to this duty to be a zealous advocate. Indeed, it would be fair to say that the basic credo of legal ethics is that the lawyer should feel free to proceed almost unrestrained as an advocate because there is a zealous advocate on the other side. This is the very basis of our adversarial system of justice. It is not a search for truth. Rather, each side struggles for an advantage, and out of the struggle the judge and jury pluck the just resolution.

The lawyers, then, have a long tradition of advocacy. It combines a notion of rights and a professional way of doing things. When their form of advocacy is applied in the political arena, it can become a formidable tool for achieving change. During the past decade, such advocacy has been the means for giving power to the powerless. Consumer advocates have given consumers who as individuals had no power the ability to assert their common demands. Civil rights advocates have done the same for minority groups. Advocates for welfare recipients and the aged have been able to have an impact on the entrenched federal bureaucracies. These advocates use the courts, the class-action suit, the media, and the political process to advance the needs and interests of the group they represent. They do so by presenting the needs and interests of their group as legal rights.

Given the success of this kind of advocacy, one can easily understand how advocacy has become a buzzword and a slogan appealing to liberals and populists alike. But it is crucial to recognize that where advocacy has really worked, it has worked because, first, the group's needs and interests could be readily defined; second, the interests could be formulated as some legal right; and third, paradoxically to us but basic to the system of law, the legal adversary had a powerful opponent, an adversary who had something to lose. Without an adversarial struggle, the judge has no real ability to find a resolution that is balanced.

Rights Versus Needs

None of these crucial elements have been present in most of the litigation in the field of mental health over the past decade. Legal advocates for the mentally ill have not been willing to consider seriously the needs of the mentally ill and to formulate those needs as legal rights. Instead they have done the reverse. They have treated rights as if they constituted the needs of the mentally ill.

And who is the powerful adversary for the mental health advocate to attack? There is none. Instead, mental health advocates, with the assistance of the radical antipsychiatrists, had to invent a powerful adversary—the psychiatric establishment. But the last decade has made it clear that psychiatrists are anything but a powerful adversary. Wherever the metal health advocate pressed, the psychiatric profession gave way. In the court rooms, there was almost never a zealous legal advocate to oppose the self-appointed patient advocate.

Consider the kind of case in which Congress wants to provide legal advocates, for the patient who may be involuntarily confined. Take for example, a prototypical patient, named Mr. Jones. He has, for the past month, been increasingly agitated. For some time he has been convinced that people at work were conspiring against him. Last week he decided people were reading his mind, and he began to hear voices accusing him of sexual perversity. Since then, he has been unable to sleep and has stopped going to work. He now refuses to communicate with his wife or children. He paces up and down with a pained expression on his face; he is obviously suffering. He is now either crazy or, as his legal advocate might argue, exercising his right to be different.

Mrs. Jones begs and cajoles her husband to come with her to the emergency room of the nearby community hospital. He reluctantly agrees. There he sees a psychiatrist who, after interviewing Mr. Jones and getting a history from Mrs. Jones, makes a diagnosis of acute paranoid schizophrenia and recommends hospitalization. Mr. Jones adamantly refuses any treatment at all. Mrs. Jones begs the doctor to do something: she is afraid her husband will lose his job, and she worries about the effect of his strange behavior on the children.

The question is, what does Mr. Jones need? What should happen now? The following is what the legal advocates believe should happen before Mr. Jones' psychiatric needs can even be considered.

First, Mr. Jones must be provided with his own lawyer, presumably paid for by the federal government, whose duty is to advocate Mr. Jones' freedom. Second, he must have a hearing before a judge within 48 hours and, no matter how disturbed he may get, the doctors are not to begin treatment until that hearing. At that hearing, his lawyer will argue that he should not be further confined and that, if confined, he has a right to refuse treatment. Third, the lawyer will insist that the psychiatrist must inform Mr. Jones of his right to remain silent and his fifth-amendment privilege against self-incrimination.

Fourth, Mr. Jones and his lawyer must be given timely notice of the charges justifying his confinement so that they can prepare a defense. Fifth, he must have notice of the right to a jury trial. Sixth, he is entitled to a full hearing, a trial with the right to cross-examine Mrs. Jones and his doctors, who must testify about the details of his illness and his dangerous behavior. Seventh, it must be proved by clear and convincing evidence that Mr. Jones is mentally ill and dangerous. And, finally, there must be inquiry into whether some less restrictive alternative can be found for Mr. Jones before involuntary inpatient care is ordered. "Less restrictive" for the lawyer will mean least loss of freedom and not "best treatment setting."

I have already mentioned that the estimated cost of these legal procedures was $60 million several years ago: it is undoubtedly much more today. That covers only the cost of lawyers for all of the Joneses; it does not include court costs, the time of the hospital staff who must testify, and the lawyers, if any, for the other side.

The total costs will far exceed $60 million, and if the federal government doesn't pay it, who will? Why should any state or prosecutor want to go to all that trouble and expense? The state is being asked to use all that money and all those legal resources to justify putting Mr. Jones in a hospital so that the state can spend still more to treat him. What is in it for the state? Prosecutors have all sorts of incentives for putting away criminals, but what is their incentive for putting away Mr. Jones? And what about the incentives of the psychiatrist? Experience demonstrates that psychiatrists have always disliked being involved in civil commitment; with these new procedures, that dislike has become abhorrence.

In sum, legal advocacy is proposed to advance the interests of the patients against a powerful adversary, but it turns our that no one but Mrs. Jones really has an incentive to confine Mr. Jones. The powerful adversary of the mental patient turns out to be a paper tiger, and the psychiatrist is soft as a grape. Nor is it clear that the advocate is concerned or will care about Mr. Jones' needs in all this rhetoric of rights.

One-Sided Advocacy

There are two important points I want to make here. The first is that the legal adversary system doesn't work well unless there are adversaries on both sides. But you won't have adversaries on both sides unless both sides have an incentive. In the ordinary psychiatric case, the state and the prosecutor have no real incentive, and the psychiatrist doesn't either. Thus in most states today, given the existing statutes and the lack of any real adversary, a conscientious legal advocate should be able to prevent all involuntary confinement. Many lawyers who work as members of the mental health bar candidly admit this to be the case, and some acknowledge that even they sometimes question the value of what they do.

Let me briefly mention another striking example of how the adversary legal model goes astray in our field. During the Supreme Court's deliberation of the need for legal advocates for children who are to be admitted to treatment facilities, a startling case was presented as an example of a violation of rights indicating the need for a lawyer. A child with Down's syndrome was being reared at home with the assistance of various professional programs. His parents, under a respite program, were to take the other children on a one-week vacation while the retarded child was placed temporarily in a facility. This kind of respite program is thought to be one good way to support families of retarded children to encourage them to keep their children at home rather than abandon them. The legal advocates insisted that the child should be provided with a lawyer whose obligation it would be to resist this one-week respite program, using most of the procedures I described for Mr. Jones.

Once again, the question arises about what incentive the state has to use its lawyers to resist such advocacy. In the end, the kind of legal advocacy the Congress wants to provide every patient would destroy the respite program in the name of children's rights, ignoring the fact that the child needs a family and the family needs the support they get from the respite program.

Some lawyers may insist that I am drawing a caricature of legal advocacy rather than a true picture. One distinguished lawyer, for example, sees the advocacy role as one that tries to place the retarded child in the best facility available during the respite. He sees the lawyer's role as getting Mr. Jones in to the best treatment setting with the least loss of freedom. His kind of advocacy is my kind of advocacy, and I can find it nowhere in the lawyers' canons of ethics. He would have the legal advocate take on the duties of the expert in access to mental health facilities. His kind of advocacy looks to needs, as well as rights.

But when I describe this kind of advocacy to the lawyers who are increasingly being recruited to the metal health bar, they generally resist it. In the first place, they don't want to be social workers, and they don't want to be responsible for taking care of clients' non-legal problems. Their vision of advocacy is the lawyer as adversary, providing a limited legal service: Mr. Jones and the retarded child have a right to be free; it is their job to see to that freedom, and what happens afterward is not their business.

When legal advocates listen to my arguments and hear them, and admit that a system of legal advocates on one side won't work, they usually come to the conclusion that it is up to psychiatrists to see that the hospitals and the state supply lawyers for the other side. Theoretically they are right, and that is why I was willing to write the congressman to ask for $120 million. That would restore the integrity of the adversarial system; the two sides of the argument could be heard.

But no one has ever said that providing lawyers for alleged criminals would reduce the problem of crime in the streets or assist in the rehabilitation of criminals. At best, it ensures that alleged criminals obtain justice from the courts. Similarly, no one can claim that providing individual legal advocates for psychiatric patients will reduce mental illness or assist in the treatment of mental patients. The best it can do is to see that alleged patients get justice in the courts. But it is not at all clear what justice is in this context.

A Crucial Distinction

When the Congress supports legal advocacy for mental patients, it ignores the distinction and the conflict between advocacy of rights and advocacy of needs. But that distinction is crucial to the future of effective mental health care in this country. How can we make that distinction clear to the courts, to the legislatures, and to the public? How can we make them realize that legal advocacy will mean that lawyers and courts will be telling us how to practice our profession?

Here we confront a paradox that many psychiatrists do not appreciate. If the American Psychiatric Association is to become an advocate for patients, then to be at all effective, we too have to hire lawyers and learn to work with them, for better or worse. There is no alternative; we will have to do it their way. We have no tradition of advocacy of our own, and without legal advocacy we are helpless. The central task of working with lawyers is to create new laws that will reverse the trend of making rights into needs. We have begun to do that in the last few years and with growing success, as illustrated by the following comment about recent Supreme Court decisions[2] in the *Mental Disability Law Reporter*, a publication that has frequently been a critic of the psychiatric establishment.

> The Supreme Court's decisions seem to be signaling de-emphasis of procedural due process and a new awareness of the right to treatment in a broad medical as well as legal sense. The Supreme Court has also discussed the tragic implications of denying proper care to those who actually need that care, saying a person who 'is suffering from a debilitating mental illness, and in need of treatment is neither wholly at liberty nor free of stigma.' Now one sees a new emphasis that promotes the need to allow psychiatrists to practice their profession unhindered by time-wasting legal procedures. There can be little doubt that the American Psychiatric Association through its amicus briefs has made a significant impact upon the legal profession.[3]

Perhaps the author goes too far in saying that we have made an impact on the legal profession, but we have made a significant impact on the future of our own profession and our capacity to treat our patients. With the help of our lawyers, we have taken our professional destiny into our own hands, and surely that is a good thing.

---

2. *Addington* v. *Texas*, 99 S.C. 1804 (1979), *Parham* v. *J.L. et al.*, 99 S.C. 2493 (1979).

3. "Historic Supreme Court Decision on the Voluntary Admission of Minors Issued," *Mental Disability Law Reporter*, Vol. 3, July–August 1979, pp. 231–234.

D. "Trusting" Clients — Lawyer as "Neutral"

Association of the Bar of the City of New York Ethics Committee

Inquiry Reference No. 80-23
[Some footnotes omitted. Remaining footnotes renumbered.]

We have been asked whether lawyers may ethically participate in a divorce mediation program organized by a non-profit organization. The organization has a staff of licensed mental health professionals who provide marital and family therapy. It now proposes to offer what is known as "structured mediation" in marital cases. Such mediation involves a trained therapist consulting with separating or divorcing couples to aid them in working out various aspects of the separation or divorce, including issues of property division, and child custody, visitation and support. We have been asked whether a lawyer could (a) become part of the mediating team, (b) give impartial legal advice to the parties, such as advice on the tax consequences of proposed separation or divorce agreements, or (c) draft a divorce or settlement agreement after the terms of such agreement have been approved by the parties. We have also been asked whether a participating lawyer could be paid, either by the parties to the mediation or by the organization.

This inquiry raises important and difficult questions concerning the participation of lawyers in non-adversarial roles in dispute resolution. The Code of Professional Responsibility provides comparatively detailed guides for the lawyer representing clients in the adversarial role of zealous advocate or confidential advisor. The Code also recognizes that lawyers may serve as "impartial arbitrators or mediators" (EC 5-20). However, the Code nowhere defines these latter roles and their responsibilities or expressly considers the role of lawyers asked to provide impartial legal assistance to parties with differing interests, in an effort to compose their differences without resort to adversary negotiation or litigation. The Committee nevertheless believes that the principles of the Code permit the extrapolation of certain guidelines for lawyers asked to participate in such non-adversarial activities.

We conclude, first, that the Code does not impose a *per se* bar to lawyer participation in divorce mediation activities, or to the provision of impartial legal assistance to parties engaged in divorce mediation. At the same time, we believe that particularly in the sensitive area of divorce, the application of labels such as "mediation" or "impartial" advice does not satisfy the Code's concerns for the administration of justice, the dangers inherent in the reliance of laymen with differing interests on the legal advice of a single lawyer, and the appearance of impropriety attendant on such situations. Rather, we conclude that a lawyer asked to participate in divorce mediation and to provide impartial legal advice or assistance in drawing up an agreement must take certain precautions, specified hereafter, to assure that the parties fully understand the lawyer's limited role and all of the risks involved and to minimize the dangers of subsequent charges that the lawyer favored the interests of one party to the detriment of the other. We also conclude that there are some situations, also discussed below, where these dangers and the potential harm to the interests of the parties are so great that it is entirely inappropriate for a lawyer to participate in mediation or to attempt to give impartial legal assistance.

The lawyer's participation in divorce mediation activities with non-lawyers raises separate ethical issues. However, some of those issues may be eliminated here, because of the non-profit status of the sponsoring organization. We conclude that if the nonlawyer mediators refrain from engaging in activities involving the practice of law and all the requirements of DR 2-103 (D)(4) are met, lawyers may participate in the divorce mediation program under the conditions discussed below. In such circumstances, the lawyer may be paid by either the organization or the parties themselves.

I

The issues raised here require the harmonization of differing policies reflected in the Code of Professional Responsibility. On the one hand, the Code provides that a lawyer may represent multiple clients only "if it is *obvious* that he can adequately represent the interest of each and if each consents to the representation after full disclosure of the possible effect of such representation on the exercise of his independent professional judgment on behalf of each." DR 5-105 (C). (Emphasis supplied) Applying this principle, it has been repeatedly held that the conflicts inherent in a matrimonial proceeding are such, that it is never appropriate to represent both spouses. Thus, New York State Opinion 258 (1972) states:

> It would be improper for a lawyer to represent both husband and wife at any stage of a marital problem, even with full disclosure and informed consent of both parties. The likelihood of prejudice is so great in this type of matter as to make impossible adequate representation of both spouses, even where the separation is "friendly" and the divorce uncontested.

This opinion further cites with approval the view that such representation is improper even if the parties consent and merely are seeking to have the lawyer reduce to writing an agreement that the parties independently arrived at.

On the other hand, EC 5-20 states that a lawyer may serve in the capacity of an "impartial arbitrator or mediator" even for present or former clients provided the lawyer makes appropriate disclosures and thereafter declines to represent any of the parties in the dispute. Accordingly, New York State Opinion 258 also acknowledges that a lawyer can serve as a "mediator" in a matrimonial dispute.

The difficulty arises because the Code nowhere explains what activities constitute "mediation," what responsibilities a lawyer has when acting as a mediator, when a lawyer is "representing" parties or whether it is possible for a lawyer to give legal guidance to all parties to a dispute—to "represent the situation"—without representing any of them or being involved in the conflicts which representing them would involve. See Hazard, *Ethics in the Practice of Law* 58–68 (1978).

Mediation, particularly in the context of divorce disputes, could have a number of meanings. It could mean acting as an intermediary between the parties to find common ground between them on such matters as who gets what piece of property or who gets custody of a child. Such activity may or may not involve the exercise of professional legal judgments.[1]

---

1. The American Arbitration Association has a program for divorce mediation in which the family mediator is not permitted to give legal advice; once the mediator produces a resolution, the parties are referred to their own attorneys. See generally, Spencer and Zammit, *Mediation-Arbitration: A Proposal for Private Resolution of Disputes Between Divorced or Separated Parents*, 1976 Duke L.J. 911, notes 34–42 and accompanying text.

The word "mediator" can:

> "imply that the lawyer is a spokesman for the position of each of the parties, as well as one who listens to the parties express their positions for themselves. It can imply that the lawyer is actively involved, indeed aggressively involved, in exploring alternative arrange-

On the other hand, mediation could mean attempting to resolve matters that involve complicated tax or other legal ramifications. As Professor Hazard has pointed out,

> Two other Bar Associations, to our knowledge, have rendered opinions in circumstances similar to those involved here. They have concluded that lawyer participation in divorce mediation—including the rendering of impartial legal advice and the preparation of a written agreement—is permissible because the Code permits mediation and because the lawyer is not "representing" either party and hence does not come within the strictures of DR 5-105 on the representation of clients with differing interests. Oregon State Bar Proposed Opinion 79-46 (1980); Boston Bar Opinion 78-1 (1978). Both opinions recognize the dangers in such situations of inequalities in the bargaining power of the parties and the potential for misunderstandings and later recrimination against the lawyer. They nevertheless conclude, with considerable reluctance, that the lawyer may undertake divorce mediation activities including the provision of impartial legal assistance, provided the lawyer makes it clear that the lawyer represents neither party, and obtains the parties' consent.

The Committee agrees in part with these opinions. However, we do not believe that participation in divorce mediation is appropriate in *all* circumstances, even if the suggested precautions are observed and consent is obtained. Nor do we believe that the issues can be resolved simply by labeling activities mediation or by advising the parties that the lawyer represents neither. Rather, as discussed below, we believe that particular circumstances, as well as particular services performed by the lawyer, must be examined in the light of the various policies of the Code, before it can be determined that the lawyer may participate in the mediation.

II

This Committee recognizes that there are circumstances where it is desirable that parties to a matrimonial dispute be afforded an alternative to the adversarial process, with its legal and emotional costs. The Code's recognition that lawyers may serve as mediators (EC 5-20), as well as ethical aspirations which recognize a lawyer's duty to assist the public in recognizing legal problems and aiding those who cannot afford the usual costs of legal assistance (EC 2-1; EC 2-25), make it inconceivable to us that the Code would deny the public the availability of non-adversary legal assistance in the resolution of divorce disputes.

At the same time, the Committee also recognizes that in some circumstances, the complex and conflicting interests involved in a particular matrimonial dispute, the difficult legal issues involved, the subtle legal ramifications of particular resolutions, and the inequality in bargaining power resulting from differences in the personalities or sophistication of the parties make it virtually impossible to achieve a just result free from later recriminations of bias or malpractice, unless both parties are represented by separate counsel. In the latter circumstances, informing the parties that the lawyer "represents" neither party and obtaining their consent, even after a full explanation of risks, may not be capable of giving truly informed consent due to the difficulty of the issues involved. In such circumstances, a party who is later advised that its interests were prejudiced in mediation or that the impartial advice offered or written agreement drawn, by the

---

ments by which the positions of the parties can be accommodated in a comprehensive resolution of the matter at hand." Hazard, *supra* at 63.

lawyer-mediator, favored the other spouse is likely to believe that it was misled into reliance on the impartiality of the lawyer-mediator. In short, we believe there are some activities and some circumstances in which a lawyer cannot undertake to compose the differences of parties to a divorce proceeding, without running afoul of the strictures and policies of DR 5-105—even if the lawyer disclaims representing the interests of any party, purports to be acting impartially and obtains the consent of the parties to the arrangement.

On the other hand, there are clearly circumstances where these difficulties are not involved and where the parties can truly understand, and the lawyer can plainly carry out, a representation that the lawyer represents neither party.

This seems likely, for example, where the lawyer is not being asked to exercise any professional legal judgment—for example where the lawyer is seeking to bring about a compromise or find a common ground for the division of articles of personal property. Such typical mediation activities can be performed by non-lawyers and we cannot conclude that the Code (which permits lawyers to serve as mediators) intended to bar lawyers from performing the same activities.

It also seems true that the lawyer can meaningfully state that he or she represents neither of the parties where the parties simply ask the lawyer to describe the legal consequences of a particular agreement they have reached. Performing such activities would not involve the lawyer in making choices between the interests of the parties.

Nevertheless, even with regard to such activities, there are likely to be situations of such complexity and difficulty that the lawyer must make the judgment that one or both of the parties' consent cannot be considered fully informed. This may be true even where the lawyer merely is asked to provide services that lay mediators may perform or where the legal question he is asked does not require him to choose between the parties' interests. For example, what may appear to be simply a resolution of a dispute about the division of property, may in fact have complicated and subtle tax consequences about which the parties are unaware. The divorce process has always been considered a special concern to the state and as such, an integral part of the administration of justice. Where the lawyer recognizes that the issues raised by a particular divorce dispute are so difficult or complex that they cannot be fairly or justly resolved unless each party is guided by its own separate counsel, the lawyer's participation in a mediation of the dispute may be prejudicial to the administration of justice. See DR 1-102 (A)(5).

Accordingly, to harmonize these various considerations, we have concluded that lawyers may participate in the divorce mediation procedure proposed in the inquiry here, only on the following conditions.

To begin with, the lawyer may *not* participate in the divorce mediation process where it appears that the issues between the parties are of such complexity or difficulty that the parties cannot prudently reach a resolution without the advice of separate and independent legal counsel.

If the lawyer is satisfied that the situation is one in which the parties can intelligently and prudently consent to mediation and the use of an impartial legal adviser, then the lawyer may undertake these roles provided the lawyer observes the following rules:

First, the lawyer must clearly and fully advise the parties of the limitations on his or her role and specifically, of the fact that the lawyer represents neither party and that accordingly, they should not look to the lawyer to protect their individual interests or to keep confidences of one party from the other.

Second, the lawyer must fully and clearly explain the risks of proceeding without separate legal counsel and thereafter proceed only with the consent of the parties and only if the lawyer is satisfied that the parties understand the risks and understand the significance of the fact that the lawyer represents neither party.

Third, a lawyer may participate with mental health professionals in those aspects of mediation which do not require the exercise of professional legal judgment and involve the same kind of mediation activities permissible to lay mediators.

Fourth, lawyers may provide impartial legal advice and assist in reducing the parties' agreement to writing only where the lawyer fully explains all pertinent considerations and alternatives and the consequences to each party of choosing the resolution agreed upon.

Fifth, the lawyer may give legal advice only to both parties in the presence of the other.

Sixth, the lawyer must advise the parties of the advantages of seeking independent legal counsel before executing any agreement drafted by the lawyer.

Seventh, the lawyer may not represent either of the parties in any subsequent legal proceedings relating to the divorce.

Underlying these guidelines is the requirement that the lawyers' participation in the mediation process be conditioned on *informed* consent by the parties. The February 6, 1981 working draft of the American Bar Association's proposed Model Rules of Professional Conduct would set specific guidelines for a lawyer acting as an "intermediary" between clients in an effort to compose their differences. Among other things, the proposal would require the lawyer to satisfy himself or herself that "each client will be able to make adequately informed decisions in the matter." The guidelines provided here would require the lawyer to make a similar judgment, and to decide that certain situations are too complex for a parties' consent to the process to be considered "informed." We recognize that such a standard does not provide a bright-line test, but it is essential if the interests of the parties are to be protected and the parties' consents are to be meaningful.

* * *

Other provisions of the Code are relevant to the participation of an attorney in a lay organization that recommends or offers to the public the services of a lawyer. DR 3-103 prohibits a lawyer from forming a partnership with a non-lawyer if any of the activities of the partnership consists of the practice of law. DR 3-102 prohibits a lawyer from sharing legal fees with a non-lawyer. EC 3-8 explains that since a lawyer should not aid or encourage a layman to practice law, DR 3-101(A), a lawyer should not practice law in association with a layman or otherwise share legal fees with a layman. Finally, DR 2-103(A) prohibits a lawyer from soliciting employment as a private practitioner "in violation of any statute or court rule." *See* New York Judiciary Law § 479 *et seq.*[2]

In 1975, a series of amendments to the Code were adopted which address the circumstances when a lawyer may be recommended by, accept employment from or cooperate with certain organizations. These changes or additions to the Code include

---

2. We do not express an opinion as to whether the United States Supreme Court's decision in *Bates v. State Bar of Arizona*, 433 U.S. 350 (1977) and the New York Court of Appeals' decision in *Matter of Koffler*, 51 N.Y. 2d 140 (1980) have affected the enforceability of any of the requirements of DR 2-103 and Section 479 of the Judiciary Law.

DR 2-101(B), DR 2-102, DR 2-103(C)(2), EC 2-33 and definitions (7) and (8) appearing after Canon 9. *See* New York State Opinion 416 (1975). Under these provisions, a lawyer may be recommended, employed or paid by or cooperate with a "bona fide organization which recommends furnishes or pays for legal services to its members or beneficiaries" (DR-2-103(D)(4)) that meets the criteria of DR 2-103(D)(4)(a)–(g), as long as the person to whom the recommendation is made is a member or beneficiary of the organization and the lawyer remains free to exercise independent professional judgment on behalf of the client (DR 2-103(C)(2)).

Accordingly, the Committee concludes that a lawyer may participate in the activities of the divorce mediation program, without violating DR 2-103(A), DR 3-101(A) or DR 3-102, if the divorce mediation program is a bona fide organization which recommends legal services to its members or beneficiaries and if all the other requirements of DR 2-103(D)(4) are met.

* * *

E. The Model Rule 4.2 Controversy

Questioning of Ex-Intern Provoked Angry Words

Don Van Natta, Jr., *The New York Times*, January 24, 1998, page A10*

WASHINGTON, Jan. 23 Monica S. Lewinsky, the fresh-faced former White House intern, was having lunch with her friend, Linda Tripp, at the Ritz Carlton in the Pentagon City mall. It was supposed to be a casual Friday tete-a-tete between two Pentagon colleagues.

Suddenly, seemingly from nowhere, six agents of the Federal Bureau of Investigation and prosecutors working for special counsel Kenneth W. Starr swooped in and confronted the 24-year-old woman.

Ms. Tripp, they told her, had taped 20 hours of intimate telephone conversations in which Ms. Lewinsky described in detail her alleged 18-month affair with President Clinton. Ms. Lewinsky was devastated. The agents asked if they could go somewhere private to talk, and Ms. Lewinsky and Ms. Tripp were escorted up to a Ritz-Carlton suite reserved by Mr. Starr's team.

For nearly 10 hours that Friday, Jan. 16, the agents tried to persuade Ms. Lewinsky into agreeing to work with them. They wanted her to help gather evidence under cover on several White House employees, including Betty W. Currie, Mr. Clinton's personal secretary. In return, the prosecutors were willing to give the former White House intern immunity from prosecution, but only if she decided to cooperate quickly, preferably that very day.

First, Ms. Lewinsky asked for her mother, Marcia Lewis, who took a train from New York. After Ms. Lewis arrived at around 10 P.M., mother and daughter went out in the hallway of the Ritz Carlton and snippets of their argument could be heard through the closed door. When they returned, Ms. Lewis phoned her ex-husband and Ms. Lewinsky's father, the Beverly Hills oncologist Bernard Lewinsky, who was divorced from Ms. Lewis a decade ago.

Before deciding whether his daughter should make a deal with Mr. Starr, Dr. Lewinsky wanted to consult a family lawyer in Los Angeles who advised Ms. Lewinsky against agreeing to cooperate with Mr. Starr's investigation.

Ms. Lewinsky's nearly 10 hours at the Ritz Carlton became the subject of angry exchanges today between the young woman's lawyer, who says the agents overstepped by questioning her without a lawyer, and Mr. Starr, who defended the conduct of his investigators. Mr. Starr added that Ms. Lewinsky thanked them before going home that evening.

Ms. Lewinsky secluded herself at a Watergate apartment as Mr. Starr's staff and her lawyer tried unsuccessfully to reach an agreement on immunity in exchange for her cooperation.

The negotiations began last Sunday between Ms. Lewinsky's lawyer, William Ginsburg, and attorneys working for Mr. Starr, according to two people familiar with the talks. Mr. Ginsburg submitted a formal proffer on Ms. Lewinsky's behalf. Late Monday, the proffer, a legal document outlining what Ms. Lewinsky would be willing to tell Mr. Starr in return for immunity, was rejected by Mr. Starr's office and no deal was brokered.

Because the heart of Mr. Starr's expanded investigation involves allegations of a conspiracy to obstruct justice by Mr. Clinton, Mr. Jordan and Ms. Lewinsky, the prosecutors refused to make a deal because the proffer provided no evidence that would support such a case, which was suggested by Ms. Lewinsky's own words on the tapes secretly recorded by Ms. Tripp.

Since the talks broke off late Monday, there has been no further discussion between the two sides.

In several televised interviews today, Mr. Ginsburg said that he would like to resume negotiations with Mr. Starr's office. "I'll be more than happy to talk with them." he said on CNN. Tonight, Mr. Starr also indicated that his office was willing to reopen the discussions.

But in several television interviews today, Mr. Ginsburg expressed irritation over the questioning of Ms. Lewinsky by the representatives from Mr. Starr's office.

"She did not get the privilege of calling counsel until late in the evening," Mr. Ginsburg said. He also challenged the way the agents swooped down on Ms. Lewinsky. "I had to ask myself," Mr. Ginsburg said, "how many F.B.I. agents and U.S. attorneys does it take to handle a 24-year-old girl."

But in a statement released tonight, Mr. Starr said there was nothing inappropriate about his office's dealings with Ms. Lewinsky.

"Recent media statements by one of her attorneys alleging that she was mistreated are wholly erroneous," Mr. Starr said.

On Jan. 7, Ms. Lewinsky provided a sworn affidavit to lawyers in the sexual harassment case brought by Paula Corbin Jones against Mr. Clinton. In that statement, given under oath, Ms. Lewinsky said, "I have never had a sexual relationship with the President. He did not propose that we have a sexual relationship."

But the following week, on Jan. 11, Ms. Tripp turned over nearly 20 hours of secretly recorded tapes of conversations with Ms. Lewinsky, who describes in graphic detail how she carried on an affair with Mr. Clinton and how both Mr. Clinton and Mr. Jordan had told her to deny it under oath to Ms. Jones' lawyers.

Ms. Tripp had approached Mr. Starr's office earlier in the week and was now, with her own grant of immunity, cooperating with his investigation. That investigation centered on whether Ms. Lewinsky was conspiring to obstruct justice by lying about her relationship with the President and encouraging Ms. Tripp to lie.

"She was repeatedly informed that she was free to leave, and she did leave several times to make calls from pay telephones," Mr. Starr said.

In fact, lawyers from Mr. Starr's office tried to accommodate Ms. Lewinsky's needs. They fetched coffee from Starbucks. Late at night, when her contact lens was bothering her, one of Mr. Starr's staffer went hunting through the Ritz-Carlton for lens solution.

In her first phone call, Ms. Lewinsky chose to call her mother, who was at her home in Manhattan. The weather was bad and Ms. Lewis did not want to fly to Washington. Instead, she took the train.

During the nearly five-hour wait, caused by delays from icy weather, Mr. Starr's lawyers held off from serious attempts to question the young Pentagon. They wiled away the hours with Ms. Lewinsky waiting for Ms. Lewis by watching movies on television, including the somewhat sultry film "Urban Cowboy." They strolled in the mall, checking out household products at a Crate & Barrel. They dined at a restaurant called Mozzarella.

But Mr. Ginsburg today painted a different portrait of how his client felt during the 10 hours she spent with Mr. Starr's staff. He said the young woman felt "squeezed," adding, "There was enough intimidation by the process, including the presence of FBI agents and U.S. attorneys, as well as words said to her about the imminence of prosecution, that she felt it was necessary to stay and not dare to leave because of the potential threat."

Mr. Starr and his staff adamantly denied that assertion tonight. "As they left the Ritz Carlton, both Ms. Lewinsky and Ms. Lewis thanked the F.B.I. agents and attorneys for their courtesy," Mr. Starr said.

Talking to Manager in Bias Suit Not Unethical

Paul D. Boynton, *Massachusetts Lawyers Weekly*
29 M.L.W. 919, December 18, 2000

A lawyer for a bias claimant did not violate ethics rules by conducting an unapproved interview with a manager for the defendant company where the employee's personal lawyer later consented to the interview, a Superior Court judge has ruled.

The defendant company argued that the employee's lawyer did not represent her for purposes of the underlying gender bias suit, and that lawyer's subsequent consent to the interview did not cure the ethics violation.

But Judge Ralph D. Gants disagreed.

"[I]t's clear that [the employee's lawyer] represented [her] 'in the matter' of [the claimant's] allegations against the [employer] of discrimination and retaliation," Gants wrote. "The [employer] can complain that it was harmed, but Comment 4 [of Rule 4.2 of the Rules of Professional Conduct] specifically makes [the employee's] private attorney, not her employer's attorney, the arbiter of whether such an interview may take place."

The 17-page decision is *Edwards v. Massachusetts Bay Transportation Authority, et al.,* Lawyers Weekly No. 12-429-00.

'Sledgehammer'

Inga S. Bernstein of Boston, counsel for the plaintiff, said the ruling will help attorneys representing discrimination claimants conduct basic pre-suit investigations.

Bernstein criticized the defense bar for using Rule of Professional Conduct 4.2 as a "legal tactic" to curb information gathering, rather than limiting it to raising legitimate concerns over ethical conduct.

"The way it's being used is to wield a sledgehammer over plaintiffs and their attorneys," she said. "They want to force your hand by having to call them to do basic investigations. This is a rule they want to establish, and they're going after it with a vengeance."

Bernstein's co-counsel, Norman S. Zalkind, pointed out that the ruling reaffirms that not all managerial employees are aligned with their employers in the context of discrimination claims.

Boston employment law expert Nina J. Kimball agreed.

"The decision says the individual employee's interests trump the company's interests when they are in conflict and not aligned," Kimball observed. "The employer's attorney does not always have the same interests as the employee. It's a plaintiff-friendly interpretation I've not seen in any other opinion."

Mark W. Batten of Boston, who represents employers, disputed the notion that plaintiffs are hampered unfairly by Rule 4.2.

Batten contended the rule limits defense attorneys, as well as plaintiffs' lawyers, from contacting parties ex parte.

"The plaintiff's bar is trying to get around the ethical rules," Batten maintained. "Instead of admitting defeat, they've chosen to ignore the rule."

Scott C. Moriearty of Boston, the defendant company's attorney, was unavailable for comment prior to deadline.

Ex Parte Interview

The plaintiff, Roberta Edwards, filed suit with the MCAD against the defendant company, the Massachusetts Bay Transportation Authority, for gender discrimination and retaliation based on her support of the earlier bias claim filed by Cynthia Gallo, who previously was the subordinate of Edwards.

In October 1996, Edwards joined the MBTA as chief administrative officer, Gallo was assistant director of medical operations and reported to Edwards.

In 1997, Gallo filed a bias complaint against the MBTA, alleging discrimination based on race and gender, and also alleging retaliation because of her advocacy of pay equality for women and minorities.

Gallo eventually settled the complaint and was later promoted to director of safety.

Edwards then filed a complaint with MCAD alleging that she had been discriminated against on the basis of her race and gender, and that she had been the victim of retaliation because of her advocacy at the MBTA against discrimination.

The MBTA eventually fired Edwards after she had been placed on administrative leave.

On Jan. 29, 1999, Edwards filed suit in Superior Court alleging race and gender employment discrimination and retaliation by the MBTA and a manager of the authority, Philip Puccia.

In her complaint, Edwards alleged she had supported Gallo when Gallo had filed her MCAD complaint, and had opposed any retaliatory actions purportedly taken against Gallo by the MBTA.

Shortly after filing the complaint, Edwards' attorney telephoned Gallo, who was still individually represented at the time, to ask if she would discuss the case. Gallo agreed to do so, and met with the attorney for about an hour.

The attorney did not notify the MBTA of the request to interview Gallo or of the actual interview. She did not ask it to consent to the interview.

The attorney also did not ask for the consent of Gallo's individual lawyer.

However, Gallo's individual lawyer later consented to the interview after it had been conducted.

Effective Cure

Gants held that even though the interview of Gallo without the individual lawyer's consent violated Rule 4.2, which prohibits ex parte contacts with managerial employees, the later consent by Gallo's lawyer cured the violation.

Since the interview could have lawfully occurred with [the individual attorney's] advance consent, there is no reason to impose sanctions when the attorney who could have given advance consent gives that consent after the fact," wrote Gants, noting that the private attorney was in the best position to determine whether Gallo's interests were injured as a result of the interview.

Gants characterized as "minimal" any danger of wholesale ex parte contacts with subsequent attempts to later obtain consent from lawyers representing individual employees.

"[F]ew attorneys will risk an ethical violation in the hope that they will later persuade the employee's private attorney to consent," he wrote. "Indeed, given the discourtesy of not asking for consent in advance, the likelihood of obtaining consent from most private attorneys is far greater before an interview than after."

Superior Interests

Gants also determined that when an employee's interests diverge from the company, and the employee is privately represented, the company can't thwart the employee from speaking with another attorney if the employee's private counsel advises the employee to do so.

While Rule 4.2 protects organizations against admissions made by employees without an attorney present, "it also recognizes that employees may have separate and distinct interests which may conflict with those of the organization," he said.

Gants pointed to Comment 4 of the rule, which states, in part, that "if an agent or employee is represented in the matter by his or her own counsel, the consent by that counsel to a communication will be sufficient for purposes of the Rule."

The judge noted that "the employee's interests may differ from those of the organization, but the employee, with the advice of his own counsel, is not barred from pursuing those interests. In short, when push comes to shove, the ethical rules favor the flesh-and-blood human being over the legal entity."

The judge noted that the private attorney is in a better position than the employer to determine whether an employee's interests are better served by speaking with another attorney or remaining silent.

Rule 4.2 "was intended to be protective of an organization's right to effective counsel but it is even more protective of an individual's right to effective counsel," the judge held. "When these interests conflict, the former must give way to the latter."

Related Matter

Gants rejected the argument of the MBTA that Gallo's private attorney did not represent her in connection with the lawsuit filed by Edwards, the plaintiff in the underlying case.

"For all practical purposes, when the need arose, Gallo looked to [her private attorney] to represent her with respect to the Edwards litigation, although for financial reasons she was sparing in her use of their time," Gants found.

"[T]his [c]ourt finds that [the private attorney] represented Gallo "in the matter of the Edwards litigation and [the plaintiff's attorney], with [the private attorney's] consent, was permitted under comment 4 of Rule 4.2 to interview Gallo without the presence or consent of the MBTA's counsel."

Messing, Rudavsky & Weliky, P.C. v. President & Fellows of Harvard College

436 Mass. 347
Supreme Judicial Court of Massachusetts, Suffolk
Argued Nov. 8, 2001
Decided March 19, 2002
[Some footnotes omitted. Remaining footnotes renumbered.]

Present: GREANEY, IRELAND, SPINA, COWIN, SOSMAN, & CORDY, JJ.

COWIN, J. The law firm of Messing, Rudavsky & Weliky, P.C. (MR & W), appeals from an order of the Superior Court sanctioning the firm for violations of Mass.R.Prof.C. 4.2, 426 Mass. 1402 (1998), and its predecessor, S.J.C. Rule 3:07, Canon 7, DR 7-104(A)(1), as appearing in 382 Mass. 786 (1981). Both versions of the rule prohibit attorneys from communicating with a represented party in the absence of that party's attorney. This appeal raises the issue whether, and to what extent, the rule prohibits an attorney from speaking ex parte to the employees of an organization represented by counsel.[1] A judge in the Superior Court interpreted the rule to prohibit communication with any employee whose statements could be used as admissions against the organization pursuant to Fed.R.Evid. 801(d)(2)(D), and sanctioned MR & W for its ethical breach. We vacate the order and remand for entry of an order denying the motion for sanctions.

---

1. We acknowledge the amicus briefs filed by Teachers of Professional Responsibility, National Employment Lawyers Association, AFL-CIO (joined by the Massachusetts AFL-CIO; the American Federation of State, County and Municipal Employees, Council 93; Service Employees International Union Local 509; and United Food & Commercial Workers Local 328), NAACP Legal Defense & Educational Fund, Inc. (joined by Lawyers' Committee for Civil Rights Under Law, Lawyers' Committee for Civil Rights Under Law of the Boston Bar Association, Coalition of Labor Union Women, Gay & Lesbian Advocates & Defenders, Maine Employment Lawyers Association, and the Disability Law Center), American Civil Liberties Union of Massachusetts, Greater Boston Legal Services (joined by Massachusetts Law Reform Institute), Boston Area Management Attorneys Group (joined by New England Legal Foundation) and the Attorney General.

On appeal, MR & W contends that the judge's construction of the rule is overly broad and results from an incorrect interpretation of the rule's commentary. In addition, MR & W contends that the judge lacked authority to issue sanctions for ethical violations, and that even if he had such authority, the attorney's fees sanction imposed by the judge constituted an abuse of discretion. Because we vacate the Superior Court judge's order on the basis that his interpretation of rule 4.2 and DR 7-104(A)(1) was overly broad, we need not address MR & W's other contentions.

1. *Facts and procedural history.* From the stipulated facts, we distill the following. In August of 1997, MR & W filed a complaint against President and Fellows of Harvard College (Harvard) with the Massachusetts Commission Against Discrimination (commission) on behalf of its client, Kathleen Stanford. Stanford, a sergeant with the Harvard University police department (HUPD), alleged that Harvard and its police chief, Francis Riley, discriminated against her on the basis of gender and in reprisal for earlier complaints of discrimination. MR & W represented Stanford, and Harvard was represented before the commission by in-house counsel, and thereafter by a Boston law firm. Following the institution of the suit, MR & W communicated ex parte with five employees of the HUPD: two lieutenants, two patrol officers, and a dispatcher. Although the two lieutenants had some supervisory authority over Stanford, it was not claimed that any of the five employees were involved in the alleged discrimination or retaliation against her or exercised management authority with respect to the alleged discriminatory or retaliatory acts.

In response to a motion by Harvard, the commission ruled that MR & W's ex parte contacts with all five employees violated rule 4.2, but declined to issue sanctions for these violations. MR & W removed the case to the Superior Court, where Harvard filed a motion seeking sanctions for the same violations of rule 4.2 on which the commission had previously ruled. The Superior Court judge then issued a memorandum of decision and order holding that MR & W violated the rule with respect to all five employees, prohibiting MR & W from using the affidavits it had procured during the interviews, and awarding Harvard the attorney's fees and costs it had expended in litigating the motion, in a later order calculated as $94,418.14.[2]

MR & W and Stanford appealed both orders to a single justice of the Appeals Court pursuant to G.L. c. 231, § 118, first par. The single justice denied the petition and declined to report the matter to the full bench of the Appeals Court. MR & W filed a complaint with the single justice of this court pursuant to G.L. c. 211, § 3, who reserved and reported the matter to the full court.

2. *Jurisdiction.* As a threshold matter, Harvard asserts that MR & W is not entitled to relief under G.L. c. 211, § 3. General Laws c. 211, § 3, provides: "The supreme judicial court shall have general superintendence of all courts of inferior jurisdiction to correct and prevent errors and abuses therein if no other remedy is expressly provided...." G.L. c. 211, § 3. This power of review is discretionary with the court and will be "exercised only in 'the most exceptional circumstances.'" *Planned Parenthood League of Mass., Inc. v. Operation Rescue*, 406 Mass. 701, 706, 550 N.E.2d 1361 (1990), quoting *Costarelli v. Commonwealth*, 374 Mass. 677, 679, 373 N.E.2d 1183 (1978).

---

2. Harvard claimed fees of $152,255.96. The judge reduced this amount after deducting fees incurred in the proceedings before the commission, and subtracting a portion of the billing rate as excessive.

* * *

3. *Interpretation of Rule 4.2 of the Massachusetts Rules of Professional Responsibility.*

a. *An overview.* Disciplinary Rule 7-104(A)(1) provides:

> "During the course of his representation of a client a lawyer shall not: ... Communicate or cause another to communicate on the subject of the representation with a party he knows to be represented by a lawyer in that matter unless he has the prior consent of the lawyer representing such other party or is authorized by law to do so."

As of January 1, 1998, DR 7-104(A)(1) was superseded by rule 4.2. Massachusetts, like most States, adopted this rule verbatim from the American Bar Association (ABA) Model Rules of Professional Conduct. Rule 4.2 provides:

> "In representing a client, a lawyer shall not communicate about the subject of the representation with a person the lawyer knows to be represented by another lawyer in the matter, unless the lawyer has the consent of the other lawyer or is authorized by law to do so."

The rule has been justified generally as "preserv[ing] the mediating role of counsel on behalf of their clients ... protect[ing] clients from overreaching by counsel for adverse interests," *Pratt v. National R.R. Passenger Corp.*, 54 F.Supp.2d 78, 79 (D.Mass.1999), and "protecting the attorney-client relationship." *In re Air Crash Disaster near Roselawn Ind.*, 909 F.Supp. 1116, 1121 (N.D.Ill.1995). See *Orlowski v. Dominick's Finer Foods, Inc.*, 937 F.Supp. 723, 727 (N.D.Ill.1996); *Brown v. St. Joseph County*, 148 F.R.D. 246, 249 (N.D.Ind.1993); *Wright v. Group Health Hosp.*, 103 Wash.2d 192, 196, 691 P.2d 564 (1984).

Neither version of the rule explicitly addresses the scope of the prohibition when the represented person is an organization. When the represented person is an individual, there is no difficulty determining when an attorney has violated the rule; the represented person is easily identifiable. In the case of an organization, however, identifying the protected class is more complicated.

Because an organization acts only through its employees, the rule must extend to some of these employees. However, most courts have rejected the position that the rule automatically prevents an attorney from speaking with all employees of a represented organization. See *Terra Int'l, Inc. v. Mississippi Chem. Corp.*, 913 F.Supp. 1306, 1320 (N.D.Iowa 1996) (noting rule banning ex parte contacts with all current employees has been rejected by courts that have considered it); *Shearson Lehman Bros. v. Wasatch Bank*, 139 F.R.D. 412, 416 (D.Utah 1991); *State v. CIBA-GEIGY*, 247 N.J.Super. 314, 323–324, 589 A.2d 180 (1991) (noting only one decision had adopted blanket rule prohibiting contact with all former and current employees, and that other cases which had applied that approach were later vacated and withdrawn); *Niesig v. Team I*, 76 N.Y.2d 363, 371, 559 N.Y.S.2d 493, 558 N.E.2d 1030 (1990); *Strawser v. Exxon Co. U.S.A.*, 843 P.2d 613, 619–620 (Wyo.1992).

Most of MR & W's contacts with the Harvard employees took place in late 1997, when DR 7-104(A)(1) was still the operative rule. However, the Superior Court found that MR & W also made "minimal communication" in early 1998, and sanctioned MR & W for violations of both the old and new versions of the rule. Rule 4.2 uses the phrase "person the lawyers knows to be represented," while DR 7-104(A)(1) uses the phrase "party [a lawyer] knows to be represented." By replacing the word "party" with "person," the drafters of rule 4.2 arguably intended to prohibit contact with a broader class than did DR 7-104(A)(1). However, both versions of the rule consider an organization to be a "person" or "party," and thus prohibit ex parte contact with at least some of the organization's employees. See, e.g., *Niesig v. Team I, supra;* Mass. R. Prof. C. 9.1(h), 426 Mass. 1432 (1998) (defining "[p]erson" to include a corporation, association, trust, partnership, and any other organization or legal entity). In the context of contact with the employees of a represented organization, courts have interpreted the two versions of the rule to prohibit the same conduct. See *Hurley v. Modern Cont. Constr. Co.,* Civil Action No. 94-11373-RBC, 1999 WL 95723 (D.Mass. Feb. 19, 1999); *Johnson v. Cadillac Plastic Group, Inc.,* 930 F.Supp. 1437, 1440 (D.Colo.1996); *Strawser v. Exxon Co., U.S.A., supra* at 617 n. 5.[3]

The comment to rule 4.2 provides guidance in the case of a represented organization. Because both versions of the rule prohibit essentially the same conduct, the comment is instructive (although not controlling) in determining the scope of both the old and new versions of the rule. See Mass. R. Prof. C. Scope [9], 426 Mass. 1305 (1998) ("The Comments are intended as guides to interpretation, but the text of each Rule is authoritative").

According to comment [4] to rule 4.2, an attorney may not speak ex parte to three categories of employees: (1) "persons having managerial responsibility on behalf of the organization with regard to the subject of the representation"; (2) persons "whose act or omission in connection with that matter may be imputed to the organization for purposes of civil or criminal liability"; and (3) persons "whose statement may constitute an admission on the part of the organization."[4] Mass. R. Prof. C. 4.2 comment [4], 426 Mass. 1403 (1998).

b. *The Superior Court judge's decision.* The judge held that all five employees interviewed by MR & W were within the third category of the comment. He reached this result by concluding that the phrase "admission" in the comment refers to statements admissible in court under the admissions exception to the rule against hearsay. The Commonwealth's version of this rule was defined in *Ruszcyk v. Secretary of Pub. Safety,* 401 Mass. 418, 517 N.E.2d 152 (1988), where we held that a court may admit a "statement by [the party's] agent or servant concerning a matter within the scope of [the] agency or employment, made during the existence of the relationship." *Id.* at 420, 517 N.E.2d 152, quoting Proposed Mass. R. Evid. 801(d)(2)(D). This rule is identical to Fed.R.Evid. 801(d)(2)(D). Because the comment includes any employee whose statement *may* constitute an admission, this interpretation would prohibit an attorney from contacting any current employees of an organization to discuss any subject within the scope of their employment. This is, as the Superior Court judge admitted, a rule that is "strikingly protective of corporations regarding employee interviews."[5]

c. *Other interpretations of rule 4.2.* Harvard contends that the third category of the comment is an unambiguous reference to the admissions exception to the hearsay rule. However, other jurisdictions that have adopted the same or similar versions of rule 4.2

---

3. All references will be to Mass. R. Prof. C. 4.2, 426 Mass. 1402 (1998), although any discussion is equally applicable to S.J.C. Rule 3:07, Canon 7, DR 7-104(A)(1), as appearing in 382 Mass. 86 (1981).

4. Massachusetts adopted the commentary to rule 4.2 proposed in the ABA Model Rules of Professional Conduct, except that the Massachusetts version adds the phrase "with regard to the subject of the representation" to the first category of the comment.

5. The judge understandably relied on and followed decisions issued by a judge and a magistrate of the United States District Court for the District of Massachusetts in reaching his decision. No prior Massachusetts State court decision had construed the scope of the rule.

are divided on whether their own versions of the rule are properly linked to the admissions exception to the hearsay rule, and disagree about the precise scope of the rule as applied to organizations. See, e.g., *Orlowski v. Dominick's Finer Foods, Inc.*, 937 F.Supp. 723, 728 (1996) ("Courts have debated at length which current corporate employees constitute represented parties ..."); *Niesig v. Team I*, 76 N.Y.2d 363, 371, 559 N.Y.S.2d 493, 558 N.E.2d 1030 (1990) ("The many courts, bar associations and commentators that have balanced the competing considerations have evolved various tests, each claiming some adherents, each with some imperfection ...").

Some jurisdictions have adopted the broad reading of the rule endorsed by the judge in this case. See, e.g., *Weibrecht v. Southern Ill. Transfer, Inc.*, 241 F.3d 875 (7th Cir.2001); *Cole v. Appalachian Power Co.*, 903 F.Supp. 975 (S.D.W.Va.1995); *Brown v. St. Joseph County*, 148 F.R.D. 246, 254 (N.D.Ind.1993). Courts reaching this result do so because, like the Superior Court, they read the word "admission" in the third category of the comment as a reference to Fed.R.Evid. 801(d)(2)(D) and any corresponding State rule of evidence. *Id.* This rule forbids contact with practically all employees because "virtually every employee may conceivably make admissions binding on his or her employer." *In re Air Crash Disaster near Roselawn, Ind.*, 909 F.Supp. 1116, 1121 (N.D.Ill. 1995). However, some of the courts that have adopted this interpretation have expressed reservations. See *Pratt v. National R.R. Passenger Corp.*, 54 F.Supp.2d 78, 80 (D.Mass.1999) ("This [c]ourt has previously highlighted some of the negative aspects of ethical rules prohibiting ex parte communications with individuals in the corporate context"); *Hurley v. Modern Cont. Constr. Co., supra* (stating that linking rule to rule of evidence may frustrate "truth-seeking process").

At the other end of the spectrum, a small number of jurisdictions has interpreted the rule narrowly so as to allow an attorney for the opposing party to contact most employees of a represented organization. These courts construe the rule to restrict contact with only those employees in the organization's "control group," defined as those employees in the uppermost echelon of the organization's management. See *Johnson v. Cadillac Plastic Group, Inc.*, 930 F.Supp. 1437, 1442 (D.Colo.1996); *Fair Automotive Repair, Inc. v. Car-X Serv. Sys., Inc.*, 128 Ill.App.3d 763, 771, 84 Ill.Dec. 25, 471 N.E.2d 554 (1984) (applying rule only to "top management persons who had the responsibility of making final decisions"); *Wright v. Group Health Hosp.*, 103 Wash.2d 192, 200, 691 P.2d 564 (1984) (applying rule only to "those employees who have the legal authority to 'bind' the corporation in a legal evidentiary sense, i.e., those employees who have 'speaking authority' for the corporation").

Other jurisdictions have adopted yet a third test that, while allowing for some ex parte contacts with a represented organization's employees, still maintains some protection of the organization. The Court of Appeals of New York articulated such a rule in *Niesig v. Team I*, 76 N.Y.2d 363, 559 N.Y.S.2d 493, 558 N.E.2d 1030 (1990), rejecting an approach that ties the rule to Fed.R.Evid. 801(d)(2)(D). Instead, the court defined a represented person to include "employees whose acts or omissions in the matter under inquiry are binding on the corporation ... or imputed to the corporation for purposes of its liability, or employees implementing the advice of counsel." *Id.* at 374, 559 N.Y.S.2d 493, 558 N.E.2d 1030. Other jurisdictions have subsequently adopted the *Niesig* test. See, e.g., *Weider Sports Equip. Co. v. Fitness First, Inc.*, 912 F.Supp. 502 (D.Utah 1996); *Branham v. Norfolk & W. Ry.*, 151 F.R.D. 67, 70–71 (S.D.W.Va.1993); *State v. CIBA-GEIGY Corp.*, 247 N.J.Super. 314, 325, 589 A.2d 180 (1991); *Dent v. Kaufman*, 185 W.Va. 171, 406 S.E.2d 68 (1991); *Strawser v. Exxon Co., U.S.A.*, 843 P.2d 613 (Wyo.1992). In addition, the Restatement (Third) of the Law Governing Lawyers endorses this rule. See

Restatement (Third) of Law Governing Lawyers § 100 Reporter's Note comment e, at 98 (1998).

d. *Our interpretation of rule 4.2.* We adopt a test similar to that proposed in *Niesig v. Team I, supra.* Although the comment's reference to persons "whose statement may constitute an admission on the part of the organization" was most likely intended as a reference to Fed.R.Evid. 801(d)(2)(D), this interpretation would effectively prohibit the questioning of all employees who can offer information helpful to the litigation. We reject the comment as overly protective of the organization and too restrictive of an opposing attorney's ability to contact and interview employees of an adversary organization.

We instead interpret the rule to ban contact only with those employees who have the authority to "commit the organization to a position regarding the subject matter of representation." See *Johnson v. Cadillac Plastic Group, Inc.,* 930 F.Supp. 1437, 1442 (D.Colo.1996); Restatement (Third) of Law Governing Lawyers, *supra* at § 100 comment e. See also Ethics 2000 Commission Draft for Public Comment Model Rule 4.2 Reporter's Explanation of Changes (Feb. 21, 2000) (recommending deletion of the third category of the comment).[6] The employees with whom contact is prohibited are those with "speaking authority" for the corporation who "have managing authority sufficient to give them the right to speak for, and bind, the corporation." *Wright v. Group Health Hosp., supra* at 201, 691 P.2d 564. Employees who can commit the organization are those with authority to make decisions about the course of the litigation, such as when to initiate suit, and when to settle a pending case. See Restatement (Third) of the Law Governing Lawyers, *supra* at § 100 comment e, at 93 (employees who have the power to make binding evidentiary admissions are "analogous to ... person[s] who possess[ ] power to settle a dispute on behalf of the organization"). We recognize that this test is a retrenchment from the broad prohibition on employee contact endorsed by the comment.

This interpretation, when read in conjunction with the other two categories of the comment, would prohibit ex parte contact only with those employees who exercise managerial responsibility in the matter, who are alleged to have committed the wrongful acts at issue in the litigation, or who have authority on behalf of the corporation to make decisions about the course of the litigation. This result is substantially the same as the *Niesig* test because it "prohibit[s] direct communication ...'with those officials ... who have the legal power to bind the corporation in the matter or who are responsible for implementing the advice of the corporation's lawyer ... or whose own interests are directly at stake in a representation.'" *Niesig v. Team I, supra* at 374, 559 N.Y.S.2d 493, 558 N.E.2d 1030, quoting C. Wolfram, Modern Legal Ethics § 11.6, at 613 (1986).

* * *

While our interpretation of the rule may reduce the protection available to organizations provided by the attorney-client privilege, it allows a litigant to obtain more meaningful disclosure of the truth by conducting informal interviews with certain employees of an opposing organization. Our interpretation does not jeopardize legitimate organizational interests because it continues to disallow contacts with those members of the organization who are so closely tied with the organization or the events at issue that it

---

6. The ABA commission established to review and make recommendations concerning improvements to the Model Rules is commonly known as the Ethics 2000 Commission.

would be unfair to interview them without the presence of the organization's counsel. Fairness to the organization does not require the presence of an attorney every time an employee may make a statement admissible in evidence against his or her employer. The public policy of promoting efficient discovery is better advanced by adopting a rule which favors the revelation of the truth by making it more difficult for an organization to prevent the disclosure of relevant evidence.

* * *

4. *Applying rule 4.2 to the employees interviewed by MR & W.* The five Harvard employees interviewed by MR & W do not fall within the third category of the comment as we have construed it. As employees of the HUPD, they are not involved in directing the litigation at bar or authorizing the organization to make binding admissions. In fact, Harvard does not argue that any of the five employees fit within our definition of this category.

The Harvard employees are also not employees "whose act or omission in connection with that matter may be imputed to the organization for purposes of civil or criminal liability." Mass. R. Prof. C. 4.2 comment [4]. Stanford's complaint does not name any of these employees as involved in the alleged discrimination. In fact, in an affidavit she states that the two lieutenants "had no role in making any of the decisions that are the subject of my complaint of discrimination and retaliation," and Harvard does not refute this averment. All five employees were mere witnesses to the events that occurred, not active participants.

We must still determine, however, whether any of the interviewed employees have "managerial responsibility on behalf of the organization with regard to the subject of the representation." Mass. R. Prof. C. 4.2 comment [4]. Although the two patrol officers and the dispatcher were subordinate to Stanford and had no managerial authority, the two lieutenants exercised some supervisory authority over Stanford. However, not all employees with some supervisory power over their coworkers are deemed to have "managerial" responsibility in the sense intended by the comment. See *Orlowski v. Dominick's Finer Foods, Inc.*, 937 F.Supp. 723, 729 (N.D.Ill.1996). "[S]upervision of a small group of workers would not constitute a managerial position within a corporation." *Id.*, quoting *Carter-Herman v. Philadelphia*, 897 F.Supp. 899, 904 (E.D.Pa. 1995). Even if the two lieutenants are deemed to have managerial responsibility, the Massachusetts version of the comment adds the requirement that the managerial responsibility be in "regard to the subject of the representation." Mass. R. Prof. C. 4.2 comment [4]. Thus, the comment includes only those employees who have supervisory authority over the events at issue in the litigation. There is no evidence in the record that the lieutenants' managerial decisions were a subject of the litigation. The affidavits of the two lieutenants indicate that they did not complete any evaluations or offer any opinions of Stanford that Chief Riley considered in reaching his decisions.

5. *Conclusion.* Because we conclude that rule 4.2 did not prohibit MR & W from contacting and interviewing the five HUPD employees, we vacate the order of the Superior Court judge and remand the case for the entry of an order denying the defendant's motion for sanctions.

So ordered.

CORDY, J. (concurring in part and dissenting in part).

I concur that the financial sanction levied against Messing, Rudavsky & Weliky, P.C., must be set aside, but do so for reasons different from those set forth in the court's opinion. I disagree with the court's interpretation of Mass. R. Prof. C. 4.2, 426 Mass. 1402 (1998), and its comment that became effective on January 1, 1998, and therefore dissent from its holding in that regard.

Rule 4.2. Whatever the merits of the interpretation that the court today gives rule 4.2, it is not consistent with the rule and the comment that we adopted in 1998, or its predecessor, S.J.C. Rule 3:07, Canon 7, DR 7-104(A)(1), as appearing in 382 Mass. 786 (1981) (DR 7-104[A][1]), and creates a troubling inconsistency in the way we treat organizations in our adversary system.

I begin with the premise that organizations have the right to be represented effectively by counsel to the same extent as individuals, while recognizing that organizations act through agents and employees, thus complicating the question of who the represented party is when it becomes, or is about to become, the subject of a legal proceeding. In this context the answer to the question has significant implications for defining and establishing the parameters of the attorney-client relationship, and for determining whether and to what extent actions and statements of individuals will be imputed to it in the legal proceedings. The answer to the same question also informs the meaning of the provision in our code of professional conduct that prohibits attorneys from having ex parte communication with opposing parties (or persons) they know to be represented by counsel (the no-contact rule), the essence of DR 7-104(A)(1) and rule 4.2.

It strikes me that the answer ought to be as close to being a single and consistent one as we can make it. This is particularly critical in the context of determining on the one hand whose actions and statements will be attributed to the organization in litigation, and on the other hand who in the organization is represented by counsel for purposes of the no-contact rule now embodied in rule 4.2. The purpose of the no-contact rule, after all, is to ensure the effective assistance of counsel by preserving counsels' mediating role on behalf of their clients, protecting clients from overreaching by counsel for adverse interests, and protecting the attorney-client relationship by preventing clients from making ill-advised statements without the advice of their attorney. There are few responsibilities more central to the effective representation of organizations (or individuals) than being in a position to advise and counsel them when they are being asked by opposing counsel to make statements that can be used against them to establish liability in litigation.

It is in this framework that, in 1982, the Committee on Professional Ethics of the Massachusetts Bar Association issued Opinion No. 82-7, interpreting DR 7-104(A)(1), as it applied to ex parte contacts by opposing counsel with employees of an organization. The opinion concluded that a lawyer could not interview current employees of such a party without the consent of opposing counsel "where the proposed interview concerns matters within the scope of the employee's employment." The ethics committee reasoned that the principal interest reflected in DR 7-104(A)(1) is the party's right to "effective representation of counsel" that can be guarded adequately only by viewing all present employees of an organization as parties where the proposed interview concerned matters within the scope of their employment. It further reasoned that effective representation requires that the attorney aid his client both to avoid procedural pitfalls and to present truthful statements in the most effective manner. Finally, it underscored that the position it was adopting was in accord with the law of evidence "which recognizes an exception to the hearsay rule as to 'a statement by [an] agent or servant concerning the matter within the scope of his agency or employment.'" "This rule binds the corporation with respect to admissions by employees far beyond the 'control group' of the corporation." Accordingly, it concluded that the definition of a "represented party" for purposes of DR 7-104(A)(1) needed to be consistent with the reach of the evidentiary rule.

This opinion, while it made eminent sense, was not fully embraced by the few Massachusetts courts (all Federal) which had occasion to consider DR 7-104(A)(1) in the context of petitions by parties to allow or prohibit ex parte communication with employees during discovery.[7] These courts, while generally acknowledging the reasoning of Opinion No. 82-7, often concluded that in the absence of specific language in the rule regarding this subject, the better test was to balance, on a case by case basis, the competing interests of "effective representation," and the need, largely by plaintiffs, to gather facts informally, unpolished or influenced by counsel for the corporate opposition. This case-by-case balancing was eventually criticized in 1990 in *Siguel v. Trustees of Tufts College,* Civ. A. No. 88-0626-Y, 1990 WL 29199 (D.Mass.1990), as being wasteful of judicial resources, running the risk of treating similarly situated parties differently, and, most important, providing no clear guidance on ethical behavior to attorneys who needed to act and rely on that guidance every day. The court called on the Supreme Judicial Court to address the issue and provide clarity to the rule.[8]

Although it took several years, this court eventually addressed the issue when, after comment and hearings, it adopted rule 4.2 and its comment. The rule was adopted with the full knowledge of Opinion No. 82-7 and its interpretation of DR 7-104(A)(1), with full knowledge of its 1988 decision in *Ruszcyk v. Secretary of Pub. Safety,* 401 Mass. 418, 517 N.E.2d 152 (1988), adopting those portions of Proposed Mass. R. Evid. 801(d)(2)(D) that made hearsay statements of employees admissible as vicarious admissions of their employers, and after hearing and considering the concerns of many lawyers (including the plaintiff law firm), that, if the court adopted rule 4.2 and its comment without amendment it would be adopting the view expounded in Opinion No. 82-7.[9] Even the court acknowledges that the adopted language in the comment prohibiting contact with persons "whose statement may constitute an admission on the part of the organization" was "most likely" intended as a reference to Fed.R.Evid. 801(d)(2)(D). *Ante* at 832.

In this context it is painful to see the court now claim that, when it adopted the commentary, it did not intend its consequence; a consequence that merely ensures that organizations are as effectively represented by counsel as individuals. We should not shrink from what is a perfectly reasonable balancing of the equities.

In its opinion, the court states that to interpret the rule and commentary as adopted would grant an advantage to organizational litigants over nonorganizational litigants because, inter alia, as concerns a nonorganizational defendant, witnesses to an event could be interviewed without court approval, but if the defendant were an organization and the witnesses were employees, those witnesses could not be interviewed without

---

7. See, e.g., Morrison v. Brandeis Univ., 125 F.R.D. 14 (D.Mass.1989); Mompoint v. Lotus Dev. Corp., 110 F.R.D. 414 (D.Mass.1986); Siguel v. Trustees of Tufts College, Civ. A. No. 88-0626-Y, 1990 WL 29199 (D.Mass.1990); Bruce v. Silber, Civ. A. No. 88-2588-H, 1989 WL 206452 (D.Mass. 1989).

8. The Local Rules of the United States District Court for the District of Massachusetts (2001) follow the disciplinary rules promulgated by the Supreme Judicial Court, formerly including DR 7-104(A)(1), as appearing in 382 Mass. 786 (1981), and now Mass. R. Prof. C. 4.2, 426 Mass. 1402 (1998).

9. Subsequent to our adoption of rule 4.2 and its comment, a Federal magistrate held that the rule now clearly prohibits contact with employees of a represented organization regarding matters within the scope of their employment. Hurley v. Modern Cont. Constr. Co., Civ. A. No. 94-11373-RBC.

court approval (assuming the interview concerned matters within the scope of their employment). *Ante* at 833–34. This observation misses the point. The reason that witnesses to an event would be, and should be, treated differently is precisely because the consequences of their interviews are treated differently. In the nonorganizational context, a witness's hearsay statement could not be a vicarious admission of the defendant, yet in the organizational context it could. The scope of the no-contact rule should be tailored to the legal consequences of the contact because the purpose of the rule is to ensure the effective legal representation of counsel. Our ruling today upsets the balance created by the rule and commentary and creates a distinct disadvantage to the organizational parties.

* * *

In these circumstances, it seems to me that we should not be so quick to adopt the position of States with very different jurisprudential landscapes, and disown a rule that makes good sense in the Commonwealth. Rather, we should work to ensure that the reach of the rule does not exceed the limits necessary to its purpose. This can be accomplished in two ways. First, by making it clear that the prohibition against communicating with persons whose statements may constitute an admission on the part of their organization (1) does not preclude counsel from contacting all employees of a represented organization and (2) only applies to communications with employees about matters within the scope of their employment that would be admissible as vicarious admissions of the organization in the particular controversy that is the subject of the representation. Second, by demonstrating that we intend narrowly to interpret the qualifying factor, i.e., what matters are within the scope of an individual's employment, for purposes of this rule and the common law rule of evidence announced in *Ruszcyk v. Secretary of Pub. Safety*, 401 Mass. 418, 517 N.E.2d 152 (1988).

Applying these limiting factors to the prohibition, I would not, for example, conclude that the plaintiff's communications with the Harvard patrol officers and dispatcher would have been impermissible. Observations by an employee of apparent wrongful conduct by other employees ought not generally be construed to be within the scope of an employee's employment unless it was their responsibility to observe or investigate such conduct.[10] Consequently, hearsay statements about such observations should not be admissible against the organization under the admissions exception to the hearsay rule.

I view the plaintiff's communications with the Harvard police lieutenants, however, as more problematic. Those employees clearly had a measure of supervisory responsibility over Stanford, whose job performance was to be a central issue in her discrimination litigation. Thus, those interviews run afoul not only of the prohibition against communicating with employees about matters within the scope of their employment but also the prohibition against communicating with employees having managerial responsibility regarding the subject of the representation.

Sanctions. I fully support the imposition of sanctions by trial judges against litigants who violate or abuse the discovery rules, obstruct the efficient exchange of discoverable information, or who take and litigate frivolous positions. The use of the

---

10. Compare Dent v. Kaufman, 185 W.Va. 171, 176, 406 S.E.2d 68 (1991) (no matter how damning, coworker's observations of improper behavior of colleagues would not constitute admission), with Ruszcyk v. Secretary of Pub. Safety, 401 Mass. 418, 420–421 n. 3, 517 N.E.2d 152 (1988) (witness's duties included receiving reports of incident investigations, therefore his hearsay statement about cause of incident was statement about matter within scope of employment).

cost of litigating such matters as a measure of the appropriate sanction also makes a great deal of sense. But DR 7-104(A)(1) and rule 4.2 are ethical rules, not discovery rules. In addition, the position taken and arguments made by the plaintiff law firm were not frivolous, and its actions were not clearly violative of the ethical rules at the time, in light of the state of the law regarding the reach and meaning of DR 7-104(A)(1).[11] Therefore, notwithstanding my view that some of the plaintiff's actions violated DR 7-104(A)(1) and rule 4.2, as I would interpret them, I would vacate the financial sanctions as an abuse of discretion. I would leave the remainder of the motion judge's order in effect.

---

11. This was the rule in effect when almost all of the ex parte communications took place.

Chapter VII

Starting a Law Practice

Problems

Problem 28

Select sides and set *Shapero* v. *Kentucky Bar Association*, 486 U.S. 466 (1988), set out at Chapter VII-3, *infra,* for argument. See Justice O'Connor's eloquent dissent, joined by Chief Justice Rehnquist and Justice Scalia. Do you agree with Justice O'Connor that "One distinguishing feature of any profession ... is that membership entails an ethical obligation to temper one's selfish pursuit of economic success by adhering to standards of conduct that could not be enforced either by legal fiat or through the discipline of the market"? If so, do you agree with the decision of the Court? Again, is there anything inherently "ethical" about advertising or solicitation restrictions?

Problem 29

Select sides and set the case of *In the Matter of Fordham*, 423 Mass. 481 (1996), set out at Chapter VII-3, *infra,* for argument. Laurence S. Fordham, Esq. is a distinguished graduate of Harvard Law School and was a partner of a major Boston firm. Along with many other members of the bar, I signed an *amicus* brief in his defense. Was I right to do so?

Problem 30

A number of lawyers and bar associations have looked into the idea of establishing "certification" examinations. According to one plan, discussed in Massachusetts, only graduation from an accredited bar school and the bar examination would be required to practice. If, however, you also passed a "certification" examination, you could also advertise yourself as a "certified specialist" in, say, employment law, or estates and trusts, or taxation etc. The Massachusetts task force even considered having a "General Practice" certification, like a "primary care" physician in medicine. What do you think of this idea? Would you have recertification tests required every five or ten years, to be sure the specialist was "up-to-date"? Would you include a further requirement of a minimum time in practice? In the end, Massachusetts chose not to go this route, but instead adopted the existing *Mass. Rule* 7.4. What do you think of that rule?

Problem 31

Assume that you are now five years out of law school. You have repaid most of your debts, and are tired of the restrictions imposed by life in the firm where you are working. You want to "strike out on your own!" How would you do that? How would you advertise your services, set your fees, and distribute earnings? What kind of law would you practice? Would you do *pro bono* work? Would you charge contingent fees? Who would you link up with? What if one of you wanted "a better quality of life," while another worked exceptionally hard, or attracted all the clients? How would you share profits? In short, create your own firm.

How are your efforts restricted by the professional rules? Does this regulation make sense, or does it favor larger, or more established, firms? Would you want some kind of certification? Would you pay and/or receive referral fees? Compare *Mass. Rule* 1.5 (e) on division of fees with *ABA Model Rule* 1.5 (e). Which is better? (This problem is variant of one originally devised by Andrew L. Kaufman. See Andrew L. Kaufman, *Problems in Professional Responsibility* (1st ed., Boston, 1996) pp. 408–409).

Problem 32

You have a great idea. Many middle class Americans are "priced out" of the market for legal services, at least for everything except contingency fee work for personal injury. While shopping at your local Walmart, it occurs to you that a high volume, low cost brand name franchise could revolutionize legal services. By leveraging paralegal assistance, using computer generated forms, and having accessible centers in atriums and malls, you could bring reasonably good tax advice, estate planning, real estate services *and more* to millions! Are there any "professional ethics" barriers? If so, are they really justifiable? See Lawrence J. Fox, "Dan's World, A Free Enterprise Dream; An Ethics Nightmare," 55 *The Business Lawyer* (August 2000), p. 1533, set out at Chapter VII-3, *supra*.

VII-1. Introduction: "On Your Own" in Law Practice

Up to now, our study of "professional ethics" could be convincingly described as a study of moral values: loyalty, confidentiality, honesty and truthful communication. But even so, some would argue that even these rules are partly about economics, such as the rules permitting a breach of client confidence to collect a bill (*Model Rule* 1.6(b)(5)) or limiting a lawyer's role in alternative dispute resolution (*Model Rule* 2.4). Now we are going to study some rules that seem openly about economics. These are the rules governing advertising, solicitation, specialization, law firm structure, and fees. Most, but not all, of these rules are grouped in the *Model Rules* in Article 5 "Law Firms and Associations" and Article 7 "Information About Legal Services." Some experts, such as Dean Daniel R. Fischel of Chicago Law School, have argued that all such professional rules distort the free market place, and are both unnecessary and harmful.[1]

Many lawyers would take a different view, and argue that these "business" rules are about values after all. In particular, rules limiting advertising and solicitations are about protecting vulnerable persons from unscrupulous exploitation. Those governing specialization have the same goal, while those governing fees protect all clients from gouging. While these may look initially like "guild" rules designed to protect the profession,

---

1. See Daniel R. Fischel, "Multidisciplinary Practice," 55 *Business Lawyer* (May, 2000) p. 951. Dean Fischel points out that, "In an unregulated marketplace, clients would have the choice of hiring a single firm that provided all of these services or have multiple firms that specialized in some subset. Service providers would have a similar choice. They could offer clients one-stop shopping, specialize in particular areas and have contractual relationships with other service providers, or simply specialize with no formal relationship with other firms." *Id.*, p. 951.

they actually protect the consumer and promote moral values sadly missing in other sectors of the economy. See Laurence J. Fox, "Dan's World: A Free Enterprise Dream; An Ethics Nightmare," 55 *The Business Lawyer* 1533 (August, 2000), set out in Chapter VII-3, *infra*.

Perhaps the hardest rule to defend on these grounds is *Model Rule* 5.4 which prohibits most sharing of fees with non-lawyers, thereby removing law firms from the equity and investment models so prevalent throughout the rest of the economy and, increasingly, in related "professions," such as accounting, health care, brokerage houses, engineering and banking. Recently, major accounting firms have attempted to provide legal services as well, in the form of "MDPs," Multidisciplinary Practices. This is permitted in the European Common Market. There was also an effort to change *Model Rule* 5.4 to permit these "MDPs," but, after much debate, this failed. Despite a favorable report from their own ABA Commission on Multidisciplinary Practice in 1999, the ABA House of Delegates voted 314 to 106 at their July, 2000 Annual Meeting to continue to bar non-lawyer partnerships or non-lawyer investments in law firms. So there will be no "MDPs," at least for now.

Notice what this means. If you want to start a chain of high volume, low price hardware stores, you can get your friends and others to invest in your enterprise. But suppose you have a great idea to provide high volume, low cost legal services to middle-income America? Non-lawyer investment is prohibited. What moral values does this protect?

Read Laurence Fox's article carefully. He argues that *Model Rule* 5.4 is required to protect client loyalty. What do you think of his reasoning? Interestingly enough, following the rejection of the suggestions of the ABA Commission on Multidisciplinary Practice, we had the major accounting scandals that destroyed Arthur Anderson and greatly injured the reputation of other accounting firms, while ruining thousands of investors. Does that prove Fox's point?[2]

Now think about your own career. Would you rather spend your professional life in a free-enterprise system, in which legal services are regulated by the same consumer-protection laws that regulate all other service industries, or do you prefer a closely regulated profession that prohibits free market equity investment? The consequences for you could be very great.

Note also that achieving efficiencies by delegating routine work to non-lawyers is limited by the unauthorized practice of law statutes and *Model Rule* 5.5(a). See *In re Sledge*, 859 So. 2d 671 (La. 2003). This can be seen as another barrier to low cost, high volume legal services.

A. Advertising and Solicitation

If you spend the first part of your career as an associate in a big, established firm, the subjects covered by this chapter will not be of pressing interest, at least until you make partner. But many of my students, usually after a few years of experience, have estab-

---

2. See Lawrence J. Fox, "MDPs Done Gone: The Silver Lining in the Very Black Enron Cloud," 44 *Arizona Law Review* (2002), p. 457.

lished their own law firms. Some are very successful. The minute you decide to go "on your own" in law practice, these rules become of great importance to you.

First, you need clients. How do you get them? Some may be referred by your old firm, if they are not angry at you for leaving. Others may be recommended to you by family and friends. But the normal answer in most businesses is to advertise and solicit customers.

Historically, the organized bar greatly curtailed both advertising and solicitation. Traditionally, British barristers could never accept a client directly, but only through a solicitor! See *In Re S. A Barrister*, 3 *Weekly Law Reports* 129 (July 10, 1981) set out at Chapter I-5, *supra*. In its original form, the ABA *Code* regulated every form of advertising, including letterheads, and prohibited almost all "in person" solicitation. See *ABA Code* DR-2-102, DR-2-103, and DR-2-104 set out at Chapter VII-2, *infra*. Certain state bars, such as Virginia, even set minimum fee schedules to avoid price competition. This, of course, would normally be an anti-trust violation, but the bar association argued that, as "a learned profession," they were exempt from such regulations, or that their rules were "state action."

In 1975, in the landmark case *Goldfarb v. Virginia State Bar*, 421 U.S. 773 (1975), these arguments were rejected. Following *Goldfarb*, a series of additional cases struck down "blanket" bars to truthful advertising, and some limitations on solicitation, as contrary to "commercial free speech" as guaranteed by the First Amendment. These cases, beginning with *Bates* v. *State Bar of Arizona* 443 U.S. 350 (1977) up to *Florida Bar* v. *Went For It, Inc.*, 515 U.S. 618 (1995), have been included in Chapter VII-3, *infra*, for your careful study. Because public advertising is easy to monitor for truthfulness, it has received the greatest constitutional protection. The more "private" and "targeted" the communication, and the more likely that the target is unsophisticated or vulnerable, the more likely the restrictions have been upheld. Nevertheless, *Model Rules* 7.1 to 7.3 are still quite restrictive, and *Model Rule* 7.3 completely bans any "in-person, live telephone or real-time electronic" solicitation "when a significant motive ... is the lawyer's pecuniary gain," with the exceptions of other lawyers, prior clients, and family or "close personal" friends.

In practice you will meet many lawyers who strongly agree with the dissenting Justices who supported the bar restrictions. These lawyers wince every time they pass a billboard, with a lawyer's face, or see a T.V. "ad" for legal services. Other lawyers think *all* restrictions should be lifted, except for rules of fair advertising and solicitation established for all businesses. Massachusetts has moved to a compromise position, permitting direct solicitation of organizations "in connection with the activities of such organizations" and of persons "engaged in trade or commerce ... in connection with such persons' trade or commerce." *Mass. Rule* 7.3(e)(4). That gives a new lawyer at least some people to phone or email.

B. Specialization

One way a new doctor or dentist can attract patients is by establishing a "Board Certified Specialty," like orthodontistry or plastic surgery. Once I went to a bar association meeting that debated having such a system in Massachusetts. There could be special certifications in trusts and estates, or domestic relations, or real estate. These could be based on fair examinations of the law. There could even be a "general practitioner" certification, that covered a number of areas more strenuously than a bar exam. Minimum amounts of experience could also be required. The idea was not to restrict practice in these specialties to only "certified" specialists, but only to permit such lawyers to list and advertise their specialties, thus attracting business and providing better information to clients. For a new lawyer, particularly one in a small firm, it provided a chance for distinction. What could be wrong with that?

There was one other big advantage to such a "certification system." Like your car inspection stickers, the certificates could expire. A client would know that a lawyer with a current certificate would have had to pass an examination regularly, say every five years. If the goal is to provide potential clients with reliable information about legal services, what could be better?

Both ABA *Code* DR-2-105 and *Model Rule* 7.4 provide for certification systems by prohibiting a lawyer from saying that he or she is "certified as a specialist in a particular field of law" unless such a system exists. But relatively few states have implemented vigorous, exam driven, renewable certificates. Massachusetts did not go this route, despite my pitiful arguments. In fact, *Mass. Rule* 7.4(a) permits all lawyers to "hold themselves out publicly as specialists in particular services, fields, and areas of law if the holding out does not include a false or misleading communication." You just cannot say you are "certified" unless you name the "certifying organization" and say it is not regulated by Massachusetts "if that is the case" or, "if the certifying organization is a governmental body, must name the governmental body." *Mass. Rule* 7.4(b).

So where are the teeth here? At first glance, there seems to be no regulation of specialties in Massachusetts. But *Mass. Rule* 7.4(c) does add some teeth in an odd, "free market" way. If you hold yourself out as an expert, you "shall be held to the standard of performance of specialists in that particular service, field or area." In short, if you say you are a "specialist" and botch up a transaction, you may be sued in malpractice and held to a higher standard than an ordinary lawyer. If you do not like that added exposure, the rule suggest that you say you "handle" or "welcome" certain cases, but not that you are a "specialist."

As a new lawyer trying to establish a law practice, what do you think about a "certification" scheme? Do you like the Massachusetts approach instead? What approach would be best for the public? In a split decision, the United States Supreme Court held that it was impossible for Illinois to prevent a lawyer from holding himself to be "certified by the National Board of Trial Advocacy," even though the Illinois Supreme Court found this to be "misleading because it tacitly attests to the qualification of [petitioner] as a civil trial advocate." See *Peel v. Attorney Registration and Discipline Comm'n of Illinois*, 496 U.S. 91 (1990). Do you agree? See discussion in *The Florida Bar v. Pape*, 981 So.2d 240 (2005) at Section VII-5, *infra*.

C. Fees

You would think "fees" would be an easy subject, at least in terms of professional ethics. In a free market, should not an appropriate "price" or "fee" be determined between a willing buyer and seller? Of course, failure to communicate clearly to a client about fees can lead to trouble, but that is governed by *Model Rule* 1.4. And it is essential that the client not be misled about the basis of the fee, or in any other way, hence the requirement that contingent fee agreements always be in writing, be signed by the client, and contain certain pieces of information, clearly stated. That is required by *Model Rule* 1.5(c), and *Model Rule* 1.5(b) strongly recommends written communication for all fees.

So let us assume a well-informed, willing client—free to go elsewhere—who agrees to a particular fee or rate. Surely, that is alright.

Not necessarily. Both the ABA *Code* DR-2-106 and *Model Rule* 1.5 prohibit fees that are "in excess of a reasonable fee" (*Code* DR-2-106(A), (B)) or "an unreasonable fee." (*Model Rule* 1.5), and set out a long list of factors to include in determining what is "unreasonable." These include things like "the fee customarily charged in the locality for similar legal services," "the nature and length of the professional relationship with the client" and "the experience, reputation, and ability of the lawyer." *Model Rule* 1.5(a)(3), (6), (7). *ABA Code* DR-2-106(B)(3), (6), (7).

Personally, I believe that most contracts involving star professional athletes and rock musicians involve "unreasonable fees." For example, I think certain baseball players and bankers make too much money under their contracts. But these contracts are freely entered into in the open market and, if free of fraud and deception, are enforced. Nobody pays attention to my views on such deals, and "comparable" deals are also irrelevant if the contract is otherwise valid. But in leading cases such as *In the Matter of Fordham*, 423 Mass. 481 (1996), set out at Chapter VII-3, *infra*, the courts have taken a different view for lawyers, and the rules clearly establish an objective "reasonableness" review that goes beyond the contract between buyer and seller of services.

There are values protected by such objective values. For example, not only are credit card interest rates regulated (barely!), but usury, now defined as predatory loans to those who can never hope to repay the interest, is seen as a sin by many religions, and is widely seen as immoral. "Unreasonable" legal fees can be seen as, likewise, sinful and immoral. In addition, massive legal fees in certain class actions have raised political and policy concerns, and have even led to the amendment of Rule 23 "Class Action" of the Federal Rules of Civil Procedure to ensure that such fees be "reasonable." See F.R.Civ.P. 23(h). But we do not apply the same rules to sports stars, entertainers, or most other commercial activities.

For the new practitioners, such issues are likely to be theoretical, as long as there is good communication with the client and special care is taken to get things in writing. You must pay particular attention to the detailed rules on contingent fees. Massachusetts even sets out a "satisfactory" contingent fee form in the rule itself, at *Mass. Rule* 1.5(F)! And the lists provided by *Model Rule* 1.5 can assist in setting the basis for a good internal fee structure. But the ultimate control of fees by something other than the fair operation of the free market sets the legal profession apart from ordinary business. In your opinion, is that good or bad?

VII-2. Law Practice: The Rules

ABA Model Rules

RULE 1.5: FEES

(a) A lawyer shall not make an agreement for, charge, or collect an unreasonable fee or an unreasonable amount for expenses. The factors to be considered in determining the reasonableness of a fee include the following:

> (1) the time and labor required, the novelty and difficulty of the questions involved, and the skill requisite to perform the legal service properly;

(2) the likelihood, if apparent to the client, that the acceptance of the particular employment will preclude other employment by the lawyer;

(3) the fee customarily charged in the locality for similar legal services;

(4) the amount involved and the results obtained;

(5) the time limitations imposed by the client or by the circumstances;

(6) the nature and length of the professional relationship with the client;

(7) the experience, reputation, and ability of the lawyer or lawyers performing the services; and

(8) whether the fee is fixed or contingent.

(b) The scope of the representation and the basis or rate of the fee and expenses for which the client will be responsible shall be communicated to the client, preferably in writing, before or within a reasonable time after commencing the representation, except when the lawyer will charge a regularly represented client on the same basis or rate. Any changes in the basis or rate of the fee or expenses shall also be communicated to the client.

(c) A fee may be contingent on the outcome of the matter for which the service is rendered, except in a matter in which a contingent fee is prohibited by paragraph (d) or other law. A contingent fee agreement shall be in a writing signed by the client and shall state the method by which the fee is to be determined, including the percentage or percentages that shall accrue to the lawyer in the event of settlement, trial or appeal; litigation and other expenses to be deducted from the recovery; and whether such expenses are to be deducted before or after the contingent fee is calculated. The agreement must clearly notify the client of any expenses for which the client will be liable whether or not the client is the prevailing party. Upon conclusion of a contingent fee matter, the lawyer shall provide the client with a written statement stating the outcome of the matter and, if there is a recovery, showing the remittance to the client and the method of its determination.

(d) A lawyer shall not enter into an arrangement for, charge, or collect:

(1) any fee in a domestic relations matter, the payment or amount of which is contingent upon the securing of a divorce or upon the amount of alimony or support, or property settlement in lieu thereof; or

(2) a contingent fee for representing a defendant in a criminal case.

(e) A division of a fee between lawyers who are not in the same firm may be made only if:

(1) the division is in proportion to the services performed by each lawyer or each lawyer assumes joint responsibility for the representation;

(2) the client agrees to the arrangement, including the share each lawyer will receive, and the agreement is confirmed in writing; and

(3) the total fee is reasonable.

Comment

Reasonableness of Fee and Expenses

[1] Paragraph (a) requires that lawyers charge fees that are reasonable under the circumstances. The factors specified in (1) through (8) are not exclusive. Nor will each fac-

tor be relevant in each instance. Paragraph (a) also requires that expenses for which the client will be charged must be reasonable. A lawyer may seek reimbursement for the cost of services performed in-house, such as copying, or for other expenses incurred in-house, such as telephone charges, either by charging a reasonable amount to which the client has agreed in advance or by charging an amount that reasonably reflects the cost incurred by the lawyer.

Basis or Rate of Fee

[2] When the lawyer has regularly represented a client, they ordinarily will have evolved an understanding concerning the basis or rate of the fee and the expenses for which the client will be responsible. In a new client-lawyer relationship, however, an understanding as to fees and expenses must be promptly established. Generally, it is desirable to furnish the client with at least a simple memorandum or copy of the lawyer's customary fee arrangements that states the general nature of the legal services to be provided, the basis, rate or total amount of the fee and whether and to what extent the client will be responsible for any costs, expenses or disbursements in the course of the representation. A written statement concerning the terms of the engagement reduces the possibility of misunderstanding.

[3] Contingent fees, like any other fees, are subject to the reasonableness standard of paragraph (a) of this Rule. In determining whether a particular contingent fee is reasonable, or whether it is reasonable to charge any form of contingent fee, a lawyer must consider the factors that are relevant under the circumstances. Applicable law may impose limitations on contingent fees, such as a ceiling on the percentage allowable, or may require a lawyer to offer clients an alternative basis for the fee. Applicable law also may apply to situations other than a contingent fee, for example, government regulations regarding fees in certain tax matters.

Terms of Payment

[4] A lawyer may require advance payment of a fee, but is obliged to return any unearned portion. See Rule 1.16(d). A lawyer may accept property in payment for services, such as an ownership interest in an enterprise, providing this does not involve acquisition of a proprietary interest in the cause of action or subject matter of the litigation contrary to Rule 1.8 (i). However, a fee paid in property instead of money may be subject to the requirements of Rule 1.8(a) because such fees often have the essential qualities of a business transaction with the client.

[5] An agreement may not be made whose terms might induce the lawyer improperly to curtail services for the client or perform them in a way contrary to the client's interest. For example, a lawyer should not enter into an agreement whereby services are to be provided only up to a stated amount when it is foreseeable that more extensive services probably will be required, unless the situation is adequately explained to the client. Otherwise, the client might have to bargain for further assistance in the midst of a proceeding or transaction. However, it is proper to define the extent of services in light of the client's ability to pay. A lawyer should not exploit a fee arrangement based primarily on hourly charges by using wasteful procedures.

Prohibited Contingent Fees

[6] Paragraph (d) prohibits a lawyer from charging a contingent fee in a domestic relations matter when payment is contingent upon the securing of a divorce or upon the amount of alimony or support or property settlement to be obtained. This provision does not preclude a contract for a contingent fee for legal representation in connection

with the recovery of post-judgment balances due under support, alimony or other financial orders because such contracts do not implicate the same policy concerns.

Division of Fee

[7] A division of fee is a single billing to a client covering the fee of two or more lawyers who are not in the same firm. A division of fee facilitates association of more than one lawyer in a matter in which neither alone could serve the client as well, and most often is used when the fee is contingent and the division is between a referring lawyer and a trial specialist. Paragraph (e) permits the lawyers to divide a fee either on the basis of the proportion of services they render or if each lawyer assumes responsibility for the representation as a whole. In addition, the client must agree to the arrangement, including the share that each lawyer is to receive, and the agreement must be confirmed in writing. Contingent fee agreements must be in a writing signed by the client and must otherwise comply with paragraph (c) of this Rule. Joint responsibility for the representation entails financial and ethical responsibility for the representation as if the lawyers were associated in a partnership. A lawyer should only refer a matter to a lawyer whom the referring lawyer reasonably believes is competent to handle the matter. See Rule 1.1.

[8] Paragraph (e) does not prohibit or regulate division of fees to be received in the future for work done when lawyers were previously associated in a law firm.

Disputes over Fees

[9] If a procedure has been established for resolution of fee disputes, such as an arbitration or mediation procedure established by the bar, the lawyer must comply with the procedure when it is mandatory, and, even when it is voluntary, the lawyer should conscientiously consider submitting to it. Law may prescribe a procedure for determining a lawyer's fee, for example, in representation of an executor or administrator, a class or a person entitled to a reasonable fee as part of the measure of damages. The lawyer entitled to such a fee and a lawyer representing another party concerned with the fee should comply with the prescribed procedure.

RULE 5.4: PROFESSIONAL INDEPENDENCE OF A LAWYER

(a) A lawyer or law firm shall not share legal fees with a nonlawyer, except that:

(1) an agreement by a lawyer with the lawyer's firm, partner, or associate may provide for the payment of money, over a reasonable period of time after the lawyer's death, to the lawyer's estate or to one or more specified persons;

(2) a lawyer who purchases the practice of a deceased, disabled, or disappeared lawyer may, pursuant to the provisions of Rule 1.17, pay to the estate or other representative of that lawyer the agreed-upon purchase price;

(3) a lawyer or law firm may include nonlawyer employees in a compensation or retirement plan, even though the plan is based in whole or in part on a profit-sharing arrangement; and

(4) a lawyer may share court-awarded legal fees with a nonprofit organization that employed, retained or recommended employment of the lawyer in the matter.

(b) A lawyer shall not form a partnership with a nonlawyer if any of the activities of the partnership consist of the practice of law.

(c) A lawyer shall not permit a person who recommends, employs, or pays the lawyer to render legal services for another to direct or regulate the lawyer's professional judgment in rendering such legal services.

(d) A lawyer shall not practice with or in the form of a professional corporation or association authorized to practice law for a profit, if:

(1) a nonlawyer owns any interest therein, except that a fiduciary representative of the estate of a lawyer may hold the stock or interest of the lawyer for a reasonable time during administration;

(2) a nonlawyer is a corporate director or officer thereof or occupies the position of similar responsibility in any form of association other than a corporation; or

(3) a nonlawyer has the right to direct or control the professional judgment of a lawyer.

Comment

[1] The provisions of this Rule express traditional limitations on sharing fees. These limitations are to protect the lawyer's professional independence of judgment. Where someone other than the client pays the lawyer's fee or salary, or recommends employment of the lawyer, that arrangement does not modify the lawyer's obligation to the client. As stated in paragraph (c), such arrangements should not interfere with the lawyer's professional judgment.

[2] This Rule also expresses traditional limitations on permitting a third party to direct or regulate the lawyer's professional judgment in rendering legal services to another. See also Rule 1.8(f) (lawyer may accept compensation from a third party as long as there is no interference with the lawyer's independent professional judgment and the client gives informed consent).

RULE 7.1: COMMUNICATIONS CONCERNING A LAWYER'S SERVICES

A lawyer shall not make a false or misleading communication about the lawyer or the lawyer's services. A communication is false or misleading if it contains a material misrepresentation of fact or law, or omits a fact necessary to make the statement considered as a whole not materially misleading.

Comment

[1] This Rule governs all communications about a lawyer's services, including advertising permitted by Rule 7.2. Whatever means are used to make known a lawyer's services, statements about them must be truthful.

[2] Truthful statements that are misleading are also prohibited by this Rule. A truthful statement is misleading if it omits a fact necessary to make the lawyer's communication considered as a whole not materially misleading. A truthful statement is also misleading if there is a substantial likelihood that it will lead a reasonable person to formulate a specific conclusion about the lawyer or the lawyer's services for which there is no reasonable factual foundation.

[3] An advertisement that truthfully reports a lawyer's achievements on behalf of clients or former clients may be misleading if presented so as to lead a reasonable person to form an unjustified expectation that the same results could be obtained for other clients in similar matters without reference to the specific factual and legal circumstances of each client's case. Similarly, an unsubstantiated comparison of the lawyer's services or fees with the services or fees of other lawyers may be misleading if presented with such specificity as would lead a reasonable person to conclude that the comparison can be substantiated. The inclusion of an appropriate disclaimer or qualifying language may preclude a finding that a statement is likely to create unjustified expectations or otherwise mislead a prospective client.

[4] See also Rule 8.4(e) for the prohibition against stating or implying an ability to influence improperly a government agency or official or to achieve results by means that violate the Rules of Professional Conduct or other law.

RULE 7.2: ADVERTISING

(a) Subject to the requirements of Rules 7.1 and 7.3, a lawyer may advertise services through written, recorded or electronic communication, including public media.

(b) A lawyer shall not give anything of value to a person for recommending the lawyer's services except that a lawyer may

    (1) pay the reasonable costs of advertisements or communications permitted by this Rule;

    (2) pay the usual charges of a legal service plan or a not-for-profit or qualified lawyer referral service. A qualified lawyer referral service is a lawyer referral service that has been approved by an appropriate regulatory authority;

    (3) pay for a law practice in accordance with Rule 1.17; and

    (4) refer clients to another lawyer or a nonlawyer professional pursuant to an agreement not otherwise prohibited under these Rules that provides for the other person to refer clients or customers to the lawyer, if

        (i) the reciprocal referral agreement is not exclusive, and

        (ii) the client is informed of the existence and nature of the agreement.

(c) Any communication made pursuant to this rule shall include the name and office address of at least one lawyer or law firm responsible for its content.

Comment

[1] To assist the public in obtaining legal services, lawyers should be allowed to make known their services not only through reputation but also through organized information campaigns in the form of advertising. Advertising involves an active quest for clients, contrary to the tradition that a lawyer should not seek clientele. However, the public's need to know about legal services can be fulfilled in part through advertising. This need is particularly acute in the case of persons of moderate means who have not made extensive use of legal services. The interest in expanding public information about legal services ought to prevail over considerations of tradition. Nevertheless, advertising by lawyers entails the risk of practices that are misleading or overreaching.

[2] This Rule permits public dissemination of information concerning a lawyer's name or firm name, address and telephone number; the kinds of services the lawyer will undertake; the basis on which the lawyer's fees are determined, including prices for specific services and payment and credit arrangements; a lawyer's foreign language ability; names of references and, with their consent, names of clients regularly represented; and other information that might invite the attention of those seeking legal assistance.

[3] Questions of effectiveness and taste in advertising are matters of speculation and subjective judgment. Some jurisdictions have had extensive prohibitions against television advertising, against advertising going beyond specified facts about a lawyer, or against "undignified" advertising. Television is now one of the most powerful media for getting information to the public, particularly persons of low and moderate income; prohibiting television advertising, therefore, would impede the flow of information about legal services to many sectors of the public. Limiting the information that may be advertised has a similar effect and assumes that the bar can accurately forecast the kind

of information that the public would regard as relevant. Similarly, electronic media, such as the Internet, can be an important source of information about legal services, and lawful communication by electronic mail is permitted by this Rule. But see Rule 7.3(a) for the prohibition against the solicitation of a prospective client through a real-time electronic exchange that is not initiated by the prospective client.

[4] Neither this Rule nor Rule 7.3 prohibits communications authorized by law, such as notice to members of a class in class action litigation.

Paying Others to Recommend a Lawyer

[5] Lawyers are not permitted to pay others for channeling professional work. Paragraph (b)(1), however, allows a lawyer to pay for advertising and communications permitted by this Rule, including the costs of print directory listings, on-line directory listings, newspaper ads, television and radio airtime, domain-name registrations, sponsorship fees, banner ads, and group advertising. A lawyer may compensate employees, agents and vendors who are engaged to provide marketing or client-development services, such as publicists, public-relations personnel, business-development staff and website designers. See Rule 5.3 for the duties of lawyers and law firms with respect to the conduct of nonlawyers who prepare marketing materials for them.

[6] A lawyer may pay the usual charges of a legal service plan or a not-for-profit or qualified lawyer referral service. A legal service plan is a prepaid or group legal service plan or a similar delivery system that assists prospective clients to secure legal representation. A lawyer referral service, on the other hand, is any organization that holds itself out to the public as a lawyer referral service. Such referral services are understood by laypersons to be consumer-oriented organizations that provide unbiased referrals to lawyers with appropriate experience in the subject matter of the representation and afford other client protections, such as complaint procedures or malpractice insurance requirements. Consequently, this Rule only permits a lawyer to pay the usual charges of a not-for-profit or qualified lawyer referral service. A qualified lawyer referral service is one that is approved by an appropriate regulatory authority as affording adequate protections for prospective clients. See, e.g., the American Bar Association's Model Supreme Court Rules Governing Lawyer Referral Services and Model Lawyer Referral and Information Service Quality Assurance Act (requiring that organizations that are identified as lawyer referral services (i) permit the participation of all lawyers who are licensed and eligible to practice in the jurisdiction and who meet reasonable objective eligibility requirements as may be established by the referral service for the protection of prospective clients; (ii) require each participating lawyer to carry reasonably adequate malpractice insurance; (iii) act reasonably to assess client satisfaction and address client complaints; and (iv) do not refer prospective clients to lawyers who own, operate or are employed by the referral service.)

[7] A lawyer who accepts assignments or referrals from a legal service plan or referrals from a lawyer referral service must act reasonably to assure that the activities of the plan or service are compatible with the lawyer's professional obligations. See Rule 5.3. Legal service plans and lawyer referral services may communicate with prospective clients, but such communication must be in conformity with these Rules. Thus, advertising must not be false or misleading, as would be the case if the communications of a group advertising program or a group legal services plan would mislead prospective clients to think that it was a lawyer referral service sponsored by a state agency or bar association. Nor could the lawyer allow in-person, telephonic, or real-time contacts that would violate Rule 7.3.

[8] A lawyer also may agree to refer clients to another lawyer or a nonlawyer professional, in return for the undertaking of that person to refer clients or customers to the lawyer. Such reciprocal referral arrangements must not interfere with the lawyer's professional judgment as to making referrals or as to providing substantive legal services. See Rules 2.1 and 5.4(c). Except as provided in Rule 1.5(e), a lawyer who receives referrals from a lawyer or nonlawyer professional must not pay anything solely for the referral, but the lawyer does not violate paragraph (b) of this Rule by agreeing to refer clients to the other lawyer or nonlawyer professional, so long as the reciprocal referral agreement is not exclusive and the client is informed of the referral agreement. Conflicts of interest created by such arrangements are governed by Rule 1.7. Reciprocal referral agreements should not be of indefinite duration and should be reviewed periodically to determine whether they comply with these Rules. This Rule does not restrict referrals or divisions of revenues or net income among lawyers within firms comprised of multiple entities.

RULE 7.3: DIRECT CONTACT WITH PROSPECTIVE CLIENTS

(a) A lawyer shall not by in-person, live telephone or real-time electronic contact solicit professional employment from a prospective client when a significant motive for the lawyer's doing so is the lawyer's pecuniary gain, unless the person contacted:

(1) is a lawyer; or

(2) has a family, close personal, or prior professional relationship with the lawyer.

(b) A lawyer shall not solicit professional employment from a prospective client by written, recorded or electronic communication or by in-person, telephone or real-time electronic contact even when not otherwise prohibited by paragraph (a), if:

(1) the prospective client has made known to the lawyer a desire not to be solicited by the lawyer; or

(2) the solicitation involves coercion, duress or harassment.

(c) Every written, recorded or electronic communication from a lawyer soliciting professional employment from a prospective client known to be in need of legal services in a particular matter shall include the words "Advertising Material" on the outside envelope, if any, and at the beginning and ending of any recorded or electronic communication, unless the recipient of the communication is a person specified in paragraphs (a)(1) or (a)(2).

(d) Notwithstanding the prohibitions in paragraph (a), a lawyer may participate with a prepaid or group legal service plan operated by an organization not owned or directed by the lawyer that uses in-person or telephone contact to solicit memberships or subscriptions for the plan from persons who are not known to need legal services in a particular matter covered by the plan.

Comment

[1] There is a potential for abuse inherent in direct in-person, live telephone or real-time electronic contact by a lawyer with a prospective client known to need legal services. These forms of contact between a lawyer and a prospective client subject the layperson to the private importuning of the trained advocate in a direct interpersonal encounter. The prospective client, who may already feel overwhelmed by the circumstances giving rise to the need for legal services, may find it difficult fully to evaluate all available alternatives with reasoned judgment and appropriate self-interest in the face of

the lawyer's presence and insistence upon being retained immediately. The situation is fraught with the possibility of undue influence, intimidation, and over-reaching.

[2] This potential for abuse inherent in direct in-person, live telephone or real-time electronic solicitation of prospective clients justifies its prohibition, particularly since lawyer advertising and written and recorded communication permitted under Rule 7.2 offer alternative means of conveying necessary information to those who may be in need of legal services. Advertising and written and recorded communications which may be mailed or autodialed make it possible for a prospective client to be informed about the need for legal services, and about the qualifications of available lawyers and law firms, without subjecting the prospective client to direct in-person, telephone or real-time electronic persuasion that may overwhelm the client's judgment.

[3] The use of general advertising and written, recorded or electronic communications to transmit information from lawyer to prospective client, rather than direct in-person, live telephone or real-time electronic contact, will help to assure that the information flows cleanly as well as freely. The contents of advertisements and communications permitted under Rule 7.2 can be permanently recorded so that they cannot be disputed and may be shared with others who know the lawyer. This potential for informal review is itself likely to help guard against statements and claims that might constitute false and misleading communications, in violation of Rule 7.1. The contents of direct in-person, live telephone or real-time electronic conversations between a lawyer and a prospective client can be disputed and may not be subject to third-party scrutiny. Consequently, they are much more likely to approach (and occasionally cross) the dividing line between accurate representations and those that are false and misleading.

[4] There is far less likelihood that a lawyer would engage in abusive practices against an individual who is a former client, or with whom the lawyer has close personal or family relationship, or in situations in which the lawyer is motivated by considerations other than the lawyer's pecuniary gain. Nor is there a serious potential for abuse when the person contacted is a lawyer. Consequently, the general prohibition in Rule 7.3(a) and the requirements of Rule 7.3(c) are not applicable in those situations. Also, paragraph (a) is not intended to prohibit a lawyer from participating in constitutionally protected activities of public or charitable legal-service organizations or bona fide political, social, civic, fraternal, employee or trade organizations whose purposes include providing or recommending legal services to its members or beneficiaries.

[5] But even permitted forms of solicitation can be abused. Thus, any solicitation which contains information which is false or misleading within the meaning of Rule 7.1, which involves coercion, duress or harassment within the meaning of Rule 7.3(b)(2), or which involves contact with a prospective client who has made known to the lawyer a desire not to be solicited by the lawyer within the meaning of Rule 7.3(b)(1) is prohibited. Moreover, if after sending a letter or other communication to a client as permitted by Rule 7.2 the lawyer receives no response, any further effort to communicate with the prospective client may violate the provisions of Rule 7.3(b).

[6] This Rule is not intended to prohibit a lawyer from contacting representatives of organizations or groups that may be interested in establishing a group or prepaid legal plan for their members, insureds, beneficiaries or other third parties for the purpose of informing such entities of the availability of and details concerning the plan or arrangement which the lawyer or lawyer's firm is willing to offer. This form of communication is not directed to a prospective client. Rather, it is usually addressed to an individual acting in a fiduciary capacity seeking a supplier of legal services for others who may, if they

choose, become prospective clients of the lawyer. Under these circumstances, the activity which the lawyer undertakes in communicating with such representatives and the type of information transmitted to the individual are functionally similar to and serve the same purpose as advertising permitted under Rule 7.2.

[7] The requirement in Rule 7.3(c) that certain communications be marked "Advertising Material" does not apply to communications sent in response to requests of potential clients or their spokespersons or sponsors. General announcements by lawyers, including changes in personnel or office location, do not constitute communications soliciting professional employment from a client known to be in need of legal services within the meaning of this Rule.

[8] Paragraph (d) of this Rule permits a lawyer to participate with an organization which uses personal contact to solicit members for its group or prepaid legal service plan, provided that the personal contact is not undertaken by any lawyer who would be a provider of legal services through the plan. The organization must not be owned by or directed (whether as manager or otherwise) by any lawyer or law firm that participates in the plan. For example, paragraph (d) would not permit a lawyer to create an organization controlled directly or indirectly by the lawyer and use the organization for the in-person or telephone solicitation of legal employment of the lawyer through memberships in the plan or otherwise. The communication permitted by these organizations also must not be directed to a person known to need legal services in a particular matter, but is to be designed to inform potential plan members generally of another means of affordable legal services. Lawyers who participate in a legal service plan must reasonably assure that the plan sponsors are in compliance with Rules 7.1, 7.2 and 7.3(b). See 8.4(a).

RULE 7.4: COMMUNICATION OF FIELDS OF PRACTICE AND SPECIALIZATION

(a) A lawyer may communicate the fact that the lawyer does or does not practice in particular fields of law.

(b) A lawyer admitted to engage in patent practice before the United States Patent and Trademark Office may use the designation "Patent Attorney" or a substantially similar designation.

(c) A lawyer engaged in Admiralty practice may use the designation "Admiralty," "Proctor in Admiralty" or a substantially similar designation.

(d) A lawyer shall not state or imply that a lawyer is certified as a specialist in a particular field of law, unless:

(1) the lawyer has been certified as a specialist by an organization that has been approved by an appropriate state authority or that has been accredited by the American Bar Association; and

(2) the name of the certifying organization is clearly identified in the communication.

Comment

[1] Paragraph (a) of this Rule permits a lawyer to indicate areas of practice in communications about the lawyer's services. If a lawyer practices only in certain fields, or will not accept matters except in a specified field or fields, the lawyer is permitted to so indicate. A lawyer is generally permitted to state that the lawyer is a "specialist," practices a "specialty," or "specializes in" particular fields, but such communications are subject to

the "false and misleading" standard applied in Rule 7.1 to communications concerning a lawyer's services.

[2] Paragraph (b) recognizes the long-established policy of the Patent and Trademark Office for the designation of lawyers practicing before the Office. Paragraph (c) recognizes that designation of Admiralty practice has a long historical tradition associated with maritime commerce and the federal courts.

[3] Paragraph (d) permits a lawyer to state that the lawyer is certified as a specialist in a field of law if such certification is granted by an organization approved by an appropriate state authority or accredited by the American Bar Association or another organization, such as a state bar association, that has been approved by the state authority to accredit organizations that certify lawyers as specialists. Certification signifies that an objective entity has recognized an advanced degree of knowledge and experience in the specialty area greater than is suggested by general licensure to practice law. Certifying organizations may be expected to apply standards of experience, knowledge and proficiency to insure that a lawyer's recognition as a specialist is meaningful and reliable. In order to insure that consumers can obtain access to useful information about an organization granting certification, the name of the certifying organization must be included in any communication regarding the certification.

RULE 7.5: FIRM NAMES AND LETTERHEADS

(a) A lawyer shall not use a firm name, letterhead or other professional designation that violates Rule 7.1. A trade name may be used by a lawyer in private practice if it does not imply a connection with a government agency or with a public or charitable legal services organization and is not otherwise in violation of Rule 7.1.

(b) A law firm with offices in more than one jurisdiction may use the same name or other professional designation in each jurisdiction, but identification of the lawyers in an office of the firm shall indicate the jurisdictional limitations on those not licensed to practice in the jurisdiction where the office is located.

(c) The name of a lawyer holding a public office shall not be used in the name of a law firm, or in communications on its behalf, during any substantial period in which the lawyer is not actively and regularly practicing with the firm.

(d) Lawyers may state or imply that they practice in a partnership or other organization only when that is the fact.

Comment

[1] A firm may be designated by the names of all or some of its members, by the names of deceased members where there has been a continuing succession in the firm's identity or by a trade name such as the "ABC Legal Clinic." A lawyer or law firm may also be designated by a distinctive website address or comparable professional designation. Although the United States Supreme Court has held that legislation may prohibit the use of trade names in professional practice, use of such names in law practice is acceptable so long as it is not misleading. If a private firm uses a trade name that includes a geographical name such as "Springfield Legal Clinic," an express disclaimer that it is a public legal aid agency may be required to avoid a misleading implication. It may be observed that any firm name including the name of a deceased partner is, strictly speaking, a trade name. The use of such names to designate law firms has proven a useful means

of identification. However, it is misleading to use the name of a lawyer not associated with the firm or a predecessor of the firm, or the name of a nonlawyer.

[2] With regard to paragraph (d), lawyers sharing office facilities, but who are not in fact associated with each other in a law firm, may not denominate themselves as, for example, "Smith and Jones," for that title suggests that they are practicing law together in a firm.

ABA Code

DR 2-106 Fees for Legal Services.

(A) A lawyer shall not enter into an agreement for, charge, or collect an illegal or clearly excessive fee.

(B) A fee is clearly excessive when, after a review of the facts, a lawyer of ordinary prudence would be left with a definite and firm conviction that the fee is in excess of a reasonable fee. Factors to be considered as guides in determining the reasonableness of a fee include the following:

> (1) The time and labor required, the novelty and difficulty of the questions involved, and the skill requisite to perform the legal service properly.

> (2) The likelihood, if apparent to the client, that the acceptance of the particular employment will preclude other employment by the lawyer.

> (3) The fee customarily charged in the locality for similar legal services.

> (4) The amount involved and the results obtained.

> (5) The time limitations imposed by the client or by the circumstances.

> (6) The nature and length of the professional relationship with the client.

> (7) The experience, reputation, and ability of the lawyer or lawyers performing the services.

> (8) Whether the fee is fixed or contingent.

(C) A lawyer shall not enter into an arrangement for, charge, or collect a contingent fee for representing a defendant in a criminal case.

DR 2-107 Division of Fees Among Lawyers.

(A) A lawyer shall not divide a fee for legal services with another lawyer who is not a partner in or associate of his law firm or law office, unless:

> (1) The client consents to employment of the other lawyer after a full disclosure that a division of fees will be made.

> (2) The division is made in proportion to the services performed and responsibility assumed by each.

> (3) The total fee of the lawyers does not clearly exceed reasonable compensation for all legal services they rendered the client.

(B) This Disciplinary Rule does not prohibit payment to a former partner or associate pursuant to a separation or retirement agreement.

VII-3. Law Practice: Cases and Materials

A. Advertising

Goldfarb v. Virginia State Bar

421 U.S. 773

U.S. Supreme Court

Argued March 25, 1975

Decided June 16, 1975

[Some footnotes deleted. Remaining footnotes renumbered.]

MR. CHIEF JUSTICE BURGER delivered the opinion of the Court.

We granted certiorari to decide whether a minimum-fee schedule for lawyers published by the Fairfax County Bar Association and enforced by the Virginia State Bar violates 1 of the Sherman Act, 26 Stat. 209, as amended, 15 U.S.C. 1. The Court of Appeals held that, although the fee schedule and enforcement mechanism substantially restrained competition among lawyers, publication of the schedule by the County Bar was outside the scope of the Act because the practice of law is not "trade or commerce," and enforcement of the schedule by the State Bar was exempt from the Sherman Act as state action as defined in Parker v. Brown, 317 U.S. 341 (1943).

I

In 1971 petitioners, husband and wife, contracted to buy a home in Fairfax County, Va. The financing agency required them to secure title insurance; this required a title examination, and only a member of the Virginia State Bar could legally perform that service. Petitioners therefore contacted a lawyer who quoted them the precise fee suggested in a minimum-fee schedule published by respondent Fairfax County Bar Association; the lawyer told them that it was his policy to keep his charges in line with the minimum-fee schedule which provided for a fee of 1% of the value of the property involved. Petitioners then tried to find a lawyer who would examine the title for less than the fee fixed by the schedule. They sent letters to 36 other Fairfax County lawyers requesting their fees. Nineteen replied, and none indicated that he would charge less than the rate fixed by the schedule; several stated that they knew of no attorney who would do so.

The fee schedule the lawyers referred to is a list of recommended minimum prices for common legal services. Respondent Fairfax County Bar Association published the fee schedule although, as a purely voluntary association of attorneys, the County Bar has no formal power to enforce it. Enforcement has been provided by respondent Virginia State Bar which is the administrative agency through which the Virginia Supreme Court regulates the practice of law in that State; membership in the State Bar is required in order to practice in Virginia. Although the State Bar has never taken formal disciplinary action to compel adherence to any fee schedule, it has published reports condoning fee schedules, and has issued two ethical opinions indicating that fee schedules cannot be ignored. The most recent opinion states that "evidence that an attorney habitually charges less than the suggested minimum fee schedule adopted by his local bar Association, raises a presumption that such lawyer is guilty of misconduct...."

Because petitioners could not find a lawyer willing to charge a fee lower than the schedule dictated, they had their title examined by the lawyer they had first contacted. They then brought this class action against the State Bar and the County Bar alleging that the operation of the minimum-fee schedule, as applied to fees for legal services relating to residential real estate transactions, constitutes price fixing in violation of 1 of the Sherman Act. Petitioners sought both injunctive relief and damages.

After a trial solely on the issue of liability the District Court held that the minimum-fee schedule violated the Sherman Act. 355 F. Supp. 491 (ED Va. 1973). The court viewed the fee-schedule system as a significant reason for petitioners' failure to obtain legal services for less than the minimum fee, and it rejected the County Bar's contention that as a "learned profession" the practice of law is exempt from the Sherman Act.

Both respondents argued that their actions were also exempt from the Sherman Act as state action. Parker v. Brown, supra. The District Court agreed that the Virginia State Bar was exempt under that doctrine because it is an administrative agency of the Virginia Supreme Court, and more important, because its "minor role in this matter ... derived from the judicial and 'legislative command of the State and was not intended to operate or become effective without that command.'" The County Bar, on the other hand, is a private organization and was under no compulsion to adopt the fee schedule recommended by the State Bar. Since the County Bar chose its own course of conduct the District Court held that the antitrust laws "remain in full force and effect as to it." The court enjoined the fee schedule, 15 U.S.C. 26, and set the case down for trial to ascertain damages. 15 U.S.C. 15.

The Court of Appeals reversed as to liability. 497 F.2d 1 (CA4 1974). Despite its conclusion that it "is abundantly clear from the record before us that the fee schedule and the enforcement mechanism supporting it act as a substantial restraint upon competition among attorneys practicing in Fairfax County," id., at 13, the Court of Appeals held the State Bar immune under Parker v. Brown, supra, and held the County Bar immune because the practice of law is not "trade or commerce" under the Sherman Act. There has long been judicial recognition of a limited exclusion of "learned professions" from the scope of the antitrust laws, the court said; that exclusion is based upon the special form of regulation imposed upon the professions by the States, and the incompatibility of certain competitive practices with such professional regulation. It concluded that the promulgation of a minimum-fee schedule is one of "those matters with respect to which an accord must be reached between the necessities of professional regulation and the dictates of the antitrust laws." The accord reached by that court was to hold the practice of law exempt from the antitrust laws.

Alternatively, the Court of Appeals held that respondents' activities did not have sufficient effect on interstate commerce to support Sherman Act jurisdiction. Petitioners had argued that the fee schedule restrained the business of financing and insuring home mortgages by inflating a component part of the total cost of housing, but the court concluded that a title examination is generally a local service, and even where it is part of a transaction which crosses state lines its effect on commerce is only "incidental," and does not justify federal regulation.

We granted certiorari, 419 U.S. 963 (1974), and are thus confronted for the first time with the question of whether the Sherman Act applies to services performed by attorneys in examining titles in connection with financing the purchase of real estate.

II

Our inquiry can be divided into four steps: did respondents engage in price fixing? If so, are their activities in interstate commerce or do they affect interstate commerce? If so, are the activities exempt from the Sherman Act because they involve a "learned profession?" If not, are the activities "state action" within the meaning of Parker v. Brown, 317 U.S. 341 (1943), and therefore exempt from the Sherman Act?

A

The County Bar argues that because the fee schedule is merely advisory, the schedule and its enforcement mechanism do not constitute price fixing. Its purpose, the argument continues, is only to provide legitimate information to aid member lawyers in complying with Virginia professional regulations. Moreover, the County Bar contends that in practice the schedule has not had the effect of producing fixed fees. The facts found by the trier belie these contentions, and nothing in the record suggests these findings lack support.

A purely advisory fee schedule issued to provide guidelines, or an exchange of price information without a showing of an actual restraint on trade, would present us with a different question, e.g., American Column Co. v. United States, 257 U.S. 377 (1921); Maple Flooring Assn. v. United States, 268 U.S. 563, 580 (1925). But see United States v. National Assn. of Real Estate Boards, 339 U.S. 485, 488–489, 495 (1950). The record here, however, reveals a situation quite different from what would occur under a purely advisory fee schedule. Here a fixed, rigid price floor arose from respondents' activities: every lawyer who responded to petitioners' inquiries adhered to the fee schedule, and no lawyer asked for additional information in order to set an individualized fee. The price information disseminated did not concern past standards, cf. Cement Mfrs. Protective Assn. v. United States, 268 U.S. 588 (1925), but rather minimum fees to be charged in future transactions, and those minimum rates were increased over time. The fee schedule was enforced through the prospect of professional discipline from the State Bar, and the desire of attorneys to comply with announced professional norms, see generally American Column Co., supra, at 411; the motivation to conform was reinforced by the assurance that other lawyers would not compete by underbidding. This is not merely a case of an agreement that may be inferred from an exchange of price information, United States v. Container Corp., 393 U.S. 333, 337 (1969), for here a naked agreement was clearly shown, and the effect on prices is plain.[1] Id., at 339 (Fortas, J., concurring).

Moreover, in terms of restraining competition and harming consumers like petitioners the price-fixing activities found here are unusually damaging. A title examination is indispensable in the process of financing a real estate purchase, and since only an attorney licensed to practice in Virginia may legally examine a title, see n. 1, supra, consumers could not turn to alternative sources for the necessary service. All attorneys, of course, were practicing under the constraint of the fee schedule. See generally United States v. Container Corp., supra, at 337. The County Bar makes much of the fact that it is a voluntary organization; however, the ethical opinions issued by the State Bar provide that any lawyer, whether or not a member of his county bar association, may be disciplined for "habitually charg[ing] less than the suggested minimum fee schedule adopted by his local bar Association...." See supra, at 777–778, and n. 4. These factors

---

1. The Court of Appeals accurately depicted the situation: "[I]t is clear from the record that all or nearly all of the [County Bar] members charged fees equal to or exceeding the fees set forth in the schedule for title examinations and other services involving real estate." 497 F.2d 1, 12 (CA4 1974). "'A significant reason for the inability of [petitioners] to obtain legal services ... for less than the fee set forth in the Minimum Fee Schedule ... was the operation of the minimum fee schedule system.'" Id., at 4. "It is abundantly clear from the record before us that the fee schedule and the enforcement mechanism supporting it act as a substantial restraint upon competition among attorneys practicing in Fairfax County." Id., at 13.

coalesced to create a pricing system that consumers could not realistically escape. On this record respondents' activities constitute a classic illustration of price fixing.

B

The County Bar argues, as the Court of Appeals held, that any effect on interstate commerce caused by the fee schedule's restraint on legal services was incidental and remote. In its view the legal services, which are performed wholly intrastate, are essentially local in nature and therefore a restraint with respect to them can never substantially affect interstate commerce. Further, the County Bar maintains, there was no showing here that the fee schedule and its enforcement mechanism increased fees, and that even if they did there was no showing that such an increase deterred any prospective homeowner from buying in Fairfax County.

These arguments misconceive the nature of the transactions at issue and the place legal services play in those transactions. As the District Court found, "a significant portion of funds furnished for the purchasing of homes in Fairfax County comes from without the State of Virginia," and "significant amounts of loans on Fairfax County real estate are guaranteed by the United States Veterans Administration and Department of Housing and Urban Development, both headquartered in the District of Columbia." Thus in this class action the transactions which create the need for the particular legal services in question frequently are interstate transactions.

* * *

Where, as a matter of law or practical necessity, legal services are an integral part of an interstate transaction, a restraint on those services may substantially affect commerce for Sherman Act purposes. Of course, there may be legal services that involve interstate commerce in other fashions, just as there may be legal services that have no nexus with interstate commerce and thus are beyond the reach of the Sherman Act.

C

The County Bar argues that Congress never intended to include the learned professions within the terms "trade or commerce" in 1 of the Sherman Act, and therefore the sale of professional services is exempt from the Act. No explicit exemption or legislative history is provided to support this contention; rather, the existence of state regulation seems to be its primary basis. Also, the County Bar maintains that competition is inconsistent with the practice of a profession because enhancing profit is not the goal of professional activities; the goal is to provide services necessary to the community. That, indeed, is the classic basis traditionally advanced to distinguish professions from trades, businesses, and other occupations, but it loses some of its force when used to support the fee control activities involved here.

In arguing that learned professions are not "trade or commerce" the County Bar seeks a total exclusion from antitrust regulation. Whether state regulation is active or dormant, real or theoretical, lawyers would be able to adopt anticompetitive practices with impunity. We cannot find support for the proposition that Congress intended any such sweeping exclusion. The nature of an occupation, standing alone, does not provide sanctuary from the Sherman Act, Associated Press v. United States, 326 U.S. 1, 7 (1945), nor is the public-service aspect of professional practice controlling in determining whether 1 includes professions. United States v. National Assn. of Real Estate Boards, 339 U.S., at 489. Congress intended to strike as broadly as it could in 1 of the Sherman Act, and to read into it so wide an exemption as that urged on us would be at odds with that purpose.

* * *

D

In Parker v. Brown, 317 U.S. 341 (1943), the Court held that an anticompetitive marketing program which "derived its authority and its efficacy from the legislative command of the state" was not a violation of the Sherman Act because the Act was intended to regulate private practices and not to prohibit a State from imposing a restraint as an act of government. Id., at 350–352; Olsen v. Smith, 195 U.S. 332, 344–345 (1904). Respondent State Bar and respondent County Bar both seek to avail themselves of this so-called state-action exemption.

Through its legislature Virginia has authorized its highest court to regulate the practice of law.[2] That court has adopted ethical codes which deal in part with fees, and far from exercising state power to authorize binding price fixing, explicitly directed lawyers not "to be controlled" by fee schedules. The State Bar, a state agency by law, argues that in issuing fee schedule reports and ethical opinions dealing with fee schedules it was merely implementing the fee provisions of the ethical codes. The County Bar, although it is a voluntary association and not a state agency, claims that the ethical codes and the activities of the State Bar "prompted" it to issue fee schedules and thus its actions, too, are state action for Sherman Act purposes.

The threshold inquiry in determining if an anticompetitive activity is state action of the type the Sherman Act was not meant to proscribe is whether the activity is required by the State acting as sovereign. Parker v. Brown, 317 U.S., at 350–352; Continental Co. v. Union Carbide, 370 U.S. 690, 706–707 (1962). Here we need not inquire further into the state-action question because it cannot fairly be said that the State of Virginia through its Supreme Court Rules required the anticompetitive activities of either respondent. Respondents have pointed to no Virginia statute requiring their activities; state law simply does not refer to fees leaving regulation of the profession to the Virginia Supreme Court; although the Supreme Court's ethical codes mention advisory fee schedules they do not direct either respondent to supply them, or require the type of price floor which arose from respondents' activities. Although the State Bar apparently has been granted the power to issue ethical opinions, there is no indication in this record that the Virginia Supreme Court approves the opinions. Respondents' arguments, at most, constitute the contention that their activities complemented the objective of the ethical codes. In our view that is not state action for Sherman Act purposes. It is not enough that, as the County Bar puts it, anticompetitive conduct is "prompted" by state action; rather, anticompetitive activities must be compelled by direction of the State acting as a sovereign.

The fact that the State Bar is a state agency for some limited purposes does not create an antitrust shield that allows it to foster anticompetitive practices for the benefit

---

2. Virginia Code Ann. 54-48 (1972) provides: "Rules and regulations defining practice of law and prescribing codes of ethics and disciplinary procedure.—The Supreme Court of Appeals may, from time to time, prescribe, adopt, promulgate and amend rules and regulations: "(a) Defining the practice of law. "(b) Prescribing a code of ethics governing the professional conduct of attorneys at law and a code of judicial ethics. "(c) Prescribing procedure for disciplining, suspending, and disbarring attorneys at law." In addition, the Supreme Court of Virginia, has inherent power to regulate the practice of law in that State. Button v. Day, 204 Va. 547, 132 S. E. 2d 292 (1963). See Lathrop v. Donohue, 367 U.S. 820 (1961).

of its members. Cf. Gibson v. Berryhill, 411 U.S. 564, 578–579 (1973). The State Bar, by providing that deviation from County Bar minimum fees may lead to disciplinary action, has voluntarily joined in what is essentially a private anticompetitive activity, and in that posture cannot claim it is beyond the reach of the Sherman Act. Parker v. Brown, supra, at 351–352. Its activities resulted in a rigid price floor from which petitioners, as consumers, could not escape if they wished to borrow money to buy a home.

III

We recognize that the States have a compelling interest in the practice of professions within their boundaries, and that as part of their power to protect the public health, safety, and other valid interests they have broad power to establish standards for licensing practitioners and regulating the practice of professions. We also recognize that in some instances the State may decide that "forms of competition usual in the business world may be demoralizing to the ethical standards of a profession." United States v. Oregon State Medical Society, 343 U.S. 326, 336 (1952). See also Semler v. Oregon State Board of Dental Examiners, 294 U.S. 608, 611–613 (1935). The interest of the States in regulating lawyers is especially great since lawyers are essential to the primary governmental function of administering justice, and have historically been "officers of the courts." See Sperry v. Florida ex rel. Florida Bar, 373 U.S. 379, 383 (1963); Cohen v. Hurley, 366 U.S. 117, 123–124 (1961); Law Students Research Council v. Wadmond, 401 U.S. 154, 157 (1971). In holding that certain anticompetitive conduct by lawyers is within the reach of the Sherman Act we intend no diminution of the authority of the State to regulate its professions.

The judgment of the Court of Appeals is reversed and the case is remanded to that court with orders to remand to the District Court for further proceedings consistent with this opinion.

Reversed and remanded.

MR. JUSTICE POWELL took no part in the consideration or decision of this case.

Bates v. State Bar of Arizona

433 U.S. 350
United States Supreme Court
Argued January 18, 1977
Decided June 27, 1977
[Some footnotes deleted. Remaining footnotes renumbered.]

MR. JUSTICE BLACKMUN delivered the opinion of the Court.

As part of its regulation of the Arizona Bar, the Supreme Court of that State has imposed and enforces a disciplinary rule that restricts advertising by attorneys. This case presents two issues: whether 1 and 2 of the Sherman Act, 15 U.S.C. 1 and 2, forbid such state regulation, and whether the operation of the rule violates the First Amendment, made applicable to the States through the Fourteenth.

I

Appellants John R. Bates and Van O'Steen are attorneys licensed to practice law in the State of Arizona.[1] As such, they are members of the appellee, the State Bar of Arizona. After admission to the bar in 1972, appellants worked as attorneys with the Maricopa County Legal Aid Society. App. 221.

In March 1974, appellants left the Society and opened a law office, which they call a "legal clinic," in Phoenix. Their aim was to provide legal services at modest fees to persons of moderate income who did not qualify for governmental legal aid. Id., at 75. In order to achieve this end, they would accept only routine matters, such as uncontested divorces, uncontested adoptions, simple personal bankruptcies, and changes of name, for which costs could be kept down by extensive use of paralegals, automatic typewriting equipment, and standardized forms and office procedures. More complicated cases, such as contested divorces, would not be accepted. Id., at 97. Because appellants set their prices so as to have a relatively low return on each case they handled, they depended on substantial volume. Id., at 122–123.

After conducting their practice in this manner for two years, appellants concluded that their practice and clinical concept could not survive unless the availability of legal services at low cost was advertised and, in particular, fees were advertised. Id., at 120–123. Consequently, in order to generate the necessary flow of business, that is, "to attract clients," id., at 121; Tr. of Oral Arg. 4, appellants on February 22, 1976, placed an advertisement (reproduced in the Appendix to this opinion, infra, at [516]) in the Arizona Republic, a daily newspaper of general circulation in the Phoenix metropolitan area. As may be seen, the advertisement stated that appellants were offering "legal services at very reasonable fees," and listed their fees for certain services.

Appellants concede that the advertisement constituted a clear violation of Disciplinary Rule 2-101 (B), incorporated in Rule 29 (a) of the Supreme Court of Arizona, 17A Ariz. Rev. Stat., p. 26 (Supp. 1976). The disciplinary rule provides in part:

> "(B) A lawyer shall not publicize himself, or his partner, or associate, or any other lawyer affiliated with him or his firm, as a lawyer through newspaper or magazine advertisements, radio or television announcements, display advertisements in the city or telephone directories or other means of commercial publicity, nor shall he authorize or permit others to do so in his behalf."

Upon the filing of a complaint initiated by the president of the State Bar, App. 350, a hearing was held before a three-member Special Local Administrative Committee, as prescribed by Arizona Supreme Court Rule 33. App. 16. Although the committee took the position that it could not consider an attack on the validity of the rule, it allowed the parties to develop a record on which such a challenge could be based. The committee recommended that each of the appellants be suspended from the practice of law for not less than six months. Id., at 482. Upon further review by the Board of Governors of the State Bar, pursuant to the Supreme Court's Rule 36, the Board recommended only a one-week suspension for each appellant, the weeks to run consecutively. App. 486–487.

---

1. Each appellant is a 1972 graduate of Arizona State University College of Law. Mr. Bates was named by the faculty of that law school as the outstanding student of his class; Mr. O'Steen graduated cum laude. App. 220–221.

ADVERTISEMENT

DO YOU NEED A LAWYER?

LEGAL SERVICES AT VERY REASONABLE FEES

⚖

° Divorce or legal separation—uncontested (both spouses sign papers)
$175 00 plus $20 00 court filing fee

° Preparation of all court papers and instructions on how to do your own simple uncontested divorce
$100 00

° Adoption—uncontested severance proceeding
$225 00 plus approximately $10.00 publication cost

° Bankruptcy—non-business, no contested proceedings
Individual
$250 00 plus $55.00 court filing fee
Wife and Husband
$300.00 plus $110.00 court filing fee

° Change of Name
$95.00 plus $20.00 court filing fee

Information regarding other types of cases furnished on request

---

Legal Clinic of Bates & O'Steen
617 North 3rd Street
Phoenix, Arizona 85004
Telephone [602] 252-8888

[The advertisement in *Bates v. State Bar of Arizona*.]

Appellants, as permitted by the Supreme Court's Rule 37, then sought review in the Supreme Court of Arizona, arguing, among other things, that the disciplinary rule violated 1 and 2 of the Sherman Act because of its tendency to limit competition, and that the rule infringed their First Amendment rights. The court rejected both claims. In re Bates, 113 Ariz. 394, 555 P.2d 640 (1976). The plurality may have viewed with some skepticism the claim that a restraint on advertising might have an adverse effect on competition. But, even if the rule might otherwise violate the Act, the plurality concluded that the regulation was exempt from Sherman Act attack because the rule "is an activity of the State of Arizona acting as sovereign." Id., at 397, 555 P.2d, at 643. The regulation thus was held to be shielded from the Sherman Act by the state-action exemption of Parker v. Brown, 317 U.S. 341 (1943).

Turning to the First Amendment issue, the plurality noted that restrictions on professional advertising have survived constitutional challenge in the past, citing, along with other cases, Williamson v. Lee Optical Co., 348 U.S. 483 (1955), and Semler v. Dental Examiners, 294 U.S. 608 (1935). Although recognizing that Virginia Pharmacy Board v. Virginia Consumer Council, 425 U.S. 748 (1976), and Bigelow v. Virginia, 421 U.S. 809 (1975), held that commercial speech was entitled to certain protection under the First Amendment, the plurality focused on passages in those opinions acknowledging that special considerations might bear on the advertising of professional services by lawyers. See Virginia Pharmacy Board v. Virginia Consumer Council, 425 U.S., at 773 n. 25; id., at 773–775 (concurring opinion); Bigelow v. Virginia, 421 U.S., at 825 n. 10. The plurality apparently was of the view that the older decisions dealing with professional advertising survived these recent cases unscathed, and held that Disciplinary Rule 2-101 (B) passed First Amendment muster. Because the court, in agreement with the Board of Governors, felt that appellants' advertising "was done in good faith to test the constitutionality of DR 2-101 (B)," it reduced the sanction to censure only. 113 Ariz., at 400, 555 P.2d, at 646.

Of particular interest here is the opinion of Mr. Justice Holohan in dissent. In his view, the case should have been framed in terms of "the right of the public as consumers and citizens to know about the activities of the legal profession," id., at 402, 555 P.2d, at 648, rather than as one involving merely the regulation of a profession. Observed in this light, he felt that the rule performed a substantial disservice to the public:

> "Obviously the information of what lawyers charge is important for private economic decisions by those in need of legal services. Such information is also helpful, perhaps indispensable, to the formation of an intelligent opinion by the public on how well the legal system is working and whether it should be regulated or even altered.... The rule at issue prevents access to such information by the public." Id., at 402–403, 555 P.2d, at 648–649.

Although the dissenter acknowledged that some types of advertising might cause confusion and deception, he felt that the remedy was to ban that form, rather than all advertising. Thus, despite his "personal dislike of the concept of advertising by attorneys," id., at 402, 555 P.2d, at 648, he found the ban unconstitutional.

We noted probable jurisdiction. 429 U.S. 813 (1976).

II
The Sherman Act

In Parker v. Brown, 317 U.S. 341 (1943), this Court held that the Sherman Act was not intended to apply against certain state action. See also Olsen v. Smith, 195 U.S. 332, 344–345 (1904). In Parker a raisin producer-packer brought suit against California officials challenging a state program designed to restrict competition among growers and thereby to maintain prices in the raisin market. The Court held that the State, "as sovereign, imposed the restraint as an act of government which the Sherman Act did not undertake to prohibit." 317 U.S., at 352. Appellee argues, and the Arizona Supreme Court held, that the Parker exemption also bars the instant Sherman Act claim. We agree.

* * *

III
The First Amendment
A

Last Term, in Virginia Pharmacy Board v. Virginia Consumer Council, 425 U.S. 748 (1976), the Court considered the validity under the First Amendment of a Virginia statute declaring that a pharmacist was guilty of "unprofessional conduct" if he advertised prescription drug prices. The pharmacist would then be subject to a monetary penalty or the suspension or revocation of his license. The statute thus effectively prevented the advertising of prescription drug price information. We recognized that the pharmacist who desired to advertise did not wish to report any particularly newsworthy fact or to comment on any cultural, philosophical, or political subject; his desired communication was characterized simply: "'I will sell you the X prescription drug at the Y price.'" Id., at 761. Nonetheless, we held that commercial speech of that kind was entitled to the protection of the First Amendment.

Our analysis began, ibid., with the observation that our cases long have protected speech even though it is in the form of a paid advertisement, Buckley v. Valeo, 424 U.S. 1 (1976); New York Times Co. v. Sullivan, 376 U.S. 254 (1964); in a form that is sold for profit, Smith v. California, 361 U.S. 147 (1959); Murdock v. Pennsylvania, 319 U.S. 105 (1943); or in the form of a solicitation to pay or contribute money, New York Times Co. v. Sullivan, supra; Cantwell v. Connecticut, 310 U.S. 296 (1940). If commercial speech is to be distinguished, it "must be distinguished by its content." 425 U.S., at 761. But a consideration of competing interests reinforced our view that such speech should not be withdrawn from protection merely because it proposed a mundane commercial transaction. Even though the speaker's interest is largely economic, the Court has protected such speech in certain contexts. See, e.g., NLRB v. Gissel Packing Co., 395 U.S. 575 (1969); Thornhill v. Alabama, 310 U.S. 88 (1940). The listener's interest is substantial: the consumer's concern for the free flow of commercial speech often may be far keener than his concern for urgent political dialogue. Moreover, significant societal interests are served by such speech. Advertising, though entirely commercial, may often carry information of import to significant issues of the day. See Bigelow v. Virginia, 421 U.S. 809 (1975). And commercial speech serves to inform the public of the availability, nature, and prices of products and services, and thus performs an indispensable role in the allocation of resources in a free enterprise system. See FTC v. Procter & Gamble Co., 386 U.S. 568, 603–604 (1967) (Harlan, J., concurring). In short, such speech serves individual and societal interests in assuring informed and reliable decision-making. 425 U.S., at 761–765.

Arrayed against these substantial interests in the free flow of commercial speech were a number of proffered justifications for the advertising ban. Central among them were claims that the ban was essential to the maintenance of professionalism among licensed pharmacists. It was asserted that advertising would create price competition that might cause the pharmacist to economize at the customer's expense. He might reduce or eliminate the truly professional portions of his services: the maintenance and packaging of drugs so as to assure their effectiveness, and the supplementation on occasion of the prescribing physician's advice as to use. Moreover, it was said, advertising would cause consumers to price-shop, thereby undermining the pharmacist's effort to monitor the drug use of a regular customer so as to ensure that the prescribed drug would not provoke an allergic reaction or be incompatible with another substance the customer was consuming. Finally, it was argued that advertising would reduce the image of the pharmacist as a skilled and specialized craftsman—an image that was said to attract talent to the profession and to reinforce the good habits of those in it—to that of a mere shopkeeper. Id., at 766–768.

Although acknowledging that the State had a strong interest in maintaining professionalism among pharmacists, this Court concluded that the proffered justifications were inadequate to support the advertising ban. High professional standards were assured in large part by the close regulation to which pharmacists in Virginia were subject. Id., at 768. And we observed that "on close inspection it is seen that the State's protectiveness of its citizens rests in large measure on the advantages of their being kept in ignorance." Id., at 769. But we noted the presence of a potent alternative to this "highly paternalistic" approach: "That alternative is to assume that this information is not in itself harmful, that people will perceive their own best interests if only they are well enough informed, and that the best means to that end is to open the channels of communication rather than to close them." Id., at 770. The choice between the dangers of suppressing information and the dangers arising from its free flow was seen as precisely the choice "that the First Amendment makes for us." Ibid. See also Linmark Associates, Inc. v. Willingboro, 431 U.S. 85, 97 (1977).

We have set out this detailed summary of the Pharmacy opinion because the conclusion that Arizona's disciplinary rule is violative of the First Amendment might be said to flow a fortiori from it. Like the Virginia statutes, the disciplinary rule serves to inhibit the free flow of commercial information and to keep the public in ignorance. Because of the possibility, however, that the differences among professions might bring different constitutional considerations into play, we specifically reserved judgment as to other professions.

In the instant case we are confronted with the arguments directed explicitly toward the regulation of advertising by licensed attorneys.

B

The issue presently before us is a narrow one. First, we need not address the peculiar problems associated with advertising claims relating to the quality of legal services. Such claims probably are not susceptible of precise measurement or verification and, under some circumstances, might well be deceptive or misleading to the public, or even false. Appellee does not suggest, nor do we perceive, that appellants' advertisement contained claims, extravagant or otherwise, as to the quality of services. Accordingly, we leave that issue for another day. Second, we also need not resolve the problems associated with in-person solicitation of clients—at the hospital room or the accident site, or in any other situation that breeds undue influence—by attorneys or their agents or "runners." Activity of that kind might well pose dangers of over-reaching and misrepresentation not encountered in newspaper announcement advertising. Hence, this issue also is not before us. Third, we note that appellee's criticism of advertising by attorneys does not apply with much force to some of the basic factual content of advertising: information as to the attorney's name, address, and telephone number, office hours, and the like. The American Bar Association itself has a provision in its current Code of Professional Responsibility that would allow the disclosure of such information, and more, in the classified section of the telephone directory. DR 2-102 (A)(6) (1976). We recognize, however, that an advertising diet limited to such spartan fare would provide scant nourishment.

The heart of the dispute before us today is whether lawyers also may constitutionally advertise the prices at which certain routine services will be performed. Numerous justifications are proffered for the restriction of such price advertising. We consider each in turn:

1. The Adverse Effect on Professionalism. Appellee places particular emphasis on the adverse effects that it feels price advertising will have on the legal profession. The key to professionalism, it is argued, is the sense of pride that involvement in the discipline generates. It is claimed that price advertising will bring about commercialization, which will undermine the attorney's sense of dignity and self-worth. The hustle of the marketplace will adversely affect the profession's service orientation, and irreparably damage the delicate balance between the lawyer's need to earn and his obligation selflessly to serve. Advertising is also said to erode the client's trust in his attorney: Once the client perceives that the lawyer is motivated by profit, his confidence that the attorney is acting out of a commitment to the client's welfare is jeopardized. And advertising is said to tarnish the dignified public image of the profession.

We recognize, of course, and commend the spirit of public service with which the profession of law is practiced and to which it is dedicated. The present Members of this Court, licensed attorneys all, could not feel otherwise. And we would have reason to pause if we felt that our decision today would undercut that spirit. But we find the postulated connection between advertising and the erosion of true professionalism to be severely strained. At its core, the argument presumes that attorneys must conceal from themselves and from their clients the real-life fact that lawyers earn their livelihood at the bar. We suspect that few attorneys engage in such self-deception. And rare is the client, moreover, even one of modest means, who enlists the aid of an attorney with the expectation that his services will be rendered free of charge. See B. Christensen, Lawyers for People of Moderate Means 152–153 (1970). In fact, the American Bar Association advises that an attorney should reach "a clear agreement with his client as to the basis of the fee charges to be made," and that this is to be done "[a]s soon as feasible after a lawyer has been employed." Code of Professional Responsibility EC 2-19 (1976). If the commercial basis of the relationship is to be promptly disclosed on ethical grounds, once the client is in the office, it seems inconsistent to condemn the candid revelation of the same information before he arrives at that office.

Moreover, the assertion that advertising will diminish the attorney's reputation in the community is open to question. Bankers and engineers advertise, and yet these professions are not regarded as undignified. In fact, it has been suggested that the failure of lawyers to advertise creates public disillusionment with the profession. The absence of advertising may be seen to reflect the profession's failure to reach out and serve the community: Studies reveal that many persons do not obtain counsel even when they perceive a need because of the feared price of services or because of an inability to locate a competent attorney. Indeed, cynicism with regard to the profession may be created by the fact that it long has publicly eschewed advertising, while condoning the actions of the attorney who structures his social or civic associations so as to provide contacts with potential clients.

It appears that the ban on advertising originated as a rule of etiquette and not as a rule of ethics. Early lawyers in Great Britain viewed the law as a form of public service, rather than as a means of earning a living, and they looked down on "trade" as unseemly. See H. Drinker, Legal Ethics 5, 210–211 (1953). Eventually, the attitude toward advertising fostered by this view evolved into an aspect of the ethics of the profession. Id., at 211. But habit and tradition are not in themselves an adequate answer to a constitutional challenge. In this day, we do not belittle the person who earns his living by the strength of his arm or the force of his mind. Since the belief that lawyers are somehow "above" trade has become an anachronism, the historical foundation for the advertising restraint has crumbled.

2. The Inherently Misleading Nature of Attorney Advertising. It is argued that advertising of legal services inevitably will be misleading (a) because such services are so individualized with regard to content and quality as to prevent informed comparison on the basis of an advertisement, (b) because the consumer of legal services is unable to determine in advance just what services he needs, and (c) because advertising by attorneys will highlight irrelevant factors and fail to show the relevant factor of skill.

We are not persuaded that restrained professional advertising by lawyers inevitably will be misleading. Although many services performed by attorneys are indeed unique, it is doubtful that any attorney would or could advertise fixed prices for services of that type. The only services that lend themselves to advertising are the routine ones: the uncontested divorce, the simple adoption, the uncontested personal bankruptcy, the change of name, and the like—the very services advertised by appellants. Although the precise service demanded in each task may vary slightly, and although legal services are not fungible, these facts do not make advertising misleading so long as the attorney does the necessary work at the advertised price. The argument that legal services are so unique that fixed rates cannot meaningfully be established is refuted by the record in this case: The appellee State Bar itself sponsors a Legal Services Program in which the participating attorneys agree to perform services like those advertised by the appellants at standardized rates. App. 459–478. Indeed, until the decision of this Court in Goldfarb v. Virginia State Bar, 421 U.S. 773 (1975), the Maricopa County Bar Association apparently had a schedule of suggested minimum fees for standard legal tasks. App. 355. We thus find of little force the assertion that advertising is misleading because of an inherent lack of standardization in legal services.

* * *

3. The Adverse Effect on the Administration of Justice. Advertising is said to have the undesirable effect of stirring up litigation. The judicial machinery is designed to serve those who feel sufficiently aggrieved to bring forward their claims. Advertising, it is argued, serves to encourage the assertion of legal rights in the courts, thereby undesirably unsettling societal repose. There is even a suggestion of barratry. See, e.g., Comment, A Critical Analysis of Rules Against Solicitation by Lawyers, 25 U. Chi. L. Rev. 674, 675–676 (1958).

But advertising by attorneys is not an unmitigated source of harm to the administration of justice. It may offer great benefits. Although advertising might increase the use of the judicial machinery, we cannot accept the notion that it is always better for a person to suffer a wrong silently than to redress it by legal action. As the bar acknowledges, "the middle 70% of our population is not being reached or served adequately by the legal profession." ABA, Revised Handbook on Prepaid Legal Services 2 (1972). Among the reasons for this under utilization is fear of the cost, and an inability to locate a suitable lawyer. See n. 22 and 23, supra. Advertising can help to solve this acknowledged problem: Advertising is the traditional mechanism in a free-market economy for a supplier to inform a potential purchaser of the availability and terms of exchange. The disciplinary rule at issue likely has served to burden access to legal services, particularly for the not-quite-poor and the unknowledgeable. A rule allowing restrained advertising would be in accord with the bar's obligation to "facilitate the process of intelligent selection of lawyers, and to assist in making legal services fully available." ABA Code of Professional Responsibility EC 2-1 (1976).

4. The Undesirable Economic Effects of Advertising. It is claimed that advertising will increase the overhead costs of the profession, and that these costs then will be passed along to consumers in the form of increased fees. Moreover, it is claimed that the additional cost of practice will create a substantial entry barrier, deterring or preventing young attorneys from penetrating the market and entrenching the position of the bar's established members.

These two arguments seem dubious at best. Neither distinguishes lawyers from others, see Virginia Pharmacy Board v. Virginia Consumer Council, 425 U.S., at 768, and neither appears relevant to the First Amendment. The ban on advertising serves to increase the difficulty of discovering the lowest cost seller of acceptable ability. As a result, to this extent attorneys are isolated from competition, and the incentive to price competitively is reduced. Although it is true that the effect of advertising on the price of services has not been demonstrated, there is revealing evidence with regard to products; where consumers have the benefit of price advertising, retail prices often are dramatically lower than they would be without advertising. It is entirely possible that advertising will serve to reduce, not advance, the cost of legal services to the consumer.

The entry-barrier argument is equally unpersuasive. In the absence of advertising, an attorney must rely on his contacts with the community to generate a flow of business. In view of the time necessary to develop such contacts, the ban in fact serves to perpetuate the market position of established attorneys. Consideration of entry-barrier problems would urge that advertising be allowed so as to aid the new competitor in penetrating the market.

5. The Adverse Effect of Advertising on the Quality of Service. It is argued that the attorney may advertise a given "package" of service at a set price, and will be inclined to provide, by indiscriminate use, the standard package regardless of whether it fits the client's needs.

Restraints on advertising, however, are an ineffective way of deterring shoddy work. An attorney who is inclined to cut quality will do so regardless of the rule on advertising. And the advertisement of a standardized fee does not necessarily mean that the services offered are undesirably standardized. Indeed, the assertion that an attorney who advertises a standard fee will cut quality is substantially undermined by the fixed-fee schedule of appellee's own prepaid Legal Services Program. Even if advertising leads to the creation of "legal clinics" like that of appellants' — clinics that emphasize standardized procedures for routine problems — it is possible that such clinics will improve service by reducing the likelihood of error.

6. The Difficulties of Enforcement. Finally, it is argued that the wholesale restriction is justified by the problems of enforcement if any other course is taken. Because the public lacks sophistication in legal matters, it may be particularly susceptible to misleading or deceptive advertising by lawyers. After-the-fact action by the consumer lured by such advertising may not provide a realistic restraint because of the inability of the layman to assess whether the service he has received meets professional standards. Thus, the vigilance of a regulatory agency will be required. But because of the numerous purveyors of services, the overseeing of advertising will be burdensome.

It is at least somewhat incongruous for the opponents of advertising to extol the virtues and altruism of the legal profession at one point, and, at another, to assert that its members will seize the opportunity to mislead and distort. We suspect that, with advertising, most lawyers will behave as they always have: They will abide by their solemn oaths to uphold the integrity and honor of their profession and of the legal system. For every attorney who overreaches through advertising, there will be thousands of others who will be candid and honest and straightforward. And, of course, it will be in the latter's interest, as in other cases of misconduct at the bar, to assist in weeding out those few who abuse their trust.

In sum, we are not persuaded that any of the proffered justifications rise to the level of an acceptable reason for the suppression of all advertising by attorneys.

* * *

IV

In holding that advertising by attorneys may not be subjected to blanket suppression, and that the advertisement at issue is protected, we, of course, do not hold that advertising by attorneys may not be regulated in any way. We mention some of the clearly permissible limitations on advertising not foreclosed by our holding.

Advertising that is false, deceptive, or misleading of course is subject to restraint. See Virginia Pharmacy Board v. Virginia Consumer Council, 425 U.S., at 771–772, and n. 24. Since the advertiser knows his product and has a commercial interest in its dissemination, we have little worry that regulation to assure truthfulness will discourage protected speech. Id., at 771–772, n. 24. And any concern that strict requirements for truthfulness will undesirably inhibit spontaneity seems inapplicable because commercial speech generally is calculated. Indeed, the public and private benefits from commercial speech derive from confidence in its accuracy and reliability. Thus, the leeway for untruthful or misleading expression that has been allowed in other contexts has little force in the commercial arena. Compare Gertz v. Robert Welch, Inc., 418 U.S. 323, 339–341 (1974), and Cantwell v. Connecticut, 310 U.S., at 310, with NLRB v. Gissel Packing Co., 395 U.S., at 618. In fact, because the public lacks sophistication concerning legal services, misstatements that might be overlooked or deemed unimportant in other advertising may be found quite inappropriate in legal advertising. For example, advertising claims as to the quality of services—a matter we do not address today—are not susceptible of measurement or verification; accordingly, such claims may be so likely to be misleading as to warrant restriction. Similar objections might justify restraints on in-person solicitation. We do not foreclose the possibility that some limited supplantation, by way of warning or disclaimer or the like, might be required of even an advertisement of the kind ruled upon today so as to assure that the consumer is not misled. In sum, we recognize that many of the problems in defining the boundary between deceptive and nondeceptive advertising remain to be resolved, and we expect that the bar will have a special role to play in assuring that advertising by attorneys flows both freely and cleanly.

As with other varieties of speech, it follows as well that there may be reasonable restrictions on the time, place, and manner of advertising. See Virginia Pharmacy Board v. Virginia Consumer Council, 425 U.S., at 771. Advertising concerning transactions that are themselves illegal obviously may be suppressed. See Pittsburgh Press Co. v. Human Relations Comm'n, 413 U.S. 376, 388 (1973). And the special problems of advertising on the electronic broadcast media will warrant special consideration. Cf. Capital Broadcasting Co. v. Mitchell, 333 F. Supp. 582 (DC 1971), summarily aff'd sub nom. Capital Broadcasting Co. v. Acting Attorney General, 405 U.S. 1000 (1972).

The constitutional issue in this case is only whether the State may prevent the publication in a newspaper of appellants' truthful advertisement concerning the availability and terms of routine legal services. We rule simply that the flow of such information may not be restrained, and we therefore hold the present application of the disciplinary rule against appellants to be violative of the First Amendment.

The judgment of the Supreme Court of Arizona is therefore affirmed in part and reversed in part.

It is so ordered.

MR. CHIEF JUSTICE BURGER, concurring in part and dissenting in part.

I am in general agreement with MR. JUSTICE POWELL'S analysis and with Part II of the Court's opinion. I particularly agree with MR. JUSTICE POWELL'S statement that "today's decision will effect profound changes in the practice of law." Post, at 389. Although the exact effect of those changes cannot now be known, I fear that they will be injurious to those whom the ban on legal advertising was designed to protect—the members of the general public in need of legal services.

Some Members of the Court apparently believe that the present case is controlled by our holding one year ago in Virginia Pharmacy Board v. Virginia Consumer Council, 425 U.S. 748 (1976). However, I had thought that we made most explicit that our holding there rested on the fact that the advertisement of standardized, prepackaged, name-brand drugs was at issue. Id., at 773 n. 25. In that context, the prohibition on price advertising, which had served a useful function in the days of individually compounded medicines, was no longer tied to the conditions which had given it birth. The same cannot be said with respect to legal services which, by necessity, must vary greatly from case to case. Indeed, I find it difficult, if not impossible, to identify categories of legal problems or services which are fungible in nature. For example, MR. JUSTICE POWELL persuasively demonstrates the fallacy of any notion that even an uncontested divorce can be "standard." Post, at 392–394. A "reasonable charge" for such a divorce could be $195, as the appellants wish to advertise, or it could reasonably be a great deal more, depending on such variables as child custody, alimony, support, or any property settlement. Because legal services can rarely, if ever, be "standardized" and because potential clients rarely know in advance what services they do in fact need, price advertising can never give the public an accurate picture on which to base its selection of an attorney. Indeed, in the context of legal services, such incomplete information could be worse than no information at all.[2] It could become a trap for the unwary.

The Court's opinion largely disregards these facts on the unsupported assumptions that attorneys will not advertise anything but "routine" services—which the Court totally fails to identify or define—or, if they do advertise, that the bar and the courts will be able to protect the public from those few practitioners who abuse their trust. The former notion is highly speculative and, of course, does nothing to solve the problems that this decision will create; as to the latter, the existing administrative machinery of both

---

2. I express no view on MR. JUSTICE POWELL'S conclusion that the advertisement of an attorney's initial consultation fee or his hourly rate would not be inherently misleading and thus should be permitted since I cannot understand why an "initial consultation" should have a different charge base from an hourly rate. Post, at 399–400. Careful study of the problems of attorney advertising—and none has yet been made—may well reveal that advertisements limited to such matters do not carry with them the potential for abuse that accompanies the advertisement of fees for particular services. However, even such limited advertisements should not be permitted without a disclaimer which informs the public that the fee charged in any particular case will depend on and vary according to the individual circumstances of that case. See ABA Code of Professional Responsibility DR 2-106 (B) (1976).

the profession and the courts has proved wholly inadequate to police the profession effectively. See ABA Special Committee On Evaluation of Disciplinary Enforcement, Problems and Recommendations in Disciplinary Enforcement (1970). To impose the enormous new regulatory burdens called for by the Court's decision on the presently deficient machinery of the bar and courts is unrealistic; it is almost predictable that it will create problems of unmanageable proportions. The Court thus takes a "great leap" into an unexplored, sensitive regulatory area where the legal profession and the courts have not yet learned to crawl, let alone stand up or walk. In my view, there is no need for this hasty plunge into a problem where not even the wisest of experts — if such experts exist — can move with sure steps.

To be sure, the public needs information concerning attorneys, their work, and their fees. At the same time, the public needs protection from the unscrupulous or the incompetent practitioner anxious to prey on the uninformed. It seems to me that these twin goals can best be served by permitting the organized bar to experiment with and perfect programs which would announce to the public the probable range of fees for specifically defined services and thus give putative clients some idea of potential cost liability when seeking out legal assistance.[3] However, even such programs should be confined to the known and knowable, e.g., the truly "routine" uncontested divorce which is defined to exclude any dispute over alimony, property rights, child custody or support, and should make clear to the public that the actual fee charged in any given case will vary according to the individual circumstances involved, see ABA Code of Professional Responsibility DR 2-106 (B) (1976), in order to insure that the expectations of clients are not unduly inflated. Accompanying any reform of this nature must be some type of effective administrative procedure to hear and resolve the grievances and complaints of disappointed clients.

Unfortunately, the legal profession in the past has approached solutions for the protection of the public with too much caution, and, as a result, too little progress has been made. However, as MR. JUSTICE POWELL points out, post, at 398–399, the organized bar has recently made some reforms in this sensitive area and more appear to be in the offing. Rather than allowing these efforts to bear fruit, the Court today opts for a Draconian "solution" which I believe will only breed more problems than it can conceivably resolve.

MR. JUSTICE POWELL, with whom MR. JUSTICE STEWART joins, concurring in part and dissenting in part.

I agree with the Court that appellants' Sherman Act claim is barred by the Parker v. Brown, 317 U.S. 341 (1943), exemption and therefore join Part II of the Court's opinion. But I cannot join the Court's holding that under the First Amendment "truthful" newspaper advertising of a lawyer's prices for "routine legal services" may not be restrained. Ante, at 384. Although the Court appears to note some reservations (mentioned below), it is clear that within undefined limits today's decision will effect profound changes in the practice of law, viewed for centuries as a learned profession. The supervisory power of the courts over members of the bar, as officers of the courts, and

---

3. The publication of such information by the organized bar would create no conflict with our holding in Goldfarb v. Virginia State Bar, 421 U.S. 773 (1975), so long as attorneys were under no obligation to charge within the range of fees described.

the authority of the respective States to oversee the regulation of the profession have been weakened. Although the Court's opinion profess to be framed narrowly, and its reach is subject to future clarification, the holding is explicit and expansive with respect to the advertising of undefined "routine legal services." In my view, this result is neither required by the First Amendment, nor in the public interest.

* * *

IV

The area into which the Court now ventures has, until today, largely been left to self-regulation by the profession within the framework of canons or standards of conduct prescribed by the respective States and enforced where necessary by the courts. The problem of bringing clients and lawyers together on a mutually fair basis, consistent with the public interest, is as old as the profession itself. It is one of considerable complexity, especially in view of the constantly evolving nature of the need for legal services. The problem has not been resolved with complete satisfaction despite diligent and thoughtful efforts by the organized bar and others over a period of many years, and there is no reason to believe that today's best answers will be responsive to future needs.

In this context, the Court's imposition of hard and fast constitutional rules as to price advertising is neither required by precedent nor likely to serve the public interest. One of the great virtues of federalism is the opportunity it affords for experimentation and innovation, with freedom to discard or amend that which proves unsuccessful or detrimental to the public good. The constitutionalizing—indeed the affirmative encouraging—of competitive price advertising of specified legal services will substantially inhibit the experimentation that has been underway and also will limit the control heretofore exercised over lawyers by the respective States.

I am apprehensive, despite the Court's expressed intent to proceed cautiously, that today's holding will be viewed by tens of thousands of lawyers as an invitation—by the public-spirited and the selfish lawyers alike—to engage in competitive advertising on an escalating basis. Some lawyers may gain temporary advantages; others will suffer from the economic power of stronger lawyers, or by the subtle deceit of less scrupulous lawyers. Some members of the public may benefit marginally, but the risk is that many others will be victimized by simplistic price advertising of professional services "almost infinite [in] variety and nature...." Virginia Pharmacy Board, 425 U.S., at 773 n. 25. Until today, in the long history of the legal profession, it was not thought that this risk of public deception was required by the marginal First Amendment interests asserted by the Court.

MR. JUSTICE REHNQUIST, dissenting in part.

I join Part II of the Court's opinion holding that appellants' Sherman Act claim is barred by the Parker v. Brown, 317 U.S. 341 (1943), state-action exemption. Largely for the reasons set forth in my dissent in Virginia Pharmacy Board v. Virginia Consumer Council, 425 U.S. 748, 781 (1976), however, I dissent from Part III because I cannot agree that the First Amendment is infringed by Arizona's regulation of the essentially commercial activity of advertising legal services. Valentine v. Chrestensen, 316 U.S. 52 (1942); Breard v. Alexandria, 341 U.S. 622 (1951). See Pittsburgh Press Co. v. Human Relations Comm'n, 413 U.S. 376 (1973).

I continue to believe that the First Amendment speech provision, long regarded by this Court as a sanctuary for expressions of public importance or intellectual interest, is demeaned by invocation to protect advertisements of goods and services. I would hold quite simply that the appellants' advertisement, however truthful or reasonable it may be, is not the sort of expression that the Amendment was adopted to protect.

* * *

YOUR
NAME
HERE
ATTORNEY AT LAW

Internet Advertising Raises Ethical Concerns
James E. Morgan, *Litigation News*
September 2001, Vol. 26, No. 6, Web Ethics

The World Wide Web may have opened new marketing avenues for lawyers, but it is filled with some old ethical potholes. Attorneys participating in online directories or similar Web sites need to be careful that their advertising does not amount to payment for referrals or aid the unauthorized practice of law, a state ethics panel warns.

Lawyers should be "extremely cautious" when contracting with a commercial Web site company for the online posting of their names and other biographical information, according to an opinion issued recently by the Ohio Supreme Court's Board of Commissioners on Grievances and Discipline.

Although limited to practitioners in Ohio, the panel's opinion should serve as a warning to lawyers nationwide because it was based on ethical rules adopted from the ABA Model Rules of Professional Conduct, says Deborah A. Coleman, Cleveland, a former Chair of the ABA Standing Committee on Ethics and Professional Responsibility.

Before participating in a third party's Web site, lawyers should consider whether the arrangement is permissible advertising or a prohibited referral arrangement, the Ohio panel says. Lawyers also need to evaluate whether their participation in the Web site will aid in the unauthorized practice of law.

The panel offered three guideposts for lawyers evaluating the advertising versus referral issue. First, lawyers should determine how the Web site provider will be compensated. When a lawyer pays a fixed amount for a specific time period of posting, the compensation arrangement is more like an advertisement, the panel suggests. Conversely, when a lawyer must pay an amount based on the number of actual new clients gained through a Web site, the arrangement is closer to an impermissible referral.

Second, lawyers should review all the services that Web sites provide. A Web site that merely posts the lawyer's information is like a typical advertisement. In contrast, a Web site provider that plays more than a ministerial role in posting the lawyers' information is more likely to be considered a prohibited source of referrals.

The panel gave the example of a Web site from which a lawyer purchases the exclusive rights to a zip code. When a person visits this hypothetical Web site and enters her zip code, she is directed only to the participating lawyer. Such exclusive direction should alert the participating lawyer to the likelihood that the arrangement runs afoul of the referral rules, the panel says.

Third, lawyers should evaluate how their information will be presented on a Web site. According to the panel, the safest advertisement contains no language suggesting that the Web site recommends lawyers or refers clients to them.

The posting should not state or even imply that a lawyer's services are part of those provided by the Web site. The Ohio panel recommends that a lawyer affirmatively take steps to have a commercial Web site identify her information as an advertisement or otherwise make clear that it is an advertisement.

While being alert to the advertising/referral issue, lawyers must also evaluate whether a Web site provider is engaged in the unauthorized practice of law, especially if the site is law-related, such as those that provide legal forms.

Before participating in any law-related commercial Web site, the Ohio panel says that a lawyer should investigate the content of the Web site and the services offered to its users. Lawyers must understand what acts constitute the unauthorized practice of law and must exercise their professional judgment to determine whether the Web site provider is engaged in that practice. If a Web site is engaged in the unauthorized practice of law, the lawyer must not aid it in any way.

Although the medium has changed, the issues addressed in the panel's opinion have existed since lawyers started to advertise in print and later in broadcast media, Coleman says. Whatever medium lawyers use to market their services, Coleman says that they "must be vigilant of the rules regulating referrals and the unauthorized practice of law anytime they contemplate a relationship with a third party, especially where the third party will be anything more than a sandwich board between the lawyer and the client."

B. Solicitation

In re Primus

436 U.S. 412
U.S. Supreme Court
Argued January 16, 1978
Decided May 30, 1978
[Some footnotes omitted. Remaining footnotes renumbered.]

MR. JUSTICE POWELL delivered the opinion of the Court.

We consider on this appeal whether a State may punish a member of its Bar who, seeking to further political and ideological goals through associational activity, including litigation, advises a lay person of her legal rights and discloses in a subsequent letter that free legal assistance is available from a nonprofit organization with which the lawyer and her associates are affiliated. Appellant, a member of the Bar of South Carolina, received a public reprimand for writing such a letter. The appeal is opposed by the State Attorney General, on behalf of the Board of Commissioners on Grievances and

Discipline of the Supreme Court of South Carolina. As this appeal presents a substantial question under the First and Fourteenth Amendments, as interpreted in NAACP v. Button, 371 U.S. 415 (1963), we noted probable jurisdiction.

I

Appellant, Edna Smith Primus, is a lawyer practicing in Columbia, S. C. During the period in question, she was associated with the "Carolina Community Law Firm," and was an officer of and cooperating lawyer with the Columbia branch of the American Civil Liberties Union (ACLU). She received no compensation for her work on behalf of the ACLU, but was paid a retainer as a legal consultant for the South Carolina Council on Human Relations (Council), a nonprofit organization with offices in Columbia.

During the summer of 1973, local and national newspapers reported that pregnant mothers on public assistance in Aiken County, S. C., were being sterilized or threatened with sterilization as a condition of the continued receipt of medical assistance under the Medicaid program. Concerned by this development, Gary Allen, an Aiken businessman and officer of a local organization serving indigents, called the Council requesting that one of its representatives come to Aiken to address some of the women who had been sterilized. At the Council's behest, appellant, who had not known Allen previously, called him and arranged a meeting in his office in July 1973. Among those attending was Mary Etta Williams, who had been sterilized by Dr. Clovis H. Pierce after the birth of her third child. Williams and her grandmother attended the meeting because Allen, an old family friend, had invited them and because Williams wanted "[t]o see what it was all about...." App. 41–42. At the meeting, appellant advised those present, including Williams and the other women who had been sterilized by Dr. Pierce, of their legal rights and suggested the possibility of a lawsuit.

Early in August 1973 the ACLU informed appellant that it was willing to provide representation for Aiken mothers who had been sterilized. Appellant testified that after being advised by Allen that Williams wished to institute suit against Dr. Pierce, she decided to inform Williams of the ACLU's offer of free legal representation. Shortly after receiving appellant's letter, dated August 30, 1973[1]—the centerpiece of this litigation—

---

1. Written on the stationery of the Carolina Community Law Firm, the letter stated:
August 30, 1973
Mrs. Marietta Williams 347 Sumter Street Aiken, South Carolina 29801
Dear Mrs. Williams:
You will probably remember me from talking with you at Mr. Allen's office in July about the sterilization performed on you. The American Civil Liberties Union would like to file a lawsuit on your behalf for money against the doctor who performed the operation. We will be coming to Aiken in the near future and would like to explain what is involved so you can understand what is going on.
Now I have a question to ask of you. Would you object to talking to a women's magazine about the situation in Aiken? The magazine is doing a feature story on the whole sterilization problem and wants to talk to you and others in South Carolina. If you don't mind doing this, call me collect at 254-8151 on Friday before 5:00, if you receive this letter in time. Or call me on Tuesday morning (after Labor Day) collect.
I want to assure you that this interview is being done to show what is happening to women against their wishes, and is not being done to harm you in any way. But I want you to decide, so call me collect and let me know of your decision. This practice must stop.
About the lawsuit, if you are interested, let me know, and I'll let you know when we will come down to talk to you about it. We will be coming to talk to Mrs. Waters at the same time; she has already asked the American Civil Liberties Union to file a suit on her behalf.

Williams visited Dr. Pierce to discuss the progress of her third child who was ill. At the doctor's office, she encountered his lawyer and at the latter's request signed a release of liability in the doctor's favor. Williams showed appellant's letter to the doctor and his lawyer, and they retained a copy. She then called appellant from the doctor's office and announced her intention not to sue. There was no further communication between appellant and Williams.

On October 9, 1974, the Secretary of the Board of Commissioners on Grievances and Discipline of the Supreme Court of South Carolina (Board) filed a formal complaint with the Board, charging that appellant had engaged in "solicitation in violation of the Canons of Ethics" by sending the August 30, 1973, letter to Williams. App. 1–2. Appellant denied any unethical solicitation and asserted, inter alia, that her conduct was protected by the First and Fourteenth Amendments and by Canon 2 of the Code of Professional Responsibility of the American Bar Association (ABA). The complaint was heard by a panel of the Board on March 20, 1975. The State's evidence consisted of the letter, the testimony of Williams, and a copy of the summons and complaint in the action instituted against Dr. Pierce and various state officials, Walker v. Pierce, Civ. No. 74-475 (SC, July 28, 1975), aff'd in part and rev'd in part, 560 F.2d 609 (CA4 1977), cert. denied, 434 U.S. 1075 (1978). Following denial of appellant's motion to dismiss, App. 77–82, she testified in her own behalf and called Allen, a number of ACLU representatives, and several character witnesses.

The panel filed a report recommending that appellant be found guilty of soliciting a client on behalf of the ACLU, in violation of Disciplinary Rules (DR) 2-103 (D)(5)(a) and (c) and 2-104 (A)(5) of the Supreme Court of South Carolina, and that a private reprimand be issued. It noted that "[t]he evidence is inconclusive as to whether [appellant] solicited Mrs. Williams on her own behalf, but she did solicit Mrs. Williams on behalf of the ACLU, which would benefit financially in the event of successful prosecution of the suit for money damages." The panel determined that appellant violated DR 2-103 (D)(5) "by attempting to solicit a client for a non-profit organization which, as its primary purpose, renders legal services, where respondent's associate is a staff counsel for the non-profit organization." Appellant also was found to have violated DR 2-104 (A)(5) because she solicited Williams, after providing unsolicited legal advice, to join in a prospective class action for damages and other relief that was to be brought by the ACLU.

After a hearing on January 9, 1976, the full Board approved the panel report and administered a private reprimand. On March 17, 1977, the Supreme Court of South Carolina entered an order which adopted verbatim the findings and conclusions of the panel report and increased the sanction, sua sponte, to a public reprimand. 268 S. C. 259, 233 S. E. 2d 301.

On July 9, 1977, appellant filed a jurisdictional statement and this appeal was docketed. We noted probable jurisdiction on October 3, 1977, sub nom. In re Smith, 434 U.S. 814. We now reverse.

II

This appeal concerns the tension between contending values of considerable moment to the legal profession and to society. Relying upon NAACP v. Button, 371 U.S. 415 (1963), and its progeny, appellant maintains that her activity involved constitution-

---

Sincerely, s/ Edna Smith Edna Smith Attorney-at-law
App. 3–4.

ally protected expression and association. In her view, South Carolina has not shown that the discipline meted out to her advances a subordinating state interest in a manner that avoids unnecessary abridgment of First Amendment freedoms. Appellee counters that appellant's letter to Williams falls outside of the protection of Button, and that South Carolina acted lawfully in punishing a member of its Bar for solicitation.

The States enjoy broad power to regulate "the practice of professions within their boundaries," and "[t]he interest of the States in regulating lawyers is especially great since lawyers are essential to the primary governmental function of administering justice, and have historically been 'officers of the courts.'" Goldfarb v. Virginia State Bar, 421 U.S. 773, 792 (1975). For example, we decide today in Ohralik v. Ohio State Bar Assn., post, p. 447, that the States may vindicate legitimate regulatory interests through proscription, in certain circumstances, of in-person solicitation by lawyers who seek to communicate purely commercial offers of legal assistance to lay persons.

Unlike the situation in Ohralik, however, appellant's act of solicitation took the form of a letter to a woman with whom appellant had discussed the possibility of seeking redress for an allegedly unconstitutional sterilization. This was not inperson solicitation for pecuniary gain. Appellant was communicating an offer of free assistance by attorneys associated with the ACLU, not an offer predicated on entitlement to a share of any monetary recovery. And her actions were undertaken to express personal political beliefs and to advance the civil-liberties objectives of the ACLU, rather than to derive financial gain. The question presented in this case is whether, in light of the values protected by the First and Fourteenth Amendments, these differences materially affect the scope of state regulation of the conduct of lawyers.

III

In NAACP v. Button, supra, the Supreme Court of Appeals of Virginia had held that the activities of members and staff attorneys of the National Association for the Advancement of Colored People (NAACP) and its affiliate, the Virginia State Conference of NAACP Branches (Conference), constituted "solicitation of legal business" in violation of state law. NAACP v. Harrison, 202 Va. 142, 116 S.E.2d 55 (1960). Although the NAACP representatives and staff attorneys had "a right to peaceably assemble with the members of the branches and other groups to discuss with them and advise them relative to their legal rights in matters concerning racial segregation," the court found no constitutional protection for efforts to "solicit prospective litigants to authorize the filing of suits" by NAACP-compensated attorneys. Id., at 159, 116 S.E.2d, at 68–69.

This Court reversed: "We hold that the activities of the NAACP, its affiliates and legal staff shown on this record are modes of expression and association protected by the First and Fourteenth Amendments which Virginia may not prohibit, under its power to regulate the legal profession, as improper solicitation of legal business violative of [state law] and the Canons of Professional Ethics." 371 U.S., at 428–429. The solicitation of prospective litigants, many of whom were not members of the NAACP or the Conference, for the purpose of furthering the civil-rights objectives of the organization and its members was held to come within the right "'to engage in association for the advancement of beliefs and ideas.'" Id., at 430, quoting NAACP v. Alabama, 357 U.S. 449, 460 (1958).

Since the Virginia statute sought to regulate expressive and associational conduct at the core of the First Amendment's protective ambit, the Button Court insisted that "government may regulate in the area only with narrow specificity." 371 U.S., at 433. The Attorney General of Virginia had argued that the law merely (i) proscribed control of the actual litigation by the NAACP after it was instituted, ibid., and (ii) sought to prevent the evils traditionally associated with common-law maintenance, champerty, and barratry, id., at 438.[2] The Court found inadequate the first justification because of an absence of evidence of NAACP interference with the actual conduct of litigation, or neglect or harassment of clients, and because the statute, as construed, was not drawn narrowly to advance the asserted goal. It rejected the analogy to the common-law offenses because of an absence of proof that malicious intent or the prospect of pecuniary gain inspired the NAACP-sponsored litigation. It also found a lack of proof that a serious danger of conflict of interest marked the relationship between the NAACP and its member and nonmember Negro litigants. The Court concluded that "although the [NAACP] has amply shown that its activities fall within the First Amendment's protections, the State has failed to advance any substantial regulatory interest, in the form of substantive evils flowing from [the NAACP's] activities, which can justify the broad prohibitions which it has imposed." Id., at 444.[3]

Subsequent decisions have interpreted Button as establishing the principle that "collective activity undertaken to obtain meaningful access to the courts is a fundamental right within the protection of the First Amendment." United Transportation Union v. Michigan Bar, 401 U.S. 576, 585 (1971). See Bates v. State Bar of Arizona, 433 U.S. 350, 376 n. 32 (1977). The Court has held that the First and Fourteenth Amendments prevent state proscription of a range of solicitation activities by labor unions seeking to provide low-cost, effective legal representation to their members. See Railroad Trainmen v. Virginia Bar, 377 U.S. 1 (1964); Mine Workers v. Illinois Bar Assn., 389 U.S. 217

---

2. Put simply, maintenance is helping another prosecute a suit; champerty is maintaining a suit in return for a financial interest in the outcome; and barratry is a continuing practice of maintenance or champerty. See generally 4 W. Blackstone, Commentaries *134–136; Zimroth, Group Legal Services and the Constitution, 76 Yale L. J. 966, 969–970 (1967); Radin, Maintenance by Champerty, 24 Calif. L. Rev. 48 (1935).

3. Whatever the precise limits of the holding in Button, the Court at least found constitutionally protected the activities of NAACP members and staff lawyers in "advising Negroes of their constitutional rights, urging them to institute litigation of a particular kind, recommending particular lawyers and financing such litigation." 371 U.S., at 447 (WHITE, J., concurring in part and dissenting in part). In the following Term, the Court noted that Button presented an "occasion to consider an ... attempt by Virginia to enjoin the National Association for the Advancement of Colored People from advising prospective litigants to seek the assistance of particular attorneys. In fact, ... the attorneys were actually employed by the association which recommended them, and recommendations were made even to nonmembers." Railroad Trainmen v. Virginia Bar, 377 U.S. 1, 7 (1964); see Mine Workers v. Illinois Bar Assn., 389 U.S. 217, 221, 222–223 (1967).

The dissent of MR. JUSTICE REHNQUIST suggests that Button is distinguishable from this case because there "lawyers played only a limited role" in the solicitation of prospective litigants, and "the Commonwealth did not attempt to discipline the individual lawyers...." Post, at 444, and n. 3. We do not think that Button can be read in this way. As the Button Court recognized, see n. 14, supra, and as the Virginia Supreme Court of Appeals had found, NAACP v. Harrison, 202 Va. 142, 154–155, 116 S. E. 2d 55, 65 (1960), NAACP staff attorneys were involved in the actual solicitation efforts. The absence of discipline in Button was not due to an absence of lawyer involvement in solicitation. Indeed, from all that appears, no one was disciplined; the case came to this Court in the posture of an anticipatory action for declaratory relief. The state court's decree made quite clear that "the solicitation of legal business by ... [NAACP] attorneys, as shown by the evidence," and the acceptance of such solicited employment by NAACP-compensated attorneys, violated the state ban and the canons of ethics. Id., at 164, 116 S. E. 2d, at 72. We therefore cannot view as dicta Button's holding that "the activities of the NAACP ... legal staff shown on this record are modes of expression and association protected by the First and Fourteenth Amendments which Virginia may not prohibit, under its power to regulate the legal profession, as improper solicitation of legal business...." 371 U.S., at 428–429.

(1967); United Transportation Union v. Michigan Bar, supra. And "lawyers accepting employment under [such plans] have a like protection which the State cannot abridge." Railroad Trainmen, supra, at 8. Without denying the power of the State to take measures to correct the substantive evils of undue influence, overreaching, misrepresentation, invasion of privacy, conflict of interest, and lay interference that potentially are present in solicitation of prospective clients by lawyers, this Court has required that "broad rules framed to protect the public and to preserve respect for the administration of justice" must not work a significant impairment of "the value of associational freedoms." Mine Workers, supra, at 222.

IV

We turn now to the question whether appellant's conduct implicates interests of free expression and association sufficient to justify the level of protection recognized in Button and subsequent cases. The Supreme Court of South Carolina found appellant to have engaged in unethical conduct because she "'solicit[ed] a client for a non-profit organization, which, as its primary purpose, renders legal services, where respondent's associate is a staff counsel for the non-profit organization.'" 268 S. C., at 269, 233 S. E. 2d, at 306. It rejected appellant's First Amendment defenses by distinguishing Button from the case before it. Whereas the NAACP in that case was primarily a "'political'" organization that used "'litigation as an adjunct to the overriding political aims of the organization,'" the ACLU "'has as one of its primary purposes the rendition of legal services.'" Id., at 268, 269, 233 S. E. 2d, at 305, 306. The court also intimated that the ACLU's policy of requesting an award of counsel fees indicated that the organization might "'benefit financially in the event of successful prosecution of the suit for money damages.'" Id., at 263, 233 S. E. 2d, at 303.

Although the disciplinary panel did not permit full factual development of the aims and practices of the ACLU, see n. 9, supra, [deleted] the record does not support the state court's effort to draw a meaningful distinction between the ACLU and the NAACP. From all that appears, the ACLU and its local chapters, much like the NAACP and its local affiliates in Button, "[engage] in extensive educational and lobbying activities" and "also [devote] much of [their] funds and energies to an extensive program of assisting certain kinds of litigation on behalf of [their] declared purposes." 371 U.S., at 419–420. See App. 177–178; n. 2, supra. The court below acknowledged that "'the ACLU has only entered cases in which substantial civil liberties questions are involved....'" 268 S. C., at 263, 233 S. E. 2d, at 303. See Button, 371 U.S., at 440 n. 19. It has engaged in the defense of unpopular causes and unpopular defendants and has represented individuals in litigation that has defined the scope of constitutional protection in areas such as political dissent, juvenile rights, prisoners' rights, military law, amnesty, and privacy. See generally Rabin, Lawyers for Social Change: Perspectives on Public Interest Law, 28 Stan. L. Rev. 207, 210–214 (1976). For the ACLU, as for the NAACP, "litigation is not a technique of resolving private differences"; it is "a form of political expression" and "political association." 371 U.S., at 429, 431.

We find equally unpersuasive any suggestion that the level of constitutional scrutiny in this case should be lowered because of a possible benefit to the ACLU. The discipline administered to appellant was premised solely on the possibility of financial benefit to the organization, rather than any possibility of pecuniary gain to herself, her associates, or the lawyers representing the plaintiffs in the Walker v. Pierce litigation. It is conceded that appellant received no compensation for any of the activities in question. It is also undisputed that neither the ACLU nor any lawyer associated with it would have shared in any monetary recovery by the plaintiffs in Walker v. Pierce. If Williams had elected to bring suit, and had been represented by staff lawyers for the ACLU, the situation would have been similar to that in Button, where the lawyers for the NAACP were "organized as a staff and paid by" that organization. 371 U.S., at 434; see id., at 457 (Harlan, J., dissenting); Mine Workers v. Illinois Bar Assn., 389 U.S., at 222–223; n. 16, supra.

* * *

Appellant's letter of August 30, 1973, to Mrs. Williams thus comes within the generous zone of First Amendment protection reserved for associational freedoms. The ACLU engages in litigation as a vehicle for effective political expression and association, as well as a means of communicating useful information to the public. See n. 32, infra; cf. Bates v. State Bar of Arizona, 433 U.S., at 364; Virginia Pharmacy Board v. Virginia Citizens Consumer Council, 425 U.S. 748, 779–780 (1976) (STEWART, J., concurring). As Button indicates, and as appellant offered to prove at the disciplinary hearing, see n. 9, supra, the efficacy of litigation as a means of advancing the cause of civil liberties often depends on the ability to make legal assistance available to suitable litigants. "'Free trade in ideas' means free trade in the opportunity to persuade to action, not merely to describe facts." Thomas v. Collins, 323 U.S. 516, 537 (1945). The First and Fourteenth Amendments require a measure of protection for "advocating lawful means of vindicating legal rights," Button, 371 U.S., at 437, including "advis[ing] another that his legal rights have been infringed and refer[ring] him to a particular attorney or group of attorneys ... for assistance," id., at 434.

V

South Carolina's action in punishing appellant for soliciting a prospective litigant by mail, on behalf of the ACLU, must withstand the "exacting scrutiny applicable to limitations on core First Amendment rights...." Buckley v. Valeo, 424 U.S. 1, 44–45 (1976). South Carolina must demonstrate "a subordinating interest which is compelling," Bates v. Little Rock, 361 U.S. 516, 524 (1960), and that the means employed in furtherance of that interest are "closely drawn to avoid unnecessary abridgment of associational freedoms." Buckley, supra, at 25.

Appellee contends that the disciplinary action taken in this case is part of a regulatory program aimed at the prevention of undue influence, overreaching, misrepresentation, invasion of privacy, conflict of interest, lay interference, and other evils that are thought to inhere generally in solicitation by lawyers of prospective clients, and to be present on the record before us. Brief for Appellee 37–49. We do not dispute the importance of these interests. This Court's decision in Button makes clear, however, that "[b]road prophylactic rules in the area of free expression are suspect," and that "[p]recision of regulation must be the touchstone in an area so closely touching our most precious freedoms." 371 U.S., at 438; see Mine Workers v. Illinois Bar Assn., 389 U.S., at 222–223. Because of the danger of censorship through selective enforcement of broad prohibitions, and "[b]ecause First Amendment freedoms need breathing space to survive, government may regulate in [this] area only with narrow specificity." Button, supra, at 433.

A

The Disciplinary Rules in question sweep broadly. Under DR 2-103 (D) (5), a lawyer employed by the ACLU or a similar organization may never give unsolicited advice to a lay person that he retain the organization's free services, and it would seem that one who merely assists or maintains a cooperative relationship with the organization also must suppress the giving of such advice if he or anyone associated with the organization will be involved in the ultimate litigation. See Tr. of Oral Arg. 32–34. Notwithstanding appellee's concession in this Court, it is far from clear that a lawyer may communicate the organization's offer of legal assistance at an informational gathering such as the July 1973 meeting in Aiken without breaching the literal terms of the Rule. Cf. Memorandum of Complainant, Apr. 8, 1975, p. 9. Moreover, the Disciplinary Rules in question permit punishment for mere solicitation unaccompanied by proof of any of the substantive evils that appellee maintains were present in this case. In sum, the Rules in their present form have a distinct potential for dampening the kind of "cooperative activity that would make advocacy of litigation meaningful," Button, supra, at 438, as well as for permitting discretionary enforcement against unpopular causes.

B

* * *

Where political expression or association is at issue, this Court has not tolerated the degree of imprecision that often characterizes government regulation of the conduct of commercial affairs. The approach we adopt today in Ohralik, post, p. 447, that the State may proscribe in-person solicitation for pecuniary gain under circumstances likely to result in adverse consequences, cannot be applied to appellant's activity on behalf of the ACLU. Although a showing of potential danger may suffice in the former context, appellant may not be disciplined unless her activity in fact involved the type of misconduct at which South Carolina's broad prohibition is said to be directed.

The record does not support appellee's contention that undue influence, overreaching, misrepresentation, or invasion of privacy actually occurred in this case. Appellant's letter of August 30, 1973, followed up the earlier meeting—one concededly protected by the First and Fourteenth Amendments—by notifying Williams that the ACLU would be interested in supporting possible litigation. The letter imparted additional information material to making an informed decision about whether to authorize litigation, and permitted Williams an opportunity, which she exercised, for arriving at a deliberate decision. The letter was not facially misleading; indeed, it offered "to explain what is involved so you can understand what is going on." The transmittal of this letter—as contrasted with in-person solicitation—involved no appreciable invasion of privacy; nor did it afford any significant opportunity for overreaching or coercion. Moreover, the fact that there was a written communication lessens substantially the difficulty of policing solicitation practices that do offend valid rules of professional conduct. See Ohralik, post, at 466–467. The manner of solicitation in this case certainly was no more likely to cause harmful consequences than the activity considered in Button, see n. 14, supra [now n. 3].

Nor does the record permit a finding of a serious likelihood of conflict of interest or injurious lay interference with the attorney-client relationship. Admittedly, there is some potential for such conflict or interference whenever a lay organization supports any litigation. That potential was present in Button, in the NAACP's solicitation of nonmembers and its disavowal of any relief short of full integration, see 371 U.S., at 420; id., at 460, 465 (Harlan, J., dissenting). But the Court found that potential insufficient in the absence of proof of a "serious danger" of conflict of interest, id., at 443, or of organizational interference with the actual conduct of the litigation, id., at 433, 444. As in Button, "[n]othing that this record shows as to the nature and purpose of [ACLU] activities permits an inference of any injurious intervention in or control of litigation which would constitutionally authorize the application," id., at 444, of the Disciplinary Rules to appellant's activity.[4] A "very distant possibility of harm," Mine Workers v. Illinois Bar Assn., 389 U.S., at 223, cannot justify proscription of the activity of appellant revealed by this record. See id., at 223–224.[5]

The State's interests in preventing the "stirring up" of frivolous or vexatious litigation and minimizing commercialization of the legal profession offer no further justification for the discipline administered in this case. The Button Court declined to accept the proffered analogy to the common-law offenses of maintenance, champerty, and barratry, where the record would not support a finding that the litigant was solicited for a malicious purpose or "for private gain, serving no public interest," 371 U.S., at 440; see id., at 439–444. The same result follows from the facts of this case. And considerations of undue commercialization of the legal profession are of marginal force where, as here, a nonprofit organization offers its services free of charge to individuals who may be in need of legal assistance and may lack the financial means and sophistication necessary to tap alternative sources of such aid.[6]

At bottom, the case against appellant rests on the proposition that a State may regulate in a prophylactic fashion all solicitation activities of lawyers because there may be some potential for overreaching, conflict of interest, or other substantive evils whenever a lawyer gives unsolicited advice and communicates an offer of representation to a layman. Under certain circumstances, that approach is appropriate in the case of speech that simply "propose[s] a commercial transaction," Pittsburgh Press Co. v. Human Relations Comm'n, 413 U.S. 376, 385 (1973). See Ohralik, post, at 455–459. In the context of political expression and association, however, a State must regulate with significantly greater precision.[7]

---

4. Although the decision whether or not to support a particular litigation is made in accordance with the ACLU's broader objectives, the organization's declared policy is to avoid all interference with the attorney-client relationship after that decision has been made. See 1976 Policy Guide of the American Civil Liberties Union, Policy #513, p. 305.

5. We are not presented in this case with a situation where the income of the lawyer who solicits the prospective litigant or who engages in the actual representation of the solicited client rises or falls with the outcome of the particular litigation....

6. Button makes clear that "regulations which reflect hostility to stirring up litigation have been aimed chiefly at those who urge recourse to the courts for private gain, serving no public interest," 371 U.S., at 440, and that "[o]bjection to the intervention of a lay intermediary ... also derives from the element of pecuniary gain," id., at 441. In recognition of the overarching obligation of the lawyer to serve the community, see Canon 2 of the ABA Code of Professional Responsibility, the ethical rules of the legal profession traditionally have recognized an exception from any general ban on solicitation for offers of representation, without charge, extended to individuals who may be unable to obtain legal assistance on their own. See, e.g., In re Ades, 6 F. Supp. 467, 475–476 (Md. 1934); Gunnels v. Atlanta Bar Assn., 191 Ga. 366, 12 S. E. 2d 602 (1940); American Bar Association, Opinions of the Committee on Professional Ethics, Formal Opinion 148, pp. 416–419 (1967).

7. Normally the purpose or motive of the speaker is not central to First Amendment protection, but it does bear on the distinction between conduct that is "an associational aspect of 'expression,'" Emerson, Freedom of Association and Freedom of Expression, 74 Yale L. J. 1, 26 (1964), and other activity subject to plenary regulation by government. Button recognized that certain forms of "cooperative, organizational activity," 371 U.S., at 430, including litigation, are part of the "freedom to engage in association for the advancement of beliefs and ideas," NAACP v. Alabama, 357 U.S. 449, 460 (1958), and that this freedom is an implicit guarantee of the First Amendment. See Healy v. James, 408 U.S. 169, 181 (1972). As shown above, appellant's speech—as part of associational activity— was expression intended to advance "beliefs and ideas." In Ohralik v. Ohio State Bar Assn., post, p. 447, the lawyer was not engaged in associational activity for the advancement of beliefs and ideas; his purpose was the advancement of his own commercial interests. The line, based in part on the motive of the speaker and the character of the expressive activity, will not always be easy to draw, cf.

VI

The State is free to fashion reasonable restrictions with respect to the time, place, and manner of solicitation by members of its Bar. See Bates v. State Bar of Arizona, 433 U.S., at 384; Virginia Pharmacy Board v. Virginia Consumer Council, 425 U.S., at 771, and cases cited therein. The State's special interest in regulating members of a profession it licenses, and who serve as officers of its courts, amply justifies the application of narrowly drawn rules to proscribe solicitation that in fact is misleading, overbearing, or involves other features of deception or improper influence.[8] As we decide today in Ohralik, a State also may forbid in-person solicitation for pecuniary gain under circumstances likely to result in these evils. And a State may insist that lawyers not solicit on behalf of lay organizations that exert control over the actual conduct of any ensuing litigation. See Button, 371 U.S., at 447 (WHITE, J., concurring in part and dissenting in part). Accordingly, nothing in this opinion should be read to foreclose carefully tailored regulation that does not abridge unnecessarily the associational freedom of nonprofit organizations, or their members, having characteristics like those of the NAACP or the ACLU.

We conclude that South Carolina's application of DR 2-103 (D) (5) (a) and (c) and 2-104 (A) (5) to appellant's solicitation by letter on behalf of the ACLU violates the First and Fourteenth Amendments. The judgment of the Supreme Court of South Carolina is

Reversed.

MR. JUSTICE BRENNAN took no part in the consideration or decision of this case.

MR. JUSTICE BLACKMUN, concurring.

Although I join the opinion of the Court, my understanding of the first paragraph of Part VI requires further explanation. The dicta contained in that paragraph are unnecessary to the decision of this case and its First Amendment overtones. I, for one, am not now able to delineate in the area of political solicitation the extent of state authority to proscribe misleading statements. Despite the positive language of the text,[*] footnote 33 explains that the Court also has refused to draw a line regarding misrepresentation:

> "We have no occasion here to delineate the precise contours of permissible state regulation. Thus, for example, a different situation might be presented if an innocent or merely negligent misstatement were made by a lawyer on behalf of an organization engaged in furthering associational or political interests."

It may well be that the State is able to proscribe such solicitation. The resolution of that issue, however, requires a balancing of the State's interests against the important First Amendment values that may lurk in even a negligent misstatement. The Court wisely has postponed this task until an appropriate case is presented and full arguments are carefully considered.

Virginia Pharmacy Board v. Virginia Consumer Council, 425 U.S. 748, 787–788 (1976) (REHNQUIST, J., dissenting), but that is no reason for avoiding the undertaking.

8. We have no occasion here to delineate the precise contours of permissible state regulation. Thus, for example, a different situation might be presented if an innocent or merely negligent misstatement were made by a lawyer on behalf of an organization engaged in furthering associational or political interests.

* "The State's special interest in regulating members of a profession it licenses, and who serve as officers of its courts, amply justifies the application of narrowly drawn rules to proscribe solicitation that in fact is misleading...." Ante, at 438.

MR. JUSTICE REHNQUIST, dissenting.

In this case and the companion case of Ohralik v. Ohio State Bar Assn., post, p. 447, the Court tells its own tale of two lawyers: One tale ends happily for the lawyer and one does not. If we were given the latitude of novelists in deciding between happy and unhappy endings for the heroes and villains of our tales, I might well join in the Court's disposition of both cases. But under our federal system it is for the States to decide which lawyers shall be admitted to the Bar and remain there; this Court may interfere only if the State's decision is rendered impermissible by the United States Constitution. We can, of course, develop a jurisprudence of epithets and slogans in this area, in which "ambulance chasers" suffer one fate and "civil liberties lawyers" another. But I remain unpersuaded by the Court's opinions in these two cases that there is a principled basis for concluding that the First and Fourteenth Amendments forbid South Carolina from disciplining Primus here, but permit Ohio to discipline Ohralik in the companion case. I believe that both South Carolina and Ohio acted within the limits prescribed by those Amendments, and I would therefore affirm the judgment in each case.

This Court said in United Transportation Union v. Michigan Bar, 401 U.S. 576, 585 (1971): "The common thread running through our decisions in NAACP v. Button, [371 U.S. 415 (1963),] Trainmen [v. Virginia Bar, 377 U.S. 1 (1964),] and United Mine Workers [v. Illinois Bar Assn., 389 U.S. 217 (1967),] is that collective activity undertaken to obtain meaningful access to the courts is a fundamental right within the protection of the First Amendment." The Court today ignores the absence of this common thread from the fabric of this case, and decides that South Carolina may not constitutionally discipline a member of its Bar for badgering a lay citizen to take part in "collective activity" which she has never desired to join.

Neither Button nor any other decision of this Court compels a State to permit an attorney to engage in uninvited solicitation on an individual basis. Further, I agree with the Court's statement in the companion case that the State has a strong interest in forestalling the evils that result "when a lawyer, a professional trained in the art of persuasion, personally solicits an unsophisticated, injured, or distressed lay person." Ohralik, post, at 465. The reversal of the judgment of the Supreme Court of South Carolina thus seems to me quite unsupported by previous decisions or by any principle which may be abstracted from them.

In distinguishing between Primus' protected solicitation and Ohralik's unprotected solicitation, the Court lamely declares: "We have not discarded the 'common-sense' distinction between speech proposing a commercial transaction, which occurs in an area traditionally subject to government regulation, and other varieties of speech." Post, at 455–456. Yet to the extent that this "common-sense" distinction focuses on the content of the speech, it is at least suspect under many of this Court's First Amendment cases, see, e.g., Police Dept. of Chicago v. Mosley, 408 U.S. 92, 96–98 (1972), and to the extent it focuses upon the motive of the speaker, it is subject to manipulation by clever practitioners. If Albert Ohralik, like Edna Primus, viewed litigation "'not [as] a technique of resolving private differences,'" but as "'a form of political expression' and 'political association,'" ante, at 428, quoting Button, supra, at 429, 431, for all that appears he would be restored to his right to practice. And we may be sure that the next lawyer in Ohralik's shoes who is disciplined for similar conduct will come here cloaked in the prescribed mantle of "political association" to assure that insurance companies do not take unfair advantage of policyholders.

This absence of any principled distinction between the two cases is made all the more unfortunate by the radical difference in scrutiny brought to bear upon state regulation in each area. Where solicitation proposes merely a commercial transaction, the Court recognizes "the need for prophylactic regulation in furtherance of the State's interest in protecting the lay public." Ohralik, post, at 468. On the other hand, in some circumstances (at least in those identical to the instant case) "[w]here political expression or association is at issue," a member of the Bar "may not be disciplined unless her activity in fact involve[s] the type of misconduct at which South Carolina's broad prohibition is said to be directed." Ante, at 434.

I do not believe that any State will be able to determine with confidence the area in which it may regulate prophylactically and the area in which it may regulate only upon a specific showing of harm. Despite the Court's assertion to the contrary, ante, at 438 n. 32, the difficulty of drawing distinctions on the basis of the content of the speech or the motive of the speaker is a valid reason for avoiding the undertaking where a more objective standard is readily available. I believe that constitutional inquiry must focus on the character of the conduct which the State seeks to regulate, and not on the motives of the individual lawyers or the nature of the particular litigation involved. The State is empowered to discipline for conduct which it deems detrimental to the public interest unless foreclosed from doing so by our cases construing the First and Fourteenth Amendments.

In Button this Court recognized the right of the National Association for the Advancement of Colored People to engage in collective activity, including the solicitation of potential plaintiffs from outside its ranks, for the purpose of instituting and maintaining litigation to achieve the desegregation of public schools. The NAACP utilized letters, bulletins, and petition drives, 371 U.S., at 422, apparently directed toward both members and nonmembers of the organization, id., at 433, to organize public meetings for the purpose of soliciting plaintiffs. As described in Button, lawyers played only a limited role in this solicitation:

> "Typically, a local NAACP branch will invite a member of the legal staff to explain to a meeting of parents and children the legal steps necessary to achieve desegregation. The staff member will bring printed forms to the meeting, authorizing him, and other NAACP or Defense Fund attorneys of his designation, to represent the signers in legal proceedings to achieve desegregation." Id., at 421.

The Court held that the organization could not be punished by the Commonwealth of Virginia for solicitation on the basis of its role in instituting desegregation litigation.

Here, South Carolina has not attempted to punish the ACLU or any laymen associated with it. Gary Allen, who was the instigator of the effort to sue Dr. Pierce, remains as free as before to solicit potential plaintiffs for future litigation. Likewise, Primus remains as free as before to address gatherings of the sort described in Button to advise potential plaintiffs of their legal rights. Primus' first contact with Williams took place at such a gathering, and South Carolina, evidently in response to Button, has not attempted to discipline her for her part in that meeting. It has disciplined her for initiating further contact on an individual basis with Williams, who had not expressed any desire to become involved in the collective activity being organized by the ACLU. While Button appears to permit such individual solicitation for political purposes by lay members of the organization, id., at 422, it nowhere explicitly permits such activity on the part of lawyers.

As the Court understands the Disciplinary Rule enforced by South Carolina, "a lawyer employed by the ACLU or a similar organization may never give unsolicited advice to a lay person that he or she retain the organization's free services." Ante, at 433. That prohibition seems to me entirely reasonable. A State may rightly fear that members of its Bar have powers of persuasion not possessed by laymen, see Ohralik, post, at 464–465, and it may also fear that such persuasion may be as potent in writing as it is in person. Such persuasion may draw an unsophisticated layman into litigation contrary to his own best interests, compare ante, at 434–438, with Ohralik, post, at 464–467, and it may force other citizens of South Carolina to defend against baseless litigation which would not otherwise have been brought. I cannot agree that a State must prove such harmful consequences in each case simply because an organization such as the ACLU or the NAACP is involved.

I cannot share the Court's confidence that the danger of such consequences is minimized simply because a lawyer proceeds from political conviction rather than for pecuniary gain. A State may reasonably fear that a lawyer's desire to resolve "substantial civil liberties questions," 268 S. C. 259, 263, 233 S. E. 2d 301, 303 (1977), may occasionally take precedence over his duty to advance the interests of his client. It is even more reasonable to fear that a lawyer in such circumstances will be inclined to pursue both culpable and blameless defendants to the last ditch in order to achieve his ideological goals. Although individual litigants, including the ACLU, may be free to use the courts for such purposes, South Carolina is likewise free to restrict the activities of the members of its Bar who attempt to persuade them to do so.

I can only conclude that the discipline imposed upon Primus does not violate the Constitution, and I would affirm the judgment of the Supreme Court of South Carolina.

Ohralik v. Ohio State Bar Assn.

436 U.S. 447
U.S. Supreme Court
Argued January 16, 1978
Decided May 30, 1978
[Some footnotes deleted. Remaining footnotes renumbered.]

MR. JUSTICE POWELL delivered the opinion of the Court.

In Bates v. State Bar of Arizona, 433 U.S. 350 (1977), this Court held that truthful advertising of "routine" legal services is protected by the First and Fourteenth Amendments against blanket prohibition by a State. The Court expressly reserved the question of the permissible scope of regulation of "in-person solicitation of clients—at the hospital room or the accident site, or in any other situation that breeds undue influence—by attorneys or their agents or 'runners.'" Id., at 366. Today we answer part of the question so reserved, and hold that the State—or the Bar acting with state authorization—constitutionally may discipline a lawyer for soliciting clients in person, for pecuniary gain, under circumstances likely to pose dangers that the State has a right to prevent.

I

Appellant, a member of the Ohio Bar, lives in Montville, Ohio. Until recently he practiced law in Montville and Cleveland. On February 13, 1974, while picking up his mail at the Montville Post Office, appellant learned from the postmaster's brother about an automobile accident that had taken place on February 2 in which Carol McClintock, a young woman with whom appellant was casually acquainted, had been injured. Appellant made a telephone call to Ms. McClintock's parents, who informed him that their daughter was in the hospital. Appellant suggested that he might visit Carol in the hospital. Mrs. McClintock assented to the idea, but requested that appellant first stop by at her home.

During appellant's visit with the McClintocks, they explained that their daughter had been driving the family automobile on a local road when she was hit by an uninsured motorist. Both Carol and her passenger, Wanda Lou Holbert, were injured and hospitalized. In response to the McClintocks' expression of apprehension that they might be sued by Holbert, appellant explained that Ohio's guest statute would preclude such a suit. When appellant suggested to the McClintocks that they hire a lawyer, Mrs. McClintock retorted that such a decision would be up to Carol, who was 18 years old and would be the beneficiary of a successful claim.

Appellant proceeded to the hospital, where he found Carol lying in traction in her room. After a brief conversation about her condition,[1] appellant told Carol he would represent her and asked her to sign an agreement. Carol said she would have to discuss the matter with her parents. She did not sign the agreement, but asked appellant to have her parents come to see her.[2] Appellant also attempted to see Wanda Lou Holbert, but learned that she had just been released from the hospital. App. 98a. He then departed for another visit with the McClintocks.

On his way appellant detoured to the scene of the accident, where he took a set of photographs. He also picked up a tape recorder, which he concealed under his raincoat before arriving at the McClintocks' residence. Once there, he re-examined their automobile insurance policy, discussed with them the law applicable to passengers, and explained the consequences of the fact that the driver who struck Carol's car was an uninsured motorist. Appellant discovered that the McClintocks' insurance policy would provide benefits of up to $12,500 each for Carol and Wanda Lou under an uninsured-motorist clause. Mrs. McClintock acknowledged that both Carol and Wanda Lou could sue for their injuries, but recounted to appellant that "Wanda swore up and down she would not do it." Ibid. The McClintocks also told appellant that Carol had phoned to say that appellant could "go ahead" with her representation. Two days later appellant returned to Carol's hospital room to have her sign a contract, which provided that he would receive one-third of her recovery.

In the meantime, appellant obtained Wanda Lou's name and address from the McClintocks after telling them he wanted to ask her some questions about the accident. He then visited Wanda Lou at her home, without having been invited. He again concealed his tape recorder and recorded most of the conversation with Wanda Lou.[3] After a brief, unproductive inquiry about the facts of the accident, appellant told Wanda Lou that he was representing Carol and that he had a "little tip" for Wanda Lou: the McClin-

---

1. Carol also mentioned that one of the hospital administrators was urging a lawyer upon her. According to his own testimony, appellant replied: "Yes, this certainly is a case that would entice a lawyer. That would interest him a great deal." App. 53a.

2. Despite the fact that appellant maintains that he did not secure an agreement to represent Carol while he was at the hospital, he waited for an opportunity when no visitors were present and then took photographs of Carol in traction. Id., at 129a.

3. Appellant maintains that the tape is a complete reproduction of everything that was said at the Holbert home. Wanda Lou testified that the tape does not contain appellant's introductory remarks to her about his identity as a lawyer, his agreement to represent Carol McClintock, and his availability and willingness to represent Wanda Lou as well. Id., at 19a–21a. Appellant disputed

tocks' insurance policy contained an uninsured-motorist clause which might provide her with a recovery of up to $12,500. The young woman, who was 18 years of age and not a high school graduate at the time, replied to appellant's query about whether she was going to file a claim by stating that she really did not understand what was going on. Appellant offered to represent her, also, for a contingent fee of one-third of any recovery, and Wanda Lou stated "O. K."[4]

Wanda's mother attempted to repudiate her daughter's oral assent the following day, when appellant called on the telephone to speak to Wanda. Mrs. Holbert informed appellant that she and her daughter did not want to sue anyone or to have appellant represent them, and that if they decided to sue they would consult their own lawyer. Appellant insisted that Wanda had entered into a binding agreement. A month later Wanda confirmed in writing that she wanted neither to sue nor to be represented by appellant. She requested that appellant notify the insurance company that he was not her lawyer, as the company would not release a check to her until he did so.[5] Carol also eventually discharged appellant. Although another lawyer represented her in concluding a settlement with the insurance company, she paid appellant one-third of her recovery[6] in settlement of his lawsuit against her for breach of contract.[7]

Both Carol McClintock and Wanda Lou Holbert filed complaints against appellant with the Grievance Committee of the Geauga County Bar Association. The County Bar Association referred the grievance to appellee, which filed a formal complaint with the Board of Commissioners on Grievances and Discipline of the Supreme Court of Ohio.[8] After a hearing, the Board found that appellant had violated Disciplinary Rules (DR) 2-103 (A) and 2-104 (A) of the Ohio Code of Professional Responsibility.[9] The Board rejected appellant's defense that his conduct was protected under the First and Fourteenth Amendments. The Supreme Court of Ohio adopted the findings of the Board,[10] reiter-

---

Wanda Lou's testimony but agreed that he did not activate the recorder until he had been admitted to the Holbert home and was seated in the living room with Wanda Lou. Id., at 58a.

4. Appellant told Wanda that she should indicate assent by stating "O.K.," which she did. Appellant later testified: "I would say that most of my clients have essentially that much of a communication.... I think most of my clients, that's the way I practice law." Id., at 81a.

In explaining the contingent-fee arrangement, appellant told Wanda Lou that his representation would not "cost [her] anything" because she would receive two-thirds of the recovery if appellant were successful in representing her but would not "have to pay [him] anything" otherwise. Id., at 120a, 125a.

5. The insurance company was willing to pay Wanda Lou for her injuries but would not release the check while appellant claimed, and Wanda Lou denied, that he represented her. Before appellant would "disavow further interest and claim" in Wanda Lou's recovery, he insisted by letter that she first pay him the sum of $2,466.66, which represented one-third of his "conservative" estimate of the worth of her claim. Id., at 26a–27a.

6. Carol recovered the full $12,500 and paid appellant $4,166.66. She testified that she paid the second lawyer $900 as compensation for his services. Id., at 38a, 42a.

7. Appellant represented to the Board of Commissioners at the disciplinary hearing that he would abandon his claim against Wanda Lou Holbert because "the rules say that if a contract has its origin in a controversy, that an ethical question can arise." Tr. 256. Yet in fact appellant filed suit against Wanda for $2,466.66 after the disciplinary hearing. Ohralik v. Holbert, Case No. 76-CV-F-66 (Chardon Mun. Ct., Geauga County, Ohio, filed Feb. 2, 1976). Appellant's suit was dismissed with prejudice on January 27, 1977, after the decision of the Supreme Court of Ohio had been filed.

8. The Board of Commissioners is an agent of the Supreme Court of Ohio. Counsel for appellee stated at oral argument that the Board has "no connection with the Ohio State Bar Association whatsoever." Tr. of Oral Arg. 24.

9. The Ohio Code of Professional Responsibility is promulgated by the Supreme Court of Ohio. The Rules under which appellant was disciplined are modeled on the same-numbered rules in the

ated that appellant's conduct was not constitutionally protected, and increased the sanction of a public reprimand recommended by the Board to indefinite suspension.

The decision in Bates was handed down after the conclusion of proceedings in the Ohio Supreme Court. We noted probable jurisdiction in this case to consider the scope of protection of a form of commercial speech, and an aspect of the State's authority to regulate and discipline members of the bar, not considered in Bates. 434 U.S. 814 (1977). We now affirm the judgment of the Supreme Court of Ohio.

II

The solicitation of business by a lawyer through direct, in-person communication with the prospective client has long been viewed as inconsistent with the profession's ideal of the attorney-client relationship and as posing a significant potential for harm to the prospective client. It has been proscribed by the organized Bar for many years.[11] Last Term the Court ruled that the justifications for prohibiting truthful, "restrained" advertising concerning "the availability and terms of routine legal services" are insufficient to override society's interest, safeguarded by the First and Fourteenth Amendments, in assuring the free flow of commercial information. Bates, 433 U.S., at 384; see Virginia Pharmacy Board v. Virginia Citizens Consumer Council, 425 U.S. 748 (1976). The balance struck in Bates does not predetermine the outcome in this case. The entitlement of in-person solicitation of clients to the protection of the First Amendment differs from that of the kind of advertising approved in Bates, as does the strength of the State's countervailing interest in prohibition.

Code of Professional Responsibility of the American Bar Association. DR 2-103 (A) of the ABA Code has since been amended so as not to proscribe forms of public advertising that would be permitted, after Bates, under amended DR 2-101 (B).

DR 2-103 (A) of the Ohio Code (1970) provides:

"A lawyer shall not recommend employment, as a private practitioner, of himself, his partner, or associate to a non-lawyer who has not sought his advice regarding employment of a lawyer."

DR 2-104 (A) (1970) provides in relevant part:

"A lawyer who has given unsolicited advice to a layman that he should obtain counsel or take legal action shall not accept employment resulting from that advice, except that:

"(1) A lawyer may accept employment by a close friend, relative, former client (if the advice is germane to the former employment), or one whom the lawyer reasonably believes to be a client."

10. The Board found that Carol and Wanda Lou "were, if anything, casual acquaintances" of appellant; that appellant initiated the contact with Carol and obtained her consent to handle her claim; that he advised Wanda Lou that he represented Carol, had a "tip" for Wanda, and was prepared to represent her, too. The Board also found that appellant would not abide by Mrs. Holbert's request to leave Wanda alone, that both young women attempted to discharge appellant, and that appellant sued Carol McClintock.

11. An informal ban on solicitation, like that on advertising, historically was linked to the goals of preventing barratry, champerty, and maintenance. See Note, Advertising, Solicitation and the Profession's Duty to Make Legal Counsel Available, 81 Yale L. J. 1181, 1181–1182, and n. 6 (1972). "The first Code of Professional Ethics in the United States was that formulated and adopted by the Alabama State Bar Association in 1887." H. Drinker, Legal Ethics 23 (1953). The "more stringent prohibitions which form the basis of the current rules" were adopted by the American Bar Association in 1908. Note, 81 Yale L. J., supra, at 1182; see Drinker, supra, at 215. The present Code of Professional Responsibility, containing DR 2-103 (A) and 2-104 (A), was adopted by the American Bar Association in 1969 after more than four years of study by a special committee of the Association. It is a complete revision of the 1908 Canons, although many of its provisions proscribe conduct traditionally deemed unprofessional and detrimental to the public.

A

* * *

Appellant does not contend, and on the facts of this case could not contend, that his approaches to the two young women involved political expression or an exercise of associational freedom, "employ[ing] constitutionally privileged means of expression to secure constitutionally guaranteed civil rights." NAACP v. Button, 371 U.S. 415, 442 (1963); see In re Primus, ante, p. 412. Nor can he compare his solicitation to the mutual assistance in asserting legal rights that was at issue in United Transportation Union v. Michigan Bar, 401 U.S. 576 (1971); Mine Workers v. Illinois Bar Assn., 389 U.S. 217 (1967); and Railroad Trainmen v. Virginia Bar, 377 U.S. 1 (1964). A lawyer's procurement of remunerative employment is a subject only marginally affected with First Amendment concerns. It falls within the State's proper sphere of economic and professional regulation. See Button, supra, at 439–443. While entitled to some constitutional protection, appellant's conduct is subject to regulation in furtherance of important state interests.

B

The state interests implicated in this case are particularly strong. In addition to its general interest in protecting consumers and regulating commercial transactions, the State bears a special responsibility for maintaining standards among members of the licensed professions. See Williamson v. Lee Optical Co., 348 U.S. 483 (1955); Semler v. Oregon State Bd. of Dental Examiners, 294 U.S. 608 (1935). "The interest of the States in regulating lawyers is especially great since lawyers are essential to the primary governmental function of administering justice, and have historically been 'officers of the courts.'" Goldfarb v. Virginia State Bar, 421 U.S. 773, 792 (1975). While lawyers act in part as "self-employed businessmen," they also act "as trusted agents of their clients, and as assistants to the court in search of a just solution to disputes." Cohen v. Hurley, 366 U.S. 117, 124 (1961).

As is true with respect to advertising, see Bates, supra, at 371, it appears that the ban on solicitation by lawyers originated as a rule of professional etiquette rather than as a strictly ethical rule. See H. Drinker, Legal Ethics 210–211, and n. 3 (1953). "[T]he rules are based in part on deeply ingrained feelings of tradition, honor and service. Lawyers have for centuries emphasized that the promotion of justice, rather than the earning of fees, is the goal of the profession." Comment, A Critical Analysis of Rules Against Solicitation by Lawyers, 25 U. Chi. L. Rev. 674 (1958) (footnote omitted). But the fact that the original motivation behind the ban on solicitation today might be considered an insufficient justification for its perpetuation does not detract from the force of the other interests the ban continues to serve. Cf. McGowan v. Maryland, 366 U.S. 420, 431, 433–435, 444 (1961). While the Court in Bates determined that truthful, restrained advertising of the prices of "routine" legal services would not have an adverse effect on the professionalism of lawyers, this was only because it found "the postulated connection between advertising and the erosion of true professionalism to be severely strained." 433 U.S., at 368 (emphasis supplied). The Bates Court did not question a State's interest in maintaining high standards among licensed professionals. Indeed, to the extent that the ethical standards of lawyers are linked to the service and protection of clients, they do further the goals of "true professionalism."

The substantive evils of solicitation have been stated over the years in sweeping terms: stirring up litigation, assertion of fraudulent claims, debasing the legal profession, and potential harm to the solicited client in the form of overreaching, overcharg-

ing, underrepresentation, and misrepresentation. The American Bar Association, as amicus curiae, defends the rule against solicitation primarily on three broad grounds: It is
said that the prohibitions embodied in DR 2-103 (A) and 2-104 (A) serve to reduce the
likelihood of overreaching and the exertion of undue influence on lay persons, to protect the privacy of individuals, and to avoid situations where the lawyer's exercise of
judgment on behalf of the client will be clouded by his own pecuniary self-interest.

We need not discuss or evaluate each of these interests in detail as appellant has conceded that the State has a legitimate and indeed "compelling" interest in preventing
those aspects of solicitation that involve fraud, undue influence, intimidation, overreaching, and other forms of "vexatious conduct." Brief for Appellant 25. We agree that
protection of the public from these aspects of solicitation is a legitimate and important
state interest.

III

* * *

The State's perception of the potential for harm in circumstances such as those presented in this case is well founded.[12] The detrimental aspects of face-to-face selling even
of ordinary consumer products have been recognized and addressed by the Federal
Trade Commission,[13] and it hardly need be said that the potential for overreaching is
significantly greater when a lawyer, a professional trained in the art of persuasion, personally solicits an unsophisticated, injured, or distressed lay person.[14] Such an individual
may place his trust in a lawyer, regardless of the latter's qualifications or the individual's
actual need for legal representation, simply in response to persuasion under circumstances conducive to uninformed acquiescence. Although it is argued that personal solicitation is valuable because it may apprise a victim of misfortune of his legal rights, the
very plight of that person not only makes him more vulnerable to influence but also
may make advice all the more intrusive. Thus, under these adverse conditions the over-
tures of an uninvited lawyer may distress the solicited individual simply because of their
obtrusiveness and the invasion of the individual's privacy,[15] even when no other harm

---

12. Although our concern in this case is with solicitation by the lawyer himself, solicitation by a
lawyer's agents or runners would present similar problems.

13. The Federal Trade Commission has identified and sought to regulate the abuses inherent in
the direct-selling industry. See 37 Fed. Reg. 22934, 22937 (1972). See also Project: The Direct Selling
Industry: An Empirical Study, 16 UCLA L. Rev. 883, 895–922 (1969). Quoted in the FTC report is an
observation by the National Consumer Law Center that "'[t]he door to door selling technique strips
from the consumer one of the fundamentals in his role as an informed purchaser, the decision as to
when, where, and how he will present himself to the market-place.... '" 37 Fed. Reg., at 22939 n. 44.

14. Most lay persons are unfamiliar with the law, with how legal services normally are procured,
and with typical arrangements between lawyer and client. To be sure, the same might be said about
the lay person who seeks out a lawyer for the first time. But the critical distinction is that in the latter
situation the prospective client has made an initial choice of a lawyer at least for purposes of a consultation; has chosen the time to seek legal advice; has had a prior opportunity to confer with family,
friends, or a public or private referral agency; and has chosen whether to consult with the lawyer
alone or accompanied.

15. Unlike the reader of an advertisement, who can "effectively avoid further bombardment of
[his] sensibilities simply by averting [his] eyes," Cohen v. California, 403 U.S., at 21, quoted in
Erznoznik v. Jacksonville, 422 U.S. 205, 211 (1975); Lehman v. Shaker Heights, 418 U.S. 298, 320
(1974) (BRENNAN, J., dissenting), the target of the solicitation may have difficulty avoiding being
importuned and distressed even if the lawyer seeking employment is entirely well meaning. Cf.
Breard v. Alexandria, 341 U.S. 622 (1951).

materializes.[16] Under such circumstances, it is not unreasonable for the State to presume that in-person solicitation by lawyers more often than not will be injurious to the person solicited.[17]

The efficacy of the State's effort to prevent such harm to prospective clients would be substantially diminished if, having proved a solicitation in circumstances like those of this case, the State were required in addition to prove actual injury. Unlike the advertising in Bates, in-person solicitation is not visible or otherwise open to public scrutiny. Often there is no witness other than the lawyer and the lay person whom he has solicited, rendering it difficult or impossible to obtain reliable proof of what actually took place. This would be especially true if the lay person were so distressed at the time of the solicitation that he could not recall specific details at a later date. If appellant's view were sustained, in-person solicitation would be virtually immune to effective oversight and regulation by the State or by the legal profession,[18] in contravention of the State's strong interest in regulating members of the Bar in an effective, objective, and self-enforcing manner. It therefore is not unreasonable, or violative of the Constitution, for a State to respond with what in effect is a prophylactic rule.

On the basis of the undisputed facts of record, we conclude that the Disciplinary Rules constitutionally could be applied to appellant. He approached two young accident victims at a time when they were especially incapable of making informed judgments or of assessing and protecting their own interests. He solicited Carol McClintock in a hospital room where she lay in traction and sought out Wanda Lou Holbert on the day she came home from the hospital, knowing from his prior inquiries that she had just been released. Appellant urged his services upon the young women and used the information he had obtained from the McClintocks, and the fact of his agreement with Carol, to induce Wanda to say "O. K." in response to his solicitation. He employed a concealed tape recorder, seemingly to insure that he would have evidence of Wanda's oral assent to the representation. He emphasized that his fee would come out of the recovery, thereby tempting the young women with what sounded like a cost-free and therefore irresistible offer. He refused to withdraw when Mrs. Holbert requested him to do so only a day after the initial meeting between appellant and Wanda Lou and continued to represent himself to the insurance company as Wanda Holbert's lawyer.

---

16. By allowing a lawyer to accept employment after he has given unsolicited legal advice to a close friend, relative, or former client, DR 2-104 (A) (1) recognizes an exception for activity that is not likely to present these problems.

17. Indeed, appellant concedes that certain types of in-person solicitation are inherently injurious. His brief states that "solicitation that is superimposed upon the physically or mentally ill patient, or upon an accident victim unable to manage his legal affairs, obviously injures the best interests of such a client." Brief for Appellant 32.

18. The problems of affording adequate protection of the public against the potential for overreaching evidenced by this case should not be minimized. The organized bars, operating under codes approved by the highest state courts pursuant to statutory authority, have the primary responsibility for assuring compliance with professional ethics and standards by the more than 400,000 lawyers licensed by the States. The means employed usually are disciplinary proceedings initially conducted by voluntary bar committees, subject to judicial review. A study of the problems of enforcing the codes of professional conduct, chaired by then retired Justice Tom C. Clark, reveals the difficulties and complexities — and the inadequacy — of disciplinary enforcement. See ABA, Special Committee on Evaluation of Disciplinary Enforcement, Problems and Recommendations in Disciplinary Enforcement (1970). No problem is more intractable than that of prescribing and enforcing standards with respect to in-person private solicitation.

The court below did not hold that these or other facts were proof of actual harm to Wanda Holbert or Carol McClintock but rested on the conclusion that appellant had engaged in the general misconduct proscribed by the Disciplinary Rules. Under our view of the State's interest in averting harm by prohibiting solicitation in circumstances where it is likely to occur, the absence of explicit proof or findings of harm or injury is immaterial. The facts in this case present a striking example of the potential for over-reaching that is inherent in a lawyer's in-person solicitation of professional employment. They also demonstrate the need for prophylactic regulation in furtherance of the State's interest in protecting the lay public. We hold that the application of DR 2-103 (A) and 2-104 (A) to appellant does not offend the Constitution.

Accordingly, the judgment of the Supreme Court of Ohio is

Affirmed.

MR. JUSTICE BRENNAN took no part in the consideration or decision of this case.

MR. JUSTICE MARSHALL, concurring in part and concurring in the judgment.*

I agree with the majority that the factual circumstances presented by appellant Ohralik's conduct "pose dangers that the State has a right to prevent," ante, at 449, and accordingly that he may constitutionally be disciplined by the disciplinary Board and the Ohio Supreme Court. I further agree that appellant Primus' activity in advising a Medicaid patient who had been sterilized that the American Civil Liberties Union (ACLU) would be willing to represent her without fee in a lawsuit against the doctor and the hospital was constitutionally protected and could not form the basis for disciplinary proceedings. I write separately to highlight what I believe these cases do and do not decide, and to express my concern that disciplinary rules not be utilized to obstruct the distribution of legal services to all those in need of them.

I

While both of these cases involve application of rules prohibiting attorneys from soliciting business, they could hardly have arisen in more disparate factual settings. The circumstances in which appellant Ohralik initially approached his two clients provide classic examples of "ambulance chasing," fraught with obvious potential for misrepresentation and overreaching. Ohralik, an experienced lawyer in practice for over 25 years, approached two 18-year-old women shortly after they had been in a traumatic car accident. One was in traction in a hospital room; the other had just been released following nearly two weeks of hospital care. Both were in pain and may have been on medication; neither had more than a high school education. Certainly these facts alone would have cautioned hesitation in pressing one's employment on either of these women; any lawyer of ordinary prudence should have carefully considered whether the person was in an appropriate condition to make a decision about legal counsel. See Note, Advertising, Solicitation and the Profession's Duty to Make Legal Counsel Available, 81 Yale L. J. 1181, 1199 (1972).

But appellant not only foisted himself upon these clients; he acted in gross disregard for their privacy by covertly recording, without their consent or knowledge, his conversations with Wanda Lou Holbert and Carol McClintock's family. This conduct, which appellant has never disputed, is itself completely inconsistent with an attorney's fiduciary obligation fairly and fully to disclose to clients his activities affecting their interests. See American Bar Association, Code of Professional Responsibility, Ethical Considera-

---

* [This opinion applies also to No. 77-56, In re Primus, ante, p. 412.]

tions 4-1, 4-5. And appellant's unethical conduct was further compounded by his pursuing Wanda Lou Holbert, when her interests were clearly in potential conflict with those of his prior-retained client, Carol McClintock. See ante, at 451.[19]

What is objectionable about Ohralik's behavior here is not so much that he solicited business for himself, but rather the circumstances in which he performed that solicitation and the means by which he accomplished it. Appropriately, the Court's actual holding in Ohralik is a limited one: that the solicitation of business, under circumstances — such as those found in this record — presenting substantial dangers of harm to society or the client independent of the solicitation itself, may constitutionally be prohibited by the State. In this much of the Court's opinion in Ohralik, I join fully.

II

The facts in Primus, by contrast, show a "solicitation" of employment in accordance with the highest standards of the legal profession. Appellant in this case was acting, not for her own pecuniary benefit, but to promote what she perceived to be the legal rights of persons not likely to appreciate or to be able to vindicate their own rights. The obligation of all lawyers, whether or not members of an association committed to a particular point of view, to see that legal aid is available "where the litigant is in need of assistance, or where important issues are involved in the case," has long been established. In re Ades, 6 F. Supp. 467, 475 (Md. 1934); see NAACP v. Button, 371 U.S. 415, 440 n. 19 (1963). Indeed, Judge Soper in Ades was able to recite numerous instances in which lawyers, including Alexander Hamilton, Luther Martin, and Clarence Darrow, volunteered their services in aid of indigent persons or important public issues. 6 F. Supp., at 475–476. The American Bar Association Code of Professional Responsibility itself recognizes that the "responsibility for providing legal services for those unable to pay ultimately rests upon the individual lawyer," and further states that "[e]very lawyer, regardless of professional prominence or professional workload, should find time to participate in serving the disadvantaged."[20]

* * *

III

Our holdings today deal only with situations at opposite poles of the problem of attorney solicitation. In their aftermath, courts and professional associations may reasonably be expected to look to these opinions for guidance in redrafting the disciplinary rules that must apply across a spectrum of activities ranging from clearly protected speech to clearly proscribable conduct. A large number of situations falling between the poles represented by the instant facts will doubtless occur. In considering the wisdom and constitutionality of rules directed at such intermediate situations, our fellow members of the Bench and Bar must be guided not only by today's decisions, but also by our decision last Term in Bates v. State Bar of Arizona, 433 U.S. 350 (1977). There, we held that truthful printed advertising by private practitioners regarding the availability and price of certain legal services was protected by the First Amendment. In that context we

---

19. Appellant's advice to Wanda Lou Holbert that she could get money from the McClintocks' insurance policy created the risk that the financial interests of his two clients would come into conflict.

20. EC 2-25. The Disciplinary Rules of the Code, moreover, while generally forbidding a lawyer from "knowingly assist[ing] a person or organization that furnishes or pays for legal services to others to promote the use of his services," makes an exception for attorney participation in, inter alia, legal aid or public defender offices. DR 2-103 (D) (1).

rejected many of the general justifications for rules applicable to one intermediate situation not directly addressed by the Court today—the commercial, but otherwise "benign" solicitation of clients by an attorney.[21]

* * *

MR. JUSTICE REHNQUIST, concurring in the judgment.

For the reasons stated in my dissenting opinion in In re Primus, ante, p. 440, I concur in the affirmance of the judgment of the Supreme Court of Ohio.

Shapero v. Kentucky Bar Assn.
486 U.S. 466
U.S. Supreme Court
Argued March 1, 1988
Decided June 13, 1988
[Most footnotes deleted. Remaining footnotes renumbered.]

JUSTICE BRENNAN announced the judgment of the Court and delivered the opinion of the Court as to Parts I and II and an opinion as to Part III in which JUSTICE MARSHALL, JUSTICE BLACKMUN, and JUSTICE KENNEDY join.

This case presents the issue whether a State may, consistent with the First and Fourteenth Amendments, categorically prohibit lawyers from soliciting legal business for pecuniary gain by sending truthful and nondeceptive letters to potential clients known to face particular legal problems.

I

In 1985, petitioner, a member of Kentucky's integrated Bar Association, see Ky. Sup. Ct. Rule 3.030 (1988), applied to the Kentucky Attorneys Advertising Commission[1] for approval of a letter that he proposed to send "to potential clients who have had a foreclosure suit filed against them." The proposed letter read as follows:

"It has come to my attention that your home is being foreclosed on. If this is true, you may be about to lose your home. Federal law may allow you to keep

---

21. By "benign" commercial solicitation, I mean solicitation by advice and information that is truthful and that is presented in a noncoercive, nondeceitful, and dignified manner to a potential client who is emotionally and physically capable of making a rational decision either to accept or reject the representation with respect to a legal claim or matter that is not frivolous. Cf. Louisville Bar Assn. v. W. Hubbard, 282 Ky. 734, 739, 139 S. W. 2d 773, 775 (1940) (attorney may personally solicit business "where he does not take advantage of the ignorance, or weakness, or suffering, or human frailties of the expected clients, and where no inducements are offered them"); see also Petition of R. Hubbard, 267 S. W. 2d 743, 744 (Ky. 1954).

1. The Attorney Advertising Commission is charged with the responsibility of "regulating attorney advertising as prescribed" in the Rules of the Kentucky Supreme Court. Ky. Sup. Ct. Rule 3.135(3) (1988). The Commission's decisions are appealable to the Board of Governors of the Kentucky Bar Association, Rule 3.135(8)(a), and are ultimately reviewable by the Kentucky Supreme Court. Rule 3.135(8)(b). "Any attorney who is in doubt as to the propriety of any professional act contemplated by him" also has the option of seeking an advisory opinion from a committee of the Kentucky Bar Association, which, if formally adopted by the Board of Governors, is reviewable by the Kentucky Supreme Court. Rule 3.530.

your home by ORDERING your creditor [sic] to STOP and give you more time to pay them.

"You may call my office anytime from 8:30 a.m. to 5:00 p.m. for FREE information on how you can keep your home.

"Call NOW, don't wait. It may surprise you what I may be able to do for you. Just call and tell me that you got this letter. Remember it is FREE, there is NO charge for calling."

The Commission did not find the letter false or misleading. Nevertheless, it declined to approve petitioner's proposal on the ground that a then-existing Kentucky Supreme Court Rule prohibited the mailing or delivery of written advertisements "precipitated by a specific event or occurrence involving or relating to the addressee or addressees as distinct from the general public." Ky. Sup. Ct. Rule 3.135(5)(b)(i).[2] The Commission registered its view that Rule 3.135(5)(b)(i)'s ban on targeted, direct-mail advertising violated the First Amendment—specifically the principles enunciated in Zauderer v. Office of Disciplinary Counsel of Supreme Court of Ohio, 471 U.S. 626 (1985)—and recommended that the Kentucky Supreme Court amend its Rules. See App. to Pet. for Cert. 11a–15a. Pursuing the Commission's suggestion, petitioner petitioned the Committee on Legal Ethics (Ethics Committee) of the Kentucky Bar Association for an advisory opinion as to the Rule's validity. See Ky. Sup. Ct. Rule 3.530; n. 1, supra. Like the Commission, the Ethics Committee, in an opinion formally adopted by the Board of Governors of the Bar Association, did not find the proposed letter false or misleading, but nonetheless upheld Rule 3.135(5)(b)(i) on the ground that it was consistent with Rule 7.3 of the American Bar Association's Model Rules of Professional Conduct (1984). App. to Pet. for Cert. 9a.

On review of the Ethics Committee's advisory opinion, the Kentucky Supreme Court felt "compelled by the decision in Zauderer to order [Rule 3.135(5)(b)(i)] deleted," 726 S. W. 2d 299, 300 (1987), and replaced it with the ABA's Rule 7.3, which provides in its entirety:

"'A lawyer may not solicit professional employment from a prospective client with whom the lawyer has no family or prior professional relationship, by mail, in-person or otherwise, when a significant motive for the lawyer's doing so is the lawyer's pecuniary gain. The term 'solicit' includes contact in person, by telephone or telegraph, by letter or other writing, or by other communication directed to a specific recipient, but does not include letters addressed or advertising circulars distributed generally to persons not known to need legal services of the kind provided by the lawyer in a particular matter, but who are so situated that they might in general find such services useful.'" 726 S. W. 2d, at 301 (quoting ABA, Model Rule of Professional Conduct 7.3 (1984)).

The court did not specify either the precise infirmity in Rule 3.135(5)(b)(i) or how Rule 7.3 cured it. Rule 7.3, like its predecessor, prohibits targeted, direct-mail solicita-

---

2. Rule 3.135(5)(b)(i) provided in full: "A written advertisement may be sent or delivered to an individual addressee only if that addressee is one of a class of persons, other than a family, to whom it is also sent or delivered at or about the same time, and only if it is not prompted or precipitated by a specific event or occurrence involving or relating to the addressee or addressees as distinct from the general public."

tion by lawyers for pecuniary gain, without a particularized finding that the solicitation is false or misleading. We granted certiorari to resolve whether such a blanket prohibition is consistent with the First Amendment, made applicable to the States through the Fourteenth Amendment, 484 U.S. 814 (1987), and now reverse.

II

Lawyer advertising is in the category of constitutionally protected commercial speech. See Bates v. State Bar of Arizona, 433 U.S. 350 (1977). The First Amendment principles governing state regulation of lawyer solicitations for pecuniary gain are by now familiar: "Commercial speech that is not false or deceptive and does not concern unlawful activities ... may be restricted only in the service of a substantial governmental interest, and only through means that directly advance that interest." Zauderer, supra, at 638 (citing Central Hudson Gas & Electric Corp. v. Public Service Comm'n of New York, 447 U.S. 557, 566 (1980)). Since state regulation of commercial speech "may extend only as far as the interest it serves," Central Hudson, supra, at 565, state rules that are designed to prevent the "potential for deception and confusion ... may be no broader than reasonably necessary to prevent the" perceived evil. In re R. M. J., 455 U.S. 191, 203 (1982).

In Zauderer, application of these principles required that we strike an Ohio rule that categorically prohibited solicitation of legal employment for pecuniary gain through advertisements containing information or advice, even if truthful and nondeceptive, regarding a specific legal problem. We distinguished written advertisements containing such information or advice from in-person solicitation by lawyers for profit, which we held in Ohralik v. Ohio State Bar Assn., 436 U.S. 447 (1978), a State may categorically ban. The "unique features of in-person solicitation by lawyers [that] justified a prophylactic rule prohibiting lawyers from engaging in such solicitation for pecuniary gain," we observed, are "not present" in the context of written advertisements. Zauderer, supra, at 641–642.

Our lawyer advertising cases have never distinguished among various modes of written advertising to the general public. See, e.g., Bates, supra (newspaper advertising); id., at 372, n. 26 (equating advertising in telephone directory with newspaper advertising); In re R. M. J., supra (mailed announcement cards treated same as newspaper and telephone directory advertisements). Thus, Ohio could no more prevent Zauderer from mass-mailing to a general population his offer to represent women injured by the Dalkon Shield than it could prohibit his publication of the advertisement in local newspapers. Similarly, if petitioner's letter is neither false nor deceptive, Kentucky could not constitutionally prohibit him from sending at large an identical letter opening with the query, "Is your home being foreclosed on?," rather than his observation to the targeted individuals that "It has come to my attention that your home is being foreclosed on." The drafters of Rule 7.3 apparently appreciated as much, for the Rule exempts from the ban "letters addressed or advertising circulars distributed generally to persons ... who are so situated that they might in general find such services useful."

The court below disapproved petitioner's proposed letter solely because it targeted only persons who were "known to need [the] legal services" offered in his letter, 726 S. W. 2d, at 301, rather than the broader group of persons "so situated that they might in general find such services useful." Generally, unless the advertiser is inept, the latter group would include members of the former. The only reason to disseminate an advertisement of particular legal services among those persons who are "so situated that they might in general find such services useful" is to reach individuals who actually "need legal services of the kind provided [and advertised] by the lawyer." But the First Amendment does not permit a ban on certain speech merely because it is more efficient; the State may not constitutionally ban a particular letter on the theory that to mail it only to those whom it would most interest is somehow inherently objectionable.

The court below did not rely on any such theory. See also Brief for Respondent 37 (conceding that "targeted direct mail advertising"—as distinguished from "solicitation"—"is constitutionally protected") (emphasis in original). Rather, it concluded that the State's blanket ban on all targeted, direct-mail solicitation was permissible because of the "serious potential for abuse inherent in direct solicitation by lawyers of potential clients known to need specific legal services." 726 S. W. 2d, at 301. By analogy to Ohralik, the court observed:

> "Such solicitation subjects the prospective client to pressure from a trained lawyer in a direct personal way. It is entirely possible that the potential client may feel overwhelmed by the basic situation which caused the need for the specific legal services and may have seriously impaired capacity for good judgment, sound reason and a natural protective self-interest. Such a condition is full of the possibility of undue influence, overreaching and intimidation." 726 S. W. 2d, at 301.

Of course, a particular potential client will feel equally "overwhelmed" by his legal troubles and will have the same "impaired capacity for good judgment" regardless of whether a lawyer mails him an untargeted letter or exposes him to a newspaper advertisement—concededly constitutionally protected activities—or instead mails a targeted letter. The relevant inquiry is not whether there exist potential clients whose "condition" makes them susceptible to undue influence, but whether the mode of communication poses a serious danger that lawyers will exploit any such susceptibility. Cf. Ohralik, supra, at 470 (MARSHALL, J., concurring in part and concurring in judgment) ("What is objectionable about Ohralik's behavior here is not so much that he solicited business for himself, but rather the circumstances in which he performed that solicitation and the means by which he accomplished it").

Thus, respondent's facile suggestion that this case is merely "Ohralik in writing" misses the mark. Brief for Respondent 10. In assessing the potential for overreaching and undue influence, the mode of communication makes all the difference. Our decision in Ohralik that a State could categorically ban all in-person solicitation turned on two factors. First was our characterization of face-to-face solicitation as "a practice rife with possibilities for overreaching, invasion of privacy, the exercise of undue influence, and outright fraud." Zauderer, 471 U.S., at 641. See Ohralik, 436 U.S., at 457–458, 464–465. Second, "unique ... difficulties," Zauderer, supra, at 641, would frustrate any attempt at state regulation of in-person solicitation short of an absolute ban because such solicitation is "not visible or otherwise open to public scrutiny." Ohralik, 436 U.S., at 466. See also ibid. ("[I]n-person solicitation would be virtually immune to effective oversight and regulation by the State or by the legal profession") (footnote omitted). Targeted, direct-mail solicitation is distinguishable from the in-person solicitation in each respect.

Like print advertising, petitioner's letter—and targeted, direct-mail solicitation generally—"poses much less risk of overreaching or undue influence" than does in-person solicitation, Zauderer, 471 U.S., at 642. Neither mode of written communication involves "the coercive force of the personal presence of a trained advocate" or the "pressure on the potential client for an immediate yes-or-no answer to the offer of representation." Ibid. Unlike the potential client with a badgering advocate breathing down his neck, the recipient of a letter and the "reader of an advertisement ... can 'effectively avoid further bombardment of [his] sensibilities simply by averting [his] eyes,'" Ohralik, supra, at 465, n. 25 (quoting Cohen v. California, 403 U.S. 15, 21 (1971)). A letter, like a printed advertisement (but unlike a lawyer), can readily be put in a drawer to be considered later, ignored, or discarded. In short, both types of written solicitation "conve[y] information about legal services [by means] that [are] more conducive to reflection and the exercise of choice on the part of the consumer than is personal solicitation by an attorney." Zauderer, supra, at 642. Nor does a targeted letter invade the recipient's privacy any more than does a substantively identical letter mailed at large. The invasion, if any, occurs when the lawyer discovers the recipient's legal affairs, not when he confronts the recipient with the discovery.

Admittedly, a letter that is personalized (not merely targeted) to the recipient presents an increased risk of deception, intentional or inadvertent. It could, in certain circumstances, lead the recipient to overestimate the lawyer's familiarity with the case or could implicitly suggest that the recipient's legal problem is more dire than it really is. See Brief for ABA as Amicus Curiae 9. Similarly, an inaccurately targeted letter could lead the recipient to believe she has a legal problem that she does not actually have or, worse yet, could offer erroneous legal advice. See, e.g., Leoni v. State Bar of California, 39 Cal. 3d 609, 619–620, 704 P.2d 183, 189 (1985), summarily dism'd, 475 U.S. 1001 (1986).

But merely because targeted, direct-mail solicitation presents lawyers with opportunities for isolated abuses or mistakes does not justify a total ban on that mode of protected commercial speech. See In re R. M. J., 455 U.S., at 203. The State can regulate such abuses and minimize mistakes through far less restrictive and more precise means, the most obvious of which is to require the lawyer to file any solicitation letter with a state agency, id., at 206, giving the State ample opportunity to supervise mailings and penalize actual abuses. The "regulatory difficulties" that are "unique" to in-person lawyer solicitation, Zauderer, supra, at 641 — solicitation that is "not visible or otherwise open to public scrutiny" and for which it is "difficult or impossible to obtain reliable proof of what actually took place," Ohralik, supra, at 466 — do not apply to written solicitations. The court below offered no basis for its "belie[f] [that] submission of a blank form letter to the Advertising Commission [does not] provid[e] a suitable protection to the public from overreaching, intimidation or misleading private targeted mail solicitation." 726 S. W. 2d, at 301. Its concerns were presumably those expressed by the ABA House of Delegates in its comment to Rule 7.3:

> "State lawyer discipline agencies struggle for resources to investigate specific complaints, much less for those necessary to screen lawyers' mail solicitation material. Even if they could examine such materials, agency staff members are unlikely to know anything about the lawyer or about the prospective client's underlying problem. Without such knowledge they cannot determine whether the lawyer's representations are misleading." ABA, Model Rules of Professional Conduct, pp. 93–94 (1984).

The record before us furnishes no evidence that scrutiny of targeted solicitation letters will be appreciably more burdensome or less reliable than scrutiny of advertisements. See Bates, 433 U.S., at 379; id., at 387 (Burger, C. J., concurring in part and dissenting in part) (objecting to "enormous new regulatory burdens called for by" Bates). As a general matter, evaluating a targeted advertisement does not require specific information about the recipient's identity and legal problems any more than evaluating a newspaper advertisement requires like information about all readers. If the targeted letter specifies facts that relate to particular recipients (e.g., "It has come to my attention that your home is being foreclosed on"), the reviewing agency has innumerable options to minimize mistakes. It might, for example, require the lawyer to prove the truth of the fact stated (by supplying copies of the court documents or material that led the lawyer to the fact); it could require the lawyer to explain briefly how he or she discovered the fact and verified its accuracy; or it could require the letter to bear a label identifying it as an advertisement, see id., at 384 (dictum); In re R. M. J., supra, at 206, n. 20, or directing the recipient how to report inaccurate or misleading letters. To be sure, a state agency or bar association that reviews solicitation letters might have more work than one that does not. But "[o]ur recent decisions involving commercial speech have been grounded in the faith that the free flow of commercial information is valuable enough to justify imposing on would-be regulators the costs of distinguishing the truthful from the false, the helpful from the misleading, and the harmless from the harmful." Zauderer, 471 U.S., at 646.

III

The validity of Rule 7.3 does not turn on whether petitioner's letter itself exhibited any of the evils at which Rule 7.3 was directed. See Ohralik, 436 U.S., at 463–464, 466. Since, however, the First Amendment overbreadth doctrine does not apply to professional advertising, see Bates, 433 U.S., at 379–381, we address respondent's contentions that petitioner's letter is particularly overreaching, and therefore unworthy of First Amendment protection. Id., at 381. In that regard, respondent identifies two features of the letter before us that, in its view, coalesce to convert the proposed letter into "high pressure solicitation, overbearing solicitation," Brief for Respondent 20, which is not protected. First, respondent asserts that the letter's liberal use of underscored, uppercase letters (e.g., "Call NOW, don't wait"; "it is FREE, there is NO charge for calling") "fairly shouts at the recipient ... that he should employ Shapero." Id., at 19. See also Brief in Opposition 11 ("Letters of solicitation which shout commands to the individual, targeted recipient in words in underscored capitals are of a different order from advertising and are subject to proscription"). Second, respondent objects that the letter contains assertions (e.g., "It may surprise you what I may be able to do for you") that "stat[e] no affirmative or objective fact," but constitute "pure salesman puffery, enticement for the unsophisticated, which commits Shapero to nothing." Brief for Respondent 20.

The pitch or style of a letter's type and its inclusion of subjective predictions of client satisfaction might catch the recipient's attention more than would a bland statement of purely objective facts in small type. But a truthful and non-deceptive letter, no matter how big its type and how much it speculates can never "shou[t] at the recipient" or "gras[p] him by the lapels," id., at 19, as can a lawyer engaging in face-to-face solicitation. The letter simply presents no comparable risk of overreaching. And so long as the First Amendment protects the right to solicit legal business, the State may claim no substantial interest in restricting truthful and nondeceptive lawyer solicitations to those least likely to be read by the recipient. Moreover, the First Amendment limits the State's authority to dictate what information an attorney may convey in soliciting legal business. "[T]he States may not place an absolute prohibition on certain types of potentially misleading information ... if the information may also be presented in a way that is not deceptive," unless the State "assert[s] a substantial interest" that such a restriction would directly advance. In re R. M. J., 455 U.S., at 203. Nor may a State impose a more particularized restriction without a similar showing. Aside from the interests that we have already rejected, respondent offers none.

To be sure, a letter may be misleading if it unduly emphasizes trivial or "relatively uninformative fact[s]," In re R. M. J., supra, at 205 (lawyer's statement, "in large capital letters, that he was a member of the Bar of the Supreme Court of the United States"), or offers overblown assurances of client satisfaction, cf. In re Von Wiegen, 63 N. Y. 2d 163, 179, 470 N. E. 2d 838, 847 (1984) (solicitation letter to victims of massive disaster informs them that "it is [the lawyer's] opinion that the liability of the defendants is clear"), cert. denied, 472 U.S. 1007 (1985); Bates, supra, at 383–384 ("[A]dvertising claims as to the quality of legal services ... may be so likely to be misleading as to warrant restriction"). Respondent does not argue before us that petitioner's letter was misleading in those respects. Nor does respondent contend that the letter is false or misleading in any other respect. Of course, respondent is free to raise, and the Kentucky courts are free to consider, any such argument on remand.

The judgment of the Supreme Court of Kentucky is reversed, and the case is remanded for further proceedings not inconsistent with this opinion.

It is so ordered.

JUSTICE WHITE, with whom JUSTICE STEVENS joins, concurring in part and dissenting in part.

I agree with Parts I and II of the Court's opinion, but am of the view that the matters addressed in Part III should be left to the state courts in the first instance.

JUSTICE O'CONNOR, with whom THE CHIEF JUSTICE and JUSTICE SCALIA join, dissenting.

Relying primarily on Zauderer v. Office of Disciplinary Counsel of Supreme Court of Ohio, 471 U.S. 626 (1985), the Court holds that States may not prohibit a form of attorney advertising that is potentially more pernicious than the advertising at issue in that case. I agree with the Court that the reasoning in Zauderer supports the conclusion reached today. That decision, however, was itself the culmination of a line of cases built on defective premises and flawed reasoning. As today's decision illustrates, the Court has been unable or unwilling to restrain the logic of the underlying analysis within reasonable bounds. The resulting interference with important and valid public policies is so destructive that I believe the analytical framework itself should now be reexamined.

I

Zauderer held that the First Amendment was violated by a state rule that forbade attorneys to solicit or accept employment through advertisements containing information or advice regarding a specific legal problem. See id., at 639–647. I dissented from this holding because I believed that our precedents permitted, and good judgment required, that we give greater deference to the State's legitimate efforts to regulate advertising by their attorneys. Emphasizing the important differences between professional services and standardized consumer products, I concluded that unsolicited legal advice was not analogous to the free samples that are often used to promote sales in other contexts. First, the quality of legal services is typically more difficult for most laypersons to evaluate, and the consequences of a mistaken evaluation of the "free sample" may be much more serious. For that reason, the practice of offering unsolicited legal advice as a means of enticing potential clients into a professional relationship is much more likely to be misleading than superficially similar practices in the sale of ordinary consumer goods. Second, and more important, an attorney has an obligation to provide clients with complete and disinterested advice. The advice contained in unsolicited "free samples" is likely to be colored by the lawyer's own interest in drumming up business, a result that is sure to undermine the professional standards that States have a substantial interest in maintaining.

Zauderer dealt specifically with a newspaper advertisement. Today's decision—which invalidates a similar rule against targeted, direct-mail advertising—wraps the protective mantle of the Constitution around practices that have even more potential for abuse. First, a personalized letter is somewhat more likely "to overpower the will and judgment of laypeople who have not sought [the lawyer's] advice." Zauderer, supra, at 678 (O'CONNOR, J., concurring in part, concurring in judgment in part, and dissenting in part). For people whose formal contacts with the legal system are infrequent, the authority of the law itself may tend to cling to attorneys just as it does to police officers. Unsophisticated citizens, understandably intimidated by the courts and their officers, may therefore find it much more difficult to ignore an apparently "personalized" letter from an attorney than to ignore a general advertisement.

Second, "personalized" form letters are designed to suggest that the sender has some significant personal knowledge about, and concern for, the recipient. Such letters are reasonably transparent when they come from somebody selling consumer goods or stock market tips, but they may be much more misleading when the sender belongs to a profession whose members are ethically obliged to put their clients' interests ahead of their own.

Third, targeted mailings are more likely than general advertisements to contain advice that is unduly tailored to serve the pecuniary interests of the lawyer. Even if such mailings are reviewed in advance by a regulator, they will rarely be seen by the bar in general. Thus, the lawyer's professional colleagues will not have the chance to observe how the desire to sell oneself to potential customers has been balanced against the duty to provide objective legal advice. An attorney's concern with maintaining a good reputation in the professional community, which may in part be motivated by long-term pecuniary interests, will therefore provide less discipline in this context than in the case of general advertising.

Although I think that the regulation at issue today is even more easily defended than the one at issue in Zauderer, I agree that the rationale for that decision may fairly be extended to cover today's case. Targeted direct-mail advertisements—like general advertisements but unlike the kind of in-person solicitation that may be banned under Ohralik v. Ohio State Bar Assn., 436 U.S. 447 (1978)—can at least theoretically be regulated by the States through prescreening mechanisms. In-person solicitation, moreover, is inherently more prone to abuse than almost any form of written communication. Zauderer concluded that the decision in Ohralik was limited by these "unique features" of in-person solicitation, see 471 U.S., at 641, and today's majority simply applies the logic of that interpretation of Ohralik to the case before us.

II

Attorney advertising generally falls under the rubric of "commercial speech." Political speech, we have often noted, is at the core of the First Amendment. See, e.g., Boos v. Barry, 485 U.S. 312, 318 (1988). One reason for the special status of political speech was suggested in a metaphor that has become almost as familiar as the principle that it sought to justify: "[W]hen men have realized that time has upset many fighting faiths, they may come to believe ... that the ultimate good desired is better reached by free trade in ideas—that the best test of truth is the power of the thought to get itself accepted in the competition of the market, and that truth is the only ground upon which their wishes safely can be carried out. That at any rate is the theory of our Constitution."

Abrams v. United States, 250 U.S. 616, 630 (1919) (Holmes, J., dissenting). Cf., e.g., Hustler Magazine, Inc. v. Falwell, 485 U.S. 46, 50–51 (1988). Traditionally, the constitutional fence around this metaphorical marketplace of ideas had not shielded the actual marketplace of purely commercial transactions from governmental regulation.

* * *

III

The roots of the error in our attorney advertising cases are a defective analogy between professional services and standardized consumer products and a correspondingly inappropriate skepticism about the States' justifications for their regulations. In Bates, for example, the majority appeared to demand conclusive proof that the country would be better off if the States were allowed to retain a rule that served "to inhibit the free flow of commercial information and to keep the public in ignorance." 433 U.S., at 365. Although the opinion contained extensive discussion of the proffered justifications for restrictions on price advertising, the result was little more than a bare conclusion that "we are not persuaded that price advertising will harm consumers." See id., at 368–379. Dismissing Justice Powell's careful critique of the implicit legislative factfinding that underlay its analysis, the Bates majority simply insisted on concluding that the benefits of advertising outweigh its dangers. Compare id., at 373, n. 28, with id., at 391–400 (Powell, J., concurring in part and dissenting in part). In my view, that policy decision was not derived from the First Amendment, and it should not have been used to displace a different and no less reasonable policy decision of the State whose regulation was at issue.

Bates was an early experiment with the doctrine of commercial speech, and it has proved to be problematic in its application. Rather than continuing to work out all the consequences of its approach, we should now return to the States the legislative function that has so inappropriately been taken from them in the context of attorney advertising. The Central Hudson test for commercial speech provides an adequate doctrinal basis for doing so, and today's decision confirms the need to reconsider Bates in the light of that doctrine.

* * *

Imbuing the legal profession with the necessary ethical standards is a task that involves a constant struggle with the relentless natural force of economic self-interest. It cannot be accomplished directly by legal rules, and it certainly will not succeed if sermonizing is the strongest tool that may be employed. Tradition and experiment have suggested a number of formal and informal mechanisms, none of which is adequate by itself and many of which may serve to reduce competition (in the narrow economic sense) among members of the profession. A few examples include the great efforts made during this century to improve the quality and breadth of the legal education that is required for admission to the bar; the concomitant attempt to cultivate a subclass of genuine scholars within the profession; the development of bar associations that aspire to be more than trade groups; strict disciplinary rules about conflicts of interest and client abandonment; and promotion of the expectation that an attorney's history of voluntary public service is a relevant factor in selecting judicial candidates.

Restrictions on advertising and solicitation by lawyers properly and significantly serve the same goal. Such restrictions act as a concrete, day-to-day reminder to the practicing attorney of why it is improper for any member of this profession to regard it as a trade or occupation like any other. There is no guarantee, of course, that the restrictions will always have the desired effect, and they are surely not a sufficient means to their proper goal. Given their inevitable anticompetitive effects, moreover, they should not be thoughtlessly retained or insulated from skeptical criticism. Appropriate modifications have been made in the light of reason and experience, and other changes may be suggested in the future.

In my judgment, however, fairly severe constraints on attorney advertising can continue to play an important role in preserving the legal profession as a genuine profession. Whatever may be the exactly appropriate scope of these restrictions at a given time and place, this Court's recent decisions reflect a myopic belief that "consumers," and thus our Nation, will benefit from a constitutional theory that refuses to recognize either the essence of professionalism or its fragile and necessary foundations. Compare, e.g., Bates, 433 U.S., at 370–372, with id., at 400–401, and n. 11 (Powell, J., concurring in part and dissenting in part). In one way or another, time will uncover the folly of this approach. I can only hope that the Court will recognize the danger before it is too late to effect a worthwhile cure.

Florida Bar v. Went For It, Inc.

515 U.S. 618
U.S. Supreme Court
Argued January 11, 1995
Decided June 21, 1995

JUSTICE O'CONNOR delivered the opinion of the Court.

Rules of the Florida Bar prohibit personal injury lawyers from sending targeted direct-mail solicitations to victims and their relatives for 30 days following an accident or disaster. This case asks us to consider whether such rules violate the First and Fourteenth Amendments of the Constitution. We hold that in the circumstances presented here, they do not.

I

In 1989, the Florida Bar completed a 2-year study of the effects of lawyer advertising on public opinion. After conducting hearings, commissioning surveys, and reviewing extensive public commentary, the Bar determined that several changes to its advertising rules were in order. In late 1990, the Florida Supreme Court adopted the Bar's proposed amendments with some modifications. The Florida Bar: Petition to Amend the Rules Regulating the Florida Bar—Advertising Issues, 571 So.2d 451 (Fla. 1990). Two of these amendments are at issue in this case. Rule 4-7.4(b)(1) provides that "[a] lawyer shall not send, or knowingly permit to be sent, ... a written communication to a prospective client for the purpose of obtaining professional employment if: (A) the written communication concerns an action for personal injury or wrongful death or otherwise relates to an accident or disaster involving the person to whom the communication is addressed or a relative of that person, unless the accident or disaster occurred more than 30 days prior to the mailing of the communication." Rule 4-7.8(a) states that "[a] lawyer shall not accept referrals from a lawyer referral service unless the service: (1) engages in no communication with the public and in no direct contact with prospective clients in a manner that would violate the Rules of Professional Conduct if the communication or contact were made by the lawyer." Together, these rules create a brief 30-day blackout period after an accident during which lawyers may not, directly or indirectly, single out accident victims or their relatives in order to solicit their business.

In March 1992, G. Stewart McHenry and his wholly owned lawyer referral service, Went For It, Inc., filed this action for declaratory and injunctive relief in the United States District Court for the Middle District of Florida challenging Rules 4.7-4(b)(1) and 4.7-8 as violative of the First and Fourteenth Amendments to the Constitution. McHenry alleged that he routinely sent targeted solicitations to accident victims or their survivors within 30 days after accidents and that he wished to continue doing so in the future. Went For It, Inc. represented that it wished to contact accident victims or their survivors within 30 days of accidents and to refer potential clients to participating Florida lawyers. In October 1992, McHenry was disbarred for reasons unrelated to this suit, The Florida Bar v. McHenry, 605 So.2d 459 (Fla. 1992). Another Florida lawyer, John T. Blakely, was substituted in his stead.

The District Court referred the parties' competing summary judgment motions to a Magistrate Judge, who concluded that the Florida Bar had substantial government interests, predicated on a concern for professionalism, both in protecting the personal privacy and tranquility of recent accident victims and their relatives and in ensuring that these individuals do not fall prey to undue influence or overreaching. Citing the Florida Bar's extensive study, the Magistrate Judge found that the rules directly serve those interests and sweep no further than reasonably necessary. The Magistrate recommended that the District Court grant the Florida Bar's motion for summary judgment on the ground that the rules pass constitutional muster.

The District Court rejected the Magistrate Judge's report and recommendations and entered summary judgment for the plaintiffs, 808 F. Supp. 1543 (MD Fla. 1992), relying on Bates v. State Bar of Arizona, 433 U.S. 350 (1977), and subsequent cases. The Eleventh Circuit affirmed on similar grounds, 21 F.3d 1038 (1994). The panel noted, in its conclusion, that it was "disturbed that Bates and its progeny require the decision" that it reached, 21 F.3d, at 1045. We granted certiorari, 512 U.S. [1289] (1994), and now reverse.

II

A

Constitutional protection for attorney advertising, and for commercial speech generally, is of recent vintage. Until the mid-1970s, we adhered to the broad rule laid out in Valentine v. Chrestensen, 316 U.S. 52, 54 (1942), that, while the First Amendment guards against government restriction of speech in most contexts, "the Constitution imposes no such restraint on government as respects purely commercial advertising." In 1976, the Court changed course. In Virginia State Bd. of Pharmacy v. Virginia Citizens Consumer Council, Inc., 425 U.S. 748, we invalidated a state statute barring pharmacists from advertising prescription drug prices. At issue was speech that involved the idea that "I will sell you the X prescription drug at the Y price." Id., at 761. Striking the ban as unconstitutional, we rejected the argument that such speech "is so removed from 'any exposition of ideas,' and from 'truth, science, morality, and arts in general, in its diffusion of liberal sentiments on the administration of Government,' that it lacks all protection." Id., at 762 (citations omitted).

In Virginia State Board, the Court limited its holding to advertising by pharmacists, noting that "[p]hysicians and lawyers ... do not dispense standardized products; they render professional services of almost infinite variety and nature, with the consequent enhanced possibility for confusion and deception if they were to undertake certain kinds of advertising." Id., at 773, n. 25. One year later, however, the Court applied the Virginia State Board principles to invalidate a state rule prohibiting lawyers from advertising in newspapers and other media. In Bates v. State Bar of Arizona, supra, the Court struck a ban on price advertising for what it deemed "routine" legal services: "the uncontested divorce, the simple adoption, the uncontested personal bankruptcy, the change of name, and the like." Id., at 372. Expressing confidence that legal advertising would only be practicable for such simple, standardized services, the Court rejected the State's proffered justifications for regulation.

Nearly two decades of cases have built upon the foundation laid by Bates. It is now well established that lawyer advertising is commercial speech and, as such, is accorded a measure of First Amendment protection. See, e.g., Shapero v. Kentucky Bar Assn., 486 U.S. 466, 472 (1988); Zauderer v. Office of Disciplinary Counsel of Supreme Court of Ohio, 471 U.S. 626, 637 (1985); In re R. M. J., 455 U.S. 191, 199 (1982). Such First Amendment protection, of course, is not absolute. We have always been careful to distinguish commercial speech from speech at the First Amendment's core. "'[C]ommercial speech [enjoys] a limited measure of protection, commensurate with its subordinate position in the scale of First Amendment values,' and is subject to 'modes of regulation that might be impermissible in the realm of noncommercial expression.'" Board of Trustees of State University of N. Y. v. Fox, 492 U.S. 469, 477 (1989), quoting Ohralik v. Ohio State Bar Assn., 436 U.S. 447, 456 (1978). We have observed that "'[t]o require a parity of constitutional protection for commercial and noncommercial speech alike could invite dilution, simply by a leveling process, of the force of the Amendment's guarantee with respect to the latter kind of speech.'" 492 U.S., at 481, quoting Ohralik, supra, at 456.

Mindful of these concerns, we engage in "intermediate" scrutiny of restrictions on commercial speech, analyzing them under the framework set forth in Central Hudson Gas & Electric Corp. v. Public Service Comm'n of N.Y., 447 U.S. 557 (1980). Under Central Hudson, the government may freely regulate commercial speech that concerns unlawful activity or is misleading. Id., at 563–564. Commercial speech that falls into neither of those categories, like the advertising at issue here, may be regulated if the government satisfies a test consisting of three related prongs: first, the government must assert a substantial interest in support of its regulation; second, the government must demonstrate that the restriction on commercial speech directly and materially advances that interest; and third, the regulation must be "'narrowly drawn,'" id., at 564–565.

B

∗ ∗ ∗

The anecdotal record mustered by the Bar is noteworthy for its breadth and detail. With titles like "Scavenger Lawyers" (The Miami Herald, Sept. 29, 1987) and "Solicitors Out of Bounds" (St. Petersburg Times, Oct. 26, 1987), newspaper editorial pages in Florida have burgeoned with criticism of Florida lawyers who send targeted direct mail to victims shortly after accidents. See Summary of Record, App. B, pp. 1–8 (excerpts from articles); see also Peltz, Legal Advertising—Opening Pandora's Box, 19 Stetson L. Rev. 43, 116 (1989) (listing Florida editorials critical of direct-mail solicitation of accident victims in 1987, several of which are referenced in the record). The study summary also includes page upon page of excerpts from complaints of direct-mail recipients. For example, a Florida citizen described how he was "'appalled and angered by the brazen attempt'" of a law firm to solicit him by letter shortly after he was injured and his fiancee was killed in an auto accident. Summary of Record, App. I(1), p. 2. Another found it "'despicable and inexcusable'" that a Pensacola lawyer wrote to his mother three days after his father's funeral. Ibid. Another described how she was "'astounded'" and then "'very angry'" when she received a solicitation following a minor accident. Id., at 3. Still another described as "'beyond comprehension'" a letter his nephew's family received the day of the nephew's funeral. Ibid. One citizen wrote, "'I consider the unsolicited contact from you after my child's accident to be of the rankest form of ambulance chasing and in incredibly poor taste.... I cannot begin to express with my limited vocabulary the utter contempt in which I hold you and your kind.'" Ibid.

In light of this showing—which respondents at no time refuted, save by the conclusory assertion that the rule lacked "any factual basis," Plaintiffs' Motion for Summary Judgment and Supplementary Memorandum of Law in No. 92-370-Civ. (MD Fla.), p. 5—we conclude that the Bar has satisfied the second prong of the Central Hudson test. In dissent, Justice Kennedy complains that we have before us few indications of the sample size or selection procedures employed by Magid Associates (a nationally renowned consulting firm) and no copies of the actual surveys employed. See post, at 6. As stated, we believe the evidence adduced by the Bar is sufficient to meet the standard elaborated in Edenfield, supra. In any event, we do not read our case law to require that empirical data come to us accompanied by a surfeit of background information. Indeed, in other First Amendment contexts, we have permitted litigants to justify speech restrictions by reference to studies and anecdotes pertaining to different locales altogether, see City of Renton v. Playtime Theatres, Inc., 475 U.S. 41, 50–51 (1986); Barnes v. Glen Theatre, Inc., 501 U.S. 560, 584–585 (1991) (Souter, J., concurring in the judgment), or even, in a case applying strict scrutiny, to justify restrictions based solely on history, consensus, and "simple common sense," Burson v. Freeman, 504 U.S. 191, 211 (1992). Nothing in Edenfield, supra, a case in which the State offered no evidence or anecdotes in support of its restriction, requires more. After scouring the record, we are satisfied that the ban on direct-mail solicitation in the immediate aftermath of accidents, unlike the rule at issue in Edenfield, targets a concrete, nonspeculative harm.

In reaching a contrary conclusion, the Court of Appeals determined that this case was governed squarely by Shapero v. Kentucky Bar Assn., 486 U.S. 466 (1988). Making no mention of the Bar's study, the court concluded that "'a targeted letter [does not] invade the recipient's privacy any more than does a substantively identical letter mailed at large. The invasion, if any, occurs when the lawyer discovers the recipient's legal affairs, not when he confronts the recipient with the discovery.'" 21 F.3d, at 1044, quoting Shapero, supra, at 476. In many cases, the Court of Appeals explained, "this invasion of privacy will involve no more than reading the newspaper." 21 F.3d, at 1044.

While some of Shapero's language might be read to support the Court of Appeals' interpretation, Shapero differs in several fundamental respects from the case before us. First and foremost, Shapero's treatment of privacy was casual. Contrary to the dissent's suggestions, post, at 3, the State in Shapero did not seek to justify its regulation as a measure undertaken to prevent lawyers' invasions of privacy interests. See generally Brief for Respondent in Shapero v. Kentucky Bar Assn., O. T. 1987, No. 87-16. Rather, the State focused exclusively on the special dangers of overreaching inhering in targeted solicitations. Ibid. Second, in contrast to this case, Shapero dealt with a broad ban on all direct-mail solicitations, whatever the time frame and whoever the recipient. Finally, the State in Shapero assembled no evidence attempting to demonstrate any actual harm caused by targeted direct mail. The Court rejected the State's effort to justify a prophylactic ban on the basis of blanket, untested assertions of undue influence and overreaching. 486 U.S., at 475. Because the State did not make a privacy-based argument at all, its empirical showing on that issue was similarly infirm.

We find the Court's perfunctory treatment of privacy in Shapero to be of little utility in assessing this ban on targeted solicitation of victims in the immediate aftermath of accidents. While it is undoubtedly true that many people find the image of lawyers sifting through accident and police reports in pursuit of prospective clients unpalatable and invasive, this case targets a different kind of intrusion. The Florida Bar has argued, and the record reflects, that a principal purpose of the ban is "protecting the personal privacy and tranquility of [Florida's] citizens from crass commercial intrusion by attorneys upon their personal grief in times of trauma." Brief for Petitioner 8; cf. Summary of Record, App. I(1) (citizen commentary describing outrage at lawyers' timing in sending solicitation letters). The intrusion targeted by the Bar's regulation stems not from the fact that a lawyer has learned about an accident or disaster (as the Court of Appeals notes, in many instances a lawyer need only read the newspaper to glean this information), but from the lawyer's confrontation of victims or relatives with such information, while wounds are still open, in order to solicit their business. In this respect, an untargeted letter mailed to society at large is different in kind from a targeted solicitation; the untargeted letter involves no willful or knowing affront to or invasion of the tranquility of bereaved or injured individuals and simply does not cause the same kind of reputational harm to the profession unearthed by the Florida Bar's study.

* * *

III

Speech by professionals obviously has many dimensions. There are circumstances in which we will accord speech by attorneys on public issues and matters of legal representation the strongest protection our Constitution has to offer. See, e.g., Gentile v. State Bar of Nevada, 501 U.S. 1030 (1991); In re Primus, 436 U.S. 412 (1978). This case, however, concerns pure commercial advertising, for which we have always reserved a lesser degree of protection under the First Amendment. Particularly because the standards and conduct of state-licensed lawyers have traditionally been subject to extensive regulation by the States, it is all the more appropriate that we limit our scrutiny of state regulations to a level commensurate with the "'subordinate position'" of commercial speech in the scale of First Amendment values. Fox, 492 U.S., at 477, quoting Ohralik, 436 U.S., at 456.

We believe that the Florida Bar's 30-day restriction on targeted direct-mail solicitation of accident victims and their relatives withstands scrutiny under the three-part Central Hudson test that we have devised for this context. The Bar has substantial interest both in protecting injured Floridians from invasive conduct by lawyers and in preventing the erosion of confidence in the profession that such repeated invasions have engendered. The Bar's proffered study, unrebutted by respondents below, provides evidence indicating that the harms it targets are far from illusory. The palliative devised by the Bar to address these harms is narrow both in scope and in duration. The Constitution, in our view, requires nothing more.

The judgment of the Court of Appeals, accordingly, is reversed.

JUSTICE KENNEDY, with whom JUSTICE STEVENS, JUSTICE SOUTER, and JUSTICE GINSBURG join, dissenting.

Attorneys who communicate their willingness to assist potential clients are engaged in speech protected by the First and Fourteenth Amendments. That principle has been understood since Bates v. State Bar of Arizona, 433 U.S. 350 (1977). The Court today undercuts this guarantee in an important class of cases and unsettles leading First Amendment precedents, at the expense of those victims most in need of legal assistance. With all respect for the Court, in my view its solicitude for the privacy of victims and its concern for our profession are misplaced and self-defeating, even upon the Court's own premises.

I take it to be uncontroverted that when an accident results in death or injury, it is often urgent at once to investigate the occurrence, identify witnesses, and preserve evidence. Vital interests in speech and expression are, therefore, at stake when by law an attorney cannot direct a letter to the victim or the family explaining this simple fact and offering competent legal assistance. Meanwhile, represented and better informed parties, or parties who have been solicited in ways more sophisticated and indirect, may be at work. Indeed, these parties, either themselves or by their attorneys, investigators, and adjusters, are free to contact the unrepresented persons to gather evidence or offer settlement. This scheme makes little sense. As is often true when the law makes little sense, it is not first principles but their interpretation and application that have gone awry.

* * *

I

* * *

To avoid the controlling effect of Shapero in the case before us, the Court seeks to declare that a different privacy interest is implicated. As it sees the matter, the substantial concern is that victims or their families will be offended by receiving a solicitation during their grief and trauma. But we do not allow restrictions on speech to be justified on the ground that the expression might offend the listener. On the contrary, we have said that these "are classically not justifications validating the suppression of expression protected by the First Amendment." Carey v. Population Services International, 431 U.S. 678, 701 (1977). And in Zauderer v. Office of Disciplinary Counsel of Supreme Court of Ohio, 471 U.S. 626 (1985), where we struck down a ban on attorney advertising, we held that "the mere possibility that some members of the population might find advertising ... offensive cannot justify suppressing it. The same must hold true for advertising that some members of the bar might find beneath their dignity." Id., at 648.

We have applied this principle to direct mail cases as well as with respect to general advertising, noting that the right to use the mails is protected by the First Amendment. See Bolger v. Youngs Drug Products Corp., 463 U.S. 60, 76 (1983) (REHNQUIST, J., concurring) (citing Blount v. Rizzi, 400 U.S. 410 (1971). In Bolger, we held that a statute designed to "shiel[d] recipients of mail from materials that they are likely to find offensive" furthered an interest of "little weight," noting that "we have consistently held that the fact that protected speech may be offensive to some does not justify its suppression." 463 U.S., at 71 (citing Carey, supra, at 701). It is only where an audience is captive that we will assure its protection from some offensive speech. See Consolidated Edison Co. of N.Y. v. Public Service Comm'n of N.Y., 447 U.S. 530, 542 (1980). Outside that context, "we have never held that the Government itself can shut off the flow of mailings to protect those recipients who might potentially be offended." Bolger, supra, at 72. The occupants of a household receiving mailings are not a captive audience, ibid., and the asserted interest in preventing their offense should be no more controlling here than in our prior cases. All the recipient of objectional mailings need do is to take "the 'short, though regular, journey from mail box to trash can.'" Ibid. (citation omitted). As we have observed, this is "an acceptable burden, at least so far as the Constitution is concerned." Ibid. If these cases forbidding restrictions on speech that might be offensive are to be overruled, the Court should say so.

In the face of these difficulties of logic and precedent, the State and the opinion of the Court turn to a second interest: protecting the reputation and dignity of the legal profession. The argument is, it seems fair to say, that all are demeaned by the crass behavior of a few. The argument takes a further step in the amicus brief filed by the Association of Trial Lawyers of America. There it is said that disrespect for the profession from this sort of solicitation (but presumably from no other sort of solicitation) results in lower jury verdicts. In a sense, of course, these arguments are circular. While disrespect will arise from an unethical or improper practice, the majority begs a most critical question by assuming that direct mail solicitations constitute such a practice. The fact is, however, that direct solicitation may serve vital purposes and promote the administration of justice, and to the extent the bar seeks to protect lawyers' reputations by preventing them from engaging in speech some deem offensive, the State is doing nothing more (as amicus the Association of Trial Lawyers of America is at least candid enough to admit) than manipulating the public's opinion by suppressing speech that informs us how the legal system works. The disrespect argument thus proceeds from the very assumption it tries to prove, which is to say that solicitations within 30 days serve no legitimate purpose. This, of course, is censorship pure and simple; and censorship is antithetical to the first principles of free expression.

* * *

IV

It is most ironic that, for the first time since Bates v. State Bar of Arizona, the Court now orders a major retreat from the constitutional guarantees for commercial speech in order to shield its own profession from public criticism. Obscuring the financial aspect of the legal profession from public discussion through direct mail solicitation, at the expense of the least sophisticated members of society, is not a laudable constitutional goal. There is no authority for the proposition that the Constitution permits the State to promote the public image of the legal profession by suppressing information about the profession's business aspects. If public respect for the profession erodes because solicitation distorts the idea of the law as most lawyers see it, it must be remembered that real progress begins with more rational speech, not less. I agree that if this amounts to mere "sermonizing," see Shapero, 486 U.S., at 490 (O'CONNOR, J., dissenting), the attempt may be futile. The guiding principle, however, is that full and rational discussion furthers sound regulation and necessary reform. The image of the profession cannot be enhanced without improving the substance of its practice. The objective of the profession is to ensure that "the ethical standards of lawyers are linked to the service and protection of clients." Ohralik, 436 U.S., at 461.

Today's opinion is a serious departure, not only from our prior decisions involving attorney advertising, but also from the principles that govern the transmission of commercial speech. The Court's opinion reflects a new-found and illegitimate confidence that it, along with the Supreme Court of Florida, knows what is best for the Bar and its clients. Self-assurance has always been the hallmark of a censor. That is why under the First Amendment the public, not the State, has the right and the power to decide what ideas and information are deserving of their adherence. "[T]he general rule is that the speaker and the audience, not the government, assess the value of the information presented." Edenfield, 507 U.S., at [767] [113 S. Ct., at 1798]. By validating Florida's rule, today's majority is complicit in the Bar's censorship. For these reasons, I dissent from the opinion of the Court and from its judgment.

The Florida Bar v. Pape
918 So.2d 240
Nov. 17, 2005
[Footnotes omitted.]

PARIENTE, C.J.

In this case we impose discipline on two attorneys for their use of television advertising devices that violate the Rules of Professional Conduct. These devices, which invoke the breed of dog known as the pit bull, demean all lawyers and thereby harm both the legal profession and the public's trust and confidence in our system of justice.

We conclude that attorneys Pape and Chandler ("the attorneys") violated Rules Regulating the Florida Bar 4-7.2(b)(3) and 4-7.2(b)(4) by using the image of a pit bull and displaying the term "pit bull" as part of their firm's phone number in their commercial. Further, because the use of an image of a pit bull and the phrase "pit bull" in the firm's advertisement and logo does not assist the public in ensuring that an informed decision is made prior to the selection of the attorney, we conclude that the First Amendment does not prevent this Court from sanctioning the attorneys based on the rule violations. We determine that the appropriate sanctions for the attorneys' misconduct are public reprimands and required attendance at the Florida Bar Advertising Workshop.

BACKGROUND AND PROCEDURAL HISTORY

On January 12, 2004, The Florida Bar filed complaints against the attorneys, alleging that their law firm's television advertisement was an improper communication concerning the services provided, in violation of the Rules of Professional Conduct. The advertisement included a logo that featured an image of a pit bull wearing a spiked collar and prominently displayed the firm's phone number, 1-800-PIT-BULL. The Bar asserted that this advertisement violated the 2004 version of Rules Regulating the Florida Bar 4-7.2(b)(3) and 4-7.2(b)(4), which state:

> (3) *Descriptive Statements.* A lawyer shall not make statements describing or characterizing the quality of the lawyer's services in advertisements and written communications; provided that this provision shall not apply to information furnished to a prospective client at that person's request or to information supplied to existing clients.

> (4) *Prohibited Visual and Verbal Portrayals.* Visual or verbal descriptions, depictions, or portrayals of persons, things, or events must be objectively relevant to the selection of an attorney and shall not be deceptive, misleading, or manipulative.

* * *

A. Violation of Attorney Advertising Rules

As a preliminary matter, the pit bull logo and 1-800-PIT-BULL telephone number in the ad by the attorneys do not comport with the general criteria for permissible attorney advertisements set forth in the comments to section 4-7 of the Rules of Professional Conduct. The rules contained in section 4-7 are designed to permit lawyer advertisements that provide objective information about the cost of legal services, the experience and qualifications of the lawyer and law firm, and the types of cases the lawyer handles. *See generally* R. Regulating Fla. Bar 4-7.1 cmt. The comment to rule 4-7.1 provides that "a lawyer's advertisement should provide only useful, factual information presented in a nonsensational manner. Advertisements using slogans ... fail to meet these standards and diminish public confidence in the legal system." The television commercial at issue here uses both a sensationalistic image and a slogan, contrary to the purpose of section 4-7.

More specifically, the attorneys' ad violated rule 4-7.2(b)(3), which prohibits the use of statements describing or characterizing the quality of the lawyer's services. In *Florida Bar v. Lange,* 711 So.2d 518, 521-22 (Fla.1998), we approved the referee's finding that an advertisement that stated "When the Best is Simply Essential" violated the predecessor provision to rule 4-7.2(b)(3) because it was self-laudatory and purported to describe the quality of the lawyer's services. In this case, the simultaneous display of the pit bull logo and the 1-800-PIT-BULL phone number conveys both the characteristics of the attorneys and the quality of the services they purport to provide. At the very least, the printed words and the image of a pit bull in the television commercial could certainly be perceived by prospective clients as characterizing the quality of the lawyers' services.

* * *

We also conclude that the ad violates rule 4-7.2(b)(4), which requires that visual or verbal depictions be "objectively relevant" to the selection of an attorney, and prohibits depictions that are "deceptive, misleading, or manipulative." The comment to this rule explains that it

> prohibits visual or verbal descriptions, depictions, or portrayals in any advertisement which create suspense, or contain exaggerations or *appeals to the emotions,* call for legal services, or create consumer problems through characterization and dialogue ending with the lawyer solving the problem. Illustrations permitted under *Zauderer v. Office of Disciplinary Counsel of the Supreme Court of Ohio,* 471 U.S. 626, 105 S.Ct. 2265, 85 L.Ed.2d 652 (1985), are informational and not misleading, and are therefore permissible. As an example, *a drawing of a fist, to suggest the lawyer's ability to achieve results, would be barred.* Examples of permissible illustrations would include a graphic rendering of the scales of justice to indicate that the advertising attorney practices law, a picture of the lawyer, or a map of the office location.

(Emphasis supplied.) The logo of the pit bull wearing a spiked collar and the prominent display of the phone number 1-800-PIT-BULL are more manipulative and misleading than a drawing of a fist. These advertising devices would suggest to many persons not only that the lawyers can achieve results but also that they engage in a combative style of advocacy. The suggestion is inherently deceptive because there is no way to measure whether the attorneys in fact conduct themselves like pit bulls so as to ascertain whether this logo and phone number convey accurate information.

In addition, the image of a pit bull and the on-screen display of the words "PIT-BULL" as part of the firm's phone number are not objectively relevant to the selection of an attorney. The referee found that the qualities of a pit bull as depicted by the logo are loyalty, persistence, tenacity, and aggressiveness. We consider this a charitable set of associations that ignores the darker side of the qualities often also associated with pit bulls: malevolence, viciousness, and unpredictability. Further, although some may associate pit bulls with loyalty to their owners, the manner in which the pit bull is depicted in the attorneys' ad in this case certainly does not emphasize this association. The dog, which is wearing a spiked collar, directly faces the viewer and is shown alone, with no indication that it is fulfilling its traditional role as "man's best friend."

Pit bulls have a reputation for vicious behavior that is borne of experience. According to a study published in the Journal of the American Veterinary Medical Association in 2000, pit bulls caused the greatest number of dog-bite-related fatalities between 1979 and 1998. Jeffery J. Saks, et al., *Breeds of Dogs Involved in Fatal Human Attacks in the United States Between 1979 and 1998,* 217 J. Am. Veterinary Med. Ass'n 836, 837 (2000), *available at http://www.cdc.gov/ncipc/duip/dogbreeds.pdf.* The dangerousness of pit bulls has also been recognized in a number of court decisions. *See, e.g., Giaculli v. Bright,* 584 So.2d 187, 189 (Fla. 5th DCA 1991) (recognizing that "[p]it bulls as a breed are known to be extremely aggressive and have been bred as attack animals"); *Hearn v. City of Overland Park,* 244 Kan. 638, 772 P.2d 758, 768 (1989) ("[P]it bull dogs represent a unique public health hazard not presented by other breeds or mixes of dogs. Pit bull dogs possess both the capacity for extraordinarily savage behavior and physical capabilities in excess of those possessed by many other breeds of dogs. Moreover, this capacity for uniquely vicious attacks is coupled with an unpredictable nature."); *Matthews v. Amberwood Assocs. Ltd. Partnership, Inc.,* 351 Md. 544, 719 A.2d 119, 127 (1998) ("The extreme dangerousness of [the pit bull] breed, as it has evolved today, is well recognized.").

In *State v. Peters,* 534 So.2d 760 (Fla. 3d DCA 1988), the Third District Court of Appeal upheld a City of North Miami ordinance imposing substantial insurance, registration, and confinement obligations on owners of pit bulls. The City of North Miami ordinance contained findings that pit bulls have a greater propensity to bite humans than all other breeds, are extremely aggressive towards other animals, and have a natural tendency to refuse to terminate an attack once it has begun. *See id.* at 764. The current Miami-Dade County ordinance provides that it is illegal to own a pit bull. *See* Miami-Dade County, Fla.Code, § 5-17 (1992).

This Court would not condone an advertisement that stated that a lawyer will get results through combative and vicious tactics that will maim, scar, or harm the opposing party, conduct that would violate our Rules of Professional Conduct. *See, e.g.,* R. Regulating Fla. Bar 4-3.4(g)-(h) (prohibiting threats to present criminal or disciplinary charges solely to gain an advantage in a civil matter). Yet this is precisely the type of unethical and unprofessional conduct that is conveyed by the image of a pit bull and the display of the 1-800-PIT-BULL. We construe the prohibitions on advertising statements that characterize the quality of lawyer services and depictions that are false or misleading to prohibit a lawyer from advertising his or her services by suggesting behavior, conduct, or tactics that are contrary to our Rules of Professional Conduct.

Further, we reject the referee's finding that the use of the words "pit bull" in the phone number is merely a mnemonic device to help potential clients remember the attorneys' number. Phrase-based phone numbers are memorable because of the images and associations they evoke. The "1-800-PIT-BULL" phone number sticks in the memory precisely because of the image of the pit bull also featured in the ad, the association of pit bulls with the characteristics discussed herein, and the "go for the jugular" style of advocacy that some persons attribute to lawyers. In short, this is a manipulative and misleading use of what would otherwise be content-neutral information to create a nefarious association.

Indeed, permitting this type of advertisement would make a mockery of our dedication to promoting public trust and confidence in our system of justice. Prohibiting advertisements such as the one in this case is one step we can take to maintain the dignity of lawyers, as well as the integrity of, and public confidence in, the legal system. Were we to approve the referee's finding, images of sharks, wolves, crocodiles, and piranhas could follow. For the good of the legal profession and the justice system, and consistent with our Rules of Professional Conduct, this type of non-factual advertising cannot be permitted. We therefore conclude that the 1-800-PIT-BULL ad aired by the attorneys violates rules 4-7.2(b)(3) and 4-7.2(b)(4).

B. First Amendment Protection of Lawyer Advertising

We also disagree with the referee's conclusion that the application of rules 4-7.2(b)(3) and 4-7.2(b)(4) to prohibit this advertisement violates the First Amendment. Lawyer advertising enjoys First Amendment protection only to the extent that it provides accurate factual information that can be objectively verified. This thread runs throughout the pertinent United State Supreme Court precedent.

The seminal lawyer advertising case is *Bates v. State Bar of Arizona,* 433 U.S. 350, 376, 97 S.Ct. 2691, 53 L.Ed.2d 810 (1977), which involved the advertising of fees for low cost legal services. In *Bates,* the Supreme Court held generally that attorney advertising "may not be subjected to blanket suppression," and more specifically that attorneys have the constitutional right to advertise their availability and fees for performing routine services. *Id.* at 383–84, 97 S.Ct. 2691. The cost of legal services, the Supreme Court concluded, would be "relevant information needed to reach an informed decision." *Id.* at 374, 97 S.Ct. 2691.

In reaching this conclusion the Supreme Court recognized that "[a]dvertising is the traditional mechanism in a free-market economy for a supplier to inform a potential purchaser of the availability and terms of exchange." *Id.* at 376, 97 S.Ct. 2691. "[C]ommercial speech serves to inform the public of the availability, nature, and prices of products and services, and thus performs an indispensable role in the allocation of resources in a free enterprise system. In short, such speech serves individual and societal interests in assuring informed and reliable decisionmaking." *Id.* at 364, 97 S.Ct. 2691 (citation omitted).

The Supreme Court emphasized that advertising by lawyers could be regulated and noted that "because the public lacks sophistication concerning legal services, misstatements that might be overlooked or deemed unimportant in other advertising may be found quite inappropriate in legal advertising." *Id.* at 383, 97 S.Ct. 2691. The Supreme Court specifically declined to address the "peculiar problems associated with advertising claims relating to the quality of legal services," but observed that "[s]uch claims *probably are not susceptible of precise measurement or verification and, under some circumstances, might well be deceptive or misleading to the public, or even false.*" *Id.* at 366, 97 S.Ct. 2691 (emphasis supplied).

After *Bates,* the Supreme Court considered a Missouri rule that restricted lawyer advertising to newspapers, periodicals, and the yellow pages, and limited the content of these advertisements to ten categories of information (name, address and telephone number, areas of practice, date and place of birth, schools attended, foreign language ability, office hours, fee for an initial consultation, availability of a schedule of fees, credit arrangements, and the fixed fee charged for specified "routine" services). *See In re R.M.J.,* 455 U.S. 191, 194, 102 S.Ct. 929, 71 L.Ed.2d 64 (1982). Even the manner of listing areas of practice was restricted to a prescribed nomenclature. *See id.* at 194–95, 102 S.Ct. 929. In violation of the state restrictions, the lawyer advertised areas of practice that did not use the prescribed terminology, listed the states in which the lawyer was licensed, specified that he was admitted to practice before the United States Supreme Court, and did not restrict the recipients of announcement cards to lawyers, clients, former clients, personal friends, and relatives. *See id.* at 198, 102 S.Ct. 929.

Writing for a unanimous Court, Justice Powell summarized the commercial speech doctrine in the context of advertising for professional services:

> Truthful advertising related to lawful activities is entitled to the protections of the First Amendment. But when the particular content or method of the advertising suggests that it is inherently misleading or when experience has proved that in fact such advertising is subject to abuse, the States may impose appropriate restrictions. Misleading advertising may be prohibited entirely. But the States may not place an absolute prohibition on certain types of potentially misleading information, *e.g.*, a listing of areas of practice, if the information also may be presented in a way that is not deceptive.

Id. at 203, 102 S.Ct. 929. In holding the Missouri restrictions per se invalid as applied to the lawyer, the Supreme Court concluded that the state had no substantial interest in prohibiting a lawyer from identifying the jurisdictions in which he or she was licensed to practice. *See id.* at 205, 102 S.Ct. 929. The Court noted that this "is *factual* and highly relevant information." *Id.* (emphasis supplied). Although the Court found the lawyer's listing in large capital letters that he was a member of the Bar of the Supreme Court of the United States to be "[s]omewhat more troubling" and in "bad taste," this alone could not be prohibited without a finding by the Missouri Supreme Court that "such a statement could be misleading to the general public unfamiliar with the requirements of admission to the Bar of this Court." *Id.* at 205, 102 S.Ct. 929. In short, the Supreme Court in *R.M.J.* was dealing with restrictions on clearly factual and relevant information that had not been found to be misleading or likely to deceive. As in *Bates*, the Supreme Court concluded that such restrictions violated the First Amendment.

In *Zauderer v. Office of Disciplinary Counsel of the Supreme Court of Ohio*, 471 U.S. 626, 629, 105 S.Ct. 2265, 85 L.Ed.2d 652 (1985), the Supreme Court addressed whether a state could discipline a lawyer who ran newspaper advertisements containing nondeceptive illustrations and legal advice. One advertisement published the lawyer's willingness to represent women injured from the use of the Dalkon Shield intrauterine device. *See id.* at 630, 105 S.Ct. 2265. The parties had stipulated that the advertisement was entirely accurate. *See id.* at 633–34, 105 S.Ct. 2265.

In holding that the lawyer could not be disciplined on the basis of the content of his advertisement, the Supreme Court observed that the advertisement did not promise results or suggest any special expertise but merely conveyed that the lawyer was representing women in Dalkon Shield litigation and was willing to represent other women with similar claims. *See id.* at 639–40, 105 S.Ct. 2265. Turning to the lawyer's use of an illustration of the Dalkon Shield, the Court first held that illustrations are entitled to the same First Amendment protection as that afforded to verbal commercial speech. *See id.* at 647, 105 S.Ct. 2265. The Court then concluded that "[b]ecause the illustration for which appellant was disciplined is an accurate representation of the Dalkon Shield and has no features that are likely to deceive, mislead, or confuse the reader, the burden is on the State to present a substantial governmental interest justifying the restriction." *Id.* at 647, 105 S.Ct. 2265.

The most recent United States Supreme Court decision to address restrictions on the content of lawyer advertising involved an attorney who held himself out as certified by the National Board of Trial Advocacy (NBTA). *See Peel v. Attorney Registration & Disciplinary Comm'n of Illinois*, 496 U.S. 91, 110 S.Ct. 2281, 110 L.Ed.2d 83 (1990). The state supreme court had concluded that the claim of NBTA certification was "misleading because it tacitly attests to the qualifications of [petitioner] as a civil trial advocate." *Id.* at 98, 110 S.Ct. 2281 (plurality opinion) (quoting *In re Peel,* 126 Ill.2d 397, 128 Ill.Dec. 535, 534 N.E.2d 980, 984 (1989)) (alteration in original). The state court had not addressed "whether NBTA certification constituted *reliable, verifiable evidence of petitioner's experience as a civil trial advocate." Id.* at 99, 128 Ill.Dec. 535, 534 N.E.2d 980 (emphasis supplied). After applauding the development of state and national certification programs, a plurality of the Supreme Court concluded that the facts as to NBTA certification were "true and verifiable." *Id.* at 100, 128 Ill.Dec. 535, 534 N.E.2d 980 (plurality opinion). The plurality pointed out the important "distinction between *statements of opinion or quality and statements of objective facts that may support an inference of quality." Id.* at 101, 128 Ill.Dec. 535, 534 N.E.2d 980 (plurality opinion) (emphasis supplied). A majority of the Court concluded that the letterhead was not actually or inherently misleading, and thus that the attorney could not be prohibited from holding himself out as a civil trial specialist certified by the NBTA. *See id.* at 106, 128 Ill.Dec. 535, 534 N.E.2d 980 (plurality opinion); *id.* at 111–12, 128 Ill.Dec. 535, 534 N.E.2d 980 (Marshall, J., concurring in the judgment).

The pit bull logo and "1-800-PIT-BULL" phone number are in marked contrast to the illustration of the Dalkon Shield intrauterine device at issue in *Zauderer,* which the United States Supreme Court found to be "an accurate representation ... and ha[ve] no features that are likely to deceive, mislead, or confuse the reader." 471 U.S. at 647, 105 S.Ct. 2265. The Dalkon Shield illustration *informed* the public that the lawyer represented clients in cases involving this device. The "pit bull" commercial produced by the attorneys in this case contains no indication that they specialize in either dog bite cases generally or in litigation arising from attacks by pit bulls specifically. Consequently, the logo and phone number do not convey objectively relevant information about the attorneys' practice. Instead, the image and words "pit bull" are intended to convey an image about the nature of the lawyers' litigation tactics. We conclude that an advertising device that connotes combativeness and viciousness without providing accurate and objectively verifiable factual information falls outside the protections of the First Amendment.

C. Discipline

Because the referee found that the attorneys were not guilty of violating rules 4-7.2(b)(3) and 4-7.2(b)(4), the referee did not address the issue of discipline. The parties do not address the issue of discipline in their briefs to this Court. However, we have in the past approved public reprimands for attorneys who have been found guilty of violating the advertising rules. *See Fla. Bar v. Herrick,* 571 So.2d 1303, 1307 (Fla.1990); *Fla. Bar v. Budish,* 421 So.2d 501, 503 (Fla.1982). We have also required that attorneys attend the Florida Bar Advertising Workshop. *See, e.g., Fla. Bar v. Zebersky,* 902 So.2d 793 (Fla.2005) (No. SC04-1907) (table report of unpublished order). We conclude that similar discipline is warranted in this case.

CONCLUSION

We disapprove the referee's finding that the television commercial at issue is constitutionally protected speech that does not violate our attorney advertising rules. We find John Robert Pape and Marc Andrew Chandler guilty of violating rules 4-7.2(b)(3) and 4-7.2(b)(4) of the Rules Regulating the Florida Bar. We order that each attorney receive a public reprimand, which shall be administered by the Board of Governors of The Florida Bar upon proper notice to appear. We also direct Pape and Chandler to attend and complete the Florida Bar Advertising Workshop within six months of the date of this opinion.

It is so ordered.

WELLS, ANSTEAD, LEWIS, QUINCE, CANTERO, and BELL, JJ., concur.

C. Specialization

Would You Know This Man If You Saw Him?
David Rattigan, *Massachusetts Bar Association Lawyers Journal*,
p. B1, B9 (October, 1999)

Would you know a head injury if you saw one? You may not know Massachusetts Bar Association member Kenneth L. Kolpan, but odds are, you've seen his ads. For years, they've appeared in Massachusetts legal publications. The ads feature the dapper William Powell-lookalike (in your movie encyclopedia, see "Loy, Myrna") posing the aforementioned question.

"We're working on a case together now and there are five or six attorneys on the other side," says Attorney Carmen L. Durso, who shares office space with Kolpan on the top floor at 100 Summer St., Boston. "We had them all here for a deposition a couple of days ago, and they were kidding Ken about the fact that his picture is always in the paper.

"That advertising has given him very high visibility ... Ken gets a great deal of work from referrals."

In fact, Kolpan estimates that more than half his work comes from other attorneys, who pass on a case to him, or hire him as co-counsel. Those attorneys often have learned about him through his advertising, and through his speeches, articles, Web site (www.kolpan.com) and other presentations on closed-head injuries, a specialty that has helped him develop a national reputation in a field that's grown significantly since he began practicing it as a specialty back in 1981.

"He's one of the most highly recognized specialists in head injury work," says attorney Mark Furcolo, a colleague at Curley & Curley, who has worked on the opposite side from Kolpan. "He's an awfully nice guy, and an honorable guy, too."

"As far as I'm concerned, we're very far down the road to the kind of specialization or compartmentalization found in the medical profession," adds Durso, a specialist in premises liability, sexual assault and incest cases. "Ken gets a lot of cases from lawyers who don't know what to do in a case, or have an idea of what to do but are nervous because of the substantial issue involved, or think the defense attorney won't respect their knowledge, or don't want to become involved because there is so much to get into. People like Ken fit that niche."

Closed-head injury cases can be very tricky, and lawyers on both sides rely heavily on medical experts, and on educating juries. Victims of closed-head injuries often appear to function normally, and have normal findings in many tests, such as an MRI, CT scan, or EEG. Attorneys for defendants often try to paint victims as malingerers. But people with closed-head injuries suffer from cognitive and memory deficits, and function far less efficiently than before the injury. Tests such as MRIs may only be "snapshots in time," Kolpan notes, and the damage may already have been done.

"Traditional diagnostic tests often come up negative," Kolpan says. "Yes, if you examined the CT scan or MRI of some of the most severely brain-injured people, they too would have normal CT scans or MRIs. What caused the damage to their brain has healed."

The damage is usually permanent.

The plaintiffs' attorney relies on the testimony or friends and family members who note the changes in the victim—who may be pouring orange juice into a coffee mug, or becoming increasingly irritable as a result of frustration—and the expert testimony of neurologists, who administer tests to measure their client's cognitive function and ability to think, to determine what Kolpan calls "the islands of deficits" they have.

Kolpan has always had a professional interest in both law (Boston College School of Law, 1972) and medicine (University of Rochester, bachelor of arts degree in psychology, 1968). He spent the early years of his professional career providing legal services to inmates in the state correctional system, advised forensic psychologists and psychiatrists as part of the staff at McLean Hospital in Belmont, and served as corporate counsel to the New England Medical Center. There, he would give seminars to physicians, rehabilitation specialists, consumers (patients) about the rights of persons with disabilities.

His career path veered when he was asked to speak on that topic to a meeting of the National Head Injury Association (now the international Brain Injury Association), where he met people such as founder Marilyn Price Spivac, whose daughter suffered severe injuries in a motor vehicle accident, and could not get services.

Kolpan saw a need, intellectual challenge, and opportunity.

"By being in the medical community you absorb through osmosis some information and knowledge about medical practice, the way physician's think and how hospitals work," says Kolpan, who got involved with the organization and in 1999 served as program co-chairman at its conference of attorneys in Arizona. "I was able to utilize this background to represent people who'd suffered traumatic brain injuries. It was very fascinating, and very challenging."

It has been rewarding in multiple ways, particularly as the field has mushroomed in the past 15 years. The verdicts and settlements in these cases often get into the millions of dollars.

One particularly significant Kolpan case was settled in 1986. It was a case in which a 30-year-old Framingham woman won a $2 million damage suit after an employee at a local K Mart closed a 400-pound mechanical garage door, striking her on the head. The woman, who had a master's degree in community health, was working as a teacher's assistant in special education and working toward full certification as a special education teacher. An economist estimated that the amount of future lost income and benefits would total $1 million. The victim testified to lack of memory, lack of concentration, disorientation, constant nightmares, fear and recurring headaches.

"I thought then, and still do, that was a watershed case," Kolpan says. "The jury had caught up with the medical understanding of the injury. They understood that despite the woman's ability to walk into the courtroom, and talk, she's suffered permanent brain injury that would not allow her to work (in her field) the rest of her life. It demonstrated that with appropriate experts and lay witnesses, the jury would appreciate the nature of the injury, despite seeing this person appearing normal."

Among the objects in Kolpan's office is a football helmet, a momento from a client whose case Kolpan didn't take.

The young man was a high school football player who suffered a head injury in a football game. Kolpan had borrowed the helmet to examine and see if it had a structural defect, but before he proceeded too far with the case, he learned that the head injury was actually the boy's second concussion within just a few weeks time. The first came during a tag football game with friends.

When a second concussion occurs within a short period of the first it has the potential to be particularly damaging.

With what is known now about head injury, if he was approached with that case now Kolpan would have investigated to see what the school's knowledge was of the first injury, and whether the coaches and trainers had acted appropriately in letting the boy suit up for the varsity. As it was, Kolpan couldn't take the case.

He keeps the helmet, he says, "as a sobering reminder of what I do.

"Hopefully, through my efforts, and people like me, people's lives are better."

D. Fees

In the Matter of Fordham

423 Mass. 481
Supreme Judicial Court of Massachusetts, Suffolk
Argued April 2, 1996
Decided Aug. 9, 1996

Before LIACOS, C.J., O'CONNOR, GREANEY and FRIED, JJ.

O'CONNOR, Justice. This is an appeal from the Board of Bar Overseers' (board's) dismissal of a petition for discipline filed by bar counsel against attorney Laurence S. Fordham. On March 11, 1992, bar counsel served Fordham with a petition for discipline alleging that Fordham had charged a clearly excessive fee in violation of S.J.C. Rule 3:07, DR 2-106, as appearing in 382 Mass. 772 (1981), for defending Timothy Clark (Timothy) in the District Court against a charge that he operated a motor vehicle while under the influence of intoxicating liquor (OUI) and against other related charges. Fordham moved that the board dismiss the petition and the board chair recommended that that be done. Bar counsel appealed from the chair's decision to the full board, and the board referred the matter to a hearing committee.

After five days of hearings, and with "serious reservations," the hearing committee concluded that Fordham's fee was not substantially in excess of a reasonable fee and that, therefore, the committee recommended against bar discipline. Bar counsel appealed from that determination to the board. By a vote of six to five, with one abstention, the board accepted the recommendation of the hearing committee and dismissed the petition for discipline. Bar counsel then filed in the Supreme Judicial Court for Suffolk County (county court) a claim of appeal from the board's action.

Fordham moved in the county court for a dismissal of bar counsel's appeal. A single justice denied Fordham's motion and reported the case to the full court. We conclude that the single justice correctly denied Fordham's motion to dismiss bar counsel's appeal. We conclude, also, that the board erred in dismissing bar counsel's petition for discipline. We direct a judgment ordering public censure be entered in the county court.

We summarize the hearing committee's findings. On March 4, 1989, the Acton police department arrested Timothy, then twenty-one years old, and charged him with OUI, operating a motor vehicle after suspension, speeding, and operating an unregistered motor vehicle. At the time of the arrest, the police discovered a partially full quart of vodka in the vehicle. After failing a field sobriety test, Timothy was taken to the Acton police station where he submitted to two breathalyzer tests which registered .10 and .12 respectively.

Subsequent to Timothy's arraignment, he and his father, Laurence Clark (Clark) consulted with three lawyers, who offered to represent Timothy for fees between $3,000 and $10,000. Shortly after the arrest, Clark went to Fordham's home to service an alarm system which he had installed several years before. While there, Clark discussed Timothy's arrest with Fordham's wife who invited Clark to discuss the case with Fordham. Fordham then met with Clark and Timothy.

At this meeting, Timothy described the incidents leading to his arrest and the charges against him. Fordham, whom the hearing committee described as a "very experienced senior trial attorney with impressive credentials," told Clark and Timothy that he had never represented a client in a driving while under the influence case or in any criminal matter, and he had never tried a case in the District Court. The hearing committee found that "Fordham explained that although he lacked experience in this area, he was a knowledgeable and hard-working attorney and that he believed he could competently represent Timothy. Fordham described himself as 'efficient and economic in the use of [his] time.'...

"Towards the end of the meeting, Fordham told the Clarks that he worked on [a] time charge basis and that he billed monthly.... In other words, Fordham would calculate the amount of hours he and others in the firm worked on a matter each month and multiply it by the respective hourly rates. He also told the Clarks that he would engage others in his firm to prepare the case. Clark had indicated that he would pay Timothy's legal fees." After the meeting, Clark hired Fordham to represent Timothy.

According to the hearing committee's findings, Fordham filed four pretrial motions on Timothy's behalf, two of which were allowed. One motion, entitled "Motion in Limine to Suppress Results of Breathalyzer Tests," was based on the theory that, although two breathalyzer tests were exactly .02 apart, they were not "within" .02 of one another as the regulations require. See 501 Code Mass.Regs. §2.56(2) (1994). The hearing committee characterized the motion and its rationale as "a creative, if not novel, approach to suppression of breathalyzer results." Although the original trial date was June 20, 1989, the trial, which was before a judge without jury, was held on October 10 and October 19, 1989. The judge found Timothy not guilty of driving while under the influence.

Fordham sent the following bills to Clark:

"1. April 19, 1989, $3,250 for services rendered in March, 1989.

"2. May 15, 1989, $9,850 for services rendered in April, 1989.

"3. June 19, 1989, $3,950 for services rendered in May, 1989.

"4. July 13, 1989, $13,300 for services rendered in June, 1989.

"5. October 13, 1989, $35,022.25 revised bill for services rendered from March 19 to June 30, 1989.

"6. November 7, 1989, $15,000 for services rendered from July 1, 1989 to October 19, 1989."

The bills totaled $50,022.25, reflecting 227 hours of billed time, 153 hours of which were expended by Fordham and seventy-four of which were his associates' time. Clark did not pay the first two bills when they became due and expressed to Fordham his concern about their amount. Clark paid Fordham $10,000 on June 20, 1989. At that time, Fordham assured Clark that most of the work had been completed "other than taking [the case] to trial." Clark did not make any subsequent payments. Fordham requested Clark to sign a promissory note evidencing his debt to Fordham and, on October 7, 1989, Clark did so. In the October 13, 1989, bill, Fordham added a charge of $5,000 as a "retroactive increase" in fees. On November 7, 1989, after the case was completed, Fordham sent Clark a bill for $15,000.

Bar counsel and Fordham have stipulated that all the work billed by Fordham was actually done and that Fordham and his associates spent the time they claim to have spent. They also have stipulated that Fordham acted conscientiously, diligently, and in good faith in representing Timothy and in his billing in this case.

* * *

In considering whether a fee is "clearly excessive" within the meaning of S.J.C. Rule 3:07, DR 2-106(B), the first factor to be considered pursuant to that rule is "the novelty and difficulty of the questions involved, and the skill requisite to perform the legal service properly." DR 2-106(B)(1). That standard is similar to the familiar standard of reasonableness traditionally applied in civil fee disputes. See *Society of Jesus of New England v. Boston Landmarks Comm'n*, 411 Mass. 754, 759 n. 10, 585 N.E.2d 326 (1992) (reasonable hours, when calculating fees pursuant to 42 U.S.C. § 1988 [1994], requires consideration as to "whether that time was reasonable in light of the difficulty of the case and the results achieved"). See also Restatement (Third) of the Law Governing Lawyers § 46 comment f (Proposed Final Draft 1996) ("The standards that apply when fees are challenged as unreasonable in fee disputes are also relevant in the discipline of lawyers for charging unreasonably high fees"). Based on the testimony of the four experts, the number of hours devoted to Timothy's OUI case by Fordham and his associates was substantially in excess of the hours that a prudent experienced lawyer would have spent. According to the evidence, the number of hours spent was several times the amount of time any of the witnesses had ever spent on a similar case. We are not unmindful of the novel and successful motion to suppress the breathalyzer test results, but that effort cannot justify a $50,000 fee in a type of case in which the usual fee is less than one-third of that amount.

The board determined that "[b]ecause [Fordham] had never tried an OUI case or appeared in the district court, [Fordham] spent over 200 hours preparing the case, in part to educate himself in the relevant substantive law and court procedures." Fordham's inexperience in criminal defense work and OUI cases in particular cannot justify the extraordinarily high fee. It cannot be that an inexperienced lawyer is entitled to charge three or four times as much as an experienced lawyer for the same service. A client "should not be expected to pay for the education of a lawyer when he spends excessive amounts of time on tasks which, with reasonable experience, become matters of routine." *Matter of the Estate of Larson*, 103 Wash.2d 517, 531, 694 P.2d 1051 (1985). "While the licensing of a lawyer is evidence that he has met the standards then prevailing for admission to the bar, a lawyer generally should not accept employment in any area of the law in which he is not qualified. However, he may accept such employment if in good faith he expects to become qualified through study and investigation, as long as such preparation would not result in unreasonable delay or expense to his client." Model Code of Professional Responsibility EC 6-3 (1982). Although the ethical considerations set forth in the ABA Code of Professional Responsibility and Canons of Judicial Ethics are not binding, they nonetheless serve as a guiding principle. See S.J.C. Rule 3:07, as appearing in 382 Mass. 768 (1981) (Ethical Considerations "are not adopted as a rule of this court, but those Ethical Considerations form a body of principles upon which the Canons of Ethics and Disciplinary Rules, as herein adopted, are to be interpreted").

DR 2-106(B) provides that the third factor to be considered in ascertaining the reasonableness of a fee is its comparability to "[t]he fee customarily charged in the locality for similar legal services." The hearing committee made no finding as to the comparability of Fordham's fee with the fees customarily charged in the locality for similar services. However, one of bar counsel's expert witnesses testified that he had never heard of a fee in excess of $15,000 to defend a first OUI charge, and the customary flat fee in an OUI case, including trial, "runs from $1,000 to $7,500." Bar counsel's other expert testified that he had never heard of a fee in excess of $10,000 for a bench trial. In his view, the customary charge for a case similar to Timothy's would vary between $1,500 and $5,000. One of Fordham's experts testified that she considered a $40,000 or $50,000 fee for defending an OUI charge "unusual and certainly higher by far than any I've ever seen before." The witness had never charged a fee of more than $3,500 for representing a client at a bench trial to defend a first offense OUI charge. She further testified that she believed an "average OUI in the bench session is two thousand [dollars] and sometimes less." Finally, that witness testified that she had "heard a rumor" that one attorney charged $10,000 for a bench trial involving an OUI charge; this fee represented the highest fee of which she was aware. The other expert witness called by Fordham testified that he had heard of a $35,000 fee for defending OUI charges, but he had never charged more than $12,000 (less than twenty-five per cent of Fordham's fee).

Although finding that Fordham's fee was "much higher than the fee charged by many attorneys with more experience litigating driving under the influence cases," the hearing committee nevertheless determined that the fee charged by Fordham was not clearly excessive because Clark "went into the relationship with Fordham with open eyes," Fordham's fee fell within a "safe harbor," and Clark acquiesced in Fordham's fee by not strenuously objecting to his bills. The board accepted the hearing committee's analysis apart from the committee's reliance on the "safe harbor" rule.

The finding that Clark had entered into the fee agreement "with open eyes" was based on the finding that Clark hired Fordham after being fully apprised that he lacked any type of experience in defending an OUI charge and after interviewing other lawyers who were experts in defending OUI charges. Furthermore, the hearing committee and the board relied on testimony which revealed that the fee arrangement had been fully disclosed to Clark including the fact that Fordham "would have to become familiar with the law in that area." It is also significant, however, that the hearing committee found that "[d]espite Fordham's disclaimers concerning his experience, Clark did not appear to have understood in any real sense the implications of choosing Fordham to represent Timothy. Fordham did not give Clark any estimate of the total expected fee or the number of $200 hours that would be required." The express finding of the hearing committee that Clark "did not appear to have understood in any real sense the implications of choosing Fordham to represent Timothy" directly militates against the finding that Clark entered into the agreement "with open eyes."

That brings us to the hearing committee's finding that Fordham's fee fell within a "safe harbor." The hearing committee reasoned that as long as an agreement existed between a client and an attorney to bill a reasonable rate multiplied by the number of hours actually worked, the attorney's fee was within a "safe harbor" and thus protected from a challenge that the fee was clearly excessive. The board, however, in reviewing the hearing committee's decision, correctly rejected the notion "that a lawyer may always escape discipline with billings based on accurate time charges for work honestly performed."

The "safe harbor" formula would not be an appropriate rationale in this case because the amount of time Fordham spent to educate himself and represent Timothy was clearly excessive despite his good faith and diligence. Disciplinary Rule 2-106(B)'s mandate that "[a] fee is clearly excessive when, after a review of the facts, a lawyer of ordinary prudence, experienced in the area of the law involved, would be left with a definite and firm conviction that the fee is substantially in excess of a reasonable fee," creates explicitly an objective standard by which attorneys' fees are to be judged. We are not persuaded by Fordham's argument that "unless it can be shown that the 'excessive' work for which the attorney has charged goes beyond mere matters of professional judgment and can be proven, either directly or by reasonable inference, to have involved dishonesty, bad faith or overreaching of the client, no case for discipline has been established." Disciplinary Rule 2-106 plainly does not require an inquiry into whether the clearly excessive fee was charged to the client under fraudulent circumstances, and we shall not write such a meaning into the disciplinary rule. See *Private Reprimand PR-87-14*, 5 Mass.Att'y Discipline Rep. 501, 502 (1987) (violation of DR 2-106[A] and [B], as appearing in 382 Mass. 772 [1981] found even where "no evidence of bad faith on the part of respondent"); *Matter of the Discipline of an Attorney*, 2 Mass. Att'y Discipline Rep. 115, 117 (1980) (violation of DR 2-106[A] and [C], as appearing in 382 Mass. 772 [1981] even though no "overreaching or improper motivation").

Finally, bar counsel challenges the hearing committee's finding that "if Clark objected to the numbers of hours being spent by Fordham, he could have spoken up with some force when he began receiving bills." Bar counsel notes, and we agree, that "[t]he test as stated in the DR 2-106(A) is whether the fee 'charged' is clearly excessive, not whether the fee is accepted as valid or acquiesced in by the client." Therefore, we conclude that the hearing committee and the board erred in not concluding that Fordham's fee was clearly excessive.

Fordham argues that our imposition of discipline would offend his right to due process. A disciplinary sanction constitutes "a punishment or penalty" levied against the respondent, and therefore the respondent is entitled to procedural due process. *In re Ruffalo*, 390 U.S. 544, 550, 88 S.Ct. 1222, 1225–26, 20 L.Ed.2d 117 (1968). *Matter of Kenney*, 399 Mass. 431, 436, 504 N.E.2d 652 (1987) ("attorney has a substantial property right in his license to practice law"). Fordham contends that the bar and, therefore, he, have not been given fair notice through prior decisions of this court or the express language of DR 2-106 that discipline may be imposed for billing excessive hours that were nonetheless spent diligently and in good faith. *Commonwealth v. Sefranka*, 382 Mass. 108, 110, 414 N.E.2d 602 (1980), quoting *Connally v. General Constr. Co.*, 269 U.S. 385, 391, 46 S.Ct. 126, 127–28, 70 L.Ed. 322 (1926) ("An essential principle of due process is that a statute may not proscribe conduct 'in terms so vague that men of common intelligence must necessarily guess at its meaning'"). It is true, as Fordham asserts, that there is a dearth of case law in the Commonwealth meting out discipline for an attorney's billing of a clearly excessive fee. There is, however, as we have noted above, case law which specifically addresses what constitutes an unreasonable attorney's fee employing virtually the identical factors contained within DR 2-106. See *Mulhern v. Roach*, 398 Mass. 18, 25–30, 494 N.E.2d 1327 (1986); *McLaughlin v. Old Colony Trust Co.*, 313 Mass. 329, 335, 47 N.E.2d 276 (1943); *Cummings v. National Shawmut Bank*, 284 Mass. 563,

569, 188 N.E. 489 (1934). See also *Beatty v. NP Corp.,* 31 Mass.App.Ct. 606, 611, 581 N.E.2d 1311 (1991) ("factors ... to be considered in determining whether a lawyer's fee is fair and reasonable have been amply discussed in the cases"). More importantly, the general prohibition in DR 2-106(A) that "[a] lawyer shall not enter into an agreement for, charge, or collect an illegal or clearly excessive fee," is followed by eight specific, and clearly expressed, factors, to be evaluated by the standard of "a lawyer of ordinary prudence," in determining the propriety of the fee. Contrast *Gentile v. State Bar of Nev.,* 501 U.S. 1030, 1049, 111 S.Ct. 2720, 2731, 115 L.Ed.2d 888 (1991), quoting *Grayned v. Rockford,* 408 U.S. 104, 112, 92 S.Ct. 2294, 2301, 33 L.Ed.2d 222 (1972) (grammatical structure of attorney disciplinary rule and lack of clarifying interpretation by State court forced attorney to "guess at [the rule's] contours" thus failing to "provide 'fair notice to those to whom [it] is directed'"). In addition, nothing contained within the disciplinary rule nor within any pertinent case law indicates in any manner that a clearly excessive fee does not warrant discipline whenever the time spent during the representation was spent in good faith. The fact that this court has not previously had occasion to discipline an attorney in the circumstances of this case does not suggest that the imposition of discipline in this case offends due process. See *Commonwealth v. Twitchell,* 416 Mass. 114, 123, 125 n. 13, 617 N.E.2d 609 (1993) (defendants not deprived of "fair warning" that particular conduct was proscribed by penal statute where criminal liability depended on "degree" of conduct); *Matter of Saab,* 406 Mass. 315, 324 n. 13, 547 N.E.2d 919 (1989) (absence of codified standards to govern attorney discipline proceedings does not offend due process). We reject Fordham's due process argument.

In charging a clearly excessive fee, Fordham departed substantially from the obligation of professional responsibility that he owed to his client. The ABA Model Standards for Imposing Lawyer Sanctions § 7.3 (1992) endorses a public reprimand as the appropriate sanction for charging a clearly excessive fee. We deem such a sanction appropriate in this case. Accordingly, a judgment is to be entered in the county court imposing a public censure. The record in this case is to be unimpounded.

So ordered.

E. Law as a Business

How to Start and Run a Successful Solo or Small-Firm Practice
Massachusetts Bar Association Continuing Legal Education Journal, May 2004
Course # LPD04
Basic Level
Thursday, May 27, 9 A.M.–5 P.M.
Western New England College School of Law
Springfield

Description:

Have you always dreamed of establishing your own practice or "hanging your shingle"? Have the recent mergers and shifts of Massachusetts law firms affected you? Are you re-evaluating your career goals and contemplating whether to strike out on your own? "How to Start and Run a Successful Solo or Small Firm Practice" features practice advice to provide you with the information that you need to become a successful lawyer-entrepreneur.

Our faculty of experienced lawyers and consultants will provide guidance and insight on every aspect of starting a new law firm, while sharing advice and candid practice pointers on their experiences creating and growing their own firms.

Some program highlights are:

The Mechanics of Setting Up Your Firm

A wide variety of topics will be covered including analyzing the costs and benefits of starting your own firm; going solo vs. associating with others; selecting a practice area; scouting out sources of business before making the move; location considerations; choice of entity; and leaving your present firm.

The Mechanics of Running Your Firm — Part I

Topics to be covered include case selection; docket control; fees and billing; accounting and bookkeeping systems; bank accounts, including IOLTA; and discrimination and harassment policies.

The Ultimate Working Lunch

Network with your colleagues.

The Mechanics of Running Your Firm — Part II

Panelists will discuss putting your technology to work; client relations; avoiding malpractice; malpractice and other insurance; and highlights of the rules of professional conduct.

The Mechanics of Marketing

Topics to be discussed include networking; speaking; lecturing; teaching; writing; getting written about; advertising; and Web sites.

Dan's World: A Free Enterprise Dream; An Ethics Nightmare

Lawrence J. Fox,* 55 *The Business Lawyer* 1533 (August, 2000)

The great Section of Business Law asking me — a mere trial lawyer — to respond to the legendary Dean Dan Fischel of that bastion of economics over law — the University of Chicago School of Multidisciplinary Practice — was an invitation too delicious to resist. Could I articulate the arguments why we as a legal profession must not succumb to the forces of economic hegemony — after economics as destiny was so persuasively presented in the May issue of this Journal by Dean Fischel? That is a question only you, gentle reader, can answer. But to observe that I enjoyed the challenge vastly understates my delight in putting this response together.[1]

Dean Fischel taught us in the May issue of this Journal that the marketplace yields far better results for our clients than any regulatory arrangement we lawyers can construct,

---

    * Partner, Drinker Biddle & Reath; Member, ABA Commission on Evaluation of the Rules of Professional Conduct (Ethics 2000); Chair, ABA Death Penalty Representation Project; Former Chair, ABA Section of Litigation; Former Chair, ABA Standing Committee on Ethics and Professional Responsibility. Professors Susan Martyn of the University of Toledo School of Law and Jonathan Macey of Cornell Law School, without endorsing any of the views of the author, were kind enough to review this paper, and provide astute editorial comments for which I am grateful. [Article reproduced with the kind permission of Lawrence J. Fox, Esq., and *The Business Lawyer.*]

    1. Though one does oppose Dean Fischel with some trepidation. *See* Karen Donovan, *Milberg Weiss' $50M Mistake*, Nat'l L. J., Apr. 26, 1999, at A1 (describing how the law firm, rather than risk an outsized punitive damage award, settled with Dean Fischel for $5,000,000 more than the initial verdict in Fischel's lawsuit against Milberg Weiss alleging abuse of process).

that mandatory principles of professional independence, conflicts of interest, confidentiality, and even professional licensure were unnecessary in a world where free enterprise was permitted to flourish, that multidisciplinary practice was an idea whose time had come and that rather than cling to our outdated ethical rules, such as Rule 5.4 which prohibits sharing legal fees with non-lawyers,[2] as a transparent subterfuge for maintaining our professional monopoly, we lawyers should embrace the new model in which anyone can offer legal services on any terms, and the clients will vote with their pocketbooks.

The brashness of Dean Fischel's approach left me weak of knee, my forehead beaded with perspiration, palpitations interrupting my ability to think straight. But then I recovered, recalling my commitment to the ideas that lawyers are not just another set of service providers, that what separates us from a world of auditors, investment bankers, and insurance salesmen is our commitment to a higher set of values, that placing lawyers in alternative practice settings in which they were mere employees or even partners of others would destroy the bulwark that has been our profession's best defense against the compromise of these values, that the laboratory of the Big 5 has demonstrated, better than any chalkboard economic calculations, how the principles Dean Fischel celebrates are destructive of the protections we offer our clients, and that if the Big 5 reflected the alternative universe which Dean Fischel considers the ideal, we should collectively pray our profession is not forced to travel there.

ACCOUNTING STORIES

PRICEWATERHOUSECOOPERS' INDEPENDENCE

My response does not start with lawyering at all. Rather I invite you into the boardroom of the closed end investment companies for which I have served for a decade as an independent director. It is early February 2000. On the agenda is the question whether we will recommend the retention of PricewaterhouseCoopers to be the independent auditors of the funds. The PricewaterhouseCoopers' slick written presentation was sent weeks before the meeting; it is annotated through an in-person appearance by the partner in charge who walks us through the information. After a discussion of audit scope, audit personnel, and audit fees, we arrive at the question of PricewaterhouseCoopers' independence. In the written materials is a disclosure of all ties between PricewaterhouseCoopers and our fund's adviser. While principles of confidentiality prevent me from sharing the details of this presentation, suffice it to say that PricewaterhouseCoopers had a multimillion dollar consulting contract, two engagements in connection with proposed transactions whose fees, in the millions, may double with the result (as we used to say in the old days, you could live on the difference), and other financial relationships with an affiliate of our adviser that were in the millions.

---

2. MODEL RULES OF PROFESSIONAL CONDUCT Rule 5.4 (1998). Rule 5.4, Professional Independence of a Lawyer, states in part:

> (a) A lawyer or law firm shall not share legal fees with a nonlawyer, except that: (1) an agreement by a lawyer with the lawyer's firm, partner, or associate may provide for the payment of money, over a reasonable period of time after the lawyer's death, to the lawyer's estate or to one or more specified persons; (2) a lawyer who purchases the practice of a deceased, disabled or disappeared lawyer may, pursuant to the provision of Rule 1.17, pay to the estate or other representative of that lawyer the agreed-upon purchase price; and (3) a lawyer or law firm may include nonlawyer employees in a compensation or retirement plan, even though the plan is based in whole or in part on a profit-sharing arrangement. (b) A lawyer shall not form a partnership with a nonlawyer if any of the activities of the partnership consist of the practice of law....

Our reliance as independent directors upon PricewaterhouseCoopers for audit services is profound. Our closed end funds hold many securities with a thin or no market. Every day those securities must be fair valued so that the world knows our funds' net asset value, and therefore the true discount or premium at which our closed end shares trade. That work is done conscientiously by our adviser and others; but knowing that independent auditors, with no axe to grind, come in annually to review our internal controls, income statement, and balance sheet gives the investing public and us directors great confidence in the integrity of our operation. With our annual audit fees of less than $40,000, however, could PricewaterhouseCoopers be considered independent given its involvement with our adviser and its affiliates?

I asked our lawyer, who wondered the same thing. Nonetheless, I was informed that even if we were inclined not to approve PricewaterhouseCoopers as our independent auditor, we would accomplish nothing because the other four Big 5 firms would reflect similar intertwining with our adviser. In other words, so long as we wanted to be audited by a Big 5 firm (an absolute necessity in a world in which only these behemoths can provide the generally accepted "Good Housekeeping" seal of approval) we had no real alternative. With only five choices, sometimes you have no choice at all.

PRICEWATERHOUSECOOPERS' INFRACTIONS

The same meeting produced a second story line. The PricewaterhouseCoopers' engagement partner in charge was required to discuss that firm's recent difficulties with the Securities and Exchange Commission (SEC) relating to firm partners, employees, and their relatives owning shares in companies PricewaterhouseCoopers audits. A press release from the SEC had announced that half the partners of PricewaterhouseCoopers, including 31 top executives, had violated the auditor independence rules that prohibit investment in audit clients of the firm. The SEC found "'widespread' noncompliance, which reflects 'serious structural and cultural problems in the firm.'"[3] The statistics regarding the PricewaterhouseCoopers' violations were just staggering. A total of 1885 staffers committed a total of 8064 violations, "owning investments in 2,159 of the firm's 3,170 SEC-registrant corporate audit clients—including almost half of all partners and 6 of the 11 senior managers who oversee the firm's independence program."[4] The SEC suggested that 52 companies hire another firm to replace PricewaterhouseCoopers.[5]

While the public response from the offending firm had been alternatively dismissive ("'the vast majority of [the] infractions resulted from an honest failure to appreciate the importance of compliance, failure to check' restricted investments, and a 'lack of understanding of the intricacies of the rules'"),[6] defensive ("[a]t no time was the integrity of our audits compromised"),[7] and apologetic (we are making "sweeping changes to our processes"),[8] our partner was clearly embarrassed that these transgressions had taken place. Forced to confront us—his clients—his remarks reflected remorse, regret, and renewed determination that PricewaterhouseCoopers was taking all the necessary steps

---

3. Elizabeth MacDonald & Michael Schroeder, *Report by SEC Says Pricewaterhouse Violated Rules on Conflicts of Interest*, WALL ST. J., Jan. 7, 2000, at A3 [hereinafter MacDonald & Schroeder].

4. Stephen Barr, *Breaking Up the Big 5*, CFO, May 1, 2000, at 43 [hereinafter Barr].

5. Elizabeth MacDonald, *Accountant Faces Salvo From SEC*, WALL ST. J., Feb. 28, 2000, at A3.

6. *See* MacDonald & Schroeder, *supra* note 3, at A3 (quoting a confidential letter to staffers from PricewaterhouseCoopers' Chairman, Nicholas Moore, and Chief Executive Officer, James Schiro).

7. *Id.* (quoting Kenton Sicchitano, PricewaterhouseCoopers' global managing partner of regulatory and independence issues).

8. *Id.*

to assure it did not happen again. I felt sorry that because of the conduct of his colleagues our PricewaterhouseCoopers partner was placed in this awkward position to have to apologize to us.

But, whatever comfort I took from that presentation quickly disappeared when I learned that while PricewaterhouseCoopers might be acting contrite, anonymous leaders of the accounting business were reacting to the SEC action against one of the colleague firms by attacking the regulations themselves as outmoded, antiquated, and annoying. The growth of the Big 5 firms, it was argued, made it ridiculous to imagine that it was important that everyone at a Big 5 firm (and their families) avoid owning shares in clients the firm audited. It was quite enough, went the litany, that those directly involved in the audit refrained from owning shares in the audited company, and that the famous accounting firm "firewalls" would safeguard independence.[9] Instead of prosecuting PricewaterhouseCoopers for its violations, these accounting industry spokespersons asserted, the SEC should be examining its regulations and revising them to comport with the reality of the modern world.[10]

In recent months, one of these individuals finally was willing to be quoted for attribution on this explosive topic. In going public, Stephen Butler, Chairman of KPMG, threw down the gauntlet. "What I see is [Arthur] Levitt, [Chairman of the SEC] waking up to the realization that these rules are outdated.... You can pound people for technical violations, but there will be a backlash if these rules are not fixed quickly."[11] What Mr. Bulter means by a "backlash" was not made clear.[12]

In other words, just like the way the accountants wish to repeal the legal profession's imputation rules governing conflicts of interest ("if we impute conflicts beyond the individuals working on the engagement we'd have to turn down so much business"),[13] which is the legal profession's core value governing loyalty, they also hope to repeal the rules governing the independence of their own profession so that no one will look askance at the millions in non-audit services they are billing their audit clients, and everyone will be comfortable with accountants and their families investing in companies their firms audit.

PRICEWATERHOUSECOOPERS' BREAK-UP

The third story line discredits one of the principal arguments invoked by the supporters of multidisciplinary practice argument: the economic forces at work are so powerful that the only choice the profession has is to lie supine on the beach, let the tsunami sweep over us, and get drenched by the new paradigm of one-stop shopping, open competition for services, and lawyers working for non-lawyers—our once great profession reduced to the lowest common denominator role as just another profit center at a department store for consulting services. Yet on February 16, 2000, as predicted by our PricewaterhouseCoopers partner, it was reported that PricewaterhouseCoopers was splitting off its tax and auditing work from its other consulting business, which in turn

---

9. *See* discussion *infra* at 1558.

10. *See* MacDonald & Schroeder, *supra* note 3, at A3.

11. *See* Barr, *supra* note 4, at 54.

12. Not long after these remarks, the rest of the Big 5 reversed an earlier decision not to fund a probe by the Public Oversight Board into their own stock ownership issues. Michael Peel & Adrian Michaels, "*Big Three" in Probe Climbdown*, Fin. Times, May 20, 2000, at 8.

13. Lawrence J. Fox, *Accountants, The Hawks of the Professional World*, 84 Minn. L. Rev. 1097, 1101 (2000) [hereinafter Fox].

might be split into two or more entities.[14] Of course, the devil is in the details, which have not been announced (and how the ownership is allocated among the principals of these new firms will determine whether what we are dealing with is form over substance); it does appear, however, that this one Big 5 firm recognizes that the SEC will not tolerate the threat to auditors' professional independence caused by its offering of so many other services to audit clients of the firm.

The second shoe dropped on March 1, 2000 when the accounting firm of Ernst & Young announced that it would be selling its non-audit business to Cap Gemini S.A. of France, a public company with its headquarters in Paris.[15] Again, we do not yet know how "independent" these various businesses will be—one from the other—but it would appear that Ernst & Young's audit clients will have to go to the great inconvenience of making a second call if they want to secure other services from the auditing firm's former colleagues.[16]

Nor have the other three firms gone untouched by these events. Everyone knows about the on-going feud between Arthur Andersen and Andersen Consulting that on August 7, 2000 ended in an arbitrator's decision that will result in a divorce.[17] KPMG Consulting will split from KPMG, LLC, the accounting house, and has filed to sell approximately $2.5 billion of its stock to the public.[18] Finally, Deloitte & Touche is said to be prepared to maintain an integrated firm unless "it was placed under extreme pressure from regulators."[19]

The lessons from these recent and planned divestitures are profound. Consolidation, we have been told, is as inevitable as it is irreversible. But these announcements prove both of those propositions wrong. There are centrifugal (albeit non-market) forces at work that are more powerful than the centripetal forces that brought all this "consulting" together.[20] And if PricewaterhouseCoopers can be split into a number of enterprises, the civil disobedience of the accounting firms in employing thousands of lawyers can be reversed as well. The *fait accompli* with which our profession has been presented ("now that we've hired 5,000 lawyers we dare you to do something about it") is far more easily undone than the splitting off of all of Ernst & Young's consulting business will turn out to be.[21]

* * *

These stories tell our profession a little about lawyers and the practice of law. But they speak volumes about Dean Fischel's "market" and about what we can expect from multidisciplinary practice if we lawyers succumb to this movement.

---

14. Elizabeth MacDonald, *Pricewaterhouse Nears Final Plan For Restructuring*, WALL ST. J., February 16, 2000, at C11.

15. John Tagliabue, *Cap Gemini to Acquire Ernst & Young's Consulting Business*, N.Y. TIMES, Mar. 1, 2000, at C1.

16. An advertisement in the June 2, 2000 *New York Times* suggests that the firms will not be totally independent from each other, for example, using the same name. N.Y. TIMES, June 2, 2000, at A11.

17. David Leonhardt, Anderson Split into Two Firms by Arbitrator, N.Y. TIMES, Aug. 8, 2000, at A1.

18. *KPMG Consulting in Filing Gives Details of Stock Offering*, N.Y. TIMES, Aug. 8, 2000, at C22.

19. Ben Griffiths & Douglas Broom, *Big 5 Launches SEC Fightback*, ACCT. AGE March 16, 2000, at 1.

20. Indeed, the SEC recently announced new proposed rules "[tightening] standards on what additional services accounting firms could sell to [those] whose books they audit." Floyd Norris, *S.E.C. Proposes Stricter Accounting Rules*, N.Y. TIMES, June 28, 2000, at C1.

21. For further thoughts on what may lie ahead for the Big 5, see Reed Abelson, *After Andersen War, Accountants Think Hard About Consulting*, N.Y. TIMES, Aug. 9, 2000, at C1.

First, we learn that without regard to its effect on independence, the Big 5 accounting firms have long ago aggressively embarked on a campaign to capitalize on their audit entree into the entire world of public companies to sell a broad range of non-audit services with little or no regard to whether the dollars generated by these other endeavors vastly outstrip the audit fees or even whether the audit partners are compensated from the consulting fees they help generate.

Second, we learn that, without any limitations on concentration, these firms have managed to consolidate, first by buying up literally hundreds of practices around the country, and then merging down from the Big 8 to the Big 5[22] so that the entire public company world is divided among them, almost like *omnia Gallia, in quinque partem.*

Third, these five firms can set the rules any way they want—on independence, on loyalty, on fees—because the consumers, as powerful as they are, have no choice. You want a Big 5 firm that provides a higher level of customer loyalty than the rules currently offer, yet even if you are in the market buying, no one is selling.

Fourth, accounting professional independence is a fragile commodity that will be seriously compromised by the announced intention that auditors and their consulting partners be permitted to buy shares in clients, a result that means if one wanted a higher level of independence one would be required to go outside the Big 5.

Fifth, we must rely on the clout of the SEC to impose a more stringent role on share ownership in audited enterprises by auditing firm employees. Indeed, the only thing that will save the current concept of independence of the accounting profession is regulation by a determined and effective SEC.

Which leads to the question, given the foregoing, will our clients be better off if we lawyers all end up as employees of Arthur Andersen or KPMG? The answer to that has to be a decided "no." If the Big 5 take such an aggressive attitude toward undermining their own important concept of professional independence, if they treat the idea of regulation with such disdain that, instead of complying with the existing rules, they ignore them and, when caught, scream that the rules should be changed, then what chance do our profession's unique principles and policies of client protection have of surviving where the law business becomes just another product extension evaluated on the sole basis of how it affects the bottom line?

Indeed, as I have argued elsewhere,[23] we do not need to extrapolate what would happen to lawyer values at the Big 5 if they became Multidisciplinary Practices (MDPs) offering legal services. These firms have already hired 5000 lawyers who systematically engage in civil disobedience, not only disingenuously arguing they are not practicing law to escape the effects of Rule 5.4's prohibition on sharing fees, but also ignoring many of our other rules, including those governing confidentiality, conflicts of interest, limitation of liability, and solicitation of clients.

Alas, this last fact does not carry the day with Dean Fischel. In his world, none of these rules or the principles they reflect are worth protecting or perpetuating. Most of his May article was dedicated to a series of sustained salvos designed to demonstrate

---

22. Some have predicted we may even see the Big Three in a few years. See Brent Shearer, *Dealing With Rifts at Accounting Firms*, M&A J., May 2000, at 6.

23. Hearings Before the Commission on Multidisciplinary Practice (Feb. 4, 1999) (written remarks of Lawrence J. Fox, Drinker Biddle & Reath LLP), available at http://www.abanet.org/cpr/foxl.html; Hearings Before the Commission on Multidisciplinary Practice (Feb. 4, 1999) (oral testimony of Lawrence J. Fox, Drinker Biddle & Reath LLP), available at http://www.abanet.org/cpr/fox3.html.

that these values, many of which he claims are simply imagined anyway, should be jettisoned along with the podiumpounding rhetoric that surrounds them. Thus to me falls their defense, an assignment I gleefully accept, starting with a discussion of professional independence.

PROFESSIONAL INDEPENDENCE: A RALLY CRY OR A SUBSTANTIVE CONCEPT?

What a treat to get an opportunity to explain professional independence to Dean Fischel. Having accused us apologists for Rule 5.4 as having "goals ... no different from any other trade union or interest group pursuing economic protectionism," but "cloaking our arguments in rhetoric about ... professional independence,"[24] I leave it to you, kind reader, to decide whether lawyer professional independence means anything or is it, as Dean Fischel suggests, simply a null set? Then, if you conclude that the former is true, you must determine whether any aspects of "professional independence" might be threatened by the MDP movement. It is my thesis that professional independence in fact reflects a number of different client-centered values and that each of those is far more at risk—some mortally at risk—if we abandon Rule 5.4.

JUST SAY NO, OR WORSE, RESIGN

"In representing a client," Rule 2.1 mandates, "a lawyer shall exercise independent professional judgment and render candid advice."[25] Some would argue that telling the client what the client may not want to hear is the very essence of the lawyer's duty. As the comment to Rule 2.1 provides:

> A client is entitled to straightforward advice expressing the lawyer's honest assessment. Legal advice often involves unpleasant facts and alternatives that a client may be disinclined to confront. In presenting advice, a lawyer endeavors to sustain the client's morale and may put advice in as acceptable a form as honesty permits. However, a lawyer should not be deterred from giving candid advice by the prospect that the advice will be unpalatable to the client.[26]

This concept has often been summed up in "the old counselors' dictum that about half the practice of a decent lawyer consists in telling would be clients that they are damned fools and should stop."[27]

Is this an easy mandate to accomplish? Practicing lawyers know that is not the case. To appreciate fully this point one must start not with the lawyer, but with the client. One of the biggest problems faced by lawyers is the clients' inclination not to tell all to their lawyers, because clients worry about the consequences of such candor. The lawyer might criticize the client; the lawyer might not show sufficient ardor for the client's cause; the lawyer might not be willing to help the client accomplish the client's goals. So the lawyer must nurture a feeling of trust, explain how much better fully informed advice from the lawyer will be for the client, and describe the importance of confidentiality and the attorney-client privilege, all to convince the client to "open up."

Having coaxed the client into sharing her greatest hopes and fears, the lawyer is not yet over the hump. The lawyer has to overcome the lawyer's reciprocal natural reluctance to share bad news with the client. The difficulty of this task is compounded when

---

24. Daniel R. Fischel, *Multidisciplinary Practice*, 55 BUS. LAW. 951, 974 (2000) [hereinafter Fischel].

25. MODEL RULES OF PROFESSIONAL CONDUCT Rule 2.1 (1998).

26. *Id.*

27. MARY ANN GLENDON, A NATION UNDER LAWYERS 75 (Farrar, Straus & Giroux 1994). The quotation is usually attributed to Elihu Root.

the lawyer recognizes (as any experienced lawyer must) that the client tends to "not to hear" that which the client does not want to hear. How many times have lawyers been confronted with the disappointed client who failed to hear (or remember) the lawyer's early warnings that the IRS might challenge the client's tax position, that a jury might reject the client's version of the facts, or that the SEC might not approve the client's public offering statement in a certain form? Thus, the obligation is not just telling the client something that will not be welcomed, but telling it convincingly and repeatedly so that it is clear that the client has in fact received and processed the message.

All of this has to be accomplished without provoking the shooting of the messenger. That, of course, is what makes fulfilling this responsibility so difficult. We do not want to deliver bad news, disappoint our clients, or lose their trust, let alone scold or remonstrate with them, and we fear the consequences of doing so. Will the client stop paying? Will the client switch lawyers? Will the client sue the lawyer for malpractice? All are possible consequences of fulfilling our duty of candor to our clients—and they come with the lawyers' territory.

Will the lawyer be less likely to fulfill this duty in the context of an MDP? The answer has to be, sad to tell, a ringing affirmative. If the client who is about to be disappointed or, worse, when the client learns bad news is also receiving a broad range of other services or products from the lawyer's MDP employer (and, of course, that will be the MDP's goal, indeed its reason for being), how much pressure will the lawyer be under to keep the client happy, pressure exerted by the lawyer's MDP colleagues who are providing the client with lucrative consulting services, investment advice, insurance, financial products, and other goods and services. Suddenly, the fulfilling of an ethical mandate becomes not just the risk of the loss of a client but the destruction of the MDP's business plan, the loss of commissions, the cutting off of the consulting fee spigot, financially jeopardizing the lawyer's non-lawyer colleagues who are not schooled in, subject to, or sensitive about, the lawyer's obligation to independently provide candid advice to the client. Perhaps Lynn Turner, the Chief Accountant of the SEC, in discussing this same problem in the context of professional independence of auditors, put it best, "When [audit partners] are a marketing channel, they can't piss off the client; otherwise they can't sell the other services."[28]

The pressure on the lawyer gets even more intense when the lawyer has to demonstrate the ultimate act of professional independence—firing the client. Our rules of professional conduct mandate lawyer withdrawal when the continued representation would result in a violation of the rules of professional conduct or law.[29] This includes, of course, when a representation becomes a violation of our rules governing conflicts of interest, when the lawyer may find her services are aiding and abetting client fraud or perjury, or when the services of the lawyer may require disclosure of client confidential information.

Again, the lawyer in an MDP will be confronted with a decision that in this case will end a representation, but one that will also result in the inevitable jettisoning of a "profit center" for the MDP, if the legal client is also a consumer of the other services and products the MDP offers. Will the pressure on the lawyer not to take such drastic action from

---

28. *See* Barr, *supra* note 4.

29. Rule 1.16(a)(1) provides: "(a) Except as stated in paragraph (c), a lawyer shall not represent a client or, where representation has commenced, shall withdraw from the representation of a client if: (1) the representation will result in violation of the rules of professional conduct or other law...." MODEL RULES OF PROFESSIONAL CONDUCT Rule 1.16 (1998).

her non-lawyer colleagues at the MDP be greater than if the lawyer were only part of a law firm that offered legal services? Anyone who thinks that will not be the case still believes in the tooth fairy.

LOYALTY

One foundation stone of professional independence is our duty of loyalty. When lawyers promise our clients professional independence, one of the guarantees we are delivering is that the zealous representation of our client will not be compromised by our obligations to other clients, third parties, or our own interests. We provide this guarantee, not just as a personal matter as to the lawyers actually working on the client's engagement, but as to all lawyers with whom we are affiliated. To implement this rule, we agree, before undertaking an engagement, to disclose to the client any possible conflicts, to seek informed consent to waive any waiveable conflict, and to abide the client's decision if a waiver is sought.

This is far from a trivial or immaterial matter. The legal profession recognizes how important it is to provide our clients with confidence that their confrontation with the confusing, complicated, and threatening world of law will be one where they can count on the unfettered advocacy of their counsel. We know all too well how clients can feel insecure and uncertain when facing a major transaction or a litigated matter. The last thing we want to add to that calculus is doubt about how committed the lawyer and law firm is to the client's matter.

Our role governing imputation is the highest embodiment of that commitment. Not only are the independent lawyers assigned to the matter free from any undisclosed outside influences, but so too are all of the other lawyers with whom the clients' lawyers practice. If punches are pulled, they are pulled because that is in the best interest of the client — not because divided loyalty is interfering with good judgment.

Does an MDP practice compromise lawyer loyalty? On this point we need not engage in prognostication in which both sides of the debate can claim the ability to predict alternative visions in the future. No, here we have already seen what would happen in the MDP setting because the Big 5 have provided us with a living laboratory for client "loyalty." And the first casualties in that endeavor are imputation of conflicts among all firm personnel, the concept of non-waiveable conflicts, and an objective standard for measuring impairment, all of which have ended, if you'll pardon the mixed metaphor, on the Big 5 cutting room floor. When clients go to the Big 5 for services they never learn whether the Big 5 firm is even performing non-audit services for adverse parties, unless the conflict is one in which the accounting firm seeks to represent both sides of a matter (a conflict that lawyers, but not accountants, consider non-waiveable). No conflicts memos are ever circulated. Each decision on loyalty is made by the individuals assigned to the matter who ask themselves, applying a totally subjective standard, "How do I feel about taking on this engagement?" While the service providers next door or across the hall or in another office are receiving huge fees from adverse enterprises, the client only gets to hope that loyalty to the other entity will not interfere with the Big 5 firm's loyalty to it. No objective standards; no imputation. How independent can these service providers be?

I should note that the accounting firm rules governing loyalty probably were precisely the correct formulation for them at a time when they were still minding their knitting, not disparaging their birthright, and just providing auditing services. For that role, conflict of interest rules should be irrelevant. Because the last thing the SEC or the investing public wants from auditors is advocacy, and the services were provided outside of the context of competition among aggressive enterprises, it should have made no difference that Peat Marwick audited all of the oil companies. Today, the Big 5's work has evolved into advising on mergers and acquisitions, consulting with enterprises competing for the same broadcast channels or cell phone franchises, litigation consulting, testifying as expert witnesses, and myriad other fields. The problem with these expanding services is that the Big 5 have sought to maintain the same rules governing loyalty even where the new services are anything but objective and advocacy is the commodity that is being purchased and the clash of competing interests is real. One recent, almost incredible example will demonstrate how tone deaf the Big 5 can be.

Without informing either client of the other representation, two lawyers from HSD Ernst & Young, the French law firm, agreed to testify as expert witnesses on French law for each side in a proceeding in the U.S. Court of Federal Claims between IBM and the federal government. When the attempt to double the firm's pleasure, double its fun, became known and the clients protested, HSD Ernst & Young promptly dropped the work for the government, for which it had been working for three years, even though the IBM expert work had only began one month earlier. This odd choice of who to drop was reached on the basis that IBM was a longstanding client of Ernst & Young, the accounting firm, though apparently, up until that point, no one had ever bothered to inform IBM that HSD Ernst & Young was working against IBM's interests.[30] On motion by the government, HSD Ernst & Young's selection of preferred client was overruled and the French law firm was disqualified from working on behalf of IBM.[31]

The case speaks volumes about the inability and unwillingness of MDPs to establish and maintain conflict checking systems and the questionable loyalty MDPs can be expected to offer their clients. In addition, it raises the curious question why any professional firm would get itself in a position where it could never bat more than .500 unless being profitable becomes a higher value than being right.

* * *

THE MYTH OF SELF-REGULATION; THE REALITY OF COURT REGULATION

Lawyers regularly invoke the mantra that one aspect of lawyer independence is the fact that we, as a profession, are self-regulated. It is true that we are self-regulating in the sense that most of our conduct is not reviewed by regulators and we rely on lawyers' natural inclination to conform their conduct to our professional rules on a voluntary basis to assure compliance. As many commentators have noted, however, that mantra of self-regulation recites what is largely a myth.[32] Lawyers only really self-regulate to the extent that state supreme courts and other members of the judiciary choose to delegate that authority to the profession. The real power to regulate lawyers is inherent in the judicial function.[33] But lawyers have generally gotten the first crack at recommending rules for professional conduct, first at the ABA level where the basic Model Code and then Model Rules that form the greater part of the rules actually adopted by every juris-

---

30. Sheryl Stratton, *Experts from E&Y's French Law Firm End Up on Both Sides of IBM Litigation*, Tax Notes Today, July 28, 2000, at 146-4.

31. International Business Machines v. United States, 95-828T (Fed. Cir. July 18, 2000), *reprinted in* Tax Notes Today, July 28, 2000, at 146–47.

32. *See, e.g.*, David B. Wilkins, *Who Should Regulate Lawyers?*, 105 Harv. L. Rev. 801 (1992); Charles W. Wolfram, *Lawyer Turf and Lawyer Regulation—the Role of the Inherent-Powers Doctrine*, 12 U. Ark. Little Rock L.J. 1 (1989).

33. Restatement of the Law, The Law Governing Lawyers § 1, comment c (Proposed Final Draft No. 2 (April 6, 1998)) [hereinafter Restatement].

diction (except California) have received their first promulgation, and then in each state where bar committees have taken the ABA "Models" and amended them to be recommended to their respective state Supreme Courts. Lawyers, too, fulfill essential tasks in the disciplinary systems of the various jurisdictions, acting as hearing officers to adjudicate alleged violations of the rules of professional conduct.[34] Thus, we do not have self-regulation in the sense that lawyers have the power to set the rules and determine violations, but an image of self-regulation in that at the sufferance of the real authorities — the highest appellate court in each jurisdiction — the profession enjoys a significant but circumscribed role.

But while the foregoing may dash the idealized version of lawyers as members of a profession that determines its own fate, it does include a point that may be even more important to our professional role — it is the court's, not the state legislature's, role to regulate the profession.[35] Admittedly the extent of that power varies from state to state,[36] and has been criticized as overstated,[37] but the effect of court regulation on the independence of the profession is profound. Lawyers are being regulated by lawyers (now judges) who recognize the role lawyers play as officers of the court, essential to the vindication of their clients' rights and just as critical to helping their clients conform their conduct to what the law requires.[38]

Could the growth of MDPs cause a loss of this professional regulation for lawyers? Once again the answer is a certain affirmative. When lawyers become just another set of service providers in a department store of financial and other services, when MDPs offer multiple profit centers — the sale of annuities, investment-advisory services, insurance, burial plots, checking accounts, and loans — and all those other services and products are regulated by executive branch agencies established by the legislature, what will be the argument why court-centered lawyer regulation should be preserved?

---

34. The legal profession's relative autonomy carries with it special responsibilities of self-government. The profession has a responsibility to assure that its regulations are conceived in the public interest and not in furtherance of parochial or self-interested concerns of the bar. Every lawyer is responsible for observance of the rules of Professional Conduct. A lawyer should also aid in securing their observance of the rules of Professional Conduct. A lawyer should also aid in securing their observance by other lawyers. Neglect of these responsibilities compromises the independence of the profession and the public interest it serves.
MODEL RULES OF PROFESSIONAL CONDUCT Preamble (1999).

35. RESTATEMENT, *supra* note 46, at § 1, comment c.

36. *Compare* Mississippi Bar v. McGuire, 647 So. 2d 706 (Miss. 1994) (striking down statute that excluded disbarment based on IRS violations as in conflict with lawyer code with no similar exception) *with* Heslin v. Connecticut Law Clinic, 461 A.2d 938 (Conn. 1983) (finding that Connecticut Unfair Trade Practices Act can be applied to the conduct of lawyers).

37. RESTATEMENT, *supra* note 46, at § 1, Reporter's Note c.

38. The Preamble to the ABA Model Rules captures the point in another way.
    The legal profession is largely self-governing. Although other professionals also have been granted powers of self-government, the legal profession is unique in this respect because of the close relationship between the profession and the processes of government and law enforcement. This connection is manifested in the fact that ultimate authority over the legal profession is vested largely in the courts. To the extent that lawyers meet the obligations of their professional calling, the occasion for government regulation is obviated. Self-regulation also helps maintain the legal profession's independence from government domination. An independent legal profession is an important force in preserving government under law, for abuse of legal authority is more readily challenged by a profession whose members are not dependent on government for the right to practice.
MODEL RULES OF PROFESSIONAL CONDUCT Preamble (1999).

In this context my obligation of candor forces me to admit that the failure to accommodate the MDP movement carries its own risks that court-centered regulation will be abolished. Many have argued that if we do not bend to the will of the Big 5, these economic (and political) behemoths will run to the legislatures for relief, just as they demonstrated their awesome political power in securing an accountant-lawyer privilege over the vigorous objection of the ABA.[39] This risk is real—despite the fact that in many states such statutes would likely be declared unconstitutional[40]—but nonetheless I conclude it is better to lose on the principle of defending professional independence than to endure a professional death by a thousand cuts as we let professional independence be taken away from us through ill-advised compromise.

UNPOPULAR CAUSES AND PRO BONO REPRESENTATION

Back in the early 1950s when McCarthyism was so rampant in the land and "Communists" were being uncovered in every area of human endeavor, Henry W. Sawyer, the late, great partner of my firm, Drinker Biddle & Reath, undertook to represent teachers in Philadelphia who had been accused of being "fellow travelers" or worse and whose jobs were in jeopardy. Sawyer was young, fearless, and articulate, and prepared to do battle on behalf of these beleaguered educators, a fact that gained wide publicity because of the paranoia of the times.

Out of the notorious nature of this representation came a protest directed to Henry Drinker, the Chairman of our firm, from a significant long-standing client. The client was outraged that his law firm was defending these "pinko commie sympathizers," and he wanted Drinker to do something about it. To call Drinker conservative would have been an understatement, and his anti-Communist sentiments were probably as strong as those of his troubled client. But Sawyer's defense of the teachers reflected a more important principle than where one's ideas fell on some political spectrum. So Drinker rejected the client's imprecations and, when the client protested further and threatened to take his business elsewhere, Drinker made it quite clear that threat would not change his mind.

Will that ferocious professional independence to rush to the defense of the unpopular be affected by MDPs? Again, we need not speculate about what a future they may bring. As Chair of the ABA Death Penalty Representation Project, I already know what that answer will be. A number of times lawyers in corporate America have told me they would love to help but their company's shareholders would be "up in arms" if it came to light that they were representing the despicable denizens of Death Row. This tells me all too well that an early casualty of the MDP movement will be the loss of this precious aspect of professional independence.

Dean Fischel, in his eloquent piece, tried to argue that this is okay because who is to say that a greater contribution to society would not be maximizing profits, paying more

---

39. *See* IRS Restructuring and Reform Act, Pub. L. No. 105-206, 1998 U.S.C.C.A.N. (112 Stat.) 685. The ABA opposed the legislation, an amendment to the Interval Revenue Code, because, *inter alia*, any such change should go through the evidence rules committee, concerns about the application and scope of the new privilege, and the inconsistency between the accountants' auditing function and the concept of confidentiality. See letter from Jerome J. Shestack, President of the ABA, and House and Senate Committee Members, dated Mar. 23, 1998 (on file with *The Business Lawyer*, University of Maryland School of Law).

40. *See, e.g.,* Commonwealth v. Stern, 701 A.2d 568 (1997) (striking penal statute that criminalized the conduct of lawyers as infringing Supreme Court's exclusive jurisdiction to regulate the professional and ethical conduct of lawyers).

in taxes, and supporting the Art Museum by serving on its board.[41] My response is this: anyone can try to increase his or her income; anyone can attend fancy, high cost parties, charity balls, glitzy benefits, supporting the orchestra or the opera; only the Henry W. Sawyers and lesser lights who seek to emulate his commitment (even if we cannot come close to his eloquence) can represent those under sentence of the ultimate sanction, or the Ku Klux Klan as it seeks to march through Skokie, Illinois, or the young student who does not want to be forced to listen to the prayers of another religion while attending a high school graduation. Just as lawyers are not merely another set of service providers, so too are they not just another set of charitable donors. Only through their dedication of time, knowledge, experience, and role as officers of the court can the poor, the down-trodden, and the despicable receive the representation they require.

A NOTE ON LAWYER INDEPENDENCE V. ACCOUNTANT INDEPENDENCE

No discussion of this topic can conclude without a short discussion of how badly the proponents of MDPs misunderstand completely any similarity between our professional independence and that of the accountants. Despite the accountants' most fervent wishes, we are not twins separated at birth, still united by our common ethical birthright. Their "independence" is independence from the client. As my discussion regarding my service as a director indicates, when we read that PricewaterhouseCoopers has opined on the financial statements of some company, we want to know that Pricewaterhouse-Coopers was free of influence from its client, able to bring healthy skepticism to its work to protect the public from relying upon financial statements that have not been prepared in accordance with generally accepted accounting principles after an audit conducted in accordance with generally accepted auditing standards. Like the SEC, we want no advocates here, but rather professional distance and objectivity.

For lawyers, professional independence is a completely different concept (as I hope this article demonstrates). Yes, it means we give our clients our best advice, even if it is not what the client wants to hear and in that sense, and in that sense alone, we adopt the accountant's version of independence. But it also means that we are as free as possible from outside influences — especially the government, other clients, third party payers, and our own self-interest — to permit us to exercise unbridled loyalty and zealous advocacy on behalf of our clients. Samuel DiPiazza, of PricewaterhouseCoopers, betrays his (and I suspect his accounting colleagues') misunderstanding when he asserts:

> To suggest that the threat to independent judgment is unacceptably higher when a non-lawyer has an economic interest in a law firm than when a lawyer is under pressure from a long-standing client to take a particular position or is encouraged by a senior partner in his own firm to accommodate a client's interests, strikes me as a doubtful proposition.[42]

It may be doubtful to him, but it is anything but that to us. Being "under pressure" from a long time client is exactly where the pressure should be. Being "encouraged" by a senior partner is exactly who should be doing the encouraging. We are quite properly beholden to our clients (so long as the suggested conduct is lawful and ethical) and we are supervised by other lawyers (whose guidance we follow unless the ethical or legal violation is clear). The former is our client to whom we are ethically committed and the latter is a lawyer, similarly conversant with our values, subject to our rules, and liable to the

---

41. Fischel, *supra* note 24, at 957.
42. Sam Di Piazza, Jr., Managing Partner, Tax Services-Americas PricewaterhouseCoopers LLP, Written Remarks to the American Bar Association Commission on Multidisciplinary Practice (Mar. 11, 1999) available in http://www.abanet.org/cpr/dipiazza.html.

same disciplinary sanctions as we. It is pressure from others that we must be ever vigilant to guard against and it is precisely those influences that will compromise our professional independence. The irony that Mr. DiPiazza's quoted statement proves this point, I trust, is not lost on those who worry about MDPs.

LAWYERS HAVE LAPSED

Have lawyers acted as committed professionals to the principle of lawyer independence? The report card is decidedly mixed. Lawyers have served as directors of their clients. Lawyers have invested in their clients and some, if recent stories are correct, have gone much further and made that a condition for providing the services.[43] Lawyers have started ancillary businesses and, though for awhile it seemed that the trendy opening of law firm subsidiaries was just a passing fancy, it now seems to have reaccelerated, perhaps in light of the fact that MDPs, like sneeze-inducing pollen in the spring, are in the air. Lawyers also have succumbed to the pressure from insurance companies. Large numbers have even gone to work as salaried employees providing legal services to insureds who, because these lawyers have stationery that to all the world represents that they work for a partnership using a fictitious firm name, remain blissfully ignorant of the relationship between their lawyers and the insurance company that employs them on salary.[44] Undoubtedly, lawyers compromise their independence every day in myriad other ways like failing to "just say no," cutting corners, overbilling, charging unreasonable fees, and otherwise failing to observe our ethical precepts.

But that is no reason to abandon the principle of professional independence or conclude there is no principle there at all. To the contrary, the courageous, quiet conduct of a great super-majority of the bar, dedicated to these principles, is a testimonial to how much we can achieve as independent professionals. Their example should provide great encouragement that we can lasso in our lapsed brethren and sisters. When one considers a profession whose ranks approach one million, we can almost be giddy with how professional independence abounds, how much it contributes to the common weal and how rewarding it could be to use the savage attack on our professional values by the Big 5 and their supporters as a way of galvanizing the rest of us into a rededication to these values and concerted action to protect them.

CONFIDENTIALITY AND PRIVILEGE: ETERNAL PROTECTIONS

News Item: WALL STREET JOURNAL, OCTOBER 4, 2002 GENERAL ENTERPRISE ANNOUNCES BOLD INITIATIVE

(New York) Wendy Fineman, General Counsel of the General Enterprise Company, announced at a press conference yesterday in front of the New York Stock Exchange that henceforth all outside counsel for General Enterprise would be encouraged to share otherwise privileged or confidential information with the financial community. Each month General Enterprise plans to publish a list of the company's outside counsel and a description

---

43. The Venture Law Group "insists on having an opportunity to buy in … at the idea stage.…" Richard B. Schmitt, *Little Law Firm Scores Big by Taking Stakes in Clients*, WALL ST. J., Mar. 22, 2000, at B1. Though investing in clients by lawyers does raise two concerns, objectivity and potential liability (See ABA Comm. On Ethics and Professional Responsibility, Formal Opinion 00-418 (July 7, 2000)), such investments can be accomplished consistent with lawyers' ethical obligations, a fact that is not true of those accountants who seek to invest in firms for which they act as auditors where pristine objectivity is the *sine qua non* of the engagement.

44. *See, e.g.*, American Insurance Ass'n v. Kentucky Bar Ass'n, 917 S.W.2d 568 (Ky. 1996); Gardner v. North Carolina State Bar, 341 S.E.2d 517 (N.C. 1986).

of the matters they are handling, to facilitate the desired disclosures. Ms. Fineman's in-house counsel staff will also be available for the purpose of divulging similar information to the press, shareholders, or the public.

When asked whether General Enterprise did not consider it dangerous to share such sensitive information outside the company, Ms. Fineman explained that she had recently read an article by Dean Daniel Fischel, of the University of Chicago Law School, that argued companies "with nothing to hide" were received better by the marketplace. "If privilege is invoked [by a company] and this is disclosed [to the public], investors will rationally conclude that negative information is being withheld because the firm has something to hide, why else withhold the information?" Since Fischel believes, like Jeremy Bentham, that the attorney-client privilege "protects the guilty," General Enterprise wanted to escape any negative implications the company's invoking the privilege or having its lawyers maintain confidentiality might convey.

General Enterprise hopes that in taking this leadership role in jettisoning antiquated notions of confidentiality, other public companies will similarly make full disclosure to the investing public, a move that will give these companies, in the view of Dean Fischel, "a comparative advantage in attracting capital."

The role of confidentiality in the practice of law is vastly overstated, Ms. Fineman observed, again relying on Dean Fischel. "The concern about information sharing is probably exaggerated. Information about business plans and strategies, for example, often depreciates rapidly and is frequently available from other sources" observes Fischel. It is in that spirit that General Enterprise has made this leadership decision.

* * *

The quotes of Dean Fischel, though not the news conference, are accurate, believe it or not.[45] The critics of MDPs asserted that, because the auditors' attest function is inconsistent with the lawyers' obligation of confidentiality, accountant-controlled MDPs threaten our clients. Dean Fischel responds not only that the advantages of the privilege are vastly overstated, but he goes further to assert that in fact, at least in the case of public company clients, the elimination of these protections would prove beneficial. Don't bemoan the auditing firm's threat to your secrets, Dean Fischel argues, you will be better off when the investment community knows you aren't hiding behind such outmoded protections.

I know Mr. Fischel put this argument in his paper just to test the limits of his approach, but it demonstrates to me how much he has lost his way. The fact that we have emphasized the importance of both the privilege and confidentiality to the health of the lawyer-client relationship for more than a century diminishes not one wit how critical it remains. Some truths are not only self-evident, but endure across time. We may be living in a world of e-commerce, e-mail, and even e-law, but to argue that as a result our fundamental values should change is as flawed as the suggestion that my rabbi should change the content of his sermons now that they are being posted on our synagogue website.

Every day major public companies consult their lawyers regarding a broad range of matters, some involving litigation, others transactions, still others tax, human resources,

---

45. Fischel, *supra* note 24, at 964, 967.

or other areas of corporate concern. The only way these representations can be effective is if the clients are free, and indeed encouraged, to share their innermost concerns with the lawyer, free from the threat that the lawyer or the client can be compelled to disclose the content of those discussions. Similarly the lawyer has to be free to explore alternatives, offer tentative advice, and candidly discuss the matter with the client. There is nothing wrong with that process nor should anyone be defensive about invoking the privilege to maintain the sanctity of the lawyer-client relationship. There is plenty of capital to be raised by companies who are wise enough to purchase Class A legal services, delivered with confidentiality and the attorney-client and attorney work product privileges intact.

Nor should anyone doubt that confidentiality would be compromised in multidisciplinary practice settings. The Big 5 provide a particular problem in that regard because of the total inconsistency between the auditor's attest function duty of disclosure and the lawyer's obligation to maintain client secrecy.[46] But other professionals, like social workers and investment bankers, have no duty of confidentiality and also, by other law, may have legal requirements of disclosure, for example to report child abuse, from which lawyers are exempt.

A recent example demonstrates the low regard other professionals might place on maintaining confidences (and loyalty). KPMG was the personal accounting firm for Garth Drabinsky, the founder and CEO of Livent, the live theatre production company. When Drabinsky sold the company to Michael Ovitz, KPMG conducted the due diligence of Ovitz. KPMG having given Livent a clean bill of health, Ovitz proceeded with the purchase and appointed a KPMG partner to the Board. When that partner heard of alleged financial irregularities at Livent, he retained a Toronto law firm which in turn hired KPMG to look into allegations. When Drabinsky complained that KPMG was not only investigating Livent, but also Drabinsky, its own client, KPMG ignored his plea and litigation ensued. On an interim ruling the Canadian court concluded that KPMG had duties not to disclose, as well as of loyalty and not to act against the interests of its ongoing client. Then on the eve of trial, KPMG was forced to accept a consent order that declared KPMG had "breached its fiduciary duty to the Plaintiff [Drabinsky] in allowing" the investigation and restrained KPMG from disclosing any confidential information of Drabinsky.[47]

THE DEATH OF LOYALTY

Not content to disparage the role of confidentiality and the critical importance of the attorney-client privilege, Dean Fischel cynically proceeds to dispatch loyalty to a similar dust heap of antiquated notions. "[I]mputed disqualification,"[48] Dean Fischel writes, "is obsolete and should be discarded," because the rule is "much costlier" in a world of very large firms (he means they have to turn down a lot of new business) and a "barrier to

---

46. Congress has also mandated auditor disclosure totally inconsistent with the attorney-client privilege and the lawyer codes' injunctions against lawyer breaches of confidentiality.

47. *KPMG, Garth Drabinsky Settle Litigation*, Canada NewsWire, Ltd., July 14, 2000, available at http:www.newswire.ca/releases/July2000/14/c3565.html; *An Executive of Livent Settles Civil Lawsuit*, N.Y. Times, July 15, 2000, at C4; Madhari Acharya, *KPMG Settles*, Toronto Star, July 15, 2000, Edition 1; Diane Francis, *Drabinsky, KPMG Case Raises Questions*, Nat'l Post, June 24, 2000, at D2.

48. Imputed disqualification, i.e. the notion that each lawyer in a practice setting is subject to the conflicts of every other lawyer, has already been discussed. *See* discussion *supra* at 1542–44.

mobility" for lawyers.[49] The Dean therefore concludes "the rule should be discarded altogether," so that "MDPs ... could then grow to their efficient size."[50]

Wow! The questions raised by this salvo, gentle reader, are multiple. First, is Dean Fischel correct that imputation is designed simply to protect confidential information? Is he correct in arguing that the rule's effect is "draconian" when it is applied to a situation in which a "junior partner" in a firm's L.A. office is hired to do a small matter" for a "minor subsidiary of a major corporation,"[51] thereby precluding a different client from hiring presumably a "senior" partner in the firm's Washington office on a major matter against the parent of the junior partner's client? Putting aside for a second, as undoubtedly a momentary lapse on his part, any suggestion that the loyalty we owe clients turns on how important in the firm their lawyer is (where, Dean Fischel, is it written that the clients of junior partners really deserve less fealty) or how large the client is (beware small clients who venture within these hallowed walls, because the loyalty you shall receive is marginal), how large the matter is (bring us your mega merger and we'll be real loyal), or whether you go to the firm's headquarters or an outlying branch, Mr. Fischel really misses the point of the rules.

While it is true imputation is designed to protect confidential information, equally important is the fact that imputation reflects the higher standard of loyalty we promise our clients. The legal profession tells our clients that we not only will protect the information they share with us by assuring that no one in the firm will have an opportunity to use it, but we also assure them that, without their informed consent, we will not take positions adverse to them even if the matter is totally unrelated. Then, if a conflict situation arises, and we wish to take on the new engagement, we promise we will call the client, seek a waiver, and abide by the client's decision whether the waiver will be granted. It is this loyalty component that the Dean ignores entirely, even to the point of never mentioning the word anywhere in his essay.

Perhaps Dean Fischel's suggestion that richer, bigger clients with more significant matters and clients of more important partners would receive a better level of loyalty stems from his unstated recognition of the real world effects of abandoning imputation. If lawyers are free to take positions directly adverse to their current clients on unrelated matters, then the only questions the law firm will ask itself (since it never, under this regime, has to tell or ask the client anything) is "How upset will the client be when it learns what we have done?" "Will we be fired?" And most important, "Do we care?" In other words, the law firm will be asking itself the totally unseemly questions that determine whether it is prepared to incur the wrath of a current client to take on a new one, questions whose answers will not turn on values like loyalty and confidentiality, but rather on the size of the respective engagements, the power within the firm of the lawyers with the competing engagements, and the future prospects for cross-selling firm services to the competing clients.

---

49. Fischel, *supra* note 24, at 966. Anticipating Dean Fischel's argument, the Section of Business Law's Ad Hoc Committee on Ethics 2000 has presented the ABA Commission evaluating the Model Rules an extraordinary proposal that would abolish imputation, permit law firms to take positions directly adverse to current clients so long as different teams undertook the work, and limit loyalty to the lawyers actually working on the client's matters, a concept the Committee characterizes as consistent with "undivided" loyalty. *See* Letter from Ad Hoc Committee to Ethics 2000 Commission dated October 5, 1999 concerning proposed Rule 1.10 (on file with the Commission). It is a good thing the Committee did not ask any clients whether they shared this cramped view on loyalty.

50. Fischel, *supra* note 24, at 966.

51. *Id.* at 965.

* * *

NO RULES FOR THE RICH AND HIGH FALUTIN'

THE RICH DON'T NEED PROTECTION

One of the problems with Dean Fischel's approach is his working assumption that clients of MDPs will be rich and sophisticated (like the enterprises who hire him (and me)) and that therefore the protections some of us value are paternalistic and unnecessary. As he writes, "[t]he need for customer protection in this market is non-existent."[52] Let the free enterprise system flourish, knock down all "barriers to entry" and only the best and the brightest will succeed because the clients are so discerning and well informed. In the Dean's view, we are to assume the University of Chicago would still produce brilliant lawyers, Illinois would still administer a bar examination and review character and fitness, mandatory CLE would be required for those duly admitted, but anyone, even those who learned law from an extension school that recruits students on matchbook covers, or who didn't learn law at all, could hold themselves out as providing legal services with the great unseen hand of Adam Smith sorting the market out.

There are multiple problems with this construct and, thus, its potential adoption presents important public policy issues for the profession and society to confront. First, we must wonder how far Dean Fischel is prepared to go. Today we license lots of occupations because we make judgments that, without specific qualifications (education, examinations, licensure, continuing education), we don't want just anyone performing open heart surgery, doing root canal, opining on financial statements, designing jet airplanes, or installing garbage disposals. Does the practice of law present any challenges in its execution and potential harm in its misdelivery that suggest we ought to have what he calls "barriers to entry," and I characterize as minimum qualifications, to undertake these difficult assignments? I would hope, despite the Dean's rhetoric, that the leader of what is one of this country's greatest law schools, one that offers a $100,000 education to the best and brightest, would lend some support to the radical notion that asking those who practice law to receive a specialized education would be viewed not as just a way to differentiate in a crowded marketplace those who are better qualified, but as a necessary prerequisite to participating in the marketplace at all.

CAN THE PROFESSION AFFORD TWO DIFFERENT SETS OF RULES?

Consenting Adults

The truth is, Mr. Fischel's hyperbole notwithstanding, that consumer protection will be required for many clients of MDPs. This means that the Dean, though he does not say so, would have us develop different rules for different clients, depending on their sophistication. This idea is deeply troubling on many levels, not the least that to go down this road represents a break from a long tradition. Our profession has had one set of rules since codes of ethics first were established. But this concept has more than history on its side; it springs from several principles. First, our rules trump what can take place between consenting adults, i.e., some protections simply cannot be waived, even by the most well informed client, or even when the client is a lawyer or separately represented by a lawyer.

A few examples can demonstrate this point. A client cannot waive a non-waiveable conflict.[53] We as a profession have concluded that some conflicts are so disabling and so

---

52. Fischel, *supra* note 24, at 961.

53. "[W]hen a disinterested lawyer would conclude that the client should not agree to the representation under the circumstances, the lawyer involved cannot properly ask for such agreement or

likely to affect the integrity of the system of justice itself that we will prohibit the lawyer from even broaching the subject. Nor can a client be asked to sign an open-ended prospective waiver.[54] Who knows where the representation will evolve over time, who knows what confidential information will be shared, and who can anticipate what the future adverse representation will be? Lawyers also may neither seek nor accede to a scope limitation of their services that is unreasonably narrow in time or subject matter.[55]

So too a lawyer may not seek waiver from the client for the lawyer's unlimited liability for malpractice.[56] As a public policy, lawyers stand behind their work as a safeguard for the public. Similarly the client cannot be asked to waive the protections of Rule 4.2.[57] Even the worldly wise represented client who initiates the communication with the other side's lawyer will be saved from the consequences of her conduct unless and until her lawyer grants permission for the unguarded contact.

The lawyer who charges an unreasonable fee will also find the defense that the client was sophisticated unavailing if the fee in fact was unreasonable.[58] This is because all lawyers may only charge all clients reasonable fees, even those who should be smart enough to know better. Preserving these values, we have decided, is far more important than providing lawyers and sophisticated clients the opportunity to create exceptions, and I would argue they ought to be preserved. What makes us a profession is the fact there are some standards that we do not compromise, no matter how successful we are in persuading the well-heeled client to do so.

* * *

ALL SERVICE PROVIDERS ARE HIGH FALUTIN'!

In Dan's world all of the service providers are high falutin'! We have Ernst & Young, Salomon Smith Barney, and American Express hiring lawyers to provide legal services to

---

provide representation on the basis of the client's consent." MODEL RULES OF PROFESSIONAL CONDUCT Rule 1.7 cmt. 5 (1999).

54. ABA Formal Opinion 93-372, observed:

> Given the importance that the Model Rules place on the ability of the client to appreciate the significance of the waiver that is being sought, it would be unlikely that a prospective waiver which did not identify either the potential opposing party or at least a class of potentially conflicting clients would survive scrutiny. Even that information might not be enough if the nature of the likely matter and its potential effect on the client were not also appreciated by the client at the time the prospective waiver was sought.

ABA Comm. On Ethics and Professional Responsibility, Formal Op. 93-372 (1993).

55. An agreement concerning the scope of representation must accord with the Rules of Professional Conduct and other law. Thus, the client may not be asked to agree to representation so limited in scope as to violate Rule 1.1 [the rule governing competence], or to surrender the right to terminate the lawyer's services or the right to settle litigation that the lawyer might wish to continue.

MODEL RULES OF PROFESSIONAL CONDUCT Rule 1.2 cmt. 5 (1999).

56. "A lawyer shall not make an agreement prospectively limiting the lawyer's liability to a client for malpractice unless permitted by law and the client is independently represented in making the agreement...." Id. 1.8(h).

57. The rule itself provides that a lawyer may not communicate with a person known to be represented in the matter "unless the lawyer has the consent of the other lawyer...." Id. 4.2.

58. The rule's admonition is unequivocal. "A lawyer's fee shall be reasonable." Id. 1.5(a).

Although a lawyer and client may have executed a written fee agreement, courts are always free to make their own inquiries about the reasonableness of legal fees as part of their inherent authority to regulate the practice of law. See Pfeifer v. Sentry Ins., 745 F. Supp. 1434 (E.D. Wis. 1990) (court has inherent power to review reasonableness of fees and to refuse to enforce any contract calling for excessive or unreasonable fees).

ANNOTATED MODEL RULES OF PROFESSIONAL CONDUCT Rule 1.5 (1999) at 48.

the customers of the MDP. But we cannot write rules that just apply to tassel-toed serv-ice providers either. If KPMG gets to have an MDP, so does Tony's Ambulance Service and Montesanto's Funeral Parlor. While I know, from our unfortunate experience with lawyers going to work for the Big 5, that even the most pretentious of MDPs has the ca-pacity to destroy our professional values, there is no reason to expect that those with less lofty airs will not act at least as badly, and perhaps even worse.

CONCLUSION

Dan Fischel and I, I hope, have joined issue. We really do describe two very different worlds. Dan Fischel's is swashbuckling, populated by behemoth multi-national enter-prises and service providers of equal scale and scope. The market will reward the good and punish the bad, and officious intermeddling by regulators has no place. Mine insists on black letter rules and effective enforcement, would reject that which the marketplace offers us as, perhaps, in the best interests of the service providers, but certainly not in the best interest of the clients. It also celebrates the lawyers as something special, not be-cause we are brighter or have an unwarranted sense of entitlement, but because we have special responsibilities and special roles to play in our society.

It is my wish, kind reader, that after you have read this far you will endorse the latter approach. But if you do so, your hard work is not at an end. Because this is not just a question of choosing one value system or another. The forces of the economic model are real. They have many adherents and those adherents are determined to tear down all that we have built. Some, like Dan Fischel, are in the academy. Others include our lapsed brethren and sisters at the Big 5 accounting firms. Still others are those who would profit from a breakdown in our system of justice, a withering away of the organized bar, a disappearance of our commitment to pro bono, an end to professional independence.

So a vote for our core values is not enough. We need to raise money, launch a cam-paign, enforce our rules, explain our position, take nothing for granted, and commit ourselves to the preservation of that which we treasure. Otherwise, just as the Grinch tried to steal Christmas, Dean Fischel and his colleagues will steal our profession. And we will have no one to blame but ourselves.

Chapter VIII

Bar Admissions

Problems

Problem 33

As a law school dean, I supervised the filing of countless equivalents of Massachusetts Form 4, Chapter VIII-3 *infra*, certifying that there was nothing "adverse in respect of the moral character or fitness to practice law of the applicant." How should I have responded in the following situations, some of which are true?

1) As a student, the applicant deliberately misfiled library books assigned for an exercise so that only he could find them.

2) While at home in the summer between terms, the applicant sold worthless investments to his old friends and neighbors. Later, he reported his employer to the SEC, but did not notify his "customers."

3) The applicant did not register for the draft "because he was a 'CO,' a conscientious objector." Would it make a difference if there was a war going on? Would it make a difference if the student had notified his draft board that he was not going to register? (In the actual case, the applicant was from a minority racial group in a state where draft exemptions were almost never granted to that group, so he never applied for "CO" status. He just did not register hoping no one would notice. Should he be admitted to the bar?)

4) The applicant was a member of an extremist conservative group that actively denounced homosexuals on the campus. (See *In re Hale*, Chapter VIII-3, *infra*). Would it make a difference if the group also denounced racial groups? Advocated racial segregation?

5) The applicant was married, but was known to be carrying on an affair with another student. Would it make a difference if the spouse knew?

6) The applicant had dozens of unpaid parking tickets, and continued to park in the faculty lot, despite dire warnings.

7) The applicant was frequently seen drunk at student parties.

8) The applicant had to seek professional psychiatric help because of a psychotic condition. This was known to the dean for students, because the student had confided in her.

9) The applicant stopped payment on his student loans. (See *Application of Gahan*, Chapter VIII-3 *infra*). Would it make a difference if the applicant were bankrupt because of poor health and lack of insurance? Would it make a difference if the applicant were bankrupt because of compulsive spending on luxury goods? Would it make a difference if the applicant were not bankrupt, but thought law school was a waste of time?

10) On graduation, the applicant struck a policeman who had come to break up a fight in a bar. He was convicted of a felony, and has served his time. He is "sorry" and is unlikely to do any such thing again. He is a now a model citizen.

11) The applicant always came late to class, failed to file papers on time, and was a general "flake." But he did graduate with a remarkably good average by borrowing notes. (See Iowa form, question 32(f), Chapter VIII-3 *infra*). (Do not try it in this class!)

12) The applicant came from a poor, struggling family. She had borrowed a great deal of money, and "panicked" midway through her first year. She purchased a term paper from a "service," and was detected. (The dean for students subscribed to all the "services"). She was suspended for a year, came back, and now will graduate with honors.

Problem 34

Examine the old Iowa and Massachusetts bar admission forms attached. Do you think the Iowa form was too tough? Do you think the Massachusetts form was too easy? What would you include on such a form? Remember, a response can only trigger further investigation by a Character Committee, and does not, in itself, bar the applicant. Thus if there is a good explanation, the applicant will be cleared. For example, should the form ask whether the applicant is seeking psychiatric help? If the answer is "Yes," the applicant can always explain the circumstances privately to the Committee, which would determine whether the problem could "impair" an ability to practice law. See Iowa Form, Question 39, and *In re Applicant*, Chapter VIII-3 *infra*. Do you like this idea? Would you feel the same way if this were an application to be a policeman carrying a gun? A nuclear plant operator? A surgeon?

Problem 35

Should reinstatement to the bar depend on contrition? What if the suspended lawyer continues to deny any guilt? See *In re Alger Hiss*, Chapter VIII-3 *infra*. What if the suspended lawyer admits to the offense but is not sorry? One of my former students turned in a client, who, in the former student's opinion, was engaged in secret, illegal acts of exceptional moral depravity. Since the acts did not fall into a category where disclosure is permitted by the rules (set out in Chapter III), he was suspended. He is not sorry. Should he be permanently excluded?

VIII-1. Introduction: The "Gatekeepers" and You

The legal profession is a gated community. Before the Civil War, Jacksonian Democrats succeeded in eliminating almost all barriers to entry in many states, but the rise of strong bar associations in the late nineteenth century restored these barriers with a vengeance. Indeed, there has always been a suspicion that the arrival in America of talented immigrants, ready to compete in the profession, contributed to the barriers.[1] There was another "concern." Women began to apply![2]

---

1. See Lawrence M. Friedman, *A History of American Law*, (2d ed., New York, 1985), pp. 633–645.

2. Myra Bradwell was turned down in her efforts to be admitted to the Illinois bar in 1869, but was eventually admitted. In California, practice of law was restricted to "any white male citizen." *Id.*, p. 639.

A. Barriers to Entry

Today, bar admission is controlled in three ways. First, with narrow exceptions, you must graduate from a three-year ABA, AALS accredited law school. Second, you must pass the bar exam. (Incidentally, that will inevitably include the professional rules of conduct, covered in this course, usually both in the state examination and through the "MPRE," the Multistate Professional Responsibility Examination.) Finally, you must be of "good character." The latter requirement usually means completing a lengthy questionnaire, of the kind included in Section VIII-3, *infra*. It may also include supplying references, "background" checks with law school deans and others, and a publication of your name in newspapers, in case there are some who would oppose you.

The professional rules do not establish these requirements. They are usually imposed by a board of bias examiners acting under the authority of the state supreme court. But the professional rules back these state requirements up. Both the ABA *Code*, DR-1-101, and the *Model Rules* 8.1 make it a professional violation to lie on a bar application form, or to fail to disclose a material fact. *Model Rule* 8.1 adds an affirmative duty, and makes failure "to disclose a fact necessary to correct a misapprehension known by the person to have arisen in the matter" a violation, except for disclosure of confidential professional information covered by *Model Rule* 1.6.

This means that if an untruth or relevant omission is discovered later, you will be subject to professional discipline, and may be suspended or disbarred. Most bar application forms are part of a public record. If you are politically active, famous, successful, or just make enemies, your application form will be looked at. If a problem exists, it could do more than just result in discipline. It could derail a confirmation hearing, or wreck a campaign.

There is no need to discuss here the issues of what should be on bar examinations, or how "tough" they should be in substance. Nor are the interesting controversies of accreditation of law schools relevant, or even whether a law graduate of an accredited school should have to take a bar examination. But "moral character" surely relates to professional ethics, particularly since so many of the professional rules must be self-enforcing.

Examine carefully the cases and bar application forms set out in Chapter VIII-3 above. What do you think should be included in determining "good moral character?" Remember, an answer that presents a "concern" does not inevitably preclude a person from admission. Rather, it will usually be referred to a "Character and Fitness" Committee, that will seek further explanation from the candidate, and others. Should psychiatric problems be included? See *In re Applicant*, 443 So. 2d 71, ret den., 443 So. 2d 77 (Fla. 1984) set out at Chapter VIII-3, *infra*. How about not paying your student loans? See *Application of Gahan*, 279 N.W. 2d 826 (Minn. 1979), set out at Chapter VIII-3, *infra*. How about use of illegal drugs? Note that some applications do not ask if you have been "indicted" or "convicted" of such illegal activity, but whether you have ever "done it." Could you take the Fifth Amendment? What should the "Character and Fitness" Committees do then? (We will discuss Fifth Amendment issues in connection with Chapter IX, *infra*). Would you take the same position with regard to a policeman who will carry a gun? The operator of a nuclear reactor?

Remember this, once a morally bad lawyer has been detected and suspended, a lot of harm will have been done. In my experience, the harm to clients and others by such a lawyer cannot be made up by malpractice actions and money damages. Lives are well and truly ruined by such people. Does this change your views about "character and fitness?"

B. Readmission and Contrition

"Admission" issues also occur on readmission of lawyers who have been disbarred. In our society, we look to punishment to deter crime. We rarely ask criminals to "say they are sorry" as a condition for release, at least once their sentence is up. But lawyers are fiduciaries with special privileges, and their clients can be very vulnerable. They are also expected to be "loyal" to our legal and constitutional system or "officers of the court." For this reason, courts look for contrition and signs of "reform" before lawyers are readmitted. But what if, like Alger Hiss, the lawyer continues to deny wrongdoing, or continues to assert that the laws violated were immoral or unconstitutional? Should we expect a lawyer to accept the "reality" of a legal ruling or conviction, even if the lawyer is innocent in fact? See *In re Alger Hiss*, 368 Mass. 447 (1975), set out at Chapter VIII-3, *infra*. Do you approve of that decision? Does it matter whether Alger Hiss really was a spy?

VIII-2. Bar Admissions: The Rules

ABA Model Rules

RULE 8.1: BAR ADMISSION AND DISCIPLINARY MATTERS

An applicant for admission to the bar, or a lawyer in connection with a bar admission application or in connection with a disciplinary matter, shall not:

(a) knowingly make a false statement of material fact; or

(b) fail to disclose a fact necessary to correct a misapprehension known by the person to have arisen in the matter, or knowingly fail to respond to a lawful demand for information from an admissions or disciplinary authority, except that this rule does not require disclosure of information otherwise protected by Rule 1.6.

Comment

[1] The duty imposed by this Rule extends to persons seeking admission to the bar as well as to lawyers. Hence, if a person makes a material false statement in connection with an application for admission, it may be the basis for subsequent disciplinary action if the person is admitted, and in any event may be relevant in a subsequent admission application. The duty imposed by this Rule applies to a lawyer's own admission or discipline as well as that of others. Thus, it is a separate professional offense for a lawyer to knowingly make a misrepresentation or omission in connection with a disciplinary investigation of the lawyer's own conduct. Paragraph (b) of this Rule also requires correction of any prior misstatement in the matter that the applicant or lawyer may have made and affirmative clarification of any misunderstanding on the part of the admissions or disciplinary authority of which the person involved becomes aware.

[2] This Rule is subject to the provisions of the fifth amendment of the United States Constitution and corresponding provisions of state constitutions. A person relying on such a provision in response to a question, however, should do so openly and not use the right of nondisclosure as a justification for failure to comply with this Rule.

[3] A lawyer representing an applicant for admission to the bar, or representing a lawyer who is the subject of a disciplinary inquiry or proceeding, is governed by the rules applicable to the client-lawyer relationship, including Rule 1.6 and, in some cases, Rule 3.3.

ABA Code

DR 1-101 Maintaining Integrity and Competence of the Legal Profession.

(A) A lawyer is subject to discipline if he has made a materially false statement in, or if he has deliberately failed to disclose a material fact requested in connection with, his application for admission to the bar.

(B) A lawyer shall not further the application for admission to the bar of another person known by him to be unqualified in respect to character, education, or other relevant attribute.

VIII-3. Bar Admissions: Cases and Materials

A. Character and Fitness

Application of Gahan
279 N.W.2d 826
Supreme Court of Minnesota
May 11, 1979
[Footnotes omitted.]

William W. Gahan, pro se.

Gislason, Dosland, Malecki, Gislason & Halvorson, C. Allen Dosland, and C. Thomas Wilson, New Ulm, for Minnesota State Board of Law Examiners.

Richard E. Klein, Director of Bar Admissions, St. Paul, for respondent.

Heard, considered, and decided by the court en banc.

TODD, Justice. William Gahan seeks admission to the bar of the State of Minnesota. After his successful completion of the bar examination, he was requested by the Board of Law Examiners to appear before them to review the circumstances surrounding the discharge in bankruptcy of certain student loans obtained by Gahan to finance his education. After formal hearing, the Board determined that Gahan did not meet the standards required of applicants for admission to practice law in Minnesota. We affirm.

The facts in this matter are not in dispute. Gahan received his law degree from the University of San Francisco, California. He was admitted to practice law in California in 1976 and subsequently was admitted to practice law in Wisconsin. Gahan is single, has never been married, and has no dependents. During the time of his education, at both the undergraduate and graduate level, Gahan required financial assistance to obtain his law degree. To achieve this goal, he obtained a series of student loans under a Federally funded guaranty program. At the time of his graduation from law school, the total amount of these loans was approximately $14,000. At the time he received the loans, Gahan agreed to repay and understood that he would be expected to repay the loans upon or shortly after graduation. Generally, student loans are amortized over a 10-year period with interest at 7 percent, and the first payment is to commence about 9 months after graduation. A monthly payment of approximately $175 would be required to repay the loans under such a repayment schedule.

In December 1976, Gahan was employed by an Oakland, California, law firm at an annual salary of $15,000. In the summer of 1977, his employer experienced financial difficulties and Gahan was not paid for 2 months, and, as a result, he terminated his employment on August 15, 1977. Shortly thereafter, he received all of his unpaid wages and expenses, except a small amount of out-of-pocket travel expenses. Gahan was unemployed until October 1977, a period of 2 months, when he obtained employment with another California law firm at an annual salary of $18,000.

Gahan claims he made some initial payments upon the loan. Subsequently, however, he defaulted. On September 27, 1977, during his period of unemployment, Gahan obtained legal counsel and filed a voluntary petition for bankruptcy in the United States District Court of the Northern District of California. Immediately prior to filing his petition for bankruptcy, Gahan mortgaged his 1959 Jaguar automobile to a friend for a loan of $2,500. He deposited $1,000 of the loan funds in an exempt account at a savings and loan institution and deposited the remaining $1,500 in an exempt account at a co-op credit union. Under California law, these deposits were the maximum amounts which could be claimed as exempt from creditors.

At the time of the filing of the bankruptcy petition, Gahan had a number of current obligations. He owed the balance on the student loans and $1,600 on a loan from the Hibernia Bank of San Francisco. These were the only debts scheduled in the bankruptcy petition. However, Gahan did disclose exempt items of $4,000, consisting of the $2,500 in the two bank deposits, the equity in the Jaguar automobile of $1,000, and $500 in household goods and wearing apparel. In addition, he disclosed the mortgage on the automobile in the amount of $2,500 and an $1,800 life insurance loan against a policy having a market value of $1,500. Gahan's bankruptcy petition showed total liabilities of $19,717.40 and $4,007 worth of assets, $4,000 of which was exempt.

After regaining employment and before his discharge in bankruptcy, Gahan reinstated his $1,600 obligation to Hibernia Bank and has paid this debt in full. He did so because he knew an officer at the bank and he believed he might need an additional loan from the bank some time in the future. Following his discharge in bankruptcy on February 7, 1978, Gahan used the balance of the $2,500 loan obtained from his friend and other funds to discharge the loan against his automobile which remained in his possession, free of encumbrances. As a result of these undertakings, the only debts actually discharged in the bankruptcy proceedings were the Federally insured student loans.

There is nothing connected with Gahan's bankruptcy to suggest that there was any fraud, deceit, or conduct which could be considered to involve moral turpitude. However, based on this evidence, the Board of Law Examiners found in part:

"XXIII.

"Procuring discharge of this indebtedness (and no other) with so little effort to repay or extend the same and with only temporary loss of employment, no exceptional financial or health problems and no major misfortunes, while neither illegal nor constituting action evincing moral turpitude, nonetheless is conduct which would cause a reasonable man to have substantial doubt concerning applicant's honesty, fairness, and respect for the rights of others and for the laws of this state and nation amounting thereby to a lack of good moral character having a rational connection with applicant's fitness or capacity to practice law.

"XXIV.

"Applicant continues to have and maintain a lack of recognition and appreciation of the underlying moral obligation and social (as opposed to legal) responsibility which arose when he was entrusted with the student loan funds in
question."

As a result of these findings, the Board found Gahan was not a person of good moral
character within the contemplation of our Rules of Admission and recommended that
he not be admitted to practice law in Minnesota. Gahan petitioned this court for review
of this recommendation.

The issue on appeal is whether, in view of the facts of this case and the applicable
Federal rights protecting those who elect to file voluntary bankruptcy, the applicant to
the Minnesota bar was properly denied admission on the grounds of insufficient moral
character.

1. Federal Bankruptcy Rights.

Initially, we observe that persons discharging their debts in bankruptcy are afforded
certain rights under Federal law. The fact of filing bankruptcy or the refusal to reinstate
obligations discharged in bankruptcy cannot be a basis for denial of admission to the
bar of the State of Minnesota. Any refusal so grounded would violate the Supremacy
Clause of the United States Constitution since applicable Federal law clearly prohibits
such a result. The leading case on this issue is Perez v. Campbell, 402 U.S. 637, 91 S.Ct.
1704, 29 L.Ed.2d 233 (1971). In that case, the Supreme Court considered the constitutionality of a state statute which precluded a person from driving if he had an unsatisfied judgment arising out of an automobile accident. In effect, a person who had such a
judgment discharged in bankruptcy could not drive unless he reaffirmed the discharged
debt. The court held the statute violated the Supremacy Clause, and overruled Kesler v.
Department of Public Safety, 369 U.S. 153, 82 S.Ct. 807, 7 L.Ed.2d 641 (1962), and Reitz
v. Mealey, 314 U.S. 33, 62 S.Ct. 24, 86 L.Ed. 21 (1941), by changing its focus from the
Purpose of the state statute to the Effect of the state statute. The court reasoned that the
effect of the statute was to coerce the person into paying a discharged debt, and that
such coercion contravened the bankruptcy act's objective of giving debtors a "'new opportunity in life and a clear field for future effort, unhampered by the pressure and dis-
couragement of pre-existing debt.'" 402 U.S. 648, 91 S.Ct. 1710, 29 L.Ed.2d 241. See,
also, Handsome v. Rutgers University, 445 F.Supp. 1362 (D.N.J.1978); Rutledge v. City of
Shreveport, 387 F.Supp. 1277 (W.D.La.1975); Matter of Loftin, 327 So.2d 543
(La.Ct.App.1976), writ denied, 331 So.2d 851 (La.1976); Grimes v. Hoschler, 12 Cal.3d
305, 115 Cal.Rptr. 625, 525 P.2d 65 (1974), certiorari denied, 420 U.S. 973, 95 S.Ct. 1364,
43 L.Ed.2d 653 (1975).

In Marshall v. District of Columbia Government, 182 U.S.App.D.C. 105, 559 F.2d 726
(1977), a Federal Circuit Court of Appeals sustained the constitutionality of a city policy
which denied an application for employment with the police force if the applicant was
an adjudicated bankrupt. The court sought to distinguish Perez, but we reject its reasoning because the effect of the policy in that case was to frustrate the purposes of the
bankruptcy act. Federal law has established the right to declare bankruptcy, and state
law may not chill the exercise of that right.

However, these constitutional limitations do not preclude a court from inquiring
into the bar applicant's responsibility or moral character in financial matters. The inquiry is impermissible only when the fact of bankruptcy is labeled "immoral" or "irre-

sponsible," and admission is denied for that reason. In other words, we cannot declare bankruptcy a wrong when Federal law has declared it a right.

Thus, in the present case, Gahan's conduct prior to bankruptcy surrounding his financial responsibility and his default on the student loans may be considered to judge his moral character. However, the fact of his bankruptcy may not be considered, nor may his present willingness or ability to pay the loans be considered because under Federal bankruptcy law, he now has a right to not pay the loans.

2. Applicant's Moral Character.

Rule II of the Rules for Admission to the bar of the State of Minnesota states in part:

"No person shall be admitted to practice law who has not established to the satisfaction of the State Board of Law Examiners:

"(2) That he is a person of good moral character;*

"* Character traits that are relevant to a determination of good moral character must have a rational connection with the applicant's present fitness or capacity to practice law, and accordingly must relate to the State's legitimate interest in protecting prospective clients and the system of justice."

A requirement of good moral character has been recognized by the Supreme Court as a constitutionally permissible condition to bar admission, provided that the Constitution is not violated in the determination of moral character. In re Stolar, 401 U.S. 23, 91 S.Ct. 713, 27 L.Ed.2d 657 (1971); Baird v. Arizona, 401 U.S. 1, 91 S.Ct. 702, 27 L.Ed.2d 639 (1971); Konigsberg v. State Bar, 353 U.S. 252, 77 S.Ct. 722, 1 L.Ed.2d 810 (1957); Schware v. Board of Bar Examiners, 353 U.S. 232, 77 S.Ct. 752, 1 L.Ed.2d 796 (1957).

The Board found that petitioner did not have good moral character because of conduct surrounding his failure to repay several student loans. No other discernible grounds for showing lack of good moral character such as fraud or dishonesty appear in the record. Consistent with the above discussion on constitutionally permissible factors, the specific question thus becomes whether petitioner showed a lack of good moral character prior to discharge in bankruptcy because he did not undertake or prepare for repayment of the student loans.

The conduct of a bar applicant in satisfying his financial obligations has been widely recognized as a relevant factor in assessing good moral character. See, In re Heller, 333 A.2d 401 (D.C.Ct.App.), certiorari denied, 423 U.S. 840, 96 S.Ct. 70, 46 L.Ed.2d 59 (1975); In re Cheek, 246 Or. 433, 425 P.2d 763 (1967). The failure of a person to honor his legal commitments adversely reflects on his ability to practice law, evincing a disregard for the rights of others. See, Matter of Connor, Ind., 358 N.E.2d 120 (1976). See, generally, Annotation, 64 A.L.R.2d 301.

The Florida court is apparently the only court to specifically consider whether a bar applicant's failure to repay his student loans demonstrates lack of good moral character so as to justify denial of admission. The Florida court has considered the issue twice, and the contrast in the cases is instructive. In the case of Florida Bd. of Bar Examiners re G. W. L., 364 So.2d 454 (Fla.1978), the applicant, G. W. L., had approximately $10,000 in student loans upon graduation from law school. As of several months before graduation, he had not obtained law-related employment. Three days before graduation, he executed a voluntary petition for bankruptcy. Approximately 7 months later, the applicant was adjudicated bankrupt and released from his debts. At approximately the same time, the applicant obtained a job as law clerk at $70 per week. He applied for admission to the Florida bar, and the Board recommended that applicant not be admitted. The Florida Supreme Court agreed with the Board, stating (364 So.2d 459):

"* * * We find that the Board had ample record evidence from which it could conclude that the principal motive of the petitioner in filing his petition for bankruptcy was to defeat creditors who had substantially funded seven years of educational training. Whether that motive was present as the debts were incurred or was formed toward the end of his law school training, the Board could fairly conclude from the petitioner's own testimony and prior behavior that he exercised his legal right to be freed of debt by bankruptcy well before the first installments on his debt became due, with absolutely no regard for his moral responsibility to his creditors. The petitioner's admittedly legal but unjustifiably precipitous action, initiated before he had obtained the results of the July bar examination, exhausted the job market, or given his creditors an opportunity to adjust repayment schedules, indicates a lack of the moral values upon which we have a right to insist for members of the legal profession in Florida. The petitioner's course of conduct in these personal affairs raises serious questions concerning the propriety of his being a counselor to others in their legal affairs, and is rationally connected to his fitness to practice law.

"To foreclose any misconstruction of this decision we must emphasize that this ruling should not be interpreted to approve any general principle concerning bankruptcies nor to hold that the securing of a discharge in bankruptcy is an act inherently requiring the denial of admission to the bar. We further do not wish this decision to be construed to hold that any comparable exercise of a clear legal right will necessarily imperil bar admission."

Three justices dissented because, even though they did not condone the applicant's actions, the applicant had a Federal right to bankruptcy and therefore the court could not constitutionally deny admission on the basis of exercising that right. The majority did not address the constitutional issue or cite the Perez case.

In the second Florida case, Florida Bd. of Bar Examiners re Groot, 365 So.2d 164 (Fla.1978), the court held that an applicant who had discharged his student loans in bankruptcy should nevertheless be admitted because the circumstances surrounding his default were justified. In distinguishing the case from Florida Bd. of Bar Examiners re G. W. L., supra, the court said (365 So.2d 168):

"Unlike G. W. L., Groot was the father and legal custodian of two children born of his recently-terminated marriage. His expenses included not only his own living costs and those of his dependents, but to some degree those of his former wife. When his personal resources became exhausted, he was forced to prevail upon family members to loan him the money, to meet current living expenses while he was without a job. Thus, unlike G. W. L., Groot had suffered unusual misfortune at the time he finally secured employment, and he had a valid present need to devote his entire employment income to his current, not past, financial responsibilities. His circumstances warranted his turning to the remedy provided by federal law for persons in just such situations, and we hold that Groot's conduct under these circumstances is not morally reprehensible or indicative of a present unfitness for admission to the bar."

In these two cases, the Florida court failed to squarely address the constitutional issue of denying employment licenses on the basis of bankruptcy. We have reservations as to whether it was constitutional for the Florida court to consider the morality of any motivations for filing bankruptcy when the Federal Government has declared the bankruptcy proceeding to be legal and presumably beneficial to the welfare of the individual and society.

Nevertheless, the Florida cases are instructive of the judicial concern over admitting to the bar those persons who disregard the rights of others and do not pay their debts even when they are reasonably able to do so. We hold that applicants who flagrantly disregard the rights of others and default on serious financial obligations, such as student loans, are lacking in good moral character if the default is neglectful, irresponsible, and cannot be excused by a compelling hardship that is reasonably beyond the control of the applicant. Such hardships might include an unusual misfortune, a catastrophe, an overriding financial obligation, or unavoidable unemployment.

We are, under the Minnesota Constitution, entrusted with the exclusive duty to assure the high moral standards of the Minnesota bar. We have no difficulty in concluding that Federal law does not preclude us from evaluating the responsibility of a bar applicant in satisfying his or her financial obligations. This is particularly true where, as here, the obligation has the significance of $14,000 in Federally insured student loans. A student loan is entrusted to a person, and is to be repaid to creditors upon graduation when and if financially able. Moreover, repayment provides stability to the student loan program and guarantees the continuance of the program for future student needs. A flagrant disregard of this repayment responsibility by the loan recipient indicates to us a lack of moral commitment to the rights of other students and particularly the rights of creditors. Such flagrant financial irresponsibility reflects adversely on an applicant's ability to manage financial matters and reflects adversely on his commitment to the rights of others, thereby reflecting adversely on his fitness for the practice of law. It is appropriate to prevent problems from such irresponsibility by denying admission, rather than seek to remedy the problem after it occurs and victimizes a client.

Applying the above principles to this case, we conclude that Gahan's failure to satisfy his obligations on the student loans cannot be excused for some compelling hardship reasonably beyond his control. During the period prior to bankruptcy, he was employed for most of the time at an annual salary of $15,000 and then $18,000. Monthly, he grossed from $1,250 to $1,500, and he accounted for monthly expenses of approximately $500. The record indicates that his monthly payments on the loans would be approximately $175. He was healthy, single, and not subject to any unusual hardship. He was reasonably able to satisfy his legal and moral obligation to prepare for repayment and continue repayment of his student loans. His failure to do so demonstrates lack of good moral character and reflects adversely on his ability to perform the duties of a lawyer.

Consistent with Gahan's Federal bankruptcy rights, we expressly state that our decision is in no way influenced by any assessment of Gahan's motivation in seeking bankruptcy. Nor are we interested in whether Gahan has any present willingness or ability to reaffirm the debts. We have based our decision solely on the circumstances surrounding Gahan's default on the student loans and the resulting failure to satisfy this important obligation. Gahan's subsequent conduct of obtaining discharge in bankruptcy and release from the default is of no concern to us.

The decision of the Board of Law Examiners to deny membership to the bar of the State of Minnesota is affirmed.

In re Applicant

443 So.2d 71

Supreme Court of Florida

Nov. 3, 1983

Rehearing Denied Jan. 25, 1984

ALDERMAN, Chief Justice. Applicant seeks review of a ruling by the Board of Bar Examiners refusing to process his application for admission to The Florida Bar until he answers item 28(b) of the applicant's questionnaire and affidavit and until he executes the authorization and release form required by the Rules of the Supreme Court Relating to Admissions to the Bar. Applicant maintains that the Board's action violates his right of privacy and his right to due process of law guaranteed by the Florida and United States Constitutions, and his rights guaranteed by section 90.503, Florida Statutes (1981), and article I, section 2 of the Florida Constitution. We find no merit to his contentions and approve the decision of the Florida Board of Bar Examiners requiring applicant to complete all portions of the questionnaire, including item 28(b), and to execute an unaltered authorization and release form before the Board will process his application for admission to The Florida Bar.

Applicant applied for admission to The Florida Bar in April 1982 by submitting application for admission form No. 1 and a modified authorization release. On his authorization release, he included a proviso that his release did not apply to his medical records. On his application, he expressly declined to answer question 28(b) on the basis that it violates his constitutional rights. In answering the questionnaire, the applicant disclosed under item 12 that he had served on active duty with the United States Marine Corps and that he had not been discharged, but rather had been transferred to a temporary retired list for medical reasons and later had been retired.

Item 28(b) asks:

> Have you ever received REGULAR treatment for amnesia, or any form of insanity, emotional disturbance, nervous or mental disorder?

> If yes, please state the names and addresses of the psychologists, psychiatrists, or other medical practitioners who treated you. (Regular treatment shall mean consultation with any such person more than two times within any 12 month period.)[1]

The authorization and release form provided by the Board in compliance with the rules of admission states:

> I, _____, having filed an application with the Florida Board of Bar Examiners and fully recognizing the responsibility to the Public, the Bench, and the Bar of this State lodged with the Florida Board of Bar Examiners by the Supreme Court of Florida under the Constitution of the State of Florida to determine that only those of high character and ability are admitted to The Bar of

---

1. By letter dated August 23, 1982, the executive director of the Board advised applicant that question 28(b) was reviewed at a recent Policy Session of the Board, and the number of visits to a psychologist, psychiatrist, or other medical practitioner was raised to four times in any twelve-month period.

Florida, hereby authorize and request every medical doctor, school official, and every other person, firm, officer, corporation, association, organization or institution having control of any documents, records or other information pertaining to me *relevant to my good moral character and fitness to perform the responsibilities of an attorney*, to furnish the originals or copies of any such documents, records and other information to said Board, or any of its representatives, and to permit said Board, or any of its representatives, to inspect and make copies of any such documents, records and other information including but not limited to any and all medical reports, laboratory reports, X-rays, or clinical abstracts which may have been made or prepared pursuant to, or in connection with, any examination or examinations, consultation or consultations, test or tests, evaluation or evaluations, of the undersigned.

I hereby authorize all such persons as set out above to answer any inquiries, questions, or interrogatories concerning the undersigned which may be submitted to them by the Florida Board of Bar Examiners or its authorized representative, and to appear before said Board, or its authorized representative, and to give full and complete testimony concerning the undersigned, including any information furnished by the undersigned. I hereby relinquish any and all rights to said reports, including but not limited to clinical abstracts, consultations, evaluations, or any other information incident in any way to cooperation with the Florida Board of Bar Examiners, or its authorized representative, and fully understand that I shall not be entitled to have disclosed to me the contents of any of the foregoing.

I hereby release and exonerate every medical doctor, school official, and every other person, firm, officer, corporation, association, organization or institution which shall comply in good faith with the authorization and request made herein from any and all liability of every nature and kind growing out of or in anywise pertaining to the furnishing or inspection of such documents, records and other information or the investigation made by said Florida Board of Bar Examiners. The undersigned further waives absolutely any privilege __ he may have *relevant to h____ good moral character and fitness to perform the responsibilities of an attorney* under Sections 90.242 and 490.32, Florida Statutes.

(Emphasis supplied.)

The executive director of the Board, on behalf of the Board, advised the applicant that processing of his application would be withheld for ten days pending receipt of an executed and unaltered authorization and release and a response to question 28(b). More correspondence between the Board and the applicant ensued for several months, concluding in the Board's decision not to process his application until he complied with the requirements of the Board.

Applicant seeks review of the Board's refusal to process his application and initially contends that to require him to answer question 28(b) and to submit an unconditional authorization and waiver violates his constitutional right of privacy under the Florida and United States Constitutions.

Article I, section 23 of the Florida Constitution provides:

Every natural person has the right to be let alone and free from governmental intrusion into his private life except as otherwise provided herein. This section shall not be construed to limit the public's right of access to public records and meetings as provided by law.

Applicant concedes and we agree that this constitutional provision was not intended to provide an absolute guarantee against all governmental intrusion into the private life of an individual.

Preliminarily, we must determine whether the requirement that applicant answer item 28(b) and execute the authorization and release falls within the governmental intrusion as contemplated by article I, section 23, and, if so, we must decide whether this intrusion violates the applicant's constitutional right of privacy. The action of the Board clearly is not within the exception proviso of article I, section 23.[2] It is just as evident that the Board's action does constitute governmental action. The exclusive jurisdiction to regulate admission of persons to the practice of law is vested in this Court. Art. V, § 15, Fla. Const. We established the Florida Board of Bar Examiners as an arm of this Court to assist us in this function.

We also find that the applicant's right of privacy is implicated by item 28(b) and the authorization and release form which allow a limited intrusion into his private life. The extent of his privacy right, however, must be considered in the context in which it is asserted and may not be considered wholly independent of those circumstances. He has chosen to seek admission into The Florida Bar. He has no constitutional right to be admitted to the Bar. Rather, the practice of law in this state is a privilege. *State ex rel. The Florida Bar v. Evans,* 94 So.2d 730 (Fla.1957). In this case, the applicant's right of privacy is circumscribed and limited by the circumstances in which he asserts that right. By making application to the Bar, he has assumed the burden of demonstrating his fitness for admission into the Bar. Fla.Sup.Ct. Bar Admiss. Rule, art. III, § 2. This encompasses mental and emotional fitness as well as character and educational fitness.

Although circumscribed and limited by the context in which it is asserted, the applicant does have a right of privacy, and we must determine whether it has been unconstitutionally intruded upon by the Board's requirements. We have not yet decided a case in which we have had to determine the appropriate standard of review in assessing a claim of unconstitutional governmental intrusion into one's privacy rights under article I, section 23. We need not make that decision in the present case since we find that the Board's action meets even the highest standard of the compelling state interest test. The compelling state interest or strict scrutiny standard imposes a heavy burden of justification upon the state to show an important societal need and the use of the least intrusive means to achieve that goal. *Carey v. Population Services International,* 431 U.S. 678, 97 S.Ct. 2010, 52 L.Ed.2d 675 (1977); *Roe v. Wade,* 410 U.S. 113, 93 S.Ct. 705, 35 L.Ed.2d 147 (1973); *In re Estate of Greenberg,* 390 So.2d 40 (Fla.1980).

Applicant concedes and we agree that the state's interest in ensuring that only those fit to practice law are admitted to the Bar is a compelling state interest. He admits that there is a legitimate need for the intrusion. His concern is not with the end sought to be achieved by the Board but is rather with the means employed by the Board to fulfill its responsibilities. He asserts that the authorization and release form and item 28(b) are unnecessarily overbroad and suggests that there should be some time limitation relative to the information sought.

That the state has a compelling state interest in regulating the legal profession has been expressly recognized by the Supreme Court of the United States. In *Goldfarb v. Virginia State Bar,* 421 U.S. 773, 95 S.Ct. 2004, 44 L.Ed.2d 572 (1975), that Court said:

---

2. The exception proviso of article I, section 23, states: "This section shall not be construed to limit the public's right of access to public records and meeting as provided by law."

[A]s part of their power to protect the public health, safety, and other valid interests [states] have broad power to establish standards for licensing practitioners and regulating the practice of professions.... The interest of the States in regulating lawyers is especially great since lawyers are essential to the primary governmental function of administering justice and have historically been "officers of the courts."

421 U.S. at 792, 95 S.Ct. at 2016.

In charging the Board with the duty to determine the character and fitness of applicants to The Florida Bar, we have required that:

> Prior to recommending an applicant for admission to practice the profession of law in Florida, the Florida Board of Bar Examiners shall conduct an investigation and otherwise inquire into and determine the character, fitness, and general qualifications of every applicant. In every such investigation and inquiry, the Board may obtain such information as bears upon the character, fitness, and general qualifications of the applicant and take and hear testimony, administer oaths and affirmations, and compel, by subpoena, the attendance of witnesses and the production of books, papers and documents. Any member of the Board may administer such oaths and affirmations. Such investigations and inquiries shall be informal, but they shall be thorough, with the object of ascertaining the truth. Technical rules of evidence need not be observed. Any investigative hearing for such purpose may be held by a division of the Board consisting of not less than three members of the Board. Each division shall record its proceedings and shall report its decisions to the full Board. Formal hearings held in response to Specifications shall be conducted before a quorum of the Board which shall consist of not less than five members.

Fla.Sup.Ct. Bar Admiss. Rule, art. III, § 3(a). It is imperative for the protection of the public that applicants to the Bar be thoroughly screened by the Board. Necessarily, the Board must ask questions in this screening process which are of a personal nature and which would not otherwise be asked of persons not applying for a position of public trust and responsibility. Because of a lawyer's constant interaction with the public, a wide range of factors must be considered which would not customarily be considered in the licensing of tradesmen and businessmen. *The Florida Bar, Petition of Rubin*, 323 So.2d 257 (Fla.1975). The inquiry into an applicant's past history of regular treatment for emotional disturbance or nervous or mental disorder requested by item 28(b) furthers the legitimate state interest since mental fitness and emotional stability are essential to the ability to practice law in a manner not injurious to the public. The pressures placed on an attorney are enormous and his mental and emotional stability should be at such a level that he is able to handle his responsibilities.

We find that the Board has employed the least intrusive means to achieve its compelling state interest. The information sought by item 28(b) is vital to the Board in evaluating an applicant's fitness. To ensure that it has all of the information necessary for its evaluation, the Board rather than the applicant must be the judge of what part of the applicant's past history is relevant.

There is no precise list of medical conditions that may affect a person's fitness to practice law and no uniformity among people who suffer from these conditions. The means employed by the Board cannot be narrowed without impinging on the Board's effectiveness in carrying out its important responsibilities. A time limitation on the information sought could preclude the Board from obtaining vitally relevant information which could impact on its decision as to an applicant's mental and emotional fitness to practice law. The fact that the information obtained in response to the Board's inquiry is held in confidence by the Board and by this Court minimizes the intrusion on an applicant's privacy. Additionally, the authorization and release form, contrary to applicant's assertion, is not a blanket release but rather is expressly limited to information *relevant* to an applicant's "good moral character and fitness to perform the responsibilities of an attorney." We hold that the Board's action does not violate article I, section 23 of the Florida Constitution.

We also hold that the Board's action does not violate applicant's federal constitutional right of privacy. In view of our disposition of this first issue, it is unnecessary for us to address, in any detail, applicant's claim that his federal constitutional privacy rights were violated. The threshold question for our analysis of that claim would be to determine which zone of privacy applicant's asserted privacy rights fell within. *Paul v. Davis,* 424 U.S. 693, 96 S.Ct. 1155, 47 L.Ed.2d 405 (1976). If we were to conclude they fell within the decision-making or autonomy zone of privacy interests we would be required to apply the compelling state interest test. The privacy interests encompassed within this zone of privacy are only those which are fundamental or implicit in the concept of ordered liberty. *Roe v. Wade,* 410 U.S. 113, 93 S.Ct. 705, 35 L.Ed.2d 147 (1973). These are matters relating to marriage, procreation, contraception, family relationships and child rearing, and education. *Paul v. Davis; Shevin v. Byron, Harless, Schaffer, Reid and Associates, Inc.,* 379 So.2d 633 (Fla.1980). The other privacy interests described by the Supreme Court of the United States in *Whalen v. Roe,* 429 U.S. 589, 97 S.Ct. 869, 51 L.Ed.2d 64 (1976), and *Nixon v. Administrator of General Services,* 433 U.S. 425, 97 S.Ct. 2777, 53 L.Ed.2d 867 (1977), involve one's interests in avoiding public disclosure of personal matters. In this area, a balancing test has been held to be the appropriate standard of review-comparing the interests served with the interests hindered. *See Plante v. Gonzalez,* 575 F.2d 1119 (5th Cir.1978).

Even applying the highest standard of review, we have already decided that the Board has demonstrated a compelling state interest and use of the least intrusive means to achieve that interest.

We likewise find no merit to applicant's claim that the Board's challenged action violates his right to due process of law or that it violates his rights guaranteed by article I, section 2 of the Florida Constitution, which provides in pertinent part that no person shall be deprived of any right because of physical handicap.

* * *

In response to applicant's reliance on the psychotherapist-patient privilege, we once again point out that it is applicant himself who placed his mental and emotional fitness as well as his moral and educational fitness in issue when he filed his applicant's questionnaire and affidavit, a preliminary step in seeking admission to practice law in Florida. Under section 90.503(4)(c), there is no privilege "[f]or communications relevant to an issue of the mental or emotional condition of the patient in any proceeding in which he relies upon the condition as an element of his claim or defense."

Accordingly, we approve the ruling of the Florida Board of Bar Examiners requiring applicant to answer item 28(b) and to file an unaltered authorization and release form. Until that time, the Board is fully warranted in not processing his application.

It is so ordered.

BOYD, OVERTON, McDONALD, EHRLICH and SHAW, JJ., concur.

ADKINS, J., dissents with an opinion.

ADKINS, Justice, dissenting.

As to the petitioner's claim predicated on the Florida Constitution, I agree with the majority that the state's interest in ensuring that only those fit to practice law are admitted to The Florida Bar is a compelling state interest. However, I must agree with the petitioner's assertion that the authorization and release form and item 28(b) are unnecessarily overbroad. I also agree with the majority's conclusion that mental fitness and emotional stability are essential to the ability to practice law in a manner not injurious to the public. However, I do not agree with the assertion that the means employed by the Board cannot be narrowed without impinging on the Board's effectiveness in carrying out its responsibilities. As petitioner argues, it is difficult to conceive of information in which an individual has a greater legitimate expectation of privacy than medical records containing communications and other information between an applicant and a psychiatrist, psychologist, or counselor. Accordingly, information which is irrelevant to an applicant's ability to practice law in this state should not come within the scope of the Board's inquiry. An applicant's past treatment for some emotional disturbance, such as loss of a parent for instance, or treatment for amnesia which occurred, say, as a child ten or fifteen years ago surely is not relevant to the potential of that applicant to be a fit and worthy member of The Florida Bar today. At a minimum I feel there must be some time frame incorporated in question 28(b) and the authorization of the release of medical records relating to treatment for emotional disturbances, etc. In addition, I feel the form of the question seeking information about regular treatment for emotional disturbances, etc., could be phrased in terms which elicit information with regard to problems which, in the judgment of the medical community, impact on one's fitness to practice law. Such an approach would be consistent with the mandate of article I, section 23 of the Florida Constitution.

For these same reasons, I would hold that the Board's action also violates the applicant's federal constitutional right of privacy. I do not believe the least intrusive means have been employed and, if a balancing test were held to be the appropriate standard, the interests served by the question as it exists do not outweigh the privacy interests of the individual hindered.

In re Hale
723 N.E.2d 206 (Ill. 1999)
Writ of Certiorari denied, 530 U.S. 1261 (2000)
Supreme Court of Illinois
Nov. 17, 1999

Justice Heiple dissents from the order of the Court of November 12, 1999, denying the petition of Matthew F. Hale, pursuant to Supreme Court Rule 708(d), requesting a full review by the Illinois Supreme Court of the findings and conclusions of the Character and Fitness Committee dated June 30, 1999, and a request for oral argument.

Justice HEIPLE, dissenting:

Petitioner Matthew F. Hale applied for admission to practice law in Illinois. The Committee on Character and Fitness concluded that his application should be denied. Petitioner now asks this court to review the Committee's decision. Thus, the question before the court at this juncture is not whether petitioner should be licensed to practice law. The question, rather, is whether the Supreme Court should consider his appeal. Because the petition raises questions of constitutional significance that should be resolved openly by this court, I dissent from the majority's refusal to hear this case.

The crux of the Committee's decision to deny petitioner's application to practice law is petitioner's open advocacy of racially obnoxious beliefs. The Hearing Panel found that petitioner's "publicly displayed views are diametrically opposed to the letter and spirit" of the Rules of Professional Conduct. The Inquiry Panel found that, in regulating the conduct of attorneys, certain "fundamental truths" of equality and nondiscrimination "must be preferred over the values found in the First Amendment." Petitioner contends that the Committee's use of his expressed views to justify the denial of his admission to the bar violates his constitutional rights to free speech. That constitutional question deserves explicit, reasoned resolution by this court. Instead, the court silently accepts the conclusion of the Committee, which asserted that "[t]his case is not about Mr. Hale's First Amendment rights." To the contrary, this case clearly impacts both the first amendment to the federal Constitution and article I, section 4, of the Illinois Constitution.

In addition, the Committee's ruling on petitioner's application presents a second important issue which this court should address. The Committee seems to hold that it may deny petitioner's application for admission to the bar without finding that petitioner has engaged in any specific conduct that would have violated a disciplinary rule if petitioner were already a lawyer. The Committee merely speculates that petitioner is "on a collision course with the Rules of Professional Conduct" and that, if admitted, he will *in the future* "find himself before the Attorney Registration and Disciplinary Commission." I believe this court should address whether it is appropriate for the Committee to base its assessment of an applicant's character and fitness on speculative predictions of future actionable misconduct.

The question also arises: If all of petitioner's statements identified by the Committee had been made after obtaining a license to practice law, would he then be subject to disbarment? That is to say, is there one standard for admission to practice and a different standard for continuing to practice? And, if the standard is the same, can already-licensed lawyers be disbarred for obnoxious speech?

The Illinois Supreme Court is the licensing authority for all Illinois lawyers. Its rules cover all aspects of admission to the bar and professional conduct thereafter. It has the power to license, regulate, and to disbar. The issues presented by Mr. Hale's petition are of such significant constitutional magnitude that they deserve a judicial review and determination by this court.

For the reasons given, I respectfully dissent from the denial of the petition for review.

B. Contrition

In re Alger Hiss

368 Mass. 447
Supreme Judicial Court of Massachusetts, Suffolk
Argued May 9, 1975
Decided Aug. 5, 1975
[Some footnotes omitted. Remaining footnotes renumbered.]

Before TAURO, C.J., and REARDON, QUIRICO, BRAUCHER, HENNESSEY, KAPLAN and WILKINS, JJ.

TAURO, Chief Justice.

Alger Hiss was struck from the roll of Massachusetts lawyers on August 1, 1952, and now seeks reinstatement. The facts as disclosed by the record before us are as follows. On January 25, 1950, Alger Hiss was convicted of two counts of perjury in his testimony before a Federal grand jury. A previous trial had resulted in a jury disagreement, and a mistrial had been declared. In particular Hiss was found to have testified falsely (1) that he had never, nor had his wife in his presence, turned over documents or copies of documents of the United States Department of State or of any other organization of the Federal government to one Whittaker Chambers or to any other unauthorized person and (2) that he thought he could say definitely that he had not seen Chambers after January 1, 1937. Chambers was the principal witness against Hiss and had been his principal accuser during hearings held prior to the grand jury investigation by the Committee on Un-American Activities of the House of Representatives.[1] After Hiss had exhausted his rights of appeal (*United States v. Hiss*, 185 F.2d 822 (2d Cir. 1950), cert. den. 340 U.S. 948, 71 S.Ct. 532, 95 L.Ed. 683 (1951); *see also United States v. Hiss*, 107 F.Supp. 128 (S.D.N.Y.1952), affd. per curiam, 201 F.2d 372 (2d Cir. 1953), cert. den. 345 U.S. 942, 73 S.Ct. 830, 97 L.Ed. 1368 (1953) (motion for a new trial)), he was committed to the United States penitentiary at Lewisburg, Pennsylvania, where he served some three and one-half years.

Following affirmance of the conviction, the Boston Bar Association filed an information with this court, setting forth the circumstances and a prayer for "such action as the Court may deem fit." The matter was duly set down for hearing before a single justice of this court, but, though given due notice of the hearing, Hiss, on the advice of counsel, failed to enter an appearance. On November 2, 1951, the single justice ordered Hiss defaulted and found the bar association's allegations to be true. On August 1, 1952, after arguments by counsel, judgment was entered by the single justice removing Hiss "from the office of Attorney-at-Law in the Courts of this Commonwealth."

On November 4, 1974, for the first time, Hiss, then age sixty-nine, filed a petition for reinstatement as an attorney and an accompanying affidavit which detailed his activities since his release from prison. The matter was referred to the Board of Bar Overseers (the board) pursuant to S.J.C. Rule 4:01, § 18(4), [365] Mass. [712] (1974). The board mem-

---

1. A more detailed history of events surrounding the trial and conviction may be found in *United States v. Hiss*, 185 F.2d 822 (2d Cir. 1950), cert. den. 340 U.S. 948, 71 S.Ct. 532, 95 L.Ed. 683 (1951).

bers[2] heard evidence and filed a report, consisting of findings and recommendations for disposition. The matter is before us now on reservation and report without decision of the single justice. Three fundamental questions are presented for our determination: (1) Were the crimes of which Hiss was convicted and for which he was disbarred so serious in nature that he is forever precluded from seeking reinstatement? (2) Are statements of repentance and recognition of guilt necessary prerequisites to reinstatement? (3) Has Hiss demonstrated his fitness to practice law in the Commonwealth?

1. At the outset, we stress that we are not here concerned with a review of the criminal case in which Hiss was tried, convicted and sentenced.[3] In his trial, he received the full measure of due process rights and opportunities to contest allegations of guilt: a trial before a jury of his peers supplemented by ample avenues of appeal. Basic respect for the integrity and finality of a prior unreversed criminal judgment demands that it be conclusive on the issue of guilt and that an attorney not be permitted to retry the result at a much later date in his reinstatement proceedings. Cf. *In the Matter of Braverman*, 271 Md. 196, 316 A.2d 246 (1974). Hiss does not contend otherwise. While, in some civil proceedings, we permit retrial of factual issues adjudicated previously in criminal cases (see, e.g., *Silva v. Silva*, 297 Mass. 217, 218, 7 N.E.2d 601 (1937)), "[s]omething different is involved ... [here].... A member of the bar whose name remains on the roll is in a sense held out by the Commonwealth, through the judicial department, as still entitled to confidence. A conviction of crime, especially of serious crime, undermines public confidence in him. The average citizen would find it incongruous for the ... [Federal government] on the one hand to adjudicate him guilty and deserving of punishment, and then, on the other hand, while his conviction and liability to punishment still stand [for the Commonwealth] to adjudicate him innocent and entitled to retain his membership in the bar." *Matter of Welansky*, 319 Mass. 205, 208–209, 65 N.E.2d 202, 204 (1946).[4] Accord, American Bar Association Special Committee on Evaluation of Disciplinary Enforcement, Problems and Recommendations in Disciplinary Enforcement, 131 (Final Draft 1970).[5] Thus, Hiss comes before us now as a convicted perjurer, whose crime, a direct and reprehensible attack on the foundations of our judicial system, is further tainted by the breach of confidence and trust which underlay his conviction. His conviction and subsequent disbarment are "conclusive evidence of his lack of moral character *at the time of his removal from office*" (emphasis supplied). *Matter of Keenan*, 313 Mass. 186, 219, 47 N.E.2d 12, 32 (1943).

2. Nevertheless, the serious nature of the crime and the conclusive evidence of past unfitness to serve as an attorney do not *necessarily* disqualify Hiss at the present time. We cannot subscribe to the arguments advanced by the chief Bar Counsel (Bar Counsel)[6] that, because the offenses committed by Hiss are so serious, they forever bar rein-

---

2. Pursuant to S.J.C. Rule 4:01, § 18(4), the board could have referred the matter to a hearing committee, but the members chose to hear the evidence themselves.

3. Hiss seeks reinstatement and not vindication.

4. In *Welansky*, we were concerned with retrial of criminal convictions in disbarment proceedings. The result follows a fortiori in reinstatement proceedings.

5. This special committee report addressed the problem of "[n]o provision making conviction of crime conclusive evidence of guilt for purposes of the disciplinary proceeding based on the conviction."

6. The Bar Counsel and assistants are appointed by the board with the approval of this court pursuant to S.J.C. Rule 4:01, § 5(3)(b), [365] Mass. [712] (1974). The Bar Counsel is charged with the responsibility of "[investigating] all matters involving alleged misconduct by an attorney" and

statement[7] irrespective of good conduct or reform.[8] Though in previous cases we intimated by way of dicta that there may be "offenses so serious that the attorney committing them can never again satisfy the court that he has become trustworthy" (*Matter of Keenan*, 314 Mass. 544, 548–549, 50 N.E.2d 785, 788 [1943]; see, e.g., *Matter of Keenan*, 313 Mass. 186, 219, 47 N.E.2d 12 [1943]; *Centracchio, petitioner*, 345 Mass. 342, 346–347, 187 N.E.2d 383 [1963]), we cannot now say that any offense is so grave that a disbarred attorney is automatically precluded from attempting to demonstrate through ample and adequate proofs, drawn from conduct and social interactions, that he has achieved a "present fitness" (*In re Kone*, 90 Conn. 440, 442, 97 A. 307 [1916]) to serve as an attorney and has led a sufficiently exemplary life to inspire public confidence once again, in spite of his previous actions.[9]

Disbarment is not a permanent punishment imposed on delinquent attorneys as a supplement to the sanctions of the criminal law — "though it may have that practical effect. Its purpose is to exclude from the office of an attorney in the courts, for the preservation of the purity of the courts and the protection of the public, one who has demonstrated that he is not a proper person to hold such office." *Keenan, petitioner*, 310 Mass. 166, 169, 37 N.E.2d 516, 519 (1941). Accord, *Bar Assn. of the City of Boston v. Greenhood*, 168 Mass. 169, 183, 46 N.E. 568, 575 (1897) ("protection of the public from attorneys who disregard their oath of office"); *Bar Assn. of the City of Boston v. Casey*, 211 Mass. 187, 192, 97 N.E. 751 (1912); *Matter of Keenan*, 314 Mass. 544, 546–547, 50 N.E.2d 785 (1943). The position of the Bar Counsel presupposes that certain disbarred attorneys,

---

"[prosecuting] all disciplinary proceedings before hearing committees, the [b]oard and this court." S.J.C. Rule 4:01, § 7(1), (3), [365] Mass. [712] (1974). The rules of this court provide that "at hearings conducted with respect to motions for reinstatement" the Bar Counsel "shall appear ... with full rights to participate as a party." S.J.C. Rule 4:01, § 7(4), [365] Mass. [712] (1974).

7. Some aspects of the board's findings and recommendations may be read to embrace this position: "With Mr. Hiss's conviction outstanding, unreversed, not subject to attack, and necessary for us to consider, all the other evidence of his present character cannot be of any weight." However, the context and remainder of the board's report make clear that the board does not subscribe to the full measure of its counsel's position.

8. In view of what we say in the opinion, we need not consider or decide whether such a ruling would amount to a *conclusive* presumption frowned on by many courts. Compare *Vlandis v. Kline*, 412 U.S. 441, 446, 93 S.Ct. 2230, 37 L.Ed.2d 63 (1973), *Leary v. United States*, 395 U.S. 6, 89 S.Ct. 1532, 23 L.Ed.2d 57 (1969), and *Barnes v. United States*, 412 U.S. 837, 93 S.Ct. 2357, 37 L.Ed.2d 380 (1973), *with Weinberger v. Salfi*, 422 U.S. 749, 95 S.Ct. 2457, 45 L.Ed.2d 522 (1975).

9. Other jurisdictions appear split on whether conviction for particularly heinous crimes will necessarily result in permanent disbarment. See generally American Bar Association Special Committee on Evaluation of Disciplinary Enforcement, Problems and Recommendations in Disciplinary Enforcement, 150 (Final Draft 1970); anno. 70 A.L.R.2d 268, 276–279 (1960). A number of States permit reinstatement on a showing of rehabilitation despite conviction for serious crimes involving moral turpitude or breaches of trust. See, e.g., *Allen v. State Bar of Cal.*, 58 Cal.2d 912, 26 Cal.Rptr. 771, 376 P.2d 835 (1962) (perjury); *In re May*, 249 S.W.2d 798 (Ky.Ct.App.1952) ("not forever ... beyond the pale of respectability"). *In re Taylor*, 330 S.W.2d 393 (Ky.Ct.App.,1959) (fraud on the court); *Ex Parte Marshall*, 165 Mass. 523, 147 So. 791 (1933) (blackmail). Cf. *March v. Committee of Bar Examiners.*, 67 Cal.2d 718, 63 Cal.Rptr. 399, 433 P.2d 191 (1967) (first admission to bar; no conviction but false testimony before Congressional committee); *Williams v. Governors of the Fla. Bar.* 173 So.2d 686 (Fla.1965) reinstatement considered and denied; conspiracy to thwart prosecution); *In re Sympson*, 322 S.W.2d 808 (Mo.1959) (criminal contempt for suborning perjury; not reinstated). Other States make conviction of certain serious crimes a ground for permanent disbarment. See, e.g., *People v. Buckles*, 167 Colo. 64, 453 P.2d 404 (1969) (statute); *In the Matter of Bennethum*, 278 A.2d 831, 833 (Del.1971); *People ex rel. Chicago Bar Assn. v. Reed*, 341 Ill. 573, 577, 173 N.E. 772 (1930); *In re Application of Van Wyck*, 225 Minn. 90, 29 N.E.2d 654 (1947); Tenn.Code Anno. § 29-310 (1955 and Supp.1974) (cf. *Cantor v. Grievance Comms.*, 189 Tenn. 536, 226 S.W.2d 283 (1949)).

guilty of particularly heinous offenses against the judicial system, are incapable of meaningful reform which would qualify them to be attorneys and, further, that the public will never be willing to revise an earlier opinion that the offender was not a proper person to function as an attorney. If adopted the rule would provide that "no matter what a disbarred attorney's subsequent conduct may be; no matter how hard and successfully he has tried to live down his past and stone for his offense; no matter how complete his reformation—the door to restoration is forever sealed against him." *In re Stump*, 272 Ky. 593, 597–598, 114 S.W.2d 1094, 1097 (1938). Such a harsh, unforgiving position is foreign to our system of reasonable, merciful justice. It denies any potentiality for reform of character. A fundamental precept of our system (particularly our correctional system is that men can be rehabilitated. "Rehabilitation ... is a 'state of mind' and the law looks with favor upon rewarding with the opportunity to serve, one who has achieved 'reformation and regeneration.'" *March v. Committee of Bar Examrs.*, 67 Cal.2d 718, 732, 63 Cal.Rptr. 399, 408, 433 P.2d 191, 200 (1967). Time and experience may mend flaws of character which allowed the immature man to err. The chastening effect of a severe sanction such as disbarment may redirect the energies and reform the values of even the mature miscreant. There is always the potentiality for reform, and fundamental fairness demands that the disbarred attorney have opportunity to adduce proofs.

The public welfare, "the true test" in all proceedings for reinstatement (*Matter of Keenan*, 314 Mass. 544, 547, 50 N.E.2d 785 (1943)), calls for no different result. There can be no harm in permitting any disbarred attorney to adduce proofs of his changed character. Certainly, the proceeding itself poses no threat to the public interest. It does not guarantee readmission. Before he again will be entered on the rolls as an attorney eligible to practice, the disbarred attorney who has committed the grave offenses to which the Bar Counsel directs attention must bear a heavy burden of proof (see, *infra*, at 438) and pass the close scrutiny to which reviewing courts subject petitions for reinstatement. Indeed, the proceeding may ultimately redound to the public benefit, for the attorney who can attain reinstatement in such a proceeding after having committed a grave offense could become a credit of the bar and an asset to those he serves.

3. In assessing Hiss's fitness for reinstatement to the bar, the Board of Bar Overseers considered itself bound by our decision in *Matter of Keenan*, 314 Mass. 544, 50 N.E.2d 785 (1943), to require admission of guilt and repentance as part of the proof of Hiss's present good moral character and rehabilitation. Accordingly, because Hiss continues to insist on his innocence, the board recommended that his petition for reinstatement be denied. The board wrote: "When the disbarment is wholly based upon the conviction of the petitioner of an offense which is clearly a 'serious crime' (perjury), which conviction has not been reversed, and the petitioner has not been pardoned, the task of a petitioner such as Mr. Hiss, who continues to assert his innocence, to satisfy this Board of his present good character, becomes logically impossible for him to meet under the law, as the Board conceives the law to be.... [S]o long as Mr. Hiss's conviction stands, and so long as he continues to deny his guilt of an offense of which he was convicted, after what was ruled to be a fair trial, the Board finds, *under the decisions by which it is bound*, that the petitioner has not satisfied us that his readmission would not be detrimental to the standing of the Bar, the administration of justice or to the public interest" (emphasis supplied).

Neither the controlling case law nor the legal standard for reinstatement to the bar requires that one who petitions for reinstatement must proclaim his repentance and affirm his adjudicated guilt. *Matter of Keenan*, 314 Mass. 544, 50 N.E.2d 785 (1943), cited by the board as dispositive, does not hold that repentance and admission of guilt are mandatory. In *Keenan, supra*, we considered a variety of factors relevant to reinstatement; repentance was but one of them. After a full review of the evidence presented, we concluded that "in view of all the factors which must be taken into account" (*id.* at 550, 50 N.E.2d at 788), Keenan should not be reinstated. The evidence held "forth no certainty that ... [the petitioner] would not again fall a victim to the same weakness that was his first undoing." *Ibid.* Particular emphasis was placed on the "unusual history and background" (*id.* at 547, 50 N.E.2d 785) of the case—the sweeping public investigation into abuses and unprofessional conduct of the tort bar—and on the precedent that the case would be for similar petitions by others exposed in the same investigation. The failure of Keenan to admit guilt or repent[10] did not, any more than the other factors considered, determine the outcome. *Centracchio, petitioner*, 345 Mass. 342, 187 N.E.2d 383 (1963), the other case from this jurisdiction cited by the board, contains no explicit holding with respect to repentance. In fact, the petitioner was denied reinstatement though, through his conduct, he had given evidence of repentance.

The legal standard for reinstatement to the bar is set forth in S.J.C. Rule 4:01, § 18 (4), [365] Mass. [712] (1974). There is no mention of repentance as a prerequisite to admission: "The respondent-attorney ... shall have the burden of demonstrating that he has the moral qualifications, competency and learning in law required for admission to practice law in this Commonwealth, and that his resumption of the practice of law will not be detrimental to the integrity and standing of the bar, the administration of justice, or to the public interest." In proceedings on petitions for reinstatement, we must ascertain that the prospective members of the bar are presently "trustworthy" (see *Bar Assn. of the City of Boston v. Greenhood*, 168 Mass. 169, 183, 46 N.E. 568 (1897); *Keenan, petitioner*, 310 Mass. 166, 168, 37 N.E.2d 516 (1941); *Kepler v. State Bar of Cal.*, 216 Cal. 52, 55, 13 P.2d 509 (1932); *In re Application of Smith*, 220 Minn. 197, 200, 19 N.W.2d 324 [1945]) and upright of character, not that they are willing to admit past mistakes. Statements of guilt and repentance may be desirable as evidence that the disbarred attorney recognizes his past wrongdoing and will attempt to avoid repetition in the future. However, to satisfy the requirements of present good moral character in the tests for reinstatement noted above, it is sufficient[11] that the petitioner adduce substantial proof that he has "such an appreciation of the distinctions between right and wrong in the conduct of men toward each other as will make him a fit and safe person to engage in the practice of law." *In re Koenig*, 152 Conn. 125, 132, 204 A.2d 33, 36 (1964). See *In re Stump*, 272 Ky. 593, 598–599, 114 S.W.2d 1094 (1938). Such an appreciation, if deeply felt and strongly anchored, will serve as a firm foundation and justification for the order of reinstatement. Mere words of repentance are easily uttered and just as easily forgotten.

The continued assertion of innocence in the face of prior conviction does not, as might be argued, constitute *conclusive* proof of lack of the necessary moral character to

---

10. Note also that the court wrote that "[t]here was little evidence of repentance or reform" (emphasis supplied). *Matter of Keenan*, 314 Mass. at 550, 50 N.E.2d at 788 (1943). Ample evidence of character reform would have been sufficient, in and of itself, to support reinstatement (though repentance alone would not have been).

11. A number of jurisdictions do not require an avowal of repentance as a prerequisite to reinstatement. See, e.g., *In re Barton*, 273 Md. 377, 382, 329 A.2d 102 (1974); *Ex Parte Marshall*, 165 Mass. 523, 551–552, 147 So. 791 (1933); *In re Eddleman*, 77 Wash.2d 42, 45, n. 1, 459 P.2d 387 (1969). But cf. *In the Matter of Bennethum*, 278 A.2d 831, 833 (Del.1971); *In re Application of Smith*, 220 Minn. 197, 202, 19 N.W.2d 324 (1945).

merit reinstatement.[12] Though we deem prior judgments dispositive of all factual issues and deny attorneys subject to disciplinary proceedings the right to relitigate issues of guilt, we recognize that a convicted person may on sincere reasoning believe himself to be innocent. We also take cognizance of Hiss's argument[13] that miscarriages of justice are possible. Basically, his underlying theory is that innocent men conceivably could be convicted, that a contrary view would place a mantle of absolute and inviolate perfection on our system of justice, and that this is an attribute that cannot be claimed for any human institution or activity. We do not believe we can say with certainty in this case, or perhaps any case, what is the true state of mind of the petitioner. Thus, we cannot say that every person who, under oath, protests his innocence after conviction and refuses to repent is committing perjury.

Simple fairness and fundamental justice demand that the person who believes he is innocent though convicted should not be required to confess guilt to a criminal *act* he honestly believes he did not commit. For him, a rule requiring admission of guilt and repentance creates a cruel quandary: he may stand mute and lose his opportunity; or he may cast aside his hard-retained scruples and, paradoxically, commit what he regards as perjury to prove his worthiness to practice law. Men who are honest would prefer to relinquish the opportunity conditioned by this rule: "Circumstances may be made to bring innocence under the penalties of the law. If so brought, escape by confession of guilt ... may be rejected,—preferring to be the victim of the law rather than its acknowledged transgressor—preferring death even to such certain infamy."[14] *Burdick v. United States*, 236 U.S. 79, 90–91, 35 S.Ct. 267, 269, 59 L.Ed. 476 (1915). Honest men would suffer permanent disbarment under such a rule. Others, less sure of their moral positions, would be tempted to commit perjury by admitting to a nonexistent offense (or to an offense they believe is nonexistent) to secure reinstatement. So regarded, this rule, intended to maintain the integrity of the bar, would encourage corruption in these latter petitioners for reinstatement and, again paradoxically, might permit reinstatement of those least fit to serve. We do not consider in this context the person who admits committing the alleged criminal act but honestly believes it is not unlawful.

Accordingly, we refuse to disqualify a petitioner for reinstatement *solely* because he continues to protest his innocence of the crime of which he was convicted. Repentance[15] or lack of repentance is evidence, like any other, to be considered in the evaluation of a petitioner's character and of the likely repercussions of his requested reinstatement.

---

12. The contrary position seems to have been adopted by the board: "Strict application of logical principles might, in fact, lead to the conclusion that the petitioner gives evidence of his present lack of moral character when he again testifies to his innocence of the original charge, in the face of a conviction which this Board, for purposes of its deliberations, must accept as establishing the fact of his guilt."

13. The Bar Counsel in his brief agrees that repentance and admission of guilt should not be conditions of reinstatement: "While an adjudication of guilt must stand as a determination of that fact, legally and judicially, binding upon the accused and all the world, all that is or can be demanded of the accused is that he shall accord full respect to and acquiescence in that finding and judgment. *It cannot be demanded that he deny his own conscience or his own knowledge, and that he assert a guilt which for him does not exist.* The *Keenan* case does not make such a demand. Repentance is only one of many factors that may be considered" (emphasis supplied). The Boston Bar Association in its amicus brief took a similar position.

14. The quotation refers to confession of guilt through acceptance of a pardon.

15. Different principles may apply to cases in which the delinquent attorney should make restitution of misappropriated funds. We do not here decide what effect failure to make restitution should have on a petition for restatement.

However, nothing we have said here should be construed as detracting one iota from the fact that in considering Hiss's petition we consider him to be guilty as charged. Our discussion relates only to the issue whether Hiss must admit his guilt as condition to reinstatement.

* * *

Considerable time (approximately twenty-three years) has elapsed since the original disbarment of Hiss. His activities since his disbarment reflect the efforts of a man who wished to abide by the court's decree of disbarment and to earn a living in other fields of endeavor while he maintained the scholarly interests he had held prior to his disbarment. In the interval between his disbarment and the present, he has scrupulously refrained from the practice of law. He has not been convicted of any crime[16] and has not been implicated in any activities which contained the slightest hint of dishonesty or moral turpitude. As the board found on ample evidence, "he has courageously and industriously set himself to earn an honest living and to support his family, without bewailing the financial loss caused by his conviction and disbarment."[17] He has pursued his scholarly interests through a program of diverse lectures and the publication of articles and books. In his lectures, delivered at a wide variety of colleges, universities and other public forums, in this country and abroad, he has generally avoided the subject of his personal tribulations in order to concentrate on subjects relating to the United Nations and American foreign policy. He has written two books and has contributed a number of book reviews to periodicals. At the request of the late Professor Mark De-Wolfe Howe of Harvard Law School, he edited the abridged edition of the Holmes-Laski letters.

The evidence regarding character supplied by Hiss's gainful employment in the business world is uniformly good. From 1956 to 1959, he was the assistant to the president of a small manufacturing concern, presumably a position of confidence. His employment was terminated by the financial difficulties suffered by his employer. After a brief period of unemployment, he obtained his current job as a salesman of stationery supplies and printing. The board found that "he has earned an excellent business reputation both for industry and honesty in this occupation." A representative of the company which employs Hiss testified that he had achieved a very close relationship with his customers and that they insisted that he alone service their accounts. She testified further that "[I]n the preparation of his billing"[18] he had "always been very, very fair and equitable and [had] never taken himself into consideration." Specifically, he had not availed himself of a bonus system through which he could have expanded his own commissions by charging a higher markup on sales. As additional proof of the high regard in which Hiss is held by his business colleagues there is in evidence a letter from the president of the corporation which is his employer's controlling stockholder. The president writes that in the event Hiss were to be become a member of the Massachusetts bar, the firm "would be glad" to engage Hiss as a legal consultant to explore the legal requirements for doing business in Massachusetts.

---

16. To be precise, he was once fined $5 for playing baseball with his son in Washington Square Park.

17. Because of restrictions on his activities, his earnings over the years have been quite modest. Since 1966, Hiss's yearly earnings from his job as a salesman have not exceeded $14,100 and have averaged only about $10,400.

18. The witness had worked with Hiss in the billing and credit aspects of the business.

At the hearing before the board, a number of talented and eminent attorneys came forward to attest to Hiss's good character.[19] Others, including a retired Justice of the United States Supreme Court and a former Solicitor General of the United States, submitted complimentary affidavits and letters.[20] We[21] have had to discount a part of this evidence because some of those giving evidence did not accept Hiss's guilt of the crime for which he had been disbarred and, thus, spoke of his good character without distinguishing the period before his conviction and disbarment from that which succeeded it.[22] See *Matter of Keenan*, 314 Mass. 544, 550, 50 N.E.2d 785 (1943).

However, several witnesses provided solid evidence of fitness for reinstatement. Professor Victor Brudney of the Harvard Law School met Hiss after his release from prison and has had regular social contacts with Hiss throughout the years. In the course of their acquaintanceship, Professor Brudney testified, they have had numerous conversations on law and law-related subjects. In those conversations, Professor Brudney found Hiss to be quite competent ("a first-rate mind") in dealing with legal problems and aware of trends and events in the law. According to Professor Brudney, "the attitudes ... [Hiss] revealed in discussion disclosed a perception and a sensitivity for the interests of others in controversial situations." Hiss was candid and direct in his dealings with people, and Professor Brudney said that he would "feel comfortable" if he received the first draft of a contract from Hiss if Hiss were acting for the other side. When asked if he would consult and confide in Hiss as a lawyer, Professor Brudney's response was enthusiastic and affirmative. Of a similar tenor was the testimony of Professor Richard Field, also of the Harvard Law School faculty. Professor Field, a noted scholar and pedagogue, currently teaches a course in "professional responsibility." His contacts with Hiss subsequent to the perjury convictions appear to have been less frequent than those of Professor Brudney, but were sufficiently numerous to provide ample basis for judgment. Professor Field testified that Hiss had retained his "deep interest" in the law and that, from their discussions, it was manifest that Hiss had "kept himself well abreast of developments" in the field of international law, his specialty. Professor Field stated further that he would have no hesitancy in employing Hiss as a legal consultant in the areas of Hiss's specialty.[23]

---

19. No witnesses came forward to oppose reinstatement. When duly notified, the Attorney General of the United States indicated that he did not "wish to be heard or to be represented at the hearing." Similar communications were received from the Massachusetts Bar Association, the Committee on Grievances of the Association of the Bar of the City of New York and the clerk of the United States Supreme Court. The prosecutor of the Hiss perjury case, the Honorable Thomas F. Murphy, did not respond to the communication of the board's counsel.

20. Erwin N. Griswold (former Solicitor General of the United States and Dean of the Harvard Law School), Eli Whitney Debevoise, Benjamin V. Cohen, Charles A. Horsky and Joseph A. Fanelli, submitted sworn affidavits recommending reinstatement. Mr. Justice Stanley Reed submitted a letter to the same effect.

21. The board did as well.

22. As noted above, some of the witnesses based their recommendations for Hiss's reinstatement on the belief that Hiss was innocent. It is true that the petitioner's record prior to the incident in question was outstanding and without blemish and that his life for the past two decades since his release from prison has been impeccable. It is equally true that nothing in the record corroborates in any way the fact of guilt and, further, that the Department of Justice, although invited, has declined to appear in these proceedings. Nonetheless, we emphasize that whether Hiss was innocent is not an issue in this matter and can receive no consideration. The record of conviction must stand without question.

23. The force of Professor Field's testimony is vitiated to an extent by his admission that he has never believed that Hiss was guilty of the crimes charged and that his opinion of Hiss's moral character was not changed by his conviction and disbarment.

* * *

Finally,[24] Hiss's own testimony must be mentioned in support of the board's finding of fitness. His testimony was both forth-right and principled. He stated that he found the charge of perjury "abhorrent" and that the perjury charge had included two other charges worse than perjury, which I regard as absolutely reprehensible in a lawyer — failure of trust and failure of confidence." He candidly gave his own impression of the development of his moral character, though that candid impression might have thwarted his reinstatement: "I have not had any complete change in moral character. I am the same person I have been, I believe, throughout my life. If that's the law of Massachusetts [requiring repentance and complete change of moral character], I am excluded." His testimony contained no hint of present animosity or grudge against those who had prosecuted and convicted him. The conviction itself had not shaken his faith in the judicial system: "[A]s far as the courts are concerned ... I have never had the slightest doubt that ours is the finest judicial system there is, and I don't just mean in the Churchill sense ... [i.e., that it's] better than any he knows about. It's good; it's fine. I think it makes mistakes, and I know it made a mistake in my case, but there is no human institution that doesn't sometimes make mistakes."

The testimony detailed above provides abundant support for the board's conclusion that Hiss is presently of good character. Though Hiss, himself, in holding fast to his contention of innocence, admits no rehabilitation of character, we believe that the evidence amply warrants the board's finding that he would not now commit the crime of which he was convicted. The considerable evidence of his present good character, his exemplary behavior over a substantial time span, and the tributes paid him by eminent practitioners who have known him well during the period convince us that, despite the gravity of the crime and his maturity at the time of its commission, "his resumption of the practice of law will not be detrimental to the integrity and standing of the bar, the administration of justice, or to the public interest." S.J.C. Rule 4:01, § 18(4), [365] Mass. [712] (1974). It is notable in this regard that the record contains no testimony in opposition to reinstatement. Indeed, the Council of the Boston Bar Association, the organization which filed the information leading to disbarment, voted to communicate the opinion to the board that Hiss's resumption of practice would not adversely affect the standing and integrity of the bar or the public interest.[25] The board could correctly find that Hiss has sustained the heavy burden of showing moral and intellectual[26] fitness by good and sufficient proofs.

The petition for reinstatement to the bar is to be granted. On subscription to the required oaths, Hiss is to be readmitted to the practice of law in the Commonwealth.

So ordered.

---

24. In the interests of brevity, we omit description of the supporting testimony of Robert Von Mehren of the New York Bar and Richard Wait of this bar.

25. In his letter, the president of the Boston Bar Association employed the language of S.J.C. Rule 4:01, § 18(4), [365] Mass. [712] (1974), in so far as it is quoted in the paragraph hereinabove.

26. As noted, many of the witnesses testified to his ability and continued attention to legal affairs. Though his recollection of Massachusetts law will not be as "sharp" as it once was, we believe he has demonstrated a competence equivalent to that of an out-of-State lawyer admitted on motion or without examination (see G.L. c. 221, § 39). In view of the finding of good moral character, we assume Hiss will have the sound discretion to restrict his consultative and advisory activities to areas of his undoubted competence.

In re Hinson-Lyles

864 So.2d 108
Supreme Court of Louisiana
Dec. 3, 2003
Rehearing Denied Jan. 16, 2004

ON APPLICATION FOR ADMISSION TO THE BAR

PER CURIAM.

This matter arises from a petition by Kelle Hinson-Lyles seeking admission to the Bar of the State of Louisiana. For the reasons that follow, we deny the petition.

UNDERLYING FACTS AND PROCEDURAL HISTORY

In her application to sit for the July 2002 Louisiana bar examination, petitioner disclosed that she was convicted of a felony sexual offense in 1999. By letter dated June 12, 2002, the Committee on Bar Admissions ("Committee") notified petitioner that in light of her conviction, she would not be certified for admission to the practice of law. A majority of this court subsequently granted petitioner permission to sit for the bar, subject to the condition that upon her successful completion of the exam, she apply to the court for the appointment of a commissioner to take character and fitness evidence.[1] *In re: Hinson-Lyles*, 02-1805 (La.7/3/02), 819 So.2d 1027. Petitioner successfully passed the essay portion of the July 2002 bar exam. We thereafter appointed a commissioner to take evidence and report to this court whether petitioner possesses the appropriate character and fitness to be admitted to the bar and allowed to practice law in the State of Louisiana. We also authorized the Office of Disciplinary Counsel to conduct an investigation into petitioner's qualifications to be admitted to the bar.

Proceedings before the Commissioner

The commissioner conducted a character and fitness hearing on February 18, 2003, pursuant to Supreme Court Rule XVII, § 9(B). The commissioner received documentary evidence and heard testimony given by petitioner and her witnesses. This record reveals that in May 1996, petitioner received an undergraduate degree in business and office education. With the assistance of her father, who was then the Superintendent of the Vernon Parish School Board, petitioner obtained a teaching position at DeRidder High School in Beauregard Parish. In May 1998, as petitioner was completing her second year of teaching at DeRidder High, she began a sexual relationship with M.C., a fourteen-year old student in her ninth-grade English class. Petitioner was twenty-three years of age at this time.

Over a period of approximately six weeks, petitioner spoke with M.C. on the telephone or saw him in person nearly every day. Because M.C. was too young to have a dri-

---

1. In cases in which the Committee has declined to recommend admission based on character and fitness concerns, it has been the court's customary practice to permit the applicant to sit for the bar examination subject to a later determination respecting character and fitness. It will frequently be necessary for this court to appoint a commissioner for the purpose of developing a record upon which we can proceed to make such a determination. The appointment of a commissioner in no way represents a finding by this court that the applicant does, in fact, possess good moral character and fitness.

ver's license, petitioner arranged to pick him up in an alley behind his home and to take him back to her house, where they engaged in sexual intercourse. In addition, petitioner and M.C. drank alcohol supplied by petitioner, and on one occasion, petitioner allowed M.C. to smoke marijuana that he had brought to her home.

On the evening of July 11, 1998, petitioner picked up M.C. and brought him back to her house, where they engaged in sexual intercourse. However, unbeknownst to petitioner or M.C., the Beauregard Parish Sheriff's Office had received a report from M.C.'s father that his son was "having a sexual affair with one of his school teachers." The officers agreed to investigate the complaint. Upon arriving at petitioner's home, the officers knocked on the door and announced themselves. Petitioner turned off the lights in the house and told M.C. to hide. Meanwhile, petitioner dressed and eventually opened the door, telling the officers she had not heard the knocking because she had been washing her hair. The officers asked whether M.C. was in the house; petitioner lied, said that he was not, and denied he had been inside her home. The officers then requested and obtained petitioner's permission to search the home. M.C. was found hiding in a bedroom closet, underneath a pile of clothes.

Petitioner was arrested and charged with five counts of carnal knowledge of a juvenile and three counts of contributing to the delinquency of a juvenile.[2] On February 25, 1999, pursuant to a plea agreement, the State filed an amended bill of information charging petitioner with two counts of felony carnal knowledge of a juvenile and one count of indecent behavior with a juvenile,[3] also a felony. Petitioner pleaded guilty to the charges in the amended bill of information and was placed on supervised probation for a period of three years with special conditions. *State v. Hinson*, No. CR-598-98 on the docket of the 36th Judicial District Court for the Parish of Beauregard.

Following her conviction, petitioner was terminated from her position at DeRidder High and she was required to forfeit her teaching certificate to the Louisiana State Department of Education.[4] Petitioner's probation concluded on February 25, 2002, and she has subsequently received an automatic first offender pardon.

At the character and fitness hearing, petitioner admitted she knew her relationship with M.C. was wrong. At the conclusion of the hearing, the commissioner issued detailed findings of fact and conclusions of law and recommended that petitioner be conditionally admitted to the practice of law in Louisiana, subject to a probationary period of two years.

The Committee timely objected to the commissioner's recommendation, and oral argument was conducted before this court pursuant to Supreme Court Rule XVII, §9(B)(3).

---

2. The carnal knowledge of a juvenile charges relate to five separate occasions on which petitioner had sexual relations with M.C.; however, petitioner candidly admitted in a sworn statement that "there's probably seven or eight, maybe even nine" occasions on which she and M.C. had sex. The contributing to the delinquency of a juvenile charges relate to the occasions on which petitioner gave alcohol to M.C. and allowed him to smoke marijuana in her presence.

3. The indecent behavior charge relates to an occasion on which petitioner and M.C. engaged in oral sexual relations. The district attorney's office dropped the contributing to the delinquency of a juvenile charges.

4. It appears from the record that no administrative proceeding was conducted; rather, petitioner surrendered her teaching certificate as a condition of her guilty plea.

DISCUSSION

This court has the exclusive and plenary power to define and regulate all facets of the practice of law, including the admission of attorneys to the Bar of this state. *Bester v. Louisiana Supreme Court Comm. on Bar Admissions,* 00-1360 (La.2/21/01), 779 So.2d 715. Among other requirements for admission to the Bar, applicants must demonstrate by competent evidence that they have "good moral character and the fitness necessary to practice law in the State of Louisiana." Supreme Court Rule XVII, § 5(E).

The primary purpose of character and fitness screening is to assure the protection of the public and to safeguard the administration of justice. Supreme Court Rule XVII, § 5(A); *In re: Singer,* 01-2776 (La.6/12/02), 819 So.2d 1017. The term "good moral character" includes, but is not limited to, the qualities of honesty, fairness, candor, trustworthiness, observances of fiduciary responsibility and of the laws of the State of Louisiana and of the United States of America, and a respect for the rights of other persons. Supreme Court Rule XVII, § 5(B). One of the specific factors to be considered in making a determination of good moral character and fitness is whether the applicant has been convicted of a felony. Supreme Court Rule XVII, § 5(C)(19).

This court has never taken the view that a prior felony conviction will automatically bar an applicant from admission to the practice of law, and we decline to adopt that approach at this time. Rather, we prefer to consider the facts of each case based on the totality of the circumstances which brings the applicant before us. *In re: Dileo,* 307 So.2d 362 (La.1975). In other words, a felony conviction is simply one of many factors to be considered in determining whether an applicant presently possesses good moral character and fitness.

After reviewing the record developed in this matter, we find that serious character and fitness concerns are present which necessitate the denial of petitioner's application for admission to the practice of law. Setting aside for a moment the gravity of any felony sexual offense,[5] particularly those involving a juvenile victim, we are extraordinarily troubled by the factual circumstances underlying the crimes of which petitioner was convicted. Petitioner occupied a position of trust as a teacher, yet she knowingly and intentionally breached that trust to gratify her own needs. Knowing full well that her conduct was immoral, inappropriate, and illegal, petitioner nevertheless carried on a sexual affair with her fourteen-year old student for nearly two months. Far from discouraging M.C.'s involvement in the relationship, petitioner in fact fostered and encouraged it. She candidly admitted during the character and fitness hearing that the affair would have continued indefinitely but for the fact that M.C.'s father called the police. On more than one occasion, petitioner supplied alcohol for consumption by a minor child, and she countenanced and permitted his use of marijuana while in her home. Finally, when confronted by law enforcement officials, petitioner lied, denied any involvement with M.C., and hid him in a closet in an effort to avoid detection by the police and his parents. Taken as a whole, we find this conduct is not an isolated instance of poor judgment on petitioner's part, but is rather evidence that she fundamentally lacks the character and fitness to be admitted to the practice of law. Accordingly, we must reject the commis-

---

5. We observe that sexual misconduct resulting in a felony criminal conviction is a ground for the permanent disbarment of an attorney who is licensed to practice law in Louisiana. See Guideline 4 of the permanent disbarment guidelines set forth in Supreme Court Rule XIX, Appendix E.

sioner's recommendation that petitioner be granted the privilege of practicing law in Louisiana.[6]

DECREE

After hearing oral argument, reviewing the evidence, and considering the law, we conclude petitioner has failed to meet her burden of proving that she has "good moral character" to be admitted to the Louisiana State Bar. Accordingly, it is ordered that Kelle Hinson-Lyles' petition for admission be and is denied.

WEIMER, J., concurs and assigns reasons.

CALOGERO, C.J., concurs for the reasons assigned by WEIMER, J.

KNOLL, J., additionally concurs and assigns reasons.

KIMBALL and TRAYLOR, JJ., dissent and assign reasons.

WEIMER, J., concurring.

I find the past criminal conduct of the petitioner reprehensible. However, I believe the per curiam fails to adequately document those facts that led the commissioner to recommend that petitioner be admitted to the bar. At some time in the future, after the lapse of a more substantial period of time from the termination of petitioner's probation and following an evaluation of petitioner's intervening conduct, this court might be called upon to consider whether petitioner has been sufficiently rehabilitated. Therefore, for the sake of completeness, the majority opinion should include the following factual findings of the commissioner which were included in a thorough, thirteen-page report to this court:

- Except for defensive postures mandated by defense counsel, petitioner never denied responsibility for the inappropriate relationship with her fourteen-year old student.

- Until the events leading up to petitioner's guilty plea, she had led an exemplary life with no moral or legal problems whatsoever.

- Petitioner was a model probationer, cooperative, understood she had done wrong, was very remorseful, did more than necessary, wanted to make changes for the good, and owned up completely to her responsibility. Both of her probation officers and counselor confirm all issues were met, she is not a re-offender threat, and all support her application.

- Psychiatric and psychological evaluations by very competent experts in those fields concluded that at the time of the incident petitioner knew right from wrong, but in an immature way. She was a budding adolescent emotionally. She was very naive and inexperienced sexually. (This was her first sexual encounter.) Dr. Harper, psychologist, found no evidence of mental predisposition to re-offend. Dr. Ware, psychiatrist, found a very low risk to re-offend (there being no absolutes).

- All witnesses and exhibits pertinent thereto have a consensus-petitioner presents one of the best examples of how one can change, her maturity is now impressive, she actually has greater resilience than usual in facing ethical demands, she will not re-offend, and they support her application.

---

6. While we afford some deference to the commissioner's recommendation, making due allowance for the commissioner's opportunity to observe and evaluate the demeanor of the applicant and the witnesses, the ultimate decision regarding admission rests with this court.

- Her only opportunity thus far in the field of law gained her an unqualified recommendation from her employer, a member of the judiciary.

- She is now married, expecting a child, and by all accounts available, is functioning as a normal young married professional.

The commissioner made particular note that at the time of the incident, petitioner was "alone, had no prior experience, [was] immature and at a vulnerable position in her life." He also concluded that petitioner has done all that can be done to achieve the rehabilitation necessary for admission to the practice of law.

In conclusion, the commissioner stated:

> This is a case of past conduct. Based simply on the cold record, the obvious seriousness of the charge, and the self evident interest of society, one would be likely to view with great suspicion an offender's application to practice law some five years after commission. Therein lies the problem. What to do when, within a five year span, by clear and convincing evidence, an applicant satisfies the requirements of admission.
>
> ...
>
> I have not found, or been cited a decision by this Court addressing our particular situation. See generally *In re: Ashy*, 721 So.2d 859 (La.1998). The Commissioner's report in the matter *In re: Michael Lawrence Bernoudy, Jr.*, No.2002-OB-2470, pending before this Court, was submitted. Though involved, carnal knowledge was only one of the complaints. Further, the recommendation was greatly influenced by a finding of lack of candor and cooperation on the part of Mr. Bernoudy, Jr., elements not found in the instant matter.
>
> This is a 1998 incident.... It would be ironic, to say the least, for society to admit to law school, with full disclosure, then permanently prevent enjoyment notwithstanding passing all scholastic requisites. Further, I don't feel the level of misconduct herein rises to the level of examples cited. Also, almost five years have elapsed. If she had been in practice and disbarred as a result, she could now apply for reinstatement.

In light of "the totality of circumstances involved," the commissioner recommended that petitioner be conditionally admitted to the practice of law in Louisiana, subject to a probationary period of two years. The commissioner further recommended that during the period of probation, petitioner be required to provide an affidavit to the Supreme Court Committee on Bar Admissions on a quarterly basis, stating that she has not committed or been accused of any misconduct; otherwise, her probationary period may be extended for an additional two years, or her conditional right to practice may be terminated or she may be subject to other discipline pursuant to the Rules for Lawyer Disciplinary Enforcement.

In summary, while I agree that petitioner should not be admitted to the practice of law at this time, I believe that it is important to chronicle all the facts, both favorable and unfavorable, reflected in the record. Therefore, I respectfully concur in the majority opinion of this court.

CALOGERO, C.J., concurs.

KNOLL, J., concurring.

I agree with the majority that petitioner fundamentally lacks the character and fitness to be admitted to the practice of law. I write separately to express my concern that this case demonstrates the need for an admission rule in tandem with permanent disbarment. In my view, it is a mockery of our rules to allow someone to apply for admission when the undisputed conduct at issue is a recommended ground for permanent disbarment.

Drafting conduct rules governing the legal profession is a very difficult and grave responsibility that we exercise with great caution. However, it is clear in my mind that when conduct is so egregious that it constitutes grounds for permanent disbarment, then the person involved should likewise be permanently prohibited from applying for admission.

The petitioner before us should never be admitted to the practice of law because her admitted and egregious conduct constitutes grounds for permanent disbarment.

KIMBALL, Justice, dissenting.

In my view, this case presents a tragic example of this court's inability to formulate definitive rules to cover these difficult character and fitness issues. In this particular case, this applicant was allowed to attend law school, notwithstanding the fact that she was on active felony probation and had surrendered her teaching certificate, thereby effectively disqualifying her from her original profession. After successfully completing her studies, this court allowed the applicant to sit for the bar examination, which she passed.

This court's rules relating to admission to the bar of the State of Louisiana exist to protect the public and to safeguard the administration of justice. The required assessment of moral character and fitness looks to an applicant's record of past conduct. Admission may be denied on the basis of an applicant's record of past conduct when such record manifests "a significant deficiency in the honesty, trustworthiness, diligence or reliability of an applicant." Supreme Court Rule XVII, § 5(B). When an applicant is found to have engaged in conduct which at that time would have constituted grounds for an unfavorable recommendation, then that applicant bears the burden of proof to affirmatively show character rehabilitation and that such inclination or instability is unlikely to recur in the future. Supreme Court Rule XVII, § 5(D).

In the instant case, the record clearly reveals that the applicant overwhelmingly proved that her character has been rehabilitated and that such inclination or instability is unlikely to recur in the future. For example, the supervisor of applicant's first five months of probation described the applicant as a model probationer and recommended her for admission to the bar. Additionally, the attorney who previously represented applicant in connection with the criminal charges that are the subject of this investigation testified that applicant took responsibility for her actions from the outset and, because the attorney had "the utmost confidence in her," wrote a strong letter of recommendation to Southern University Law Center and, later, the National Conference of Bar Examiners. He also assisted the applicant in obtaining a position as a law clerk in the Ninth Judicial District Court. A Shreveport psychiatrist who evaluated the applicant opined there is a very low risk that the applicant will commit a sexual offense in the future. The director of the clinical education department at Southern University Law Center who supervised the applicant's class work testified that the applicant was very dedicated, extremely committed, and worked all the time to make "sure that it's right." The judge for whom applicant worked as a law clerk reported that her work has been excellent, that she is very conscientious, and that she gets along well with others in the court. The judge highly recommended the applicant for admission to the bar "regardless of her past situation or the circumstances." After hearing all the evidence in this case, the commissioner found the applicant understood her past behavior was wrong, was remorseful, and wanted to make positive changes in her life. The commissioner found that psychiatric and psychological evaluations showed applicant knew right from wrong, but in an immature way such that she was emotionally a budding adolescent when the behavior at issue occurred. Finally, the commissioner found that the applicant is now married, expecting a child, and by all accounts is functioning as a normal young married professional.

Although this appears to be an unusual case with extraordinary facts, it is clear to me that the applicant has produced an impressive amount of evidence proving that she has good moral character and the fitness necessary to practice law in the State of Louisiana. The medical evidence consistently reveals that there is a very low risk the applicant will re-offend. In concluding that this case presents serious character and fitness concerns that necessitate the denial of the petitioner's application for admission to the practice of law, the majority disingenuously focuses solely on the applicant's past deplorable conduct and fails to consider or even mention the overwhelming evidence that the applicant has turned her life around. The retired judge appointed as a commissioner by this court to hear evidence in this case found as a matter of fact that the applicant has done all that can be done to achieve the rehabilitation necessary for admission to the practice of law. In reaching its decision to deny the applicant admission, the majority simply ignores the factual findings made by the appointed commissioner.

The case before us illustrates the need for clear rules detailing what conduct will likely prevent an applicant from being admitted to the bar of our state. In my view, potential law students should be given notice of the types of conduct that will probably preclude them from practicing law before they undertake the challenge of law school and, in many cases, incur substantial debt to acquire a legal education. This court should work with Louisiana's law schools to ensure potential students are given clear information so they can make informed choices.

Under the facts of this particular case, I believe the applicant should be conditionally admitted to the practice of law, subject to a probationary period of two years. As the commissioner found, the applicant has done everything she can to show the necessary rehabilitation. Because the applicant has complied with every requirement presently contained in our rules, it is simply unjust to deny her admission at this juncture.

TRAYLOR, J., dissenting.

In July of last year, Kelle Hinson-Lyles applied to sit for the Louisiana Bar Examination. Her application was opposed by the Committee on Bar Admissions based upon her three 1999 felony convictions. This Court, in its collective wisdom, allowed the petitioner to take the bar examination, upon the condition that she apply to the court for the appointment of a commissioner to take character and fitness evidence. I opposed allowing the petitioner to take the examination and voted, along with Justices Kimball and Knoll, to deny her application.

Ms. Hinson-Lyles took and passed the bar examination and subsequently requested the appointment of a commissioner to take character and fitness evidence. The commissioner held a hearing, took evidence, and found that petitioner possessed the requisite character and fitness to be conditionally admitted to the bar based upon her rehabilitation. This Court now determines that the petitioner should not be admitted to the bar, even though the only new evidence we have before us supports her conditional admission, as recommended by the commissioner that this Court appointed for that purpose.

I do not take the position that Ms. Hinson-Lyles possesses the character and fitness required to be admitted to the bar and, in fact, adhere to my previous determination that she should not have been allowed to sit for the bar examination. I do, however, believe that when this Court allows a person to take the bar examination upon condition, and then that person passes the examination and meets the conditions set before them, it is disingenuous for the Court to then decide that more conditions must be met, especially without stating what those conditions are.

In this case what can the petitioner do that she has not done? Wait and apply later? When or what is the "magic moment" which will show that rehabilitation has occurred? If Ms. Hinson-Lyles applies five years from now, will that be long enough? Ten years? Will she ever be able to show successful rehabilitation? If not, why was she allowed to take the bar examination at all?

Supreme Court Rule XVII contains the factors to be considered when assessing past conduct and rehabilitation in relation to an applicant's character and fitness to practice law. These factors include the applicant's age since the conduct, the time elapsed since the conduct, the reliability of the information concerning the conduct, the seriousness of the conduct, factors underlying the conduct, the cumulative effect of the conduct, the applicant's social contributions, the applicant's candor and cooperation, the materiality of any omissions or misrepresentations, and the evidence of rehabilitation. Sup.Ct. R. XVII, § 5(D). None of these factors is determinative and all are subjective and give little guidance to either applicants for admission to the bar or to the commissioners we appoint to make findings of fact and determinations of law. In fact, according to these factors, *no* conduct, including murder, disqualifies a candidate from admission to the bar. This Court must develop definitive rules as to what conduct may be rehabilitated and what conduct is a bar to admission, both to give useful guidance to applicants and to avoid wasting valuable time and resources.

Bar Application Form, Iowa (2010)

[**Note:** This form is given for example only, and may be changed.]

SECTION C: CONFIDENTIAL

34. SOCIAL SECURITY NUMBER: _____ - _____ - _____

Providing your social security number is voluntary, pursuant to the Federal Privacy Act of 1974. However, providing it assists in expediting the character review process. Your social security number will be used for purposes of investigation and verification, so as to avoid errors of identity which might introduce problems and delays into the certification and licensure process.

35. _____ DISABILITY STATUS: Do you have any disability for which you are requesting reasonable testing accommodations?

If YES, you will need to file an ELIGIBILITY QUESTIONNAIRE FOR REASONABLE ACCOMMODATIONS (Form A) with the Office of Professional Regulation. This form can be found on the Supreme Court's website at: http://www.iowacourts.gov/Professional_Regulation/Bar_Admission__Practice_Rules/Bar_Exam_Schedule_Fees__Applications/.

36. _____ CHILD SUPPORT/ALIMONY: Have you ever been required to make child support or alimony payments?

_____ Have you ever been more than 30 days past due in the payment of any child support obligation or alimony (spousal maintenance) obligation?

If YES, what is the status of your compliance with the child support or alimony order? What is the name and last known mailing address of your former spouse(s)? If you answer yes to any of the above questions, LIST DETAILS, giving names and addresses, amounts, dates, and the reason for nonpayment.

37. _____ UNSATISFIED JUDGMENTS: Are there any unsatisfied judgments against you?

If YES, list details, giving names and addresses of creditors, amounts, dates and the nature of debts or judgments, and the reason for nonpayment.

38. MISCONDUCT: Have you ever been formally or informally investigated, reprimanded, disciplined, discharged, or asked to resign by an employer or educational institution for misconduct including:

a. Acts of dishonesty, fraud, or deceit;

b. Lying or misrepresentations on a resume or prior application or registration;

c. Academic misconduct, such as cheating or plagiarism;

d. Misconduct involving student activities;

e. Theft;

f. Excessive absences;

g. Failure to complete assignments in a timely manner;

h. Actions in disregard for health, safety, and welfare of others;

i. Discrimination or harassment based upon sex, religion, age, disability, race, or national or ethnic origin;

j. Neglect of financial responsibilities;

k. Conduct related to the use of alcohol or any other drug in the last ten years?

If the answer to any of the above is YES, describe the specific facts of each occurrence, including date of the action, by whom taken, the name and address of the employment supervisor or academic advisor involved, if applicable, and any person involved in the investigation of your conduct. If you need additional space, please attach sheets to the end of this document.

39. MILITARY SERVICE: _____ A. Are you now or have you ever been a member of the United States Armed Yes/No Forces (including the reserve components and the National Guard)?

If YES, give the branch of service and the period of duty. If you are no longer active, provide a certificate of discharge. If you no longer have a copy of your discharge, you must have a new copy forwarded to the Office of Professional Regulation.

_____ B. As a member of the armed forces, have any charges ever been made or any proceedings been instituted against you (court martial, Article 15, etc.)?

If YES, give complete details below (or on an ATTACHED sheet), including the date, the charge, the disposition of the matter, and the address and designation of the military establishment where the proceedings took place.

_____C. Have you ever received a discharge other than an honorable discharge from the armed forces?

If YES, give complete details below (or on an ATTACHED sheet), including the reason for discharge, and ATTACH a copy of the other-than-honorable discharge.

40. _____ CRIMINAL PROCEEDINGS: Have you ever been arrested, cited for, or charged with a crime or a delinquent act, INCLUDING ANY TRAFFIC VIOLATIONS, but excluding parking tickets?

If YES, provide a complete and detailed explanation of each occurrence. Include in the chart below the date of the arrest or charge, the arresting agency, the nature of the charge, the name and location of the court, and the disposition. Do NOT attach your DMV driving record or a print-out from the Court's website, but you should consult those sources in completing this application.

NOTE: You must disclose EVERY occurrence even if the charge was dismissed, the judgment was deferred, or the record was sealed or expunged, etc.

41. _____ ILLEGAL DRUGS: Are you currently, or have you been in the last three years, engaged in the illegal use of drugs?

If YES, give complete details below (or on an ATTACHED sheet).

"Illegal Use of Drugs" means the use of controlled substances obtained illegally as well as the use of controlled substances which are not obtained pursuant to a valid prescription or taken in the accordance with the directions of a licensed health care practitioner. "Currently" does not mean on the day of, or even the weeks or months preceding the completion of this application. Rather, it means recently enough so that the condition or impairment may have an ongoing impact.

You have a right to elect not to answer those portions of the above questions which inquire as to the illegal use of controlled substances or activity if you have reasonable cause to believe that answering may expose you to the possibility of criminal prosecution. In that event, you may assert the Fifth Amendment privilege against self-incrimination. Any claim of the Fifth Amendment privilege must be made in good faith. If you choose to assert the Fifth Amendment privilege, you must do so in writing. You must fully respond to all other questions on the application. Your application for licensure will be processed if you claim the Fifth Amendment privilege against self-incrimination.

42. _____ FRAUD: Have you ever, under any circumstances not explained elsewhere on this form, been accused of fraud?

If YES, give complete details below (or on an ATTACHED sheet), including the dates.

43. _____ CONDITIONS OR IMPAIRMENTS: Do you have any condition or impairment that currently impairs your ability to practice law?

If YES, set forth the specifics, including dates, the name and the address of treating physician or mental health counselor.

"Condition or impairment" means any physiological, mental, or psychological condition, impairment or disorder, including drug addiction and alcoholism. "Ability to Practice Law" is to be construed to include the following:

a. The cognitive capacity to undertake fundamental lawyering skills such as problem solving, legal analysis and reasoning, legal research, factual investigation, organization and management of legal work, making appropriate reasoned legal judgments, and recognizing and resolving ethical dilemmas, for example.

b. The ability to communicate legal judgments and legal information to clients, other attorneys, judicial and regulatory authorities with or without the use of aids or devices; and

c. The capability to perform legal tasks in a timely manner.

The Board understands that mental health counseling or treatment is a normal part of many persons' lives and such counseling or treatment does not of itself disqualify an applicant from the practice of law. Furthermore, the Board does not wish to pry into the private affairs of applicants. However, the Board is obligated by the Supreme Court of Iowa's rules governing admission to the Bar to determine whether an applicant is physically and mentally fit to practice law, and therefore, must inquire into such matters to the extent necessary to make such determination. <u>The Board is not seeking disclosure of counseling or treatment for a traumatic or upsetting event such as death, break-up of a relationship, or a personal assault, even if such event does affect the applicant's ability to practice law for a limited time.</u>

44. _____ CHARACTER: A. Have you ever been prohibited from applying for, or applied for but been denied, a position, certificate, or license which required proof of good character?

_____ B. Have you ever held a position, certificate, or license which required proof of good character, but then you were removed from the position or had the certificate or license suspended or revoked? If you answered YES to either of the foregoing two questions, give complete details below (or on an ATTACHED sheet), including the date, the name and mailing address of the issuing agency, and the reasons for the action. If there was a suspension or revocation order, ATTACH a copy.

45. PREVIOUS APPLICATIONS FOR ADMISSION TO THE BAR:

_____ A. Have you ever before applied for admission to the bar or for permission to take the bar examination in Iowa?

_____ B. Have you ever before applied for admission to the bar or for permission to take the bar in any other state or jurisdiction?

If YES to either of the above, give the date of each application, the state or jurisdiction to which applied, and the disposition of the application, including the dates and results of any bar examination taken. All applications must be listed, even if the application was withdrawn prior to the disposition.

46. _____ INCOME TAX RETURNS: Have you filed federal and state income tax returns for all years when your income warranted such filings?

47. _____ MISCELLANEOUS ISSUES: If there is any information (event, incident, occurrence, etc.) that was not specifically addressed or asked of you in this application that could be considered to reflect on your character or fitness to practice law, you are required to provide a detailed explanation for each event, incident, or occurrence. Given this requirement, do you have any additional information to disclose?

SECTION D: CONFIDENTIAL

48. LEGAL DISCIPLINE:

_____ Have you ever been disbarred, suspended from practice, reprimanded, censured, or otherwise disciplined?

_____ Have any complaints or charges, formal or informal, including any now pending, ever been made or proceedings instituted against you?

_____ Have you ever appeared, formally or informally, before a grievance or other similar committee of any bar association or other law group?

If you answered YES to any of the foregoing three questions, give full details, including the date of the charge, the nature of the charge, the facts, the disposition of the matter and the name and mailing address of the person in possession of the records thereof.

SECTION E

STATE OF _____)

COUNTY OF _____)

Under penalty of perjury, I do hereby make the foregoing application. I have read the questions and have answered them completely and truthfully. I have not omitted any information that might have a bearing on my application. I understand that if any changes occur after the application is filed which affect my answers, I must amend my application by a letter to the Office of Professional Regulation.

_____
Applicant's Signature

Sworn to and subscribed before me this _____ day of _____, 20 ____.

_____

(Notary Seal)   Notary Public for

State of _____

The Commonwealth of Massachusetts Bar Application Forms (2011)

Suffolk, SS.   FORM 2   Supreme Judicial Court
                                                         For Suffolk County

[**Note:** This form is given for example only, and may be changed.]

In   the   matter   of

_____

(*Applicant for admission as an attorney at law taking the Massachusetts Bar Examination for the first time*)

By examination to be held _____
                          (Date)

APPLICANT'S STATEMENT TO THE BOARD OF BAR EXAMINERS

* * *

7. List employment you have held since your 18th birthday or any business or profession engaged in on your own account. Enclose additional 8.5•11 white sheets if necessary.

(a) Month & Year of Beginning & Ending Period of Employment (most recent) _____

Name & Address of Employer & Nature of Business _____
                                                DO NOT ABBREVIATE

Position Held _____

Reason for Leaving _____

(b) Month & Year of Beginning & Ending Period of Employment (most recent) _____

Name & Address of Employer & Nature of Business _____
                                                DO NOT ABBREVIATE

Position Held _____

Reason for Leaving _____

(c) Month & Year of Beginning & Ending Period of Employment (most recent) _____

Name & Address of Employer & Nature of Business _____
                                                DO NOT ABBREVIATE

Position Held _____

Reason for Leaving _____

ATTACH RIDER PAGE(S) IF NECESSARY (information must be provided in same format as above)

_____
Applicant's Name (Type or Print Clearly)

8. Name jurisdictions and courts other than Massachusetts in which you have applied (this should include application or reinstatement and any applications subsequently withdrawn) or been admitted to practice law. Give dates of application and admission to practice (if applicable), or <u>disposition (do not leave blank or answer "n/a"). Attach a certificate (dated within 90 days of this application), evidencing your admission and good standing from each state to which you are admitted to practice law.</u>

(a) Date of Application (b) Jurisdiction (include Court) (c) Date of Admission/ Disposition

_____	_____	_____
_____	_____	_____
_____	_____	_____

(*You must respond to all questions by writing "yes" or "no" in the space provided. "N/A" is not an acceptable answer.*)

9. Have you ever been reprimanded, sanctioned, disciplined or suspended or expelled from a college, university or law school? _____. If yes, state the facts fully including date(s)

10. (a) Have you ever been disbarred, suspended, reprimanded, censured, admonished or otherwise disciplined or disqualified as an attorney, or as a member of any other profession, or as a holder of any public office? _____

If yes, state the dates, the details and the name and address of the authority in possession of the record thereof.

(b) Have any charges or complaints been made concerning your conduct as an attorney, or as a member of any profession, or as a holder of any public office? _____

If yes, state the dates, the details and the name and address of the authority in possession of the record thereof. (*Attach rider pages if necessary.*)

_____

Applicant's Name (Type or Print Clearly)

(*You must respond to all questions by writing "yes" or "no" in the space provided. "N/A is not an acceptable answer.*)

11. (a) Are there any unsatisfied judgments or court orders continuing effect against you? _____

(b) If yes, state the facts fully, giving names and addresses of creditors, amounts, dates, and nature of debts, judgments or court orders, and the reason for nonpayment of unsatisfied judgments or any non-compliance with court orders (attach additional pages if necessary).

12. (a) Have you ever been charged with or been the subject of any investigation for a felony or misdemeanor other than a minor traffic charge? _____ If yes, state the dates, courts, details, and results.

(b) Have you ever been a party on either side in a civil action or proceeding involving a claim of fraud, conversion, breach of fiduciary duty, professional malpractice or other wrongful conduct? _____ If yes, please explain and include dates.

(c) Have you been a party in any other legal or administrative proceedings? _____ If yes, please explain and include dates.

(d) Have you ever been adjudged bankrupt or insolvent? _____ If yes, please explain and include dates.

GIVE <u>FULL</u> DETAILS for affirmative responses to Questions 12 (a), (b), (c), and (d) including *date(s)*, exact name and location of court, if any, case numbers, references to court records, if any, the facts, the disposition of the matter; if no court records are available, give to the best of your ability the names and addresses of all persons involved, including counsel. (Attach additional sheets if necessary.)

_____

Applicant's Name (<u>Type or Print Clearly</u>)

13. Enclose two current letters of recommendation, addressed to the Board of Bar Examiners, stating facts relative to your character by persons who know you <u>other</u> than family members. Please call to the attention of the author that the statements should not be conclusions but should contain facts tending to help the Board of Bar Examiners reach conclusions about your character and fitness to be admitted to the bar. (See Information for Letters of Recommendation).

14. When did you sit for the Multistate Professional Responsibility Examination (MPRE)?

_____

MONTH AND YEAR

15. Provide your MPRE score below (*and attach a copy of your MRPE Score Report*).

_____   _____

Raw Score   Scaled Score

I agree to inform the Supreme Judicial Court Clerk's Office for Suffolk County, in writing, of any changed or additions to answers that I have made on this application. I understand that this obligation shall continue until I am admitted to the practice of law in the Commonwealth of Massachusetts, or until such time as my application is withdrawn or denied by the Supreme Judicial Court.

CERTIFICATE

I, the applicant, certify that each of the foregoing answers is true, complete and candid and that I have not altered the wording of any question.

Dated   this   _____   day   of   _____ ,

_____
             (day)   (month)   (year)

                                          _____
                                          Applicant's Signature

                                          _____
                                          Applicant's Name (<u>Type or Print Clearly</u>)

Commonwealth of Massachusetts (2011)

Board of Bar Examiners
<u>FORM 3—AUTHORIZATION</u>

I,*(name)*

_____,

residing at*(address, city, state, zip code)* _____

_____

and

born on*(date of birth)* _____, having filed an application

for admission to the bar of the Commonwealth of Massachusetts, hereby consent to have

any investigation made as to my moral character, professional reputation, and fitness for

the practice of law.

I hereby authorize every person, firm, company, corporation, governmental agency, law enforcement agency, court, bar association, or institution having control of any documents or records regarding charges or complaints filed against me, including any complaints expunged by law, whether formal or informal, pending or closed, or any other pertinent data to provide them to the Massachusetts Board of Bar Examiners.

Signature of Applicant: _____

Dated: _____

[Author's note: This authorization is both very broad in scope and unlimited by any time period. Do you agree with that?]

The Commonwealth of Massachusetts (2011)

Suffolk, ss.

Supreme Judicial Court
for Suffolk County

LAW SCHOOL CERTIFICATE—FORM 4

(to be completed by the law school from which the applicant <u>graduated</u>. Improperly completed certificates will not be accepted and will be returned to the law school.)

In the matter of the application for admissions as attorney of:

_____ DATE OF BIRTH_____
(Name)

_____
(Address)

I certify that the above-named applicant:

A) was a member of the: _____(Law School)

which is _____ *is not* _____ *approved by the American Bar Association.*

B) attended the   Day_____ Evening_____ program

From _____ to _____
(month, day, year)   (month, day, year)

C) to the best of my belief the applicant was in regular attendance at school during that period.

D) has furnished evidence to this school of a <u>college education</u> as follows:

_____(Undergraduate Degree)

E) has graduated from _____ Law School,
the _____ day of _____, with the degree of (LLB or JD) _____
(day)   (month & year)   (degree)

F) I understand that you expect me to report to you by simultaneous <u>separate</u> communication anything which appears to me to be adverse in respect of the moral character or fitness to practice law of the applicant or anything which, in my opinion, should be investigated by the Board with respect thereto.

_____
(Signature)   (Title)   (State Registration #—if any)

_____
(Name and Address of School)

Dated: _____

THIS FORM MUST BE AN ORIGINAL AND MAY <u>NOT BE FAXED, PRE-DATED OR AMENDED</u>.

If the applicant has graduated prior to May 1, 2004, the law school certificate must be filed with their bar application. If the applicant's degree has not been conferred by that date, the law school certificate may be submitted separately to the Clerk of the Supreme Judicial Court for Suffolk County on or before July 2, 2004. In order for the applicants to be eligible to sit the bar examination to the Supreme Judicial Court must receive their law school certificate *<u>no later than July 2, 2004</u>*.

Chapter IX

Bar Discipline and Malpractice

Problems

Problem 36

Select sides and set the case of *State Bar of Arizona* v. *Richard G. Kleindienst*, Section IX-3, *infra*, for oral argument. Would the rule system in effect make any difference? Does it make any difference that Kleindienst's perjury was not pursuant to any law practice? What about the fact that Kleindienst was just trying to protect the President, having succeeded in persuading the President, of the United States in the end, to do the right thing? Would it make any difference if the perjury were totally unrelated to any government service, say a lie about an affair with an intern to protect one's spouse and daughter? Should the fact that Kleindienst was a high ranking government official make a difference? How?

Problem 37

Do you agree with the result in *Spevack* v. *Klein*, *infra*? Would you agree that practicing law is a privilege, not a right? If so, shouldn't asserting a Fifth Amendment privilege give rise to a presumption that you are unfit to practice law? (Remember, this is about suspension or disbarment, not going to jail, or even criminal fines). Every year the Massachusetts Client Security Board spends millions of dollars to reimburse private clients. Should lawyers be able to "hide behind the Fifth" and continue to practice? Is there a "compromise" position?

Problem 38

Are not lawyers "officers of the court?" If so, shouldn't they be required to treat judges, courts and the legal system with courteous respect? What First Amendment rights should be curtailed for lawyers? See *Matter of Erdman*, Section IX-3, *infra*, and *In re Wilkins*, Section IX-3, *infra*.

Problem 39

Assume that a lawyer is charged with failing to pay income tax, but is acquitted by a jury. Should that lawyer be subject to bar discipline proceedings? (Assume the alleged tax misfeasance was not connected in any way with the lawyer's practice, which was handled in an exemplary way).

Problem 40

One of my former students became a famous advocate for animal rights. Assume, for argument, that he was suspended from the practice of law in Massachusetts for six months for allegedly "turning in" one of his own clients for animal rights violations in Texas, in violation of *Mass. Rule* 1.6. At the time, the Massachusetts version of the "choice of law" rule, *Mass. Rule* 8.5, made Massachusetts lawyers always subject to Massachusetts rules, no matter where the violation occured. Was that right? Suppose the Texas rule was different, and my former student was a member of the Texas bar as well? What do you think of the *ABA Mode Rule* 8.5? Mass. Comment [1B] to the new Mass. Rule 8.5, states that "[t]here is no completely satisfactory solution to the choice of law question so long as different states have different rules ..." Do you agree? By the way, should such a case be treated more leniently on the grounds that the alleged violation was a matter of conscience? That the lawyer's "judgment was clouded ... by his devotion to the cause of animal rights?" Should the Board of Bar Overseers ask if he is "sorry"? Suppose the lawyer insists that he conducted himself "in the first tradition of the Massachusetts bar?" See Problem 33, *supra*. See also *In the Matter of Steven Mark Wise*, No. SJC-08254 (December 19, 2000), where the actual facts, which are more complex, are set out.

Problem 41

The Supreme Judicial Court set argument on whether *Mass. Rule* 8.3 (the so-called "snitch" rule) should be permissive ("should") or mandatory ("shall"). I was asked to argue for "shall." Most of the Massachusetts bar associations took the opposite position. What do you think? Do you think it should be mandatory for doctors to report another doctor for violations of professional rules that raise "a substantial question" as to that doctor's fitness to practice medicine? If doctors have no such duties, will the patients be likely to detect unfit doctors? Go back to Problem 21, the "lowballing" problem in Chapter V *supra*. What version of Rule 8.3 would lead to the best result for the client? For the bar? For the public?

IX-1. Introduction: The "Watchdogs" and You

Those who advocate relatively lenient standards for bar admission usually point to the fact that lawyers are carefully regulated, and that every state has the rough equivalent of the Massachusetts Board of Bar Overseers. This is a court appointed "watchdog" body with the power to discipline lawyers, subject to court review. Thus, they argue, the "bad apples" who escape the "gatekeepers" can be suspended or disbarred later by the "watch dogs." But when disciplinary actions are actually brought against lawyers, another set of arguments are made by their defenders. These lawyers become "devoted professionals with their careers at stake." They have "invested a great deal in their professional education and their practice, sometimes over the course of many years." They often have "dependent families." For them, it is argued, disbarment or suspension can be "worse than conviction of a crime." Thus, similar burdens of proof should apply, including constitutional rights against self-incrimination. Often "problems" are blamed on alcoholism, or other substance abuse or psychological problems. The defendants promise to undergo "rehabilitation" programs. They promise "to go straight." But often, by now, their clients have suffered severe harm.

As we will see, the bar counsel officers that screen complaints and the hearing panels that initially "try" them, consist mostly of other lawyers. They can be naturally sympathetic to the defendant. After all, they see client "problems" from a similar perspective. Defendant lawyers are often well represented, and the complainants may be naive, inexperienced, or easily intimidated. In my experience, the defendant lawyers also will try to "settle" with the complainants on the side, to avoid discipline. In short, it is not easy to remove a "bad apple" from the bar, once admitted. And by the time it is done, there can be much damage and expense.

That is not to say that all complaints are well founded. And some complainants are well represented by plaintiff malpractice lawyers, who will be amply rewarded by contingency fees if successful in civil tort actions. Proceedings before a board of bar overseers can be used to establish a record for a subsequent civil malpractice action. Plaintiff lawyers who specialize in legal malpractice, are affectionately called "the cannibals" because they devour their own. Thanks to them, the malpractice system is an often more efficient protector of client rights than the discipline system. In any event, the two systems are interrelated and, despite the disclaimers in the *Model Rules* that "violation of a Rule should not itself give rise of a cause of action against a lawyer" and that "they are not designed to be a basis for civil liability," there are many cases holding that "a lawyer's violations of a Rule may be evidence of breach of the applicable standard of conduct" in malpractice. "Violations of the rules governing the legal profession are evidence of legal malpractice ..." *Sears, Roebuck & Co.* v. *Goldstone & Sudalter, P.C.*, 128 F. 3d (1st Cir. 1997), 19. See "Preamble," *Model Rules* [20]. See also "Preamble" to the ABA *Code*.

A. The Process

Most states have a rough equivalent of the Massachusetts Bar Counsel, who is essentially a prosecutor of lawyers in disciplinary cases. The Bar Counsel can have a very large office. For example, as of 2011 in Massachusetts there were two "First Assistant Bar Counsels" and eighteen "Assistant Bar Counsels," plus investigators and administrative support. In addition, there is a "General Counsel" to assist the Board of Bar Overseers in its judicial capacity, plus an "Associate General Counsel," and two "Assistant General Counsels." There are twelve board members under the direction of a Chair and Vice Chair, and dozens of specially appointed hearing committees. This very extensive system is supported by annual fees paid by Massachusetts lawyers when they renew their bar membership.

This is not the only cost that bad or incompetent lawyers impose on other lawyers. Again, let us use Massachusetts as an example. Massachusetts has a Client Security Board (the "CSB"), founded by the Supreme Judicial Court in 1974. This Board is also funded by a portion of your annual registration fee, often more than 20%. While the CSB tries to recover money from the lawyers who cause the damage, most of the payments come from the fees of honest lawyers. In fiscal 2000, one lawyer alone was responsible for $1.3 million in CSB payments, and the annual total is always in the millions. See Dick Dahl, "Payouts to Victims of Lawyer Theft Reach All Time High," 8 *Mass. Bar Assoc. Lawyers J.* (no. 10, June, 2001), p. 1. Of course, the cost is reflected in your premiums to your malpractice insurer, as well, and there is always the subtle, but very real, cost to your personal reputation from every "bad apple" in the same profession.

Continuing to use Massachusetts as a typical example, anyone can initiate a Massachusetts Board of Bar Overseers complaint by filing a "BBO-1" form. Complaints can be filed by judges and other lawyers, as well as clients, and, as we will see, *Mass. Rule* 8.3, the "Reporting Professional Misconduct" rule, requires such complaints in some circumstances. The Bar Counsel's office reviews the complaint, and will seek a reply from the lawyer in most cases. See Massachusetts Supreme Judicial Court Rule 4:01, Section 2.6. The Bar Counsel can then close the matter, or recommend an admonition, public reprimand or prosecution of formal charges. *Id.*, Section 2.8. These recommendations then go to a Reviewing Board Member. If that Member believes that the charges would warrant public discipline if proved by a preponderance of the evidence, a Hearing Committee is established. That Committee is subject to review by the Board and, where appropriate, by the Supreme Judicial Court itself.

Boards of Bar Overseers have a wide range of possible sanctions. In my experience, they can give a lawyer a private letter of reprimand that is just a gentle reminder, or just require a few "review" classes in professional ethics. Or they can disbar a lawyer for life, or suspend a lawyer for years. They can require that all clients be notified of the discipline, or require rehabilitation programs. But it is important to remember these are not criminal proceedings, and there is a fundamental question whether being a lawyer is a "right" or a "privilege." Many of the controversies in the area turn on this issue.

B. Scope

Disciplinary actions are not just limited to abuse of clients or client matters. They are also designed to protect the justice system (the "officer of the court" ideal, again) and the profession (the "guild ideal"). English barristers were traditionally expected never to criticize judges or the bar in public. As an English law student, I was a student member of Gray's Inn, one of the four Inns of Court that govern the English bar. I was also editor of a little law journal called *Verdict*, published by Oxford students. One day we published an article by a disbarred barrister criticizing the criminal defense system. The next day I was invited to tea, along with the other editors, by the academic representative of the Inns of Court at the University, and warned not to do it again. I managed some comment about "First Amendment rights" before I remembered I was in the wrong country!

First Amendment rights can be involved in bar discipline. See *In re Wilkins*, 782 NE 2d 985 (Ind. 2003), *In re Hinds*, 90 N.J. 604, 449 A. 2d 483 (1982) and *Matter of Erdmann*, 33 N.Y. 2d 599, 301 N.E. 2d 426 (1973) set out in Chapter IX-3, *infra*. These cases apply basic guidelines established by the Supreme Court in the famous case of *In re Sawyer*, 360 U.S. 622 (1959). The ABA *Code* has many provisions that directly curtail a lawyer's free speech, apart from commercial speech. For example, DR-7-107 restricts what you can say publicly while criminal or civil cases are pending; DR-8-102 and 8-103 restricts false statements about a judge or candidates for judicial office, and DR-9-101 restricts your ability to say you can influence officials on improper or irrelevant grounds. The *Model Rules* have retained similar rules on trial publicity, *Model Rule* 3.6, and statements about judges, *Model Rule* 8.2, and have a general rule protecting the "impartiality and decrees of the tribunal, including a prohibition against "conduct intended to disrupt a tribunal," *Model Rule* 3.5. Even *Rule* 4.2 is "a prohibition on speech and Acts as a prior restraint on speech." Clark, p. 75, *supra*, Section VI-1.

The court in *In re Wilkins*, *infra*, reduced the discipline of the lawyer from suspension to a public reprimand because he apologized for calling a court opinion so "factually and legally inaccurate" as to raise questions as to the court's integrity. Should he be treated less harshly than a lawyer who stuck by what he said?

In addition, discipline can be imposed for purely personal conduct, unrelated to representing a client or law practice. Neither ABA *Code* DR-1-102 nor the *Model Rule* 8.4, the general "honesty" rules, are limited to representation of a client. *State Bar of Arizona v. Richard G. Kleindienst* (1974), set out at Chapter IX-3 *infra*, involves purely personal conduct, testimony during a confirmation hearing. President Clinton's acts, that led to his suspension in Arkansas, were entirely in a personal capacity! See *Neal* v. *Clinton*, set out at Chapter IX-3, *infra*. Comment [2] to *Model Rule* 8.4 does indicate that "some matters of personal morality, such as adultery and comparable offenses ... have no specific connection to the practice of law" and that "[a]lthough a lawyer is personably answerable to the entire criminal law, a lawyer should be professionally answerable only for offenses that indicate lack of those characteristics relevant to law practice." Since *Model Rule* 8.4(c) includes "conduct involving dishonesty, fraud, deceit or misrepresentation," it could be assumed that honest, open adultery is what the Comment [2] has in mind!

Note also that Comment [2] specifically includes "willful failure to file an income tax return" or conduct that reflects "adversely on fitness to practice law," even though that may have nothing to do with law practice. Note also that *Mass. Rule* 8.4 adds two additional misconduct grounds, 8.4(g) failure "without good cause to cooperate with the Bar Counsel or the Board of Bar Overseers" and 8.4(h), "engage in any other conduct that adversely reflects on his or her fitness to practice law," the latter being the old DR-1-102(A)(6) of the *Code*.

These rules are very broad. So are *Model Rule* and *Mass. Rule* 8.4(d), which prohibit "conduct prejudicial to the administration of justice." These are "catch all" provisions. Do you think they would meet the constitutional notice requirements described by Justice White in *In Re Ruffalo*, 390 U.S. 554 (1968), set out in Chapter I-5, *supra*?

C. Jurisdiction and Choice of Law

Not only do these rules cover much conduct outside actual law practice, they also can have a broad jurisdictional scope. This is covered by *Model Rule* 8.5. It states that a lawyer admitted to practice in a jurisdiction "is subject to the disciplinary authority of this jurisdiction, regardless of where the lawyer's conduct occurs." *Model Rule* 8.5(a). But what if you are admitted in two or more jurisdictions? The rule helpfully adds that "a lawyer may be subject to the disciplinary authority of both this jurisdiction and another jurisdiction for the same conduct." Great! But we have already seen that the rules may differ between states, or even between federal courts and state courts in the same state. See the discussion at Chapter I-1, *supra*, "Introduction: What Are Professional Ethics?" So what if a lawyer is subject to conflicting or different professional rules?

This is the problem *Model Rule* 8.5(b) tries to solve. It states:

(b) *Choice of Law.* In any exercise of the disciplinary authority of this jurisdiction, the rules of professional conduct to be applied shall be as follows:

(1) for conduct in connection with a matter pending before a tribunal, the rules of the jurisdiction in which the tribunal sits, unless the rules of the tribunal provide otherwise; and

(2) for any other conduct, the rules of the jurisdiction in which the lawyer's conduct occurred, or, if the predominant effect of the conduct is in a different jurisdiction, the rules of that jurisdiction shall be applied to the conduct. A lawyer shall not be subject to discipline if the lawyer's conduct conforms to the rules of a jurisdiction in which the lawyer reasonably believes the predominant effect of the lawyer's conduct will occur.

But does this really solve the problem? Massachusetts has now adopted the ADA version of Rule 8.5, after having a different version for many years. But Massachusetts also added its own comment [1B] to Mass. 8.5 stating, "There is no completely satisfactory solution to the choice of law question so long as different states have different rules of professional responsibility." Certainly, lawyers admitted to several state bars still have to be very careful.

D. Self-Incrimination

We have noted that there is serious tension between some of the professional rules and the constitutional guarantees of the First Amendment, both in a commercial context and with regard to personal political speech. See the discussion at Chapters VIII-1 and IX-1, *supra*. But there have also been serious problems with the Fifth Amendment. What if a lawyer "takes the Fifth" in response to Bar Counsel questions? In *Spevack* v. *Klein*, 385 U.S. 511 (1967), set out at Chapter IX-3, *infra*, a New York lawyer "refused to produce the demanded financial records and refused to testify at the judicial inquiry." A minority opinion of the court, written by Justice Douglas and concurred in by Chief Justice Warren, Black and Brennan, held that "[t]he threat of disbarment and the loss of professional standing, professional reputation, and of livelihood are powerful forms of compulsion to make a lawyer relinquish the privilege" and were comparable to "fine or imprisonment." See *Id.*, p. 628. Justice Fortas concurred, but left open the question of whether a lawyer "might be disbarred for refusing to keep or to produce ... records which the lawyer was lawfully and properly required to keep by the state ..." See *Id.*, p. 631. Justice Harlan wrote a powerful dissent, joined by Justice Clark and Stewart, beginning with "This decision, made in the name of the Constitution, permits a lawyer suspected of professional misconduct to thwart direct official inquiry of him without fear of disciplinary action. What is done today will be disheartening and frustrating to courts and bar associations throughout the country in their efforts to maintain high standard at the bar." *Id.*, p. 631.

Read *Spevack* v. *Klein* carefully, as well as *Debock* v. *State*, 512 So. 2d 164 (Fla. 1987), *cert. denied* 484 U.S. 1025 (1988), also set out at Chapter IX-3, *infra*. In *Spevack*, the lawyer was disbarred *solely* for invoking the privilege. Does that allow Bar Counsel to weigh "taking the Fifth" in connection with other incriminating evidence? What if the lawyer is given a grant of immunity and is required to testify. Can that testimony be used in a disciplinary proceeding? The Florida Court in *Debock*, *supra* said "yes." Do you agree? For that matter, do you agree with *Spevack* at all? Self-incrimination remains a troublesome issue in the context of professional discipline. See Geoffrey Hazard and Cameron Beard, "A Lawyer's Privilege Against Self-Incrimination Disciplinary Proceedings," 96 *Yale L. J.* 1060 (1987). Would you extend the Fifth Amendemtn privilege to Bar Application forms like the ones set out in Chapter VIII-3, *infra*? Again, Massachusetts added a new Rule 8.4(g) to the *Mass. Rules* making it misconduct to "fail without good cause to cooperate with the Bar Counsel or the Board of Bar Overseers." When should the Fifth Amendment be "good cause" not to cooperate?

E. Self-Enforcement: The "Snitch" Rule, Model Rule 8.3

Now we come to the most controversial areas of all. Think of another profession, such as medicine. Who is most likely to know if there is "a substantial question" as to whether a doctor is fit to practice medicine? It might be the patients, but they will probably lack the expertise to judge. More likely it would be the other professionals that surround the doctor: hospital staff, nurses and—other doctors. What if a doctor commits a violation of a professional rule that "raises a substantial question ... as to that doctor's honesty, trust worthiness or fitness as a doctor in other respects" and another doctor *knows about it*? Should not that other doctor report the violation to "the appropriate professional authority?" If he does not, should not that second doctor also be punished? Lives could be at stake!

Model Rule 8.3 requires the same of lawyers. But it is very controversial. Almost all lawyers agree that there should be the discretion to report a serious violation of a professional rule that raises a "substantial question" as to another lawyer's fitness to practice, assuming no *Model Rule* 1.6 confidentiality is involved. Most would further agree that, as a matter of moral responsibility, a lawyer "should" report such a violation, particularly because the rule exempts confidential client information and information gained "while participating in an approved lawyers assistance program." See *Model Rule* 8.3(c). The debate is over whether to make the duty mandatory, i.e., not "may" or "should," but "shall." If it is mandatory, failure to report will, in itself, be professional misconduct on the part of any lawyer who learns of such a violation, and fails to report it.

The ABA *Code* had a similar provision, DR-1-103(A), "A lawyer possessing unprivileged knowledge of a violation of DR-1-102 shall report such knowledge to a tribunal or other authority ..." After much debate, Massachusetts Supreme Judicial Court Justice John V. Spalding, as Special Master, filed a report on April 13, 1972 recommending that the rule *not* be adopted, and DR-1-103(A) was not adopted in Massachusetts. See the Spalding Report set out in Chapter IX-3, *infra*. Later, at the time Massachusetts moved to a "*Model Rule*" format, the matter was debated again, and I was asked to make an oral argument for adopting the *mandatory Model Rule* 8.3, on September 9, 1997. All the representatives of the major bar associations were against me, and made arguments *against* a mandatory *Model Rule* 8.3. The Supreme Judicial Court decided my way. A large number of Massachusetts lawyers, however, disagreed, and call *Mass. Rule* 8.3 the "snitch rule." My argument, which is set out at Chapter IX-3, *infra*, was certainly not popular with them!

There is no doubt that a vigorous enforcement of a mandatory *Mass. Rule* 8.3, which Bar Counsel has promised, will create problems for practicing lawyers. Imagine that you practice in a big firm with hundreds of lawyers, and you learn of such a *Mass. Rule* 8.3 violation. You report it to the firm management, but they do nothing. *Mass. Rule* 5.2 ("Responsibilities of a Subordinate Lawyer") gives an associate a little protection, if the result is a "Supervisory lawyer's reasonable resolution of an arguable question of professional duty." But even associates are personally responsible for clear violations, no matter what the partners say. See *Daniels* v. *Alexander* 844 A.2d 182 (Conn. 2003). *Mass. Rule* 5.1 (Responsibilities of a Partner or Supervising Lawyer") makes partners completely responsible. If the violation comes out, all of the lawyers who knew of it could be in trouble under *Mass. Rule* 8.3. What if Bar Counsel made it a policy that, whenever such a rule violation is discovered, every effort be made to see if any other lawyers knew about it? But think again about what you expect from other professions that are largely self-regulating, including medicine. The privilege of self-regulation brings difficult duties. There is, of course, an alternative, being regulated by others. As Justice Lewis F. Powell, then President of the American Bar Association, said.

> "Surely no one wants punitive action, but it must be remembered that the bar
> has a privilege of disciplining itself to a greater extent than any other profession
> or calling. This imposes on the bar a higher responsibility, one which the bar

must discharge with greater determination." See the ABA Committee on Evaluation of Disciplinary Enforcement, etc., (1970) set out at Chapter IX-3, *infra*.

What do you think?

IX-2. Bar Discipline: The Rules

ABA Model Rules

RULE 5.1: RESPONSIBILITIES OF A PARTNER OR SUPERVISORY LAWYER

(a) A partner in a law firm, and a lawyer who individually or together with other lawyers possesses comparable managerial authority in a law firm, shall make reasonable efforts to ensure that the firm has in effect measures giving reasonable assurance that all lawyers in the firm conform to the Rules of Professional Conduct.

(b) A lawyer having direct supervisory authority over another lawyer shall make reasonable efforts to ensure that the other lawyer conforms to the Rules of Professional Conduct.

(c) A lawyer shall be responsible for another lawyer's violation of the Rules of Professional Conduct if:

(1) the lawyer orders or, with knowledge of the specific conduct, ratifies the conduct involved; or

(2) the lawyer is a partner or has comparable managerial authority in the law firm in which the other lawyer practices, or has direct supervisory authority over the other lawyer, and knows of the conduct at a time when its consequences can be avoided or mitigated but fails to take reasonable remedial action.

Comment

[1] Paragraph (a) applies to lawyers who have managerial authority over the professional work of a firm. See Rule 1.0(c). This includes members of a partnership, the shareholders in a law firm organized as a professional corporation, and members of other associations authorized to practice law; lawyers having comparable managerial authority in a legal services organization or a law department of an enterprise or government agency; and lawyers who have intermediate managerial responsibilities in a firm. Paragraph (b) applies to lawyers who have supervisory authority over the work of other lawyers in a firm.

[2] Paragraph (a) requires lawyers with managerial authority within a firm to make reasonable efforts to establish internal policies and procedures designed to provide reasonable assurance that all lawyers in the firm will conform to the Rules of Professional Conduct. Such policies and procedures include those designed to detect and resolve conflicts of interest, identify dates by which actions must be taken in pending matters, account for client funds and property and ensure that inexperienced lawyers are properly supervised.

[3] Other measures that may be required to fulfill the responsibility prescribed in paragraph (a) can depend on the firm's structure and the nature of its practice. In a small firm of experienced lawyers, informal supervision and periodic review of compliance with the required systems ordinarily will suffice. In a large firm, or in practice situations in which difficult ethical problems frequently arise, more elaborate measures may be necessary. Some firms, for example, have a procedure whereby junior lawyers can make

confidential referral of ethical problems directly to a designated senior partner or special committee. See Rule 5.2. Firms, whether large or small, may also rely on continuing legal education in professional ethics. In any event, the ethical atmosphere of a firm can influence the conduct of all its members and the partners may not assume that all lawyers associated with the firm will inevitably conform to the Rules.

[4] Paragraph (c) expresses a general principle of personal responsibility for acts of another. See also Rule 8.4(a).

[5] Paragraph (c)(2) defines the duty of a partner or other lawyer having comparable managerial authority in a law firm, as well as a lawyer who has direct supervisory authority over performance of specific legal work by another lawyer. Whether a lawyer has supervisory authority in particular circumstances is a question of fact. Partners and lawyers with comparable authority have at least indirect responsibility for all work being done by the firm, while a partner or manager in charge of a particular matter ordinarily also has supervisory responsibility for the work of other firm lawyers engaged in the matter. Appropriate remedial action by a partner or managing lawyer would depend on the immediacy of that lawyer's involvement and the seriousness of the misconduct. A supervisor is required to intervene to prevent avoidable consequences of misconduct if the supervisor knows that the misconduct occurred. Thus, if a supervising lawyer knows that a subordinate misrepresented a matter to an opposing party in negotiation, the supervisor as well as the subordinate has a duty to correct the resulting misapprehension.

[6] Professional misconduct by a lawyer under supervision could reveal a violation of paragraph (b) on the part of the supervisory lawyer even though it does not entail a violation of paragraph (c) because there was no direction, ratification or knowledge of the violation.

[7] Apart from this Rule and Rule 8.4(a), a lawyer does not have disciplinary liability for the conduct of a partner, associate or subordinate. Whether a lawyer may be liable civilly or criminally for another lawyer's conduct is a question of law beyond the scope of these Rules.

[8] The duties imposed by this Rule on managing and supervising lawyers do not alter the personal duty of each lawyer in a firm to abide by the Rules of Professional Conduct. See Rule 5.2(a).

RULE 5.2: RESPONSIBILITIES OF A SUBORDINATE LAWYER

(a) A lawyer is bound by the Rules of Professional Conduct notwithstanding that the lawyer acted at the direction of another person.

(b) A subordinate lawyer does not violate the Rules of Professional Conduct if that lawyer acts in accordance with a supervisory lawyer's reasonable resolution of an arguable question of professional duty.

Comment

[1] Although a lawyer is not relieved of responsibility for a violation by the fact that the lawyer acted at the direction of a supervisor, that fact may be relevant in determining whether a lawyer had the knowledge required to render conduct a violation of the Rules. For example, if a subordinate filed a frivolous pleading at the direction of a supervisor, the subordinate would not be guilty of a professional violation unless the subordinate knew of the document's frivolous character.

[2] When lawyers in a supervisor-subordinate relationship encounter a matter involving professional judgment as to ethical duty, the supervisor may assume responsibility for

making the judgment. Otherwise a consistent course of action or position could not be taken. If the question can reasonably be answered only one way, the duty of both lawyers is clear and they are equally responsible for fulfilling it. However, if the question is reasonably arguable, someone has to decide upon the course of action. That authority ordinarily reposes in the supervisor, and a subordinate may be guided accordingly. For example, if a question arises whether the interests of two clients conflict under Rule 1.7, the supervisor's reasonable resolution of the question should protect the subordinate professionally if the resolution is subsequently challenged.

RULE 8.3: REPORTING PROFESSIONAL MISCONDUCT

(a) A lawyer who knows that another lawyer has committed a violation of the Rules of Professional Conduct that raises a substantial question as to that lawyer's honesty, trustworthiness or fitness as a lawyer in other respects, shall inform the appropriate professional authority.

(b) A lawyer who knows that a judge has committed a violation of applicable rules of judicial conduct that raises a substantial question as to the judge's fitness for office shall inform the appropriate authority.

(c) This Rule does not require disclosure of information otherwise protected by Rule 1.6 or information gained by a lawyer or judge while participating in an approved lawyers assistance program.

Comment

[1] Self-regulation of the legal profession requires that members of the profession initiate disciplinary investigation when they know of a violation of the Rules of Professional Conduct. Lawyers have a similar obligation with respect to judicial misconduct. An apparently isolated violation may indicate a pattern of misconduct that only a disciplinary investigation can uncover. Reporting a violation is especially important where the victim is unlikely to discover the offense.

[2] A report about misconduct is not required where it would involve violation of Rule 1.6. However, a lawyer should encourage a client to consent to disclosure where prosecution would not substantially prejudice the client's interests.

[3] If a lawyer were obliged to report every violation of the Rules, the failure to report any violation would itself be a professional offense. Such a requirement existed in many jurisdictions but proved to be unenforceable. This Rule limits the reporting obligation to those offenses that a self-regulating profession must vigorously endeavor to prevent. A measure of judgment is, therefore, required in complying with the provisions of this Rule. The term "substantial" refers to the seriousness of the possible offense and not the quantum of evidence of which the lawyer is aware. A report should be made to the bar disciplinary agency unless some other agency, such as a peer review agency, is more appropriate in the circumstances. Similar considerations apply to the reporting of judicial misconduct.

[4] The duty to report professional misconduct does not apply to a lawyer retained to represent a lawyer whose professional conduct is in question. Such a situation is governed by the Rules applicable to the client-lawyer relationship.

[5] Information about a lawyer's or judge's misconduct or fitness may be received by a lawyer in the course of that lawyer's participation in an approved lawyers or judges assistance program. In that circumstance, providing for an exception to the reporting requirements of paragraphs (a) and (b) of this Rule encourages lawyers and judges to seek

treatment through such a program. Conversely, without such an exception, lawyers and judges may hesitate to seek assistance from these programs, which may then result in additional harm to their professional careers and additional injury to the welfare of clients and the public. These Rules do not otherwise address the confidentiality of information received by a lawyer or judge participating in an approved lawyers assistance program; such an obligation, however, may be imposed by the rules of the program or other law.

RULE 8.5: DISCIPLINARY AUTHORITY; CHOICE OF LAW

(a) Disciplinary Authority. A lawyer admitted to practice in this jurisdiction is subject to the disciplinary authority of this jurisdiction, regardless of where the lawyer's conduct occurs. A lawyer not admitted in this jurisdiction is also subject to the disciplinary authority of this jurisdiction if the lawyer provides or offers to provide any legal services in this jurisdiction. A lawyer may be subject to the disciplinary authority of both this jurisdiction and another jurisdiction for the same conduct.

(b) Choice of Law. In any exercise of the disciplinary authority of this jurisdiction, the rules of professional conduct to be applied shall be as follows:

> (1) for conduct in connection with a matter pending before a tribunal, the rules of the jurisdiction in which the tribunal sits, unless the rules of the tribunal provide otherwise; and

> (2) for any other conduct, the rules of the jurisdiction in which the lawyer's conduct occurred, or, if the predominant effect of the conduct is in a different jurisdiction, the rules of that jurisdiction shall be applied to the conduct. A lawyer shall not be subject to discipline if the lawyer's conduct conforms to the rules of a jurisdiction in which the lawyer reasonably believes the predominant effect of the lawyer's conduct will occur.

Comment

Disciplinary Authority

[1] It is longstanding law that the conduct of a lawyer admitted to practice in this jurisdiction is subject to the disciplinary authority of this jurisdiction. Extension of the disciplinary authority of this jurisdiction to other lawyers who provide or offer to provide legal services in this jurisdiction is for the protection of the citizens of this jurisdiction. Reciprocal enforcement of a jurisdiction's disciplinary findings and sanctions will further advance the purposes of this Rule. See, Rules 6 and 22, ABA *Model Rules for Lawyer Disciplinary Enforcement*. A lawyer who is subject to the disciplinary authority of this jurisdiction under Rule 8.5(a) appoints an official to be designated by this Court to receive service of process in this jurisdiction. The fact that the lawyer is subject to the disciplinary authority of this jurisdiction may be a factor in determining whether personal jurisdiction may be asserted over the lawyer for civil matters.

Choice of Law

[2] A lawyer may be potentially subject to more than one set of rules of professional conduct which impose different obligations. The lawyer may be licensed to practice in more than one jurisdiction with differing rules, or may be admitted to practice before a particular court with rules that differ from those of the jurisdiction or jurisdictions in which the lawyer is licensed to practice. Additionally, the lawyer's conduct may involve significant contacts with more than one jurisdiction.

[3] Paragraph (b) seeks to resolve such potential conflicts. Its premise is that minimizing conflicts between rules, as well as uncertainty about which rules are applicable, is in the best interest of both clients and the profession (as well as the bodies having authority to regulate the profession). Accordingly, it takes the approach of (i) providing that any particular conduct of a lawyer shall be subject to only one set of rules of professional conduct, (ii) making the determination of which set of rules applies to particular conduct as straightforward as possible, consistent with recognition of appropriate regulatory interests of relevant jurisdictions, and (iii) providing protection from discipline for lawyers who act reasonably in the face of uncertainty.

[4] Paragraph (b)(1) provides that as to a lawyer's conduct relating to a proceeding pending before a tribunal, the lawyer shall be subject only to the rules of the jurisdiction in which the tribunal sits unless the rules of the tribunal, including its choice of law rule, provide otherwise. As to all other conduct, including conduct in anticipation of a proceeding not yet pending before a tribunal, paragraph (b)(2) provides that a lawyer shall be subject to the rules of the jurisdiction in which the lawyer's conduct occurred, or, if the predominant effect of the conduct is in another jurisdiction, the rules of that jurisdiction shall be applied to the conduct. In the case of conduct in anticipation of a proceeding that is likely to be before a tribunal, the predominant effect of such conduct could be where the conduct occurred, where the tribunal sits or in another jurisdiction.

[5] When a lawyer's conduct involves significant contacts with more than one jurisdiction, it may not be clear whether the predominant effect of the lawyer's conduct will occur in a jurisdiction other than the one in which the conduct occurred. So long as the lawyer's conduct conforms to the rules of a jurisdiction in which the lawyer reasonably believes the predominant effect will occur, the lawyer shall not be subject to discipline under this Rule.

[6] If two admitting jurisdictions were to proceed against a lawyer for the same conduct, they should, applying this rule, identify the same governing ethics rules. They should take all appropriate steps to see that they do apply the same rule to the same conduct, and in all events should avoid proceeding against a lawyer on the basis of two inconsistent rules.

[7] The choice of law provision applies to lawyers engaged in transnational practice, unless international law, treaties or other agreements between competent regulatory authorities in the affected jurisdictions provide otherwise.

IX-3. Bar Discipline: Cases and Materials

A. Fitness

In re Gilman
Supreme Court of Kansas
280 Kan. 962
No. 95,133
Feb. 3, 2006

ORIGINAL PROCEEDING IN DISCIPLINE

PER CURIAM:

This is an original proceeding in discipline filed by the office of the Disciplinary Administrator against David R. Gilman, of Overland Park, an attorney admitted to the practice of law in Kansas. The formal complaint filed against the Respondent alleged violations of KRPC 8.4(d) (2005 Kan. Ct. R. Annot. 504) (misconduct); KRPC 3.4(d) (2005 Kan. Ct. R. Annot 467) (fairness to opposing party and counsel); KRPC 3.5(c) (2005 Kan. Ct. R. Annot. 471) (impartiality and decorum to the tribunal); and KRPC 8.4(g) (2005 Kan. Ct. R. Annot. 504) (misconduct), but as will be clarified in the opinion, the hearing panel and this court found the evidence was sufficient only as to KRPC 8.4(d).

* * *

CONCLUSIONS OF LAW

1. Based upon the findings of fact, the Hearing Panel concludes as a matter of law that the Respondent violated KRPC 8.4(d). 'It is professional misconduct for a lawyer to ... engage in conduct that is prejudicial to the administration of justice.' KRPC 8.4(d). In this case, the Respondent engaged in conduct that is prejudicial to the administration of justice when he appeared in court after having consumed several drinks of whiskey. Because the Respondent appeared to be impaired, Judge Baird continued Ms. Brandel's trial and had to call a recess to address the Respondent's condition.

2. In addition to alleging that the Respondent violated KRPC 8.4(d), the Deputy Disciplinary Administrator alleged that the Respondent violated KRPC 3.4(d), KRPC 3.5(c), and KRPC 8.4(g). The Hearing Panel concludes that the Deputy Disciplinary Administrator failed to present clear and convincing evidence that the Respondent violated those rules.

3. KRPC 3.4(c) provides, in pertinent part, as follows:

'A lawyer shall not ... knowingly disobey an obligation under the rules of a tribunal except for an open refusal based on an assertion that no valid obligation exists.'

The Deputy Disciplinary Administrator argued that Respondent knowingly disobeyed an order of the Court when he drove his vehicle from the Lenexa Municipal Court. The Hearing Panel concludes that Judge Baird did not have the authority to order the Respondent to refrain from driving his vehicle. Accordingly, Judge Baird's direction, ordering the Respondent to refrain from driving his vehicle, was not a valid obligation of the tribunal. As such the Hearing Panel concludes that the Respondent did not violate KRPC 3.4(d).

4. Lawyers shall not 'engage in undignified or discourteous conduct degrading to a tribunal.' KRPC 3.5(d). The Deputy Disciplinary Administrator argued that by appearing in court impaired by the use of alcohol, the Respondent engaged in 'undignified or discourteous conduct.' The Hearing Panel agrees that appearing in Court after having consumed 'several' drinks of whiskey, the Respondent engaged in 'undignified' conduct. However, the Respondent's 'undignified' conduct was not degrading to the tribunal. No testimony was presented that he was disrespectful or discourteous to the Court. Accordingly, the Hearing Panel concludes that the Respondent did not violate KRPC 3.5(d).

5. Finally, the Deputy Disciplinary Administrator alleged that the Respondent engaged in 'other conduct that adversely reflects on the lawyer's fitness to practice law.' KRPC 8.4(g). It is the position of the Hearing Panel that the 'catch-all' provision of KRPC 8.4(g) does not apply if another provision of the Kansas Rules of Professional Conduct does apply. As such, because the Hearing Panel concludes that KRPC 8.4(d) applies, the Hearing Panel concludes that the provisions of KRPC 8.4(g) do not apply.

* * *

RECOMMENDATION

"The Respondent recommended that the allegations that the Respondent violated the Kansas Rules of Professional Conduct be dismissed, arguing that the rules which govern our profession do not prohibit attorneys from appearing in court after having consumed alcohol.

"While the Hearing Panel acknowledges that none of the Kansas Rules of Professional Conduct specifically prohibit attorneys from appearing in court after having consumed alcohol, the rules prohibit many of the consequences which may be expected from appearing in Court after consuming alcohol. When the Respondent appeared in Court after having consumed several drinks of whiskey, he caused the Court to grant his request for a continuance and recess so that the question of his impairment could be further examined and the rights of his client protected. The Respondent's conduct interfered with the administration of justice and violated KRPC 8.4(d). Accordingly, the Hearing Panel declines to dismiss the allegations as requested by the Respondent.

"The Deputy Disciplinary Administrator recommended that the Respondent be suspended from the practice of law. The Deputy Disciplinary Administrator based his recommendation on the serious nature of the misconduct and the fact that the Respondent has been previously disciplined in six cases. While the Respondent's conduct is serious and requires appropriate discipline, the Hearing Panel does not believe that the Respondent's conduct warrants a suspension from the practice of law. Since the only consequences of the drinking appear to have been to cause the Court to grant a continuance which it may not have otherwise granted, the Hearing Panel does not believe it appropriate to discipline on the basis of possible consequences which did not occur.

"The Hearing Panel is concerned, however, that the Respondent does not appreciate the seriousness of his misconduct. The Respondent acknowledged no wrongdoing and made no promises of reform, other than in his initial written response to the investigator. No evidence was presented that the Respondent did, in fact, contact Don Zemites [of the Kansas Impaired Lawyers Assistance Program] or seek any professional help. Because the Respondent does not appear to appreciate the serious nature of his misconduct, the Hearing Panel believes that some form of public discipline is appropriate. Given the remote nature of the Respondent's prior discipline, the Hearing Panel finds it of limited relevance and recommends that censure, to be published in the Kansas Reports, is the appropriate discipline in this case.

"Costs are assessed against the Respondent in an amount to be certified by the Office of the Disciplinary Administrator."

DISCUSSION

Respondent did not file exceptions to the final hearing report of the panel. Accordingly, pursuant to Supreme Court Rule 212(d) (2005 Kan. Ct. R. Annot. 297), the panel's findings of fact are deemed admitted. These findings of fact are supported by clear and convincing evidence and also support the panel's conclusions of law. We adopt the findings and conclusions of the panel.

A majority of this court agrees with the panel's recommendation for discipline in this case. However, a minority of this court would discipline Respondent by imposing a suspension of his license to practice law in this state.

All members of the court express the same concerns of the panel in this case: Respondent does not appreciate the seriousness of his misconduct and the record supports the conclusion that Respondent minimized, rationalized, and excused his drinking misconduct.

We note that Respondent appeared in the Lenexa Municipal Court on December 9th with "an odor of alcohol coming from the Respondent" and that his "speech was slurred." The municipal judge believed Respondent to be impaired because of his use of alcohol.

After granting a continuance to Respondent's client, the court took a recess to address Respondent's condition. Respondent was asked to take a preliminary breath test which Respondent submitted to. The court was shocked with the result of the test and directed Respondent not to drive from the courthouse. Notwithstanding this admonition, Respondent administered himself a field sobriety test and left in his automobile after he passed his test.

Approximately 2 months later, Respondent was present in the same courthouse when the prosecutor smelled alcohol on his breath. She confirmed the presence of alcohol based upon an agreed to preliminary breath test. At the time, the prosecutor was concerned about Respondent's ability to drive a car. The similarity of the two charges adds weight to the court's concern that Respondent may have a serious alcohol problem that should be addressed.

There is no indication in the record that Respondent has taken any action to address the above concern. Instead, Respondent demonstrates no remorse, acknowledges no wrongdoing, and has taken no steps to address what may be a serious problem. Yet, the record supports the findings and conclusions by clear and convincing evidence that Respondent violated the provisions of KRPC 8.4(d) [2005 Kan. Ct. R. Annot. 504]: "It is professional misconduct for a lawyer to … engage in conduct that is prejudicial to the administration of justice." Respondent engaged in such conduct when he appeared in court after having consumed several drinks of alcohol. The court had to continue the case Respondent was appearing on because the court concluded that Respondent was impaired by reason of the alcohol. Additionally, a recess had to be called to address the condition of Respondent.

Thus, in addition to imposing the panel's recommended discipline, this court urges Respondent to contact Mr. Don Zemites, Executive Director, Kansas Impaired Lawyers Assistance Program, for advice and help with what may be a serious problem for the Respondent. See Supreme Court Rule 206 (2005 Kan. Ct. R. Annot. 268). Based upon the discipline imposed, this court is not in a position to order Respondent to seek the above help. The recommendation, however, is made for the benefit of Respondent, his clients, the courts in which he practices, and his continued practice of law in this state.

IT IS THEREFORE ORDERED that Respondent, David R. Gilman, be and he is hereby disciplined by published censure in accordance with Supreme Court Rule 203(a)(3) (2005 Kan. Ct. R. Annot. 247) for violation of KRPC 8.4(d).

* * *

Attorney Grievance Commission of Maryland v. Reinhardt
Court of Appeals of Maryland
391 Md. 209
Feb. 10, 2006
[Some footnotes deleted. Remaining footnotes renumbered.]

Dolores O. Ridgell, Asst. Bar Counsel (Melvin Hirshman, Bar Counsel, Atty. Grievance Com'n), for petitioner.

J. Calvin Jenkins, Jr., Towson, for respondent.

Argued before BELL, C.J., RAKER, WILNER, CATHELL, HARRELL, BATTAGLIA and GREENE, JJ.

RAKER, J.

The Attorney Grievance Commission of Maryland filed a petition with this Court for disciplinary action against Richard J. Reinhardt, alleging violations of the Maryland Rules of Professional Conduct.[1] The Commission charged respondent with violating Maryland Rules of Professional Conduct: (1) Rule 1.1 Competence, (2) Rule 1.2 Scope of Representation, (3) Rule 1.3 Diligence, (4) Rule 1.4 Communication, (5) Rule 3.2 Expediting Litigation, and (6) Rule 8.4 Misconduct. Pursuant to Maryland Rule 16-752(a), we referred the matter to Judge Ruth Jakubowski of the Circuit Court for Baltimore County to make findings of fact and proposed conclusions of law. Judge Jakubowski held an evidentiary hearing and concluded that respondent had violated Rules 1.1, 1.2(a), and 1.4(b). Respondent admitted to violating Maryland Rules of Professional Conduct 1.3, 1.4(a) and 3.2.

I.

"The Petitioner has charged Respondent with violating the following rules of Maryland Rules of Professional Conduct.

Rule 1.1. Competence.

A lawyer shall provide competent representation to a client. Competent representation requires the legal knowledge, skill, thoroughness and preparation reasonably necessary for the representation.

Rule 1.2. Scope of Representation.

(a) A lawyer shall abide by a client's decisions concerning the objectives of representation, subject to paragraphs (c), (d) and (e), and, when appropriate, shall consult with the client as to the means by which they are to be pursued. A lawyer shall abide by a client's decision whether to accept an offer of settlement of a matter. In a crim-

---

1. The version of the Maryland Rules of Professional Conduct applicable to this case is the version of the Maryland Rules in effect prior to July 1, 2005.

inal case, the lawyer shall abide by the client's decision, after consultation with the lawyer, as to a plea to be entered, whether to waive jury trial and whether the client will testify.

(b) A lawyer's representation of a client, including representation by appointment does not constitute an endorsement of the client's political, economic, social or moral views or activities.

(c) A lawyer may limit the objectives of the representation if the client consents after consultation.

(d) A lawyer shall not counsel a client to engage, or assist a client, in conduct that the lawyer knows is criminal or fraudulent, but a lawyer may discuss the legal consequences of any proposed course of conduct with a client and may counsel or assist a client to make a good faith effort to determine the validity, scope, meaning or application of the law.

(e) When a lawyer knows that a client expects assistance not permitted by the rules of professional conduct or other law, the lawyer shall consult with the client regarding the relevant limitations on the lawyer's conduct.

Rule 1.3. Diligence.

A lawyer shall act with reasonable diligence and promptness in representing a client.

Rule 1.4. Communication.

(a) A lawyer shall keep a client reasonably informed about the status of a matter and promptly comply with reasonable requests for information.

(b) A lawyer shall explain a matter to the extent reasonably necessary to permit the client to make informed decisions regarding the representation.

Rule 3.2. Expediting Litigation.

A lawyer shall make reasonable efforts to expedite litigation consistent with the interests of the client.

Rule 8.4. Misconduct.

It is professional misconduct for a lawyer to: ...

(c) engage in conduct involving dishonesty, fraud, deceit or misrepresentation;

(d) engage in conduct that is prejudicial to the administration of justice; ...

"The parties entered into a Stipulation (Joint Exhibit 1) in which most of the allegations of Petitioner's Complaint have been admitted.

"All the Petitioner's charges against the Respondent arise out of the Respondent's handling of a personal injury claim of his client, Ms. Bernice Cohen, who was involved in an automobile accident on August 2, 1996. The evidence was undisputed that Ms. Cohen was injured in a multi-vehicle automobile accident in Maryland on August 2, 1996. At the time of the accident, Ms. Cohen was a resident of New York and the accident occurred in Maryland. The evidence is also undisputed that within about two days of Ms. Cohen's release from Johns Hopkins Hospital, sometime in August of 1996, she engaged the Respondent to represent her in any claims resulting from the automobile accident. It is further undisputed that the Respondent assisted Ms. Cohen in making a claim against her spouse's auto insurance carrier for personal injury protection (PIP) benefits and actually obtained these benefits for

Ms. Cohen. It is also undisputed that the Respondent obtained the investigative report, conducted his own investigation and obtained medical reports and bills from Ms. Cohen's health care provider. Respondent admits that he was unable to obtain a financial settlement from the party and/or parties who caused the accident.

"It is further undisputed that on or about July 30, 1999, the Respondent filed a lawsuit in the Circuit Court for Baltimore County on behalf of Ms. Cohen where he named five Defendants including a corporate entity. It is further undisputed that on or about July 30, 1999, the Circuit Court for Baltimore County did issue summons to the Defendants named in the action. It is further undisputed and admitted by the Respondent that he failed to serve said Defendants and failed to take any further action on Ms. Cohen's claim. The Respondent further admits that Ms. Cohen wrote to him on January 14, 2000, requesting a status on her case. The Respondent admitted that he did not respond to this letter and in fact lost the file. According to the testimony, he placed the file in a briefcase and later put that briefcase in a closet, obtained a new briefcase, and did not realize that he had left the file in the old briefcase. It is further admitted by the Respondent that on or about February 20, 2001, Ms. Cohen wrote to the Respondent again requesting information about the status of the case and the Respondent admits to not responding to her letter.

"The evidence further showed that on September 27, 2001, the Clerk of the Circuit Court for Baltimore County issued a Notice of Contemplated Dismissal pursuant to Maryland Rule 2-507. The exhibits presented by the Petitioner indicated that the notification was sent by mail to the Respondent at his Bosley Road address. In testimony before this Court the Respondent indicated that he does not recall ever receiving the 2-507 notice. Although he admits that he failed to take any action to prevent the dismissal of the Circuit Court lawsuit, he does state that if he had received this notice he would have immediately filed a Motion to Stay the Dismissal under Rule 2-507.

"Furthermore, in reviewing the Respondent's file that was admitted into evidence in Petitioner's Exhibit 1, there is no evidence that the 2-507 notification is in the Respondent's file for Ms. Cohen.

"It is further undisputed that on or about April of 2003, Ms. Cohen asked a friend, who is an attorney, to contact the Respondent to gain additional information about the status of her case. On or about May 15, 2003, it is admitted that Elizabeth O'Leary, a New York attorney, spoke with the Respondent by phone and indicated that he was trying to determine the status of her case and promised to contact Ms. Cohen in a few days. Respondent failed to contact Ms. Cohen following the May, 2003, telephone conversation. It is also admitted that on or about July 8, 2003, Ms. O'Leary, counsel in New York, sent Respondent a letter as a follow-up again requesting follow-up.

"Respondent testified that sometime around July or August of 2003, he conducted an aggressive search for the file. He also testified that although he had been searching for the file since January of 2002, that at this point in time he underwent a more rigorous search and ultimately found the lost file in a briefcase in the closet. It is further undisputed that on August 27, 2003, the Respondent sent Ms. Cohen a letter enclosing a copy of the lawsuit.

"Respondent admits that he never told Ms. Cohen that he had lost her file and that he had taken no action on her case since 1999. He did, however, indicate in his letter that there was an issue about securing service on multiple Defendants and advised her to forward any additional medical expenses for further processing. Respondent testified that at the time he sent this letter he did not know that the case had been dismissed on or about September 27, 2001. It is undisputed by the Respondent that following the letter of August 27, 2003, he did not take any action on Ms. Cohen's case. It is further admitted that Ms. Cohen wrote another letter to the Respondent on or about December 3, 2003, informing that she had neither received mail or telephone communications and wanted a response within thirty days. Respondent admitted to not responding to Ms. Cohen's letter of December 3, 2003.

"It is further admitted that on or about April 7, 2004, Ms. Cohen contacted the Attorney Grievance Commission of Maryland concerning Respondent's conduct. Respondent admitted in his testimony that he lost the file and continued to search for it over an eighteen month period to no avail until August of 2003. He denies that he ever knew that the case was dismissed and testified that he first learned of the dismissal when meeting with a representative of the Attorney Grievance Commission. He testified that he was "overwhelmed" when he found out that the case was dismissed.

* * *

Respondent was dishonest and misrepresented the truth when he told his client that he was working on the case when, in fact, he had lost the file and was not working on the case at all. In dealing with his client, respondent exhibited a lack of probity, integrity and straightforwardness, and, therefore, his actions were dishonest in that sense. *See Attorney Grievance v. Sheridan,* 357 Md. 1, 25–26, 741 A.2d 1143, 1156 (1999). Respondent confuses intent with motive. Although respondent may have acted in a certain manner because he was "embarrassed," he unquestionably told the client a lie. Accordingly, we sustain petitioner's exception to the hearing judge's finding as to Rule 8.4(c).

Respondent's admission as to violation of Rules 1.3, 1.4(a), and 3.2, along with the court's finding by clear and convincing evidence that respondent violated Rules 1.1, 1.2, 1.4(b), and this Court's holding that respondent violated 8.4(c), establish a violation of Rule 8.4(d). Behavior that may seriously impair public confidence in the entire profession, without extenuating circumstances, may be conduct prejudicial to the administration of justice. *See Attorney Grievance v. Childress,* 360 Md. 373, 381, 758 A.2d 117, 121 (2000). An attorney's material misrepresentation to the client, his failure to act on the client's case for over three years and failure to expedite litigation, to the client's detriment, is conduct prejudicial to the administration of justice. Failure to represent a client in an adequate manner and lying to a client constitute a violation of Rule 8.4(d). *See Attorney Grievance v. Zdravkovich,* 362 Md. 1, 31, 762 A.2d 950, 966 (2000); *Attorney Grievance v. Mooney,* 359 Md. 56, 83, 753 A.2d 17, 31 (2000); *Attorney Grievance v. Brugh,* 353 Md. 475, 478–79, 727 A.2d 913, 914–15 (1999).

III.

We now turn to the appropriate sanction. The sanction for a violation of the Maryland Rules of Professional Conduct depends on the facts and circumstances of each case, including a consideration of any mitigating factors. *Attorney Grievance v. Zuckerman,* 386 Md. 341, 375, 872 A.2d 693, 713 (2005). In determining the appropriate sanction to be imposed, we are guided by our interest in protecting the public and its attendant confidence in the legal profession. *Attorney Grievance v. Pennington,* 387 Md. 565, 595, 876 A.2d 642, 660 (2005). The purpose of attorney disciplinary proceedings is not to punish the lawyer, but to protect the public as well as to deter other lawyers from violating the Rules of Professional Conduct. *Id.* at 596, 876 A.2d at 660. In order to protect the public, we impose a sanction commensurate with the nature and gravity of the violations and the intent with which the violations were committed. *See Attorney Grievance v. Goodman,* 381 Md. 480, 497, 850 A.2d 1157, 1167 (2004).

Bar Counsel maintains that disbarment is the appropriate sanction because respondent has engaged in a "continuing course and pattern of dishonest and deceitful conduct" absent any compelling, extenuating circumstances. Respondent contends that a suspension of between fifteen and thirty days would be appropriate.

* * *

Respondent's conduct related to one client and one case. Significantly, this is not a case of misappropriation of funds or criminal conduct. Considering all of the circumstances, we conclude that the appropriate sanction is an indefinite suspension from the practice of law.

HARRELL, BATTAGLIA and GREENE, JJ. dissent.

Dissenting Opinion by HARRELL, J., which BATTAGLIA and GREENE, JJ., Join.

I respectfully dissent as to the sanction only. Rather than an indefinite suspension, disbarment is more appropriate.

* * *

State Bar of Arizona v. Richard G. Kleindienst

74-1-S11 (Board of Governors of the State Bar of Arizona,
unpublished opinion by Jesse Adisson Udall,
former Chief Justice of the Arizona Supreme Court, 1974)

I concur with the recommendations of the Board of Governors, but differ on some matters of importance. I have therefore decided to set forth my views separately. Admittedly, such a procedure is unusual, but so is the case. To me, this case involves issues which go to the heart of the legal profession. I feel, therefore, that the Board's report should not be transmitted to the Supreme Court without expressing reasons for the decision in more detail than that which the Board majority adopted.

In writing this, I do not speak for the Board, or even its majority. I state my own opinions, with which some members of the Board might agree, and others would not.

By vote of eight to six, one member not voting, the Board of Governors recommended that Respondent be found guilty of a violation of Disciplinary Rule 1-102(A)(6). The majority voted to censure Respondent for that violation. Of the six who voted against those findings and recommendations, three specifically indicated that they did so because they thought the punishment recommended was insufficient to fit the offense. I tended to agree with them, but voted for the motion to censure because otherwise it would have been impossible to reach a decision, a "majority of the entire Board" being required on disciplinary matters.

The facts of this matter are found in the volumes of the transcript of the testimony given by Respondent before the Senate Judiciary Committee. Those facts are amplified and explained by the statement Respondent made before the Special Local Administrative Committee of the State Bar, by the summary letter authored by the office of the Watergate Prosecutor, by a letter written by Respondent and filed in this case, and by Respondent's answers to questions put to him at the hearing before the Board of Governors. The entire problem must also be placed within the context of the political situation which existed at the time of the offense, for no one could fairly consider the matter without reference to the political partisanship which colored the questioning put to Respondent before the Senate Judiciary Committee and the reactions of anyone placed in Respondent's position.

Despite all this, the *operative facts* are clear and mostly uncontroverted. During the period 1969 to 1970, Respondent was Deputy Attorney General of the United States. Before that he had actively practiced law in Arizona. He has a reputation as a competent, honest practitioner. He had been involved in politics and had run for the office of Governor of Arizona. He had worked hard for the election of Richard Nixon as President of the United States. His stature in the Bar, and his efforts on behalf of the Republican Party, had resulted in his being offered the position of Deputy Attorney General; his acceptance of that position cast him as a participant in a Byzantine political drama.

While Respondent was Deputy Attorney General of the United States, Richard McLaren was Assistant Attorney General with direct responsibility for handling three proposed anti-trust cases wherein the United States proposed to challenge the acquisition by International Telephone and Telegraph of Canteen Corporation, Hartford Insurance and Grinnell Corporation. Regulations of the Justice Department required the Attorney General's approval for filing of anti-trust cases. The Attorney General, John Mitchell, had recused himself and Mr. Kleindienst was therefore responsible for granting or denying approval of the filing of the ITT cases. Mr. McLaren requested and was given approval to file.

As of April, 1971, the United States had filed all three cases. The trial courts had ruled against the United States in Grinnell, had refused to issue a preliminary injunction in Hartford. The Government was awaiting the decision of the court in Canteen. The appeal process had been commenced in Grinnell and the Government's jurisdictional statement in that case was due in the Supreme Court on April 20, 1971.

On April 16, 1971, an attorney for ITT filed a written request with Mr. Kleindienst asking that the government seek an extension of time for filing the jurisdictional statement. Mr. McLaren opposed this request. Mr. Kleindienst told ITT's attorney on April 19, 1971, that it was not likely that the Government would seek an extension. That same day, Mr. Kleindienst received a call from Mr. Ehrlichman, who said he was calling on behalf of President Nixon and was instructing Mr. Kleindienst not to file the Grinnell appeal. Mr. Kleindienst replied that filing could not be withheld. A few minutes later, Mr. Kleindienst received a call from the President, who ordered him to drop the case and not to file the appeal.

Mr. Kleindienst then called Mr. Mitchell and protested the President's orders, threatened resignation and asked Mr. Mitchell to intercede with the President and persuade him to change the orders. Before Mr. Mitchell called back, Respondent talked to Mr. McLaren and the Solicitor General, informed them of the situation and they all agreed not to file the jurisdictional statement but instead to seek an extension. They did so on April 19, 1971. Mr. Mitchell later told Respondent the President ("your friend at the White House") would let Mr. Kleindienst handle it his own way. In effect, the President rescinded his orders to drop the case. Mr. Kleindienst had thus refused the direct orders of the President, withstood the pressure and preserved the Government's position. The cases were thereafter settled by Mr. McLaren's office and on terms favorable to the Government.

During his confirmation hearing in March, 1972, Respondent testified under oath to the Senate Judiciary Committee that he had never "discussed" any aspect of the ITT case with Mr. Mitchell or with anyone on the White House staff; that he had received no suggestions from the White House regarding the cases, and had not been pressured or directed by anyone at the White House; he testified that he had changed his mind and instructed Mr. McLaren and the solicitor General to obtain the extension of time within which to file the jurisdictional statement because of the request from ITT's attorney and the lack of prejudice to the Government in granting that request. Respondent failed to mention his conversations with John Ehrlichman, John Mitchell and Richard M. Nixon. Respondent did not disclose that the true reason for filing the request for the extension was to allow for time to get the President to change his mind or, if he did not, to resign.

On May 16, 1974, Richard G. Kleindienst entered a plea of guilty to an information accusing him of the misdemeanor of violating Title 2, Section 192, United States Code, by refusing or failing to give accurate and complete answers to questions propounded to him while he was testifying under oath before the Senate Judiciary Committee in regard to the matters hereinabove set forth.

The transcripts of the proceedings before the Senate Judiciary Committee, before the Special Local Administrative Committee and before the Board of Governors, together with analysis of the documents forming part of the file (including the comments of Judge Hart at the time of sentencing of Respondent on the misdemeanor conviction, the comments of Mr. Jaworski and of Justice Udall in the dissenting opinion before the Special Local Administrative Committee) all lead to the compelling conclusion that we are dealing with a situation which, while simple from a factual standpoint, is more complex from a moral standpoint.

Factually, Mr. Kleindienst found himself in an untenable situation at the hearings on his confirmation. He felt that the *settlement* of the ITT anti-trust case had been accomplished free from pressure and in a manner advantageous to the Government. He felt he had withstood an intense amount of political pressure and had performed in an exemplary manner by refusing the President's order to dismiss the cases and by proceeding to work out the best settlement obtainable from the United States' viewpoint. He felt, probably correctly, that he deserved commendation for refusing an improper order from the President. On the other hand, he was loyal to his political party and was especially loyal to Richard Nixon, a man for whom he had worked, in whom he believed, and who was then a popular President. He knew the President's attempt to pressure him was wrong; he felt that it had produced no harm and that, for reasons unknown to him, the President had backed off. He also knew that if he revealed the attempt of the President and his counsel to bring pressure on the Attorney General's office on behalf of ITT he would have precipitated a political storm, damaging to the President, though it would certainly have helped insure Mr. Kleindienst's confirmation as Attorney General.

In the final analysis, Respondent tried to protect the President and the Administration by adopting a policy of non-disclosure, unless direct questions were asked. In other words, he did not intend to commit perjury, only to come as close to the line as necessary in order to protect the Administration, but to stop short of perjury. The problem is that it is difficult in the heat of interrogation to tell just where the line between non-disclosure and lying by non-disclosure exists. Whether Respondent's non-disclosure constituted perjury or not is a nice question which, in my mind, is not answered in the record, and perhaps is unanswerable. Certainly it is fair to say that respondent probably did not *consciously* intend to commit perjury.

So, we have a man who has been nominated for the office of Attorney General of the United States, whose qualifications are unquestioned, who has resisted serious political pressure in order to protect the Government's interests but who, it must be said, misled a Senate inquiry in order to protect those in whom he had political faith and to whom he owed political loyalty.

Respondent's answers to questions from the Senate Judiciary Committee, while arguably not perjury, were certainly short of a full and frank description of the events which had occurred. If we take the oath which was administered literally, i.e.: "tell the truth, the whole truth and nothing but the truth," we must find that Respondent failed to tell "the whole truth." He himself admits he answered incompletely, although, he claims, not inaccurately. I would say that his answers were so incomplete as to be inaccurate.

The best method for a witness to keep out of trouble is to tell the whole truth as he knows it. Of course, if Respondent had done that, he would have brought political troubles on the Administration. However, he would not have found himself in his present position. In the long run, he, like Archibald Cox and Elliott Richardson, would have preserved both personal honor and the honor of his profession. If his loyalty motivated him to resist disclosure, his alternative course could well have been to claim executive privilege. If the claim of executive privilege was one which he was unwilling or unable to take, he could simply ask that his name be withdrawn from consideration and pass up the opportunity to become Attorney General. Instead, he chose to take his chances on a policy of non-disclosure and made answers which were incomplete, despite the fact he took the oath to tell " ... the whole truth ..." and despite the fact he was a lawyer, being examined under oath with regard to his qualifications to become Attorney General of the United States.

I think it not overly idealistic to feel that Respondent's acts under those circumstances involved moral turpitude and, regardless of moral turpitude, also involved a violation of several portions of Disciplinary Rule 1-102(A). One must consider the situation *and the duty thereby created:* [The opinion then quotes EC 8-5.].

Under Rule 29(c), conviction of the offense is proof of commission of the act, and, with respect to a misdemeanor, the only inquiry is whether that misdemeanor was one involving moral turpitude. The Special Local Administrative Committee found that it was. A majority of the Board of Governors disagreed and is of the opinion that no moral turpitude can be found because the legal definition of that term requires motives which are absent from this case.

> "Moral turpitude is an elusive concept incapable of precise definition. One dramatic exposition of the term ... has since been consistently followed: An act of baseness, vileness or depravity in the private and social duties which a man owes to his fellow men or to society in general...." In Re Higbie, 99 Cal. Rptr. 865, 493 P.2d 97.

I do not concur with the majority on their finding of an absence of moral turpitude. It is true that we deal with understandable human frailty rather than evil or base motives. However, the definition of moral turpitude must vary somewhat with the circumstances. Non-disclosure may be acceptable between two businessmen dealing at arm's length and with equal means of knowledge. If not acceptable in such circumstances, it would ordinarily not involve moral turpitude. On the other hand, non-disclosure between attorney and client may well involve moral turpitude, a non-disclosure between a man who has been nominated for the highest legal office in the country and the elected representatives of the people of that country is, to my mind, sufficient moral turpitude to warrant imposition of discipline.

Of course, even if the misdemeanor of which Respondent was convicted did not involve moral turpitude, he may be disciplined for breach of some of the disciplinary rules which members of our profession must observe. Here we have an even more interesting concept. Respondent was not an ordinary lawyer involved in an ordinary situation. He was the acting Attorney General at the time of the hearings before the Senate Judiciary Committee, and he was the nominee for the position of Attorney General of the United States. His acts must be judged by the office to which he aspired. Some members of the Board were of the opinion that to be fair to Respondent we must take cognizance of the fact that he was involved in "politics" (and certainly one must admit that any Cabinet position is in a greater or lesser sense "political," and some members of the Board thought that some additional allowance must be made to Respondent because of that fact. Pragmatically, that may be right. However, my view is diametrically opposed. I feel that simply because he was a lawyer, and was the nominee for the highest legal office of the country the duty he owed was higher and not lower; I am unwilling, as a matter of principle, to make any allowance.

Thus, like the majority of the Special Administrative Committee and at least ten members of the Board of Governors, I feel that discipline should be imposed.

The question of what that discipline should be is to my mind considerably less clear. I am cognizant that there is considerable public clamor for disbarment and that many of those who have little knowledge of the facts are most vocal in their recommendation. Interestingly enough, no member of the Board of Governors was in favor of disbarment and I think that even a minimal degree of human understanding of Respondent's predicament would make it impossible to impose such punishment. After all, in the final analysis, Respondent is not convicted of failing to show the degree of candor and honesty of the normal person, but rather of failing to display that greater amount which is to be expected of a person in a much higher position than normal. Punishment for that failure will come from the history books and from Respondent's own feelings of remorse. The basic purpose of the Bar's disciplinary proceedings is not to punish but to protect the public from those lawyers who may fail to properly represent their clients or who may practice in a dishonest manner. No such danger exists with respect to the Respondent.

The problem, however, is that while one can understand, one cannot justify Respondent's failure to disclose and lack of candor; because he was a lawyer in a high place he, of all people, should have been completely candid. To impose no discipline would be to condone, and this the profession cannot do. To disbar the Respondent would be to mete punishment unsuited to the situation. To some extent the same could be said about suspension of Respondent. Somewhere between public censure and a brief suspension the principle is established, the importance of the matter is confirmed and, to my mind, justice is done. I would, therefore, have suspended Respondent for a short period, not for the purpose of "punishing" him, since history has already done that, but for the purpose of establishing a precedent and making it clear that the profession demands more of itself than of other people and that it demands most of those members who seek high office. I think that censure is not enough to establish that precedent; I voted for it since otherwise there would have been insufficient votes to find for imposition of any discipline. However, I felt unable to agree to censure in the absence of some explanation of what was being done and why.

James A. Neal v. William Jefferson Clinton

2001 WL 34355768 (Ark.Cir.)
Circuit Court of Arkansas, Pulaski County, Fifth Division
No. CIV 2000-5677
Jan. 19, 2001

AGREED ORDER OF DISCIPLINE

Come now the parties hereto and agree to the following Order of this Court in settlement of the pending action:

The formal charges of misconduct upon which this Order is based arose out of information referred to the Committee on Professional Conduct ("the Committee") by the Honorable Susan Webber Wright, Chief United States District Judge for the Eastern District of Arkansas. The information pertained to William Jefferson Clinton's deposition testimony in a civil case brought by Ms. Paula Jones in which he was a defendant, *Jones v. Clinton,* No. LR-C-94-290 (E.D.Ark.).

Mr. Clinton was admitted to the Arkansas bar on September 7, 1973. On June 30, 1990, he requested that his Arkansas license be placed on inactive status for continuing legal education purposes, and this request was granted. The conduct at issue here does not arise out of Mr. Clinton's practice of law. At all times material to this case, Mr. Clinton resided in Washington, D.C., but he remained subject to the Model Rules of Professional Conduct for the State of Arkansas.

On April 1, 1998, Judge Wright granted summary judgment to Mr. Clinton, but she subsequently found him in Civil contempt in a 32-page Memorandum Opinion and Order (the "Order") issued on April 12, 1999, ruling that he had "deliberately violated this Court's discovery orders and thereby undermined the integrity of the judicial system." Order, at 31. Judge Wright found that Mr. Clinton had "responded to plaintiff's questions by giving false, misleading and evasive answers that were designed to obstruct the judicial process.... [concerning] whether he and Ms. [Monica] Lewinsky had ever been alone together and whether he had ever engaged in sexual relations with Ms. Lewinsky." Order, at 16 (footnote omitted). Judge Wright offered Mr. Clinton a hearing, which he declined by a letter from his counsel, dated May 7, 1999. Mr. Clinton was subsequently ordered to pay, and did pay, over $90,000, pursuant to the Court's contempt findings. Judge Wright also referred the matter to the Committee "for review and any action it deems appropriate." Order, at 32.

Mr. Clinton's actions which are the subject of this Agreed Order have subjected him to a great deal of public criticism. Twice elected President of the United States, he became only the second President ever impeached and tried by the Senate, where he was acquitted. After Ms. Jones took an appeal of the dismissal of her case, Mr. Clinton settled with her for $850,000, a sum greater than her initial *ad damnum* in her complaint. As already indicated, Mr. Clinton was held in civil contempt and fined over $90,000.

Prior to Judge Wright's referral, Mr. Clinton had no prior disciplinary record with the Committee, including any private warnings. He had been a member in good standing of the Arkansas Bar for over twenty-five years. He has cooperated fully with the Committee in its investigation of this matter and has furnished information to the Committee in a timely fashion.

Mr. Clinton's conduct, as described in the Order, caused the court and counsel for the parties to expend unnecessary time, effort, and resources. It set a poor example for other litigants, and this damaging effect was magnified by the fact that at the time of his deposition testimony, Mr. Clinton was serving as President of the United States.

Judge Wright ruled that the testimony concerning Ms. Lewinsky "was not essential to the core issues in this case and, in fact, that some of this evidence might even be inadmissible...." *Jones v. Clinton*, 993 F.Supp. 1217, 1219 (E.D.Ark.1998). Judge Wright dismissed the case on the merits by granting Mr. Clinton summary judgment, declaring that the case was "lacking in merit—a decision that would not have changed even had the President been truthful with respect to his relationship with Ms. Lewinsky." Order, at 24–25 (footnote omitted). As Judge Wright also observed, as a result of Mr. Clinton's paying $850,000 in settlement, "plaintiff was made whole, having agreed to a settlement in excess of that prayed for in the complaint." Order, at 13. Mr. Clinton also paid to plaintiff $89,484 as the "reasonable expenses, including attorney's fees, caused by his willful failure to obey the Court's discovery orders." Order, at 31; *Jones v. Clinton*, 57 F.Supp.2d 719, 729 (E.D.Ark.1999).

On May 22, 2000, after receiving complaints from Judge Wright and the Southeastern Legal Foundation, the Committee voted to initiate disbarment proceedings against Mr. Clinton. On June 30, 2000, counsel for the Committee filed a complaint seeking disbarment in Pulaski County Circuit Court, *Neal v. Clinton*, Civ. No. 2000-5677. Mr. Clinton filed an answer on August 29, 2000, and the case is in the early stages of discovery.

In this Agreed Order Mr. Clinton admits and acknowledges, and the Court, therefore, finds that:

A. That he knowingly gave evasive and misleading answers, in violation of Judge Wright's discovery orders, concerning his relationship with Ms. Lewinsky, in an attempt to conceal from plaintiff Jones' lawyers the true facts about his improper relationship with Ms. Lewinsky, which had ended almost a year earlier.

B. That by knowingly giving evasive and misleading answers, in violation of Judge Wright's discovery orders, he engaged in conduct that is prejudicial to the administration of justice in that his discovery responses interfered with the conduct of the *Jones* case by causing the court and counsel for the parties to expend unnecessary time, effort, and resources, setting a poor example for other litigants, and causing the court to issue a thirty-two page Order civilly sanctioning Mr. Clinton.

Upon consideration of the proposed Agreed Order, the entire record before the Court, the advice of counsel, and the Arkansas Model Rules of Professional Conduct (the "Model Rules"), the Court finds:

1. That Mr. Clinton's conduct, heretofore set forth, in the *Jones* case violated Model Rule 8.4(d), when he gave knowingly evasive and misleading discovery responses concerning his relationship with Ms. Lewinsky, in violation of Judge Wright's discovery orders. Model Rule 8.4(d) states that it is professional misconduct for a lawyer to "engage in conduct that is prejudicial to the administration of justice."

WHEREFORE, it is the decision and order of this Court that William Jefferson Clinton, Arkansas Bar ID # 73019, be, and hereby is, SUSPENDED for FIVE YEARS for his conduct in this matter, and the payment of fine in the amount of $ 25,000. The suspension shall become effective as of the date of January 19, 2001.

IT IS SO ORDERED.

B. Speech

In re Hinds

90 N.J. 604
Supreme Court of New Jersey
Argued Feb. 9, 1982
Decided Aug. 4, 1982
[Some footnotes omitted.]

HANDLER, J. This case requires us to determine the constitutional scope of rules disciplining an attorney for making out-of-court statements publicly criticizing the trial judge's conduct of an ongoing criminal trial. Lennox Hinds, the appellant, claims that as a matter of constitutional right under the First Amendment, an attorney cannot be disciplined for making such statements unless they present a "clear and present danger" to the fairness of the judicial proceeding. The primary disciplinary standard sought to be applied in this case, however, requires discipline of an attorney if his extrajudicial statements are "reasonably likely" to interfere with a criminal trial. *DR 7-107(D)*.

We now affirm the constitutionality of the "reasonable likelihood" standard of *DR 7-107(D)* for restricting attorney extrajudicial speech in the specific setting of a criminal trial. We further hold that the determination of whether a particular statement is likely to interfere with a fair trial involves a careful balancing of factors, including consideration of the status of the attorney, the nature and timing of the statement, as well as the context in which it was uttered. In addition, we hold that *DR 7-107(D)* applies not only to an attorney of record in a criminal case but also to an attorney who cooperates with the defense on a regular and continuing basis, provides legal assistance in connection with the defense of a criminal charge, and holds himself out to be a member of the defense team. However, because this opinion represents the first time that we have interpreted the proper scope of *DR 7-107(D)* and the standard to be followed in applying this disciplinary rule to extrajudicial statements, we deem it appropriate to give our determination prospective effect only. Consequently, we dismiss these charges against Hinds, as well as related charges under *DR 1-102(A)(5)*, which sanctions attorney conduct that is "prejudicial to the administration of justice."

I

We deal first with the procedural and factual background of the case. Hinds has been a member of the New Jersey Bar since 1973. He has been active and prominent as a lawyer in civil rights causes and has a national reputation for his work as Director of the National Conference of Black Lawyers (hereinafter "NCBL"), a capacity in which he served for five years until 1978. In 1973 Joanne Chesimard, a black woman reputed to be a militant radical, was accused of killing a New Jersey State trooper. Following her arrest, Chesimard was brought to trial after a long series of delays. Hinds represented Chesimard during this pretrial period in several federal civil actions concerning the legality and general conditions of her incarceration by the State. Hinds apparently did not, however, represent Chesimard at her criminal trial.

Chesimard finally went on trial for murder in 1977 in the Superior Court, Law Division, in New Brunswick. After observing the initial phases of the trial and while the jury was still being impaneled, Hinds called a press conference at his New Brunswick office on January 20, 1977. In an article appearing January 21, 1977, in the *New York Daily*

News under the headline, "Joanne Loses 2 Rounds in Trial Transfer," it was reported that:

> ... Lenox [sic] Hinds, an attorney also representing Mrs. Chesimard, said the defense team wanted the case moved to another court because in New Brunswick "what we are seeing is legalized lynching."

> He said he was speaking for the defense team because its members were "gagged" by [the trial judge] whom he accused of asking prospective jurors self-serving questions which he said were leading to "the creation of a hang-man's court."

An article appearing in the *Newark Star-Ledger* on the same date reported that Hinds had referred to the Chesimard trial as "a travesty." The article further quoted Hinds as saying that the trial judge "does not have the judicial temperament or the racial sensitivity to sit as an impartial judge" in Chesimard's trial, and that "[i]t was only after the trial began that we began to have fears that what we are seeing is a legalized lynching."

Also, a television reporter covering the press conference for the New Jersey Public Broadcasting Authority (Channel 52) recorded the following exchange:

> Hinds: "We feel that it is a kangaroo—it will be a kangaroo court unless the judge recluses [sic] himself and that will be the very minimum.

> Reporter: "And a kangaroo court means a guilty verdict?"

> Hinds: "That's correct."

The Middlesex County Ethics Committee (now the District VIII Ethics Committee) authorized an investigation to determine whether Hinds' statements constituted a violation of any disciplinary rules. The investigation was stayed until completion of Chesimard's trial. Chesimard was eventually convicted of murder in the first degree and sentenced to a mandatory term of life imprisonment. Thereafter, the disciplinary proceedings were renewed, and as a result of the investigation, it was recommended that Hinds be charged with violating two disciplinary rules: *DR* 1-102(A)(5), which prohibits attorneys from "[e]ngag[ing] in conduct ... prejudicial to the administration of justice;" and *DR* 7-107(D), which provides that

> [d]uring the selection of a jury or a trial of a criminal matter, a lawyer or law firm associated with the prosecution or defense of a criminal matter shall not make or participate in making an extra-judicial statement that he expects to be disseminated by means of public communication and that relates to the trial, parties, or issues in the trial or other matters that are reasonably likely to interfere with a fair trial....

In December 1977 the Ethics Committee adopted this recommendation and approved the filing of charges against Hinds for violating these disciplinary rules. On January 3, 1978, Hinds was served with the charges and informed that a hearing would be held. Instead of responding, however, Hinds filed a suit in federal court on February 10, 1978, seeking to enjoin the State disciplinary proceedings and to obtain a judgment declaring these particular disciplinary rules unconstitutional. The State proceedings were then stayed during the early stages of the federal litigation.

The United States District Court eventually denied the injunction and dismissed the complaint on grounds of abstention. *Garden State Bar Ass'n v. Middlesex Cty. Ethics Com.*, No. 78-273 (D.C.N.J. June 6, 1978 and Dec. 13, 1979). On appeal, the Third Circuit reversed, finding the abstention doctrine inapplicable because it felt the State procedure effectively denied Hinds the right to present his constitutional claims in a timely manner before a competent State tribunal. *Garden State Bar Ass'n v. Middlesex Cty. Ethics Com.*, 643 *F.*2d 119, rehearing den., 651 *F.*2d 154 (3 Cir. 1981) (en banc).

This Court, on its own motion, then ordered certification of the complaint against Hinds, pursuant to *R.* 2:12-1, and directed that "the entire record, including but not limited to, the constitutional challenges to *DR* 1-102 and *DR* 7-197(D) raised by respondent, be considered by this Court." We also granted leave for the American Civil Liberties Union of New Jersey and the Association of Black Women Lawyers of New Jersey to participate in the case as *amici curiae*. In the meantime, the United States Supreme Court granted *certiorari* in the federal case. In a decision dated June 21, 1982, the Supreme Court reversed the Circuit Court, unanimously holding that the federal courts should abstain from interfering with this State's ongoing disciplinary proceedings. *Middlesex Ethics Comm. v. Garden St. Bar Ass'n*, [457] *U.S.* [423], 102 *S.Ct.* 2515, 73 *L.Ed.*2d 116. The Court reasoned that New Jersey's attorney disciplinary proceedings are considered "judicial in nature," *id.* at [433–34], 102 *S.Ct.* at 2522, the State has an "extremely important interest" in regulating the professional conduct of attorneys, *id.*, and the State's system afforded Hinds "abundant opportunity" to raise his federal constitutional claims, *id.* at [453–36], 102 *S.Ct.* at 2523.

II

Disciplinary Rule 7-107(D) restricts the speech of attorneys who are associated with pending criminal litigation by sanctioning such attorneys for making any extrajudicial statement that they expect to be disseminated to the public and that is "reasonably likely" to interfere with a fair trial.

Appellant Hinds claims that *DR* 7-107(D) is unconstitutionally vague and overbroad under the First Amendment. He asserts that the rule can be applied to restrict speech only when an attorney's out-of-court statements create a "clear and present danger" to the trial and that, applying this constitutional standard to these facts, his remarks regarding the conduct of the judge at the Chesimard trial did not violate the disciplinary rule or otherwise warrant sanction.

We note at the outset that the freedom to engage in robust public debate is at the very heart of the First Amendment. See *Maressa v. New Jersey Monthly*, 89 *N.J.* 176, 200–201, 445 *A.*2d 376 (1982); *Kotlikoff v. Community News*, 89 *N.J.* 62, 73, 444 *A.*2d 1086 (1982). The Constitution unquestionably guarantees the right of citizens to criticize public officials, including judges. See *Brown v. United States*, 356 *U.S.* 148, 153, 78 *S.Ct.* 622, 625, 2 *L.Ed.*2d 589, 596 (1958); *Craig v. Harney*, 331 *U.S.* 367, 376, 67 *S.Ct.* 1249, 1255, 91 *L.Ed.* 1546, 1552 (1946). In our constitutional democracy, expressional activity enjoys the fullest and firmest protection. See *Brandenburg v. Ohio*, 395 *U.S.* 444, 89 *S.Ct.* 1827, 23 *L.Ed.*2d 430 (1969); *Bridges v. California*, 314 *U.S.* 252, 62 *S.Ct.* 190, 86 *L.Ed.* 192 (1941).

A restriction on free speech can survive judicial scrutiny under the First Amendment only if certain fundamental and stringent conditions are satisfied. First, the limitation must "further an important or substantial governmental interest unrelated to the suppression of expression." *Procunier v. Martinez*, 416 *U.S.* 396, 413, 94 *S.Ct.* 1800, 1811, 40 *L.Ed.*2d 224, 240 (1974). Second, the restriction must be "no greater than is necessary or essential to the protection of the particular governmental interest involved." *Id.* These two conditions are interrelated in the sense that the restriction must not only further a substantial governmental interest unrelated to the suppression of speech but it must also go no further than is necessary and essential to protect that substantial governmental interest. The judicial inquiry into whether these conditions have been met involves a balancing process. The court must weigh the gravity and probability of the harm caused by freely allowing the expression against the extent to which free speech rights would be inhibited or circumscribed by suppressing the expression. See *Nebraska Press Association v. Stuart*, 427 *U.S.* 539, 562, 96 *S.Ct.* 2791, 2804, 49 *L.Ed.*2d 683, 699 (1976), citing *United States v. Dennis*, 183 *F.*2d 201, 212 (2 Cir. 1950) (Hand, J.), aff'd, 341 *U.S.* 494, 71 *S.Ct.* 857, 95 *L.Ed.* 1137 (1951).

Like other citizens, attorneys are entitled to the full protection of the First Amendment, even as participants in the administration of justice. See *R.M.J.*, [455] *U.S.* [191, 198–205], 102 *S.Ct.* 929, 935–38, 71 *L.Ed.*2d 64, 70–75 (1982); *Konigsberg v. State Bar*, 353 *U.S.* 252, 273, 77 *S.Ct.* 722, 733, 1 *L.Ed.*2d 810, 825 (1957). *Cf. Richmond Newspapers, Inc. v. Virginia*, 448 *U.S.* 555, 100 *S.Ct.* 2814, 65 *L.Ed.*2d 973 (1980) (reaffirming right of public access to trials). Since *DR* 7-107 purports to restrict the free speech rights of attorneys, its validity turns upon the application of conventional First Amendment standards. Under these demanding tests, we must first examine the nature and importance of the governmental interest assertedly advanced by the restriction.

There can be no doubt that the State has a substantial interest in ensuring the fairness of judicial proceedings. See *State v. Kavanaugh*, 52 *N.J.* 7, 243 *A.*2d 225, *cert.* den., 393 *U.S.* 924, 89 *S.Ct.* 254, 21 *L.Ed.*2d 259 (1968); *State v. Van Duyne*, 43 *N.J.* 369, 204 *A.*2d 841 (1964), *cert.* den., 380 *U.S.* 987, 85 *S.Ct.* 1359, 14 *L.Ed.*2d 279 (1965); *Sheppard v. Maxwell*, 384 *U.S.* 333, 86 *S.Ct.* 1507, 16 *L.Ed.*2d 600 (1966); *Singer v. United States*, 380 *U.S.* 24, 36, 85 *S.Ct.* 783, 790, 13 *L.Ed.*2d 630, 638, 646–47; *In re Sawyer*, 360 *U.S.* 622, 666, 79 *S.Ct.* 1376, 1397, 3 *L.Ed.*2d 1473, 1499 (1959) (Frankfurter, J., dissenting); *Hirschkop v. Snead*, 594 *F.*2d 356, 366 (4 Cir. 1979) (en banc); *Chicago Council of Lawyers v. Bauer*, 522 *F.*2d 242 (7 Cir. 1975), *cert.* den., *sub nom. Chicago Council of Lawyers v. Cunningham*, 427 *U.S.* 912, 96 *S.Ct.* 3201, 49 *L.Ed.*2d 1204 (1976); *United States v. Tijerina*, 412 *F.*2d 661, 667 (10 Cir. 1969). This interest does not belong to the defendant alone. The public also has an interest in a fair trial that cannot be imperiled or diminished by out-of-court assertions by either defense or prosecution lawyers. See *Kavanaugh*, 52 *N.J.* at 19–20, 243 *A.*2d 225; *Van Duyne*, 43 *N.J.* at 389, 204 *A.*2d 841; *State v. Carter*, 143 *N.J.Super.* 405, 408, 363 *A.*2d 366 (App.Div.), rev'd on other grounds, 71 *N.J.* 348, 364 *A.*2d 1079 (1976). Thus, courts have recognized that restricting the extra-judicial statements of criminal defense attorneys relates to the government's substantial interest in preserving the proper administration of justice and the basic integrity of the judicial process. See *Singer*, 380 *U.S.* at 36, 85 *S.Ct.* at 790, 13 *L.Ed.*2d at 638.

Attorneys occupy a special status and perform an essential function in the administration of justice. Because attorneys are "officers of the court" with a special responsibility to protect the administration of justice, courts have recognized the need for the imposition of some reasonable speech restrictions upon attorneys. "The interest of the states in regulating lawyers is especially great since lawyers are essential to the primary governmental function of administering justice, and have historically been 'officers of the courts.'" *Goldfarb v. Virginia State Bar*, 421 *U.S.* 773, 792, 95 *S.Ct.* 2004, 2016, 44 *L.Ed.*2d 572, 588 (1975). *Cf. Standards Relating to Fair Trial and Free Press*, ABA Project on Minimum Standards for Criminal Justice at 82 (1968) (hereinafter "ABA Project") (lawyers have a "fiduciary obligation to the courts"). Thus, in resolving Hinds' federal action, the Supreme Court recently noted that "[t]he State of New Jersey has an extremely important interest in maintaining and assuring the professional conduct of the attorneys it licenses." *Middlesex Ethics Comm.*, [457] *U.S.* at [433], 102 *S.Ct.* at 2522.

In their unique and special capacity as judicial officers, lawyers differ from ordinary citizens. This was aptly expressed by Justice Frankfurter in his dissent in *In re Sawyer*:

> Of course, a lawyer is a person and he too has a constitutional freedom of utterance and may exercise it to castigate courts and their administration of justice. But a lawyer actively participating in a trial, particularly an emotionally charged criminal prosecution, is not merely a person and not even merely a lawyer.... He is an intimate and trusted and essential part of the machinery of justice, an "officer of the court" in the most compelling sense. [360 *U.S.* at 666, 79 *S.Ct.* at 1397, 3 *L.Ed.*2d at 1499–1500].

Justice Stewart, concurring in that case, agreed that an attorney who uses a public forum to obstruct justice and interfere with a fair trial cannot invoke the protection of the First Amendment to avoid disciplinary sanctions. 360 *U.S.* at 646, 79 *S.Ct.* at 1388, 3 *L.Ed.*2d at 1489.

This interest in trial fairness is particularly acute in the criminal context. There, the problem of preserving the basic fairness and integrity of the proceeding is of constitutional dimension because the defendant's right to a fair trial is guaranteed in the Sixth Amendment of the federal Constitution. Some courts, including the Supreme Court, have even held that the criminal defendant's constitutional right to a fair trial must take precedence over free speech. See, *e.g., Estes v. Texas*, 381 *U.S.* 532, 540, 85 *S.Ct.* 1628, 1632, 14 *L.Ed.*2d 543, 549 (1965) (defendant's right to a fair trial is "the most fundamental of all freedoms"); *Bauer*, 522 *F.*2d at 248; *Tijerina*, 412 *F.*2d at 667; *Hirschkop v. Virginia State Bar*, 421 *F.Supp.* 1137, 1146–47 (E.D.Va.1976). Cf. *Gannett Co., Inc. v. DePasquale*, 443 *U.S.* 368, 99 *S.Ct.* 2898, 61 *L.Ed.*2d 608 (1979) (press may sometimes be excluded from pretrial hearings in a criminal case); *Branzburg v. Hayes*, 408 *U.S.* 665, 92 *S.Ct.* 2646, 33 *L.Ed.*2d 626 (1972) (journalists have no absolute First Amendment right to refuse to disclose their sources or other confidential information when asked to do so by a grand jury). More than in any other context, the criminal trial setting requires our most diligent effort to ensure that the truth emerges and that the right result is reached. See *In re Farber*, 78 *N.J.* 259, 394 *A.*2d 330 (1978). A criminal case involves the highest of stakes because the defendant stands to lose his most precious of freedoms—his personal liberty—if convicted. The fairness of the trial is integral to reaching a just and proper result. Therefore, there are compelling reasons for making every effort to preserve trial fairness in the criminal context. See *Middlesex Ethics Comm.*, [457] *U.S.* at [433], 102 *S.Ct.* at 2522.

* * *

These considerations, in our view, require ethical constraints upon attorneys. These must include reasonable restrictions upon their extrajudicial speech to discourage and prevent extraneous matters from being insinuated into a criminal case. Such outside influences, if left unchecked, could divert the search for truth and wreck the intricate machinery of the criminal justice system. The reasonable likelihood test expressed in *DR* 7-107(D) is necessary and essential to the achievement of these objectives and, therefore, does not suffer from constitutional overbreadth.[3]

---

3. An overbreadth analysis also necessarily involves consideration of whether the government's substantial interest could be adequately protected through some means other than a speech restriction. If an alternative form of regulation would combat the danger without infringing upon First Amendment rights, then a speech restriction would be unnecessary and, therefore, unconstitutional. See Sherbert v. Verner, 374 U.S. 398, 83 S.Ct. 1790, 10 L.Ed.2d 965 (1963). A variety of alternatives to attorney speech restrictions exist for protecting a fair trial, including: (1) exclusion of the public

* * *

VI

Thus, we conclude that the reasonable likelihood standard of *DR* 7-107(D) is constitutional as applied to the extrajudicial statements of an attorney who is associated with a criminal trial, where the statements are about the trial and are intended to be disseminated publicly.

We limit this holding to the criminal context only. With the personal liberty of the defendant at stake and the need to reach the right result so vital, a criminal case presents unique problems of trial fairness that compel us to take every step possible to protect the integrity of that process. Therefore, our decision today should not be interpreted as approving of the reasonable likelihood standard to restrict attorney speech in any other context but a criminal trial.

We decline, however, to find Hinds in violation of any ethical rule. We do so for several reasons. First, because the District Ethics Committee conducted no hearing on this case, we are presented with an inadequate factual record on which to base a decision. Second, because this case involves the application of an ethical precept rather than a criminal law, we view the decision itself as a sufficient explanation of the ethical responsibility of attorneys and find no need for punishment. Third, because this opinion represents the first opportunity we have had to define the proper scope of *DR* 7-107(D), the primary disciplinary rule sought to be applied in this case, we deem it appropriate to give that rule prospective effect only. Finally, there being no present basis for imposing discipline under *DR* 7-107(D), the related charges under *DR* 1-102(A)(5) should likewise be dismissed.

Accordingly, the charges against Hinds are dismissed.

PASHMAN, J., concurring.

I concur with the majority's conclusion that the "reasonable likelihood" test of DR 7-107(D) does not violate the constitutionally protected free speech rights of attorneys while they are participating in criminal trials. I do so because the majority has construed this standard to require a "showing by clear and convincing evidence that an attorney's extrajudicial speech truly jeopardized trial fairness...." *Ante* at 495. This test precludes the Court from disciplining an attorney based on the vague feeling that his statement could possibly, or even foreseeably, have affected the trial. Rather, before dis-

---

from those hearings during trial held in the absence of jury; (2) continuances; (3) change of venue; (4) jury waiver; (5) searching voir dire; (6) selection of jury from locality outside area of extensive news coverage; (7) sequestration of jury; (8) admonitions to jury to avoid news reports relating to trial; (9) cautionary instructions to media regarding critical matters; (10) examination of jurors regarding possible exposure to prejudicial information during trial; (11) declaring a mistrial, and (12) granting a new trial. Cf. State v. Allen, 73 N.J. 132, 160–61, 373 A.2d 377 (1977) (court should attempt other protective devices before imposing "gag" order on press).

These other options, taken singly or together, do not preclude the imposition of attorney free speech restrictions because, in the criminal trial setting, courts have an overriding obligation to "prevent ... prejudice at its inception," Sheppard, 384 U.S. at 363, 86 S.Ct. at 1522, 16 L.Ed.2d at 620, rather than to wait until after the fact to attempt remedial action. Hirschkop, 594 F.2d at 365. Certain of these measures, such as change of venue, continuances and searching voir dire, simply are not effective alternatives. Moreover, ready resort to these alternative steps might impinge upon other constitutional guarantees, such as the defendant's right to a speedy trial or trial by jury. 594 F.2d at 366–67. Thus, while alternative approaches to dealing with the problem of prejudicial publicity exist, they do not obviate the need for properly fashioned restrictions on the extrajudicial speech of attorneys participating in criminal trials.

cipline may be imposed, the Court must have a firm conviction that the statement created an immediate danger of jeopardizing the fairness of the trial. Moreover, the restriction on speech is narrowly limited to attorneys associated with the prosecution or defense of criminal trials. It does not extend to civil trials; nor does it encompass attorneys who are not associated with the case.

I also agree with the majority's conclusion that an "attorney with no supervening professional responsibilities in a pending criminal case would seemingly enjoy the same free speech rights as any other citizen." *Ante* at 498. I therefore concur that the Constitution prohibits the discipline of attorneys for exercising their right to free speech when they are not directly associated with a criminal trial unless that speech creates a clear and present danger of prejudicing the administration of justice. *Ante* at 499.

I write because I believe that the justification for applying the clear and present danger test to attorneys not associated with a criminal case requires fuller elaboration. I also think that the application of that clear and present danger test to this case requires greater discussion so that our decision today does not chill protected speech by attorneys.

* * *

fosters the criticism of official conduct that is necessary to make government responsive to citizens. That is why democracies do not punish inaccurate speech. *Maressa v. New Jersey Monthly*, 89 *N.J.* 176 at 201, 445 *A.2d* 376 (1982)

Judges are public officials. As part of the state government, they are subject to public criticism like any other official. *In re Sawyer*, 360 *U.S.* 622, 666, 79 *S.Ct.* 1376, 1397, 3 *L.Ed.*2d 1473, 1499 (1959) (Stewart, J., concurring). Public debate about courts, and even the performance of specific judges, has long been part of our political and legal system.

Like other citizens, attorneys are entitled to speak freely. This right is guaranteed by the First Amendment to the Constitution. *Ante* at 489. See *R.M.J.*, [455] *U.S.* [191, 198–205], 102 *S.Ct.* 929, 935–38, 71 *L.Ed.*2d 64, 70–75 (1982); *Konigsberg v. State Bar*, 353 *U.S.* 252, 273, 77 *S.Ct.* 722, 733, 1 *L.Ed.*2d 810, 825 (1957). Since attorneys are officers of the courts, they may be constitutionally subject to certain limitations on their speech to protect the fairness of criminal trials, *see ante* at 489–490. However, when attorneys are not direct participants in the criminal proceedings there is little, if any, justification for imposing greater limits on their speech than those limits that apply to the general public. I believe that the Constitution demands such a result. Lawyers do not possess any inside information about a trial in which they are not participating; nor do they speak for any of the parties. The only difference between such attorneys and the general public is that attorneys may know more about trials and the conduct of specific judges. Because of this knowledge, their statements may be more valuable to the public or have a greater impact on public opinion. However, their expertise does not by itself create an increased danger of prejudice to the fairness of the trial.

Justice Stewart has distinguished between lawyers actively participating in criminal trials and those who are not. *In re Sawyer*, 360 *U.S.* at 666, 79 *S.Ct.* at 1397, 3 *L.Ed.*2d at 1499 (concurring opinion). He suggested that the Constitution did not permit the same restrictions on attorneys not immediately engaged in the litigation. "Of course, a lawyer is a person and he too has a constitutional freedom of utterance and may exercise it to castigate courts and their administration of justice." *Id.* I agree with this distinction.

Ordinarily, restrictions on speech are prohibited by the Constitution unless they are limited to speech that creates a "clear and present danger" of harming a compelling state interest unrelated to the suppression of speech. *See ante* at 491; *Brandenburg v. Ohio*, 395 *U.S.* 444, 89 *S.Ct.* 1827, 33 *L.Ed.*2d 430 (1969); *Bridges v. California*, 314 *U.S.* 252, 62 *S.Ct.* 190, 86 *L.Ed.* 192 (1941). This standard is the only appropriate one for determining whether this Court may discipline an attorney for statements critical of a criminal trial judge when that attorney is not directly associated with the case. See *ante* at 498–499. Attorneys cannot be disciplined under DR 1-102(A)(5) for out-of-court statements unless their speech presents a clear and present danger of interfering with the administration of justice or otherwise harming a compelling state interest.

In this case, Hinds called a press conference to state that the trial of Joanne Chesimard was "legalized lynching," a "travesty," and a "kangaroo court." He claimed that the judge lacked "racial sensitivity." *Ante* at 487. Hinds did not make his statements inside the courtroom. He did not address it to any juror or potential witness. His statements had nothing to do with the specific merits of the case. Hinds spoke as Director of the National Conference of Black Lawyers about a case which had national significance. I do not believe that these statements posed a clear and present danger of threatening the fairness of Joanne Chesimard's trial. There is no question that an ordinary citizen would be absolutely free to make these statements in public. I do not think any lawyer can be forbidden from making such statements if he is not associated with the case. This is not the type of conduct that is encompassed by the prohibition against prejudicing the administration of justice. Because these statements did not pose a clear and present danger of prejudicing the administration of justice, Hinds did not violate DR 1-102(A)(5).

I recognize, of course, that public criticism of judges might reduce respect for the legal system. This criticism, and the possible loss of respect, may sometimes be undeserved. Yet the Constitution does not permit us to coerce citizens, including attorneys, to silently acquiesce in official acts that they deplore. As we stated in *Maressa v. New Jersey Monthly, supra*:

> Sometimes published statements will hurt. Sometimes they will turn out to be untrue. Nevertheless, those regrettable consequences must yield to the need for an informed citizenry. [89 *N.J.* at 200, 445 *A.2d* 376]

Preventing a potential loss of respect by citizens for our legal institutions is not a sufficiently compelling government interest to justify restrictions on speech. *Bridges v. California*, 314 *U.S.* at 270, 62 *S.Ct.* at 197, 86 *L.Ed.* at 207. The lawyer's role as officer of the court is to protect the fairness of trials. While attorneys also have some responsibility for ensuring public confidence in the legal system, the system's public image cannot be protected at the cost of shielding judges from criticism. As Justice Black stated in *Bridges v. California, supra*:

> The assumption that respect for the judiciary can be won by shielding judges from published criticism wrongly appraises the character of American public opinion. For it is a prized American privilege to speak one's mind, although not always with perfect good taste, on all public institutions. And an enforced silence, however limited, solely in the name of preserving the dignity of the bench, would probably engender resentment, suspicion, and contempt much more than it would enhance respect. [314 *U.S.* at 270–71, 62 *S.Ct.* at 197–198, 86 *L.Ed.* at 207]

It is also possible that criticisms of judges may turn out to be deserved. If this is so, then public criticism will in fact improve, rather than prejudice, the administration of justice. It will remind judges that they are officials of the state and that their actions, like those of other officials, will be reviewed and judged by the citizenry. There is no reason

to believe that public statements about the official behavior of judges, even when not accurate, reduce the ability of our legal system to protect rights and do justice. There is
every reason to believe that public scrutiny and debate about the conduct of public officials is a necessary element of our system of government. *See* Shattuck and Byers, "An
Egalitarian Interpretation of the First Amendment," 16 *Harv.C.R.-C.L.L.Rev.* 377,
379–81 (1981). Unlike authoritarian governments that stifle both participation in politics and public debate, our system of government encourages citizens to speak their
minds on issues of public importance. We do not fear criticism of officials. We welcome
it and we expect it to be vigorous and forthright. We want active and informed citizens,
not timid subjects.

Attorneys are more knowledgeable than other citizens about the official conduct of
judges. Preventing attorneys from criticizing judges would go a long way toward insulat-
ing judges from public scrutiny. This is not a result that a democracy could tolerate.

CLIFFORD, J., concurring in result.

The Court concludes that the "reasonable likelihood" standard of *DR 7-107(D)*, dealing with one phase of trial publicity, is the appropriate standard by which to test a
lawyer's extrajudicial comments where the speech is intended to be disseminated to the
public. I agree. It is only to the extent that the majority holds back from a determination
on whether Hinds violated that standard that I depart from Justice Handler's thoughtful
opinion.

The pertinent part of the Rule bears repeating:

> During the selection of a jury or a trial of a criminal matter, a lawyer or law
> firm associated with the prosecution or defense of a criminal matter shall not
> make or participate in making any extra-judicial statement that he expects to
> be disseminated by means of public communication and that relates to the
> trial, parties, or issues in the trial or other matters that are reasonably likely to
> interfere with a fair trial * * *.

Hinds's remarks were deplorable in their absence of professionalism. But how is it
reasonably likely that they could have "interfered with a fair trial"? They were directed
solely at the trial judge, who commented, "I don't think it had any impact on the trial
whatsoever," thereby displaying a desirable degree of epidermal impenetrability: the trial
courtroom is no haven for the thin-skinned, either as lawyer or as judge. There was
nothing in what respondent said that was likely to influence either the judge or a jury,
which was still being selected. Had he announced, say, that a defendant's confession had
been extracted by law enforcement officials' brutality, then a situation fraught with prejudice would have been presented. But these remarks, critical of the trial judge's alleged
racial insensitivity, did not touch upon any substantive issues in the case. I think we
should say that today, so that the bench and bar will understand what kind of content
we would pour into the Disciplinary Rule.

Merle L. Meacham said that "[t]he trouble with being tolerant is that people think
you don't understand the problem." I understand the problem. I just refuse to get exercised about respondent's lapse into uncivil sloganeering.

SCHREIBER, J., dissenting.

* * *

I agree with the majority that *DR 7-107(D)* is constitutional.

* * *

The policy underlying this Disciplinary Rule is that the defendant and the State are entitled to and should have a fair trial. The attorney's right to speak is not completely prohibited. He may make appropriate argument in the courtroom. *See State v. Van Duyne,* 43 *N.J.* 369, 389, 204 *A.*2d 841 (1964), *cert.* denied, 380 *U.S.* 987, 85 *S.Ct.* 1359, 14 *L.Ed.*2d 279 (1965). He may after the case has been completed properly comment on the matter. What he may not do is intentionally disseminate to the public statements relating to the trial which are "reasonably likely to interfere with a fair trial."

The majority contends that the charge should be dismissed for two reasons, neither of which is valid. First it claims that its interpretation of *DR* 7-107(D) involves some new concept. I submit that application of the stated test — reasonably likely to interfere with a fair trial — does not involve any new or unforeseen dogma. The so-called "balancing test" referred to by the majority, *ante* at 495, is nothing more than the usual weighing which any fact finder must do when evaluating facts to reach a conclusion. Nor do I foresee any unfairness to the respondent. The Rule was written "by and for lawyers." *In re Keiler*, 380 *A.*2d 119, 126 (D.C.1977). As stated in that case: "The language of a rule setting guidelines for members of the bar need not meet the precise standards of clarity that might be required of rules of conduct for laymen." *Id.* at 126.

The second reason advanced is even more curious. It is that the charge should be dismissed because the factual dispute concerning the respondent's relationship to the defendant has never been resolved. Thus the respondent has successfully evaded a hearing to resolve whether he was "associated with the ... defense" by instituting a constitutional attack — which the Court finds is unsuccessful.

Lastly, I disagree with the majority's opinion that it seems quite certain that the First Amendment would require application of a "clear and present danger" standard to conduct under *DR* 1-102(A)(5).

* * *

This Disciplinary Rule on its face requires that the conduct must be shown to be prejudicial. There must be clear and convincing evidence that the attorney's conduct did in fact hinder, block or obstruct the administration of justice. I envisage no constitutional impediment to that standard. Assuredly attorneys whether directly related or not to an ongoing trial should not be permitted to frustrate a fair trial. *See Sheppard v. Maxwell,* 384 *U.S.* 333, 363, 86 *S.Ct.* 1507, 1522, 16 *L.Ed.*2d 600, 620 (1966). In truth it is conceivable that an attorney who is not associated with the defense may have such standing in the community that his words may have a substantially greater impact on the fairness of a trial than those of the attorney of record. This is not to say that attorneys may not criticize courts, judges, their decisions, and the judicial system. There is a proper time and place for such criticism.

We shall not know whether the respondent's conduct was "prejudicial to the administration of justice or whether respondent was associated with the defense and violated *DR* 7-107(D)" due to the improper aborting of this proceeding. Innovative arguments advanced in support of the contention that a rule has not been violated may at times be relevant in determining the sanction to be applied. However, they should not serve as vehicles to evade due disciplinary proceedings. I would remand the matter to the District VIII Ethics Committee to process the complaint and proceed pursuant to R. 1:20-2.

Matter of Erdmann

33 N.Y.2d 559
Court of Appeals of New York
July 2, 1973

PER CURIAM.

Without more, isolated instances of disrespect for the law, Judges and courts expressed by vulgar and insulting words or other incivility, uttered, written, or committed outside the precincts of a court are not subject to professional discipline (cf. Code of Professional Responsibility, EC 8-6; cf., generally, Ann., Attorneys—Criticizing Court, 12 A.L.R.3d 1408). Nor is the matter substantially altered if there is hyperbole expressed in the impoverished vocabulary of the street. On this view, no constitutional issue of privileged expression is involved in the conduct ascribed to appellant.

Perhaps persistent or general courses of conduct, even if parading as criticism, which are degrading to the law, the Bar, and the courts, and are irrelevant or grossly excessive, would present a different issue. No such issue is presented now.

As for the self-laudatory content of the magazine article to which appellant contributed, the petition charged misconduct but the Appellate Division did not ground its action on that allegation.

Since appellant's out-of-court conduct was not censurable, it would not be appropriate to characterize further that conduct on the score of taste, civility, morality, or ethics.

Accordingly, the order of the Appellate Division, 39 A.D.2d 223, 333 N.Y.S.2d 863, should be reversed and the petition dismissed.

BURKE, Judge (dissenting) This appeal involves an order of the Appellate Division, Third Department, which decided, with two Justices dissenting, that the appellant was guilty of professional misconduct and censured him.

The charge was based on statements and language used in an article entitled 'I Have Nothing To Do With Justice', which appeared in the March 12, 1971 issue of Life magazine. Lawyer Erdmann said of and concerning the courts within the First Judicial Department: 'There are so few trial judges who just judge, who rule on questions of law, and leave guilt or innocence to the jury. And Appellate Division judges aren't any better. They're the whores who became madams. I would like to (be a judge) just to see if I could be the kind of judge I think a judge should be. But the only way you can get it is to be in politics or buy it — and I don't even know the going price.'

The article stated: 'He defends killers, burglars, rapists, robbers—the men people mean when they talk about crime in the streets. Martin Erdmann's clients are crime in the streets. In 25 years, Martin Erdmann has defended more than 100,000 criminals. He has saved them tens of thousands of years in prison and in those years they have robbed, raped, burglarized and murdered tens upon tens of thousands of people. The idea of having had a very personal and direct hand in all that mayhem strikes him as boring and irrelevant. 'I have nothing to do with justice,' he says. 'Justice is not even part of the equation. If you say I have no moral reaction to what I do, you are right.' * * *

'He is disgusted when people accuse him of dedication. 'That's just plain nonsense. The one word that does not describe me is dedicated. I reserve that word for people who do something that requires sacrifice. I don't sacrifice anything. The only reason I'm any good is because I have an ego. I like to win.'

* * *

'To play the game well, a lawyer must be ruthless. He is working within, but against a system that has been battered to its knees. He must not hesitate to kick it when it's down, and to take every advantage of its weakness. No one is better at the game than Martin Erdmann. * * *

'He laughs, 'The exultation of winning dampens any moral feelings you have.' * * *

'Erdmann talks with the defendant and gets the plea quickly accepted. Five months for homicide. As he leaves the courtroom, a DA says, 'Marty, you got away with murder.'

'Erdmann is gleeful. 'I always get away with murder.''

The entire article is nothing more than a treatise upon the ability, cunning and expertise of the appellant.

It is difficult to read the article from the point of view of giving credence to the moralizing of the appellant, without coming to the conclusion that neither the legal system nor the legal profession possesses integrity and without having one's confidence therein shaken.

As a judicial report very recently noted 'To a great degree the complainant (victim) has not received the measure of protection and care he deserves' (New York Times, May 31, 1973) due, it would appear, to the above self-described activities of the appellant.

Justices Greenblott and Simons dissented and voted to dismiss the petition being of the opinion that the majority found appellant innocent of all charges of having violated Disciplinary Rules and censured appellant as a result of their conclusion that he was guilty of a violation of ethical consideration; that ethical considerations cannot result in censure as they are aspirational in character.

The article in *Life* magazine containing the vulgar and insulting language as far as Erdmann is concerned is not protected by the First and Fourteenth Amendments of the United States Constitution and article I of the New York State Constitution. The article, as well as the remarks, violate restrictions placed on attorneys which they impliedly assume when they accept admission to the Bar. The Supreme Court of the State of Nevada, in Matter of Raggio, 87 Nev. 369, 487 P.2d 499 described the duty of an attorney to the courts and judicial officers very well when it stated (pp. 371, 372, 487 P.2d pp. 500, 501): 'The inner motivation which caused Mr. Raggio to speak out in such intemperate fashion is unknown to us and we shall not indulge in presumptions or inferences adverse to him. We are never surprised when persons, not intimately involved with the administration of justice, speak out in anger or frustration about our work and the manner in which we perform it, and we shall protect their right to so express themselves. A member of the bar, however, stands in a different position by reason of his oath of office and the standards of conduct which he is sworn to uphold. Conformity with those standards has proven essential to the administration of justice in our courts. Mr. Raggio offended them, and, as recommended by the Board of Governors, we reprimand him therefor.'

It has long been the law that in cases of claims of First Amendment rights States still have the power to regulate conduct which offends, is inappropriate under the circumstance or could lead to disorder unless regulated (Matter of Trans-Lux Distr. Corp. v. Board of Regents, 14 N.Y.2d 88, 90, 91, 248 N.Y.S.2d 857, 858, 859, 198 N.E.2d 242, 243, 244; People v. Stover, 12 N.Y.2d 462, 240 N.Y.S.2d 734, 191 N.E.2d 272; Thornhill v. Alabama, 310 U.S. 88, 60 S.Ct. 736, 84 L.Ed. 1093; Local Union No. 10 etc., Plumbers etc. v. Graham, 345 U.S. 192, 73 S.Ct. 585, 97 L.Ed. 946). The proscription of the behavior herein bears no necessary relationship to a lawyer's freedom to speak, write or distribute information or critical opinions couched in civil language.

In other words, freedom of speech is not abridged by a reprimand for incivility to the judiciary or disparagement of the legal system Indeed, Mr. Erdmann could have been censured for co-operating in the publication of the article which described him as one of the best defense lawyers in the United States. In the Matter of Connelly, 18 A.D.2d 466 (1963), 240 N.Y.S.2d 126, the court noted that lawyers and law firms may not publicize themselves in the media through self-laudatory statements calculated to draw the plaudits of public through the use of self-serving statements.

* * *

GABRIELLI, Judge (dissenting).

I subscribe to the holding of the majority that no constitutional issue of privileged expression is involved.

However, I otherwise dissent, and agree with the determination of the Appellate Division (39 A.D.2d 223, 333 N.Y.S.2d 863) that appellant was guilty of professional misconduct when, knowing that his statements would be published in Life magazine, he announced that: 'There are so few trial judges who just judge, who rule on questions of law, and leave guilt or innocence to the jury. And Appellate Division judges aren't any better. They're the whores who became madams. I would like to (be a judge) just to see if I could be the kind of judge I think a judge should be. But the only way you can get it is to be in politics or buy it—and I don't even know the going price.' It is appropriate to here point out that appellant admitted not only the making of these statements but also that he participated in the preparation of the magazine article which appeared in the March 12, 1971 issue of Life. The unabashed use of intemperate, vulgar and insulting language—certainly an offense against the integrity and dignity of the courts—tended to create disrespect for the law, the courts and judicial officers as well as lessening public confidence in the courts.

[The] appellant's statement was made with the knowledge that it would be published in a weekly magazine, having a Nationwide and foreign circulation of several million copies.[1] In that sense, his utterance may not be characterized as one of those 'isolated instances of disrespect for law, Judges and courts'. Since his conduct was a designed and calculated act we are required, as a practical matter, to equate his act as intending to have been uttered the innumerable times represented by the copies sold and distributed, not only at newsstands, but by individual subscriptions as well as placement in public and school libraries, for millions to read.

However one may desire to parochialize this statement or, in fact, to now defensively limit its application, a fair reading of it leads to the inescapable conclusion that the vulgarity of Erdmann's undocumented and baseless charges that 'Appellate Division judges aren't any better. They're the whores who became madams,' was directed to all such Judges, wherever located.

His conduct may well be characterized as morally and ethically reprehensible; and his widely published statement, couched in such scandalous terms, is bound to have the effect of bringing discredit upon the administration of justice amongst the citizenry, an act which ought not be permitted.

* * *

---

1. The weekly domestic circulation at the time of the publication was 6,936,865 copies.

I am of the firm belief that one who occupies the responsible position of an attorney upon whose good faith, sense of propriety and ethical standards the public is entitled to rely, is still cloaked with the duty of abstaining from using offensive, insulting and abusive language as here depicted.

The order censuring appellant should be affirmed.

FULD, C.J., and BREITEL, JASEN, JONES and WACHTLER, JJ., concur in Per Curiam opinion.

BURKE, J., dissents and votes to affirm in an opinion.

GABRIELLI, J., dissents and votes to affirm in a separate opinion in which BURKE, J., also concurs.

Order reversed, without costs, and petition dismissed.

In re Wilkins

782 N.E.2d 985
Supreme Court of Indiana
Feb. 4, 2003

DISCIPLINARY ACTION ON PETITION FOR REHEARING

DICKSON, Justice.

The respondent in this attorney discipline matter seeks rehearing following our *per curiam* opinion, *Matter of Wilkins,* 777 N.E.2d 714 (Ind.2002), which held that certain remarks in the respondent's brief supporting his petition for transfer in a prior case violated Indiana Professional Conduct Rule 8.2(a) and warranted his suspension from the practice of law for thirty days. His petition requests reconsideration of (1) the application of the First Amendment protection to the offending remarks, and (2) the appropriate sanction to be imposed.

We dispose of these requests largely on the difference between sound advocacy and defamation. Lawyers are completely free to criticize the decisions of judges. As licensed professionals, they are not free to make recklessly false claims about a judge's integrity.

I.

We decline to grant rehearing as to the First Amendment issue. Aside from First Amendment considerations, however, we acknowledge that important interests of judicial administration require considerable latitude regarding the content of assertions in judicial pleadings, motions, and briefs. Just as we must seek to preserve the public respect and confidence in the judiciary, in prescribing practice and procedures for the proper administration of justice we must also preserve the right of a party to access and use the judicial system to present a "good faith argument for an extension, modification, or reversal of existing law." Ind. Professional Conduct Rule 3.1. The Comment to Rule 3.1 observes: "[T]he law is not always clear and never is static. Accordingly, in determining the proper scope of advocacy, account must be taken of the law's ambiguities and potential for change."

In *Orr v. Turco Mfg. Co., Inc.,* 512 N.E.2d 151 (Ind.1987), this Court emphasized the need for an appellate tribunal to use extreme restraint in stifling appellate advocacy: "[W]e cannot fail to recognize that the imposition of punitive sanctions does have significant negative consequences.... It will have a chilling effect upon the exercise of the right to appeal. It will discourage innovation and inhibit the opportunity for periodic reevaluation of controlling precedent." *Id.* at 152. Concluding that "we must invite, not inhibit, the presentation of new and creative argument[,]" we held in *Orr* that "punitive sanctions may not be imposed to punish lack of merit unless an appellant's contentions and argument are utterly devoid of all plausibility." *Id.* at 153.

These considerations are limited, however, by Indiana Professional Conduct Rule 8.2(a), which provides in relevant part: "A lawyer shall not make a statement that the lawyer knows to be false or with reckless disregard as to its truth or falsity concerning the ... integrity of a judge...." Our *per curiam* opinion noted that the respondent's brief suggested that the decision of the judges on the Court of Appeals resulted from unethical motivations. The offending language consisted of footnote 2 to his brief, stating:

> Indeed, the [Court of Appeals] Opinion is so factually and legally inaccurate that one is left to wonder whether the Court of Appeals was determined to find for Appellee Sports, Inc., and then said whatever was necessary to reach that conclusion (regardless of whether the facts or the law supported its decision).

Wilkins, 777 N.E.2d at 716.

The language of footnote 2 does not merely argue that the Court of Appeals decision is factually or legally inaccurate. Such would be permissible advocacy. The footnote goes further and ascribes bias and favoritism to the judges authoring and concurring in the majority opinion of the Court of Appeals, and it implies that these judges manufactured a false rationale in an attempt to justify their pre-conceived desired outcome. These aspersions transgress the wide latitude given appellate argument, and they clearly impugn the integrity of a judge in violation of Professional Conduct Rule 8.2(a). We decline to revise our determination that the respondent violated Rule 8.2(a).

II.

We grant rehearing in part, however, as to the particular issue of the appropriate sanction to be imposed for this violation. Upon further reconsideration we are persuaded to revise the nature of the discipline.

As noted in our *per curiam* opinion, the respondent timely contacted the offices of both the Chief Judge of the Indiana Court of Appeals and the Chief Justice of Indiana, and thereafter wrote to both the Chief Judge and the Chief Justice "offering to apologize in person and to acknowledge that the footnote was 'overly-aggressive and inappropriate and should never have made its way into our Brief.'" *Wilkins,* 777 N.E.2d at 716.

We also give renewed consideration to the Hearing Officer's findings that the respondent has maintained an outstanding and exemplary record for honesty, integrity, and truthfulness among his peers in the Bar, and among members of the judiciary. This warrants substantial weight. Furthermore, although the respondent's role in signing and filing the brief constitutes joint responsibility pursuant to Indiana Admission and Discipline Rule 3(2)(d), we note that the language of the footnote was not authored by the respondent but by an out-of-state co-counsel.

We find unpersuasive, however, assertions that some other prominent American lawyers or judges may have engaged in similar techniques of argument. Such unfortunate occasional resorts to uncivil dialogue should not be our standard for acceptable Indiana pleading and practice.

Upon rehearing as to the sanction, we conclude that the respondent's penalty in this disciplinary proceeding should not consist of a period of suspension but rather only the public reprimand already effected by the content of our initial *per curiam* opinion.

Rehearing is granted in part and denied in part, and the respondent's sanction is revised from a thirty-day suspension from the practice of law to a public reprimand. Because we are only granting rehearing on a particular point, rather than a general rehearing, our *per curiam* opinion remains in effect except as modified herein. *See Griffin v. State*, 763 N.E.2d 450, 451 (Ind.2002).

SHEPARD, C.J., concurs; BOEHM, J., concurs in result with separate opinion; RUCKER, J., not participating; SULLIVAN, J., dissents, believing respondent's conduct was speech protected by the First Amendment and so no sanction is permissible. *See In re Wilkins*, 777 N.E.2d 714 (Ind.2002) (Sullivan, J., dissenting).

BOEHM, Justice, concurring in result.

I continue to adhere to the view that the respondent did nothing that this Court should find sanctionable. Specifically, I believe the statements attributed to the respondent are protected by both the First Amendment to the Constitution of the United States and by Article I, Section 9 of the Indiana Constitution. Even if these statements were not constitutionally protected, for the reasons given in my original dissent, I would not find them to violate the Rules of Professional Responsibility. Therefore, I would grant rehearing on all aspects of the Court's initial opinion. However, there is no majority to grant rehearing on the sanction unless a public reprimand remains in place. For that reason, I concur in the result to impose a public reprimand rather than leave in place the thirty-day suspension already imposed.

The respondent's petition to rehear this matter arrives in an extremely unusual procedural posture. Although the full court addressed the case initially, only four Justices remain to consider the petition to reconsider. If a majority votes to grant rehearing, the effect is to recall the former opinion, and Wilkins' case would be before us "as if it had never been decided." 2 Arch N. Bobbitt, *Indiana Appellate Practice and Procedure*, 62:11, at 625 (1972); *see also Bally v. Guilford Township Sch. Corp.*, 234 Ind. 273, 275, 126 N.E.2d 13, 15 (1955); *Booher v. Goldsborough*, 44 Ind. 490, 496 (1873); Terrance L. Smith and Anthony DeBonis, Jr., *Appellate Handbook for Indiana Lawyers*, 19:8, at 302 (1987). If rehearing is granted on a single issue — in this case the proper sanction — the original opinion stands as to all other issues, and only the sanction is vacated. *Griffin v. State*, 763 N.E.2d 450 (Ind.2002).

The votes of the Chief Justice and Justice Dickson are to grant rehearing as to the sanction only, and to impose a public reprimand. Justice Sullivan and I would vote for no sanction at all. But if neither of us joins in the result reached by Justice Dickson and the Chief Justice, we have no majority to grant rehearing as to any aspect of the original opinion and Wilkins' thirty-day suspension stands. Lewis Carroll would love that result: half the Court believes no sanction is appropriate, and half would impose a small sanction, so the result is a major penalty. Only those who love the law could explain that to their children. To free parents everywhere from that burden, I concur in the result of granting rehearing as to the sanction and reducing it to a public reprimand.

C. Privilege against Self-Incrimination

Spevack v. Klein

385 U.S. 511
U.S. Supreme Court
Argued November 7, 1966
Decided January 16, 1967
[Some footnotes deleted. Remaining footnotes renumbered.]

MR. JUSTICE DOUGLAS announced the judgment of the Court and delivered an opinion in which THE CHIEF JUSTICE, MR. JUSTICE BLACK and MR. JUSTICE BRENNAN concur.

This is a proceeding to discipline petitioner, a member of the New York Bar, for professional misconduct. Of the various charges made, only one survived, viz., the refusal of petitioner to honor a subpoena duces tecum served on him in that he refused to produce the demanded financial records and refused to testify at the judicial inquiry. Petitioner's sole defense was that the production of the records and his testimony would tend to incriminate him. The Appellate Division of the New York Supreme Court ordered petitioner disbarred, holding that the constitutional privilege against self-incrimination was not available to him in light of our decision in Cohen v. Hurley, 366 U.S. 117. See 24 App. Div. 2d 653. The Court of Appeals affirmed, 16 N. Y. 2d 1048, 213 N. E. 2d 457, 17 N. Y. 2d 490, 214 N. E. 2d 373. The case is here on certiorari which we granted to determine whether Cohen v. Hurley, supra, had survived Malloy v. Hogan, 378 U.S. 1.

Cohen v. Hurley was a five-to-four decision rendered in 1961. It is practically on all fours with the present case. There, as here, an attorney relying on his privilege against self-incrimination refused to testify and was disbarred. The majority of the Court allowed New York to construe her own privilege against self-incrimination so as not to make it available in judicial inquiries of this character (366 U.S., at 125–127) and went on to hold that the Self-Incrimination Clause of the Fifth Amendment was not applicable to the States by reason of the Fourteenth. Id., at 127–129. The minority took the view that the full sweep of the Fifth Amendment had been absorbed into the Fourteenth and extended its protection to lawyers as well as other persons.

In 1964 the Court in another five-to-four decision held that the Self-Incrimination Clause of the Fifth Amendment was applicable to the States by reason of the Fourteenth. Malloy v. Hogan, 378 U.S. 1. While Cohen v. Hurley was not overruled, the majority indicated that the principle on which it rested had been seriously eroded. 378 U.S., at 11. One minority view espoused by MR. JUSTICE HARLAN and MR. JUSTICE CLARK stated that Cohen v. Hurley flatly decided that the Self-Incrimination Clause of the Fifth Amendment was not applicable against the States (id., at 17) and urged that it be followed. The others in dissent—MR. JUSTICE WHITE and MR. JUSTICE STEWART—thought that on the facts of the case the privilege was not properly invoked and that the state trial judge should have been sustained in ruling that the answers would not tend to incriminate. Id., at 33–38.

The Appellate Division distinguished Malloy v. Hogan on the ground that there the petitioner was not a member of the Bar. 24 App. Div. 2d, at 654. And the Court of Appeals rested squarely on Cohen v. Hurley as one of the two grounds for affirmance.

And so the question emerges whether the principle of Malloy v. Hogan is inapplicable because petitioner is a member of the Bar. We conclude that Cohen v. Hurley should be overruled, that the Self-Incrimination Clause of the Fifth Amendment has been absorbed in the Fourteenth, that it extends its protection to lawyers as well as to other individuals, and that it should not be watered down by imposing the dishonor of disbarment and the deprivation of a livelihood as a price for asserting it. These views, expounded in the dissents in Cohen v. Hurley, need not be elaborated again.

We said in Malloy v. Hogan:

> "The Fourteenth Amendment secures against state invasion the same privilege that the Fifth Amendment guarantees against federal infringement—the right of a person to remain silent unless he chooses to speak in the unfettered exercise of his own will, and to suffer no penalty … for such silence." 378 U.S., at 8.

In this context "penalty" is not restricted to fine or imprisonment. It means, as we said in Griffin v. California, 380 U.S. 609, the imposition of any sanction which makes assertion of the Fifth Amendment privilege "costly." Id., at 614. We held in that case that the Fifth Amendment, operating through the Fourteenth, "forbids either comment by the prosecution on the accused's silence or instructions by the court that such silence is evidence of guilt." Id., at 615. What we said in Malloy and Griffin is in the tradition of the broad protection given the privilege at least since Boyd v. United States, 116 U.S. 616, 634–635, where compulsory production of books and papers of the owner of goods sought to be forfeited was held to be compelling him to be a witness against himself.

> "It may be that it is the obnoxious thing in its mildest and least repulsive form; but illegitimate and unconstitutional practices get their first footing in that way, namely, by silent approaches and slight deviations from legal modes of procedure. This can only be obviated by adhering to the rule that constitutional provisions for the security of person and property should be liberally construed. A close and literal construction deprives them of half their efficacy, and leads to gradual depreciation of the right, as if it consisted more in sound than in substance. It is the duty of courts to be watchful for the constitutional rights of the citizen, and against any stealthy encroachments thereon." 116 U.S., at 635.

The threat of disbarment and the loss of professional standing, professional reputation, and of livelihood are powerful forms of compulsion to make a lawyer relinquish the privilege. That threat is indeed as powerful an instrument of compulsion as "the use of legal process to force from the lips of the accused individual the evidence necessary to convict him…." United States v. White, 322 U.S. 694, 698. As we recently stated in Miranda v. Arizona, 384 U.S. 436, 461, "In this Court, the privilege has consistently been accorded a liberal construction." It is in that tradition that we overrule Cohen v. Hurley. We find no room in the privilege against self-incrimination for classifications of people so as to deny it to some and extend it to others. Lawyers are not excepted from the words "No person … shall be compelled in any criminal case to be a witness against himself"; and we can imply no exception. Like the school teacher in Slochower v. Board of Education, 350 U.S. 551, and the policemen in Garrity v. New Jersey,[1] ante, p. 493, lawyers also enjoy first-class citizenship.

---

1. Whether a policeman, who invokes the privilege when his conduct as a police officer is questioned in disciplinary proceedings, may be discharged for refusing to testify is a question we did not reach.

The Court of Appeals alternately affirmed the judgment disbarring petitioner on the ground that under Shapiro v. United States, 335 U.S. 1, and the required records doctrine he was under a duty to produce the withheld records. The Court of Appeals did not elaborate on the point; nor did the Appellate Division advert to it. At the time in question the only Rule governing the matter was entitled "Preservation of records of actions, claims and proceedings." It provided that in cases involving "contingent fee compensation" attorneys for all the parties shall preserve "the pleadings, records and other papers pertaining to such action, claim and proceeding, and also all data and memoranda of the disposition thereof, for the period of at least five years after any settlement or satisfaction of the action, claim or proceeding or judgment or final order thereon, or after the dismissal or discontinuance of any action or proceeding brought."

The documents sought in the subpoena were petitioner's daybook, cash receipts book, cash disbursements book, checkbook stubs, petty cashbook and vouchers, general ledger and journal, canceled checks and bank statements, passbooks and other evidences of accounts, record of loans made, payroll records, and state and federal tax returns and worksheets relative thereto.

The Shapiro case dealt with a federal price control regulation requiring merchants to keep sales records. The Court called them records with "public aspects," as distinguished from private papers (335 U.S., at 34); and concluded by a divided vote that their compelled production did not violate the Fifth Amendment. We are asked to overrule Shapiro. But we find it unnecessary to reach it.

Rule 5, requiring the keeping of records, was broad and general — "the pleadings, records and other papers pertaining to such action, claim and proceeding, and also all data and memoranda of the disposition thereof." The detailed financial aspects of contingent-fee litigation demanded might possibly by a broad, generous construction of the Rule be brought within its intendment. Our problem, however, is different. Neither the referee of the inquiry, nor counsel for the inquiry, nor the Appellate Division of the New York Supreme Court questioned the applicability of the privilege against self-incrimination to the records. All proceeded on the basis that petitioner could invoke the privilege with respect to the records, but that the price he might have to pay was disbarment. The Court of Appeals was the first to suggest that the privilege against self-incrimination was not applicable to the records. Petitioner, however, had been disbarred on the theory that the privilege was applicable to the records, but that the invocation of the privilege could lead to disbarment. His disbarment cannot be affirmed on the ground that the privilege was not applicable in the first place. Cole v. Arkansas, 333 U.S. 196, 201. For that procedure would deny him all opportunity at the trial to show that the Rule, fairly construed and understood, should not be given a broad sweep[2] and to make a record

---

2. Counsel for respondent conceded on oral argument that the subpoena was broader than Rule 5:

"Q. Is this subpoena coextensive with the provisions of the order about keeping the financial records or does the subpoena go beyond?
"A. I would say in my judgment it goes beyond.... There is room for reasonable argument that some of the items called for in the subpoena might perhaps be argued to not come within the required records I am talking about.
"Q. Would you mind relating those to us? Tell us what those are.... Cash disbursements?
"A. I would say do come under the records.... I would exclude as not coming within the statute the federal and state tax returns for example....
"Q. How about worksheets ... ?
"A. Worksheets? Out....
"Q. You mean all of item 12 ... would be out?

that the documents demanded by the subpoena had no "public aspects" within the required records rule but were private papers.

Reversed.

MR. JUSTICE FORTAS, concurring in the judgment.

I agree that Cohen v. Hurley, 366 U.S. 117 (1961), should be overruled. But I would distinguish between a lawyer's right to remain silent and that of a public employee who is asked questions specifically, directly, and narrowly relating to the performance of his official duties as distinguished from his beliefs or other matters that are not within the scope of the specific duties which he undertook faithfully to perform as part of his employment by the State. This Court has never held, for example, that a policeman may not be discharged for refusal in disciplinary proceedings to testify as to his conduct as a police officer. It is quite a different matter if the State seeks to use the testimony given under this lash in a subsequent criminal proceeding. Garrity v. New Jersey, ante, p. 493.

But a lawyer is not an employee of the State. He does not have the responsibility of an employee to account to the State for his actions because he does not perform them as agent of the State. His responsibility to the State is to obey its laws and the rules of conduct that it has generally laid down as part of its licensing procedures. The special responsibilities that he assumes as licensee of the State and officer of the court do not carry with them a diminution, however limited, of his Fifth Amendment rights. Accordingly, I agree that Spevack could not be disbarred for asserting his privilege against self-incrimination.

If this case presented the question whether a lawyer might be disbarred for refusal to keep or to produce, upon properly authorized and particularized demand, records which the lawyer was lawfully and properly required to keep by the State as a proper part of its functions in relation to him as licensor of his high calling, I should feel compelled to vote to affirm, although I would be prepared in an appropriate case to re-examine the scope of the principle announced in Shapiro v. United States, 335 U.S. 1 (1948). I am not prepared to indicate doubt as to the essential validity of Shapiro. However, I agree that the required records issue is not appropriately presented here, for the

---

"A. Item 12—copies of federal and state tax returns, accountants' worksheets, and all other ... I do not include them.

"Q. They would all be outside the rules?

"A. Yes....

"Q. But the demand was for records beyond the records that he was required to keep....

"A. [T]he New York Court of Appeals, speaking for the State of New York, says these are required records.

"Q. I suppose that if he produced just the records that were required—that he was required to keep—that that might very well constitute a waiver as to other records.

"A. No, no it would not....

"Q. Why not?

"A. Because if the other records were held not to come within the required records doctrine he would have the privilege to do that, but he has no privilege.

"Q. I am not sure. Are you sure about that? ... I would say that the common understanding is that if he produces some of the records relating to a given subject matter, that is a waiver of privilege as to the balance of the records relating to the subject matter. Am I wrong about that?

"A. I would not agree with that. It is an argument that could be made but I would disagree with it for this reason. Under the doctrine of Shapiro v. United States, he has no Fifth Amendment privilege as to records that are required to be kept. He does have Fifth Amendment privilege as to records he is not required to keep and also as to refusal to give oral testimony."

reasons stated by my Brother DOUGLAS. On this basis I join in the judgment of the Court.

MR. JUSTICE HARLAN, whom MR. JUSTICE CLARK and MR. JUSTICE STEWART join, dissenting.

This decision, made in the name of the Constitution, permits a lawyer suspected of professional misconduct to thwart direct official inquiry of him without fear of disciplinary action. What is done today will be disheartening and frustrating to courts and bar associations throughout the country in their efforts to maintain high standards at the bar.

It exposes this Court itself to the possible indignity that it may one day have to admit to its own bar such a lawyer unless it can somehow get at the truth of suspicions, the investigation of which the applicant has previously succeeded in blocking. For I can perceive no distinction between "admission" and "disbarment" in the rationale of what is now held. The decision might even lend some color of support for justifying the appointment to the bench of a lawyer who, like petitioner, prevents full inquiry into his professional behavior. And, still more pervasively, this decision can hardly fail to encourage oncoming generations of lawyers to think of their calling as imposing on them no higher standards of behavior than might be acceptable in the general market-place. The soundness of a constitutional doctrine carrying such denigrating import for our profession is surely suspect on its face.

Six years ago a majority of this Court, in Cohen v. Hurley, 366 U.S. 117, set its face against the doctrine that now prevails, bringing to bear in support of the Court's holding, among other things, the then-established constitutional proposition that the Fourteenth Amendment did not make applicable to the States the Fifth Amendment as such. Three years later another majority of the Court, in Malloy v. Hogan, 378 U.S. 1, decided to make the Fifth Amendment applicable to the States and in doing so cast doubt on the continuing vitality of Cohen v. Hurley. The question now is whether Malloy requires the overruling of Cohen in its entirety. For reasons that follow I think it clear that it does not.

It should first be emphasized that the issue here is plainly not whether lawyers may "enjoy first-class citizenship." Nor is the issue whether lawyers may be deprived of their federal privilege against self-incrimination, whether or not criminal prosecution is undertaken against them. These diversionary questions have of course not been presented or even remotely suggested by this case either here or in the courts of New York. The plurality opinion's vivid rhetoric thus serves only to obscure the issues with which we are actually confronted, and to hinder their serious consideration. The true question here is instead the proper scope and effect of the privilege against self-incrimination under the Fourteenth Amendment in state disciplinary proceedings against attorneys. In particular, we are required to determine whether petitioner's disbarment for his failure to provide information relevant to charges of misconduct in carrying on his law practice impermissibly vitiated the protection afforded by the privilege. This important question warrants more complete and discriminating analysis than that given to it by the plurality opinion.

* * *

It cannot be claimed that the purposes served by the New York rules at issue here, compendiously aimed at "ambulance chasing" and its attendant evils, are unimportant or unrelated to the protection of legitimate state interests. This Court has often held that the States have broad authority to devise both requirements for admission and standards of practice for those who wish to enter the professions. E. g., Hawker v. New York, 170 U.S. 189; Dent v. West Virginia, 129 U.S. 114; Barsky v. Board of Regents, 347 U.S. 442. The States may demand any qualifications which have "a rational connection with the applicant's fitness or capacity," Schware v. Board of Bar Examiners, 353 U.S. 232, 239, and may exclude any applicant who fails to satisfy them. In particular, a State may require evidence of good character, and may place the onus of its production upon the applicant. Konigsberg v. State Bar of California, 366 U.S. 36. Finally, a State may without constitutional objection require in the same fashion continuing evidence of professional and moral fitness as a condition of the retention of the right to practice. Cohen v. Hurley, 366 U.S. 117. All this is in no way questioned by today's decision.

As one prerequisite of continued practice in New York, the Appellate Division, Second Department, of the Supreme Court of New York has determined that attorneys must actively assist the courts and the appropriate professional groups in the prevention and detection of unethical legal activities. The Second Department demands that attorneys maintain various records, file statements of retainer in certain kinds of cases, and upon request provide information, all relevant to the use by the attorneys of contingent fee arrangements in such cases. These rules are intended to protect the public from the abuses revealed by a lengthy series of investigations of malpractices in the geographical area represented by the Second Department. It cannot be said that these conditions are arbitrary or unreasonable, or that they are unrelated to an attorney's continued fitness to practice. English courts since Edward I have endeavored to regulate the qualification and practice of lawyers, always in hope that this might better assure the integrity and evenhandedness of the administration of justice.[3] Very similar efforts have been made in the United States since the 17th century.[4] These efforts have protected the systems of justice in both countries from abuse, and have directly contributed to public confidence in those systems. Such efforts give appropriate recognition to the principle accepted both here and in England that lawyers are officers of the court who perform a fundamental role in the administration of justice.[5] The rules at issue here are in form and spirit a continuation of these efforts, and accordingly are reasonably calculated to serve the most enduring interests of the citizens of New York.

* * *

The petitioner here does not contend, and the plurality opinion does not suggest, that the state courts have derived any inference of guilt from petitioner's claim of the privilege. The state courts have expressly disclaimed all such inferences. 24 App. Div. 2d 653, 654. Nor is it suggested that the proceedings against petitioner were not an effort in good faith to assess his qualifications for continued practice in New York, or that the information sought from petitioner was not reasonably relevant to those qualifications. It would therefore follow that under the construction consistently given by this Court both to the privilege under the Fifth Amendment and to the Due Process Clause of the Fourteenth Amendment, petitioner's disbarment is constitutionally permissible.

---

3. The history of these efforts is outlined in Cohen, A History of the English Bar and Attornatus to 1450, 277 et seq., 2 Holdsworth, A History of English Law 317, 504 et seq.; 6 id., 431 et seq.

4. These efforts are traced in Warren, History of the American Bar, passim.

5. Evidences of this principle may be found in the opinions of this Court. See, e. g., Ex parte Bradley, 7 Wall. 364; Powell v. Alabama, 287 U.S. 45; Gideon v. Wainwright, 372 U.S. 335.

The plurality opinion does not pause either to acknowledge the previous handling of these issues or to explain why the privilege must now be supposed to forbid all consequences which may result from privileged silence. This is scarcely surprising, for the plurality opinion would create a novel and entirely unnecessary extension of the privilege which would exceed the needs of the privilege's purpose and seriously inhibit the protection of other public interests. The petitioner was not denied his privilege against self-incrimination, nor was he penalized for its use; he was denied his authority to practice law within the State of New York by reason of his failure to satisfy valid obligations imposed by the State as a condition of that authority. The only hazard in this process to the integrity of the privilege is the possibility that it might induce involuntary disclosures of incriminating materials; the sanction precisely calculated to eliminate that hazard is to exclude the use by prosecuting authorities of such materials and of their fruits. This Court has, upon proof of involuntariness, consistently forbidden their use since Brown v. Mississippi, 297 U.S. 278, and now, as my Brother WHITE has emphasized, the plurality has intensified this protection still further with the broad prohibitory rule it has announced today in Garrity v. New Jersey, ante, p. 493. It is true that this Court has on occasion gone a step further, and forbidden the practices likely to produce involuntary disclosures, but those cases are readily distinguishable. They have uniformly involved either situations in which the entire process was thought both to present excessive risks of coercion and to be foreign to our accusatorial system, as in Miranda v. Arizona, 384 U.S. 436, or situations in which the only possible purpose of the practice was thought to be to penalize the accused for his use of the constitutional privilege, as in Griffin v. California, 380 U.S. 609. Both situations are plainly remote from that in issue here. None of the reasons thought to require the prohibitions established in those cases have any relevance in the situation now before us; nothing in New York's efforts in good faith to assure the integrity of its judicial system destroys, inhibits, or even minimizes the petitioner's constitutional privilege. There is therefore no need to speculate whether lawyers, or those in any other profession or occupation, have waived in some unspecified fashion a measure of the protection afforded by the constitutional privilege; it suffices that the State is earnestly concerned with an urgent public interest, and that it has selected methods for the pursuit of that interest which do not prevent attainment of the privilege's purposes.

I think it manifest that this Court is required neither by the logic of the privilege against self-incrimination nor by previous authority to invalidate these state rules, and thus to overturn the disbarment of the petitioner. Today's application of the privilege serves only to hamper appropriate protection of other fundamental public values.[6]

In view of these conclusions, I find it unnecessary to reach the alternative basis of the Court of Appeals' decision, the "required records doctrine." See Shapiro v. United States, 335 U.S. 1.

I would affirm the judgment of disbarment.

---

6. It should be noted that the principle that a license or status may be denied to one who refuses, under the shelter of the constitutional privilege, to disclose information pertinent to that status or privilege, has been adopted in a variety of situations by statute. See, e. g., 12 U.S.C. 481; 47 U.S.C. 308 (b), 312 (a) (4): 5 U.S.C. 2283.

Debock v. State

512 So.2d 164 (Fla. 1987)
Supreme Court of Florida
July 16, 1987
Rehearing Denied Sept. 4, 1987
Stay Denied Nov. 2, 1987
See 108 S.Ct. 282
cert. denied 484 U.S. 1025 (1988)
[Some footnotes omitted. Remaining footnotes renumbered.]

EHRLICH, Justice. We have for our review *State v. Rendina,* 467 So.2d 734 (Fla. 4th DCA 1985). We have jurisdiction pursuant to article V, section 3(b)(3) and article V, section 15, Florida Constitution, and approve the decision of the district court below.

The petitioner, DeBock, was served with a subpoena by the state attorney's office for the Seventeenth Judicial Circuit. DeBock's testimony was sought in connection with criminal charges pending against Richard F. Rendina, an attorney, for offering unlawful compensation to DeBock while DeBock was an assistant state attorney. DeBock asserted his fifth amendment privilege and refused to answer questions at a deposition, contending that the immunity flowing from section 914.04, Florida Statutes (1983), was insufficient to immunize him from bar disciplinary proceedings. DeBock alleged that immunity from bar disciplinary proceedings could only come from this Court and the state had the burden of obtaining such immunity before DeBock could be required to testify. The trial court agreed with DeBock and entered an order finding that he was entitled to invoke his fifth amendment privilege until being granted immunity from bar proceedings, and that the state had to obtain this immunity for him before DeBock could be compelled to testify in the criminal case.

The district court reversed, holding that the witness seeking immunity from bar discipline is the one who has the burden of obtaining it from this Court. The district court reasoned that section 914.04 immunizes a witness solely from criminal prosecution and since bar disciplinary proceedings are remedial and not penal, the immunized witness cannot invoke his fifth amendment privilege and refuse to testify in a criminal case because of the "potentially adverse use of his testimony in bar disciplinary proceedings." 467 So.2d at 736.

DeBock petitioned this Court for review, alleging that the district court's opinion was in conflict with our decision in *Ciravolo v. The Florida Bar,* 361 So.2d 121 (Fla.1978), which dealt with two attorneys who had been granted immunity from criminal prosecution pursuant to section 914.04 and who claimed that this immunity also extended to bar disciplinary proceedings. DeBock raises numerous issues here. He claims first that bar disciplinary proceedings are penal and, therefore, in order to protect his Fifth Amendment privilege against compulsory self-incrimination, the grant of statutory immunity must also extend to bar disciplinary proceedings. In support of this contention, DeBock's second claim is that *Ciravolo* left intact previous decisions of this Court which held that a grant of statutory immunity to a non-attorney witness also immunized the witness from professional license revocation proceedings. According to DeBock, these prior cases support his position that professional disciplinary proceedings are considered penal in Florida. DeBock's third claim is that given our holdings in these prior cases, equal protection demands that an attorney-witness granted statutory immunity be treated the same as an immunized non-attorney witness. We reject each of these suggestions. Because DeBock's claims are all at least partially based on an erroneous view of our decision in *Ciravolo*, it is with that case that our discussion begins.

Two attorneys, Ciravolo and Feldman, had been subpoenaed to appear before a grand jury; both were granted immunity pursuant to the provisions of section 914.04. Counsel for both the state and the attorneys were of the opinion that the statutory grant of immunity extended to bar disciplinary proceedings, and the attorneys testified before the grand jury pursuant to this understanding. The Florida Bar subsequently instituted disciplinary proceedings against the attorneys based upon the transactions testified to before the grand jury. Ciravolo and Feldman sought a writ of prohibition from this Court in order to stop the bar from taking any disciplinary action. 361 So.2d at 122.

After discussing several of our prior decisions dealing with the immunity statute, *Lurie v. Florida State Board of Dentistry*, 288 So.2d 223 (Fla.1973), *Headley v. Baron*, 228 So.2d 281 (Fla.1969), *Florida Bar v. Massfeller*, 170 So.2d 834 (Fla.1964), and *Florida State Board of Architecture v. Seymour*, 62 So.2d 1 (Fla.1952), we concluded that counsel for the state and the attorneys had justifiably relied on our "unfortunate" reference to attorneys in *Lurie* which had suggested that a grant of immunity to an attorney would also extend to bar disciplinary matters. Therefore, we held:

> Since the testimony given in this case was predicated on a justifiable interpretation of this court's strong language in *Lurie*, and the court's imperfect handling of precedents, we are bound by the understanding reached by counsel in this case.

361 So.2d at 124. We explicitly receded from the unfortunate reference to attorneys in *Lurie*, and recognized that because of the separation of powers doctrine and this Court's exclusive jurisdiction over attorneys pursuant to article V, section 15 of the Florida Constitution, a state attorney under the executive branch of government had no authority to confer immunity on an attorney-witness from bar discipline; such immunity could only come from this Court. *Id.* at 124–125.

DeBock's first claim, that bar discipline is penal and therefore, that the grant of statutory immunity must also extend to a bar inquiry in order to protect his Fifth Amendment privilege, is incorrect. Our decision in *The Florida Bar v. Massfeller* is controlling. In *Massfeller* we recognized not only the inherent power of a court to discipline an attorney, but also rejected the idea that an inquiry into an attorney's fitness to practice law is penal, *i.e.*, is designed to punish an attorney. This Court explicitly embraced the reasoning of (then) Judge Cardozo in *In re: Rouss*, 221 N.Y. 81, 84–85, 116 N.E. 782, 783 (N.Y.1917), *cert. denied*, 246 U.S. 661, 38 S.Ct. 332, 62 L.Ed. 927 (1918):

> Membership in the bar is a privilege burdened with conditions. A fair private and professional character is one of them. Compliance with that condition is essential at the moment of admission; but it is equally essential afterwards. Whenever the condition is broken the privilege is lost. To refuse admission to an unworthy applicant is not to punish him for past offenses. The examination into character, like the examination into learning, is merely a test of fitness. To strike the unworthy lawyer from the roll is not to add to the pains and penalties of crime. The examination into character is renewed; and the test of fitness is no longer satisfied. For these reasons courts have repeatedly said that disbarment is not punishment. (citations omitted).170 So.2d at 839. We reaffirm here our holding in *Massfeller* that bar disciplinary proceedings are remedial, and are designed for the protection of the public and the integrity of the courts. An attorney as an officer of the Court and a member of the third branch of gov-

ernment occupies a unique position in our society. Because attorneys are in a position where members of the public must place their trust, property and liberty, and at times even their lives, in a member of the bar, society rightfully demands that an attorney must possess a fidelity to truth and honesty that is beyond reproach. When an attorney breaches this duty, the public is harmed. Not only is the individual citizen harmed by the unethical practitioner, all of society suffers when confidence in our system of law and justice is eroded by the unethical conduct of an officer of the Court. To protect the public the bar is mandated to inquire into an attorney's conduct when even the *appearance* of impropriety exists. For these reasons, the vast weight of judicial authority recognizes that bar discipline exists to protect the public, and not to "punish" the lawyer.

DeBock's second and third claims must logically be dealt with together. DeBock alleges that *Ciravolo* left intact our prior decisions, specifically *Lurie,* which held that a grant of immunity from criminal prosecution extends to professional license revocation proceedings. From this premise DeBock argues that equal protection demands that an attorney be treated the same as non-lawyer professionals. We reject both suggestions.

First, we point out that the underpinnings of both *Lurie* and *Seymour,* upon which DeBock relies, were effectually gutted when section 914.04 was amended by 82-393, section 1, Laws of Florida (1982). Prior to the amendment, the statute provided not only for transactional immunity "which accords full immunity from [criminal] prosecution for the offense to which the compelled testimony relates," *Kastigar v. United States,* 406 U.S. 441, 453, 92 S.Ct. 1653, 1661, 32 L.Ed.2d 212 (1972), but also provided that "no person shall be prosecuted *or subjected to any penalty or forfeiture for or on account of any transaction, matter, or thing concerning which he may so testify …*" 914.04, Fla.Stat. (1981) (emphasis added). As interpreted by this Court, a grant of transactional immunity under the prior statute provided that once a witness was immunized, *no* penalty would follow on account of *the transaction* testified about; we specifically held in *Seymour* that whether the penalty was criminal or civil was immaterial. 62 So.2d at 3.

However, the 1982 amendment narrowed the scope of the grant and the statute now provides for only use and derivative use immunity. The Supreme Court in *Kastigar* held that this is as broad as is constitutionally required to encompass the Fifth Amendment's protection against compulsory self-incrimination. 406 U.S. at 453, 92 S.Ct. at 1661.[1] By its plain terms, section 914.04 now is limited strictly to "any criminal investigation or proceeding."

Even accepting arguendo DeBock's assertion that *Ciravolo* left intact *Lurie* and *Seymour,* the 1982 amendment to section 914.04 now renders *Lurie* and *Seymour* inapposite. Since bar disciplinary proceedings are not penal, the grant of use and derivative use immunity conferred on DeBock extends only to the "criminal investigation or proceeding" concerning Rendina. Therefore, strictly under an analysis of the applicable statutory provision, DeBock had no right sub judice to invoke his Fifth Amendment privilege until immunized from bar discipline.

---

1. The Supreme Court held that use and derivative use immunity "prohibits the prosecutorial authorities from using the compelled testimony in any respect," 406 U.S. at 453, 92 S.Ct. at 1661 (emphasis in original), and "it imposes on the prosecution the affirmative duty to prove that the evidence it proposes to use is derived from a legitimate source wholly independent of the compelled testimony." Id. at 460, 92 S.Ct. at 1665.

However, regardless of this statutory analysis, DeBock's reading of *Ciravolo* is incorrect. We *explicitly* limited the "unfortunate" reference to lawyers made in *Lurie,* and held that a grant of immunity under section 914.04 does not immunize an attorney from bar disciplinary proceedings. 361 So.2d at 124.

Still relying on the validity of *Lurie* and *Seymour* DeBock raises an equal protection claim and states that there is "simply no rational basis for applying constitutional guarantees differently to the loss of the license of a certified public accountant, for example, than to the loss of a lawyer's license." As stated, the immunity statute involved in *Lurie* and *Seymour* has been significantly narrowed, thus bringing the continued validity of those cases into doubt. Further, in order to dispel the implication nascent in DeBock's argument that he somehow has a "right" to practice law, we point out what should be obvious to all members of the bar: "[a] license to practice law confers no vested right to the holder thereof, but is a conditional privilege which is revocable for cause." Rule 3-1.1, Rules Regulating The Florida Bar.

DeBock further argues, in support of his equal protection claim, that *Ciravolo* cannot be read to set forth different standards for attorneys than for other regulated professionals. Not only did we explicitly limit *Lurie's* rational as it applied to attorneys, our opening paragraph in *Ciravolo* belies DeBock's argument: The question we considered in that case was "whether or not evidence given by an attorney, following a grant of immunity under section 914.04, Florida Statutes (1975), may be used against him in a disciplinary proceeding brought by The Florida Bar;" we answered this question in the *affirmative.* 361 So.2d at 121.

The 1975 version of section 914.04 at issue in *Ciravolo* provided for the broad grant of transactional immunity and, as stated, extended to any penalty, whether civil or criminal. By our answer to the question presented in *Ciravolo* we recognized that an immunized attorney's testimony in a criminal proceeding *could* be used in a bar inquiry. This clearly sets forth the proposition that attorneys can be held to different standards than other regulated professions. The reasons cited above to explain why bar proceedings are designed to protect the public is also a "rational basis" for holding attorneys to different standards: the unique role of attorneys as officers of the court mandates that attorneys be held to the highest of ethical standards. This difference has been recognized by centuries of jurisprudential thought and is manifested in article V, section 15 of our constitution.

Relying on our separation of powers holding in *Ciravolo,* DeBock's final argument is that the burden is on the state to seek from this Court bar immunity for an attorney-witness. We reject this suggestion. In *Ciravolo* we held that an immunized attorney may be granted immunity from bar disciplinary proceedings by order of this Court, "[w]here it appears that the greater good to society will be served by granting immunity from disciplinary action to an attorney ..." *Id.* at 125. Who would have the burden of obtaining such immunity from this Court was not explicitly addressed in *Ciravolo*. However, our holdings here and in *Ciravolo* that the immunity conferred by 914.04 does not extend to bar disciplinary proceedings because they are remedial, not penal, and our recognition in *Ciravolo* that a state attorney is powerless to interfere with this Court's exclusive jurisdiction over members of the bar, easily leads us to conclude that it is the attorney seeking bar immunity who must so persuade this Court. As we stated in *Ciravolo:*

> The court is concerned about the practice of law by those involved in wrong doings of a criminal nature, but, we are also mindful that this court and the

profession should not place a stumbling block in the path of the citizens of this state who strive mightily to uncover and rid our communities of criminal acts.

Id. at 125. It would not only be inconsistent with our separation of powers concerns to place this burden on a state attorney, it would also needlessly "place a stumbling block in the path" of those whose duty is to investigate and prosecute criminal wrongdoing.

Once immunity was granted to DeBock pursuant to section 914.04, he was fully protected from having his testimony used against him in any criminal proceeding. That is the extent of both the statute's reach and the Fifth Amendment's privilege against compulsory self-incrimination. Should DeBock now refuse to testify in the criminal proceeding below he, like any other similarly situated witness, can be held in contempt of court.

Accordingly, we approve the decision of the district court below.

It is so ordered.

McDONALD, C.J., and OVERTON, SHAW and GRIMES, JJ., concur.

BARKETT, J., dissents with an opinion, in which KOGAN, J., concurs.

BARKETT, Justice, dissenting.

I dissent. I cannot agree with the premise from which the majority's conclusion derives. To say that bar disciplinary proceedings are remedial in order to protect the public and are not penal in nature is pure semantic tomfoolery. It totally ignores the numerous cases which have imposed discipline when the conduct involved had no connection with the protection of the public, e.g., in cases where a felony conviction *automatically* results in discipline without any analysis of the specific crime as it relates to the protection of the public.

I agree, rather, with the United States Supreme Court which has recognized that where the accused attorney asserted his constitutional privilege against self-incrimination and refused to testify, the attorney should "'suffer no penalty ... for such silence.'" *Spevack v. Klein,* 385 U.S. 511, 514, 87 S.Ct. 625, 628, 17 L.Ed.2d 574 (1967) (quoting *Malloy v. Hogan,* 378 U.S. 1, 8, 84 S.Ct. 1489, 1494, 12 L.Ed.2d 653 (1964)). The Supreme Court stated further that in this context "penalty" is not restricted to fine or imprisonment, rather it means the imposition of any sanction which makes the assertion of the fifth amendment privilege "costly." 385 U.S. at 515, 87 S.Ct. at 628. The Court concluded that the self-incrimination clause extends to lawyers as well as other individuals and "it should not be watered down by imposing the dishonor of disbarment and the deprivation of a livelihood as a price for asserting it." *Id.* at 514, 87 S.Ct. at 627. In *In re Ruffalo,* 390 U.S. 544, 550, 88 S.Ct. 1222, 1226, 20 L.Ed.2d 117 (1968), the Court said "[d]isbarment, designed to protect the public, is a punishment or penalty imposed on the lawyer." In *Gardner v. Broderick,* 392 U.S. 273, 277, 88 S.Ct. 1913, 1916, 20 L.Ed.2d 1082 (1968), when comparing a police officer's right against self-incrimination with that of an attorney, the Supreme Court agreed with the premise that "a lawyer could not constitutionally be confronted with Hobson's choice between self-incrimination and forfeiting his means of livelihood."

Moreover, the United States Supreme Court ruling in *Supreme Court of New Hampshire v. Piper,* 470 U.S. 274, 281, 105 S.Ct. 1272, 1277, 84 L.Ed.2d 205 (1985), has cast considerable doubt on this Court's prior statements that the opportunity to practice law is not a right protected by the Constitution:

> The lawyer's role in the national economy is not the only reason that the opportunity to practice law should be considered a "fundamental right."

Although *Piper* used this rationale to void a residency requirement restricting the practice of law to those who live within a state, this dictum nonetheless suggests that the United States Supreme Court is starting to view the practice of law in a far different light than that suggested by the majority. If the opportunity to practice law indeed is a "fundamental right," I see no justification for the majority's holding that bar disciplinary proceedings are not penal in nature. Any proceeding that may strip someone of a fundamental right by definition is "penal" and therefore subject to all the strictures of the Fifth Amendment.

I therefore must respectfully dissent.

D. Process

"How to File a Complaint"
Massachusetts Board of Bar Overseers (2005)
(www.mass.gov/obcbbo/complaint.htm)

- What You Should Know before Filing a Complaint
- How to File a Complaint
- What Happens when You File a Complaint
- What Sanctions Are Available
- What to Expect
- What not to Expect
- Confidentiality

Inquiries concerning the professional conduct of an attorney admitted to practice in Massachusetts are initially handled by the Attorney and Consumer Assistance Program (ACAP) of the Office of the Bar Counsel. The ACAP staff is available to discuss your concerns by telephone during normal business hours and can be reached at (617) 728-8750. If you would prefer to communicate your problem in writing, you can contact ACAP by fax at (617) 357-1866 or by letter at the Office of Bar Counsel. ACAP cannot accept inquiries over the internet.

Where possible, ACAP will attempt to assist in resolving attorney-client disputes by providing information, calling the lawyer, or suggesting alternative ways of dealing with the problem. Please see the ACAP link for more information about how ACAP may be of assistance to you. If the matter brought to the attention of ACAP involves potentially serious misconduct on the part of the lawyer warranting prompt investigation by the Office of Bar Counsel, ACAP will immediately issue a complaint form.

What You Should Know before Filing a Complaint

- All lawyers admitted to practice in Massachusetts are bound by the *Rules of Professional Conduct* adopted by the Massachusetts Supreme Judicial Court. The purpose of the Rules is to set forth minimum ethical standards for the practice of law. It is the responsibility of the Board of Bar Overseers and the Office of the Bar Counsel to see that the Rules of Professional Conduct are observed.

- Inquiries concerning the professional conduct of an attorney admitted to practice in Massachusetts may be initially handled by the Attorney and Consumer Assistance Program (ACAP) of the Office of the Bar Counsel. ACAP issues all complaint forms and can be reached at **(617) 728-8750**.

- In order for a lawyer to be found to have committed misconduct, it must be shown that his acts have violated the Rules of Professional Conduct. Charges of misconduct must be supported by the facts.
- Examples of attorney practices clearly prohibited by the Rules include:
  - Serious neglect of a client's case or a client. Examples would be a lawyer's failure to file papers or documents with the court within time periods prescribed by law, or unreasonable failure to communicate with clients on a timely basis.
  - Failure to account to clients, as required by the Rules of Professional Conduct, concerning the status of funds or property being held by the lawyer.
  - Commingling, or failure to keep a client's funds separate from a lawyer's own funds.
  - Use of a client's funds by a lawyer for his own purposes.
  - Failure to reduce to writing an attorney-client Contingent Fee Agreement. This is an agreement between a lawyer and a client stating that the lawyer's fee depends in whole or in part on the lawyer's success on behalf of a client.
  - Engaging in work for a client notwithstanding the existence of a conflict of interest, as defined and prohibited by the Rules of Professional Conduct.

How to File a Complaint

Complaint forms can be obtained by telephoning the Attorney and Consumer Assistance Program (ACAP), as explained above. Because of the confidentiality requirements complaints **cannot be accepted via e-mail**. Send complaints to the address below.

Office of the Bar Counsel
99 High Street
Boston, Massachusetts 02110
(617) 728-8750

What Your Complaint Should Contain

In order for the investigation to proceed, it will be necessary that you provide as many facts and as much documentation as possible. Although you may feel certain that the acts complained of constitute misconduct, a simple statement that misconduct has occurred is not enough. You should set forth the facts surrounding your complaint. Include dates, the nature of the legal matter, and specific information about what you feel the lawyer did wrong. If you have documents, including a fee agreement, court papers, letters or notes, that you think are helpful to understand the complaint, send copies. **DO NOT SEND ORIGINAL DOCUMENTS**.

Clients should not hesitate to ask their lawyers about anything concerning their cases, including costs and fees. Before filing a complaint, the client should try to discuss the problem candidly and openly with the lawyer. Clients may become dissatisfied with their lawyers for many reasons, but unless there is a violation of the Rules of Professional Conduct, discipline will not be imposed.

If you have any doubts about whether to proceed, the Office of the Bar Counsel will try to answer any questions you may have. The address and telephone number are listed above.

What Happens when You File a Complaint

After screening by ACAP, complaint forms are submitted to the Office of the Bar Counsel for investigation. Sometimes a complaint does not fit within the area that is regulated by the Rules of Professional Conduct. Please read the section entitled What

Not to Expect. If Bar Counsel determines that your complaint falls into one of these categories, the complaint will be closed and notice will be sent to you. You may request review of this decision by a member of the Board. However, there is no appeal from a decision by the Board not to bring disciplinary charges against an attorney.

If a lawyer is found to have committed a relatively minor infraction of the rules, the lawyer may receive an admonition. If there appears to be serious misconduct, the matter is referred to a local Hearing Committee appointed by the Board. All the evidence is reviewed and considered. Each side is heard. The Hearing Committee then submits a written report to the Board with its recommendation as to discipline.

If Bar Counsel and the lawyer reach agreement as to discipline, the recommendation may be submitted directly to the Board without referral to a Hearing Committee.

The Board may accept or modify the recommendation for discipline. If the Board feels it needs additional information, it may return the case to the Hearing Committee for further hearing, or conduct hearings of its own before making a final determination.

What Sanctions Are Available

The types of discipline that may be imposed by the Board are:

- **Admonition**, which means that the lawyer is reproved. A record is made of the reproval, but the name of the lawyer is not made public.

- **Public Reprimand**, which means that the lawyer is publicly reproved. Public reprimands are published in Lawyer's Weekly and other publications, and are compiled in the bound volumes of the Massachusetts Attorney Discipline Reports.

- If the Board determines that more severe discipline is required, it sends the matter, together with its recommendation, to the Supreme Judicial Court. The types of discipline which only the Court can impose are:

- **Suspension**, which means that the lawyer may not practice law for a period of time. Suspension can be for either a specified term or for an indefinite period. A lawyer who is suspended for an indefinite period may not apply for reinstatement for five years.

- **Disbarment**, which means that the lawyer's license to practice is revoked and the lawyer's name is stricken from the list of licensed lawyers.

Sometimes one of the above disciplines may be imposed with terms of probation. An attorney may also resign from the bar rather than face disciplinary action, but only with the Court's consent.

Decisions of the Board and the Court with respect to public discipline are released for publication. Recently-published decisions and orders are available on this website.

What to Expect

Complaints are not dismissed lightly, nor are they prosecuted without justification. The protection of the public is paramount in considering every complaint filed.

You may expect ...

A prompt reply from the Office of the Bar Counsel acknowledging receipt of your complaint.

A fair and impartial investigation. This means listening not only to your side of the story, but to the lawyer's side as well. It also means that whatever independent investigation may be necessary in order to establish the facts will also be conducted.

As speedy a disposition as is possible of your complaint. Depending on the complexity of the matter, this can take from a month to a year or longer.

To be called as a witness, if necessary, and to provide additional information for the investigation of your complaint.

That even though a matter is resolved between you and your attorney, your continued cooperation may be necessary to discipline the attorney.

Disciplinary action, commensurate with the offense, against any lawyer found to have violated the Rules of Professional Conduct.

Advice concerning where you may go if the subject of your complaint does not fall within the jurisdiction of the Board.

To be kept informed of the progress of the investigation and to be notified of the final disposition of the complaint.

There are no charges or other costs to you by the Office of the Bar Counsel or the Board of Bar Overseers.

What not to Expect

You should not expect the Office of the Bar Counsel or the Board of Bar Overseers to provide legal services or advice. If you wish to be referred to a lawyer you might contact the Massachusetts Bar Association Lawyer Referral Service at (617) 654-0400 in Boston or (866) MASSLRS which is (866) 627-7577 or the Boston Bar Association Lawyer Referral Service at (617) 742-0625. The lawyers at the Office of the Bar Counsel do not and cannot represent you personally in the matters of which you complain.

Although a lawyer may take corrective steps to avoid disciplinary action after he receives a complaint, the Board of Bar Overseers does not have power to compel a lawyer to refund money, release your case, or return files. The Board has only the power to discipline attorneys or recommend discipline to the Court.

You may have a civil claim against your lawyer that can be pursued in the courts, a fee dispute that can be resolved by a bar association fee arbitration board, or a claim that will be considered by the Clients' Security Board. The Office of the Bar Counsel will tell you where to explore these other possibilities in appropriate cases.

Confidentiality

Under Court rules, the Board of Bar Overseers and the Office of the Bar Counsel must treat complaints as confidential matters. Until public discipline has been imposed by the Court, the Board and Bar Counsel may not disclose that a complaint has been filed, except in certain cases as specified in the rules. You are immune from liability based upon your complaint.

E. Duty to Inform on Other Lawyers

["The Spalding Report"]
Petition of Boston Bar Association to Adopt the Canons and the Disciplinary Rules in the Code of Professional Responsibility Adopted by the American Bar Association

Report of Special Master [The Honorable John V. Spalding]

Pursuant to an order of the Supreme Judicial Court of November 17, 1971, the above-entitled matter was referred to me "as special master and commissioner (a) for study and consideration of the record and briefs, (b) to hear arguments … on the legal and policy questions raised by the briefs and otherwise, (c) to formulate any amendments or revisions of the proposed code which [I] may deem advisable and to receive and hear comments upon the same in [my] discretion, and (d) to prepare and submit [my] recommendations for action by this court."

* * *

1

Canon 1
Disciplinary Rule 1-102
Misconduct

(A) A Lawyer shall not:

(1) Violate a Disciplinary Rule.

(2) Circumvent a Disciplinary Rule through actions of another.

(3) Engage in illegal conduct involving moral turpitude.

(4) Engage in conduct involving dishonesty, fraud, deceit, or misrepresentation.

(5) Engage in conduct that is prejudicial to the administration of justice.

(6) Engage in any other conduct that adversely reflects on his fitness to practice law. (Code pamphlet, 3)

None of the parties before the court, with the exception of Brown, appear to have any objection to the adoption of Disciplinary Rule 1-102. Brown's objection seems to be that the rule is "far to encompassing, ambiguous … and employs standards which are words of conclusion." (Brown brief, page 7). Expressions such as "illegal conduct involving moral turpitude" (3), "dishonesty, fraud or misrepresentation" (4) and "conduct that adversely reflects on his fitness to practice law" are, according to Brown, too vague to constitute the basis for disciplinary action.

The arguments in support of the rule are set forth in Boston's brief (Boston brief, pages 18–21). I will not undertake to set them forth at length. Doubtless, there are expressions in the rule that are not susceptible of precise definition, such as, "illegal conduct involving moral turpitude." Boston concedes that this expression is troublesome and points to the fact that Professor Weckstein, who appears to favor this portion of the Code in general, has accused the framers of the Code of "overkill" in proscribing "illegal conduct involving moral turpitude." He suggests that this provision either be deleted or a more expressive provision substituted. See Weckstein: Maintaining the Integrity and Competence of the Legal Profession, 48 *Tex. L. Rev.* 267, 280. It is the writer's view that unless this provision can be made more precise, and none has been suggested and I can think of none, it should be deleted.

Recommendation

I therefore recommend that Disciplinary Rule 1-102 (A) be adopted except for sub-paragraph (3) which reads "Engage in illegal conduct involving moral turpitude."

Disciplinary Rule 1-103 (A)
Disclosure of Information to Authorities

(A) A lawyer possessing unprivileged knowledge of a violation of DR 1-102 shall report such knowledge to a tribunal or other authority empowered to investigate or act upon such violation. (Code Pamphlet, 3)

This rule is opposed by Mass. Bar, Brown and Professor Hall. The arguments against the rule are that it would create a profession of informants and would breed distrust among members of the Bar. (Mass Bar brief, page 4)

Professor Hall argues that disciplining lawyers for failure to report the misconduct of others, as would be required by Rule 1-103(A), is too harsh. It would be tantamount to reviving the common law crime of misprision of felony, a concept that has not gained favor in this country. He points out that most states have either rejected the offense completely, or have modified it. No court in the United States, he says, has held that a mere failure to disclose knowledge of a felony is itself punishable. (Hall brief, pages 3–5). In this Commonwealth it is not certain that the crime exists but if it does, there must be proof of "an evil motive to prevent or delay administration of justice." *Commonwealth v. Lopes*, 318 Mass. 453, 459. In the Lopes case Lummus, J. quoted Chief Justice Marshall in *Marbury v. Brooks* 7 Wheat. 556, 575, where in discussing misprision of felony he said, "It may be the duty of a citizen to accuse every offender, and to proclaim every offense which comes to his knowledge; but the law which would punish him in every case for not performing that duty is too harsh for man."

The analogy of Rule 1-103(A) to the crime of misprision of felony, I submit, is close and the arguments against that offence are equally applicable against Rule 101(A).

The position of Boston appears to be that while it thinks that Rule 1-103(A) goes too far, it ought not be eliminated in its entirety. (Boston brief, page 22). Boston proposes amending 1-103(A) as follows: "A lawyer possessing unprivileged knowledge of a violation of DR 1-102(A)*(3) or (4)* shall report this knowledge to a tribunal or other authority empowered to investigate or act upon such violation." (Proposed amendment is underscored).

Under this proposal a lawyer is subject to discipline only if he fails to report another lawyer who has "(3) [engaged] in illegal conduct involving moral turpitude" or "(4) [engaged] in conduct involving dishonesty, fraud, deceit, or misrepresentation." Boston's arguments in favor of retaining 1-103(A) with the proposed amendment are set forth in its brief at pages 22–25. Since Boston strenuously urges that Rule 1-103(A) be retained with the proposed amendment, I have considered their arguments with care. The question is by no means free from difficulty. The amendment would subject an attorney to discipline for failure to inform against a fellow lawyer only in situations involving moral turpitude, dishonesty, fraud, deceit, or misrepresentation. While the rule, with the amendment, is an improvement, and Boston's argument in favor of it is appealing, (Boston brief, pages 22–25), I am inclined to agree with the position taken by Mass. Bar and Professor Hall.

Recommendation

I therefore recommend that Rule 1-103(A) be eliminated in its entirety.

Respectfully submitted,

Justice John V. Spalding (retired)

Special Master

[NOTE: The Special Master's recommendations on DR 1-102 and DR 1-103(A) were accepted by the Massachusetts Supreme Judicial court when it adopted the ABA Code as part of its *Rules of Court*. See Rule 3:07, *Rules of the Supreme Judicial Court, Massachusetts Rules of Court*, 271 (1975)].

ABA Committee on Evaluation of Disciplinary Enforcement, Problems and Recommendations in Disciplinary Enforcement (1970)

"Problem 31—Reluctance on the Part of Judges to Report Instances of Professional Misconduct" Recommendation

Greater emphasis in law school and continuing legal education courses on the individual attorney's responsibility to assist the profession's efforts to police itself by reporting instances of professional misconduct to the appropriate disciplinary agency; sanctions, in appropriate circumstances, against attorneys and judges who fail to report attorney misconduct of which they are aware.

Discussion

In an address at the 1965 annual meeting of the American Bar Association, then President Lewis F. Powell stated:

> Surely no one wants punitive action, but it must be remembered that the bar has the privilege of disciplining itself to a greater extent than any other profession or calling. This imposes upon the bar a higher responsibility, one which the bar must discharge with greater determination.

If individual attorneys and judges shirk that responsibility, permitting wrongdoers in their midst to escape disciplinary action unless the circumstances are reported by laymen, the public may conclude that "self-policing" is in reality "self protection." The failure of attorneys and judges to report instances of misconduct, while undoubtedly the result of the almost universal reluctance to inform, hampers effective enforcement and does a disservice to the bench, the bar and the public.

The client who retains an unethical practitioner may form his opinion of the entire profession from a single experience. If other attorneys who have become aware of the misconduct take prompt action against the violator, the client's respect for the integrity of the bar may be restored. If, on the other hand, the other attorneys close their eyes and do nothing, the client may conclude that the bar is engaged in a conspiracy to protect its own. Moreover, the attorney who takes no action when he becomes aware of apparent misconduct on the part of another often subjects future clients of the unethical practitioner to serious harm. For example, disciplinary agencies occasionally receive complaints of conversion by an attorney and discover, on investigation, that the monies were converted in order to make restitution of monies previously converted from another client. Not infrequently, the second conversion will have occurred after a demand by a new attorney consulted by the first client that restitution be made so that a complaint to the appropriate disciplinary agency will be unnecessary. By not reporting the conversion of the first client's fund immediately, and agreeing not to do so if restitution is made, the new attorney not only permits the unethical practitioner to continue to practice but may encourage subsequent conversion of another's client's funds....

The adverse effect on the reputation of the bar and the danger to the public stemming from this reluctance of attorneys and judges require that strong measures be taken. The individual attorney's responsibility to report instances of misconduct as a necessary element of the self-policing privilege should be stressed in law school so that it is impressed on the lawyer during his formative years. Bar associations should engage in extensive educational campaigns as part of their continuing legal education programs to call the attention of the profession to the harmful effects of its silence in the face of misconduct.

A former chairman of a court disciplinary commission expressed the opinion that prompt reporting by attorneys of instances of misconduct of which they become aware may even prove beneficial to the wrongdoers:

> It seems to me somewhere in our profession we have to try to get the rank and file of the bar to realize that when they sense there is something wrong with one of their fellow attorneys, they are really not doing the public any favor, by sitting back and allowing this to go unnoticed in one way or another.

> I have a hunch that some of these cases that then blow up into major cases could have been nipped in the bud if we just could get a little more sense of responsibility in trying to call these things to attention of the proper disciplinary bodies at an early stage, so that private censure or warning, or whatever you might call it, might well have some effect.

Consideration should also be given to sanctions against attorneys and judges who fail to report misconduct to the proper disciplinary agency in appropriate cases. Such sanctions are fully justified in light of the obligation imposed by Disciplinary Rule 1-103(A) of the Code of Professional Responsibility ("A lawyer possessing unprivileged knowledge of a violation of DR 1-102 shall report such knowledge to a tribunal or other authority empowered to investigate or act upon such violation"); ... and Canon 11 of the Canons of Judicial Ethics ("A judge should utilize his opportunities to criticize and correct unprofessional conduct of attorneys and counselors, brought to his attention; and, if adverse comment is not a sufficient corrective, should send the matter at once to the proper investigating and disciplinary authorities").

The existence and proposed use of sanctions, together with a restatement of the obligations of lawyers and judges, should be emphasized in bar publications. The chairman of a state disciplinary commission concluded that this action is absolutely necessary if the profession is to be jarred out its complacency into the sense of concern and responsibility necessary for effective professional self-discipline:

> I frankly feel, based on experience both at the grievance level and with respect to the disciplinary commission, that we are going to be wasting our time unless lawyers as a group—not just those of us who are concerned with grievance matters—unless lawyers as a profession become more concerned with and more sensitive to our responsibilities as individuals and to the collective responsibility of the profession.

> I think that we have developed a "live and let live" philosophy. We really do not care much about what our colleagues are doing unless they cross us. There is a

good deal of talk among us about how we covet professionalism, but there is really not much indication to me that we have any overwhelming concern for the public interest in relation, at least, to the activities of our fellow lawyers.

Argument — Supreme Judicial Court

Daniel R. Coquillette
September 9, 1997

Mr. Chief Justice and May It Please the Court,

Almost exactly 26 years ago today I began work for this Court as a law clerk to Justice Robert Braucher. I will never forget my first assignment. The Justice walked into my room and announced, "There's a man up in single justice session who claims there's a conspiracy against him. Find out all you can about it, so that I can join in!" My second assignment was the special order of 1971 establishing Justice John V. Spalding as special master to recommend whether or not to adopt an ABA mandatory lawyer reporting rule, the old DR-1-103(A). Today we have before us a version of another mandatory ABA reporting rule, Rule 8.3. As Yogi Berra said, "It's *déjà vu*, all over again!"

While some of the issues are the same as 25 years ago, the new Rule 8.3 — as reviewed and revised by your special Committee, is significantly improved, in part by adopting some of the very recommendations made by Justice Spalding in 1972. In particular, the new Rule 8.3 is limited to lawyers having knowledge that another lawyer has committed a violation of the professional rules that "raises a *substantial question* as to that lawyer's honesty, trustworthiness or fitness as a lawyer." The word "substantial" already has a body of case law making it a high threshold. The new rule also does not authorize disclosure of client information protected by Rule 1.6. These changes avoid the so-called "Himmel" problem presented by Rule 1-103 A.[1] The issue today is simply whether this very narrow rule, already adopted in some version in 43 states, should be mandatory or permissive — "shall" or "should."

I am here, at your request, to put the case for a mandatory Rule 8.3. I am delighted to do so. Whatever situation that faced this Court 25 years ago, today there is a radically changed legal profession and a very different public environment. These changes call out for increased responsibility by the bar. The great majority of states adopting Rule 8.3 have recognized this fact and adopted the mandatory version.

Professionally, I wear three hats, and I believe each hat can provide some assistance to this Court. First, "Hat 1." I am a judicial rulemaker by trade. For 14 years I have been Reporter to the statutory Standing Committee on Rules for the Judicial Conference of the U.S., the chief federal rulemaking body. As a rulemaker I have just two points to make: 1) court rules should not be pious hopes; they should establish enforceable duties, or be put somewhere else. The *ABA Model Rules* deliberately eliminated purely aspirational guidelines and exhortations. A professional rule of conduct should be enforced by Bar Counsel or omitted, altogether, as this Court did with Rule 1-103(A) in 1972. There is a statute that says that the chickadee is the state bird of Massachusetts, but it would not make a good rule in court. 2) Court rulemaking is not like deciding cases. Rulemaking is prospective, not retroactive. This Court can promulgate a rule and see how it works. If it isn't perfect, it can be amended later, as the federal courts do frequently. Just look at Rule 11 or Rule 26 of the Federal Rules of Civil Procedure. But to

---

1. See *In Re Himmel*, 125 Ill. 2d 531, 533 N.E. 2d 790 (1988).

do nothing is to make no progress. The "Chicken Littles" will claim that a mandatory Rule 8.3 will make the sky fall. The Board of Bar Overseers' Counsel, Mr. Frederickson, disagrees, and so do the Illinois Bar Overseers, the Arizona Bar Overseers and many others. "Nothing Ventured—Nothing Gained" is the motto of rulemaking. In addition, unlike most cases, important constituents are frequently not heard in the rulemaking process, and this Court should be alert as to who they are. Here, the most directly interested party is the lay public, the consumers of legal services that this rule was designed to protect. Their interests must be protected by this Court, or there will be a big price to pay.

"Hat 2." For twenty years I have taught in the Commonwealth's law schools, including BC, Harvard and BU. My students, some of whom are here today, are deeply anxious that the profession has become just another special interest group pursuing its own economic and political interests, indifferent to higher duties to the public and the justice system. The recently released Report of the Boston Bar Association Task Force on Professionalism, a superb piece of work, asks for a recommitment to these higher duties. This Court is now making rules for the lawyers of the 21st century. Flinching from an absolute standard of duty will feed growing suspicion and cynicism. It just does not send the right message to the next generation.

"Hat 3." Since the early Jurassic period I have been a member of the bar of this court, and as an ancient member of the bar I would like to conclude with a profoundly conservative argument. Very few things are as important to American freedom as an independent bar, subject only to regulation by an independent judiciary. But this great tradition requires both the fact and appearance of genuine, publicly responsible self-regulation. Already the United States Congress is expressing deep concern about recent activities of the legal profession, and state legislators will not be far behind. We must not claim that our public duties are less than those we would urge for doctors, dentists, engineers, judges,[2] government officers and other groups which—like us—are specially entrusted with the public welfare. Our mandatory duties are, ultimately, at the head of our ancient and great profession. Do not make me and other teachers stand up before the future lawyers and judges of this Commonwealth and teach a half-baked rule that breeds cynicism and disrespect. Justice Lewis F. Powell, in urging the ABA to adopt a mandatory rule, said:

> "[I]t must be remembered that the bar has the privilege of disciplining itself to a greater extent than any other profession or calling. This imposes upon the bar a higher responsibility, one which the bar must discharge with greater determination. If individual attorneys and judges shirk that responsibility, permitting wrongdoers in their midst to escape disciplinary action unless the circumstances are reported by laymen, the public may conclude that 'self-policing' is in reality 'self-protection.'"[3]

I urge you to adopt a mandatory Rule 8.3. It will be a code of honor for our profession and for the profession of the future.

Thank you.

---

2. See SJC Rule 3:09, Canon 3-B (3).

3. *ABA Committee on Evaluation of Disciplinary Enforcement, Problems and Recommendations in Disciplinary Enforcement* (1970).

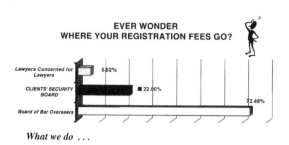

Massachusetts Client Security Board Announcement (2004)

Lawyer's Duty to Report Rule Violations by Another Lawyer Who May Suffer from Disability or Impairment

American Bar Association
Formal Opinion 03-431
August 8, 2003

A lawyer who believes that another lawyer's known violations of disciplinary rules raise substantial questions about her fitness to practice must report those violations to the appropriate professional authority. A lawyer who believes that another lawyer's mental condition materially impairs her ability to represent clients, and who knows that that lawyer continues to do so, must report that lawyer's consequent violation of Rule 1.16(b)(2), which requires that she withdraw from the representation of clients.

In this opinion, we examine the obligation of a lawyer who acquires knowledge that another lawyer, not in his firm, suffers from a mental condition that materially impairs the subject lawyer's ability to represent a client.[1] Under Rule 1.16(a)(2) of the Model Rules of Professional Conduct,[2] a lawyer must not undertake or continue representation of a client when that lawyer suffers from a mental condition that "materially impairs the

---

1. In ABA Standing Committee on Professional Responsibility Formal Opinion 03-429 (Obligations With Respect to Mentally Impaired Lawyer in the Firm) (June 11, 2003), we addressed the obligations of lawyers within a firm when another lawyer within that firm violates the Model Rules of Professional Conduct due to mental impairment. Like that opinion, this opinion deals only with mental impairment, which may be either temporary or permanent. Physical impairments are beyond the scope of this opinion unless they also result in the impairment of mental faculties. In addition to Alzheimer's disease and other mental conditions that are age-related and affect the entire population, lawyers have been found to suffer from alcoholism and substance abuse at a rate at least twice as high as the general population. See George Edward Bailly, Impairment, The Profession and Your Law Partner, 11 No. 1 PROF. LAW. 2 (1999).

2. This opinion is based on the Model Rules of Professional Conduct as amended by the ABA House of Delegates in February 2002 and, to the extent indicated, the predecessor Model Code of Professional Responsibility of the American Bar Association. The laws, court rules, regulations, rules of professional responsibility, and opinions promulgated in the individual jurisdictions are controlling.

lawyer's ability to represent the client."[3] That requirement reflects the conclusion that allowing persons who do not possess the capacity to make the professional judgments and perform the services expected of a lawyer is not only harmful to the interests of clients, but also undermines the integrity of the legal system and the profession.

Under Rule 8.3(a), a lawyer with knowledge[4] that another lawyer's conduct has violated the Model Rules in a way that "raises a substantial question as to that lawyer's honesty, trustworthiness or fitness as a lawyer in other respects" must inform the appropriate professional authority.[5] Although not all violations of the Model Rules are reportable events under Rule 8.3, as they may not raise a substantial question about a lawyer's fitness to practice law, a lawyer's failure to withdraw from representation while suffering from a condition materially impairing her ability to practice, as required by Rule 1.16(a)(2), ordinarily would raise a substantial question requiring reporting under Rule 8.3.[6]

When considering his obligation under Rule 8.3(a), a lawyer should recognize that, in most cases, lack of fitness will evidence itself through a pattern of conduct that makes clear that the lawyer is not meeting her obligations under the Model Rules, for example, Rule 1.1 (Competence) or Rule 1.3 (Diligence). A lawyer suffering from an impairment may, among other things, repeatedly miss court deadlines, fail to make filings required to complete a transaction, fail to perform tasks agreed to be performed, or fail to raise issues that competent counsel would be expected to raise. On occasion, however, a single act by a lawyer may evidence her lack of fitness.[7]

A lawyer may be impaired by senility or dementia due to age or illness or because of alcoholism, drug addiction,[8] substance abuse, chemical dependency, or mental illness.[9]

---

3. Rule 1.16(a)(2) states that a lawyer shall not represent a client or, where representation has commenced, shall withdraw from the representation of a client if "the lawyer's physical or mental condition materially impairs the lawyer's ability to represent the client." See, e.g., In re Morris, 541 S.E.2d 844 (S.C. 2001) (lawyer failed to notify clients that he would be unavailable while being treated at in-patient drug and alcohol rehabilitation program); State ex rel. Oklahoma Bar Ass'n v. Southern, 15 P.3d 1 (Okla. 2000) (lawyer had been suffering severe, untreated vitamin B-12 illness that essentially destroyed his short-term memory and exacerbated his depression; lawyer neglected five clients and their cases); In re Francis, 4 P.3d 579 (Kan. 2000) (lawyer's depression resulted in misconduct, including failure to comply with discovery requests, to prosecute civil suit, to return telephone calls, and to withdraw from representing client); People v. Heilbrunn, 814 P.2d 819 (Colo. 1991) (lawyer who neglected, deceived, and abandoned clients due to drugs, alcohol, and depression failed to withdraw); State v. Ledvina, 237 N.W.2d 683 (Wis. 1976) (lawyer with compulsive personality disorder with paranoid trends engaged in hostile and aggressive conduct).

4. "Knows" denotes actual knowledge, which may be inferred from the circumstances. Rule 1.0(f). Thus, the duty to report the violation caused by the mental impairment of another lawyer will likely arise only in very limited situations.

5. Note that the disclosure obligation does not apply to information protected by Rule 1.6 or acquired by the lawyer from his participation in an approved lawyers assistance program. Rule 8.3(c).

6. As noted in Comment [3] to Rule 8.3, the rule "limits the reporting obligation to those offenses that a self-regulating profession must vigorously endeavor to prevent. A measure of judgment is, therefore, required in complying with the provisions of this Rule."

7. A single act of aberrant behavior may be part of a pattern of conduct affecting the lawyer while under the influence of drugs or alcohol or while displaying the symptoms of a mental illness that manifest themselves only on occasion. As noted in Comment [1] to Rule 8.3, "[a]n apparently isolated violation may indicate a pattern of misconduct that only a disciplinary investigation can uncover."

8. In certain cases, the conduct of the lawyer may involve violation of applicable criminal law. In such cases, Rule 8.4(b) is implicated. That rule provides that it is professional misconduct for a lawyer to "commit a criminal act that reflects adversely on the lawyer's honesty, trustworthiness or fitness as a lawyer in other respects."

9. See ABA Formal Opinion 03-429 for discussion of mental impairments that affect a lawyer only on occasion.

Because lawyers are not health care professionals, they cannot be expected to discern when another lawyer suffers from mental impairment with the precision of, for example, a psychiatrist, clinical psychologist, or therapist.[10] Nonetheless, a lawyer may not shut his eyes to conduct reflecting generally recognized symptoms of impairment (e.g., patterns of memory lapse or inexplicable behavior not typical of the subject lawyer, such as repeated missed deadlines).

Each situation, therefore, must be addressed based on the particular facts presented. A lawyer need not act on rumors or conflicting reports about a lawyer. Moreover, knowing that another lawyer is drinking heavily or is evidencing impairment in social settings is not itself enough to trigger a duty to report under Rule 8.3. A lawyer must know that the condition is materially impairing the affected lawyer's representation of clients.[11]

In deciding whether an apparently impaired lawyer's conduct raises a substantial question of her fitness to practice, a lawyer might consider consulting with a psychiatrist, clinical psychologist, or other mental health care professional about the significance of the conduct observed or of information the lawyer has learned from third parties.[12] He might consider contacting an established lawyer assistance program.[13] In addition, the lawyer also might consider speaking to the affected lawyer herself about his concerns. In some circumstances, that may help a lawyer understand the conduct and why it occurred, either confirming or alleviating his concerns. In such a situation, however, the affected lawyer may deny that any problem exists or maintain that although it did exist, it no longer does. This places the lawyer in the position of assessing the affected lawyer's response, rather than the affected lawyer's conduct itself. Care must be taken when acting on the affected lawyer's denials or assertions that the problem has been resolved. It is the knowledge of the impaired conduct that provides the basis for the lawyer's obligations under Rule 8.3; the affected lawyer's denials alone do not make the lawyer's knowledge non-reportable under Rule 8.3.

If the affected lawyer is practicing within a firm, the lawyer should consider speaking with the firm's partners or supervising lawyers.[14] If the affected lawyer's partners or supervising lawyers take steps to assure that the affected lawyer is not representing clients

---

10. There is a wealth of information about impairments available for the general reader. For an initial overview, see such sources as David R. Goldmann, AMERICAN COLLEGE OF PHYSICIANS COMPLETE HOME MEDICAL GUIDE WITH INTERACTIVE HUMAN ANATOMY CD-ROM (DK Publishing 1999); Charles R. Clayman, THE AMERICAN MEDICAL ASSOCIATION FAMILY MEDICAL GUIDE (3rd ed. Random House 1994); and Anthony L. Komaroff, THE HARVARD MEDICAL SCHOOL FAMILY HEALTH GUIDE (Simon & Schuster 1999). Websites for various organizations also can be a good starting point for information. The American Medical Association's website at http://www.ama-assn.org has links to various sites, as does the website of the National Institutes of Health, http://www.nih.gov. For Alzheimer's disease and related conditions, see the websites of the Alzheimer's Disease Education and Referral Center, http://www.alzheimers.org, and the American Association of Geriatric Psychiatry, http://www.aagpgpa.org.

11. See Rule 1.16(a)(2).

12. The reporting lawyer may become aware of the impaired lawyer's conduct either from personal observation or from a third party, such as a client of the lawyer who complains of the impaired lawyer's conduct.

13. In most states, lawyer assistance programs are operated through the state or major metropolitan bar associations. Information about these systems is available from the staff of the ABA Commission on Lawyer Assistance Programs. See http://www.abanet.org/legalservices/colap/home.html.

14. Such contact is solely discretionary. Although partners and supervising lawyers have a responsibility to ensure that lawyers in their own firms comply with the rules of professional conduct, see ABA Formal Opinion 03-429, no lawyer is obligated under the Model Rules to take any action to ensure compliance with the rules by lawyers in other firms.

while materially impaired, there is no obligation to report the affected lawyer's past failure to withdraw from representing clients. If, on the other hand, the affected lawyer's firm is not responsive to the concerns brought to their attention, the lawyer must make a report under Rule 8.3. We note that there is no affirmative obligation to speak with either the affected lawyer or her firm about her conduct or condition before reporting to the appropriate authority.

If a lawyer concludes there is material impairment that raises a substantial question about another lawyer's fitness to practice, his obligation ordinarily is to report to the appropriate professional authority.[15] As we said in ABA Formal Opinion 03-429, however, if information relating to the representation of one's own client would be disclosed in the course of making the report to the appropriate authority, that client's informed consent to the disclosure is required. In the usual case, information gained by a lawyer about another lawyer is unlikely to be information protected by Rule 1.6, for example, observation of or information about the affected lawyer's conduct in litigation or in the completion of transactions. Given the breadth of information protected by Rule 1.6,[16] however, the reporting lawyer should obtain the client's informed consent to the disclosure in cases involving information learned in the course of representation through interaction with the affected lawyer.

Whether the lawyer is obligated under Model Rule 8.3 to make a report or not, he may report the conduct in question to an approved lawyers assistance program, which may be able to provide the impaired lawyer with confidential education, referrals, and other assistance. Indeed, that may well be in the best interests of the affected lawyer, her family, her clients. and the profession. Nevertheless, such a report is not a substitute for reporting to a disciplinary authority with responsibility for assessing the fitness of lawyers licensed to practice in the jurisdiction.

In conclusion, a lawyer should review the situation and determine his responsibilities under Rule 8.3 when he has information that another lawyer has failed to meet her obligation to withdraw from the representation of client when suffering from a mental condition materially impairing her ability to represent her clients.

---

15. Rule 8.3 cmt. 3. There is no duty to report information learned from participation in an approved lawyers assistance program.

16. Rule 1.6 cmts. 3 and 4.

Appendix

Massachusetts Rules of Professional Conduct

Supreme Judicial Court Rule 3:07

Massachusetts Rules of Professional Conduct
[Including amendments through 3/15/11]
[Warning: These rules are subject to periodic revision.]

Index to the Rules

Preamble: A Lawyer's Responsibilities

Scope

Rule

PREAMBLE AND SCOPE

PREAMBLE: A LAWYER'S RESPONSIBILITIES

A lawyer is a representative of clients, an officer of the legal system, and a public citizen having special responsibility for the quality of justice.

1. As a representative of clients, a lawyer performs various functions. As advisor, a lawyer provides a client with an informed understanding of the client's legal rights and obligations and explains their practical implications. As advocate, a lawyer zealously asserts the client's position under the rules of the adversary system. As negotiator, a lawyer seeks a result advantageous to the client but consistent with requirements of honest dealing with others. A lawyer acts as evaluator by examining a client's legal affairs and reporting about them to the client or to others.

2. In all professional functions a lawyer should be competent, prompt, and diligent. A lawyer should maintain communication with a client concerning the representation. A lawyer should keep in confidence information relating to representation of a client except so far as disclosure is required or permitted by the Rules of Professional Conduct or other law.

3. A lawyer's conduct should conform to the requirements of the law, both in professional service to clients and in the lawyer's business and personal affairs. A lawyer should use the law's procedures only for legitimate purposes and not to harass or intimidate others. A lawyer should demonstrate respect for the legal system and for those who serve it, including judges, other lawyers, and public officials. While it is a lawyer's duty, when necessary, to challenge the rectitude of official action, it is also a lawyer's duty to uphold legal process.

4. As a public citizen, a lawyer should seek improvement of the law, the administration of justice, and the quality of service rendered by the legal profession. As a member of a learned profession, a lawyer should cultivate knowledge of the law beyond its use for clients, employ that knowledge in reform of the law, and work to strengthen legal education. A lawyer should be mindful of deficiencies in the administration of justice and of the fact that the poor, and sometimes persons who are not poor, cannot afford adequate legal assistance, and should therefore devote professional time and civic influence in their behalf. A lawyer should aid the legal profession in pursuing these objectives and should help the bar regulate itself in the public interest.

5. Many of a lawyer's professional responsibilities are prescribed in the Rules of Professional Conduct, as well as in substantive and procedural law. However, a lawyer is also guided by personal conscience and the approbation of professional peers. A lawyer should strive to attain the highest level of skill, to improve the law and the legal profession, and to exemplify the legal profession's ideals of public service.

6. A lawyer's responsibilities as a representative of clients, an officer of the legal system, and a public citizen are usually harmonious. Thus, when an opposing party is well represented, a lawyer can be a zealous advocate on behalf of a client and at the same time assume that justice is being done. So also, a lawyer can be sure that preserving client confidences ordinarily serves the public interest because people are more likely to seek legal advice, and thereby heed their legal obligations, when they know their communications will be private.

7. In the nature of law practice, however, conflicting responsibilities are encountered. Virtually all difficult ethical problems arise from conflict between a lawyer's responsibilities to clients, to the legal system, and to the lawyer's own interest in remaining an upright person while earning a satisfactory living. The Rules of Professional Conduct prescribe terms for resolving such conflicts. Within the framework of these Rules, many difficult issues of professional discretion can arise. Such issues must be resolved through the exercise of sensitive professional and moral judgment guided by the basic principles underlying the Rules.

8. The legal profession is largely self-governing. Although other professions also have been granted powers of self-government, the legal profession is unique in this respect because of the close relationship between the profession and the processes of government and law enforcement. This connection is manifested in the fact that ultimate authority over the legal profession is vested largely in the courts.

9. To the extent that lawyers meet the obligations of their professional calling, the occasion for government regulation is obviated. Self-regulation also helps maintain the legal profession's independence from government domination. An independent legal profession is an important force in preserving government under law, for abuse of legal authority is more readily challenged by a profession whose members are not dependent on government for the right to practice.

10. The legal profession's relative autonomy carries with it special responsibilities of self-government. The profession has a responsibility to assure that its regulations are conceived in the public interest and not in furtherance of parochial or self-interested concerns of the bar. Every lawyer is responsible for observance of the Rules of Professional Conduct. A lawyer should also aid in securing their observance by other lawyers. Neglect of these responsibilities compromises the independence of the profession and the public interest which it serves.

11. Lawyers play a vital role in the preservation of society. The fulfillment of this role requires an understanding by lawyers of their relationship to our legal system. The Rules of Professional Conduct, when properly applied, serve to define that relationship.

SCOPE

[1] The Rules of Professional Conduct are rules of reason. They should be interpreted with reference to the purposes of legal representation and of the law itself. Some of the Rules are imperatives, cast in the terms "shall" or "shall not." These define proper conduct for purposes of professional discipline. Others, generally cast in the term "may" are permissive and define areas under the Rules in which the lawyer has professional discretion. No disciplinary action should be taken when the lawyer chooses not to act or acts within the bounds of such discretion. Other Rules define the nature of relationships between the lawyer and others. The Rules are thus partly obligatory and disciplinary and partly constitutive and descriptive in that they define a lawyer's professional role. Many of the Comments use the term "should." Comments do not add obligations to the Rules but provide guidance for practicing in compliance with the Rules.

[2] The Rules presuppose a larger legal context shaping the lawyer's role. That context includes court rules and statutes relating to matters of licensure, laws defining specific obligations of lawyers, and substantive and procedural law in general. Compliance with the Rules, as with all law in an open society, depends primarily on understanding and voluntary compliance, secondarily on reinforcement by peer and public opinion, and, finally, when necessary, on enforcement through disciplinary proceedings. The Rules do not, however, exhaust the moral and ethical considerations that should inform a lawyer, for no worthwhile human activity can be completely defined by legal rules. The Rules simply provide a framework for the ethical practice of law.

[3] Furthermore, for purposes of determining the lawyer's authority and responsibility, principles of substantive law external to these Rules determine whether a client-lawyer relationship exists. Most of the duties flowing from the client-lawyer relationship attach only after the client has requested the lawyer to render legal services and the lawyer has agreed to do so. But there are some duties, such as that of confidentiality under Rule 1.6, that may attach when the lawyer agrees to consider whether a client-lawyer relationship shall be established. Whether a client-lawyer relationship exists for any specific purpose can depend on the circumstances and may be a question of fact.

[4] Under various legal provisions, including constitutional, statutory, and common law, the responsibilities of government lawyers may include authority concerning legal matters that ordinarily reposes in the client in private client-lawyer relationships. For example, a lawyer for a government agency may have authority on behalf of the government to decide upon settlement or whether to appeal from an adverse judgment. Such authority in various respects is generally vested in the Attorney General, and Federal counterparts, and the same may be true of other government law officers. Also, lawyers under the supervision of these officers may be authorized to represent several government agencies in intragovernmental legal controversies in circumstances where a private

lawyer could not represent multiple private clients. They also may have authority to represent the "public interest" in circumstances where a private lawyer would not be authorized to do so. These rules are not meant to address the substantive statutory and constitutional authority of the Attorney General when appearing for the Commonwealth to assume primary control over the litigation and to decide matters of legal policy on behalf of the Commonwealth.

[5] Failure to comply with an obligation or prohibition imposed by a Rule is a basis for invoking the disciplinary process. The Rules presuppose that disciplinary assessment of a lawyer's conduct will be made on the basis of the facts and circumstances as they existed at the time of the conduct in question and in recognition of the fact that a lawyer often has to act on uncertain or incomplete evidence of the situation. Moreover, the Rules presuppose that whether or not discipline should be imposed for a violation, and the severity of a sanction, depend on all the circumstances, including the wilfulness and seriousness of the violation, extenuating factors, and whether there have been previous violations.

[6] "A violation of a canon of ethics or a disciplinary rule ... is not itself an actionable breach of duty to a client." Fishman v. Brooks, 396 Mass. 643, 649 (1986). The Rules are designed to provide guidance to lawyers and to provide a structure for regulating conduct through disciplinary agencies. The fact that a Rule is just a basis for a lawyer's self-assessment, or for sanctioning a lawyer under the administration of a disciplinary authority, does not necessarily mean that an antagonist in a collateral proceeding or transaction may rely on a violation of a Rule. "As with statutes and regulations, however, if a plaintiff can demonstrate that a disciplinary rule was intended to protect one in his position, a violation of that rule may be some evidence of the attorney's negligence." Id. at 649.

[7] Moreover, these Rules are not intended to govern or affect judicial application of either the attorney-client or work product privilege. Those privileges were developed to promote compliance with law and fairness in litigation. In reliance on the attorney-client privilege, clients are entitled to expect that communications within the scope of the privilege will be protected against compelled disclosure. The attorney-client privilege is that of the client and not of the lawyer. The fact that in exceptional situations the lawyer under the Rules has a limited discretion to disclose a client confidence does not vitiate the proposition that, as a general matter, the client has a reasonable expectation that information relating to the client will not be voluntarily disclosed and that disclosure of such information may be judicially compelled only in accordance with recognized exceptions to the attorney-client and work product privileges.

[8] [RESERVED]

[9] The Comment accompanying each Rule explains and illustrates the meaning and purpose of the Rule. The Preamble and this note on Scope provide general orientation. The Comments are intended as guides to interpretation, but the text of each Rule is authoritative.

CLIENT-LAWYER RELATIONSHIP

RULE 1.1 COMPETENCE

A lawyer shall provide competent representation to a client. Competent representation requires the legal knowledge, skill, thoroughness, and preparation reasonably necessary for the representation.

Comment

Legal Knowledge and Skill

[1] In determining whether a lawyer employs the requisite knowledge and skill in a particular matter, relevant factors include the relative complexity and specialized nature of the matter, the lawyer's general experience, the lawyer's training and experience in the field in question, the preparation and study the lawyer is able to give the matter and whether it is feasible to refer the matter to, or associate or consult with, a lawyer of established competence in the field in question. In many instances, the required proficiency is that of a general practitioner. Expertise in a particular field of law may be required in some circumstances. See Rule 7.4.

[2] A lawyer need not necessarily have special training or prior experience to handle legal problems of a type with which the lawyer is unfamiliar. A newly admitted lawyer can be as competent as a practitioner with long experience. Some important legal skills, such as the analysis of precedent, the evaluation of evidence and legal drafting, are required in all legal problems. Perhaps the most fundamental legal skill consists of determining what kind of legal problems a situation may involve, a skill that necessarily transcends any particular specialized knowledge. A lawyer can provide adequate representation in a wholly novel field through necessary study. Competent representation can also be provided through the association of a lawyer of established competence in the field in question.

[3] In an emergency a lawyer may give advice or assistance in a matter in which the lawyer does not have the skill ordinarily required where referral to or consultation or association with another lawyer would be impractical. Even in an emergency, however, assistance should be limited to that reasonably necessary in the circumstances, for ill-considered action under emergency conditions can jeopardize the client's interest.

[4] A lawyer may accept representation where the requisite level of competence can be achieved by reasonable preparation. This applies as well to a lawyer who is appointed as counsel for an unrepresented person. See also Rule 6.2.

Thoroughness and Preparation

[5] Competent handling of a particular matter includes inquiry into and analysis of the factual and legal elements of the problem, and use of methods and procedures meeting the standards of competent practitioners. It also includes adequate preparation. The required attention and preparation are determined in part by what is at stake; major litigation and complex transactions ordinarily require more elaborate treatment than matters of lesser consequence.

Maintaining Competence

[6] To maintain the requisite knowledge and skill, a lawyer should engage in continuing study and education. While the Supreme Judicial Court has not established a formal system of peer review, some of the bar associations have informal systems, and the lawyer should consider making use of them in appropriate circumstances.

Corresponding ABA Model Rule. Identical to Model Rule 1.1.

Corresponding Former Massachusetts Rule. DR 6-101.

RULE 1.2 SCOPE OF REPRESENTATION

(a) A lawyer shall seek the lawful objectives of his or her client through reasonably available means permitted by law and these rules. A lawyer does not violate this rule, however, by acceding to reasonable requests of opposing counsel which do not prejudice the rights of his or her client, by being punctual in fulfilling all professional commitments, by avoiding offensive tactics, or by treating with courtesy and consideration all persons involved in the legal process. A lawyer shall abide by a client's decision whether to accept an offer of settlement of a matter. In a criminal case, the lawyer shall abide by the client's decision, after consultation with the lawyer, as to a plea to be entered, whether to waive jury trial, and whether the client will testify.

(b) A lawyer's representation of a client, including representation by appointment, does not constitute an endorsement of the client's political, economic, social, or moral views or activities.

(c) A lawyer may limit the objectives of the representation if the client consents after consultation.

(d) A lawyer shall not counsel a client to engage, or assist a client, in conduct that the lawyer knows is criminal or fraudulent, but a lawyer may discuss the legal consequences of any proposed course of conduct with a client and may counsel or assist a client to make a good faith effort to determine the validity, scope, meaning, or application of the law.

(e) When a lawyer knows that a client expects assistance not permitted by the rules of professional conduct or other law, the lawyer shall consult with the client regarding the relevant limitations on the lawyer's conduct.

Comment

Scope of Representation

[1] A lawyer should seek to achieve the lawful objectives of a client through permissible means. This does not prevent a lawyer from observing such rules of professional courtesy as those listed in Rule 1.2(a). The specification of decisions subject to client control is illustrative, not exclusive. In general, the client's wishes govern the conduct of a matter, subject to the lawyer's professional obligations under these Rules and other law, the general norms of professional courtesy, specific understandings between the lawyer and the client, and the rules governing withdrawal by a lawyer in the event of conflict with the client. The lawyer and client should therefore consult with one another about the general objectives of the representation and the means of achieving them. As the Rule implies, there are circumstances, in litigation or otherwise, when lawyers are required to act on their own with regard to legal tactics or technical matters and they may and should do so, albeit within the framework of the objectives of the representation.

[2] In a case in which the client appears to be suffering mental disability, the lawyer's duty to abide by the client's decisions is to be guided by reference to Rule 1.14.

Independence from Client's Views or Activities

[3] Legal representation should not be denied to people who are unable to afford legal services, or whose cause is controversial or the subject of popular disapproval. By the same token, representing a client does not constitute approval of the client's views or activities.

Services Limited in Objectives or Means

[4] The objectives or scope of services provided by a lawyer may be limited by agreement with the client or by the terms under which the lawyer's services are made available to the client. For example, a retainer may be for a specifically defined purpose. Rep-

resentation provided through a legal aid agency may be subject to limitations on the types of cases the agency handles. When a lawyer has been retained by an insurer to represent an insured, the representation may be limited to matters related to the insurance coverage. The terms upon which representation is undertaken may exclude specific objectives or means. Such limitations may exclude objectives or means that the lawyer regards as repugnant or imprudent.

[5] An agreement concerning the scope of representation must accord with the Rules of Professional Conduct and other law. Thus, the client may not be asked to agree to representation so limited in scope as to violate Rule 1.1, or to surrender the right to terminate the lawyer's services or the right to settle litigation that the lawyer might wish to continue.

Criminal, Fraudulent and Prohibited Transactions

[6] A lawyer is required to give an honest opinion about the actual consequences that appear likely to result from a client's conduct. The fact that a client uses advice in a course of action that is criminal or fraudulent does not, of itself, make a lawyer a party to the course of action. However, a lawyer may not knowingly assist a client in criminal or fraudulent conduct. There is a critical distinction between presenting an analysis of legal aspects of questionable conduct and recommending the means by which a crime or fraud might be committed with impunity.

[7] When the client's course of action has already begun and is continuing, the lawyer's responsibility is especially delicate. The lawyer is not permitted to reveal the client's wrongdoing, except where permitted by Rule 1.6. or required by Rule 3.3, 4.1, or 8.3. However, the lawyer is required to avoid furthering the purpose, for example, by suggesting how it might be concealed. A lawyer may not continue assisting a client in conduct that the lawyer originally supposes is legally proper but then discovers is criminal or fraudulent. See the discussion of the meaning of "assisting" in Comment 3 to Rule 4.1 and the special meaning in Comment 2A to Rule 3.3. Withdrawal from the representation, therefore, may be required. But see Rule 3.3(e).

[8] Where the client is a fiduciary, the lawyer may be charged with special obligations in dealings with a beneficiary.

[9] Paragraph (d) applies whether or not the defrauded party is a party to the transaction. Hence, a lawyer should not participate in a sham transaction; for example, a transaction to effectuate criminal or fraudulent escape of tax liability. Paragraph (d) does not preclude undertaking a criminal defense incident to a general retainer for legal services to a lawful enterprise. The last clause of paragraph (d) recognizes that determining the validity or interpretation of a statute or regulation may require a course of action involving disobedience of the statute or regulation or of the interpretation placed upon it by governmental authorities.

Corresponding ABA Model Rule. Identical to Model Rule 1.2, except the first two sentences of (a) replace the first sentence of the Model Rule.

Corresponding Former Massachusetts Rule. (a) and (b) no counterpart, except that the first sentence of (a) comes from DR 7-101 (A); (c) DR 7-101 (B) (1); (d) DR 7-102 (A) (6) and (7), DR 7-106, S.J.C. Rule 3:08, DF 7; (e) DR 2-110 (C) (1) (c), DR 9-101 (C).

RULE 1.3 DILIGENCE

A lawyer shall act with reasonable diligence and promptness in representing a client. The lawyer should represent a client zealously within the bounds of the law.

Comment

[1] A lawyer should pursue a matter on behalf of a client despite opposition, obstruction or personal inconvenience to the lawyer, and may take whatever lawful and ethical measures are required to vindicate a client's cause or endeavor. A lawyer should act with commitment and dedication to the interests of the client and with zeal in advocacy upon the client's behalf. However, a lawyer is not bound to press for every advantage that might be realized for a client. A lawyer has professional discretion in determining the means by which a matter should be pursued subject to Rule 1.2. A lawyer's work load should be controlled so that each matter can be handled adequately.

[1A] It is implicit in the second sentence of the rule that a lawyer may not intentionally prejudice or damage his client during the course of the professional relationship.

[2] Perhaps no professional shortcoming is more widely resented than procrastination. A client's interests often can be adversely affected by the passage of time or the change of conditions; in extreme instances, as when a lawyer overlooks a statute of limitations, the client's legal position may be destroyed. Even when the client's interests are not affected in substance, however, unreasonable delay can cause a client needless anxiety and undermine confidence in the lawyer's trustworthiness.

[3] Unless the relationship is terminated as provided in Rule 1.16, a lawyer should carry through to conclusion all matters undertaken for a client. If a lawyer's employment is limited to a specific matter, the relationship terminates when the matter has been resolved. If a lawyer has served a client over a substantial period in a variety of matters, the client sometimes may assume that the lawyer will continue to serve on a continuing basis unless the lawyer gives notice of withdrawal. Doubt about whether a client-lawyer relationship still exists should be clarified by the lawyer, preferably in writing, so that the client will not mistakenly suppose the lawyer is looking after the client's affairs when the lawyer has ceased to do so. For example, if a lawyer has handled a judicial or administrative proceeding that produced a result adverse to the client but has not been specifically instructed concerning pursuit of an appeal, the lawyer should advise the client of the possibility of appeal before relinquishing responsibility for the matter.

Corresponding ABA Model Rule. Identical to Model Rule 1.3 with the addition of the clause at the end of the Rule.

Corresponding Former Massachusetts Rule. DR 6-101 (A) (3); DR 7-101.

RULE 1.4 COMMUNICATION

(a) A lawyer shall keep a client reasonably informed about the status of a matter and promptly comply with reasonable requests for information.

(b) A lawyer shall explain a matter to the extent reasonably necessary to permit the client to make informed decisions regarding the representation.

Comment

[1] The client should have sufficient information to participate intelligently in decisions concerning the objectives of the representation and the means by which they are to be pursued, to the extent the client is willing and able to do so. For example, a lawyer negotiating on behalf of a client should provide the client with facts relevant to the matter, inform the client of communications from another party and take other reasonable steps that permit the client to make a decision regarding a serious offer from another party. A lawyer who receives from opposing counsel an offer of settlement in a civil controversy or a proffered plea bargain in a criminal case should promptly inform the client

of its substance unless prior discussions with the client have left it clear that the proposal will be unacceptable. See Rule 1.2(a). Even when a client delegates authority to the lawyer, the client should be kept advised of the status of the matter.

[2] Adequacy of communication depends in part on the kind of advice or assistance involved. For example, in negotiations where there is time to explain a proposal, the lawyer should review all important provisions with the client before proceeding to an agreement. In litigation a lawyer should explain the general strategy and prospects of success and ordinarily should consult the client on tactics that might injure or coerce others. On the other hand, a lawyer ordinarily cannot be expected to describe trial or negotiation strategy in detail. The guiding principle is set forth in the comment to Rule 1.2(a).

[3] Ordinarily, the information to be provided is that appropriate for a client who is a comprehending and responsible adult. However, fully informing the client according to this standard may be impracticable, for example, where the client is a child or suffers from mental disability. See Rule 1.14. When the client is an organization or group, it is often impossible or inappropriate to inform every one of its members about its legal affairs; ordinarily, the lawyer should address communications to the appropriate officials of the organization. See Rule 1.13. Where many routine matters are involved, a system of limited or occasional reporting may be arranged with the client. Practical exigency may also require a lawyer to act for a client without prior consultation.

Withholding Information

[4] In some circumstances, a lawyer may be justified in delaying transmission of information when the client would be likely to react imprudently to an immediate communication. Thus, a lawyer might withhold a psychiatric diagnosis of a client when the examining psychiatrist indicates that disclosure would harm the client. A lawyer may not withhold information to serve the lawyer's own interest or convenience. Rules or court orders governing litigation may provide that information supplied to a lawyer may not be disclosed to the client. Rule 3.4(c) directs compliance with such rules or orders.

Alternate Dispute Resolution

[5] There will be circumstances in which a lawyer should advise a client concerning the advantages and disadvantages of available dispute resolution options in order to permit the client to make informed decisions concerning the representation.

Corresponding ABA Model Rule. Identical to Model Rule 1.4.

Corresponding Former Massachusetts Rule. None.

RULE 1.5 FEES

(a) A lawyer shall not enter into an agreement for, charge, or collect an illegal or clearly excessive fee or collect an unreasonable amunt for expenses. The factors to be considered in determining whether a fee is clearly excessive include the following:

    (1) the time and labor required, the novelty and difficulty of the questions involved, and the skill requisite to perform the legal service properly;

    (2) the likelihood, if apparent to the client, that the acceptance of the particular employment will preclude other employment by the lawyer;

    (3) the fee customarily charged in the locality for similar legal services;

    (4) the amount involved and the results obtained;

    (5) the time limitations imposed by the client or by the circumstances;

(6) the nature and length of the professional relationship with the client;

(7) the experience, reputation, and ability of the lawyer or lawyers performing the services; and

(8) whether the fee is fixed or contingent.

(b) The scope of the representation and the basis or rate of the fee and expenses for which the client will be responsible shall be communicated to the client, preferably in writing, before or within a reasonable time after commencing the representation, except when the lawyer will charge a regularly represented client on the same basis or rate. Any changes in the basis or rate of the fee or expenses shall also be communicated to the client.

(c) A fee may be contingent on the outcome of the matter for which the service is rendered, except in a matter in which a contingent fee is prohibited by paragraph (d) or other law. Except for contingent fee arrangements concerning the collection of commercial accounts and of insurance company subrogation claims, a contingent fee agreement shall be in writing and signed in duplicate by both the lawyer and the client within a reasonable time after the making of the agreement. One such copy (and proof that the duplicate copy has been delivered or mailed to the client) shall be retained by the lawyer for a period of seven years after the conclusion of the contingent fee matter. The writing shall state:

(1) the name and address of each client;

(2) the name and address of the lawyer or lawyers to be retained;

(3) the nature of the claim, controversy, and other matters with reference to which the services are to be performed;

(4) the contingency upon which compensation will be paid, whether and to what extent the client is to be liable to pay compensation otherwise than from amounts collected for him or her by the lawyer, and if the lawyer is to be paid any fee for the representation that will not be determined on a contingency, the method by which this fee will be determined;

(5) the method by which the fee is to be determined, including the percentage or percentages that shall accrue to the lawyer out of amounts collected, and unless the parties otherwise agree in writing, that the lawyer shall be entitled to the greater of (i) the amount of any attorney's fees awarded by the court or included in the settlement or (ii) the percentage or other formula applied to the recovery amount not including such attorney's fees; and

(6) the method by which litigation and other expenses are to be deducted from the recovery and whether such expenses are to be deducted before or after the contingent fee is calculated.

(7) if the lawyer intends to pursue such a claim, the client's potential liability for expenses and reasonable attorney's fees if the attorney-client relationship is terminated before the conclusion of the case for any reason, including a statement of the basis on which such expenses and fees will be claimed, and, if applicable, the method by which such expenses and fees will be calculated; and

(8) if the lawyer is the successor to a lawyer whose representation has terminated before the conclusion of the case, whether the client or the successor lawyer is to be responsible for payment of former counsel's attorney's fees and expenses, if any such payment is due.

Upon conclusion of a contingent fee matter for which a writing is required under this paragraph, the lawyer shall provide the client with a written statement stating the outcome of the matter and, if there is a recovery, showing the remittance to the client and the method of its determination.

(d) A lawyer shall not enter into an arrangement for, charge, or collect:

> (1) any fee in a domestic relations matter, the payment or amount of which is contingent upon the securing of a divorce or upon the amount of alimony or support, or property settlement in lieu thereof; or

> (2) a contingent fee for representing a defendant in a criminal case.

(e) A division of a fee between lawyers who are not in the same firm may be made only if, the client is notified before or at the time the client enters into a fee agreement for the matter that a division of fees will be made and consents to the joint participation in writing and the total fee is reasonable. This limitation does not prohibit payment to a former partner or associate pursuant to a separation or retirement agreement.

(f) (1) The following forms of contingent fee agreement may be used to satisfy the requirements of paragraphs (c) and (e) if they accurately and fully reflect the terms of the engagement.

CONTINGENT FEE AGREEMENT, FORM A

To be Executed in Duplicate

Date:_____, 20_____

The Client _____

             (Name)   (Street & Number)   (City or Town)

retains the Lawyer _____

             (Name)   (Street & Number)   (City or Town)

to perform the legal services mentioned in paragraph (1) below. The lawyer agrees to perform them faithfully and with due diligence.

(1) The claim, controversy, and other matters with reference to which the services are to be performed are.

(2) The contingency upon which compensation is to be paid is recovery of damages, whether by settlement, judgment or otherwise.

(3) The lawyer agrees to advance, on behalf of the client, all out-of-pocket costs and expenses. The client is not to be liable to pay court costs and expenses of litigation other than from amounts collected for the client by the lawyer.

(4) Compensation (including that of any associated counsel) to be paid to the lawyer by the client on the foregoing contingency shall be the following percentage of the (gross) (net) [indicate which] amount collected. [Here insert the percentages to be charged in the event of collection. These may be on a flat rate basis or in a descending or ascending scale in relation to amount collected.] The percentage shall be applied to the amount of the recovery not including any attorney's fees awarded by a court or included in a settlement. The lawyer's compensation shall be such attorney's fees or the amount determined by the percentage calculation described above, whichever is greater.

(5) [IF APPLICABLE] The client understands that a portion of the compensation payable to the lawyer pursuant to paragraph 4 above shall be paid to [Name of Attorney entitled to a share of compensation] and consents to this division of fees.

(6) [IF APPLICABLE] If the attorney-client relationship is terminated before the conclusion of the case for any reason, the attorney may seek payment for the work done and expenses advanced before the termination. Whether the lawyer will receive any payment for the work done before the termination, and the amount of any payment, will depend on the benefit to the client of the services performed by the lawyer as well as the timing and circumstances of the termination. Such payment shall not exceed the lesser of (i) the fair value of the legal services rendered by the lawyer, or (ii) the contingent fee to which the lawyer would have been entitled upon the occurrence of the contingency. This paragraph does not give the lawyer any rights to payment beyond those conferred by existing law.

(7) [USE IF LAWYER IS SUCCESSOR COUNSEL] The lawyer is responsible for payment of former counsel's reasonable attorney's fees and expenses and the cost of resolving any dispute between the client and prior counsel over fees or expenses.

This agreement and its performance are subject to Rule 1.5 of the Rules of Professional Conduct adopted by the Massachusetts Supreme Judicial Court.

WE EACH HAVE READ THE ABOVE AGREEMENT BEFORE SIGNING IT.

Witnesses to signatures   Signatures of client and lawyer

(To client) _____   _____

                                        (Signature of Client)

(To lawyer _____   _____

                                        (Signature of Lawyer)

CONTINGENT FEE AGREEMENT, FORM B

To be Executed in Duplicate

Date:_____, 20____

The Client _____

                      (Name)   (Street & Number)   (City or Town)

retains the Lawyer _____

                      (Name)   (Street & Number)   (City or Town)

to perform the legal services mentioned in paragraph (1) below. The lawyer agrees to perform them faithfully and with due diligence.

(1) The claim, controversy, and other matters with reference to which the services are to be performed are:

(2) The contingency upon which compensation is to be paid is:

(3) Costs and Expenses. The client should initial next to the option selected.

   (i)   The lawyer agrees to advance, on behalf of the client, all out-of-pocket costs and expenses. The client is not to be liable to pay court costs and expenses of litigation, other than from amounts collected for the client by the lawyer; or

   (ii) The client is not to be liable to pay compensation or court costs and expenses of litigation otherwise than from amounts collected for the client by the lawyer, except as follows:

(4) Compensation (including that of any associated counsel) to be paid to the lawyer by the client on the foregoing contingency shall be the following percentage of the (gross) (net) [indicate which] amount collected. [Here insert the percentages to be charged in

the event of collection. These may be on a flat rate basis or in a descending or ascending scale in relation to the amount collected.] The percentage shall be applied to the amount of the recovery not including any attorney's fees awarded by a court or included in a settlement. The lawyer's compensation shall be such attorney's fees or the amount determined by the percentage calculation described above, whichever is greater. [Modify the last two sentences as appropriate if the parties agree on some other basis for calculation.]

(5) [IF APPLICABLE] The client understands that a portion of the compensation payable to the lawyer pursuant to paragraph 4 above shall be paid to [Name of Attorney entitled to a share of compensation] and consents to this division of fees.

(6) [IF APPLICABLE] If the attorney-client relationship is terminated before the conclusion of the case for any reason, the attorney may seek payment for the work done and expenses advanced before the termination. Whether the lawyer will be entitled to receive any payment for the work done before the termination, and the amount of any payment, will depend on the benefit to the client of the services performed by the lawyer as well as the timing and circumstances of the termination. Such payment shall not exceed the lesser of (i) the fair value of the legal services rendered by the lawyer, or (ii) the contingent fee to which the lawyer would have been entitled upon the occurrence of the contingency. This paragraph does not give the lawyer any rights to payment beyond those conferred by existing law.

(7) [USE IF LAWYER IS SUCCESSOR COUNSEL] Payment of any fees owed to former counsel. The client should initial next to the option selected.

> (i) The lawyer is responsible for payment of former counsel's reasonable attorney's fees and expenses and the cost of resolving any dispute between the client and prior counsel over fees or expenses; or
>
> (ii) The client is responsible for payment of former counsel's reasonable attorney's fees and expenses and the cost of resolving any dispute between the client and prior counsel over fees or expenses.

This agreement and its performance are subject to Rule 1.5 of the Rules of Professional Conduct adopted by the Massachusetts Supreme Judicial Court.

WE EACH HAVE READ THE ABOVE AGREEMENT BEFORE SIGNING IT.

Witnesses to signatures   Signatures of client and lawyer

(To client) _____   _____

                                           (Signature of Client)

(To lawyer _____   _____

                                           (Signature of Lawyer)

Comment

Basis or Rate of Fee

[1] When the lawyer has regularly represented a client, they ordinarily will have evolved an understanding concerning the basis or rate of the fee and the expenses for which the client will be responsible. In a new client-lawyer relationship, however, an understanding as to the fees and expenses must be promptly established. It is not necessary to recite all the factors that underlie the basis of the fee, but only those that are directly involved in its computation. It is sufficient, for example, to state that the basic rate is an hourly charge or a fixed amount or an estimated amount,or to identify the factors that may be taken into account in finally fixing the fee. When developments occur during the repre-

sentation that render an earlier estimate substantially inaccurate, a revised estimate should be provided to the client. A written statement concerning the fee reduces the possibility of misunderstanding. Furnishing the client with a simple memorandum or a copy of the lawyer's customary fee schedule is sufficient if the basis or rate of the fee is set forth.

[1A] Rule 1.5(a) departs from Model Rule 1.5(a) by retaining the standard of former DR2-106(A) that a fee must be illegal or clearly excessive to constitute a violation of this rule. However, it does not affect the substantive law that fees must be reasonable to be enforceable against the client.

[1B] Paragraph (a) also requires that expenses for which the client will be charged must be reasonable. As such, the standard differs from that for fees, as described in Comment 1A. A lawyer may seek reimbursement for the cost of services performed in-house, such as telephone charges,either by charging a reasonable amount to which the client has agreed in advance or by charging an amount that reasonably reflects the cost incurred by the lawyer.

[2] Rule 1.5(b) states, as the ABA Model Rule does, that the basis or rate of a fee shall be communicated "preferably in writing." Appropriate caution and ease of proof of compliance with Rule 1.5(b) indicate that the presentation of a fee agreement to the client in writing is desirable.

[3] Contingent fees, like any other fees, are subject to the not-clearly-excessive standard of paragraph (a) of this rule. In determining whether a particular contingent fee is clearly excessive, or whether it is reasonable to charge any form of contingent fee, a lawyer must consider the factors that are relevant under the circumstances. Applicable law may impose limitations on contingent fees, such as a ceiling on the percentage allowable, or may require a lawyer to offer clients an alternative basis for the fee. Applicable law also may apply to situations other than a contingent fee, for example, government regulations regarding fees in certain matters. When there is doubt whether a contingent fee is consistent with the client's best interest, the lawyer should inform the client of alternative bases for the fee and explain their implications.

[3A] A lawyer must inform the client at the time representation is undertaken if there is a possibility that a legal fee or other payments will be owed under other circumstances. A lawyer may pursue a quantum meruit recovery or payment for expenses advanced only if the contingent fee agreement so provides.

[3B] The "fair value" of the legal services rendered by the attorney before the occurrence of a contingency in a contingent fee case is an equitable determination designed to prevent a client from being unjustly enriched if no fee is paid to the attorney. Because a contingent fee case does not require any certain amount of labor or hours worked to achieve its desired goal, a lodestar method of fee calculation is of limited use in assessing a quantum meruit fee. A quantum meruit award should take into account the benefit actually conferred on the client. Other factors relevant to determining "fair value" in any particular situation may include those set forth in Rule 1.5(a), as well as the circumstances of the discharge or withdrawal, the amount of legal work required to bring the case to conclusion after the discharge or withdrawal, and the contingent fee to which the lawyer would have been entitled upon the occurrence of the contingency. Unless otherwise agreed in writing, the lawyer will ordinarily not be entitled to receive a fee unless the contingency has occurred. Nothing in this Rule is intended to create a presumption that a lawyer is entitled to a quantum meruit award when the representation is terminated before the contingency occurs.

[3C] When the attorney-client relationship in a contingent fee case terminates before completion, and the lawyer makes a claim for fees or expenses, the lawyer is required to state in writing the fee claimed and to enumerate the expenses incurred, providing supporting justification if requested. In circumstances where the lawyer is unable to identify the precise amount of the fee claimed because the matter has not been resolved, the lawyer is required to identify the amount of work performed and the basis employed for calculating the fee due. This statement of claim will help the client and any successor attorney to assess the financial consequences of a change in representation.

[3D] A lawyer who does not intend to make a claim for fees in the event the representation is terminated before the occurrence of the contingency entitling the lawyer to a fee under the terms of a contingent fee agreement would not be required to use paragraph (6) of the model forms of contingent fee agreement specified in Rule 1.5(f)(1) and (2). However, if a lawyer expects to make a claim for fees if the representation is terminated before the occurrence of the contingency, the lawyer must advise the client of his or her intention to retain the option to make a claim by including the substance of paragraph (6) of the model form of contingent fee agreement in the engagement agreement and would be expected to be able to provide records of work performed sufficient to support such a claim.

Terms of Payment

[4] A lawyer may require advance payment of a fee, but is obliged to return any unearned portion. See Rule 1.16(d). A lawyer may accept property in payment for services, such as an ownership interest in an enterprise, providing this does not involve acquisition of a proprietary interest in the cause of action or subject matter of the litigation contrary to Rule 1.8(j). However, a fee paid in property instead of money may be subject to the requirements of Rule 1.8(a) because such fees often have the essential qualities of a business transaction with the client.

[5] An agreement may not be made whose terms might induce the lawyer improperly to curtail services for the client or perform them in a way contrary to the client's interest. For example, a lawyer should not enter into an agreement whereby services are to be provided only up to a stated amount when it is foreseeable that more extensive services probably will be required, unless the situation is adequately explained to the client. Otherwise, the client might have to bargain for further assistance in the midst of a proceeding or transaction. However, it is proper to define the extent of services in light of the client's ability to pay. A lawyer should not exploit a fee arrangement based primarily on hourly charges by using wasteful procedures.

Prohibited Contingent Fees

[6] Paragraph (d) prohibits a lawyer from charging a contingent fee in a domestic relations matter when payment is contingent upon the securing of a divorce or upon the amount of alimony or support or property settlement to be obtained. This provision does not preclude a contract for a contingent fee for legal representation in connection with the recovery of post-judgment balances due under support, alimony or other financial orders because such contracts do not implicate the same policy concerns.

Division of Fee

[7] A division of fee is a single billing to a client covering the fee of two or more lawyers who are not in the same firm. A division of fee facilitates association of more than one lawyer in a matter in which neither alone could serve the client as well, and most often is used when the fee is contingent and the division is between a referring lawyer and a

trial specialist. Paragraph (e) permits the lawyers to divide a fee if the client has been informed that a division of fees will be made and consents in writing. A lawyer should only refer a matter to a lawyer whom the referring lawyer reasonably believes is competent to handle the matter. See Rule 1.1.

[7A] Paragraph (e), unlike ABA Model Rule 1.5(e), does not require that the division of fees be in proportion to the services performed by each lawyer unless, with a client's written consent, each lawyer assumes joint responsibility for the representation. The Massachusetts rule does not require disclosure of the fee division that the lawyers have agreed to, but if the client requests information on the division of fees, the lawyer is required to disclose the share of each lawyer.

[8] Paragraph (e) does not prohibit or regulate division of fees to be received in the future for work done when lawyers were previously associated in a law firm.

Disputes over Fees

[9] In the event of a fee dispute not otherwise subject to arbitration, the lawyer should conscientiously consider submitting to mediation or an established fee arbitration service. If such procedure is required by law or agreement, the lawyer shall comply with such requirement. Law may prescribe a procedure for determining a lawyer's fee, for example, in representation of an executor or administrator, a class or a person entitled to a reasonable fee as part of the measure of damages. The lawyer entitled to such a fee and a lawyer representing another party concerned with the fee should comply with the prescribed procedure. For purposes of paragraph 1.5(f)(3), a provision requiring that fee disputes be resolved by arbitration is a provision that differs materially from the forms of contingent fee agreement set forth in this rule and is subject to the prerequisite that the lawyer explain the provision and obtain the client's consent, confirmed in writing.

Form of Fee Agreement

[10] Paragraph (f) provides model forms of contingent fee agreements and identifies explanations that a lawyer must provide to a client, except where the client is an organization, including a non-profit or governmental entity.

[11] Paragraphs (f)(1) and (f)(2) provide two forms of contingent fee agreement that may be used. Because paragraphs (3) and (7) of Form A do not contain alternative provisions, a lawyer who uses Form A does not need to provide any special explanation to the client. Paragraphs (2), (3), and (7) of Form B differ from Form A. While in most contingency cases, the contingency upon which compensation will be paid is recovery of damages, paragraph (2) of Form B permits lawyers and clients to agree to other lawful contingencies. A lawyer is not required to provide any special explanation when using paragraph (2). Paragraphs (3) and (7) of Form B allow options for the payment of costs and expenses and the payment of reasonable attorney's fees and expenses to former counsel. To ensure that a client gives informed consent to the agreed-upon option, a lawyer who uses Form B must retain in the form both options contained in paragraphs (3) and, where applicable, paragraph (7); show and explain these options to the client; and obtain the client's informed consent confirmed in writing to the selected option.

[12] Paragraph (f)(3) permits the lawyer and client to agree to modifications to Forms A and B, including modifications which are more favorable to the lawyer, to the extent permitted by this rule. However, a lawyer using a modified form of fee agreement must explain to the client any provisions that materially differ from or add to those contained in Forms A and B, and obtain the client's informed written consent. For purposes of this rule, an agreement that does not contain option (i) in paragraph (3) and, where applicable, option (i) in paragraph (7) of Form B is materially different, and a lawyer must

explain those different or added provisions to the client, and obtain the client's informed written consent.

[13] When attorney's fees are awarded by a court or included in a settlement, a question arises as to the proper method of calculating a contingent fee. Rule 1.5(c)(5) and paragraph (4) of the form agreement s contained in Rule 1.5(f) state the default rule, but the parties may agree on a different basis for such calculation, such as applying the percentage to the total recovery, including attorneys fees.

RULE 1.6 CONFIDENTIALITY OF INFORMATION

(a) A lawyer shall not reveal confidential information relating to representation of a client unless the client consents after consultation, except for disclosures that are impliedly authorized in order to carry out the representation, and except as stated in paragraph (b).

(b) A lawyer may reveal, and to the extent required by Rule 3.3, Rule 4.1(b), or Rule 8.3 must reveal, such information:

(1) to prevent the commission of a criminal or fraudulent act that the lawyer reasonably believes is likely to result in death or substantial bodily harm, or in substantial injury to the financial interests or property of another, or to prevent the wrongful execution or incarceration of another;

(2) to the extent the lawyer reasonably believes necessary to establish a claim or defense on behalf of the lawyer in a controversy between the lawyer and the client, to establish a defense to a criminal charge or civil claim against the lawyer based upon conduct in which the client was involved, or to respond to allegations in any proceeding concerning the lawyer's representation of the client;

(3) to the extent the lawyer reasonably believes necessary to rectify client fraud in which the lawyer's services have been used, subject to Rule 3.3 (e);

(4) when permitted under these rules or required by law or court order.

(c) A lawyer participating in a lawyer assistance program, as hereinafter defined, shall treat the person so assisted as a client for the purposes of this rule. Lawyer assistance means assistance provided to a lawyer, judge, other legal professional, or law student by a lawyer participating in an organized nonprofit effort to provide assistance in the form of (a) counseling as to practice matters (which shall not include counseling a law student in a law school clinical program) or (b) education as to personal health matters, such as the treatment and rehabilitation from a mental, emotional, or psychological disorder, alcoholism, substance abuse, or other addiction, or both. A lawyer named in an order of the Supreme Judicial Court or the Board of Bar Overseers concerning the monitoring or terms of probation of another attorney shall treat that other attorney as a client for the purposes of this rule. Any lawyer participating in a lawyer assistance program may require a person acting under the lawyer's supervision or control to sign a nondisclosure form approved by the Supreme Judicial Court. Nothing in this paragraph (c) shall require a bar association-sponsored ethics advisory committee, the Office of Bar Counsel, or any other governmental agency advising on questions of professional responsibility to treat persons so assisted as clients for the purpose of this rule.

Comment

[1] The lawyer is part of a judicial system charged with upholding the law. One of the lawyer's functions is to advise clients so that they avoid any violation of the law in the proper exercise of their rights.

[2] The observance of the ethical obligation of a lawyer to hold inviolate confidential information of the client not only facilitates the full development of facts essential to proper representation of the client but also encourages people to seek early legal assistance.

[3] Almost without exception, clients come to lawyers in order to determine what their rights are and what is, in the maze of laws and regulations, deemed to be legal and correct. The common law recognizes that the client's confidences must be protected from disclosure.

[4] A fundamental principle in the client-lawyer relationship is that the lawyer maintain confidentiality of information relating to the representation. The client is thereby encouraged to communicate fully and frankly with the lawyer even as to embarrassing or legally damaging subject matter.

[5] The principle of confidentiality is given effect in two related bodies of law, the attorney-client privilege (and the related work product doctrine) in the law of evidence and the rule of confidentiality established in professional ethics. The attorney-client privilege applies in judicial and other proceedings in which a lawyer may be called as a witness or otherwise required to produce evidence concerning a client. The rule of client-lawyer confidentiality applies in situations other than those where evidence is sought from the lawyer through compulsion of law. The confidentiality rule applies not merely to matters communicated in confidence by the client but also to virtually all information relating to the representation, whatever its source. The term "confidential information" relating to representation of a client therefore includes information described as "confidences" and "secrets" in former DR 4-101(A) but without the limitation in the prior rules that the information be "embarrassing" or "detrimental" to the client. Former DR 4-101(A) provided: 'Confidence' refers to information protected by the attorney-client privilege under applicable law, and 'secret' refers to other information gained in the professional relationship that the client has requested be held inviolate or the disclosure of which would be embarrassing or would likely be detrimental to the client." See also Scope.

[5A] The word "virtually" appears in the fourth sentence of paragraph 5 above to reflect the common sense understanding that not every piece of information that a lawyer obtains relating to a representation is protected confidential information. While this understanding may be difficult to apply in some cases, some information is so widely available or generally known that it need not be treated as confidential. The lawyer's discovery that there was dense fog at the airport at a particular time does not fall within the rule. Such information is readily available. While a client's disclosure of the fact of infidelity to a spouse is protected information, it normally would not be after the client publicly discloses such information on television and in newspaper interviews. On the other hand, the mere fact that information disclosed by a client to a lawyer is a matter of public record does not mean that it may not fall within the protection of this rule. A client's disclosure of conviction of a crime in a different state a long time ago or disclosure of a secret marriage would be protected even if a matter of public record because such information was not generally known.

[5B] The exclusion of generally known or widely available information from the information protected by this rule explains the addition of the word "confidential" before the word "information" in Rule 1.6(a) as compared to the comparable ABA Model Rule. It also explains the elimination of the words "or is generally known" in Rule 1.9(c)(1) as compared to the comparable ABA Model Rule. The elimination of such information from the concept of protected information in that subparagraph has been achieved more generally throughout the rules by the addition of the word "confidential" in this rule. It might be misleading to repeat the concept in just one specific subparagraph. Moreover, even information that is generally known may in some circumstances be protected, as when the client instructs the lawyer that generally known information, for example, spousal infidelity, not be revealed to a specific person, for example, the spouse's parent who does not know of it.

[6] The requirement of maintaining confidentiality of information relating to representation applies to government lawyers who may disagree with the policy goals that their representation is designed to advance.

Authorized Disclosure

[7] A lawyer is authorized to make disclosures about a client when appropriate in carrying out the representation, except to the extent that the client's instructions or special circumstances limit that authority. In litigation, for example, a lawyer may disclose information by admitting a fact that cannot properly be disputed, or in negotiation by making a disclosure that facilitates a satisfactory conclusion. Rule 1.6(b)(4) has been added to make clear the purpose to carry forward the explicit statement of former DR 4-101(C)(2).

[8] Lawyers in a firm may, in the course of the firm's practice, disclose to each other information relating to a client of the firm, unless the client has instructed that particular information be confined to specified lawyers. Before accepting or continuing representation on such a basis, the lawyers to whom such restricted information will be communicated must assure themselves that the restriction will not contravene firm governance rules or prevent them from discovering disqualifying conflicts of interests.

Disclosure Adverse to Client

[9] One premise of the confidentiality rule is that to the extent a lawyer is required or permitted to disclose a client's confidential information, the client will be inhibited from revealing facts that would enable the lawyer to counsel against a wrongful course of action. The implication of that premise is that generally the public will be better protected if full and open communication by the client is encouraged than if it is inhibited. Nevertheless, there are instances when the confidentiality rule is subject to exceptions.

[9A] Rule 1.6(b)(1) is derived from the original Kutak Commission proposal for the ABA Model Rules which permitted disclosure of confidential information to prevent criminal or fraudulent acts likely to result in death or substantial bodily harm or in substantial injury to the financial interests or property of another. The former Massachusetts Disciplinary Rules permitted revelation of confidential information with respect to all crimes and all injuries, no matter how trivial. The use of the term "substantial" harm or injury restricts permitted revelation by limiting the permission granted to instances when the harm or injury is likely to be more than trivial or small. The reference to bodily harm is not meant to require physical injury as a prerequisite. Acts of statutory rape, for example, fall within the concept of bodily harm. Rule 1.6(b)(1) also permits a lawyer to reveal confidential information in the specific situation where such information discloses that an innocent person has been convicted of a crime and has been sentenced to imprisonment or execution. This language has been included to permit disclosure of confidential information in these circumstances where the failure to disclose may not involve the commission of a crime.

[10] Several situations must be distinguished.

[11] First, the lawyer may not counsel or assist a client in conduct that is criminal or fraudulent. See Rule 1.2(d). Similarly, a lawyer has a duty under Rule 3.3(a)(4) not to use false evidence. This duty is essentially a special instance of the duty prescribed in Rule 1.2(d) to avoid assisting a client in criminal or fraudulent conduct.

[12] Second, the lawyer may have been innocently involved in past conduct by the client that was criminal or fraudulent. In such a situation the lawyer has not violated Rule 1.2(d), because to "counsel or assist" criminal or fraudulent conduct requires knowing that the conduct is of that character. See Rule 4.1, Comment 3. With regard to conduct before a tribunal, however, see the special meaning of the concept of assisting in Rule 3.3, Comment 2A.

[12A] When the lawyer's services have been used by the client to perpetrate a fraud, that is a perversion of the lawyer-client relationship and Rule 1.6(b)(3) permits the lawyer to reveal confidential information necessary to rectify the fraud.

[13] Third, the lawyer may have confidential information whose disclosure the lawyer reasonably believes is necessary to prevent the commission of a crime that is likely to re-sult in death or substantial bodily or financial harm. As stated in paragraph (b)(1), the lawyer has professional discretion to reveal such information. Before disclosure is made, the lawyer should have a reasonable belief that a crime is likely to be committed and that disclosure of confidential information is necessary to prevent it. The lawyer should not ignore facts that would lead a reasonable person to conclude that disclosure is per-missible.

[13A] The language of paragraph (b)(1) has been changed from the ABA Model Rules version to permit disclosure of a client's confidential information when the harm will be the result of the activities of third parties as well as of the client.

[14] The lawyer's exercise of discretion requires consideration of such factors as the na-ture of the lawyer's relationship with the client and with those who might be injured by the client, the lawyer's own involvement in the transaction, and factors that may extenu-ate the conduct in question. Where practical, the lawyer should seek to persuade the client to take suitable action. In any case, a disclosure adverse to the client's interest should be no greater than the lawyer reasonably believes necessary to the purpose. A lawyer's decision not to take preventive action permitted by paragraph (b)(1) does not violate this rule, but in particular circumstances, it might violate Rule 3.3(e) or Rule 4.1.

Withdrawal

[15] If the lawyer's services will be used by the client in materially furthering a course of criminal or fraudulent conduct, the lawyer must withdraw, as stated in Rule 1.16(a)(1). If the client has already used the lawyer's services to commit fraud, the lawyer may re-veal confidential information to rectify the fraud in accordance with Rule 1.6(b)(3).

[16] After withdrawal the lawyer is required to refrain from making disclosure of the client's confidences, except as otherwise provided in Rule 1.6, Rule 3.3, Rule 4.1, and Rule 8.3. Neither this rule nor Rule 1.8(b) nor Rule 1.16(d) prevents the lawyer from giving notice of the fact of withdrawal, and the lawyer may also withdraw or disaffirm any opinion, document, affirmation, or the like.

[17] Where the client is an organization, the lawyer may be in doubt whether contem-plated conduct will actually be carried out by the organization. Where necessary to guide conduct in connection with this rule, the lawyer may make inquiry within the or-ganization as indicated in Rule 1.13(b).

Dispute Concerning a Lawyer's Conduct

[18] Where a legal claim or disciplinary charge alleges complicity of the lawyer in a client's conduct or other misconduct of the lawyer involving representation of the client, the lawyer may respond to the extent the lawyer reasonably believes necessary to establish a defense. The same is true with respect to a claim involving the conduct or representation of a former client. The lawyer's right to respond arises when an assertion of such complicity has been made. Paragraph (b)(2) does not require the lawyer to await the commencement of an action or proceeding that charges such complicity, so that the defense may be established by responding directly to a third party who has made such an assertion. The right to defend, of course, applies where a proceeding has been commenced. Where practicable and not prejudicial to the lawyer's ability to establish the defense, the lawyer should advise the client of the third party's assertion and request that the client respond appropriately. In any event, disclosure should be no greater than the lawyer reasonably believes is necessary to vindicate innocence, the disclosure should be made in a manner which limits access to the information to the tribunal or other persons having a need to know it, and appropriate protective orders or other arrangements should be sought by the lawyer to the fullest extent practicable.

[19] If the lawyer is charged with wrongdoing in which the client's conduct is implicated, the rule of confidentiality should not prevent the lawyer from defending against the charge. Such a charge can arise in a civil, criminal, or professional disciplinary proceeding, and can be based on a wrong allegedly committed by the lawyer against the client, or on a wrong alleged by a third person, for example, a person claiming to have been defrauded by the lawyer and client acting together. A lawyer entitled to a fee is permitted by paragraph (b)(2) to prove the services rendered in an action to collect it. This aspect of the rule expresses the principle that the beneficiary of a fiduciary relationship may not exploit it to the detriment of the fiduciary. As stated above, the lawyer must make every effort practicable to avoid unnecessary disclosure of information relating to a representation, to limit disclosure to those having the need to know it, and to obtain protective orders or make other arrangements minimizing the risk of disclosure.

Notice of Disclosure to Client

[19A] Whenever the rules permit or require the lawyer to disclose a client's confidential information, the issue arises whether the lawyer should, as a part of the confidentiality and loyalty obligation and as a matter of competent practice, advise the client beforehand of the plan to disclose. It is not possible to state an absolute rule to govern a lawyer's conduct in such situations. In some cases, it may be impractical or even dangerous for the lawyer to advise the client of the intent to reveal confidential information either before or even after the fact. Indeed, such revelation might thwart the reason for creation of the exception. It might hasten the commission of a dangerous act by a client or it might enable clients to prevent lawyers from defending themselves against accusations of lawyer misconduct. But there will be instances, such as the intended delivery of whole files to prosecutors to convince them not to indict the lawyer, where the failure to give notice would prevent the client from making timely objection to the revelation of too much confidential information. Lawyers will have to weigh the various policies and make reasonable judgments about the demands of loyalty, the requirements of competent practice, and the policy reasons for creating the exception to confidentiality in order to decide whether they should give advance notice to clients of the intended disclosure.

Disclosures Otherwise Required or Authorized

[20] If a lawyer is called as a witness to give testimony concerning a client, absent waiver by the client, paragraph (a) requires the lawyer to invoke the privilege when it is applicable. The lawyer must comply with the final orders of a court or other tribunal of competent jurisdiction requiring the lawyer to give information about the client. Whether a lawyer should consider an appeal before complying with a court order depends on such considerations as the gravity of the harm to the client from compliance and the likelihood of prevailing on appeal.

[21] These rules in various circumstances permit or require a lawyer to disclose information relating to the representation. See Rules 2.3, 3.3, 4.1, and 8.3. The reference to Rules 3.3, 4.1(b), and 8.3 in the opening phrase of Rule 1.6(b) has been added to emphasize that Rule 1.6(b) is not the only provision of these rules that deals with the disclosure of confidential information and that in some circumstances disclosure of such information may be required and not merely permitted. In addition to these provisions, a lawyer may be obligated or permitted by other provisions of law to give information about a client. Whether another provision of law supersedes Rule 1.6 is a matter of interpretation beyond the scope of these rules.

Former Client

[22] The duty of confidentiality continues after the client-lawyer relationship has terminated.

Corresponding ABA Model Rule. (a) identical to Model Rule 1.6(a) except that the information must be confidential information; (b) different, in part taken from DR 4-101 (C); (c) based on DR 4-101 (E).

Corresponding Former Massachusetts Rule. DR 4-101 (C), see also DR 7-102 (B).

Cross-reference: See definition of "consultation" in Rule 9.1 (c).

RULE 1.7 CONFLICT OF INTEREST: GENERAL RULE

(a) A lawyer shall not represent a client if the representation of that client will be directly adverse to another client, unless:

(1) the lawyer reasonably believes the representation will not adversely affect the relationship with the other client; and

(2) each client consents after consultation.

(b) A lawyer shall not represent a client if the representation of that client may be materially limited by the lawyer's responsibilities to another client or to a third person, or by the lawyer's own interests, unless:

(1) the lawyer reasonably believes the representation will not be adversely affected; and

(2) the client consents after consultation. When representation of multiple clients in a single matter is undertaken, the consultation shall include explanation of the implications of the common representation and the advantages and risks involved.

Comment

Loyalty to a Client

[1] Loyalty is an essential element in the lawyer's relationship to a client. An impermissible conflict of interest may exist before representation is undertaken, in which event the representation should be declined. The lawyer should adopt reasonable procedures, ap-

propriate for the size and type of firm and practice, to determine in both litigation and non-litigation matters the parties and issues involved and to determine whether there are actual or potential conflicts of interest.

[2] If such a conflict arises after representation has been undertaken, the lawyer should withdraw from the representation. See Rule 1.16. Where more than one client is involved and the lawyer withdraws because a conflict arises after representation, whether the lawyer may continue to represent any of the clients is determined by Rule 1.9. As to whether a client-lawyer relationship exists or, having once been established, is continuing, see Comment to Rule 1.3 and Scope.

[3] As a general proposition, loyalty to a client prohibits undertaking representation directly adverse to that client without that client's consent. Paragraph (a) expresses that general rule. Thus, a lawyer ordinarily may not act as advocate against a person the lawyer represents in some other matter, even if it is wholly unrelated. On the other hand, simultaneous representation in unrelated matters of clients whose interests are only generally adverse, such as competing economic enterprises, does not require consent of the respective clients. Paragraph (a) applies only when the representation of one client would be directly adverse to the other.

[4] Loyalty to a client is also impaired when a lawyer cannot consider, recommend or carry out an appropriate course of action for the client because of the lawyer's other responsibilities or interests. The conflict in effect forecloses alternatives that would otherwise be available to the client. Paragraph (b) addresses such situations. A possible conflict does not itself preclude the representation. The critical questions are the likelihood that a conflict will eventuate and, if it does, whether it will materially interfere with the lawyer's independent professional judgment in considering alternatives or foreclose courses of action that reasonably should be pursued on behalf of the client. Consideration should be given to whether the client wishes to accommodate the other interest involved.

Consultation and Consent

[5] A client may consent to representation notwithstanding a conflict. However, as indicated in paragraph (a)(1) with respect to representation directly adverse to a client, and paragraph (b)(1) with respect to material limitations on representation of a client, when a disinterested lawyer would conclude that the client should not agree to the representation under the circumstances, the lawyer involved cannot properly ask for such agreement or provide representation on the basis of the client's consent. When more than one client is involved, the question of conflict must be resolved as to each client. Moreover, there may be circumstances where it is impossible to make the disclosure necessary to obtain consent. For example, when the lawyer represents different clients in related matters and one of the clients refuses to consent to the disclosure necessary to permit the other client to make an informed decision, the lawyer cannot properly ask the latter to consent.

Lawyer's Interests

[6] The lawyer's own interests should not be permitted to have an adverse effect on representation of a client. For example, a lawyer's need for income should not lead the lawyer to undertake matters that cannot be handled competently and at a reasonable fee. See Rules 1.1 and 1.5. If the probity of a lawyer's own conduct in a transaction is in serious question, it may be difficult or impossible for the lawyer to give a client detached advice. A lawyer may not allow related business interests to affect representation, for example, by referring clients to an enterprise in which the lawyer has an undisclosed inter-

est. Likewise, a lawyer should not accept referrals from a referral source, including law enforcement or court personnel, if the lawyer's desire to continue to receive referrals from that source or the lawyer's relationship to that source would discourage or would reasonably be viewed as discouraging the lawyer from representing the client zealously.

Conflicts in Litigation

[7] Paragraph (a) prohibits representation of opposing parties in litigation. Simultaneous representation of parties whose interests in litigation may conflict, such as coplaintiffs or codefendants, is governed by paragraph (b). An impermissible conflict may exist by reason of substantial discrepancy in the parties' testimony, incompatibility in positions in relation to an opposing party or the fact that there are substantially different possibilities of settlement of the claims or liabilities in question. Such conflicts can arise in criminal cases as well as civil. In criminal cases, the potential for conflict of interest in representing multiple defendants is so grave that ordinarily a lawyer should decline to act for more than one codefendant, or more than one person under investigation by law enforcement authorities for the same transaction or series of transactions, including any investigation by a grand jury. On the other hand, common representation of persons having similar interests is proper if the lawyer reasonably believes the risk of adverse effect is minimal and all persons have given their informed consent to the multiple representation, as required by paragraph (b).

[8] Ordinarily, a lawyer may not act as advocate against a client the lawyer represents in some other matter, even if the other matter is wholly unrelated. However, there are circumstances in which a lawyer may act as advocate against a client. For example, a lawyer representing an enterprise with diverse operations may accept employment as an advocate against the enterprise in an unrelated matter if doing so will not adversely affect the lawyer's relationship with the enterprise or conduct of the suit and if both clients consent upon consultation. A lawyer representing the parent or a subsidiary of a corporation is not automatically disqualified from simultaneously taking an adverse position to a different affiliate of the represented party, even without consent. There may be situations where such concurrent representation will be possible because the effect of the adverse representation is insignificant with respect to the other affiliate or the parent and the management of the lawsuit is handled at completely different levels of the enterprise. But in many, perhaps most, cases, such concurrent representation will not be possible without consent of the parties.

[8A] The situation with respect to government lawyers is special, and public policy considerations may permit representation of conflicting interests in some circumstances where representation would be forbidden to a private lawyer.

[9] A lawyer may ordinarily represent parties having antagonistic positions on a legal question that has arisen in different matters. However, the antagonism may relate to an issue that is so crucial to the resolution of a matter as to require that the clients be advised of the conflict and their consent obtained. On rare occasions, such as the argument of both sides of a legal question before the same court at the same time, the conflict may be so severe that a lawyer could not continue the representation even with client consent.

Interest of Person Paying for a Lawyer's Service

[10] A lawyer may be paid from a source other than the client, if the client is informed of that fact and consents and the arrangement does not compromise the lawyer's duty of loyalty to the client. See Rule 1.8(f). For example, when an insurer and its insured have conflicting interests in a matter arising from a liability insurance agreement, and

the insurer is required to provide special counsel for the insured, the arrangement should assure the special counsel's professional independence. So also, when a corporation and its directors or employees are involved in a controversy in which they have conflicting interests, the corporation may provide funds for separate legal representation of the directors or employees, if the clients consent after consultation and the arrangement ensures the lawyer's professional independence.

Other Conflict Situations

[11] Conflicts of interest in contexts other than litigation sometimes may be difficult to assess. Relevant factors in determining whether there is potential for adverse effect include the duration and intimacy of the lawyer's relationship with the client or clients involved, the functions being performed by the lawyer, the likelihood that actual conflict will arise and the likely prejudice to the client from the conflict if it does arise. The question is often one of proximity and degree.

[12] For example, a lawyer may not represent multiple parties to a negotiation whose interests are fundamentally antagonistic to each other, but common representation is permissible where the clients are generally aligned in interest even though there is some difference of interest among them. Thus, a lawyer may seek to establish or to adjust a relationship between clients on an amicable and mutually advantageous basis, for example, in helping to organize a business in which two or more clients are entrepreneurs, working out the financial reorganization of an enterprise in which two or more clients have an interest, or arranging a property distribution in settlement of an estate. The lawyer seeks to resolve potentially conflicting interests by developing the parties' mutual interests. Otherwise, each party might have to obtain separate representation, with the possibility of incurring additional cost, complication, or even litigation. Given these and other relevant factors, the clients may prefer that the lawyer act for all of them.

[12A] In considering whether to represent clients jointly, a lawyer should be mindful that if the joint representation fails because the potentially conflicting interests cannot be reconciled, the result can be additional cost, embarrassment, and recrimination. In some situations the risk of failure is so great that joint representation is plainly impossible. For example, a lawyer cannot undertake common representation of clients between whom contentious litigation is imminent or who contemplate contentious negotiations. A lawyer who has represented one of the clients for a long period and in a variety of matters might have difficulty being impartial between that client and one to whom the lawyer has only recently been introduced. More generally, if the relationship between the parties has already assumed definite antagonism, the possibility that the clients' interests can be adjusted by joint representation is not very good. Other relevant factors are whether the lawyer subsequently will represent both parties on a continuing basis and whether the situation involves creating a relationship between the parties or terminating one.

Confidentiality and Privilege

[12B] A particularly important factor in determining the appropriateness of joint representation is the effect on lawyer-client confidentiality and the attorney-client privilege. With regard to the evidentiary attorney-client privilege, the prevailing rule is that as between commonly represented clients the privilege does not attach. Hence, it must be assumed that if litigation eventuates between the clients, the privilege will not protect any such communications, and the client should be so advised.

[12C] As to the duty of confidentiality, while each client may assert that the lawyer keep something in confidence between the lawyer and the client, which is not to be disclosed to the other client, each client should be advised at the outset of the joint representation that making such a request will, in all likelihood, make it impossible for the lawyer to continue the joint representation. This is so because the lawyer has an equal duty of loyalty to each client. Each client has a right to expect that the lawyer will tell the client anything bearing on the representation that might affect that client's interests and that the lawyer will use that information to that client's benefit. But the lawyer cannot do this if the other client has sworn the lawyer to secrecy about any such matter. Thus, for the lawyer to proceed would be in derogation of the trust of the other client. To avoid this situation, at the outset of the joint representation the lawyer should advise both (or all) clients that the joint representation will work only if they agree to deal openly and honestly with one another on all matters relating to the representation, and that the lawyer will have to withdraw, if one requests that some matter material to the representation be kept from the other. The lawyer should advise the clients to consider carefully whether they are willing to share information openly with one another because above all else that is what it means to have one lawyer instead of separate representation for each.

[12D] In limited circumstances, it may be appropriate for a lawyer to ask both (or all) clients, if they want to agree that the lawyer will keep certain information confidential, i.e., from the other client. For example, an estate lawyer might want to ask joint clients if they each want to agree that in the eventuality that one becomes mentally disabled the lawyer be allowed to proceed with the joint representation, appropriately altering the estate plan, without the other's knowledge. Of course, should that eventuality come to pass, the lawyer should consult Rule 1.14 before proceeding. However, aside from such limited circumstances, the lawyer representing joint clients should emphasize that what the clients give up in terms of confidentiality is twofold: a later right to claim the attorney-client privilege in disputes between them; and the right during the representation to keep secrets from one another that bear on the representation.

Consultation

[12E] When representing clients jointly, the lawyer is required to consult with them on the implications of doing so, and proceed only upon consent based on such a consultation. The consultation should make clear that the lawyer's role is not that of partisanship normally expected in other circumstances. When the lawyer is representing clients jointly, the clients ordinarily must assume greater responsibility for decisions than when each client is independently represented.

Withdrawal

[12F] Subject to the above limitations, each client in the joint representation has the right to loyal and diligent representation and the protection of Rule 1.9 concerning obligations to a former client. The client also has the right to discharge the lawyer as stated in Rule 1.16.

[13] Conflict questions may also arise in estate planning and estate administration. A lawyer may be called upon to prepare wills for several family members, such as husband and wife, and, depending upon the circumstances, a conflict of interest may arise. In estate administration the lawyer should make clear the relationship to the parties involved.

[14] A lawyer for a corporation or other organization who is also a member of its board of directors should determine whether the responsibilities of the two roles may conflict. The lawyer may be called on to advise the corporation in matters involving actions of the directors. Consideration should be given to the frequency with which such situa-

tions may arise, the potential intensity of the conflict, the effect of the lawyer's resignation from the board and the possibility of the corporation's obtaining legal advice from another lawyer in such situations. If there is material risk that the dual role will compromise the lawyer's independence of professional judgment, the lawyer should not serve as a director.

[14A] A lawyer who undertakes to represent a class should make an initial determination whether subclasses within the class should have separate representation because their interests differ in material respects from other segments of the class. Moreover, the lawyer who initially determines that subclasses are not necessary should revisit that determination as the litigation or settlement discussions proceed because as discovery or settlement talks proceed the interests of subgroups within the class may begin to diverge significantly. The class lawyer must be constantly alert to such divergences and to whether the interests of a subgroup of the class are being sacrificed or undersold in the interests of the whole. The lawyer has the responsibility to request that separate representation be provided to protect the interests of subgroups within the class. In general, the lawyer for a class should not simultaneously represent individuals, not within the class, or other classes, in actions against the defendant being sued by the class. Such simultaneous representation invites defendants to propose global settlements that require the class lawyer to trade off the interest of the class against the interests of other groups or individuals. Given the difficulty of obtaining class consent and the difficulty for the class action court of monitoring the details of the other settlements, such simultaneous representation should ordinarily be avoided. In some limited circumstances, it may be reasonable for class counsel to represent simultaneously the class and another party or parties against a common party if the other matter is not substantially related to the class representation and there is an objective basis for believing that the lawyer's representation will not be materially affected at any stage of either matter. For example, a lawyer might reasonably proceed if the common defendant were the government and the government's decision making in the class action was entrusted to a unit of the government highly unlikely to be affected by the decision maker for the government in the other matter.

Conflict Charged by an Opposing Party

[15] Resolving questions of conflict of interest is primarily the responsibility of the lawyer undertaking the representation. In litigation, a court may raise the question when there is reason to infer that the lawyer has neglected the responsibility. In a criminal case, inquiry by the court is generally required when a lawyer represents multiple defendants. Where the conflict is such as clearly to call in question the fair or efficient administration of justice, opposing counsel may properly raise the question. Such an objection should be viewed with caution, however, for it can be misused as a technique of harassment. See Scope.

Corresponding ABA Model Rule. Identical to Model Rule 1.7.

Corresponding Former Massachusetts Rule. DR 5-101 (A), 5-105 (A) and (C), 5-107 (B).

Cross-reference: See definition of "consultation" in Rule 9.1 (c).

RULE 1.8 CONFLICT OF INTEREST: PROHIBITED TRANSACTIONS

(a) A lawyer shall not enter into a business transaction with a client or knowingly acquire an ownership, possessory, security, or other pecuniary interest adverse to a client unless:

(1) the transaction and terms on which the lawyer acquires the interest are fair and reasonable to the client and are fully disclosed and transmitted in writing to the client in a manner which can be reasonably understood by the client;

(2) the client is given a reasonable opportunity to seek the advice of independent counsel in the transaction; and

(3) the client consents in writing thereto.

(b) A lawyer shall not use confidential information relating to representation of a client to the disadvantage of the client or for the lawyer's advantage or the advantage of a third person, unless the client consents after consultation, except as Rule 1.6 or Rule 3.3 would permit or require.

(c) A lawyer shall not prepare an instrument giving the lawyer or a person related to the lawyer as parent, child, sibling, or spouse any substantial gift from a client, including a testamentary gift, except where the client is related to the donee.

(d) Prior to the conclusion of representation of a client, a lawyer shall not make or negotiate an agreement giving the lawyer literary or media rights to a portrayal or account based in substantial part on information relating to the representation.

(e) A lawyer shall not provide financial assistance to a client in connection with pending or contemplated litigation, except that:

(1) a lawyer may advance court costs and expenses of litigation, the repayment of which may be contingent on the outcome of the matter; and

(2) a lawyer representing an indigent client may pay court costs and expenses of litigation on behalf of the client.

(f) A lawyer shall not accept compensation for representing a client from one other than the client unless:

(1) the client consents after consultation;

(2) there is no interference with the lawyer's independence of professional judgment or with the client-lawyer relationship; and

(3) information relating to representation of a client is protected as required by Rule 1.6.

(g) A lawyer who represents two or more clients shall not participate in making an aggregate settlement of the claims of or against the clients, or in a criminal case an aggregated agreement as to guilty or nolo contendere pleas, unless each client consents after consultation, including disclosure of the existence and nature of all the claims or pleas involved and of the participation of each person in the settlement.

(h) A lawyer shall not make an agreement prospectively limiting the lawyer's liability to a client for malpractice unless permitted by law and the client is independently represented in making the agreement, or settle a claim for such liability with an unrepresented client or former client without first advising that person in writing that independent representation is appropriate in connection therewith.

(i) A lawyer related to another lawyer as parent, child, sibling, or spouse shall not represent a client in a representation directly adverse to a person whom the lawyer knows is represented by the other lawyer except upon consent by the client after consultation regarding the relationship.

(j) A lawyer shall not acquire a proprietary interest in the cause of action or subject matter of litigation the lawyer is conducting for a client, except that the lawyer may:

(1) acquire a lien granted by law to secure the lawyer's fee or expenses; and

(2) contract with a client for a reasonable contingent fee in a civil case.

Comment

Transactions Between Client and Lawyer

[1] As a general principle, all transactions between client and lawyer should be fair and reasonable to the client. In such transactions a review by independent counsel on behalf of the client is often advisable. Furthermore, a lawyer may not exploit information relating to the representation to the client's disadvantage. For example, a lawyer who has learned that the client is investing in specific real estate may not, without the client's consent, seek to acquire nearby property where doing so would adversely affect the client's plan for investment. Paragraph (a) does not, however, apply to standard commercial transactions between the lawyer and the client for products or services that the client generally markets to others, for example, banking or brokerage services, medical services, products manufactured or distributed by the client, and utilities' services. In such transactions, the lawyer has no advantage in dealing with the client, and the restrictions in paragraph (a) are unnecessary and impracticable.

[1A] Paragraph (b) continues the former prohibition contained in DR 4-101(B)(3) against a lawyer's using a client's confidential information not only to the disadvantage of the client but also to the advantage of the lawyer or a third person.

[2] A lawyer may accept a gift from a client, if the transaction meets general standards of fairness. For example, a simple gift such as a present given at a holiday or as a token of appreciation is permitted. If effectuation of a substantial gift requires preparing a legal instrument such as a will or conveyance, however, the client should have the detached advice that another lawyer can provide. Paragraph (c) recognizes an exception where the client is a relative of the donee or the gift is not substantial.

Literary Rights

[3] An agreement by which a lawyer acquires literary or media rights concerning the conduct of the representation creates a conflict between the interests of the client and the personal interests of the lawyer. Measures suitable in the representation of the client may detract from the publication value of an account of the representation. Paragraph (d) does not prohibit a lawyer representing a client in a transaction concerning literary property from agreeing that the lawyer's fee shall consist of a share in ownership in the property, if the arrangement conforms to Rule 1.5 and paragraph (j).

Person Paying for a Lawyer's Services

[4] Paragraph (f) requires disclosure of the fact that the lawyer's services are being paid for by a third party. Such an arrangement must also conform to the requirements of Rule 1.6 concerning confidentiality and Rule 1.7 concerning conflict of interest. Where the client is a class, consent may be obtained on behalf of the class by court-supervised procedure.

Limiting Liability

[5] Paragraph (h) is not intended to apply to customary qualifications and limitations in legal opinions and memoranda.

Family Relationships Between Lawyers

[6] Paragraph (i) applies to related lawyers who are in different firms. Related lawyers in the same firm are governed by Rules 1.7, 1.9, and 1.10. The disqualification stated in

paragraph (i) is personal and is not imputed to members of firms with whom the lawyers are associated.

Acquisition of Interest in Litigation

[7] Paragraph (j) states the traditional general rule that lawyers are prohibited from acquiring a proprietary interest in litigation. This general rule, which has its basis in common law champerty and maintenance, is subject to specific exceptions developed in decisional law and continued in these Rules, such as the exception for reasonable contingent fees set forth in Rule 1.5 and the exception for certain advances of the costs of litigation set forth in paragraph (e).

Corresponding ABA Rule. Identical to Model Rule 1.8 except for paragraph (b).

Corresponding Former Massachusetts Rule. DR 4-101 (B) (2), DR 4-101 (B) (3), DR 5-103, DR 5-104, DR 5-106, DR 5-107 (A) and (B), DR 5-108, DR 6-102.

Cross-reference: See definition of "consultation" in Rule 9.1 (c).

RULE 1.9 CONFLICT OF INTEREST: FORMER CLIENT

(a) A lawyer who has formerly represented a client in a matter shall not thereafter represent another person in the same or a substantially related matter in which that person's interests are materially adverse to the interests of the former client unless the former client consents after consultation.

(b) A lawyer shall not knowingly represent a person in the same or a substantially related matter in which a firm with which the lawyer formerly was associated had previously represented a client

(1) whose interests are materially adverse to that person; and

(2) about whom the lawyer had acquired information protected by Rules 1.6 and 1.9(c) that is material to the matter, unless the former client consents after consultation.

(c) A lawyer who has formerly represented a client in a matter or whose present or former firm has formerly represented a client in a matter shall not thereafter, unless the former client consents after consultation:

(1) use confidential information relating to the representation to the disadvantage of the former client, to the lawyer's advantage, or to the advantage of a third person, except as Rule 1.6, Rule 3.3, or Rule 4.1 would permit or require with respect to a client; or

(2) reveal confidential information relating to the representation except as Rule 1.6 or Rule 3.3 would permit or require with respect to a client.

Comment

[1] After termination of a client-lawyer relationship, a lawyer may not represent another client except in conformity with this Rule. The principles in Rule 1.7 determine whether the interests of the present and former client are adverse. Thus, a lawyer could not properly seek to rescind on behalf of a new client a contract drafted on behalf of the former client. So also a lawyer who has prosecuted an accused person could not properly represent the accused in a subsequent civil action against the government concerning the same transaction.

[2] The scope of a "matter" for purposes of this Rule may depend on the facts of a particular situation or transaction. The lawyer's involvement in a matter can also be a ques-

tion of degree. When a lawyer has been directly involved in a specific transaction, subsequent representation of other clients with materially adverse interests clearly is prohibited. On the other hand, a lawyer who recurrently handled a type of problem for a former client is not precluded from later representing another client in a wholly distinct problem of that type even though the subsequent representation involves a position adverse to the prior client. Similar considerations can apply to the reassignment of military lawyers between defense and prosecution functions within the same military jurisdiction. The underlying question is whether the lawyer was so involved in the matter that the subsequent representation can be justly regarded as a changing of sides in the matter in question.

Lawyers Moving Between Firms

[3] When lawyers have been associated within a firm but then end their association, the question of whether a lawyer should undertake representation is more complicated. There are several competing considerations. First, the client previously represented by the former firm must be reasonably assured that the principle of loyalty to the client is not compromised. Second, the rule should not be so broadly cast as to preclude other persons from having reasonable choice of legal counsel. Third, the rule should not unreasonably hamper lawyers from forming new associations and taking on new clients after having left a previous association. In this connection, it should be recognized that today many lawyers practice in firms, that many lawyers to some degree limit their practice to one field or another, and that many move from one association to another several times in their careers. If the concept of imputation were applied with unqualified rigor, the result would be radical curtailment of the opportunity of lawyers to move from one practice setting to another and of the opportunity of clients to change counsel.

[4] Reconciliation of these competing principles in the past has been attempted under two rubrics. One approach has been to seek per se rules of disqualification. For example, it has been held that a partner in a law firm is conclusively presumed to have access to all confidences concerning all clients of the firm. Under this analysis, if a lawyer has been a partner in one law firm and then becomes a partner in another law firm, there may be a presumption that all confidences known by the partner in the first firm are known to all partners in the second firm. This presumption might properly be applied in some circumstances, especially where the client has been extensively represented, but may be unrealistic where the client was represented only for limited purposes. Furthermore, such a rigid rule exaggerates the difference between a partner and an associate in modern law firms.

[5] The other rubric formerly used for dealing with disqualification is the appearance of impropriety proscribed in Canon 9 of the ABA Model Code of Professional Responsibility. This rubric has a two-fold problem. First, the appearance of impropriety can be taken to include any new client-lawyer relationship that might make a former client feel anxious. If that meaning were adopted, disqualification would become little more than a question of subjective judgment by the former client. Second, since "impropriety" is undefined, the term "appearance of impropriety" is question-begging. It therefore has to be recognized that the problem of disqualification cannot be properly resolved either by simple analogy to a lawyer practicing alone or by the very general concept of appearance of impropriety.

Confidentiality

[6] Preserving confidentiality is a question of access to information. Access to information, in turn, is essentially a question of fact in particular circumstances, aided by infer-

ences, deductions or working presumptions that reasonably may be made about the way in which lawyers work together. A lawyer may have general access to files of all clients of a law firm and may regularly participate in discussions of their affairs; it should be inferred that such a lawyer in fact is privy to all information about all the firm's clients. In contrast, another lawyer may have access to the files of only a limited number of clients and participate in discussions of the affairs of no other clients; in the absence of information to the contrary, it should be inferred that such a lawyer in fact is privy to information about the clients actually served but not those of other clients.

[7] Application of paragraph (b) depends on a situation's particular facts. In such an inquiry, the burden of proof should rest upon the firm whose disqualification is sought.

[8] Paragraph (b) operates to disqualify the lawyer only when the lawyer involved has actual knowledge of information protected by Rules 1.6 and 1.9(b). Thus, if a lawyer while with one firm acquired no knowledge or information relating to a particular client of the firm, and that lawyer later joined another firm, neither the lawyer individually nor the second firm is disqualified from representing another client in the same or a related matter even though the interests of the two clients conflict. See Rule 1.10(b) for the restrictions on a firm once a lawyer has terminated association with the firm.

[9] Independent of the question of disqualification of a firm, a lawyer changing professional association has a continuing duty to preserve confidentiality of information about a client formerly represented. See Rules 1.6 and 1.9.

Adverse Positions

[10] The second aspect of loyalty to a client is the lawyer's obligation to decline subsequent representations involving positions adverse to a former client arising in substantially related matters. This obligation requires abstention from adverse representation by the individual lawyer involved, but does not properly entail abstention of other lawyers through imputed disqualification. Hence, this aspect of the problem is governed by Rule 1.9(a). Thus, if a lawyer left one firm for another, the new affiliation would not preclude the firms involved from continuing to represent clients with adverse interests in the same or related matters, so long as the conditions of paragraphs (b) and (c) concerning confidentiality have been met.

[11] Information acquired by the lawyer in the course of representing a client may not subsequently be used or revealed by the lawyer to the disadvantage of the client or to the advantage of the lawyer or a third party. See Rule 1.8(b) and Comment 1A to that Rule. However, the fact that a lawyer has once served a client does not preclude the lawyer from using generally known information about that client when later representing another client.

[12] Disqualification from subsequent representation is for the protection of former clients and can be waived by them. A waiver is effective only if there is disclosure of the circumstances, including the lawyer's intended role in behalf of the new client.

[13] With regard to an opposing party's raising a question of conflict of interest, see Comment to Rule 1.7. With regard to disqualification of a firm with which a lawyer is or was formerly associated, see Rule 1.10.

Corresponding ABA Model Rule. Identical to Model Rule 1.9 except for (c).

Corresponding Former Massachusetts Rule. DR 4-101 (B) and (C), DR 5-105; (c) no counterpart.

Cross-reference: See definition of "consultation" in Rule 9.1 (c).

RULE 1.10 IMPUTED DISQUALIFICATION: GENERAL RULE

(a) While lawyers are associated in a firm, none of them shall knowingly represent a client when any one of them practicing alone would be prohibited from doing so by Rule 1.7, 1.8(c), or 1.9. A lawyer employed by the Public Counsel Division of the Committee for Public Counsel Services and a lawyer assigned to represent clients by the Private Counsel Division of that Committee are not considered to be associated. Lawyers are not considered to be associated merely because they have each individually been assigned to represent clients by the Committee for Public Counsel Services through its Private Counsel Division.

(b) When a lawyer has terminated an association with a firm, the firm is not prohibited from thereafter representing a person with interests materially adverse to those of a client represented by the formerly associated lawyer and not currently represented by the firm, unless:

(1) the matter is the same or substantially related to that in which the formerly associated lawyer represented the client; and

(2) any lawyer remaining in the firm has information protected by Rules 1.6 and 1.9(c) that is material to the matter.

(c) A disqualification prescribed by this rule may be waived by the affected client under the conditions stated in Rule 1.7.

(d) When a lawyer becomes associated with a firm, the firm may not undertake to or continue to represent a person in a matter that the firm knows or reasonably should know is the same or substantially related to a matter in which the newly associated lawyer (the "personally disqualified lawyer"), or a firm with which that lawyer was associated, had previously represented a client whose interests are materially adverse to that person unless:

(1) the personally disqualified lawyer has no information protected by Rule 1.6 or Rule 1.9 that is material to the matter ("material information"); or

(2) the personally disqualified lawyer (i) had neither substantial involvement nor substantial material information relating to the matter and (ii) is screened from any participation in the matter in accordance with paragraph (e) of this Rule and is apportioned no part of the fee therefrom.

(e) For the purposes of paragraph (d) of this Rule and of Rules 1.11 and 1.12, a personally disqualified lawyer in a firm will be deemed to have been screened from any participation in a matter if:

(1) all material information which the personally disqualified lawyer has been isolated from the firm;

(2) the personally disqualified lawyer has been isolated from all contact with the client relating to the matter, and any witness for or against the client;

(3) the personally disqualified lawyer and the firm have been precluded from discussing the matter with each other;

(4) the former client of the personally disqualified lawyer or of the firm with which the personally disqualified lawyer was associated receives notice of the conflict and an affidavit of the personally disqualified lawyer and the firm describing the procedures being used effectively to screen the personally disqualified lawyer, and attesting that (i) the personally disqualified lawyer will not participate in the matter and will not discuss the matter or the representation with any other lawyer or employee

of his or her current firm, (ii) no material information was transmitted by the personally disqualified lawyer before implementation of the screening procedures and notice to the former client; and (iii) during the period of the lawyer's personal disqualification those lawyers or employees who do participate in the matter will be apprised that the personally disqualified lawyer is screened from participating in or discussing the matter; and

(5) the personally disqualified lawyer and the firm with which he is associated reasonably believe that the steps taken to accomplish the screening of material information are likely to be effective in preventing material information from being disclosed to the firm and its client.

In any matter in which the former client and the person being represented by the firm with which the personally disqualified lawyer is associated are not before a tribunal, the firm, the personally disqualified lawyer, or the former client may seek judicial review in a court of general jurisdiction of the screening procedures used, or may seek court supervision to ensure that implementation of the screening procedures has occurred and that effective actual compliance has been achieved.

Comment

Definition of "Firm"

[1] For purposes of the Rules of Professional Conduct, the term "firm" includes lawyers in a private firm, and lawyers in the legal department of a corporation or other organization, or in a legal services organization. Whether two or more lawyers constitute a firm within this definition can depend on the specific facts. For example, two practitioners who share office space and occasionally consult or assist each other ordinarily would not be regarded as constituting a firm. However, if they present themselves to the public in a way suggesting that they are a firm or conduct themselves as a firm, they should be regarded as a firm for the purposes of the Rules. The terms of any formal agreement between associated lawyers are relevant in determining whether they are a firm, as is the fact that they have mutual access to information concerning the clients they serve. Furthermore, it is relevant in doubtful cases to consider the underlying purpose of the Rule that is involved. A group of lawyers could be regarded as a firm for purposes of the rule that the same lawyer should not represent opposing parties in litigation, while it might not be so regarded for purposes of the rule that information acquired by one lawyer is attributed to the other.

[2] With respect to the law department of an organization, there is ordinarily no question that the members of the department constitute a firm within the meaning of the Rules of Professional Conduct. However, there can be uncertainty as to the identity of the client. For example, it may not be clear whether the law department of a corporation represents a subsidiary or an affiliated corporation, as well as the corporation by which the members of the department are directly employed. A similar question can arise concerning an unincorporated association and its local affiliates.

[3] Similar questions can also arise with respect to lawyers in legal aid. Lawyers employed in the same unit of a legal service organization constitute a firm, but not necessarily those employed in separate units. As in the case of independent practitioners, whether the lawyers should be treated as associated with each other can depend on the particular rule that is involved, and on the specific facts of the situation.

[4] Where a lawyer has joined a private firm after having represented the government, the situation is governed by Rule 1.11 (a) and (b); where a lawyer represents the government after having served private clients, the situation is governed by Rule 1.11(c)(1).

The individual lawyer involved is bound by the Rules generally, including Rules 1.6, 1.7 and 1.9.

[5] Reserved.

Principles of Imputed Disqualification

[6] The rule of imputed disqualification stated in paragraph (a) gives effect to the principle of loyalty to the client as it applies to lawyers who practice in a law firm. Such situations can be considered from the premise that a firm of lawyers is essentially one lawyer for purposes of the rules governing loyalty to the client, or from the premise that each lawyer is vicariously bound by the obligation of loyalty owed by each lawyer with whom the lawyer is associated. Paragraph (a) operates only among the lawyers currently associated in a firm. When a lawyer moves from one firm to another, the situation is governed by Rules 1.9(b) and 1.10(b), (d) and (e).

[7] Rule 1.10(b) operates to permit a law firm, under certain circumstances, to represent a person with interests directly adverse to those of a client represented by a lawyer who formerly was associated with the firm. The Rule applies regardless of when the formerly associated lawyer represented the client. However, the law firm may not represent a person with interests adverse to those of a present client of the firm, which would violate Rule 1.7. Moreover, the firm may not represent the person where the matter is the same or substantially related to that in which the formerly associated lawyer represented the client and any other lawyer currently in the firm has material information protected by Rules 1.6 and 1.9(c).

[8] Paragraphs (d) and (e) of Rule 1.10 are new. They apply when a lawyer moves from a private firm to another firm and are intended to create procedures similar in some cases to those under Rule 1.11(b) for lawyers moving from a government agency to a private firm. Paragraphs (d) and (e) of Rule 1.10, unlike the provisions of Rule 1.11, do not permit a firm, without the consent of the former client of the disqualified lawyer or of the disqualified lawyer's firm, to handle a matter with respect to which the disqualified lawyer was personally and substantially involved, or had substantial material information, as noted in Comment 11 below. Like Rule 1.11, however, Rule 1.10(d) can only apply if the lawyer no longer represents the client of the former firm after the lawyer arrives at the lawyer's new firm.

[9] If the lawyer has no confidential information about the representation of the former client, the new firm is not disqualified and no screening procedures are required. This would ordinarily be the case if the lawyer did no work on the matter and the matter was not the subject of discussion with the lawyer generally, for example at firm or working group meetings. The lawyer must search his or her files and recollections carefully to determine whether he or she has confidential information. The fact that the lawyer does not immediately remember any details of the former client's representation does not mean that he or she does not in fact possess confidential information material to the matter.

[10] If the lawyer does have material information about the representation of the client of his former firm, the firm with which he or she is associated may represent a client with interests adverse to the former client of the newly associated lawyer only if the personally disqualified lawyer had no substantial involvement with the matter or substantial material information about the matter, the personally disqualified lawyer is apportioned no part of the fee, and all of the screening procedures are followed, including the requirement that the personally disqualified lawyer and the new firm reasonably believe that the screening procedures will be effective. For example, in a very small firm, it may

be difficult to keep information screened. On the other hand, screening procedures are more likely to be successful if the personally disqualified lawyer practices in a different office of the firm from those handling the matter from which the personally disqualified lawyer is screened.

[11] In situations where the personally disqualified lawyer was substantially involved in a matter, or had substantial material information, the new firm will generally only be allowed to handle the matter if the former client of the personally disqualified lawyer or of the law firm consents and the firm reasonably believes that the representation will not be adversely affected, all as required by Rule 1.7. This differs from the provisions of Rule 1.11, in that Rule 1.11(a) permits a firm to handle a matter against a government agency, without the consent of the agency, with respect to which one of its associated lawyers was personally and substantially involved for that agency, provided that the procedures of Rule 1.11(a)(1) and (2) are followed. Likewise, Rule 1.11(b) permits a firm to handle a matter against a government agency, without the consent of the agency, with respect to which one of its associated lawyers had substantial material information even if that lawyer was not personally and substantially involved for that agency, provided that the lawyer is screened and not apportioned any part of the fee.

[12] The former client is entitled to review of the screening procedures if the former client believes that the procedures will not be or have not been effective. If the matter involves litigation, the court before which the litigation is pending would be able to decide motions to disqualify or to enter appropriate orders relating to the screening, taking cognizance of whether the former client is seeking the disqualification of the firm upon a reasonable basis or without a reasonable basis for tactical advantage or otherwise. If the matter does not involve litigation, the former client can seek judicial review of the screening procedures from a trial court.

Corresponding ABA Model Rule. (a) similar to Model Rule 1.10 (a) and last two sentences added; (b) and (c) identical to Model Rule 1.10(b) and (c); (d) & (e) new.

Corresponding Former Massachusetts Rule. See DR 5-105 (D) for last two sentences in (a); (b)–(e) no counterpart.

RULE 1.11 SUCCESSIVE GOVERNMENT AND PRIVATE EMPLOYMENT

(a) Except as law may otherwise expressly permit, a lawyer shall not represent a private client in connection with a matter in which the lawyer participated personally and substantially as a public officer or employee, unless the appropriate government agency consents after consultation. No lawyer in a firm with which that lawyer is associated may knowingly undertake or continue representation in such a matter unless:

> (1) the disqualified lawyer is screened from any participation in the matter and is apportioned no part of the fee therefrom; and

> (2) written notice is promptly given to the appropriate government agency to enable it to ascertain compliance with the provisions of this rule.

(b) Except as law may otherwise expressly permit, a lawyer having information that the lawyer knows is confidential government information about a person acquired when the lawyer was a public officer or employee, may not represent a private client whose interests are adverse to that person in a matter in which the information could be used to the material disadvantage of that person. A firm with which that lawyer is associated may undertake or continue representation in the matter only if the disqualified lawyer is screened from any participation in the matter and is apportioned no part of the fee therefrom.

(c) Except as law may otherwise expressly permit, a lawyer serving as a public officer or employee shall not:

(1) participate in a matter in which the lawyer participated personally and substantially while in private practice or nongovernmental employment, unless under applicable law no one is, or by lawful delegation may be, authorized to act in the lawyer's stead in the matter; or

(2) negotiate for private employment with any person who is involved as a party or as lawyer for a party in a matter in which the lawyer is participating personally and substantially, except that a lawyer serving as a law clerk to a judge, other adjudicative officer, arbitrator, or mediator may negotiate for private employment as permitted by Rule 1.12(b) and subject to the conditions stated in Rule 1.12(b).

(d) As used in this rule, the term "matter" includes:

(1) any judicial or other proceeding, application, request for a ruling or other determination, contract, claim, controversy, investigation, charge, accusation, arrest, or other particular matter involving a specific party or parties, and

(2) any other matter covered by the conflict of interest rules of the appropriate government agency.

(e) As used in this rule, the term "confidential government information" means information which has been obtained under governmental authority and which, at the time this rule is applied, the government is prohibited by law from disclosing to the public or has a legal privilege not to disclose, and which is not otherwise available to the public.

Comment

[1] This Rule prevents a lawyer from exploiting public office for the advantage of a private client. It is a counterpart of Rule 1.10(b), which applies to lawyers moving from one firm to another.

[2] A lawyer representing a government agency, whether employed or specially retained by the government, is subject to the Rules of Professional Conduct, including the prohibition against representing adverse interests stated in Rule 1.7 and the protections afforded former clients in Rule 1.9. See Comment 8 to Rule 1.7. In addition, such a lawyer is subject to Rule 1.11 and to statutes and government regulations regarding conflict of interest. Such statutes and regulations may circumscribe the extent to which the government agency may give consent under this Rule.

[3] Where the successive clients are a public agency and a private client, the risk exists that power or discretion vested in public authority might be used for the special benefit of a private client. A lawyer should not be in a position where benefit to a private client might affect performance of the lawyer's professional functions on behalf of public authority. Also, unfair advantage could accrue to the private client by reason of access to confidential government information about the client's adversary obtainable only through the lawyer's government service. However, the rules governing lawyers presently or formerly employed by a government agency should not be so restrictive as to inhibit transfer of employment to and from the government. The government has a legitimate need to attract qualified lawyers as well as to maintain high ethical standards. The provisions for screening and waiver are necessary to prevent the disqualification rule from imposing too severe a deterrent against entering public service.

[4] When the client is an agency of one government, that agency should be treated as a private client for purposes of this Rule if the lawyer thereafter represents an agency of

another government, as when a lawyer represents a city and subsequently is employed by a federal agency.

[5] Paragraphs (a)(1) and (b) do not prohibit a lawyer from receiving a salary or partnership share established by prior independent agreement. They prohibit directly relating the lawyer's compensation to the fee in the matter in which the lawyer is disqualified.

[6] Paragraph (a)(2) does not require that a lawyer give notice to the government agency at a time when premature disclosure would injure the client; a requirement for premature disclosure might preclude engagement of the lawyer. Such notice is, however, required to be given as soon as practicable in order that the government agency will have a reasonable opportunity to ascertain that the lawyer is complying with Rule 1.11 and to take appropriate action if it believes the lawyer is not complying.

[7] Paragraph (b) operates only when the lawyer in question has knowledge of the information, which means actual knowledge; it does not operate with respect to information that merely could be imputed to the lawyer.

[8] Paragraphs (a) and (c) do not prohibit a lawyer from jointly representing a private party and a government agency when doing so is permitted by Rule 1.7 and is not otherwise prohibited by law.

[9] Paragraph (c) does not disqualify other lawyers in the agency with which the lawyer in question has become associated.

Corresponding ABA Model Rule. Similar to Model Rule 1.11.

Corresponding Former Massachusetts Rule. (b) and (e) no counterpart; DR 9-101 (B).

Cross-reference: See definition of "person" in Rule 9.1(h).

RULE 1.12 FORMER JUDGE OR ARBITRATOR

(a) Except as stated in paragraph (d), a lawyer shall not represent anyone in connection with a matter in which the lawyer participated personally and substantially as a judge or other adjudicative officer, arbitrator, mediator, or law clerk to such a person, unless all parties to the proceeding consent after consultation.

(b) A lawyer shall not negotiate for employment with any person who is involved as a party or as lawyer for a party in a matter in which the lawyer is participating personally and substantially as a judge or other adjudicative officer, arbitrator, or mediator. A lawyer serving as a law clerk to a judge, other adjudicative officer, arbitrator or mediator may negotiate for employment with a party or lawyer involved in a matter in which the clerk is participating personally and substantially, but only after the lawyer has notified the judge, other adjudicative officer, arbitrator, or mediator.

(c) If a lawyer is disqualified by paragraph (a), no lawyer in a firm with which that lawyer is associated may knowingly undertake or continue representation in the matter unless:

(1) the disqualified lawyer is screened from any participation in the matter and is apportioned no part of the fee therefrom; and

(2) written notice is promptly given to the appropriate tribunal to enable it to ascertain compliance with the provisions of this rule.

(d) An arbitrator selected as a partisan of a party in a multimember arbitration panel is not prohibited from subsequently representing that party.

Comment

[1] This Rule generally parallels Rule 1.11. The term "personally and substantially" signifies that a judge who was a member of a multimember court, and thereafter left judicial office to practice law, is not prohibited by these Rules from representing a client in a matter pending in the court, but in which the former judge did not participate. So also the fact that a former judge exercised administrative responsibility in a court does not prevent the former judge from acting as a lawyer in a matter where the judge had previously exercised remote or incidental administrative responsibility that did not affect the merits. Compare the Comment to Rule 1.11. The lawyer should also consider applicable statutes and regulations, e.g. M.G.L. Ch. 268A. The term "adjudicative officer" includes such officials as magistrates, referees, special masters, hearing officers and other parajudicial officers. Canon 8A(2) of the Code of Judicial Conduct (S.J.C. Rule 3:09) provides that a retired judge recalled to active service "should not enter an appearance nor accept an appointment to represent any party in any court of the Commonwealth for a period of six months following the date of retirement, resignation or most recent service as a retired judge pursuant to G.L. c. 32, §§ 65E–65G."

[2] Law clerks who serve before they are admitted to the bar are subject to the limitations stated in Rule 1.12 (b).

Corresponding ABA Model Rule. Similar to Model Rule 1.12.

Corresponding Former Massachusetts Rule. See DR 9-101 (A).

Cross-reference: See definition of "consultation" in Rule 9.1 (c).

RULE 1.13 ORGANIZATION AS CLIENT

(a) A lawyer employed or retained by an organization represents the organization acting through its duly authorized constituents.

(b) If a lawyer for an organization knows that an officer, employee, or other person associated with the organization is engaged in action, intends to act or refuses to act in a matter related to the representation that is a violation of a legal obligation to the organization, or a violation of law that reasonably might be imputed to the organization, and that is likely to result in substantial injury to the organization, then the lawyer shall proceed as is reasonably necessary in the best interest of the organization. Unless the lawyer reasonably believes that it is not necessary in the best interest of the organization to do so, the lawyer shall refer the matter to higher authority in the organization, including, if warranted by the circumstances, to the highest authority that can act on behalf of the organization as determined by applicable law.

(c) Except as provided in paragraph (d), if

(1) despite the lawyer's efforts in accordance with paragraph (b) the highest authority that can act on behalf of the organization insists upon or fails to address in a timely and appropriate manner an action, or a refusal to act, that is clearly a violation of law and

(2) the lawyer reasonably believes that the violation is reasonably certain to result in substantial injury to the organization, then the lawyer may reveal information relating to the representation whether or not Rule 1.6 permits such disclosure, but only if and to the extent the lawyer reasonably believes necessary to prevent substantial injury to the organization.

(d) Paragraph (c) shall not apply with respect to information relating to a lawyer's representation of an organization to investigate an alleged violation of law, or to defend the organization or an officer, employee or other constituent associated with the organization against a claim arising out of an alleged violation of law.

(e) A lawyer who reasonably believes that he or she has been discharged because of the lawyer's actions taken pursuant to paragraphs (b) or (c), or who withdraws under circumstances that require or permit the lawyer to take action under either of those paragraphs, shall proceed as the lawyer reasonably believes necessary to assure that the organization's highest authority is informed of the lawyer's discharge or withdrawal.

(f) In dealing with an organization's directors, officers, employees, members, shareholders, or other constituents, a lawyer shall explain the identity of the client when the lawyer knows or reasonably should know that the organization's interests are adverse to those of the constituents with whom the lawyer is dealing.

(g) A lawyer representing an organization may also represent any of its directors, officers, employees, members, shareholders, or other constituents, subject to the provisions of Rule 1.7. If the organization's consent to the dual representation is required by Rule 1.7, the consent shall be given by an appropriate official of the organization other than the individual who is to be represented, or by the shareholders.

Comment

The Entity as the Client

[1] An organizational client is a legal entity, but it cannot act except through its officers, directors, employees, shareholders and other constituents. Officers, directors, employees and shareholders are the constituents of the corporate organizational client. The duties defined in this Comment apply equally to unincorporated associations. "Other constituents" as used in this Comment means the positions equivalent to officers, directors, employees and shareholders held by persons acting for organizational clients that are not corporations.

[2] When one of the constituents of an organizational client communicates with the organization's lawyer in that person's organizational capacity, the communication is protected by Rule 1.6. Thus, by way of example, if an organizational client requests its lawyer to investigate allegations of wrongdoing, interviews made in the course of that investigation between the lawyer and the client's employees or other constituents are covered by Rule 1.6. This does not mean, however, that constituents of an organizational client are the clients of the lawyer. The lawyer may not disclose to such constituents information relating to the representation except for disclosures explicitly or impliedly authorized by the organizational client in order to carry out the representation or as otherwise permitted by Rule 1.6.

[3] When constituents of the organization make decisions for it, the decisions ordinarily must be accepted by the lawyer even if their utility or prudence is doubtful. Decisions concerning policy and operations, including ones entailing serious risk, are not as such in the lawyer's province. Paragraph (b) makes clear, however, that when the lawyer knows that the organization is likely to be substantially injured by action of an officer or other constituent that violates a legal obligation to the organization or is in violation of law that might be imputed to the organization, the lawyer must proceed as is reasonably necessary in the best interest of the organization. As defined in Rule 9.1(f), knowledge can be inferred from circumstances, and a lawyer cannot ignore the obvious.

[4] In determining how to proceed under paragraph (b), the lawyer should give due consideration to the seriousness of the violation and its consequences, the responsibility in the organization and the apparent motivation of the person involved, the policies of

the organization concerning such matters, and any other relevant considerations. Ordinarily, referral to a higher authority would be necessary. In some circumstances, however, it may be appropriate for the lawyer to ask the constituent to reconsider the matter; for example, if the circumstances involve a constituent's innocent misunderstanding of law and subsequent acceptance of the lawyer's advice, the lawyer may reasonably conclude that the best interest of the organization does not require that the matter be referred to higher authority. If a constituent persists in conduct contrary to the lawyer's advice, it will be necessary for the lawyer to take steps to have the matter reviewed by a higher authority in the organization. If the matter is of sufficient seriousness and importance or urgency to the organization, referral to higher authority in the organization may be necessary even if the lawyer has not communicated with the constituent. Any measures taken should, to the extent practicable, minimize the risk of revealing information relating to the representation to persons outside the organization. Even in circumstances where a lawyer is not obligated by Rule 1.13 to proceed, a lawyer may bring to the attention of an organizational client, including its highest authority, matters that the lawyer reasonably believes to be of sufficient importance to warrant doing so in the best interest of the organization.

[5] Paragraph (b) also makes clear that when it is reasonably necessary to enable the organization to address the matter in a timely and appropriate manner, the lawyer must refer the matter to higher authority, including, if warranted by the circumstances, the highest authority that can act on behalf of the organization under applicable law. The organization's highest authority to whom a matter may be referred ordinarily will be the board of directors or similar governing body. However, applicable law may prescribe that under certain conditions the highest authority reposes elsewhere, for example, in the independent directors of a corporation.

Relation to Other Rules

[6] The authority and responsibility provided in this Rule are concurrent with the authority and responsibility provided in other Rules. In particular, this Rule does not limit or expand the lawyer's responsibility under Rules 1.8, 1.16, 3.3, 4.1, or 8.3. Moreover, the lawyer may be subject to disclosure obligations imposed by law or court order as contemplated by Rule 1.6(b)(4). Paragraph (c) of this Rule supplements Rule 1.6(b) by providing an additional basis upon which the lawyer may reveal information relating to the representation, but does not modify, restrict, or limit the provisions of Rule 1.6(b)(1)–(4). Under paragraph (c) the lawyer may reveal such information only when the organization's highest authority insists upon or fails to address threatened or ongoing action that is clearly a violation of law, and then only to the extent the lawyer reasonably believes necessary to prevent reasonably certain substantial injury to the organization. It is not necessary that the lawyer's services be used in furtherance of the violation, but it is required that the matter be related to the lawyer's representation of the organization. If the lawyer's services are being used by an organization to further a crime or fraud by the organization, Rule 1.6(b)(1) may permit the lawyer to disclose confidential information. In such circumstances Rule 1.2(d) may also be applicable, in which event, withdrawal from the representation under Rule 1.16(a)(1) may be required.

[7] Paragraph (d) makes clear that the authority of a lawyer to disclose information relating to a representation in circumstances described in paragraph (c) does not apply with respect to information relating to a lawyer's engagement by an organization to investigate an alleged violation of law or to defend the organization or an officer, employee or other person associated with the organization against a claim arising out of an

alleged violation of law. This is necessary in order to enable organizational clients to enjoy the full benefits of legal counsel in conducting an investigation or defending against a claim.

[8] A lawyer who reasonably believes that he or she has been discharged because of the lawyer's actions taken pursuant to paragraph (b) or (c), or who withdraws in circumstances that require or permit the lawyer to take action under either of these paragraphs, must proceed as the lawyer reasonably believes necessary to assure that the organization's highest authority is informed of the lawyer's discharge or withdrawal. Nothing in these rules prohibits the lawyer from disclosing what the lawyer reasonably believes to be the basis for his or her discharge or withdrawal.

Government Agency

[9] The duty defined in this Rule applies to governmental organizations. Defining precisely the identity of the client and prescribing the resulting obligations of such lawyers may be more difficult in the government context and is a matter beyond the scope of these Rules. See Scope [4]. Although in some circumstances the client may be a specific agency, it may also be a branch of government, such as the executive branch, or the government as a whole. For example, if the action or failure to act involves the head of a bureau, either the department of which the bureau is a part or the relevant branch of government may be the client for purposes of this Rule. Moreover, in a matter involving the conduct of government officials, a government lawyer may have authority under applicable law to question such conduct more extensively than that of a lawyer for a private organization in similar circumstances. Thus, when the client is a governmental organization, a different balance may be appropriate between maintaining confidentiality and assuring that the wrongful act is prevented or rectified, for public business is involved. In addition, duties of lawyers employed by the government or lawyers in military service may be defined by statutes and regulation. This Rule does not limit that authority. See Scope.

Clarifying the Lawyer's Role

[10] There are times when the organization's interest may be or become adverse to those of one or more of its constituents. In such circumstances the lawyer should advise any constituent, whose interest the lawyer finds adverse to that of the organization of the conflict or potential conflict of interest, that the lawyer cannot represent such constituent, and that such person may wish to obtain independent representation. Care must be taken to assure that the individual understands that, when there is such adversity of interest, the lawyer for the organization cannot provide legal representation for that constituent individual, and that discussions between the lawyer for the organization and the individual may not be privileged.

[11] Whether such a warning should be given by the lawyer for the organization to any constituent individual may turn on the facts of each case.

Dual Representation

[12] Paragraph (g) recognizes that a lawyer for an organization may also represent a principal officer or major shareholder.

Derivative Actions

[13] Under generally prevailing law, the shareholders or members of a corporation may bring suit to compel the directors to perform their legal obligations in the supervision of the organization. Members of unincorporated associations have essentially the same

right. Such an action may be brought nominally by the organization, but usually is, in fact, a legal controversy over management of the organization.

[14] The question can arise whether counsel for the organization may defend such an action. The proposition that the organization is the lawyer's client does not alone re-solve the issue. Most derivative actions are a normal incident of an organization's affairs, to be defended by the organization's lawyer like any other suit. However, if the claim in-volves serious charges of wrongdoing by those in control of the organization, a conflict may arise between the lawyer's duty to the organization and the lawyer's relationship with the board. In those circumstances, Rule 1.7 governs who should represent the di-rectors and the organization.

Corresponding ABA Model Rule. Identical to Model Rule 1.13.

Corresponding Former Massachusetts Rule. No counterpart.

RULE 1.14 CLIENT WITH DIMINISHED CAPACITY

(a) When a client's capacity to make adequately considered decisions in connection with a representation is diminished, whether because of minority, mental impairment or for some other reason, the lawyer shall, as far as reasonably possible, maintain a normal client lawyer relationship with the client.

(b) When the lawyer reasonably believes that the client has diminished capacity that prevents the client from making an adequately considered decision regarding a specific issue that is part of the representation, is at risk of substantial physical, financial or other harm unless action is taken, and cannot adequately act in the client's own interest, the lawyer may take reasonably necessary protective action in connection with the rep-resentation, including consulting with individuals or entities that have the ability to take action to protect the client and, in appropriate cases, seeking the appointment of a guardian ad litem, conservator, or guardian.

(c) Information relating to the representation of a client with diminished capacity is protected by Rule 1.6. When taking protective action pursuant to paragraph (b), the lawyer is impliedly authorized under Rule 1.6(a) to reveal information about the client, but only to the extent reasonably necessary to protect the client's interests.

Comment

[1] The normal client-lawyer relationship is based on the assumption that the client, when properly advised and assisted, is capable of making decisions about important matters. When the client has diminished capacity, however, maintaining the ordinary client-lawyer relationship may not be possible in all respects. In particular, a severely in-capacitated person may have no power to make legally binding decisions. Nevertheless, a client with diminished capacity often has the ability to understand, deliberate upon, and reach conclusions about matters affecting the client's own well-being. For example, children as young as five or six years of age, and certainly those of ten or twelve, are re-garded as having opinions that are entitled to weight in legal proceedings concerning their custody. So also, it is recognized that some persons of advanced age can be quite capable of handling routine financial matters while needing special legal protection concerning major transactions.

[2] The fact that a client has diminished capacity does not lessen the lawyer's obligation to treat the client with attention and respect. Even if the person has a legal representa-tive, the lawyer should as far as possible accord the represented person the status of client, particularly in maintaining communication.

[3] The client may wish to have family members or other persons participate in discussions with the lawyer. The lawyer may also consult family members even though they may be personally interested in the situation. Before the lawyer discloses confidential information of the client, the lawyer should consider whether it is likely that the person or entity to be consulted will act adversely to the client's interests. Decisions under Rule 1.14(b) whether and to what extent to consult or to disclose confidential information are matters of professional judgment on the lawyer's part.

[4] If a legal representative has already been appointed for the client, the lawyer should ordinarily look to the representative for decisions on behalf of the client. If the lawyer represents the guardian as distinct from the ward, and is aware that the guardian is acting adversely to the ward's interest, the lawyer may have an obligation to prevent or rectify the guardian's misconduct. See Rules 1.2(d), 1.6, 3.3 and 4.1.

Taking Protective Action

[5] If a lawyer reasonably believes that a client is at risk of substantial physical, financial or other harm unless action is taken, and that a normal client-lawyer relationship cannot be maintained as provided in paragraph (a) because the client lacks sufficient capacity to communicate or to make adequately considered decisions in connection with the representation, then paragraph (b) permits the lawyer to take protective measures deemed necessary. Such measures could include: consulting with family members, using a reconsideration period to permit clarification or improvement of circumstances, using voluntary surrogate decision-making tools such as durable powers of attorney or consulting with support groups, professional services, adult-protective agencies or other individuals or entities that have the ability to protect the client. In taking any protective action, the lawyer should be guided by such factors as the wishes and values of the client to the extent known, the client's best interests and the goals of intruding into the client's decision-making autonomy to the least extent feasible, maximizing client capacities and respecting the client's family and social connections.

[6] In determining whether a client has diminished capacity that prevents the client from making an adequately considered decision regarding a specific issue that is part of the representation, the lawyer should consider and balance such factors as: the client's ability to articulate reasoning leading to a decision, variability of state of mind and ability to appreciate consequences of a decision; the substantive fairness of a decision; and the consistency of a decision with the known long-term commitments and values of the client. In appropriate circumstances, the lawyer may seek guidance from an appropriate diagnostician.

[7] If a client is unable to make an adequately considered decision regarding an issue, and if achieving the client's expressed preferences would place the client at risk of a substantial harm, the attorney has four options. The attorney may:

    i.   advocate the client's expressed preferences regarding the issue;

    ii.   advocate the client's expressed preferences and request the appointment of a guardian ad litem or investigator to make an independent recommendation to the court;

    iii.   request the appointment of a guardian ad litem or next friend to direct counsel in the representation; or

    iv.   determine what the client's preferences would be if he or she were able to make an adequately considered decision regarding the issue and represent the client in accordance with that determination.

In the circumstances described in clause (iv) above where the matter is before a tribunal and the client has expressed a preference, the lawyer will ordinarily inform the tribunal of the client's expressed preferences. However, there are circumstances where options other than the option in clause (i) above will be impermissible under substantive law or otherwise inappropriate or unwarranted. Such circumstances arise in the representation of clients who are competent to stand trial in criminal, delinquency and youthful offender, civil commitment and similar matters.

Counsel should follow the client's expressed preference if it does not pose a risk of substantial harm to the client, even if the lawyer reasonably determines that the client has not made an adequately considered decision in the matter.

Disclosure of the Client's Condition

[8] Disclosure of the client's diminished capacity could adversely affect the client's interests. For example, raising the question of diminished capacity could, in some circumstances, lead to proceedings for involuntary commitment. Information relating to the representation is protected by Rule 1.6. Therefore, unless authorized to do so, the lawyer may not disclose such information. When taking protective action pursuant to paragraph (b), the lawyer is impliedly authorized to make the necessary disclosures, even when the client directs the lawyer to the contrary. Nevertheless, given the risks of disclosure, paragraph (c) limits what the lawyer may disclose in consulting with other individuals or entities or seeking the appointment of a legal representative. At the very least, the lawyer should determine whether it is likely that the person or entity consulted with will act adversely to the client's interests before discussing matters related to the client. The lawyer's position in such cases is an unavoidably difficult one.

Emergency Legal Assistance

[9] In an emergency where the health, safety or a financial interest of a person with seriously diminished capacity is threatened with imminent and irreparable harm, a lawyer may take legal action on behalf of such a person even though the person is unable to establish a client-lawyer relationship or to make or express considered judgments about the matter, when the person or another acting in good faith on that person's behalf has consulted with the lawyer. Even in such an emergency, however, the lawyer should not act unless the lawyer reasonably believes that the person has no other lawyer, agent or other representative available. The lawyer should take legal action on behalf of the person only to the extent reasonably necessary to maintain the status quo or otherwise avoid imminent and irreparable harm. A lawyer who undertakes to represent a person in such an exigent situation has the same duties under these Rules as the lawyer would with respect to a client.

[10] A lawyer who acts on behalf of a person with seriously diminished capacity in an emergency should keep the confidences of the person as if dealing with a client, disclosing them only to the extent necessary to accomplish the intended protective action. The lawyer should disclose to any tribunal involved and to any other counsel involved the nature of his or her relationship with the person. The lawyer should take steps to regularize the relationship or implement other protective solutions as soon as possible. Normally, a lawyer would not seek compensation for such emergency actions taken.

Corresponding ABA Model Rule. Identical to Model Rule 1.14(a) and (c); (b) different.

Corresponding Former Massachusetts Rule. No counterpart.

RULE 1.15 SAFEKEEPING PROPERTY

(a) Definitions:

(1) "Trust property" means property of clients or third persons that is in a lawyer's possession in connection with a representation and includes property held in any fiduciary capacity in connection with a representation, whether as trustee, agent, escrow agent, guardian, executor, or otherwise. Trust property does not include documents or other property received by a lawyer as investigatory material or potential evidence. Trust property in the form of funds is referred to as "trust funds."

(2) "Trust account" means an account in a financial institution in which trust funds are deposited. Trust accounts must conform to the requirements of this rule.

(b) Segregation of Trust Property. A lawyer shall hold trust property separate from the lawyer's own property.

(1) Trust funds shall be held in a trust account, except that advances for costs and expenses may be held in a business account.

(2) No funds belonging to the lawyer shall be deposited or retained in a trust account except that:

(i) Funds reasonably sufficient to pay bank charges may be deposited therein, and

(ii) Trust funds belonging in part to a client or third person and in part currently or potentially to the lawyer shall be deposited in a trust account, but the portion belonging to the lawyer must be withdrawn at the earliest reasonable time after the lawyer's interest in that portion becomes fixed. A lawyer who knows that the right of the lawyer or law firm to receive such portion is disputed shall not withdraw the funds until the dispute is resolved.If the right of the lawyer or law firm to receive such portion is disputed within a reasonable time after notice is given that the funds have been withdrawn, the disputed portion must be restored to a trust account until the dispute is resolved.

(3) Trust property other than funds shall be identified as such and appropriately safeguarded.

(c) Prompt Notice and Delivery of Trust Property to Client or Third Person. Upon receiving trust funds or other trust property in which a client or third person hasan interest, a lawyer shall promptly notify the client or third person. Except as stated in this rule or as otherwise permitted by law or by agreement with the client or third person on whose behalf a lawyer holds trust property, a lawyer shall promptly deliver to the client or third person any funds or other property that the client or third person is entitled to receive.

(d) Accounting.

(1) Upon final distribution of any trust property or upon request by the client or third person on whose behalf a lawyer holds trust property, the lawyer shall promptly render a full written accounting regarding such property.

(2) On or before the date on which a withdrawal from a trust account is made for the purpose of paying fees due to a lawyer, the lawyer shall deliver to the client in writing (i) an itemized bill or other accounting showing the services rendered, (ii) written notice of amount and date of the withdrawal, and (iii) a statement of the balance of the client's funds in the trust account after the withdrawal.

(e) Operational Requirements for Trust Accounts.

(1) All trust accounts shall be maintained in the state where the lawyer's office is situated, or elsewhere with the consent of the client or third person on whose behalf the trust property is held, except that all funds required by this rule to be deposited in an IOLTA account shall be maintained in this Commonwealth.

(2) Each trust account title shall include the words "trust account," "escrow account," "client funds account," "conveyancing account," "IOLTA account," or words of similar import indicating the fiduciary nature of the account. Lawyers maintaining trust accounts shall take all steps necessary to inform the depository institution of the purpose and identity of such accounts.

(3) No withdrawal from a trust account shall be made by a check which is not prenumbered. No withdrawal shall be made in cash or by automatic teller

machine or any similar method. No withdrawal shall be made by a check payable to "cash" or "bearer" or by any other method which does not identify the recipient of the funds.

(4) Every withdrawal from a trust account for the purpose of paying fees to a lawyer or reimbursing a lawyer for costs and expenses shall be payable to the lawyer or the lawyer's law firm.

(5) Each lawyer who has a law office in this Commonwealth and who holds trust funds shall deposit such funds, as appropriate, in one of two types of interest-bearing accounts: either (i) a pooled account ("IOLTA account") for all trust funds which in the judgment of the lawyer are nominal in amount, or are to be held for a short period of time, or (ii) for all other trust funds, an individual account with the interest payable as directed by the client or third person on whose behalf the trust property is held. The foregoing deposit requirements apply to funds received by lawyers in connection with real estate transactions and loan closings, provided, however, that a trust account in a lending bank in the name of a lawyer representing the lending bank and used exclusively for depositing and disbursing funds in connection with that particular bank's loan transactions, shall not be required but is permitted to be established as an IOLTA account. All IOLTA accounts shall be established in compliance with the provisions of paragraph (g) of this rule.

(6) Property held for no compensation as a custodian for a minor family member is not subject to the Operational Requirements for Trust Accounts set out in this paragraph (e) or to the Required Accounts and Records in paragraph (f) of this rule. As used in this subsection, "family member" refers to those individuals specified in section (e)(2) of rule 7.3.

(f) Required Accounts and Records: Every lawyer who is engaged in the practice of law in this Commonwealth and who holds trust property in connection with a representation shall maintain complete records of the receipt, maintenance, and disposition of that trust property, including all records required by this subsection.Records shall be preserved for a period of six years after termination of the representation and after distribution of the property. Records may be maintained by computer subject to the requirements of subparagraph 1G of this paragraph (f) or they may be prepared manually.

(1) **Trust Account Records.** The following books and records must be maintained for each trust account:

A. **Account Documentation.** A record of the name and address of the bank or other depository; account number; account title; opening and closing dates;

and the type of account, whether pooled, with net interest paid to the IOLTA Committee (IOLTA account), or account with interest paid to the client or third person on whose behalf the trust property is held (including master or umbrella accounts with individual subaccounts).

B. Check Register. A check register recording in chronological order the date and amount of all deposits; the date, check or transaction number, amount, and payee of all disbursements, whether by check, electronic transfer, or other means; the date and amount of every other credit or debit of whatever nature; the identity of the client matter for which funds were deposited or disbursed; and the current balance in the account.

C. Individual Client Records. A record for each client or third person for whom the lawyer received trust funds documenting each receipt and disbursement of the funds of the client or third person, the identity of the client matter for which funds were deposited or disbursed, and the balance held for the client or third person, including a subsidiary ledger or ledger for each client matter for which the lawyer receives trust funds documenting each receipt and disbursement of the funds of the client or third person with respect to such matter. A lawyer shall not disburse funds from the trust account that would create a negative balance with respect to any individual client.

D. Bank Fees and Charges. A ledger or other record for funds of the lawyer deposited in the trust account pursuant to paragraph (b)(2)(i) of this rule to accommodate reasonably expected bank charges. This ledger shall document each deposit and expenditure of the lawyer's funds in the account and the balance remaining.

E. Reconciliation Reports. For each trust account, the lawyer shall prepare and retain a reconciliation report on a regular and periodic basis but in any event no less frequently than every sixty days. Each reconciliation report shall show the following balances and verify that they are identical:

(i) The balance which appears in the check register as of the reporting date.

(ii) The adjusted bank statement balance, determined by adding outstanding deposits and other credits to the bank statement balance and subtracting outstanding checks and other debits from the bank statement balance.

(iii) For any account in which funds are held for more than one client matter, the total of all client matter balances, determined by listing each of the individual client matter records and the balance which appears in each record as of the reporting date, and calculating the total. For the purpose of the calculation required by this paragraph, bank fees and charges shall be considered an individual client record. No balance for an individual client may be negative at any time.

F. Account Documentation. For each trust account, the lawyer shall retain contemporaneous records of transactions as necessary to document the transactions. The lawyer must retain:

(i) bank statements.

(ii) all transaction records returned by the bank, including canceled checks and records of electronic transactions.

(iii) records of deposits separately listing each deposited item and the client or third person for whom the deposit is being made.

G. Electronic Record Retention. A lawyer who maintains a trust account record by computer must maintain the check register, client ledgers, and reconciliation reports in a form that can be reproduced in printed hard copy. Electronic records must be regularly backed up by an appropriate storage device.

(2) Business Accounts. Each lawyer who receives trust funds must maintain at least one bank account, other than the trust account, for funds received and disbursed other than in the lawyer's fiduciary capacity.

(3) Trust Property Other than Funds. A lawyer who receives trust property other than funds must maintain a record showing the identity, location, and disposition of all such property.

(g) Interest on Lawyers' Trust Accounts.

(1) The IOLTA account shall be established with any bank, savings and loan association, or credit union authorized by Federal or State law to do business in Massachusetts and insured by the Federal Deposit Insurance Corporation or similar State insurance programs for State-chartered institutions. At the direction of the lawyer, funds in the IOLTA account in excess of $100,000 may be temporarily reinvested in repurchase agreements fully collateralized by U.S. Government obligations. Funds in the IOLTA account shall be subject to withdrawal upon request and without delay.

(2) Lawyers creating and maintaining an IOLTA account shall direct the depository institution:

(i) to remit interest or dividends, net of any service charges or fees, on the average monthly balance in the account, or as otherwise computed in accordance with an institution's standard accounting practice, at least quarterly, to the IOLTA Committee;

(ii) to transmit with each remittance to the IOLTA Committee a statement showing the name of the lawyer who or law firm which deposited the funds; and

(iii) at the same time to transmit to the depositing lawyer a report showing the amount paid, the rate of interest applied, and the method by which the interest was computed.

(3) Lawyers shall certify their compliance with this rule as required by S.J.C. Rule 4:02, subsection (2).

(4) This court shall appoint members of a permanent IOLTA Committee to fixed terms on a staggered basis. The representatives appointed to the committee shall oversee the operation of a comprehensive IOLTA program, including:

(i) the receipt of all IOLTA funds and their disbursement, net of actual expenses, to the designated charitable entities, as follows: sixty-seven percent(67%) to the Massachusetts Legal Assistance Corporation and the remaining thirty-three percent (33%) to other designated charitable entities in such proportions as the Supreme Judicial Court may order;

(ii) the education of lawyers as to their obligation to create and maintain IOLTA accounts under Rule 1.15(h);

(iii) the encouragement of the banking community and the public to support the IOLTA program;

(iv) the obtaining of tax rulings and other administrative approval for a comprehensive IOLTA program as appropriate;

(v) the preparation of such guidelines and rules, subject to court approval, as may be deemed necessary or advisable for the operation of a comprehensive IOLTA program;

(vi) establishment of standards for reserve accounts by the recipient charitable entities for the deposit of IOLTA funds which the charitable entity intends to preserve for future use; and

(vii) reporting to the court in such manner as the court may direct.

(5) The Massachusetts Legal Assistance Corporation and other designated charitable entities shall receive IOLTA funds from the IOLTA Committee and distribute such funds for approved purposes. The Massachusetts Legal Assistance Corporation may use IOLTA funds to further its corporate purpose and other designated charitable entities may use IOLTA funds either for (a) improving the administration of justice or (b) delivering civil legal services to those who cannot afford them.

(6) The Massachusetts Legal Assistance Corporation and other designated charitable entities shall submit an annual report to the court describing their IOLTA activities for the year and providing a statement of the application of IOLTA funds received pursuant to this rule.

(h) Dishonored Check Notification.

All trust accounts shall be established in compliance with the following provisions on dishonored check notification:

(1) A lawyer shall maintain trust accounts only in financial institutions which have filed with the Board of Bar Overseers an agreement, in a form provided by the Board, to report to the Board in the event any properly payable instrument is presented against any trust account that contains insufficient funds, and the financial institution dishonors the instrument for that reason.

(2) Any such agreement shall apply to all branches of the financial institution and shall not be cancelled except upon thirty days notice in writing to the Board.

(3) The Board shall publish annually a list of financial institutions which have signed agreements to comply with this rule, and shall establish rules and procedures governing amendments to the list.

(4) The dishonored check notification agreement shall provide that all reports made by the financial institution shall be identical to the notice of dishonor customarily forwarded to the depositor, and should include a copy of the dishonored instrument, if such a copy is normally provided to depositors. Such reports shall be made simultaneously with the notice of dishonor and within the time provided by law for such notice, if any.

(5) Every lawyer practicing or admitted to practice in this Commonwealth shall, as a condition thereof, be conclusively deemed to have consented to the reporting and production requirements mandated by this rule.

(6) The following definitions shall be applicable to this subparagraph:

(i) "Financial institution" includes (a) any bank, savings and loan association, credit union, or savings bank, and (b) with the written consent of the client or third person on whose behalf the trust property is held, any other business or person which accepts for deposit funds held in trust by lawyers.

(ii) "Notice of dishonor" refers to the notice which a financial institution is required to give, under the laws of this Commonwealth, upon presentation of an instrument which the institution dishonors.

(iii) "Properly payable" refers to an instrument which, if presented in the normal course of business, is in a form requiring payment under the laws of this Commonwealth.

Comment

[1] A lawyer should hold property of others with the care required of a professional fiduciary. Securities should be kept in a safe deposit box, except when some other form of safekeeping is warranted by special circumstances. Separate trust accounts are warranted when administering estate monies or acting in similar fiduciary capacities.

[2] In general, the phrase "in connection with a representation" includes all situations where a lawyer holds property as a fiduciary, including as an escrow agent. For example, an attorney serving as a trustee under a trust instrument or by court appointment holds property "in connection with a representation." Likewise, a lawyer serving as an escrow agent in connection with litigation or a transaction holds that property "in connection with a representation." However, a lawyer serving as a fiduciary who is not actively practicing law does not hold property "in connection with a representation."

[3] Lawyers often receive funds from third parties from which the lawyer's fee will be paid. If there is risk that the client may divert the funds without paying the fee, the lawyer is not required to remit the portion from which the fee is to be paid. However, a lawyer may not hold funds to coerce a client into accepting the lawyer's contention. The disputed portion of the funds must be kept in trust and the lawyer should suggest means for prompt resolution of the dispute, such as arbitration. The undisputed portion of the funds shall be promptly distributed.

[4] Third parties, such as a client's creditors, may have just claims against funds or other property in a lawyer's custody. A lawyer may have a duty under applicable law to protect such third-party claims against wrongful interference by the client, and accordingly may refuse to surrender the property to the client. However, a lawyer should not unilaterally assume to arbitrate a dispute between the client and the third party.

[5] The obligations of a lawyer under this Rule are independent of those arising from activity other than rendering legal services. For example, a lawyer who serves as an escrow agent is governed by the applicable law relating to fiduciaries even though the lawyer does not render legal services in the transaction.

[6] How much time should elapse between the receipt of funds by the lawyer and notice to the client or third person for whom the funds are held depends on the circumstances. By example, notice must be furnished immediately upon receipt of funds in settlement of a disputed matter, but a lawyer acting as an escrow agent or trustee routinely collecting various items of income may give notice by furnishing a complete statement of receipts and expenses on a regular periodic basis satisfactory to the client or third person. Notice to a client or third person is not ordinarily required for payments of interest and dividends in the normal course, provided that the lawyer properly includes all such payments in regular periodic statements or accountings for the funds held by the lawyer.

[7] Paragraph (e)(3) states the general rule that all withdrawals and disbursements from trust account must be made in a manner which permits the recipient or payee

of the withdrawal to be identified. It does not prohibit electronic transfers or fore-close means of withdrawal which may be developed in the future, provided that the recipient of the payment is identified as part of the transaction. When payment is made by check, the check must be payable to a specific person or entity. A prenum-bered check must be used, except that starter checks may be used for a brief period between the opening of a new account and issuance of numbered checks by the bank or depository.

[8] Paragraph (f) lists records that a lawyer is obliged to keep in order to comply with the requirement that "complete records" be maintained. Additional records may be re-quired to document financial transactions with clients or third persons. Depending on the circumstances, these records could include retainer, fee, and escrow agreements and accountings, including RESPA or other real estate closing statements, accountings in contingent fee matters, and any other statement furnished to a client or third person to document receipt and disbursement of funds.

[9] The "Check Register," "Individual Client Ledger" and "Ledger for Bank Fees and Charges" required by paragraph (f)(1) are all chronological records of transactions. Each entry made in the check register must have a corresponding entry in one of the ledgers. This requirement is consistent with manual record keeping and also comports with most software packages. In addition to the data required by paragraph (f)(1)(B), the source of the deposit and the purpose of the disbursement should be recorded in the check register and appropriate ledger. For non-IOLTA accounts, the dates and amounts of interest accrual and disbursement, including disbursements from accrued interest to defray the costs of maintaining the account, are among the transactions which must be recorded. Check register and ledger balances should be calculated and recorded after each transaction or series of related transactions.

[10] Periodic reconciliation of trust accounts is also required. Generally, trust accounts should be reconciled on a monthly basis so that any errors can be corrected promptly. Active, high-volume accounts may require more frequent reconciliations. A lawyer must reconcile all trust accounts at least every sixty days. The three-way reconciliation de-scribed in paragraph (f)(1)(E) must be performed for any account in which funds re-lated to more than one client matter are held. The reconciliation described in paragraph (f)(1)(E)(iii) need not be performed for accounts which only hold the funds of a single client or third person, but the lawyer must be sure that the balance in that account cor-responds to the balance in the individual ledger maintained for that client or third per-son. The method of preparation and form of the periodic reconciliation report will de-pend upon the volume of transactions in the accounts during the period covered by the report and whether the lawyer maintains records of the account manually or electroni-cally. By example, for an inactive single client account for which the lawyer keeps records manually, a written record that the lawyer has reconciled the account statement from the financial institution with the check register maintained by the lawyer may be sufficient.

[11] Lawyers who maintain records electronically should back up data on a regular basis. For moderate to high-volume trust accounts, weekly or even daily backups may be appropriate.

Corresponding ABA Model Rule. Different from Model Rule 1.15.

Corresponding Former Massachusetts Rule. DR 9-102, DR 9-103.

RULE 1.16 DECLINING OR TERMINATING REPRESENTATION

(a) Except as stated in paragraph (c), a lawyer shall not represent a client or, where representation has commenced, shall withdraw from the representation of a client if:

(1) the representation will result in violation of the rules of professional conduct or other law;

(2) the lawyer's physical or mental condition materially impairs the lawyer's ability to represent the client; or

(3) the lawyer is discharged.

(b) Except as stated in paragraph (c), a lawyer may withdraw from representing a client if withdrawal can be accomplished without material adverse effect on the interests of the client, or if:

(1) the client persists in a course of action involving the lawyer's services that the lawyer reasonably believes is criminal or fraudulent;

(2) the client has used the lawyer's services to perpetrate a crime or fraud;

(3) a client insists upon pursuing an objective that the lawyer considers repugnant or imprudent;

(4) the client fails substantially to fulfil an obligation to the lawyer regarding the lawyer's services and has been given reasonable warning that the lawyer will withdraw unless the obligation is fulfilled;

(5) the representation will result in an unreasonable financial burden on the lawyer or has been rendered unreasonably difficult by the client; or

(6) other good cause for withdrawal exists.

(c) If permission for withdrawal from employment is required by the rules of a tribunal, a lawyer shall not withdraw from employment in a proceeding before that tribunal without its permission.

(d) Upon termination of representation, a lawyer shall take steps to the extent reasonably practicable to protect a client's interests, such as giving reasonable notice to the client, allowing time for employment of other counsel, surrendering papers and property to which the client is entitled, and refunding any advance payment of fee that has not been earned.

(e) A lawyer must make available to a former client, within a reasonable time following the client's request for his or her file, the following:

(1) all papers, documents, and other materials the client supplied to the lawyer. The lawyer may at his or her own expense retain copies of any such materials.

(2) all pleadings and other papers filed with or by the court or served by or upon any party. The client may be required to pay any copying charge consistent with the lawyer's actual cost for these materials, unless the client has already paid for such materials.

(3) all investigatory or discovery documents for which the client has paid the lawyer's out-of-pocket costs, including but not limited to medical records, photographs, tapes, disks, investigative reports, expert reports, depositions, and demonstrative evidence. The lawyer may at his or her own expense retain copies of any such materials.

(4) if the lawyer and the client have not entered into a contingent fee agreement, the client is entitled only to that portion of the lawyer's work product (as defined in subparagraph (6) below) for which the client has paid.

(5) if the lawyer and the client have entered into a contingent fee agreement, the lawyer must provide copies of the lawyer's work product (as defined in subparagraph (6) below). The client may be required to pay any copying charge consistent with the lawyer's actual cost for the copying of these materials.

(6) for purposes of this paragraph (e), work product shall consist of documents and tangible things prepared in the course of the representation of the client by the lawyer or at the lawyer's direction by his or her employee, agent, or consultant, and not described in paragraphs (2) or (3) above. Examples of work product include without limitation legal research, records of witness interviews, reports of negotiations, and correspondence.

(7) notwithstanding anything in this paragraph (e) to the contrary, a lawyer may not refuse, on grounds of nonpayment, to make available materials in the client's file when retention would prejudice the client unfairly.

Comment

[1] A lawyer should not accept representation in a matter unless it can be performed competently, promptly, without improper conflict of interest and to completion.

Mandatory Withdrawal

[2] A lawyer ordinarily must decline or withdraw from representation if the client demands that the lawyer engage in conduct that is illegal or violates the Rules of Professional Conduct or other law. The lawyer is not obliged to decline or withdraw simply because the client suggests such a course of conduct; a client may make such a suggestion in the hope that a lawyer will not be constrained by a professional obligation. Paragraph (c), taken from DR 2-110(A)(1) of the Code of Professional Conduct, has been substituted for ABA Model Rule 1.16(c) because it better states the principle of the need to obtain leave to withdraw.

[3] When a lawyer has been appointed to represent a client, withdrawal ordinarily requires approval of the appointing authority. See also Rule 6.2.

Discharge

[4] A client has a right to discharge a lawyer at any time, with or without cause, subject to liability for payment for the lawyer's services. Where future dispute about the withdrawal may be anticipated, it may be advisable to prepare a written statement reciting the circumstances.

[5] An appointed lawyer should advise a client seeking to discharge the appointed lawyer of the consequences of such an action, including the possibility that the client may be required to proceed pro se.

[6] If the client is mentally incompetent, the client may lack the legal capacity to discharge the lawyer, and in any event the discharge may be seriously adverse to the client's interests. The lawyer should make special effort to help the client consider the consequences under the provisions of Rule 1.14.

Optional Withdrawal

[7] A lawyer may withdraw from representation in some circumstances. The lawyer has the option to withdraw if it can be accomplished without material adverse effect on the

client's interests. Withdrawal is also justified if the client persists in a course of action that the lawyer reasonably believes is criminal or fraudulent, for a lawyer is not required to be associated with such conduct even if the lawyer does not further it. Withdrawal is also permitted if the lawyer's services were misused in the past even if that would materially prejudice the client. The lawyer also may withdraw where the client insists on a repugnant or imprudent objective.

[8] A lawyer may withdraw if the client refuses to abide by the terms of an agreement relating to the representation, such as an agreement concerning fees or court costs or an agreement limiting the objectives of the representation.

Assisting the Client upon Withdrawal

[9] Even if the lawyer has been unfairly discharged by the client, a lawyer must take all reasonable steps to mitigate the consequences to the client. Whether or not a lawyer for an organization may under certain unusual circumstances have a legal obligation to the organization after withdrawing or being discharged by the organization's highest authority is beyond the scope of these Rules.

[10] Paragraph (e) preserves from DR 2-110(A)(4) detailed obligations that a lawyer has to make materials available to a former client.

Corresponding ABA Model Rule. Identical to Model Rule 1.16 (a) and (b); (c) is from DR 2-110 (A) (1); (d) is from the Model Rule but the last sentence is eliminated; (e) new, taken from DR 2-110 (A) (4).

Corresponding Former Massachusetts Rule. DR 2-109, DR 2-110.

RULE 1.17 SALE OF LAW PRACTICE

A lawyer or legal representative may sell, and a lawyer or law firm may purchase, with or without consideration, a law practice, including good will, if the following conditions are satisfied:

(a) [RESERVED]

(b) [RESERVED]

(c) Actual written notice is given to each of the seller's clients regarding:

> (1) the proposed sale;

> (2) the terms of any proposed change in the fee arrangement authorized by paragraph (d);

> (3) the client's right to retain other counsel or to take possession of the file; and

> (4) the fact that the client's consent to the transfer of that client's representation will be presumed if the client does not take any action or does not otherwise object within ninety (90) days of receipt of the notice.

If a client cannot be given notice, the representation of that client may be transferred to the purchaser only upon entry of an order so authorizing by a court having jurisdiction. The seller may disclose to the court in camera information relating to the representation only to the extent necessary to obtain an order authorizing the transfer of a file.

(d) The fees charged clients shall not be increased by reason of the sale. The purchaser may, however, refuse to undertake the representation unless the client consents to pay the purchaser fees at a rate not exceeding the fees charged by the purchaser for rendering substantially similar services prior to the initiation of the purchase negotiations.

Comment

[1] The practice of law is a profession, not merely a business. Clients are not commodities that can be purchased and sold at will. Pursuant to this Rule, when a lawyer or an entire firm ceases to practice and another lawyer or firm takes over the representation, the selling lawyer or firm may obtain compensation for the reasonable value of the practice as may withdrawing partners of law firms. See Rules 5.4 and 5.6.

[2] Reserved

[3] Reserved

[4] Reserved

[5] Reserved

Client Confidences, Consent and Notice

[6] Negotiations between seller and prospective purchaser prior to disclosure of information relating to a specific representation of an identifiable client no more violate the confidentiality provisions of Rule 1.6 than do preliminary discussions concerning the possible association of another lawyer or mergers between firms, with respect to which client consent is not required. Providing the purchaser access to client-specific information relating to the representation and to the file, however, requires client consent. The Rule provides that before such information can be disclosed by the seller to the purchaser the client must be given actual written notice of the contemplated sale, including the identity of the purchaser and any proposed change in the terms of future representation, and must be told that the decision to consent or make other arrangements must be made within 90 days. If nothing is heard from the client within that time, consent to the sale is presumed.

[7] A lawyer or law firm ceasing to practice cannot be required to remain in practice because some clients cannot be given actual notice of the proposed purchase. Since these clients cannot themselves consent to the purchase or direct any other disposition of their files, the Rule requires an order from a court having jurisdiction authorizing their transfer or other disposition. The Court can be expected to determine whether reasonable efforts to locate the client have been exhausted, and whether the absent client's legitimate interests will be served by authorizing the transfer of the file so that the purchaser may continue the representation. Preservation of client confidences requires that the petition for a court order be considered in camera.

[8] All the elements of client autonomy, including the client's absolute right to discharge a lawyer and transfer the representation to another, survive the sale of the practice.

Fee Arrangements Between Client and Purchaser

[9] The sale may not be financed by increases in fees charged the clients of the practice. Existing agreements between the seller and the client as to fees and the scope of the work must be honored by the purchaser, unless the client consents after consultation. The purchaser may, however, advise the client that the purchaser will not undertake the representation unless the client consents to pay the higher fees the purchaser usually charges. To prevent client financing of the sale, the higher fee the purchaser may charge must not exceed the fees charged by the purchaser for substantially similar service rendered prior to the initiation of the purchase negotiations.

[10] Reserved

Other Applicable Ethical Standards

[11] Lawyers participating in the sale of a law practice are subject to the ethical standards applicable to involving another lawyer in the representation of a client. These include, for example, the seller's obligation to exercise competence in identifying a purchaser qualified to assume the practice and the purchaser's obligation to undertake the representation competently (see Rule 1.1); the obligation to avoid disqualifying conflicts, and to secure client consent after consultation for those conflicts which can be agreed to (see Rule 1.7); and the obligation to protect information relating to the representation (see Rules 1.6 and 1.9).

[12] If approval of the substitution of the purchasing lawyer for the selling lawyer is required by the rules of any tribunal in which a matter is pending, such approval must be obtained before the matter can be included in the sale (see Rule 1.16).

Applicability of the Rule

[13] This Rule applies to the sale of a law practice by representatives of a deceased, disabled or disappeared lawyer. Thus, the seller may be represented by a non-lawyer representative not subject to these Rules. Since, however, no lawyer may participate in a sale of a law practice which does not conform to the requirements of this Rule, the representatives of the seller as well as the purchasing lawyer can be expected to see to it that they are met.

[14] Admission to or retirement from a law partnership or professional association, retirement plans and similar arrangements, and a sale of tangible assets of a law practice, do not constitute a sale or purchase governed by this Rule.

[15] This Rule does not apply to the transfers of legal representation between lawyers when such transfers are unrelated to the sale of a practice.

[16] ABA Model Rule 1.17(a) would require the seller to cease to engage in the practice of law in a geographical area. This is a matter for agreement between the parties to the transfer and need not be dictated by rule.

[17] ABA Model Rule 1.17(b) would require the sale of the entire practice. Under Rule 1.17, a lawyer may sell all or part of the practice.

[18] The language of the ABA Model Rule has also been changed to make clear that a law practice may be transferred and acquired without the necessity of a sale and that the client's consent referred to in Rule 1.17(c)(4) is only to the transfer of that client's representation.

[19] The rule permits the estate or representative of a lawyer to make a transfer of the lawyer's practice to one or more purchasers.

Corresponding ABA Model Rule. Substantially similar to Model Rule 1.17, except (a) and (b) eliminated.

Corresponding Former Massachusetts Rule. No counterpart.

COUNSELOR

RULE 2.1 ADVISOR

In representing a client, a lawyer shall exercise independent professional judgment and render candid advice. In rendering advice, a lawyer may refer not only to law but to other considerations, such as moral, economic, social, and political factors, that may be relevant to the client's situation.

Comment

Scope of Advice

[1] A client is entitled to straightforward advice expressing the lawyer's honest assessment. Legal advice often involves unpleasant facts and alternatives that a client may be disinclined to confront. In presenting advice, a lawyer endeavors to sustain the client's morale and may put advice in as acceptable a form as honesty permits. However, a lawyer should not be deterred from giving candid advice by the prospect that the advice will be unpalatable to the client.

[2] Advice couched in narrowly legal terms may be of little value to a client, especially where practical considerations, such as cost or effects on other people, are predominant. Purely technical legal advice, therefore, can sometimes be inadequate. It is proper for a lawyer to refer to relevant moral and ethical considerations in giving advice. Although a lawyer is not a moral advisor as such, moral and ethical considerations impinge upon most legal questions and may decisively influence how the law will be applied.

[3] A client may expressly or impliedly ask the lawyer for purely technical advice. When such a request is made by a client experienced in legal matters, the lawyer may accept it at face value. When such a request is made by a client inexperienced in legal matters, however, the lawyer's responsibility as advisor may include indicating that more may be involved than strictly legal considerations.

[4] Matters that go beyond strictly legal questions may also be in the domain of another profession. Family matters can involve problems within the professional competence of psychiatry, clinical psychology or social work; business matters can involve problems within the competence of the accounting profession or of financial specialists. Where consultation with a professional in another field is itself something a competent lawyer would recommend, the lawyer should make such a recommendation. At the same time, a lawyer's advice at its best often consists of recommending a course of action in the face of conflicting recommendations of experts.

Offering Advice

[5] In general, a lawyer is not expected to give advice until asked by the client. However, when a lawyer knows that a client proposes a course of action that is likely to result in substantial adverse legal consequences to the client, duty to the client under Rule 1.4 may require that the lawyer act if the client's course of action is related to the representation. A lawyer ordinarily has no duty to initiate investigation of a client's affairs or to give advice that the client has indicated is unwanted, but a lawyer may initiate advice to a client when doing so appears to be in the client's interest.

Corresponding ABA Model Rule. Identical to Model Rule 2.1.

Corresponding Former Massachusetts Rule. No counterpart.

RULE 2.2 INTERMEDIARY [RESERVED]

Comment

[1] ABA Model Rule 2.2 sets forth circumstances in which a lawyer may act as an intermediary between clients. The court concluded that a lawyer representing more than one client should be governed by the conflict of interest principles stated in Rule 1.7. Specific Massachusetts Comments 12 through 12F to Rule 1.7 provide guidance concerning the joint representation of clients.

[2] Special Massachusetts Comment. See Special Massachusetts Comment to Rule 1.7 concerning joint representation.

RULE 2.3 EVALUATION FOR USE BY THIRD PERSONS

(a) A lawyer may undertake an evaluation of a matter affecting a client for the use of someone other than the client if:

(1) the lawyer reasonably believes that making the evaluation is compatible with other aspects of the lawyer's relationship with the client; and

(2) the client consents after consultation.

(b) Except as disclosure is required in connection with a report of an evaluation, information relating to the evaluation is otherwise protected by Rule 1.6.

Comment

Definition

[1] An evaluation may be performed at the client's direction but for the primary purpose of establishing information for the benefit of third parties; for example, an opinion concerning the title of property rendered at the behest of a vendor for the information of a prospective purchaser, or at the behest of a borrower for the information of a prospective lender. In some situations, the evaluation may be required by a government agency; for example, an opinion concerning the legality of the securities registered for sale under the securities laws. In other instances, the evaluation may be required by a third person, such as a purchaser of a business.

[2] Lawyers for the government may be called upon to give a formal opinion on the legality of contemplated government agency action. In making such an evaluation, the government lawyer acts at the behest of the government as the client but for the purpose of establishing the limits of the agency's authorized activity. Such an opinion is to be distinguished from confidential legal advice given agency officials. The critical question is whether the opinion is to be made public.

[3] A legal evaluation should be distinguished from an investigation of a person with whom the lawyer does not have a client-lawyer relationship. For example, a lawyer retained by a purchaser to analyze a vendor's title to property does not have a client-lawyer relationship with the vendor. So also, an investigation into a person's affairs by a government lawyer, or by special counsel employed by the government, is not an evaluation as that term is used in this Rule. The question is whether the lawyer is retained by the person whose affairs are being examined. When the lawyer is retained by that person, the general rules concerning loyalty to client and preservation of confidences apply, which is not the case if the lawyer is retained by someone else. For this reason, it is essential to identify the person by whom the lawyer is retained. This should be made clear not only to the person under examination, but also to others to whom the results are to be made available.

Duty to Third Person

[4] When the evaluation is intended for the information or use of a third person, a legal duty to that person may or may not arise. That legal question is beyond the scope of this Rule. However, since such an evaluation involves a departure from the normal client-lawyer relationship, careful analysis of the situation is required. The lawyer must be satisfied as a matter of professional judgment that making the evaluation is compatible with other functions undertaken in behalf of the client. For example, if the lawyer is acting as advocate in defending the client against charges of fraud, it would normally be incompatible with that responsibility for the lawyer to perform an evaluation for others concerning the same or a related transaction. Assuming no such impediment is appar-

ent, however, the lawyer should advise the client of the implications of the evaluation, particularly the lawyer's responsibilities to third persons and the duty to disseminate the findings.

Access to and Disclosure of Information

[5] The quality of an evaluation depends on the freedom and extent of the investigation upon which it is based. Ordinarily a lawyer should have whatever latitude of investigation seems necessary as a matter of professional judgment. Under some circumstances, however, the terms of the evaluation may be limited. For example, certain issues or sources may be categorically excluded, or the scope of search may be limited by time constraints or the noncooperation of persons having relevant information. Any such limitations which are material to the evaluation should be described in the report. If after a lawyer has commenced an evaluation, the client refuses to comply with the terms upon which it was understood the evaluation was to have been made, the lawyer's obligations are determined by law, having reference to the terms of the client's agreement and the surrounding circumstances.

Financial Auditors' Requests for Information

[6] When a question concerning the legal situation of a client arises at the instance of the client's financial auditor and the question is referred to the lawyer, the lawyer's response may be made in accordance with procedures recognized in the legal profession. Such a procedure is set forth in the American Bar Association Statement of Policy Regarding Lawyers' Responses to Auditors' Requests for Information, adopted in 1975.

Corresponding ABA Model Rule. Identical to Model Rule 2.3.

Corresponding Former Massachusetts Rule. No counterpart.

Cross-reference: See definition of "consultation" in Rule 9.1 (c).

RULE 2.4 LAWYER SERVING AS THIRD-PARTY NEUTRAL

(a) A lawyer serves as a third-party neutral when the lawyer assists two or more persons who are not clients of the lawyer to reach a resolution of a dispute or other matter that has arisen between them. Service as a third-party neutral may include service as an arbitrator, a mediator or in such other capacity as will enable the lawyer to assist the parties to resolve the matter.

(b) A lawyer serving as a third-party neutral shall inform unrepresented parties that the lawyer is not representing them. When the lawyer knows or reasonably should know that a party does not understand the lawyer's role in the matter, the lawyer shall explain the difference between the lawyer's role as a third-party neutral and a lawyer's role as one who represents a client.

Comment

[1] Alternative dispute resolution has become a substantial part of the civil justice system. Aside from representing clients in dispute-resolution processes, lawyers often serve as third-party neutrals. A third-party neutral is a person, such as a mediator, arbitrator, conciliator or evaluator, who assists the parties, represented or unrepresented, in the resolution of a dispute or in the arrangement of a transaction. Whether a third-party neutral serves primarily as a facilitator, evaluator or decisionmaker depends on the particular process that is either selected by the parties or mandated by a court.

[2] The role of a third-party neutral is not unique to lawyers, although, in some court-connected contexts, only lawyers are allowed to serve in this role or to handle certain

types of cases. In performing this role, the lawyer may be subject to court rules or other law that apply either to third-party neutrals generally or to lawyers serving as third-party neutrals. Lawyer-neutrals may also be subject to various codes of ethics, such as the Code of Ethics for Arbitration in Commercial Disputes prepared by a joint committee of the American Bar Association and the American Arbitration Association or the Model Standards of Conduct for Mediators jointly prepared by the American Bar Association, the American Arbitration Association and the Society of Professionals in Dispute Resolution. In particular, lawyers in Massachusetts may be subject to the Uniform Rules of Dispute Resolution set forth as Supreme Judicial Court Rule 1.18.

[3] Unlike nonlawyers who serve as third-party neutrals, lawyers serving in this role may experience unique problems as a result of differences between the role of a third-party neutral and a lawyer's service as a client representative. The potential for confusion is significant when the parties are unrepresented in the process. Thus, paragraph (b) requires a lawyer-neutral to inform unrepresented parties that the lawyer is not representing them. For some parties, particularly parties who frequently use dispute-resolution processes, this information will be sufficient. For others, particularly those who are using the process for the first time, more information will be required. Where appropriate, the lawyer should inform unrepresented parties of the important differences between the lawyer's role as third-party neutral and a lawyer's role as a client representative, including the inapplicability of the attorney-client evidentiary privilege. The extent of disclosure required under this paragraph will depend on the particular parties involved and the subject matter of the proceeding, as well as the particular features of the dispute-resolution process selected.

[4] A lawyer who serves as a third-party neutral subsequently may be asked to serve as a lawyer representing a client in the same matter. The conflicts of interest that arise for both the individual lawyer and the lawyer's law firm are addressed in Rule 1.12. See also Uniform Rule of Dispute Resolution 9(e) set forth in S.J.C. Rule 1.18.

[5] Lawyers who represent clients in alternative dispute-resolution processes are governed by the Rules of Professional Conduct. When the dispute-resolution process takes place before a tribunal, as in binding arbitration (see Rule 1.0(o)), the lawyer's duty of candor is governed by Rule 3.3. Otherwise, the lawyer's duty of candor toward both the third-party neutral and other parties is governed by Rule 4.1.

Corresponding ABA Model Rule. Identical to Model Rule 2.4.

Corresponding Former Massachusetts Rule. No counterpart.

ADVOCATE

RULE 3.1 MERITORIOUS CLAIMS AND CONTENTIONS

A lawyer shall not bring or defend a proceeding, or assert or controvert an issue therein, unless there is a basis for doing so that is not frivolous, which includes a good faith argument for an extension, modification, or reversal of existing law. A lawyer for the defendant in a criminal proceeding, or the respondent in a proceeding that could result in incarceration, may nevertheless so defend the proceeding as to require that every element of the case be established.

Comment

[1] The advocate has a duty to use legal procedure for the fullest benefit of the client's cause, but also a duty not to abuse legal procedure. The law, both procedural and substantive, establishes the limits within which an advocate may proceed. However, the law

is not always clear and never is static. Accordingly, in determining the proper scope of advocacy, account must be taken of the law's ambiguities and potential for change.

[2] The filing of an action or defense or similar action taken for a client is not frivolous merely because the facts have not first been fully substantiated or because the lawyer expects to develop vital evidence only by discovery. Such action is not frivolous even though the lawyer believes that the client's position ultimately will not prevail. The action is frivolous, however, if the client desires to have the action taken primarily for the purpose of harassing or maliciously injuring a person, or, if the lawyer is unable either to make a good faith argument on the merits of the action taken or to support the action taken by a good faith argument for an extension, modification or reversal of existing law.

[3] The principle underlying the provision that a criminal defense lawyer may put the prosecution to its proof in all circumstances often will have equal application to proceedings in which the involuntary commitment of a client is in issue. The option granted to a criminal defense lawyer to defend the proceeding so as to require proof of every element of a crime does not impose an obligation to do so. Sound judgment and reasonable trial tactics may reasonably indicate a different course.

Corresponding ABA Model Rule. Identical to Model Rule 3.1.

Corresponding Former Massachusetts Rule. DR 7-102 (A) (1-2), DR 7-106.

RULE 3.2 EXPEDITING LITIGATION

A lawyer shall make reasonable efforts to expedite litigation consistent with the interests of the client.

Comment

[1] Dilatory practices bring the administration of justice into disrepute. Delay should not be indulged merely for the convenience of the advocates, or for the purpose of frustrating an opposing party's attempt to obtain rightful redress or repose. It is not a justification that similar conduct is often tolerated by the bench and bar. The question is whether a competent lawyer acting in good faith would regard the course of action as having some substantial purpose other than delay. Realizing financial or other benefit from otherwise improper delay in litigation is not a legitimate interest of the client.

Corresponding ABA Model Rule. Identical to Model Rule 3.2.

Corresponding Former Massachusetts Rule. DR 7-102 (A) (1); see also DR 7-101, S.J.C. Rule 3:08, PF 2, DF 2.

RULE 3.3 CANDOR TOWARD THE TRIBUNAL

(a) A lawyer shall not knowingly:

(1) make a false statement of material fact or law to a tribunal;

(2) fail to disclose a material fact to a tribunal when disclosure is necessary to avoid assisting a criminal or fraudulent act by the client, except as provided in Rule 3.3 (e);

(3) fail to disclose to the tribunal legal authority in the controlling jurisdiction known to the lawyer to be directly adverse to the position of the client and not disclosed by opposing counsel; or

(4) offer evidence that the lawyer knows to be false, except as provided in Rule 3.3 (e). If a lawyer has offered, or the lawyer's client or witnesses testifying on behalf of

the client have given, material evidence and the lawyer comes to know of its falsity, the lawyer shall take reasonable remedial measures.

(b) The duties stated in paragraph (a) continue to the conclusion of the proceeding, including all appeals, and apply even if compliance requires disclosure of information otherwise protected by Rule 1.6.

(c) A lawyer may refuse to offer evidence that the lawyer reasonably believes is false.

(d) In an ex parte proceeding, a lawyer shall inform the tribunal of all material facts known to the lawyer which will enable the tribunal to make an informed decision, whether or not the facts are adverse.

(e) In a criminal case, defense counsel who knows that the defendant, the client, intends to testify falsely may not aid the client in constructing false testimony, and has a duty strongly to discourage the client from testifying falsely, advising that such a course is unlawful, will have substantial adverse consequences, and should not be followed. If a lawyer discovers this intention before accepting the representation of the client, the lawyer shall not accept the representation; if the lawyer discovers this intention before trial, the lawyer shall seek to withdraw from the representation, requesting any required permission. Disclosure of privileged or prejudicial information shall be made only to the extent necessary to effect the withdrawal. If disclosure of privileged or prejudicial information is necessary, the lawyer shall make an application to withdraw ex parte to a judge other than the judge who will preside at the trial and shall seek to be heard in camera and have the record of the proceeding, except for an order granting leave to withdraw, impounded. If the lawyer is unable to obtain the required permission to withdraw, the lawyer may not prevent the client from testifying. If a criminal trial has commenced and the lawyer discovers that the client intends to testify falsely at trial, the lawyer need not file a motion to withdraw from the case if the lawyer reasonably believes that seeking to withdraw will prejudice the client. If, during the client's testimony or after the client has testified, the lawyer knows that the client has testified falsely, the lawyer shall call upon the client to rectify the false testimony and, if the client refuses or is unable to do so, the lawyer shall not reveal the false testimony to the tribunal. In no event may the lawyer examine the client in such a manner as to elicit any testimony from the client the lawyer knows to be false, and the lawyer shall not argue the probative value of the false testimony in closing argument or in any other proceedings, including appeals.

Comment

[1] The advocate's task is to present the client's case with persuasive force. Performance of that duty while maintaining confidences of the client is qualified by the advocate's duty of candor to the tribunal. However, an advocate does not vouch for the evidence submitted in a cause; the tribunal is responsible for assessing its probative value.

Representations by a Lawyer

[2] An advocate is responsible for pleadings and other documents prepared for litigation, but is usually not required to have personal knowledge of matters asserted therein, for litigation documents ordinarily present assertions by the client, or by someone on the client's behalf, and not assertions by the lawyer. Compare Rule 3.1. However, an assertion purporting to be on the lawyer's own knowledge, as in an affidavit by the lawyer or in a statement in open court, may properly be made only when the lawyer knows the assertion is true or believes it to be true on the basis of a reasonably diligent inquiry. There are circumstances where failure to make a disclosure is the equivalent of an affirmative misrepresentation. The obligation prescribed in Rule 1.2(d) not to counsel a

client to commit, or assist the client in committing, a fraud applies in litigation. Regarding compliance with Rule 1.2(d), see the Comment to that Rule. See also the Comment to Rule 8.4(b).

Special Meaning of "Assistance"

[2A] Comment 3 to Rule 4.1 states the general rule that the word "assisting" refers to that level of assistance that would render a third party liable for another's crime or fraud, i.e., assistance sufficient to render one liable as an aider or abettor under criminal law or as a joint tortfeasor under principles of tort and agency law. However, the concept of assisting has a special meaning in Rule 3.3 because it deals with a lawyer's conduct before a tribunal. The term assisting in Rule 3.3 is not limited to conduct that makes the lawyer liable as an aider, abettor or joint tortfeasor. Rule 3.3(a) is intended to guide the conduct of the lawyer as an officer of the court as a prophylactic measure to protect against the contamination of the judicial process. Thus, for example, a lawyer who knows that a client has committed fraud on a tribunal and has refused to rectify it must disclose that fraud to avoid assisting the client's fraudulent act.

Misleading Legal Argument

[3] Legal argument based on a knowingly false representation of law constitutes dishonesty toward the tribunal. A lawyer is not required to make a disinterested exposition of the law, but must recognize the existence of pertinent legal authorities. Furthermore, as stated in paragraph (a)(3), an advocate has a duty to disclose directly adverse authority in the controlling jurisdiction which has not been disclosed by the opposing party. The underlying concept is that legal argument is a discussion seeking to determine the legal premises properly applicable to the case.

False Evidence

[4] When evidence that a lawyer knows to be false is provided by a person who is not the client, the lawyer must refuse to offer it regardless of the client's wishes.

[5] When false evidence is offered by the client, however, a conflict may arise between the lawyer's duty to keep the client's revelations confidential and the duty of candor to the court. Upon ascertaining that material evidence is false, the lawyer should seek to persuade the client that the evidence should not be offered or, if it has been offered, that its false character should immediately be disclosed. If the persuasion is ineffective, the lawyer must take reasonable remedial measures.

[6] Except in the defense of a criminal accused, an advocate must disclose, if necessary to rectify the situation, the existence of the client's deception to the court or to the other party. The lawyer's obligation to disclose also extends to material evidence given by others on behalf of the client. Such a disclosure can result in grave consequences to the client, including not only a sense of betrayal but also loss of the case and perhaps a prosecution for perjury. But the alternative is that the lawyer cooperate in deceiving the court, thereby subverting the truth-finding process which the adversary system is designed to implement. See Rule 1.2(d). Furthermore, unless it is clearly understood that the lawyer will act upon the duty to disclose the existence of false evidence, the client can simply reject the lawyer's advice to reveal the false evidence and insist that the lawyer keep silent. Thus the client could in effect coerce the lawyer into being a party to fraud on the court.

Perjury by a Criminal Defendant

[7] In the defense of a criminally accused, the lawyer's duty to disclose the client's intent to commit perjury or offer of perjured testimony is complicated by state and federal

constitutional provisions relating to due process, right to counsel, and privileged communications between lawyer and client. While there has been intense debate over a lawyer's duty in such situations in criminal cases, this rule proposes to accommodate these special constitutional concerns in a criminal case by providing specific procedures and restrictions to be followed in the rare situations in which the client states his intention to, or does, offer testimony the lawyer knows to be perjured in a criminal trial.

[8] In such cases, it is the clear duty of the lawyer first to seek to persuade the client to refrain from testifying perjuriously. That persuasion should include, at a minimum, advising the client that such a course of action is unlawful, may have substantial adverse consequences, and should not be followed. If that persuasion fails, and the lawyer has not yet accepted the case, the lawyer must not agree to the representation. If the lawyer learns of this intention after the lawyer has accepted the representation of the client, but before trial, and is unable to dissuade the client of his or her intention to commit perjury, the lawyer must seek to withdraw from the representation. The lawyer must request the required permission to withdraw from the case by making an application ex parte before a judge other than the judge who will preside at the trial. The lawyer must request that the hearing on this motion to withdraw be heard in camera, and that the record of the proceedings, except for an order granting a motion to withdraw, be impounded.

[9] Once the trial has begun, the lawyer may seek to withdraw from the representation but no longer has an obligation to withdraw if the lawyer reasonably believes that to do so would prejudice the client. If the lawyer learns of the client's intention to commit perjury during the trial, and is unable to dissuade the client from testifying falsely, the lawyer may not stand in the way of the client's absolute right to take the stand and testify. If, during a trial, the lawyer knows that his or her client, while testifying, has made a perjured statement, and the lawyer reasonably believes that any immediate action taken by the lawyer will prejudice the client, the lawyer should wait until the first appropriate moment in the trial and then attempt to persuade the client confidentially to correct the perjury.

[10] In any of these circumstances, if the lawyer is unable to convince the client to correct the perjury, the lawyer must not assist the client in presenting the perjured testimony and must not argue the false testimony to a judge, or jury or appellate court as true or worthy of belief. Except as provided in this rule, the lawyer may not reveal to the court that the client intends to perjure or has perjured himself or herself in a criminal trial.

[11] Reserved.

[12] Reserved.

Duration of Obligation

[13] A practical time limit on the obligation to rectify the presentation of false evidence has to be established. The conclusion of the proceeding is a reasonably definite point for the termination of the obligation.

Refusing to Offer Proof Believed to Be False

[14] Generally speaking, a lawyer has authority to refuse to offer testimony or other proof that the lawyer believes is untrustworthy. Offering such proof may reflect adversely on the lawyer's ability to discriminate in the quality of evidence and thus impair the lawyer's effectiveness as an advocate. Whether constitutional requirements affect the resolution of this issue is beyond the scope of these comments.

Ex Parte Proceedings

[15] Ordinarily, an advocate has the limited responsibility of presenting one side of the matters that a tribunal should consider in reaching a decision; the conflicting position is expected to be presented by the opposing party. However, in any ex parte proceeding, such as an application for a temporary restraining order, there is no balance of presentation by opposing advocates. The object of an ex parte proceeding is nevertheless to yield a substantially just result. The judge has an affirmative responsibility to accord the absent party just consideration. The lawyer for the represented party has the correlative duty to make disclosures of material facts known to the lawyer and that the lawyer reasonably believes are necessary to an informed decision. Rule 3.3(d) does not change the rules applicable in situations covered by specific substantive law, such as presentation of evidence to grand juries, applications for search or other investigative warrants and the like.

[16] When adversaries present a joint petition to a tribunal, such as a joint petition to approve the settlement of a class action suit or the settlement of a suit involving a minor, the proceeding loses its adversarial character and in some respects takes on the form of an ex parte proceeding. The lawyers presenting such a joint petition thus have the same duties of candor to the tribunal as lawyers in ex parte proceedings and should be guided by Rule 3.3(d).

Corresponding ABA Model Rule. Identical in (a) to (d) to Model Rule 3.3 except in (a) (2) and (4); in (b) phrase "including all appeals" added; (e) new.

Corresponding Former Massachusetts Rule. DR 7-102, DR 7-106 (B), S.J.C. Rule 3:08, PF 12, DF 13.

RULE 3.4 FAIRNESS TO OPPOåSING PARTY AND COUNSEL

A lawyer shall not:

(a) unlawfully obstruct another party's access to evidence or unlawfully alter, destroy, or conceal a document or other material having potential evidentiary value. A lawyer shall not counsel or assist another person to do any such act;

(b) falsify evidence, counsel or assist a witness to testify falsely, or offer an inducement to a witness that is prohibited by law;

(c) knowingly disobey an obligation under the rules of a tribunal except for an open refusal based on an assertion that no valid obligation exists;

(d) in pretrial procedure, make a frivolous discovery request or fail to make reasonably diligent effort to comply with a legally proper discovery request by an opposing party;

(e) in trial, allude to any matter that the lawyer does not reasonably believe is relevant or that will not be supported by admissible evidence, assert personal knowledge of facts in issue except when testifying as a witness, or state a personal opinion as to the justness of a cause, the credibility of a witness, the culpability of a civil litigant, or the guilt or innocence of an accused;

(f) request a person other than a client to refrain from voluntarily giving relevant information to another party unless:

(1) the person is a relative or an employee or other agent of a client; and

(2) the lawyer reasonably believes that the person's interests will not be adversely affected by refraining from giving such information;

(g) pay, offer to pay, or acquiesce in the payment of compensation to a witness contingent upon the content of his or her testimony or the outcome of the case. But a lawyer may advance, guarantee, or acquiesce in the payment of:

(1) expenses reasonably incurred by a witness in attending or testifying

(2) reasonable compensation to a witness for loss of time in attending or testifying

(3) a reasonable fee for the professional services of an expert witness;

(h) present, participate in presenting, or threaten to present criminal or disciplinary charges solely to obtain an advantage in a private civil matter; or

(i) in appearing in a professional capacity before a tribunal, engage in conduct manifesting bias or prejudice based on race, sex, religion, national origin, disability, age, or sexual orientation against a party, witness, counsel, or other person. This paragraph does not preclude legitimate advocacy when race, sex, religion, national origin, disability, age, or sexual orientation, or another similar factor is an issue in the proceeding.

Comment

[1] The procedure of the adversary system contemplates that the evidence in a case is to be marshalled competitively by the contending parties. Fair competition in the adversary system is secured by prohibitions against destruction or concealment of evidence, improperly influencing witnesses, obstructive tactics in discovery procedure, and the like.

[2] Documents and other items of evidence are often essential to establish a claim or defense. Subject to evidentiary privileges, the right of an opposing party, including the government, to obtain evidence through discovery or subpoena is an important procedural right. The exercise of that right can be frustrated if relevant material is altered, concealed or destroyed. Applicable law in many jurisdictions makes it an offense to destroy material for purpose of impairing its availability in a pending proceeding or one whose commencement can be foreseen. Falsifying evidence is also generally a criminal offense. Paragraph (a) applies to evidentiary material generally, including computerized information.

[3] With regard to paragraph (b), it is not improper to pay a witness's expenses or to compensate an expert witness on terms permitted by law.

[4] Paragraph (f) permits a lawyer to advise employees of a client to refrain from giving information to another party, for the employees may identify their interests with those of the client. See also Rule 4.2.

[5] Paragraph (g) carries over the provision of former DR 7-109(C) concerning the payment of funds to a witness. Compensation of a witness may not be based on the content of the witness's testimony or the result in the proceeding. A lawyer may pay a witness reasonable compensation for time lost and for expenses reasonably incurred in attending the proceeding. A lawyer may pay a reasonable fee for the professional services of an expert witness.

[6] Paragraph (h) is taken from former DR 7-105(A), but it prohibits filing or threatening to file disciplinary charges as well as criminal charges solely to obtain an advantage in a private civil matter. The word "private" has been added to make clear that a government lawyer may pursue criminal or civil enforcement, or both criminal and civil enforcement, remedies available to the government. This rule is never violated by a report

under Rule 8.3 made in good faith because the report would not be made "solely" to gain an advantage in a civil matter.

[7] Paragraph (i) is taken from former DR 7-106(C)(8) concerning conduct before a tribunal that manifests bias or prejudice based on race, sex, religion, national origin, disability, age, or sexual orientation of any person. When these factors are an issue in a proceeding, paragraph (i) does not bar legitimate advocacy.

Corresponding ABA Model Rule. Identical to Model Rule 3.4(a), (b), (c), (d), (e), and (f); (g) from DR 7-109 (C), (h) from DR 7-105, and (i) from DR 7-106 (C) (8) are new.

Corresponding Former Massachusetts Rule. DR 7-102 (A) (6); DR 7-105; DR 7-106 (A) and (C), DR 7-109, S.J.C. Rule 3:08 PF 4, DF 9; See also DR 7-103 (B), DR 7-104 (A)(2).

RULE 3.5 IMPARTIALITY AND DECORUM OF THE TRIBUNAL

A lawyer shall not:

(a) seek to influence a judge, juror, prospective juror, or other official by means prohibited by law;

(b) communicate ex parte with such a person except as permitted by law;

(c) engage in conduct intended to disrupt a tribunal; or

(d) after discharge of the jury from further consideration of a case with which the lawyer was connected, initiate any communication with a member of the jury without leave of court granted for good cause shown. If a juror initiates a communication with such a lawyer, directly or indirectly, the lawyer may respond provided that the lawyer shall not ask questions of or make comments to a member of that jury that are intended only to harass or embarrass the juror or to influence his or her actions in future jury service. In no circumstances shall such a lawyer inquire of a juror concerning the jury's deliberation processes.

Comment

[1] Many forms of improper influence upon a tribunal are proscribed by criminal law. Others are specified in S.J.C. Rule 3:09, the Code of Judicial Conduct, with which an advocate should be familiar. A lawyer is required to avoid contributing to a violation of such provisions.

[2] The advocate's function is to present evidence and argument so that the cause may be decided according to law. Refraining from abusive or obstreperous conduct is a corollary of the advocate's right to speak on behalf of litigants. A lawyer may stand firm against abuse by a judge but should avoid reciprocation; the judge's default is no justification for similar dereliction by an advocate. An advocate can present the cause, protect the record for subsequent review and preserve professional integrity by patient firmness no less effectively than by belligerence or theatrics.

Corresponding ABA Model Rule. Identical to Model Rule 3.5(a), (b) and (c); (d) added from DR 7-108 (D).

Corresponding Former Massachusetts Rule. DR 7-106, DR 7-108 (D), DR 7-110 (B), S.J.C. Rule 3:08, PF 1, DF 1.

RULE 3.6 TRIAL PUBLICITY

(a) A lawyer who is participating or has participated in the investigation or litigation of a matter shall not make an extrajudicial statement that a reasonable person would expect to be disseminated by means of public communication if the lawyer knows or reasonably should know that it will have a substantial likelihood of materially prejudicing an adjudicative proceeding in the matter.

(b) Notwithstanding paragraph (a), a lawyer may state:

(1) the claim, offense, or defense involved, and, except when prohibited by law, the identity of the persons involved;

(2) the information contained in a public record;

(3) that an investigation of the matter is in progress;

(4) the scheduling or result of any step in litigation;

(5) a request for assistance in obtaining evidence and information necessary thereto;

(6) a warning of danger concerning the behavior of a person involved, when there is reason to believe that there exists the likelihood of substantial harm to an individual or to the public interest; and

(7) in a criminal case, in addition to subparagraphs (1) through (6): (i) the identity, residence, occupation, and family status of the accused; (ii) if the accused has not been apprehended, information necessary to aid in apprehension of that person; (iii) the fact, time, and place of arrest; and (iv) the identity of investigating and arresting officers or agencies and the length of the investigation.

(c) Notwithstanding paragraph (a), a lawyer may make a statement that a reasonable lawyer would believe is required to protect a client from the substantial undue prejudicial effect of recent publicity not initiated by the lawyer or the lawyer's client. A statement made pursuant to this paragraph shall be limited to such information as is necessary to mitigate the recent adverse publicity.

(d) No lawyer associated in a firm or government agency with a lawyer subject to paragraph (a) shall make a statement prohibited by paragraph (a).

(e) This rule does not preclude a lawyer from replying to charges of misconduct publicly made against him or her or from participating in the proceedings of a legislative, administrative, or other investigative body.

Comment

[1] It is difficult to strike a balance between protecting the right to a fair trial and safeguarding the right of free expression. Preserving the right to a fair trial necessarily entails some curtailment of the information that may be disseminated about a party prior to trial, particularly where trial by jury is involved. If there were no such limits, the result would be the practical nullification of the protective effect of the rules of forensic decorum and the exclusionary rules of evidence. On the other hand, there are vital social interests served by the free dissemination of information about events having legal consequences and about legal proceedings themselves. The public has a right to know about threats to its safety and measures aimed at assuring its security. It also has a legitimate interest in the conduct of judicial proceedings, particularly in matters of general public concern. Furthermore, the subject matter of legal proceedings is often of direct significance in debate and deliberation over questions of public policy.

[2] Special rules of confidentiality may validly govern proceedings in juvenile, domestic relations and mental disability proceedings, and perhaps other types of litigation. Rule 3.4(c) requires compliance with such rules.

[3] The Rule sets forth a basic general prohibition against a lawyer's making statements that the lawyer knows or should know will have a substantial likelihood of materially prejudicing an adjudicative proceeding. Recognizing that the public value of informed commentary is great and the likelihood of prejudice to a proceeding by the commentary of a lawyer who is not involved in the proceeding is small, the rule applies only to lawyers who are, or who have been involved in the investigation or litigation of a case, and their associates.

[4] Paragraph (b) identifies specific matters about which a lawyer's statements would not ordinarily be considered to present a substantial likelihood of material prejudice, and should not in any event be considered prohibited by the general prohibition of paragraph (a). Paragraph (b) is not intended to be an exhaustive listing of the subjects upon which a lawyer may make a statement, but statements on other matters may be subject to paragraph (a).

[5] There are, on the other hand, certain subjects which are more likely than not to have a material prejudicial effect on a proceeding, particularly when they refer to a civil matter triable to a jury, a criminal matter, or any other proceeding that could result in incarceration. These subjects relate to:

[6] (1) the character, credibility, reputation or criminal record of a party, suspect in a criminal investigation or witness, or the identity of a witness, or the expected testimony of a party or witness;

[7] (2) in a criminal case or proceeding that could result in incarceration, the possibility of a plea of guilty to the offense or the existence or contents of any confession, admission, or statement given by a defendant or suspect or that person's refusal or failure to make a statement;

[8] (3) the performance or results of any examination or test or the refusal or failure of a person to submit to an examination or test, or the identity or nature of physical evidence expected to be presented;

[9] (4) any opinion as to the guilt or innocence of a defendant or suspect in a criminal case or proceeding that could result in incarceration;

[10] (5) information that the lawyer knows or reasonably should know is likely to be inadmissible as evidence in a trial and that would, if disclosed, create a substantial risk of prejudicing an impartial trial; or

[11] (6) the fact that a defendant has been charged with a crime, unless there is included therein a statement explaining that the charge is merely an accusation and that the defendant is presumed innocent until and unless proven guilty.

[12] Another relevant factor in determining prejudice is the nature of the proceeding involved. Criminal jury trials will be most sensitive to extrajudicial speech. Civil trials may be less sensitive. Non-jury hearings and arbitration proceedings may be even less affected. The Rule will still place limitations on prejudicial comments in these cases, but the likelihood of prejudice may be different depending on the type of proceeding.

[13] Finally, extrajudicial statements that might otherwise raise a question under this Rule may be permissible when they are made in response to statements made publicly by another party, another party's lawyer, or third persons, where a reasonable lawyer would believe a public response is required in order to avoid prejudice to the lawyer's client. When prejudicial statements have been publicly made by others, responsive statements may have the salutary effect of lessening any resulting adverse impact on the adjudicative proceeding. Such responsive statements should be limited to contain only

such information as is necessary to mitigate undue prejudice created by the statements made by others.

Corresponding ABA Model Rule. Almost identical to Model Rule 3.6 except paragraph (e) is derived from DR 7-107 (I).

Corresponding Former Massachusetts Rule. DR 7-107.

RULE 3.7 LAWYER AS WITNESS

(a) A lawyer shall not act as advocate at a trial in which the lawyer is likely to be a necessary witness except where:

    (1) the testimony relates to an uncontested issue;

    (2) the testimony relates to the nature and value of legal services rendered in the case; or

    (3) disqualification of the lawyer would work substantial hardship on the client.

(b) A lawyer may act as advocate in a trial in which another lawyer in the lawyer's firm is likely to be called as a witness unless precluded from doing so by Rule 1.7 or Rule 1.9.

Comment

[1] Combining the roles of advocate and witness can prejudice the opposing party and can involve a conflict of interest between the lawyer and client.

[2] The opposing party has proper objection where the combination of roles may prejudice that party's rights in the litigation. A witness is required to testify on the basis of personal knowledge, while an advocate is expected to explain and comment on evidence given by others. It may not be clear whether a statement by an advocate-witness should be taken as proof or as an analysis of the proof.

[3] Paragraph (a)(1) recognizes that if the testimony will be uncontested, the ambiguities in the dual role are purely theoretical. Paragraph (a)(2) recognizes that where the testimony concerns the extent and value of legal services rendered in the action in which the testimony is offered, permitting the lawyers to testify avoids the need for a second trial with new counsel to resolve that issue. Moreover, in such a situation the judge has firsthand knowledge of the matter in issue; hence, there is less dependence on the adversary process to test the credibility of the testimony.

[4] Apart from these two exceptions, paragraph (a)(3) recognizes that a balancing is required between the interests of the client and those of the opposing party. Whether the opposing party is likely to suffer prejudice depends on the nature of the case, the importance and probable tenor of the lawyer's testimony, and the probability that the lawyer's testimony will conflict with that of other witnesses. Even if there is risk of such prejudice, in determining whether the lawyer should be disqualified, due regard must be given to the effect of disqualification on the lawyer's client. It is relevant that one or both parties could reasonably foresee that the lawyer would probably be a witness. The principle of imputed disqualification stated in Rule 1.10 has no application to this aspect of the problem.

[5] Whether the combination of roles involves an improper conflict of interest with respect to the client is determined by Rule 1.7 or 1.9. For example, if there is likely to be substantial conflict between the testimony of the client and that of the lawyer or a member of the lawyer's firm, the representation is improper. The problem can arise whether the lawyer is called as a witness on behalf of the client or is called by the opposing party. Determining whether or not such a conflict exists is primarily the responsibility of the

lawyer involved. See Comment to Rule 1.7. If a lawyer who is a member of a firm may not act as both advocate and witness by reason of conflict of interest, Rule 1.10 disqualifies the firm also.

Corresponding ABA Model Rule. Identical to Model Rule 3.7.

Corresponding Former Massachusetts Rule. DR 5-101 (B), DR 5-102 (A).

RULE 3.8 SPECIAL RESPONSIBILITIES OF A PROSECUTOR

The prosecutor in a criminal case shall:

(a) refrain from prosecuting a charge that the prosecutor knows is not supported by probable cause;

(b) make reasonable efforts to assure that the accused has been advised of the right to, and the procedure for obtaining, counsel and has been given reasonable opportunity to obtain counsel;

(c) not seek to obtain from an unrepresented accused a waiver of important pretrial rights, such as the right to a preliminary hearing, unless a court first has obtained from the accused a knowing and intelligent written waiver of counsel;

(d) make timely disclosure to the defense of all evidence or information known to the prosecutor that tends to negate the guilt of the accused or mitigates the offense, and, in connection with sentencing, disclose to the defense and to the tribunal all unprivileged mitigating information known to the prosecutor, except when the prosecutor is relieved of this responsibility by a protective order of the tribunal;

(e) exercise reasonable care to prevent investigators, law enforcement personnel, employees, or other persons assisting or associated with the prosecutor in a criminal case from making an extrajudicial statement that the prosecutor would be prohibited from making under Rule 3.6;

(f) not subpoena a lawyer in a grand jury or other criminal proceeding to present evidence about a past or present client unless:

  (1) the prosecutor reasonably believes:

   (i) the information sought is not protected from disclosure by any applicable privilege; (ii) the evidence sought is essential to the successful completion of an ongoing investigation or prosecution; and

   (iii) there is no other feasible alternative to obtain the information; and

  (2) the prosecutor obtains prior judicial approval after an opportunity for an adversarial proceeding; (g) except for statements that are necessary to inform the public of the nature and extent of the prosecutor's action and that serve a legitimate law enforcement purpose, refrain from making extrajudicial comments that have a substantial likelihood of heightening public condemnation of the accused;

(h) not assert personal knowledge of the facts in issue, except when testifying as a witness;

(i) not assert a personal opinion as to the justness of a cause, as to the credibility of a witness, as to the culpability of a civil litigant, or as to the guilt or innocence of an accused; but the prosecutor may argue, on analysis of the evidence, for any position or conclusion with respect to the matters stated herein; and

(j) not intentionally avoid pursuit of evidence because the prosecutor believes it will damage the prosecution's case or aid the accused.

Comment

[1] A prosecutor has the responsibility of a minister of justice and not simply that of an advocate. This responsibility carries with it specific obligations to see that the defendant is accorded procedural justice and that guilt is decided upon the basis of sufficient evidence. See also S.J.C. Rule 3:08, Disciplinary Rules Applicable to Practice as a Prosecutor or as a Defense Lawyer. Applicable law may require other measures by the prosecutor and knowing disregard of those obligations or a systematic abuse of prosecutorial discretion could constitute a violation of Rule 8.4.

[2] Unlike the language of ABA Model Rule 3.8(c), paragraph (c) permits a prosecutor to seek a waiver of pretrial rights from an accused if the court has first obtained a knowing and intelligent written waiver of counsel from the accused. The use of the term "accused" means that paragraph (c) does not apply until the person has been charged. Paragraph (c) also does not apply to an accused appearing pro se with the approval of the tribunal. Nor does it forbid the lawful questioning of a suspect who has knowingly waived the rights to counsel and silence.

[3] The exception in paragraph (d) recognizes that a prosecutor may seek an appropriate protective order from the tribunal if disclosure of information to the defense could result in substantial harm to an individual or to the public interest.

[4] Paragraph (f) is intended to limit the issuance of lawyer subpoenas in grand jury and other criminal proceedings to those situations in which there is a genuine need to intrude into the client-lawyer relationship.

[5] Paragraph (g) supplements Rule 3.6, which prohibits extrajudicial statements that have a substantial likelihood of prejudicing an adjudicatory proceeding. In the context of a criminal prosecution, a prosecutor's extrajudicial statement can create the additional problem of increasing public condemnation of the accused. Although the announcement of an indictment, for example, will necessarily have severe consequences for the accused, a prosecutor can, and should, avoid comments which have no legitimate law enforcement purpose and have a substantial likelihood of increasing public opprobrium of the accused. Nothing in this Comment is intended to restrict the statements which a prosecutor may make which comply with Rule 3.6(b) or 3.6(c).

[6] Paragraphs (h) and (i), which do not appear in the ABA Model Rules, are taken from DR 7-106(C)(3) and (4), respectively. They state limitations on a prosecutor's assertion of personal knowledge of facts in issue and the assertion of a personal opinion on matters before a trier of fact, but under paragraph (i) a prosecutor may contend, based on the evidence, that the trier of fact should reach particular conclusions.

Corresponding ABA Model Rule. Model Rule 3.8, paragraphs (a)–(g) except for (c) (written waiver) and (f) (2) which is from former Model Rule 3.8 (f) (2) and S.J.C. Rule 3:08, PF 15; paragraphs (h) and (i) are taken from DR 7-106 (C) (3) and (4). Paragraph (j) is taken from Rule 3.08, PF 7(b)

Corresponding Massachusetts Rule. See S.J.C. Rule 3:08, Standards Relating to the Prosecution Function.

RULE 3.9 ADVOCATE IN NONADJUDICATIVE PROCEEDINGS

A lawyer representing a client before a legislative or administrative tribunal in a nonadjudicative proceeding shall disclose that the appearance is in a representative capacity and shall conform to the provisions of Rules 3.3(a) through (c), 3.4(a) through (c), and 3.5(a) through (c).

Comment

[1] In representation before bodies such as legislatures, municipal councils, and executive and administrative agencies acting in a rule-making or policy-making capacity, lawyers present facts, formulate issues and advance argument in the matters under consideration. The decision-making body, like a court, should be able to rely on the integrity of the submissions made to it. A lawyer appearing before such a body should deal with the tribunal honestly and in conformity with applicable rules of procedure.

[2] Lawyers have no exclusive right to appear before nonadjudicative bodies, as they do before a court. The requirements of this Rule therefore may subject lawyers to regulations inapplicable to advocates who are not lawyers. However, legislatures and administrative agencies have a right to expect lawyers to deal with them as they deal with courts.

[3] This Rule does not apply to representation of a client in a negotiation or other bilateral transaction with a governmental agency; representation in such a transaction is governed by Rules 4.1 through 4.4.

[4] Unless otherwise expressly prohibited, ex parte contacts with legislators and other persons acting in a legislative capacity are not prohibited.

Corresponding ABA Model Rule. Identical to Model Rule 3.9, except for reference to paragraphs (a)–(c) of Rule 3.5.

Corresponding Former Massachusetts Rule. DR 7-106 (B) (2).

TRANSACTIONS WITH PERSONS OTHER THAN CLIENTS

RULE 4.1 TRUTHFULNESS IN STATEMENTS TO OTHERS

In the course of representing a client a lawyer shall not knowingly:

> (a) make a false statement of material fact or law to a third person; or

> (b) fail to disclose a material fact to a third person when disclosure is necessary to avoid assisting a criminal or fraudulent act by a client, unless disclosure is prohibited by Rule 1.6.

Comment

Misrepresentation

[1] A lawyer is required to be truthful when dealing with others on a client's behalf, but generally has no affirmative duty to inform an opposing party of relevant facts. A misrepresentation can occur if the lawyer incorporates or affirms a statement of another person that the lawyer knows is false. Misrepresentations can also occur by failure to act.

Statements of Fact

[2] This Rule refers to statements of fact. Whether a particular statement should be regarded as one of fact can depend on the circumstances. Under generally accepted conventions in negotiation, certain types of statements ordinarily are not taken as statements of material fact. Estimates of price or value placed on the subject of a transaction and a party's intentions as to an acceptable settlement of a claim are in this category, and so is the existence of an undisclosed principal except where nondisclosure of the principal would constitute fraud.

Fraud by Client

[3] Paragraph (b) recognizes that substantive law may require a lawyer to disclose certain information to avoid being deemed to have assisted the client's crime or fraud. In paragraph (b) the word "assisting" refers to that level of assistance which would render a

third party liable for another's crime or fraud, i.e., assistance sufficient to render one liable as an aider or abettor under criminal law or as a joint tortfeasor under principles of tort and agency law. The requirement of disclosure in this paragraph is not intended to broaden what constitutes unlawful assistance under criminal, tort or agency law, but instead is intended to ensure that these rules do not countenance behavior by a lawyer that other law marks as criminal or tortious. But see the special meaning of "assistance" in the context of a lawyer's appearance before a tribunal in Comment 2A to Rule 3.3.

Corresponding ABA Model Rule. Identical to Model Rule 4.1.

Corresponding Former Massachusetts Rule. DR 1-102, DR 7-102; see also DR 1-103.

RULE 4.2 COMMUNICATION WITH PERSON REPRESENTED BY COUNSEL

In representing a client, a lawyer shall not communicate about the subject of the representation with a person the lawyer knows to be represented by another lawyer in the matter, unless the lawyer has the consent of the other lawyer or is authorized by law to do so.

Comment

[1] This Rule does not prohibit communication with a represented person, or an employee or agent of such a person, concerning matters outside the representation. For example, the existence of a controversy between a government agency and a private party, or between two organizations, does not prohibit a lawyer for either from communicating with nonlawyer representatives of the other regarding a separate matter. Also, parties to a matter may communicate directly with each other and a lawyer having independent justification or legal authorization for communicating with a represented person is permitted to do so. Communications authorized by law include, for example, the right of a party to a controversy with a government agency to speak with government officials about the matter. Counsel could also prepare and send written default notices and written demands required by such laws as Chapter 93A of the General Laws.

[2] Communications authorized by law also include constitutionally permissible investigative activities of lawyers representing governmental entities, directly or through investigative agents, prior to the commencement of criminal or civil enforcement proceedings, when there is applicable judicial precedent that either has found the activity permissible under this Rule or has found this Rule inapplicable. However, the Rule imposes ethical restrictions that go beyond those imposed by constitutional provisions.

[3] This rule applies to communications with any person, whether or not a party to a formal adjudicative proceeding, contract or negotiation, who is represented by counsel concerning the matter to which the communication relates. See the definition of "person" in Rule 9.1(h).

[4] In the case of an organization, this Rule prohibits communications by a lawyer for another person or entity concerning the matter in representation only with those agents or employees who exercise managerial responsibility in the matter, who are alleged to have committed the wrongful acts at issue in the litigation, or who have authority on behalf of the organization to make decisions about the course of the litigation. If an agent or employee of the organization is represented in the matter by his or her own counsel, the consent by that counsel to a communication will be sufficient for purposes of this Rule. Compare Rule 3.4(f).

[5] The prohibition on communications with a represented person only applies, however, in circumstances where the lawyer knows that the person is in fact represented in

the matter to be discussed. This means that the lawyer has knowledge of the fact of the representation; but such knowledge may be inferred from the circumstances. See the definition of "knowledge" in Rule 9.1(f). Such an inference may arise in circumstances where there is substantial reason to believe that the person with whom communication is sought is represented in the matter to be discussed. Thus, a lawyer cannot evade the requirement of obtaining the consent of counsel by closing eyes to the obvious.

[6] In the event the person with whom the lawyer communicates is not known to be represented by counsel in the matter, the lawyer's communications are subject to Rule 4.3.

[7] Nothing in this rule prohibits a lawyer from seeking and acting in accordance with a court order permitting communication with a person known to be represented by counsel.

Corresponding ABA Model Rule. Identical to Model Rule 4.2.

Corresponding Former Massachusetts Rule. DR 7-104 (A) (1).

Cross-reference: See definition of "person" in Rule 9.1.

RULE 4.3 DEALING WITH UNREPRESENTED PERSON

(a) In dealing on behalf of a client with a person who is not represented by counsel, a lawyer shall not state or imply that the lawyer is disinterested. When the lawyer knows or reasonably should know that the unrepresented person misunderstands the lawyer's role in the matter, the lawyer shall make reasonable efforts to correct the misunderstanding.

(b) During the course of representation of a client, a lawyer shall not give advice to a person who is not represented by a lawyer, other than the advice to secure counsel, if the interests of such person are or have a reasonable possibility of being in conflict with the interests of the client.

Comment

[1] An unrepresented person, particularly one not experienced in dealing with legal matters, might assume that a lawyer is disinterested in loyalties or is a disinterested authority on the law even when the lawyer represents a client. Therefore Rule 4.3 continues the prohibition contained in former DR 1-104(A)(2) against giving advice to an unrepresented person, other than the advice to obtain counsel, when that person's interests are, or reasonably might be, in conflict with the interests of the lawyer's client. Nothing in this Rule, however, should be understood as precluding the lawyer from functioning in the normal representational role of advancing the client's position. Explaining the lawyer's own view of the meaning of a contract, for example, does not involve the giving of "advice" to an unrepresented person. Lawyers should be careful, however, to explain their roles to unrepresented persons to avoid the possibility of misunderstanding.

Corresponding ABA Model Rule. Paragraph (a) identical to Model Rule 4.3.

Corresponding Former Massachusetts Rule. No counterpart except (b) is taken from DR 7-104 (A) (2).

RULE 4.4 RESPECT FOR RIGHTS OF THIRD PERSONS

In representing a client, a lawyer shall not use means that have no substantial purpose other than to embarrass, delay, or burden a third person, or use methods of obtaining evidence that violate the legal rights of such a person.

Comment

[1] Responsibility to a client requires a lawyer to subordinate the interests of others to those of the client, but that responsibility does not imply that a lawyer may disregard the rights of third persons. It is impractical to catalogue all such rights, but they include legal restrictions on methods of obtaining evidence from third persons.

Corresponding ABA Model Rule. Identical to Model Rule 4.4.

Corresponding Former Massachusetts Rule. DR 7-106 (C) (2); see also DR 1-102, 7-102(A).

LAW FIRMS AND ASSOCIATIONS

RULE 5.1 RESPONSIBILITIES OF A PARTNER OR SUPERVISORY LAWYER

(a) A partner in a law firm shall make reasonable efforts to ensure that the firm has in effect measures giving reasonable assurance that all lawyers in the firm conform to the Rules of Professional Conduct.

(b) A lawyer having direct supervisory authority over another lawyer shall make reasonable efforts to ensure that the other lawyer conforms to the Rules of Professional Conduct.

(c) A lawyer shall be responsible for another lawyer's violation of the Rules of Professional Conduct if:

(1) the lawyer orders or, with knowledge of the specific conduct, ratifies the conduct involved; or

(2) the lawyer is a partner in the law firm in which the other lawyer practices, or has direct supervisory authority over the other lawyer, and knows of the conduct at a time when its consequences can be avoided or mitigated but fails to take reasonable remedial action.

Comment

[1] Paragraphs (a) and (b) refer to lawyers who have supervisory authority over the professional work of a firm or legal department of a government agency. This includes members of a partnership and the shareholders in a law firm organized as a professional corporation; lawyers having supervisory authority in the law department of an enterprise or government agency; and lawyers who have intermediate managerial responsibilities in a firm.

[2] The measures required to fulfill the responsibility prescribed in paragraphs (a) and (b) can depend on the firm's structure and the nature of its practice. In a small firm, informal supervision and occasional admonition ordinarily might be sufficient. In a large firm, or in practice situations in which intensely difficult ethical problems frequently arise, more elaborate procedures may be necessary. Some firms, for example, have a procedure whereby junior lawyers can make confidential referral of ethical problems directly to a designated senior partner or special committee. See Rule 5.2. Firms, whether large or small, may also rely on continuing legal education in professional ethics. In any event, the ethical atmosphere of a firm can influence the conduct of all its members and a lawyer having authority over the work of another may not assume that the subordinate lawyer will inevitably conform to the Rules.

[3] Paragraph (c)(1) expresses a general principle of responsibility for acts of another. See also Rule 8.4(a).

[4] Paragraph (c)(2) defines the duty of a lawyer having direct supervisory authority over performance of specific legal work by another lawyer. Whether a lawyer has such

supervisory authority in particular circumstances is a question of fact. Partners of a private firm have at least indirect responsibility for all work being done by the firm, while a partner in charge of a particular matter ordinarily has direct authority over other firm lawyers engaged in the matter. Appropriate remedial action by a partner would depend on the immediacy of the partner's involvement and the seriousness of the misconduct. The supervisor is required to intervene to prevent avoidable consequences of misconduct if the supervisor knows that the misconduct occurred. Thus, if a supervising lawyer knows that a subordinate misrepresented a matter to an opposing party in negotiation, the supervisor as well as the subordinate has a duty to correct the resulting misapprehension. Professional misconduct by a lawyer under supervision could reveal a violation of paragraph (b) on the part of the supervisory lawyer even though it does not entail a violation of paragraph (c) because there was no direction, ratification or knowledge of the violation.

[5] Apart from this Rule and Rule 8.4(a), a lawyer does not have disciplinary liability for the conduct of a partner, associate or subordinate. Whether a lawyer may be liable civilly or criminally for another lawyer's conduct is a question of law beyond the scope of these Rules.

Corresponding ABA Model Rule. Identical to Model Rule 5.1.

Corresponding Former Massachusetts Rule. None; but see DR 4-101 (D) and DR 7-107 (J).

RULE 5.2 RESPONSIBILITIES OF A SUBORDINATE LAWYER

(a) A lawyer is bound by the Rules of Professional Conduct notwithstanding that the lawyer acted at the direction of another person.

(b) A subordinate lawyer does not violate the Rules of Professional Conduct if that lawyer acts in accordance with a supervisory lawyer's reasonable resolution of an arguable question of professional duty.

Comment

[1] Although a lawyer is not relieved of responsibility for a violation by the fact that the lawyer acted at the direction of a supervisor, that fact may be relevant in determining whether a lawyer had the knowledge required to render conduct a violation of the Rules. For example, if a subordinate filed a frivolous pleading at the direction of a supervisor, the subordinate would not be guilty of a professional violation unless the subordinate knew of the document's frivolous character.

[2] When lawyers in a supervisor-subordinate relationship encounter a matter involving professional judgment as to ethical duty, the supervisor may assume responsibility for making the judgment. Otherwise a consistent course of action or position could not be taken. If the question can reasonably be answered only one way, the duty of both lawyers is clear and they are equally responsible for fulfilling it. However, if the question is reasonably arguable, someone has to decide upon the course of action. That authority ordinarily reposes in the supervisor, and a subordinate may be guided accordingly. For example, if a question arises whether the interests of two clients conflict under Rule 1.7, the supervisor's reasonable resolution of the question should protect the subordinate professionally if the resolution is subsequently challenged.

Corresponding ABA Model Rule. Identical to Model Rule 5.2.

Corresponding Former Massachusetts Rule. None.

RULE 5.3 RESPONSIBILITIES REGARDING NONLAWYER ASSISTANTS

With respect to a nonlawyer employed or retained by or associated with a lawyer:

(a) a partner in a law firm shall make reasonable efforts to ensure that the firm has in effect measures giving reasonable assurance that the person's conduct is compatible with the professional obligations of the lawyer;

(b) a lawyer having direct supervisory authority over the nonlawyer shall make reasonable efforts to ensure that the person's conduct is compatible with the professional obligations of the lawyer; and

(c) a lawyer shall be responsible for conduct of such a person that would be a violation of the Rules of Professional Conduct if engaged in by a lawyer if:

(1) the lawyer orders or, with the knowledge of the specific conduct, ratifies the conduct involved; or

(2) the lawyer is a partner in the law firm in which the person is employed, or has direct supervisory authority over the person, and knows of the conduct at a time when its consequences can be avoided or mitigated but fails to take reasonable remedial action.

Comment

[1] Lawyers generally employ assistants in their practice, including secretaries, investigators, law student interns, and paraprofessionals. Such assistants, whether employees or independent contractors, act for the lawyer in rendition of the lawyer's professional services. A lawyer should give such assistants appropriate instruction and supervision concerning the ethical aspects of their employment, particularly regarding the obligation not to disclose information relating to representation of the client, and should be responsible for their work product. The measures employed in supervising nonlawyers should take account of the fact that they do not have legal training and are not subject to professional discipline.

Corresponding ABA Model Rule. Identical to Model Rule 5.3.

Corresponding Former Massachusetts Rule. None; but see DR 4-101 (D), DR 7-107 (J).

RULE 5.4 PROFESSIONAL INDEPENDENCE OF A LAWYER

(a) A lawyer or law firm shall not share legal fees with a nonlawyer, except that:

(1) an agreement by a lawyer with the lawyer's firm, partner, or associate may provide for the payment of money, over a reasonable period of time after the lawyer's death, to the lawyer's estate or to one or more specified persons;

(2) a lawyer who purchases the practice of a deceased, disabled, or disappeared lawyer may, pursuant to the provisions of Rule 1.17, pay to the estate or other representative of that lawyer the agreed-upon purchase price;

(3) a lawyer or law firm may include nonlawyer employees in a compensation or retirement plan, even though the plan is based in whole or in part on a profit-sharing arrangement; and

(4) a lawyer or law firm may agree to share a statutory or tribunal-approved fee award, or a settlement in a matter eligible for such an award, with a qualified legal assistance organization that referred the matter to the lawyer or law firm, if (i) the organization is one that is not for profit, (ii) the organization is tax-exempt under federal law, (iii) the fee award or settlement is made in connection with a proceeding to advance one or more of the purposes by virtue of which the organization is

tax-exempt, and (iv) the client consents, after being informed that a division of fees will be made, to the sharing of the fees and the total fee is reasonable.

(b) A lawyer shall not form a partnership or other business entity with a nonlawyer if any of the activities of the entity consist of the practice of law.

(c) A lawyer shall not permit a person who recommends, employs, or pays the lawyer to render legal services for another to direct or regulate the lawyer's professional judgment in rendering such legal services.

(d) A lawyer shall not practice with or in the form of a limited liability entity authorized to practice law for a profit, if:

> (1) a nonlawyer owns any interest therein, except that a fiduciary representative of the estate of a lawyer may hold the stock or interest of the lawyer for a reasonable time during administration;

> (2) a nonlawyer is an officer, or a corporate director or limited liability company manager thereof; or

> (3) a nonlawyer has the right to direct or control the professional judgment of a lawyer.

Comment

[1] The provisions of this Rule express traditional limitations on sharing fees. These limitations are to protect the lawyer's professional independence of judgment. Where someone other than the client pays the lawyer's fee or salary, or recommends employment of the lawyer, that arrangement does not modify the lawyer's obligation to the client. As stated in paragraph (c), such arrangements must not interfere with the lawyer's professional judgment. See Comment 10 to Rule 1.17.

[2] Rule 5.4(a)(4) explicitly permits a lawyer, with the client's consent to agree, to share certain fees with a tax-exempt, non-profit qualified legal assistance organization that has referred the matter to the lawyer. The interest that such a charitable or public purpose organization has in the successful pursuit of litigation advancing an aim of the organization related to its tax exemption lessens significantly the danger of the abuses of fee-sharing between lawyers and nonlawyers that this Rule is designed to prevent. The financial needs of these organizations, which serve important public ends, justify a limited exception to the prohibition against fee-sharing with nonlawyers. Should abuses occur in the carrying out of such arrangements, they may constitute a violation of Rule 5.4(c) or Rule 8.4(d) or (h). The permission to share fees granted by this Rule is not intended to restrict the ability of those qualified legal assistance organizations that engage in the practice of law themselves to receive a share of another lawyer's legal fees pursuant to Rule 1.5(e). The permission granted by this Rule does not extend to fees generated in connection with proceedings not related to the purpose for which the organization is tax-exempt, such as generating business income for the organization.

Corresponding ABA Model Rule. Identical to Model Rule 5.4, except for subclause (4) of paragraph (a) which is new, and except for changes to paragraphs (b) and (d).

Corresponding Former Massachusetts Rule. DR 3-102, DR 3-103, DR 5-107(B) and (C); see also DR 3-101(A).

RULE 5.5 UNAUTHORIZED PRACTICE OF LAW; MULTIJURISDICTIONAL PRACTICE OF LAW

(a) A lawyer shall not practice law in a jurisdiction in violation of the regulation of the legal profession in that jurisdiction, or assist another in doing so.

(b) A lawyer who is not admitted to practice in this jurisdiction shall not:

(1) except as authorized by these Rules or other law, establish an office or other systematic and continuous presence in this jurisdiction for the practice of law; or

(2) hold out to the public or otherwise represent that the lawyer is admitted to practice law in this jurisdiction.

(c) A lawyer admitted in another United States jurisdiction, and not disbarred or suspended from practice in any jurisdiction, may provide legal services on a temporary basis in this jurisdiction that:

(1) are undertaken in association with a lawyer who is admitted to practice in this jurisdiction and who actively participates in the matter;

(2) are in or reasonably related to a pending or potential proceeding before a tribunal in this or another jurisdiction, if the lawyer, or a person the lawyer is assisting, is authorized by law or order to appear in such proceeding or reasonably expects to be so authorized;

(3) are in or reasonably related to a pending or potential arbitration, mediation, or other alternative dispute resolution proceeding in this or another jurisdiction, if the services arise out of or are reasonably related to the lawyer's practice in a jurisdiction in which the lawyer is admitted to practice and are not services for which the forum requires pro hac vice admission; or

(4) are not within paragraphs (c)(2) or (c)(3) and arise out of or are reasonably related to the lawyer's practice in a jurisdiction in which the lawyer is admitted to practice.

(d) A lawyer admitted in another United States jurisdiction, and not disbarred or suspended from practice in any jurisdiction, may provide legal services in this jurisdiction that:

(1) are provided to the lawyer's employer or its organizational affiliates and are not services for which the forum requires pro hac vice admission; or

(2) are services that the lawyer is authorized to provide by federal law or other law of this jurisdiction.

Comment

[1] A lawyer may practice law in this jurisdiction only if admitted to practice generally or if authorized by court rule or order or by law to practice for a limited purpose or on a restricted basis. Paragraph (a) applies to unauthorized practice of law by a lawyer, whether through the lawyer's direct action or by the lawyer assisting another person.

[2] Limiting the practice of law to members of the bar protects the public against rendition of legal services by unqualified persons. This Rule does not prohibit a lawyer from employing the services of paraprofessionals and delegating functions to them, so long as the lawyer supervises the delegated work and retains responsibility for their work. See Rule 5.3.

[3] A lawyer may provide professional advice and instruction to nonlawyers whose employment requires knowledge of law; for example, claims adjusters, employees of financial or commercial institutions, social workers, accountants and persons employed in government agencies.

[4] Other than as authorized by law or this Rule, a lawyer who is not admitted to practice generally in this jurisdiction violates paragraph (b) if the lawyer establishes an office or other systematic and continuous presence in this jurisdiction for the practice of law.

Presence may be systematic and continuous, for example by placing a name on the office door or letterhead of another lawyer without qualification, even if the lawyer is not physically present here. A lawyer not admitted to practice in this jurisdiction must not hold out to the public or otherwise represent that the lawyer is admitted to practice law in this jurisdiction. See also Rules 7.1(a) and 7.5(b).

[5] There are occasions in which a lawyer admitted to practice in another United States jurisdiction, and not disbarred or suspended from practice in any jurisdiction, may provide legal services on a temporary basis in this jurisdiction under circumstances that do not create an unreasonable risk to the interests of the lawyer's clients, the public or the courts. Paragraph (c) identifies four such circumstances. The fact that conduct is not so identified does not imply that the conduct is or is not authorized. With the exception of paragraphs (d)(1) and (d)(2), this Rule does not authorize a lawyer to establish an office or other systematic and continuous presence in this jurisdiction without being admitted to practice generally here.

[6] There is no single test to determine whether a lawyer's services are provided on a "temporary basis" in this jurisdiction, and may therefore be permissible under paragraph (c). Services may be "temporary" even though the lawyer provides services in this jurisdiction on a recurring basis, or for an extended period of time, as when the lawyer is representing a client in a single lengthy negotiation or litigation.

[7] Paragraphs (c) and (d) apply to lawyers who are admitted to practice law in any United States jurisdiction, which includes the District of Columbia and any state, territory or commonwealth of the United States. The word "admitted" in paragraph (c) and (d) means the lawyer is authorized to practice in the jurisdiction in which the lawyer is admitted and excludes a lawyer who while technically admitted is not authorized to practice, because, for example, the lawyer is on inactive status.

[8] Paragraph (c)(1) recognizes that the interests of clients and the public are protected if a lawyer admitted only in another jurisdiction associates with a lawyer licensed to practice in this jurisdiction. For this paragraph to apply, however, the lawyer admitted to practice in this jurisdiction must actively participate in and share responsibility for the representation of the client.

[9] Lawyers not admitted to practice generally in this jurisdiction may be authorized by law or order of a tribunal or an administrative agency to appear before the tribunal or agency. This authority may be granted pursuant to formal rules governing admission pro hac vice or pursuant to informal practice of the tribunal or agency. Under paragraph (c)(2), a lawyer does not violate this Rule when the lawyer appears before a tribunal or agency pursuant to such authority. To the extent that a court rule or other law of this jurisdiction requires a lawyer who is not admitted to practice in this jurisdiction to obtain admission pro hac vice before appearing before a tribunal or administrative agency, this Rule requires the lawyer to obtain that authority.

[10] Paragraph (c)(2) also provides that a lawyer rendering services in this jurisdiction on a temporary basis does not violate this Rule when the lawyer engages in conduct in anticipation of a proceeding or hearing in a jurisdiction in which the lawyer is authorized to practice law or in which the lawyer reasonably expects to be admitted pro hac vice. Examples of such conduct include meetings with the client, interviews of potential witnesses, and the review of documents. Similarly, a lawyer admitted only in another jurisdiction may engage in conduct temporarily in this jurisdiction in connection with pending litigation in another jurisdiction in which the lawyer is or reasonably expects to be authorized to appear, including taking depositions in this jurisdiction.

[11] When a lawyer has been or reasonably expects to be admitted to appear before a court or administrative agency, paragraph (c)(2) also permits conduct by lawyers who are associated with that lawyer in the matter, but who do not expect to appear before the court or administrative agency. For example, subordinate lawyers may conduct research, review documents, and attend meetings with witnesses in support of the lawyer responsible for the litigation.

[12] Paragraph (c)(3) permits a lawyer admitted to practice law in another jurisdiction to perform services on a temporary basis in this jurisdiction if those services are in or reasonably related to a pending or potential arbitration, mediation, or other alternative dispute resolution proceeding in this or another jurisdiction, if the services arise out of or are reasonably related to the lawyer's practice in a jurisdiction in which the lawyer is admitted to practice. The lawyer, however, must obtain admission pro hac vice in the case of a court-annexed arbitration or mediation or otherwise if court rules or law so require.

[13] Paragraph (c)(4) permits a lawyer admitted in another jurisdiction to provide certain legal services on a temporary basis in this jurisdiction that arise out of or are reasonably related to the lawyer's practice in a jurisdiction in which the lawyer is admitted but are not within paragraphs (c)(2) or (c)(3). These services include both legal services and services that nonlawyers may perform but that are considered the practice of law when performed by lawyers.

[14] Paragraphs (c)(3) and (c)(4) require that the services arise out of or be reasonably related to the lawyer's practice in a jurisdiction in which the lawyer is admitted. A variety of factors evidence such a relationship. The lawyer's client may have been previously represented by the lawyer, or may be resident in or have substantial contacts with the jurisdiction in which the lawyer is admitted. The matter, although involving other jurisdictions, may have a significant connection with that jurisdiction. In other cases, significant aspects of the lawyer's work might be conducted in that jurisdiction or a significant aspect of the matter may involve the law of that jurisdiction. The necessary relationship might arise when the client's activities or the legal issues involve multiple jurisdictions, such as when the officers of a multinational corporation survey potential business sites and seek the services of their lawyer in assessing the relative merits of each. In addition, the services may draw on the lawyer's recognized expertise developed through the regular practice of law on behalf of clients in matters involving a particular body of federal, nationally-uniform, foreign, or international law.

[15] Paragraph (d) identifies two circumstances in which a lawyer who is admitted to practice in another United States jurisdiction, and is not disbarred or suspended from practice in any jurisdiction, may establish an office or other systematic and continuous presence in this jurisdiction for the practice of law as well as provide legal services on a temporary basis. Except as provided in paragraphs (d)(1) and (d)(2), a lawyer who is admitted to practice law in another jurisdiction and who establishes an office or other systematic or continuous presence in this jurisdiction must become admitted to practice law generally in this jurisdiction.

[16] Paragraph (d)(1) applies to a lawyer who is employed by a client to provide legal services to the client or its organizational affiliates, i.e., entities that control, are controlled by, or are under common control with the employer. This paragraph does not authorize the provision of personal legal services to the employer's officers or employees that are unrelated to their employment. The paragraph applies to in-house corporate lawyers, government lawyers and others who are employed to render legal services to the

employer. The nature of the relationship between the lawyer and client provides a sufficient safeguard that the lawyer is competent to advise regarding the matters for which the lawyer is employed.

[17] If an employed lawyer establishes an office or other systematic presence in this jurisdiction for the purpose of rendering legal services to the employer, the lawyer may be subject to registration or other requirements, including assessments for appropriate fees and charges.

[18] Paragraph (d)(2) recognizes that a lawyer may provide legal services in this jurisdiction even though not admitted when the lawyer is authorized to do so by federal or other law, which includes statute, court rule, executive regulation or judicial precedent.

[19] A lawyer who practices law in this jurisdiction pursuant to paragraphs (c) or (d) or otherwise is subject to the disciplinary authority of this jurisdiction. See Rule 8.5(a).

[20] In some circumstances, a lawyer who practices law in this jurisdiction pursuant to paragraphs (c) or (d) may have to inform the client that the lawyer is not admitted to practice law in this jurisdiction. For example, that may be required when the representation occurs primarily in this jurisdiction and requires knowledge of the law of this jurisdiction. See Rule 1.4(b).

[21] Paragraphs (c) and (d) do not authorize communications advertising legal services to prospective clients in this jurisdiction by lawyers who are admitted to practice in other jurisdictions. Whether and how lawyers may communicate the availability of their services to prospective clients in this jurisdiction is governed by Rules 7.1 to 7.5.

Corresponding ABA Model Rule. Identical to Model Rule 5.5, as amended in 2002; comments substantially similar.

Corresponding Former Massachusetts Rule. DR 3-101.

RULE 5.6 RESTRICTIONS ON RIGHT TO PRACTICE

A lawyer shall not participate in offering or making:

> (a) a partnership or employment agreement that restricts the right of a lawyer to practice after termination of the relationship, except an agreement concerning benefits upon retirement; or

> (b) an agreement in which a restriction on the lawyer's right to practice is part of the settlement of a controversy.

Comment

[1] An agreement restricting the right of partners or associates to practice after leaving a firm not only limits their professional autonomy but also limits the freedom of clients to choose a lawyer. Paragraph (a) prohibits such agreements except for restrictions incident to provisions concerning retirement benefits for service with the firm.

[2] Paragraph (b) prohibits a lawyer from agreeing not to represent other persons in connection with settling a claim on behalf of a client. The prohibition applies to matters in which the government is a party as well as to purely private disputes.

[3] This Rule does not apply to prohibit restrictions that may be included in the terms of the sale of a law practice pursuant to Rule 1.17.

Corresponding ABA Model Rule. Identical to Model Rule 5.6, except reference to private parties deleted at the end of paragraph (b).

Corresponding Former Massachusetts Rule. DR 2-108.

RULE 5.7 RESPONSIBILITIES REGARDING LAW-RELATED SERVICES

(a) A lawyer shall be subject to the Rules of Professional Conduct with respect to the provision of law-related services, as defined in paragraph (b), if the law-related services are provided:

(1) by the lawyer in circumstances that are not distinct from the lawyer's provision of legal services to clients; or

(2) by a separate entity controlled by the lawyer individually or with others if the lawyer fails to take reasonable measures to assure that a person obtaining the law-related services knows that the services of the separate entity are not legal services and that the protections of the client-lawyer relationship do not exist.

(b) The term "law-related services" denotes services that might reasonably be performed in conjunction with and in substance are related to the provision of legal services, and that are not prohibited as unauthorized practice of law when provided by a nonlawyer.

Comment

[1] When a lawyer performs law-related services or controls an organization that does so, there exists the potential for ethical problems. Principal among these is the possibility that the person for whom the law-related services are performed fails to understand that the services may not carry with them the protections normally afforded as part of the client-lawyer relationship. The recipient of the law-related services may expect, for example, that the protection of client confidences, prohibitions against representation of persons with conflicting interests, and obligations of a lawyer to maintain professional independence apply to the provision of law-related services when that may not be the case.

[2] Rule 5.7 applies to the provision of law-related services by a lawyer even when the lawyer does not provide any legal services to the person for whom the law-related services are performed. The Rule identifies the circumstances in which all of the Rules of Professional Conduct apply to the provision of law-related services. Even when those circumstances do not exist, however, the conduct of a lawyer involved in the provision of law-related services is subject to those Rules that apply generally to lawyer conduct, regardless of whether the conduct involves the provision of legal services. See, e.g., Rule 8.4.

[3] When law-related services are provided by a lawyer under circumstances that are not distinct from the lawyer's provision of legal services to clients, the lawyer in providing the law-related services must adhere to the requirements of the Rules of Professional Conduct as provided in Rule 5.7(a)(1).

[4] Law-related services also may be provided through an entity that is distinct from that through which the lawyer provides legal services. If the lawyer individually or with others has control of such an entity's operations, the Rule requires the lawyer to take reasonable measures to assure that each person using the services of the entity knows that the services provided by the entity are not legal services and that the Rules of Professional Conduct that relate to the client-lawyer relationship do not apply. A lawyer's control of an entity extends to the ability to direct its operation. Whether a lawyer has such control will depend upon the circumstances of the particular case.

[5] When a client-lawyer relationship exists with a person who is referred by a lawyer to a separate law-related service entity controlled by the lawyer, individually or with others, the lawyer must comply with Rule 1.8(a).

[6] In taking the reasonable measures referred to in paragraph (a)(2) to assure that a person using law-related services understands the practical effect or significance of the inapplicability of the Rules of Professional Conduct, the lawyer should communicate to the person receiving the law-related services, in a manner sufficient to assure that the person understands the significance of the fact, that the relationship of the person to the business entity will not be a client-lawyer relationship. The communication should be made before entering into an agreement for provision of or providing law-related services, and preferably should be in writing.

[7] The burden is upon the lawyer to show that the lawyer has taken reasonable measures under the circumstances to communicate the desired understanding. For instance, a sophisticated user of law-related services, such as a publicly held corporation, may require a lesser explanation than someone unaccustomed to making distinctions between legal services and law-related services, such as an individual seeking tax advice from a lawyer-accountant or investigative services in connection with a lawsuit.

[8] Regardless of the sophistication of potential recipients of law-related services, a lawyer should take special care to keep separate the provision of law-related and legal services in order to minimize the risk that the recipient will assume that the law-related services are legal services. The risk of such confusion is especially acute when the lawyer renders both types of services with respect to the same matter. Under some circumstances the legal and law-related services may be so closely entwined that they cannot be distinguished from each other, and the requirement of disclosure and consultation imposed by paragraph (a)(2) of the Rule cannot be met. In such a case a lawyer will be responsible for assuring that both the lawyer's conduct and, to the extent required by Rule 5.3, that of nonlawyer employees in the distinct entity which the lawyer controls complies in all respects with the Rules of Professional Conduct.

[9] A broad range of economic and other interests of clients may be served by lawyers' engaging in the delivery of law-related services. Examples of law-related services include providing title insurance, financial planning, accounting, trust services, real estate counseling, legislative lobbying, economic analysis social work, psychological counseling, tax preparation, and patent, medical or environmental consulting.

[10] When a lawyer is obliged to accord the recipients of such services the protections of those Rules that apply to the client-lawyer relationship, the lawyer must take special care to heed the proscriptions of the Rules addressing conflict of interest (Rules 1.7 through 1.11, especially Rules 1.7(b) and 1.8(a),(b) and (f)), and to scrupulously adhere to the requirements of Rule 1.6 relating to disclosure of confidential information. The promotion of the law-related services must also in all respects comply with Rules 7.1 through 7.5, dealing with advertising and solicitation. In that regard, lawyers should take special care to identify the obligations that may be imposed as a result of a jurisdiction's decisional law.

[11] When the full protections of all of the Rules of Professional Conduct do not apply to the provision of law-related services, principles of law external to the Rules, for example, the law of principal and agent, govern the legal duties owed to those receiving the services. Those other legal principles may establish a different degree of protection for the recipient with respect to confidentiality of information, conflicts of interest and permissible business relationships with clients. See also Rule 8.4 (Misconduct).

Corresponding ABA Model Rule. Identical to Model Rule 5.7.

Corresponding Former Massachusetts Rule. None.

PUBLIC SERVICE

RULE 6.1 VOLUNTARY PRO BONO PUBLICO SERVICES

A lawyer should provide annually at least 25 hours of *pro bono publico* legal services for the benefit of persons of limited means. In providing these professional services, the lawyer should:

(a) provide all or most of the 25 hours of *pro bono publico* legal services without compensation or expectation of compensation to persons of limited means, or to charitable, religious, civic, community, governmental, and educational organizations in matters that are designed primarily to address the needs of persons of limited means. The lawyer may provide any remaining hours by delivering legal services at substantially reduced compensation to persons of limited means or by participating in activities for improving the law, the legal system, or the legal profession that are primarily intended to benefit persons of limited means; or,

(b) contribute from $250 to 1% of the lawyer's annual taxable, professional income to one or more organizations that provide or support legal services to persons of limited means.

Comment

[1] Every lawyer, regardless of professional prominence or professional work load, should provide legal services to persons of limited means. This rule sets forth a standard which the court believes each member of the Bar of the Commonwealth can and should fulfill. Because the rule is aspirational, failure to provide the pro bono publico services stated in this rule will not subject a lawyer to discipline. The rule calls on all lawyers to provide a minimum of 25 hours of pro bono publico legal services annually. Twenty-five hours is one-half of the number of hours specified in the ABA Model Rule 6.1 because this Massachusetts rule focuses only on legal activity that benefits those unable to afford access to the system of justice. In some years a lawyer may render greater or fewer than 25 hours, but during the course of his or her legal career, each lawyer should render annually, on average, 25 hours. Also, it may be more feasible to act collectively, for example, by a firm's providing through one or more lawyers an amount of pro bono publico legal services sufficient to satisfy the aggregate amount of hours expected from all lawyers in the firm. Services can be performed in civil matters or in criminal or quasi-criminal matters for which there is no government obligation to provide funds for legal representation.

[2] The purpose of this rule is to make the system of justice more open to all by increasing the pro bono publico legal services available to persons of limited means. Because this rule calls for the provision of 25 hours of pro bono publico legal services annually, instead of the 50 hours per year specified in ABA Model Rule 6.1, the provision of the ABA Model Rule regarding service to non-profit organizations was omitted. This omission should not be read as denigrating the value of the voluntary service provided to non-profit community and civil rights organizations by many lawyers. Such services are valuable to the community as a whole and should be continued. Service on the boards of non-profit arts and civic organizations, on school committees, and in local public office are but a few examples of public service by lawyers. Such activities, to the extent they are not directed at meeting the legal needs of persons of limited means, are not within the scope of this rule. While the American Bar Association Model Rule 6.1 also does not credit general civic activities, it explicitly provides that some of a lawyer's pro bono publico obligation may be met by legal services provided to vindicate "civil rights,

civil liberties and public rights." Such activities, when undertaken on behalf of persons of limited means, are within the scope of this rule.

[3] Paragraph (a) describes the nature of the pro bono publico legal services to be rendered annually under the rule. Such legal services consist of a full range of activities on behalf of persons of limited means, including individual and class representation, the provision of legal advice, legislative lobbying, administrative rule making, community legal education, and the provision of free training or mentoring to those who represent persons of limited means.

[4] Persons eligible for pro bono publico legal services under this rule are those who qualify for publicly-funded legal service programs and those whose incomes and financial resources are above the guidelines used by such programs but who, nevertheless, cannot afford counsel. Legal services can be rendered to individuals or to organizations composed of low-income people, to organizations that serve those of limited means such as homeless shelters, battered women's centers, and food pantries or to those organizations which pursue civil rights, civil liberties, and public rights on behalf of persons of limited means. Providing legal advice, counsel and assistance to an organization consisting of or serving persons of limited means while a member of its board of directors would be pro bono publico legal services under this rule.

[5] In order to be pro bono publico services under the first sentence of Rule 6.1 (a), services must be provided without compensation or expectation of compensation. The intent of the lawyer to render free legal services is essential for the work performed to fall within the meaning of this paragraph. Accordingly, services rendered cannot be considered pro bono if an anticipated fee is uncollected. The award of statutory attorneys' fees in a case accepted as a pro bono case, however, would not disqualify such services from inclusion under this section.

[6] A lawyer should perform pro bono publico services exclusively or primarily through activities described in the first sentence of paragraph (a). Any remaining hours can be provided in the ways set forth in the second sentence of that paragraph, including instances in which an attorney agrees to receive a modest fee for furnishing legal services to persons of limited means. Acceptance of court appointments and provision of services to individuals when the fee is substantially below a lawyer's usual rate are encouraged under this sentence.

[7] The variety of activities described in Comment [3] should facilitate participation by government and corporate attorneys, even when restrictions exist on their engaging in the outside practice of law. Lawyers who by the nature of their positions are prohibited from participating in the activities described in the first sentence of paragraph (a) may engage in the activities described in the second sentence of paragraph (a) or make a financial contribution pursuant to paragraph (b).

[8] The second sentence of paragraph (a) also recognizes the value of lawyers engaging in activities, on behalf of persons of limited means, that improve the law, the legal system, or the legal profession. Examples of the many activities that fall within this sentence, when primarily intended to benefit persons of limited means, include: serving on bar association committees, serving on boards of pro bono or legal services programs, taking part in Law Day activities, acting as a continuing legal education instructor, a mediator or an arbitrator, and engaging in legislative lobbying to improve the law, the legal system, or the profession.

[9] Lawyers who choose to make financial contributions pursuant to paragraph (b) should contribute from $250 to 1% of the lawyer's adjusted net Massachusetts income

from legal professional activities. Each lawyer should take into account his or her own specific circumstances and obligations in determining his or her contribution.

Corresponding ABA Model Rule. Different from Model Rule 6.1.

Corresponding Former Massachusetts Rule. None.

RULE 6.2 ACCEPTING APPOINTMENTS

A lawyer shall not seek to avoid appointment by a tribunal to represent a person except for good cause, such as:

(a) representing the client is likely to result in violation of the Rules of Professional Conduct or other law;

(b) representing the client is likely to result in an unreasonable financial burden on the lawyer; or

(c) the client or the cause is so repugnant to the lawyer as to be likely to impair the client-lawyer relationship or the lawyer's ability to represent the client.

Comment

[1] A lawyer ordinarily is not obliged to accept a client whose character or cause the lawyer regards as repugnant. The lawyer's freedom to select clients is, however, qualified. For example, a lawyer may be subject to appointment by a court to serve unpopular clients or persons unable to afford legal services.

Appointed Counsel

[2] For good cause a lawyer may seek to decline an appointment to represent a person who cannot afford to retain counsel or whose cause is unpopular. Good cause exists if the lawyer could not handle the matter competently, see Rule 1.1, or if undertaking the representation would result in an improper conflict of interest, for example, when the client or the cause is so repugnant to the lawyer as to be likely to impair the client-lawyer relationship or the lawyer's ability to represent the client. A lawyer may also seek to decline an appointment if acceptance would be unreasonably burdensome, for example, when it would impose a financial sacrifice so great as to be unjust.

[3] An appointed lawyer has the same obligations to the client as retained counsel, including the obligations of loyalty and confidentiality, and is subject to the same limitations on the client-lawyer relationship, such as the obligation to refrain from assisting the client in violation of the Rules.

Corresponding ABA Model Rule. Identical to Model Rule 6.2.

Corresponding Former Massachusetts Rule. None.

RULE 6.3 MEMBERSHIP IN LEGAL SERVICES ORGANIZATION

A lawyer may serve as a director, officer, or member of a legal services organization, apart from the law firm in which the lawyer practices, notwithstanding that the organization serves persons having interests adverse to a client of the lawyer. The lawyer shall not knowingly participate in a decision or action of the organization:

(a) if participating in the decision or action would be incompatible with the lawyer's obligations to a client under Rule 1.7; or

(b) where the decision or action could have a material adverse effect on the representation of a client of the organization whose interests are adverse to a client of the lawyer.

Comment

[1] Lawyers should be encouraged to support and participate in legal service organizations. A lawyer who is an officer or a member of such an organization does not thereby have a client-lawyer relationship with persons served by the organization. However, there is potential conflict between the interests of such persons and the interests of the lawyer's clients. If the possibility of such conflict disqualified a lawyer from serving on the board of a legal services organization, the profession's involvement in such organizations would be severely curtailed.

[2] It may be necessary in appropriate cases to reassure a client of the organization that the representation will not be affected by conflicting loyalties of a member of the board. Established, written policies in this respect can enhance the credibility of such assurances.

Corresponding ABA Model Rule. Identical to Model Rule 6.3.

Corresponding Former Massachusetts Rule. None.

RULE 6.4 LAW REFORM ACTIVITIES AFFECTING CLIENT INTERESTS

A lawyer may serve as a director, officer, or member of an organization involved in reform of the law or its administration notwithstanding that the reform may affect the interests of a client of the lawyer. When the lawyer knows that the interests of a client may be materially benefitted by a decision in which the lawyer participates, the lawyer shall disclose that fact but need not identify the client.

Comment

[1] Lawyers involved in organizations seeking law reform generally do not have a client-lawyer relationship with the organization. Otherwise, it might follow that a lawyer could not be involved in a bar association law reform program that might indirectly affect a client. See also Rule 1.2(b). For example, a lawyer specializing in antitrust litigation might be regarded as disqualified from participating in drafting revisions of rules governing that subject. In determining the nature and scope of participation in such activities, a lawyer should be mindful of obligations to clients under other Rules, particularly Rule 1.7. A lawyer is professionally obligated to protect the integrity of the program by making an appropriate disclosure within the organization when the lawyer knows a private client might be materially benefitted.

Corresponding ABA Model Rule. Identical to Model Rule 6.4.

Corresponding Former Massachusetts Rule. None. But see G. L. c. 211D, § 1, as to members of the Committee for Public Counsel Services.

RULE 6.5 NONPROFIT AND COURT-ANNEXED LIMITED LEGAL SERVICES PROGRAMS

(a) A lawyer who, under the auspices of a program sponsored by a nonprofit organization or court, provides short-term limited legal services to a client without expectation by either the lawyer or the client that the lawyer will provide continuing representation in the matter:

(1) is subject to Rules 1.7 and 1.9(a) only if the lawyer knows that the representation of the client involves a conflict of interest; and

(2) is subject to Rule 1.10 only if the lawyer knows that another lawyer associated with the lawyer in a law firm is disqualified by Rule 1.7 or 1.9(a) with respect to the matter.

(b) Except as provided in paragraph (a)(2), Rule 1.10 is inapplicable to a representation governed by this Rule.

Comment

[1] Legal services organizations, courts and various nonprofit organizations have established programs through which lawyers provide short-term limited legal services—such as advice or the completion of legal forms—that will assist persons to address their legal problems without further representation by a lawyer. In these programs, such as legal-advice hotlines, advice-only clinics or pro se counseling program ms, a client-lawyer relationship is established, but there is no expectation that the lawyer's representation of the client will continue beyond the limited consultation. Such programs are normally operated under circumstances in which it is not feasible for a lawyer to systematically screen for conflicts of interest as is generally required before undertaking a representation. See, e.g., Rules 1.7, 1.9 and 1.10.

[2] A lawyer who provides short-term limited legal services pursuant to this Rule must secure the client's informed consent to the limited scope of the representation. See Rule 1.2(c). If a short-term limited representation would not be reasonable under the circumstances, the lawyer may offer advice to the client but must also advise the client of the need for further assistance of counsel. Except as provided in this Rule, the Rules of Professional Conduct, including Rules 1.6 and 1.9(c), are applicable to the limited representation.

[3] Because a lawyer who is representing a client in the circumstances addressed by this Rule ordinarily is not able to check systematically for conflicts of interest, paragraph (a) requires compliance with Rules 1.7 or 1.9(a) only if the lawyer knows that the representation presents a conflict of interest for the lawyer, and with Rule 1.10 only if the lawyer knows that another lawyer in the lawyer's firm is disqualified by Rules 1.7 or 1.9(a) in the matter.

[4] Because the limited nature of the services significantly reduces the risk of conflicts of interest with other matters being handled by the lawyer's firm, paragraph (b) provides that Rule 1.10 is inapplicable to a representation governed by this Rule except as provided by paragraph (a)(2). Paragraph (a)(2) requires the participating lawyer to comply with Rule 1.10 when the lawyer knows that the lawyer's firm is disqualified by Rules 1.7 or 1.9(a). By virtue of paragraph (b), however, a lawyer's participation in a short-term limited legal services program will not preclude the lawyer's firm from undertaking or continuing the representation of a client with interests adverse to a client being represented under the program's auspices. Nor will the personal disqualification of a lawyer participating in the program be imputed to other lawyers participating in the program.

[5] If, after commencing a short-term limited representation in accordance with this Rule, a lawyer undertakes to represent the client in the matter on an ongoing basis, Rules 1.7, 1.9(a) and 1.10 become applicable.

Corresponding ABA Model Rule. Identical to Model Rule 6.5.

Corresponding Former Massachusetts Rule. No counterpart.

INFORMATION ABOUT LEGAL SERVICES

RULE 7.1 COMMUNICATIONS CONCERNING A LAWYER'S SERVICES

A lawyer shall not make a false or misleading communication about the lawyer or the lawyer's services. A communication is false or misleading if it contains a material misrepresentation of fact or law, or omits a fact necessary to make the statement considered as a whole not materially misleading.

Comment

[1] This Rule governs all communications about a lawyer's services, including advertising permitted by Rule 7.2. Whatever means are used to make known a lawyer's services, statements about them should be truthful. Statements that compare a lawyers services with another lawyer's services and statements that create unjustified expectations about the results the lawyer can achieve would violate Rule 7.1 if they constitute "false or misleading" communications under the Rule.

Corresponding ABA Model Rule. Identical to Model Rule 7.1.

Corresponding Former Massachusetts Rule. DR 2-101(A).

RULE 7.2 ADVERTISING

(a) Subject to the requirements of Rule 7.1, a lawyer may advertise services through public media, such as a telephone directory, legal directory including an electronic or computer-accessed directory, newspaper or other periodical, outdoor advertising, radio or television, or through written, electronic, computer-accessed or similar types of communication not involving solicitation prohibited in Rule 7.3.

(b) A copy or recording of an advertisement or written communication of services offered for a fee shall be kept for two years after its last dissemination along with a record of when and where it was used.

(c) A lawyer shall not give anything of value to a person for recommending the lawyer's services, except that a lawyer may:

> (1) pay the reasonable costs of advertisements or communications permitted by this Rule;

> (2) pay the usual charges of a not-for-profit lawyer referral service or legal service organization;

> (3) pay for a law practice in accordance with Rule 1.17;

> (4) pay referral fees permitted by Rule 1.5(e); and

> (5) share a statutory fee award or court-approved settlement in lieu thereof with a qualified legal assistance organization in accordance with Rule 5.4(a)(4).

(d) Any communication made pursuant to this rule shall include the name of the lawyer, group of lawyers, or firm responsible for its content.

Comment

[1] To assist the public in obtaining legal services, lawyers should be allowed to make known their services not only through reputation but also through organized information campaigns in the form of advertising.

[2] [Reserved]

[3] Questions of effectiveness and taste in advertising are matters of speculation and subjective judgment. Television and other electronic media, including computer-accessed communications, are now among the most powerful media for getting information to the public. Prohibiting such advertising, therefore, would impede the flow of information about legal services to many sectors of the public. Limiting the information that may be advertised has a similar effect and assumes that the bar can accurately forecast the kind of information that the public would regard as relevant.

[3A] The advertising and solicitation rules can generally be applied to computer-accessed or other similar types of communications by analogizing the communication to its hard-copy form. Thus, because it is not a communication directed to a specific recipient, a web site or home page would generally be considered advertising subject to this rule, rather than solicitation subject to Rule 7.3. For example, when a targeted e-mail solicitation of a person known to be in need of legal services contains a hot-link to a home page, the e-mail message is subject to Rule 7.3, but the home page itself need not be because the recipient must make an affirmative decision to go to the sender's home page. Depending upon the circumstances, posting of comments to a newsgroup, bulletin board or chat group may constitute targeted or direct contact with prospective clients known to be in need of legal services and may therefore be subject to Rule 7.3. Depending upon the topic or purpose of the newsgroup, bulletin board, or chat group, the posting might also constitute an association of the lawyer or law firms name with a particular service, field, or area of law amounting to a claim of specialization under Rule 7.4 and would therefore be subject to the restrictions of that rule. In addition, if the lawyer or law firm uses an interactive forum such as a chat group to solicit for a fee professional employment that the prospective client has not requested, this conduct may constitute prohibited personal solicitation under Rule 7.3(d).

[4] Neither this Rule nor Rule 7.3 prohibits communications authorized by law, such as notice to members of a class in class action litigation.

Record of Advertising

[5] Paragraph (b) requires that a record of the content and use of advertising be kept in order to facilitate enforcement of this Rule. It does not require that advertising be subject to review prior to dissemination. Such a requirement would be burdensome and expensive relative to its possible benefits, and may be of doubtful constitutionality.

Paying Others to Recommend a Lawyer

[6] A lawyer is allowed to pay for advertising permitted by this Rule and for the purchase of a law practice in accordance with the provisions of Rule 1.17, but otherwise is not permitted to pay another person for channeling professional work. However, a legal aid agency or prepaid legal services plan may pay to advertise legal services provided under its auspices. Likewise, a lawyer may participate in not-for-profit lawyer referral programs and pay the usual fees charged by such programs. Paragraph (c) does not prohibit paying regular compensation to an assistant, such as a secretary, to prepare communications permitted by this Rule. Paragraph (c) also excepts from its prohibition the referral fees permitted by Rule 1.5(e).

Corresponding ABA Model Rule. Substantially similar to Model Rule 7.2, except minor differences in (a) and (b), subclauses (4) and (5) were added to paragraph (c), and paragraph (d) was modified.

Corresponding Former Massachusetts Rule. DR 2-101(B); see DR 2-103.

RULE 7.3 SOLICITATION OF PROFESSIONAL EMPLOYMENT

(a) In soliciting professional employment, a lawyer shall not coerce or harass a prospective client and shall not make a false or misleading communication.

(b) A lawyer shall not solicit professional employment if:

(1) the lawyer knows or reasonably should know that the physical, mental, or emotional state of the prospective client is such that there is a substantial potential that the person cannot exercise reasonable judgment in employing a lawyer, provided, however, that this prohibition shall not apply to solicitation not for a fee; or

(2) the prospective client has made known to the lawyer a desire not to be solicited.

(c) Except as provided in paragraph (e), a lawyer shall not solicit professional employment for a fee from a prospective client known to be in need of legal services in a particular matter by written communication, including audio or video cassette or other electronic communication, unless the lawyer retains a copy of such communication for two years.

(d) Except as provided in paragraph (e), a lawyer shall not solicit professional employment for a fee from a prospective client in person or by personal communication by telephone, electronic device, or otherwise.

(e) The following communications shall be exempt from the provisions of paragraphs (c) and (d) above:

   (1) communications to members of the bar of any state or jurisdiction;

   (2) communications to individuals who are

      (A) the grandparents of the lawyer or the lawyer's spouse,

      (B) descendants of the grandparents of the lawyer or the lawyer's spouse, or

      (C) the spouse of any of the foregoing persons;

   (3) communications to prospective clients with whom the lawyer had a prior attorney-client relationship; and

   (4) communications with (i) organizations, including non-profit and governmental entities, in connection with the activities of such organizations, and (ii) with persons engaged in trade or commerce as defined in G.L. c. 93A, § 1(b), in connection with such persons' trade or commerce.

(f) A lawyer shall not give anything of value to any person or organization to solicit professional employment for the lawyer from a prospective client. However, this rule does not prohibit a lawyer or a partner or associate or any other lawyer affiliated with the lawyer or the lawyer's firm from requesting referrals from a lawyer referral service operated, sponsored, or approved by a bar association or from cooperating with any qualified legal assistance organization. Such requests for referrals or cooperation may include a sharing of fee awards as provided in Rule 5.4(a)(4).

Comment

[1] This rule applies to solicitation, the obtaining of business through letter, e-mail, telephone, in-person or other communications directed to particular prospective clients. It does not apply to non-targeted advertising, the obtaining of business through communications circulated more generally and more indirectly than that, such as through web sites, newspapers or placards in mass transit vehicles. This rule allows lawyers to conduct some form of solicitation of employment from all prospective clients, except in a small number of very special circumstances, and hence permits prospective clients to receive information about legal services that may be useful to them. At the same time it recognizes the possibility of undue influence, intimidation, and overreaching presented by personal solicitation in the circumstances prohibited by this rule and seeks to limit them by regulating the form and manner of solicitation by rules that reach no further than the danger that is perceived.

[2] Paragraphs (a) and (b) apply whenever a lawyer is engaging in solicitation that is not prohibited under another paragraph of this Rule. In determining whether a contact is permissible under Rule 7.3(b)(1), it is relevant to consider the times and circumstances under which the contact is initiated. For example, a person undergoing active medical

treatment for traumatic injury is unlikely to be in an emotional state in which reasonable judgment about employing a lawyer can be exercised. The reference to the "physical, mental, or emotional state of the prospective client" is intended to be all-inclusive of the condition of such person and includes a prospective client who for any reason lacks sufficient sophistication to be able to select a lawyer. A proviso in subparagraph (b)(1) makes clear that it is not intended to reduce the ability possessed by non-profit organizations to contact the elderly and the mentally disturbed or disabled. Abuse of the right to solicit such persons by non-profit organizations would probably constitute a violation of paragraph (a) of the rule or Rule 8.4(c), (d), or (h). The references in paragraph (b)(1), (c), and (d) of the rule to solicitation "for a fee" are intended to carry forward the exemption in former DR 2-103 for non-profit organizations. Where such an organization is involved, the fact that there may be a statutory entitlement to a fee is not intended by itself to bring the solicitation within the scope of the rule. There is no blanket exemption from regulation for all solicitation that is not done "for a fee." Non-profit organizations are subject to the general prohibitions of paragraphs (a) and (f) and subparagraph (b)(2).

[3] Paragraph (c) imposes minimum regulations on solicitation by written and other communication that is not interactive. Copies of such solicitations must be retained for two years. Paragraph (c) applies only in situations where the person is known to be in need of services in a particular matter. For purposes of paragraph (c) a prospective client is "known to be in need of legal services in a particular matter" in circumstances including, but not limited to, all instances in which the communication by the lawyer concerns an event specific to the person solicited that is pending or has already occurred, such as a personal injury, a criminal charge, or a real estate purchase or foreclosure.

[4] While paragraph (c) permits written and other nondirect solicitation of any prospective client, except under the special circumstances set forth in paragraphs (a) and (b), paragraph (d) prohibits solicitation in person or by personal communication, except in the situations described in paragraph (e). See also Comment 3A to Rule 7.2, discussing prohibited personal solicitation through chat groups or other interactive computer-accessed or similar types of communications. The prohibitions of paragraph (d) do not of course apply to in-person solicitation after contact has been initiated by the prospective client.

[4A] Paragraph (e) acknowledges that there are certain situations and relationships in which concerns about overreaching and undue influence do not have sufficient force to justify banning all in-person solicitation. The risk of overreaching and undue influence is diminished where the prospective client is a former client or a member of the lawyer's immediate family. The word "descendant" is intended to include adopted and step-members of the family. Similarly, other lawyers and those who manage commercial, non-profit, and governmental entities generally have the experience and judgment to make reasonable decisions with respect to the importunings of trained advocates soliciting legal business Subparagraph (e)(4) permits in-person solicitation of organizations, whether the organization is a non-profit or governmental organization, in connection with the activities of such organizations, and of individuals engaged in trade or commerce, in connection with the trade or commerce of such individuals.

[5] Paragraph (f) prohibits lawyers from paying a person or organization to solicit on their behalf. The provision should be read together with Rule 8.4(a), which prohibits a lawyer from violating these rules through the acts of another. The rule contains an exception for requests for referrals from described organizations.

Corresponding ABA Model Rule. Different from Model Rule 7.3.

Corresponding Former Massachusetts Rule. DR 2-103.

RULE 7.4 COMMUNICATION OF FIELDS OF PRACTICE

(a) Lawyers may hold themselves out publicly as specialists in particular services, fields, and areas of law if the holding out does not include a false or misleading communication. Such holding out includes

(1) a statement that the lawyer concentrates in, specializes in, is certified in, has expertise in, or limits practice to a particular service, field, or area of law,

(2) directory listings, including electronic, computer-accessed or other similar types of directory listings, by particular service, field, or area of law, and

(3) any other association of the lawyer's name with a particular service, field, or area of law.

(b) Lawyers who hold themselves out as "certified" in a particular service, field, or area of law must name the certifying organization and must state that the certifying organization is "a private organization, whose standards for certification are not regulated by the Commonwealth of Massachusetts," if that is the case, or, if the certifying organization is a governmental body, must name the governmental body.

(c) Except as provided in this paragraph, lawyers who associate their names with a particular service, field, or area of law imply an expertise and shall be held to the standard of performance of specialists in that particular service, field, or area. Lawyers may limit responsibility with respect to a particular service, field, or area of law to the standard of an ordinary lawyer by holding themselves out in a fashion that does not imply expertise, such as by advertising that they "handle" or "welcome" cases, "but are not specialists in" a specific service, field, or area of law.

Comment

[1] This Rule is substantially similar to DR 2-105 which replaced a rule prohibiting lawyers, except for patent, trademark, and admiralty lawyers, from holding themselves out as recognized or certified specialists. The Rule removes prohibitions against holding oneself out as a specialist or expert in a particular field or area of law so long as such holding out does not include any false or misleading communication but provides a broad definition of what is included in the term "holding out." See also Comment 3A to Rule 7.2, discussing computer-accessed or other similar types of newsgroups, bulletin boards, and chat groups. The phrase "false or misleading communication," defined in Rule 7.1, replaces the phrase "deceptive statement or claim" in DR 2-105 to conform to the terminology of Rules 7.1 and 7.3. The Rule merely expands to all claims of expertise the language of the former rule, which permitted nondeceptive statements about limiting practice to, or concentrating in, specified fields or areas of law. There is no longer any need to deal specifically with patent, trademark, or admiralty specialization. To the extent that such practices have fallen within federal jurisdiction, they will continue to do so.

[2] The Rule deals with the problem that the public might perceive that the Commonwealth is involved in certification of lawyers as specialists. It therefore requires lawyers holding themselves out as certified to identify the certifying organization with specifically prescribed language when it is a private organization and to name the certifying governmental organization when that is the case. Nothing in the Rule prevents lawyers from adding truthful language to the prescribed language.

[3] The Rule also specifies that lawyers who imply expertise in a particular field or area of law should be held to the standard of practice of a recognized expert in the field or area. It gives specific examples of commonly used forms of advertising that fall within that description. The Rule also recognizes that there may be good reasons for lawyers to wish to associate their names with a particular field or area of law without wishing to imply expertise or to accept the responsibility of a higher standard of conduct. Such a situation might describe, for example, a lawyer who wishes to develop expertise in a particular or field area without yet having it. The Rule identifies specific language that might be used to avoid any implication of expertise that would trigger the imposition of a higher standard of conduct.

Corresponding ABA Model Rule. Different from Model Rule 7.4.

Corresponding Former Massachusetts Rule. DR 2-105.

RULE 7.5 FIRM NAMES AND LETTERHEADS

(a) A lawyer shall not use a firm name, letterhead, or other professional designation that violates Rule 7.1. A trade name may be used by a lawyer in private practice if it does not imply a connection with a government agency or with a public or charitable legal services organization and is not otherwise in violation of Rule 7.1.

(b) A law firm with offices in more than one jurisdiction may use the same name in each jurisdiction, but identification of the lawyers in an office of the firm shall indicate the jurisdictional limitations on those not licensed to practice in the jurisdiction where the office is located.

(c) The name of a lawyer holding a public office shall not be used in the name of a law firm, or in communications on its behalf, during any substantial period in which the lawyer is not actively and regularly practicing with the firm.

(d) Lawyers may state or imply that they practice in a partnership or other organization only when that is the fact.

Comment

[1] A firm may be designated by the names of all or some of its members, by the names of deceased or retired members where there has been a continuing succession in the firm's identity or by a trade name such as the "ABC Legal Clinic." Use of such names in law practice is acceptable so long as it is not misleading. If a private firm uses a trade name that includes a geographical name such as "Springfield Legal Clinic," an express disclaimer that it is a public legal aid agency may be required to avoid a misleading implication. It may be observed that any firm name including the name of a deceased or retired partner is, strictly speaking, a trade name. The use of such names to designate law firms has proven a useful means of identification. However, it is misleading to use the name of a lawyer not associated with the firm or a predecessor of the firm.

[2] With regard to paragraph (d), lawyers who are not in fact partners, such as those who are only sharing office facilities, may not denominate themselves as, for example, "Smith and Jones," or "Smith and Jones, A Professional Association," for those titles, in the absence of an effective disclaimer of joint responsibility, suggest partnership in the practice of law. Likewise, the use of the term "associates" by a group of lawyers implies practice in either a partnership or sole proprietorship form and may not be used by a group in which the individual members disclaim the joint or vicarious responsibility inherent in such forms of business in the absence of an effective disclaimer of such responsibility.

[3] S.J.C. Rule 3:06 imposes further restrictions on trade names for firms that are professional corporations, limited liability companies or limited liability partnerships.

Corresponding ABA Model Rule. Identical to Model Rule 7.5.

Corresponding Former Massachusetts Rule. DR 2-102.

MAINTAINING THE INTEGRITY OF THE PROFESSION

RULE 8.1 BAR ADMISSION AND DISCIPLINARY MATTERS

An applicant for admission to the bar, or a lawyer in connection with a bar admission application or in connection with a disciplinary matter, shall not:

    (a) knowingly make a false statement of material fact; or

    (b) fail to disclose a fact necessary to correct a misapprehension known by the person to have arisen in the matter, or knowingly fail to respond to a lawful demand for information from an admissions or disciplinary authority, except that this rule does not require disclosure of information otherwise protected by Rule 1.6.

Comment

[1] The duty imposed by this Rule extends to persons seeking admission to the bar as well as to lawyers. Hence, if a person makes a material false statement in connection with an application for admission, it may be the basis for subsequent disciplinary action if the person is admitted, and in any event may be relevant in a subsequent admission application. The duty imposed by this Rule applies to a lawyer's own admission or discipline as well as that of others. Thus, it is a separate professional offense for a lawyer to knowingly make a misrepresentation or omission in connection with a disciplinary investigation of the lawyer's own conduct. This Rule also requires affirmative clarification of any misunderstanding on the part of the admissions or disciplinary authority of which the person involved becomes aware.

[2] This Rule is subject to the provisions of the fifth amendment of the United States Constitution and Article 12 of the Massachusetts Declaration of Rights. A person relying on such a provision in response to a question, however, should do so openly and not use the right of nondisclosure as a justification for failure to comply with this Rule.

[3] A lawyer representing an applicant for admission to the bar, or representing a lawyer who is the subject of a disciplinary inquiry or proceeding, is governed by the rules applicable to the client-lawyer relationship.

Corresponding ABA Model Rule. Identical to Model Rule 8.1.

Corresponding Former Massachusetts Rule. DR 1-101; see also DR 1-102.

RULE 8.2 JUDICIAL AND LEGAL OFFICIALS

A lawyer shall not make a statement that the lawyer knows to be false or with reckless disregard as to its truth or falsity concerning the qualifications or integrity of a judge or a magistrate, or of a candidate for appointment to judicial or legal office.

Comment

[1] Assessments by lawyers are relied on in evaluating the professional or personal fitness of persons being considered for election or appointment to judicial or legal offices. Expressing honest and candid opinions on such matters contributes to improving the administration of justice. Conversely, false statements by a lawyer can unfairly undermine public confidence in the administration of justice.

[2] ABA Model Rule 8.2(b) is inapplicable in Massachusetts since judges are not elected.

Corresponding ABA Model Rule. Different from Model Rule 8.2.

Corresponding Former Massachusetts Rule. DR 8-102.

RULE 8.3 REPORTING PROFESSIONAL MISCONDUCT

(a) A lawyer having knowledge that another lawyer has committed a violation of the Rules of Professional Conduct that raises a substantial question as to that lawyer's honesty, trustworthiness or fitness as a lawyer in other respects, shall inform the Bar Counsel's office of the Board of Bar Overseers.

(b) A lawyer having knowledge that a judge has committed a violation of applicable rules of judicial conduct that raises a substantial question as to the judge's fitness for office shall inform the Commission on Judicial Conduct.

(c) This rule does not require disclosure of information otherwise protected by Rule 1.6 or information gained by a lawyer or judge while serving as a member of a lawyer assistance program as defined in Rule 1.6(c), to the extent that such information would be confidential if it were communicated by a client.

Comment

[1] This rule requires lawyers to report serious violations of ethical duty by lawyers and judges. Even an apparently isolated violation may indicate a pattern of misconduct that only a disciplinary investigation can uncover. Reporting a violation is especially important where the victim is unlikely to discover the offense.

[2] A report about misconduct is not required or permitted where it would involve violation of Rule 1.6. However, a lawyer should encourage a client to consent to disclosure where prosecution would not substantially prejudice the client's interests.

[3] While a measure of judgment is required in complying with the provisions of this Rule, a lawyer must report misconduct that, if proven and without regard to mitigation, would likely result in an order of suspension or disbarment, including misconduct that would constitute a "serious crime" as defined in S.J.C. Rule 4:01, § 12(3). Precedent for determining whether an offense would warrant suspension or disbarment may be found in the Massachusetts Attorney Discipline Reports. Section 12(3) of Rule 4:01 provides that a serious crime is "any felony, and ... any lesser crime a necessary element of which ... includes interference with the administration of justice, false swearing, misrepresentation, fraud, willful failure to file income tax returns, deceit, bribery, extortion, misappropriation, theft, or an attempt or a conspiracy, or solicitation of another to commit [such a crime]." In addition to a conviction of a felony, misappropriation of client funds or perjury before a tribunal are common examples of reportable conduct. The term "substantial" refers to the seriousness of the possible offense and not the quantum of evidence of which the lawyer is aware. A lawyer has knowledge of a violation when he or she possesses supporting evidence such that a reasonable lawyer under the circumstances would form a firm opinion that the conduct in question had more likely occurred than not. A report should be made to Bar Counsel's office or to the Judicial Conduct Commission, as the case may be. Rule 8.3 does not preclude a lawyer from reporting a violation of the Massachusetts Rules of Professional Conduct in circumstances where a report is not mandatory.

[3A] In most situations, a lawyer may defer making a report under this Rule until the matter has been concluded, but the report should be made as soon as practicable thereafter. An immediate report is ethically compelled, however, when a client or third person will likely be injured by a delay in reporting, such as where the lawyer has knowledge that another lawyer has embezzled client or fiduciary funds and delay may impair the ability to recover the funds.

[4] The duty to report past professional misconduct does not apply to a lawyer retained to represent a lawyer whose professional conduct is in question. Such a situation is governed by the Rules applicable to the client-lawyer relationship.

[5] Information about a lawyer's or judge's misconduct or fitness may be received by a lawyer in the course of that lawyer's participation in a lawyer assistance program. In that circumstance, providing for the confidentiality of such information encourages lawyers and judges to seek treatment through such programs. Conversely, without such confidentiality, lawyers and judges may hesitate to seek assistance from these programs. Failure to do so may then result in additional harm to their professional careers and additional injury to the welfare of clients and the public. The Rule, therefore, exempts the lawyer from the reporting requirements of paragraphs (a) and (b) with respect to information that would be protected by Rule 1.6 if the relationship between the impaired lawyer or judge and the recipient of the information were that of a client and a lawyer.

Corresponding ABA Model Rule. Different from Model Rule 8.3.

Corresponding Former Massachusetts Rule. None. [DR 1-103 (A) was not adopted in Massachusetts].

RULE 8.4 MISCONDUCT

It is professional misconduct for a lawyer to:

(a) violate or attempt to violate the Rules of Professional Conduct, knowingly assist or induce another to do so, or do so through the acts of another;

(b) commit a criminal act that reflects adversely on the lawyer's honesty, trustworthiness, or fitness as a lawyer in other respects;

(c) engage in conduct involving dishonesty, fraud, deceit, or misrepresentation;

(d) engage in conduct that is prejudicial to the administration of justice;

(e) state or imply an ability to influence improperly a government agency or official;

(f) knowingly assist a judge or judicial officer in conduct that is a violation of applicable rules of judicial conduct or other law;

(g) fail without good cause to cooperate with the Bar Counsel or the Board of Bar Overseers as provided in Supreme Judicial Court Rule 4:01, § 3; or

(h) engage in any other conduct that adversely reflects on his or her fitness to practice law.

Comment

[1] Many kinds of illegal conduct reflect adversely on fitness to practice law, such as offenses involving fraud and the offense of willful failure to file an income tax return. However, some kinds of offense carry no such implication. Traditionally, the distinction was drawn in terms of offenses involving "moral turpitude." That concept can be construed to include offenses concerning some matters of personal morality, such as adultery and comparable offenses, that have no specific connection to fitness for the practice

of law. Although a lawyer is personally answerable to the entire criminal law, a lawyer should be professionally answerable only for offenses that indicate lack of those characteristics relevant to law practice. Offenses involving violence, dishonesty, breach of trust, or serious interference with the administration of justice are in that category. A pattern of repeated offenses, even ones of minor significance when considered separately, can indicate indifference to legal obligation.

[2] A lawyer may refuse to comply with an obligation imposed by law upon a good faith belief that no valid obligation exists. The provisions of Rule 1.2(d) concerning a good faith challenge to the validity, scope, meaning or application of the law apply to challenges of legal regulation of the practice of law.

[3] Lawyers holding public office assume legal responsibilities going beyond those of other citizens. A lawyer's abuse of public office can suggest an inability to fulfill the professional role of lawyer. The same is true of abuse of positions of private trust such as trustee, executor, administrator, guardian, agent and officer, director or manager of a corporation or other organization.

[4] Paragraph (c) prohibits the acceptance of referrals from a referral source, such as court or agency personnel, if the lawyer states or implies, or the client could reasonably infer, that the lawyer has an ability to influence the court or agency improperly.

[5] Paragraph (h) carries forward the provision of Former DR 1-102(A)(6) prohibiting conduct that adversely reflects on that lawyer's fitness to practice law, even if the conduct does not constitute a criminal, dishonest, fraudulent or other act specifically described in the other paragraphs of this rule.

Corresponding ABA Model Rule. Clauses (a), (b), (c), (d), (e), and (f) identical to Model Rule 8.4; clause (g) incorporates obligations set forth in S.J.C. Rule 4:01, §3; clause (h) comes from DR 1-102 (A) (6).

Corresponding Former Massachusetts Rule. DR 1-102, DR 9-101 (C). See S.J.C. Rule 4:01, §3.

RULE 8.5 DISCIPLINARY AUTHORITY; CHOICE OF LAW

(a) **Disciplinary Authority.** A lawyer admitted to practice in this jurisdiction is subject to the disciplinary authority of this jurisdiction, regardless of where the lawyer's conduct occurs. A lawyer not admitted in this jurisdiction is also subject to the disciplinary authority of this jurisdiction if the lawyer provides or offers to provide any legal services in this jurisdiction. A lawyer may be subject to the disciplinary authority of both this jurisdiction and another jurisdiction for the same conduct.

(b) **Choice of Law.** In any exercise of the disciplinary authority of this jurisdiction, the rules of professional conduct to be applied shall be as follows:

(1) for conduct in connection with a matter pending before a governmental tribunal, the rules of the jurisdiction in which the tribunal sits, unless the rules of the tribunal provide otherwise; and

(2) for any other conduct, the rules of the jurisdiction in which the lawyer's principal office is located shall be applied, unless the predominant effect of the conduct is in a different jurisdiction, in which case the rules of that jurisdiction shall be applied. A lawyer shall not be subject to discipline if the lawyer's conduct conforms to the rules of a jurisdiction in which the lawyer reasonably believes the predominant effect of the lawyer's conduct will occur.

other jurisdictions. Second, lawyers are likely to be more familiar with the rules of the jurisdiction where they principally practice than with rules of another jurisdiction, even if licensed in that other jurisdiction. Indeed, most lawyers will be licensed in the jurisdiction where they principally practice, and familiarity with a jurisdiction's ethical rules is commonly made a condition of licensure. Third, in many situations, a representation will affect many jurisdictions, such as a transaction among multiple parties who reside in different jurisdictions involving performance in yet other jurisdictions. The selection of any of the jurisdictions that are affected by the representation will often be problematic.

[4B] There will be some circumstances, however, where the predominant effect of the lawyer's conduct will clearly be in a jurisdiction than the jurisdiction in which the lawyer maintains his or her principal office. Accordingly, paragraph (b)(2) provides that when the predominant effect of lawyer's conduct is in a jurisdiction other than the jurisdiction in which the lawyer's principal office is located, the ethical rules of such other jurisdiction apply to such conduct. For example, when litigation is contemplated but not yet instituted in another in jurisdiction, a lawyer whose principal office is in this jurisdiction may well find that the rules of that jurisdiction govern the lawyer's ability to interview a former employee of a potential opposing party in that jurisdiction. Likewise, under Rule 8.5(b), when litigation is contemplated and not yet begun in this jurisdiction, a lawyer whose principal office is in another jurisdiction may well find that the rules of this jurisdiction govern the lawyer's ability to interview a former employee of a potential opposing party in this jurisdiction.

[4C] A lawyer who serves as in-house counsel in this jurisdiction pursuant to Rule 5.5, and whose principal office is in this jurisdiction will be subject to the rules of this jurisdiction unless the predominant effect of his or her conduct is clearly in another jurisdiction.

[5] The application of these rules will often involve the exercise of judgment in situations in situations in which reasonable people may disagree. So long as the lawyer's conduct reflects an objectively reasonable application of the choice of law principles set forth in paragraph (b), the lawyer shall not be subject to discipline under this Rule.

[6] If this jurisdiction and another jurisdiction were to proceed against a lawyer for the same conduct, they should identify and apply the same governing ethics rules. Disciplinary authorities in this jurisdiction should take all appropriate steps to see that they do apply the same rule to the same conduct as authorities in other jurisdictions, and in all events should avoid proceeding against a lawyer on the basis of two inconsistent rules.

[7] The choice of law provision applies to lawyers engaged in transnational practice, unless international law, treaties or other agreements between competent regulatory authorities in the affected jurisdictions provide otherwise. Moreover, no lawyer should be subject to discipline in this jurisdiction for violating the regulations governing advertising or solicitation of a non-U.S. jurisdiction where the conduct would be constitutionally protected if performed in this jurisdiction.

Corresponding ABA Model Rule. Rule 8.5 is identical to Model Rule 8.5 (a).

Corresponding Former Massachusetts Rule. S.J.C. Rule 4:01 (Bar Discipline), § 1.

DEFINITIONS; TITLE

RULE 9.1 DEFINITIONS

The following definitions are applicable to the Rules of Professional Conduct:

Comment

Disciplinary Authority

[1] It is longstanding law that the conduct of a lawyer admitted to practice in diction is subject to the disciplinary authority of this jurisdiction. Extension ciplinary authority of this jurisdiction to other lawyers who provide or offer legal services in this jurisdiction is for the protection of the citizens of this jur

[1A] In adopting Rule 5.5, Massachusetts has made it clear that out-of-state law engage in practice in this jurisdiction are subject to the disciplinary authori state. A great many states have rules that are similar to, or identical with, Rule Massachusetts lawyers therefore need to be aware that they may become subje disciplinary rules of another state in certain circumstances. Rule 8.5 deals with lated question of the conflict of law rules that are to be applied when a lawyer's affects multiple jurisdictions. Comments 2-7 state the particular principles that

[1B] There is no completely satisfactory solution to the choice of law question so different states have different rules of professional responsibility. When a lawyer duct has an effect in another jurisdiction, that jurisdiction may assert that its law fessional responsibility should govern, whether the lawyer was physically present jurisdiction or not.

Choice of Law

[2] A lawyer may be potentially subject to more than one set of rules of profes conduct which impose different obligations. The lawyer may be licensed to pract more than one jurisdiction with differing rules, or may be admitted to practice bet particular court with rules that differ from those of the jurisdiction or jurisdictio which the lawyer is licensed to practice. Additionally, the lawyer's conduct may in significant contacts with more than one jurisdiction.

[3] Paragraph (b) seeks to resolve such potential conflicts. Minimizing conflicts betw rules, as well as uncertainty about which rules are applicable, is in the best interes both clients and the profession (as well as the bodies having authority to regulate profession). Accordingly,paragraph (b) provides that any particular act of a lawyer sl be subject to only one set of rules of professional conduct, makes the determination which set of rules applies to particular conduct as straightforward as possible, consiste with recognition of the appropriate regulatory interests of relevant jurisdictions, a provides protection from discipline for lawyers who act reasonably in the face of unce tainty.

[4] Paragraph (b)(1) provides that as to a lawyer's conduct relating to a proceedin pending before a government tribunal, the lawyer shall be subject only to the rules o the government tribunal, if any, or of the jurisdiction in which the government tribuna sits unless the rules of that tribunal, including its choice of law rule, provide otherwise. By limiting application of the rule to matters before a government tribunal, e.g. a court or administrative agency, parties may establish which disciplinary rules will apply in private adjudications such as arbitration.

[4A] As to all other conduct, including conduct in anticipation of a proceeding not yet pending before a tribunal, the choice of law is governed by paragraph (b)(2). Paragraph (b)(2) creates a"default" choice of the rules of the jurisdiction in which the lawyer's principal office is located. There are several reasons for identifying such a default rule. First, the jurisdiction where the lawyer principally practices has a clear regulatory inter-est in the conduct of such lawyer, even in situations where the lawyer's conduct affects

(a) "Bar association" includes an association of specialists in particular services, fields, and areas of law.

(b) "Belief" or "believes" denotes that the person involved actually supposed the fact in question to be true. A person's belief may be inferred from circumstances.

(c) "Consult" or "consultation" denotes communication of information reasonably sufficient to permit the client to appreciate the significance of the matter in question.

(d) "Firm" or "law firm" denotes a lawyer or lawyers in a private firm, lawyers employed in the legal department of a corporation or other organization, and lawyers employed in a legal services organization. The term includes a partnership, including a limited liability partnership, a corporation, a limited liability company, or an association treated as a corporation, authorized by law to practice law for profit.

(e) "Fraud" or "fraudulent" denotes conduct having a purpose to deceive and not merely negligent misrepresentation or failure to apprise another of relevant information.

(f) "Knowingly," "known," or "knows" denotes actual knowledge of the fact in question. A person's knowledge may be inferred from circumstances.

(g) "Partner" denotes a member of a partnership and a shareholder in a law firm organized as a professional corporation.

(h) "Person" includes a corporation, an association, a trust, a partnership, and any other organization or legal entity.

(i) "Qualified legal assistance organization" means a legal aid, public defender, or military assistance office; or a bona fide organization that recommends, furnishes or pays for legal services to its members or beneficiaries, provided the office, service, or organization receives no profit from the rendition of legal services, is not designed to procure financial benefit or legal work for a lawyer as a private practitioner, does not infringe the individual member's freedom as a client to challenge the approved counsel or to select outside counsel at the client's expense, and is not in violation of any applicable law.

(j) "Reasonable" or "reasonably" when used in relation to conduct by a lawyer denotes the conduct of a reasonably prudent and competent lawyer.

(k) "Reasonable belief" or "reasonably believes" when used in reference to a lawyer denotes that the lawyer believes the matter in question and that the circumstances are such that the belief is reasonable.

(l) "Reasonably should know" when used in reference to a lawyer denotes that a lawyer of reasonable prudence and competence would ascertain the matter in question.

(m) "State" includes the District of Columbia, Puerto Rico, and federal territories or possessions.

(n) "Substantial" when used in reference to degree or extent denotes a material matter of clear and weighty importance.

(o) "Tribunal" includes a court or other adjudicatory body.

Comment

[1] See Comments 1-3 to Rule 1.10 for further information on the definition of "firm."

[2] In addition to the terms defined in this rule, there are two other important concepts whose meaning is discussed at some length at other places in these rules. The terms "assist" and "assisting" appear in Rules 1.2(d), 3.3(a)(2) and 4.1(b). Comment 3 to Rule 4.1 sets forth the meaning of these terms with respect to conduct proscribed in Rules 1.2(d) and 4.1(b), and Comment 2A to Rule 3.3 sets forth the special meaning of those terms in the context of a lawyer's appearance before a tribunal. The term "confidential information" is also used in the rules to describe the information that lawyers shall not reveal unless required or permitted under these rules. As Comment 5, 5A and 5B to Rule 1.6 indicate, confidential information includes "virtually" all information relating to the representation whatever its scope. It therefore includes information described as confidences and secrets under the prior Massachusetts Disciplinary Rules without the limitation in the prior rules that the information be "embarrassing" or "detrimental" to the client. As pointed out in Comment 5A, however, a lawyer may learn some information in the course of representation that is so widely known that it ought not be considered confidential.

[3] The final category of qualified legal assistance organization requires that the organization "receives no profit from the rendition of legal services." That condition refers to the entire legal services operation of the organization; it does not prohibit the receipt of a court-awarded fee that would result in a 'profit" from that particular lawsuit.

Corresponding ABA Model Rule. The definitions are largely taken from the "Terminology" of the ABA Model Rules which is not a numbered rule.

These rules may be known and cited as the Massachusetts Rules of Professional Conduct (Mass. R. Prof. C.).

Corresponding ABA Model Rule. None.

Index